Langensche

Pocket

Merriam-We

Thesaur

Langenscheidt's
Pocket
Merriam-Webster
Thesaurus

LANGENSCHEIDT
NEW YORK • BERLIN • MUNICH • VIENNA • ZURICH

Preface

THE MERRIAM-WEBSTER THESAURUS is based on Webster's Collegiate Thesaurus and is designed especially to meet the day-to-day needs of those who want a compact and handy thesaurus. In this book we have been able to eliminate much of the bulk and weight of the larger volume while retaining the basic features that distinguish Webster's Collegiate Thesaurus.

The basic premise behind both books is that the user of a thesaurus is seeking a more appropriate term than the one he has in mind. This very broad concept is scarcely consonant with the typical thesaurus presentation of "synonyms" and sometimes "antonyms". In point of fact, the user may be seeking a synonym, a word stronger or weaker in force, one of slightly different meaning, a more starchy or more folksy word, an idiomatic phrase that conveys the same idea, or a word that to a greater or lesser degree contrasts with his starting point. Patently, all these possible uses cannot be subsumed reasonably under the rather unitary notions of "synonym" and "antonym". Perhaps the longevity of Roget's *Thesaurus* rests on the simple fact that in spite of its complexity and lack of guidance, it does spread before the user a greater body of material to browse through than any comparable book heretofore available. The Merriam-Webster Thesaurus is designed to present a similar range of material but in a readily available and highly structured form that minimizes the consultant's need to grope and guess.

In earlier Merriam-Webster® publications the pattern of supplementing synonym lists with lists of related and contrasted words, words that were relevant to the group under study yet not quite synonyms or antonyms respectively, was extensively tested. This favorably received feature not only allowed more precise delineation of synonyms and antonyms but provided the user with much additional significant and pertinent assistance. The same plan of supplementing synonyms and antonyms with genuinely germane collateral material has been made a feature of this thesaurus.

Additional features of The Merriam-Webster Thesaurus designed to facilitate its use are the provision at each main entry of a concise statement of the segment of denotation in which a group of words can be construed as synonyms, a strictly alphabetical organization, and the entry at its own alphabetical place of each word that appears as a synonym at a main entry. The absence or inadequate handling of the first of these features is a major flaw in most existent thesauruses. Though many justifications have been offered for avoiding the second, they all boil down to the implausible notion that the members of a group of words are synonymous but some are more synonymous than others! Perhaps unfairly, one can't help feeling that the only valid explanation for non-alphabetical listing of properly chosen synonyms appears in one specialized dictionary of synonyms whose author comments: "Apologies are in order, however, for my inability to maintain alphabetical order within the categories, the plea being of course lack of time." Finally, since no one can anticipate where the user's search may start, it seems only logical to enter each synonym in such a way that it can serve as a convenient starting point in his searching.

Though The Merriam-Webster Thesaurus is based on Webster's Collegiate Thesaurus, its ultimate authority lies in Webster's Third New International Dictionary and the Merriam-Webster research file of nearly 13,000,000 instances of words in actual use by a wide range of writers and speakers. In preparing The Merriam-Webster Thesaurus the chief organizational change was the replacement of the synonym list at each secondary entry with a cross-reference to the appropriate main entry. In addition a few specialized or abstruse entries were eliminated and a few synonyms not likely to be of general interest were dropped.

The Merriam-Webster Thesaurus was prepared by Kathleen M. Doherty, assistant editor, under the immediate supervision of E. Ward Gilman, senior editor.

Explanatory Notes

How to Use The Merriam-Webster Thesaurus

Every thesaurus user should read these Explanatory Notes because a thorough understanding of the scope, content, and structure of the book is essential to its effective employment. The key lines at the bottom of the text pages direct the user to these Explanatory Notes.

Since the English lexicon contains an incalculable number of fixed combinations, senses, subsenses, and nuances of meaning (for example, Webster's Third New International Dictionary records some 251 distinguishable meanings for the verb *set* and its fixed combinations), *it is essential that the thesaurus be used in conjunction with an adequate dictionary.*

Scope of The Merriam-Webster Thesaurus

This book is concerned with the general vocabulary of the English language. Since the user may actually be hindered rather than helped by a vocabulary diluted with obsolete, archaic, or extremely rare terms or with specialized or technical jargon, such words have been omitted.

Structure and Content

Entry Order   The body of the book consists of main and secondary entries introduced by alphabetically ordered boldface headwords, as

> **raid** *vb* **1** to make a raid on <Indians *raided* the
> settlers frequently>
> *syn* foray, harass, harry, maraud
> *rel* despoil, devastate, ravage, sack, spoliate,
> waste; loot, plunder, rifle, rob
> **2** *syn* see INVADE 1
>
> **raider** *n syn* see MARAUDER
>
> **rail** *n syn* see RAILING

where *raid, raider,* and *rail* are the headwords introducing either a main entry (as **raid** *vb* **1**), or a secondary entry (as **raid** *vb* **2, raider** *n,* or **rail** *n*).

Homograph headwords are entered in historical order: the one first used in English is entered first, as

> **till** *prep*
> **till** *conj*
> **till** *vb*

Verbs used predominantly with one or two prepositions or adverbs may be headwords introducing main or secondary entries; in this case, they are entered with the verb segment in boldface type followed by the parenthetical element or elements in lightface type. Such verb + particle combinations immediately follow their base verb in alphabetical order:

> **put** *vb* —————————— base-verb homograph
> **put** (back) *vb*
> **put** (on) *vb* ⎫ verb + particle combinations
> **put** (on *or* upon) *vb* ⎭
> **put** *n* ————————————— noun homograph

Fixed verb + adverb collocations commonly entered in dictionaries as two-word verbs have boldface entry at their appropriate alphabetical positions in this book. However, they follow any verb + particle combinations occurring in the same alphabetical sequence:

> **take** *vb* ————————— base verb
> **take** (from) *vb* ———— verb + particle combinations
> **take** (to) *vb*
> **take away** *vb* ⎫
> **take back** *vb* ⎪
> **take down** *vb* ⎬ two-word verb collocations
> **take in** *vb* ⎪
> **take off** *vb* ⎭

Headwords ordinarily conform to normal dictionary practices: for instance, they are styled as singular nouns or infinitive verbs. Special situations (as plural usage or variant spellings) are signaled by the use of boldface subheads, as

> **crossroad** *n, usu* **crossroads** *pl but sing or pl in constr syn see* JUNCTURE 2
>
> **woe** *n . . .* **3** *usu* **woes** *pl syn see* DISASTER
>
> **catercorner** (*or* **catty-corner** *or* **kitty-corner**) *adv syn see* DIAGONALLY

where **crossroads** and **woes** are subheads indicating plural usage, and **catty-corner** and **kitty-corner** are subheads showing variant spellings of the headwords.

The Main Entry and Its Basic Elements Each main entry consists of a headword followed by a part-of-speech label, a sense number when needed, a meaning core with a brief verbal illustration, and a list of synonyms. Lists of related words, idiomatic equivalents, contrasted words, and antonyms follow the synonym list if they are called for.

A typical main entry is

> **calm** *adj* **1** free from storm or rough activity <the
> wind died and the sea became *calm*>
> *syn* halcyon, hushed, placid, quiet, still, stilly,
> untroubled
> *rel* inactive, quiescent, reposing, resting; pacific,
> smooth, tranquil, unruffled
> *idiom* calm as a millpond, still as death
> *con* agitated, disturbed, perturbed, restless,
> turbulent, uneasy
> *ant* stormy

where the italic part-of-speech label *adj* indicates that the headword is an
adjective. Other such labels used in the book are: *adv* (adverb), *conj* (conjunction), *interj* (interjection), *n* (noun), *prep* (preposition), *pron* (pronoun),
and *vb* (verb).

Individual senses of multisense entries (as **calm** *adj*) are introduced by a
boldface sense number (as **1**).

The meaning core, as at **calm 1**

> free from storm or rough activity

indicates the area of meaning in which a group of words (in this case *calm,
halcyon, hushed, placid, quiet, still, stilly,* and *untroubled*) are considered to be
synonymous.

In other words, the meaning core pinpoints the exact relationship between
the main-entry headword and its synonyms.

A meaning core may be supplemented by a usage note introduced by a
lightface dash when additional information or comments on syntax or usage
are required:

> **yet** *adv* **1** beyond this — used as an intensive to
> stress the comparative degree

Some interjections express feelings but otherwise are untranslatable into
substitutable meaning; in such cases, the meaning core itself may be replaced
by a usage note:

> **good-bye** *interj* — used as a conventional expression
> of good wishes at parting

Each meaning core is followed by a verbal illustration enclosed by angle
brackets, as

> <the wind died and the sea became *calm*>

that exemplifies a typical use of the headword (here, **calm**) in its pertinent
sense (**1**). The verbal illustration also offers the thesaurus user a frame for
testing the suitability of the synonyms and/or related words with regard to
his particular needs. Two verbal illustrations may appear after a meaning
core that is broad enough to subsume alternatives (as both a literal and an
extended use):

> **see** *vb* **1** to take cognizance of by physical
> or mental vision <*saw* that the boat was being
> driven ashore> <the only one who *saw* the truth>

Such double illustrations have been chosen with discretion and are used spar-
ingly in this book.

The boldface italic abbreviation *syn* introduces a synonym list that appears
at each main entry on a line below the meaning core and the verbal illustration. This list may consist of only one synonym (as *here* at **hitherto** *adv* **2**) or
of many (as *halcyon, hushed, placid, quiet, still, stilly,* and *untroubled* at **calm**
adj **1**). Each synonym in a main-entry list has a boldface entry at its own
alphabetical place.

A compare cross-reference may appear at the end of a main-entry *syn* list.
This cross-reference introduced by the italic word *compare* is used (1) when
two or more groups of synonyms are very closely related and it is felt that the
user examining one list should be aware of the existence of the other list or
lists:

> **assassin** *n* a person hired or hirable to
> commit murder <found out who paid the *assassin*>
> *syn* bravo, cutthroat, gun, gunman, ‖gunsel, gunslinger,
> hatchet man, hit man, torpedo, triggerman; *compare* MURDERER

> **murderer** *n* one who kills a human being
> <a *murderer* who wouldn't hesitate to kill in cold blood>
> *syn* homicide, killer, manslayer, slayer; *compare* ASSASSIN

and (2) when the user should be warned that certain words have evolved
derivative senses that tend to blur precise sense boundaries and consequently
cause an overlapping of senses or of meaning, thus making those words
somewhat less desirable choices for the user in terms of preciseness than
other words in their lists. A comparison of the main entries

> **ration** *n* an amount allotted or made available
> especially from a limited supply <saved up their gasoline
> *ration* for a vacation trip>
> *syn* allotment, allowance, apportionment, measure,
> meed, part, portion, quantum, quota, share; *compare* SHARE 1

> **share** *n* **1** something belonging to, assumed by, or falling to
> one (as in division or apportionment) <wanted his *share* of
> the prize money>
> *syn* allotment, allowance, bite, cut, lot,
> part, partage, portion, quota, slice; *compare* RATION

reveals the usage overlap of the synonyms *allotment, allowance, part, portion,*
quota, and *share,* which are indeed valid synonyms at both entries.

The Secondary Entry and Its Basic Elements   A secondary entry consists
of a boldface headword followed by a part-of-speech label, a boldface sense
number when needed, and a *syn* see cross-reference in small capitals directing
the user to the appropriate main entry in whose *syn* list the secondary entry
appears (followed when needed by a lightface sense number of the main entry). Lists of related words, idiomatic equivalents, contrasted words, or antonyms that are specifically applicable to the secondary-entry headword in the
relationship indicated by the *syn* see cross-reference may be included as well.

A typical secondary entry is

> **placid** *adj* **1** *syn* see CALM 1
>   *rel* irenic, peaceful, serene, unagitated, unstirring
>   *ant* roiled

where **placid** is the headword, *adj* is the part-of-speech label, **1** is the sense number of the secondary entry, and *syn* see CALM 1 is the *syn* cross-reference directing the user to the main entry **calm 1** where *placid* is a synonym.

Main and Secondary Entries: Elements Common to Both   All, some, or none of the following lists may appear at both main and secondary entries in this order: related words, idiomatic equivalents, contrasted words, and antonyms.

The boldface abbreviation *rel* introduces a list of related words. The related words — words that are almost but not quite synonymous with the headword — are included at an entry next after the synonym list. For example, at the main entry

> **splendid** *adj* . . .
>   **2** extraordinarily or transcendently impressive . . .
>   *syn* glorious, gorgeous, magnificent, proud,
>   resplendent, splendiferous, splendorous, sublime, superb
>   *rel* eminent, illustrious; grand, impressive, lavish,
>   luxurious, royal, sumptuous; divine, exquisite,
>   lovely; incomparable, matchless, peerless,
>   superlative, supreme, unparalleled, unsurpassed;
>   surpassing, transcendent

the *rel* list is composed of twenty terms separated into five subgroups that each share a common likeness or relation with the headword and its synonyms. On the other hand, at the secondary entry

> **splendiferous** *adj syn* see SPLENDID 2
>   *rel* dazzling, marvelous; smashing, walloping;
>   rattling, ripping, screaming, terrific

three subgroups of eight terms were selected as being distinctively related to *splendiferous* rather than to the whole synonym group in the context indicated by the *syn* see cross-reference to **splendid 2.** Related words appearing at a main entry are not ordinarily repeated at the secondary entries. The user should therefore check the main entry when seeking the most complete groupings of related words. Related words as such are not entered in boldface at their own alphabetical places. They may, of course, be synonyms in other lists or head their own main entries.

The boldface italic abbreviation *idiom* introduces a list of idiomatic equivalents that are essentially the same in meaning as the members of a synonym group. An *idiom* list at a main entry includes phrases that are generally pertinent to the entire *syn* list and the headword, as the ones at

> **speak** *vb* **1** to articulate words in order to express
>   thoughts . . .
>   *syn* talk, utter, verbalize, vocalize, voice
>   *rel* . . .
>   *idiom* break silence, give voice (*or* tongue *or* utterance) to,

> let fall, make public (*or* known), open
> one's mouth (*or* lips), put in (*or* into) words, say one's say,
> speak one's piece

while a secondary-entry list, as the one at

> **retaliate** *vb syn* see RECIPROCATE
> *rel* . . .
> *idiom* even the score, get back at, get
> even with, give in kind, give one a
> dose of his own medicine, give one tit for
> tat, pay one in his own coin, settle (*or*
> square) accounts, turn the tables on

features idioms that are particularly appropriate equivalents of its headword
in the context indicated by the *syn* see cross-reference. Idiomatic equivalents,
including those fixed verb + preposition combinations that function as idioms rather than as literal meanings of the verb, are not entered in boldface at
their own alphabetical places in this book.

The boldface italic abbreviation *con* introduces a list of contrasted words
— words that are strongly contrastable but not quite antonymous with the
headword — that may appear at an entry:

> **watchful** *adj* paying close attention usually
> with a view to anticipating approaching
> danger or opportunity . . .
> *syn* . . .
> *rel* . . .
> *idiom* . . .
> *con* careless, heedless, thoughtless;
> inadvertent; absentminded, abstracted,
> faraway

> **alert** *adj* **1** *syn* see WATCHFUL
> *rel* . . .
> *idiom* . . .
> *con* inattentive, unmindful; aloof,
> detached, indifferent, unconcerned

At the main entry **watchful** *adj* the *con* list is composed of seven words separated into three subgroups that each share at least one aspect of contrast to
the headword and its *syn* list, while the *con* list at the secondary entry **alert 1**
comprises six words separated into two such subgroups. Contrasted words
appearing at a main entry are not ordinarily repeated at the secondary
entries. The thesaurus user should therefore check the main entry when seeking the most complete groupings of contrasted words. Contrasted words as
such are not entered in boldface at their own alphabetical places. They may,
of course, be synonyms in other lists or head their own main entries.

The boldface italic abbreviation *ant* introduces the last possible element of
a main or secondary entry: an antonym or list of antonyms, as at the entry

> **perfect** *adj* . . . **2** . . .
> *ant* imperfect

or at the entry

quiet *adj* . . . **4** not showy or obtrusive . . .
    ant gaudy, loud

When antonyms are drawn from different classes of opposites, members of
the two groups are separated by a semicolon, as at the entry

assistance *n syn* see HELP 1 | antonyms that are opposites
 rel . . . | with intermediates
 con . . . |
 ant impediment, impeding; | antonyms that are reverse
 obstructing, obstruction | opposites

Like related and contrasted words, antonyms as such are not entered in boldface at their own alphabetical places. They may, of course, be synonyms in
other lists or head their own main entries.

Main and Secondary Entries: The One Arbitrary Rule Ideally, a book such
as this should be free of all arbitrary restraints and curtailments. In practice,
however, its editors found that one rule was essential: *No word may appear in
more than one list at a main or secondary entry.* For example, *nice* is a synonym at **pleasant** *adj* **1.** The applicable sense of *nice* is found in Webster's
Third New International Dictionary at the entry **¹nice** . . . *adj* . . . **7** (binding substitute) + **7b,** where the definitions are

 : pleasant and satisfying: as . . . **b** : ENJOYABLE. . . .
 PLEASING, DELIGHTFUL <a *nice* time at
 the party> <*nice* and warm by the fire> <we have
 four *nice* bedrooms upstairs to make them
 comfortable —Willa Cather>

However, one might reasonably construe senses **7e** (: MILD, CLEMENT, PLEAS-
ING <the *nice* weather of late spring> <the *nice* old days of the past>) and **7g**
(: FITTING, APPROPRIATE, SUITABLE <the *nice* clothes she wears> <not a *nice*
word for use in church>) as a basis for entering *nice* as a related word as well
as a synonym at **pleasant 1,** while sense **8** in Webster's Third New International Dictionary

 : most inappropriate : UNPLEASANT, UNATTRACTIVE. . . .
 TREACHEROUS — used ironically <a chronic
 alcoholic is certainly a *nice* one to talk about
 temperance> <a *nice* friend, who would have
 me . . . cover myself with eternal infamy —J.A.
 Froude> <got himself in a *nice* fix>

could be construed as evidence for entering *nice* as both a contrasted word
and an antonym at **pleasant 1.** Obviously, the thesaurus user would not be
helped by an entry showing any word in such an involved relationship with
itself.

Labels, Punctuation, and Symbols

Labels Words that are labeled *cap* or *usu* [ally] *cap* in Webster's Third New
International Dictionary are capitalized in this book. Thus, the synonyms
Gehenna, Pandemonium, Sheol, and *Tophet* are so styled at the main entry
hell *n* as are the related words *Styx* and *Tartarus.* A term that is capitalized

in a main-entry *syn* list is also capitalized when it appears as a boldface secondary entry at its own alphabetical position:

Gehenna *n syn* see HELL

If only one entered sense of a word is capitalized, an italic *cap* label followed by a boldface capitalized subhead is attached to the affected sense:

pandemonium *n* **1** *cap* **Pandemonium** *syn* see HELL
  2 *syn* see SINK 1
  3 *syn* see DIN

In addition to the part-of-speech label, an italic plural label may be added when a word or a sense of a word is sometimes, often, usually, or always used in the plural. Typical examples of these labels are found at

years *n pl syn* see OLD AGE

where *pl* indicates that the headword **years** is always plural in form and construction in this particular application, and at

road *n* **1** *often* **roads** *pl syn* see HARBOR 3
  2 *syn* see WAY 1
  3 *syn* see WAY 2

where sense **1** (and only that sense) of the headword **road** is often but not always used in the plural, and at

minutia *n, usu* **minutiae** *pl* **1** *syn* see
  INS AND OUTS
  2 *syn* see TRIVIA

where the label preceding both senses indicates that the headword **minutia** is usually used in the plural in both of these applications, and at the main entry

trivia *n pl but sometimes sing in constr*

where the label is qualified to show that this plural noun may sometimes be used with a singular verb, and at

common *n* **1** **commons** *pl but sing or pl in*
  constr syn see COMMONALTY

which indicates that **common** occurs as a plural noun in sense **1** but may occur with either singular or plural verbs, and at

outdoors *n pl but sing in constr* the space where
  air is unconfined <every night he let the dog
  run in the *outdoors*>

whose label indicates that while the word *outdoors* is a plural noun, it consistently takes a singular verb. Use of these labels conforms to the treatment of plurals in Webster's Third New International Dictionary.

An italic subject guide phrase pointing to something with which the headword is associated may precede a meaning core in a very few instances, as at

set *vb* . . . **11** *of a fowl* to incubate eggs
  by crouching upon them . . .

Punctuation A comma links items (as synonyms, idiomatic equivalents, members of a single group or subgroup of related or contrasted words or of antonyms) that are alike in their relation to the headword, as at

> **conservative** *adj* . . . **2** . . .
>   *syn* controlled, discreet, moderate, reasonable,
>   restrained, temperate, unexcessive, unextreme
>   *rel* cautious, chary, wary; circumspect, politic, proper,
>   prudent
>   *con* expansive, unconstrained; excessive, freewheeling,
>   uncontrolled, unrestrained

A semicolon signals a break in continuity and is used in *rel* and *con* lists (as between the two subgroups in the *rel* and *con* lists at **conservative 2** above) to separate subgroups of words which differ in their relation to the headword. A semicolon is also used to separate antonyms that belong to different classes of opposites, as

> **arise** *vb* **1** *syn* see RISE 4
>   *ant* recline; slump

where the two antonyms are so separated. A semicolon may also appear at the end of a main-entry *syn* list to introduce a compare cross-reference, as shown at **honorable** *adj* **1**:

> *syn* estimable, high-principled, noble,
> sterling, worthy; *compare* VENERABLE 1

Parentheses enclose variant spellings, as at the main entry **cake** *vb* **1** where

> encrust (*or* incrust)

is a synonym, and at the secondary entries, where that particular synonym is styled

> **encrust** (*or* **incrust**) *vb* *syn* see CAKE 1

Parentheses also enclose a particle or particles usually associated with a base word, as

> **adore** *vb* . . . **3** to love, admire, or enjoy excessively . . .
>   *syn* dote (on *or* upon), idolize, worship
>
> **dote** (on *or* upon) *vb* *syn* see ADORE 3

Similarly, parentheses may indicate usage alternatives in idiomatic expressions, as at **slavery** *n* **2** where

> *idiom* . . . the yoke (*or* chains) of slavery

alerts the user that he may choose one of two noun elements when employing this particular idiom. Parentheses are also used in main-entry *syn* lists to enclose plural suffixes of words that are sometimes, often, or usually but not always used in the plural:

> **scad** *n, usu* **scads** *pl* a great number or abundance . . .
>   *syn* gob(s), heap, jillion, load(s), million,
>   oodles, quantities, . . .

Parentheses enclose material indicating a typical or, occasionally, a sole object of reference, as in the meaning core of **express** *vb* **2**

> to give expression to (as a thought, an opinion,
> or an emotion)

where they enclose an adjunct, or at entries such as **abrogate** *vb* **2**

> *ant* establish, fix (*as a right, a quality, or*
>   *a custom*)

where an antonym or a group of antonyms is associated with a particular object or objects of reference — a restriction or limitation to which the thesaurus user should be alerted.

Symbols   A warning symbol is used in this book in the form of the double bars ‖.

The double bars prefixing some terms warn the user that the employment of such a term may involve a problem of diction too complex for presentation in a thesaurus, or a restriction in usage. Consequently, the thesaurus user should consult a dictionary if he is in doubt about the stylistic level or appropriateness of the word or if he is unfamiliar with its meaning. For example, ‖**fat cat** (a synonym of **notable** *n* **1**), ‖**chuff** (a synonym of **sullen** *adj*), and ‖**puxy** (a synonym of **swamp** *n*) are all double-barred in this book because they carry stigmatizing or regional labels in Webster's Third New International Dictionary.

Langenscheidt's
Pocket
Merriam-Webster
Thesaurus

A
Thesaurus
of the
English Language

A

aback *adv syn* see UNAWARES

abaft *adv* toward or at the stern (of a vessel) <headed *abaft* for a smoke>
syn aft, astern
rel after, back, behind
ant forward

abaft *prep* to the rear of <huddled in a nook *abaft* the chimney>
syn back of, behind

abalienate *vb syn* see TRANSFER 4

abandon *vb* **1** to give up without intent to return or reclaim <*abandoned* his family>
syn chuck, desert, forsake, quit, renounce, throw over
rel cast (off), discard, disuse, drop, junk, scrap; reject, repudiate
idiom have done with, leave flat, quit cold, run out on, turn one's back on (*or* upon), walk out on
con hold, keep, possess, retain; redeem, rescue, save; acquire, gain, get, procure, win; cherish, foster
ant reclaim
2 *syn* see RELINQUISH
ant retain

abandon *n* **1** *syn* see UNCONSTRAINT
2 carefree disregard for consequences <behave with *abandon*>
syn impulsiveness, uninhibitedness, unrestraint; *compare* UNCONSTRAINT
rel freedom, liberty, license; exuberance, heedlessness, laxity, laxness, looseness, unruliness, wildness; incontinence, licentiousness, wantonness; fun, games, play, sport
con constraint, inhibitedness, inhibition, restraint; repression, suppression
ant self-restraint

abandoned *adj* **1** *syn* see DERELICT 1
2 free from moral restraint <led a thoroughly *abandoned* life>
syn dissolute, licentious, profligate, reprobate, self-abandoned, unprincipled
rel debased, debauched, depraved, perverted, riotous; incorrigible; lascivious, lecherous, lewd, wanton; corrupt, degenerate

idiom dead to honor, gone to the bad, lost to shame, rotten (to *or* at) the core
con ethical, high-principled, moral, reputable, virtuous; correct, decent, decorous, proper, seemly
ant scrupulous, upright

abase *vb syn* see HUMBLE
rel demote, diminish, downgrade, reduce; fawn, grovel, toady; cower, cringe, truckle
con elevate, lift, raise
ant exalt; extol

abash *vb syn* see EMBARRASS 1
rel abase, demean, humble, humiliate
idiom make one eat humble pie
ant embolden, reassure

abashment *n syn* see EMBARRASSMENT

abate *vb* **1** *syn* see ABOLISH 1
2 *syn* see ANNIHILATE 2
3 *syn* see DECREASE
4 to lessen in force or intensity <the storm *abated* slowly>
syn ‖bate, die (down *or* away), ease off, ebb, fall, let up, lull, moderate, relent, slacken, subside, wane
rel decrease, diminish, dwindle, lessen, weaken
idiom run its course
con augment, expand, extend, increase; mount, rage, soar, surge
ant revive; rise

abatement *n syn* see DEDUCTION 1
con enlargement, increase
ant addition

abbreviate *vb syn* see SHORTEN
rel attenuate, extenuate
con enlarge, increase; amplify, dilate, expand
ant lengthen; extend

ABC *n* **1** *usu* **ABC's** *pl syn* see ALPHABET 1
2 *often* **ABC's** *pl syn* see ALPHABET 2

abdicate *vb* **1** to part formally or definitely with a position of honor or power <the king *abdicated* the throne in order to marry a commoner>
syn demit, renounce, resign; *compare* RELINQUISH

rel abandon, leave, relinquish, surrender; drop; withdraw
con appropriate, arrogate, confiscate; grab, seize, take over, wrest
ant assume, usurp
2 *syn* see DISCARD
con keep, retain, treasure

abdomen *n* the part of the body between the chest and the pelvis <intense pain in the lower *abdomen*>
syn belly, ‖gut, paunch, stomach, tummy, venter
rel bay window, ‖breadbasket, corporation, pod, pot, potbelly; middle, midriff, midsection

abduct *vb syn* see KIDNAP
rel grab, seize

abecedarian *n syn* see AMATEUR 2

aberrant *adj* **1** *syn* see ABNORMAL 1
rel different, disparate, divergent; eccentric, odd, peculiar, strange; exceptional, unusual
con natural, normal, regular, typical; customary, usual, wonted
ant true (*to a type*)
2 *syn* see ERRANT 2

aberration *n* **1** *syn* see DEVIATION 1
rel abnormality; mistake, slip; curiosity, oddity, prodigy, rarity
con average, mean, norm; normality
ant conformity; regularity
2 *syn* see INSANITY 1
ant soundness (*of mind*)

abet *vb* **1** *syn* see INCITE
rel egg, exhort, goad, prod, spur, urge; advocate, countenance, encourage, endorse
con forbid, prevent, prohibit; debar, deter, discourage
2 *syn* see HELP 1

abettor *n syn* see CONFEDERATE

abeyance *n* a state of temporary inactivity <the warm dry weather kept his asthma in *abey- ance*>
syn abeyancy, cold storage, doldrums, dormancy, intermission, interruption, latency, quiescence, quiescency, suspension
rel break, interval, pause, respite
con activeness, activity, stir
ant continuance

abeyancy *n syn* see ABEYANCE
ant continuancy

abeyant *adj syn* see LATENT
rel deferred, intermitted, postponed, stayed, suppressed; repressed
con refreshed, renewed, restored
ant active, operative; revived

abhor *vb* **1** *syn* see HATE
2 *syn* see DESPISE
con dote (on *or* upon), like, love
ant admire

abhorrence *n syn* see ABOMINATION 2
rel distaste, repellency; dismay, horror
con affection, attachment, love
ant admiration; enjoyment

abhorrent *adj* **1** *syn* see HATEFUL 2
ant admirable

2 *syn* see REPUGNANT 1
rel antipathetic; uncongenial, unsympathetic
con alluring, attractive, captivating; enticing, seductive, tempting
ant congenial

abide *vb* **1** *syn* see STAY 2
rel adhere, cleave, cling, stick; dwell, live, reside
con go, leave, quit; move, remove, shift
ant depart
2 *syn* see CONTINUE 1
rel linger; exist, subsist
con avoid, elude, escape, evade
ant pass
3 *syn* see BEAR 10
rel accept, receive; accede, consent
idiom put up with
4 *syn* see RESIDE 1

abiding *adj syn* see SURE 2
rel durable, lasting, perdurable, persistent
con ephemeral, impermanent, short-lived, transient, transitory

ability *n* **1** physical, mental, or legal power to perform <he has the *ability* to accomplish whatever he sets his mind to>
syn adequacy, capability, capacity, competence, might, qualification, qualifiedness
rel address, adroitness, cleverness, dexterity; aptitude, aptness, facility, knack
idiom what it takes
con impotence, inadequacy, incapability, incompetence
ant inability
2 natural or acquired proficiency especially in a particular activity <he has unusual *ability* in planning and designing>
syn command, expertise, expertism, expertness, knack, know-how, mastership, mastery, skill
rel adroitness, deftness, efficiency, handiness, proficiency; ingenuity, resourcefulness; talent
con inadequacy, incompetence, ineffectualness, unfitness; futility, futility, inanity

abject *adj syn* see DOWNTRODDEN

abjure *vb* to give up (something formerly adhered to) irrevocably and usually solemnly or formally <an immigrant solemnly *abjuring* allegiance to his former country>
syn forswear, palinode, recall, recant, retract, take back, unsay, withdraw
rel disavow, disown, renounce, repudiate; abandon, desert, forsake; cede, relinquish, surrender
idiom eat one's words

ablaze *adj* **1** *syn* see BURNING 1
2 *syn* see ALIGHT 2

able *adj* possessed of or marked by a high level of efficiency and ability <an *able* student always near the head of his class>
syn au fait, capable, competent, good, proper, qualified, wicked
rel effective, effectual, efficient; expert, proficient, skilled, skillful; alert, clever, keen, sharp; brainy, brilliant, intelligent, smart; enterprising, go-ahead, up-and-coming
con ineffective, ineffectual, inefficient; incapable, incompetent, unqualified; fair, indifferent, mediocre; lackluster, maladroit

---

syn synonym(s)   *rel* related word(s)
ant antonym(s)   *con* contrasted word(s)
idiom idiomatic equivalent(s)
‖ use limited; if in doubt, see a dictionary

ant inept; unable

abnegation *n syn see* RENUNCIATION

abnormal *adj* **1** departing significantly from the normal or a norm <the *abnormal* rains caused flooding>

syn aberrant, anomalous, atypical, deviant, deviative, heteroclite, preternatural, unrepresentative, untypical

rel divergent, offtype; irregular, unnatural; uncustomary, unusual, unwonted; heteromorphic; paratypic

con common, familiar, natural, ordinary, regular, typical; customary, usual, wonted

ant normal

2 *syn see* IRREGULAR 1

abode *n syn see* HABITATION 2

abolish *vb* **1** to bring to an end often by formal or concerted action <*abolish* a tax>

syn abate, abrogate, annihilate, annul, circumduct, invalidate, negate, nullify, quash, undo, vitiate

rel cancel, disallow, disannul, repeal, rescind, revoke, vacate

idiom bring to naught, make void, set aside

con conserve, preserve, save; keep, retain

2 *syn see* ANNIHILATE 2

con found, institute

ant establish

abominable *adj syn see* HATEFUL 2

rel accursed, cursed; loathsome, offensive, repugnant, revolting

con applaudable, commendable

ant laudable (*as practices, customs*); delightful, enjoyable

abominate *vb syn see* HATE

rel curse, damn, objurgate

idiom hold in abomination, take an aversion to

con admire, regard

ant enjoy; esteem

abomination *n* **1** one that is a source of utter disgust or intense dislike <found the new tax form an *abomination* of confused complexity>

syn anathema, bête noire, black beast, bugbear, detestation, hate

rel annoyance, pest, plague, trial; bogey, bugaboo, incubus

con delectation, delight, joy, pleasure; treasure

2 a feeling of extreme disgust and dislike <they hold every indulgence in *abomination*>

syn abhorrence, aversion, detestation, hate, hatred, horror, loathing, repugnance, repugnancy, repulsion, revulsion

rel contempt, despite, disdain, scorn; disfavor, dislike, disrelish, distaste

con admiration, regard, respect; fondness, liking, relish, taste; approbation, approval, countenance, favor; acceptance, tolerance

ant esteem; enjoyment

aboriginal *adj syn see* NATIVE 2

rel primeval, primitive, primordial, pristine; barbarian, barbaric, barbarous, savage

con advanced, progressive; civilized, cultured; sequent, successive

abort *vb syn* CANCEL 2

rel end, terminate; scrap, scratch

abortion *n syn see* FREAK 2

abortive *adj syn see* FUTILE

rel unformed; immature, unmatured, unripe

con accomplished, completed, concluded, finished

ant consummated

abound *vb syn see* TEEM

abounding *adj syn see* ALIVE 5

rel full, jammed, packed, stuffed

about *adv* **1** in every direction <looked carefully *about*>

syn around, round, round about

2 in a circuitous way or course <took the long way *about*>

syn circuitously, round about

3 *syn see* NEARLY

4 here or there without plan or order <left his tools lying *about*>

syn anyhow, any which way, anywise, around, at random, haphazard, haphazardly, helter-skelter, random, randomly

rel back and forth, hither and thither, to and fro; aimlessly, carelessly, casually

5 in the vicinity <talked to the people standing *about*>

syn near, near-at-hand, nearby

idiom close by

6 in the opposite direction <he turned *about* and saw her>

syn again, around, back, backward, in reverse, round, round about

idiom in one's course

about *prep* **1** in the vicinity of <*about* five miles to go>

syn around, circa, close on, near, nearby, nigh

idiom hard by, not far from

2 *syn see* APROPOS

idiom in point of, with regard to

3 *syn see* OVER 3

4 here and there upon or within <traveled *about* the country>

syn round, through, throughout

idiom all over

about–face *n syn see* REVERSAL 1

above *adv* **1** *syn see* OVER 4

ant below

2 higher on the same page or on a preceding page <earlier examples appear *above*>

syn supra

ant below, infra

above *prep* **1** *syn see* OVER 1

ant below

2 *syn see* BEYOND 2

aboveboard *adj syn see* STRAIGHTFORWARD 2

rel open, scrupulous; artless, ingenuous, unsophisticated

con clandestine, covert, furtive, secret, surreptitious; deceitful; crooked, devious, oblique

ant underhand, underhanded

abracadabra *n syn see* GIBBERISH 3

rel mystification; argot, cant, jargon

abrade *vb* **1** to injure or flaw by frictional action <wind-driven sand *abraded* the glass>

syn chafe, corrade, erode, gall, graze, rub, ruffle, wear

rel corrode, eat away, fret; grate, rasp, scrape

2 syn see CHAFE 3
rel burn
3 syn see ANNOY 1
rel disorganize, disturb, flurry, rattle; confuse, distract, perturb
con calm, relieve, soothe

Abraham's bosom *n syn* see HEAVEN 2

abreast *adj* **1 syn** see UP-TO-DATE
2 syn see FAMILIAR 3

abridge *vb* **1** to make less by in some manner restricting <laws that *abridge* freedom of speech>
syn curtail, diminish, lessen, minify
rel limit, narrow, reduce, restrict; minimize
con augment, broaden, enlarge, extend
ant amplify
2 syn see SHORTEN
con amplify, augment, enlarge, increase
ant expand, extend

abridgment *n* a shortened version of a larger work or treatment produced by condensing and omitting without basic alteration of intent and language <an *abridgment* of a dictionary>
syn abstract, boildown, breviary, breviate, brief, condensation, conspectus, epitome, synopsis
rel aperçu, compendium, digest, outline, précis, sketch, syllabus; capsule, summary; sum, summation, summing-up
con elaboration; paraphrase
ant expansion

abroad *adv syn* see OVERSEAS

abrogate *vb* **1 syn** see ANNUL 4
rel abate, extinguish
con establish, found; confirm, ratify
ant institute (*as by enacting or decreeing*)
2 syn see ABOLISH 1
rel extinguish; blot out, cancel, obliterate; ruin, wreck
con support, uphold
ant establish, fix (*as a right, a quality, or a custom*)

abrupt *adj* **1 syn** see PRECIPITATE 1
rel hastened; casual, informal, unceremonious; quick, speedy
con dilatory, laggard; easy, relaxed
ant deliberate, leisurely
2 syn see BLUFF
rel brisk, crisp, sharp; impetuous, quick, ready
con calm, easy, relaxed
3 syn see STEEP 1
rel perpendicular, plumb, vertical
con inclined, slanting; flat, level, plane, smooth
ant sloping

abruptly *adv syn* see SHORT 1

abscess *n* a localized swollen area of infection containing pus <had an *abscess* on his leg>
syn boil, carbuncle, furuncle, pimple, pustule
rel lesion, sore, trauma; botch, ulcer

abscond *vb syn* see ESCAPE 1

rel go, leave, quit, withdraw
idiom do the disappearing act, skip out, take French leave
con render, surrender, yield
ant give (oneself) up

absence *n* the state of being absent or missing <the *absence* of news was disturbing>
syn dearth, default, defect, lack, ‖miss, privation, want; *compare* FAILURE 3
rel deficiency, drought, inadequacy, insufficiency; exigency, necessity, need; vacuum, void; nonappearance, nonattendance
con abundance, copiousness, plenty
ant presence

absent *adj* **1** not now present <all missed their *absent* friend>
syn away, gone, lacking, missing, omitted, wanting
ant present
2 syn see ABSTRACTED
rel absorbed; forgetful, heedless
con attending, hearkening, listening; considerate, thoughtful
ant attentive

absentminded *adj syn* see ABSTRACTED
rel unnoticing, unobserving, unperceiving, unseeing; heedless, inattentive
idiom lost in thought
con alert; aware
ant wide-awake

absolute *adj* **1 syn** see PERFECT 2
rel pure, sheer, simple
con circumscribed, limited, partial, restricted
2 syn see PURE 2
rel abstract, ideal; real, true
con imperfect, incomplete
ant mixed, qualified
3 syn see UTTER
4 exercising power or authority without external restraint <an *absolute* monarch>
syn arbitrary, autarchic, autocratic, despotic, monocratic, tyrannical, tyrannous; *compare* TOTALITARIAN 1
rel dictatorial, magisterial; authoritarian, totalitarian; domineering, imperious, masterful; plenipotential, plenipotentiary, unlimited
con circumscribed, limited, restrained, restricted; constitutional, lawful
5 syn see ACTUAL 2
6 syn see ULTIMATE 3
rel ideal, transcendent, transcendental; autonomous, free, independent, sovereign; boundless, eternal, infinite
con circumscribed, limited, restricted; conditional, contingent, dependent

absolutely *adv syn* see EASILY 2

absolution *n syn* see PARDON
rel condonation
con censure, reprehension, reprobation
ant condemnation

absolve *vb* **1 syn** see EXEMPT
2 syn see EXCULPATE
rel discharge, free, release
con condemn, doom, sentence; chasten, discipline, punish
ant charge (with), hold (to)

absorb *vb* **1** to take in and make a part of one's being <*absorb* knowledge from reading>

---

syn assimilate, imbibe, incorporate, inhaust, insorb

rel embody, imbue, impregnate, infuse, permeate

con disgorge, eject, expel, vomit; discharge, eliminate, emit, give off, pass

ant exude, give out

2 *syn* see MONOPOLIZE

rel concern, engage, immerse, involve, preoccupy

con diffuse, disperse, scatter

ant dissipate (*as time, attention*)

absorbed *adj syn* see INTENT

rel involved

idiom caught up in, up to the elbows (*or* ears) in

con apathetic, disinterested, indifferent, unconcerned; uninterested; absent, abstracted

ant distracted

absorbing *adj syn* see ENGROSSING

ant irksome

abstain *vb* **1** *syn* see DENY 3

rel abnegate, eschew, forgo; decline, refuse, reject, spurn

idiom dispense with, do without, let alone

con pamper; gratify, regale; sate, satiate, surfeit

ant indulge

2 *syn* see REFRAIN 1

abstemious *adj* marked by restraint in satisfying desires (as for food, drink, or pleasure) <an *abstemious* man, little given to self-indulgence>

syn abstentious, abstinent, continent, self-restraining, sober, temperate; *compare* SOBER 3

rel self-abnegating, self-denying; ascetic, austere; sparing

con greedy, rapacious, voracious; epicurean, sybaritic, voluptuous

ant gluttonous

abstentious *adj syn* see ABSTEMIOUS

ant gluttonous

abstinence *n syn* see TEMPERANCE 2

rel renunciation

con gorging, sating, surfeiting; immoderateness, overdoing, unrestraint; crapulence, excess, extravagance

ant self-indulgence

abstinent *adj syn* see ABSTEMIOUS

ant gluttonous

abstract *adj* **1** having conceptual rather than concrete existence <the *abstract* perfect society>

syn hypothetical, ideal, theoretical, transcendent, transcendental

rel academic, impractical, utopian, visionary; speculative, undemonstrable; conceptual, notional; inconcrete

con corporeal, material, objective, phenomenal, physical; actual, factual, real

ant concrete

2 *syn* see NEUTRAL

abstract *n syn* see ABRIDGMENT

con enlargement, expansion

ant amplification

abstract *vb* **1** *syn* see DETACH

rel divide, part, separate

con insinuate, interpolate, interpose

ant insert, introduce

2 *syn* see STEAL 1

abstracted *adj* withdrawn in mind and inattentive to external matters <seemed *abstracted* and remote>

syn absent, absentminded, bemused, distrait, faraway, inconscient, lost, preoccupied

rel engrossed, intent, rapt; oblivious, unmindful, unminding; heedless, inattentive

idiom in a brown study, lost in thought, lost to the world

con attentive, vigilant, watchful, wide-awake; noticing, noting, observant, seeing

ant alert

abstruse *adj syn* see RECONDITE

rel complex, complicated, intricate, knotty; abstract, hypothetical, ideal

con clear, evident, manifest, palpable; clear, lucid, perspicuous; easy, facile, simple

ant obvious, plain

absurd *adj syn* see FOOLISH 2

rel comic, droll, funny; asinine, fatuous, simple; irrational, unreasonable

con logical, ratiocinative, subtle

ant rational, sensible

absurdity *n syn* see FOOLISHNESS

abundance *n syn* see PROSPERITY 2

rel adequacy, competence, enough, plenty, sufficiency; lavishness, prodigality

idiom enough and to spare

con deficiency, inadequacy, insufficiency, lack, paucity

abundant *adj syn* see PLENTIFUL

rel lavish, lush, luxuriant, profuse; crammed, crowded, thick; common

idiom in good supply

con infrequent, rare, uncommon; inadequate, scanty

ant scarce

abuse *vb* **1** *syn* see DECRY 2

ant praise

2 to put to a bad or improper use <*abuse* the prerogatives of office>

syn misapply, misemploy, mishandle, misimprove, misuse, pervert, prostitute

rel mar, spoil; corrupt, debase, desecrate, profane

idiom make ill use of

con esteem, respect

3 *syn* see EXPLOIT 2

4 to treat without compassion and usually in a hurtful manner <parents who *abuse* children>

syn ill-treat, ill-use, maltreat, mistreat, misuse, outrage

rel damage, harm, hurt, impair, injure; oppress, persecute, wrong; manhandle, mess (up)

idiom do one dirt, do violence to

con cherish, prize, treasure; esteem, revere, reverence, venerate

ant honor, respect

abuse *n* vehemently and usually coarsely expressed condemnation or disapproval <had an unequal vocabulary of *abuse*>

syn billingsgate, contumely, invective, obloquy, scurrility, vituperation

rel calumny, defamation, malignment, mud, vilification; cursing, profanity, swearing; berating, railing, rating, reviling

con acclaim, laudation, praise; applause, commendation, compliment
ant adulation

abusive *adj* coarse, insulting, and contemptuous in character or utterance <an *abusive* denunciation>
syn contumelious, invective, opprobrious, scurrile, scurrilous, truculent, vituperative, vituperatory, vituperous
rel affronting, insulting, offending, outraging; dirty, odious, offensive; aspersing, maligning, vilifying
con acclaiming, extolling, lauding, praising; eulogistic, panegyrical; flattering
ant complimentary; respectful

abut *vb syn* see ADJOIN

abutting *adj syn* see ADJACENT 3
rel connecting, joining; impinging
con detached, disengaged; disassociated, disconnected, disjoined, parted, separated

abysm *n syn* see GULF 2

abysmal *adj* 1 *syn* see BOTTOMLESS 2
2 *syn* see DEEP 1
rel illimitable, infinite

abyss *n* 1 *syn* see HELL
2 *syn* see GULF 2
3 *syn* see DEPTH 2

academic *adj* 1 *syn* see PEDANTIC
con ignorant, illiterate, unlettered; down-to-earth, everyday, practical, realistic, straightforward
2 *syn* see THEORETICAL 1
rel impractical, utopian, visionary; chimerical, imaginary

accede *vb syn* see ASSENT
rel concur, cooperate; allow, let, permit
con decline; balk, shy, stick; expostulate, kick, object, protest; fight, oppose, resist, withstand
ant demur

accelerate *vb syn* see SPEED 3
rel drive, impel
idiom get going, make up for lost time
con clog, hamper; delay, detain, slow; decelerate, retard

accent *n* 1 *syn* see INFLECTION
2 *syn* see EMPHASIS
rel cadence, meter, rhythm; beat, pulsation, pulse, throb

accentuation *n syn* see EMPHASIS
con evenness, sameness, steadiness, uniformity
ant inaccentuation

accept *vb* 1 *syn* see APPROVE 1
rel fancy, like, relish; admire, esteem
con discountenance, disesteem, dislike, disrelish
ant reject
2 to take or sustain without protest or repining <a losing candidate must *accept* the decision of the electorate>
syn bear (with), endure, pocket, swallow, tolerate, tough (out); *compare* BEAR 10
rel acquiesce (in), agree (to *or* with), assent (to); subscribe (to); respect; bow, capitulate, yield

idiom abide by, put up with
con disavow, disown; brush (aside), deny, reject, repudiate
3 *syn* see BELIEVE 1
4 *syn* see APPREHEND 1

acceptable *adj syn* see DECENT 4
rel average, commonplace, ordinary; bearable, endurable, supportable
con insupportable, intolerable, unbearable, unendurable
ant unacceptable

acceptably *adv syn* see WELL 4

acceptant *adj syn* see RECEPTIVE 1

acceptation *n syn* see MEANING 1

accepted *adj* 1 *syn* see USUAL 1
rel conventional, established, recognized; correct, orthodox, proper, right
idiom according to custom (*or* use)
con irregular, questionable, unacceptable, unconventional; incongruent, unconformable, unorthodox
2 *syn* see ORTHODOX 1

acceptive *adj syn* see RECEPTIVE 1

access *n* 1 *syn* see ATTACK 3
rel onset; taking; pang, stitch, twinge
2 *syn* see OUTBURST 1
3 *syn* see DOOR 2
rel passage, route
con departure, retreat, withdrawal
ant egress; outlet

accessible *adj* 1 *syn* see OPEN 4
rel approachable
con limited, restricted; remote
2 *syn* see OPEN 5
ant inaccessible

accession *n syn* see ADDITION
ant discard

accessory *n* 1 *syn* see APPENDAGE
rel accompaniment, concomitant; accretion, addition, increment
2 *syn* see CONFEDERATE
ant principal

accessory *adj syn* see AUXILIARY
rel secondary, subordinate, tributary; coincident, concomitant, concurrent; adventitious, incidental
con constitutional, ingrained, inherent, intrinsic; cardinal, fundamental, vital; essential, indispensable, necessary
ant constituent, integral

accident *n* 1 absence of positive plan or intent <we stopped there by *accident*>
syn chance, fortuity, hap, luck
rel fluke, fortune, hazard
con design, premeditation
ant intent
2 a chance event bringing injury, loss, or distress <the school was closed by an *accident* to the heating system>
syn casualty, misadventure, mischance, mishap
rel calamity, catastrophe, disaster, tragedy; misfortune; chance, destiny, fate, kismet
con foreordination, predestination

accidental *adj* resulting from chance <an *accidental* meeting>
syn casual, chance, contingent, fluky, fortuitous, incidental, odd; *compare* RANDOM. UNINTENTIONAL
rel conditional, dependent; coincident, coincidental; inadvertent, undesigned, unin-

---

syn synonym(s)   *rel* related word(s)
ant antonym(s)   *con* contrasted word(s)
idiom idiomatic equivalent(s)
‖ use limited; if in doubt, see a dictionary

tended, unintentional, unmeant, unplanned, unpurposed, unwitting

con designed, intended, purposed; constitutional, inherent, intrinsic; innate

ant planned; essential

accidentally *adv syn* see INCIDENTALLY 1

acclaim *vb syn* see COMMEND 2

rel cheer, root (for); exalt, magnify; glorify, honor

con berate, rate, revile; damn, execrate, objurgate; censure, denounce

ant vituperate

acclaim *n syn* see APPLAUSE

rel homage, honor, reverence; éclat, glory

con abuse, invective, obloquy; censure, condemnation, denunciation, reprobation

ant vituperation

acclamation *n syn* see APPLAUSE

acclimate *vb syn* see HARDEN 2

acclimatize *vb syn* see HARDEN 2

accolade *n syn* see HONOR 2

accommodate *vb* **1** *syn* see ADAPT

rel bow, defer, submit, yield; alter, change, modify, vary

con alienate, estrange

ant constrain

2 *syn* see HARMONIZE 3

3 *syn* see OBLIGE 2

rel cater (to), humor, indulge

con annoy, harass, harry; irk, vex, worry

ant incommode

4 *syn* see CONTAIN 2

rel encase, enclose

5 *syn* see HARBOR 2

accommodations *n pl* shelter, food, and services (as at a hotel) <searched for *accommodations* as night drew near>

syn lodging, lodgment, room and board

rel bed, room; keep; housing, shelter

idiom bed and breakfast

accompaniment *n* **1** something added to a principal thing usually to increase its impact or effectiveness <her song had a soft orchestral *accompaniment*>

syn augmentation, complement, enhancement, enrichment

rel accessory, addition, supplement; aid, assistance, help

2 an accompanying individual, situation, or occurrence <smog is an inevitable *accompaniment* of excessive numbers of automobiles>

syn associate, companion, concomitant, consort, fellow, mate

rel attendant, colleague, comrade, partner; corollary, equivalent

accompany *vb* to go or be together with <*accompanied* his wife to the theater>

syn attend, bear, ‖bring, ‖carry, chaperon, companion, company, conduct, consort (with), convoy, escort

rel associate, combine, join, link; defend, guard, protect, safeguard, shield; guide, lead, pilot, steer

idiom bear one company, go along with, go hand in hand with

con leave, quit, withdraw; abandon, forsake

accompanying *adj syn* see CONCOMITANT

accomplice *n syn* see CONFEDERATE

rel aider, assistant, helper; flunky, stooge

accomplish *vb syn* see GAIN 1

accomplished *adj syn* see CONSUMMATE 1

rel adept, expert, masterly, proficient; all-around, many-sided, versatile

accomplishment *n* **1** *syn* see ACQUIREMENT

rel art, craft, skill; adeptness, expertise, expertness, proficiency

2 *syn* see ACTION 1

accord *vb* **1** *syn* see AGREE 4

rel coincide, concur; blend, coalesce, fuse, merge

con differ, disagree; compare, contrast

ant conflict

2 *syn* see GRANT 1

rel allot

con deny, gainsay; refuse; detain, hold, reserve

ant withhold

3 *syn* see GIVE 2

accord *n* **1** *syn* see HARMONY 2

rel affinity, attraction, empathy, sympathy; solidarity, union

idiom community of interest(s)

con conflict, contention, difference; animosity, antipathy, hostility

ant dissension, strife; antagonism

2 *syn* see AGREEMENT 2

3 *syn* see HARMONY 1

accordant *adj syn* see HARMONIOUS 2

accordingly *adv syn* see THEREFORE

idiom by reason of that (or this), for that (or this) reason

according to *prep syn* see BY 5

accost *vb* **1** *syn* see ADDRESS 7

rel buttonhole

con ignore, overlook, slight; avoid, elude, evade, shun

2 to approach boldly or in a challenging or sometimes a defensive manner <*accosted* by a beggar who demanded money>

syn confront, face, front

rel affront, insult, offend, outrage; annoy, bother; challenge, dare, outface

idiom come face to face with, meet face to face

3 *syn* see ADDRESS 4

rel call (to), hail, halloo; buttonhole; dog, hound, pester, worry

accouchement *n syn* see CONFINEMENT 2

account *n* **1** *syn* see BILL 1

2 *syn* see USE 3

con immateriality, inconsequence, insignificance, unimportance; bootlessness, fruitlessness, futility

3 *syn* see WORTH 1

4 *syn* see REGARD 4

rel consequence, dignity, distinction, note; reputation, repute

5 *syn* see EXPLANATION 2

6 *syn* see SCORE 4

7 a statement of real or purported events, occurrences, or conditions <wrote an *account* of his travels>

syn chronicle, history, narrative, report, story, version; *compare* STORY 2

account *vb* **1** *syn* see CONSIDER 3

rel appraise, assess, estimate, evaluate, rate; esteem

con underestimate, underrate, undervalue

2 syn see EXPLAIN 3
rel answer, elucidate, expound, interpret
accountable *adj syn* see RESPONSIBLE
con absolute, arbitrary, autocratic; imperious, magisterial, masterful
ant unaccountable
accouter *vb syn* see FURNISH 1
rel attire, dress; adorn, deck, decorate, embellish; fix (up), prepare, ready
accouterment *n, usu* **accouterments** *pl syn* see EQUIPMENT
rel appointment(s); furnishing(s); bravery, regalia, trappings
accredit *vb* **1 syn** see APPROVE 2
rel commend, recommend; attest, certify, vouch (for)
con belittle, deprecate, depreciate, disapprove; reject, repudiate
2 syn see ASCRIBE
3 syn see AUTHORIZE 1
rel introduce, present
accretion *n syn* see ADDITION
rel enlargement; attachment, joining, uniting; adjunct, appendage
accroach *vb* **1 syn** see ARROGATE 1
2 syn see APPROPRIATE 1
accumulate *vb* to bring together and form a store of <*accumulate* knowledge>
syn amass, cumulate, garner, hive, lay up, roll up, stockpile, store (up), uplay; *compare* HOARD
rel assemble, collect, gather, lay by, lay down, lay in; heap, mass, pile, stock; fund, hoard, treasure
idiom squirrel away
con decrease, diminish, lessen; deal, dispense, distribute, dole (out); dispel, disperse, scatter; consume, expend, spend, use, use up
ant dissipate
accumulation *n* a mass, quantity, or number that has accumulated <an *accumulation* of rubbish>
syn agglomeration, aggregation, amassment, collection, conglomeration, cumulation, hoard, trove
rel bank, heap, mass, pile; cumulus, reserve, stock, store
con dispersal, dispersion, scattering
accumulative *adj syn* see CUMULATIVE
rel aggregative, conglomerative; augmentative, multiplicative
con contractile, contractive, reducing, reductive; dispelling, dispersing, dispersive, dissipative, scattering
accuracy *n syn* see PRECISION
accurate *adj* **1 syn** see CORRECT 2
con slipshod, slovenly; careless, heedless, lax
ant inaccurate
2 syn see CERTAIN 3
accurately *adv syn* see JUST 1
accursed *adj syn* see EXECRABLE 1
rel abhorrent, abominable, detestable, hateful, odious; offensive, repugnant, revolting

con admirable, estimable; honorable; divine, holy, sacred
ant blessed
accuse *vb* to declare one guilty of a fault or offense <*accused* her daughter of neglecting her children>
syn arraign, charge, criminate, impeach, incriminate, inculpate, indict, tax
rel blame, censure, criticize, denounce, reprobate; complain
idiom bring charges (against), point the finger at, prefer charges (against)
con absolve, acquit, exonerate, vindicate; accept, approve, endorse, sanction
ant exculpate
accustom *vb* to make something familiar or acceptable through use or experience <*accustom* oneself to city life>
syn familiarize, habituate, inure, use, wont
rel accommodate, adapt, adjust; acclimatize, harden, season
con alienate, estrange, wean; abjure, reject, repudiate; rebuff, repel, repulse, scorn
ant disaccustom
accustomed *adj* **1 syn** see HABITUAL 2
2 syn see USUAL 1
rel commonplace, everyday; conventional, regulation, standard
con infrequent, occasional, uncommon; erratic, odd, peculiar, queer, singular
ant unaccustomed
ace *n* **1 syn** see HAIR
2 syn see PARTICLE
acedia *n syn* see SLOTH 2
acerb *adj* **1 syn** see SOUR 1
2 syn see SARCASTIC
acerbate *vb syn* see EXACERBATE
acerbic *adj* **1 syn** see SOUR 1
2 syn see SARCASTIC
acerbity *n* **1 syn** see ACRIMONY
rel acidity, sourness, tartness; crabbedness, dourness, saturninity, surliness; acridity, bitterness; harshness, roughness
con blandness, gentleness, mildness, smoothness; amiability, complaisance, good nature
ant mellowness
2 syn see SARCASM
acetose *adj syn* see SOUR 1
ache *vb* **1 syn** see HURT 4
2 syn see COMPASSIONATE
rel deplore; sorrow (over); comfort, console, solace
3 syn see LONG
ache *n syn* see PAIN 1
rel injury; rack
con alleviation, assuagement, mitigation, relief; comfort, ease
acheronian *adj syn* see GLOOMY 3
acherontic *adj syn* see GLOOMY 3
achieve *vb* **1 syn** see PERFORM 2
rel complete, conclude, finish; conquer, overcome, surmount
idiom bring to a happy issue, bring to pass
con begin, commence, start
ant fail (in *or* to do)
2 syn see GAIN 1
rel acquire, get, obtain, secure; actualize; arrive, come
idiom gain one's end

---

syn synonym(s)   *rel* related word(s)
ant antonym(s)   *con* contrasted word(s)
idiom idiomatic equivalent(s)
‖ use limited; if in doubt, see a dictionary

con depart, deviate, swerve; avoid, elude, escape, shun
ant miss
achievement n 1 syn see FEAT 2
   con omission, slighting
   ant failure
   2 syn see ACQUIREMENT
Achilles' heel n syn see SOFT SPOT 2
aching adj syn see PAINFUL 1
   rel achy
acicular adj syn see POINTED 1
aciculate adj syn see POINTED 1
acid adj syn see SOUR 1
   con bland, mild, neutral
   ant sweet; alkaline, basic
acidulous adj syn see SOUR 1
   rel biting, cutting, sharp; piquant, pungent
   con bland, mild, neutral; mellow, smooth, suave
   ant saccharine
acknowledge vb 1 to show often grudgingly by word or deed that one knows of and agrees to or with something <*acknowledge* the justice of a complaint>
   syn admit, allow, avow, concede, confess, fess (up), grant, let on, own, own up
   rel disclose, divulge, reveal, tell; announce, declare, proclaim, publish
   con disallow, disavow, disown, ‖nix, reject; contradict, gainsay, impugn, negate, negative
   ant deny
   2 to take notice of and accept as being as stated <he is generally *acknowledged* to be the leader in his profession>
   syn admit, agree, recognize
   rel accept, receive; concede, consider, deem, hold, view
   con disregard, neglect, slight; reject, repudiate, spurn
   ant ignore
acknowledgment n syn see CREDIT 4
acme n syn see APEX 2
acoustic adj syn see AUDITORY
acquaint vb 1 syn see INTRODUCE 4
   idiom make acquainted
   2 syn see INFORM 2
   rel disclose, divulge, reveal; accustom, habituate
   con hold, hold back, reserve, withhold; conceal, hide
acquaintance n 1 knowledge of something based on personal exposure <had a considerable *acquaintance* with modern poetry>
   syn experience, familiarity, intimacy, inwardness
   rel apprehension, grasp, ken; appreciation, awareness, consciousness
   con inexperience, unfamiliarity; greenness, verdancy
   2 syn see FRIEND
   rel associate, companion, comrade, crony
   con outsider, stranger
acquainted adj syn see FAMILIAR 3
acquiesce vb syn see ASSENT
   rel accommodate, adapt, adjust, reconcile; bow, coincide, concur
   con balk, demur, shy (away); kick, protest, remonstrate; differ, dissent
   ant object

acquiescence n weak or passive agreement to what is asked or demanded <his childish *acquiescence* to all claims on his time>
   syn compliance, conformity, resignation
   rel complaisance; submissiveness; deference
   con contumaciousness, insubordination; independence, self-assurance
   ant rebellion, rebelliousness
acquiescent adj syn see PASSIVE 2
acquire vb 1 syn see GET 1
   rel achieve, reach; add
   con alienate, convey, transfer; abandon, relinquish, surrender, yield
   ant forfeit
   2 syn see EARN 1
   rel accumulate, amass, collect, cumulate, garner
   3 syn see DEVELOP 4
acquirement n a power or skill that results from persistent endeavor and cultivation <proud of his scholastic *acquirements*>
   syn accomplishment, achievement, acquisition, attainment, finish
   rel accretion, addition; advance, advancement; education, erudition, knowledge
   con dearth, defect, lack, privation, want
acquisition n syn see ACQUIREMENT
   rel accession, increment; assets, belongings, means, possessions
acquisitive adj syn see COVETOUS
   rel demanding, exacting, exigent
   con eschewing, forbearing, forgoing; sacrificing
   ant abnegating, self-denying
acquit vb 1 syn see EXCULPATE
   rel discharge, free, liberate, release; justify
   con condemn, damn, doom, proscribe, sentence
   ant convict
   2 syn see BEHAVE 1
acres n pl syn see ESTATE 3
acrid adj having or being a noticeable, persistent, and usually unpleasant flavor or sometimes odor <the tonic had an *acrid* aftertaste>
   syn amaroidal, astringent, austere, bitter, harsh, sharp
   rel biting, caustic, cutting; piquant, pungent; cloying, oversweet, saccharine
   con palatable, sapid, tasty, toothsome; delectable, delicious, luscious
   ant savory
acrimonious adj syn see ANGRY
   rel cranky, cross, irascible, splenetic, testy; belligerent, contentious, quarrelsome
   con benign, benignant, kind, kindly
   ant irenic, peaceable
acrimony n sharpness or rancor manifested in words, manner, or disposition <the dispute was renewed with increasing *acrimony*>
   syn acerbity, asperity, mordancy
   rel bitterness, ill will, malevolence, malice, malignity, spite, spleen; animosity, animus, antipathy, rancor
   con civility, courtesy, graciousness, politeness; diplomacy, urbanity
   ant suavity
acroamatic adj syn see RECONDITE
across adv 1 so as to intersect the length of something <cut the board *across*>

syn athwart, crossways, crosswise
2 *syn* see OVER 1

across *prep* from one side to the other <drew the curtain *across* the window>
syn athwart, cross, over

act *vb* **1** to present a role or performance on or as if on the stage <*acted* the part of Hamlet's father>
syn discourse, do, enact, impersonate, perform, personate, play, playact
rel characterize, portray, represent; masquerade; counterfeit, feign, sham, simulate
2 *syn* see ASSUME 4
idiom act a part, put on an act (of)
3 *syn* see BEHAVE 1
rel perform
4 to perform the duties or function of <he *acted* as president for over a year>
syn function, officiate, serve
idiom do duty (as), discharge the office (of), serve in the office (*or* capacity) of
5 to perform especially in an indicated way <the laxative *acted* quickly>
syn behave, function, operate, perform, react, take, work
idiom take effect
6 *syn* see FUNCTION 3

act *n syn* see ACTION 1
rel exploit, feat

actify *vb syn* see VITALIZE

acting *adj syn* see TEMPORARY

action *n* **1** something done or effected <a kindly *action*>
syn accomplishment, act, deed, doing, thing
rel discharge, effectuation, execution, fulfillment, performance; activity, behavior, operation, reaction, work; procedure, proceeding, process
2 *syn* see BATTLE
rel affray, combat, conflict, fray
3 *syn* see SERVICE 1
4 *syn* see SUIT 1

activate *vb syn* see VITALIZE
rel arouse, awaken, rally, rouse, stir, wake, waken
ant arrest

active *adj* **1** being at work or in effective operation <marginal mines that are *active* only when prices are high>
syn alive, dynamic, functioning, live, operative, running, working
rel assiduous, busy, diligent, industrious; energetic, strenuous, vigorous; alert, wide-awake; rushing
con dormant, latent, quiescent; idle, inert, passive, supine; dead, dull, slow
ant inactive; abeyant
2 *syn* see AGILE
rel animated, spirited, vivacious; flexible, graceful, supple
con inert, lumpish, torpid
ant inactive
3 *syn* see ENERGETIC 2
rel expeditious, prompt, ready
con disinterested, indifferent, unconcerned

actively *adv syn* see SERIOUSLY 1
activity *n syn* see EXERCISE 2
activize *vb syn* see VITALIZE
actor *n* **1** one who takes part in an exhibition simulating happenings in real life <had been an *actor* on the stage and in television>
syn impersonator, mime, mimic, mummer, performer, playactor, player, thespian, trouper
2 *syn* see PARTICIPANT
rel mainstay, supporter, sustainer, upholder
con abettor, backer, patron, promoter

actual *adj* **1** existing in act <our *actual* intentions>
syn existent, extant
ant possible, potential
2 existing in or based on fact <problems of *actual* life>
syn absolute, factual, genuine, hard, positive, sure-enough
rel commonplace, everyday, ordinary, routine, usual; concrete, real, tangible
con conjectural, hypothetical, theoretical; putative, reputed, supposititious
ant apparent, nominal
3 *syn* see REAL 3
rel material, objective, phenomenal, physical; authentic, bona fide, legitimate
con abstract, transcendent, transcendental; academic, speculative, theoretical; fabulous, fictitious, mythical
ant ideal; imaginary

actuality *n* **1** *syn* see EXISTENCE 1
rel actualization, externalization, incarnation, materialization; achievement, attainment
con abstraction, ideality, transcendence
ant possibility, potentiality
2 something that has existence <a predicted downturn in the stock market was received as if it were an *actuality*>
syn materiality, reality
rel basis, essence, substance; embodiment, incarnation
3 *syn* see FACT 1

actually *adv syn* see VERY 2
actuate *vb* **1** *syn* see MOVE 5
2 *syn* see MOBILIZE 1
rel excite, galvanize, provoke; arouse, rouse, stir; vitalize

act up *vb syn* see CUT UP 2
acumen *n syn* see WIT 3
rel acuteness, sharpness
con denseness, density, slowness
ant obtuseness, obtusity
acuminate *adj syn* see POINTED 1
acuminous *adj syn* see POINTED 1
acute *adj* **1** *syn* see POINTED 1
rel barbed, prickly, spiky, spined, spiny
ant blunt
2 *syn* see SHARP 4
rel cutting, incisive, trenchant; piercing
con crass, dense, dull, slow, stupid
ant obtuse
3 perceiving clearly and sensitively <an *acute* ear>
syn keen, perceptive, sensitive, sharp
rel observant, penetrating, probing; accurate, meticulous, precise
con imperceptive, insensitive; imprecise, inaccurate; inexact, uncritical

---

syn synonym(s)   *rel* related word(s)
ant antonym(s)   *con* contrasted word(s)
idiom idiomatic equivalent(s)
‖ use limited; if in doubt, see a dictionary

ant dull

4 elevated in pitch <an *acute* note>
syn argute, high, piercing, piping, sharp, shrill, thin, treble

rel penetrating; reedy, screechy, shrieky, shrilly, squeaky; tinny

con bass, deep, low

ant grave

5 *syn* see SHARP 8

6 serious to the point of approaching a crisis <an *acute* housing shortage>
syn climacteric, critical, crucial, desperate, dire

rel afflictive, grave, serious; aggravated, intensified; dangerous, hazardous, menacing, perilous, precarious, threatening; exigent, urgent

adage *n syn* see SAYING

adamant *adj syn* see INFLEXIBLE 2

rel immobile, immovable; unsubmitting

con placable, relenting; submitting; complaisant, obliging; subdued, submissive

ant yielding

adamantine *adj syn* see INFLEXIBLE 2

rel immobile, immovable; unsubmitting

con placable, relenting; submitting; complaisant, obliging; subdued, submissive

ant yielding

adapt *vb* to bring into correspondence or make suitable <*adapted* himself easily to the company he found himself with>
syn accommodate, adjust, conform, fit, quadrate, reconcile, square, suit, tailor, tailor-make

rel qualify, temper; acclimate, acclimatize

ant unfit

adaptable *adj* 1 *syn* see VERSATILE

2 *syn* see PLASTIC

con intractable, irreconcilable, nonconforming, refractory, unaccommodating

ant inadaptable, unadaptable

adapted *adj syn* see ASSORTED 2

add *vb* 1 to bring in or join on something more so as to form a larger or more inclusive whole <*added* music to his accomplishments>
syn annex, append, subjoin, superadd, take on

rel affix, attach, fasten, superimpose, tack (on); augment, enlarge, increase; burden, clutter, cumber, encumber, saddle

con abstract, detach; curtail, decrease, diminish, lessen, reduce

ant deduct, subtract

2 to combine numbers or quantities into one sum <*add* up a column of figures>
syn cast, figure, foot, sum, summate, tot, total, totalize, tote

rel calculate, compute, estimate, reckon; score, tally

added *adj syn* see ADDITIONAL

addendum *n, sometimes* **addenda** *pl but sing or pl in constr syn* see APPENDIX 1

addict *vb syn* see HABITUATE 2

rel bias, dispose, incline, predispose; address, apply, direct

con alienate, estrange; detach, disengage, disincline, indispose

ant wean

addict *n* a person who by habit or strong inclination indulges in something <a science fiction *addict*>
syn aficionado, buff, devotee, fan, habitué, hound, lover, votary

rel enthusiast, fanatic, zealot; hobbyist, putterer, tinkerer

addition *n* something that tends to increase something else (as in size, number, or content) <there are several new *additions* to our staff>
syn accession, accretion, augmentation, increase, increment, raise, rise

rel accessory, adjunct, appanage, appurtenance, supplement; continuation, extension, rider; accrual, accruement, accumulation

con deduction, lessening, reduction

additional *adj* being or coming by way of addition <gave *additional* reasons to justify his position>
syn added, another, else, farther, fresh, further, more, new, other

rel accessory, adscititious, collateral, extra, supplemental, supplementary

additionally *adv* 1 *syn* see ALSO 2

2 *syn* see AGAIN 4

additive *adj syn* see CUMULATIVE

rel component, constituent, elemental

additory *adj syn* see CUMULATIVE

addle *vb syn* see CONFUSE 2

rel confound, dumbfound, nonplus; amaze, astound, flabbergast

idiom addle one's wits

con animate, enliven, quicken, vivify

ant refresh (*mentally*)

address *vb* 1 *syn* see DIRECT 2

2 *syn* see SEND 1

3 to occupy (oneself or one's attention or efforts) with something <*addressed* himself to the job and soon finished it>
syn apply, bend, buckle (down), devote, direct, give, throw, turn

rel associate, connect, couple, link, relate; aim, level, point

idiom bring (oneself) into relation with something, tax (one's energies) with something

con disregard, ignore, overlook

4 to communicate directly to or with <*addressed* the governor with his petition>
syn accost, apply (to), approach, bespeak, memorialize

rel speak (to), talk (with); appeal (to); apostrophize; petition

con ignore, overlook, pass up, slight; avoid, cut, disregard

5 *syn* see TALK 7

6 to affix directions for delivery <*address* a letter>
syn direct, superscribe

7 to seek the attention of usually orally and in order to gain recognition <*address* a stranger to ask directions>
syn accost, call (to), greet, hail, salute

rel converse, speak, talk

idiom attract one's attention

8 to direct one's attention to in the role of a suitor <ready to marry the first man that *addressed* her>
syn court, make up (to), pursue, spark, sue, sweetheart, woo

rel attend, escort, squire; neck, pet, romance, rush, smooch, spoon
idiom make a play for, pay (one's) addresses to, run after

address *n* **1** the quality or state of being ready or skillful <to bring off such a coup requires *address*>
syn adroitness, deftness, dexterity, dexterousness, prowess, readiness, skill, sleight; compare TACT
rel competence, efficiency, expertise, knowhow, proficiency; craft, finesse; ingeniousness, ingenuity, resourcefulness
con inadequacy, ineptitude, ineptness, unskillfulness; awkwardness, clumsiness, gawkiness, lubberliness, stupidity
2 *syn* see TACT
rel dexterity, ease, facility; cleverness, readiness; affability, graciousness
con awkwardness, clumsiness, gaucheness; boorishness, churlishness
ant maladroitness
3 *syn* see BEARING 1
4 *syn* see SPEECH 2

adduce *vb* to bring forward for consideration <*adduce* evidence in support of a hypothesis>
syn advance, allege, cite, lay, offer, present
rel animadvert, comment, commentate, remark; document, exemplify, illustrate; prefer, proffer, propose, submit, suggest, tender

add up *vb syn* see AMOUNT 1
add up (to) *vb syn* see MEAN 2
adept *n syn* see EXPERT
ant bungler, incompetent
adept *adj syn* see PROFICIENT
rel clever; adroit, deft, dexterous
con amateurish, dabbling, dilettantish; awkward, clumsy, maladroit
ant bungling, inapt, inept

adequacy *n* **1** *syn* see ABILITY 1
rel equality, satisfactoriness, sufficiency
idiom enough on the ball
ant inadequacy, inadequateness
2 *syn* see ENOUGH

adequate *adj* **1** *syn* see SUFFICIENT 1
con meager, scanty, sparse
ant inadequate, unadequate
2 *syn* see DECENT 4

adequately *adv* **1** *syn* see ENOUGH 1
2 *syn* see WELL 4

adequation *n syn* see EQUIVALENCE

adhere *vb syn* see STICK 2
rel combine, join, link, unite
con disjoin, disunite

adherence *n* **1** a physical adhering <the close *adherence* of scales to a plant bud>
syn adhesion, bond, cling, clinging, coherence, cohesion, stickage, sticking
rel agglutination, cementation, concretion, conglutination; congelation, set, setting, solidification
con detachment, disjunction, parting, separation

2 *syn* see ATTACHMENT 1
con fickleness, inconstancy

adherent *n syn* see FOLLOWER
rel backer, champion, upholder
con apostate, recreant; deserter, forsaker; adversary, antagonist, opponent
ant renegade

adhesion *n* **1** *syn* see ADHERENCE 1
ant nonadhesion
2 *syn* see ATTACHMENT 1
con fickleness, inconstancy

adhesive *adj syn* see STICKY 1
adieu *interj syn* see GOOD-BYE
adieu *n syn* see PARTING
ad interim *adj syn* see TEMPORARY
ant permanent
adipose *adj syn* see FATTY 1
adiposity *n syn* see OBESITY
adit *n syn* see DOOR 2
adjacent *adj* **1** *syn* see NEIGHBORING
ant remote
2 *syn* see CONVENIENT 2
3 having a common border <the brothers built on *adjacent* lots>
syn abutting, adjoining, approximal, bordering, conterminous, contiguous, juxtaposed, touching
rel closest, nearest, next; consecutive, successive; attached, connected, joined, linked
con distant, far, remote, removed; parted, separated
ant nonadjacent

adjoin *vb* to be contiguous or adjacent to <the new suburb *adjoins* farmland>
syn abut, border, butt (on *or* against), communicate, join, line, march, neighbor, touch, verge
rel meet, run (into); end

adjoining *adj syn* see ADJACENT 3
ant detached

adjourn *vb* **1** *syn* see DEFER
rel curb, hold back, restrain
con advance, expedite, further, promote
2 to bring to a formal close <*adjourn* the legislature>
syn dissolve, prorogate, prorogue, recess, rise, terminate
rel break up, close, disband, discontinue, disperse; stay, suspend
con open; mobilize, muster, rally
ant convene, convoke

adjudge *vb syn* see JUDGE 1
rel accord, allot, assign, award, grant
adjudicate *vb syn* see JUDGE 1

adjunct *n syn* see APPENDAGE
rel accretion, addition; appanage; affix, attachment, fixture

adjust *vb* **1** *syn* see ADAPT
rel accord, correspond; attune, harmonize
2 to alter so as to make more efficient or more efficient <*adjust* a carburetor>
syn fix, regulate, tune (up)
rel correct, rectify, right; balance, stabilize, steady, trim, true; arrange, order, rig
idiom make right, put (*or* set) in order, put right (*or* to rights), set right (*or* to rights)
con disarrange, disorder, disturb, upset
ant derange
3 *syn* see HABITUATE 2

adjuvant *adj syn* see AUXILIARY

---

syn synonym(s)   *rel* related word(s)
ant antonym(s)   *con* contrasted word(s)
idiom idiomatic equivalent(s)
‖ use limited; if in doubt, see a dictionary

rel synergistic

con antagonistic, negating, negativing, neutralizing; hindering, impeding, obstructing

ant counteractive

ad-lib *vb syn* see IMPROVISE

admeasure *vb syn* see ALLOT

admeasurement *n syn* see SIZE 1

adminicular *adj syn* see CORROBORATIVE

administer *vb* **1** to supervise the affairs or the provision, use, or conduct of especially in the capacity of an agent or steward <*administer* justice>

syn administrate, carry out, execute, govern, render

rel conduct, direct, manage, run, supervise **2** to provide in appropriate amount <*administer* a laxative>

syn apportion, deal (out), dispense, dole (out), mete (out), portion (out), share out

rel distribute, give, give out; issue; allot, assign, consign; allocate, ration

3 *syn* see GIVE 10

administrate *vb syn* see ADMINISTER 1

administrator *n syn* see EXECUTIVE

admirable *adj syn* see WORTHY 1

admiration *n* **1** *syn* see WONDER 2

rel surprise; ecstasy, rapture, transport

con aloofness, indifference, unconcern

2 *syn* see REGARD 4

rel appreciation; adoration, reverence, veneration, worship

con detestation, hate, hatred, loathing; dislike, disrelish, distaste

ant abhorrence

admire *vb* **1** to view with an elevated feeling of pleasure <*admired* the scene that spread out before them>

syn appreciate, cherish, delight (in), relish; *compare* APPRECIATE 1

rel adore, revere, reverence, venerate, worship

idiom go into raptures over, take delight in

con disesteem, disfavor, dislike, disrelish, mislike

ant disdain

2 to hold in high esteem <*admired* his ability to get things done>

syn consider, esteem, regard, respect

rel appreciate, cherish, prize, treasure, value

idiom have (or hold) a high opinion of, rate highly, set (great) store by, think much (or highly) of

con abominate, detest, hate, loathe; contemn, despise, disdain, scorn

ant abhor

admirer *n syn* see AMATEUR 1

admissible *adj syn* see PERMISSIBLE

admission *n syn* see DOOR 2

admit *vb* **1** *syn* see TAKE 10

rel allow, permit, suffer; entertain, harbor, house, lodge, shelter

con debar, exclude, shut out; bar, block, hinder, obstruct

ant eject, expel

2 *syn* see ACKNOWLEDGE 1

rel acquiesce, agree, assent, subscribe

ant gainsay

3 *syn* see ENTER 2

rel induct, initiate, install; insert, interject, interpose

con debar, shut out; eject, expel, oust

ant exclude

4 *syn* see ACKNOWLEDGE 2

admittance *n syn* see DOOR 2

admix *vb syn* see MIX 1

admixture *n* **1** an added ingredient that alters the character of something <her love had a marring *admixture* of selfishness>

syn adulterant, alloy, denaturant

rel doctor, fortification, taint; accretion, addition; bit, dash, shade, smack, spice, tinge

2 *syn* see MIXTURE

admonish *vb syn* see REPROVE

rel caution, forewarn, warn

idiom have a word with

con applaud, approve, compliment

ant commend

admonishing *adj syn* see MONITORY

admonishment *n syn* see REBUKE

admonition *n* **1** *syn* see REBUKE

2 *syn* see WARNING

admonitory *adj syn* see MONITORY

ado *n syn* see STIR 1

rel effort, exertion, pains, trouble; confusion, hurly-burly, turmoil, uproar

con calm, peace, serenity, tranquillity; quiet, silence, stillness

adolescence *n syn* see YOUTH 1

ant senescence

adopt *vb* to make one's own what in some fashion one owes to another <*adopt* a new style>

syn embrace, espouse, take on, take up

rel affect, assume; appropriate, arrogate, take, usurp; domesticate, naturalize

idiom adapt to one's own ends, go in for

con reject, spurn; abjure, forswear, renounce

ant discard; repudiate

adoption *n syn* see ESPOUSAL 4

adorable *adj* **1** *syn* see LOVABLE

2 *syn* see DELIGHTFUL

adoration *n* deep, ardent, and often excessive attachment or love <the *adoration* given popular heroes>

syn idolatry, idolization, worship

rel affection, attachment, devotion, love; crush, infatuation, passion; weakness

con antipathy, aversion; disfavor, dislike, distaste

ant detestation

adore *vb* **1** *syn* see REVERE

rel extol, laud, praise

con curse, execrate

2 *syn* see LOVE 2

3 to love, admire, or enjoy excessively <she *adores* and spoils her grandchildren>

syn dote (on *or* upon), idolize, worship

rel admire, esteem, love; coddle, indulge, pamper, spoil

idiom be silly over

con abhor, abominate, hate, loathe; contemn, despise, disdain, scorn

ant detest

4 *syn* see LOVE 1

adorn *vb* to add something nonessential to enhance the appearance or beauty of <a hat *adorned* with feathers>

syn beautify, bedeck, deck, decorate, dress (up), embellish, garnish, ornament, prank, trim

rel enrich, furbish, smarten, spruce (up); bedizen, dandify, fancy up; enhance, heighten, intensify

con clear, divest, expose, strip, uncover; deface, mar, scar, spoil

ant disfigure

ad rem *adj syn* see RELEVANT

adroit *adj* **1** *syn* see DEXTEROUS 1
    ant maladroit
2 *syn* see SKILLFUL 2
3 *syn* see CLEVER 4
    rel astute, perspicacious, shrewd; intelligent, quick-witted, smart; artful, subtle
    con dense, dull, stupid; apathetic, heavy, impassive, phlegmatic, stodgy
    ant stolid

adroitness *n* **1** *syn* see ADDRESS 1
2 *syn* see ART 1

adscititious *adj syn* see ADVENTITIOUS

adulation *n syn* see FLATTERY
    rel acclaim, applause
    ant abuse

adult *adj syn* see MATURE 1
    rel aged
    con adolescent, pubescent
    ant juvenile, puerile

adulterant *n syn* see ADMIXTURE 1

adulterate *vb* to alter fraudulently usually for profit <sausage *adulterated* with cereal products>
    syn debase, doctor, dope (up), load, sophisticate, weight
    rel cut, dilute; denaturalize, denature, manipulate, tamper (with); defile, impurify, pollute, taint; deacon
    con better, improve; augment, fortify, supplement
    ant refine

adumbrate *vb* **1** to give a hint or indication of something to come <social unrest that *adumbrated* the revolt>
    syn foreshadow, hint, prefigurate, prefigure, shadow (forth); *compare* SUGGEST 5
    rel augur, bode, forebode, foretell, presage; lower, menace, threaten; symbolize, typify
    idiom cast its shadow before
2 *syn* see FORETELL
    rel argue, bespeak, betoken, indicate
3 *syn* see SKETCH
4 *syn* see SUGGEST 5
    rel denote, mean, signify
5 *syn* see OBSCURE

adumbration *n syn* see SHADE 1
    rel hint, intimation, suggestion; sign, symptom, token; emblem, symbol, type
    con disclosure, discovery, divulgence
    ant revelation

advance *vb* **1** to cause to proceed or progress toward a goal <warm rains *advanced* the crops>
    syn encourage, forward, foster, further, promote, serve

rel aid, assist; help; accelerate, quicken, speed
    con hinder, impede; delay, slow; curb, restrain
    ant retard; check
2 to raise in rank or position <was *advanced* to the presidency>
    syn elevate, prefer, promote, upgrade
    rel aggrandize, exalt, raise, uplift; glorify, immortalize, magnify
    ant hold back; reduce (*in rank*)
3 *syn* see LEND
4 *syn* see ADDUCE
    rel air, broach, expose
5 to go forward in space or time or toward an objective <prices *advanced* sharply>
    syn get along, get on, march, move, proceed, progress
    rel heighten, increase, intensify; develop, mature
    idiom forge ahead, gain ground, get ahead, make headway (*or* progress), make one's way, make rapid strides
    con retire, retreat, retrograde, withdraw
    ant recede

advance *n* **1** *syn* see PROGRESS 2
2 forward movement especially on a course of action or development <the recent *advance* of technology>
    syn advancement, anabasis, headway, march, ongoing, proficiency, progress
    rel betterment, furtherance, improvement; development, evolution; breakthrough
    con retreat, retrogression; ebbing, retiring, withdrawal
    ant recession
3 *syn* see OVERTURE 1
    rel offer, proffer

advanced *adj* **1** *syn* see PRECOCIOUS
    con retrograde, retrogressive
    ant backward
2 *syn* see LIBERAL 3
    rel adventurous, daring, venturesome
    ant conservative

advancement *n* **1** the act of raising or the status of being raised in grade, rank, or dignity <his *advancement* in his profession was rapid>
    syn elevation, preference, preferment, prelation, promotion, upgrading
    rel aggrandizement, dignification, magnification, raising, uplifting
    con demotion, downgrading, reduction
    ant degradation
2 *syn* see ADVANCE 2

advantage *n* **1** *syn* see BETTER 2
2 *syn* see WELFARE
3 something giving one person or side a position of superiority (as in a contest) <he had the *advantage* of greater height>
    syn allowance, bulge, ‖deadwood, draw, edge, handicap, head start, odds, ‖overhand, start, vantage; *compare* BETTER 2
    rel drop, jump, lead, running start; ascendancy, domination, leadership; mastery, superiority, upper hand, whip hand
    idiom ace in the hole, inside track
    con embarrassment, hamper, hindrance, impediment, inconvenience
    ant disadvantage

---

syn synonym(s)   *rel* related word(s)
ant antonym(s)   *con* contrasted word(s)
idiom idiomatic equivalent(s)
‖ use limited; if in doubt, see a dictionary

4 syn see USE 3
rel betterment, improvement; enhancement; heightening
con damage, harm, hurt, injury
ant detriment
5 syn see GOOD 1

advantage *vb syn* see BENEFIT

advantageous *adj* **1** yielding a profit <sold on very *advantageous* terms>
syn gainful, good, lucrative, moneymaking, paying, profitable, remunerative, well-paying, worthwhile
rel acceptable, agreeable, desirable, pleasing, satisfactory, satisfying
idiom in the black, paying its (own) way
con disadvantageous, unfavorable, unprofitable; damaging, hurtful
2 syn see GOOD 1
rel remedial, salutary; conducive, contributory, implemental, instrumental; advisable, expedient
con unfavorable; inconvenient; deleterious, detrimental
ant disadvantageous

advenient *adj syn* see ADVENTITIOUS

advent *n syn* see ARRIVAL 1
rel approach, nearing
ant exit

advential *adj syn* see ADVENTITIOUS

adventitious *adj* coming from without and not participating in the fundamental nature of something <*adventitious* notions that have corrupted the primitive doctrine>
syn adscititious, advenient, advential, supervenient
rel accidental, casual, contingent, fortuitous, incidental
con constitutional, essential, intrinsic; inborn, inbred, innate
ant inherent

adventure *n* an undertaking or experience that involves hazard and requires boldness <recounted the *adventures* of his solitary voyage>
syn emprise, enterprise, exploit, feat, gest, venture
rel hazard, peril, risk; quest; achievement

adventure *vb syn* see VENTURE 1

adventuresome *adj syn* see ADVENTUROUS
ant unadventurous; cautious

adventurous *adj* courting danger or exposing oneself to danger beyond the call of duty or courage <*adventurous* boys scrambled over the cliff face>
syn adventuresome, audacious, daredevil, daring, foolhardy, rash, reckless, temerarious, venturesome, venturous
rel bold, doughty, intrepid; brash, harebrained, hotheaded, impetuous, imprudent, madcap, overconfident
con shrinking, timid, timorous; afraid, alarmed, fearful, scared; apprehensive, uneasy
ant unadventurous; cautious

adversary *n syn* see OPPONENT
rel assaulter, attacker
con backer, supporter, upholder
ant ally

adverse *adj* **1** acting against or in a contrary direction <hindered by *adverse* forces>
syn antagonistic, anti, antipathetic, opposed, opposing, oppugnant
rel contrary, counter, counteractive; hindering, impeding, obstructive; hostile, unfriendly
con coactive, collaborative, cooperative; adjuvant, synergistic; favorable, propitious
2 being opposed to one's interests <an *adverse* balance of trade>
syn detrimental, negative, unfavorable
rel deleterious, harmful, hurtful, injurious; disadvantageous, prejudicial, unpropitious, unsatisfactory
con advantageous, favorable, positive, propitious, satisfactory

adversity *n syn* see MISFORTUNE
rel distress, misery, suffering; deprivation, destitution, indigence, poverty
con bliss, felicity, happiness; comfort, ease
ant prosperity

advert *vb syn* see REFER 3
rel animadvert, note, notice, observe, remark
con disregard, ignore, neglect, overlook

advertent *adj syn* see ATTENTIVE 1

advertise *vb* **1 syn** see DECLARE 1
rel recount, relate, report; communicate, impart; ballyhoo, promote, propagandize, publicize
con conceal, repress, suppress; bury, hide, obscure
2 syn see PUBLICIZE
3 syn see PROMOTE 3

advertisement *n syn* see DECLARATION
rel ballyhoo, promotion, propaganda, publicity

advertising *n syn* see PUBLICITY

advice *n* **1** recommendation regarding a decision or course of conduct <benefited from his *advice* on study habits>
syn advisement, counsel
rel direction, guidance, instruction, teaching; input; admonition; caution, cautioning, forewarning, warning
2 syn see NEWS

advisable *adj syn* see EXPEDIENT
rel commendable, desirable; becoming, seemly, suitable; sensible
ant inadvisable

advise *vb* **1 syn** see COUNSEL
rel caution, forewarn, warn; coax, induce, persuade, win (over)
con bedazzle, misadvise, mislead
2 syn see CONFER 2
rel deliberate
3 syn see INFORM 2
rel disclose, let out, reveal; communicate, impart

advised *adj syn* see DELIBERATE 1
rel intended, intentional, meant; knowing, purposeful, willful

advisement *n syn* see ADVICE 1

advocate *n syn* see EXPONENT

advocate *vb* **1 syn** see ENCOURAGE 2
2 syn see SUPPORT 2
rel justify, vindicate; advance, forward, promote
idiom hold a brief for
con assail, attack; combat, fight, oppose
ant impugn

aegis *n* **1 syn** see DEFENSE 1
  2 syn see BACKING

aeneous *adj* **syn** see BRAZEN 4

aeon *n* **syn** see AGE 2

aerial *adj* **1 syn** see AIRY 1
  2 syn see LOFTY 6
  3 syn see AIRY 3
  rel immaterial, incorporeal; impalpable,
  imperceptible, imponderable

aesthete *n* **syn** see CONNOISSEUR
  rel perfectionist, stickler; fussbudget, old
  maid
  con barbarian; clod, lout, oaf

affable *adj* **1 syn** see GRACIOUS 1
  rel courteous, polite; suave, urbane; loquacious, talkative
  con crabbed, glum, surly; reticent, withdrawn; silent, taciturn, uncommunicative
  ant reserved
  2 syn see GENTLE 2

affair *n* **1** something done or dealt with <try-
  ing to get at the truth of the *affair*>
  syn business, concern, matter, shooting
  match, thing
  rel care, lookout, responsibility; pie, proceeding
  idiom cup of tea
  2 syn see BUSINESS 8
  3 syn see LOVE AFFAIR
  4 syn see AMOUR 2

affect *vb* **1 syn** see ASSUME 4
  2 syn see FREQUENT

affect *vb* to produce a usually mental or
  emotional effect on one capable of reaction
  <much *affected* by the touching scene>
  syn carry, get, impress, influence, inspire,
  move, strike, sway, touch
  rel actuate, draw, drive, impel; penetrate,
  pierce
  idiom work on

affectation *n* **syn** see POSE 2
  rel ostentation, pretentiousness
  con ingenuousness, naiveté, naturalness,
  simplicity, unsophistication
  ant artlessness

affected *adj* **1 syn** see INTERESTED
  2 syn see SELF-CONSCIOUS
  3 syn see GENTEEL 3
  4 syn see PRECIOUS 4
  5 syn see ARTIFICIAL 3

affecting *adj* **syn** see MOVING 2
  rel piteous, pitiable, pitiful; distressful,
  distressing, disturbing, troubling

affection *n* **1 syn** see FEELING 3
  rel leaning, penchant, propensity; bias,
  predilection; bent, faculty, turn
  con aversion, hate, hatred; dislike, distaste
  ant antipathy
  2 syn see LOVE 1
  rel sympathy, tenderness, warmth; attention, concern, interest; doting, enjoying
  con coolness, frigidity
  ant coldness

affection *vb* **syn** see LOVE 2

affection *n* **1 syn** see DISEASE 1

rel access, attack, paroxysm, spell; derangement, disordering, disturbance
  2 syn see QUALITY 1

affectionate *adj* **syn** see LOVING
  rel sympathetic, tender, warm
  con apathetic, impassive, stolid; remote,
  uninterested, withdrawn
  ant cold; undemonstrative

affective *adj* **syn** see EMOTIONAL 2

affectivity *n* **syn** see FEELING 3

affianced *adj* **syn** see ENGAGED 2

affianced *n* **syn** see BETROTHED

affiche *n* **syn** see POSTER

affiliated *adj* **syn** see RELATED
  con autonomous, free, independent
  ant unaffiliated

affiliation *n* **syn** see ASSOCIATION 1

affinity *n* **1 syn** see ATTRACTION 1
  con antipathy, aversion; dislike, distaste;
  repugnance, repellency, repulsion
  2 syn see LIKENESS
  rel accord

affirm *vb* **syn** see ASSERT 1
  rel attest, certify, guarantee, vouch, witness;
  say, state
  con debate

affirmative *adj* **syn** see POSITIVE 6

affix *vb* **syn** see FASTEN 1
  rel add, annex, append, subjoin
  con disengage, disjoin
  ant detach

afflation *n* **syn** see INSPIRATION

afflatus *n* **syn** see INSPIRATION

afflict *vb* to inflict upon one something hard
  to endure <he was *afflicted* with boils>
  syn agonize, crucify, excruciate, harrow,
  martyr, martyrize, rack, smite, strike, torment, torture, try, wring
  rel annoy, harass, harry, pester, plague,
  press, worry; bother, irk, vex; lacerate,
  wound
  con console, delight, gladden, please, rejoice; ease, relieve, solace
  ant comfort

afflicted *adj* **syn** see WOEFUL 1

affliction *n* **1 syn** see TRIAL 1
  rel mischance, mishap
  con alleviation, assuagement, easement,
  relief
  ant consolation, solace
  2 syn see SORROW
  3 syn see SICKNESS 1

afflictive *adj* **syn** see PAINFUL 1
  2 syn see DEPLORABLE
  3 syn see BITTER 2

affluent *adj* **syn** see RICH 1
  rel acquisitive, grasping
  con poor; bankrupt, impoverished
  ant impecunious; straitened

affranchise *vb* **syn** see ENFRANCHISE

affray *n* **1 syn** see BRAWL 2
  2 syn see CLASH 2

affright *vb* **syn** see FRIGHTEN
  rel bewilder, confound
  con animate, fire, inspire
  ant embolden, nerve

affront *vb* **1 syn** see OFFEND 3
  rel criticize, dispraise
  con compliment; laud, praise; dignify,
  honor

---

syn synonym(s)   **rel** related word(s)
ant antonym(s)   **con** contrasted word(s)
idiom idiomatic equivalent(s)
‖ use limited; if in doubt, see a dictionary

2 *syn* see CONFRONT 1

affront *n* a speech or an action designed to impugn the honor or worth of someone or something <her costume was an *affront* to the solemnity of the occasion>
syn contumely, despite, indignity, insult, slap
rel dishonor, flouting, offense, outrage, slight; aspersion, barb, defamation, dig
idiom slap in the face
con deference, homage, honor; adulation, compliment, flattery

aficionado *n syn* see ADDICT

afield *adj syn* see AMISS 2

afire *adj* **1** *syn* see BURNING 1
2 *syn* see ALIGHT 2

aflame *adj* **1** *syn* see BURNING 1
2 *syn* see ALIGHT 2

aflicker *adj syn* ALIGHT 2, ablaze, afire, aflame, aglow

à fond *adv syn* see WELL 3

aforementioned *adj syn* see SUCH 1

aforesaid *adj syn* see SUCH 1

aforethought *adj syn* see DELIBERATE 1

afraid *adj* **1** suffering the effects of apprehension, fear, or terror <too *afraid* to even cry for help>
syn aghast, anxious, ‖ascared, fearful, frightened, scared, scary, terrified; *compare* FEARFUL 2
rel shrinking, shy, timid, timorous; cautious, chary, wary; jumpy, skittish
idiom frightened out of one's wits, in a (blue) funk, scared to death, terror stricken
con confident, dauntless, fearless; assured, collected, poised, self-possessed
ant unafraid
2 *syn* see FEARFUL 2
idiom all of a twitter (*or* flutter)
ant unafraid; sanguine
3 *syn* see DISINCLINED

afresh *adv* **1** *syn* see OVER 7
2 *syn* see NEW

‖African dominoes *n pl syn* see DICE

aft *adv syn* see ABAFT
rel hind, posterior
con ahead, before, forward
ant fore

after *adv* so as to follow in time or space <*after*, we turned toward home>
syn afterward, afterwhile, behind, by and by, infra, later, latterly, next, subsequently
rel abaft, aft, astern
idiom after a time (*or* while), in the wake of
con ahead, forward
ant before

after *prep* **1** so as to resemble or follow in some respect <named *after* his father>
syn for, from
2 later in time or lower in place or rank <*after* our discussion>
syn behind, below, following, next, since, subsequent to
con ante, ere, in advance of, preceding, prior to
ant before
3 *syn* see BEYOND 1

after *adj* **1** *syn* see SUBSEQUENT 1
2 *syn* see POSTERIOR 2
con antecedent, preceding, prior

after all *adv syn* see HOWEVER

aftereffect *n syn* see EFFECT 1
rel remainder, residual, residuum

afterlife *n* **1** *syn* see ETERNITY 2
2 *syn* see HEREAFTER 2

afterlight *n syn* see REVIEW 5

aftermath *n syn* see EFFECT 1
rel remainder, residual, residuum

aftertime *n syn* see FUTURE

afterward *adv syn* see AFTER

afterward *n syn* see FUTURE

afterwhile *adv syn* see AFTER

afterword *n syn* see EPILOGUE 1

afterworld *n syn* see HEREAFTER 2

again *adv* **1** *syn* see ABOUT 6
2 *syn* see OVER 7
3 *syn* see THEN 1
4 as another point, fact, or instance <*again*, consider taxes>
syn additionally, also, besides, further, in addition, then; *compare* ALSO 2
idiom by the same token, into the bargain, on top of that
5 as an alternative and especially a converse <he may win and *again* he may not>
syn contra, contrariwise, contrary, contrawise, conversely, oppositely, vice versa; *compare* HOWEVER
idiom at the same time, be that as it may, just the same, on the other hand

again and again *adv syn* see OFTEN

against *prep* **1** directly opposite <stood *against* the crowd and shouted for order>
syn contra, facing, fronting, over against, toward, vis-à-vis
idiom counter to, face to face with
2 so as to touch <vines trained *against* the wall>
syn to, touching
idiom in contact with, next to
3 *syn* see VERSUS 1
4 without being prevented or obstructed by <succeeded *against* grave handicaps>
syn despite, in spite of, notwithstanding, regardless of
idiom in the face of
5 *syn* see FROM 2
6 *syn* see APROPOS

agape *adj syn* see AGHAST 2

age *n* **1** *syn* see OLD AGE
ant youth
2 *often* **ages** *pl* a long or seemingly long period of time <haven't seen her for *ages*>
syn aeon, blue moon, coon's age, dog's age, donkey's years, eternity, long
idiom month of Sundays, ‖right smart spell
con flash, instant, minute, moment, second, split second, trice
3 *syn* see PERIOD 2

age *vb syn* see MATURE

aged *adj* **1** being in the declining phase of life <*aged* pensioners>
syn ancient, elderly, old, olden
rel pensioned (off), retired, superannuated; senior; hoary, patriarchal, venerable; doddering, senescent, senile, tottery
idiom along in years, getting on, getting on (*or* along) in years, gray with age, on one's last legs, stricken with years
con juvenile, puerile

ant youthful
2 syn see ANCIENT 1
3 syn see RIPE 3
ageless *adj syn* see ETERNAL 4
agency *n syn* see MEAN 2
rel antecedent, cause, determinant; gear
agenda *n syn* see PROGRAM 1
agent *n* **1 syn** see MEAN 2
rel doer, executive, executor, performer;
actor, worker; activator, energizer
2 one who acts for another <diplomatic
agents serving abroad>
syn assignee, attorney, deputy, factor,
proxy; *compare* DELEGATE
rel go-between, middleman; instrument,
minister, tool; commissioner, proctor, procurator, representative, steward; buyer, com-
missionary
ant principal
3 syn see SPY
age–old *adj syn* see ANCIENT 1
agglomerate *n syn* see AGGREGATE 1
rel heap, mass, pile
agglomeration *n* **1 syn** see ACCUMULA-
TION
rel association, combination
2 syn see AGGREGATE 1
aggrandize *vb* **1 syn** see INCREASE 1
rel amplify, build up
2 syn see EXALT 1
ant belittle
aggrandizement *n syn* see APOTHEOSIS 2
aggravate *vb* **1 syn** see INTENSIFY
rel augment, enlarge, increase, multiply;
aggrandize
con extenuate, palliate
ant alleviate
2 syn see IRRITATE
rel disturb, perturb, upset; annoy, bedevil
con calm, tranquilize
ant appease
aggravation *n syn* see ANNOYANCE 2
aggregate *vb syn* see AMOUNT 1
aggregate *n* **1** a mass or body formed of
particles or parts that retain their individuality <an *aggregate* of ill-planned arguments>
syn agglomerate, agglomeration, aggregation, conglomerate, conglomeration; *compare* ACCUMULATION
ant constituent, element
2 syn see BODY 5
ant individual, unit; particular
3 syn see WHOLE 1
aggregation *n* **1 syn** see AGGREGATE 1
ant constituent, element
2 syn see ACCUMULATION
rel backlog, reserve, stockpile
3 syn see GATHERING 2
aggress *vb syn* see ATTACK 1
aggression *n* **1 syn** see ATTACK 1
2 syn see ATTACK 2
rel incursion, inroad, invasion, raid; irruption
ant resistance

---

syn synonym(s)   *rel* related word(s)
ant antonym(s)   *con* contrasted word(s)
idiom idiomatic equivalent(s)
‖ use limited; if in doubt, see a dictionary

aggressive *adj* marked by bold determination and readiness for conflict <an *aggressive*
fighter>
syn assertive, assertory, militant, pushful,
pushing, pushy, self-assertive
rel belligerent, combative, contentious,
scrappy; domineering, imperious, masterful,
tough; energetic, hard-hitting, strenuous,
vigorous
con passive, unassertive; meek, submissive,
yielding
aggressiveness *n syn* see ATTACK 2
aggrieve *vb* **1 syn** see DISTRESS 2
rel abuse, misuse, outrage; pain
con delight, gladden, please
2 syn see WRONG
rel afflict, torment, try; annoy, harass,
harry, plague, worry
con benefit, profit
aghast *adj* **1 syn** see AFRAID 1
rel appalled, horrified, horror-struck; undone, unmanned
idiom scared stiff (or white)
2 struck by an intense emotional reaction (as
surprise, disgust, or bewilderment) <*aghast*
at the lack of discipline>
syn agape, confounded, dismayed, dumbfounded, overwhelmed, shocked, thunderstruck
rel agog, amazed, startled; awed, awe-
stricken; astonished, flabbergasted, surprised
idiom struck all of a heap, taken aback,
unable to believe one's eyes (or senses)
con acceptant, acquiescent, tolerant
agile *adj* acting or moving with easy alacrity
<an *agile* athlete with superior flexibility>
syn active, brisk, brisky, catty, lively, nimble, sprightly, spry, volant, yare, zippy
rel adroit, deft, dexterous; fleet, quick,
speedy; limber, lissome, lithe, supple; light-
footed, tripping
con inactive, inert, sluggish; heavy, lethargic,
logy; dull, slow, sluggish
ant torpid
agitable *adj syn* see EXCITABLE
agitate *vb* **1 syn** see SHAKE 4
rel bounce, joggle, jounce; actuate, drive,
impel, move
con lull, quiet, still
2 syn see DISCOMPOSE 1
rel exasperate, irritate, peeve, provoke, rile,
ruffle
ant calm, tranquilize
3 syn see DISCUSS 1
rel air, broach, ventilate; consider; assail,
attack
agitation *n syn* see COMMOTION 2
rel ado, bustle, disturbance, stir
ant tranquillity
agitator *n syn* see INSTIGATOR
aglow *adj syn* see ALIGHT 2
rel gleaming, glowing, shining; lucent,
luminous, radiant
agnate *adj* **1 syn** see RELATED
2 syn see LIKE
agog *adj syn* see EAGER
rel aroused, roused, stirred; excited, galvanized, stimulated; restive; zestful
ant aloof

agonize *vb* **1** *syn* see AFFLICT
rel distress, trouble; chafe, fret, gall
2 *syn* see WRITHE 1
rel bear, endure, suffer

agonizing *adj syn* see EXCRUCIATING
rel exquisite, fierce, intense, vehement, violent

agony *n syn* see DISTRESS
con repose, rest

agrarian *adj syn* see WILD 1

agree *vb* **1** *syn* see ACKNOWLEDGE 2
rel allow, concede, grant, own
con except, exclude
ant deny
2 *syn* see ASSENT
rel allow, concede, grant; receive; acknowledge, admit
con expostulate, kick, object, remonstrate; balk, demur, jib; oppose, resist, withstand
ant protest (against); differ (with)
3 to achieve harmony (as of opinion, feeling, or purpose) <they *agreed* finally on all major issues>
syn coincide, concert, concord, concur, harmonize
rel coact, cooperate, unite
idiom fall in with, hit it off with
con bicker, quarrel, squabble, wrangle; argue, debate, dispute, hassle
ant differ; disagree
4 to exist or go together without conflict or incongruity <his conclusion *agrees* with the evidence>
syn accord, check, check out, cohere, comport, conform, consist, consort, correspond, dovetail, fit (in), ‖gee, go, harmonize, jibe, march, quadrate, rhyme, square, suit, tally
rel approach, equal, match, rival, touch; complete, fulfill, round out, supplement
idiom go hand in hand
con negate, negative, nullify; clash, conflict, jar
ant differ (from)

agree (with) *adj syn* see SUIT 4

agreeability *n syn* see AMENITY 1

agreeable *adj* **1** *syn* see PLEASANT 1
rel delectable, delightful
ant disagreeable
2 *syn* see CONSONANT 1
con conflicting, inharmonious, jarring, uncongenial

agreeableness *n syn* see AMENITY 1

agreed *adv syn* see YES 1

agreement *n* **1** *syn* see HARMONY 2
ant disagreement
2 a settlement reached by parties to a dispute or negotiation <the company has reached an *agreement* with the striking workers>
syn accord, deal, understanding; *compare* CONTRACT
rel cartel, concordat, convention, entente, pact; compact, contract, covenant, treaty; engagement; consensus
3 *syn* see TREATY
4 *syn* see CONTRACT

agrestal *adj syn* see WILD 1

agrestic *adj syn* see RURAL

agriculture *n* the science or business of raising useful plants and animals <opening the country for *agriculture*>

syn farming, husbandry

aground *adj* being or becoming forced onto the ground or shore <the boat is *aground* and breaking up>
syn beached, grounded, stranded
idiom high and dry, on the rocks
ant afloat

ahead *adv* **1** *syn* see BEFORE 1
con after
ant behind
2 further on in the direction in question <the road stretched *ahead* toward the west>
syn alee, forth, forward, onward

ahead of *prep syn* see BEFORE 1

aid *vb syn* see HELP 1
rel alleviate, lighten, mitigate, relieve
ant impede

aid *n* **1** *syn* see HELP 1
2 *syn* see HELP 2
rel alleviation, assuagement, mitigation; backing, support
idiom a leg up
con check, curb, restraint; bar, obstacle, obstruction
ant impediment
3 *syn* see HELPER
4 *syn* see ASSISTANT 2
rel aider, befriender, benefactor, ministrant, succorer; striker

aidant *adj syn* see HELPFUL 1

aide *n syn* see ASSISTANT 2

aide–de–camp *n syn* see ASSISTANT 2

aiding *adj syn* see HELPFUL 1

ail *vb syn* see TROUBLE 1
rel afflict, try
idiom be the matter (with), give one trouble
con alleviate, ease, relieve; comfort, console, solace

ailing *adj syn* see UNWELL
rel debilitated, enfeebled, gone, strengthless, weak; droopy, limp, sapless, spiritless
con hale, lusty, robust, rugged, vigorous

ailment *n* **1** *syn* see DISEASE
2 *syn* see UNREST

aim *vb* **1** *syn* see DIRECT 2
rel concentrate, fix, focus
idiom draw a bead on, take aim
2 to have as a controlling desire something that transcends one's present capacity for attainment <from a boy he had *aimed* at high office>
syn aspire, pant
rel attempt, endeavor, essay, strive, try; design, intend, propose, purpose; covet, crave, yearn (for)
idiom have an eye to, reach for the stars, set one's eyes upon
3 *syn* see INTEND 2
rel choose, desire, want, wish; expect
idiom have (or keep) in view, promise oneself (to)
4 *syn* see SLANT 2

aim *n syn* see AMBITION 2
rel desideratum, desire, idol, urge
idiom end in view

aimless *adj syn* see RANDOM

air *n* **1** *syn* see BEARING 1
rel manner, style
2 *usu* **airs** *pl syn* see POSE 2

rel loftiness, ostentation, pretentiousness, show; complacency, self-importance, vainglory, vanity

3 a pervading influence that colors outward appearance or apparent character <the village had an *air* of decay>
syn atmosphere, aura, feel, feeling, mood, semblance
rel character, property, quality
con basis, essence, reality
4 *syn* see MELODY

air *vb syn* see EXPRESS 2
rel discover, divulge, reveal; broadcast, declare, proclaim, publish
idiom make public, noise (*or* sound) abroad, spread far and wide

airless *adj syn* see STUFFY 1

airman *n syn* see PILOT 2

airy *adj* 1 of or relating to air <clouds drifting on *airy* currents>
syn aerial, atmospheric, pneumatic
rel gaseous, vaporous
2 *syn* see LOFTY 6
rel exposed, windswept; supernal
3 resembling or suggesting air especially in lightness or lack of substance <*airy* persiflage>
syn aerial, ethereal, vaporous, vapory
rel frivolous, light, volatile; rare, rarefied, tenuous, thin; dainty, delicate, diaphanous, exquisite, spirituel
con corporeal, material, physical; bulky, massive, massy
ant substantial
4 *syn* see ELASTIC 2
rel animated, high-spirited, spirited
5 *syn* see WINDY 1

akin *adj* 1 *syn* see RELATED
2 *syn* see LIKE
rel kindred; according, agreeing, conforming, harmonizing
con extraneous, foreign
ant alien

alacrity *n* promptness in responding or acting <accepted the invitation with *alacrity*>
syn dispatch, expedition, goodwill, promptitude, readiness
rel briskness, eagerness; enthusiasm, fervor, heartiness, zeal; promptness, quickness
con hesitation, procrastination, temporization, vacillation; apathy, indifference, lethargy, phlegm, sluggishness
ant dilatoriness

a la mode *adj syn* see STYLISH

alarm *n* 1 a signal that warns or calls to action <the *alarm* consisted of two quick flashes of light>
syn alert, SOS, tocsin
rel caution, forewarning, prenotice, warning
2 *syn* see FEAR 1
rel upset; strain, stress, tension
con calm, calmness, serenity, tranquillity; equanimity, sangfroid

ant assurance; composure

alarm *vb syn* see FRIGHTEN
rel amaze, astonish, surprise
idiom give one a turn
con comfort, console, solace
ant assure, relieve

alarmable *adj syn* see EXCITABLE

albeit *conj syn* see THOUGH

album *n syn* see ANTHOLOGY

alcohol *n syn* see LIQUOR 2

alcoholic *adj syn* see SPIRITUOUS

alcoholized *adj syn* see INTOXICATED 1

alcove *n syn* see SUMMERHOUSE

alee *adv syn* see AHEAD 2

alehouse *n* an establishment serving primarily beer and ale <an *alehouse* specializing in beers actually brewed on the premises>
syn beer garden, beer hall, ‖beerhouse, bierstube, mughouse, stube; *compare* BAR 5
rel barrelhouse, bistro, bottle club, brasserie, cabaret, café, honky-tonk, nightclub, rathskeller, roadhouse, wineshop

alembicated *adj syn* see PRECIOUS 4

alert *adj* 1 *syn* see WATCHFUL
rel attentive, heedful, mindful; careful
idiom all eyes and ears, on (one's) guard, on the alert
con inattentive, unmindful; aloof, detached, indifferent, unconcerned
2 *syn* see INTELLIGENT 2
rel apt, prompt, quick, ready
con lackadaisical, languid, listless
3 *syn* see LIVELY 1
rel frisky; mercurial
idiom full of life
con inactive, indolent
ant inert

alert *n syn* see ALARM 1

alfresco *adj syn* see OUTDOOR

algetic *adj syn* see PAINFUL 1

alias *n syn* see PSEUDONYM

alibi *n syn* see EXCUSE 1

alien *adj syn* see EXTRINSIC
rel exotic, outlandish, strange; incompatible, incongruous, inconsonant
con cognate, kindred, related; compatible, congenial, congruous, consonant; germane, material, pertinent, relevant
ant akin; assimilable

alien *n syn* see STRANGER
con national, subject
ant citizen

alien *vb* 1 *syn* see ESTRANGE
rel alter, change, convert
con accommodate, adjust, conform, reconcile
ant unite; reunite
2 *syn* see TRANSFER 4
rel give up, hand over, relinquish

alienate *vb* 1 *syn* see TRANSFER 4
rel give up, hand over, relinquish
2 *syn* see ESTRANGE
rel alter, change, convert
con accommodate, adjust, conform, reconcile
ant unite; reunite

alienation *n* 1 *syn* see ESTRANGEMENT
2 *syn* see INSANITY 1

alight *vb* to come to rest after or as if after a flight, a descent, or a fall <snowflakes *alighting* on the bare trees>

---

syn synonym(s)   *rel* related word(s)
ant antonym(s)   *con* contrasted word(s)
idiom idiomatic equivalent(s)
‖ use limited; if in doubt, see a dictionary

syn land, light, perch, roost, set down, settle, sit down, touch down
rel drop, fall, tumble
con arise, ascend, rise, soar

alight *adj* 1 *syn* see BURNING 1
2 made bright by or as if by fire <her face *alight* with joy>
syn ablaze, afire, aflame, aflicker, aglow
rel bright, effulgent, fulgent, refulgent; blazing, flaming, flaring, glowing
con dark, dusky, gloomy, heavy, lowery, shadowed, shadowy

align *vb* 1 *syn* see LINE 1
rel adjust, fix, regulate
con unsettle

alike *adj* *syn* see LIKE
con separate
ant unlike; different

alikeness *n* *syn* see LIKENESS

aliment *n* *syn* see FOOD 2

alimentary *adj* *syn* see NUTRITIVE 1

alimentation *n* *syn* see LIVING

alimentative *adj* *syn* see NUTRITIVE 1

alimony *n* *syn* see LIVING

alive *adj* 1 *syn* see LIVING 1
con inactive, inert
ant dead, defunct
2 *syn* see EXTANT 1
3 *syn* see ACTIVE 1
rel fresh, green, verdant
con dormant, inactive, quiescent
ant dead, extinct
4 *syn* see AWARE
rel vigilant, watchful, wide-awake; intelligent, quick, quick-witted
con heedless, inattentive, oblivious, unmindful; careless, negligent, negligent
ant blind (to)
5 full of vigorous life, animation, or activity <the streets were *alive* with shoppers>
syn abounding, overflowing, replete, rife, swarming, teeming, thronged
rel crowded, populous, thick; filled, flush, full
con barren, empty, vacant, void; unoccupied, unpopulated, untenanted

all *adj* 1 *syn* see WHOLE 4
rel full, plenary
2 each member or individual of <*all* my friends came with me>
syn each, every
ant no

all *adv* 1 without exception <the money was *all* spent>
syn all in all, altogether, exactly, in toto, just, purely, quite, stick, totally, utterly, wholly
idiom in its entirety
2 *syn* see APIECE

all *pron* 1 *syn* see EVERYTHING
2 *syn* see EVERYBODY

all *n* *syn* see WHOLE 1

all–around *adj* 1 *syn* see VERSATILE
rel complete, consummate
2 not narrowly particularized <taking an *all-around* view of the problem>
syn comprehensive, general, global, inclusive, overall, sweeping
rel broad, extensive, panoramic, wide; all-inclusive, unexcluding, unexclusive, wide-ranging; synoptic

con express, particular, specific; narrow, precise, restricted; individual, singular

allay *vb* 1 *syn* see RELIEVE 1
con arouse, rouse, stir; excite, provoke, stimulate; aggravate, enhance
ant intensify
2 *syn* see CALM
rel ease, soften, subdue; deaden, dull, temper; disburden, disembarrass, disencumber; deliver, free, release
con aggravate, enhance, heighten, magnify, worsen
ant intensify

all but *adv* 1 *syn* see NEARLY
2 *syn* see ALMOST 2

allege *vb* 1 *syn* see ADDUCE
rel affirm, assert, avouch, avow, declare, profess; recite, recount, rehearse, state
con contradict, deny, gainsay, impugn, negate, negative; controvert, disprove, rebut, refute
ant contravene

alleged *adj* of questionable truth or genuineness <had doubts of the *alleged* miracle>
syn ostensible, pretended, professed, purported, so-called, supposed; *compare* SUPPOSED 1
rel credible, plausible, specious; doubtful, dubious, questionable; self-styled, soi-disant, would-be
idiom in name only
con authentic, bona fide, genuine, veritable; actual, real, true; delusory, erroneous, fallacious, false, illusory, imaginary, unreal

allegiance *n* *syn* see FIDELITY 1
rel firmness, consecration, dedication; deference, homage, honor
con alienation, disaffection; disloyalty, treason

allegiant *adj* *syn* see FAITHFUL 1

allegory *n* 1 a method of indirect representation (as in literature or art) of ideas or truths <by *allegory* such abstractions as love and fear can be depicted>
syn figuration, symbolism, symbolization, typification
2 a literary form that tells a story to present a truth or enforce a moral <Orwell's *Animal Farm* is a well-known English *allegory*>
syn apologue, fable, myth, parable; *compare* MYTH 1

allergy *n* *syn* see ANTIPATHY 2
rel rejection, repulsion, revulsion
con affinity, attraction, sympathy

alleviate *vb* *syn* see RELIEVE 1
rel cure, remedy
idiom temper the wind to the shorn lamb
con augment, heighten, intensify
ant aggravate

alleviation *n* *syn* see EASE 3

all–fired *adj* *syn* see UTTER

alliance *n* 1 *syn* see ASSOCIATION 1
2 an association (as of nations) for a common object <a world *alliance* in support of peace>
syn anschluss, coalition, confederacy, confederation, federation, league, union; *compare* UNIFICATION
rel association, club, order, society

allied *adj* *syn* see RELATED

rel linked, united; parallel, similar
con alien, extraneous, foreign; discrete, separate, several
ant unallied
all in *adj syn see* EFFETE 2
  idiom at last gasp
all in all *adv* **1** *syn see* ALL 1
  2 *syn see* ALTOGETHER 3
allineate *vb syn see* LINE 1
allness *n syn see* ENTIRETY 1
allocate *vb* **1** *syn see* ALLOT
  con reserve, sequester, stockpile
  2 *syn see* DESIGNATE 3
allocution *n syn see* SPEECH 2
allot *vb* to give as one's share, portion, role, or place <*allotted* himself a daily hour for exercise>
  syn admeasure, allocate, allow, apportion, assign, give, lot, mete (out)
  rel deal (out), dispense, distribute, dole (out); equip, fit out, furnish; accord, grant, vouchsafe; appoint, ordain, prescribe
  con detain, hold, hold back, keep, retain, withhold; appropriate, arrogate, confiscate
allotment *n* **1** *syn see* SHARE 1
  2 *syn see* RATION
all–out *adj syn see* TOTAL 5
all over *adv syn see* EVERYWHERE 1
allover *adj syn see* OMNIPRESENT
‖all–overs *n pl syn see* JITTERS
allow *vb* **1** *syn see* ALLOT
  rel bestow, confer
  con refuse
  2 *syn see* ACKNOWLEDGE 1
  rel accede, acquiesce, assent
  con confute, refute, reject
  ant disallow
  3 *syn see* LET 2
  rel brook, endure, stand, tolerate; defer, submit, yield
  con avert, prevent, ward (off)
  ant inhibit
allowable *adj syn see* PERMISSIBLE
allowance *n* **1** *syn see* RATION
  rel assignment; appropriation, grant, subsidy
  2 *syn see* SHARE 1
  3 *syn see* ADVANTAGE 3
  rel aid, assistance, help; bounty, grant, subsidy
  4 *syn see* PERMISSION
  rel countenance, favor; indulgence, toleration
  con refusal, rejection; contradiction, contravention, negation
  5 a taking into account of extenuating circumstances or of contingencies <we must make *allowance* for the inexperience of youth>
  syn concession
  rel accommodation, adaptation, adjustment; extenuation, mitigation, palliation
alloy *n* **1** *syn see* ADMIXTURE 1
  2 *syn see* MIXTURE
all–powerful *adj syn see* OMNIPOTENT

all right *adv syn see* YES 1
all right *adj syn see* DECENT 4
all round (*or* all around) *adv syn see* EVERYWHERE 1
all there *adj syn see* SANE 2
all told *adv syn see* ALTOGETHER 3
allude *vb syn see* REFER 3
  rel hint, imply, intimate, suggest
allure *vb* **1** *syn see* ATTRACT 1
  rel delude; woo
  con avoid, elude, eschew, shun; alienate, disaffect, estrange, wean
  2 *syn see* LURE
allure *n syn see* CHARM 3
allurement *n* **1** *syn see* ATTRACTION 1
  2 *syn see* LURE 2
alluring *adj syn see* ATTRACTIVE 1
  rel appetizing; beguiling, delusive
  con repellent; disagreeable, displeasing, uninviting, unlikable, unpleasant
  ant repulsive
almighty *adj syn see* OMNIPOTENT
almost *adv* **1** *syn see* NEARLY
  2 not actually but in effect <he paid *almost* nothing for it>
  syn all but, as good as, as much as, essentially, practically, well–nigh; *compare* VIRTUALLY
  idiom for all practical purposes, in effect, just about, to all intents and purposes
alms *n pl syn see* DONATION
aloft *adv syn see* OVER 4
  rel high; skyward, upward
  idiom in the clouds
alone *adj* **1** separated from others <the house was *alone* on a windy ridge>
  syn apart, detached, isolate, isolated, removed, unaccompanied
  rel out-of-the-way, private, remote, retired, secluded, withdrawn
  idiom off the beaten track
  con adjacent, close-by, near-at-hand, nearly, neighboring, nigh
  2 *syn see* LONE 1
  3 having no equal or rival and being single in kind or excellence <a drug *alone* in its curative powers>
  syn matchless, only, peerless, unequaled, unique, unmatched, unparalleled, unrivaled; *compare* SUPREME
  rel inimitable; incomparable, unexcelled, unsurpassed; excellent, good, superior
  idiom second to none
  con common, commonplace, everyday, ordinary, usual; accustomed, conventional, customary, regular
  4 *syn see* ONLY 2
alone *adv syn see* ONLY 1
aloneness *n syn see* SOLITUDE
along *adv* **1** so as to make forward progress <hurrying *along* toward town>
  syn forth, forward, on, onward; *compare* AHEAD 2
  2 *syn see* ALSO 2
alongside *prep syn see* BESIDE 1
aloof *adj* **1** *syn see* INDIFFERENT 2
  rel arrogant, disdainful, haughty, proud; chilly, cold, cool, frigid; constrained, reserved, restrained, reticent, standoffish
  con affable, companionable, gregarious, sociable, social; friendly, neighborly

---

syn synonym(s)   *rel* related word(s)
ant antonym(s)   *con* contrasted word(s)
idiom idiomatic equivalent(s)
‖ use limited; if in doubt, see a dictionary

ant familiar; outgoing
2 syn see UNSOCIABLE

alp *n syn* see MOUNTAIN 1

alpha *n syn* see BEGINNING
ant omega

alphabet *n* **1** a set of characters in which a language can be written <the Greek *alphabet*>
syn ABC(s), christcross-row, letters
2 the simplest fundamental part or level <learning the *alphabet* of computer science>
syn ABC's, elements, fundamentals, grammar, principles, rudiments
rel beginning, commencement, start; outset
idiom first steps
con entirety, total, whole; details, minutiae, trivia

already *adv* **1 syn** see BEFORE 2
2 syn see EVEN 2

also *adv* **1** in the same manner <they *also* serve who nurse the wounded soldiers>
syn correspondingly, likewise, similarly, so
idiom in like manner
2 in addition to that <he was stern but *also* just>
syn additionally, along, as well, besides, furthermore, item, likewise, more, moreover, still, too, withal, yea, yet
idiom into the bargain, on top of that, to boot
3 syn see AGAIN 4

alter *vb* **1 syn** see CHANGE 1
rel accommodate, adapt, adjust, moderate, modulate, temper; doctor
idiom work a change (in)
con conserve, keep, preserve, retain
ant fix
2 syn see STERILIZE

alteration *n* **1 syn** see CHANGE 1
rel accommodation, adaptation, adjustment; conversion, metamorphosis, transformation; fluctuation, shilly-shally, vacillation, wavering
con perdurability, permanence, stability; continuance, endurance, persistence
ant fixation, fixity
2 syn see TRANSITION
3 syn see CONVERSION 2

altercate *vb syn* see QUARREL
rel agitate, argue, debate, dispute
con accord, get along; accommodate, adapt, adjust, conform
ant concur

altercation *n syn* see QUARREL
rel argument; combat, contest
con agreement, concord, consonance, harmony; empathy, like-mindedness, sympathy, understanding
ant accord; concurrence

alterity *n syn* see DISSIMILARITY

alternate *adj* **1 syn** see INTERMITTENT
rel alternant, alternating, rotating; complementary, corresponding, reciprocal
con sequent, successive
ant consecutive
2 syn see SUBSTITUTE 1
rel equivalent, proxy, replacing; exchangeable, interchangeable; makeshift, provisional, tentative

alternate *vb syn* see ROTATE 2

rel fluctuate, oscillate, sway, waver; recur, return, revert
con follow, succeed

alternate *n syn* see SUBSTITUTE

alternately *adv syn* see INSTEAD

alternation *n syn* see SUCCESSION 2
rel recurrence, return, reversion; reappearance, repetition

alternative *adj syn* see SUBSTITUTE 1
rel equivalent, proxy, replacing; exchangeable, interchangeable; makeshift, provisional, tentative

alternative *n syn* see CHOICE 1
rel attainable, contingency, possibility

alternatively *adv syn* see INSTEAD

although *conj syn* see THOUGH

altitude *n syn* see HEIGHT
rel apex, eminence, peak, summit
con depth

altitudinous *adj syn* see HIGH 1

altogether *adv* **1 syn** see WELL 3
2 syn see ALL 1
3 as a total <*altogether* it cost over a thousand dollars>
syn all told, in all, quite
idiom taken together
4 with minor exceptions or flaws <*altogether* the party was a success>
syn all in all, by and large, en masse, generally, on the whole
idiom all things considered, as a whole, for the most part, generally speaking, in the main

altruistic *adj syn* see CHARITABLE 1
rel considerate, kind, unselfish; bounteous, bountiful, generous, liberal, openhanded; bighearted, magnanimous, noble-minded
con egotistic, self-centered, selfish, self-seeking; illiberal, mean, niggardly, stingy, ungenerous
ant egoistic

always *adv* **1** on every relevant occasion <*always* made the same mistake>
syn constantly, continuously, ever, invariably, perpetually
rel frequently, often, regularly, usually
idiom in every case (or instance), without exception
con rarely, seldom
ant never
2 syn see EVER 2

‖**amah** *n syn* see NURSEMAID

amalgam *n syn* see MIXTURE

amalgamate *vb syn* see MIX 1
rel compact, consolidate, unify
con crumble, decompose, disintegrate; disperse, dissipate, scatter

amalgamation *n* **1 syn** see MIXTURE
2 syn see CONSOLIDATION 2

amaranthine *adj syn* see EVERLASTING 1

amaroidal *adj syn* see ACRID

amass *vb syn* see ACCUMULATE
ant distribute

amassment *n syn* see ACCUMULATION

amateur *n* **1** one having a marked and usually informed taste or liking for something <an *amateur* of fine fabrics>
syn admirer, devotee, fan, fancier, votary
rel crank, enthusiast, faddist, infatuate, ‖nut, zealot; aesthete, cognoscente, connoisseur, dilettante; illuminato, illuminist

con abecedarian, dabbler, tyro; adept, expert

2 one who follows a pursuit without attaining mastery or professional status <a nation handicapped by *amateurs* in high office>
syn abecedarian, dabbler, dilettante, nonprofessional, smatterer, tyro, uninitiated
rel beginner, greenhorn, neophyte; apprentice, novice, probationer; potterer, putterer, tinker
con adept, virtuoso, wizard
ant expert, master; professional

amateurish *adj* lacking or marked by lack of expert skill or finish <an *amateurish* actor>
syn dabbling, dilettante, dilettantish, dilettantist, jackleg, unaccomplished, unfinished, ungifted, unskilled
rel clumsy, crude, green, raw, untutored; defective, deficient, faulty, flawed
con accomplished, expert, gifted, skilled
ant professional

amative *adj syn* see EROTIC

amatory *adj syn* see EROTIC
rel admiring, attracted, yearning

amaze *vb syn* see SURPRISE 2
rel affect, impress, move, strike, touch

amaze *n syn* see WONDER 2
rel confoundment; surprise

amazement *n syn* see WONDER 2
rel confoundment; surprise

amazing *adj syn* see MARVELOUS 1

amazon *n syn* see VIRAGO

ambidextrous *adj* **1** *syn* see TWO-HANDED 2
2 *syn* see VERSATILE
3 *syn* see INSINCERE

ambience *n syn* see ENVIRONMENT

ambient *n syn* see ENVIRONMENT

ambiguity *n* expression or an expression obscure because subject to more than one interpretation <a speech full of *ambiguities*>
syn amphibology, double entendre, double meaning, equivocality, equivocation, equivoque, tergiversation
rel dodge, evasion, hedge, quibble, shift, subterfuge; cavil, haggling, hairsplitting, quibbling; obscurity, uncertainty, vagueness
con definiteness, expressness, specificity; clearness, exactness, precision
ant explicitness; lucidity

ambiguous *adj* **1** *syn* see OBSCURE 3
rel doubtful, dubious, questionable
con clear, lucid, perspicuous; categorical, express, specific
ant explicit
2 *syn* see DOUBTFUL 1

ambit *n* **1** *syn* see CIRCUMFERENCE
2 *syn* see RANGE 2

ambition *n* **1** strong desire for advancement <a life ruled by *ambition*>
syn ambitiousness, aspiration, pretension
rel drive, go-ahead, push; anxiety, avidity, eagerness, keenness; energy, enterprise, spirit; goad, incentive, motive, spur
con contentment, satisfaction; faineance, indolence, lethargy, sloth

2 an object of desire or intent <his *ambition* was to have enough to live on without working>
syn aim, goal, mark, objective, quaesitum, target; *compare* INTENTION
rel design, intent, purpose; desire, fancy, hope, wish; dream, ideal, nirvana
3 *syn* see ENTERPRISE 4

ambitious *adj* **1** marked by intense desire for advancement (as in power, fame, or wealth) <a ruthlessly *ambitious* politician>
syn aspiring, emulous, vaulting
rel aggressive, enterprising, go-ahead, pushing, up-and-doing; energetic, hardworking, indefatigable; anxious, avid, eager, keen
con apathetic, phlegmatic, stolid; faineant, indolent, lazy, slothful
2 of a kind to try or exceed one's powers of performance <an *ambitious* scheme to corner the gold market>
syn grandiose, lofty, pretentious, utopian, visionary
rel audacious, bold, daring; chimerical, extravagant, high-flown, impractical, quixotic, unrealistic
con easy, plain, straightforward; feasible, practicable, realistic; unpretentious
ant modest

ambitiousness *n syn* see AMBITION 1

ambivalent *adj syn* see EQUIVOCAL 2

amble *vb syn* see SAUNTER
rel dally, dawdle, dillydally, loiter

ambrosial *adj* **1** *syn* see DELIGHTFUL
2 *syn* see SWEET 2

ambulant *adj syn* see ITINERANT
ant bedfast, bedridden

ambulate *vb syn* see WALK 1

ambulatory *adj syn* see ITINERANT

ambuscade *n syn* see AMBUSH

ambush *vb syn* see SURPRISE 1
rel assail, assault, attack; ensnare, entrap, snare, trap

ambush *n* a device to entrap an enemy by lying in hiding until a surprise attack is feasible <planned an *ambush* on the cliff above the trail>
syn ambuscade, ambushment
rel lure, snare, trap; blind, cover, hideout, retreat

ambushment *n syn* see AMBUSH

ameliorate *vb* **1** *syn* see IMPROVE 1
rel alleviate, lighten, mitigate, relieve
con damage, harm, hurt, impair, injure, mar, spoil; aggravate, intensify
ant worsen; deteriorate
2 *syn* see IMPROVE 3

amenable *adj* **1** *syn* see RESPONSIBLE
rel open, subject; dependent, subordinate
con autarchic, free
ant independent (of); autonomous
2 *syn* see OBEDIENT
rel subdued, tame; receptive, responsive, willing; adaptable, impressionable, malleable, plastic, pliable, pliant
con fierce, mulish, obstinate, stubborn, truculent
ant recalcitrant, refractory

amend *vb* **1** *syn* see CORRECT 1
rel repair; elevate, lift, raise
con corrupt, debauch, deprave, pervert, vitiate

---

ant debase

2 syn see IMPROVE 1

rel advance, forward, promote

ant worsen; impair

amends *n pl syn* see REPARATION

amenity *n* **1** the quality of being pleasant or agreeable <a discussion conducted in perfect *amenity*><the *amenity* of the climate>

syn agreeability, agreeableness, amiability, cordiality, enjoyableness, geniality, gratefulness, pleasance, pleasantness, sweetness and light

rel attractiveness, charm, delightfulness; fascination, pleasingness

con disagreeableness, distastefulness, unattractiveness, unpleasantness

2 a feature that makes for pleasantness or ease <among the *amenities* of the house is central air-conditioning>

syn comfort, convenience, facility

rel betterment, enhancement, enrichment, improvement; excellence, merit, quality, virtue

con difficulty, hardship, trial, vicissitude

3 *pl amenities syn* see MANNER 5

4 syn see LUXURY

5 syn see COURTESY 1

rel civility, courteousness, politeness; affability, cordiality, geniality, graciousness, sociability

con discourtesy, impoliteness, incivility; affront, indignity, insult; acrimony

ant rudeness

ament *n syn* see FOOL 4

amerce *vb syn* see PENALIZE

amercement *n syn* see FINE

amiability *n syn* see AMENITY 1

amiable *adj* **1** of a generally agreeable nature especially in social interaction <the meeting ended on an *amiable* note>

syn complaisant, easy, good-humored, good-natured, good-tempered, lenient, mild, obliging

rel affable, cordial, genial, gracious; courteous, mannerly, benign, benignant, kind, kindly; responsive, warm, warmhearted

idiom easy to get along with

con discourteous, ill-mannered, ill-natured, impolite, rude; crabbed, dour, unsociable

ant unamiable; surly

2 syn see GENTLE 2

amicable *adj* **1** characterized by peaceableness and goodwill <the negotiators joined in *amicable* discussion>

syn friendly, neighborly

rel empathic, like-minded, sympathetic, understanding; accordant, agreeing, concordant, frictionless, harmonious; pacific, peaceable, peaceful

con bellicose, belligerent, combative, contentious, pugnacious, quarrelsome; antipathetic, hostile, suspicious, uncooperative

2 syn see HARMONIOUS 3

amical *adj syn* see HARMONIOUS 3

amid *prep* **1** in or into the central part of <the bomb burst *amid* the crowd>

syn among, mid, midst

idiom in (*or* into) the middle of, in (*or* into) the midst of, in (*or* into) the thick of

2 syn see AMONG 1

3 syn see DURING

amigo *n syn* see FRIEND

amiss *adv* **1** in a mistaken, inappropriate, or reprehensible way <I feel you judge him *amiss*>

syn faultily, incorrectly, wrongly

rel inaccurately; indiscreetly, unwisely

con accurately, correctly, properly, rightly; cleverly, wisely

ant right

2 out of the proper course <our planning had gone *amiss*>

syn afield, astray, awry, badly, unfavorably, wrong; compare HARD 5

idiom beside (*or* off) the mark

con auspiciously, famously, favorably, promisingly, propitiously, well

ant aright

amiss *adj* **1 syn** see BAD 1

2 syn see FAULTY

3 syn see BLAMEWORTHY

amity *n syn* see GOODWILL 1

rel accord, agreement, concord, harmony; amicableness, neighborliness

con animosity, antagonism, antipathy, hostility; conflict, contention, discord, dissension, strife

ant enmity

amnesty *n syn* see PARDON

among *prep* **1** surrounded by <the valley nestled *among* high mountains>

syn amid, mid, midst

2 syn see AMID 1

3 syn see BETWEEN

amorist *n syn* see GALLANT 2

amorous *adj syn* see EROTIC

rel enamored, infatuated; lustful

con aloof, detached, indifferent; cold, cool; apathetic, impassive, unconcerned

ant frigid

amorousness *n syn* see LOVE 2

amorphous *adj syn* see FORMLESS

amount *vb* **1** to make up as a total <their expenses *amounted* to just a hundred dollars>

syn add up, aggregate, come, number, run (to *or* into), sum (to *or* into), total

rel comprehend, comprise, embody, include, incorporate, reach, subsume

2 to be essentially equivalent <that utter terror that *amounts* to madness>

syn approach, correspond (to), equal, match, partake (of), rival, touch

rel hint, imply, intimate, smack (of), suggest

idiom be near to, come to the same thing as, have all the earmarks (*or* features) of

amount *n* **1 syn** see BODY 5

2 syn see SUBSTANCE 2

amour *n* **1 syn** see LOVE AFFAIR

2 an illicit or informal sexual relation <memoirs devoted to accounts of his *amours*>

syn affair, intrigue, liaison

rel entanglement, intimacy, relationship; love affair, romance

3 syn see LOVE AFFAIR

amour propre *n* **1 syn** see PRIDE 2

2 syn see CONCEIT 2

rel complacency, self-complacency, self-satisfaction, smugness; pride

amphibological *adj syn* see OBSCURE 3

amphibology *n syn* see AMBIGUITY

ample *adj* **1** *syn* see SPACIOUS
rel distended, expanded, inflated, swollen
con scant, skimpy, spare; cramped, exiguous, narrow, strait
ant meager; circumscribed
2 *syn* see PLENTIFUL
rel lavish, prodigal, profuse; handsome
idiom enough and to spare
con scrimpy, spare, sparse; beggarly, miserable, niggardly
ant meager, scant

amplify *vb* **1** *syn* see EXPAND 4
rel augment, extend, increase; unfold
con abbreviate, shorten
ant abridge, condense
2 *syn* see EXPAND 3

amplitude *n* **1** *syn* see SIZE 2
2 *syn* see BREADTH 2
con closeness, limitation, restriction, straitness
ant narrowness
3 *syn* see EXPANSE
rel bigness, greatness, largeness; capaciousness, commodiousness, roominess, spaciousness
con circumscription, restriction
ant straitness; limitation

amply *adv syn* see WELL 4

amulet *n syn* see CHARM 2
rel lucky piece, rabbit-foot

amuse *vb* to pass or cause to pass time in pleasant or agreeable activity <simple toys to *amuse* children on long trips>
syn divert, entertain, recreate
rel absorb, distract, engross; animate, enliven, fleet, quicken; beguile, charm, delight, enchant, fascinate, wile; while
con fatigue, irk, jade, pall (on), tire, wear (on), weary; bore, ennui

amusement *n syn* see ENTERTAINMENT

ana *n syn* see ANTHOLOGY

anabasis *n syn* see ADVANCE 2

anachronism *n* **1** a chronological error <*anachronisms* of several centuries mar some earlier chronicles>
syn misdate, misdating, mistiming, parachronism
rel antedate, anticipation, prochronism, prolepsis; postdate
2 one that is inappropriately situated especially in time <born centuries too late, he was an *anachronism* in modern urban society>
syn solecism
rel faux pas, gaffe; defect, flaw, mistake, slip

anagogic *adj syn* see MYSTICAL 1
rel esoteric, occult, recondite; allegorical, symbolical

analects *n pl syn* see ANTHOLOGY

analgesic *n syn* see ANODYNE 1
ant irritant

analogous *adj syn* see LIKE
rel convertible, corresponding, interchangeable; kindred

analogue *n syn* see PARALLEL
rel cognate, congener

analogy *n* **1** *syn* see LIKENESS
2 expression or an expression involving explicit or implied comparison of things basically unlike but with some striking similarities <God can be described only by *analogy*>
syn metaphor, simile, similitude
rel ambiguity, equivocation, equivoque, tergiversation
con demonstration, description, formulation

analphabet *n syn* see ILLITERATE

analysis *n* **1** separation of a whole into its fundamental elements or constituent parts <*analysis* of a problem>
syn breakdown, breakup, dissection, resolution
rel division, separation; decomposition, disintegration
con combination, union; concatenation, integration, unification
ant synthesis
2 *syn* see EXAMINATION

analytic *adj syn* see LOGICAL 2
rel deep, profound; acute, keen, sharp; penetrating, piercing
con constructive, creative, inventive

analytical *adj syn* see LOGICAL 2

analyze *vb* to divide a complex whole into its constituent parts or elements <*analyze* the plot of a novel>
syn anatomize, break down, decompose, decompound, dissect, resolve
rel divide, part, separate; assort, classify, pigeonhole; examine, inspect, investigate, scrutinize
con articulate, concatenate, integrate
ant compose, compound; construct

anamnesis *n syn* see MEMORY 2

Ananias *n syn* see LIAR

anarch *n syn* see REBEL

anarchism *n* **1** a political theory opposed to all forms of government and advocating voluntary cooperation and interaction of individuals and groups in satisfying their common needs <the doubtful premises of *anarchism* about human nature>
syn anarchy
rel utopianism; communism, Marxism, syndicalism
con absolutism, authoritarianism, dictatorship; elitism
2 *syn* see DISORDER 2

anarchist *n syn* see REBEL

anarchy *n* **1** absence of effective government or the resulting social disorder <complete *anarchy* followed the breakdown of communications>
syn chaos, lawlessness, mobocracy, ochlocracy
rel confusion, disorder, disorganization
idiom mob rule (*or* law), reign of terror
2 *syn* see ANARCHISM
3 *syn* see DISORDER 2

anastomose *vb syn* see INTERJOIN

anathema *n* **1** *syn* see CURSE 1
rel censure, condemnation, denunciation, reprehension, reprobation, reproof

---

syn synonym(s)	*rel* related word(s)
ant antonym(s)	*con* contrasted word(s)
idiom idiomatic equivalent(s)	

‖ use limited; if in doubt, see a dictionary

con eulogy, laudation, praise
2 syn see ABOMINATION 1
rel leper, pariah, outcast, untouchable

anathematize *vb syn* see EXECRATE 1
rel impugn, reproach
con approbate, approve, countenance,
endorse, favor

anatomize *vb syn* see ANALYZE

ancestor *n* **1** a person from whom one is
descended <proud of his pioneer *ancestors*>
syn antecedent (s), ascendant, forebear,
forefather, primogenitor, progenitor
ant descendant
2 syn see FORERUNNER 2

ancestry *n* one's progenitors or their character or quality as a whole <a man of noble
ancestry>
syn blood, descent, extraction, lineage,
origin, pedigree
rel family, kindred, line, race, stock; derivation, source; breed, breeding
ant descendants; posterity

anchor *vb syn* see FASTEN 1
rel imbed, plant
idiom make fast (*or* secure)

anchorage *n syn* see HARBOR 3

ancient *adj* **1** persisting from the distant past
<an *ancient* monument>
syn aged, age-old, antediluvian, antique,
hoary, Noachian, old, timeworn, venerable;
compare OBSOLETE
rel primal, primeval, primordial, pristine;
forgotten, immemorial, remote, traditional;
ageless, dateless
idiom old as time, older than God (*or* the
hills), out of the dim past
con current, fresh, new, novel, prevailing,
up-to-date
ant modern
2 syn see AGED 1
rel doddering, doting, fading, sinking,
waning, wasting
idiom old as Methuselah (*or* the hills)

ancient *n syn* see OLDSTER

ancilla *n syn* see HELPER

ancillary *adj* **1** *syn* see AUXILIARY
2 syn see CONCOMITANT

androgynous *adj syn* see BISEXUAL

android *n syn* see ROBOT 1

anecdote *n syn* see STORY 2
rel recital, relation; episode, event, incident

anemic *adj syn* see PALE 2

anent *prep syn* see APROPOS

anesthetic *adj syn* see INSENSIBLE 5
rel impenetrable, impermeable, impervious;
obtuse
con responsive, sensitive

anesthetic *n syn* see ANODYNE 1
ant stimulant

anesthetized *adj syn* see NUMB 1

anew *adv* **1** *syn* see OVER 7
2 syn see NEW

anfractuous *adj syn* see WINDING

angel *n syn* see SPONSOR
rel ‖butter-and-egg man

angelic *adj syn* see SAINTLY

anger *n* emotional excitement induced by
intense displeasure <a man easily aroused to
anger>
syn fury, indignation, ire, mad, rage, wrath

rel ‖dander, dudgeon, ‖Dutch, huff, ‖mon-
key, pet, pique, ‖temper; annoyance, exasperation, infuriation, irritation
ant forbearance

anger *vb* **1** to make angry <their constant
heedless interruptions *angered* her>
syn enrage, incense, infuriate, ire, mad,
madden, steam up, umbrage
rel annoy, irk, vex; aggravate, exasperate,
irritate, nettle, provoke, rile; affront, offend,
outrage
idiom burn one up, make one hot under the
collar, put (*or* get) one's dander up, set one
by the ears
con appease, conciliate, mollify, placate,
propitiate, soothe
ant gratify; pacify
2 to be or become angry <he *angers* easily>
syn blow up, boil, boil over, bristle, burn,
flare (up), fume, rage, seethe
rel chafe, fret, stew; rant, rave, storm
idiom breathe fire, fly into a rage, get hot
under the collar, get one's blood (*or* dander)
up, hit the ceiling, lose one's temper, see red
ant calm (down)

angle *vb syn* see HINT 4

angle *n* **1** *syn* see VIEWPOINT 2
2 syn see PHASE
rel detail, item, particular
3 syn see TURN 4

angle *vb* **1** *syn* see SLANT 2
2 syn see SLANT 3

angry *adj* feeling or showing strong displeasure or bad temper <*angry* at the children's
lack of consideration>
syn acrimonious, choleric, heated, indignant, irate, ireful, mad, ‖pissed, ‖pissed-off,
shirty, waxy, wrathful, wrathy, wroth,
wrothful, wrothy
rel aggravated, exasperated, perturbed, put
out, riley, upset, uptight, worked up,
wrought (up); angered, enraged, incensed,
infuriate, infuriated, maddened, sore, vexed;
orey-eyed, red-faced, wild-eyed
idiom foaming at the mouth, hot under the
collar, in a taking, in a temper (*or* rage), mad
as a hornet (*or* wet hen)
con calm, placid, tolerant; content, pleased,
satisfied

anguish *n syn* see SORROW
rel anxiety, worry; ache, pain, pang, throe;
torment, torture
con comfort, consolation, solace; alleviation, assuagement, mitigation
ant relief

angular *adj* **1** *syn* see RUDE 1
2 syn see LEAN
rel lathy, ribby, weedy
con chubby, chuffy
ant rotund

anima *n syn* see SOUL 1

animadversion *n* a remark or statement
that constitutes an adverse and usually
uncharitable criticism <her spiteful *animad-
versions* on her neighbors' children>
syn aspersion, obloquy, reflection, slam,
slur, stricture
rel censure, criticism, reprehension; accusation, imputation, insinuation; captiousness,
carping, caviling, faultfinding

con acclaim, extolling, laudation, praise; approbation, approval
ant commendation

animadvert *vb* 1 *syn* see REMARK 2
rel declare, say, state, tell, utter; descant, dilate, expatiate, perorate; adduce, offer, present
con disregard, ignore, overlook

animal *n* 1 *syn* see BEAST

animal *adj* 1 *syn* see BRUTISH
2 *syn* see CARNAL 2
rel bestial, brutal, brutish
con intellectual, mental, psychic; reasoning, thinking; nonphysical, spiritual
ant rational

animalism *n* 1 *syn* see ANIMALITY
rel lasciviousness, lecherousness, lechery, licentiousness, lustfulness, unchastity; sensualism, sensuality, voluptuousness

animality *n* the animal aspect or quality of human beings or human nature <his violent reaction was sheer *animality*>
syn animalism, carnality, fleshliness
rel maleness, masculinity, virility; sensuality; brutishness, coarseness, grossness
ant spirituality

animalize *vb* *syn* see DEBASE 1

animate *adj* 1 *syn* see LIVING 1
rel breathing, viable
ant inanimate
2 *syn* see LIVELY 1
rel active, dynamic, live; activated, energized, vitalized
con dead, inanimate, lifeless; passive
ant inert

animate *vb* 1 *syn* see ENCOURAGE 1
rel invigorate, refresh, renew; fortify, reinforce, strengthen
idiom give a lift (to), put on (*or* upon) one's mettle, raise the spirits of
2 *syn* see QUICKEN 1
3 *syn* see FIRE 2
rel activate, actuate, motivate; drive, impel, move
con check, curb, restrain; frustrate, thwart
ant inhibit

animated *adj* 1 *syn* see LIVING 1
rel activated, energized, vitalized
con passive
ant inert
2 *syn* see LIVELY 1
rel exuberant, high-spirited, zestful
con enervated, spiritless; comatose
ant dejected, depressed

animating *adj* *syn* see INVIGORATING

animation *n* *syn* see SPIRIT 5

animosity *n* *syn* see ENMITY
con amity; esteem
ant goodwill

animus *n* 1 *syn* see INTENTION
2 *syn* see SOUL 2
3 *syn* see ENMITY
rel grudge; bias, discrimination, prejudice
con partiality, predilection; sympathy
ant favor

annals *n pl syn* see HISTORY 2

annex *vb* 1 *syn* see ADD 1
rel associate, connect, join, link, unite
con disengage; divorce, part, separate
2 *syn* see GET 1
3 *syn* see APPROPRIATE 1
4 *syn* see STEAL 1

annex *n* a subsidiary structure associated with a main building <built an *annex* to the museum to hold a new collection>
syn arm, block, ell, extension, wing
rel addition, continuation

annihilate *vb* 1 *syn* see ABOLISH 1
2 to destroy utterly <matter cannot be *annihilated*>
syn abate, abolish, blot out, eradicate, exterminate, extinguish, extirpate, murder, root out, uncreate, uproot, wipe (out)
rel cancel, efface, erase, expunge, obliterate
con renew, restore; create, discover, invent; fashion, forge, form, make, shape
3 *syn* see DESTROY 1
4 *syn* see SLAUGHTER 3
rel rout
5 *syn* see CRUSH 5

annihilative *adj* *syn* see DESTRUCTIVE

annotate *vb* to add or append comment <*annotate* a volume of poems>
syn gloss
rel construe, elucidate, explain, expound; comment, commentate, remark

announce *vb* 1 *syn* see DECLARE 1
rel communicate, impart
con hush (up), smother, stifle, suppress
2 to point to as a future occurrence or development <the shortening days *announce* the coming of winter>
syn forerun, foreshow, harbinger, herald, preindicate, presage
rel augur, forebode, forecast, foretell, predict
3 *syn* see INDICATE 2
rel present, set forth, show (forth)

announcement *n* *syn* see DECLARATION
rel affirmation, assertion, averment, statement

annoy *vb* 1 to disturb and upset nervously <her persistent prying soon *annoyed* her hostess>
syn abrade, bother, ‖bug, chafe, exercise, fret, gall, irk, provoke, ruffle, vex; *compare* IRRITATE
rel agitate, disturb, perturb, upset
idiom get in one's hair
con comfort, console, solace; content, gratify, please, satisfy
ant soothe
2 *syn* see WORRY 1
rel badger, bait, chivy, heckle, hector; chafe, distress, gall, rub
idiom get (*or* grate) on one's nerves, rub one the wrong way
con disregard, ignore, overlook; appease, calm, dulcify, mollify; cool, lull, subdue

annoyance *n* 1 the act of annoying <devoted himself to the *annoyance* of his patient wife>
syn bothering, harassment, irking, provocation, vexation, vexing
rel pestering, teasing

---

syn synonym(s)   *rel* related word(s)
ant antonym(s)   *con* contrasted word(s)
idiom idiomatic equivalent(s)
‖ use limited; if in doubt, see a dictionary

2 the state or feeling of being annoyed <her *annoyance* increased as he continued to pester her>

syn aggravation, bother, botheration, exasperation, pother

rel anger, indignation, ire, wrath; aversion, repugnance, repulsion, revulsion; disgust, dislike, distaste

con appreciation, enjoyment, liking, pleasure

3 something that causes an annoyed state or feeling <his constant baiting was an *annoyance* to her>

syn besetment, bother, botheration, botherment, exasperation, irritant, nuisance, pest, pester, ‖pesterment, plague

rel affliction, aggravation, distress, provocation, trial; riding

annual *n syn* see YEARBOOK

annuary *n syn* see YEARBOOK

annul *vb* 1 *syn* see ERASE

rel abstract, dispose (of), eliminate, remove

2 *syn* see NEUTRALIZE

rel outweigh, overbalance

3 *syn* see ABOLISH 1

rel counteract, negative, neutralize; blot out, cancel, efface, obliterate; extinguish

idiom make void, set aside

con enact, ordain, pass

4 to deprive of legal validity, force, or authority <*annul* a marriage>

syn abrogate, discharge, dissolve, quash, vacate, void

rel abolish, cancel, countermand, invalidate, nullify, undo

idiom make void

annunciate *vb syn* see DECLARE 1

rel affirm, assert, asseverate, aver; profess, protest; pronounce, state

anodyne *n* 1 something used to relieve or prevent pain <opium and its derivatives are still our most potent *anodynes*>

syn analgesic, anesthetic, pain-killer

rel calmative, depressant, sedative, tranquilizer; hypnotic, somnifacient, soporific, stupefacient

2 something that soothes or, often, dulls or deadens the senses or sensibilities <the kind of religion that is no more than an *anodyne*>

syn narcotic, nepenthe, opiate

ant energizer, stimulant; irritant

anomalous *adj* 1 *syn* see IRREGULAR 1

rel monstrous, prodigious

2 *syn* see ABNORMAL 1

rel foreign, peculiar, singular, strange; monstrous, prodigious

con accustomed, customary, usual, wonted

anon *adv* 1 *syn* see PRESENTLY 1

2 *syn* see THEN 1

anonym *n syn* see PSEUDONYM

anonymous *adj* not identified by name <saved by an *anonymous* hero>

syn innominate, nameless, undesignated, unnamed

rel incognito, unidentified, unknown, unrecognized, unspecified

ant named, onymous

another *adj* 1 *syn* see THAT 1

2 *syn* see ADDITIONAL

rel second

anschauung *n syn* see INTUITION

anschluss *n syn* see ALLIANCE 2

answer *n* 1 something spoken or written by way of return to a question or demand <a sullen *answer*>

syn antiphon, rejoinder, reply, respond, response, retort, return

rel comment, observation, remark; defense, justification; rebuttal, refutation; replication

con inquiry, interrogation, query, question, quiz

2 something attained by mental effort and especially by computation <got the *answer* by trial-and-error methods>

syn result, solution

answer *vb* 1 to say, write, or do something in response (as to a question) <*answered* his critics with documented facts>

syn come in, rejoin, reply, respond, retort, return

rel acknowledge, recognize; disprove, rebut, refute; countercharge, recriminate

idiom come back (at), make reply (to)

con ask, inquire, interrogate, query, question, quiz

2 *syn* see SATISFY 5

answerable *adj syn* see RESPONSIBLE

rel bound, compelled, constrained, dutybound, obligated, obliged

Antaean *adj syn* see HUGE

antagonism *n* 1 *syn* see ENMITY

rel opposition, oppugnancy, resistance, withstanding; clashing, conflict, difference, disagreement, discord, friction

con concord, consonance, harmony; agreement, understanding

ant accord; comity

2 an opposing state, action, or position <the natural *antagonism* of predators and prey>

syn antithesis, con, contradistinction, contraposition, contrariety, opposition, opposure

rel disagreement, discrepancy, disparity, incongruity; annulling, negation, nullification; counteraction

con agreement, congruity; alliance, association, rapport; empathy, sympathy

antagonist *n syn* see OPPONENT

con adherent, henchman, partisan

ant supporter

antagonistic *adj* 1 *syn* see BITTER 3

2 *syn* see ADVERSE 1

rel discordant, incompatible, inconsonant; averse, disinclined, indisposed, unwilling; conflicting, hostile

con advantageous, beneficial; auspicious, benign, propitious

ant favorable

3 *syn* see ANTIPATHETIC 1

rel adverse, counter, counteractive, reactive; discordant; antonymous, opposing, oppugnant

ante *adv* 1 *syn* see BEFORE 1

ante *prep syn* see BEFORE 1

ante *n syn* see BET

antecede *vb syn* see PRECEDE 2

antecedence *n syn* see PRIORITY

antecedent *n* 1 *syn* see CAUSE 1

rel forebear, forerunner, precursor; agency, instrumentality, means

con sequel; upshot
  ant consequence
2 *syn* see FORERUNNER 2
3 antecedents *pl syn* see ANCESTOR 1
antecedent *adj syn* see PRECEDING
  ant consequent; subsequent
antecedently *adv syn* see BEFORE 1
antecessor *n syn* see FORERUNNER 2
antedate *vb syn* see PRECEDE 2
antediluvian *adj syn* see ANCIENT 1
antediluvian *n syn* see FOGY
anterior *adj syn* see PRECEDING
  con after, back, hind, hinder, rear
  ant posterior
anthology *n* a collection of selected artistic and especially literary pieces or passages <an *anthology* of sacred music>
  syn album, ana, analects, florilegium, garland, miscellany, omnibus, posy
  rel collection, compilation; delectus, treasure-house, treasury
anthropoid *adj* resembling man <*anthropoid* extraterrestrials>
  syn anthropomorphic, anthropomorphous, humanoid, manlike
anthropomorphic *adj syn* see ANTHROPOID
anthropomorphous *adj syn* see ANTHROPOID
anti *n syn* see OPPONENT
anti *adj syn* see ADVERSE 1
  ant pro
antic *n syn* see PRANK
  rel artifice, wile; romp
antic *adj* **1** *syn* see FANTASTIC 2
  rel foolish; comic, comical, farcical, laughable, ludicrous
  con prudent, sensible, wise; conventional, formal; grave, sedate, serious, solemn, somber
2 characterized by a light gay quality <a briskly *antic* and delightful tale>
  syn frolicsome, playful, rollicking, sprightly
  rel gay, lively, spirited; light, whimsical; casual, easy, suave
  con constrained, controlled, curbed, guarded, inhibited, restrained
3 *syn* see PLAYFUL 1
anticipant *adj syn* see EXPECTANT 1
anticipate *vb* **1** *syn* see PREVENT 1
  rel forecast, foretell, presage
  idiom be one step ahead of
  con disregard, ignore, neglect, overlook, slight
2 *syn* see FORESEE
  rel await, contemplate, expect; foretaste
  idiom be on the lookout (*or* watch) for, look forward to, look (*or* watch) out for
anticipation *n syn* see EXPECTANCY 1
anticipative *adj syn* see EXPECTANT 1
anticipatory *adj syn* see EXPECTANT 1
antidote *n syn* see REMEDY 1
  rel negator, neutralizer, nullifier, offset; backfire
antipasto *n syn* see APPETIZER

antipathetic *adj* **1** having a natural or inherent opposition <national needs *antipathetic* to peace>
  syn antagonistic, clashing, conflicting, contrariant, contrary, discordant
  rel antipodal, antithetical, antonymous, contradictory, opposite
  idiom at cross purposes, at daggers drawn, at war with one another
  con agreeing, consonant, correspondent, harmonious; coactive, collaborative, cooperative
  ant concordant
2 arousing marked aversion or dislike <found his sister's husband in every way *antipathetic*>
  syn aversive, kindless, repellent, repugnant, uncongenial, ungenial, unsympathetic
  rel abhorrent, obnoxious; disgustful, disgusting, distasteful, loathsome, repulsive
  con compatible, consonant, sympathetic; alluring, attractive, charming; agreeable, pleasant, pleasing, satisfying, soothing
  ant congenial
3 *syn* see ADVERSE 1
antipathy *n* **1** *syn* see ENMITY
  rel disrelish, distaste, repellency, repugnance; avoidance, escape, eschewal, evasion
  con liking, partiality, predilection, prepossession; attachment, love; attraction, taste (for)
  ant affection (for)
2 the state of mind induced by what is antipathetic <a strong *antipathy* to modern art>
  syn allergy, aversion, dyspathy
  rel abhorrence, dislike, disrelish, distaste, repellency, repugnance; avoidance, escape, eschewal, evasion
  con liking, partiality, predilection, prepossession; affection, attachment, love; attraction
  ant taste (for)
antiphon *n syn* see ANSWER 1
antipodal *adj syn* see OPPOSITE
antipode *n syn* see OPPOSITE
antipodean *adj syn* see OPPOSITE
antipole *n syn* see OPPOSITE
antiquate *vb syn* see OUTDATE
antiquated *adj syn* see OLD-FASHIONED
  con modern, new, novel
  ant modernistic
antique *adj* **1** *syn* see ANCIENT 1
  rel ancestral, dateless, immemorial, legendary, time-honored, traditional
  con advanced, current, recent
2 *syn* see OLD-FASHIONED
antisocial *adj* averse to the society of others <a pure scholar, remote and *antisocial*>
  syn eremitic, misanthropic, reclusive, reserved, solitary, standoffish
  rel ascetic, austere, cold, remote; cynical, introverted, withdrawn
  con affable, friendly, gregarious; communicative, outgoing, sociable
  ant social
antithesis *n* **1** *syn* see ANTAGONISM 2
2 *syn* see OPPOSITE
antithetical *adj syn* see OPPOSITE
anxiety *n syn* see CARE 2
  rel doubt, mistrust, uncertainty; distress, misery, suffering; dread; panic

---

syn synonym(s)	*rel* related word(s)
ant antonym(s)	*con* contrasted word(s)
idiom idiomatic equivalent(s)	
‖ use limited; if in doubt, see a dictionary	

con composure, equanimity, sangfroid; aplomb, confidence, self-possession; certainty, certitude, faith, trust
ant security

anxious *adj syn* see AFRAID 1
rel agitated, apprehensive, jittery, perturbed, upset, worried; alarmed, bothered, disquieted, troubled, uneasy
idiom ill at ease
con calm, collected, cool, easy, imperturbable, unruffled; assured, confident, sanguine, sure
2 *syn* see EAGER
rel importunate, pressing, urgent
idiom all agog, bursting to
con averse, disinclined, hesitant, indisposed, reluctant
ant loath

anyhow *adv syn* see ABOUT 4
anytime *adv syn* see EVER 4
anyway *adv syn* see EVER 5
any which way *adv syn* see ABOUT 4
anywise *adv* **1** *syn* see ABOUT 4
2 *syn* see EVER 5
A1 *adj syn* see EXCELLENT
apace *adv syn* see FAST 2
apart *adv* **1** as a discrete item <taken *apart*, his view seemed sound enough>
syn independently, individually, one by one, separately, severally, singly
idiom one at a time
2 excluded from consideration <these slips *apart*, he had done very well>
syn aside
idiom to one side
3 in or into parts <tore the sheets *apart*>
syn asunder, sky-high
idiom all to pieces, to bits (*or* flinders)

apart *adj syn* see ALONE 1
apart from *prep syn* see EXCEPT
apartheid *n syn* see SEGREGATION
apartment *n* **1** a set of rooms (as in a private house or a block) rented or leased for use as a dwelling place <had a tiny top-floor *apartment*>
syn ‖chambers, flat, lodging(s), rental, rooms, suite, tenement
2 *syn* see ROOM 1

apathetic *adj syn* see IMPASSIVE 1
rel dull, inert, languid, sluggish, torpid; anesthetic, impassible, insensible, insensitive; callous, unmoved, untouched; limp, spiritless
con aroused, awake, aware, conscious, impressionable, perceptive, receptive; vigilant, watchful, wide-awake
ant alert

apathy *n* **1** lack of emotional responsiveness <hid her sorrow behind a dull brooding *apathy*>
syn impassivity, insensibility, phlegm, stoicism, stolidity, unresponsiveness
rel inertness, passivity, supineness; aloofness, detachment, indifference, unconcern; lethargy, torpidity, torpor; listlessness, numbness, stupefaction, stupor
con ardor, fervor, passion, responsiveness, warmth; alertness, awareness, concern, solicitude
ant zeal; enthusiasm

2 lack of interest or concern <public *apathy* toward the school crisis>
syn disinterest, disregard, heedlessness, indifference, insouciance, lassitude, lethargy, listlessness, unconcern, unmindfulness
rel callousness, hardness, insensitivity, obduracy, unawareness; coldness, halfheartedness, lukewarmness; calmness, dispassion, dispassionateness
con attentiveness, concern, heedfulness, interest; awareness, mindfulness, sensitivity, solicitude; ardency, fervency, passion, warmth, zeal

ape *vb syn* see MIMIC
rel caricature; emulate, rival
idiom make like

aperçu *n syn* see COMPENDIUM 1
aperitive *adj syn* see PALATABLE
aperture *n* a discontinuity allowing passage <the mouse squeezed through a narrow *aperture* in the wall>
syn hole, opening, orifice, outlet, vent
rel discontinuity, gap, hiatus, interstice; bore, perforation, pinhole, prick, puncture; chasm, cleft, cut, gash, slash, slit; breach, break, rupture

apery *n syn* see MIMICRY
apex *n* **1** *syn* see TOP 1
rel extremity, limit, spire
ant nadir
2 the culminating point <the *apex* of his career>
syn acme, apogee, capsheaf, capstone, climax, comble, crescendo, crest, crown, culmen, culmination, meridian, ne plus ultra, noon, noontide, peak, pinnacle, sublimity, summit, zenith
rel last word, prime, quintessence, ultimate; achievement, attainment, consummation, realization
ant nadir
3 *syn* see POINT 9
rel cap, crest, peak, prominence, spire

aphorism *n syn* see MAXIM
aphrodisia *n syn* see LUST 2
aphrodisiac *adj syn* see EROTIC
ant anaphrodisiac

apiarist *n syn* see BEEKEEPER
apical *adj syn* see TOP 1
apiculturist *n syn* see BEEKEEPER
apiece *adv* by, for, or to each one <gave the boys a dollar *apiece*>
syn all, aside, each, ‖per, per capita, per caput
rel individually, one by one, respectively, severally, singly, successively

apish *adj syn* see SLAVISH 3
aplomb *n syn* see CONFIDENCE 2
rel poise, savoir faire; coolness, imperturbability, levelheadedness, nonchalance; composure, ease, easiness, equanimity, sangfroid
idiom presence of mind
con bewilderment, distraction, perplexity; befuddlement, confusion, fluster, fuddlement; discomfiture, embarrassment, perturbation
ant shyness

apocalypse *n syn* see REVELATION
rel envisioning, foresight, precognition, prevision

apocalyptic *adj* **1** *syn* see PROPHETIC
2 *syn* see OMINOUS

apocryphal *adj* *syn* see SPURIOUS 3
rel false, erroneous, inaccurate, incorrect, untrue, wrong; doubtful, dubious, questionable
idiom open to question
con accurate, correct, established, factual, true, truthful, veracious; authentic

apogee *n* *syn* see APEX 2
Apollyon *n* *syn* see DEVIL 1
apologetic *adj* *syn* see REMORSEFUL
apologetic *n* *syn* see APOLOGY 1
apologia *n* *syn* see APOLOGY 1
rel clarification, elucidation, explanation, interpretation
apologue *n* *syn* see ALLEGORY 2
apology *n* **1** a presentation intended to justify or defend something <the white paper is essentially an *apology* for recent foreign policy>
syn apologetic, apologia, defense, justification; *compare* EXCUSE 1
rel excuse, extenuation, mitigation, palliation; advocating, advocation, championing, espousal, espousing, support
idiom pleading one's cause, putting in a good word for, speaking up for
con blame, censure, condemnation, decrial, reprehension, reprobation
2 an acknowledgment expressing regret for a wrong, improper, or discommoding act <murmured a brief *apology* for her lateness>
syn excuse, regrets; *compare* EXCUSE 1
rel amends, atonement; acknowledgment, admission, concession, confession, mea culpa; reparation, redress, satisfaction
3 *syn* see EXCUSE 3

aporetic *adj* *syn* see INCREDULOUS
apostasy *n* *syn* see DEFECTION
rel perfidy, treacherousness
apostate *n* *syn* see RENEGADE
rel bolter; dissenter, nonconformist, recusant
con adherent, follower, partisan; convert, proselyte
apostatize *vb* *syn* see DEFECT 1
a posteriori *adj* *syn* see INDUCTIVE
apostle *n* *syn* see MISSIONARY
apothecary *n* *syn* see DRUGGIST
apothegm *n* *syn* see MAXIM
apotheosis *n* **1** the consummate form, example, or instance (as of a quality) <the *apotheosis* of vulgarity>
syn epitome, last word, quintessence, ultimate; *compare* EMBODIMENT
rel acme, culmination, height, peak, summit
idiom ‖the living end
2 a raising to a state of eminent triumph or glory <the *apotheosis* of a folk hero>
syn aggrandizement, deification, dignification, exaltation, glorification
rel elevation, ennoblement, enshrinement, idolization, immortalization, lionization
con debasement, defamation, degradation, denigration, sullying

appall *vb* *syn* see DISMAY 1
rel awe, faze, overawe
con brace (up), buck up, cheer (up); assure, hearten, inspire, inspirit
ant embolden, nerve
appalling *adj* *syn* see FEARFUL 3
rel daunting, dismaying, horrifying; bewildering, confounding, dumbfounding
con assuring, heartening, inspiriting
ant reassuring
appanage *n* *syn* see RIGHT 2
apparatus *n* *syn* see EQUIPMENT
rel implement, instrument, tool, utensil; furnishings, provisions, supplies
apparel *vb* *syn* see CLOTHE
rel appoint
con bare, denude
ant divest
apparel *n* *syn* see CLOTHES
apparent *adj* **1** *syn* see CLEAR 5
rel ponderable; noticeable, prominent; discernible, observable, perceivable
idiom plain as day, plain to be seen
con ambiguous, hidden, obscure
ant inapparent
2 being other than seems to be the case <her *apparent* goodwill masked an inner loathing>
syn Barmecidal, illusive, illusory, ostensible, seeming, semblant
rel deceptive, delusive, delusory, misleading; credible, plausible, specious; factitious, fake, false, pseudo, sham, supposititious
con genuine, true, valid; basic, essential, fundamental, inherent, intrinsic
ant actual, real
apparently *adv* *syn* see OSTENSIBLY
apparition *n* a visible appearance of something not present and especially of a dead person <illusions that the superstitious see as *apparitions*>
syn bogey, eidolon, ghost, ‖haunt, phantasm, phantom, revenant, shade, shadow, specter, spectrum, spirit, ‖spook, umbra, wraith
rel delusion, hallucination, illusion; corposant, fox fire, ignis fatuus, jack-o'-lantern, marshfire, Saint Elmo's fire, will-o'-the-wisp
appeal *n* **1** *syn* see PRAYER
rel asking, requesting, solicitation
con claim, demand, exaction; kick, objection, protest
2 *syn* see ATTRACTION 1
3 *syn* see CHARM 3
rel draw; pleasantness
con disagreeableness, unpleasantness
appeal *vb* **1** *syn* see BEG
2 *syn* see PETITION
3 *syn* see INTEREST
appealing *adj* *syn* see ATTRACTIVE 1
appear *vb* **1** to become visible <the sun *appeared* from behind a cloud>
syn emerge, loom, show
rel arrive, come; arise, emanate, issue, materialize, outcrop, rise, spring
idiom come in sight, come into view, meet (or strike) the eye, show one's face
con go, leave; depart, retire, withdraw

---

syn synonym(s)	*rel* related word(s)
ant antonym(s)	*con* contrasted word(s)
idiom idiomatic equivalent(s)	
‖ use limited; if in doubt, see a dictionary	

ant disappear, vanish

2 *syn* see SEEM

idiom give an appearance of, strike one as

appearance *n* **1** the state or form in which one appears <his disheveled *appearance* surprised his guests>
syn aspect, look, mien, seeming
rel air, bearing, countenance, demeanor, manner

2 *usu* **appearances** *pl* outward and often deceptive indication or look <to all *appearances* he was guilty>
syn face, guise, seeming, semblance, show, showing, simulacrum; *compare* MASK
rel fiction, make-believe, pretense, pretension; disguise, facade, front, masquerade, outside, pose
idiom outward show
con fact, reality, truth

appease *vb* **1** *syn* see PACIFY
rel calm (down), ease, soothe; extenuate, gloss (over), palliate, whitewash
con annoy, bother, irk, vex; anger, enrage, incense, infuriate; discompose, disturb, perturb, upset
ant exasperate

2 *syn* see SATISFY 3
rel ease, relieve; cater (to), coddle, pamper, spoil
ant aggravate

appellation *n syn* see NAME 1
appellative *n syn* see NAME 1
append *vb syn* see ADD 1
appendage *n* something accompanying or attached to another thing to which it is usually subordinate or nonessential <people to whom culture is a mere *appendage* to life>
syn accessory, adjunct, appendix, appurtenance
rel auxiliary, incidental, subsidiary, supplement; collateral, extra, nonessential

appendix *n* **1** additional material subjoined to a writing and especially a book <a dictionary with an *appendix* of new words>
syn addendum, codicil, rider, supplement
2 *syn* see APPENDAGE

apperception *n syn* see RECOGNITION 1
rel apprehension, grasp, perception; comprehension, understanding

appertain *vb syn* **1** *syn* see BELONG 2
2 *syn* see BEAR (on *or* upon)

appetence *n syn* see APPETITE 1
appetent *adj syn* see EAGER
rel craving, desirous, lusting, yearning
idiom consumed with desire

appetite *n* **1** a natural enjoyment of food <all fell to with a hearty *appetite*>
syn appetence, stomach, taste
rel gluttony, greed, hunger, voracity; epicurism, gourmandise
2 *syn* see DESIRE 1
rel cupidity, greed, urgency
con abnegation, asceticism, renunciation, self-denial; distaste, revulsion
3 an attraction toward something <had a great *appetite* for gossip>
syn fondness, inclination, liking, soft spot, taste, weakness
rel bent, bias, flair, leaning, penchant, proclivity, propensity

con disinclination, dislike, distaste; disinterest, unconcern

appetition *n syn* see DESIRE 1
appetizer *n* food or drink served before a meal to stimulate appetite <*appetizers* such as cocktails and canapé>
syn antipasto, hors d'oeuvre, whet, zakuska
rel dainty, delicacy, goody, tidbit; savory

appetizing *adj syn* see PALATABLE
ant disgusting, nauseating

applaud *vb* **1** *syn* see COMMEND 2
rel boost, plug
ant admonish; censure
2 to express enthusiastic approval <*applauded* wildly when his team won a point>
syn cheer, rise (to), root
rel acclaim, extol, laud, praise; eulogize, glorify, magnify, panegyrize
con deride, mock, ridicule, taunt; contemn, disdain, scorn, scout
ant boo, hiss

applause *n* public expression of approbation <her appearance was greeted with *applause*>
syn acclaim, acclamation, plaudit(s)
rel cheers, hand, ovation, round; cheering, clapping, rooting
con derision, mockery, ridicule, taunting; Bronx cheer, raspberry
ant booing, hissing

‖**apple knocker** *n syn* see RUSTIC
apple-polish *vb syn* see FAWN
apple-polisher *n syn* see SYCOPHANT
‖**applesauce** *n syn* see NONSENSE 2
appliance *n syn* see USE 1
applicability *n syn* see USE 3
con irrelevance, unsuitability
ant inapplicability

applicable *adj* **1** *syn* see RELEVANT
rel alliable, associable, compatible, congenial, connective
con incompatible, uncongenial; inappropriate, unfit, unsuitable
ant inapplicable
2 *syn* see FIT 1
rel correct, good, seemly
idiom as it ought to be, as it should be
con improper, incorrect

applicant *n syn* see CANDIDATE
application *n* **1** *syn* see ATTENTION 1
rel busyness, zeal; energy, indefatigability
con bemusement, wool-gathering; faineance, laziness, sloth
ant indolence
2 *syn* see USE 1
3 *syn* see EXERCISE 1
4 *syn* see PRAYER

applicative *adj syn* see RELEVANT
applicatory *adj syn* see RELEVANT
apply *vb* **1** *syn* see ADDRESS 3
rel set about, take on, undertake; drudge, grind, toil
idiom burn the midnight oil, keep one's nose to the grindstone, work like a horse (*or* dog); concern (oneself) with something, set (one's hand) to something
con let slide, neglect, pass over, slight
2 *syn* see BEAR (on *or* upon)
idiom come into relation with
3 *syn* see RESORT 2

rel appeal, petition; beg, beseech, entreat, implore, supplicate; importune, press, urge
idiom make application to
4 *syn* see USE 2

apply (to) *vb syn* see ADDRESS 4

appoint *vb* **1** *syn* see DESIGNATE 1
rel accredit, authorize, commission
con cashier, discharge, dismiss; debar, exclude, reject
2 *syn* see FURNISH 1
rel embellish, enrich, furbish, garnish; dress up, set off, spruce (up)
con denude, dismantle, divest, strip

appointment *n* **1** *syn* see JOB 2
2 *syn* see ENGAGEMENT 3

apportion *vb* **1** *syn* see ALLOT
rel divide, partition, share
con assemble, collect, gather
2 to separate something into shares with care and accuracy and distribute it among a number <Christ *apportioned* the loaves and fishes>
syn divide, ‖divvy, parcel, portion, prorate, quota, ration, share, ‖shift
rel accord, award, bestow, distribute; give, grant, present; part, separate, split
3 *syn* see ADMINISTER 2
rel dish out, serve

apportionment *n syn* see RATION

apposite *adj syn* see RELEVANT
rel felicitous, happy; opportune, pat, seasonable, timely
idiom to the point (*or* purpose)
con awkward, inept; casual, haphazard, hit-or-miss, random
ant inapposite, inapt

appositeness *n syn* see ORDER 11

appraisal *n* **1** *syn* see ESTIMATE 1
2 *syn* see ESTIMATION 1

appraise *vb syn* see ESTIMATE 1
rel adjudge, deem, esteem, judge; audit, examine, inspect, scrutinize
idiom set (*or* place) a value on, take the measure of

appraisement *n* **1** *syn* see ESTIMATE 1
2 *syn* see ESTIMATION 1

appreciable *adj syn* see PERCEPTIBLE
rel noticeable; apparent, clear, evident, manifest, obvious, plain; concrete, material, real, substantial
con impalpable, imperceptible, imponderable, insensible, intangible
ant inappreciable

appreciate *vb* **1** to hold in high estimation <*appreciate* the kindness of a friend>
syn apprize, cherish, esteem, prize, treasure, value; *compare* ADMIRE 1
rel admire, regard, respect; adore, ‖eat up, enjoy, like, love, relish
idiom rate highly, set great store by, think much (*or* well) of
con contemn, disapprove, disdain, scorn; decry, depreciate, disparage
ant despise
2 *syn* see ADMIRE 1

---

syn synonym(s)   *rel* related word(s)
ant antonym(s)   *con* contrasted word(s)
idiom idiomatic equivalent(s)
‖ use limited; if in doubt, see a dictionary

---

rel enjoy, like, savor
con contemn, disdain, scorn
3 *syn* see KNOW 1
rel catch, seize, take in

appreciation *n syn* see TESTIMONIAL 2

apprehend *vb* **1** to recognize the existence or meaning of <as a child learns to *apprehend* the relation between naughtiness and punishment>
syn accept, catch, compass, comprehend, conceive, cotton (to *or* on to), ‖dig, follow, grasp, make out, see, take, take in, tumble (to), twig, understand
rel realize, recognize, sense; absorb, digest, seize; catch on, wise (up); penetrate
idiom catch (*or* get) the drift of, get the idea, get through one's head, make head or tail of
ant misapprehend
2 *syn* see ARREST 2
3 *syn* see FORESEE
rel dread, fear
idiom be on pins and needles, have one's heart in one's mouth, wait with bated breath
4 *syn* see KNOW 1
idiom be acquainted with, be cognizant of

apprehensible *adj syn* see UNDERSTANDABLE

apprehension *n* **1** *syn* see IDEA
2 *syn* see ARREST
3 fear that something is going or will go wrong <had the strongest *apprehension* about her sister's health>
syn apprehensiveness, foreboding, misgiving, premonition, prenotion, presage, presentiment
rel agitation, angst, anxiety, care, concern, disquiet, disquietude, solicitude, unease, uneasiness, worry; alarm, dread, fear, panic
idiom the anxious seat
con assurance, composure, equanimity, sangfroid, self-possession; faith, reliance, trust
ant confidence

apprehensive *adj* **1** *syn* see AWARE
2 *syn* see FEARFUL 2
ant confident

apprehensiveness *n syn* see APPREHENSION 3

apprentice *n syn* see NOVICE
rel starter; amateur
con adept, expert; specialist

apprenticed *adj syn* see BOUND 2

apprise *vb syn* see INFORM 2
rel announce, communicate, declare, proclaim, publish; disclose, discover, divulge, reveal, tell
idiom make known to, serve (one) notice

apprize *vb syn* see APPRECIATE 1

approach *vb* **1** to come or go near or nearer <as a boy *approaches* manhood>
syn approximate, near, nigh
rel achieve, arrive (at), attain, gain, hit, make, reach; draw on
idiom come to close quarters with
con recede, retire, retreat, withdraw; depart, go, leave
2 *syn* see ADDRESS 4
rel advise, confer, consult, counsel, negotiate, parley; beg, beseech, entreat, implore, plead, supplicate

3 *syn* see REACH 3

4 *syn* see AMOUNT 2

con depart, deviate, digress; differ, disaccord, disharmonize, vary

5 *syn* see BORDER 3

approach *n syn* see OVERTURE 1

rel attempt, endeavor, essay, try; call, invitation

ant withdrawal

approaching *adj syn* see FORTHCOMING

approbate *vb syn* see APPROVE 1

approbation *n* warmly commending acceptance or agreement <expressed *approbation* of their prog- ress>

syn approval, benediction, blessing, favor, OK (*or* okay)

rel commendation, countenance, goodwill, sanction; admiration, esteem, liking, regard, respect; pleasure, satisfaction

con censure, condemnation, criticism, disapproval, disfavor, reprehension; annoyance, disgust, irritation; distress, regret, sorrow

ant disapprobation

approbative *adj syn* see FAVORABLE 1

approbatory *adj syn* see FAVORABLE 1

appropinquity *n syn* see PROXIMITY

appropriate *vb* **1** to take over as if by preeminent right <limitations on the right of the state to *appropriate* private property>

syn accroach, annex, arrogate, commandeer, confiscate, expropriate, preempt, seize, sequester, take; *compare* ARROGATE 1

rel grab, grasp, snatch; claim, exact, extort, wrench; conscript, draft, press

idiom help oneself to, lay hold of, make free with, take possession of

2 *syn* see STEAL 1

rel despoil, spoil; forage, raid

3 *syn* see ARROGATE 1

appropriate *adj* **1** *syn* see FIT 1

rel apposite, germane, pertinent, relevant; opportune, pat, seasonable, timely

con incompatible, incongruous, inconsonant

ant inappropriate

2 *syn* see GOOD 2

rel agreeable, desirable, enjoyable, pleasant; acceptable, admissible, eligible, entitled, right, worthy

con disagreeable undesirable, unpleasant; inadmissible, ineligible, unworthy, wrong

ant inappropriate

3 *syn* see JUST 3

con unfair, unjustified, unmerited, unreasonable; unsuitable

ant inappropriate

4 *syn* see TRUE 7

ant inappropriate

appropriately *adv syn* see WELL 4

appropriateness *n* **1** *syn* see USE 3

2 *syn* see ORDER 11

appropriation *n* property (as money) set apart or given by official or formal action for a predetermined use by others <an increased *appropriation* for public housing>

syn grant, subsidy, subvention

rel allotment, allowance, stipend; aid, assistance, grant-in-aid, help

approval *n syn* see APPROBATION

rel applause, commendation, compliment; acceptance, endorsement, sanction, suffrage

con depreciation, derogation, disparagement

ant disapproval

approve *vb* **1** to find acceptable <they don't *approve* of their daughter's life-style>

syn accept, approbate, countenance, favor, go (for), hold (with)

rel back (up), stand by, support, sustain, uphold; bear, endure, put up (with), tolerate

idiom be in favor of, pat on the back, take kindly to, think well (*or* highly) of, view with approval (*or* favor)

con deprecate, disfavor, dislike, frown (on *or* upon); object (to), oppose

ant disapprove

2 to give an formal expression of approval and support <the committee *approved* the plans for the new clubhouse>

syn accredit, certify, endorse, OK (*or* okay), sanction

rel applaud, commend, compliment; confirm, initial, ratify; clear

con refuse, reject, repudiate, spurn; censure, condemn, criticize, reprehend, reprobate

ant disapprove

approving *adj syn* see FAVORABLE 1

approximal *adj syn* see ADJACENT 3

approximate *adj* **1** *syn* see COMPARATIVE 2 *syn* see RUDE 3

approximate *vb* **1** *syn* see APPROACH 1

idiom be in the neighborhood of

2 *syn* see ESTIMATE 3

approximately *adv syn* see NEARLY

idiom in round numbers, right about

ant exactly, precisely

appulse *n syn* see IMPACT 1

appurtenance *n syn* see APPENDAGE

rel appointment (*usu* appointments *pl*), equipment, furnishings; furniture

appurtenant *adj syn* see AUXILIARY

a priori *adj syn* see DEDUCTIVE

apriorism *n syn* see ASSUMPTION 2

apropos *adj syn* see RELEVANT

rel meet, proper

con clumsy, gauche, inappropriate, inept

ant malapropos

apropos *prep* in reference to <it is impossible to reach a decision *apropos* this matter at present>

syn about, against, anent, as for, as regards, as respects, as to, concerning, in re, in respect to, re, regarding, respecting, touching, toward, with respect to

apt *adj* **1** having a tendency or inclination <it is *apt* to be cool late in the evening>

syn given, inclined, liable, likely, prone

rel disposed, minded, predisposed

con averse, disinclined, indisposed, loath; doubtful, improbable, unlikely

2 *syn* see FIT 1

rel apposite, apropos, pertinent, relevant; compelling, convincing, telling; exact, nice, precise

con awkward, clumsy, maladroit

ant inapt, inept

3 *syn* see QUICK 2

rel alert, brainy, bright; gifted, talented

con laggard

aptness n 1 syn see ORDER 11
rel helpfulness, propitiousness
2 syn see GIFT 2

‖**apurpose** adv syn see INTENTIONALLY

apyrous adj syn see NONCOMBUSTIBLE

aquake adj syn see TREMULOUS

aqua vitae n syn see LIQUOR 2

aqueduct n syn see CHANNEL 1

aquiculture n syn see HYDROPONICS

aquiver adj syn see TREMULOUS

arab n 1 syn see VAGABOND
‖2 syn see PEDDLER

arable adj suitable for tilling and for growing crops <used their *arable* land intensively>
syn cultivable, cultivatable, tillable
rel fat, fertile, fruitful, productive
con barren, sterile, unfertile, unfruitful, unproductive

arbiter n syn see JUDGE 1
rel moderator

arbitrary adj 1 characterized by or given to willful and often unwise or irrational choices and demands <a proud fitful *arbitrary* nature>
syn capricious, erratic, freakish, vagarious, wayward, whimsical, whimsied
rel undisciplined, unruly, wild, willful; arrogant, unconstrained, unreasonable; careless, heedless, impetuous, indiscreet, precipitate, rash; kooky, screwball, zany
con circumspect, discreet, heedful, judicious, politic, reflective; calculating, discriminative, judicial, prudent, well-advised
2 syn see ABSOLUTE 4
rel authoritarian, dictatorial, magisterial, oracular
con lawful, legal, licit, rightful
ant legitimate

arbitrate vb syn see JUDGE 1
rel intermediate, intervene, mediate; appease, placate, soothe

arbitrator n 1 syn see MODERATOR
2 syn see JUDGE 1

arbor n a shelter (as in a garden) formed of vines or branches or of latticework covered with climbing shrubs or vines <the children picnicked under the *arbor*>
syn bower, pergola
rel belvedere, casino, gazebo, summerhouse

arc n syn see CURVE

arcadia n syn see UTOPIA

arcane adj syn see MYSTERIOUS
rel eerie, uncanny, weird; anagogic, mystical

arced adj syn see CURVED

arch n syn see CURVE

arch adj 1 syn see FIRST 3
rel conspicuous, notable, noteworthy; extraordinary, preeminent, extreme
2 syn see SAUCY 1
rel impish, mischievous, playful, roguish, waggish; bold, cheeky, cocky, flippant, fresh; derisive, mocking, twitting
con modest, quiet, respectful, submissive
3 syn see COY 2

archaic adj 1 syn see OLD-FASHIONED
idiom behind the times, of the old school
con fresh, modern, new, novel; fashionable
ant up-to-date
2 syn see PRIMITIVE 3

arched adj syn see CURVED

archetypal adj syn see TYPICAL 1

archetype n 1 syn see ORIGINAL 1
2 syn see MODEL 2

archfiend n syn see DEVIL 2

archilochian adj syn see SARCASTIC

archimage n syn see MAGICIAN 1

architect n syn see FATHER 2

architecture n syn see MAKEUP 1

archive n, usu **archives** pl 1 syn see LIBRARY
2 syn see DOCUMENT 1
rel papers, parchments, scrolls, writings; clippings, cuttings, excerpts, extracts, fragments, gleanings, remains

arciform adj syn see CURVED

arctic adj syn see COLD 1
rel bitter, boreal, hyperborean; numbing, rigorous; hibernal, hiemal
idiom cold as charity, cold enough to freeze a brass monkey
ant torrid

ardent adj 1 syn see IMPASSIONED
rel enthusiastic, urgent; avid, desirous, eager, keen
con calm, composed, imperturbable, nonchalant; apathetic, impassive, phlegmatic; disinterested, dispassionate, impartial, uninterested
ant cool
2 very deep or moving <had an *ardent* longing for knowledge>
syn extreme, intense
rel crying, importunate, insistent, urgent; great, mighty, powerful, strong
con feeble, minimal, slight, trivial
3 syn see EAGER
rel hasty, impetuous, impulsive, precipitate; fervid, fiery, hectic, hot; uncontrolled, ungoverned; earnest, intent, urgent, vehement
con dull, heavy, inert, leaden, lumpish; languid, lethargic, listless; apathetic, impassive, phlegmatic
ant easygoing
4 syn see FAITHFUL 1
5 syn see HOT 1
6 syn see SPIRITUOUS

ardor n 1 syn see PASSION 6
rel avidity, gusto, spirit, verve, zest; excitement, galvanization, quickening, stimulation
con aloofness, detachment, disinterest, unconcern; apathy, lackadaisy, languor, listlessness
ant coolness; indifference
2 syn see EAGERNESS
rel ardency, fervor, warmth
3 syn see FIDELITY 1
rel adoration, love, worship

arduous adj 1 syn see HARD 6
2 syn see STEEP 1
3 syn see TIGHT 4

arduously adv syn see HARD 8
con easily, facilely
ant effortlessly

---

syn synonym(s)　　　**rel** related word(s)
ant antonym(s)　　　**con** contrasted word(s)
idiom idiomatic equivalent(s)
‖ use limited; if in doubt, see a dictionary

area *n* **1** a distinguishable extent of surface and especially of the earth's surface <a large wooded *area*>
syn belt, region, territory, tract, zone
rel expanse, stretch; district, locality, place; lot, plot, section; terrain; circuit
2 *syn* see LOCALITY 1

arena *n syn* see SCENE 4

arete *n syn* see EXCELLENCE

argent *adj syn* see SILVERY

argentate *adj syn* see SILVERY

argenteous *adj syn* see SILVERY

argentine *adj syn* see SILVERY

argot *n syn* see DIALECT 2

arguable *adj syn* see MOOT

argue *vb* **1** *syn* see DISCUSS 1
rel analyze, investigate, review, sift, study, ventilate; expostulate, object, protest, remonstrate
2 to contend in words <*arguing* about who should answer the phone>
syn argufy, bicker, dispute, hassle, quibble, squabble, wrangle; *compare* QUARREL
rel differ, disaccord, disagree, dissent; balk, demur, jib; clash, conflict
idiom bandy words, have it out, join (*or* take) issue
con accord, agree, concur
3 *syn* see INDICATE 2
4 *syn* see MAINTAIN 2

argue (into) *vb syn* see INDUCE 1

argufy *vb syn* see ARGUE 2

argument *n* **1** *syn* see REASON 3
rel basis, foundation; position, posture, stance, standpoint
2 a vigorous often heated discussion of a moot question <their continuing *argument* over household expenses>
syn contention, controversy, dispute, hurrah, rumpus
rel argumentation, debate, disputation, polemic; disagreement, dissension, squabbling; embroilment, fuss, hassle, wrangle
3 *syn* see SUBJECT 2
rel position, proposition, statement, thesis

argumentation *n* the act or art or an exercise of one's powers of argument <noted for his skill in *argumentation*>
syn debate, dialectic, disputation, forensic, mooting
rel argument, controversy, dispute; declamation, elocution, eloquence, oratory, rhetoric

argumentative *adj syn* see CONTENTIOUS 2

argute *adj* **1** *syn* see SHREWD
2 *syn* see ACUTE 4

aria *n syn* see SONG 2

arid *adj* **1** *syn* see DRY 1
rel barren, infertile, sterile, unfruitful
con fecund, fertile, fruitful
2 lacking in interest or liveliness <some of the most *arid* prose ever written>
syn bromidic, dry, dryasdust, dull, dusty, insipid, tedious, uninteresting, wearful, wearisome; *compare* TEPID 2, UNORIGINAL
rel drab, dreary, flat, heavy, lackluster, leaden, unanimated, unlively; academic, bookish, pedantic; boring, humdrum, monotonous, unimaginative, uninspired
con appealing, bright, lively, sparkling, stimulating, vigorous, vivid

aright *adv syn* see WELL 1

arise *vb* **1** *syn* see RISE 4
ant recline; slump
2 *syn* see ROLL OUT
3 *syn* see SPRING 1
rel ensue, follow, succeed
4 *syn* see BEGIN 2

aristarch *n syn* see CRITIC

‖**aristo** *n syn* see GENTLEMAN 1

aristocracy *n* the highest stratum of a society <the self-centered attitude of some *aristocracies*>
syn aristoi, blue blood, carriage trade, crème de la crème, elite, flower, gentility, gentry, haut monde, optimacy, patriciate, quality, society, upper class, upper crust, who's who
rel nobility, noblesse, patricians; county; beau monde, bon ton, jet set, smart set
con canaille, mob, rabble, riffraff; commoners, commons, masses, people, plebeians

aristocrat *n syn* see GENTLEMAN 1
ant commoner

aristoi *n syn* see ARISTOCRACY

arithmetic *n syn* see COMPUTATION

arm *n* **1** *syn* see INLET
2 *syn* see ANNEX
3 *syn* see POWER 4

arm *vb syn* see FURNISH 1
rel prepare, ready
idiom put in (*or* into) shape
ant disarm

armament *n syn* see DEFENSE 1

armamentarium *n syn* see SUPPLY

armed forces *n pl syn* see TROOP 2

armistice *n syn* see TRUCE

armor *n syn* see DEFENSE 1
rel cloak, mantle, shroud, veil; buckler, cover, screen, shelter

armory *n* a place where military arms and supplies are stored <the problem of weapon theft from *armories*>
syn arsenal, depot, dump, magazine

army *n syn* see MULTITUDE 1
rel crush, horde, mob, press, throng

aroma *n* **1** *syn* see FRAGRANCE
2 *syn* see SMELL 1
rel fetor, mephitis, reek, stench, stink

aromal *adj syn* see SWEET 2
rel penetrating, piquant, pungent
ant acrid

aromatic *adj syn* see SWEET 2
ant acrid

aromatize *vb syn* see SCENT 2

around *adv* **1** *syn* see ABOUT 1
2 *syn* see THROUGH 1
3 *syn* see ABOUT 4
4 *syn* see ABOUT 6

around *prep syn* see ABOUT 1

around *adj syn* see EXTANT 1

around–the–clock *adj syn* see CONTINUAL

arouse *vb syn* see STIR 1
rel alert, excite, work up; electrify, thrill; fire, inflame
idiom fan the fire (*or* flame), raise to fever heat, set on fire, stir one's blood (*or* feelings)
con allay, alleviate, assuage, ease, mitigate, relieve; mollify, pacify, placate
ant calm, quiet

arraign vb syn see ACCUSE
  rel cite, summon; test, try
  idiom bring to book, call to account
  con absolve, acquit, exculpate, exonerate, vindicate; defend, justify
arrange vb 1 syn see ORDER 1
  rel assort, categorize, pigeonhole, sort
  con disorder, disorganize, disturb, unsettle; confuse, jumble, muddle, tumble; disperse, scatter
  ant derange, disarrange
  2 syn see DESIGN 3
  3 syn see PLAN 2
  4 syn see NEGOTIATE 1
  rel design, plan, project, scheme
  5 syn see HARMONIZE 4
arrangement n syn see ORDER 3
  rel layout, lineup, setup; method, system
  ant disarrangement
arrant adj 1 syn see UTTER
  rel plain, pure, regular, sheer
  2 syn see SHAMELESS
array vb 1 syn see ORDER 1
  ant disarray
  2 syn see CLOTHE
array n 1 syn see GROUP 3
  2 syn see DISPLAY 2
  rel exhibition, exposing, showing; arranging, marshaling, ordering
arrear n, usu **arrears** pl syn see DEBT 3
arrearage n 1 syn see DEBT 3
  2 syn see INDEBTEDNESS 1
arrect adj 1 syn see ERECT
  2 syn see ATTENTIVE 1
arrest vb 1 to bring to a halt <science cannot yet *arrest* the process of aging>
  syn check, halt, interrupt, stall, stay; *compare* STOP 3
  rel balk, frustrate, thwart; choke, obstruct, stop (up); delay, detain, hamper, hinder, restrain, retard; interfere, interpose, intervene; contain, stem, withstand
  idiom bring to a halt (*or* stand *or* standstill), bring up short, check in full career, cut short
  con advance, forward, further, promote; expedite, hasten, quicken, speed
  2 to take and hold in custody under authority of the law <*arrested* for murder>
  syn apprehend, ‖bust, detain, nab, pick up, pinch, pull in, run in; *compare* CATCH 1
  rel immure, imprison, incarcerate, jail, lock (up), ‖slough; attach
  idiom lay by the heels, lay hands on
  con discharge, free, liberate, release
arrest n the taking and holding of a person in custody under authority of the law <unwilling to submit to *arrest*>
  syn apprehension, arrestation, arrestment, ‖bust, detention, ‖nab, pickup, pinch
  rel capture, catch, collar, seizure, taking
  con discharge, freeing, liberation, release
arrestation n syn see ARREST
arresting adj syn see NOTICEABLE
  rel attractive, enchanting, fascinating; affective, appealing, impressive, moving, touching

idiom enough to make one stop and take notice
  con common, familiar, ordinary, run-of-the-mill; hackneyed, stereotyped, trite
arrestive adj syn see NOTICEABLE
arrestment n syn see ARREST
arride vb syn see PLEASE 2
  rel beguile, divert, entertain, recreate
  idiom tickle one's fancy
  con bore, ennui, jade, weary
arrival n 1 the reaching of a destination <the train was late in its *arrival*>
  syn advent, coming
  rel appearance, emergence, entrance, issuance, manifestation
  con disappearance, going, leaving, withdrawal; recession, retirement, retreat
  ant departure
  2 syn see SUCCESS
arrive vb 1 syn see COME 1
  con get away, go, retire
  ant depart
  2 syn see SUCCEED 3
arriviste n syn see UPSTART
arrogance n syn see PRIDE 3
  ant humility
arrogant adj 1 syn see PROUD 1
  rel domineering, imperative, peremptory; affected, artificial, highfalutin, mannered, showy
  idiom too big for one's britches
  con humble; deferential, submissive; abject, obsequious, subservient, truckling
  ant meek
  2 syn see POMPOUS 1
arrogate vb 1 to claim or take over in a high-handed manner <*arrogated* to himself the right to make all decisions>
  syn accroach, appropriate, assume, commandeer, preempt, usurp; *compare* APPROPRIATE 1
  rel annex, preempt, preoccupy, sequester; grab, seize, take, take over
  idiom help oneself to, make free with, take into one's own hands
  con cede, relinquish, resign, surrender, yield
  ant renounce
  2 syn see APPROPRIATE 1
arrondi adj syn see CURVED
arroyo n syn see RAVINE
arsenal n 1 syn see ARMORY
  2 syn see DEPOT 2
arsonist n syn see INCENDIARY
arsy-varsy adj syn see UPSIDE-DOWN 2
art n 1 a usually acquired proficiency in doing or performing <there's an *art* to competent public speaking>
  syn adroitness, craft, cunning, dexterity, expertise, know-how, skill
  rel capability, competence, handiness, proficiency; address, finesse, ‖savvy
  con clumsiness, maladroitness
  2 syn see CUNNING 2
  rel acuteness, astuteness
  con candor, frankness, sincerity; directness, straightforwardness, bluffness, bluntness
  3 syn see TRADE 2
artery n syn see WAY 1
artful adj syn see SLY 2
  rel diplomatic, oily, politic, smooth, suave; facile, specious, superficial; adroit, dexterous

---

syn synonym(s)   *rel* related word(s)
ant antonym(s)   *con* contrasted word(s)
idiom idiomatic equivalent(s)
‖ use limited; if in doubt, see a dictionary

ant artless

artfulness *n syn* see CUNNING 2
article *n* 1 *syn* see POINT 1
rel division, section, segment
2 *syn* see ESSAY 2
rel critique, manifesto, report, statement, study, survey
3 *syn* see THING 3
rel detail, particular
articled *adj syn* see BOUND 2
articulate *adj* 1 *syn* see VOCAL 1
rel clear, distinct, intelligible
ant inarticulate; dumb
2 *syn* see VOCAL 3
rel meaningful, significant; garrulous, prolix, talkative; uttering, venting
ant inarticulate
articulate *vb* 1 *syn* see INTEGRATE 3
rel connect, join, relate; methodize, order, organize, systematize; adjust, coordinate, harmonize, regulate; assemble, collect, gather; unify
con dissect, resolve; divide, part, separate
2 to form speech sounds <regional differences in *articulating* the letter *r*>
syn enunciate, phonate, pronounce, say
rel sound, utter
articulation *n syn* see VOCALIZATION
artifice *n* 1 *syn* see CUNNING 2
rel ingenuity, inventiveness, originality; adroitness, cleverness, keenness, quickness, shrewdness; adeptness, proficiency
2 *syn* see TRICK 1
rel chicane, chicanery, trickery; knavery, rascality, skulduggery; deceit, dissimulation, duplicity, guile
artificial *adj* 1 *syn* see SYNTHETIC
rel fabricated, fashioned, made
con native
ant natural
2 taking the place of something else and especially of something finer or more costly <*artificial* diamonds>
syn dummy, ersatz, false, imitation, mock, sham, simulated, spurious, substitute; *compare* FICTITIOUS 2, SPURIOUS 3
rel fake, papier-mâché, ‖pretend, unreal; hollow, painted
con authentic, bona fide, genuine, real, sure‑enough, true, veritable
3 lacking in spontaneity and genuineness <exchanged *artificial* smiles>
syn affected, assumed, feigned, put-on, spurious
rel histrionic, insincere, overdone, quaint, stagy, theatrical, unnatural; cute, cutesy, goody-goody, mincing, overrefined, simpering; contrived, forced, labored
con genuine, sincere, spontaneous, unaffected
artist *n syn* see EXPERT
rel ace, crackerjack, first-rater, shark, top-notcher; genius, prodigy, wonder
artiste *n syn* see EXPERT
artless *adj syn* see NATURAL 5
rel free, relaxed; aboveboard, forthright, straightforward; childlike, trusting, unsuspicious; untouched, virginal
con cunning, insidious, sly, wily; calculating, designing, intriguing, scheming; artificial, insincere

ant artful; affected

arty *adj syn* see PRETENTIOUS 3
arty–crafty *adj syn* see PRETENTIOUS 3
as *conj syn* see BECAUSE
as a rule *adv syn* see USUALLY 2
‖**ascared** *adj syn* see AFRAID 1
ascend *vb* 1 to move upward to or toward a summit <*ascend* a mountain>
syn climb, escalade, escalate, mount, scale, upclimb, upgo
rel clamber, get up, scramble, shin; crest, surmount, top
idiom scale the heights, work one's way up
ant descend
2 *syn* see RISE 4
ascendancy *n syn* see SUPREMACY
ascendant *n* 1 *syn* see SUPREMACY
2 *syn* see ANCESTOR 1
rel forerunner, precursor, predecessor
ant descendant
ascendant *adj syn* see DOMINANT 1
ascension *n syn* see ASCENT
ascent *n* a moving upward or an upward movement <the slow *ascent* of the creaky old elevator>
syn ascension, rise, rising
rel elevation, raising, uplifting
ant descent
ascertain *vb syn* see DISCOVER 3
rel ask, inquire, interrogate, query, question; appraise, inspect, observe, survey, view; consider, contemplate, study, weigh
con assume, presume; conjecture, guess, surmise
ascetic *adj syn* see SEVERE 1
rel abstemious, abstinent, forbearing; self‑abasing, self-abnegating, self-denying, self‑forgetful, selfless; disciplined, restrained, schooled, trained
con epicurean, sensual, sensuous, sybaritic; abandoned, dissolute, licentious, self-indulgent
ant luxurious, voluptuous
ascribe *vb* to refer especially to a supposed cause, source, or author <a manuscript commonly *ascribed* to Saint Augustine>
syn accredit, assign, attribute, charge, credit, impute, lay, refer
rel attach (to), connect (with), fix (on or upon), pin (on), saddle (on or upon or with); affix, fasten; conjecture, guess, surmise; adduce, advance, allege, cite
aseptic *adj syn* see UNDEMONSTRATIVE
as for *prep syn* see APROPOS
as good as *adv* 1 *syn* see NEARLY
2 *syn* see ALMOST 2
ash *n* the residue left when material is consumed by fire <cold whitened *ash* on the hearth>
syn ashes, cinders, clinkers
rel dross, scoria, slag; charcoal, coal(s), coke, ember(s); fumes, smoke, soot
ashake *adj syn* see TREMULOUS
ashamed *adj* humiliated or disconcerted usually by feelings of guilt, disgrace, or impropriety <*ashamed* of her brother's noisy boasting>
syn chagrined, mortified, shamed
rel abashed, discomfited, embarrassed; abased, humbled, humiliated; abject, hang-dog, mean; contrite, penitent, repentant

idiom unable to show one's face
con arrogant, assured, overbearing, self=
assured; vain, vainglorious
ant proud

ashen *adj syn* see PALE 1
rel corpselike, ghostly, macabre; blanched,
bleached, decolorized, faded

ashes *n pl syn* see ASH

ashiver *adj syn* see TREMULOUS

ashy *adj syn* see PALE 1

aside *adv* **1** in a slanting or sloping direction
<his head hung *aside* as if he lacked the
strength to hold it up>
syn aslant, aslope, obliquely, sideways,
sidewise, slant, slantingly, slantingways,
slantly, slantways, slantwise, ‖slaunchways,
slopeways; *compare* SIDEWAYS 1
rel askance, askant, askew, awry; downgrade, downhill
con erectly, uprightly, vertically
2 *syn* see APART 2
3 *syn* see APIECE

‖**aside** *prep syn* see NEAR 2

aside *n syn* see DIGRESSION

aside from *prep syn* see EXCEPT

asinine *adj syn* see SIMPLE 3
rel puerile; absurd, irrational, unreasonable
con prudent, sage, sane, sapient, wise;
clever, intelligent, knowing, smart; rational,
reasonable
ant judicious, sensible

ask *vb* **1** to call upon for an answer or information <*asked* him to explain his behavior>
syn catechize, examine, inquire, interrogate,
query, question, quiz
rel argue, canvass, debate, deliberate, discuss, review, talk (over)
con answer, rejoin, reply, respond, retort
2 to seek to obtain by making one's needs or
desires known <*asked* for time to consider
the problem>
syn bespeak, desire, request, solicit
rel claim, demand, exact, require; beg,
beseech, entreat, implore, importune
idiom put in for
3 *syn* see DEMAND 2
4 *syn* see INVITE
rel canvass, request, seek

askance *adv* **1** *syn* see AWRY 1
ant directly
2 with absence of approval or trust <a proceeding one must view more than a little
askance>
syn distrustfully, doubtfully, mistrustfully,
skeptically, suspiciously
rel captiously, critically, cynically, doubt-
ingly; deprecatingly, depreciatively, dispar-
agingly
con approvingly, favorably

askant *adv syn* see AWRY 1
ant directly

asker *n syn* see SUPPLIANT

askew *adv syn* see AWRY 1
ant straight

aslant *adv syn* see ASIDE 1

asleep *adj* **1** *syn* see DEAD 1
2 *syn* see NUMB 1
3 *syn* see INACTIVE

as long as *conj syn* see BECAUSE

aslope *adv syn* see ASIDE 1

as much as *adv syn* see ALMOST 2

asomatous *adj syn* see IMMATERIAL 1

aspect *n* **1** *syn* see APPEARANCE 1
rel countenance, face, visage; air, bearing,
port, presence
2 *syn* see PHASE
rel point of view, slant, standpoint

asperity *n* **1** *syn* see DIFFICULTY 1
rel austerity, bitterness, grimness, harshness, inclemency, severity, stringency
con blandness, gentleness, mildness, softness
2 *syn* see INEQUALITY 1
3 *syn* see ACRIMONY
rel harshness, keenness, roughness, sharpness; irritability, snappishness, tartness,
waspishness
con blandness, smoothness, suavity, urbanity; courtesy, gallantry
ant amenity

asperous *adj syn* see ROUGH 1

asperse *vb* **1** *syn* see MALIGN
rel deride, mock, taunt; affront, insult,
offend
con applaud, commend, compliment
2 *syn* see BAPTIZE

aspersion *n syn* see ANIMADVERSION
rel abuse, invective, muck, vituperation;
backbiting, calumny, detraction, scandal,
slander; lampoon, libel, pasquinade, skit,
squib
con eulogy, extolling, laudation, praise;
acclaim, acclamation, applause, plaudits;
commendation, compliment

asphyxiate *vb syn* see SUFFOCATE

aspirant *n syn* see CANDIDATE

aspiration *n syn* see AMBITION 1
rel aim, direction, goal, objective; desire,
lust, passion, urge

aspire *vb* **1** *syn* see AIM 2
rel hunger, long, pine, thirst; bid (for),
strain (for *or* after), struggle (for), try (for)
idiom cry for the moon, have at heart, have
one's heart set on, reach for (*or* keep one's
eyes on) the stars
con condescend, deign, look down (on);
grovel, stoop, wallow
2 *syn* see RISE 4

aspiring *adj syn* see AMBITIOUS 1
rel desirous, impassioned, urgent; wanting,
wishful, yearning

as regards *prep syn* see APROPOS

as respects *prep syn* see APROPOS

ass *n* **1** *syn* see DONKEY 1
2 *syn* see FOOL 1

assail *vb syn* see ATTACK 2
rel beat, belabor, buffet, pound, pummel
idiom round on

assailment *n syn* see ATTACK 1

assassin *n* a person hired or hirable to commit murder <found out who paid the *assassin*>
syn bravo, cutthroat, gun, gunman, ‖gunsel,
gunslinger, hatchet man, hit man, torpedo,
triggerman; *compare* MURDERER

---

syn synonym(s)   *rel* related word(s)
ant antonym(s)   *con* contrasted word(s)
idiom idiomatic equivalent(s)
‖ use limited; if in doubt, see a dictionary

rel apache, desperado, goon, ‖gorilla, high-binder, strong arm, thug

assassinate *vb syn* see MURDER 1

assault *n syn* see ATTACK 1
rel brush, clash, invasion, melee, skirmish; brawl, contest, fracas, set-to

assault *vb syn* see ATTACK 1
rel battle, fight, war; clash, collide, encounter, engage; skirmish

assay *vb* 1 *syn* see TRY 5
rel venture
idiom make an effort to
2 *syn* see ESTIMATE 1
rel demonstrate, prove, test, try; analyze, resolve; calculate, compute, reckon

assemblage *n syn* see GATHERING 1

assemble *vb* 1 *syn* see CONVOKE
2 *syn* see GATHER 6
rel associate, combine, unite; convene, convoke
con dispel, dissipate, scatter; leave, part, quit, separate
ant disperse
3 *syn* see GROUP 1
rel accumulate, aggregate, amass, garner; bunch, clump; bank, heap, mound, pile, stack
con dispel, dissipate, scatter; leave, part, quit, separate; break up, disband
ant disperse
4 *syn* see MAKE 3

assembly *n* 1 *syn* see GATHERING 2
rel association, band, conclave, party, troupe
2 *syn* see GROUP 1
rel crowd, push; faction, interest, sect, wing; brotherhood, fellowship, fraternity
con masses, multitude; canaille, rabble, riffraff, ruck, trash

assent *vb* to give or express one's consent or concurrence <*assented* grudgingly to her plans for the evening>
syn accede, acquiesce, agree, consent, subscribe, yes
rel adopt, embrace, espouse; accept; abide, bear (with), endure, stand, suffer, tolerate; down, stomach, swallow, take; defer, relent, submit, yield
idiom be at one with, cast one's vote for, give the nod of approval, go along with, see eye to eye with
con rebuff, refuse, reject, scorn, scout, spurn; deny, gainsay
ant dissent

assert *vb* 1 to state firmly, positively, or assuredly <he continued to *assert* his innocence>
syn affirm, aver, avouch, avow, constate, declare, depose, predicate, profess, protest
rel adduce, advance, allege, cite, claim, pretend; announce, broadcast, disseminate, proclaim, promulgate, publish, spread
idiom have it
con contradict, contravene, dispute, gainsay, negate, negative, traverse; confute, disprove, rebut, refute
ant deny; controvert
2 *syn* see MAINTAIN 2
rel declare, express, utter, voice; advance, state, stipulate, submit

assertive *adj* 1 *syn* see EMPHATIC
2 *syn* see AGGRESSIVE
rel affirmative; arbitrary, dogmatic, peremptory, positive; assured, certain, cocksure, opinionated, opinionative, self-assured, sure; confident, presumptuous, sanguine, self-confident
con bashful, diffident, modest, shy; amenable, biddable, docile, submissive
ant retiring; acquiescent

assertory *adj syn* see AGGRESSIVE

assess *vb* 1 *syn* see LEVY
2 *syn* see ESTIMATE 1
rel calculate, compute; account, consider, deem, reckon, weigh

assessment *n* 1 *syn* see ESTIMATION 1
2 *syn* see ESTIMATE 1
3 *syn* see TAX 1

asset *n* 1 assets *pl syn* see MEAN 3
rel bankroll, money; equity; principal
ant liabilities
2 *syn* see CREDIT 3
rel distinction, glory, honor, ornament
con detriment, disadvantage, discredit, liability
ant handicap

asshead *n syn* see FOOL 1

assiduous *adj* marked by careful attention or persistent application <learned to speak French fluently by *assiduous* practice>
syn diligent, industrious, operose, sedulous; *compare* BUSY 1
rel hardworking, laborious, moiling; indefatigable, tireless, untiring, unwearied, zealous
idiom hard at it
con casual, haphazard, happy-go-lucky, hit-or-miss, intermittent, random; careless, lax, remiss, slack, sloppy, slovenly; indolent, lazy, slothful
ant desultory

assiduously *adv syn* see HARD 3

assign *vb* 1 *syn* see TRANSFER 4
2 *syn* see ALLOT
rel establish, fix, set, settle
3 *syn* see ASCRIBE
rel associate, link, relate; classify, pigeonhole
4 *syn* see PRESCRIBE 2
rel decide, determine; commit, consign, entrust, relegate

assignation *n syn* see ENGAGEMENT 3
rel agreement, arrangement, understanding; get-together

assignee *n syn* see AGENT 2

assignment *n syn* see TASK 1
rel incumbency, liability, obligation, responsibility

assimilate *vb* 1 *syn* see ABSORB 1
rel imbue, infuse, ingrain, inoculate, leaven, suffuse; adopt, embrace, espouse; corner, engross, monopolize
2 *syn* see EQUATE 2

assimilation *n syn* see RECOGNITION 1
rel awareness, consciousness, mindfulness

assist *vb syn* see HELP 1
rel accompany, attend, escort; concur, cooperate
con clog, fetter, trammel; forestall, prevent; burden, encumber, handicap, tax, weigh down

ant hamper; impede

assist *n syn* see HELP 1

assistance *n syn* see HELP 1
rel backing, supporting, upholding; advantage, avail, profit, use; appropriation, grant, subsidy, subvention
con checking, hampering, hindering, hindrance; balking, foiling, frustration, thwarting
ant impediment, impeding; obstructing, obstruction

assistant *n* **1** *syn* see HELPER
2 a person who takes over part of the duties of a superior <started as *assistant* to the secretary>
syn aid, aide, aide-de-camp, coadjutant, coadjutor, lieutenant
rel acolyte, attendant, second; flunky, henchman, minion, stooge; girl Friday, right-hand man; agent, attorney, deputy, factor, proxy; fall guy, patsy; co-worker, workfellow, yokemate

assistive *adj syn* see HELPFUL 1

assize *n* **1** *syn* see LAW 1
2 *syn* see STANDARD 4

associate *vb syn* see JOIN 1
rel amalgamate, blend, coalesce, merge, mingle, mix; ally, confederate, federate, league
con alienate, estrange; divide, divorce, part

associate *n* **1** *syn* see PARTNER
rel affiliate, ally, confederate, leaguer; abettor, accomplice, collaborator
2 *syn* see COLLEAGUE
3 a person regularly frequenting the company of another <a man is judged by the *associates* he keeps>
syn buddy, chum, comate, companion, comrade, crony, ‖cully, pal, running mate; *compare* FRIEND
rel acquaintance, friend, sympathizer; confidant, familiar, intimate; brother-in-arms, comrade-in-arms
4 *syn* see ACCOMPANIMENT 2
rel complement, correlate, correlative, counterpart, match; correspondent
con competitor, rival; adversary, antagonist, opponent

association *n* **1** the quality or state of being associated <worked in close *association* with the courts>
syn affiliation, alliance, cahoots, combination, conjointment, conjunction, connection, hookup, partnership, tie-up, togetherness
rel coaction, collaboration, concert, cooperation, teamwork; conviviality, gaiety, joviality, sociability
con aloofness, apartness, disjunction, disunion, isolation, separation
ant disassociation, dissociation
2 an organization of persons sharing a common interest or purpose <a buyers' *association*>

syn brotherhood, club, congress, fellowship, fraternity, guild, league, order, society, sodality, union
rel alliance, axis, bloc, coalition, federation, organization; faction, interest, sect, wing; combine, gang, machine, ring
3 *syn* see LEAGUE 4
4 something (as a feeling or recollection) associated in the mind with a particular person or thing <the thought of her childhood home always carried an *association* of loving warmth>
syn connotation, hint, implication, overtone, suggestion, undertone
rel image, picture, vision; appearance, fantasy, illusion, mirage

assort *vb* to arrange systematically <*assort* yarn by color>
syn categorize, class, classify, group, pigeonhole
rel arrange, methodize, order, systematize; distribute, divide, separate; screen, sift; stratify
con derange, disarrange, disorder, disorganize; commingle, jumble, mingle, mix, scramble

assorted *adj* **1** *syn* see MISCELLANEOUS
con chosen, picked, preferred, selected
2 corresponding in such manner or degree as to be appropriately associated <they made a well-*assorted* pair>
syn adapted, conformable, fitted, matched, suited
rel chosen, picked, preferred, selected; associated, bracketed, coupled, linked
con confused, disordered, fouled-up, haywire, jumbled, muddled, scrambled

assortment *n* **1** *syn* see VARIETY 2
2 *syn* see MISCELLANY 1

assuage *vb* **1** *syn* see RELIEVE 1
rel placate
con augment, increase, recruit, reinforce; enhance, exaggerate, heighten, intensify, magnify, strengthen
ant exacerbate
2 *syn* see PACIFY
rel calm, ease, relax, slack, slacken, soothe
con annoy, inflame, nettle, provoke, ruffle, vex

as such *adv syn* see PER SE

assumably *adv syn* see PRESUMABLY

assume *vb* **1** *syn* see DON 2
2 *syn* see DON 1
3 *syn* see ARROGATE 1
rel grab, seize, snatch, take
idiom take over the helm, take possession (or command)
4 to take on or present a false or deceptive appearance <their gaiety was *assumed*>
syn act, affect, bluff, counterfeit, fake, feign, pretend, put on, sham, simulate
rel camouflage, cloak, conceal, disguise, dissemble, hide, mask
idiom make believe
5 *syn* see PRESUPPOSE
rel affirm, assert, aver, predicate, profess; allow, concede, grant
6 *syn* see UNDERSTAND 3

assumed *adj syn* see ARTIFICIAL 3
rel factitious, synthetic; deceptive, delusory, illusory, insubstantial, unreal

---

syn synonym(s)   *rel* related word(s)
ant antonym(s)   *con* contrasted word(s)
idiom idiomatic equivalent(s)
‖ use limited; if in doubt, see a dictionary

con authentic, bona fide, genuine, veritable; real, true

assumption *n* **1** *syn* see PRESUPPOSITION
2 something that is taken for granted or advanced as fact <decisions based on *assumptions* about the nature of society>
syn apriorism, posit, postulate, postulation, premise, presumption, presupposition, supposition, thesis
rel conjecture, guess, surmise; hypothesis, theory; axiom, fundamental, law, principle, theorem

assurance *n* **1** *syn* see WORD 8
rel parole, promise, troth; plight; agreement, compact, covenant, pact, understanding
2 *syn* see CERTAINTY
rel credit, dependence, reliance, trust
con suspicion, uncertainty; disbelief, incredulity, unbelief
ant mistrust; dubiousness
3 *syn* see SAFETY
4 *syn* see CONFIDENCE 2
rel composure, equanimity, sangfroid
con agitation, disquiet, jumpiness, nervousness, shakiness, skittishness; anxiety, doubt, foreboding, funk, perturbation, trepidation
ant alarm
5 *syn* see TEMERITY
rel brazenness, cockiness, presumption; conceit, self-conceit, self-importance, vanity
con diffidence, modesty, shyness, timidity; self-depreciation, self-effacement, unassumingness, unpretentiousness

assure *vb* **1** *syn* see ENSURE
con abash, discomfit, embarrass; buffalo, bulldoze, cow, daunt, intimidate, shake; demoralize, disquiet, unman, unnerve
ant alarm
2 to make one sure or certain of something <pinched his arm to *assure* himself he was awake>
syn convince, persuade, satisfy
idiom bring (*or* drive) home to, lead one to believe, sell one on something

assured *adj* **1** *syn* see CONFIDENT 1
rel collected, composed, cool, imperturbable, unflappable, unruffled; game, plucky, resolute, spunky
con abashed, discomfited, disconcerted, embarrassed, rattled; hesitant, insecure, reluctant, uncertain; apprehensive, timorous
2 *syn* see DECIDED 1
rel certain, fixed, set
con ambiguous, uncertain; enigmatic, mysterious, obscure

assuredness *n* *syn* see CERTAINTY

astern *adv* *syn* see ABAFT
rel rear
con ahead, before, forward

as to *prep* **1** *syn* see APROPOS
2 *syn* see BY 5

astonish *vb* *syn* see SURPRISE 2
rel overwhelm; affright, alarm, terrify

astonishing *adj* *syn* see MARVELOUS 1

astound *vb* *syn* see SURPRISE 2

astounding *adj* *syn* see MARVELOUS 1

astral *adj* **1** *syn* see STELLAR 1
2 *syn* see DREAMY 1
3 *syn* see EXALTED 1

astray *adv* *syn* see AMISS 2

astricted *adj* *syn* see CONSTIPATED

astringent *adj* **1** *syn* see ACRID
rel puckery
con bland, mellow, mild
2 *syn* see SEVERE 1
rel biting, cutting, incisive, penetrating, piercing, stabbing; brisk, caustic, keen, sharp
con lax, loose, relaxed, slack, weak; unexacting
3 *syn* see TONIC 1

astucious *adj* *syn* see SHREWD

astucity *n* *syn* see WIT 3

astute *adj* **1** *syn* see SHREWD
rel discreet, foresighted, prudent; cunning, sly, wily
con ingenuous, naive, simple, unsophisticated; dull, heavy, obtuse, slow; arid, barren, staid, stuffy, uninspired
ant gullible
2 *syn* see SLY 2
rel subtile, subtle; keen, knowing, sharp
idiom slippery as an eel, too clever by half
con aboveboard, forthright, straightforward; ingenuous, naive, simple, unsophisticated

astuteness *n* *syn* see WIT 3

asudden *adv* *syn* see SHORT 1

asunder *adv* *syn* see APART 3
idiom all to pieces, one part from the other, to shreds

as usual *adv* *syn* see USUALLY 1

asweat *adj* *syn* see SWEATY

as well *adv* **1** *syn* see ALSO 2
idiom over and above
2 *syn* see EVEN 1

as well as *prep* *syn* see BESIDES 1

as yet *adv* *syn* see HITHERTO 1

asylum *n* **1** *syn* see SHELTER 1
2 *syn* see REFUGE 1
rel inviolability; security
3 an institution for the care of the insane <demand for improved *asylums*>
syn booby hatch, ‖bughouse, crazy house, ‖funny farm, loony bin, madhouse, ‖nuthouse
rel farm, home, institution, sanatorium
idiom insane (*or* lunatic) asylum, mental hospital (*or* institution), state hospital

asymmetric *adj* *syn* see LOPSIDED

at all *adv* **1** *syn* see EVER 5
2 *syn* see EVER 4

ataraxy *n* *syn* see EQUANIMITY

atavism *n* *syn* see REVERSION 1

ataxia *n* *syn* see CONFUSION 3

at close hand *adv* *syn* see CLOSE

atelier *n* *syn* see STUDIO

athenaeum *n* *syn* see LIBRARY

athirst *adj* **1** *syn* see THIRSTY 1
rel dehydrated, desiccated, dried up
2 *syn* see EAGER
con lackadaisical, languid, listless; autistic, withdrawn

athletic *adj* *syn* see MUSCULAR 2
rel active, energetic, strenuous, vigorous
con delicate; decadent, effete, flabby, soft

athletics *n pl* physical activities engaged in for exercise or pleasure <went in heavily for *athletics*>

syn games, sports
rel calisthenics, exercise, gymnastics; drill, practice, workout; amusement, diversion, entertainment, pastime, recreation

athwart *adv* **1** *syn* see ACROSS 1
2 *syn* see OVER 1

athwart *prep* *syn* see ACROSS

atiptoe *adj* *syn* see EXPECTANT 1

atmosphere *n* **1** *syn* see AIR 3
rel character, flavor, property, quality; characteristic, individuality, peculiarity; impression, suggestion
2 *syn* see ENVIRONMENT

atmospheric *adj* *syn* see AIRY 1

atom *n* *syn* see PARTICLE
rel dash, touch, trace; shade, smack, spice, soupçon, suggestion, suspicion, tincture, tinge

atomize *vb* *syn* see DESTROY 1

at once *adv* **1** *syn* see TOGETHER 1
2 *syn* see AWAY 2

atone *vb* *syn* see EXPIATE
rel compensate, pay, recompense, satisfy; appease, conciliate, propitiate
idiom set one's house in order

atone (for) *vb* *syn* see COMPENSATE 1

atramentous *adj* *syn* see BLACK 1

at random *adv* *syn* see ABOUT 4

atrocious *adj* **1** *syn* see OUTRAGEOUS 2
rel flagitious, infamous, iniquitous, vicious; barbarous, savage; glaring, rank; abominable, contemptible, despicable, execrable, odious, vile
con fine, righteous, upright, virtuous; benign, gentle, kindly
ant humane
2 *syn* see OFFENSIVE
rel displeasing, distasteful
con alluring, magnetic

atrociousness *n syn* see ENORMITY 1

atrocity *n syn* see ENORMITY 1

atrophy *n syn* see DETERIORATION 1

attach *vb syn* see FASTEN 1
rel associate; add, annex, append; bind, tie
con disassociate, dissociate; disembarrass, disencumber, disengage, disentangle
ant detach

attachment *n* **1** the state of being firmly attached to someone or something (as by affection, sympathy, or self-interest) <his *attachment* to an outworn code>
syn adherence, adhesion, constancy, faithfulness, fidelity, loyalty
rel firmness, staunchness, steadfastness; allegiance, devotion, fealty
con disloyalty, faithlessness, infidelity, unfaithfulness; aloofness, distance, remoteness; disinterest, disregard, unconcern, unmindfulness
ant detachment
2 *syn* see LOVE 1
rel piety; devotedness
con antipathy, disinclination, dislike; alienation, disaffection, estrangement
ant aversion

---

syn synonym(s)   *rel* related word(s)
ant antonym(s)   *con* contrasted word(s)
idiom idiomatic equivalent(s)
|| use limited; if in doubt, see a dictionary

attack *vb* **1** to act in violent opposition <cavalry *attacked* the Indian camp>
syn aggress, assail, assault, beset, fall (on or upon), storm, strike
rel invade, irrupt; charge, raid, rush; besiege, blockade, encompass, invest; beleaguer, beset, harass, harry, press; turn (on)
idiom gang up on, light into, sail into, set upon, take the offensive
con defend, guard, protect, shield; combat, oppose, resist, withstand
2 to begin to work vigorously (as at a task) <*attack* a problem>
syn bang away (at), tackle
rel buckle (to or down or down to), fall to, pitch in, wade (in or into)
idiom address (or apply or devote) oneself to, give oneself up to
con dawdle, lag, poke, putter

attack *n* **1** an act of attacking especially in the form of an attempt to injure, destroy, or defame <insecticides that are essential for successful *attack* on insect pests>
syn aggression, assailment, assault, offense, offensive, onfall, onset, onslaught
rel charge, descent, drive, foray, push, raid, sally, sortie; blitz, incursion, inroad, surprise; action, battle
con championing, justification, protection, support, vindication; opposition, resistance; defending, guarding, protecting, sheltering
ant defense
2 action or an attitude in a struggle that calls for or is opposed by defense <his policy had always been one of *attack*>
syn aggression, aggressiveness, belligerence, combativeness, fight, pugnacity
rel bellicosity, chauvinism, jingoism, warmongering; activation, militarization, mobilization, muster
con submissiveness, yielding
3 an episode of bodily or mental disorder <a sudden *attack* of dizziness>
syn access, fit, seizure, spell, throe, turn;
compare SIEGE
rel outbreak, paroxysm, spasm; affection, ailment, complaint, disease, disorder

attain *vb syn* see GAIN 1
idiom gain one's end, make good

attainable *adj syn* see AVAILABLE 1

attainment *n syn* see ACQUIREMENT

attempt *vb syn* see TRY 5
rel begin, commence, inaugurate, initiate, start; venture
idiom give (something) a try, take a crack (or whack) at
con accomplish, achieve, effect, execute, fulfill, perform; attain, compass, gain, reach
ant succeed

attempt *n* an effort made to do or accomplish something <made a determined *attempt* to improve her writing>
syn endeavor, essay, hassle, striving, struggle, trial, try, undertaking
rel care, effort, pains, trouble; beginning, commencement, initiation, offer, shy, start
con accomplishment, achievement, attainment, finish, fulfillment

attend *vb* **1** *syn* see LISTEN
idiom be attentive (to), give heed (to)

2 *syn* see TEND 2
rel govern, oversee, supervise; direct, handle, manage, regulate, run; aid, assist, help
3 *syn* see ACCOMPANY
rel associate, fraternize, join, mingle, mix
attendant *adj syn* see CONCOMITANT
attendant *n syn* see HELPER
attending *adj syn* see CONCOMITANT
attention *n* **1** a focusing of the mind on something <gave the problem careful *attention*>
syn application, concentration, consideration, debate, deliberation, heed, study
rel assiduity, diligence, industry, sedulity, sedulousness; notice, observation, regard, remark; absorption, engrossment, immersion, intentness
con absence, absentmindedness, abstraction, detachment, remoteness, withdrawal; disinterest, indifference, unconcern, unmindfulness
ant inattention
2 *syn* see NOTICE 1
rel awareness, consciousness, mindfulness, sensibility
con disregard, heedlessness, insensibility, unawareness, unconsciousness
3 *syn* see COURTESY 1
rel deference, homage, honor, reverence; benignity; considerateness, consideration, kindliness, solicitude
con neglect, negligence; aloofness, indifference, unconcern; discourtesy
attentive *adj* concentrating one's attention on something <listeners *attentive* to the speaker's appeal>
syn advertent, arrect, heedful, intentive, observant, regardful
rel alert, aware, mindful; agog, eager, interested, keen; concentrating, earnest, intent; open-eared, open-eyed
idiom all ears (or eyes), on the ball, paying attention
con absorbed, abstracted, bemused; preoccupied; absentminded, daydreaming, faraway, oblivious, wandering, woolgathering
ant absent; inattentive
2 *syn* see THOUGHTFUL 3
con aloof, indifferent
ant inattentive; neglectful
attenuate *vb* **1** *syn* see THIN 1
rel lessen; sap; dissipate; constrict, contract, deflate, shrink
con amplify, dilate, distend, expand, inflate, swell; augment, enlarge, increase; enrich
2 *syn* see WEAKEN 1
3 *syn* see THIN 2
attenuate *adj* **1** *syn* see THIN 1
2 *syn* see THIN 2
attenuated *adj syn* see THIN 2
attest *vb* **1** *syn* see CERTIFY 1
rel confirm, corroborate, substantiate, verify; support, sustain, uphold, warrant; affirm, asseverate, depone, swear, testify
con confute, controvert, disprove, refute; contradict, deny, gainsay
2 *syn* see INDICATE 2
rel authenticate, confirm, substantiate
con falsify, misrepresent; distort, garble, pervert, twist, warp

2 *syn* see TESTIFY 1
attestation *n syn* see TESTIMONY
at times *adv syn* see SOMETIMES
attire *vb syn* see CLOTHE
rel accouter, appoint, arm, equip, outfit
con bare, denude, dismantle, strip
ant divest
attire *n syn* see CLOTHES
attirement *n syn* see CLOTHES
attitude *n* **1** *syn* see POSTURE 1
rel air, demeanor, port, presence
2 *syn* see POSITION 1
rel point of view; bias, predilection, prejudice, prepossession
attitudinize *vb syn* see POSE 4
attorney *n* **1** *syn* see AGENT 2
rel alternate, locum tenens, stand-in, substitute, supply
2 *syn* see LAWYER
attorney-at-law *n syn* see LAWYER
attract *vb* **1** to exert an irresistible or compelling influence on <her beauty *attracted* all eyes>
syn allure, bewitch, captivate, charm, draw, enchant, fascinate, magnetize, take, wile
rel entice, lure, seduce, tempt; beguile, draw (in), intrigue, inveigle, suck (in); enrapture, entrance; court, invite, solicit
con fend (off), hold (off or away), rebuff, repulse; disgust, offend, revolt
ant repel
2 *syn* see INTEREST
attracting *adj syn* see ATTRACTIVE 1
attraction *n* **1** a quality that elicits admiration or pleased responsiveness <yielding to the *attraction* of the balmy afternoon>
syn allurement, appeal, attractiveness, call, draw, drawing power, lure, pull, seduction
rel charm, glamour, interest; delight, pleasure; bait, hook, snare
con offensiveness, repulsiveness, ugliness
2 a relationship characteristic of individuals that are drawn together naturally and involuntarily and exert a degree of influence on one another <the *attraction* between iron and the magnet>
syn affinity, sympathy
rel accord, concord, harmony
idiom drawing together
con conflict, discord, friction, tension
attractive *adj* **1** having the power to attract <an area *attractive* to wildlife>
syn alluring, appealing, attracting, bewitching, captivating, charming, drawing, enchanting, engaging, fascinating, glamorous, magnetic, mesmeric, prepossessing, seductive, siren
rel beautiful, bonny, comely, fair, lovely, pretty; Circean, enticing, fetching, luring, tempting; interesting, taking, winning; beckoning, come-hither, inviting, provocative, tantalizing, teasing; likable, simpatico
con abhorrent, distasteful, obnoxious, repugnant; loathsome, offensive, repulsive, revolting; antipathetic, unsympathetic
ant repellent, repelling; forbidding
2 *syn* see BEAUTIFUL
rel agreeable, goodly, ‖likely, pleasing, sightly

con homely, ill-favored, plain, uncomely, unprepossessing
ant unattractive

attractiveness *n syn* see ATTRACTION 1

attribute *n* **1** *syn* see QUALITY 1
rel particularity, singularity, specialty; brand, earmark, impress, stamp
2 *syn* see SYMBOL 1

attribute *vb syn* see ASCRIBE
rel calendar, chronologize, date, place

attrition *n syn* see PENITENCE

attritional *adj syn* see REMORSEFUL

attune *vb syn* see HARMONIZE 3
rel balance, compensate, counterbalance; accord, agree; fix, rectify, regulate
idiom put in tune, set to rights (*or* in order)
con divide, separate, wean

‖**atween** *prep syn* see BETWEEN 2

‖**atwixt** *prep syn* see BETWEEN 2

atypical *adj syn* see ABNORMAL 1
rel irregular, unnatural; different, divergent; exceptional, odd, peculiar, queer, strange
con customary, usual
ant typical; representative

auberge *n syn* see HOTEL

au courant *adj* **1** *syn* see AWARE
2 *syn* see UP-TO-DATE
3 *syn* see FAMILIAR 3

audacious *adj* **1** *syn* see BRAVE 1
rel adventurous, daredevil, daring, foolhardy, rash, reckless, venturesome; brash, brazen, shameless
con calculating, cautious, chary, wary; judicious, prudent, sane, wise; careful, circumspect, discreet
2 *syn* see ADVENTUROUS
rel fearless, valiant, valorous
con careful, circumspect, discreet; calculating, cautious, chary, wary
3 *syn* see INSOLENT 2
4 free from constraint and formality <found life an *audacious* ever-changing adventure>
syn uncurbed, ungoverned, unhampered, uninhibited, unrestrained, untrammeled
rel emancipated, free, independent; easy, relaxed; careless, heedless, thoughtless; self-absorbed, self-centered, selfish
con checked, curbed, governed, hampered, inhibited, restrained, trammeled; careful, cautious, heedful, mindful, thoughtful; considerate, generous, self-abnegating, self-effacing; drab, dull, pedestrian

audacity *n syn* see TEMERITY
rel cheek, effrontery, face, gall; brass, brazenness, cockiness; forwardness, impudence, resolution; courage, mettle, spirit
con calculation, caution, wariness; shyness, timidity, timorousness; agitation, disquiet, nervousness, perturbation; trepidation
ant circumspection

audible *adj syn* see AURAL 1
ant inaudible

audience *n* **1** *syn* see HEARING 2
rel attention, consideration, ear
2 *syn* see FOLLOWING 2

rel admirers, devotees, fanciers, fans, votaries

audile *adj syn* see AUDITORY

audit *n syn* see EXAMINATION
rel investigation, probe; check, control, corrective

audition *n syn* see HEARING 2

auditory *adj* of, relating to, or experienced through the sense of hearing <*auditory* disorders>
syn acoustic, audile, aural; *compare* AURAL 1

au fait *adj* **1** *syn* see ABLE
2 *syn* see FAMILIAR 3
3 *syn* see DECOROUS 1

au fond *adv syn* see ESSENTIALLY 1

Augean stable *n syn* see SINK 1

aught (*or* ought) *n syn* see ZERO 1

augment *vb* **1** *syn* see INCREASE 1
2 *syn* see INCREASE 2

augment *n syn* see INCREASE 1
rel exalt, hike, raise
con attenuate, decrease, dwindle; abridge; alleviate, assuage, relieve
ant abate

augmentation *n* **1** *syn* see ACCOMPANIMENT 1
rel adjunct, annex, attachment, fixture, reinforcement; bonus, boot, extra, plus
2 *syn* see ADDITION
con subtraction

augur *n syn* see PROPHET

augur *vb* **1** *syn* see FORETELL
rel argue, bespeak, indicate
2 to indicate or suggest a future probability <their enthusiasm *augurs* well for the success of the enterprise>
syn betoken, bode, forebode, foreshadow, foreshow, foretoken, omen, portend, presage, promise
rel hint, imply, intimate, suggest; prefigure, shadow (forth)
idiom bid fair to, give promise (*or* fair promise) of, hold out hope of, lead one to believe (*or* expect)

augury *n syn* see FORETOKEN
rel anticipation, premonition, presentiment
con accomplishment, effecting, effectuation, fulfillment; actualization, materialization, realization; appearance, emergence, forthcoming, issuance

august *adj syn* see GRAND 1
rel splendid, sublime, superb; impressive, moving, striking; awe-inspiring, awful, fearful, overwhelming

au naturel *adj syn* see NUDE 2

aura *n syn* see AIR 3
rel appearance, aspect, suggestion; aureole, radiance

aural *adj* **1** heard or perceived with the ear <responded to *aural* stimuli>
syn audible, auricular; *compare* AUDITORY
2 *syn* see AUDITORY

aureate *adj syn* see RHETORICAL
rel baroque, rococo
con moderate, quiet, restrained, sober, temperate
ant austere

auricular *n syn* see AURAL 1

aurora *n syn* see DAWN 1

---

syn synonym(s)   **rel** related word(s)
ant antonym(s)   **con** contrasted word(s)
idiom idiomatic equivalent(s)
‖ use limited; if in doubt, see a dictionary

auslander n syn see STRANGER
auspex n syn see PROPHET
auspices n pl syn see BACKING
auspicious adj 1 syn see FAVORABLE 5
  rel hopeful; golden, halcyon, roseate, rosy
  con ominous, portentous; unpropitious;
  adverse, antagonistic
  ant inauspicious; ill-omened
  2 syn see TIMELY 1
austere adj 1 syn see SEVERE 1
  rel bald, bare, simple, unadorned, undecorated, unembellished, unornamented;
  earnest, grave, serious, sober, somber
  con complicated, elaborate, fancy, flamboyant, fussy, ornate; frivolous, light, light≈
  minded, shallow, superficial
  2 syn see ACRID
  rel biting, keen, rough
  con bland, mellow, smooth, soft
  3 syn see GRIM 2
autarchic adj 1 syn see ABSOLUTE 4
  rel commanding, dogmatic, imperious;
  nonconstitutional, undemocratic
  2 syn see FREE 1
  rel self-dependent, self-reliant, self-sufficient
autarkic adj syn see FREE 1
  rel self-dependent, self-reliant, self-sufficient
authentic adj 1 worthy of acceptance because of accuracy <an *authentic* portrayal of
  ancient customs>
  syn convincing, credible, faithful, trustworthy, trusty
  rel accurate, dependable, factual, reliable,
  sure; solid, sound, straight, valid; authoritative, cathedral, official, standard
  idiom all wool and a yard wide; to be depended (or relied) on
  con incredible, unconvincing, untrustworthy; equivocal, obscure, uncertain,
  vague; hypothetical, purported, putative,
  supposed, supposititious; debatable, doubtful, questionable; nonstandard
  ant inauthentic
  2 being exactly as appears or is claimed <an
  authentic masterpiece>
  syn blown-in-the-bottle, bona fide, genuine,
  indubitable, pukka, questionless, real, right,
  simon-pure, sure-enough, true, undoubted,
  undubitable, unquestionable, veritable, very
  rel cognizable, identifiable, knowable, recognizable; honest, pure, unadulterated,
  unalloyed
  con deceptive, delusive, delusory, false,
  misleading, wrong; unidentifiable, unrecognizable
  ant spurious
  3 syn see CERTAIN 3
authenticate vb 1 syn see CONFIRM 2
  rel accredit, approve, endorse; demonstrate,
  prove, test, try; avouch, vouch (for)
  con reject, repudiate, spurn; contradict,
  deny, negate
  ant impugn
author n syn see FATHER 2
  rel origin, source; ancestor, parent, procre-
  ator
authoritarian adj 1 syn see DICTATORIAL
  rel heavy-handed, high-handed, oppressive,
  strict, stringent

ant libertarian; anarchistic
  2 syn see TOTALITARIAN 1
  rel fascistic, nazi; patriarchal
  ant democratic
authoritative adj 1 syn see OFFICIAL
  2 syn see TRUE 9
  rel attested, authenticated, circumstanti-
  ated, confirmed, proven, validated, verified;
  convincing, indisputable, irrefutable, sure,
  unrefutable; cathedral, cathedratic
  con contestable, controversial, debatable,
  disputable, refutable; dubious, questionable,
  suspect, unreliable
  3 syn see DICTATORIAL
  4 syn see ORTHODOX 1
authority n 1 syn see EXPERT
  2 syn see POWER 1
  rel governance, government, rule
  3 syn see INFLUENCE 1
  rel example, exemplar, ideal, model, pattern, standard; force, power, pressure
authorization n syn see PERMISSION
authorize vb 1 to invest with power or the
  right to act <I did not *authorize* him to speak
  for me>
  syn accredit, commission, empower, enable,
  license
  rel approve, countenance, endorse; aid,
  assist, help, support, subserve; advance,
  facilitate, forward, further, promote
  con bar, disallow, enjoin, forbid, interdict,
  prohibit
  2 syn see ENTITLE 2
  rel allow, let, permit; approve, countenance,
  endorse
  idiom give one the right to
  3 syn see INVEST 2
auto n syn see CAR
auto vb 1 syn see DRIVE 5
  2 syn see RIDE 1
autobiographer n syn see BIOGRAPHER
autobiographist n syn see BIOGRAPHER
autobiography n syn see BIOGRAPHY
  rel diary, journal, letters
autocar n syn see CAR
autochthonous adj syn see NATIVE 2
  con alien, extraneous, extrinsic, foreign;
  imported, introduced
  ant naturalized
autocracy n syn see TYRANNY
autocratic adj syn see ABSOLUTE 4
  rel arrogant, haughty, overbearing, overweening
  con deferential, submissive, yielding; forbearing, indulgent, lenient, tolerant
autodidactic adj syn see SELF-TAUGHT
autograph vb syn see SIGN 1
autognosis n syn see SELF-KNOWLEDGE
autoist n syn see MOTORIST
automatic adj 1 syn see SPONTANEOUS
  rel prompt, quick, ready; accustomed,
  confirmed, habitual, habituated
  2 syn see PERFUNCTORY
automaton n 1 syn see ROBOT 1
  2 syn see ROBOT 2
automobile n syn see CAR
automobilist n syn see MOTORIST
autonomous adj syn see FREE 1
  rel self-governed; unconstrained, uncontrolled, unsubordinated

con controlled, subordinated; governed, ruled; affiliated, allied

autopsy *n* examination of the body after death usually to determine the cause of death <the *autopsy* of a murder victim>
syn necropsy, ‖post, postmortem, postmortem examination

autoschediasm *n syn* see IMPROVISATION

autoschediastic *adj syn* see EXTEMPORANEOUS

auxiliary *adj* capable of supplying or intended to supply aid or support <an *auxiliary* police unit>
syn accessory, adjuvant, ancillary, appurtenant, collateral, contributory, subservient, subsidiary
rel complementary, supplementary; peripheral, secondary, subordinate, tributary; backing, supporting, upholding; aiding, assisting, helping
con chief, leading, main, principal; sole, solitary, unique

avail *vb syn* see BENEFIT
rel answer, fill, fulfill, meet, satisfy
con damage, harm, hurt, injure

avail *n syn* see USE 3
rel interest; appositeness, suitability
con inappropriateness, unsuitableness

available *adj* **1** that is accessible or may be obtained <the best pen *available* at the present time>
syn attainable, disponible, gettable, obtainable, procurable, securable
rel accessible, convenient, handy
idiom to be had
con unattainable, unobtainable; absent, deficient, lacking, missing
ant unavailable
2 *syn* see PURCHASABLE 1

avarice *n syn* see CUPIDITY
rel frugality, parsimony, thrift; miserliness, niggardliness, parsimoniousness, stinginess; acquisitiveness, covetousness, graspingness, piggishness
con extravagance; bountifulness, bounty, generosity, liberality, munificence, openhandedness
ant prodigality

avariciousness *n syn* see CUPIDITY

avenge *vb* to inflict punishment by way of repayment for <*avenge* an insult>
syn redress, revenge, venge, vindicate
rel compensate, pay (back), pay out, recompense, repay, requite, retaliate, retribute; chasten, chastise, punish; correct, right
idiom get an eye for an eye, get even with, settle accounts, wreak one's vengeance
con condone, disregard, ignore, overlook; absolve, amnesty, forgive, pardon, remit; bear, endure, stand, suffer, tolerate

avengement *n syn* see RETALIATION

avenging *n syn* see RETALIATION

avenue *n* **1** *syn* see WAY 1
‖**2** *syn* see DRIVEWAY

aver *vb syn* see ASSERT 1

---

rel defend, hold, justify, maintain
con deny

average *n* something (as a number, quantity, or condition) that represents a middle point between extremes <somewhat sweeter than *aver- age*>
syn mean, median, norm, par
ant maximum; minimum

average *adj syn* see MEDIUM
rel common, familiar, ordinary; customary, usual
idiom common or garden variety
con choice, excellent, exceptional, prime, superior; conspicuous, noticeable, outstanding, prominent; bad, inferior, low-grade, poor, punk

averagely *adv syn* see ENOUGH 2

avernal *adj syn* see INFERNAL 2

averse *adj syn* see DISINCLINED
rel balky, contrary, perverse; flinching, quailing, recoiling, resistant, shrinking; uncongenial, unsympathetic
ant avid (of *or* for)

aversion *n* **1** *syn* see DISLIKE
rel antagonism, antipathy, hostility; dread, fear, horror
con bias, partiality; leaning, propensity, taste
ant predilection
2 *syn* see ANTIPATHY 2
rel abhorrence, distaste, repellency, repugnance, repulsion, revulsion; disgust, dread, loathing
con bias, partiality, penchant; flair, inclination, leaning, taste
ant attachment; predilection
3 *syn* see ABOMINATION 2
ant delight

aversive *adj syn* see ANTIPATHETIC 2

avert *vb* **1** *syn* see TURN 6
rel remove, transfer
2 *syn* see PREVENT 2
rel anticipate; balk, foil, frustrate, thwart; check, halt, stay, stop
con advance, further, promote

aviary *n* a house, enclosure, or large cage for confining live birds <the zoo's *aviary*>
syn birdhouse
rel dovecote, dovehouse; columbary, pigeon house

aviator *n syn* see PILOT 2

avid *adj syn* see EAGER
rel covetous, craving, desirous, wanting, wishful; importunate, insistent, pressing, urgent; gluttonous, omnivorous
con aloof, disinterested, uninterested; disinclined, indisposed, loath
ant indifferent; averse

avidity *n syn* see CUPIDITY

avoid *vb syn* see ESCAPE 2
rel avert, deflect, divert, obviate, prevent, ward (off); debar, exclude, preclude; forbid, prohibit
idiom give a miss (or a wide berth), have no truck with, set one's face against, steer clear of, turn one's back on
con court, invite, solicit
ant face; meet

avoidance *n syn* see ESCAPE 2

avouch *vb syn* see ASSERT 1

---

syn synonym(s)   *rel* related word(s)
ant antonym(s)   *con* contrasted word(s)
idiom idiomatic equivalent(s)
‖ use limited; if in doubt, see a dictionary

rel confirm, corroborate; acknowledge, admit, confess, own

con deny, impugn

avow *vb* **1** *syn* see ASSERT 1

rel defend, maintain, vindicate; asseverate, swear, testify

2 *syn* see ACKNOWLEDGE 1

con repudiate, withdraw

avowry *n* *syn* see PATRON SAINT

await *vb* **1** *syn* see EXPECT 1

rel abide, stay, wait

idiom bide one's time, sweat (*or* tough) it out

awake *vb* **1** *syn* see WAKE 1

awake *adj* *syn* see AWARE

rel vigilant, watchful; aroused, awakened, roused, stirred up; excited

con drowsy, sleepy, slumberous, somnolent; inactive, inert, supine

awaken *vb* **1** *syn* see WAKE 1

2 *syn* see STIR 1

rel fire, inflame; alert

idiom stir the feelings (*or* blood) of

con arrest, check, retard, subdue; calm, compose, restrain

awanting *prep* *syn* see WITHOUT 2

award *vb* **1** *syn* see GRANT 1

rel allocate, allot, apportion, assign; dower, endow, endue

2 *syn* see GIVE 2

award *n* *syn* see HONOR 2

aware *adj* marked by realization, perception, or knowledge often of something not generally realized, perceived, or known <*aware* of her own inner weakness>

syn alive, apprehensive, au courant, awake, cognizant, conscious, conversant, knowing, mindful, sensible, sentient, ware, witting

rel acquainted, apprised, informed; alert, heedful; impressionable, perceptive, receptive

con anesthetic, impassible, insensible, insensitive; ignorant, unknowing

ant unaware

awash *adj* *syn* see FULL 1

away *adv* **1** from this or that place <come *away* at once>

syn hence, thence

rel forth, out, therefrom

2 at some distance from a place expressed or implied <he lived several blocks *away*>

syn off, over

rel afar, far; apart, aside

3 without hesitation or delay <fire *away* when you see the target>

syn at once, directly, first off, forthwith,

immediately, instanter, instantly, now, PDQ, right, right away, right off, straight, straight away, straight off, straightway

rel momentarily, promptly, ‖pronto, punctually; expeditiously, quickly, speedily, swiftly

away *adj* *syn* see ABSENT 1

awe *n* *syn* see REVERENCE 2

rel esteem, regard, respect, veneration, worship; admiration, amazement, wonder, wonderment

con despite, scorn; arrogance, insolence, superciliousness

awe *vb* *syn* see FRIGHTEN

aweless *adj* *syn* see BRAVE 1

awful *adj* *syn* see FEARFUL 3

rel impressive, moving; august, imposing, majestic; splendid, superb; grave, serious, solemn; ominous, portentous

‖**awful** *adv* *syn* see VERY 1

awfully *adv* *syn* see VERY 1

awkward *adj* **1** *syn* see CLUMSY 1

rel blundering, bumbling, bungling; clownish, lubberly, oafish; cumbrous, hulking, ponderous

idiom all thumbs

2 marked by a lack of grace, ease, skill, or fitness (as in action or speech) <his *awkward* approach to the problem>

syn bumbling, clumsy, gauche, halting, ham-handed, heavy-handed, inept, lumbering, maladroit, unhandy, unhappy, wooden; *compare* CLUMSY 1

rel rigid, stiff; discomfited, disconcerted, embarrassed; bunglesome, bungling, inefficient, inexpert, unskillful

con adept, adroit, dexterous, expert, finished, polished, proficient, skilled, skillful, smooth; easy, effortless, facile, simple

ant graceful

3 *syn* see INCONVENIENT

4 *syn* see INFELICITOUS

awry *adv* (*or adj*) **1** deviating from a straight line or direction <the coverlet was pulled *awry*>

syn askance, askant, askew, ‖cam, cock-a≠ hoop, cockeyed, crookedly

rel aside, aslant, obliquely, slantways

con even, straight, true; directly, undeviatingly

2 *syn* see AMISS 2

rel erroneously, faultily, untruly; aside

ax *vb* *syn* see DISMISS 3

axiom *n* **1** *syn* see PRINCIPLE 1

2 *syn* see MAXIM

‖**ayah** *n* *syn* see NURSEMAID

aye *adv* *syn* see YES 1

B

Babbitt n syn see PHILISTINE
babblative adj syn see TALKATIVE
babble vb 1 syn see GIBBER
    2 to talk nonsensically <silly people *babbling* on about trivia>
    syn blabber, blather, drivel, drool, gabble, prate, prattle, twaddle, ‖waffle
    rel clack, jaw, rattle, run on, yak, yammer, yap
    idiom run off at the mouth
    3 syn see CHAT 1
babble n 1 syn see CHATTER
    2 syn see GIBBERISH 1
babe n 1 syn see BABY 1
    2 syn see WOMAN 1
babel n syn see DIN
    con hush, noiselessness; peace, quiet, silence
babushka n syn see KERCHIEF 1
baby n 1 a very young child especially in the first year of life <the love of a mother for her *baby*>
    syn babe, bantling, infant, neonate, newborn
    rel bambino, little one, toddler, tot; nursling, suckling, weanling; bratling
    idiom babe in arms
    2 syn see WEAKLING
    ‖**3** syn see GIRL FRIEND 2
baby vb to treat with special, excessive, or fond care <*baby* a sick husband>
    syn cater (to), cocker, coddle, cosset, cotton, humor, indulge, mollycoddle, pamper, spoil
    rel dry-nurse, wet-nurse; dote (on *or* upon), favor; gratify, please, satisfy
    con control, discipline, restrain; abuse, illtreat, ill-use, mistreat, oppress; neglect, overlook, slight
baby buggy n syn see BABY CARRIAGE
baby carriage n a four-wheeled push carriage with a folding top for a baby <a park popular with young mothers pushing *baby carriages*>
    syn baby buggy, bassinet, ‖perambulator, ‖pram
babyhood n syn see INFANCY 1
babyish adj syn see CHILDISH
bacchanal n syn see ORGY 2
bacchanalia n syn see ORGY 2
back n 1 the surface or part most remote from the front <the *back* of his neck>
    syn posterior, rear, rearward
    rel extremity, tail; reverse
    con anterior
    ant front
    2 syn see SPINE

back adv syn see ABOUT 6
back adj 1 distant from settled areas <*back* regions in the hill country>
    syn frontier, outlandish, remote, unsettled
    rel uncultivated, uninhabited, unoccupied, unpopulated, wild
    con built-up, settled, urban
    2 syn see POSTERIOR 2
    ant front
back vb 1 syn see SUPPORT 2
    rel aid, assist, help; abet
    2 syn see CAPITALIZE
    3 syn see MOUNT 5
    4 syn see RECEDE 1
    con advance, progress
back answer n syn see RETORT 2
backbiting n syn see DETRACTION
    rel animadversion, reflection, stricture; abuse, invective, obloquy, vituperation
    con accolade, commendation, encomium, eulogy, laudation, paean, panegyric, praise, tribute; adulation, blarney, compliment, flattery, soft soap
backbiting adj syn see LIBELOUS
backbone n 1 syn see SPINE
    2 syn see FORTITUDE
    rel hardihood; heart
    con irresoluteness, irresolution
    ant backbonelessness, spinelessness
    3 syn see MAINSTAY
backchat n syn see BANTER
backcountry n syn see FRONTIER 2
‖**backdoor trots** n pl but sing or pl in constr
    syn see DIARRHEA
back down vb to withdraw from a previous agreement or stand <a politician *backing down* on an earlier promise>
    syn back off, back out, backpedal, backwater, cop out, crawfish (out), cry off, declare off, renege, resile, welsh
    rel disavow, recall, recant, retract, take back, withdraw; backtrack; beg off, weasel (out); balk, demur, hold back, stickle
    idiom get out of, go back on
backer n syn see SPONSOR
    rel ally, protagonist; bankroller, ‖grubstaker, ‖meal ticket, promoter
backer–up n syn see SPONSOR
backfire vb to have the reverse of the desired effect <the new policy *backfired* disastrously>
    syn backlash, boomerang, bounce (back), kick back
    rel fall (through), fizzle, miscarry, miss, ricochet
    idiom come to grief, go on the rocks, ‖lay an egg
    con come off, succeed, work out
backhouse n syn see PRIVY 1
backing n aid or support given to an undertaking <the project had the *backing* of the city fathers>

---

syn synonym(s)   *rel* related word(s)
ant antonym(s)   *con* contrasted word(s)
idiom idiomatic equivalent(s)
‖ use limited; if in doubt, see a dictionary

syn aegis, auspices, patronage, sponsorship
rel championship, cooperation, fosterage; guidance, tutelage; encouragement; assistance, help, support

backland *n syn* see FRONTIER 2
backlash *vb syn* see BACKFIRE
backlog *n syn* see RESERVE
back of *prep syn* see ABAFT
back off *vb syn* see BACK DOWN
back out *vb syn* see BACK DOWN
backpack *n* a carrying case (as of canvas or nylon) held on the back by shoulder straps <carried his supplies in a *backpack*>
syn haversack, knapsack, pack, packsack, rucksack
backpedal *vb syn* see BACK DOWN
rel dodge, duck, elude, evade, get around, shirk, sidestep
backset *n syn* see SETBACK
backside *n syn* see BUTTOCKS
backslide *vb syn* see LAPSE
rel regress, retrovert, return, revert; defect, desert, tergiversate, turn
idiom fall away, fall (*or* sink *or* slide *or* slip) back into, give in to
backsliding *n syn* see LAPSE 2
backstabbing *n syn* see DETRACTION
backstage *adj or adv* off or away from the part of the stage visible to the audience <*backstage* sounds that gave the impression of a storm>
syn offstage
idiom behind the scenes
ant onstage
backstop *vb syn* see SUPPORT 2
back talk *n* impudent and insolent talk <do as you're told and no *back talk*>
syn guff, ||jaw, ||lip, mouth, sass, sauce
rel cheek, impudence, insolence
backup *n syn* see SUBSTITUTE 1
backup *adj syn* see SUBSTITUTE 1
||**backveld** *n syn* see FRONTIER 2
backward *adv syn* see ABOUT 6
backward *adj* 1 directed, turned, or executed backward <the *backward* swimming of the crayfish>
syn retral, retrograde
rel inverted, reversed
ant advance, forward
2 *syn* see DISINCLINED
rel bashful, diffident
3 *syn* see SHY 1
4 *syn* see RETARDED
5 holding to outworn or traditional views, ideas, or principles <had a *backward* attitude toward social inferiors>
syn benighted, ignorant, unenlightened, unprogressive
rel conservative, reactionary; obtuse, stupid, thickheaded; bigoted, hidebound, narrow; blind; unenlightened, uninformed
con advanced, aware, enlightened, forward≠ looking, progressive; unbenighted
6 not developing or progressing especially in economic and social areas <*backward* nations using primitive farming methods>
syn behindhand, underdeveloped, undeveloped, unprogressive
rel poor, struggling; medieval; benighted, retarded, uncultivated, uncultured

idiom behind the times
con forward-looking, progressive; civilized, cultivated, cultured; modern
ant advanced
backwash *n syn* see FRONTIER 2
backwater *n syn* see FRONTIER 2
backwater *vb syn* see BACK DOWN
rel dodge, duck, elude, evade, get around, shirk, sidestep
backwoods *n pl but sing or pl in constr syn* see FRONTIER 2
||**backwoodser** *n syn* see RUSTIC
backwoodsman *n syn* see RUSTIC
bad *adj* 1 falling short of a standard of what is satisfactory <a *bad* repair job>
syn amiss, ||bum, ||crappy, dissatisfactory, poor, ||punk, rotten, unsatisfactory, up, wrong
rel deficient, inadequate, inferior; careless, slipshod; defective, disordered, off, unsound; execrable, ||lousy, miserable, wretched; inadmissible, objectionable, unacceptable; insufferable, intolerable
idiom below par, not up to snuff (*or* scratch)
con excellent, fine, meritorious; acceptable, adequate, sound
2 *syn* see WRONG 1
rel arrant, peccant; graceless, improper, indecorous, untoward; disorderly, misbehaving, naughty, rowdy, ruffianly, unruly; froward, perverse
ant good
3 *syn* see EVIL 5
4 *syn* see EVIL 6
5 having undergone decay <one *bad* apple can spoil the barrel>
syn decayed, putrid, rotten, spoiled
rel fusty, stale; mildewed, moldered, moldy, moth-eaten, musty, rancid, worm-eaten, decomposed, putrefied, putridacted; tainted, turned
con crisp, dewy, fresh, sweet, unspoiled; choice, picked, prime
ant good
6 *syn* see NAUGHTY 1
7 *syn* see TOUGH 8
8 arousing discomfort or distaste <a *bad* smell>
syn ||chisely, disagreeable, displeasing, rotten, sour, unhappy, unpleasant
rel disgusting, foul, nauseating, noisome, noxious, offensive, repulsive, sickening; abhorrent, hateful, loathsome, obnoxious; uneasy; thankless, ungrateful; distasteful, distressing, sticky; ungracious, unhandsome
con agreeable, pleasant, pleasing, refreshing, soothing; unoffensive
9 *syn* see HARMFUL
10 *syn* see DOWNCAST
11 *syn* see NULL
bad actor *n syn* see TROUBLEMAKER
bad books *n pl syn* see DISLIKE
badge *n* 1 *syn* see INSIGNIA
2 *syn* see HONOR 2
badger *vb syn* see BAIT 2
rel plague, tease, worry
badinage *n syn* see BANTER
rel chaffing, guying, japery, joshing, kidding, sport
badland *n syn* see WASTE 1

‖**bad lot** n syn see WASTREL 1
badly adv 1 syn see HARD 5
2 syn see AMISS 2
ant well

badman n syn see OUTLAW
rel criminal, villain; hood, hoodlum, hooligan, thug; blackguard, devil, knave, rapscallion, rascal, rascallion, rogue, scoundrel

bad–mouth vb syn see DECRY 2
bad–tempered adj syn see ILL-TEMPERED
rel cantankerous, cranky, crusty, temperamental, touchy
con forbearing, long-suffering, patient
ant good-tempered

Baedeker n syn see HANDBOOK
baffle vb syn see FRUSTRATE 1
rel confound, dumbfound, flummox, mystify, nonplus, puzzle; addle, ball up, befuddle, confuse, fog, mix up, muddle; discomfit, disconcert, embarrass, faze, rattle
con enlighten, illuminate

bag n 1 a container made of a flexible material and open or opening at the top <a grocery *bag*>
syn ‖poke, pouch, sack
‖2 syn see HAG 2

bag vb syn see CATCH 1
rel clench, ‖cop, ‖glom, hook, land, nab, net, sack, scoop
idiom lay by the heels

baggage n syn see WANTON
‖**bagged** adj syn see INTOXICATED 1
bagnio n syn see BROTHEL
bail n syn see GUARANTEE 1
bail vb syn see DIP 2
bailiwick n syn see FIELD
rel district, jurisdiction, neighborhood, place, quarter, realm; beat, circuit, round, walk

bait vb 1 syn see MOLEST
2 to persist in tormenting or harassing another <*baiting* him with gibes about his humble origin>
syn badger, bullyrag, chivy, heckle, hector, hound, ride
rel annoy, bother, bedevil, devil, rag, worry; harass, harry, haze, vex; ‖bug, nag, pester, push around
3 syn see LURE

bait n 1 syn see LURE 2
‖2 syn see SNACK
bake vb 1 syn see BURN 3
2 syn see FIRE 6
baking adj syn see HOT 1
balance n 1 the stability resulting from the equalization of opposing forces <keeping his emotional *balance* when under stress>
syn counterpoise, equilibrium, equipoise, poise, stasis
rel collectedness, composure, cool, coolness, coolth, equanimity, repose, sangfroid; aplomb, assurance, self-assurance, self-possession; control, self-control, stability, steadiness; stagnancy, stagnation
con imbalance, unbalance; instability, nervousness, shakiness, uncontrol, unsteadiness

2 syn see SYMMETRY
rel congruity, consistency, correspondence, sameness
con disbalance, disharmony, disproportion, incongruity, inconsistency, irregularity, overbalance, unbalance
ant imbalance
3 syn see REMAINDER

balance vb syn see COMPENSATE 1
rel adjust, attune, harmonize, tune; accord, agree, correspond; even, level, square
idiom strike a balance

bald adj 1 syn see HAIRLESS
rel bobbed, clipped, cropped, polled, shaven, sheared
con bushy, hairy, hirsute, shaggy; unshaven, unshorn; fleecy, furry, woolly; downy, fuzzy, pilose, pubescent
2 syn see BARE 1
rel austere, severe; plain, unadorned, undecorated, unembellished, ungarnished, unornamented; colorless, lackluster, lifeless, lusterless, uncolored

balderdash n syn see NONSENSE 2
baldhead n one who has a bald head
syn baldpate, ‖baldy, ‖skinhead
baldpate n syn see BALDHEAD
‖**baldy** n syn see BALDHEAD
balefire n syn see BEACON 1
baleful adj syn see SINISTER
rel deadly, evil, harmful, pernicious; bodeful, foreboding, unfavorable, unpromising
con auspicious, benign, favorable, promising, propitious; advantageous, beneficial
ant beneficent
2 syn see OMINOUS

balk n syn see TIMBER 2
balk vb 1 syn see FRUSTRATE 1
idiom stand in the way of
con back, support, uphold; aid, assist, help
ant forward
2 syn see DEMUR
rel decline, refuse, turn down; flinch, hang back, quail, recoil, shrink
con capitulate, give in

balky adj syn see CONTRARY 3
rel immovable, inflexible, unbending, unmanageable; averse, disinclined, hesitant, indisposed, loath, reluctant
con subdued, submissive, tame

ball n a more or less spherical body or mass <a *ball* of string>
syn globe, orb, rondure, round, sphere
rel egg, oval, ovoid

ball vb to form into a more or less spherical body or mass <*balled* the cookie dough with her hands>
syn conglobate, conglobe, ensphere, round, sphere
rel bead, pill; clot, wad

balladmonger n syn see POETASTER
ball and chain n 1 syn see RESTRICTION 1
‖2 syn see WIFE
ballast vb syn see STABILIZE
ballerina n syn see DANCER
ballet girl n syn see DANCER
ballot n 1 a piece of paper used to cast a vote in an election <deliberately spoiled his *ballot*>
syn ticket, vote

---

syn synonym(s)   rel related word(s)
ant antonym(s)   con contrasted word(s)
idiom idiomatic equivalent(s)
‖ use limited; if in doubt, see a dictionary

rel Australian ballot, Indiana ballot, Massachusetts ballot, office-block ballot, office-group ballot, party-column ballot, secret ballot
2 *syn* see SUFFRAGE
ballot *vb syn* see ELECT 2
‖**ballup** *n syn* see CONFUSION 3
ball up *vb syn* see CONFUSE 2
ballyhoo *vb syn* see TOUT
balm *n* **1 *syn*** see OINTMENT
2 *syn* see FRAGRANCE
balm *vb syn* see CALM
balmy *adj* **1 *syn*** see SWEET 2
rel musky; refreshing, rejuvenating, restorative; pleasant, pleasing
2 *syn* see GENTLE 1
rel agreeable, delightful, gratifying, pleasant, pleasing; allaying, assuaging, balsamic, easing, lightening, relieving, soothing
con annoying, bothering, bothersome, irking, irksome, vexing
‖**3 *syn*** see FOOLISH 2
‖**baloney** *n syn* see NONSENSE 2
balustrade *n syn* see RAILING
bamboozle *vb syn* see DUPE
rel bilk, diddle, swindle
ban *vb syn* see FORBID
rel illegalize, outlaw
con approve, authorize; suffer, tolerate
ban *n syn* see TABOO
banal *adj syn* see INSIPID 3
rel hackneyed, pedestrian, trite, warmed-over; bromidic, commonplace, corny, platitudinous, stock; bewhiskered, hoary, old; asinine, fatuous, silly, simple
con fresh, new, novel; different, uncommon, unusual; stimulating, zesty; choice, rare, recherché
ant original
banality *n syn* see COMMONPLACE
bananas *adj syn* see INSANE 1
banausic *adj* **1 *syn*** see DULL 9
2 *syn* see MATERIALISTIC
band *n syn* see STRIP 1
rel belt, border, edge, line; tape; fascia, taenia; streak, vein
band *vb* **1 *syn*** see BELT 1
2 *syn* see UNITE 2
rel amalgamate, unionize; consociate; club, team (up)
con disintegrate, disperse, dissolve, separate
ant break up, disband
band *n* **1 *syn*** see COMPANY 4
rel assembly, bevy, body, bunch, covey, group; detachment, detail
2 *syn* see GROUP 1
3 *syn* see ORCHESTRA
bandage *vb* to cover with a bandage <*bandage* wounds>
syn bind, dress
bandanna *n syn* see KERCHIEF 1
bandar-log *n syn* see CHATTERBOX
bandbox *adj syn* see DAPPER
bandeau *n syn* see STRIP 1
banderole *n syn* see FLAG
‖**bandido** *n syn* see OUTLAW
rel brigand, footpad, highwayman, holdup man; bravo, cutthroat, gunman, villain; gangster, mobster, racketeer
banding *n syn* see STRIP 1

bandit *n* **1 *syn*** see OUTLAW
rel brigand, footpad, highwayman, holdup man; bravo, cutthroat, villain; gangster, mobster, racketeer; jayhawker
2 *syn* see MARAUDER
bandwagon *n syn* see FASHION 3
bandy *vb syn* see EXCHANGE 3
rel chuck, flip, pitch, throw, toss; banter; answer, repay, retort
idiom bat (*or* beat) back and forth
bandy *adj syn* see BOWLEGGED
bandy-legged *adj syn* see BOWLEGGED
bane *n* **1 *syn*** see POISON
2 *syn* see DOWNFALL 2
baneful *adj* **1 *syn*** see PERNICIOUS
rel injurious; insalubrious, noisome, unhealthy, unwholesome
con benign, favorable, propitious; advantageous, helpful, profitable; healthful, salubrious, salutary, wholesome
ant beneficial
2 *syn* see OMINOUS
bang *vb syn* see SURPASS 1
bang *n* **1 *syn*** see BLOW 1
2 a loud percussive or explosive noise <slammed the book shut with a *bang*>
syn blast, boom, burst, clap, crack, crash, slam, smash, wham
rel noise, report, sound; discharge, explosion, pop, shot; howl, roar, roll, rumble, thunder
3 *syn* see THRILL
4 *syn* see SMASH 6
5 *syn* see VIGOR 2
bang *adv syn* see JUST 1
bang away (at) *vb syn* see ATTACK 2
bang-up *adj syn* see EXCELLENT
banish *vb* to eject by force or authority from a country, state, or sovereignty <*banish* an enemy of the king>
syn cast out, deport, displace, exile, expatriate, expel, expulse, ‖lag, ostracize, oust, relegate, run out, transport; *compare* EJECT 1
rel disfellowship, excommunicate, rusticate; debar, exclude, shut out; drive out, eject, evict, turn out; bump, can, cashier, discharge, dismiss, fire, put out, sack; blackball, blacklist, boycott
banishment *n syn* see EXILE 1
banister *n syn* see RAILING
bank *n* **1 *syn*** see PILE 1
rel snowbank, snowdrift; cloudage, fogbank
2 *syn* see SHORE
rel bankside, levee, riverfront, streamside; lakefront, lakeshore, lakeside; margin; oceanfront, seabank, seabeach, seaboard, seafront, sea frontage, sea line, sea sands, shingle
idiom water's edge
bank *vb syn* see HEAP 1
rel compact, concentrate
bank *vb* to place money in a bank <*banks* half his paycheck every week>
syn deposit
rel invest, lay aside, lay away, salt away, salt down, save, set aside, sock away; cache, coffer, hoard, squirrel (away), stash
con draw out, take out, withdraw; disburse, expend, fork (over *or* out), lay out, pay (out), spend

bank (on *or* upon) *vb syn* see RELY (on *or* upon)

rel intend, plan; bet (on), gamble (on), stake, venture, wager

idiom bank the rent on, bet one's bottom dollar on, go bail on, lay money on

bankroll *vb syn* see CAPITALIZE

bankrupt *vb* **1** *syn* see DEPLETE

rel break, impair, incapacitate

con rebuild, repair, restore, revive; augment, bolster, fortify, strengthen

2 *syn* see STRIP 2

3 *syn* see RUIN 3

4 *syn* see RUIN 2

banned *adj* **1** *syn* see FORBIDDEN

2 *syn* see CONTRABAND

banner *n syn* see FLAG

rel banneret

banner *adj syn* see EXCELLENT

bannerol *n syn* see FLAG

banquet *n syn* see DINNER

rel bridale, feed, ||gaudy, harvest home, repast, ||tuck, tuck-in, ||tuck-out

bantam *adj* **1** *syn* see SMALL 1

2 *syn* see SAUCY 1

banter *vb* **1** to make fun of good-naturedly <the students resented their teacher's *bantering* them about mistakes>

syn chaff, fool, fun, jest, ||jive, joke, jolly, josh, kid, rag, razz, rib

rel deride, guy, mock, quiz, rally, ridicule, satirize, taunt, tease, twit

idiom make fun of, make merry with, poke fun at

||**2** *syn* see FACE 3

||**3** *syn* see COAX

banter *n* an animated back-and-forth exchange of remarks <entertained the group with their jolly *banter*>

syn backchat, badinage, ||cross talk, persiflage, repartee, snip-snap

rel chitchat, gossip, gossipry, small talk; rallying, teasing; exchange, give-and-take

con debate, deliberation, discussion

bantling *n syn* see BABY 1

baptismal name *n syn* see GIVEN NAME

baptize *vb* **1** to administer the rite of baptism <a child *baptized* in the Catholic Church>

syn asperse, christen, immerse, sprinkle

rel cleanse, purify, regenerate

2 *syn* see NAME 1

bar *n* **1** a solid piece of material usually rectangular and considerably longer than it is wide <a *bar* of gold>

syn billet, ingot, rod, slab, stick, strip

2 something that stands in the way of some objective <his religion was a *bar* to membership in that exclusive club>

syn barricade, barrier, blank wall, block, blockade, fence, roadblock, stop, wall

rel clog, encumbrance, hamper, hindrance, impediment; hurdle, obstacle, obstruction, stumbling block; check, checkrein, control, curb; bamboo curtain, iron curtain; difficulty, hardship, vicissitude

3 *syn* see OBSTACLE

rel check, checkrein, control, curb

con accommodation, convenience, facility, service

ant advantage

4 *syn* see COURT 2

5 a room or public establishment where alcoholic beverages are served <nightly discussions in the *bar*>

syn barroom, ||boozer, ||bucket shop, buvette, cantina, cocktail lounge, drinkery, drunkery, ||gin mill, ||groggery, ||grogshop, lounge, pothouse, pub, ||public house, ||rumhole, rummery, ||rum-mill, rumshop, saloon, tap, taproom, tavern, watering hole, watering place; *compare* ALEHOUSE

rel barrelhouse, bistro, bottle club, cabaret, café, dive, honky-tonk, nightclub, rathskeller, roadhouse, wineshop

bar *vb* **1** *syn* see LIMIT 2

2 *syn* see EXCLUDE

rel block, hinder; leave out, omit, pass over; banish, deport, exile, ostracize

con accept, receive, welcome; allow, let, permit

ant admit, include

3 *syn* see HINDER

rel halt, stop

con back, support, uphold

bar *prep syn* see EXCEPT

barathrum *n syn* see HELL

barb *n syn* see SHAFT 2

barbarian *adj* **1** of, relating to, or characteristic of people that are not fully civilized <the *barbarian* tribes that sacked Rome>

syn barbaric, barbarous, Gothic, Hunnic, Hunnish, rude, savage, uncivil, uncivilized, uncultivated, wild

rel heathenish, vandal, vandalic; backward, coarse, crude, ill-mannered, primitive, rough; untamed; uncouth, uncultured; beastish, bloodthirsty, brutal, cruel, ferocious, inhuman

con gentle, peaceful, subdued, submissive, tame; cultured, enlightened, humane, sophisticated; genteel, refined, well-bred, well-mannered

ant civilized

2 *syn* see BARBARIC 1

barbaric *adj* **1** marked by a lack of restraint, cultivated taste, and refinement <the *barbaric* use of color and ornament>

syn barbarian, barbarous, graceless, outlandish, tasteless, vulgar, wild

rel coarse, crude, rough, rude, uncouth; flamboyant, florid, ornate, ostentatious, showy; blatant, flashy, garish, gaudy, loud, tawdry; cacophonous, harsh, raucous; aggressive

con quiet, restrained, soft, subdued; concinnous, cultivated, elegant, polished, refined; smooth, sophisticated, urbane

2 *syn* see BARBARIAN 1

barbarism *n* a word or expression which in form or use offends against contemporary standards of correctness or purity in a language <many writers consider *irregardless* a *barbarism*>

syn corruption, impropriety, slangism, solecism, vernacularism, vernacularity, vulgarism

---

syn synonym(s)   *rel* related word(s)
ant antonym(s)   *con* contrasted word(s)
idiom idiomatic equivalent(s)
|| use limited; if in doubt, see a dictionary

rel neologism; colloquialism; foreignism; shibboleth; Goldwyn- ism, Irish bull, malaprop, malapropism, spoonerism; caconym; error, lapse, misuse, slip

barbarous *adj* **1** *syn* see BARBARIAN 1

2 *syn* see OUTRAGEOUS 1

3 *syn* see BARBARIC 1

rel backward, benighted, cretinous, ignorant, illiterate, lowbrow, philistine, uneducated, unlettered, unread, unschooled, untaught, untutored

con aware, informed, sophisticated, with-it; finished, polished, rounded; well-bred, well-mannered; educated, intelligent, learned, schooled; erudite, well-read

4 *syn* see FIERCE 1

rel heartless, uncompassionate, unmerciful; atrocious, monstrous, outrageous; bloody, butcherly, sanguinary; fiendish, sadistic

con forbearing, lenient, merciful, tolerant; compassionate, sympathetic, tender; benevolent, humane, humanitarian

ant clement

barbate *adj syn* see BEARDED

barber *n* one whose occupation is primarily cutting hair

syn haircutter

rel coiffeur, coiffeuse, friseur, hairdresser, hair stylist; beautician, cosmetologist; clipper, cropper, shaver

bard *n* **1** a poet-singer who sang or recited verse to the accompaniment of a stringed instrument (as a harp) <*bards* were the theater of olden times>

syn jongleur, minstrel, troubadour

rel meistersinger, minnesinger, rhapsodist; gleeman; skald; conteur

2 *syn* see POET

bardlet *n syn* see POETASTER

bardling *n syn* see POETASTER

bare *adj* **1** lacking a natural or usual cover or finish <the room looked *bare* without curtains and pictures>

syn bald, naked, nude

rel denuded, dismantled, divested, peeled, stripped, uncovered; baldish, depilated, hairless; unattired, unclad, unclothed, undressed, unrobed; arid, bleak, desert, desolate

con attired, clad, clothed, dressed, garbed; furry, hairy; green, leafy, luxuriant, verdant; complete, consummate, finished, perfect

ant covered

2 *syn* see OPEN 2

3 *syn* see EMPTY 1

rel barren, depleted, destitute, dried-up, emptied, exhausted; unfilled, unstocked, unsupplied

con bountiful, bursting, chock-full, complete, crammed, laden, overflowing, overfull, replete, stuffed; full, stocked, supplied

4 *syn* see VERY 4

bare *vb syn* see STRIP 2

rel disclose, exhibit, expose, reveal, show, unveil

con camouflage, cloak, disguise, dissemble, mask; apparel, attire, dress, garb, invest, robe

ant cover

barefaced *adj syn* see SHAMELESS

rel blunt, candid, frank, open, plain, temerarious; indecent, indecorous, unseemly

con covert, secret, secretive, stealthy; cautious, circumspect, discreet, tactful

ant furtive

barefisted *adj or adv syn* see BARE≈HANDED

barefoot *adj* **1** wearing no shoes or stockings <always went *barefoot* in the summer>

syn shoeless, unsandaled, unshod

con socked, stockinged; sockless; booted, sandaled, shod

2 *syn* see DISCALCED

bare–handed *adj or adv* without covering on the hands <box *bare-handed*>

syn barefisted, bareknuckle

ant gloved

bareknuckle *adj or adv syn* see BARE≈HANDED

barely *adv syn* see JUST 2

con amply; adequately, enough, sufficiently

barf *vb syn* see VOMIT

bargain *n* **1** an advantageous purchase <at that price the car is a *bargain*>

syn buy, closeout, pennyworth, steal

rel deal; giveaway

con cheat, flimflam, gouge, sticking, sting

2 *syn* see CONTRACT

bargain *vb* **1** *syn* see HAGGLE 2

rel arrange, confer, negotiate; compromise

2 *syn* see TRADE 1

barge *vb syn* see LUMBER

bark *vb syn* see SNAP 1

barkeeper *n* **1** *syn* see SALOONKEEPER

2 *syn* see BARTENDER

barmaid *n syn* see BARTENDER

barman *n syn* see BARTENDER

Barmecidal *adj syn* see APPARENT 2

barnacle *n syn* see PARASITE

barney *n syn* see QUARREL

barnyard *adj syn* see OBSCENE 2

baron *n syn* see MAGNATE

baronial *adj syn* see GRAND 1

baroque *adj syn* see ORNATE

rel embellished, gilt, ornamented, scrolled

con austere, gray

barrage *n* a vigorous expulsion or projection of many things at once <the announcement was met with a *barrage* of protests>

syn bombardment, broadside, burst, cannonade, drumfire, fusillade, hail, salvo, shower, storm, volley

rel burst, eruption, flare, outburst, stream, surge, tornado

barrel *n* **1** *syn* see CASK

2 *syn* see MUCH

barrel *vb syn* see HURRY 2

barrelhouse *n syn* see DIVE

barrelhouse *vb syn* see HURRY 2

barren *adj* **1** *syn* see STERILE 1

rel childless, fallow, heirless, issueless

con pregnant; fertile

ant fecund

2 deficient in production of vegetation and especially crops <*barren* deserts and wastelands>

syn hardscrabble, infertile, unbearing, unfertile, unproductive

rel fallow; irreclaimable, uncultivable, unhusbanded, untillable, wild; bleak, depleted, impoverished, poor, worn-out; vegetationless, verdureless; arid, desert, dry, parched

con arable, fruitful, productive; fat, rich; lush, luxuriant; green, verdant, verdurous

ant fertile

barren *n syn* see WASTE 1

barricade *n syn* see BAR 2

barrier *n syn* see BAR 2

barring *prep syn* see EXCEPT

barroom *n syn* see BAR 5

bar sinister *n syn* see STIGMA

bartender *n* one who serves alcoholic beverages at a bar <worked for some years as a *bartender*>

syn barkeeper, barmaid, barman, mixologist, tapster; *compare* SALOONKEEPER

barter *vb syn* see TRADE 1

basal *adj* 1 *syn* see FUNDAMENTAL 1

rel pedimental; bottommost, lowermost, lowest, nethermost, undermost

con highest, uppermost

2 *syn* see ELEMENTARY 1

base *n* 1 something on which another thing is reared or built or by which it is supported or fixed in place <the *base* of a lamp>

syn basement, basis, bed, bedrock, bottom, footing, foundation, ground, groundwork, hardpan, infrastructure, rest, seat, seating, substratum, substruction, substructure, underpinning, understructure; *compare* BASIS 1

rel bolster, buttress, framework, prop, stand, stay, support; foot

2 *syn* see BASIS 1

3 *syn* see BOTTOM 3

base *vb* to supply or to serve as a basis <based his accusation on sound evidence>

syn bottom, establish, found, ground, predicate, rest, stay

rel build, construct, fix, plant, seat, set up

base *adj* 1 *syn* see IGNOBLE 1

2 *syn* see CHEAP 2

3 contemptible because beneath minimal standards of human decency <a *base* lying cheat>

syn despicable, ignoble, low, low-down, servile, sordid, squalid, ugly, vile, wretched; *compare* CONTEMPTIBLE

rel beggarly, lousy, sorry; abominable, disgraceful, loathsome; bad, evil, wicked; base-minded, low-minded, meanspirited; caitiff, cowardly, dastardly, recreant; unworthy; dirty, filthy; degrading, humiliating, ignominious

con honest, honorable, upright; virtuous; ethical, moral, righteous; fair, forbearing, open-minded, patient, reasonable, tolerant, understanding

ant noble

baseborn *adj* 1 *syn* see IGNOBLE 1

2 *syn* see ILLEGITIMATE 1

baseless *adj* being without cause or occasion <anxious old ladies with their *baseless* fears>

syn bottomless, foundationless, gratuitous, groundless, uncalled-for, unfounded, ungrounded, unwarranted

rel false, wrong; indefensible, reasonless, unjustifiable, unsolid, unsupported, unsustained, untenable; empty, idle, vain; needless, pointless, senseless, unnecessary, unneeded

con actual, real, reasonable, true; authentic, bona fide, genuine, valid

basement *n syn* see BASE 1

bash *n* 1 *syn* see BLOW 1

2 *syn* see SHINDIG 1

bashful *adj syn* see SHY 1

rel timorous; recoiling, shrinking; mousy; abashed, embarrassed; blushful

con assured, bold, intrepid; arrogant, barefaced, brazen, impudent, shameless; loquacious, talkative

ant brash, forward

basic *adj* 1 *syn* see FUNDAMENTAL 1

rel capital, chief, main, principal

2 *syn* see ELEMENTAL 1

basic *n syn* see ESSENTIAL 1

basically *adv syn* see ESSENTIALLY 1

basin *n syn* see DEPRESSION 2

basis *n* 1 something that supports or sustains anything immaterial <his argument rested on a *basis* of conjecture>

syn base, bedrock, footing, foundation, ground, groundwork, infrastructure, root, substratum, underpinning; *compare* BASE 1

rel axiom, fundamental, law, principle, theorem; assumption, postulate, premise, presumption, presupposition; essence, heart

2 *syn* see BASE 1

3 something serving as a reason or justification for an action or opinion <resented such a challenge without *basis* or reason>

syn foundation, warrant

rel call, justification, right; ground(s), reason

bask *vb* 1 *syn* see SUN

2 *syn* see WALLOW 3

bassinet *n syn* see BABY CARRIAGE

bastard *n* 1 one born out of wedlock <bore a *bastard* before she was fifteen>

syn by-blow, catch colt, chance child, come-by-chance, filius nullius, filius populi, illegitimate, love child, mamzer (*or* momzer *or* momser), natural child, whoreson, woods colt

2 *syn* see HYBRID

bastard *adj* 1 *syn* see ILLEGITIMATE 1

2 *syn* see SPURIOUS 3

bastardize *vb syn* see DEBASE 1

bastardy *n syn* see ILLEGITIMACY 1

baste *vb* 1 *syn* see BEAT 1

rel clobber, ‖larrup, mill, whip

2 *syn* see SCOLD 1

bastille *n syn* see JAIL

bastille *vb syn* see IMPRISON

bastinado *n syn* see BLOW 1

bastion *n syn* see BULWARK

bat *n* 1 *syn* see BLOW 1

2 *syn* see CUDGEL

‖3 *syn* see SPEED 2

4 *syn* see BINGE 1

‖**bat** *n syn* see HAG 2

bat *vb syn* see WANDER 1

bat *vb syn* see WINK

batch *n syn* see GROUP 3

bate *vb* ‖**1** *syn* see ABATE 4
‖**2** *syn* see DECREASE
3 *syn* see EXCLUDE

bath *n, usu* **baths** *pl syn* see SPA 1
‖**bath** *vb syn* see BATHE 1

bathe *vb* **1** to clean oneself with a bath <*bathed* only on Saturday nights>
syn ‖bath, shower, tub, wash
rel soap; douse, soak
2 to flow or splash against <waves *bathed* the rocky shore>
syn lap, lave, lip, wash
rel drench, soak, sop, souse; flush

bathetic *adj* **1** *syn* see TRITE
2 *syn* see SENTIMENTAL

bathtub gin *n syn* see MOONSHINE 2

bating *prep syn* see EXCEPT

baton *n syn* see CUDGEL

batter *vb* **1** to affect (as by repeated blows) so severely as to disfigure or damage <so *battered* in the fight he couldn't even crawl away> <a boat *battered* to pieces by stormy seas>
syn ‖bung up, mangle, maul
rel disable, disfigure; maim, mutilate; cripple, lame; bruise, contuse, lacerate; baste, clobber, pummel; shatter, wreck
idiom beat black and blue, beat to pieces (or shreds), beat within an inch of one's life
2 *syn* see BEAT 1

battery *n syn* see GROUP 3

battle *n* a hostile meeting between opposing military forces <the *battle* continued until nightfall>
syn action, engagement
rel brush, clash, encounter, pitched battle, scrimmage, skirmish; assault, attack, onset, onslaught, sortie; combat, conflict, contest, fight; hostilities

battle *vb syn* see CONTEND 1
rel clash, scrimmage; assail, assault, attack, bombard

battle cry *n* a word or phrase used as a slogan by a faction <"death to the invader" was the *battle cry*>
syn cry, motto, rallying cry, war cry; *compare* CATCHWORD

battlesome *adj syn* see QUARRELSOME 2

‖**batty** *adj syn* see INSANE 1

bauble *n syn* see KNICKKNACK

bavardage *n syn* see SMALL TALK

bawd *n syn* see PROSTITUTE

bawdy house *n syn* see BROTHEL

bawl *vb* **1** *syn* see ROAR
rel holler, scream, screech, shout, shriek, squall, yammer, yell
2 to cry and weep loudly or lustily especially from distress <the baby *bawled* and kicked when its bottle was taken away>
syn howl, squall, wail, yowl; *compare* CRY 2, ROAR
rel blubber, boohoo, cry, sob, weep

bawl out *vb syn* see SCOLD 1
rel condemn, denounce
idiom read a lecture (or lesson)

bay *n, usu* **bays** *pl syn* see HONOR 2

bay *vb syn* see HOWL 1

bay *n syn* see INLET

baygall *n syn* see SWAMP

bayou *n syn* see INLET

bay window *n syn* see POTBELLY

bazoo *n* ‖**1** *syn* see MOUTH 1
2 *syn* see RASPBERRY

be *vb* to have actuality or reality <I think, therefore I *am*>
syn breathe, exist, live, move, subsist
rel hold, obtain, stand; abide, continue, endure, go on, persist, prevail, remain; come

beach *n syn* see SHORE
rel oceanfront; lakeshore, lakeside

beach *vb syn* see SHIPWRECK 1

beached *adj syn* see AGROUND

beacon *n* **1** a signal fire usually on an elevated place <a *beacon* on the hill to warn of danger>
syn balefire, watchfire
rel flare; bonfire
2 *syn* see LIGHTHOUSE

beak *n* **1** *syn* see BILL 1
2 *syn* see NOSE 1
3 *syn* see PROMONTORY
‖**4** *syn* see JUDGE 2

beak *vb syn* see PECK 1

be–all and end–all *n* **1** *syn* see ESSENCE 2
2 *syn* see WHOLE 1

beam *n* **1** *syn* see TIMBER 2
2 *syn* see RAY 1
3 *syn* see BUTTOCKS

beam *vb* **1** *syn* see SHINE 1
2 *syn* see SMILE

beaming *adj syn* see BRIGHT 1

‖**bean** *n syn* see HEAD 1

beanery *n syn* see EATING HOUSE

beany *adj syn* see SPIRITED 2

bear *vb* **1** *syn* see CARRY 1
rel shoulder
2 *syn* see BEHAVE 1
3 to have attached to one <the bottle *bears* the label "poisonous">
syn carry, have, possess
rel display, exhibit, show
con lack, need, want
4 *syn* see ACCOMPANY
5 to give birth to offspring <she has *borne* several children>
syn ‖birth, ‖born, bring forth, deliver
idiom bring abed, bring to bed, bring to birth, give birth to, have a baby
con abort, miscarry
6 *syn* see PRESS 8
7 *syn* see PRESS 1
8 *syn* see PROCREATE 1
9 to bring forth a product <the apple trees *bear* every year>
syn produce, turn out, yield
rel breed, engender, generate, propagate, reproduce; fructify, fruit; fabricate, fashion, form, make, shape; create, invent
10 to put up with something trying or difficult <can't *bear* the tension of the work>
syn abide, brook, digest, endure, go, lump, stand, ‖stick, stick out, stomach, suffer, support, sustain, swallow, sweat out, take, tolerate; *compare* ACCEPT 2
rel afflict, torment, torture, try; allow, condone, countenance, permit; acquiesce, bow, defer, submit; yield
idiom make do, put up with, take lying down

con decline, refuse, reject, spurn; avoid, bypass, elude, evade, shun

11 *syn* see HEAD 3

bear (on *or* upon) *vb* to have a connection especially logically <this situation *bears* directly upon the question under discussion>
syn appertain, apply, pertain, relate
rel refer; affect, concern, involve, touch; correspond, parallel
idiom have to do with, tie in with

bear (with) *vb syn* see ACCEPT 2

bearable *adj* capable of being borne <his outrageous behavior is hardly *bearable*>
syn endurable, livable, sufferable, supportable, sustainable, tolerable
rel acceptable, admissible, allowable, satisfactory
con insufferable, insupportable, intolerable, unendurable, unsupportable
ant unbearable

beard *n* the natural growth of hair on a man's face <some look better with *beards*>
syn beaver, whiskers; *compare* SIDE-WHISKERS
rel charley, galways, goatee, imperial, spade beard, Vandyke; fuzz

beard *vb syn* see FACE 3
idiom beard the lion in his den

bearded *adj* having a beard <an old *bearded* philosopher>
syn barbate, bewhiskered, whiskered
rel beardy; goateed; hairy; stubbed, stubbly, unshaven
con barefaced, clean-faced, clean-shaven, shaven, smooth-faced, whiskerless
ant beardless

bear down *vb syn* see CONQUER 1

bearer *n* 1 *syn* see MESSENGER
2 a man who carries baggage and supplies for travelers <native *bearers* serving the safari>
syn carrier, drogher, porter
rel boy, cargador, coolie; redcap, skycap

bearing *n* 1 the way in which or the quality by which a person outwardly manifests his personality <a dowager with a regal *bearing*>
syn address, air, comportment, demeanor, deportment, mien, port, presence, set
rel aspect, brow, look; attitude, carriage, pose, posture, stand; poise; display, front; behavior, conduct
2 *syn* see BIRTH 1

bearish *adj syn* see CANTANKEROUS

bear out *vb syn* see CONFIRM 2

bear up *vb syn* see SUPPORT 4

beast *n* a lower animal as distinguished from man <*beasts* of the field>
syn animal, brute, creature, ‖critter
rel beastie, varmint; quadruped

beastly *adj syn* see BRUTISH

beat *vb* 1 to strike repeatedly <robbed and *beaten* by thugs>
syn baste, batter, belabor, buffet, drub, ‖dump, hammer, lam, lambaste, paste, pelt,

pound, pummel, thrash, tromp, wallop, whop
rel bastinado, baton, bludgeon, cudgel, fustigate, pistol-whip; flog, lace, lash, tan, whip; lay on, maul, muss up, rough (up)
idiom give one beans, rain blows on
2 *syn* see WHIP 2
3 *syn* see SCOUR 2
4 *syn* see WHIP 3
5 *syn* see WAG
6 *syn* see HAMMER 1
7 *syn* see SURPASS 1
idiom beat (all) hollow
8 *syn* see NONPLUS 1
9 *syn* see CHEAT
10 *syn* see FRUSTRATE 1
11 *syn* see SCOOP 3
12 *syn* see PULSATE
13 *syn* see WIN 1

beat *n* 1 *syn* see RHYTHM
2 *syn* see SCOOP

beat down *vb syn* see CONQUER 1

beating *n syn* see DEFEAT 1
rel lump(s)

beatitude *n syn* see HAPPINESS
rel ecstasy, rapture, transport
con affliction, trial, tribulation; anguish, grief, sorrow, woe; agony, suffering
ant despair, dolor

beau *n* 1 *syn* see BOYFRIEND 1
2 *syn* see BOYFRIEND 2

Beau Brummel *n syn* see FOP

beau ideal *n syn* see MODEL 2
idiom shining example

‖**beaut** *n syn* see BEAUTY

beauteous *adj syn* see BEAUTIFUL

beautiful *adj* very pleasing or delightful to look at <the most *beautiful* woman in the world>
syn attractive, beauteous, ‖bonny, comely, dishy, fair, foxy, good-looking, handsome, lovely, pretty, pulchritudinous, stunning, well-favored
rel choice, elegant, exquisite; glorious, resplendent, splendid, superb; eye-appealing, eye-filling, ‖proper; personable, pleasing
con offensive, repugnant, repulsive, revolting; homely, ordinary, plain, unattractive, unbeauteous, uncomely, unhandsome, unlovely, unpretty
ant ugly, unbeautiful

beautiful people *n pl syn* see SMART SET

beautify *vb syn* see ADORN
rel glamorize, prettify
con deface, disfigure; damage, mar, spoil
ant uglify

beauty *n* a physically attractive woman <a charming woman and a *beauty* to boot>
syn ‖beaut, bunny, eyeful, knockout, looker, lovely, stunner
rel charmer, dazzler, dream, eye-opener, good-looker, peach; belle, toast
idiom raving beauty
con dog, gorgon, hag, slattern, witch

beaver *n syn* see BEARD

becalm *vb syn* see CALM

because *conj* for the reason that <I left *because* I was bored>

---

syn synonym(s)   *rel* related word(s)
ant antonym(s)   *con* contrasted word(s)
idiom idiomatic equivalent(s)
‖ use limited; if in doubt, see a dictionary

syn as, as long as, ‖being, 'cause, considering, for, inasmuch as, now, seeing, since, whereas

idiom in view of the fact

because of *prep syn* see OVER 6

becloud *vb* 1 *syn* see OBSCURE
rel befuddle, confuse, perplex, puzzle
con illuminate
2 *syn* see CONFUSE 4

become *vb* 1 to commence to be <*became* sick yesterday>
syn come, ‖come over, get, go, grow, run, turn, wax
rel arise, mount, rise, soar
idiom get to be, turn out to be
2 *syn* see SUIT 4
3 *syn* see FLATTER

becoming *adj syn* see DECOROUS 1
rel attractive, flattering, tasteful
con unattractive, unflattering; distasteful; inappropriate, unfitting, unrespectable, unsuitable
ant unbecoming

becomingly *adv syn* see WELL 4

becrush *vb syn* see CRUSH 2

bed *n syn* see BASE 1

bed *vb* 1 to put to bed <getting the children *bedded*>
syn tuck (in)
rel cradle
2 *syn* see RETIRE 4

bedamn *vb syn* see SWEAR 3

bedaub *vb syn* see SMEAR 1

bedaze *vb syn* see DAZE 2

bedazzle *vb syn* see DAZE 1

bedcover *n syn* see BEDSPREAD

bedeck *vb syn* see ADORN
rel bedaub, bedizen

bedevil *vb syn* see WORRY 1

bedfast *adj syn* see BEDRIDDEN

bedim *vb syn* see OBSCURE
con highlight, illuminate

bedlamite *n syn* see LUNATIC 1

bedlamite *n syn* see INSANE 1

bedog *vb syn* see TAIL

bedraggled *adj syn* see SHABBY 1

bedridden *adj* confined to one's bed by illness or injury <a *bedridden* invalid>
syn bedfast
rel confined, incapacitated, laid up; feeble, infirm, sickly, weak
idiom flat on one's back
con healed, well; hale, healthy, whole
ant ambulant, ambulatory

bedrock *n* 1 *syn* see BASE 1
2 *syn* see BASIS 1

bedspread *n* an often ornamental outer covering for a bed <an appliquéd *bedspread*>
syn bedcover, counterpane, coverlet, ‖coverlid, spread

bee *n syn* see CAPRICE
rel idea; impulse

beef *n* 1 *syn* see MUSCLE 1
2 *syn* see POWER 4
3 *syn* see QUARREL

‖**beef** *vb syn* see GRIPE

beef (up) *vb syn* see INCREASE 1

beefheaded *adj syn* see STUPID 1

beef–witted *adj syn* see STUPID 1

beefy *adj syn* see HUSKY 1

beekeeper *n* one who engages in the production of and caring for bees and honey <special masks and gloves for *beekeepers*>
syn apiarist, apiculturist, beeman, beemaster

beeline *vb syn* see HURRY 2

Beelzebub *n syn* see DEVIL 1

beeman *n syn* see BEEKEEPER

beemaster *n syn* see BEEKEEPER

beer garden *n syn* see ALEHOUSE

beer hall *n syn* see ALEHOUSE

‖**beerhouse** *n syn* see ALEHOUSE

beetle *vb* 1 *syn* see HANG 4
2 *syn* see BULGE

beetlehead *n syn* see DUNCE

beetleheaded *adj syn* see STUPID 1

‖**beezer** *n syn* see NOSE 1

befall *vb syn* see HAPPEN 1

befit *vb syn* see SUIT 4

befitting *adj* 1 *syn* see FIT 1
ant unbefitting
2 *syn* see DECOROUS 1

befittingly *adv syn* see WELL 4

befog *vb* 1 *syn* see OBSCURE
2 *syn* see CONFUSE 4
3 *syn* see PUZZLE

befool *vb syn* see DUPE

before *adv* 1 so as to precede something in order or time <racing on *before* to give warning>
syn ahead, ante, antecedently, beforehand, fore, forward, in advance, precedently, previous
con behind; abaft, aft, astern
ant after
2 in time past <had heard that joke *before*>
syn already, earlier, erstwhile, formerly, heretofore, once, previously; *compare* THEN 1
ant after
3 until now or then <you'll get it tomorrow and not *before*>
syn beforehand, earlier, sooner

before *prep* 1 coming before in space or time <be home *before* dark>
syn ahead of, ante, ere, in advance of, preceding, prior to, to; *compare* UNTIL
con since, subsequent to
ant after
2 in the presence of <stood *before* the court>
syn confronting, facing
idiom face to face with
3 *syn* see UNTIL

beforehand *adv* 1 *syn* see BEFORE 1
2 *syn* see BEFORE 3

befoul *vb* 1 *syn* see CONTAMINATE 2
2 *syn* see MALIGN

befuddle *vb syn* see CONFUSE 2
rel daze

befuddlement *n syn* see HAZE 2
rel confusion, mix-up
con clearheadedness, lucidity

beg *vb* to ask for or ask one for something urgently <*beg* one's life from an attacker> <*beg* a stranger for help>
syn appeal, beseech, brace, conjure, crave, entreat, implore, importune, invoke, plead, pray, supplicate
rel ask, call (on), request, solicit; petition, sue; besiege, demand, press; nag, worry

idiom throw oneself at the feet of (*or* on the mercy of)
con hint, intimate, suggest

‖**begats** *n pl* **1** *syn* see GENEALOGY
2 *syn* see OFFSPRING

begem *vb syn* see BEJEWEL

beget *vb* **1** *syn* see FATHER
2 *syn* see PROCREATE 1

beggar *n* **1** one who begs especially habitually or as a livelihood <*beggars* crying out to tourists>
syn bummer, cadger, moocher, panhandler, ‖schnorrer
rel deadbeat, freeloader, sponge, sponger; ‖bindle stiff, hobo, tramp
2 *syn* see SUPPLIANT
3 *syn* see PAUPER

beggared *adj syn* see POOR 1

beggarly *adj syn* see CONTEMPTIBLE
rel wretched; ‖cheesy, trashy; measly, paltry

beggary *n* **1** *syn* see POVERTY 1
2 *syn* see MENDICANCY

begin *vb* **1** to carry out the first act or step of an action or operation <*began* his lecture with a joke>
syn commence, embark (on *or* upon), enter, get off, inaugurate, initiate, jump (off), kick off, launch, lead off, open, set to, start, take up, tee off
rel establish, found, institute; introduce, usher in; broach; attack, tackle; prepare; break in; dig in
idiom get the show on the road, get to work, get underway
con cease, desist, discontinue, quit, stop; close, complete, conclude, finish, terminate; abandon, forsake, leave, quit; back out, renege, withdraw
ant end
2 to come into existence <not since civilization *began* has there been such distress>
syn arise, commence, originate, start; *compare* SPRING 1
rel spring; open
idiom raise its head
con end, finish, terminate

beginner *n syn* see NOVICE

beginning *n* the first part or stage of a process or development <the first few chapters at the *beginning* of the novel>
syn alpha, birth, commencement, dawn, dawning, day spring, genesis, onset, opening, opening gun, outset, outstart, setout, start
rel creation, inception, origin, origination, root, source, spring; anlage, rudiment, sprout; prologue; appearance, emergence, rise; incipiency, infancy
idiom the word go
con consummation, termination; closing, completion, conclusion; omega
ant end, ending

beginning *adj* **1** *syn* see INITIAL 1
2 *syn* see ELEMENTARY 1

begird *vb* **1** *syn* see BELT 1

2 *syn* see SURROUND 1

begirdle *vb syn* see BELT 1

begone *vb syn* see GET OUT 1

begrime *vb syn* see SOIL 2

begrudge *vb syn* see ENVY

beguile *vb* **1** *syn* see MANIPULATE 2
2 *syn* see DECEIVE
rel entice, lure, seduce
3 *syn* see WHILE

beguiling *adj syn* see MISLEADING

béguin *n syn* see INFATUATION

behave *vb* **1** to act in a specified way <*behave* as people of good breeding should>
syn acquit, act, bear, carry, comport, conduct, demean, deport, disport, do, go on, move, quit
rel control, direct, manage
idiom make as if (*or* though); be on one's best behavior, mind one's p's and q's
ant misbehave, misconduct
2 *syn* see ACT 5

behavior *n* one's actions in general or on a particular occasion <his flustered *behavior* before women>
syn comportment, conduct, deportment, tenue
rel bearing, demeanor, mien; action, manner, way
con misbehavior, misconduct

behead *vb* to sever the head <nobles *beheaded* for treason>
syn decapitate, decollate, guillotine, head, neck
idiom bring to the block

behemoth *n syn* see GIANT

behemothic *adj syn* see HUGE

behest *n syn* see COMMAND 1
rel demand; prompting, request, solicitation

behind *adv syn* see AFTER

behind *prep* **1** *syn* see ABAFT
2 *syn* see AFTER 2

behind *n syn* see BUTTOCKS

behindhand *adj* **1** *syn* see NEGLIGENT
2 *syn* see BACKWARD 6
3 *syn* see TARDY
ant beforehand

behold *vb syn* see SEE 1

beholden *adj syn* see INDEBTED

beholder *n syn* see SPECTATOR

being *n* **1** *syn* see EXISTENCE 1
rel character, individuality, personality
ant nonbeing
2 *syn* see THING 5
3 *syn* see ENTITY 1
4 *syn* see ESSENCE 1
5 *syn* see HUMAN

‖**being** *conj syn* see BECAUSE

bejewel *vb* to ornament with or as if with jewels <a *bejeweled* headdress> <cobwebs all *bejeweled* with glittering morning dew>
syn begem, beset, enjewel, gem, jewel
rel bespangle, spangle; diamond; encrust

belabor *vb syn* see BEAT 1

belated *adj* **1** *syn* see TARDY
2 *syn* see OLD-FASHIONED

belch *vb* to expel gas suddenly from the stomach through the mouth <ate and ate until he *belched*>
syn burp, eruct, eructate

---

syn synonym(s)   *rel* related word(s)
ant antonym(s)   *con* contrasted word(s)
idiom idiomatic equivalent(s)
‖ use limited; if in doubt, see a dictionary

2 *syn* see ERUPT 1

beldam *n* 1 a woman of advanced years <a crotchety *beldam* hunched over the fire>
syn dame, gammer, grandam; *compare* GAFFER, OLDSTER
rel grandmother, granny; grand dame; matron; matriarch
idiom old girl
con damsel, lass, maid, miss
2 *syn* see HAG 2

beleaguer *vb* 1 *syn* see BESIEGE
rel siege, storm
idiom set upon from all sides
2 *syn* see WORRY 1

belfry *n* 1 *syn* see BELL TOWER
‖2 *syn* see HEAD 1

belie *vb* *syn* see MISREPRESENT
rel contradict, contravene, negative; controvert, disprove; conceal, disguise, hide
con bespeak, betoken, indicate; disclose, discover, reveal
ant attest

belief *n* 1 the act of assenting intellectually to something proposed as true or the state of mind of one who so assents <offered ready *belief* to anyone he trusted>
syn credence, credit, faith
rel assurance, certainty, certitude, conviction, sureness; acquiescence, assent; trust; credibility, trustworthiness
con distrust, doubt, mistrust, uncertainty; incredulity; question
ant disbelief, unbelief
2 *syn* see OPINION
rel doctrine, dogma, fundamental, law, precept, principle; concept, idea

believable *adj* worthy of belief <the author's bizarre characterizations are hardly *believable*>
syn colorable, credible, creditable, plausible
rel likely, possible, probable, tenable; conceivable, rational, reasonable; presumable, supposable; unquestionable; convincing, impressive, persuasive, satisfying; meaningful, solid, substantial
con improbable, unlikely; doubtable, doubtful, dubious, fishy, questionable, specious; implausible, incredible; inconceivable, untenable; fabulous, mythological
ant unbelievable

believe *vb* 1 to have a firm conviction in the reality of something <*believes* in ghosts>
syn accept, ‖buy, swallow
rel accredit, credit, trust; admit
idiom have no doubts about, hold the belief that, take (*or* accept) as gospel, take at one's word, take one's word for
con discredit, distrust, doubt, mistrust, question, suspect; challenge, dispute, reject, turn down
ant disbelieve, misbelieve
2 *syn* see FEEL 3
3 *syn* see UNDERSTAND 3

belittle *vb* 1 *syn* see DECRY 3
rel criticize, discredit; underestimate, underrate, undervalue
con intensify; boast, crow
ant aggrandize; magnify

belittlement *n* *syn* see DETRACTION

bell *vb* *syn* see RING

‖**bell cow** *n* *syn* see LEADER 1

bellicose *adj* *syn* see BELLIGERENT
rel aggressive, assertive; factious, fighting, rebellious
idiom full of fight
con gentle, moderate, temperate
ant amicable; pacific

belligerence *n* *syn* see ATTACK 2

belligerent *adj* having or taking an aggressive or fighting attitude <a *belligerent* reply to a diplomatic note>
syn bellicose, combative, contentious, gladiatorial, militant, pugnacious, quarrelsome, ‖ructious, scrappy, truculent, warlike; *compare* QUARRELSOME 2
rel battling, fighting, warring; attacking, invading; aggressive, antagonistic, fierce, hostile; ardent, hot, hot-tempered
con neutral; pacific, pacifist, peaceable, peaceful; conciliatory; amicable
ant friendly

‖**belling** *n* *syn* see SHIVAREE

bellow *vb* *syn* see ROAR
rel bark, bay, yelp; cry, wail; low, moo

bell ringer *n* *syn* see SMASH 6

bell tower *n* a tower that supports or shelters a bell or group of bells <a *bell tower* stood free from the church>
syn belfry, campanile, carillon

bellwether *n* *syn* see LEADER 1

belly *n* *syn* see ABDOMEN

bellyache *n* *syn* see STOMACHACHE

‖**bellyache** *vb* *syn* see GRIPE

‖**bellyacher** *n* *syn* see GROUCH

belong *vb* 1 to be suitable, appropriate, or advantageous or to be in a proper or fitting place or situation <the boxes *belong* in the attic>
syn fit, go, set
rel become, befit, suit; accord, agree, chime, harmonize; correspond, match, tally
idiom have one's place
2 to be the property of (a person or thing) <the books *belong* to the library>
syn appertain, pertain, vest
3 to be an attribute, part, adjunct, or function (of a person or thing) <good humor and wit *belong* to his personality>
syn indwell, inhere
idiom run in one's blood (*or* family)

belongings *n pl syn* see POSSESSION 2

beloved *adj* *syn* see FAVORITE 1

beloved *n* 1 *syn* see SWEETHEART 1
2 *syn* see GIRL FRIEND 2
3 *syn* see BOYFRIEND 2

below *adv* 1 in or at a lower position than something expressed or implied <several business establishments were situated *below*>
syn beneath, under, underneath
ant above
2 lower on the same page or on a following page <for additional examples see *below*>
syn infra
ant above, supra

below *prep* 1 in a lower position relative to some other object or place <lives just *below* me>
syn beneath, under, underneath
con over

ant above
2 **syn** see AFTER 2

belt *n* **1** a strip of flexible material worn around the waist <a leather *belt*>
syn ceinture, cincture, girdle, sash, waistband
rel baldric, cummerbund; band
2 **syn** see AREA 1
rel stretch, strip

belt *vb* **1** to bind about or around with or as if with a belt <gold lamé *belting* the gown>
syn band, begird, begirdle, cincture, encincture, engird, engirdle, gird, girdle
rel tie (up); loop; sash; circle, encircle, ring
2 **syn** see SLAM 1

belt *n* **syn** see BLOW 1

belvedere *n* **syn** see SUMMERHOUSE

bemean *vb* **syn** see HUMBLE

bemedaled *adj* having or wearing decorations especially as awarded by the military <the general's *bemedaled* uniform>
syn beribboned, decorated

bemired *adj* **syn** see MUDDY 1

bemoan *vb* **syn** see DEPLORE 1
rel regret; complain
con applaud, cheer, huzzah; delight, jubilate, rejoice
ant exult

bemuse *vb* **syn** see DAZE 2
rel addle; perplex, puzzle
con enlighten, illuminate

bemused *adj* **syn** see ABSTRACTED

benchmark *n* **syn** see STANDARD 3

bend *vb* **1** **syn** see CURVE
rel arch, curl, double, hook
ant straighten
2 **syn** see GIVE 12
3 **syn** see INCLINE 3
4 **syn** see ADDRESS 3

bend (over) *vb* **syn** see HANG 4

bend *n* **1** **syn** see TURN 2
2 **syn** see TURN 4
3 **syn** see CURVE

bender *n* **syn** see BINGE 1

bending *adj* **syn** see CROOKED 1

beneath *adv* **syn** see BELOW 1

beneath *prep* **syn** see BELOW 1
ant above, over

benediction *n* **1** **syn** see BLESSING 1
2 **syn** see GRACE 1
3 **syn** see APPROBATION
4 **syn** see GOOD 1

benefact *vb* **syn** see HELP 1

benefaction *n* **syn** see DONATION

benefic *adj* **syn** see GOOD 1
rel desirable, pleasing, satisfying
con damaging, harmful, injurious
ant malefic

beneficence *n* **syn** see DONATION

beneficial *adj* **syn** see GOOD 1
rel salutary, wholesome
con baneful, deleterious, noxious, pernicious
ant detrimental, harmful

benefit *n* **1** **syn** see GOOD 1

2 **syn** see WELFARE
rel account, behalf, sake; gain, profit
con catastrophe, disaster, misfortune; detriment
ant harm, ill

benefit *vb* to be useful or profitable to <medicines that *benefit* mankind>
syn advantage, avail, profit, serve, work (for)
rel advance, ameliorate, better, contribute (to), favor, improve; relieve, succor; build, further, promote; aid, assist, help
idiom do a world of good
con hinder, impede; damage, impair, injure; distress, upset; afflict, anguish; oppose
ant harm, hurt

benet *vb* **syn** see CATCH 3

benevolence *n* **1** **syn** see GOODWILL 1
con animosity, bitterness, ill will; antagonism, hostility; inimicality, unkindliness; stinginess
2 **syn** see GIFT 1

benevolent *adj* **1** **syn** see GENEROUS 1
rel beneficent; charitable; humane; compassionate, tenderhearted
con cruel, inhuman, malicious, spiteful
ant malevolent
2 **syn** see CHARITABLE 1
rel bighearted, freehearted, generous, greathearted, largehearted, liberal, openhanded; public-spirited; do-good
con niggardly, stingy; callous, indifferent, insensitive, unconcerned, unfeeling

benighted *adj* **1** **syn** see IGNORANT 1
rel backward, unenlightened; uninformed
idiom in the dark
con informed, intelligent
2 **syn** see BACKWARD 5

benightedness *n* **syn** see IGNORANCE 1

benign *adj* **1** **syn** see KIND
rel gracious
con malevolent, malicious, malignant, spiteful; acrid, caustic, mordant
ant malign
2 **syn** see FAVORABLE 5
rel gentle, mild; benevolent, charitable, humane; clement, forbearing, merciful
con menacing, threatening
ant malign

benignant *adj* **syn** see KIND
rel mild; gracious
con malevolent, malicious, spiteful; relentless
ant malignant

benison *n* **syn** see BLESSING 1

bent *n* **1** **syn** see LEANING 2
2 **syn** see GIFT 2
con antipathy, aversion; inability, incapacity

bent *adj* **1** **syn** see CURVED
2 **syn** see DECIDED 2

benumb *vb* **1** **syn** see DEADEN 1
2 **syn** see DAZE 2

benumbed *adj* **syn** see NUMB 1

bequeath *vb* **1** **syn** see WILL
con disinherit, exheridate
2 **syn** see HAND DOWN

bequest *n* **syn** see LEGACY 1

berate *vb* **syn** see SCOLD 1
con acclaim, praise; applaud; commend, compliment

---

syn synonym(s)   **rel** related word(s)
ant antonym(s)   **con** contrasted word(s)
idiom idiomatic equivalent(s)
‖ use limited; if in doubt, see a dictionary

berceuse n syn see LULLABY

bereave vb syn see DEPRIVE 2

bereaved adj suffering the death of a loved one <the *bereaved* family>
syn bereft
rel distressed, sorrowing

bereft adj syn see BEREAVED

beribboned adj syn see BEMEDALED

berth n 1 syn see WHARF
   2 syn see JOB 2

beseech vb syn see BEG

beset vb 1 syn see BEJEWEL
   2 syn see ATTACK 1
   3 syn see BESIEGE
   4 syn see INFEST 1
   5 syn see SURROUND 1
   idiom come at from all directions (or sides)

besetment n syn see ANNOYANCE 3

beside prep 1 at or by the side of <left the car *beside* the road>
   syn alongside, by, ∥fornent, next to
   rel near, opposite
   2 syn see NEAR 2
   3 syn see BESIDES 1
   4 syn see EXCEPT

besides adv 1 syn see ALSO 2
   idiom at that
   2 syn see AGAIN 4

besides prep 1 in addition to <*besides* being tall, he's thin>
   syn as well as, beside, beyond, over and above
   idiom along with, together with
   2 syn see EXCEPT

besides adj syn see ADDITIONAL

besiege vb to surround an enemy in a fortified or strong position so as to prevent ingress and egress <Troy was *besieged* by Greeks for ten years>
   syn beleaguer, beset, blockade, invest
   rel encircle, encompass, hem (in); surround; trap; assail, assault, attack

besmear vb 1 syn see SMEAR 1
   2 syn see TAINT 1

besmirch vb syn see TAINT 1

besoil vb syn see SOIL 2

besotted adj syn see INFATUATED

bespangle vb syn see SPANGLE 1

bespatter vb 1 syn see SPOT 1
   2 syn see MALIGN

bespeak vb 1 syn see RESERVE 2
   2 syn see ADDRESS 4
   3 syn see ASK 2
   idiom put in for
   4 syn see INDICATE 2

bespeckle vb syn see SPECKLE 1

bespot vb syn see SPOT 1

besprinkle vb syn see SPRINKLE 1

best adj much more than half <passed the *best* part of a month at the shore>
   syn better, ∥bettermost, greater, largest, most

best vb 1 syn see CONQUER 2
   2 syn see SURPASS 1
   3 syn see DEFEAT 2

best n the choicest one or part <always gave the *best* that she had>

syn choice, cream, elite, fat, flower, pick, pride, prime, primrose, prize, top
   rel gem; nonesuch, nonpareil; exemplar, model, paragon, pattern
   idiom cock of the walk, flower of the flock, one in a thousand (or million)
   ant worst

bestain vb syn see STAIN 1

∥**best bib and tucker** n syn see FINERY

best girl n syn see GIRL FRIEND 1

bestial adj syn see BRUTISH

bestialize vb syn see DEBASE 1

bestir vb syn see STIR 1

bestow vb 1 syn see USE 2
   2 syn see STOW
   3 syn see HARBOR 2
   4 syn see GIVE 1

bestower n syn see DONOR

bestrew vb syn see STREW 1

bestride vb 1 syn see MOUNT 5
   2 to sit with one leg on each side <boys *bestriding* a fallen log>
   syn straddle, ∥striddle, stride

bet n something of value (as money) staked on a winner-take-all basis on the outcome of an uncertainty <laid a *bet* at three to one on the champion>
   syn ante, pot, stake, wager

bet vb syn see GAMBLE 1

bête noire n syn see ABOMINATION 1

bethink vb syn see REMEMBER

betide vb syn see HAPPEN 1

betimes adv 1 syn see EARLY 1
   2 syn see EARLY 2
   ∥3 syn see SOMETIMES

betoken vb 1 syn see INDICATE 2
   2 syn see AUGUR 2

betray vb 1 syn see DECEIVE
   rel ensnare, entrap, snare, trap
   2 to prove faithless or treacherous <*betrayed* his own people by going over to the enemy>
   syn cross, double-cross, sell, sell out, ∥split
   rel desert, renegade; give away, inform, turn in; collaborate; apostatize
   idiom act (or play) the traitor, break faith, round on, sell down the river
   3 syn see REVEAL 1
   rel demonstrate, evidence, evince, manifest, show; betoken, indicate
   con defend, guard, protect, safeguard, shield

betrayer n syn see INFORMER

betrothal n syn see ENGAGEMENT 2

betrothed n either member of a couple engaged to be married
   syn affianced, intended
   rel fiancé, husband-to-be; bride-to-be, fiancée, wife-to-be

betrothed adj syn see ENGAGED 2

betrothing n syn see ENGAGEMENT 2

betrothment n syn see ENGAGEMENT 2

better adj 1 syn see BEST
   2 more worthy or pleasing than an alternative <it is *better* to lose gracefully than to win arrogantly>
   syn ∥bettermost, preferable, superior; *compare* GOOD
   rel exceeding, exceptional, surpassing; choice, desirable, excellent
   idiom more than a match for

ant worse

better *adv syn* see MORE 2
ant worse

better *n* **1** *syn* see SUPERIOR
2 a superior or winning position <had the *better* of the argument>
syn advantage, superiority, upper hand, victory, whip hand; *compare* ADVANTAGE 3
rel success, triumph, win
con collapse, defeat, disadvantage, loss; beating, drubbing, licking
ant worse

better *vb* **1** *syn* see IMPROVE 1
ant worsen
2 *syn* see SURPASS 1

‖**bettermost** *adj* **1** *syn* see BETTER 2
2 *syn* see BEST

between *prep* **1** in common to (as in position, in a distribution, or in participation) <a treaty *between* three powers>
syn among
2 in the space, time, space, or interval that separates <*between* the ages 12 and 20>
syn ‖atween, ‖atwixt, ‖betwixt, in between, tween, twixt

‖**betwixt** *prep syn* see BETWEEN 2

bevel *adj syn* see DIAGONAL

beveled *adj syn* see DIAGONAL

‖**bever** *n syn* see SNACK

beverage *n syn* see DRINK 1

bevy *n syn* see GROUP 1

bewail *vb syn* see DEPLORE 1
ant rejoice

beware *vb* to be cautious <*beware* of the dog>
syn look out, mind, watch out
rel attend, heed, notice, watch
idiom be on one's guard, be on the lookout (*or* watch), keep at a safe distance, take care (*or* heed)
con disregard, ignore, neglect

bewhiskered *adj syn* see BEARDED

bewilder *vb* **1** *syn* see PUZZLE
rel baffle, fuddle, muddle
2 *syn* see CONFUSE 2

bewitch *vb* **1** to practice witchcraft on <medicine men who *bewitch* ignorant tribesmen>
syn charm, enchant, ensorcell, hex, spell, voodoo, witch
rel bedevil, demonize, overlook, possess, sorcerize; beglamour, dazzle, trick
idiom cast a spell on (*or* over), give (*or* cast) the evil eye, put a curse on
2 *syn* see ATTRACT 1
rel beglamour, ‖snow

bewitched *adj syn* see ENAMORED 3

bewitching *adj syn* see ATTRACTIVE 1
con forbidding, grim

bewitchment *n syn* see MAGIC 1

beyond *adv* **1** on or to the farther side <a house with mountains *beyond*>
syn farther, further, ‖yon, yonder
2 *syn* see OVER 1

beyond *prep* **1** on or to the farther side of <the store is just *beyond* the next house>

syn after, outside, past, without
2 out of the reach, sphere, or comprehension of <it's *beyond* me how he did it>
syn above, past
idiom beyond one's depth (*or* power), over (*or* above) one's head, too deep (*or* much) for
3 *syn* see BESIDES 1

beyond *adj syn* see ADDITIONAL

beyond *n syn* see HEREAFTER 2

‖**b'hoy** *n syn* see TOUGH

bias *n* **1** *syn* see LEANING 2
2 *syn* see PREJUDICE
rel inclination, predisposition; slant, standpoint, viewpoint
con dispassionateness; fairness, justness

bias *adj syn* see DIAGONAL

bias *vb* **1** *syn* see SLANT 3
2 *syn* see INCLINE 3
3 *syn* see PREJUDICE 2

biased *adj syn* see DIAGONAL
2 exhibiting or characterized by a highly personal and unreasoned distortion of judgment <a *biased* estimate of the book's worth>
syn colored, jaundiced, one-sided, partial, partisan, prejudiced, prepossessed, tendentious, unindifferent, unneutral, warped
rel bent, disposed, inclined, predisposed; influenced, interested, swayed; opinionated
con detached, dispassionate, impartial, neutral, open-minded; fair, honest, just
ant unbiased

bibber *n syn* see DRUNKARD

bibble–babble *n syn* see CHATTER

bibelot *n syn* see KNICKKNACK

Bible *n* the sacred volume of Christians <students of the *Bible*>
syn Book, Holy Writ, Sacred Writ, Scripture
idiom Book of Books, Good Book, Word of God

bibliopole *n syn* see BOOKDEALER

bicker *vb* **1** *syn* see ARGUE 2
rel battle, contend, fight, war
2 *syn* see QUARREL
3 *syn* see RATTLE 1

bickering *n syn* see QUARREL

bicycle *n* a pedal-propelled vehicle with two wheels tandem, a steering handle, and a saddle seat <ten-speed *bicycles*>
syn bike, cycle, two-wheeler, velocipede

bid *vb* **1** *syn* see COMMAND
rel summon
con interdict, prohibit
ant forbid
2 *syn* see INVITE
rel request

biddable *adj syn* see OBEDIENT
rel amiable, good-natured, obliging
con mulish, obstinate, stiff-necked, stubborn
ant recalcitrant

bidding *n syn* see COMMAND 1
rel call, summoning

biddy *n* **1** *syn* see MAID 2
2 *syn* see HAG 2

bide *vb* **1** *syn* see STAY 2
rel continue
2 *syn* see RESIDE 1

bierstube *n syn* see ALEHOUSE

---

syn synonym(s)   *rel* related word(s)
ant antonym(s)   *con* contrasted word(s)
idiom idiomatic equivalent(s)
‖ use limited; if in doubt, see a dictionary

biff *n syn* see BLOW 1

‖**biff** *vb syn* see STRIKE 2

‖**biffy** *n syn* see PRIVY 1

bifold *adj syn* see TWOFOLD 1

big *adj* 1 of significant size or scope <a *big* expanse of mud> <*big* plans>
syn considerable, extensive, hefty, large, large-scale, major, sizable
rel bumper, hulking, whacking, whopping; clumsy, unwieldy; ample, biggish, capacious, commodious, comprehensive, copious, roomy, spacious, voluminous; distended, inflated, swollen
con paltry, piddling, trivial; slight, small; insignificant; minute, tiny, wee
ant little
2 *syn* see LARGE 1
3 *syn* see PREGNANT 1
4 *syn* see FULL 1
rel flushed, overflowing; cloyed, glutted, sated, satiated, satisfied
idiom full to bursting (*or* overflowing), full to the ears, stuffed to the gills
con empty
5 *syn* see IMPORTANT 1
6 *syn* see PRETENTIOUS 3
7 *syn* see GENEROUS 1

‖**big** *adv syn* see VERY 1

big *n syn* see NOTABLE 1

big boy *n syn* see NOTABLE 1

‖**big bug** *n syn* see NOTABLE 1

big cheese *n syn* see NOTABLE 1

‖**big chief** *n syn* see NOTABLE 1

‖**biggety** *adj syn* see WISE 5

‖**biggie** *n syn* see NOTABLE 1

big gun *n syn* see NOTABLE 1

‖**big house** *n syn* see JAIL

bight *n syn* see INLET

big name *n syn* see CELEBRITY 2

bigness *n syn* see SIZE 1

‖**big noise** *n syn* see NOTABLE 1

bigot *n syn* see ENTHUSIAST
rel approver, liker, relisher; mumpsimus, racist, segregationist
con depreciator, disparager, knocker; disliker, disrelisher, hater, loather, misliker

bigoted *adj syn* see ILLIBERAL
rel lily-white; conservative

big shot *n syn* see NOTABLE 1

big-timer *n syn* see NOTABLE 1

‖**big wheel** *n syn* see NOTABLE 1

bigwig *n syn* see NOTABLE 1

bike *n syn* see BICYCLE

bilge *n syn* see NONSENSE 2

bilk *vb* 1 *syn* see FRUSTRATE 1
con fulfill
2 *syn* see CHEAT
3 *syn* see ESCAPE 2
rel dodge, shake

bill *n* 1 the jaws of a bird with their projecting horny covering <the huge *bill* of the toucan>
syn beak, neb, nib, pecker
2 *syn* see PROMONTORY
3 *syn* see VISOR 1

bill *n* a statement of the amount due a creditor <*bills* from the grocer and doctor>
syn account, invoice, reckoning, score, statement, tab
rel charges, damage

idiom statement of account
2 *syn* see CHECK 2
3 *syn* see POSTER
4 *syn* see DOLLAR

billet *n syn* see JOB 2

billet *vb* 1 to assign quarters to soldiers <the troops were *billeted* in private homes>
syn canton, quarter
rel bed, house, lodge, put up; bestow
2 *syn* see HARBOR 2

billet *n syn* see BAR 1

billet–doux *n syn* see LOVE LETTER

billingsgate *n syn* see ABUSE

billy *n syn* see CUDGEL

billy club *n syn* see CUDGEL

‖**bim** *n syn* see WANTON

bimanal *adj syn* see TWO-HANDED 2

bimanual *adj syn* see TWO-HANDED 1

‖**bimbo** *n syn* see WANTON

binary *adj syn* see TWOFOLD 1

bind *vb* 1 *syn* see TIE 1
con release
ant unloose
2 *syn* see BANDAGE

bindle stiff *n syn* see VAGABOND

bing *n syn* see PILE 1

binge *n* 1 a drunken revel <hung over after a weekend *binge*>
syn bat, bender, blowoff, booze, brannigan, bum, bust, carousal, carouse, compotation, drunk, jag, orgy, ran-tan, rowdydow, soak, souse, tear, ‖time, toot, wassail
rel bacchanal, bacchanalia, debauch; blast, ‖blowout; ‖bun
2 *syn* see SPREE 1

bio *n syn* see BIOGRAPHY

biocide *n syn* see PESTICIDE

biographer *n* one who writes a biography <irresponsible *biographers* whose work is more fiction than fact>
syn autobiographer, autobiographist, Boswell, memoirist

biography *n* a more or less detailed account of the events and circumstances of a person's life <wrote a *biography* of his grandfather>
syn autobiography, bio, confessions, life, memoir
rel diary, journal, letters; adventures, history, story; profile; obit, obituary

biologic *n syn* see DRUG 1

bird *n* 1 *syn* see RASPBERRY
‖2 *syn* see GIRL 1

birdbrain *n syn* see SCATTERBRAIN

birdhouse *n syn* see AVIARY

birdman *n syn* see PILOT 2

bird–witted *adj syn* see GIDDY 1

birr *n syn* see ENERGY 2

birth *n* 1 the act or process of bringing forth young from the womb <had a very hard *birth* after a prolonged labor>
syn bearing, ‖birthing, childbearing, childbirth, delivery, parturition
rel abortion, miscarriage, slip
2 *syn* see BEGINNING

birth *vb* ‖1 *syn* see BEAR 5
2 *syn* see SPRING 1

birth control *n* control of the number of children born especially by preventing or lessening the frequency of conception <cultural and religious aspects of *birth control*>

syn contraception
rel rhythm method; planned parenthood; vasectomy; (the) pill
‖**birthing** *n syn* see BIRTH 1
birthmark *n* **1** a congenital pigmented area on the skin <*birthmarks* often appear on the neck>
syn mole, nevus
2 *syn* see CHARACTERISTIC 1
birth pang *n, usu* **birth pangs** *pl syn* see LABOR 1
birthright *n* **1** *syn* see RIGHT 2
2 *syn* see HERITAGE 1
bisexual *adj* being structurally and functionally both male and female <many lower animals are *bisexual*>
syn androgynous, hermaphrodite, hermaphroditic
bistered *adj syn* see DARK 3
bistro *n syn* see NIGHTCLUB
bit *n* **1** *syn* see MORSEL 1
2 *syn* see PARTICLE
3 *syn* see END 4
4 *syn* see WHILE 1
bit *vb syn* see RESTRAIN 1
bit by bit *adv syn* see GRADUALLY
‖**bitch** *vb* **1** *syn* see GRIPE
2 *syn* see DECEIVE
bitch (up) *vb syn* see BOTCH
bitchy *adj syn* see MALICIOUS
bite *vb* **1** to seize with the teeth so that they enter <*bite* into a pear>
syn champ, chomp
rel gnaw, nibble, tooth; ‖chaw, chew, crunch, masticate, munch; eat
idiom sink one's teeth into
2 *syn* see EAT 3
3 *syn* see SMART
bite *n* **1** *syn* see MORSEL 1
2 *syn* see SNACK
3 *syn* see SHARE 1
biting *adj syn* see INCISIVE
‖**bitsy** *adj syn* see TINY
bitter *adj* **1** *syn* see ACRID
rel acerb, acid, bitterish
con delicious; bland, flat, insipid
2 difficult to accept mentally <the *bitter* truth>
syn afflictive, distasteful, galling, grievous, painful, unpalatable
rel annoying, distressing, disturbing, woeful; bad, disagreeable, displeasing, offensive, unpleasant; galling, provoking, vexatious
con agreeable, gratifying, satisfying
3 marked by intense animosity <*bitter* contempt>
syn antagonistic, hostile, rancorous, virulent, vitriolic
rel alienated, divided, estranged; irreconcilable
4 *syn* see SEVERE 3
con mild, springlike, summery
bitter–ender *n syn* see DIEHARD 1
bitterly *adv syn* see HARD 6
bivouac *vb syn* see CAMP

syn synonym(s)   *rel* related word(s)
ant antonym(s)   *con* contrasted word(s)
idiom idiomatic equivalent(s)
‖ use limited; if in doubt, see a dictionary

‖**bivvy** *vb syn* see CAMP
bizarre *adj* **1** *syn* see STRANGE 4
2 *syn* see FANTASTIC 2
con normal, ordinary, regular
blab *n syn* see CHATTER
blab *vb syn* see GOSSIP
blab (out) *vb syn* see REVEAL 1
blabber *vb syn* see BABBLE 2
blabber *n syn* see CHATTER
blabber *n syn* see CHATTERBOX
blabbermouth *n syn* see CHATTERBOX
blabmouth *n syn* see CHATTERBOX
black *adj* **1** having the color of soot or coal <a *black* hearse>
syn atramentous, ebon, ebony, inky, jet, jetty, onyx, pitch-black, pitch-dark, pitchy, raven, sable
rel blackish; charcoal, slate; piceous; dusky, swart, swarthy; brunet
idiom black as a crow (or a shoe or the ace of spades), black as hell (or night)
ant white
2 *syn* see DIRTY 1
3 *syn* see GLOOMY 3
4 *syn* see UTTER
black *vb syn* see BRUISE 1
black (out) *vb syn* see ERASE
black and white *n syn* see PRINT 2
black–a–vised *adj syn* see DARK 3
black beast *n syn* see ABOMINATION 1
‖**blackcoat** *n syn* see CLERGYMAN
black dog *n syn* see SADNESS
blacken *vb syn* see MALIGN
idiom blacken one's good name, give one a black eye, throw mud at
black eye *n* **1** a bruise about the eye <got a *black eye* in a fight>
syn mouse, shiner
rel contusion
2 *syn* see STIGMA
blackguard *n syn* see VILLAIN 1
black out *vb syn* see FAINT
blackout *n syn* see FAINT
blague *n syn* see NONSENSE 2
blah *n syn* see NONSENSE 2
blah *adj syn* see DULL 9
blamable *adj syn* see BLAMEWORTHY
blame *vb syn* see CRITICIZE
rel accuse, charge; impute
idiom lay at one's door (or doorstep), lay (or put) the blame on
con exculpate, vindicate; praise
blame *n* responsibility for misdeed or delinquency <accepted the *blame* for his foolish act>
syn culpability, fault, guilt, onus
rel accountability, answerability, liability; accusation, charge, imputation; censure, condemnation, denunciation, reprehension
idiom burden of guilt
con commendation, compliment; acclaim, applause, praise
blamed *adj* **1** *syn* see DAMNED 2
2 *syn* see UTTER
blameful *adj syn* see BLAMEWORTHY
blameless *adj* **1** *syn* see INNOCENT 2
2 *syn* see GOOD 11
rel unimpeachable
ant blameworthy

blameworthy *adj* deserving reproach and punishment <though not criminal, his behavior was certainly *blameworthy*>
syn amiss, blamable, blameful, censurable, culpable, demeritorious, guilty, reprehensible, sinful, unholy
rel illaudable, uncommendable, unpraiseworthy, unpretty; delinquent, faultful; punishable; foolish, irresponsible, reckless
idiom at fault, to blame
con faultless, flawless, impeccable, irreproachable, unimpeachable; guiltless, innocent, sinless; creditable, high-principled, upright
ant blameless; unblamable

blanch *vb syn* see WHITEN 1
blanch (over) *vb syn* see PALLIATE
blanch *vb syn* see RECOIL
blanched *adj syn* see PALE 1
bland *adj* **1** *syn* see SUAVE
rel good-natured, ingratiating
con bluff, crusty, gruff
ant brusque
2 *syn* see GENTLE 1
3 *syn* see INSIPID 3
con pungent, savory, spicy, zestful

blandish *vb syn* see COAX
rel flatter; beguile, charm
con threaten

blandishment *n syn* see FLATTERY

blank *adj* **1** *syn* see EXPRESSIONLESS
2 *syn* see UTTER
blank *n syn* see OMISSION
blank check *n syn* see CARTE BLANCHE
blanket *vb syn* see COVER 3
blankety-blank *adj* **1** *syn* see DAMNED 2
2 *syn* see UTTER
blankness *n syn* see VACUITY 2
blank wall *n syn* see BAR 2
blare *vb* **1** *syn* see BLAZE
2 *syn* see SCREAM 4
blaring *adj syn* see LOUD 1
blarney *vb syn* see COAX
blarney *n syn* see FLATTERY
blasé *adj syn* see SOPHISTICATED 2
con awed, wide-eyed; artless, naive, natural, unsophisticated
blasphemous *adj syn* see SACRILEGIOUS
blasphemy *n* **1** impious or irreverent language <cursing God is *blasphemy*>
syn cursing, cussing, execration, imprecation, profanity, swearing
rel affront, indignity, insult; abuse, billingsgate, scurrility, vituperation
con reverence, veneration, worship
ant adoration
2 *syn* see PROFANATION
rel abuse, befouling, shaming
blast *n syn* see BANG 2
blast *vb* **1** to ruin or to injure severely, suddenly, or surprisingly <we'll have no peaches; frost *blasted* the blossoms this year>
syn blight, dash, nip
rel destroy, ruin, wreck; damage, injure, spoil; shrivel, stunt, wither
2 *syn* see SLAM 1
3 *syn* see WHIP 2
blasted *adj* **1** *syn* see DAMNED 2
2 *syn* see UTTER

blat *vb syn* see EXCLAIM
blatant *adj* **1** *syn* see VOCIFEROUS
rel screaming; obtrusive
con modest, soft-spoken
2 *syn* see GAUDY
3 *syn* see SHAMELESS
blather *vb syn* see BABBLE 2
blather *n syn* see NONSENSE 2
blatherskite *n syn* see NONSENSE 2
blatter *n syn* see CHATTER
blaze *vb* to burn or appear to burn brightly <the hot sun *blazed* down>
syn blare, flame, flare, glare, glow
rel illuminate, illumine, light; radiate, shine; coruscate, fulgurate, scintillate, sparkle; incandesce
blaze (abroad) *vb syn* see DECLARE 1
blazes *n pl syn* see HELL
blazing *adj* **1** *syn* see BURNING 1
2 *syn* see IMPASSIONED
blazon *vb syn* see DECLARE 1
bleach *vb syn* see WHITEN 1
bleak *adj* **1** *syn* see GRIM 2
2 *syn* see GLOOMY 3
blear *vb syn* see DULL 4
blear *adj syn* see FAINT 2
blear-eyed *adj syn* see STUPID 1
blear-witted *adj syn* see STUPID 1
bleary *adj* **1** *syn* see FAINT 2
2 *syn* see EFFETE 2
bleat *vb syn* see GRIPE
bleed *vb* **1** *syn* see EXUDE
2 *syn* see FLEECE 2
bleeding *adj* **1** *syn* see DAMNED 2
2 *syn* see UTTER
blemish *vb syn* see INJURE 1
blemish *n* an imperfection (as a spot or crack) <a *blemish* on the face>
syn defect, flaw, vice
rel fault, scar; blister, blotch, disfigurement, pockmark, wart; catch, snag, tear
blench *vb syn* see RECOIL
blench *vb syn* see WHITEN 1
blend *vb* **1** *syn* see MIX 1
rel combine, integrate
con resolve, separate
2 *syn* see HARMONIZE 4
blend *n syn* see MIXTURE
blending *adj syn* see HARMONIOUS 1
bless *vb* **1** to make holy by religious rite or word <the priest *blessed* the water and wine>
syn consecrate, hallow, sanctify
rel dedicate
con defile, desecrate, profane
2 *syn* see PRAISE 2
blessed *adj* **1** *syn* see HOLY 1
2 *syn* see DAMNED 2
3 *syn* see UTTER
blessedness *n syn* see HAPPINESS
con agony, suffering
ant misery
blessing *n* **1** an expression or utterance of good wishes <on departing, he received his father's *blessing*>
syn benediction, benison
rel Godspeed, valediction
2 *syn* see APPROBATION
3 *syn* see GOOD 1
4 *syn* see GRACE 1

‖**bless out** vb syn see SCOLD 1
blight vb syn see BLAST 1
blighted adj **1** syn see DAMNED 2
  2 syn see UTTER
‖**blighter** n syn see WRETCH 1
blimp n **1** syn see FATTY
  2 cap syn see REACTIONARY
  3 cap syn see STUFFED SHIRT
blind adj **1** lacking the power to see <kittens are *blind* at birth>
  syn ‖dark, eyeless, sightless, stone-blind, visionless
  rel dim-sighted; purblind, short-sighted; blindish; blindfolded; unseeing
  idiom blind as a bat
  con seeing, sighted; keen, sharp
  2 syn see INTOXICATED 1
  3 syn see DULL 7
blind vb syn see DAZE 1
blind n **1** syn see FRONT 3
  2 syn see DECOY 1
blind alley n syn see DEAD END
blinding adj **1** syn see DAMNED 2
  2 syn see UTTER
blink vb **1** syn see WINK
  2 to shine intermittently <we'll signal by *blinking* the headlights>
  syn flash, flicker, twinkle
  rel glimmer, scintillate, shimmer
blink (at) vb syn see CONNIVE 1
blink (at or away) vb syn see NEGLECT 1
‖**blinking** adj **1** syn see DAMNED 2
  2 syn see UTTER
blip vb **1** syn see SLAP 1
  2 syn see CENSOR
bliss n **1** syn see HAPPINESS
  con dolor, misery, woe
  ant anguish
  2 syn see HEAVEN 2
blissfulness n syn see HAPPINESS
  rel ecstasy, euphoria, exaltation; heaven, paradise
blister vb syn see LAMBASTE 3
blistering adj **1** syn see HOT 1
  ‖**2** syn see DAMNED 2
blithe adj **1** syn see CHEERFUL 1
  2 syn see MERRY
  ant atrabilious, morose
blithering adj syn see UTTER
blithesome adj syn see MERRY
blitz vb syn see BOMBARD
‖**bloat** n syn see DRUNKARD
bloated adj syn see POMPOUS 1
bloc n syn see COMBINATION 2
block n **1** syn see BAR 2
  2 syn see ANNEX
block vb **1** syn see HINDER
  2 syn see INTERCEPT
  3 syn see FILL 1
block (out) vb syn see SKETCH
blockade n **1** syn see BAR 2
  ‖**2** syn see MOONSHINE 2
blockade vb syn see BESIEGE
block and block adj syn see FULL 1
blockhead n syn see DUNCE

blockheaded adj syn see STUPID 1
blockish adj syn see STUPID 1
block out vb syn see SCREEN 3
‖**bloke** n syn see MAN 3
blond adj **1** of a pale soft yellow color <*blond* hair>
  syn flaxen, golden, straw
  rel blondish; platinum; champagne, tow-headed
  con dark; brunet
  2 syn see FAIR 3
blood n **1** the fluid that circulates in the heart, arteries, capillaries, and veins of a vertebrate animal <*blood* covered the battlefield>
  syn ‖claret, gore
  rel ichor; humor
  2 syn see ANCESTRY
  3 syn see MURDER
  4 syn see FOP
blood-and-guts adj syn see INTENSIVE
bloodbath n syn see MASSACRE
bloodless adj **1** syn see PALE 2
  rel colorless; lifeless
  con alive; vigorous; florid
  ant plethoric; sanguine
  2 syn see INSENSIBLE 5
bloodshed n syn see MASSACRE
bloodstained adj syn see BLOODY 1
bloodsucker n syn see PARASITE
bloodthirsty adj syn see MURDEROUS
bloody adj **1** affected by or involving the shedding of blood <a *bloody* knife> <when will this long and *bloody* conflict cease?>
  syn bloodstained, ensanguined, gory, imbrued, sanguinary, sanguine, sanguineous
  rel bloodthirsty, grim, murderous, slaughterous; cutthroat, red-handed
  2 syn see MURDEROUS
bloom n **1** syn see FLOWER 1
  2 a state or time of beauty, freshness, and vigor <the *bloom* of youth>
  syn blossom, flush
  rel glow
  3 a rosy appearance of the cheeks <recovered all her health and *bloom*>
  syn blossom, blush, flush, glow
bloom vb syn see BLOSSOM
‖**blooming** adj **1** syn see DAMNED 2
  2 syn see UTTER
blooper n **1** syn see ERROR 2
  2 syn see FAUX PAS
blossom n **1** syn see FLOWER 1
  rel capitulum, corymb, cyme, inflorescence, panicle, raceme, spike, umbel
  2 syn see BLOOM 2
  3 syn see BLOOM 3
blossom vb to produce flowers or be in flower <lilacs *blossom* in the spring>
  syn bloom, blow, burgeon, effloresce, flower, outbloom
  rel bud; leaf; shoot; open, unfold
  idiom burst into bloom, come into flower, put forth blossoms (or flowers or bloom)
  con fade, fall, wither
blot n syn see STIGMA
  rel blemish, flaw, defect
blot vb syn see STAIN 1
blotch vb syn see SPLOTCH
blot out vb **1** syn see ERASE
  2 syn see ANNIHILATE 2

---

syn synonym(s)   rel related word(s)
ant antonym(s)   con contrasted word(s)
idiom idiomatic equivalent(s)
‖ use limited; if in doubt, see a dictionary

blotter *n syn* see DRUNKARD
blotto *adj syn* see INTOXICATED 1
bloviate *vb syn* see ORATE
blow *vb* **1** to produce a current of air on <let the wind *blow* your hair dry>
syn fan, ruffle, wind, winnow
2 *syn* see BOAST
3 *syn* see PANT 1
4 *syn* see WASTE 2
5 *syn* see TREAT 3
6 *syn* see BOTCH
7 *syn* see GO 2
blow *n syn* see BREAK 4
blow *vb syn* see BLOSSOM
blow *n* **1** a forceful sharp stroke (as with the fist or an instrument) <struck him a sudden *blow*>
syn bang, bash, bastinado, bat, belt, biff, bop, crack, ‖ding, ‖douse, pound, slam, slosh, smack, smash, swap, ‖swat, wallop, ‖welt, whack, whop; *compare* CUFF, HIT 1
rel recumbentibus, slug, ‖souse; clip, pelt, plug, punch, swat
2 *syn* see IMPACT 1
blow-by-blow *adj syn* see CIRCUMSTAN-TIAL
blowen *n syn* see HARLOT 1
blower *n syn* see BRAGGART
blowhard *n syn* see BRAGGART
blow in *vb syn* see COME 1
blown-in-the-bottle *adj adj syn* see AU-THENTIC 2
blow off *vb syn* see GRIPE
blowoff *n syn* see BINGE 1
blowout *n syn* see SHINDIG 1
blowsy *adj syn* see SLATTERNLY
ant spruce
blow up *vb* **1** *syn* see EXPLODE 1
2 *syn* see DISCREDIT 2
3 *syn* see ANGER 2
blowy *adj syn* see WINDY 1
blub *vb syn* see CRY 2
blubber *vb syn* see CRY 2
bludgeon *n syn* see CUDGEL
bludgeon *vb syn* see INTIMIDATE
blue *adj* **1** *syn* see DOWNCAST
2 *syn* see RISQUÉ
3 *syn* see UTTER
blue *n syn* see OCEAN
blue blood *n* **1** *syn* see GENTLEMAN 1
2 *syn* see ARISTOCRACY
‖**bluebottle** *n syn* see POLICEMAN
bluecoat *n syn* see POLICEMAN
blue-eyed *adj syn* see FAVORITE 1
blue moon *n syn* see AGE 2
bluenose *n syn* see PRUDE
bluenosed *adj syn* see PRIM 1
blueprint *n syn* see PLAN 1
rel outline, sketch
blueprint *vb syn* see PLAN 2
blue-ribbon *adj syn* see EXCELLENT
blues *n pl but sometimes sing in constr syn* see SADNESS
bluff *adj* direct and unceremonious in speech or manner <*bluff* aggressive questions>
syn abrupt, blunt, breviloquent, brief, brusque, crusty, curt, gruff, rough, short, short-spoken, snippety, snippy
rel hearty, honest, sincere; barefaced, candid, direct, forthright, frank, no-nonsense,

outspoken, plainspoken, straightforward; bearish, rude, tactless; sharp, tart; laconic, terse
idiom to the point
con civil, courteous, courtly, gallant, polite; diplomatic, urbane
ant smooth, suave
bluff *vb* **1** *syn* see DECEIVE
rel fool, joke, trick
2 *syn* see ASSUME 4
blunder *vb* **1** *syn* see STUMBLE 3
2 *syn* see WALLOW 2
3 *syn* see BOTCH
blunder (away) *vb syn* see WASTE 2
blunder *n syn* see ERROR 2
blunderbuss *n syn* see STUMBLEBUM
blunderer *n syn* see STUMBLEBUM
blunt *adj* **1** *syn* see DULL 6
rel unpointed, unsharp; insensitive
con acuminate, acute
ant keen, sharp
2 *syn* see BLUFF
con politic, smooth, suave
ant subtle; tactful
blunt *vb* **1** *syn* see DULL 3
2 *syn* see DEADEN 1
3 *syn* see DULL 5
4 *syn* see WEAKEN 1
‖**blunt** *n syn* see MONEY
blur *n syn* see STIGMA
blur *vb* **1** *syn* see TAINT 1
2 *syn* see CONFUSE 4
3 *syn* see DULL 4
blurb *n syn* see PUFF 3
blurt (out) *vb syn* see EXCLAIM
blush *vb* to turn or glow red in the face <*blushed* from embarrassment>
syn color, crimson, flush, glow, mantle, pink, pinken, redden, rose, rouge
blush *n syn* see BLOOM 3
bluster *vb* **1** *syn* see ROAR
rel blast, storm, rage
2 *syn* see INTIMIDATE
blustering *adj syn* see WILD 6
blustery *adj syn* see WILD 6
board *vb* **1** to get aboard of <*boarded* the wrong bus>
syn embark
rel embus, emplane, entrain
idiom get on
con debus, deplane, detrain; land
ant debark, disembark, get off
2 *syn* see HARBOR 2
rel care (for); cherish, nurture, tend
board *n* **1** boards *pl syn* see DRAMA
2 *syn* see TABLE 1
boast *vb* to express pride in oneself or one's accomplishments <*boasting* about all the girl friends he had>
syn blow, brag, cock-a-doodle-doo, crow, gasconade, mouth, prate, puff, rodomontade, vaunt
rel pique, plume, preen, pride, quack; gush, vapor; aggrandize, exalt, glory, triumph; bluster, ‖bounce, bully, ruffle, swash, swashbuckle, swagger; flaunt, parade, show off
idiom blow one's horn, congratulate oneself, hug oneself, pat oneself on the back
con belittle, decry, degrade, disparage, knock, minimize, run down

ant depreciate

boaster *n syn* see BRAGGART

boastful *adj* given to or characterized by boasting <a *boastful* old windbag>
  syn braggadocian, braggart, braggy, rodomontade, self-glorifying, vaunting
  rel arrogant, pretentious; cock-a-hoop, exultant; big-headed, conceited, swelled-headed; self-aggrandizing, self-applauding, self-flattering, vainglorious
  idiom having a high opinion of oneself, seeing oneself larger than life
  con self-depreciating, self-effacing, unassuming; bashful, demure, sheepish, shy, timid; quiet, reserved, restrained, retiring
  ant modest

bob *vb syn* see TAP 1

bobbery *n syn* see BRAWL 2

bobble *vb syn* see BOTCH

‖**bobby** *n syn* see POLICEMAN

‖**bodacious** *adj syn* see NOTEWORTHY

bode *vb syn* see AUGUR 2

bodement *n syn* see FORETOKEN

bodiless *adj syn* see IMMATERIAL 1

bodily *adj* of or relating to the human body <*bodily* pain>
  syn carnal, corporal, corporeal, fleshly, physical, somatic
  rel animal, sensual
  con intellectual, mental, psychic, psychological; spiritual, unworldly

boding *n syn* see FORETOKEN

body *n* 1 *syn* see HUMAN
  2 *syn* see CORPSE
  3 the main, central, or essential part <the *body* of the discussion dealt with ways to ensure equal opportunities for all>
  syn bulk, core, corpus, mass, staple, substance; *compare* ESSENCE 2, SUBSTANCE 2, TENOR 1
  rel majority; sum, total, whole; basis, crux, fundamental, gravamen; gist, pith
  con angle, aspect, facet, feature, side; accessory, extension, offshoot, side issue
  4 a discrete portion of matter <unknown *bodies* in space>
  syn bulk, mass, object, volume
  5 a determinable or measurable whole <collected a large *body* of evidence>
  syn aggregate, amount, budget, bulk, quantity, quantum, total
  rel input; extent, range; number, stock, sum, whole
  6 *syn* see GROUP 3
  7 *syn* see SUBSTANCE 2

body (forth) *vb syn* see REPRESENT 2

boeotian *n syn* see PHILISTINE

bog *n syn* see SWAMP

bog (down) *vb syn* see DELAY 1

bogey *n syn* see APPARITION

boggle *vb* 1 *syn* see DEMUR
  2 *syn* see BOTCH
  3 *syn* see STAGGER 5

bogus *adj syn* see COUNTERFEIT
  rel forged; imitation

---

con bona fide, good
  ant authentic, genuine, real

Bohemian *n* a person (as an artist) who has an unconventional life-style that often reflects protest against or indifference to convention <a gathering place for radicals and *Bohemians*>
  syn maverick, nonconformist
  rel beat, beatnik, dropout, hippie; iconoclast; eccentric, original; recusant
  con conformer, conventionalist, formalist, pedant

bohunk *n syn* see OAF 2

boil *n syn* see ABSCESS

boil *vb* 1 *syn* see SEETHE 4
  2 to prepare (as food) in a liquid heated to the point that it begins to give off steam <*boil* eggs>
  syn parboil, seethe, simmer, stew
  rel coddle, poach; decoct; steam
  3 *syn* see ANGER 2
  4 *syn* see RUSH 1

boil down *vb syn* see SIMPLIFY

boildown *n syn* see ABRIDGMENT

‖**boiled** *adj syn* see INTOXICATED 1

boiling *adj syn* see HOT 1

boil over *vb syn* see ANGER 2

boisterous *adj* 1 *syn* see TURBULENT 1
  2 *syn* see VOCIFEROUS
  rel brawling, noisy, riotous, rollicking, rowdy
  con sedate, sober, staid; noiseless

‖**boko** *n syn* see NOSE 1

bold *adj* 1 *syn* see BRAVE 1
  con pusillanimous, shrinking, timid, timorous
  ant cowardly
  2 *syn* see WISE 5
  rel audacious; bluff
  con mousy, quiet, shy
  3 *syn* see INSOLENT 2

‖**boldacious** *adj syn* see INSOLENT 2

bold-faced *adj syn* see WISE 5

boldhearted *adj syn* see BRAVE 1

boldness *n syn* see INSOLENCE

bollix *vb syn* see BOTCH

Bolshevik *n syn* see COMMUNIST

‖**Bolshie** *n syn* see COMMUNIST

bolster *vb* 1 *syn* see SUPPORT 4
  rel reinforce, strengthen
  2 *syn* see SUPPORT 5

bolt *n syn* see THUNDERBOLT

bolt *vb* 1 *syn* see START 1
  2 *syn* see RUSH 1
  3 *syn* see RUN 2
  4 *syn* see EXCLAIM
  5 *syn* see GULP

bomb *n* 1 *syn* see FAILURE 5
  ‖2 *syn* see FORTUNE 4

bomb *vb* 1 *syn* see BOMBARD
  2 *syn* see FAIL 4

bombard *vb* to assault with bombs or shells <cities *bombarded* by planes and artillery>
  syn blitz, bomb, cannonade, shell
  rel barrage, strafe, strike
  idiom open up on, pour a broadside into

bombardment *n syn* see BARRAGE

bombast *n* pretentious inflated speech or writing <adolescent *bombast* about Youth and Destiny>

---

syn fustian, highfalutin, rant, rhapsody, rhetoric, rodomontade

rel grandiloquence, magniloquence; flatulence, orotundity, tumidity, turgidity; heroics, pyrotechnics, sesquipedality; Johnsonese; spread-eagleism; nonsense

idiom purple prose

bombastic *adj syn* see RHETORICAL
rel flatulent
con unimpassioned; unaffected

‖**bombed** *adj syn* see INTOXICATED 1

bombinate *vb syn* see HUM

bona fide *adj syn* see AUTHENTIC 2

bona fides *n syn* see GOOD FAITH

bonanza *n* a place of great abundance or a source of great wealth or opportunity <the town proved to be a *bonanza* for entrepreneurs>
syn eldorado, Golconda, gold mine, mine, treasure-house, treasure trove, treasury

bond *n* 1 *usu* **bonds** *pl syn* see SHACKLE
2 *syn* see CONTRACT
3 a uniting or binding element or force <the *bonds* of friendship>
syn knot, ligament, ligature, link, nexus, tie, vinculum, yoke
rel bridge, connection, connective, liaison; interrelationship, relationship
4 *syn* see ADHERENCE 1
5 *syn* see GUARANTEE 1

bondage *n* the state of subjection to an owner or master <prisoners sold into *bondage*>
syn enslavement, helotry, peonage, serfage, serfdom, servility, servitude, slavery, thrall, thralldom, villenage, yoke
rel subjection, subjugation
con freedom, independence, liberty

bondman *n syn* see SLAVE 1

bondslave *n syn* see SLAVE 1

bondsman *n syn* see SLAVE 1

bone *n* 1 **bones** *pl syn* see DICE
‖2 *syn* see DOLLAR

bone (up) *vb syn* see CRAM 4

bone–dry *adj* 1 *syn* see DRY 1
2 *syn* see DRY 3

bonehead *n syn* see DUNCE

boneless *adj syn* see WEAK 4

boner *n* 1 *syn* see ERROR 2
2 *syn* see FAUX PAS

‖**boneyard** *n syn* see CEMETERY

bong *vb syn* see RING

boniface *n syn* see SALOONKEEPER

‖**bonkers** *adj syn* see INSANE 1

bonne bouche *n syn* see DELICACY

‖**bonnet** *n syn* see DECOY 1

‖**bonny** *adj syn* see BEAUTIFUL

bon vivant *n syn* see EPICURE
rel bon viveur, boulevardier, high liver, high roller, man-about-town, sport

bony *adj syn* see LEAN

boo *n syn* see RASPBERRY

boo *n syn* see MARIJUANA

boob *n* 1 *syn* see DUNCE
2 *syn* see PHILISTINE

‖**boo–boo** *n syn* see FAUX PAS

boob tube *n syn* see TELEVISION

booby *n syn* see DUNCE

booby hatch *n syn* see ASYLUM 3

booby trap *n syn* see PITFALL

boodle *n* 1 *syn* see FORTUNE 4
2 *syn* see SPOIL

boodle *vb syn* see CHEAT

boohoo *vb syn* see CRY 2

book *n* 1 a collection of folded, cut, bound, and usually printed sheets <a *book* of poems>
syn tome, volume
rel publication, work, writing; scroll; booklet, brochure, folder, leaflet, magazine, pamphlet; compendium, handbook, manual, monograph, textbook, tract, treatise; codex; novel
2 *cap* **Book** *syn* see BIBLE

book *vb* 1 *syn* see LIST 3
2 *syn* see TIME 1
3 *syn* see RESERVE 2

bookdealer *n* one who deals in books <sold his library to a *bookdealer*>
syn bibliopole, bookman, bookseller
rel bouquiniste

bookie *n syn* see BOOKMAKER

bookish *adj syn* see PEDANTIC
rel booksy, highbrow

book–learned *adj syn* see PEDANTIC

bookmaker *n* one who determines odds and receives and pays off bets <*bookmakers* who welsh on paying off winners>
syn bookie, layer
rel pricemaker; runner

bookman *n syn* see BOOKDEALER

bookseller *n syn* see BOOKDEALER

booky *adj syn* see PEDANTIC

boom *n* 1 *syn* see BANG 2
2 *syn* see PROSPERITY 4

boomerang *vb syn* see BACKFIRE

booming *adj syn* see FLOURISHING

boon *n* 1 *syn* see GIFT 1
2 *syn* see GOOD 1

boon *adj syn* see MERRY

‖**boondocks** *n pl syn* see FRONTIER 2

‖**boonies** *n pl syn* see FRONTIER 2

boor *n* an uncouth ungainly fellow <an ill-mannered *boor*>
syn ‖bosthoon, chuff, churl, clodhopper, clown, grobian, mucker
rel barbarian, vulgarian; looby, lubber; farmer, loon, rustic, swain; ‖carl; bohunk; boob, buffoon, oaf
con slicker, smoothy; gentleman; cosmopolitan, cosmopolite, sophisticate

boorish *adj* uncouth in manner or appearance <a *boorish* fellow lacking all grace>
syn churlish, cloddish, clodhopping, clownish, ill-bred, loutish, lowbred, lubberly, lumpish, robustious, rugged, swainish, uncivilized, uncultured, unpolished, unrefined; *compare* COARSE 3
rel barbarian, barbaric, outlandish, tasteless, vulgar; bucolic, countrified, inurbane, provincial, rustic, yokelish; ill-mannered, impolite, rude, uncivil, ungracious; graceless, unpoised
con cultivated, cultured, refined; suave, urbane; courteous, courtly, genteel, polite, well-bred; graceful, gracious, poised

boost *vb syn* see RAISE 9
2 *syn* see INCREASE 1
3 *syn* see PROMOTE 3
‖4 *syn* see SHOPLIFT

boost n syn see RISE 3
‖**booster** n syn see DECOY 2
boot n 1 syn see THRILL
　2 syn see NOVICE
boot (out) vb 1 syn see EJECT 1
　2 syn see DISMISS 3
‖**boot hill** n syn see CEMETERY
bootleg n syn see MOONSHINE 2
bootleg vb syn see SMUGGLE
bootless adj syn see FUTILE
　rel frustrating; profitless, worthless
bootlick vb syn see FAWN
bootlick n syn see SYCOPHANT
bootlicker n syn see SYCOPHANT
bootlicking adj syn see FAWNING
booty n syn see SPOIL
booze n syn see DRINK 3
booze n 1 syn see LIQUOR 2
　2 syn see BINGE 1
‖**boozed** adj syn see INTOXICATED 1
boozehound n syn see DRUNKARD
boozer n 1 syn see DRUNKARD
　‖2 syn see BAR 5
‖**boozy** adj syn see INTOXICATED 1
bop n syn see BLOW 1
borasca n syn see POVERTY 1
bordello n syn see BROTHEL
border n 1 a line or relatively narrow space
　that marks the outermost bound of some-
　thing <the *border* of the rug>
　syn brim, brink, edge, fringe, hem, margin,
　perimeter, periphery, rim, selvage, skirt,
　verge; compare CIRCUMFERENCE
　rel butts and bounds, lines, metes and
　bounds; bound, circumference, confine, end,
　extremity, limit, termination, boundary,
　frontier, march, pale; beginning, door, en-
　trance, threshold; sideline; lip
　con inside, interior; recesses; center; body,
　bulk, mass, whole
　2 syn see FRONTIER 1
border vb 1 to form a border to <hedges
　border the park>
　syn bound, define, edge, fringe, hem, mar-
　gin, outline, rim, skirt, surround, verge
　rel circumscribe, encircle, enclose, frame;
　contour, delineate, mark (off), outline, set
　off; flank, line, side; trim
　2 syn see ADJOIN
　3 to come to be closely similiar to a specified
　thing <ideas that *border* on the absurd>
　syn approach, trench, verge
　rel approximate, compare, near
　idiom come close (or near) to
bordering adj syn see ADJACENT 3
borderland n syn see FRONTIER 1
borderline adj syn see DOUBTFUL 1
bore vb 1 syn see PERFORATE
　2 syn see GAZE 1
bore vb to induce a state of boredom in
　<*bored* to death by his endless sermon>
　syn ennui, pall, tire, weary
　rel jade; fatigue, wear; annoy, irk, irritate;
　afflict, bother, discomfort
　idiom put one to sleep

con amuse, entertain; excite, fascinate,
intrigue; absorb, beguile, engross, enthrall,
grip; enliven, freshen, invigorate, quicken,
stimulate
ant interest
bore n someone or something that is boring
<cocktail parties frequented mainly by
bores>
　syn drag, ‖dullsville, ‖pill
　rel bad news; downer; soporific
　idiom crashing bore
boreal adj syn see COLD 1
boredom n syn see TEDIUM
　rel fatigue, weariness; disgust, distaste
　con amusement, diversion, entertainment;
　excitement, fascination; engrossment, en-
　thrallment
boresome adj syn see IRKSOME
　rel deadly, dreary, dull, humdrum, monoto-
　nous
　con amusing, entertaining; exciting, fasci-
　nating, intriguing; absorbing, engrossing,
　enthralling, gripping, stimulating
　ant interesting
boring adj syn see IRKSOME
born adj syn see INHERENT
‖**born** vb syn see BEAR 5
borné adj syn see LITTLE 2
bosh n syn see NONSENSE 2
bosom n syn see HEART 1
bosomy adj syn see BUXOM
boss n syn see LEADER 2
‖**boss** adj syn see EXCELLENT
boss vb syn see SUPERVISE
bossy adj syn see MASTERFUL 1
‖**bosthoon** n syn see BOOR
Boswell n syn see BIOGRAPHER
botch vb to do or proceed ineffectively or
　badly through clumsiness, stupidity, or lack
　of ability <a complete incompetent —
　botches everything he puts his hand to>
　syn bitch (up), ‖blow, blunder, bobble,
　boggle, bollix, bugger up, bumble, bungle,
　cobble, dub, flub, fluff, foozle, fumble, goof
　(up), gum (up), louse up, mess, ‖muck,
　mucker, muff, ‖screw (up)
　rel butcher, mangle, murder, mutilate; mar,
　ruin, spoil; destroy, wreck; hash; tinker;
　misconduct, mishandle, mismanage; con-
　fuse, disorder
　idiom ‖drop a clanger, play (or wreak)
　havoc with, play hell with, pull a boner (or
　rock)
botch n syn see MESS 3
botchery n syn see MESS 3
botchy adj syn see SLIPSHOD 1
bother vb 1 syn see DISCOMPOSE 1
　2 syn see ANNOY 1
bother n 1 syn see ANNOYANCE 2
　2 syn see ANNOYANCE 3
　3 syn see INCONVENIENCE
botheration n 1 syn see ANNOYANCE 2
　2 syn see ANNOYANCE 3
bothering n syn see ANNOYANCE 1
botherment n syn see ANNOYANCE 3
bothersomeness n syn see INCONVE-
NIENCE
bottega n syn see STUDIO
bottle (up) vb 1 syn see RESTRAIN
　2 syn see CORNER

---

syn synonym(s)　　rel related word(s)
ant antonym(s)　　con contrasted word(s)
idiom idiomatic equivalent(s)
‖ use limited; if in doubt, see a dictionary

bottom n **1** the under surface as opposed to the top surface <gum was stuck to the *bottom* of her shoe>
syn sole, underneath, underside, undersurface
rel belly, underbelly, underbody; base, floor, foot, ground
con acme, apex, cap, crest, crown, tip, upper
ant top
2 *syn* see BUTTOCKS
3 the lower or lowest point <the *bottom* of the page>
syn base, foot, nadir
rel basement, floor, ground; end; low
con acme, apex, pinnacle, zenith
ant top
4 *syn* see BASE 1
5 *syn* see ESSENCE 2
bottom vb *syn* see BASE
bottom adj **1** *syn* see BOTTOMMOST
2 see FUNDAMENTAL 1
bottom dog n *syn* see VICTIM 2
bottomless adj **1** *syn* see BASELESS
rel reasonless, unjustifiable, unsupportable
2 extremely deep <the *bottomless* sea>
syn abysmal, fathomless, plumbless, plummetless, soundless, unfathomable; *compare* DEEP 1
rel endless, infinite
bottommost adj that is at the very bottom <the ladder's *bottommost* rung>
syn bottom, lowermost, lowest, nethermost, rock-bottom, undermost
con top, upper, uppermost
ant topmost
bough n *syn* see LIMB
bought adj *syn* see READY-MADE
‖**boughten** adj *syn* see READY-MADE
boulevard n *syn* see WAY 1
bounce vb **1** *syn* see JUMP 1
2 *syn* see DISMISS 3
‖**3** *syn* see INTIMIDATE
bounce (back) vb **1** *syn* see RECOVER 3
2 *syn* see BACKFIRE
bouncer n ‖**1** *syn* see LIE
rel exaggeration, hyperbole, overstatement
idiom tall tale
2 a person employed to restrain or eject disorderly persons (as at a bar) <tossed out by the *bouncer*>
syn chucker, ‖chucker-out, houseman
rel goon, muscleman, strong arm
bouncy adj *syn* see ELASTIC 2
bound n **1** *usu* bounds *pl syn* see ENVIRONS 1
2 *syn* see LIMIT 1
bound vb **1** *syn* see DEMARCATE 1
2 *syn* see BORDER 1
bound adj **1** *syn* see FINITE
2 obliged to serve a master or in a clearly defined capacity for a certain length of time by the terms of a contract or mutual agreement <brought to the American colonies as a *bound* servant>
syn apprenticed, articled, indentured
rel contracted; enslaved
con free, freed
3 *syn* see CONSTIPATED
bound vb *syn* see JUMP 1
boundary n *syn* see ENVIRONS 1
bounded adj *syn* see FINITE

ant unbounded
bounder n *syn* see CAD
boundless adj *syn* see LIMITLESS
bounteous adj **1** *syn* see LIBERAL 1
con cheap, illiberal, scant
ant niggardly
2 *syn* see PLENTIFUL
con insufficient, scant, sparse
bountiful adj **1** *syn* see LIBERAL 1
2 *syn* see PLENTIFUL
bouquet n **1** cut flowers arranged for wear or display <a *bouquet* of spring flowers>
syn nosegay, posy
rel arrangement; boutonniere, corsage; spray; wreath; garland, festoon; lei
2 *syn* see COMPLIMENT 1
3 *syn* see FRAGRANCE
Bourbon n *syn* see REACTIONARY
bout n **1** *syn* see SPELL 1
2 *syn* see SIEGE
boutade n *syn* see CAPRICE
bow vb *syn* see YIELD 2
bow n **1** *syn* see CURVE
2 *syn* see TURN 4
bow vb *syn* see CURVE
bowdlerize vb *syn* see CENSOR
bowed adj **1** *syn* see CURVED
2 *syn* see BOWLEGGED
bowel vb *syn* see EVISCERATE
bower n *syn* see ARBOR
bowery n *syn* see SKID ROW
bowl n *syn* see STADIUM
‖**bowl** (down *or* out) vb *syn* see WHIP 2
bowl (down *or* over) vb *syn* see FELL 1
bowlegged adj having legs bent outward <a *bowlegged* cowboy>
syn bandy, bandy-legged, bowed
rel bent, crooked, curved, misshapen
bowwow n *syn* see DOG 1
box n ‖**1** *syn* see HUT
‖**2** *syn* see PREDICAMENT
3 *syn* see TELEVISION
box n *syn* see CUFF
box vb *syn* see SLAP 1
boxing n the art of attack and defense with the fists practiced as a sport <he liked *boxing*—at least as a spectator sport>
syn fisticuffs, prizefighting, pugilism, ring
boy n **1** a male person not fully matured <a *boy* of nine>
syn lad, laddie, shaveling, son, stripling, tad
rel gamin, ragamuffin, street arab, urchin; hobbledehoy, whippersnapper; schoolboy
idiom little shaver, small fry
2 *syn* see MAN 3
boyfriend n **1** a man who is a woman's usual or preferred escort or companion <went to the movies with her *boyfriend*>
syn beau, gentleman friend, swain, young man
rel admirer
2 a man who shares with a woman a strong and usually sexually oriented mutual attraction <moved in with her *boyfriend*>
syn beau, beloved, flame, inamorato, lover, steady, sweetheart, truelove
rel crush, heartthrob; fiancé
3 *syn* see LOVER 1
brabble vb *syn* see QUARREL
brabble n **1** *syn* see QUARREL

2 *syn* see CHATTER
brace *n* 1 *syn* see COUPLE
  2 *syn* see SUPPORT 3
  3 **braces** *pl syn* see SUSPENDERS
brace *vb* 1 *syn* see GIRD 3
  2 *syn* see SUPPORT 4
  3 *syn* see BEG
bracing *adj syn* see INVIGORATING
bracket *vb* 1 *syn* see JOIN 1
  2 *syn* see COMPARE 2
brag *vb syn* see BOAST
  con apologize, deprecate
braggadocian *adj syn* see BOASTFUL
braggadocio *n syn* see BRAGGART
braggart *n* one who boasts <too much of a *braggart* about his strength>
  syn blower, blowhard, boaster, braggadocio, bragger, ‖gasbag, puckfist, rodomont, rodomontade, vaunter
  rel bluffer, blusterer, loudmouth, miles gloriosus, ranter, raver, windbag
  con Milquetoast
braggart *adj syn* see BOASTFUL
bragger *n syn* see BRAGGART
braggy *adj syn* see BOASTFUL
Brahmin *n* 1 *syn* see INTELLECTUAL 2
brain *n* 1 *syn* see MIND 1
  2 *syn* see INTELLECT 2
  3 *often* **brains** *pl syn* see INTELLIGENCE 1
brainchild *n syn* see INVENTION
brainless *adj syn* see SIMPLE 3
brainpower *n syn* see INTELLIGENCE 1
brainsick *adj syn* see INSANE 1
brainwork *n syn* see THOUGHT 1
brainy *adj syn* see INTELLIGENT 2
brake *vb syn* see HINDER
  rel slow, stop
branch *n* 1 *syn* see LIMB
  rel branchlet
  2 *syn* see CREEK 2
brand *n* 1 *syn* see MARK 7
  2 *syn* see STIGMA
brandish *vb syn* see SHOW 4
brand name *n syn* see MARK 7
brand–new *adj* conspicuously new and unused <a *brand-new* car right out of the showroom>
  syn fire-new, mint, spang-new, spanking-new, span-new, spick-and-span
  rel untouched, unused; clean, fresh, pristine
  con hand-me-down, secondhand, used; outworn, shabby, worn, worn-out
  ant old
brannigan *n* 1 *syn* see BINGE 1
  2 *syn* see QUARREL
brash *adj* 1 *syn* see RASH 1
  2 *syn* see EXUBERANT 1
  3 *syn* see TACTLESS
  4 *syn* see PRESUMPTUOUS
  rel bold, brazen; rash, reckless; headlong, impetuous; cocksure
brashness *n* 1 *syn* see TEMERITY
  2 *syn* see EFFRONTERY
brass *n* ‖1 *syn* see MONEY
  2 *syn* see EFFRONTERY

brassbound *adj* 1 *syn* see ILLIBERAL
  2 *syn* see INFLEXIBLE 2
  3 *syn* see PRESUMPTUOUS
brass hat *n syn* see SUPERIOR
brassy *adj* 1 *syn* see SHAMELESS
  2 *syn* see BRAZEN 2
brave *adj* 1 having or showing no fear when faced with something dangerous, difficult, or unknown <made a *brave* attempt to save the burning house>
  syn audacious, aweless, bold, boldhearted, bravehearted, chin-up, courageous, dauntless, doughty, fearless, gallant, game, greathearted, ‖gutsy, heroic, intrepid, lionhearted, manful, manly, ‖plucked, plucky, soldierly, spunky, stalwart, stout, stouthearted, unafraid, unblenched, unblenching, undauntable, undaunted, unfearful, unfearing, valiant, valorous
  rel daring, defiant, gritty, hardy, mettlesome, resolute, spirited, steadfast, unapprehensive, undismayed, unflinching, unfrightened, unquailing, unshrinking, unswerving, unwincing, unyielding, venturesome; chivalrous, noble, preux; confident
  con cringing, flinching, frightened, pusillanimous, scared, shrinking, timid; chickenhearted, fainthearted, lily-livered, nerveless, soft, spineless, unmanly, weakhearted, weak-kneed, yellow
  ant cowardly, craven
  2 *syn* see COLORFUL
  3 *syn* see GOOD 1
brave *vb syn* see FACE 3
  con avoid
bravehearted *adj syn* see BRAVE 1
bravery *n syn* see FINERY
bravo *n syn* see ASSASSIN
brawl *vb syn* see QUARREL
brawl *n* 1 *syn* see QUARREL
  2 a rough, noisy, and often prolonged hand-to-hand fight usually involving several people <windows and furniture were broken in the barroom *brawl*>
  syn affray, bobbery, broil, dogfight, donnybrook, fight, fracas, fray, free-for-all, knock-down-and-drag-out, maul, melee, mellay, ‖muss, rough-and-tumble, row, rowdydow, ruction, scrap, scrimmage, scuffle, set-to; *compare* QUARREL
  rel fistfight, fisticuffs, slugfest; struggle, tussle; conflict, contention, contest, riot; altercation, embroilment, imbroglio, quarrel, wrangle; commotion, disturbance, eruption, hubbub, pandemonium, ruckus, rumpus, turn-to, ‖turnup, upheaval, uproar; incident, ‖rumble
  idiom a coming to blows, exchange of blows
brawling *adj syn* see QUARRELSOME 2
brawlsome *adj syn* see QUARRELSOME 2
brawly *adj syn* see QUARRELSOME 2
brawn *n syn* see MUSCLE 1
brawny *adj syn* see MUSCULAR 2
  rel lusty, red-blooded, vigorous, vital; tough
  con lanky, lean, rawboned, skinny, thin
  ant scrawny
bray *vb syn* see PULVERIZE 1
brazen *adj* 1 *syn* see INSOLENT 2
  2 *syn* see SHAMELESS

---

syn synonym(s)   *rel* related word(s)
ant antonym(s)   *con* contrasted word(s)
idiom idiomatic equivalent(s)
‖ use limited; if in doubt, see a dictionary

3 syn see GAUDY
4 of the color of polished brass <a *brazen* sky at sunset>
syn aeneous, brassy
rel bronze
brazenfaced *adj syn* see SHAMELESS
breach *n* **1** the act or offense of failing to keep the law or to do what law, duty, or obligation requires <sued for *breach* of contract> <his behavior was a gross *breach* of good manners>
syn contravention, infraction, infringement, transgression, trespass, violation
rel disregard, nonobservance; delinquency, dereliction, neglect
con conformance, conformity, observance
ant observance
2 syn see GAP 1
3 an interruption of accustomed friendly relations <a trivial misunderstanding caused a *breach* between the brothers>
syn break, fissure, fracture, rent, rift, rupture, schism, split; *compare* SCHISM 3
rel division, separation, severance; alienation, estrangement; difference, discord, disharmony, dissension, disunity, strife, variance, secession, withdrawal; falling-out, quarrel
idiom parting of ways
con integrity, solidarity, union, unity; communion, community; accord, concord, harmony
4 syn see GAP 2
breach *vb* **1 syn** see OPEN 3
rel bore, penetrate
2 syn see VIOLATE 1
bread *n* **1 syn** see FOOD 1
2 syn see LIVING
‖**3 syn** see MONEY
bread and butter *n syn* see LIVING
breadth *n* **1 syn** see EXPANSE
2 spaciousness of extent <the *breadth* of his knowledge on the subject is awesome>
syn amplitude, comprehensiveness, fullness, scope, wideness
rel compass, gamut, orbit, range, reach, sweep; expanse, spread, stretch
con limitation, restriction
ant narrowness
breadthen *vb syn* see BROADEN
break *vb* **1 syn** see GIVE 12
2 syn see PLOW
3 syn see VIOLATE 1
ant observe
4 syn see ESCAPE 1
5 syn see FAIL 5
idiom go broke
6 syn see RUIN 3
7 syn see DEGRADE 1
8 syn see DISPROVE 1
9 syn see COMMUNICATE 1
10 syn see SOLVE 2
11 syn see DECODE
12 syn see HAPPEN 1
13 syn see GET OUT 2
‖**14 syn** see CLEAR 9
break *n* **1 syn** see GAP 1
2 syn see GAP 3
3 syn see INTERLUDE
4 a usually short rest period <took a *break* for coffee>

syn blow, breath, breather, breathing space (*or* spell), respite, ten; *compare* PAUSE
5 syn see BREACH 3
6 syn see FAUX PAS
7 syn see OPPORTUNITY
breakable *adj syn* see FRAGILE 1
break down *vb* **1 syn** see ANALYZE
2 syn see DECAY
3 syn see COLLAPSE 2
breakdown *n* **1 syn** see NERVOUS BREAKDOWN
2 syn see COLLAPSE 2
3 syn see ANALYSIS 1
break in *vb* **1 syn** see HOUSEBREAK
idiom break and enter
2 syn see INTERRUPT 2
breakneck *adj syn* see FAST 3
break out *vb syn* see ERUPT 2
breakout *n syn* see ESCAPE 1
breakthrough *n syn* see RISE 3
break up *vb* **1 syn** see SEPARATE 1
2 syn see DISBAND
breakup *n syn* see ANALYSIS 1
breast *n syn* see HEART 1
breast-feed *vb syn* see NURSE 1
breastwork *n syn* see BULWARK
breath *n* **1 syn** see HINT 2
2 syn see BREAK 4
breathe *vb* **1 syn** see BE
2 syn see REST 3
3 to draw (as air) into and expel from the lungs <*breathe* clean air>
syn respire
rel exhale, inhale
4 syn see CONFIDE 1
breathe (in) *vb syn* see INHALE
breathe (out) *vb syn* see EXHALE
breather *n syn* see BREAK 4
breathing *n syn* see INSTANT 1
breathing space (*or* spell) *n syn* see BREAK 4
breathless *adj* **1 syn** see EAGER
2 syn see STUFFY 1
bred-in-the-bone *adj syn* see INVETERATE 1
breech *n syn* see BUTTOCKS
breed *vb* **1 syn** see PROCREATE 1
2 syn see FATHER 1
3 syn see GENERATE 3
4 syn see GROW 1
breed *n syn* see TYPE
breeding *n syn* see CULTURE
rel civility, courtesy, gentility, grace
con barbarism, boorishness; coarseness, grossness; discourtesy, rudeness
ant vulgarity
breeding ground *n* a place or environment which favors growth <the slum was a *breeding ground* for crime>
syn forcing bed, forcing house, hotbed, hothouse
breeze *n syn* see SNAP 1
breeze *vb* to proceed quickly and easily <*breezed* through customs>
syn waltz, zip
rel skim, slide, slip
con drag, falter, flag, lag, trail
breezy *adj* **1 syn** see WINDY 1
2 syn see EASYGOING 3
breviary *n syn* see ABRIDGMENT

breviate *n syn* see ABRIDGMENT
breviloquent *adj* **1** *syn* see CONCISE
  2 *syn* see BLUFF
brew *vb syn* see LOOM 2
brew *n syn* see MISCELLANY 1
bribable *adj syn* see VENAL 1
bribe *vb* to give or promise money or favor to a person in a position of trust to influence his judgment or conduct <*bribed* a building inspector>
  syn buy, buy off, fix, have, ‖lubricate, sop, square, tamper (with)
  rel approach; corrupt, instigate, suborn; soften (up), sweeten
  idiom grease the palm (*or* hand), oil the palm (*or* hand), tickle the palm
bridal *n syn* see WEDDING
bridewell *n syn* see JAIL
bridle *vb syn* see RESTRAIN 1
  rel repress, suppress; control, manage; govern, rule
  con air, express, utter, ventilate, voice
  ant vent
brief *adj* **1** *syn* see SHORT 1
  rel fleeting, momentary, passing, transient
  ant long
  2 *syn* see CONCISE
  3 *syn* see BLUFF
brief *n syn* see ABRIDGMENT
briefly *adv* in a few words <he answered *briefly* and to the point>
  syn concisely, in brief, in short, laconically, shortly, succinctly, tersely
  rel accurately, crisply, exactly, precisely
  idiom in a capsule, in a nutshell, in a word, to make a long story short
  con diffusely, long-windedly, profusely, prolixly, protractedly, verbosely, wordily; at length, comprehensively, fully
‖**brig** *n syn* see JAIL
brigand *n syn* see MARAUDER
bright *adj* **1** shining or glowing with light <the *bright* sun>
  syn beaming, brilliant, effulgent, fulgent, incandescent, lambent, lucent, lucid, luminous, lustrous, radiant, refulgent
  rel clear, light, undimmed; illuminated, lighted; coruscating, flashing, gleaming, glistening, glittering, scintillating, shimmering, sparkling; blazing, flaming, glowing; burnished, polished, shiny; sunshiny
  con dark, dusky, gloomy, murky, tenebrous; colorless, drab, dreary, lackluster, leaden; somber; cloudy, gray, overcast, shadowy; moonless, starless, sunless; faint, pale, weak
  ant dim; dull
  2 *syn* see COLORFUL
  3 *syn* see GLAD 2
  4 *syn* see FAVORABLE 5
  5 *syn* see INTELLIGENT 2
  rel advanced, precocious
  con retarded
  ant dense, dull
  6 *syn* see LIVELY 1

brilliant *adj* **1** *syn* see BRIGHT 1
  ant subdued
  2 *syn* see INTELLIGENT 2
  rel erudite, learned; sage, wise
brim *n syn* see BORDER 1
brimful *adj* **1** *syn* see FULL 1
  2 *syn* see BIG 3
brimming *adj* **1** *syn* see FULL 1
  2 *syn* see BIG 3
brine *n syn* see OCEAN
bring *vb* **1** *syn* see CONVERT 1
  ‖**2** *syn* see ACCOMPANY
  3 *syn* see SELL 4
bring about *vb syn* see EFFECT 1
bring around *vb syn* see INDUCE 1
bring down *vb syn* see FELL 1
bring forth *vb syn* see BEAR 5
bring in *vb* **1** *syn* see YIELD 5
  2 *syn* see SELL 4
  3 *syn* see EARN 1
bring off *vb syn* see EFFECT 2
bring out *vb syn* see SAY 1
bring up *vb* **1** to give a child a parent's fostering care <the orphan was *brought up* by his aunt>
  syn ‖fetch up, raise, rear
  rel breed, cultivate, foster, nurture; feed, nourish, provide (for); discipline, educate, train
  con abuse, ill-use, maltreat; neglect
  2 *syn* see STOP 4
  3 *syn* see REFER 3
  4 *syn* see BROACH 3
  5 *syn* see VOMIT
brink *n* **1** *syn* see BORDER 1
  2 *syn* see VERGE 2
‖**briny** *n syn* see OCEAN
brio *n syn* see SPIRIT 5
brisk *adj syn* see AGILE
  rel adroit; quick
  con inactive, torpid
  ant sluggish
brisky *adj syn* see AGILE
bristle *vb syn* see ANGER 2
brittle *adj syn* see SHORT 6
broach *n syn* see BROOCH
broach *vb* to open up (a subject) for discussion <would be awkward to *broach* the matter now>
  syn bring up, introduce, moot, ventilate
  rel interject, interpose; mention, speak (about); propose, suggest
  con hush (up), quash, stifle, suppress; black out, censor
broad *adj* **1** *syn* see LIBERAL 3
  2 *syn* see EXTENSIVE 1
  3 *syn* see RISQUÉ
‖**broad** *n syn* see WOMAN 1
broadcast *n syn* see DECLARATION
broadcast *vb* **1** *syn* see STREW 1
  2 *syn* see DECLARE 1
  rel communicate, radio, televise, transmit
  idiom spread a report, spread far and wide
broaden *vb* to grow or become broad or broader <the street *broadens* into an avenue>
  syn breadthen, widen
  rel expand; spread (out); open
  con contract, shrink; slim, thin
  ant narrow

---

syn synonym(s)   *rel* related word(s)
ant antonym(s)   *con* contrasted word(s)
idiom idiomatic equivalent(s)
‖ use limited; if in doubt, see a dictionary

broad–minded *adj syn* see LIBERAL 3
broadside *n syn* see BARRAGE
Brobdingnagian *adj syn* see HUGE
brocard *n syn* see MAXIM
∥**brogue** *n syn* see IDLE
broil *vb syn* see BURN 3
broil *n syn* see BRAWL 2
broiling *adj syn* see HOT 1
broke *adj syn* see POOR 1
broken–down *adj syn* see SHABBY 1
broker *n syn* see GO-BETWEEN 2
bromide *n syn* see COMMONPLACE
bromidic *adj syn* see ARID 2
∥**Bronx cheer** *n syn* see RASPBERRY
brooch *n* an ornament with a pin or clasp now worn usually by women <a diamond *brooch*>
  syn broach, clip, pin
brood *n syn* see OFFSPRING
brood *vb* **1** *syn* see SET 11
  2 *syn* see MOPE 1
brook *vb syn* see BEAR 10
brook *n syn* see CREEK 2
brothel *n* an establishment where prostitutes ply their trade <madam of the local *brothel*>
  syn bagnio, bawdy house, bordello, call house, cathouse, crib, disorderly house, fancy house, ∥hookshop, ∥joyhouse, lupanar, parlor house, seraglio, sporting house, stew, whorehouse
  idiom house of ill fame (*or* repute), house of prostitution
brotherhood *n syn* see ASSOCIATION 2
brouhaha *n* **1** *syn* see DIN
  2 *syn* see COMMOTION 3
brow *n syn* see FOREHEAD
browbeat *vb syn* see INTIMIDATE
browbeater *n syn* see BULLY 1
brownie *n syn* see FAIRY
∥**brownnose** *vb syn* see FAWN
∥**brownnose** *n syn* see SYCOPHANT
∥**brownnoser** *n syn* see SYCOPHANT
brown study *n syn* see REVERIE
browse *vb* to read through, study, or examine cursorily <*browsed* through the book looking for illustrations>
  syn dip (into), flip (through), glance (at *or* over), leaf (through), riff (through), riffle (through), run (through *or* over), scan, skim (through), thumb (through)
  rel go (through *or* over), look (over), peruse, skip (through)
  idiom give the once over, run the eye over
  con examine, study; delve (into), dig (into)
  ant pore (over)
bruise *n* an injury involving rupture of small blood vessels and discoloration without break in the overlying skin <got an ugly *bruise* when he fell>
  syn contusion; *compare* BLACK EYE
  rel ∥boo-boo, abrasion, scrape, scratch
  idiom black-and-blue spot (*or* mark)
bruise *vb* **1** to inflict a bruise on <fell down and *bruised* his hip>
  syn black, contuse
  rel batter, ∥bung up
  2 *syn* see CRUSH 3
bruit (about) *vb syn* see DECLARE 1
  rel hint, intimate, rumor, suggest
bruja *n syn* see WITCH 1

brume *n syn* see HAZE 1
brummagem *adj syn* see COUNTERFEIT
brunet *adj syn* see DARK 3
brush *vb* to touch or strike lightly (as in passing) <they *brushed* fenders but no real damage was done>
  syn glance, graze, kiss, shave, skim
  rel bump, clash, collide, sideswipe; clip, contact, scrape, touch
brush *n* **1** *syn* see ENCOUNTER
  rel clash, engagement
  2 *syn* see CLASH 2
brush up *vb syn* see TOUCH UP
brusque *adj syn* see BLUFF
brutal *adj* **1** *syn* see BRUTISH
  2 *syn* see SEVERE 3
brutalize *vb syn* see DEBASE 1
brute *adj syn* see BRUTISH
brute *n syn* see BEAST
brutish *adj* marked by animal traits and by a lack of man's dignity or refinement <a graceless *brutish* hulk of a man>
  syn animal, beastly, bestial, brutal, brute, feral, ferine, swinish
  rel animalistic; coarse, crude; base, low, mean, scurvy, vile
bubble *vb* **1** *syn* see SLOSH 1
  2 *syn* see SEETHE 4
bubble *n syn* see PIPE DREAM
buccaneer *n syn* see PIRATE
buck *n* **1** *syn* see MAN 3
  2 *syn* see FOP
  ∥**3** *syn* see DOLLAR
  4 *syn* see SAWHORSE
buck *vb* **1** *syn* see RESIST
  2 *syn* see CARRY 1
  3 *syn* see PASS 9
buck (off) *vb syn* see THROW 2
buck *vb syn* see PULVERIZE 1
∥**bucket** *n syn* see JAIL
bucket *vb syn* see HURRY 2
∥**bucket shop** *n syn* see BAR 5
buckle (down) *vb* **1** *syn* see ADDRESS 3
  2 *syn* see PITCH IN 1
buckle (under) *vb syn* see YIELD 2
buckram *adj syn* see STIFF 4
buck up *vb syn* see COMFORT
bucolic *adj syn* see RURAL
  ant urbane
bucolic *n syn* see RUSTIC
bud *n* **1** *syn* see CHILD 1
  2 *syn* see SEED 2
buddy *n syn* see ASSOCIATE 3
∥**buddy–buddy** *adj syn* see INTIMATE 4
∥**budge** *n syn* see LIQUOR 2
budget *n syn* see BODY 5
budtime *n syn* see SPRING 5
buff *n syn* see ADDICT
buff *vb syn* see POLISH 1
buffalo *vb* **1** *syn* see FRUSTRATE 1
  2 *syn* see NONPLUS 1
buff–bare *adj syn* see NUDE 2
buffet *n syn* see CUFF
buffet *vb* **1** *syn* see SLAP 1
  2 *syn* see BEAT 1
∥**buffet** *n syn* see EATING HOUSE
∥**bufflehead** *n syn* see DUNCE
buffle–headed *adj syn* see SIMPLE 3
buffoon *n syn* see CLOWN 3
∥**buffy** *adj syn* see INTOXICATED 1

bug *n syn* see ENTHUSIAST
‖**bug** *vb syn* see ANNOY 1
bugbear *n syn* see ABOMINATION 1
‖**bugger** *n syn* see SNOT 1
‖**bugger** *vb syn* see EXHAUST 4
bugger up *vb syn* see BOTCH
‖**buggy** *adj* 1 *syn* see ENTHUSIASTIC
    2 *syn* see INSANE 1
‖**buggy** *n syn* see CAR
bughouse *n syn* see ASYLUM 3
bughouse *adj syn* see INSANE 1
bug off *vb syn* see GET OUT 1
‖**bugs** *adj* 1 *syn* see INSANE 1
    2 *syn* see ENTHUSIASTIC
build *vb* 1 to form or fashion a structure
    <will *build* either a garage or carport>
    syn construct, erect, put up, raise, rear,
    upraise; *compare* ERECT 3, MAKE 3
    rel fabricate, fashion, frame, manufacture;
    run up, throw up; prefabricate
    con demolish, destroy, dismantle, level, pull
    down, raze, take down, tear down, wreck
    2 *syn* see MAKE 3
    3 *syn* see INCREASE 1
    4 *syn* see INCREASE 2
build (on) *vb syn* see RELY (on *or* upon)
build *n syn* see PHYSIQUE
    rel conformation
building *n* a usually roofed and walled struc-
    ture built for permanent use <a *building*
    with four apartments>
    syn fabric, structure; *compare* EDIFICE,
    HUT
build up *vb* 1 *syn* see ERECT 5
    2 *syn* see PUBLICIZE
buildup *n syn* see PUBLICITY
‖**built** *adj* 1 *syn* see CURVACEOUS
    2 *syn* see BUXOM
built-in *adj syn* see INHERENT
bulge *vb* to extend outward beyond the usual
    or normal line <the box was so full that the
    sides *bulged*>
    syn beetle, jut, overhang, poke, pouch,
    pout, project, protrude, protuberate, stand
    out, stick out
    rel bag, belly, dilate, distend, expand, swell
bulge *n* 1 *syn* see PROJECTION 1
    rel bump, lump, swelling
    con depression, hollow, pit
    2 *syn* see ADVANTAGE 3
bulk *n* 1 a body of usually material substance
    that constitutes a thing or unit <his industry
    was proven by the *bulk* of his accomplish-
    ment> <a great dark *bulk* blocked the al-
    ley>
    syn mass, volume
    rel bigness, greatness, largeness, magnitude,
    quantity, totality
    2 *syn* see BODY 4
    3 *syn* see BODY 5
    4 *syn* see BODY 3
bulk *vb syn* see LOOM 3
bull *n* 1 *syn* see ERROR 2
    ‖2 *syn* see NONSENSE 2
    ‖3 *syn* see POLICEMAN

bull *adj syn* see LARGE 1
‖**bull band** *n syn* see SHIVAREE
bulldoze *vb* 1 *syn* see INTIMIDATE
    rel menace, threaten; harass, harry
    2 *syn* see PUSH 2
bulldozer *n syn* see BULLY 1
bullet *vb syn* see HURRY 2
bullfighter *n* one who fights bulls <moved
    with the grace of an experienced *bullfighter*>
    syn matador, toreador, torero
    rel banderillero; cuadrillero; cua-
    drilla
bullheaded *adj syn* see OBSTINATE
bullwork *n syn* see WORK 2
bully *n* 1 an insolent, overbearing person
    who persists in tormenting another <a big
    bully who picked on little kids>
    syn browbeater, bulldozer, harasser, har-
    rier, hector, intimidator; *compare* TOUGH
    rel annoyer, antagonizer, heckler, persecu-
    tor, pest, tease, tormenter
    2 *syn* see PIMP 1
bully *adj syn* see EXCELLENT
bully *vb syn* see INTIMIDATE
    rel torment, torture; menace, threaten
    ant coax
bullyboy *n syn* see TOUGH
bullyrag *vb* 1 *syn* see INTIMIDATE
    2 *syn* see BAIT 2
bulwark *n* an aboveground defensive struc-
    ture that forms part of a fortification <the
    bulwarks were woefully undermanned>
    syn bastion, breastwork, parapet, rampart
    rel citadel, fort, fortress, stronghold
    con bunker, dugout
bulwark *vb syn* see DEFEND 1
‖**bum** *vb syn* see HUM
bum *vb syn* see IDLE
bum *n* 1 *syn* see VAGABOND
    2 *syn* see SLUGGARD
‖**bum** *adj syn* see BAD 1
bum *n syn* see BINGE 1
bumble *vb syn* see HUM
bumble *vb* 1 *syn* see BOTCH
    2 *syn* see STUMBLE 3
bumbling *adj syn* see AWKWARD 2
‖**bumfuzzle** *vb syn* see CONFUSE 2
bummel *vb syn* see SAUNTER
bummer *n* 1 *syn* see BEGGAR 1
    2 *syn* see MARAUDER
    3 *syn* see FAILURE 5
bumming *n syn* see MENDICANCY
bump *vb* 1 to meet with or come up against
    forcibly <the two cars *bumped* with a great
    crumpling of fenders>
    syn clash, collide, ‖prang
    rel bang, carom, crash, hit, knock, slam,
    strike; impinge; jar, jolt
    idiom whang together
    2 *syn* see HAPPEN 2
    3 *syn* see DEGRADE 1
bump *n* 1 *syn* see IMPACT 1
    2 a swelling of tissue usually resulting from a
    blow <fell and got a *bump* on his head>
    syn bunch, knot, lump, ‖pumpknot
    rel protuberance, swelling
    3 a marked unevenness in a road surface
    likely to jolt a passing vehicle
    syn ‖cahot, thank-you-ma'am
    rel chuckhole, mudhole, pothole, rut

---

syn synonym(s)   *rel* related word(s)
ant antonym(s)   *con* contrasted word(s)
idiom idiomatic equivalent(s)
‖ use limited; if in doubt, see a dictionary

4 *syn* see GIFT 2

bumpkin *n syn* see RUSTIC

bump off *vb syn* see MURDER 1

‖**bump–off** *n syn* see MURDER

bunch *n* **1** *syn* see BUMP 2

  2 *syn* see GROUP 3

  3 *syn* see SET 5

  4 *syn* see GROUP 1

bunco steerer *n syn* see SWINDLER

bundle *n* **1** *syn* see GROUP 3

  2 *syn* see FORTUNE 4

bundle up *vb* to dress warmly <*bundle up,* it's cold outside>

  syn ‖hap, muffle, wrap (up)

  rel envelop, mummify, swaddle, swathe

‖**bung** *vb syn* see THROW 1

‖**bung–full** *adj syn* see FULL 1

bungle *vb syn* see BOTCH

bungle *n syn* see ERROR 2

bungler *n syn* see STUMBLEBUM

‖**bung up** *vb syn* see BATTER 1

‖**bunk** *vb syn* see HARBOR 2

‖**bunk** *vb syn* see ESCAPE 1

bunk *n syn* see NONSENSE 2

‖**bunk** *vb syn* see DECEIVE

bunkum *n syn* see NONSENSE 2

‖**bunkum** *adj* **1** *syn* see EXCELLENT

  2 *syn* see HEALTHY 1

bunny *n syn* see BEAUTY

  rel bimbo

buns *n pl syn* see BUTTOCKS

Bunyanesque *adj syn* see HUGE

buoy (up) *vb syn* see SUPPORT 5

buoyancy *n syn* see EBULLIENCE

buoyant *adj syn* see ELASTIC 2

burble *vb* **1** *syn* see SLOSH 1

  2 *syn* see CHAT 1

burden *n* **1** *syn* see LOAD 1

  2 *syn* see LOAD 3

burden *vb* to lay a heavy load on or to lie like a heavy load on a person or thing <*burdened* his men with needless heavy work><I won't *burden* you with this lengthy story>

  syn charge, clog, cumber, encumber, lade, load, lumber, saddle, task, tax, weigh, weight

  rel overburden, overload, overweigh; handicap; afflict, oppress

  idiom bear down on (*or* upon)

  con alleviate, ease, lighten, relieve, unload; disburden, disencumber

  ant unburden

burden *n syn* see SUBSTANCE 2

burdensome *adj syn* see ONEROUS

burdensomely *adv syn* see HARD 8

bureaucrat *n* a member of a bureaucracy <*bureaucrats* were blamed for the error>

  syn mandarin

  rel civil servant, functionary, official

burg *n* a small, insignificant, remote town <the *burg* had only two stores and one gas station>

  syn hick town, jerkwater town, mudhole, one-horse town, Podunk, tank town, whistle-stop

  rel cowtown; crossroads; jumping-off place; hamlet, village

  con city, metropolis

burgee *n syn* see FLAG

burgeon *vb* **1** *syn* see INCREASE 2

  2 *syn* see BLOSSOM

burghal *adj syn* see URBAN

burgher *n syn* see TOWNSMAN

burglarize *vb* to commit an act of breaking open and entering with a felonious purpose the dwelling house of another by night <that night several homes were *burglarized*>

  syn burgle; *compare* HOUSEBREAK, ROB 1

  rel knock over, rob; ransack, rifle; screw

burgle *vb syn* see BURGLARIZE

burial *n* **1** *syn* see GRAVE

  2 the act or ceremony of burying <his *burial* took place yesterday>

  syn entombment, inhumation, interment, sepulture

  rel burying, exequies, funeral, obsequies; deposition; deep six

  con disinterment, exhumation

burial ground *n syn* see CEMETERY

buried *adj syn* see ULTERIOR

burke *vb* **1** *syn* see SUPPRESS 3

  2 *syn* see SKIRT 3

burlesque *n* **1** *syn* see MOCKERY 2

  2 *syn* see CARICATURE 2

burlesque *vb syn* see MIMIC

burly *adj syn* see HUSKY 1

‖**burn** *n syn* see CREEK 2

burn *vb* **1** *syn* see SHINE 1

  2 to undergo combustion <the wood is too green to *burn*>

  syn combust

  rel fire, flame, ignite, incinerate, kindle, light; consume, use; smolder, sputter

  3 to be hot as if on fire <sand *burning* in the blazing sun>

  syn bake, broil, cook, melt, roast, scorch, swelter

  rel parch, toast, warm; char

  con chill, cool, freeze

  4 *syn* see ANGER 2

  5 *syn* see SMART

  6 *syn* see FIRE 6

  ‖**7** *syn* see CHEAT

burn (up) *vb syn* see IRRITATE

burnable *adj syn* see COMBUSTIBLE 1

burning *adj* **1** on fire <the *burning* house>

  syn ablaze, afire, aflame, alight, blazing, conflagrant, fiery, flaming, flaring, ignited, lighted

  rel aglow, glowing, incandescent

  idiom in flames

  con burned-out, cold

  2 *syn* see HOT 1

  ant icy

  3 *syn* see FEVERISH 2

  4 *syn* see IMPASSIONED

  5 *syn* see PRESSING

burnish *vb syn* see POLISH 1

burnished *adj syn* see LUSTROUS 1

burn off *vb syn* see CLEAR 9

burnsides *n pl syn* see SIDE-WHISKERS

burp *vb syn* see BELCH 1

burro *n syn* see DONKEY 1

burrow *n* **1** *syn* see LAIR 1

  2 *syn* see HOVEL

burrow *vb syn* see SNUGGLE

burst *vb* **1** *syn* see EXPLODE 1

  2 *syn* see SHATTER 1

  3 *syn* see PLUNGE 2

burst (forth) *vb syn* see ERUPT 2

burst *n* 1 *syn* see OUTBREAK 1

2 *syn* see OUTBURST 1

3 *syn* see BANG 2

4 *syn* see BARRAGE

bury *vb* 1 to deposit (a corpse) in or as if in the earth <the pharaohs were *buried* in pyramids><*buried* at sea>
syn entomb, inhume, inter, lay away, plant, put away, sepulcher, sepulture, tomb; *compare* ENTOMB 1
rel inurn; coffin
idiom consign to the grave, lay to rest, put six feet under
con dig (up), disentomb, disinter, exhume, untomb; burn, cremate

2 *syn* see HIDE

burying ground *n syn* see CEMETERY

||**bus** *n syn* see CAR

bush *n syn* see FRONTIER 2

bush *adj syn* see MINOR 2

bush–league *adj syn* see MINOR 2

||**bush up** *vb syn* see HIDE

bushwa *n syn* see NONSENSE 2

business *n* 1 *syn* see FUNCTION 1

2 *syn* see PATRONAGE 2

3 *syn* see WORK 1

4 activity concerned with the supplying and distribution of commodities <the lumber *business* depends heavily on the housing *business*>
syn commerce, industry, trade, traffic

5 *syn* see ENTERPRISE 3

6 *syn* see AFFAIR 1

7 *syn* see DOODAD

8 something personal to oneself <that is none of your *business*>
syn affair, concern, lookout, occasions, palaver

businessman *n syn* see MERCHANT

buss *vb syn* see KISS 1

bust *vb* 1 *syn* see RUIN 3

2 *syn* see DEGRADE 1
ant promote

3 *syn* see FAIL 5

||**4** *syn* see ARREST 2

bust *n* ||**1** *syn* see CUFF

2 *syn* see FAILURE 5

3 *syn* see BINGE 1

4 *syn* see RAID 2

||**5** *syn* see ARREST

||**busthead** *n syn* see MOONSHINE 2

bustle *vb syn* see HURRY 2

bustle *n* 1 *syn* see STIR 1

2 *syn* see COMMOTION 4

bustling *adj* full of activity <a *bustling* frontier town>
syn busy, fussy, hopping, humming, hustling, lively, popping
rel active, brisk, energetic
idiom on its way, on the go (*or* move), up and doing

busty *adj syn* see BUXOM

busy *adj* 1 engaged in activity <I can't stop to talk. I'm *busy*>
syn employed, engaged, occupied, working; *compare* ASSIDUOUS

idiom at work, on the fly
con idle, inactive
ant free

2 *syn* see BUSTLING

3 *syn* see IMPERTINENT 2

busy *vb syn* see ENGAGE 4

busybody *n* one who concerns himself with affairs not his own <a meddlesome *busybody* who saw all and tattled all she saw>
syn butt-in, ||buttinsky, intermeddler, kibitzer, meddler, Meddlesome Mattie, nose, nosey Parker, Paul Pry, polypragmatist, pragmatic, pragmatist, prier (*or* pryer), quidnunc, rubber, rubberneck, snoop, ||stickybeak; *compare* GOSSIP 1, INFORMER
rel gossip, gossipmonger, newsmonger, rumormonger, scandalmonger, tabby, talebearer, telltale
idiom curiosity shop, question box

busybody *vb* 1 *syn* see SNOOP

2 *syn* see MEDDLE

but *conj* 1 *syn* see ONLY

2 *syn* see EXCEPT 1

but *prep syn* see EXCEPT

but *adv* 1 *syn* see ONLY 1

2 *syn* see JUST 3

butcher *vb* 1 *syn* see SLAUGHTER 1

2 *syn* see SLAUGHTER 2

butchery *n syn* see MASSACRE

butt *n* 1 *syn* see TARGET 1

2 *syn* see LAUGHINGSTOCK

3 *syn* see FOOL 3

butt (on *or* against) *vb syn* see ADJOIN

||**butt** *n* 1 *syn* see BUTTOCKS

||**2** *syn* see CIGARETTE

butt *n syn* see CASK

butterball *n syn* see FATTY

butt in *vb* 1 *syn* see INTRUDE 1
con abstain, forbear, restrain

2 *syn* see MEDDLE

butt–in *n syn* see BUSYBODY

||**buttinsky** *n syn* see BUSYBODY

buttocks *n pl* the part of the back on which a person sits <gave the boy a whack across the *buttocks*>
syn backside, beam, behind, bottom, breech, buns, ||butt, ||can, cheeks, derriere, ||duff, fanny, fundament, hams, haunches, heinie (*or* hiney), hind end, ||hinder, hunkers, ||keister, nates, podex, posterior, rear, rear end, rump, seat, ||stern, tail, tail end, ||tokus, ||twat
idiom seat of one's pants

button–down *adj syn* see CONVENTIONAL 1

buttress *n syn* see SUPPORT 3

buttress *vb syn* see SUPPORT 4

buvette *n syn* see BAR 4

buxom *adj* having an amply developed bosom <a *buxom* young woman>
syn bosomy, ||built, busty, chesty, full≈bosomed, ||stacked; *compare* CURVACEOUS
rel full-figured, Junoesque, shapely, well-developed, well-proportioned

buy *vb* 1 to acquire something for money or the equivalent <*bought* a new car>
syn purchase, take
rel acquire, get, obtain, procure
ant sell

2 *syn* see RANSOM

---

syn synonym(s)   *rel* related word(s)
ant antonym(s)   *con* contrasted word(s)
idiom idiomatic equivalent(s)
|| use limited; if in doubt, see a dictionary

3 *syn* see BRIBE
‖**4 syn** see BELIEVE 1
buy *n syn* see BARGAIN 1
buyable *adj syn* see VENAL 1
buyer *n syn* see PURCHASER
buy off *vb syn* see BRIBE
buzz *vb* 1 *syn* see HUM
  2 *syn* see HISS
  ‖**3 syn** see TELEPHONE
buzz *n syn* see REPORT 1
‖**buzzed** *adj syn* see INTOXICATED 1
buzz off *vb syn* see GET OUT 1
by *prep* 1 *syn* see BESIDE 1
  2 *syn* see NEAR 2
  3 *syn* see VIA 1
  4 *syn* see VIA 2
  5 with reference to <sorted *by* color>
  syn according to, as to
by *adv syn* see OVER 5
by *interj syn* see GOOD-BYE
by all odds *adv syn* see FAR AND AWAY
by a long shot *adv syn* see FAR AND AWAY
by and by *adv* 1 *syn* see AFTER
  2 *syn* see PRESENTLY 1
by-and-by *n syn* see FUTURE
by and large *adv syn* see ALTOGETHER 3
by-blow *n syn* see BASTARD 1
by dint of *prep syn* see VIA 2

bye–bye *interj syn* see GOOD-BYE
by far *adv syn* see FAR AND AWAY
bygone *adj* 1 *syn* see FORMER 2
  2 *syn* see OLD-FASHIONED
  3 *syn* see EXTINCT 2
by long odds *adv syn* see FAR AND AWAY
by means of *prep syn* see VIA 2
byname *n syn* see NICKNAME
by odds *adv syn* see FAR AND AWAY
by ordinary *adv syn* see USUALLY 2
bypass *vb* 1 *syn* see SKIRT 2
  2 *syn* see SKIRT 3
byplace *n syn* see NOOK
by-product *n syn* see OUTGROWTH 2
by–sitter *n syn* see SPECTATOR
bystander *n syn* see SPECTATOR
by stealth *adv syn* see SECRETLY
by–talk *n syn* see SMALL TALK
the bye *adv syn* see INCIDENTALLY 2
by the way *adv syn* see INCIDENTALLY 2
by–the–way *adj syn* see INDIFFERENT 2
by virtue of *prep syn* see VIA 2
by way of *prep* 1 *syn* see VIA 1
  2 *syn* see VIA 2
byword *n* 1 *syn* see SAYING
  2 *syn* see CATCHWORD
  3 *syn* see NICKNAME
Byzantine *adj syn* see COMPLEX 2

C

cab *n syn* see TAXICAB
‖**cab** *n syn* see CRUD
cabal *n* 1 *syn* see CLIQUE
  2 *syn* see PLOT 2
cabalistic *adj syn* see MYSTERIOUS
cabaret *n syn* see NIGHTCLUB
‖**cabbage** *n syn* see MONEY
cabbage *vb syn* see STEAL 1
cabbagehead *n syn* see DUNCE
cabin *n syn* see HUT
‖**caboose** *n syn* see HUT
‖**caboose** *n syn* see JAIL
‖**ca' canny** *n syn* see SLOWDOWN 2
cache *vb syn* see HIDE
  con discover, unearth
cachet *n syn* see STATUS 1
‖**cack** *vb syn* see VOMIT
cackle *vb syn* see CHAT 1
cackle *n syn* see CHATTER
cacophonic *adj syn* see DISSONANT 1
cacophonous *adj syn* see DISSONANT 1
cad *n* a person without gentlemanly instincts
  <gloated over his rival's distress like the *cad*
  that he was>
  syn bounder, cur, rotter, yellow dog
  rel boor, churl, clown, lout; guttersnipe,

mucker, vulgarian; ‖creep; bastard, heel,
louse, rat, stinker
  idiom Jack Nasty
  ant gentleman
cadaver *n syn* see CORPSE
cadaverous *adj* 1 *syn* see GHASTLY 2
  2 *syn* see EMACIATED
  rel careworn, haggard, pinched, worn
cadence *n syn* see RHYTHM
  rel accent, accentuation, emphasis, stress;
  pulsation, pulse, throb
cadency *n syn* see RHYTHM
‖**cadet** *n syn* see PIMP 1
cadger *n syn* see BEGGAR 1
cadging *n syn* see MENDICANCY
caducity *n syn* see OLD AGE
  rel dotage, dotingness, second childhood
café *n* 1 *syn* see EATING HOUSE
  2 *syn* see NIGHTCLUB
‖**caff** *n syn* see EATING HOUSE
cage *vb syn* see ENCLOSE 1
  rel imprison, incarcerate, jail
cagey *adj syn* see SHREWD
cageyness *n syn* see CUNNING 2
cahoots *n pl syn* see ASSOCIATION 1
‖**cahot** *n syn* see BUMP 3

cajole *vb syn* see COAX
  rel beguile, deceive, delude; tantalize; crowd, push

cake *vb* **1** to cover with a surface layer <the floor was *caked* with filth>
  syn crust, encrust (*or* incrust), incrustate, rime
  rel besmear, coat, smear, spread; cover, daub
  2 *syn* see HARDEN 1
  rel compress, condense, contract, shrink

cakewalk *n syn* see RUNAWAY

‖**calaboose** *n syn* see JAIL

calamitous *adj* **1** *syn* see FATAL 2
  2 *syn* see DEPLORABLE

calamity *n syn* see DISASTER
  rel collapse, ruin, wreck; affliction, cross, trial, tribulation, visitation
  con fortune, luck; benefaction; favor, gift
  ant boon

calamity howler *n syn* see PESSIMIST

calculate *vb* to determine or approximate a mathematical value (as speed, cost, or quantity) <*calculate* the cost of a new car>
  syn cipher, compute, estimate, figure, reckon
  rel consider, study, weigh; ascertain, determine, discover; appraise, evaluate, price, value; assess, prize, rate
  con conjecture, guess, surmise

calculate (on *or* upon) *vb syn* see RELY (on *or* upon)

calculating *adj syn* see CAUTIOUS
  rel artful, crafty, cunning, guileful, sly, wily
  con improvident, imprudent, indiscreet
  ant rash, reckless

calculation *n syn* see COMPUTATION

calembour *n syn* see PUN

calendar *n syn* see PROGRAM 1

calenture *n syn* see PASSION 6

caliber *n* **1** *syn* see QUALITY 2
  rel ability, capability, capacity; force, power
  2 *syn* see QUALITY 3

caliginous *adj syn* see DARK 1

call *vb* **1** to speak or utter in a loud distinct carrying voice <*call* for help>
  syn cry, hallo, holler, hollo, shout, vociferate, yell; *compare* SHOUT 1
  rel bawl, bellow, hoot, howl, roar, scream, screech, shriek, shrill, whoop, yowl
  con murmur, whisper
  2 *syn* see DEMAND 1
  3 *syn* see SUMMON 2
  rel assemble, collect, gather, round up; bid, invite
  4 *syn* see CONVOKE
  5 *syn* see TELEPHONE
  6 *syn* see NAME 1
  7 *syn* see PREDICT 2
  8 *syn* see ESTIMATE 3
  9 *syn* see FORETELL
  10 *syn* see VISIT 2

call (for) *vb syn* see DEMAND 2

call (to) *vb syn* see ADDRESS 7

call *n* **1** the natural vocal sound of an animal and especially a bird <the clear *call* of a bellbird>
  syn cry, note, song
  rel cheep, chirp, peep, twitter, warble
  2 *syn* see ATTRACTION 1
  3 *syn* see OCCASION 3
  4 *syn* see VISIT 1

call down *vb syn* see REPROVE

caller *n syn* see VISITOR 1

‖**callet** *n syn* see PROSTITUTE

call girl *n syn* see PROSTITUTE

call house *n syn* see BROTHEL

calligraphy *n syn* see HANDWRITING

call in *vb syn* see SUMMON 2

calling *n* **1** *syn* see MISSION
  2 *syn* see TRADE 1
  3 *syn* see WORK 1

‖**callithump** *n syn* see SHIVAREE

call off *vb syn* see CANCEL 2

callous *adj syn* see UNFEELING 2
  rel indurated, set

callow *adj* **1** *syn* see YOUNG 1
  2 *syn* see INEXPERIENCED

callowness *n syn* see INEXPERIENCE

call up *vb* to summon for active military duty <*called up* the army reserves>
  syn order up; *compare* DRAFT 1
  rel mobilize
  idiom call to the colors
  ant discharge, muster out

calm *n syn* see QUIET 1

calm *adj* **1** free from storm or rough activity <the wind died and the sea became *calm*>
  syn halcyon, hushed, placid, quiet, still, stilly, untroubled
  rel inactive, quiescent, reposing, resting; pacific, smooth, tranquil, unruffled
  idiom calm as a millpond, still as death
  con agitated, disturbed, perturbed, restless, turbulent, uneasy
  ant stormy
  2 free from mental or emotional distress or agitation <a man who remained *calm* under stress>
  syn collected, composed, easy, easygoing, placid, poised, possessed, self-composed, self-possessed, serene, tranquil
  rel cool, imperturbable, laid-back, nonchalant, unflappable, unruffled; even-tempered, impassive, phlegmatic, steady; firm, stable, staunch
  con discomposed, disturbed, perturbed, upset; anxious, bothered, confused, nervous; fidgety, jittery, jumpy, shaky, tense
  ant agitated

calm *vb* to relieve from or bring to an end whatever distresses, agitates, or disturbs <that inner faith that *calms* the troubled spirit>
  syn allay, balm, becalm, compose, lull, quiet, ‖quieten, settle, soothe, ‖soother, still, tranquilize
  rel alleviate, assuage, mitigate, relieve; appease, mollify, pacify, placate; relax, steady
  con bother, discompose, disquiet, disturb, flurry, perturb, stir up, upset
  ant arouse

calmant *n syn* see SEDATIVE

---

syn synonym(s)   *rel* related word(s)
ant antonym(s)   *con* contrasted word(s)
idiom idiomatic equivalent(s)
‖ use limited; if in doubt, see a dictionary

calmative *n syn* see SEDATIVE
calmness *n syn* see EQUANIMITY
calumniate *vb syn* see MALIGN
   ant eulogize; vindicate
calumnious *adj syn* see LIBELOUS
calumny *n syn* see DETRACTION
   rel animadversion, reflection, stricture
   con encomium, panegyric, tribute; adulation, compliment, flattery
   ant eulogy; vindication
calvary *n syn* see TRIAL 1
‖**cam** *adv syn* see AWRY 1
camaraderie *n* a spirit of friendly goodwill typical of comrades <the easy *camaraderie* of a cozy neighborhood bar>
   syn comradery, good-fellowship
   rel affability, friendliness, gregariousness, sociability; cheer, conviviality, jollity
   con aloofness, coldness, frigidity, inaccessibility, reclusiveness, remoteness, self-containment; exclusiveness, self-sufficiency, unsociability
camarilla *n syn* see CLIQUE
cameraman *n syn* see PHOTOGRAPHER
camerist *n syn* see PHOTOGRAPHER
camouflage *vb syn* see DISGUISE
   rel becloud, befog, dim
camp *n* 1 a place where a number of people (as vacationers or soldiers) live temporarily together in usually more or less casual housing <planned to summer at a fishing *camp* in Maine>
   syn campground, encampment
   2 *syn* see CLIQUE
   3 *syn* see HUT
camp *vb* to live temporarily in a camp or the outdoors <*camped* under the trees for the night>
   syn bivouac, ‖bivvy, encamp, ‖laager, ‖maroon, tent
   idiom rough it
   con decamp
campanile *n syn* see BELL TOWER
camper *n syn* see TRAILER
campestral *adj syn* see RURAL
camp follower *n syn* see PROSTITUTE
campground *n syn* see CAMP 1
‖**cample** *vb syn* see SCOLD 1
‖**can** *n* 1 *syn* see JAIL
   2 *syn* see TOILET
   3 *syn* see BUTTOCKS
‖**can** *vb syn* see DISMISS 3
Canaan *n syn* see HEAVEN 2
canaille *n syn* see RABBLE 2
canal *n syn* see CHANNEL 1
canard *n syn* see LIE
   rel hoax, humbug, mare's nest, sell, spoof; artifice, dodge, trick
‖**canary** *n syn* see INFORMER
cancel *vb* 1 *syn* see ERASE
   2 to give up something previously arranged or agreed on <decided to *cancel* his appointment with the dentist>
   syn abort, call off, drop, scrub
   rel end, terminate; annul, invalidate, rescind, revoke; give up, relinquish, surrender
cancel (out) *vb syn* see NEUTRALIZE
candid *adj* 1 *syn* see FAIR 4
   rel aboveboard, forthright, straightforward; honest, scrupulous, upright

   2 *syn* see FRANK
   ant evasive
candidate *n* one who seeks an office, honor, position, or award <examining *candidates* for editorial positions>
   syn applicant, aspirant, hopeful, seeker
   rel nominee; dark horse; also-ran, has-been; campaigner, electioneerer, stumper, whistle-stopper
candy *vb syn* see SUGARCOAT 1
canine *n syn* see DOG 1
canker *vb syn* see DEBASE 1
cankered *adj syn* see CANTANKEROUS
cannabis *n syn* see MARIJUANA
canned *adj* 1 *syn* see CONDENSED
   ‖2 *syn* see INTOXICATED 1
cannibalic *adj syn* see FIERCE 1
canniness *n* 1 *syn* see PRUDENCE 1
   2 *syn* see CUNNING 2
‖**cannon** *n syn* see PICKPOCKET
cannonade *n syn* see BARRAGE
cannonade *vb syn* see BOMBARD
canny *adj* 1 *syn* see CLEVER 4
   2 *syn* see SPARING
   3 *syn* see WISE 4
canon *n* 1 *syn* see LAW 1
   2 *syn* see DOCTRINE
canonical *adj syn* see ORTHODOX 1
‖**cant** *adj syn* see LIVELY 1
cant *vb syn* see SLANT 1
cant *n* 1 *syn* see DIALECT 2
   rel diction, language, phraseology, vocabulary; idiom, speech
   2 *syn* see TERMINOLOGY
   3 *syn* see HYPOCRISY
cantankerous *adj* habitually ill-humored, irritable, and disagreeable <one of our more *cantankerous* fellow workers>
   syn bearish, cankered, cranky, cross-grained, crotchety, ornery, rantankerous, vinegarish, vinegary, waspish, waspy; *compare* IRASCIBLE, IRRITABLE
   rel dour, morose, sour; crabbed, cross, crusty, huffy, petulant, prickly, snappish; dyspeptic, ill-conditioned, ill-natured; liverish
   idiom like a bear with a sore paw
   con benign, kindly, mellow, mild; amiable, congenial, friendly, pleasant, well-disposed; benevolent, gracious, kind
canter *n syn* see VAGABOND
cantina *n syn* see BAR 5
canting *adj syn* see HYPOCRITICAL
canton *vb syn* see BILLET 1
‖**canty** *adj syn* see LIVELY 1
canvass *vb* 1 *syn* see SCRUTINIZE 1
   2 *syn* see DISCUSS 1
   3 *syn* see SOLICIT 1
cap *vb* 1 *syn* see SURMOUNT 3
   ‖2 *syn* see PUZZLE
   3 *syn* see COVER 3
   4 *syn* see SURPASS 1
   5 *syn* see CLIMAX
capability *n* 1 *syn* see ABILITY 1
   rel art, craft, cunning, skill
   con inability, disability
   ant incapability, incompetence
   2 *syn* see EFFICACY 1
capable *adj syn* see ABLE
   ant incapable

capacious *adj syn* see SPACIOUS
   rel dilatable, distensible, expandable, expansive, extensible; abundant, copious, plentiful
   ant exiguous
capacity *n* **1** *syn* see ABILITY 1
   rel bent, faculty, gift, knack, talent, twin; caliber, stature
   con impotence, ineffectiveness, powerlessness
   ant incapacity
   2 *syn* see STATUS 1
cape *n* *syn* see PROMONTORY
caper *vb syn* see GAMBOL
   idiom cut capers
caper *n* **1** *syn* see ESCAPADE
   2 *syn* see PRANK
   rel devilment, impishness, mischief, roguery, waggishness
‖**capernoited** *adj syn* see INTOXICATED 1
capital *adj* **1** *syn* see EGREGIOUS
   2 *syn* see CHIEF 2
   rel cardinal, essential, vital; basic, fundamental, underlying
   3 *syn* see EXCELLENT
capital *n* *syn* see MEAN 3
capitalize *vb* to supply capital for or to
   <agreed to *capitalize* the venture>
   syn back, bankroll, finance, grubstake, stake
   rel aid, assist, help, subsidize, support; fund; promote, sponsor
capitulate *vb syn* see YIELD 2
capitulation *n* *syn* see SURRENDER
capper *n* *syn* see DECOY 2
caprice *n* an arbitrary, impulsive, and often illogical notion or change of mind <given to sudden *caprices* and random fancies>
   syn bee, boutade, conceit, crank, crotchet, fancy, freak, humor, maggot, megrim, notion, vagary, whigmaleerie, whim, whimsy
   rel mood, temper, vein; contrariety, inconsistency, perversity; characteristic, foible, habit, mannerism, peculiarity, trait, trick
capricious *adj* **1** *syn* see ARBITRARY 1
   2 *syn* see INCONSTANT 1
   rel humorsome, moody; effervescent
   con constant, steady
   ant steadfast
   3 *syn* see UNCERTAIN 1
capsheaf *n* *syn* see APEX 2
capstone *n* *syn* see APEX 2
capsule *adj syn* see CONDENSED
caption *n* an explanatory or identifying comment accompanying a pictorial illustration <the *captions* were under the wrong figures>
   syn legend, underline
captious *adj syn* see CRITICAL 1
   rel demanding, exacting, finicky; contrary, perverse; irritable, peevish, petulant, snappish, snappy, testy
   con judicious, sensible, wise; rational, reasonable; knowing, knowledgeable
   ant appreciative

captivate *vb syn* see ATTRACT 1
   rel delight, gratify, please; enthrall, grip, hold, mesmerize, spellbind
   ant repulse
captivated *adj syn* see ENAMORED 3
captivating *adj syn* see ATTRACTIVE 1
capture *vb syn* see CATCH 1
Capuan *adj syn* see LUXURIOUS 3
car *n* a usually private passenger-carrying automotive vehicle <drove a shabby old car>
   syn auto, autocar, automobile, buggy, ‖bus, machine, motor, motorcar
   rel beach wagon, coach, compact, convertible, coupe, fastback, hardtop, hatchback, limousine, notchback, phaeton, roadster, runabout, sedan, station wagon, subcompact, touring car; ‖clunker, ‖crate, ‖heap, ‖jalopy, junker, ‖wreck
‖**caravan** *n* *syn* see TRAILER
caravansary *n* *syn* see HOTEL
carbon *n* *syn* see REPRODUCTION
carbon copy *n* *syn* see REPRODUCTION
carbuncle *n* *syn* see ABSCESS
carcass *n* *syn* see CORPSE
‖**carcel** *n* *syn* see JAIL
card *n* **1** *syn* see WAG 1
   2 *syn* see PROGRAM 1
   3 *syn* see MENU
card *vb syn* see SCHEDULE 1
cardboard *adj syn* see STIFF 4
   rel unlifelike, unreal, unrealistic
cardinal *adj* **1** *syn* see ESSENTIAL 2
   2 *syn* see CENTRAL 1
care *n* **1** *syn* see SORROW
   rel strain, stress, tension
   2 a burdened or disquieted state of mind <a mind full of *care* and sadness>
   syn anxiety, concern, concernment, disquiet, disquietude, solicitude, unease, uneasiness, worry
   rel apprehension, foreboding, misgiving, suspense; agitation, disturbance, perturbation; alarm, consternation, dismay, fear
   con calm, ease, peace, quietude; assurance, comfort, easiness
   3 *syn* see TRIAL 2
   4 serious and heedful attentiveness <attended his words with *care*>
   syn carefulness, concern, consciousness, heed, heedfulness, regard; *compare* ATTENTION 1
   rel curiosity; enthusiasm, interest; consideration, solicitude, thoughtfulness; effort, exertion, pains, trouble; alertness, vigilance, watchfulness
   con carelessness, disregard, heedlessness, unconcern; boredom, disinterest, ennui
   5 *syn* see OVERSIGHT 1
   6 *syn* see CUSTODY
care (for) *vb* **1** *syn* see TEND 2
   2 *syn* see MINISTER (to)
   idiom take care of
careen *vb syn* see LURCH 2
career *vb syn* see COURSE
carefree *adj* **1** *syn* see HAPPY-GO-LUCKY
   2 *syn* see IRRESPONSIBLE
careful *adj* **1** *syn* see CAUTIOUS
   rel attentive, heedful, observant
   2 closely attentive to details or showing such attention <*careful* workmanship>

---

syn conscientious, conscionable, exact, fussy, heedful, meticulous, painstaking, punctilious, punctual, scrupulous

rel accurate, nice, precise; deliberate, studied; foresighted, provident, prudent; critical, discriminating, finical, finicky; observant, particular, religious; duteous, dutiful, intent

con disorderly, lax, negligent, slack, slipshod, slovenly; heedless, neglectful, remiss

ant careless

carefulness *n syn see* CARE 4

careless *adj* **1** lacking in or showing lack of care and attention <*careless* of the harm his neglect might do to others> <unwilling to accept such *careless* shoddy work>

syn feckless, heedless, inadvertent, irreflective, thoughtless, uncaring, unheeding, unrecking, unreflective, unthinking; *compare* INCAUTIOUS, RASH 1

rel forgetful, inattentive, oblivious, unmindful; lax, neglectful, negligent, slack, unconcerned, uninterested; inadequate, incapable, unfit, unqualified

con careful, heedful, thoughtful; concerned, considerate, punctilious, scrupulous

ant careful

2 *syn see* IRRESPONSIBLE

3 *syn see* NEGLIGENT

4 *syn see* SLIPSHOD 3

5 *syn see* SLOVENLY 1

caress *vb* to express interest, affection, or love by touching or handling <*caress* a frightened child>

syn cosset, cuddle, dandle, fondle, love, pet

rel cocker, coddle, indulge, pamper; coquet, dally, flirt, toy, trifle; nuzzle, pat, stroke

careworn *adj syn see* HAGGARD

rel distressed, troubled; exhausted, fagged, jaded, tuckered

ant carefree

cargo *n syn see* LOAD 1

caricature *n* **1** *syn see* MOCKERY 2

2 a grotesque or bizarre imitation <a doting attentiveness that was a sickly *caricature* of motherhood>

syn burlesque, parody, takeoff, travesty

rel lampoon, libel, pasquinade; laughingstock, mockery; cheat, fake, imitation, phony, sham; bosh, bunk, gammon, hokum, moonshine; clinquant, pinchbeck, shoddy, tinsel

carillon *n syn see* BELL TOWER

caritas *n syn see* MERCY

cark *vb* **1** *syn see* TROUBLE 1

2 *syn see* WORRY 3

carnage *n syn see* MASSACRE

carnal *adj* **1** *syn see* BODILY

rel material, substantial; earthly, earthy

2 characterized by physical rather than intellectual or spiritual day-to-day <giving too much heed to the *carnal* aspects of day-to-day life>

syn animal, fleshly, sensual; *compare* SENSUOUS

rel bodily, corporal, corporeal, physical; coarse, gross, obscene, vulgar; earthly, earthy, mundane, temporal, worldly; lascivious, lewd, lustful, wanton; Pandemic, sensuous

con ethical, moral, noble, righteous, virtuous; aerial, ethereal, otherworldly, supernal; chaste, decent, modest, pure

ant spiritual; intellectual

carnality *n syn see* ANIMALITY

carom *vb syn see* GLANCE 1

carousal *n syn see* BINGE 1

carouse *n syn see* BINGE 1

carouse *vb syn see* REVEL 1

carp (at) *vb syn see* NAG

carper *n syn see* CRITIC

‖**carpet** *vb syn see* SCOLD 1

idiom call on the carpet, take to task

carpet knight *n syn see* HEDONIST

carping *adj syn see* CRITICAL 1

rel blaming, criticizing, reprehending, reprobating; jawing, railing, upbraiding; blameful, condemnatory, damnatory, objurgatory, reproachful, reprobatory

con applauding, commendatory, complimentary; approving, endorsing; extolling, laudatory, praiseful

ant fulsome

carriage *n* **1** *syn see* TRANSPORTATION 1

2 *syn see* POSTURE 1

carriageable *adj syn see* PORTABLE

carriage trade *n syn see* ARISTOCRACY

carrier *n* **1** *syn see* BEARER 2

2 *syn see* MESSENGER

3 *syn see* VECTOR

carrot *n syn see* REWARD

carry *vb* **1** to be the agent or means by which someone or something is shifted from one place to another <*carried* the child on his shoulder>

syn bear, buck, convey, ferry, ‖hump, ‖jag, lug, pack, tote, transport

rel bring, fetch, take; move, remove, shift, transfer; send, transmit

‖**2** *syn see* ACCOMPANY

3 *syn see* AFFECT

4 *syn see* BEAR 3

5 *syn see* CONDUCT 4

6 *syn see* BEHAVE 1

7 *syn see* SUPPORT 4

8 *syn see* STOCK

carrying *n syn see* TRANSPORTATION 1

carry off *vb syn see* KILL 1

carry on *vb* **1** *syn see* CONDUCT 3

2 *syn see* CUT UP 2

3 *syn see* PERSEVERE

carry out *vb syn see* ADMINISTER 1

rel complete, finalize; discharge, effect, effectuate, fulfill; prosecute, transact

idiom put in force (*or* into effect); sign, seal, and deliver

2 *syn see* EFFECT 2

carrytale *n syn see* GOSSIP 1

carry through *vb* **1** *syn see* EFFECT 2

2 *syn see* CONTINUE 1

carte blanche *n* full discretionary power <was given *carte blanche* to build, landscape, and furnish the house>

syn blank check, free hand

rel license, prerogative, right; authority, power; say, say-so

idiom power of attorney

carte d'entrée *n syn see* TICKET 2

carte du jour *n syn see* MENU

cartel *n* **1** *syn see* DEFIANCE 1

rel gage, gauntlet, glove; blow, slap

2 syn see SYNDICATE

rel corporation; multinational; consortium, merger

carve *vb* **1 syn** see CUT 5

2 syn see SCULPTURE

Casanova *n* **1 syn** see GALLANT 2

2 syn see WOLF

cascade *n syn* see WATERFALL

‖**cascade** *vb syn* see VOMIT

case *n* **1 syn** see EVENT 4

2 syn see ORDER 9

3 syn see SUIT 1

4 syn see INSTANCE

rel circumstance, episode, event, incident, occurrence; condition, situation, state

5 syn see ECCENTRIC

case *vb syn* see HULL

‖**case** *vb syn* see SCRUTINIZE 1

case history *n syn* see INSTANCE

cash *n syn* see MONEY

cashier *vb* **1 syn** see DISMISS 3

rel eject, expel, oust; bar, eliminate, exclude; pass over, shelve

con appoint, designate, elect, name; employ, engage, hire

2 syn see DISCARD

cash in *vb syn* see DIE 1

cask *n* a vessel made of staves, headings, and hoops <a *cask* of cider>

syn barrel, butt, hogshead, keg, pipe, tun

Cassandra *n syn* see PESSIMIST

cassock *n syn* see CLERGYMAN

cast *vb* **1 syn** see THROW 1

rel broadcast, disperse, distribute, scatter

2 syn see DIRECT 2

3 syn see DISCARD

rel abandon, leave, relinquish, surrender, yield; dismiss, drop

‖**4 syn** see VOMIT

5 syn see ADD 2

6 syn see PLAN 2

cast *n* **1 syn** see LOOK 2

2 syn see PREDICTION

3 syn see COLOR 1

4 syn see HINT 2

5 syn see TYPE

6 syn see FORM 1

cast about *vb syn* see SEEK 1

cast away *vb* **1 syn** see WASTE 2

2 syn see SHIPWRECK 1

castaway *n syn* see OUTCAST

cast down *vb syn* see HUMBLE

cast down *adj syn* see DOWNCAST

castigate *vb* **1 syn** see PUNISH 1

rel baste, beat, belabor, drub, pummel, thrash; berate, rail, rate, tongue-lash, upbraid, wig; penalize

2 syn see LAMBASTE 3

castigation *n syn* see PUNISHMENT

castigatory *adj syn* see PUNITIVE

castle *n syn* see MANSION

castle-builder *n syn* see DREAMER

cast out *vb* **1 syn** see BANISH

‖**2 syn** see QUARREL

castrate *vb* **1 syn** see STERILIZE

2 syn see UNNERVE

rel bleed, drain, empty, exhaust

casual *adj* **1 syn** see ACCIDENTAL

rel unplanned, unpremeditated; extemporaneous, extempore, impromptu, improvised, offhand; impulsive, spontaneous

con advised, considered, deliberate, intentional, planned, premeditated, studied

ant deliberate

2 syn see INDIFFERENT 2

3 syn see EASYGOING 3

con ceremonial, conventional, formal

4 syn see LITTLE 3

casually *adv syn* see INCIDENTALLY 1

casualty *n* **1 syn** see ACCIDENT 2

2 syn see FATALITY 2

3 syn see VICTIM 2

casuistry *n syn* see FALLACY 2

‖**cat** *n syn* see MAN 3

‖**cat** *vb syn* see VOMIT

cataclysm *n* **1 syn** see FLOOD 2

2 syn see DISASTER

cataclysmic *adj syn* see FATAL 2

catacomb *n syn* see CRYPT

catalog *n syn* see LIST

rel program, prospectus, syllabus

catalog *vb* **1 syn** see INVENTORY

2 syn see LIST 3

rel admit, enter, introduce; count, enumerate, number

catalyst *n syn* see STIMULUS

cataplasm *n syn* see POULTICE

cataract *n* **1 syn** see WATERFALL

2 syn see FLOOD 2

catastrophe *n syn* see DISASTER

catastrophic *adj syn* see FATAL 2

catcall *n syn* see RASPBERRY

catch *vb* **1** to obtain physical mastery and possession of <the cat *caught* a mouse>

syn bag, capture, collar, ‖cotch, get, nail, prehend, secure, take; *compare* ARREST 2, SEIZE 2

rel clutch, grab, snatch; clasp, grasp, grip; ensnare, entangle, entrap, snare, tangle, trap

con free, release

ant miss

2 syn see SEIZE 2

3 to put at a disadvantage or bring under control by or as if by enmeshing in a net <*caught* in the fallacy of his own argument>

syn benet, catch up, ensnare, entangle, entrap, snare, tangle, trap; *compare* ENTANGLE 3

rel baffle, confound, nonplus, perplex, stick, stump; abash, disturb, embarrass, put out; confuse, flurry, fluster, rattle

4 syn see DUPE

5 syn see FIND 1

6 syn see MARRY 1

7 to come up with often unexpectedly <the storm *caught* them unawares>

syn ‖cotch, overhaul, overtake, take

rel reach

idiom come upon

8 syn see SEIZE 3

9 syn see INTERCEPT

10 syn see CONTRACT 1

idiom fall ill (*or* with), fall victim to

11 syn see FASTEN 2

---

syn synonym(s)   *rel* related word(s)
ant antonym(s)   *con* contrasted word(s)
idiom idiomatic equivalent(s)
‖ use limited; if in doubt, see a dictionary

12 *syn* see STRIKE 2

13 *syn* see APPREHEND 1

catch colt *n syn* see BASTARD

catching *adj* **1** *syn* see INFECTIOUS 2

2 *syn* see INFECTIOUS 3

catch on *vb syn* see DISCOVER 3

catchphrase *n syn* see CATCHWORD

catchpole *n syn* see DELEGATE

catch up *vb* **1** *syn* see CATCH 3

2 *syn* see ENTHRALL 2

catchword *n* a word or phrase that catches the eye or ear and is repeated so often that it becomes representative of a political party, school of thought, or point of view <"new deal" became the *catchword* of supporters and critics of Franklin Roosevelt>
syn byword, catchphrase, phrase, shibboleth, slogan, watchword; *compare* BATTLE CRY
rel household word; maxim, motto

catchy *adj syn* see FITFUL

catechize *vb syn* see ASK 1

categorical *adj* **1** *syn* see ULTIMATE 3
con conjectural, hypothetical, supposititious; conditional, contingent, dependent, relative
2 *syn* see EXPLICIT
rel certain, positive, sure; direct, downright, forthright
con ambiguous; doubtful, dubious, problematic, questionable
3 *syn* see POSITIVE 1

categorically *adv syn* see EXPRESSLY 1

categorize *vb syn* see ASSORT
rel identify, nail down, peg, put down

category *n syn* see CLASS 1

cater (to) *vb* **1** *syn* see BABY
idiom make much of
2 *syn* see INDULGE 1

cateran *n syn* see MARAUDER

catercorner (*or* **catty-corner** *or* **kitty-corner**) *adv syn* see DIAGONALLY

cater–cousin *n syn* see FRIEND

caterwaul *vb syn* see QUARREL

catharsis *n syn* see PURIFICATION

catholic *adj* **1** *syn* see UNIVERSAL 2
rel comprehensive, inclusive; general, generic, indeterminate; extensive, large-scale
ant parochial; provincial
2 *syn* see ECLECTIC 2

catholicon *n syn* see PANACEA

cathouse *n syn* see BROTHEL

catlike *adj syn* see STEALTHY 2

catnap *n syn* see NAP

catnap *vb syn* see NAP

‖**catouse** *n syn* see COMMOTION 3

cat's–paw *n syn* see TOOL 2

catty *adj* **1** *syn* see STEALTHY 2
2 *syn* see AGILE
3 *syn* see MALICIOUS

‖**caulk** (off) *vb syn* see NAP

‖**caulker** *n syn* see DRAM

causatum *n syn* see EFFECT 1

cause *n* **1** that (as a person, fact, or condition) which is responsible for an effect <the storm was the *cause* of all our difficulties>
syn antecedent, determinant, occasion, reason
rel goad, impulse, incentive, inducement, motive, spring; origin, prime mover, root,

source; author, creator, generator, originator
con consequence, effect, issue, outcome, result
2 *syn* see MOTIVE 1
3 *syn* see OCCASION 3
4 *syn* see SUIT 1

cause *vb* **1** *syn* see GENERATE 3
2 *syn* see EFFECT 1
rel elicit, evoke, provoke
idiom be at the root of, give origin to, set on foot

'cause *conj syn* see BECAUSE

causerie *n syn* see CHAT 2

caustic *adj* **1** marked by sharp and often witty incisiveness <a *caustic* critic>
syn mordacious, mordant, salty, scathing, trenchant; *compare* SARCASTIC
rel biting, cutting, incisive; acrid, bitter, pungent, tart; acute, keen, sharp; ironic, sarcastic, satiric, stinging; harsh, rough, severe, stringent; crisp, pithy, succinct, terse
con gentle, mild; cordial, gracious; bland, diplomatic, suave, urbane
ant genial
2 *syn* see SARCASTIC

causticity *n syn* see SARCASM

caution *n* **1** *syn* see WARNING
2 *syn* see PRUDENCE 1

caution *vb syn* see WARN 1

cautionary *adj syn* see MONITORY

cautioning *adj syn* see MONITORY

cautious *adj* marked by careful prudence especially in reducing or avoiding risk or danger <a *cautious* approach to marriage>
syn calculating, careful, chary, circumspect, considerate, discreet, gingerly, guarded, safe, wary
rel alert, vigilant, watchful; cagey, canny, cozy, foresighted, precautious, shrewd; forethoughtful, prethoughtful, provident, prudent; calculating, scheming, shrewd; expedient, judicious, politic
idiom on one's guard, on the safe side, playing it safe
con daring, rash, reckless, venturesome; headlong, impetuous, precipitate
ant adventurous, temerarious

cavalier *adj syn* see PROUD 1

cave *n* a usually natural underground chamber <the limestone *caves* of Kentucky>
syn cavern, grotto, subterrane, subterranean

cave *vb* **1** *syn* see GIVE 12
2 *syn* see YIELD 2

cave (in) *vb syn* see COLLAPSE 2

caveat *n syn* see WARNING

cavern *n syn* see CAVE

cavernous *adj* suggestive of a cave <a *cavernous* fireplace that gulped in wood>
syn chasmal, gaping, yawning
rel commodious, vast
2 *syn* see HOLLOW 1

cavil *vb syn* see QUIBBLE 1

caviler *n syn* see CRITIC

caviling *adj syn* see CRITICAL 1
rel contrary, perverse; demanding, exacting; finicky, fussy, picky; mean, petty, small; hairsplitting, niggling, nitpicking
con amiable, complaisant, good-natured, tolerant; accommodating, easy, obliging

cavillous *adj syn* see CRITICAL 1

cavity *n syn* see HOLE 3

cavort *vb syn* see GAMBOL
rel carry on, cut up, horse (around), horse-play, roughhouse

caw *vb syn* see SQUALL 1

cease *vb syn* see STOP 3
rel close, conclude, end, finish, terminate; intermit
con continue, persist; extend, prolong, protract; arise, originate, rise, spring

cease *n syn* see END 2

cease-fire *n syn* see TRUCE

ceaseless *adj* 1 *syn* see CONTINUAL
2 *syn* see EVERLASTING 1

cede *vb* 1 *syn* see RELINQUISH
rel accord, concede, grant, vouchsafe
con hold, hold back, keep back, retain, withhold
2 *syn* see TRANSFER 4

ceinture *n syn* see BELT 1

‖**celeb** *n syn* see CELEBRITY 2

celebrate *vb* 1 *syn* see KEEP 2
2 *syn* see PRAISE 2

celebrated *adj syn* see FAMOUS 2

celebrious *adj syn* see FAMOUS 2

celebrity *n* 1 *syn* see FAME 1
ant obscurity
2 a widely known and popularly esteemed person <youngsters making a great to-do over sports *celebrities*>
syn big name, ‖celeb, luminary, name, notability, notable, somebody
rel hero, immortal, mahatma, star, superstar; lion; personage, worthy; cynosure
idiom center of attraction, person of note (*or* mark)
con back number; nobody

celerity *n* 1 *syn* see HASTE 1
rel alacrity, briskness, legerity
2 *syn* see SPEED 2

celestial *adj* of, relating to, or befitting heaven or the heavens <*celestial* music from an angelic choir>
syn empyreal, empyrean, heavenly
rel ethereal, supernal, transcendental; otherworldly, unearthly, transmundane; beatific, blessed, elysian, Olympian
con earthly, earthy, mundane, sublunary, worldly; chthonian, hellish, infernal
ant terrestrial, uncelestial

cemetery *n* a piece of land used for burying the dead <the quiet peace of a country *cemetery*>
syn ‖boneyard, ‖boot hill, burial ground, burying ground, God's acre, graveyard, memorial park, necropolis, polyandrium, potter's field
rel churchyard; catacomb
idiom city of the dead

censor *vb* to remove matter considered objectionable by expurgation or alteration <*censor* a movie>
syn blip, bowdlerize, expurgate, screen

rel cut out, excise, exscind; blue-pencil, delete, edit, red-pencil; bleach, clean (up), purge, purify; narrow, restrain, restrict

censorious *adj syn* see CRITICAL 1
rel chiding, reproachful, reproaching; condemnatory, condemning, denouncing, denunciatory, reprehending; accusatory, culpatory
con acclaiming, acclamatory, extolling, laudatory, lauding, praising; adulatory, complimentary, flattering
ant eulogistic

censurable *adj syn* see BLAMEWORTHY
rel improper, incorrect, objectionable, wrong, wrongful; discreditable, doubtful, questionable; inadmissible, unacceptable
con correct, proper, right; acceptable, admissible; creditable
ant uncensurable

censure *vb syn* see CRITICIZE
rel rebuke, reprimand, reproach, reprove; contemn, disdain, scorn, scout, strafe; disallow, disapprove, oppose, reject, stigmatize
con applaud, compliment, recommend; allow, support
ant commend

center *n* 1 a point or part in a surface or solid more or less equidistant from the periphery <the *center* of the earth>
syn core, middle, midpoint, midst
rel inside, interior
con circumference, compass, perimeter, periphery; bounds, confines, limits
2 one eminent in or central to a particular activity, condition, or interest <a *center* of international trade>
syn focal point, focus, heart, hub, nerve center, polestar, seat; *compare* ESSENCE 2
3 a source or point of origin (as of an influence, pressure, or effect) <the group proved a *center* of discontent>
syn core, heart, pith, quick, root
rel activator, dynamo, energizer, stimulant

center *adj* 1 *syn* see MIDDLE 1
2 *syn* see MIDDLE 2

centermost *adj syn* see MIDDLE 1

central *adj* 1 occupying a dominant or supremely important position <the *central* theme of American foreign policy>
syn cardinal, overriding, overruling, pivotal, ruling
rel dominant, paramount, predominant, preponderant; important, significant; outstanding, salient, signal; chief, essential, foremost, leading, main; all-absorbing, controlling, master; focal, key; basic, fundamental, primary, radical
con insignificant, minor, trivial, unimportant; borderline, marginal
ant peripheral
2 *syn* see MIDDLE 2

centralizing *adj syn* see INTEGRATIVE

centripetal *adj syn* see INTEGRATIVE

‖**cep** *prep syn* see EXCEPT

cerate *n syn* see OINTMENT

cerberus *n syn* see CUSTODIAN

cerebral *adj* 1 *syn* see MENTAL 1
2 *syn* see INTELLECTUAL 2

cerebrate *vb syn* see THINK 5

cerebration *n syn* see THOUGHT 1

---

syn synonym(s)	*rel* related word(s)
ant antonym(s)	*con* contrasted word(s)
idiom idiomatic equivalent(s)	
‖ use limited; if in doubt, see a dictionary	

ceremonial *adj* stressing or concerned with careful attention to form and detail <his *ceremonial* approach to everyday life>
  syn ceremonious, conventional, formal, solemn, stately
  rel mannered, studied, stylized; liturgical, ritual, ritualistic; august, courtly, imposing, lofty; fixed, rigid, set, starchy, stiff
  con casual, easy, informal, relaxed; artless, ingenuous, open, sincere

ceremonial *n* 1 *syn* see FORM 2
  2 *syn* see RITE 2

ceremonious *adj syn* see CEREMONIAL
  rel decorous, proper, seemly; impressive, moving, striking; grandiose, imposing, majestic
  ant unceremonious

ceremony *n* 1 *syn* see FORM 2
  2 *syn* see RITE 2

certain *adj* 1 *syn* see FIRM 4
  rel assured, certified, guaranteed, warranted; ensured, insured, sure
  2 constituting an indeterminate and otherwise unidentified part of a group or whole <*certain* students dispute this finding>
  syn some, various
  rel a, an; one; many, numerous; divers, several, sundry
  con no; all
  3 being such beyond a doubt <no *certain* likeness of this saint survives>
  syn accurate, authentic, dependable, reliable
  rel credible, plausible, well-grounded
  con counterfeit, false, spurious; controversial, doubtful, dubious, questionable
  ant uncertain
  4 *syn* see INFALLIBLE 2
  5 *syn* see POSITIVE 3
  rel confirmable, demonstrable, establishable, provable, verifiable; doubtless, trustworthy, unerring
  con controversial, iffy
  ant uncertain
  6 *syn* see INEVITABLE
  rel indefeasible, irrevocable, unalterable, written; fated, predestinated, predetermined
  ant uncertain
  7 *syn* see SURE 5
  rel assured, confident, sanguine
  con hesitant, indecisive, vague, wavering; doubtful, dubious, questionable
  ant uncertain

certainty *n* a state of mind in which one is free from doubt <answered with complete *certainty*>
  syn assurance, assuredness, certitude, confidence, conviction, sureness, surety
  rel belief, credence, faith; absoluteness, definiteness, dogmatism, positiveness, positivism; firmness, staunchness, steadiness
  con doubt, mistrust, skepticism, unsureness; fluctuation, irresolution, shifting, trimming, vacillation, wavering; obscurity, vagueness
  ant uncertainty

certification *n syn* see CREDENTIALS

certify *vb* 1 to testify usually formally and in writing to the truth or genuineness of something <*certify* a student's college transcript>

  syn attest, vouch, witness
  rel assert, aver, avouch, avow, profess
  2 *syn* see WARRANT 2
  3 *syn* see APPROVE 2
  rel authorize, commission, license
  con antagonize, counter, oppose

certitude *n syn* see CERTAINTY
  rel cocksureness
  con uncertainty
  ant doubt

‖**cess** *n syn* see TAX 1

cessation *n syn* see END 2

cesspit *n syn* see SINK 1

cesspool *n syn* see SINK 1

‖**chack** *n syn* see SNACK

chafe *vb* 1 *syn* see ANNOY 1
  2 *syn* see ABRADE 1
  3 to make sore or raw through friction <the high stiff collar *chafed* his neck>
  syn abrade, excoriate, fret, gall, rub
  rel damage, hurt, impair, injure; flay, peel, skin; inflame, irritate; graze, scrape, scratch
  con ease, relieve, soothe

chaff *vb syn* see BANTER 1
  idiom make merry over

chaffer *vb syn* see HAGGLE 2
  rel beg, coax, plead

chafing *adj syn* see IMPATIENT 1

chagrined *adj syn* see ASHAMED
  rel crushed, disconcerted; discomposed, perturbed, upset
  idiom put out of countenance

chain *n* 1 chains *pl syn* see SHACKLE
  2 *syn* see SUCCESSION 2
  3 *syn* see SYNDICATE

chain *adj* 1 *syn* see CUMULATIVE
  2 *syn* see TRITE

chair *vb syn* see PRESIDE

chair car *n syn* see PARLOR CAR

chalk (out) *vb syn* see SKETCH

chalk up *vb syn* see GET 1

challenge *vb* 1 *syn* see DEMAND 1
  2 *syn* see QUESTION 2
  3 *syn* see FACE 3
  rel question; dispute; strive, struggle, try
  idiom throw down the (*or* one's) gage
  con bypass, evade
  4 *syn* see STIR 1

challenge *n* 1 *syn* see DEMUR 2
  2 *syn* see DEFIANCE 1
  rel calling, claiming, demanding, exacting; importuning, insistence

chamber *n* 1 *syn* see ROOM 1
  ‖2 chambers *pl syn* see APARTMENT 1

chamber *vb syn* see HARBOR 1

champ *vb* 1 *syn* see CHEW 1
  rel crush, macerate, mash, smash
  2 *syn* see BITE 1
  rel nibble, nip; gum, mouth, mumble; peck, pick

champaign *n syn* see FIELD

champion *n syn* see EXPONENT

champion *vb syn* see SUPPORT 2
  rel battle, contend, fight (for)
  idiom put in a good word for, stand behind (*or* back of), stand up for
  con condemn, denounce
  ant combat

champion *adj* 1 *syn* see EXCELLENT
  rel distinguished, illustrious, outstanding, splendid

2 *syn* see FIRST 3

chance *n* 1 *syn* see ACCIDENT 1
con certainty, inevitability, necessity; destiny, fate, foreordination, predestination
ant law
2 an unpurposed, unpredictable, and uncontrollable master force <the folly of depending on *chance* for success in life>
syn fortune, hazard, luck
rel advantage, break, fluke; fate, lot; contingency
3 *syn* see OPPORTUNITY
rel likelihood, possibility, probability; outlook, prospect
chance *vb* 1 *syn* see HAPPEN 1
2 *syn* see HAPPEN 2
3 *syn* see GAMBLE 2
4 *syn* see VENTURE 1
idiom put at (or in) hazard
con cherish, protect, safeguard, secure
chance *adj syn* see ACCIDENTAL
rel careless, heedless, offhand
chance child *n syn* see BASTARD 1
chancy *adj* 1 *syn* see UNCERTAIN 1
rel hazardous, risky, speculative, unsound; precarious, ticklish, touchy, tricky
idiom hanging by a thread, on thin ice (or slippery ground)
con safe, secure, sound, stable
2 *syn* see DANGEROUS 1
change *vb* 1 to make or become different <*changed* her will again and again> <our needs *change* as we grow older>
syn alter, modify, mutate, refashion, turn, vary; *compare* TRANSFORM
rel convert, metamorphose, transform, transmute; diversify, variegate; exchange, interchange
idiom go (or pass through) a change
con establish, fix, set
2 *syn* see TRANSFORM
3 *syn* see REVERSE 1
4 *syn* see STERILIZE
5 to make substitution for or among <it's time to *change* the subject>
syn replace, shift
rel exchange, swap, trade; substitute
6 *syn* see EXCHANGE 2
change *n* 1 a making different <saw a gradual *change* of attitude in the community>
syn alteration, modification, mutation, turn, variation
rel aberration, deviation, divergence; diversification; shift; innovation
ant uniformity
2 a result of such change <amazed at the *changes* in the town>
syn innovation, mutation, novelty, permutation, sport, vicissitude
rel conversion, metamorphosis, transformation, transmutation; shift, substitute, surrogate; avatar
changeable *adj* 1 alterable or changing under slight provocation <*changeable* April weather>

syn changeful, fluid, mobile, mutable, protean, unsettled, unstable, unsteady, variable, weathery; *compare* INCONSTANT 1, MUTABLE 2
rel adaptable, impressionable, plastic, pliant; ever-changing, kaleidoscopic; restless, unfixed; inconstant, uncertain, vicissitudinous
con constant, invariable, permanent; certain, fixed, immutable, unalterable, unmodifiable; abiding, enduring, persistent
ant unchangeable; unchanging
2 *syn* see MUTABLE 2
3 *syn* see INCONSTANT 1
changeabout *n syn* see REVERSAL 1
changeful *adj syn* see CHANGEABLE 1
rel active, dynamic, live; lively, vigorous
con durable, lasting, perdurable, stable; steady, uniform
ant changeless, unchanging
changeover *n syn* see CONVERSION 2
channel *n* 1 passage through which a fluid (as water) flows or is led <the river cut a new *channel* to the sea>
syn aqueduct, canal, conduit, course, duct, watercourse
rel pass, passage, way
2 *syn* see MEAN 2
3 *syn* see PIPELINE
channel *vb syn* see CONDUCT 4
chant *vb syn* see SING 1
chaos *n* 1 *syn* see CONFUSION 3
2 *syn* see ANARCHY 1
rel misrule, unruliness
chap *n syn* see MAN 3
chaperon *vb* 1 *syn* see ACCOMPANY
rel guide, overlook, oversee, supervise
2 *syn* see SUPERVISE
chapfallen *adj syn* see DOWNCAST
chaplet *n syn* see WREATH
character *n* 1 an arbitrary or conventional device used in writing or printing <an inscription in runic *characters*>
syn mark, sign, symbol
rel cipher, device, monogram; letter
2 *syn* see CHARACTERISTIC 1
3 *syn* see QUALITY 1
rel distinction, uniqueness, uniquity
4 *syn* see TYPE
5 *syn* see DISPOSITION 3
rel soul, spirit; courage, mettle, resolution; intellect, intelligence, mind
6 *syn* see ROLE 1
7 *syn* see STATUS 1
8 *syn* see NOTABLE 1
9 *syn* see ECCENTRIC
‖10 *syn* see HUMAN
11 *syn* see REPUTATION 2
character assassination *n syn* see DETRACTION
characteristic *adj* being or revealing a quality specific or identifying to an individual or group <her *characteristic* down-to-earth approach to a problem>
syn diacritic, diagnostic, distinctive, idiosyncratic, individual, peculiar, proper
rel especial, particular, special, specific; natural, normal, regular, typical
con general, generic, universal
ant uncharacteristic

characteristic *n* **1** something that marks or sets apart <*characteristics* that distinguish man from lower primates>
syn birthmark, character, feature, point, trait; *compare* QUALITY 1
rel badge, mark, sign, token; flavor, odor, savor, smack, tang; differentia; singularity
2 *syn* see QUALITY 1

characterize *vb* **1** *syn* see SKETCH
2 to be a peculiar or significant quality or feature of something <a man *characterized* by quiet dignity>
syn distinguish, individualize, individuate, mark, qualify, signalize, singularize
rel define, describe, differentiate, identify; peculiarize, personalize
idiom be a feature of

characterless *adj* lacking in character or solid qualities <a drab *characterless* little man that no one ever seemed to notice>
syn namby-pamby, pantywaist, wishy≠washy
rel childish, infantile; sissified, sissy, unmanly; futile, weak; impotent, powerless
con manly, strong, vigorous, virile

charade *n* *syn* see PRETENSE 2

chare *n* *syn* see TASK 1

charge *vb* **1** *syn* see BURDEN
2 *syn* see LOAD 3
3 *syn* see PERMEATE
4 *syn* see ENTRUST 1
5 *syn* see COMMAND
rel ask, request, solicit; adjure
6 *syn* see ACCUSE
rel impugn, reprehend, reproach
idiom bring (*or* prefer) charges
con excuse, forgive, pardon, remit; acquit
ant absolve
7 *syn* see ASCRIBE
8 *syn* see RUSH 1

charge *n* **1** *syn* see LOAD 3
rel business, devoir, place
2 *syn* see OBLIGATION 2
3 *syn* see OVERSIGHT 1
4 *syn* see COMMAND 1
5 *syn* see PRICE 1

chargeless *adj* *syn* see FREE 5

charger *n* *syn* see COURSER

charioteer *vb* *syn* see DRIVE 5

charisma *n* *syn* see CHARM 3

charitable *adj* **1** having or showing interest in or concern for the welfare of others <spent generously for *charitable* aid to the needy>
syn altruistic, benevolent, eleemosynary, good, humane, humanitarian, philanthropic
rel accommodating, helpful, obliging; benign, kindhearted, kindly, sympathetic
2 *syn* see FORBEARING
rel benevolent, considerate, kindly, thoughtful
con cold, harsh, heartless, unfeeling
ant uncharitable

charity *n* **1** *syn* see MERCY
rel affection, attachment, love; altruism, benevolence, humaneness; kindliness; amity, friendliness, goodwill
con malevolence, malignancy, malignity, spite, spleen
ant ill will, malice

2 *syn* see DONATION

charivari *n* *syn* see SHIVAREE

charlatan *n* one who pretends unscrupulously to knowledge or skill <the medical establishment called him a *charlatan*>
syn mountebank, quack, quacksalver, quackster, saltimbanque; *compare* IMPOSTOR
rel bluff, four-flusher, sham

Charlie McCarthy *n* *syn* see STOOGE 1

charm *n* **1** *syn* see SPELL
2 an object worn or cherished to ward off evil or attract good fortune <the American Indian medicine bag is essentially a *charm*>
syn amulet, fetish, juju, luck, mascot, periapt, phylactery, talisman, zemi
3 a quality or combination of qualities that is wholly attractive and irresistible <the *charm* of her smile>
syn allure, appeal, charisma, fascination, glamour, magnetism, witchcraft, witchery
rel allurement, attraction, attractiveness, lure; agreeableness, delightfulness, gratefulness
con hatefulness, obnoxiousness, odiousness, repulsiveness; distastefulness, unpleasantness

charm *vb* **1** *syn* see ATTRACT 1
2 *syn* see BEWITCH 1

charmed *adj* *syn* see ENAMORED 3

charmer *n* *syn* see MAGICIAN 1

charming *adj* *syn* see ATTRACTIVE 1
ant charmless

chart *n* **1** a stylized or symbolic depiction of something incapable of direct verbal or pictorial representation (as because of complexity or abstractness) <a *chart* of anticipated economic progress>
syn graph, map
rel plan, plat, plot, scheme
2 *syn* see TABLE 2

chart *vb* *syn* see PLAN 2

charter *n* *syn* see DEED 3

charter *vb* *syn* see HIRE 1

chary *adj* **1** *syn* see CAUTIOUS
rel disinclined, hesitant, loath, reluctant; economical, frugal, sparing, thrifty; constrained, inhibited, restrained
2 *syn* see SPARING

chase *vb* **1** *syn* see FOLLOW 2
con flee, fly
2 *syn* see HUNT 1
3 *syn* see EJECT 1
4 *syn* see RUSH 1
5 *syn* see COURSE

chase *n* *syn* see HUNTING
2 *syn* see GAME 3

chaser *n* *syn* see WOLF

chasm *n* **1** *syn* see GULF 2
2 *syn* see RAVINE
3 *syn* see OMISSION
4 *syn* see SCHISM 3

chasmal *adj* *syn* see CAVERNOUS 1

chaste *adj* free from every trace of the lewd or salacious <was as *chaste* in language as in conduct>
syn clean, decent, immaculate, modest, pure, spotless, stainless, unblemished, undefiled, unsullied

rel ethical, moral, righteous, virtuous; maidenly, virgin, virginal; becoming, decorous, proper, seemly; abstinent, continent
con coarse, gross, obscene, ribald, vulgar; lascivious, lecherous, licentious, lustful; gluttonous, incontinent, self-indulgent
ant unchaste

chasten *vb syn* see PUNISH 1
rel abase, humble, humiliate; afflict, try
con baby, humor, indulge, spoil
ant pamper

chastise *vb syn* see PUNISH 1
rel baste, beat, belabor, pummel, thrash

chastisement *n syn* see PUNISHMENT

chat *vb* **1** to emit a ready flow of inconsequential talk <*chats* on the phone for hours>
syn babble, burble, cackle, chatter, chin‐chin, clack, clatter, ‖dish, dither, gab, gabble, ‖gas, jaw, ‖natter, patter, prate, prattle, rattle, run on, smatter, talk, tinkle, twaddle, twiddle, twitter, yak, yakety-yak, yammer, yatter; *compare* CONVERSE
rel yap; blab, gossip; gush, lallygag; confabulate
idiom beat one's gums, ‖chew the fat (*or* rag), ‖shoot (*or* bat) the breeze, ‖shoot (*or* sling) the bull
con discourse, expound; declaim, harangue, hold forth, orate, preach
2 *syn* see CONVERSE

chat *n* **1** *syn* see CHATTER
2 an informal conversation <had a satisfactory little *chat* with the new assistant>
syn causerie, chin, prose, rap, talk, yarn; *compare* CONVERSATION 2
rel gossip, tête-à-tête
idiom bull session, rap session
con debate, deliberation, discussion
3 *syn* see CONVERSATION 1

chateau *n syn* see MANSION

chattel *n* **1** chattels *pl syn* see POSSESSION 2
2 *syn* see SLAVE 1

chatter *vb* **1** *syn* see GIBBER
2 *syn* see CHAT 1

chatter *n* idle and often loud and incessant talk <schoolgirl *chatter*>
syn babble, bibble-babble, blab, blabber, ‖blatter, brabble, cackle, chat, chin-chin, chin music, chitchat, chitter-chatter, clack, gab, gabble, gibble-gabble, jabber, palaver, prate, prattle, stultiloquence, talkee-talkee, tittle-tattle, yak, yakety-yak, yak-yak, yatter
rel ‖bull, gossip, small talk
idiom tongue wagging

chatterbox *n* one who engages in chatter <that old *chatterbox* will talk your arm off>
syn bandar-log, blabber, blabbermouth, blabmouth, chatterer, chewet, gabber, jabberer, magpie, prater, prattler
rel busybody, gossip, newsmonger, quidnunc, scandalmonger, tabby, tattletale

chatterer *n syn* see CHATTERBOX

chatty *adj syn* see TALKATIVE

‖**chaw** *vb* **1** *syn* see CHEW 1
2 *syn* see PONDER 2

---

chawbacon *n syn* see RUSTIC

cheap *adj* **1** costing little <produce is usually *cheaper* in summer>
syn inexpensive, low, low-cost, low-priced, popular, reasonable, uncostly, undear
rel bargain-basement, bargain-counter, cut‐rate, reduced; dirt-cheap
con dear, high, high-priced
ant costly, expensive
2 of inferior quality <*cheap* furniture is never a bargain>
syn base, cheesy, common, mean, ‖ornery, paltry, poor, rubbishing, rubbishly, rubbishy, shoddy, sleazy, tatty, trashy, trumpery; *compare* INFERIOR 2
rel cheap-jack, valueless, worthless; flashy, garish, meretricious, tawdry; brummagem, fake, phony, sham; bad, rotten, terrible
con capital, excellent, fine, good; first-class, first-rate, high-class, high-grade, superior, tip-top, top-notch
ant precious
3 *syn* see CONTEMPTIBLE
rel wrong; base, low, vile; measly, petty, trifling
ant noble
4 *syn* see STINGY

cheapen *vb syn* see DEPRECIATE 1

cheap–jack (*or* cheap-john) *n syn* see PEDDLER

cheapskate *n syn* see MISER

cheat *n* **1** *syn* see DECEPTION 1
2 *syn* see IMPOSTURE
rel bamboozlement, cozening, hoaxing; chicane, chicanery, trickery
3 *syn* see SWINDLER

cheat *vb* to obtain something (as money) from or an advantage over by dishonesty and trickery <*cheated* out of his inheritance by a grasping lawyer>
syn beat, bilk, boodle, ‖burn, chisel, chouse, cozen, ‖crook, defraud, diddle, do, ‖doodle, ‖dry-shave, ‖duff, flimflam, gyp, ‖mace, ‖mump, overreach, ream, ‖screw, sucker, swindle, take; *compare* EXTORT 1, FLEECE 1
rel befool, dupe, fool, gull, slick; bunco, con, fudge, short; beguile, deceive, delude, double-cross, mislead

cheater *n syn* see SWINDLER

check *vb* **1** *syn* see ARREST 1
rel cease, desist, discontinue, stop; repress, suppress; circumvent, foil, frustrate, thwart
ant expedite
2 *syn* see RESTRAIN 1
rel baffle, balk; obviate, preclude, prevent
ant accelerate (*of speed*); advance (*as of hopes, plans*); release (*of feelings, energies*)
3 *syn* see TRY 1
4 *syn* see AGREE 4

check *n* **1** *syn* see SETBACK
2 a statement of charges for food and drink consumed (as at a restaurant) <shocked at the size of the *check*>
syn bill, tab
rel damage, score

check out *vb* ‖**1** *syn* see DIE 1
2 *syn* see AGREE 4

check over *vb syn* see SCRUTINIZE 1

check–over *n syn* see EXAMINATION

check up *vb syn* see SCRUTINIZE 1

---

checkup *n syn* see EXAMINATION

cheek *n* 1 **cheeks** *pl syn* see BUTTOCKS
  2 *syn* see EFFRONTERY

cheeky *adj syn* see WISE 5

cheep *vb syn* see CHIRP

cheer *vb* 1 *syn* see COMFORT
  2 *syn* see ENCOURAGE 1
  3 *syn* see APPLAUD 2

cheerful *adj* 1 marked by or suggestive of lighthearted ease of mind and spirit <a *cheerful* smile>
  syn blithe, cheery, ‖chirk, chirpy, chirrupy, lightsome, sunbeamy, sunny; *compare* LIVELY 1
  rel airy, carefree, debonair, jaunty; animated, gay, lighthearted, lively, vivacious; buoyant, corky
  idiom in good (*or* high) spirits, of good cheer
  con blue, dejected, depressed, melancholy; dispirited, heavyhearted, joyless, mournful, sorrowful, woeful; dour, morose, saturnine, sullen; doleful, lugubrious; austere, forbidding, grim, stern
  ant gloomy, glum
  2 *syn* see GLAD 2
  ant cheerless

‖**cheerio** *interj syn* see GOOD-BYE

cheerless *adj syn* see GLOOMY 3
  rel dejecting
  ant cheerful

cheery *adj* 1 *syn* see GLAD 2
  2 *syn* see CHEERFUL 1

cheeseparer *n syn* see MISER

cheeseparing *adj syn* see STINGY
  rel cheap, grudging, mean, shabby; illiberal

cheesy *adj syn* see CHEAP 2

chef d'oeuvre *n* 1 *syn* see MASTERPIECE 1
  2 *syn* see SHOWPIECE

‖**chemist** *n syn* see DRUGGIST

cherish *vb* 1 *syn* see NURSE 2
  rel conserve, preserve, save; entertain, harbor, keep, shelter; defend, guard, safeguard, shield
  con reject, repudiate, scorn
  ant abandon
  2 *syn* see APPRECIATE 1
  rel revere, reverence, venerate
  idiom hold in high esteem
  con disregard, forget, ignore, overlook, slight
  ant neglect
  3 *syn* see ADMIRE 1

‖**cherry** *n syn* see VIRGINITY

chest *n syn* see TREASURY 2

chesty *adj syn* see BUXOM

chew *vb* 1 to crush or grind with the teeth <*chew* your food well>
  syn champ, ‖chaw, chomp, ‖chonk, chumble, chump, crunch, masticate, munch, ruminate, scrunch
  rel bite; gnaw, nibble; consume, devour, eat; gum, mumble
  ‖2 *syn* see SCOLD 1

chewet *n syn* see CHATTERBOX

‖**chew out** *vb syn* see SCOLD 1

chiaus *n syn* see SWINDLER

chic *n syn* see FASHION 3

chic *adj syn* see STYLISH

chicane *vb* 1 *syn* see QUIBBLE 1

  2 *syn* see DUPE

chicane *n syn* see DECEPTION 1
  rel artifice, feint, gambit, maneuver, ploy, ruse, stratagem, trick, wile; furtiveness, surreptitiousness, underhandedness
  con forthrightness, straightforwardness

chicanery *n syn* see DECEPTION 1
  rel intrigue, machination, plot; furtiveness, surreptitiousness, underhandedness
  con forthrightness, straightforwardness; honesty, honor, integrity, probity

chichi *adj* 1 *syn* see SHOWY
  2 *syn* see PRECIOUS 4

chick *n* 1 *syn* see CHILD 1
  ‖2 *syn* see GIRL FRIEND 1

chickabiddy *n syn* see CHILD 1

chicken *n syn* see COWARD

‖**chicken** *adj syn* see COWARDLY

chide *vb syn* see REPROVE
  rel berate, rate, scold, upbraid
  con applaud, compliment; approve, endorse, sanction
  ant commend

chiding *n syn* see REBUKE

chief *n* 1 *syn* see LEADER 2
  rel dictator, duce, führer
  2 *syn* see NOTABLE 1

chief *adj* 1 *syn* see FIRST 3
  2 standing apart by reason of superior importance, significance, or influence <his *chief* claim to consideration is his unquestionable uprightness>
  syn capital, ‖cock, dominant, main, major, number one, outstanding, predominant, preeminent, principal, star, stellar
  rel primal, primary, prime; important, prominent, significant, consequential, momentous, weighty; effective, potent, telling; controlling, master, ruling
  con inconsequential, minor, trivial, unimportant; collateral, contingent, secondary

chiefly *adv syn* see GENERALLY 1

chieftain *n syn* see LEADER 2

chiffer *n syn* see NUMBER

child *n* 1 a young person <a movie for both *children* and adults>
  syn bud, chick, chickabiddy, chit, juvenile, kid, moppet, ‖nipper, puss, youngling, young one, youngster, youth
  rel minor; adolescent, teenager, teener, teenybopper; brat, bratling, dickens, runabout; cherub, innocent, lamb, sweeting
  idiom a slip of a boy (*or* girl), small fry, young hopeful
  ant adult, grown-up
  2 **children** *pl syn* see OFFSPRING

childbearing *n* 1 *syn* see BIRTH 1
  2 *syn* see LABOR 2

childbed *n syn* see CONFINEMENT 2

childbirth *n* 1 *syn* see BIRTH 1
  2 *syn* see LABOR 2

childing *adj* 1 *syn* see PREGNANT 1
  2 *syn* see FERTILE

childish *adj* significantly deficient in maturity <a *childish* and spiteful attitude>
  syn babyish, immature, infantile, infantine, prekindergarten, puerile
  rel asinine, fatuous, foolish, silly, simple; naive, unsophisticated; arrested, backward, moronic, retarded, slow, ‖wanting

ant adult

child's play *n syn* see SNAP 1

chill *vb syn* see DISCOURAGE 1

chill *adj* **1** *syn* see COLD 1
2 *syn* see COLD 2
rel distant, formal, reserved, solitary, stand-offish, uncompanionable, withdrawn; abstracted, disinterested, uninterested
con easy, gregarious, informal; sociable

chiller *n syn* see THRILLER

chillsome *adj syn* see COLD 1

chilly *adj syn* see COLD 1

chime *n syn* see HARMONY 2

chime *vb syn* see RING

chime in *vb* **1** *syn* see INTERRUPT 2
2 *syn* see SAY 1

chimera *n syn* see PIPE DREAM

chimerical *adj syn* see FICTITIOUS 1
rel ambitious, pretentious, utopian; deceptive, delusive, delusory; fabulous, mythical; absurd, preposterous
con believable, plausible, rational, reasonable; possible, practicable
ant feasible

chiming *adj syn* see HARMONIOUS 1

chin *n syn* see CHAT 2

chin *vb syn* see CONVERSE

chin–chin *vb syn* see CHAT 2

chin–chin *n syn* see CHATTER

‖**chinchy** *adj syn* see STINGY

chine *n syn* see RIDGE 1

Chinese puzzle *n syn* see MYSTERY

Chinese wall *n syn* see OBSTACLE

chink *n syn* see CRACK 3
rel interruption

chink *vb syn* see JINGLE

‖**chink** *n syn* see MONEY

‖**chinkle** *vb syn* see JINGLE

‖**chin music** *n syn* see CHATTER

chintzy *adj* **1** *syn* see GAUDY
2 *syn* see STINGY

chin–up *adj syn* see BRAVE 1

chip *vb syn* see CHIRP

chip in *vb* **1** *syn* see CONTRIBUTE 1
2 *syn* see INTERRUPT 2

chipper *vb syn* see CHIRP

chipper *adj* **1** *syn* see LIVELY 1
2 *syn* see NEAT 2

‖**chippy** *n syn* see DOXY 1

chips *n pl syn* see MONEY

‖**chirk** *adj* **1** *syn* see LIVELY 1
2 *syn* see CHEERFUL 1

chirk (up) *vb syn* see ENCOURAGE 1

‖**chirm** *n syn* see DIN

‖**chirm** *vb syn* see CHIRP

chirography *n syn* see HANDWRITING

chirp *vb* to make a short, sharp, and usually repeating sound <sparrows *chirping* on the lawn>
syn cheep, chip, chipper, ‖chirm, chirrup, clutter, peep, tweedle, tweet, twitter

chirpy *adj syn* see CHEERFUL 1

chirrup *vb syn* see CHIRP

chirrupy *adj syn* see CHEERFUL 1

chisel *vb* **1** *syn* see SCULPTURE

2 *syn* see CHEAT

chisel (in) *vb syn* see INTRUDE 1

‖**chiselly** *adj syn* see BAD 8

chit *n syn* see CHILD 1

chit *n syn* see NOTE 2

chitchat *n* **1** *syn* see CHATTER
2 *syn* see SMALL TALK

chitter *vb syn* see CHIRP

chitter–chatter *n* **1** *syn* see CHATTER
2 *syn* see SMALL TALK

chivalrous *adj syn* see GENEROUS 1
rel knightly, manly, noble
con churlish common, low

chivy *vb* **1** *syn* see FOLLOW 2
2 *syn* see BAIT 2
rel afflict, torment, try; chase, pursue, trail

choate *adj syn* see WHOLE 3

chockablock *adj syn* see FULL 1

chock–full *adj syn* see FULL 1

choice *n* **1** the act, right, opportunity, or faculty of choosing or deciding <the *choice* lies with the electorate>
syn alternative, ‖druthers, election, option, preference, selection
rel decision, determination, finding, judgment, verdict; appraisal, evaluation, rating
2 *syn* see BEST

choice *adj* having qualities that appeal to a fine or highly refined taste <a few *choice* spirits gathered nightly to discuss the day's events>
syn dainty, delicate, elegant, exquisite, rare, recherché, select, superior
rel incomparable, peerless, preeminent, prime, superlative, supreme, surpassing, transcendent, unsurpassed; chosen, culled, picked, selected
con common, ordinary; average, fair, mediocre, medium, middling, run-of-the-mill, second-rate; drab, dull, lackluster, lusterless
ant indifferent

‖**choicy** *adj syn* see NICE 1

choke *vb* **1** to check normal breathing especially by compressing or obstructing the windpipe <*choked* by a bone in the throat>
syn strangle, throttle; *compare* SUFFOCATE
2 *syn* see SUFFOCATE
3 *syn* see FILL 1
4 *syn* see LOAD 3

choke (off) *vb syn* see SILENCE

‖**chokey** *n syn* see JAIL

choking *n syn* see REPRESSION 1

choleric *adj* **1** *syn* see IRASCIBLE
rel acrimonious, angry, fiery, indignant, irate, mad, spunky, wrathful, wroth; captious, carping, faultfinding
con calm, serene, tranquil; composed, cool, nonchalant
ant placid
2 *syn* see ANGRY

chomp *vb* **1** *syn* see CHEW 1
2 *syn* see BITE 2

‖**chonk** *vb syn* see CHEW 1

choose *vb* **1** to fix upon one among alternatives as the one to be taken, accepted, or adopted <*chose* the largest apple but found it sour>
syn cull, elect, mark, opt (for), optate, pick, pick out, prefer, select, single (out), take
rel adopt, embrace, espouse; crave, desire, love, want, wish

---

con decline, refuse, repudiate, spurn; abnegate, forbear, forgo
ant reject; eschew
2 *syn* see WILL
rel favor, prefer
‖3 *syn* see DESIRE 1

choosy *adj syn* see NICE 1
chop *vb* 1 *syn* see FELL 2
2 to cut into fragments by repeated strokes
<*chop* meat and onions for hash>
syn hash, mince
rel cut up, dice, fragment
idiom cut to bits, make mincemeat of
chop *n syn* see CUFF
chop–chop *adv syn* see FAST 2
chore *n* 1 *syn* see TASK 1
2 *syn* see TASK 2
rel trial, tribulation
chortle *vb syn* see LAUGH
chorus *n syn* see HARMONY 1
chosen *adj syn* see SELECT 1
chouse *n syn* see TRICK 1
chouse *vb syn* see CHEAT
‖**chow** ‖1 *syn* see FOOD 1
2 *syn* see MEAL
chowchow *adj syn* see MISCELLANEOUS
chowchow *n syn* see MISCELLANY 1
chowderhead *n syn* see DUNCE
chrism *n syn* see OINTMENT
christcross–row *n syn* see ALPHABET 1
christen *vb* 1 *syn* see BAPTIZE
2 *syn* see NAME 1
Christian *adj syn* see DECOROUS 1
Christian name *n syn* see GIVEN NAME
Christmas *n* a festival or holiday commemorating the birth of Christ <gave presents on *Christmas*>
syn Nativity, noel, Xmas, yule, yuletide
chronic *adj* 1 *syn* see HABITUAL 2
2 *syn* see USUAL 1
chronicle *n* 1 *syn* see HISTORY 2
2 *syn* see ACCOUNT 7
rel narration, recital, recountal
chthonian *adj syn* see INFERNAL 1
chthonic *adj syn* see INFERNAL 1
chubby *adj syn* see ROTUND 2
ant slim
chuck *vb* 1 *syn* see DISCARD
2 *syn* see EJECT 1
3 *syn* see ABANDON 1
4 *syn* see THROW 1
‖**chuck** *n syn* see HARBOR 3
chucker *n syn* see BOUNCER 2
‖**chucker–out** *n syn* see BOUNCER 2
chuckhole *n syn* see POTHOLE
chuckle *vb syn* see LAUGH
chucklehead *n syn* see DUNCE
chuckleheaded *adj syn* see STUPID 1
chuff *n* 1 *syn* see BOOR
2 *syn* see MISER
‖**chuff** *adj syn* see SULLEN
‖**chuffy** *adj syn* see STOCKY
‖**chuffy** *adj syn* see SULLEN
chum *n syn* see ASSOCIATE 3
chumble *vb syn* see CHEW 1
chummy *adj* 1 *syn* see FAMILIAR 1
2 *syn* see INTIMATE 4
chump *n* ‖1 *syn* see HEAD 1
2 *syn* see DUNCE
3 *syn* see FOOL 3

chump *vb syn* see CHEW 1
‖**chumpy** *adj syn* see STOCKY
chunk *n syn* see LUMP 1
chunky *adj syn* see STOCKY
rel chubby, rotund
‖**chunter** *vb syn* see MUMBLE
church *n* 1 *syn* see HOUSE OF WORSHIP
2 *syn* see RELIGION 2
church *adj syn* see ECCLESIASTICAL
churchly *adj syn* see ECCLESIASTICAL
churchman *n syn* see CLERGYMAN
churchmanly *adj syn* see ECCLESIASTICAL
churl *n syn* see BOOR
ant aristocrat, gentleman
churlish *adj syn* see BOORISH
rel crude, discourteous; blunt, brusque, crusty, curt, gruff; dour, surly; naive, unschooled
con bland, politic, smooth; polished, sophisticated
ant courtly
churn *vb syn* see SEETHE 4
chute *n syn* see WATERFALL
chutzpah *n syn* see EFFRONTERY
cicatrix *n syn* see SCAR
cicatrize *vb syn* see SCAR
‖**cig** *n syn* see CIGARETTE
cigarette *n* a paper-wrapped tube of finely cut smoking tobacco <dependence on *cigarettes*>
syn ‖butt, ‖cig, ‖coffin nail, fag, ‖gasper, ‖pill, ‖skag, smoke
cimmerian *adj syn* see INFERNAL 2
cinch *n syn* see SNAP 1
cinch *vb syn* see ENSURE
cincture *n syn* see BELT 1
cincture *vb syn* see BELT 1
cinders *n pl syn* see ASH
cine *n syn* see MOVIE
‖**cinema** *n syn* see MOVIE
cipher *n* 1 *syn* see ZERO 1
2 *syn* see NUMBER
3 *syn* see MONOGRAM
4 *syn* see NONENTITY
cipher *vb* 1 *syn* see CALCULATE
‖2 *syn* see SOLVE 2
ciphering *n syn* see COMPUTATION
circa *prep syn* see ABOUT 1
Circean *adj syn* see ENTICING
circle *n* 1 *syn* see RANGE 2
2 *syn* see CYCLE 1
3 *syn* see SET 5
rel acquaintance; cronies, friends, intimates; associates, companions, comrades
4 *syn* see CLIQUE
circle *vb* 1 *syn* see SURROUND 1
2 *syn* see TURN 1
circuit *n* 1 *syn* see CIRCUMFERENCE
rel course, route, way; journey, tour, travels, trip
2 *syn* see REVOLUTION 1
3 *syn* see TOUR 2
4 *syn* see LEAGUE 4
circuitous *adj syn* see INDIRECT 1
ant straight
circuitously *adv syn* see ABOUT 1
circular *adj* 1 *syn* see ROUND 1
2 *syn* see INDIRECT 1
circulate *vb* 1 *syn* see SPREAD 1
rel exchange, interchange; flow; revolve, rotate

2 *syn* see MOBILIZE 1

circulation *n syn* see REVOLUTION 1

circulator *n syn* see GOSSIP 1

circumambages *n pl syn* see VERBIAGE 1

circumambulate *vb syn* see WANDER 1

circumbendibus *n syn* see VERBIAGE 1

circumduct *vb syn* see TURN 1

2 *syn* see ABOLISH 1

circumference *n* a continuous line or course about an area <strolled along the *circumference* of the reservoir>
  syn ambit, circuit, compass, perimeter, periphery; *compare* BORDER 1
  rel boundary, bounds, confines, limits; border, margin, rim

circumlocution *n syn* see VERBIAGE 1
  con conciseness, concision, pithiness, succinctness, terseness; compactness

circumnavigate *vb syn* see SKIRT 2

circumscribe *vb syn* see LIMIT 2
  rel fetter, hamper, trammel
  con amplify, distend, inflate, swell; enlarge
  ant dilate, expand

circumscribed *adj syn* see DEFINITE 1
  rel bound, bounded, finite; confined, cramped, strait

circumscription *n* 1 *syn* see RESTRICTION 1

2 *syn* see RESTRICTION 2

circumspect *adj syn* see CAUTIOUS
  rel meticulous, punctilious, scrupulous
  con adventurous, daredevil, foolhardy; careless, heedless; bold
  ant audacious

circumstance *n* 1 *syn* see OCCURRENCE
  rel detail, item, particular; component, constituent, element, factor

2 *syn* see FATE

circumstantial *adj* marked by careful attention to relevant details <gave a *circumstantial* account of his adventure>
  syn blow-by-blow, clocklike, detailed, full, itemized, minute, particular, particularized, thorough
  rel accurate, exact, nice, precise; complete, replete; close, strict
  con compendious, concise, laconic, pithy, short, succinct, terse; abbreviated, curtailed, cut, pruned, shortened, trimmed
  ant abridged; summary

circumvent *vb* 1 *syn* see FRUSTRATE 1
  rel befool, dupe, hoodwink, trick; avoid, elude, escape, evade
  ant conform (*to laws, orders*); cooperate (*with persons*)

2 *syn* see SKIRT 2

3 *syn* see SKIRT 3

circumvolution *n syn* see REVOLUTION 1

cit *n syn* see TOWNSMAN

citadel *n syn* see FORT

citation *n syn* see ENCOMIUM
  rel award, guerdon, reward

cite *vb* 1 *syn* see REMEMBER

2 *syn* see MENTION

3 *syn* see ADDUCE

  rel count, enumerate, number, tell

citizen *n* 1 *syn* see TOWNSMAN
  2 a person regarded as a member of a sovereign state, entitled to its protection, and subject to its laws <the subtle bond between the *citizen* and the nation>
  syn national, subject
  con foreigner, stranger
  ant alien

city *adj syn* see URBAN

civic *adj syn* see PUBLIC 1

civil *adj* 1 *syn* see PUBLIC 1
  2 adequate in courtesy <made a *civil* inquiry about their health>
  syn courteous, genteel, mannerly, polite, well-mannered; *compare* COURTLY
  rel cultivated, refined, well-bred; accommodating, affable, cordial, obliging; bland, diplomatic, gracious, politic, suave, urbane
  con boorish, churlish, loutish, uncouth; discourteous, ill-mannered, impolite, ungracious
  ant uncivil; rude

civilities *n pl syn* see MANNER 5

civilized *adj* 1 *syn* see DECOROUS 1

2 *syn* see SUAVE

Civitas Dei *n syn* see HEAVEN 2

‖**clabber** *vb syn* see CURDLE

clack *vb* 1 *syn* see CHAT 1

2 *syn* see RATTLE 1

clack *n* 1 *syn* see CHATTER

2 *syn* see GOSSIP 1

clad *vb* 1 *syn* see CLOTHE

2 *syn* see SHEATHE

‖**claggy** *adj* 1 *syn* see STICKY 1

‖ *syn* see MUDDY 1

claim *vb* 1 *syn* see DEMAND 1
  rel adduce, advance, allege; assert, defend, justify, maintain, vindicate
  con abnegate, forgo; refuse, reject, repudiate; disavow, disown
  ant disclaim; renounce

2 *syn* see MAINTAIN 2

claim *n* 1 a real or assumed right to demand something as one's own or one's due <his genial wit was his greatest *claim* to fame>
  syn ‖dibs, pretense, pretension, title
  rel birthright, prerogative, privilege, right; affirmation, assertion, declaration, protestation

2 *syn* see INTEREST 1

clamant *adj syn* see PRESSING

clamber *vb syn* see SCRAMBLE 1

clamor *n* 1 *syn* see COMMOTION 4

2 *syn* see DIN

3 *syn* see COMMOTION 1

clamor *vb syn* see ROAR
  rel claim, demand; agitate, debate, dispute
  idiom make the welkin ring, raise the roof

clamorous *adj* 1 *syn* see VOCIFEROUS
  rel articulate, eloquent, vocal, voluble; adjuring, begging, imploring, importunate
  ant taciturn

2 *syn* see PRESSING

clamp *n syn* see HOLD

clampdown *n syn* see REPRESSION 2

clan *n* 1 *syn* see FAMILY 1

2 *syn* see CLIQUE

clandestine *adj syn* see SECRET 1
  rel illegitimate, illicit; artful, foxy, sly

---

syn synonym(s)   *rel* related word(s)
ant antonym(s)   *con* contrasted word(s)
idiom idiomatic equivalent(s)
‖ use limited; if in doubt, see a dictionary

con aboveboard, forthright, straightforward
clandestinely *adv syn* see SECRETLY
||**clanger** *n syn* see ERROR 2
clangorous *adj syn* see NOISY
clap *n syn* see BANG 2
||**clapped–out** *adj* 1 *syn* see EFFETE 2
  2 *syn* see TIRED 1
claptrap *n syn* see NONSENSE 2
claret *n syn* see BLOOD 1
clarify *vb* 1 *syn* see PURIFY 1
  2 to make clear and understandable <felt a need to *clarify* his position on the question>
  syn clear, clear up, elucidate, explain, illuminate, illustrate; *compare* EXPLAIN 1
  rel settle, straighten out; define, delineate, formulate; analyze, break down, simplify
  idiom make plain
  con befog, cloud, obfuscate, obscure; confuse, foul up, muddle, ||snafu
clarion *adj syn* see FAIR 2
clarity *n* notable precision of thought or expression <*clarity* of expression depends on use of exactly the right words in precisely the right way>
  syn clearness, limpidity, lucidity, perspicuity, plainness
  rel articulateness, articulation; care, exactitude, fussiness, meticulousness, nicety, precision; accuracy, correctitude, propriety
  con haziness, imprecision, indefiniteness, unclearness, vagueness; inexactness, laxity, looseness, sloppiness, slovenliness
  ant obscurity
||**clarty** *adj* 1 *syn* see MUDDY 1
  2 *syn* see STICKY 1
clash *vb* 1 *syn* see BUMP 1
  2 to be markedly out of harmony <garish colors that *clashed* almost painfully>
  syn conflict, disaccord, discord, disharmonize, jangle, jar, mismatch
  rel fret, gall, grate, try
  idiom swear at one another
  con accord, blend, conform, correspond; fit, meet, suit
  ant harmonize
clash *n* 1 *syn* see IMPACT 1
  2 a sharp and usually brief conflict especially between military units <recurrent border *clashes*>
  syn affray, brush, fray, melee, mellay, scrimmage, skirmish
  rel brawl, broil, fracas, riot, row, rumpus, scrap, set-to; action, battle, conflict, engagement; embroilment, encounter
  idiom clash of arms, passage at (or of) arms
clashing *adj syn* see ANTIPATHETIC 1
clasp *n syn* see HOLD
clasp *vb* 1 *syn* see EMBRACE 1
  2 *syn* see TAKE 4
class *n* 1 a unit or a subunit of a larger whole made up of members sharing one or more characteristics <miniaturization of circuitry made possible a whole new *class* of small computers and calculators>
  syn category, grade, group, grouping, league, pigeonhole, tier
  rel brand, color, description, feather, genre, grain, ilk, kidney, kind, nature, order, sort, stamp, style, type; bracket, branch, denomi-

nation, division, head, section; genus, species
  2 *syn* see QUALITY 3
  3 *syn* see TYPE
class *vb* 1 *syn* see ASSORT
  2 to put into an appropriate class <he is generally *classed* among our leading theoretical physicists>
  syn classify, evaluate, grade, rank, rate
  rel appraise, gauge, judge; divide, part, separate; allot, assign; account, assess, consider, hold, reckon, regard; mark, score
classic *adj* 1 *syn* see EXCELLENT
  2 *syn* see VINTAGE 1
  3 *syn* see TYPICAL 1
classic *n syn* see MASTERPIECE 1
classical *adj* 1 *syn* see EXCELLENT
  2 *syn* see VINTAGE 1
  3 *syn* see TYPICAL 1
classify *vb* 1 *syn* see ASSORT
  2 *syn* see CLASS 2
||**classy** *adj syn* see STYLISH
clatter *vb* 1 *syn* see RATTLE 1
  2 *syn* see CHAT 1
clatter *n syn* see COMMOTION 4
clattery *adj syn* see NOISY
claviger *n syn* see CUSTODIAN
||**clawback** *n syn* see SYCOPHANT
clean *adj* 1 free from dirt <kept a *clean* house in a dirty neighborhood>
  syn cleanly, immaculate, spotless, taintless, unsoiled, unsullied
  rel bright, shining, sparkling; fresh, pure, untainted, wholesome
  idiom clean as a whistle (or new penny)
  con dingy, grimy, grubby, messy, mussy, slovenly; filthy, foul, noisome
  ant dirty, unclean
  2 *syn* see INNOCENT 2
  3 *syn* see CHASTE
  ant unclean
  4 *syn* see FAIR 5
clean *vb* 1 *syn* see PURIFY 1
  2 to make clean <*cleaned* his car every week>
  syn cleanse, clean up
  rel do, neaten, order, police, spruce, straighten (up), tidy, trim; brighten, freshen, furbish, recondition; renew, renovate
  idiom make spick-and-span
  con begrime, daub, dirty, sully; besmirch, defile, foul, pollute
  ant soil
  3 *syn* see DRESS 3
clean–cut *adj syn* see EXPLICIT
clean–limbed *adj syn* see SHAPELY
cleanly *adj syn* see CLEAN 1
  rel neat, orderly, spick-and-span, tidy, trim; dainty, fastidious, fussy, nice
  con disheveled, disorderly, slipshod, sloppy, slovenly, unkempt
  ant uncleanly
cleanse *vb* 1 *syn* see CLEAN 2
  rel disinfect, sanitize, sterilize
  2 *syn* see PURIFY 1
  3 *syn* see PURIFY 2
cleansing *n syn* see PURIFICATION
clean up *vb* 1 *syn* see CLEAR 6
  2 *syn* see CLEAN 2
  3 *syn* see SETTLE 7

‖**clean up** (on) *vb syn* see WHIP 2

clear *adj* 1 *syn* see FAIR 2
2 *syn* see TRANSPARENT 1
3 *syn* see TRANSLUCENT 3
rel milky, opalescent
4 free from obscurity or ambiguity <his account of the accident was perfectly *clear*>
syn clear-cut, crystal, lucent, lucid, luculent, luminous, pellucid, perspicuous, translucent, transparent, transpicuous, unambiguous, unblurred; *compare* UNDERSTANDABLE
rel apprehensible, comprehensible, graspable, knowable, understandable; plain, simple, straightforward, uncomplicated, unperplexed; defined, definite
idiom clear as day (*or* crystal), plain as the nose on one's face
con clouded, dark, mysterious, unclear; hazy, ill-defined, vague
ant obscure
5 readily perceived or apprehended <a *clear* case of embezzlement>
syn apparent, conspicuous, distinct, evident, manifest, obvious, open-and-shut, openhanded, palpable, patent, plain, straightforward, unambiguous, unequivocal, univocal, unmistakable; *compare* SELF-EXPLANATORY, UNDERSTANDABLE
rel appreciable, perceptible, recognizable, sensible, tangible; overt, public, published, unhidden, unobscured; exact, precise
con dim, dusky, gloomy, murky; cryptic, dark, enigmatical, equivocal, indistinct, vague; arcane, esoteric, mysterious, occult
ant obscure
6 *syn* see EMPTY 1

clear *adv syn* see WELL 3

clear *vb* 1 *syn* see EXCULPATE
2 *syn* see CLARIFY 2
3 *syn* see VACATE 2
4 *syn* see RID
rel eliminate, rule out; clean, cleanse
5 to make right by presenting what is due <*clear* one's accounts>
syn clear off, discharge, liquidate, pay, pay up, quit, satisfy, settle, square
rel close, pay off, repay, sink, solve
6 to obtain as a profit or return <he *cleared* several thousand on the deal>
syn clean up, gain, make, net
rel acquire, get, obtain, secure; earn, win; accumulate, gather, glean, pick up
7 *syn* see EXTRICATE 2
8 to pass over or by <*cleared* the hurdle with perfect form>
syn hurdle, leap, negotiate, over, overleap, surmount, vault
9 to become fair <the weather *cleared* later in the day>
syn ‖break, burn off
rel ameliorate, better, improve, meliorate; settle, stabilize
10 *syn* see VANISH

clear away *vb* 1 *syn* see REMOVE 4

---

syn synonym(s)   *rel* related word(s)
ant antonym(s)   *con* contrasted word(s)
idiom idiomatic equivalent(s)
‖ use limited; if in doubt, see a dictionary

---

2 *syn* see EXTRICATE 2
clear-cut *adj* 1 *syn* see CLEAR 4
2 *syn* see EXPLICIT
3 *syn* see INCISIVE
rel clear, distinct, manifest, plain; definite, explicit, express; exact, nice, precise
con fogged, hazy, misty; confused, muddled; obscured, overcast
4 *syn* see DECIDED 1
rel indubitable, undisputed, undoubted, unquestioned
idiom beyond a shade (*or* shadow) of doubt, past dispute

clearness *n syn* see CLARITY

clear off *vb syn* see CLEAR 5

clear out *vb syn* see GET OUT 1

clear-sightedness *n syn* see WIT 3

clear up *vb* 1 *syn* see CLARIFY 2
2 *syn* see SOLVE 2

cleavage *n syn* see SCHISM 3

cleave *vb syn* see STICK 2
rel associate, combine, conjoin, join, link, unite
con alienate, disaffect, disunite, estrange, separate

cleave *vb* 1 *syn* see CUT 5
2 *syn* see TEAR 1
rel divide, divorce, separate; chop, hew
con join, link, unite; attach, fasten

cleft *n* 1 *syn* see CRACK 3
2 *syn* see RAVINE
3 *syn* see SCHISM 3

clemency *n* 1 *syn* see MERCY
rel gentleness, mildness; equitableness, fairness, justness
con austerity, severity, sternness; rigidity, rigorousness, strictness; inexorableness, inflexibility, obduracy
ant harshness
2 *syn* see FORBEARANCE 2
rel endurance, sufferance
con firmness, hardness, inflexibility, obdurateness, relentlessness, rigidity
ant harshness

clement *adj syn* see FORBEARING
rel compassionate, sympathetic, tender; benign, benignant, kind, kindly; benevolent, charitable, humane
con austere, severe, stern; rigid, rigorous, strict, stringent
ant harsh; barbarous

clench *n syn* see HOLD

clergyman *n* one duly ordained to the service of God in the Christian church <the responsibility of the *clergyman* to the whole community>
syn ‖blackcoat, cassock, churchman, cleric, clerical, cleric, ‖devil-dodger, divine, ‖dominie, ecclesiast, ecclesiastic, ‖Holy Joe, minister, parson, preacher, pulpitarian, pulpiteer, pulpiter, reverend, sermonizer, sky pilot
rel evangelist, missionary; chaplain, curate, pastor, vicar; father, priest, shepherd; predicant
idiom man of God, man of the cloth

cleric *n syn* see CLERGYMAN

clerical *n syn* see CLERGYMAN

clerisy *n syn* see INTELLIGENTSIA

clerk *n syn* see CLERGYMAN

clerkish *adj syn* see NICE 1

clever *adj* **1** *syn* see SKILLFUL 2

2 *syn* see DEXTEROUS 1

3 *syn* see INTELLIGENT 2

rel apt, prompt, quick, ready; able, capable, competent; all-around, many-sided, versatile

idiom quick as a flash, sharp (*or* smart) as a whip

con asinine, fatuous, foolish, simple

ant dull

4 highly skilled in devising or contriving <very *clever* about getting her own way>

syn adroit, canny, ‖coony, cunning, dexterous, ingenious, ‖sleighty, slim, sly; *compare* SKILLFUL 2

rel able, adept, expert, handy, masterly, proficient, skilled, skillful; capable, competent, qualified; crafty, deceitful, slick, tricky

con awkward, clumsy, gauche, inept, maladroit; dilatory, laggard, slow, sluggish; incapable, incompetent, inept, unqualified

5 pleasing because of aptness, sparkle, and usually wit <delighted her audience with a series of *clever* comparisons>

syn good, scintillating, smart, sprightly

rel bright, brilliant, coruscating, dazzling, sparkling; piquant, racy, salty; fanciful, whimsical; amusing, entertaining, pleasing; facetious, funny, humorous, witty; laughable, risible

con drab, dull, humdrum, monotonous, stodgy; barren, empty, inane; fatuous, pointless; absurd, foolish, nonsensical, ridiculous

ant stupid

‖**cleverly** *adv* *syn* see WELL 3

cliché *n* *syn* see COMMONPLACE

cliché *adj* *syn* see TRITE

clichéd *adj* *syn* see TRITE

click *vb* *syn* see SUCCEED 2

client *n* *syn* see CUSTOMER

clientage *n* *syn* see FOLLOWING 2

clientele *n* *syn* see FOLLOWING 2

climacteric *adj* *syn* see ACUTE 6

climate *n* *syn* see ENVIRONMENT

climatize *vb* *syn* see HARDEN 2

climax *n* *syn* see APEX 2

climax *vb* to bring to or come to a satisfying termination <the feast was *climaxed* by a glorious plum pudding>

syn cap, crown, culminate, finish off, round off, top off

rel content, please, satisfy; conclude, end, finish, terminate

climb *vb* *syn* see ASCEND 1

‖**clinch** *vb* *syn* see EMBRACE 1

‖**clinch** *n* *syn* see HOLD

clincher *n* *syn* see TRUMP CARD

cling *vb* *syn* see STICK 2

cling *n* *syn* see ADHERENCE 1

clinging *n* *syn* see ADHERENCE 1

clink *vb* *syn* see JINGLE

‖**clink** *n* *syn* see JAIL

clinkers *n pl* *syn* see ASH

‖**clip** *vb* *syn* see EMBRACE 1

clip *n* *syn* see BROOCH

clip *vb* **1** *syn* see CUT 6

2 *syn* see MOW

3 *syn* see REDUCE 2

4 *syn* see OVERCHARGE 1

clique *n* a narrowly exclusive group of people usually held together by a common often

selfish interest or purpose <there was a politically minded *clique* on the campus>

syn cabal, camarilla, camp, circle, clan, coterie, in-group, mob, ring; *compare* SET 5

clitter *vb* *syn* see RATTLE 1

cloak *n* *syn* see MASK 2

cloak *vb* *syn* see DISGUISE

rel blanket, curtain, screen, shroud, veil

ant uncloak

clobber *vb* ‖**1** *syn* see WHIP 2

2 *syn* see SLAM 1

clochard *n* *syn* see VAGABOND

clock *vb* *syn* see TIME 2

‖**clock** *vb* *syn* see SET 11

clocklike *adj* *syn* see CIRCUMSTANTIAL

clockwise *adj* *syn* see RIGHT-HANDED

clod *n* **1** *syn* see LUMP 1

2 *syn* see DUNCE

cloddish *adj* *syn* see BOORISH

clodhopper *n* **1** *syn* see RUSTIC

2 *syn* see BOOR

clodhopping *adj* *syn* see BOORISH

clodpate *n* *syn* see DUNCE

clodpoll *n* *syn* see DUNCE

clog *n* *syn* see ENCUMBRANCE

clog *vb* **1** *syn* see BURDEN

2 *syn* see HAMPER

3 *syn* see FILL 1

cloggy *adj* *syn* see STICKY 1

cloister *vb* *syn* see SECLUDE

cloistered *adj* *syn* see SECLUDED

clonk *vb* *syn* see THUD

‖**Cloot** *n*, *usu* **Cloots** *pl* *syn* see DEVIL 1

‖**Clootie** *n* *syn* see DEVIL 1

close *vb* **1** to fill an opening with an appropriate closure <be sure to *close* the gate>

syn ‖put to, shut

rel bang, clap, slam; block, choke, clog, obstruct, occlude, stop; debar, exclude

ant open

2 *syn* see SCREEN 3

3 to bring or come to a limit or to a natural or appropriate stopping point <*closed* the meeting as soon as the discussion was over>

syn complete, conclude, consummate, determine, do, end, finish, halt, terminate, ultimate, wind up, wrap up

rel cease, desist, quit, stop; finalize, write off

idiom call it a day, set a period to

con begin, commence, enter (on *or* upon), inaugurate, initiate, start

4 *syn* see FILL 1

5 *syn* see DECREASE

6 *syn* see MEET 6

close *n* **1** *syn* see END 2

2 *syn* see FINALE

ant opening

‖**close** *n* *syn* see COURT 1

close *adj* **1** *syn* see SILENT 3

idiom close as a clam

con candid, frank, plain

ant open

2 *syn* see STUFFY 1

rel humid, muggy, sticky

3 *syn* see STINGY

ant liberal

4 having the constituent parts massed closely together <a paper of fine *close* texture>

syn compact, crowded, dense, thick, tight

rel compacted, compressed, condensed, consolidated, constricted, contracted; firm, solid, substantial; impenetrable, impermeable; close-grained
con lax, loose, slack; unconsolidated
5 *syn* see TIGHT 3
6 not far removed (as in space, time, or relationship) from something stipulated or understood <true and veritable are *close* synonyms> <the park is very *close* to the river> <it is *close* to closing time>
syn immediate, near, near-at-hand, nearly, nigh, proximate; *compare* NEIGHBORING
rel abutting, adjacent, adjoining, contiguous; convenient, handy; nearest, nearmost, next
idiom at hand, at one's fingers' ends (*or* fingertips), under one's nose
con distant, far, faraway, far-off, removed
ant remote
7 *syn* see FAMILIAR 1
con cool, remote, withdrawn
ant aloof

close *adv* into proximity with respect to space, time, or approach <hoping to come *closer* to the truth of the matter>
syn at close hand, hard, near, nearby, nigh
rel almost, nearabout, nearly
idiom as near as no matter (*or* never mind), in hailing (*or* spitting) distance, within an inch (*or* an ace) of, within a stone's throw
con afar, distantly, far
ant remotely

close-at-hand *adj* **1** *syn* see NEIGHBORING
2 *syn* see CONVENIENT 2
close-by *adj* **1** *syn* see NEIGHBORING
2 *syn* see CONVENIENT 2
closed *adj* *syn* see SELF-SUFFICIENT
closed book *n* *syn* see MYSTERY
closed-minded *adj* *syn* see OBSTINATE
closefisted *adj* *syn* see STINGY
rel clinging, clutching, grasping, keeping, tenacious
close in *vb* *syn* see ENCLOSE 1
close-lipped *adj* *syn* see SILENT 3
closely *adv* *syn* see HARD 4
rel carefully, heedfully, mindfully, thoughtfully; meticulously, minutely, punctiliously, scrupulously
con carelessly, heedlessly, thoughtlessly
closemouthed *adj* *syn* see SILENT 3
close off *vb* *syn* see ISOLATE
close on *prep* *syn* see ABOUT 3
close out *vb* *syn* see SELL OUT 1
closeout *n* *syn* see BARGAIN 1
‖**closet** *n* *syn* see PRIVY 1
closet *adj* **1** *syn* see PRIVATE 2
2 *syn* see THEORETICAL 1
close-tongued *adj* *syn* see SILENT 3
closing *n* *syn* see END 2
closing *adj* *syn* see LAST
closure *n* *syn* see END 2
clot *n* *syn* see GROUP 3
clot *vb* *syn* see COAGULATE

clothe *vb* to cover with or as if with garments <forests *clothe* the rocky slopes>
syn apparel, array, attire, clad, dress, enclothe, garb, garment, raiment
rel costume, do up, dress up, tog (up *or* out); cloak, mantle, robe; accouter, equip, outfit, rig (out); bedrape, drape, swathe; endue, invest
con dismantle, divest, strip
ant unclothe
clothes *n pl* a person's garments as a whole <dressed in new *clothes* from the skin out>
syn apparel, attire, attirement, clothing, dress, duds, habiliment(s), rags, raiment, rigging, things, togs
rel array, garb, toggery, vestments, vesture; costume, getup, outfit, rig
clothing *n* **1** *syn* see CLOTHES
2 *syn* see ROLE 1
cloud *n* *syn* see MULTITUDE 1
cloud *vb* **1** *syn* see OBSCURE
rel addle, befuddle, confuse, muddle; distract, perplex, puzzle
2 *syn* see CONFUSE 4
3 *syn* see TAINT 1
clouded *adj* *syn* see DOUBTFUL 1
cloudless *adj* *syn* see FAIR 2
cloudy *adj* **1** *syn* see OVERCAST
2 *syn* see HAZY
3 *syn* see MURKY 3
clough *n* *syn* see RAVINE
clout *n* **1** *syn* see CUFF
2 *syn* see PULL 2
clout *vb* **1** *syn* see STRIKE 2
‖**2** *syn* see STEAL 1
clove *n* *syn* see RAVINE
clown *n* **1** *syn* see RUSTIC
2 *syn* see BOOR
3 a performer (as in a circus) who entertains by grotesque appearance and actions <children delighted by the antics of the *clowns*>
syn buffoon, harlequin, merry-andrew, zany
rel comedian; fool, jester, mountebank; mime, mummer
4 *syn* see ZANY 2
clownish *adj* *syn* see BOORISH
rel awkward, clumsy, gauche; green, raw, rough, rude, uncouth
ant urbane
cloy *vb* *syn* see SATIATE
con excite, pique, provoke, stimulate
ant whet
club *n* **1** *syn* see CUDGEL
2 *syn* see ASSOCIATION 2
club car *n* *syn* see PARLOR CAR
‖**cluck** *n* *syn* see DUNCE
clue *n* *syn* see HINT 1
clue (*or* **clew**) *vb* *syn* see INFORM 2
clump *n* **1** *syn* see GROUP 3
rel clutter, hodgepodge, jumble, omnium≠gatherum
2 *syn* see LUMP 1
clump *vb* *syn* see LUMBER
clumsy *adj* **1** lacking in physical ease and grace usually because of coarse cumbersome build or poor coordination <a *clumsy* boy constantly stumbling over his own feet> <the *clumsy* gait of a young puppy>
syn awkward, gawky, lumbering, lumpish, splathering, splay, ungainly; *compare* AWKWARD 2

---

syn synonym(s)   *rel* related word(s)
ant antonym(s)   *con* contrasted word(s)
idiom idiomatic equivalent(s)
‖ use limited; if in doubt, see a dictionary

rel butterfingered, heavy-handed, left-handed, unhandy; graceless, inelegant, uncouth; bulky, hulking, unwieldy
idiom all thumbs, fingers all thumbs
con comely, shapely, well-formed, well-proportioned; apt, deft, handy, quick, ready
2 *syn see* AWKWARD 1

clunk *vb syn see* THUD
clunker *n syn see* JALOPY
cluster *n* **1** *syn see* GROUP 3
2 *syn see* GROUP 1
cluster *vb syn see* GROUP 1
rel accumulate, aggregate, associate, cumulate; bundle, package, parcel
clutch *vb syn see* SEIZE 2
rel clench, clinch, gripe; cherish, harbor, hold, keep
clutch *n syn see* HOLD
clutch *n syn see* GROUP 3
clutter *n* **1** *syn see* CONFUSION 3
2 a disordered nondescript mass or group <a *clutter* of ornaments on the mantel>
syn hash, hugger-mugger, jumble, jungle, litter, mash, mishmash, muddle, rummage, scramble, shuffle, tumble
rel hodgepodge, macédoine, medley, mélange; disarray, mess, muss, ruck
con arrangement, array, order; grouping, ordering, pigeonholing, ranking, sorting
‖**cly** *vb syn see* STEAL 1
coact *vb syn see* INTERACT
coacting *adj syn see* COOPERATIVE
coactive *adj syn see* COOPERATIVE
coadjutant *n syn see* ASSISTANT 2
coadjute *vb syn see* UNITE 1
coadjutor *n syn see* ASSISTANT 2
coadunate *vb syn see* JOIN 1
coadunation *n syn see* UNIFICATION
coagment *vb syn see* JOIN 1
coagulate *vb* to alter by chemical reaction from a liquid to a more or less firm jelly <the blood *coagulated* and closed the wound>
syn clot, congeal, gel, gelate, gelatinize, jell, jellify, jelly, set
rel concrete, harden, solidify; curdle, inspissate; compact, concentrate, consolidate; coalesce; freeze; dehydrate, dry; condense, thicken
con deliquesce, fluidify, liquefy, liquesce; flux, fuse, melt, run
coalesce *vb syn see* JOIN 1
rel adhere, cleave, cling, stick; blend, fuse, merge, mingle, mix
coalition *n* **1** *syn see* UNIFICATION
2 *syn see* COMBINATION 2
3 *syn see* ALLIANCE 2
coarct *vb syn see* RESTRAIN 1
coarse *adj* **1** made up of relatively large particles <*coarse* sand>
syn grainy, granular
rel caked, cakey, lumpy, particulate
2 *syn see* CRUDE 5
3 deficient in refinement of manner and delicacy of feeling <a *coarse* practical man lacking all social graces>
syn crass, crude, gross, incult, inelegant, low, raw, rough, rude, uncouth, uncultivated, uncultured, unrefined, vulgar; *compare* BOORISH
rel raffish, roughneck, rowdy, vulgarian; common, tacky

con considerate, courtly, gracious; cultivated, polished, refined
4 *syn see* OBSCENE 2
‖**5** *syn see* WILD 6
coast *n syn see* SHORE
coast *vb syn see* SLIDE 6
coax *vb* to influence or persuade by artful ingratiation <*coaxed* her friend to help her with her work>
syn ‖barter, blandish, blarney, cajole, con, soft-soap, sweet-talk, wheedle
rel pester, plague, tease; importune, press, urge; get, induce, persuade, prevail; entice, inveigle, lure, tempt; butter (up)
con coerce, compel, constrain, force, oblige; browbeat, bulldoze, cow, intimidate
ant bully
cob *vb syn see* SURPASS 1
cobble *vb syn see* BOTCH
rel confuse, foul up, snafu, snarl (up)
‖**cobblers** *n syn see* NONSENSE 2
cobweb *n syn see* WEB 2
cock *n* **1** *syn see* FAUCET
2 *syn see* LEADER 2
‖**3** *syn see* NONSENSE 2
‖**cock** *adj syn see* CHIEF 2
cock *vb syn see* LORD
cock *n syn see* PILE 1
cock *vb syn see* HEAP 1
cock-a-doodle-doo *vb syn see* BOAST
cock-a-hoop *adj* **1** *syn see* EXULTANT
2 *syn see* AWRY 1
Cockaigne *n syn see* UTOPIA
cockamamie *adj syn see* FOOLISH 2
cock-and-bull story *n syn see* LIE
cock-a-whoop *adj syn see* EXULTANT
cockcrow *n syn see* DAWN 1
cockcrowing *n syn see* DAWN 1
cocker *vb syn see* BABY
‖**cocket** *adj syn see* SAUCY 1
cockeyed *adj* **1** *syn see* AWRY 1
2 *syn see* INTOXICATED 1
cockle *vb syn see* RIPPLE
cocksure *adj syn see* SURE 5
cocktail lounge *n syn see* BAR 5
‖**coco** *n syn see* HEAD 1
coconspirator *n syn see* CONFEDERATE
‖**coconut** *n syn see* HEAD 1
cocotte *n syn see* PROSTITUTE
coddle *vb syn see* BABY
codicil *n syn see* APPENDIX 1
‖**codswallop** *n syn see* NONSENSE 2
coefficient *adj syn see* COOPERATIVE
coerce *vb syn see* FORCE 2
rel beset, push, urge; browbeat, bulldoze, bully, cow, intimidate; menace, terrorize, threaten
coercion *n syn see* FORCE 4
rel menace, menacing, threat, threatening
coetaneous *adj syn see* CONTEMPORARY 1
coeval *adj syn see* CONTEMPORARY 1
coexistent *adj syn see* CONTEMPORARY 1
coexisting *adj syn see* CONTEMPORARY 1
coffee shop *n syn see* EATING HOUSE
coffer *n syn see* TREASURY 2
‖**coffin nail** *n syn see* CIGARETTE
cogency *n syn see* POINT 3
rel pertinence, relevance; bearing, concern, connection
cogent *adj* **1** *syn see* VALID

rel compelling, constraining, forceful, forcible, potent, powerful, puissant; inducing, persuasive; justified, well-founded, well-grounded
con ineffective, ineffectual, inefficacious; feeble, forceless, impotent, powerless, weak
2 *syn* see WELL-FOUNDED
rel consequential, influential, momentous, weighty; meaningful, significant
cogitable *adj syn* see THINKABLE 1
cogitate *vb* 1 *syn* see THINK 5
rel conceive, envisage, envision, imagine
2 *syn* see PLOT
cogitation *n syn* see THOUGHT 1
cogitative *adj syn* see THOUGHTFUL 1
cognate *adj syn* see RELATED
rel common, general, generic, universal
con different, disparate, divergent, diverse, various
cognizance *n syn* see NOTICE 1
cognizant *adj syn* see AWARE
con forgetful, oblivious, unmindful; heedless, ignoring, neglectful, slighting, unmindful
ant ignorant
cognize *vb syn* see KNOW 1
cognomen *n syn* see NAME 1
cognoscente *n syn* see CONNOISSEUR
rel ∥dab, proficient, specialist; authority, critic, judge
cohere *vb* 1 *syn* see STICK 2
rel blend, coalesce, fuse, merge; associate, combine, connect, join, unite
con disembarrass, disentangle, untangle
2 *syn* see AGREE 4
coherence *n* 1 *syn* see ADHERENCE 1
rel integrity, solidarity, union, unity
ant incoherence
2 *syn* see CONSISTENCY
cohesion *n* 1 *syn* see ADHERENCE 1
ant incohesion
2 *syn* see SOLIDARITY
cohort *n* 1 *syn* see PARTNER
2 *syn* see FOLLOWER
coil *n syn* see COMMOTION 3
coil *vb syn* see WIND 2
rel revolve, rotate, turn
∥**coin** *n syn* see MONEY
idiom coin of the realm
coinage *n syn* see INVENTION
coincide *vb syn* see AGREE 3
rel accord, correspond, jibe, tally; equal, match
con deviate, divagate, divaricate, diverge; bias, skew, twist, warp
ant differ
coincident *adj syn* see CONCOMITANT
coincidentally *adv syn* see TOGETHER 1
coincidently *adv syn* see TOGETHER 1
coinstantaneously *adv syn* see TOGETHER 1
cojones *n pl syn* see COURAGE
cold *adj* 1 marked by a deficiency of warmth <a *cold* day>

---

syn synonym(s)   *rel* related word(s)
ant antonym(s)   *con* contrasted word(s)
idiom idiomatic equivalent(s)
∥ use limited; if in doubt, see a dictionary

syn arctic, chill, chillsome, chilly, cool, freezing, frigid, frore, frosty, gelid, glacial, icy, nippy, shivery
rel biting, bleak, chilling, cutting, nipping, polar, raw, sharp; frozen, iced, wintry; bracing, brisk, crisp, snappy
con genial, mild
ant warm
2 lacking cordiality or emotional warmth <a *cold* greeting>
syn chill, emotionless, frigid, glacial, icy, indifferent, unemotional
rel unenthusiastic, unresponsive, unsympathetic
con cordial, friendly, genial, hearty, warm; empathic, sympathetic
3 *syn* see MATTER-OF-FACT 3
4 *syn* see FRIGID 3
ant hot
5 *syn* see GLOOMY 3
6 *syn* see DEAD 1
7 *syn* see INSENSIBLE 2
cold–blooded *adj* 1 *syn* see UNFEELING 2
2 *syn* see MATTER-OF-FACT 3
cold feet *n syn* see FEAR 1
coldhearted *adj syn* see UNFEELING 2
ant warmhearted
∥**cold meat** *n syn* see CORPSE
cold–shoulder *vb syn* see CUT 7
cold storage *n syn* see ABEYANCE
colic *n syn* see STOMACHACHE
coliseum *n syn* see STADIUM
∥**coll** *vb syn* see EMBRACE 1
collapse *vb* 1 *syn* see GIVE 12
rel break up, disintegrate, shatter
idiom fall to pieces
2 to lose energy, stamina, or control under stress <exhausted to the point of *collapsing* helplessly on the bed>
syn break down, cave (in), drop, ∥flake out, give out, peg out, succumb, wilt
rel droop, fail, languish, weaken; exhaust, fag, flag, play out, tire, weary
con enliven, invigorate, stimulate
collapse *n* 1 *syn* see NERVOUS BREAKDOWN
2 a sudden and grave failure <the *collapse* of an overextended market>
syn breakdown, crack-up, crash, debacle, smash, smashup, wreck
rel breakup, disorganization, disruption, undoing; cataclysm, catastrophe; destruction, ruination, ruining; failure
collar *vb* 1 *syn* see CORNER
2 *syn* see CATCH 1
3 *syn* see STEAL 1
collate *vb syn* see COMPARE 2
collateral *adj* 1 *syn* see CONCOMITANT
2 *syn* see INDIRECT 1
3 *syn* see CORROBORATIVE
4 *syn* see SUBORDINATE
rel allied, cognate, kindred, related; complementary, corresponding, reciprocal
con major, prominent
5 *syn* see AUXILIARY
∥**collateral** *n syn* see REFUSE
colleague *n* one affiliated with another usually through a common office or profession <he claims to speak for his *colleagues* in the Senate>

syn associate, compatriot, compeer, confrere

rel consociate, copartner, fellow, partner; co-worker, workfellow; buddy, chum, companion, crony, pal; aide, assistant, helper

collect *vb* 1 *syn* see GATHER 6
   con assort, sort; sever, sunder; deal, dispense, divide, dole
   ant disperse; distribute
   2 *syn* see INFER
   3 *syn* see COMPOSE 4
   4 *syn* see GROUP 1
   rel align, array, dispose, marshal, order, rank
   con broadcast, disperse, distribute, scatter

collected *adj* 1 *syn* see CALM 2
   rel peaceful, quiet, still
   ant distraught
   2 *syn* see COOL 2
   rel assured, confident, sanguine, sure; complacent, self-satisfied, smug
   con disordered, troubled

collection *n* 1 *syn* see GATHERING 2
   rel band, crew, outfit, party
   2 *syn* see ACCUMULATION
   rel assortment, medley, miscellany, variety; bunch, clump, cluster, group; armamentarium; caboodle, kit, lot

‖**college** *n* *syn* see JAIL

collide *vb* *syn* see BUMP 1
   rel atomize, fragment, pulverize, shatter, smash, splinter; break up, crunch, scrap

collimate *vb* *syn* see PARALLEL 2

collision *n* *syn* see IMPACT 1
   rel dilapidation, ruin, wreck; demolishment, destruction

collocate *vb* *syn* see PARALLEL 2

collogue *vb* ‖1 *syn* see PLOT
   2 *syn* see CONFER 2

colloque *vb* *syn* see CONVERSE

colloquial *adj* *syn* see VERNACULAR 1

colloquial *adj* *syn* see VERNACULAR 3

colloquium *n* *syn* see CONFERENCE 2

colloquy *n* 1 *syn* see CONVERSATION 1
   2 *syn* see CONVERSATION 2
   3 *syn* see CONFERENCE 2

collude *vb* *syn* see PLOT

collusion *n* *syn* see COMPLICITY

colluvies *n* *syn* see MISCELLANY 1

collywobbles *n pl but sing or pl in constr syn* see STOMACHACHE

Colonel Blimp *n* 1 *syn* see STUFFED SHIRT
   2 *syn* see REACTIONARY

color *n* 1 a property of a visible thing recognizable only when rays of light fall upon it and serving to distinguish things otherwise visually identical (as in size, shape, or texture) <the green *color* of foliage turns red and gold in autumn>
   syn cast, hue, shade, tinge, tint, tone
   2 *syn* see MASK 2
   3 *syn* see VERISIMILITUDE
   4 *syn* see POSITION 1
   5 *syn* see FLAG
   6 something used to impart visible color to something <dyed her curtains with one of the new easy-to-use *colors*>
   syn colorant, dye, dyestuff, pigment, stain, tincture

color *vb* 1 *syn* see EMBROIDER

rel disguise, distort, fake, misrepresent
   con constrain, minimize, reduce, soften, temper; blue-pencil, censor, edit
   2 *syn* see MISREPRESENT
   3 *syn* see BLUSH

colorable *adj* *syn* see BELIEVABLE
   rel cogent, compelling, convincing, sound, telling, valid

colorant *n* *syn* see COLOR 6

colored *adj* *syn* see BIASED 2

colorful *adj* making a fine display of usually showy color <a *colorful* bed of asters>
   syn brave, bright, colory, gay, vivid
   rel blatant, florid, garish, gaudy, loud; flashy, showy, splashy
   con blanched, bleached, pallid, wan; dim, dull, faint, pale, weak
   ant colorless

coloring *n* 1 *syn* see MASK 2
   2 *syn* see EXAGGERATION

colorless *adj* 1 *syn* see PALE 1
   2 lacking in sparkle and vitality <an accurate but *colorless* recital of facts>
   syn drab, dull, flat, lackluster, lifeless, lusterless, prosaic, prosy
   rel blurry, hazy, obscure, vague; feeble, insipid, milk-and-water, namby-pamby, weak, wishy-washy; unimaginative, uninspired
   con clear, concise, exact, precise; exciting, provocative, rousing, stimulating, stirring
   ant colorful
   3 *syn* see NEUTRAL
   rel aloof, remote, withdrawn

colory *adj* *syn* see COLORFUL

colossal *adj* *syn* see HUGE

colporteur *n* *syn* see MISSIONARY

colt *n* *syn* see NOVICE

coltish *adj* *syn* see PLAYFUL 1

columbary *n* *syn* see DOVECOTE

column *n* 1 *syn* see PILLAR 1
   2 *syn* see SUPPORT 3

coma *n* 1 *syn* see FAINT
   2 *syn* see LETHARGY 1

comate *n* *syn* see ASSOCIATE 3

comatose *adj* 1 *syn* see INSENSIBLE 2
   2 *syn* see LETHARGIC
   rel anesthetic, impassible, insensitive
   ant awake

comb *vb* 1 *syn* see SORT 2
   2 *syn* see SCOUR 2
   rel examine, inspect, scrutinize; investigate, probe, sift

combat *vb* *syn* see RESIST
   rel battle, contend, war

combat *n* *syn* see SERVICE 1

combative *adj* *syn* see BELLIGERENT
   rel energetic, strenuous, vigorous; manful, manly, virile
   ant pacifistic

combativeness *n* *syn* see ATTACK 2

‖**combe** *n* *syn* see VALLEY

combination *n* 1 *syn* see UNIFICATION
   2 individuals or organized interests banded together to further a common end <a *combination* of citizens devoted to holding down taxes>
   syn bloc, coalition, combine, faction, party, ring
   rel cartel, pool, syndicate, trust; cabal, circle, clique, coterie, set

3 syn see ASSOCIATION 1

combine *vb* **1 syn** see JOIN 1
rel amalgamate, blend, commingle, fuse, mingle, mix; consolidate, unify
con divide, divorce, part
ant separate
2 syn see EMBODY 2
3 syn see UNITE 1
rel agree, coincide; merge, pool
combine *n* **1 syn** see COMBINATION 2
2 syn see SYNDICATE
comble *n* **syn** see APEX 2
combust *vb* **syn** see BURN 1
combustible *adj* **1** capable of catching or being set on fire <*combustible* materials should be stored away from open fire>
syn burnable, flammable, ignitable, inflammable
rel comburent, combustive; burning, firing, igniting, kindling
con fireproof; flameproof, nonflammable; fire-resistant, fire-resistive, fire-retardant
ant incombustible, noncombustible
2 syn see EXCITABLE

come *vb* **1** to attain to a destination <when will they *come*>
syn arrive, ‖blow in, get, get in, reach, show, show up, turn up
rel approach, near, nigh
con depart, leave, quit, retreat, withdraw
ant go
2 syn see AMOUNT 1
3 syn see HAPPEN 1
4 syn see BECOME 1
come (from) *vb* **1 syn** see SPRING 1
2 syn see ORIGINATE 5
come (in) *vb* **syn** see ENTER 1
comeback *n* **syn** see RETORT 2
come by *vb* **syn** see VISIT 2
come-by-chance *n* **syn** see BASTARD 1
comedian *n* **1 syn** see HUMORIST 2
2 syn see WAG 1
come down (with) *vb* **syn** see CONTRACT 1
comedown *n* a loss of status <bitter over their *comedown* in the world>
syn descent, discomfiture, down; *compare* SETBACK
rel collapse, crash, downfall, fall, ruin, smash, undoing, wreck
con advance, headway, progress
ant rise
comedy *n* **syn** see HUMOR 4
come in *vb* **syn** see ANSWER 1
comely *adj* **1 syn** see BEAUTIFUL
ant homely
2 syn see DECOROUS 1
come off *vb* **1 syn** see SUCCEED 2
2 syn see HAPPEN 1
come-off *n* **syn** see ESCAPE 2
come-on *n* **1 syn** see LURE 2
‖**2 syn** see FOOL 3
3 syn see SWINDLER
come out *vb* **1 syn** see GET OUT 2
2 syn see DEBUT
come out (with) *vb* **syn** see SAY 1

come over *vb* **1 syn** see VISIT 2
2 syn see BECOME 1
come round *vb* **syn** see RECOVER 2
comestible *adj* **syn** see EDIBLE
comestibles *n pl* **syn** see FOOD 1
come through *vb* **1 syn** see SURVIVE 2
2 syn see CONTRIBUTE 1
comeuppance *n* **syn** see DUE 1
comfort *n* **1 syn** see HELP 1
2 syn see AMENITY 2
comfort *vb* to cheer or try to cheer a person overcome by grief or misery <*comforting* her widowed sister with words of hope>
syn buck up, cheer, console, solace, upraise
rel brighten, gladden, lighten; allay, alleviate, assuage, mitigate, relieve; refresh, renew, restore; reassure; commiserate, condole, sympathize
idiom give a lift to
con torment, torture, try; distress, trouble, worry; annoy, irk, vex
ant afflict; bother
comfortable *adj* **1 syn** see SUFFICIENT 1
2 enjoying or providing conditions that make for comfort and security <lived in a *comfortable* home on a quiet street>
syn comfy, cozy, cushy, easeful, easy, snug, soft
rel agreeable, grateful, gratifying, welcome; pleasant, pleasing; restful; comforting, consoling, solacing; content, pleased, satisfied
con distressing, perturbing, troubling; annoying, bothering, irking, vexing; inferior, miserable, poor, substandard, wretched
ant uncomfortable
3 syn see PROSPEROUS 3
idiom in comfortable circumstances
‖**comfortable** *n* **syn** see QUILT
comforter *n* **syn** see QUILT
comfortless *adj* **syn** see UNCOMFORTABLE
comfy *adj* **syn** see COMFORTABLE 2
comic *adj* **syn** see LAUGHABLE
rel antic, fantastic, grotesque; mocking, ridiculing
ant tragic
comic *n* **syn** see HUMORIST 2
comical *adj* **syn** see LAUGHABLE
rel absurd, foolish, silly; impish, roguish, sportive, waggish
con doleful, dolorous, lugubrious, melancholy
ant pathetic
comicality *n* **syn** see HUMOR 4
comicalness *n* **syn** see HUMOR 4
coming *n* **syn** see ARRIVAL 1
coming *adj* **1 syn** see FORTHCOMING
2 syn see NEXT
coming in *n, usu* **comings in** *pl* **syn** see REVENUE
comingle *vb* **syn** see MIX 1
comity *n* **syn** see GOODWILL 1
rel accord, concord, harmony; camaraderie, companionship, comradeship, good-fellowship
comma *n* **syn** see PAUSE
command *vb* to issue orders or an order to <the general *commanded* the troops to advance>
syn bid, charge, direct, enjoin, instruct, order, tell, warn

---

syn synonym(s)   *rel* related word(s)
ant antonym(s)   *con* contrasted word(s)
idiom idiomatic equivalent(s)
‖ use limited; if in doubt, see a dictionary

rel demand, exact, require; coerce, compel, constrain, force, oblige; conduct, control, manage; ask, call (on), request, say

ant comply, obey

command *n* **1** a direction that must or should be obeyed <failure to obey a direct *command* subjects the soldier to grave penalties>

syn behest, bidding, charge, dictate, injunction, mandate, order, word

rel direction, directive, instruction; canon, law, ordinance, precept, rule, statute; devoir, duty, obligation, responsibility

2 *syn* see POWER 1

rel rule

3 *syn* see ABILITY 2

rel aplomb, assurance, confidence, poise

con incertitude, insecurity, uncertainty, unsureness; indecisiveness, vagueness

commandeer *vb* **1** *syn* see APPROPRIATE 1

2 *syn* see ARROGATE 1

comme il faut *adj syn* see DECOROUS 1

commemorate *vb* **1** *syn* see KEEP 2

2 *syn* see MEMORIALIZE 2

commemorative *adj syn* see MEMORIAL

commemoratory *adj syn* see MEMORIAL

commence *vb* **1** *syn* see BEGIN 1

2 *syn* see BEGIN 2

idiom come into being (*or* existence)

commencement *n syn* see BEGINNING

commend *vb* **1** *syn* see COMMIT 1

rel resign, yield; proffer, tender

2 to indicate one's warm approval <the teacher *commended* her pupils' studious attitude>

syn acclaim, applaud, compliment, hail, kudize, praise, recommend, ‖roose

rel eulogize, extol; approve, countenance, endorse, support

con blame, criticize, reprehend, reprobate; chide, rebuke, reprimand, reproach, reprove

ant censure; admonish

commendable *adj syn* see WORTHY 1

commensurable *adj* *syn* see PROPORTIONAL

commensurate *adj* *syn* see PROPORTIONAL

comment *n* **1** *syn* see REMARK 2

2 *syn* see CRITICISM 1

comment *vb syn* see REMARK 2

rel construe, elucidate, explain, explicate, expound; annotate, gloss

commentary *n syn* see REMARK 2

commentate *vb syn* see REMARK 2

commerce *n* **1** *syn* see CONTACT 2

2 a situation characterized by mutual exchange (as of ideas) <those who feel that art should have no *commerce* with morality>

syn communion, dealings, intercourse, traffic, truck

rel communication, congress, contact, exchange, interchange, intercommunication; basis, common ground, takeoff

3 *syn* see BUSINESS 4

commie *n syn* see COMMUNIST

commination *n syn* see CURSE 1

commingle *vb syn* see MIX 1

rel integrate, unify

comminute *vb syn* see PULVERIZE 1

commiserable *adj syn* see PITIFUL 1

commiserate *vb syn* see COMPASSIONATE

commiseration *n syn* see PITY

commission *vb* **1** *syn* see AUTHORIZE 1

rel appoint, designate, name, nominate; bid, charge, command, enjoin, instruct, order

2 *syn* see DELEGATE

commit *vb* **1** to assign (as to a person) especially for use or safekeeping <it is unwise to *commit* all power and authority to one man> <sainted beings who *commit* their spirits to God>

syn commend, confide, consign, entrust, hand over, relegate, turn over

rel allocate, allot, assign, destine, ordain; move, remove, shift, transfer; deliver, give, offer, submit; delegate, deputize

idiom give into the charge (*or* hands) of

2 to be responsible for or guilty of (an offense or wrongdoing) <*commit* a crime>

syn perpetuate, pull

rel accomplish, achieve, do, effectuate, execute, perform, pull off; contravene, transgress, trespass, violate; offend, scandalize, sin

commitment *n syn* see OBLIGATION 2

committal *n syn* see OBLIGATION 2

commix *vb syn* see MIX 1

commixture *n syn* see MIXTURE

commodious *adj syn* see SPACIOUS

con cramped, narrow, strait

ant incommodious

commodities *n pl syn* see MERCHANDISE

rel articles, items, things

common *adj* **1** generally shared in or participated in by members of a community <our *common* civic responsibilities>

syn communal, conjoint, conjunct, intermutual, joint, mutual, public, shared

rel general, generic, universal; like, reciprocal, similar; corporate

con personal, private, restricted

ant individual

2 *syn* see GENERAL 2

rel popular, public

3 *syn* see IMPURE 3

4 taking place often <a *common* occurrence>

syn customary, everyday, familiar, frequent

rel repetitious, routine, usual

con infrequent, occasional, unfrequent; casual, chance, incidental

ant rare, uncommon

5 *syn* see GENERAL

6 conforming to a type without noteworthy excellences or faults <just a *common* everyday sort trying to get by in life>

syn commonplace, ordinary, prosaic, uneventful, unexceptional, unnoteworthy

rel down-to-earth, matter-of-fact, prosy, unexciting; dull, flat, trite, stale, uninteresting

con exceptional, noteworthy, remarkable, excellent, marvelous, prodigious, wonderful; aberrant, divergent, eccentric

ant extraordinary

7 *syn* see DECENT 4

8 *syn* see CHEAP 2

9 *syn* see INFERIOR 2

‖**10** *syn* see EASYGOING 3

common *n* **1** **commons** *pl* but *sing* or *pl* in *constr syn* see COMMONALTY

2 an often improved and ornamentally planted open space for public use in a built-up area <in summer a band played on the village *common*>
syn green, plaza, square
rel garden, park, pleasance, pleasure ground

commonage *n syn* see COMMONALTY

commonalty *n* persons without rank or authority or the political estate made up of these <laws that both the gentles and the *commonalty* recognized as just>
syn commonage, commoners, common men, commune, people, plebeians, plebes, plebs, populace, rank and file, third estate
rel masses, mob, multitude, proletariat, public
con aristocracy, elite, gentility, nobility; classes, gentry, nobs

commoners *n pl syn* see COMMONALTY

commonition *n syn* see WARNING

commonly *adv syn* see USUALLY 2
idiom more often than not

common men *n pl syn* see COMMONALTY

commonplace *n* an idea or expression deficient in originality or freshness <lazily exchanging *commonplaces* over their beer>
syn banality, bromide, cliché, platitude, prosaicism, prosaism, rubber stamp, shibboleth, tag, truism
rel chestnut, corn, prose, stereotype; inanity, shallowness, wishy-washiness; threadbareness, triteness
ant profundity

commonplace *adj 1 syn* see COMMON 6
2 *syn* see GENERAL 1
3 *syn* see PROSAIC 3
4 *syn* see TRITE
idiom a dime a dozen, as everyday as breakfast

common sense *n syn* see SENSE 6

commorancy *n syn* see HABITATION 2

commotion *n* **1** a state of often disorderly civic unrest <the whole city was in *commotion* over the new restrictions>
syn clamor, convulsion, ferment, outcry, tumult, upheaval, upturn
rel insurgence, insurrection, mutiny, rebellion, revolt, riot, uprising
2 a state of usually mental or emotional excitement <this challenge threw him into great *commotion* of mind>
syn agitation, confusion, dither, flap, lather, pother, stew, tumult, turbulence, turmoil
rel discomposure, disquiet, flurry, fluster, perturbation, upset; annoyance, bother, irritation, vexation; strain, tension
con calm, placidity, quietude, relaxation, serenity
3 a noisy and often unruly disturbance <the children created a *commotion* over missing the circus>
syn brouhaha, ‖catouse, coil, foofaraw, furore, fuss, hurrah, ruckus, rumpus, shindig, shindy, to-do, uproar

rel din, hubbub, hullabaloo, pandemonium; racket; fracas, ruction, row
4 a state of noisy confusion <never saw such *commotion* as the time the old sow got out and knocked the preacher into the midden>
syn bustle, clamor, clatter, hassle, hubbub, hurly-burly, lather, moil, pother, rowdy-dow, ruction, storm, to-do, tow-row, tumult, turmoil, uproar, whirl, whoopla; *compare* DIN, STIR 1
con calmness, order, peace, quiet

commove *vb syn* see ELATE

communal *adj syn* see COMMON 1

commune *n syn* see COMMONALTY

communicable *adj 1 syn* see INFECTIOUS 2
2 *syn* see COMMUNICATIVE

communicate *vb* **1** to make known <*communicated* the whole story under a pledge of secrecy>
syn break, convey, impart, pass on, transmit
rel betray, disclose, discover, divulge, ‖let out, reveal, tell; hint, imply, let on, suggest; broadcast, disseminate, publicize
con conceal, hide, obscure, screen, veil; dissemble; distort, garble, twist, warp; camouflage, disguise
2 *syn* see ADJOIN

communication *n* **1** *syn* see MESSAGE 1
2 *syn* see CONTACT 2
3 interchange of thoughts or opinions through shared symbols <the difficulties of *communication* between people of different cultural backgrounds>
syn communion, converse, intercommunication, intercourse
rel exchange, interchange; conversing, discussing, talking; conversation, discussion, talk; advice, intelligence, news, tidings

communicative *adj* inclined to talk freely and sometimes indiscreetly <too *communicative* to be trusted with a secret>
syn communicable, expansive; *compare* FRANK
rel garrulous, loquacious, talkable, voluble; conversational; demonstrative, effusive, gushing
con constrained, guarded, inhibited, restrained; bridled, controlled, curbed

communion *n* **1** *syn* see COMMERCE 2
2 *syn* see COMMUNICATION 3
3 *syn* see CONTACT 2
4 *syn* see RELIGION 2

Communist *n* a member of the Russian Communist party <restructuring of Russia by the *Communists*>
syn Bolshevik, ‖Bolshie, commie, comrade, Red
rel fellow traveler, pink, pinko; Leninist, Marxist, Stalinist, Trotskyist; apparatchik

community *n syn* see SOCIETY 3

commutable *adj syn* see INTERCHANGEABLE

commute *vb syn* see TRANSFORM

compact *adj 1 syn* see PITHY
2 *syn* see CLOSE 4
rel hard; appressed, bunched, packed
con loose, slack, unconstrained; rare, tenuous, thin

compact *vb syn* see UNIFY 1

rel compress, condense, contract; combine, unite; set, solidify
con disperse, ~~dissipate~~; fluff, loosen

compact *n syn* see CONTRACT
compacting *adj syn* see INTEGRATIVE
companion *n* 1 *syn* see ASSOCIATE 3
rel colleague, fellow, partner; chaperon, escort
2 *syn* see MATE 5
3 *syn* see ACCOMPANIMENT 2
companion *vb syn* see ACCOMPANY
companionable *adj syn* see SOCIAL 1
rel amiable, complacent, good-natured
con uncongenial, unsympathetic; reserved, taciturn, uncommunicative
companionship *n syn* see COMPANY 1
company *n* 1 association between individuals especially on pleasant or intimate terms <we always enjoyed his *company*>
syn companionship, fellowship, society
rel camaraderie, comradeship, consociation
2 persons visiting especially in one's house <invited *company* for dinner>
syn guests, visitors; *compare* VISITOR 1
3 *syn* see GATHERING 2
4 a group of persons associated in a joint effort or for a common purpose <a *company* of thieves lay in wait by the highway>
syn band, corps, outfit, party, troop, troupe; *compare* GROUP 1
rel crew, gang, pack, team; circle, clique, coterie, set; association, club, order, society; crowd, horde, mob, throng; group
5 *syn* see ENTERPRISE 3
company *vb syn* see ACCOMPANY
comparable *adj syn* see LIKE
ant disparate
comparative *adj* being such in comparison with an expressed or implied standard or absolute <living in *comparative* poverty>
syn approximate, near, relative
rel equivalent, like, similar
con genuine, real, true
ant absolute
compare *vb* 1 *syn* see EQUATE 2
2 to examine side by side or point by point in order to establish likenesses and differences <*compare* the effects of two diets on weight loss>
syn bracket, collate, contrast
rel approach, equal, match, rival, touch; examine, inspect, observe, scan, scrutinize, size (up); consider, contemplate, ponder, study, weigh
comparison *n syn* see LIKENESS
compass *vb* 1 *syn* see SURROUND 1
2 *syn* see GET 1
3 *syn* see APPREHEND 1
compass *n* 1 *syn* see CIRCUMFERENCE
rel domain, field, sphere; enclosure
2 *syn* see ENVIRONS 1
3 *syn* see RANGE 2
rel bounds, limits; circumscription, limitation, restriction
compassion *n syn* see SYMPATHY 2
rel charity, clemency, grace, lenity, mercy; benevolence, humaneness, humanity
con aloofness, indifference, unconcern; cruelty, harshness, mercilessness; implacability, relentlessness

2 *syn* see PITY
compassionate *adj syn* see TENDER
rel clement, forbearing; piteous, pitiful
con grim, implacable, merciless, relentless, unrelenting; adamant, inexorable, inflexible, obdurate
compassionate *vb* to feel or express compassion for <a kindly man who *compassionated* all human misery>
syn ache, commiserate, feel (for), pity, sympathize (with)
rel grieve (over), regret, repine; lament, mourn, sorrow (for *or* over); deplore
con accept, endure, tolerate; disregard, ignore, overlook, pass over
compassionless *adj syn* see UNFEELING 2
compatible *adj syn* see CONSONANT 1
rel appropriate, fit, fitting, meet, proper, suitable
ant incompatible
compatriot *n syn* see COLLEAGUE
compeer *n syn* see COLLEAGUE
compel *vb syn* see FORCE 2
compellation *n syn* see NAME 1
compendiary *adj syn* see CONCISE
compendious *adj syn* see CONCISE
rel close, compact
con amplified, elaborated, expanded, inflated; complete, full
compendium *n* 1 a condensed treatment of a subject <prepared a *compendium* of the state laws dealing with education>
syn aperçu, digest, pandect, précis, sketch, survey, syllabus, sylloge
rel abridgment, abstract, brief, conspectus, epitome; overview
con elaboration, expansion
2 *syn* see HANDBOOK
compenetrate *vb syn* see PERMEATE
compensate *vb* 1 to make good the defects of <her kind heart *compensated* for her nosy ways>
syn atone (for), balance, counterbalance, counterpoise, countervail, make up, offset, outweigh, redeem, set off
rel abrogate, annul, invalidate, negate, nullify; counteract, negative, neutralize; better, fix (up), improve, repair; redress
idiom make amends (*or* reparations), make matters right
2 *syn* see PAY 1
3 to make proper payment to (as for injury, loss, or damage) <*compensated* a worker injured on the job>
syn indemnify, pay, recompense, reimburse, remunerate, repay, requite
rel recoup; refund
idiom make restitution (*or* reparation)
compensation *n syn* see REPARATION
compete *vb* 1 to strive to gain mastery or obtain a prize <students *competing* for a scholarship>
syn contend, contest, rival, vie
rel dispute; battle, fight, strive, struggle; attempt, essay, try
2 *syn* see RIVAL 2
rel approach, equal, match, touch
competence *n* 1 *syn* see ENOUGH
2 *syn* see ABILITY 1
rel appropriateness, fitness, suitability

ant incompetence
competent *adj* **1** *syn* see ABLE
  rel adept, finished, masterly, polished
  ant incompetent
  2 *syn* see SUFFICIENT 1
competition *n* **1** *syn* see CONTEST 1
  2 *syn* see CONTEST 2
  3 *syn* see RIVAL
competitor *n* *syn* see RIVAL
complacence *n* *syn* see CONCEIT 2
complacency *n* *syn* see CONCEIT 2
complacent *adj* feeling or showing an often excessive or unjustified satisfaction and pleasure in one's status, possessions, or attainments <had the *complacent* air of superiority that often mars an ignorant self‡ made man>
  syn priggish, self-complacent, self-contented, self-pleased, self-satisfied, smug
  rel assured, confident, self-assured, self‡ confident, self-possessed; conceited, egoistic, egotistic
  con humble, modest; diffident, shy
complain *vb* to express discontent, resentment, or regret usually peaceably and as if seeking sympathy <a nice girl but given to *complaining* over trifles>
  syn fuss, kick, murmur, repine, wail, whine; *compare* GRIPE 2, GRUMBLE 1
  rel fret, worry; nag, pester
  idiom air a grievance, find fault, register a complaint, sing (*or* cry) the blues
  con accept, condone, countenance, tolerate
complainer *n* *syn* see GROUCH
complaint *n* *syn* see DISEASE 1
complaisant *adj* *syn* see AMIABLE 1
  rel accommodating, agreeable, generous, indulgent; submissive
  con harsh, rigorous, stern; determined, firm, masterful
complement *n* **1** something that makes up a deficiency in another thing <bought the farm with its *complement* of equipment and livestock>
  syn supplement
  rel correlate, counterpart; makeweight
  2 *syn* see ACCOMPANIMENT 1
  3 *syn* see COUNTERPART 1
complete *adj* **1** *syn* see WHOLE 3
  2 *syn* see UNABRIDGED
  3 *syn* see WHOLE 2
  4 brought to completion <each *complete* revolution of the earth>
  syn completed, concluded, done, down, ended, finished, terminated, through
  rel accomplished, achieved, effected, executed, realized; attained, compassed
  idiom all over, done with, set at rest
  ant incomplete
  5 *syn* see EXHAUSTIVE
  ant incomplete
  6 *syn* see UTTER
complete *vb* **1** *syn* see CLOSE 3
  rel accomplish, achieve, discharge, effect, execute, fulfill, perform

  idiom carry through, go through with
  2 *syn* see FULFILL 1
completed *adj* *syn* see COMPLETE 4
completely *adv* **1** *syn* see DOWN 2
  idiom down to the ground
  2 *syn* see THOROUGHLY 2
  3 *syn* see WELL 3
completeness *n* **1** *syn* see ENTIRETY 1
  2 *syn* see INTEGRITY 2
complex *adj* **1** made up of two or more separable or identifiable elements <the *complex* vascular system of higher plants>
  syn composite, compound
  rel blended, compounded, mingled, mixed; heterogeneous, varied; elaborate, intricate, involved; complicated, confused, mixed-up
  con homogeneous, uniform
  ant simple
  2 difficult to comprehend because of a multiplicity of interrelated elements <a *complex* plot to undermine the government by discrediting its leaders>
  syn Byzantine, complicated, daedal, elaborate, gordian, intricate, involved, knotty, labyrinthine, sophisticated
  rel bewildering, confusing, distracting, disturbing; baffling, confounding, mysterious, mystifying, perplexing, puzzling; equivocal, obscure, vague; involute, involuted, reticular
  con clear, defined, definite, distinct, plain, recognizable, uncomplicated, uninvolved; comprehensible, explicable, intelligible, knowable
  ant simple
complex *n* *syn* see SYSTEM 1
  con constituent, element, factor; member, part, piece, portion; detail, item, particular
  ant component
complexion *n* *syn* see DISPOSITION 3
  rel kind, sort, style, type
complexion *vb* *syn* see TINT
complexionless *adj* *syn* see PALE 1
compliance *n* *syn* see ACQUIESCENCE
  rel amenability, docility, obedience, tractability; deference, submission, submissiveness
  con contumacy, obstinacy, stubbornness
  ant frowardness
complicate *vb* to make complex, involved, or difficult <a disagreement *complicated* by intense personal animosities>
  syn entangle, ‖muck, muddle, perplex, ravel, snarl, tangle
  rel jumble, ‖snafu; derange, disarrange, disorder, mix up, upset
  con arrange, order; disentangle, straighten (out), untangle
  ant simplify
complicated *adj* **1** *syn* see ELABORATE 2
  2 *syn* see COMPLEX 2
  rel arduous, difficult, hard; abstruse, recondite
  con easy, facile, light; clear-cut, precise, straightforward
  ant simple
complicity *n* association with an improper or unlawful activity <failed to prove his *complicity* in the cover-up>
  syn collusion, connivance
  rel implication, involvement; engineering, machination, manipulation, wire-pulling

---

syn synonym(s)   *rel* related word(s)
ant antonym(s)   *con* contrasted word(s)
idiom idiomatic equivalent(s)
‖ use limited; if in doubt, see a dictionary

compliment n 1 an expression of regard or praise <a man meriting the *compliments* and homage of his fellows>
syn bouquet, kudo, orchid(s)
rel trade-last; laud, laudation, praise; accolade, commendation, honor; blessing(s), congratulation(s), felicitation(s); encomium, eulogy, tribute
con dig, gibe, jeer, slam
ant taunt
‖2 *syn* see GIFT 1

compliment vb *syn* see COMMEND 2
idiom take off one's hat to
con belittle, decry, denigrate, depreciate, disparage, run down

complimentary adj *syn* see FREE 5

comply vb *syn* see OBEY

component n *syn* see ELEMENT 2
con admixture, amalgam, blend, compound, mixture
ant composite; complex

comport vb 1 *syn* see AGREE 4
2 *syn* see BEHAVE 1

comportment n 1 *syn* see BEARING 1
2 *syn* see BEHAVIOR

compose vb 1 *syn* see CONSTITUTE 1
rel consist (of)
2 to bring into being by mental and especially artistic effort <*compose* a ballad or a history of England>
syn create
rel devise, invent, make up, originate; dream up
3 *syn* see CALM
rel ease, lessen, soften; comfort, console, solace
con agitate, embroil, trouble, unsettle
ant discompose
4 to bring oneself or one's emotions under control <*composed* himself and turned to face the new attack>
syn collect, contain, control, cool, re-collect, rein, repress, restrain, simmer down, smother, suppress
rel down, mitigate, moderate, modulate, pocket, temper, tune down; bottle (up), check, hold in; ease (off or up), let up, relax, slacken
idiom calm down, control one's feelings (or emotions), get hold of oneself, master one's feelings, pull oneself together

composed adj 1 *syn* see CALM 2
2 *syn* see COOL 2
rel quiet, still; sedate, serious, staid; repressed, suppressed
con concerned, worried
ant discomposed, ruffled

composite adj *syn* see COMPLEX 1

composite n *syn* see MIXTURE
rel combination, union

composition n 1 *syn* see MAKEUP 1
2 *syn* see COMPROMISE
3 *syn* see ESSAY 2

compos mentis adj *syn* see SANE 2

compost n *syn* see MIXTURE

composure n *syn* see EQUANIMITY
ant discomposure, perturbation

compotation n *syn* see BINGE 1

compound vb 1 *syn* see JOIN 1
2 *syn* see MIX 1

3 *syn* see INCREASE 1

compound adj *syn* see COMPLEX 1

compound n *syn* see MIXTURE

comprehend vb 1 *syn* see APPREHEND 1
2 *syn* see KNOW 1
rel envisage, envision, see
3 *syn* see INCLUDE

comprehendible adj *syn* see UNDERSTANDABLE
ant incomprehensible

comprehensible adj *syn* see UNDERSTANDABLE
ant incomprehensible

comprehensive adj 1 *syn* see ENCYCLOPEDIC
2 *syn* see ALL-AROUND 2
idiom in depth

comprehensiveness n *syn* see BREADTH 2

compress vb 1 *syn* see CONTRACT 3
rel compact, consolidate; cram, crowd, press, squeeze
con disperse, dissipate, scatter
ant stretch; spread
2 *syn* see PRESS 1

comprise vb *syn* see CONSTITUTE 1

compromise n a settlement reached by mutual concession <the company and the union agreed to a *compromise* on fringe benefits>
syn composition
rel golden mean, mean, middle ground, middle way; agreement, compact, contract, pact; arrangement, bargain, understanding
idiom happy medium

compromise vb *syn* see ENDANGER
rel blast, blight, mar, queer, ruin, spoil
idiom cook one's goose; play havoc (or hob) with, settle one's hash

compulsatory adj *syn* see MANDATORY

compulsion n *syn* see FORCE 4
rel driving, impelling, pressing; exigency, necessity, need; pressure, stress
con coaxing, inducing, persuasion; choice, election, option, preference

compulsory adj *syn* see MANDATORY

compunction n 1 *syn* see PENITENCE
rel conscience, conscientiousness, punctiliousness, scrupulosity, scrupulousness
con brazenness, callousness, hardness, insensitivity; disinterest, indifference, unconcern; obduracy, recalcitrance
2 *syn* see QUALM
rel disinclination; hesitancy, hesitation

compunctious adj *syn* see REMORSEFUL

computation n the act or action of calculating mathematically <by his *computation* they could not possibly afford a new car>
syn arithmetic, calculation, ciphering, estimation, figuring, reckoning

compute vb *syn* see CALCULATE

comrade n 1 *syn* see ASSOCIATE 3
rel consort, fellow, mate; adjunct, ally, auxiliary
2 *syn* see COMMUNIST

comradery n *syn* see CAMARADERIE

comstock n *syn* see PRUDE

con vb 1 *syn* see SCRUTINIZE 1
2 *syn* see MEMORIZE

con n 1 *syn* see OPPONENT
ant pro

2 *syn* see ANTAGONISM 2

con *vb* **1** *syn* see DUPE
  2 *syn* see COAX
‖**con** *n* *syn* see CONVICT
concatenate *vb* *syn* see INTEGRATE 3
concavity *n* *syn* see DEPRESSION 2
conceal *vb* *syn* see HIDE
  rel camouflage, disguise, dissemble
  idiom keep (something) dark
  con betray, divulge; evidence, evince, manifest
  ant reveal
concealed *adj* *syn* see ULTERIOR
concede *vb* **1** *syn* see ACKNOWLEDGE 1
  rel cede, relinquish, waive
  con agitate, argue, debate, discuss; answer, confute, refute; controvert
  ant dispute
  2 *syn* see GRANT 1
  con refuse, reject
  ant deny
conceit *n* **1** *syn* see IDEA
  2 an attitude of regarding oneself with favor <his constant boasting was an indication of *conceit*>
  syn amour propre, complacence, complacency, conceitedness, consequence, egoism, egotism, narcissism, outrecuidance, pride, self-admiration, self-complacency, self-conceit, self-consequence, self-esteem, self-exaltation, self-glory, self-importance, self-love, self-opinion, self-pride, swelled head, swellheadedness, vainglory, vainness, vanity
  rel assurance, pomposity, self-partiality, smugness, stuffiness
  con humbleness, humility, self-depreciation, unpretentiousness
  ant modesty
  3 *syn* see CAPRICE
‖**conceit** *vb* *syn* see UNDERSTAND 3
conceited *adj* *syn* see VAIN 3
conceitedness *n* *syn* see CONCEIT 2
‖**conceity** *adj* *syn* see VAIN 3
conceivable *adj* **1** *syn* see THINKABLE 2
  2 *syn* see PROBABLE
conceive *vb* **1** *syn* see THINK 1
  rel excogitate; cogitate, speculate; meditate, ponder, ruminate
  2 *syn* see APPREHEND 1
  rel heed, mark, note, notice, observe, remark
  3 *syn* see UNDERSTAND 3
  rel judge; deem, feel
concenter *vb* **1** *syn* see FASTEN 3
  2 *syn* see CONVERGE
concentrate *vb* **1** *syn* see FASTEN 3
  rel establish, set, settle
  2 *syn* see UNIFY 1
  rel assemble, collect, gather; heap, mass, pile
  con dispel, disperse; attenuate, dilute, extenuate, rarefy, thin; dispense, distribute
  ant dissipate
  3 *syn* see CONTRACT 3
  4 *syn* see CONVERGE

---

syn synonym(s)   *rel* related word(s)
ant antonym(s)   *con* contrasted word(s)
idiom idiomatic equivalent(s)
‖ use limited; if in doubt, see a dictionary

concentrated *adj* **1** *syn* see STRONG 3
  2 *syn* see WHOLE 5
  rel complete, entire, total
  3 *syn* see INTENSE 1
concentrating *adj* *syn* see INTEGRATIVE
concentration *n* *syn* see ATTENTION 1
  rel enthrallment, raptness
  ant distraction
concept *n* *syn* see IDEA
  con percept, sensation, sense-datum, sensum
conception *n* *syn* see IDEA
conceptual *adj* existing or dealing with what exists only in the mind <*conceptual* analysis of a problem>
  syn ideal, ideational, notional
  rel abstract, transcendent, transcendental; absolute, categorical, ultimate; obscure, remote; fanciful, imaginary, visionary
  con practical, pragmatic, realistic; concrete, material, substantial, tangible
concern *n* **1** *syn* see INTEREST 3
  2 *syn* see AFFAIR 1
  3 *syn* see BUSINESS 8
  4 *syn* see CARE 4
  5 *syn* see CONSIDERATION 3
  6 *syn* see UNCERTAINTY
  rel faltering, irresolution; apprehension, misgiving; inquietude, suspense
  7 *syn* see CARE 2
  rel attention, consideration, thoughtfulness
  con aloofness, incuriousness, indifference
  ant unconcern
  8 *syn* see ENTERPRISE 3
  9 *syn* see GADGET 1
concerned *adj* *syn* see INTERESTED
concerning *prep* *syn* see APROPOS
concernment *n* *syn* see CARE 2
concert *vb* **1** *syn* see NEGOTIATE 1
  rel argue, debate, discuss; concur, cooperate, unite
  2 *syn* see AGREE 2
concert *n* *syn* see HARMONY 1
concession *n* *syn* see ALLOWANCE 5
conciliate *vb* *syn* see PACIFY
  rel intervene, mediate; persuade, prevail; calm, quiet, soothe, tranquilize
  con alienate, disaffect, estrange; foment, incite; excite, pique, provoke, stimulate
  ant antagonize
concise *adj* presented with or given to brevity of expression <a *concise* statement of the problem> <a very *concise* thinker>
  syn breviloquent, brief, compendiary, compendious, curt, laconic, short, short and sweet, succinct, summary, terse; *compare* PITHY
  rel abridged, compressed, condensed; marrowy, meaty, pithy; lean
  con diffuse, long-winded, prolix, rambling, voluble, wordy
  ant redundant; verbose
concisely *adv* *syn* see BRIEFLY
conclude *vb* **1** *syn* see DECIDE
  2 *syn* see CLOSE 3
  idiom ring down the curtain
  ant open
  3 *syn* see INFER
concluded *adj* *syn* see COMPLETE 4
concluding *adj* *syn* see LAST

ant opening
conclusion *n* **1** *syn* see INFERENCE 2
2 *syn* see FINALE
3 *syn* see END 2
4 *syn* see DECISION 1
conclusive *adj* putting an end to debate or question usually by reason of irrefutability <the evidence was *conclusive* and no defense was possible>
syn definitive
rel cogent, compelling, convincing, telling; incontrovertible, irrefragable, irrefrangible, irrefutable, unanswerable; deciding, decisive, determinant, determinate, determinative; clear, precise, unambiguous
con doubtful, dubious, problematic, questionable; credible, plausible, specious; ambiguous, cryptic, enigmatic, obscure
ant inconclusive
concoct *vb* *syn* see CONTRIVE 2
rel conceive, envisage, envision; create, discover, originate
concomitant *adj* occurring in company with <good manners are likely to be *concomitant* with good behavior>
syn accompanying, ancillary, attendant, attending, coincident, collateral, incident, satellite
rel accessory, adjuvant, supplementary; correlative, corresponding
concomitant *n* *syn* see ACCOMPANIMENT 2
concord *n* **1** *syn* see HARMONY 2
rel amity, comity, friendship, goodwill; calmness, peace, placidity, serenity, tranquillity
con conflict, contention, difference, dissension, strife, variance
ant discord
2 *syn* see HARMONY 3
3 *syn* see HARMONY 1
4 *syn* see TREATY
concord *vb* *syn* see AGREE 3
concordance *n* *syn* see HARMONY 2
concordant *adj* *syn* see HARMONIOUS 2
concours *n* *syn* see CONTEST 2
concourse *n* a coming, flocking, or flowing together <they doubt the universe originated in a chance *concourse* of atoms>
syn concursion, confluence, gathering, junction, meeting
rel association, joining, linkage
con disassociation, parting, separation
concrete *vb* **1** *syn* see HARDEN 1
2 *syn* see JOIN 1
concupiscence *n* *syn* see LUST 2
concupiscent *adj* *syn* see LUSTFUL 2
concur *vb* **1** *syn* see UNITE 2
rel accord, agree, harmonize, jibe
2 *syn* see AGREE 3
rel accede, acquiesce, assent, consent
ant contend; altercate
concurrent *adj* *syn* see CONTEMPORARY 1
concurrently *adv* *syn* see TOGETHER 1
concursion *n* *syn* see CONCOURSE
concuss *vb* **1** *syn* see SHAKE 4
2 *syn* see FORCE 2
concussion *n* *syn* see IMPACT 1
rel beating, buffeting, jarring, jolting, pounding, shaking; blow, clip, clout

condemn *vb* **1** *syn* see CRITICIZE
rel belittle, decry, depreciate, disparage; deprecate, disapprove
idiom damn with faint praise, find fault with
con applaud, commend, compliment; acclaim, eulogize, extol, laud, praise; condone, excuse, forgive, pardon
2 *syn* see SENTENCE
con deliver, redeem, rescue, save
condemned *adj* *syn* see DAMNED 1
rel fallen, fated
condensation *n* *syn* see ABRIDGMENT
condense *vb* **1** *syn* see CONTRACT 3
rel compact, consolidate; curtail, minimize
con amplify
2 *syn* see EPITOMIZE 1
con broaden, expand, extend, widen
ant amplify
condensed *adj* made shorter and typically simpler <a *condensed* biography>
syn canned, capsule, epitomized, pocket, potted
rel abbreviated, abridged, bobbed, bobtail, bobtailed, curtailed, shortened
con elaborated, polished, refined; amplified, enlarged, expanded
condescend *vb* *syn* see STOOP 1
condign *adj* *syn* see JUST 3
rel grim, rigorous, stern, strict, stringent; atrocious, awful, dreadful, horrible
condition *n* **1** something that limits or qualifies an agreement or offer <included the *condition* that any heir contesting the will would be automatically disinherited>
syn provision, proviso, reservation, stipulation, strings, terms
rel prerequisite, requirement, requisite; exception, exemption, limitation, modification, qualification, restriction, saving clause
2 *syn* see ESSENTIAL 2
3 *syn* see STATE 1
4 *syn* see ORDER 9
5 *syn* see ORDER 10
6 *syn* see DISEASE 1
conditional *adj* **1** containing or dependent on a condition <our agreement is *conditional* on your raising the needed funds>
syn provisional, provisionary, provisory, tentative
rel iffy, obscure, uncertain; limited, modified, qualified, restricted
con fixed, set, sure
ant unconditional
2 *syn* see DEPENDENT 1
rel provisional, tentative; problematic, questionable; fortuitous, incidental
ant unconditional
condonable *adj* *syn* see JUSTIFIABLE
rel acceptable, tolerable
condone *vb* *syn* see EXCUSE 1
rel disregard, forget, ignore, overlook
con deplore, deprecate, disapprove; impugn, reproach
conduce *vb* *syn* see CONTRIBUTE 2
conduct *n* **1** *syn* see OVERSIGHT 1
2 *syn* see BEHAVIOR
rel bearing, demeanor, mien, posture, stance
conduct *vb* **1** *syn* see GUIDE
2 *syn* see ACCOMPANY

rel convey, transmit

3 to have the direction of and responsibility for <he had *conducted* a small market for many years>
syn carry on, direct, keep, manage, operate, ordain, run
rel administer, handle, head, oversee, supervise; arrange, control, keep up, order, regulate, rule; engineer, lead, pilot, steer

4 to act as a conduit for <*shady* transactions that *conducted* profits away from the stockholders>
syn carry, channel, convey, funnel, pipe, siphon, traject, transmit
rel remove, separate, take away, withdraw

5 *syn* see BEHAVE 1

conduit *n* **1** *syn* see CHANNEL 1

2 *syn* see PIPELINE

confab *vb syn* see CONFER 2

confabulate *vb syn* see CONFER 2

confabulation *n* **1** *syn* see CONVERSATION 1

2 *syn* see CONVERSATION 2

3 *syn* see CONFERENCE 1

confederacy *n syn* see ALLIANCE 2

confederate *n* one associated with another or others in a wrong or unlawful act <conspiring with his *confederates* to overthrow the government>
syn abettor, accessory, accomplice, coconspirator, conspirator
rel collaborator, fellow traveler; associate, colleague, fellow, partner

confederation *n syn* see ALLIANCE 2

confer *vb* **1** *syn* see GIVE 2
rel allot, provide; vouchsafe

2 to carry on a conversation or discussion usually directed toward reaching a decision or settlement <the President *conferred* with his cabinet about the scandal>
syn advise, collogue, confab, confabulate, consult, huddle, parley, powwow, treat
rel bargain, chaffer, deal, negotiate; argue, debate, discuss; converse, speak, talk
idiom put one's head together with

conference *n* **1** an interchanging of views <took several hours of *conference* to find a solution to the problem>
syn confabulation, deliberation, discussion, rap, ventilation

2 a meeting for the purpose of serious discussion and interchange of views <the association held a *conference* on the problems of aging>
syn colloquium, colloquy, palaver, rap session, seminar
rel round robin, round table

3 *syn* see TALK 4

4 *syn* see LEAGUE 4

conferrer *n syn* see DONOR

confess *vb syn* see ACKNOWLEDGE 1
idiom make a clean breast, open one's heart

confessions *n pl syn* see BIOGRAPHY

confidant *n syn* see FRIEND

confide *vb* **1** to tell confidentially <shyly *confided* her secret>
syn breathe, whisper
rel hint, insinuate, intimate, suggest
con advertise, broadcast, proclaim, publish

2 *syn* see COMMIT 1
rel bestow, present

confidence *n* **1** *syn* see TRUST 1
con distrust, mistrust; despair, hopelessness
ant doubt; apprehension

2 a feeling or showing of adequacy and reliance on oneself and one's powers <had serene *confidence* in his own ability to win>
syn aplomb, assurance, self-assurance, self-assuredness, self-confidence, self-trust;
compare EQUANIMITY
rel courage, mettle, resolution, spirit, tenacity; brashness, impudence, presumption
con apprehension, incertitude, misgiving, self-depreciation, self-doubt, uncertitude
ant diffidence

3 *syn* see CERTAINTY

4 *syn* see EFFRONTERY

confidence man *n syn* see SWINDLER

confident *adj* **1** marked by a strong, fearless, and bold belief in oneself and one's capacities <faced his accusers with a *confident* air>
syn assured, sanguine, secure, self-assured, self-confident, undoubtful
rel certain, cocksure, cocky, perky, positive, sure; self-possessed, self-reliant; bold, brave, courageous, dauntless, fearless, intrepid, unafraid, undaunted, valiant
con jittery, nervous, uneasy; afraid, daunted, fearful; doubtful, dubious
ant apprehensive

2 *syn* see SURE 5

3 *syn* see PRESUMPTUOUS

confidential *adj* **1** *syn* see PRIVATE 2

2 *syn* see FAMILIAR 1
rel secret; tried, trustworthy, trusty

configuration *n syn* see FORM 1

confine *vb* **1** *syn* see LIMIT 2

2 *syn* see IMPRISON

confine *n, usu* confines *pl* **1** *syn* see ENVIRONS 1

2 *syn* see LIMIT 1
rel circumference, compass, periphery

3 *syn* see RANGE 2

confined *adj syn* see CRAMPED

confinement *n* **1** *syn* see RESTRICTION 2

2 the state attending and consequent to childbirth <had a long difficult *confinement*>
syn accouchement, childbed, lying-in
rel parturition; labor, travail

confirm *vb* **1** *syn* see RATIFY
rel accede, acquiesce, assent, consent, subscribe; validate
idiom make good
con decline, refuse, reject

2 to attest to the truth, genuineness, accuracy, or validity of something <a surprise witness *confirmed* his account of the incident>
syn authenticate, bear out, corroborate, justify, substantiate, validate, verify
rel attest, certify, vouch, witness; back, support, underpin, uphold, warrant; check, check out
con confute, controvert, disprove, refute; contravene, gainsay, impugn, negative, traverse

---

syn synonym(s)   *rel* related word(s)
ant antonym(s)   *con* contrasted word(s)
idiom idiomatic equivalent(s)
‖ use limited; if in doubt, see a dictionary

ant deny; contradict

confirm (in) vb syn see HABITUATE 2

confirmation n syn see TESTIMONY

confirmative adj syn see CORROBORATIVE

confirmatory adj syn see CORROBORATIVE

confirmed adj 1 syn see HABITUAL 2
2 syn see INVETERATE 1

confiscate vb syn see APPROPRIATE 1

confiture n syn see JAM

conflagrant adj syn see BURNING 1

conflagration n syn see FIRE 1

conflict n 1 syn see CONTEST 1
rel argument, controversy, dispute
2 syn see CONTEST 2
3 syn see DISCORD

conflict vb syn see CLASH 2
rel differ, disagree, vary; disturb, interfere
idiom run against the tide

conflicting adj 1 syn see ANTIPATHETIC 1
2 syn see INCONSONANT 1

confluence n syn see CONCOURSE

conform vb 1 syn see ADAPT 1
rel attune, harmonize, tune
2 syn see AGREE 4
con conflict, differ, disagree
ant diverge
3 syn see HARMONIZE 3
4 syn see OBEY
idiom toe the line

conformable adj syn see ASSORTED 2
rel appropriate, fitting, suitable; applicable, usable

conformation n syn see FORM 1

conforming adj syn see DECOROUS 1

conformity n 1 syn see CONSISTENCY
2 syn see ACQUIESCENCE

confound vb 1 syn see PUZZLE
idiom take aback
2 syn see MISTAKE 1
ant discriminate, distinguish
3 syn see EMBARRASS
4 syn see DISPROVE 1

confounded adj 1 syn see AGHAST 2
2 syn see DAMNED 2
3 syn see UTTER

confoundedly adv syn see EVER 6

confrere n 1 syn see COLLEAGUE
2 syn see PARTNER

confront vb 1 to stand over against in the role of an adversary or enemy <he *confronted* his accusers with perfect aplomb>
syn affront, encounter, face, meet; *compare* MEET 6
rel beard, brave, challenge, defy; flout, scorn, scout; oppose, resist, withstand
idiom come to close quarters with, come up against
con avoid, elude, evade
2 syn see ACCOST 2

confronting prep syn see BEFORE 2

confuse vb 1 syn see EMBARRASS
2 to make unclear in mind or purpose <found the city hustle and noise very *confusing*>
syn addle, ball up, befuddle, bewilder, ‖bumfuzzle, discombobulate, distract, dizzy, fluster, fuddle, mix up, ‖mizzle, ‖momble, muddle, mull, throw off, throw out
rel misguide, mislead; agitate, bother, discompose, disquiet, flurry, perturb, upset

3 syn see PUZZLE
4 to make indistinct the elements or true character of (as a discussion) <*confuse* an issue in a debate>
syn becloud, befog, blur, cloud, fog, muddy
rel complicate, confound, involve, mix up
idiom lose in a fog
con clarify, elucidate; simplify
5 to throw into disorder <surging waves *confused* the waters> <her accounts were totally *confused*>
syn foul up, jumble, mix up, muddle, ‖snafu, snarl up, tumble; *compare* DISORDER 1
rel derange, disarrange, disorder, disorganize, disturb, mess (up), unsettle
idiom put in a flutter, throw into confusion
6 syn see MISREPRESENT
7 syn see MISTAKE 1
ant differentiate

confusion n 1 syn see RUIN 3
2 syn see EMBARRASSMENT
3 a condition in which things are out of their normal or proper places or relationships <the room was in complete *confusion*>
syn ataxia, ‖ballup, chaos, clutter, disarray, disorder, huddle, misorder, muddle, ‖mullock, pell-mell, snarl, topsy-turviness
rel derangement, disarrangement, disturbance; foul-up, mess, mix-up, muck, ‖mux, ‖snafu; babel, din, hullabaloo, pandemonium
con methodization, ordering, organization, systematization; method, order, system
4 syn see COMMOTION 2
rel disorder, disorganization, disturbance; discomfiture, embarrassment

confute vb syn see DISPROVE 1

congé n syn see PARTING

congeal vb 1 syn see HARDEN 1
rel chill, cool, freeze
2 syn see COAGULATE

congenial adj 1 syn see HARMONIOUS 3
ant uncongenial
2 syn see CONSONANT 1
rel companionable, cooperative, social; affable, cordial, genial, gracious, sociable; pleasant, pleasing
ant uncongenial; antipathetic (*of persons*); abhorrent (*of tasks, responsibilities*)
3 syn see PLEASANT 1
4 syn see GRACIOUS 1

congenital adj 1 syn see INNATE 1
2 syn see INHERENT

congeries n syn see GATHERING 2

congest vb syn see FILL 1

conglobate vb syn see BALL

conglobe vb syn see BALL

conglomerate adj syn see MISCELLANEOUS

conglomerate n 1 syn see AGGREGATE 1
2 syn see SYNDICATE

conglomeration n 1 syn see ACCUMULATION
2 syn see AGGREGATE 1

congratulate vb to express to another one's pleasure on his good fortune or success <*congratulate* a friend when he wins a race>
syn felicitate
rel applaud, laud, praise; bless, compliment

idiom pat one on the back, tender (*or* offer) congratulation, wish one joy, wish one well
con belittle, depreciate, disparage, knock, run down, slur

congregate *vb syn* see GATHER 6
rel swarm, teem
ant disperse

congregation *n syn* see GATHERING 2
rel audience, disciples, following, public

congress *n syn* see ASSOCIATION 2

congress *vb syn* see GATHER 6

congruity *n syn* see CONSISTENCY

congruous *adj syn* see CONSONANT 1
rel appropriate, fit, fitting, meet; proper, seemly
ant incongruous
2 *syn* see HARMONIOUS 2

conjectural *adj syn* see SUPPOSED 1
con demonstrated; unquestionable

conjecture *n syn* see THEORY 2
ant fact

conjecture *vb* to draw an inference from slight or inadequate evidence <when he failed to arrive on time she *conjectured* that he was drinking again>
syn guess, presume, pretend, suppose, surmise, think; *compare* INFER, UNDERSTAND 3
rel assume, expect, suspect; believe, deem, feel; conceive, fancy, imagine; conclude, estimate, gather, glean, infer, judge
idiom hazard a guess, take for granted
con demonstrate, prove, test, try; ascertain, determine, discover, learn

conjoin *vb* **1** *syn* see JOIN 1
2 *syn* see UNITE 2

conjoint *adj* **1** *syn* see COMMON 1
2 *syn* see COOPERATIVE

conjointly *adv syn* see TOGETHER 3

conjointment *n syn* see ASSOCIATION 1

conjugal *adj syn* see MATRIMONIAL

conjugality *n syn* see MARRIAGE 1

conjugate *vb syn* see JOIN 1

conjunct *adj syn* see COMMON 1

conjunction *n syn* see ASSOCIATION 1

conjuration *n syn* see SPELL

conjure *vb syn* see BEG

conjurer *n* **1** *syn* see MAGICIAN 1
2 *syn* see MAGICIAN 2

conjuring *n* **1** *syn* see MAGIC 1
2 *syn* see MAGIC 2

conjury *n syn* see MAGIC 1

‖**conk** *n* **1** *syn* see NOSE 1
2 *syn* see HEAD 1

‖**conk** *n syn* see HIT 1

conk *vb syn* see DIE 1

con man *n syn* see SWINDLER
rel shill
con mark, sucker, victim; greenhorn

connate *adj syn* **1** *syn* see INNATE 1
2 *syn* see INHERENT
3 *syn* see RELATED

connatural *adj* **1** *syn* see INNATE 1
2 *syn* see RELATED

connect *vb syn* see JOIN 1

---

syn synonym(s)   *rel* related word(s)
ant antonym(s)   *con* contrasted word(s)
idiom idiomatic equivalent(s)
‖ use limited; if in doubt, see a dictionary

ant disconnect

connection *n* **1** *syn* see ASSOCIATION 1
2 *syn* see JOINT 1
3 *syn* see JOB 2
4 *syn* see RELIGION 2

connivance *n syn* see COMPLICITY

connive *vb* **1** to secretly favor or sympathize with something improper or illicit <*connive* at treason>
syn blink (at), wink (at)
rel condone, disregard, ignore, overlook, tolerate
idiom close (*or* shut) one's eyes to, let go by (*or* get by) one's eye, regard with indulgence
con disapprove, disfavor, frown (at *or* upon); disallow, reject, repudiate; disdain, scorn, scout, spurn
2 *syn* see PLOT

connoisseur *n* a person who enjoys with discrimination and appreciation of subtleties and details especially in matters of culture or art <a *connoisseur* of fine wines>
syn aesthete, cognoscente, dilettante
rel bon vivant, epicure, gourmet; adept, authority, critic, expert
con abecedarian, amateur, dabbler, tyro

connotation *n syn* see ASSOCIATION 4

connote *vb* **1** *syn* see MEAN 2
2 *syn* see SUGGEST 1

connubial *adj syn* see MATRIMONIAL

connubiality *n syn* see MARRIAGE 1

conquer *vb* **1** to overcome or gain dominion over by force of arms <leaders who have tried and failed to *conquer* the world>
syn bear down, beat down, crush, defeat, overpower, reduce, subdue, subjugate, vanquish; *compare* DEFEAT 2, OVERTHROW 2, WHIP 2, WIN 1
rel baffle, balk, circumvent, foil, frustrate, outwit, override, thwart; bend, control, master, overmaster, subject, worst
idiom bring one to one's knees, trample in the dust, trample underfoot
con bow, cave, give up, succumb, yield; capitulate, submit, surrender
2 to gain mastery over something by getting the better of obstacles and difficulties <trials faced by the men who *conquered* Mount Everest>
syn best, master, overcome, prevail, triumph; *compare* OVERCOME 1
3 *syn* see OVERCOME 1

conqueror *n syn* see VICTOR 1

conquest *n syn* see VICTORY 1
rel defeating, overthrow, rout, routing, subdual

consanguine *adj syn* see RELATED

‖**consarned** *adj* **1** *syn* see DAMNED 2
2 *syn* see UTTER

conscience *n syn* see QUALM

conscienceless *adj syn* see UNSCRUPULOUS
rel devious, shifty, tricky, unfair
ant conscientious

conscientious *adj* **1** *syn* see UPRIGHT 2
ant conscienceless
2 *syn* see CAREFUL 2

consciable *adj syn* see CAREFUL 2

conscious *adj* **1** *syn* see AWARE
rel noticing, noting, observing, perceiving, remarking; vigilant, watchful

con forgetful, oblivious, unmindful; disregarding, ignoring, overlooking
ant unconscious
2 *syn* see SELF-CONSCIOUS
consciousness *n syn* see CARE 4
conscribe *vb syn* see DRAFT 1
conscript *vb syn* see DRAFT 1
consecrate *vb* 1 *syn* see DEVOTE 1
con desecrate, profane; defile, pollute
2 *syn* see BLESS 1
consecrated *adj syn* see HOLY 1
consecution *n* 1 *syn* see ORDER 5
2 *syn* see SUCCESSION 2
consecutive *adj* following one after another
in orderly fashion <it rained for five *consecutive* days>
syn sequent, sequential, serial, subsequent, subsequential, succedent, succeeding, successional, successive; *compare* NEXT
rel after, ensuing, following, later; enlarging, increasing, progressive
con antecedent, preceding, prior
consecutively *adv syn* see TOGETHER 2
consent *vb syn* see ASSENT
rel allow, let, permit; approve, sanction; concur
con decline; balk, demur, stick, stickle
consent *n* 1 *syn* see PERMISSION
2 *syn* see AGREEMENT 2
consentaneous *adj syn* see UNANIMOUS
consentient *adj syn* see UNANIMOUS
consequence *n* 1 *syn* see EFFECT 1
con origin, root, source
ant antecedent
2 *syn* see IMPORTANCE
rel exigency, need; fame, honor, renown, reputation, repute
3 *syn* see STATUS 2
4 *syn* see CONCEIT 2
consequent *adj syn* see RATIONAL
consequential *adj syn* see IMPORTANT 1
consequently *adv syn* see THEREFORE
conservancy *n syn* see CONSERVATION 1
conservation *n* 1 a deliberate planned
guarding and protecting of something felt as precious <*conservation* of our natural resources>
syn conservancy, husbanding, preserval, preservation, salvation, saving
rel attention, care, cherishing, protection; control, directing, governing, management, managing, supervising, supervision
con neglect, squandering, waste
2 *syn* see PRESERVATION 1
conservative *adj* 1 tending to resist or oppose change <took a very *conservative* stance politically>
syn die-hard, fogyish, old-line, orthodox, reactionary, right, tory, traditionalistic
con modern, progressive, radical
ant advanced
2 kept or keeping within bounds <equally *conservative* in speech and action>
syn controlled, discreet, moderate, reasonable, restrained, temperate, unexcessive, unextreme
rel cautious, chary, wary; circumspect, politic, proper, prudent
con expansive, unconstrained; excessive, freewheeling, uncontrolled, unrestrained

conservative *n syn* see DIEHARD 1
conservatory *n syn* see GREENHOUSE
conserve *vb syn* see SAVE 1
rel keep up, maintain, support, sustain
con dissipate, fritter, squander, waste
conserve *n syn* see JAM
consider *vb* 1 to give serious thought to
<*consider* the risk you would be taking>
syn contemplate, excogitate, mind, perpend, ponder, study, think (out *or* over), weigh
rel meditate, muse, ruminate; cogitate, reason, reflect, speculate; think; examine, inspect, look (at), scan, scrutinize, see
idiom bestow thought to, chew the cud over, revolve (*or* turn over) in one's mind
con disregard, ignore, neglect, overlook, slight
2 *syn* see EYE 1
rel envisage, envision
3 to come to view, judge, or classify <he *considered* thrift essential to success>
syn account, deem, reckon, regard, view; *compare* FEEL 3
rel conceive, fancy, imagine, think; conclude, gather, infer, judge, rule
4 *syn* see ADMIRE 2
5 *syn* see FEEL 3
considerable *adj* 1 *syn* see IMPORTANT 1
2 tending more to the large than the small
<buckled down with his ax and made a *considerable* impression on the woodpile>
syn good, respectable, ‖right smart, sensible, sizable, ‖smart
rel able, capable, competent; active, effective, efficacious; important, notable, significant; goodly, pretty, substantial, tidy
con insignificant, meager, slight, trivial; big, grand, great, huge
3 *syn* see BIG 1
considerably *adv syn* see WELL 8
considerate *adj* 1 *syn* see CAUTIOUS
2 *syn* see THOUGHTFUL 3
rel kind, kindly; compassionate, sympathetic, tender, warmhearted; amiable, complaisant, obliging
ant inconsiderate
3 *syn* see GENEROUS 1
considerately *adv syn* see WELL 2
rel solicitously, tenderly; altruistically, benevolently, charitably
con austerely, harshly, severely, strictly
considerateness *n syn* see CONSIDERATION 3
consideration *n* 1 *syn* see ATTENTION 1
2 *syn* see MOTIVE 1
3 thoughtful and sympathetic attention
<showed great *consideration* to the needs of others>
syn concern, considerateness, regard, solicitude
rel awareness, heed, heedfulness, mindfulness; forbearance, mercy, quarter
con disregard, heedlessness, unconcern, unmindfulness; inconsiderateness; contempt, despite, disdain, disinterest, scorn
4 *syn* see REGARD 4
considered *adj syn* see DELIBERATE 1
rel intentional, voluntary, willful
con impulsive, instinctive, spontaneous; headlong, impetuous, precipitate

ant unconsidered

considering *conj syn* see BECAUSE

consign *vb* **1** *syn* see COMMIT 1
rel resign, surrender, yield
2 *syn* see SEND 1

consist *vb* **1** to have existence or a place <our national strength *consists* not solely in military readiness>
syn dwell, exist, inhere, lie, reside
rel be, subsist; abide, repose, rest
idiom have one's (*or* a) place
2 *syn* see AGREE 4

consistency *n* agreement or harmony of parts, traits, or features <his adversary had to admit the *consistency* of his position>
syn coherence, conformity, congruity, correspondence; *compare* HARMONY 2
rel agreement, concord, consonance; likeness, similarity; apposition, aptness, felicity, fitness, suitability
con incoherence, incongruity; impropriety, inappropriateness, unsuitability
ant inconsistency

consistent *adj* **1** *syn* see SAME 3
2 *syn* see CONSONANT 1

consistently *adv syn* see USUALLY 1

consociate *n syn* see PARTNER

console *vb syn* see COMFORT
rel calm, relieve, tranquilize; animate, hearten, inspirit
idiom lift the spirits of
con agitate, discompose, disquiet, disturb, perturb, upset

consolidate *vb syn* see UNIFY 1
rel amalgamate, blend, fuse, merge; set, solidify
con part, sever, sunder; liquefy, melt

consolidating *adj syn* see INTEGRATIVE

consolidation *n* **1** *syn* see UNIFICATION
2 a union of two or more businesses <*consolidation* is often accompanied by a new corporate name>
syn amalgamation, merger
ant dissolution

consonance *n* **1** *syn* see HARMONY 2
con discrepancy, incompatibility, incongruousness
ant discord
2 *syn* see HARMONY 1
ant dissonance

consonant *adj* **1** conforming (as to a pattern, a standard, or a relationship) without discord or difficulty <his performance was seldom *consonant* with his very real abilities>
syn agreeable, compatible, congenial, congruous, consistent, sympathetic; *compare* HARMONIOUS 2
rel accordant, conformable, harmonious; coincident, concurrent; en rapport
con discordant, discrepant; incompatible, incongruous, inconsistent
ant inconsonant
2 *syn* see HARMONIOUS 1
ant dissonant

3 *syn* see LIKE
4 *syn* see RESONANT

consort *n* **1** *syn* see ACCOMPANIMENT 2
2 *syn* see SPOUSE

consort *vb syn* see AGREE 4

consort (with) *vb syn* see ACCOMPANY

consortium *n syn* see ASSOCIATION 2

conspectus *n syn* see ABRIDGMENT

conspicuous *adj* **1** *syn* see CLEAR 5
2 *syn* see NOTICEABLE
rel celebrated, eminent, illustrious; showy
con common, everyday, ordinary; covert, secret; concealed, hidden
ant inconspicuous

conspiracy *n syn* see PLOT 2
rel sedition, treason; disloyalty, faithlessness, falsity, perfidiousness, perfidy, treacherousness, treachery
con faith, faithfulness, fealty, loyalty

conspirator *n syn* see CONFEDERATE

conspire *vb syn* see PLOT

‖**constable** *n syn* see POLICEMAN

constancy *n syn* see ATTACHMENT 1

constant *adj* **1** *syn* see FAITHFUL 1
rel abiding, clinging, enduring, lasting, persistent, persisting
con capricious, mercurial
ant fickle, inconstant
2 *syn* see INFLEXIBLE 3
con fluctuant, fluctuating, fluctuational, unstable
ant inconstant, variable
3 *syn* see SAME 3
4 *syn* see STEADY 2
5 *syn* see CONTINUAL
rel chronic, confirmed, inveterate; dogged, obstinate, pertinacious; persevering
con alternate, intermittent, recurrent; infrequent, occasional, sporadic
ant fitful

constantly *adv syn* see ALWAYS 1
idiom day after day, day in, day out
ant occasionally

constate *vb syn* see ASSERT 1

consternate *vb syn* see DISMAY 1

consternation *n syn* see FEAR 1
rel confusion, muddle, muddlement; bewilderment, distraction, perplexity
con composure, equanimity, phlegm, sangfroid; aplomb, poise, self-command, self=possession

constipate *vb syn* see STULTIFY

constipated *adj* being unable to defecate regularly and without difficulty <complained that she was constantly *constipated*>
syn astricted, bound, costive, obstipated

constituent *n syn* see ELEMENT 2
rel division, fraction, part, portion
con complex, economy, organism, system; amalgam, blend, composite, compound
ant aggregate, whole

constitute *vb* **1** to be all or a fundamental part of the substance of <water *constitutes* the greater part of the human body>
syn compose, comprise, form, make, make up
rel embody, incorporate, integrate; complement, complete, fill out, flesh (out)
2 *syn* see ENACT 1
3 *syn* see FOUND 2

---

syn synonym(s)   *rel* related word(s)
ant antonym(s)   *con* contrasted word(s)
idiom idiomatic equivalent(s)
‖ use limited; if in doubt, see a dictionary

constitution n 1 syn see PHYSIQUE
  2 syn see MAKEUP 1
constitutional adj syn see INHERENT
  con anomalous, irregular, unnatural
  ant adventient
constitutional n syn see WALK 1
  rel ambulation, footwork, legwork, perambulation
constitutive adj syn see ESSENTIAL 2
constrain vb 1 syn see FORCE 2
  2 syn see RESTRAIN 1
  3 syn see DENY 3
  rel abridge, curtail, deprive; ban, bar, disallow, enjoin
  4 syn see IMPRISON
  5 syn see PRESS 1
  6 syn see DISTRESS 2
constrained adj syn see RESERVED 1
constrainment n syn see RESTRICTION 2
constraint n 1 syn see FORCE 4
  rel repression, suppression; driving, impelling, impulsion; goad, motive, spring, spur
  2 syn see RESTRICTION 2
constrict vb 1 syn see CONTRACT 3
  rel curb, restrain; circumscribe, confine, limit, restrict
  con enlarge, expand, increase, maximize
  2 to make narrow or narrower <the muscles that constrict the sphincter>
  syn constringe, narrow
  rel gather, plait, pucker; compress, constrain, squeeze; astringe
  con broaden, dilate, distend, widen
  ant expand
constringe vb syn see CONSTRICT 2
construal n syn see EXPLANATION 1
construct vb 1 syn see MAKE 3
  2 syn see BUILD 1
  3 syn see ERECT 5
construction n 1 syn see MAKEUP 1
  2 syn see EXPLANATION 1
constructive adj syn see IMPLICIT 2
  rel inferential, ratiocinative; construable, interpretable, renderable
  con clear, evident, obvious, patent
  ant manifest
construe vb syn see EXPLAIN 1
consuetude n syn see HABIT 1
consult vb syn see CONFER 2
  rel cogitate, counsel, deliberate; consider, examine, review
consume vb 1 to bring to an end by or as if by the action of a destroying force <the village was consumed by fire>
  syn devour, eat, eat up, exhaust, use up
  rel destroy, raze, ruin, wreck; annihilate, extinguish; crush, overwhelm, suppress
  con bolster, brace, buttress, hold up, prop, stay, support, sustain; build, construct, create, make, produce; renew, restore
  2 syn see WASTE 2
  3 syn see GO 4
  4 syn see EAT 1
  5 to eat or drink usually gluttonously or without measure <consumed dozens of burgers and a case of beer>
  syn polish off, punish, put away, put down, shift, swill; compare EAT 1
  rel absorb, ingest; devour, gobble (up), gorge, wolf; down, gulp, guzzle, inhale, swallow

  idiom dispose of
  6 syn see MONOPOLIZE
consumedly adv syn see EVER 6
consuming adj syn see ENGROSSING
consummate adj 1 brought to the highest possible point of perfection <the difficult allegro passages displayed her consummate skill>
  syn accomplished, finished, perfected, ripe, virtuosic; compare PERFECT 2
  rel faultless, flawless, impeccable, perfect; practiced, skilled, trained; able, gifted, talented; inimitable, peerless, superb, superlative, supreme, transcendent, unsurpassable
  con callow, crude, green, raw, rough, uncouth; defective, deficient, inadequate
  2 syn see UTTER
consummate vb syn see CLOSE 3
consumption n syn see TUBERCULOSIS
contact n 1 the state of being in or coming into close association or connection <shuddered at the contact of his icy hand>
  syn contingence, touch
  rel closeness, contiguity, nearness, propinquity, proximity; impingement, taction, touching; association, connection, relation; oneness, union, unity
  con breach, break, rift, rupture, split; insularity, isolation, seclusion, segregation, separation; distance, farness, remoteness
  2 a situation permitting exchange of ideas and opinions <tried for several days to get in contact with her brother>
  syn commerce, communication, communion, intercommunication, intercourse
  rel association, companionship, fellowship; oneness, union, unity; accord, concord, harmony, rapport; empathy, sympathy, understanding
contact vb syn see REACH 4
contagion n syn see POISON
  rel contamination, corruption, pollution, taint; miasma
contagious adj 1 syn see INFECTIOUS 2
  2 syn see INFECTIOUS 3
contain vb 1 syn see COMPOSE 4
  2 to have or be capable of having within <the box contained family papers> <a mug that will contain a quart of ale>
  syn accommodate, hold
  rel harbor, house, lodge, shelter; admit, receive, take, take in
  3 syn see INCLUDE
contaminate vb 1 to debase by making impure or unclean <feared her child's morals would be contaminated by others>
  syn defile, pollute, soil, taint; compare TAINT 1
  rel corrupt, debase, debauch, deprave, pervert, vitiate; harm, injure, spoil
  con better, elevate, improve
  ant purify
  2 to render unfit for use by the introduction of unwholesome or undesirable elements <water contaminated by sewage>
  syn befoul, foul, pollute
  rel infect; poison; dirty, soil
  ant purify
contemn vb syn see DESPISE
contemplate vb 1 syn see EYE 1

rel ponder, reflect, study; examine, inspect, scan, scrutinize

2 *syn* see CONSIDER 1
rel drift, roam

3 *syn* see INTEND 2
idiom have in view

contemplative *adj syn* see THOUGHTFUL 1
rel musing, weighing; reasoning
idiom in a brown study

contemporaneous *adj syn* see CONTEMPORARY 1

contemporary *adj* **1** existing or occurring at the same time <the story has come down from several *contemporary* sources>
syn coetaneous, coeval, coexistent, coexisting, concurrent, contemporaneous, simultaneous, synchronal, synchronic, synchronous
rel accompanying, attendant, attending, coincident, concomitant; current, existing, present; associated, connected, linked, related
con antecedent, foregoing, preceding, previous, prior; ensuing, following, succeeding

2 *syn* see PRESENT

3 *syn* see UP-TO-DATE

contempt *n* **1** *syn* see DESPITE 1
rel antipathy, aversion; distaste, repugnance
con awe, fear, reverence
ant regard

2 *syn* see DISGRACE

3 *syn* see DEFIANCE 2

contemptible *adj* arousing or meriting scorn or disdain <a *contemptible* attempt to blame his wife for his failure>
syn beggarly, cheap, despicable, despisable, mean, pitiable, pitiful, scummy, scurvy, shabby, sorry; *compare* BASE 3
rel abhorrent, abominable, detestable, hateful, odious; abject, ignoble, sordid; bad, inferior, poor, sad; disgusting, scrimy, shameful; outcast
con creditable, estimable, honorable, noble; high-minded, high-principled, principled, true, upright; honest, square, straight
ant admirable

contend *vb* **1** to strive in opposition to someone or something <*contending* against the temptation to look behind him>
syn battle, fight, oppugn, tug, war
rel combat, oppose, resist, withstand; contest, cope (with), vie

2 *syn* see MAINTAIN 2
rel report, say, tell; charge, enjoin, urge; dictate, prescribe

3 *syn* see COMPETE 1
rel combat, oppose, resist, withstand; confront, encounter, face, meet, stand

content *vb* *syn* see SATISFY 3
rel delight, thrill, tickle; bewitch, captivate, charm, enrapture
con disappoint, dishearten, displease
ant discontent

contention *n* **1** *syn* see DISCORD
rel altercation, quarrel, squabble, wrangle; argument, controversy, dispute

con agreement, coincidence, concurrence

2 *syn* see ARGUMENT 2

3 *syn* see THESIS 1

contentious *adj* **1** *syn* see BELLIGERENT
rel contrary, froward, perverse; captious, carping, caviling, faultfinding
con calm, serene, tranquil; amiable, complaisant, good-natured, obliging
ant peaceable

2 prone to wordy contention <a *contentious* old chap, always ready for an argument>
syn argumentative, controversial, disputatious, litigious, polemical
rel fiery, hasty, hotheaded, impetuous, peppery; bellicose, belligerent, scrappy
con amiable, complaisant, good-natured, obliging; agreeable, cooperative, understanding

conterminous *adj syn* see ADJACENT 3

contest *vb* **1** *syn* see COMPETE 1
rel endeavor

2 *syn* see RESIST

contest *n* **1** an earnest struggle for superiority or victory <the rival factions continued in *contest* for several years>
syn competition, conflict, emulation, rivalry, strife, striving, tug-of-war, warfare
rel brush, encounter, skirmish; action, battle, engagement

2 a competitive encounter between groups or individuals <there were *contests* of skill and endurance>
syn competition, concours, conflict, meet, meeting, rencontre
rel proving, testing, trial, trying

contestation *n syn* see THESIS 1

contiguity *n syn* see PROXIMITY

contiguous *adj* **1** *syn* see ADJACENT 3
rel close, near, nearby, nigh
con apart, separate; distant, remote

2 *syn* see NEIGHBORING

contiguously *adv syn* see IMMEDIATELY 1

contiguousness *n syn* see PROXIMITY

continence *n syn* see TEMPERANCE 2
rel self-restraint; moderation, temperateness; chasteness, chastity, purity
con self-indulgence; excessiveness, inordinateness; lasciviousness, lecherousness, lewdness, licentiousness, wantonness
ant incontinence

continent *adj syn* see ABSTEMIOUS
rel bridled, curbed, inhibited, restrained; chaste, pure
con self-indulgent, spoiled
ant incontinent

contingence *n syn* see CONTACT 1

contingency *n syn* see JUNCTURE 2
rel break, chance, occasion, opportunity

contingent *adj syn* see ACCIDENTAL
rel unanticipated, unforeseeable, unforeseen; likely, possible, probable
con certain, inevitable, necessary

2 *syn* see DEPENDENT 1

continual *adj* continuing without intermission and seemingly without end <they were tired of her *continual* nagging>
syn around-the-clock, ceaseless, constant, continuous, endless, everlasting, incessant, interminable, minutely, perpetual, timeless, unceasing, unending, unintermitted, unintermittent, uninterrupted, unremitting

rel abiding, enduring, persistent, persisting, staying; unvarying; unchanging, unfailing, unflagging, unwaning; relentless, running, steady

con ephemeral, evanescent, impermanent, short-lived, temporary, transient, transitory

continually *adv syn* see TOGETHER 2

continuance *n syn* see RUN 2
rel constancy, longevity, permanence; survival

continuation *n* **1** uninterrupted existence or succession <the *continuation* of political disorder in Northern Ireland>
syn continuity, duration, endurance, persistence
rel extension, prolongation, protraction
ant termination
2 *syn* see RUN 2
ant cessation

continue *vb* **1** to remain indefinitely in existence or in a particular state or course <many traditional beliefs still *continue*> <do you expect to *continue* in school for the rest of your life?>
syn abide, carry through, endure, last, perdure, persist
rel carry on, carry over, ride, run on; outlast, outlive, survive; remain, stay
con cease, desist, discontinue, quit; arrest, check, interrupt; defer, intermit, postpone, stay, suspend
ant discontinue
2 *syn* see RESUME 2

continuing *adj syn* see OLD 2

continuity *n syn* see CONTINUATION 1

continuous *adj syn* see CONTINUAL
ant discontinuous

continuously *adv* **1** *syn* see TOGETHER 2
2 *syn* see ALWAYS 1

contort *vb syn* see DEFORM
rel bend, curve, twist

contour *n syn* see OUTLINE

contra *prep syn* see AGAINST 1

contra *adv syn* see AGAIN 5

contra *n syn* see OPPOSITE

contraband *adj* prohibited or excluded by law or treaty <fur or feathers from endangered species are *contraband* in advanced nations>
syn banned, hot
rel disapproved, proscribed, taboo; forbidden, prohibited; excluded, shut out

contraband *vb syn* see SMUGGLE

contraception *n syn* see BIRTH CONTROL

contract *n* a usually legally enforceable arrangement between two or more parties <a *contract* for a new roof>
syn agreement, bargain, bond, compact, convention, covenant, pact, transaction; *compare* AGREEMENT 2, TREATY

contract *vb* **1** to become affected by a disease or disorder <*contracted* a severe cold that later turned into pneumonia>
syn catch, come down (with), get, sicken (with *or* of), take
rel acquire, obtain; decline, fail, sink, weaken; afflict, derange, disorder, indispose, upset; bring on, cause, induce; succumb (to)
idiom be laid by the heels by, fall (a) victim to

2 *syn* see INCUR
3 to make or become smaller in bulk or volume <*contract* a muscle>
syn compress, concentrate, condense, constrict, shrink
rel decrease, diminish, dwindle, lessen, reduce
con dilate, distend, inflate, swell
ant expand

contracted *adj syn* see ENGAGED 2

contradict *vb syn* see DENY 4
rel dispute; belie, falsify, garble
con authenticate, substantiate, verify
ant corroborate; confirm

contradiction *n syn* see DENIAL 2

contradictory *n syn* see OPPOSITE

contradictory *adj syn* see OPPOSITE
rel negating, nullifying; adverse, antagonistic, counteractive
con agreeing, jibing, squaring, tallying
ant corroboratory; confirmatory

contradistinction *n syn* see ANTAGONISM 2

contraposition *n syn* see ANTAGONISM 2

contraption *n syn* see DEVICE 2

contrariant *n syn* see ANTIPATHETIC 1

contrariety *n syn* see ANTAGONISM 2

contrariwise *adv syn* see AGAIN 5
idiom on (*or* to) the contrary

contrary *n syn* see OPPOSITE

contrary *adj* **1** *syn* see OPPOSITE
2 *syn* see ANTIPATHETIC 1
3 obstinately self-willed in refusing to concur, conform, or submit <why be *contrary* about something that you cannot change>
syn balky, cross-grained, froward, ornery, perverse, restive, wayward, wrongheaded
rel headstrong, intractable, recalcitrant, refractory, unruly; contumacious, insubordinate, rebellious; dissentient, dissident, nonconforming, nonconformist, recusant; obstinate, stubborn
con amenable, biddable, docile, obedient, tractable; amiable, obliging; acquiescent, compliant; forbearing, long-suffering, tolerant
ant complaisant

contrary *adv syn* see AGAIN 5

contrast *vb syn* see COMPARE 2

contravene *vb* **1** *syn* see VIOLATE 1
rel encroach, intrude, overstep, trespass
2 *syn* see DENY 4
rel combat, fight, oppose, resist; abjure, disclaim, disown, exclude, reject, repudiate, spurn
con accept, agree, subscribe (to); admit, allow, own
ant uphold (*as a principle*); allege (*as a right or claim*)

contravention *n syn* see BREACH 1
rel crime, offense, sin, vice

contrawise *adv syn* see AGAIN 5

contretemps *n syn* see MISFORTUNE

contribute *vb* **1** to give in common with others <*contribute* to a fund for handicapped children>
syn chip in, come through, kick in, pitch in, subscribe; *compare* GIVE 1
idiom put something in the pot, sweeten the kitty

2 to have a share in something (as an act or effect) <careful planning *contributed* greatly to the success of the project>
syn conduce, redound, tend
rel aid, help, assist; add (to), augment, supplement; fortify, recruit, reinforce, strengthen
idiom do one's bit, have a hand in
con detract, minus, subtract, take away
contribution *n syn* see DONATION
contributory *adj syn* see AUXILIARY
contrite *adj syn* see REMORSEFUL
contriteness *n syn* see PENITENCE
contrition *n syn* see PENITENCE
contriturate *vb syn* see PULVERIZE 1
contrivance *n* **1** see DEVICE 2
2 *syn* see INVENTION
contrive *vb* **1** *syn* see PLOT
rel develop, elaborate, work out
2 to use ingenuity in making or doing or achieving an end <*contrived* a useful camp stove from a few bricks and a piece of screen>
syn concoct, cook (up), devise, dream up, formulate, frame, hatch (up), invent, make up, vamp (up)
rel plan, plot, project, scheme; fabricate, fashion, make, manufacture; handle, manipulate, move; rig
control *vb* **1** *syn* see COMPOSE 4
rel adjust, regulate; curb, master, quell, subdue
2 *syn* see GOVERN 3
rel regulate, supervise; discipline
idiom put through the mill (or a course of sprouts), take in hand
control *n syn* see POWER 1
controlled *adj syn* see CONSERVATIVE 2
controversial *adj syn* see CONTENTIOUS 2
controversy *n* **1** *syn* see ARGUMENT 2
2 *syn* see QUARREL
controvert *vb syn* see DISPROVE 1
rel challenge, oppugn, question
contumacious *adj syn* see INSUBORDINATE
rel contrary, froward, perverse; alienated, disaffected, estranged, irreconcilable
con acquiescent, compliant, resigned
ant obedient
contumacy *n syn* see DEFIANCE 2
contumelious *adj* **1** *syn* see ABUSIVE
2 *syn* see INSOLENT 2
ant obsequious
contumely *n* **1** *syn* see ABUSE
rel animadversion, aspersion, reflection, stricture
idiom hard (or bitter) words
2 *syn* see AFFRONT
contuse *vb syn* see BRUISE 1
contusion *n syn* see BRUISE
conundrum *n syn* see MYSTERY
convalesce *vb syn* see IMPROVE 3
convenance *n syn* see FORM 3
convene *vb* **1** to begin a session (as of a legislature or conference) <the council *convened* at 10 o'clock>

syn meet, open, sit
idiom hold a meeting (or session)
2 *syn* see SUMMON 2
rel convoke, muster
3 *syn* see CONVOKE
convenience *n* **1** *syn* see AMENITY 2
2 *syn* see TOILET
convenience *vb syn* see OBLIGE 2
convenient *adj* **1** *syn* see GOOD 2
2 situated within easy reach <left his glasses *convenient* to his book>
syn adjacent, close-at-hand, close-by, handy, near-at-hand, nearby
rel close, near, nigh; immediate, next
idiom at one's beck and call, at one's fingertips, in one's immediate neighborhood, under one's nose
ant inconvenient
convention *n* **1** *syn* see TREATY
2 *syn* see CONTRACT
rel accord, understanding
3 *syn* see FORM 3
rel canon, law, precept, rule; custom, practice
conventional *adj* **1** according with or based on generally accepted and well-established usage <took a very *conventional* view of his duty>
syn button-down, orthodox, square, straight; *compare* TRADITIONAL 1
rel moderate, sober, temperate; constrained, restrained; dependable, reliable, responsible; conscientious, fastidious, nice, punctilious, scrupulous; conservative, traditionalistic
ant unconventional
2 *syn* see TRADITIONAL 1
3 *syn* see CEREMONIAL
rel decent, decorous, proper, seemly; correct, precise, right
con lax, negligent, remiss, slack; artless, ingenuous, naive, natural, simple, unsophisticated
ant unconventional
converge *vb* to come to or trend toward a common point <the main streets *converge* on a central square>
syn concenter, concentrate, focus, meet
idiom come to a center, come (or run) together
conversant *adj* **1** *syn* see AWARE
ant ignorant
2 *syn* see FAMILIAR 3
rel sensible; up-to-date; apprehending, comprehending, perceptive, percipient
con unfamiliar; nescient
ant unconversant
conversation *n* **1** oral exchange of information or ideas <leaned against the fence in casual *conversation*>
syn chat, colloquy, confabulation, converse, dialogue, parley
rel discussion; discourse, speech, talk
2 an instance of conversational exchange <had a long *conversation* about family problems>
syn colloquy, confabulation, dialogue, talk; *compare* CHAT 2
rel debate, deliberation, discussion, ventilation; comment, observation, remark; cross talk, repartee

---

syn synonym(s)   *rel* related word(s)
ant antonym(s)   *con* contrasted word(s)
idiom idiomatic equivalent(s)
‖ use limited; if in doubt, see a dictionary

conversation piece *n syn* see CURIOSITY 2

converse *vb* to engage in conversation <they *conversed* quietly while waiting for their friend>
syn chat, chin, colloque, talk, visit, yarn; *compare* CHAT 1

converse (in) *vb syn* see SPEAK 3

converse *n* **1** *syn* see CONVERSATION 1
2 *syn* see COMMUNICATION 3

converse *adj syn* see OPPOSITE

converse *n syn* see OPPOSITE

conversely *adv syn* see AGAIN 5

conversion *n* **1** fundamental alteration in one's system of beliefs <Judaism does not encourage *conversion* of gentiles>
syn metanoia, rebirth
rel about-face, reversal, turning; reclamation, regeneration
idiom change of heart
2 change of one thing to another usually by substitution <*conversion* of locomotives from steam to diesel power>
syn alteration, changeover, shift, transformation
rel change, modification, qualification; metamorphosis, mutation, permutation, transmutation; innovation, novelty

convert *vb* **1** to induce (another or others) to accept the validity of something (as a belief, course of action, or point of view) <Chinese missionaries *converted* many Japanese to Buddhism>
syn bring, lead, move, persuade
rel redeem, reform, save; bend, bias, incline, sway; actuate, budge, impel; proselyte, proselytize
2 *syn* see TRANSFORM
rel fabricate, forge, make, manufacture; apply, employ, use, utilize

convey *vb* **1** *syn* see CARRY 1
2 *syn* see COMMUNICATE 1
rel project, put across
3 *syn* see TRANSFER 4
rel commit, consign, relegate
4 *syn* see CONDUCT 4

conveyance *n* **1** *syn* see TRANSPORTATION 1
2 *syn* see DEED 3
3 *syn* see VEHICLE 3

convict *n* a person serving time in prison after conviction as a criminal <mixing hardened *convicts* with juvenile offenders>
syn ||con, jailbird, ||lag, loser, prison bird
rel long-termer, longtimer; ||stir bug; recidivist, repeater

conviction *n* **1** *syn* see CERTAINTY 1
con dubiety, dubiosity, uncertainty; disbelief, incredulity, unbelief
2 *syn* see OPINION
rel doctrine, dogma, tenet

convince *vb* **1** *syn* see ASSURE 2
2 *syn* see INDUCE 1

convincing *adj* **1** *syn* see AUTHENTIC 1
2 *syn* see VALID

convivial *adj syn* see SOCIAL 1
rel lively, vivacious; jocund, jolly, merry
con grave, sedate, serious, sober, solemn, somber; reserved, reticent, silent
ant taciturn; stolid

convoke *vb* to bring together by or as if by summons <the ruler *convoked* his council>
syn assemble, call, convene, summon; *compare* SUMMON 2
rel collect, congregate, gather; ask, bid, invite, request; meet, sit
con adjourn, close, dissolve, prorogue, recess, suspend; disperse, scatter

convoluted *adj syn* see WINDING

convoy *vb syn* see ACCOMPANY
rel defend, guard, protect, safeguard, shield

convulse *vb syn* see SHAKE 4

convulsion *n syn* see COMMOTION 1
rel cataclysm, disaster; quaking, rocking, shaking, tottering, trembling

cook *vb* **1** to make ready or fit for eating by the use of heat <liked everything well= *cooked*>
syn do
2 *syn* see BURN 3

cook (up) *vb syn* see CONTRIVE 2

cookshop *n syn* see EATING HOUSE

cool *adj* **1** *syn* see COLD 1
ant warm
2 freed or giving the impression of freedom from all agitation or excitement <they looked *cool* and very formidable>
syn collected, composed, disimpassioned, imperturbable, nonchalant, unflappable, unruffled; *compare* HAPPY-GO-LUCKY
rel calm, placid, serene, tranquil; aloof, detached, indifferent; impassive, phlegmatic, stolid; assured, confident, self-possessed
con fervent, fervid, impassioned, passionate, perfervid; discomposed, disturbed, flurried, flustered, perturbed, upset
ant ardent; agitated
3 *syn* see UNSOCIABLE
||**4** *syn* see MARVELOUS 2

cool *vb* **1** *syn* see COMPOSE 4
2 *syn* see MURDER 1

cooler *n syn* see JAIL

coolness *n syn* see EQUANIMITY

||**coon** *vb syn* see STEAL 1

coon's age *n syn* see AGE 2

||**coony** *adj syn* see CLEVER 4

coop *n syn* see JAIL

coop *vb syn* see ENCLOSE 1
rel bar, block, hinder, impede, obstruct

cooperate *vb syn* see UNITE 2
rel agree, coincide
con annul, negate, nullify; negative, neutralize
ant counteract

cooperative *adj* involving joint action in producing a result <the need of *cooperative* efforts to effect lasting social change>
syn coacting, coactive, coefficient, conjoint, synergetic, synergic
rel collaborative, concerted; noncompetitive, uncompetitive
con competitive, emulous, rivaling, vying; antagonistic, conflicting, oppugnant
ant counteractive

coordinate *vb syn* see HARMONIZE 3

coordinate *n* **1** *syn* see OPPOSITE NUMBER
2 *syn* see MATE 5

||**cop** *vb syn* see STEAL 1

cop *n syn* see POLICEMAN

copartner *n syn* see PARTNER

copious *adj syn* see PLENTIFUL
rel exuberant, lush, luxuriant

con exiguous, scant, scanty, scrimpy, spare, sparse; slender, slight, slim, tenuous, thin
ant meager

cop out *vb* ‖**1** *syn* see DIE 1
2 *syn* see BACK DOWN

‖**copper** *n syn* see POLICEMAN

copy *n* **1** *syn* see IMITATION
2 *syn* see REPRODUCTION
rel counterpart, parallel; impress, impression, imprint, print; effigy, image, likeness
ant original

copy *vb* to make a copy of <*copied* the speech word for word>
syn duplicate, imitate, reduplicate, replicate, reproduce
rel ditto, repeat; counterfeit, fake, sham, simulate; ape, burlesque, mock, parody, take off, travesty
ant originate

coquet *vb syn* see TRIFLE 1
coquette *n syn* see FLIRT
coquettish *adj syn* see COY 2
cordial *adj syn* see GRACIOUS 1
rel responsive, sympathetic, tender, warm, warmhearted; heartfelt, hearty, sincere, wholehearted
con cold, cool, frigid, frosty; aloof, detached, disinterested, indifferent; reserved, silent, taciturn

cordiality *n syn* see AMENITY 1
rel responsiveness, sympathy, understanding, warmth, mutuality, reciprocity; approbation, approval, favor
con cross-purposes, difference, disagreement, misunderstanding, odds, variance; disapprobation, disapproval, disfavor

core *n* **1** *syn* see CENTER 1
2 *syn* see BODY 3
3 *syn* see SUBSTANCE 2
rel consequence, import, importance, significance
4 *syn* see CENTER 3
rel base, basis, foundation; beginning, commencement, origin, start

‖**corker** *n syn* ‖DILLY, crackerjack, ‖daisy, dandy, humdinger, jim-dandy, knockout, ‖lalapalooza, ‖lulu, nifty

corkscrew *vb syn* see WIND 2
corner *n* **1** *syn* see PREDICAMENT
2 *syn* see MONOPOLY
corner *vb* to get into one's control or a position from which escape is difficult <*cornered* him at a party and tried to borrow a hundred dollars>
syn bottle (up), collar, tree
rel bother, disturb, put out, trouble; capture, catch, nab, seize, trap
idiom chase up a tree, drive (*or* run) into a corner, get (*or* have) on the ropes

cornerwise *adv syn* see DIAGONALLY
corny *adj syn* see TRITE
corollary *n syn* see EFFECT 1
coronal *n syn* see WREATH
coronet *n syn* see WREATH
corporal *adj syn* see BODILY

corporation *n syn* see POTBELLY
corporeal *adj* **1** *syn* see BODILY
2 *syn* see MATERIAL 1
corps *n syn* see COMPANY 4
corpse *n* a dead body especially of a human being <concealed the *corpse* under some rubbish>
syn body, cadaver, carcass, ‖cold meat, ‖deader, mort, remains, stiff
rel carrion; bones

corpselike *adj* **1** *syn* see DEATHLY 1
2 *syn* see GHASTLY 2
corpsy *adj syn* see DEATHLY 1
corpulence *n syn* see OBESITY
corpulent *adj syn* see FAT 2
corpus *n* **1** *syn* see BODY 3
2 *syn* see OEUVRE
corrade *vb syn* see ABRADE 1
corral *vb syn* see ENCLOSE 1
correct *vb* **1** to set right something that is wrong <*correct* a misstatement>
syn amend, emend, mend, rectify, right
rel ameliorate, better, improve; redress, remedy, revise; make over, reform; adjust, fix, regulate
con damage, harm, hurt, impair, injure, mar, spoil
2 *syn* see PUNISH 1
con baby, coddle, cosset, humor, indulge, pamper, spoil

correct *adj* **1** *syn* see DECOROUS 1
rel careful, meticulous, punctilious, scrupulous
2 conforming to or agreeing with fact <the *correct* solution to the problem>
syn accurate, exact, nice, precise, proper, right, rigorous
rel faithful, true, undistorted, veracious, veridical; faultless, flawless, impeccable, perfect
con fallacious, false, wrong; defective, faulty, flawed, imperfect
ant incorrect

correction *n syn* see PUNISHMENT
correctitude *n syn* see ORDER 7
corrective *n syn* see REMEDY 2
correctly *adv syn* see WELL 1
correctness *n* **1** *syn* see ORDER 7
2 *syn* see PRECISION
correlate *n* **1** *syn* see COUNTERPART 1
2 *syn* see PARALLEL
correspond *vb syn* see AGREE 4
correspond (to) *vb syn* see AMOUNT 2
correspondence *n syn* see CONSISTENCY
ant divergence
correspondent *n syn* see PARALLEL
corresponding *adj syn* see LIKE
correspondingly *adv syn* see ALSO 1
corridor *n syn* see PASSAGE 4
corrival *n syn* see RIVAL
corroborate *vb syn* see CONFIRM 2
con invalidate, negate, nullify
ant contradict
corroborative *adj* serving or tending to corroborate <*corroborative* evidence>
syn adminicular, collateral, confirmative, confirmatory, corroboratory, verificatory
rel ancillary, auxiliary, supplementary, supportive; assisting, helping
con confutative, refutative, refutatory; contradictory, negatory

---

syn synonym(s)   *rel* related word(s)
ant antonym(s)   *con* contrasted word(s)
idiom idiomatic equivalent(s)
‖ use limited; if in doubt, see a dictionary

corroboratory *adj syn* see CORROBORA-TIVE

corrode *vb syn* see EAT 1

corrosive *adj syn* see SARCASTIC

corrosiveness *n syn* see SARCASM

corrugation *n syn* see WRINKLE

corrupt *vb* **1** *syn* see DEBASE 1
  rel abase, degrade; ruin, wreck
  con amend, correct, reform
  2 *syn* see DECAY
  rel befoul, defile, foul; smirch, tarnish

corrupt *adj* **1** *syn* see VICIOUS 2
  rel crooked, devious, oblique; baneful, deleterious, detrimental, noxious, pernicious; abased, degraded, low
  2 seeking sordid advantage with little regard to moral or legal bars <a *corrupt* politician>
  syn mercenary, praetorian, unethical, unprincipled, unscrupulous, venal; *compare* CROOKED 2, VENAL 1
  rel undependable, unreliable, untrustworthy; faithless, inconstant, unfaithful; double-dealing, perfidious, treacherous, two-faced; bribable, corruptible; blackguardly, knavish, reprobate
  con ethical, principled, scrupulous, upright; dependable, reliable, trustworthy, trusty
  3 *syn* see CROOKED 2

corrupted *adj syn* see DEBASED

corruptible *adj syn* see VENAL 1

corruption *n* **1** *syn* see VICE 1
  2 *syn* see BARBARISM

corsair *n syn* see PIRATE

coruscate *vb syn* see FLASH 1

coruscation *n syn* see FLASH 1

corybantic *adj syn* see FURIOUS 2

coryphée *n syn* see DANCER

cosmic *adj syn* see UNIVERSAL 2

cosmopolitan *adj* **1** exhibiting or characterized by a sophistication and savoir faire arising from cultured urban life and wide travel <had a thoroughly *cosmopolitan* outlook on life>
  syn metropolitan, urbane; *compare* SOPHISTICATED 2
  rel civilized, polished, smooth; sophisticated, worldly-wise; cultivated, cultured
  con boorish, cloddish, rude, rustic; insular, parochial, provincial
  2 *syn* see UNIVERSAL 2

cosmos (*or* kosmos) *n syn* see UNIVERSE

cosset *vb* **1** *syn* see CARESS
  2 *syn* see BABY

cost *n* **1** *syn* see PRICE 1
  2 *syn* see EXPENSE 1
  3 *syn* see EXPENSE 2

costive *adj* **1** *syn* see CONSTIPATED
  2 *syn* see STINGY

costless *adj syn* see FREE 5

costly *adj* **1** commanding or being a large price <the scarcer an item becomes the more *costly* it is>
  syn dear, expensive, high; *compare* PRECIOUS 1
  rel excessive, exorbitant, extravagant, inordinate, steep, stiff; fancy, premium, top
  con inexpensive, low, low-priced, reasonable
  ant cheap
  2 *syn* see PRECIOUS 1

costume *n* style of clothing and adornment <her *costume* was always suitable to the occasion>
  syn dress, getup, guise, outfit, rig, setout, turnout
  rel fashion, mode, style

cot *n syn* see HUT

‖**cotch** *vb* **1** *syn* see SEIZE 2
  2 *syn* see CATCH 1
  3 *syn* see CATCH 7

coterie *n syn* see CLIQUE

cottage *n syn* see HUT

cotton *vb* **1** *syn* see BABY
  2 *syn* see FAWN

cotton (to *or* on to) *vb syn* see APPREHEND 1

cottony *adj syn* see SOFT 3

couch *vb* **1** *syn* see WORD
  2 *syn* see LOWER 3

couch *n syn* see LAIR 1

couleur de rose *adj syn* see HOPEFUL 2

couloir *n syn* see PASSAGE 4

counsel *n syn* see ADVICE 1

counsel *vb* to give advice to or about <*counseled* him to wait for a more propitious occasion>
  syn advise, recommend
  rel admonish, reprehend, warn; direct, order, prescribe; charge, enjoin, prompt, urge; advocate, suggest

count *vb* **1** to ascertain the total of units in a collection by noting one after another <*counted* the sheep in the pasture>
  syn enumerate, number, numerate, tale, tally, tell
  rel add, cast, figure, foot, sum, tot, total; calculate, compute, estimate, reckon; tell off
  2 *syn* see MATTER
  3 *syn* see WEIGH 3

count (on) *vb syn* see RELY (on *or* upon)

count (on *or* upon) *vb syn* see EXPECT 1

countenance *n* **1** *syn* see LOOK 2
  idiom (the) cut of one's jib
  2 *syn* see FACE 1

countenance *vb* **1** *syn* see ENCOURAGE 2
  rel applaud, commend; back, champion, support, uphold
  con deride, ridicule; criticize, reprehend, reprobate; reproach, reprove
  ant discountenance
  2 *syn* see APPROVE 1

counter *vb syn* see OPPOSE 1
  rel baffle, balk, beat, bilk, circumvent, dash, disappoint, foil, frustrate, ruin

counter *n syn* see OPPOSITE

counter *adj syn* see OPPOSITE
  rel hostile, inimical; adverse, antagonistic, anti, oppugnant; hindering, impeding, obstructive

counteract *vb syn* see NEUTRALIZE
  rel correct, fix, rectify, right
  con cooperate, coordinate, synergize; back, reinforce, support

counteractant *n syn* see REMEDY 2

counteractive *n syn* see REMEDY 2

counteragent *n syn* see REMEDY 2

counterbalance *vb syn* see COMPENSATE 1
  rel amend, correct; rectify
  con overbalance, unbalance

counterblow *n syn* see RETALIATION

countercheck *vb syn* see NEUTRALIZE

counterfactual *adj syn* see FALSE 1
counterfeit *vb syn* see ASSUME 4
    rel ape, copy, imitate, mimic
counterfeit *adj* being an imitation intended to mislead or deceive <*counterfeit* money> <*counterfeit* sympathy>
    syn bogus, brummagem, fake, false, phony, pinchbeck, pseudo, sham, snide, spurious; *compare* SPURIOUS 3
    rel feigned, pretended, simulated; deceptive, delusive, delusory, misleading; fraudulent
    con authentic, veritable; actual, real, true; unquestionable, valid
    ant bona fide, genuine
counterfeit *n syn* see IMPOSTURE
    rel copy, facsimile, reproduction; dummy, simulacrum
countermeasure *n syn* see REMEDY 2
counterpane *n syn* see BEDSPREAD
counterpart *n* 1 something that completes or complements <export controls as a *counterpart* of domestic distribution controls>
    syn complement, correlate, pendant; *compare* PARALLEL
    rel analogue, correlate, correspondent; equal, equivalent, like, match
    con counterpoint, opposite
    2 *syn* see PARALLEL
    3 *syn* see EQUAL
    4 *syn* see OPPOSITE NUMBER
counterpoise *n syn* see BALANCE 1
counterpoise *vb syn* see COMPENSATE 1
    rel ballast, poise, stabilize, steady, trim
    con capsize, overturn, upset
counterpole *n syn* see OPPOSITE
countersign *n syn* see PASSWORD 1
counterstep *n syn* see REMEDY 2
countertype *n syn* see PARALLEL
countervail *vb syn* see COMPENSATE 1
    rel amend, correct, rectify; foil, frustrate, thwart; overcome, surmount
countless *adj syn* see INNUMERABLE
count out *vb syn* see EXCLUDE
countrified *adj syn* see RURAL
country *n* the nation-state to which one belongs or from which one originated <returned to his own *country* after years of exile>
    syn fatherland, home, homeland, land, mother country, motherland, soil
country *adj syn* see RURAL
country jake *n syn* see RUSTIC
countryman *n syn* see RUSTIC
couple *vb* 1 *syn* see JOIN 1
    2 *syn* see HITCH 2
    rel hook up, ‖inspan
couple *n* two individuals of the same or a similar kind that occur, function, or are considered together <a *couple* of ideas for improving the book> <the happiest *couple* I know>
    syn brace, doublet, duo, dyad, pair, twosome
    rel span, team, yoke
coupling *n syn* see JOINT 1

courage *n* a quality of mind or temperament that enables one to stand fast in the face of opposition, hardship, or danger <had the kind of *courage* that could appreciate a danger yet steadfastly face it>
    syn cojones, dauntlessness, guts, heart, mettle, ‖moxie, pluck, resolution, spirit, spunk; *compare* FORTITUDE
    rel audacity, boldness, bravery, doughtiness, fearlessness, intrepidity; gallantry, heroism, valor; backbone, fortitude, grit, sand; assurance, determination, firmness, persistence, tenacity
    con chickenheartedness, faintheartedness, unmanliness, yellowness; baseness, cravenness, poltroonery, pusillanimity; timidity, timorousness
    ant cowardice
courageous *adj syn* see BRAVE 1
    rel fiery, high-spirited; strong, tenacious
    con afraid, apprehensive, fearful
    ant pusillanimous
courier *n syn* see MESSENGER
course *n* 1 *syn* see WAY 2
    rel circuit, orbit, range, scope
    2 *syn* see CHANNEL 1
    3 way of acting or proceeding <hard to decide on the best *course* to follow>
    syn line, policy, polity, procedure, program
    rel design, pattern, plan, platform, scheme; manner, system, way
    idiom course of action
    4 *syn* see PROGRESS 2
    5 *syn* see SUCCESSION 2
course *vb* to proceed with great celerity (as in pursuing or competing) <the fox *coursed* after the hare>
    syn career, chase, race, rush, speed, tear; *compare* RUSH 1
    rel hasten, hurry, hustle; dart, dash, scamper, scoot, scurry; run, sprint
    idiom step on the gas, stir one's stumps
courser *n* a strong vigorous horse formerly used in mounted combat <heroes mounted on great fiery *coursers*>
    syn charger, war-horse
court *n* 1 an open space wholly or partly enclosed (as by buildings or walls) <the apartment overlooks the *court*>
    syn ‖close, courtyard, curtilage, enclosure, quad, quadrangle, yard
    2 a place or the persons assembled for the administration of justice <the *court* was called to order>
    syn bar, lawcourt, tribunal
    3 *syn* see JUDGE 2
court *vb syn* see ADDRESS 8
    rel allure, attract, captivate, charm
courteous *adj syn* see CIVIL 2
    rel attentive, considerate, thoughtful
    con blunt, brusque, curt, gruff; insolent, overbearing, supercilious
    ant discourteous
courtesan *n syn* see HARLOT 1
courtesy *n* 1 courteous behavior or a courteous act <noted for her *courtesy* and graciousness> <such little *courtesies* take little time but often brighten lonely lives>
    syn amenity, attention, gallantry
    rel affability, cordiality, geniality, graciousness; comity, complaisance; chivalry, civil-

---

syn synonym(s)   *rel* related word(s)
ant antonym(s)   *con* contrasted word(s)
idiom idiomatic equivalent(s)
‖ use limited; if in doubt, see a dictionary

ity, courteousness, courtliness; attentiveness, considerateness, consideration, thoughtfulness
con boorishness, churlishness; impoliteness, incivility, rudeness, ungraciousness
ant discourtesy
2 *syn* see FAVOR 4

courtly *adj* marked by elaborate and often ceremonious courtesy <a *courtly* gentleman of the old school>
syn gallant, gracious, preux, stately; *compare* CIVIL 2
rel august, dignified, imposing, lofty; prim, starchy, stiff, stilted, studied; ceremonious, conventional, formal; civilized
con discourteous, ill-mannered, impolite, rude, uncivil, ungracious; boorish, coarse, gross, loutish, uncouth, vulgar
ant churlish

courtyard *n syn* see COURT 1
cousinhood *n syn* see KIN 2
cousinhood *n syn* see KIN 2
cove *n syn* see INLET
covenant *n syn* see CONTRACT
covenant *vb syn* see VOW
rel agree, concur

cover *vb* **1** *syn* see DEFEND 1
2 *syn* see HIDE
3 to spread over or put something over <fog *covered* the ground> <*covered* the bed with a quilt>
syn blanket, cap, crown, overcast, overlay, overspread
rel conceal, hide, screen; defend, protect, shield; enclose, enfold, envelop, shroud, wrap; superimpose, superpose
con display, exhibit, expose
ant bare, uncover
4 *syn* see TRAVEL 2
5 *syn* see SET 11

cover *n* **1** *syn* see SHELTER 1
rel concealment, hiding, screen; safety, security
ant exposure
2 *syn* see MASK 2

coverlet *n syn* see BEDSPREAD
‖**coverlid** *n syn* see BEDSPREAD
covert *adj* **1** *syn* see SECRET 1
rel camouflaged, cloaked, disguised, dissembled, masked
con candid, frank, open
ant overt
2 *syn* see ULTERIOR
con direct, forthright; honest, square, straight

covert *n syn* see SHELTER 1
covertly *adv syn* see SECRETLY
covet *vb syn* see DESIRE 1
con abjure, forswear
ant renounce

covetous *adj* having or marked by an urgent and often unscrupulous desire for possessions <the *covetous* eye of an avid collector>
syn acquisitive, desirous, grabby, grasping, greedy, itchy, prehensile
rel esurient, gluttonous, rapacious, ravenous, voracious; hoggish, lickerish, piggish, swinish; avid, eager, keen; envious, jealous; grudging, selfish

con generous, liberal, munificent; ungrudging, unselfish; abstemious, abstinent, ascetic, austere; moderate, restrained, temperate

covey *n syn* see GROUP 1
covin *n syn* see PLOT 2
cow *vb syn* see INTIMIDATE
rel appall, daunt, dismay; abash, discomfit, disconcert, embarrass, faze, rattle
con cower, cringe, fawn, toady, truckle

coward *n* one who shows or yields to ignoble fear <a treacherous *coward* who betrayed his friends to save his own skin>
syn chicken, craven, dastard, funk, funker, poltroon, quitter, yellowbelly
rel baby, fraidycat, invertebrate, jellyfish, milksop, scaredy-cat; caitiff, recreant
con gallant, hero, palladin, stalwart; ideal, model, pattern, standard

coward *adj syn* see COWARDLY
cowardly *adj* marked by or arising from a base lack of courage <a *cowardly* desertion>
syn ‖chicken, coward, cowhearted, craven, gutless, lily-livered, milk-livered, poltroon, poltroonish, poor-spirited, pusillanimous, spunkless, unmanly, white-livered, yellow
rel afraid, chickenhearted, fainthearted, fearful, timid, timorous; funky, panicky; caitiff, dastardly, recreant, vile, worthless
con courageous, fearless, intrepid, valiant; daring, reckless, temerarious
ant brave

cower *vb syn* see FAWN
rel blench, flinch, quail, recoil, shrink, wince
con browbeat, bulldoze, bully, cow, intimidate; bristle, strut, swagger

cowering *adj syn* see FAWNING
cowhearted *adj syn* see COWARDLY
coxcomb *n syn* see FOP
coy *adj* **1** *syn* see SHY 1
rel decent, decorous, nice, proper, seemly
con brash, brazen, impudent
2 marked by a light playful artlessness <glanced up with a *coy* twinkle in her eye>
syn arch, coquettish, roguish
rel capricious, kittenish, lively, mischievous, playful, skittish
con serious, sober, thoughtful

cozen *vb* **1** *syn* see CHEAT
2 *syn* see DECEIVE
cozy *adj* **1** *syn* see COMFORTABLE 2
rel safe, secure
2 *syn* see INTIMATE 4

crab *vb syn* see GRIPE
idiom fret and fume
crab *n syn* see GROUCH
crabbed *adj syn* see SULLEN
rel blunt, brusque, crusty, gruff; choleric, cranky, splenetic, testy, huffy, irascible, irritable, snappish
con amiable, complaisant, good-natured, obliging; benign, benignant, kind, kindly; agreeable, pleasing; affable, genial, gracious
crabber *n syn* see GROUCH
crabby *adj syn* see SULLEN
crabwise *adv syn* see SIDEWAYS 1
crack *vb syn* see DECODE
rel puzzle out
crack *n* **1** *syn* see BANG 2
rel splintering, splitting; percussion

2 *syn* see JOKE 1
rel dig, fling, potshot
idiom flash of wit
3 a usually narrow opening, break, or discontinuity made by splitting and rupture <a *crack* in the ice>
syn chink, cleft, fissure, rift, rima, rimation, rime, split
rel rent; discontinuity, interstice, interval; cranny, niche; crevasse, crevice
4 *syn* see INSTANT 1
idiom flash of lightning
5 *syn* see BLOW 1
6 *syn* see FLING 1
crack *adj syn* see PROFICIENT
rel excellent, superior
crackbrain *n syn* see CRACKPOT
idiom cracked wit
crackbrained *adj syn* see INSANE 1
crackdown *n syn* see REPRESSION 2
rel quashing
idiom lowering the boom
cracked *adj syn* see INSANE 1
idiom ‖off in the upper story
crackerjack *n syn* see ‖DILLY
crackerjack *adj syn* see PROFICIENT
‖crackers *adj syn* see INSANE 1
cracking *adj syn* see MONSTROUS 1
crackpot *n* one given to extremely eccentric or lunatic ideas or actions <a *crackpot* who wrote threatening letters to public figures>
syn crackbrain, crank, cuckoo, ding-a-ling, harebrain, kook, lunatic, nut, screwball
rel case, character, ‖dingbat, eccentric, oddball, oddity, ‖wack; loon, loony, madman, maniac
crack–up *n* **1** *syn* see NERVOUS BREAKDOWN
2 *syn* see CRASH 3
3 *syn* see COLLAPSE 2
rel decline, deterioration
‖cracky *adj syn* see INSANE 1
cradlesong *n syn* see LULLABY
craft *n* **1** *syn* see ART 1
2 *syn* see TRADE 1
rel job
3 *syn* see CUNNING 2
craftiness *n syn* see CUNNING 2
crafty *adj syn* see SLY 2
rel adroit, clever, tidy; acute, keen, sharp; deceitful, fawning, ‖sleekit, ‖sleeky
cragged *adj syn* see ROUGH 1
craggy *adj syn* see ROUGH 1
cram *vb* **1** to fill (a limited space) forcibly with more than is practicable or fitting <*crammed* the suitcase chock-full and had to sit on it to close it>
syn jam, jam-pack, ‖pang, ram, stuff, tamp; *compare* LOAD 3, PRESS 7
rel pack, stive; fill, heap; chock, choke; press, shove, thrust; drive, force; squeeze, wedge
2 *syn* see PRESS 7
3 *syn* see GULP
rel overeat

---

syn synonym(s)   *rel* related word(s)
ant antonym(s)   *con* contrasted word(s)
idiom idiomatic equivalent(s)
‖ use limited; if in doubt, see a dictionary

idiom pack it in
4 to study intensively or under pressure <had to *cram* all night before the exam>
syn bone (up), ‖mug (up)
rel study; review
idiom burn the midnight oil
cram–full *adj syn* see FULL 1
crammed *adj syn* see FULL 1
idiom crammed full, crammed to the bursting point, fit (*or* ready) to burst
ant emptied
cramp *n* **1** *syn* see RESTRICTION 1
rel shackle
2 *syn* see RESTRICTION 2
rel constipation, stultification
cramp *adj syn* see CRAMPED
cramped *adj* having insufficient size or capacity <a *cramped* cubbyhole of an office>
syn confined, cramp, incommodious, squeezy, ‖tucked up
rel close, narrow, tight, two-by-four; little, mi- nute, small, tiny
con commodious, unconfined
ant spacious
crank *n* **1** *syn* see CAPRICE
2 *syn* see CRACKPOT
rel freak
3 *syn* see GROUCH
cranky *adj* **1** *syn* see INSANE 1
2 *syn* see CANTANKEROUS
rel contrary, difficult, froward, perverse
3 *syn* see IRASCIBLE
rel bad-humored, ill-humored; disagreeable; ugly
idiom out of sorts
cranny *n syn* see NOOK
‖crap *n syn* see NONSENSE 2
‖crap out *vb syn* see FAINT
‖crappy *adj syn* see BAD 1
crash *vb syn* see FAIL 5
ant skyrocket
crash *n* **1** *syn* see BANG 2
2 *syn* see IMPACT 1
3 a wrecking or smashing especially of a vehicle <an air *crash*>
syn crack-up, pileup, ‖prang, smash, smashup, ‖stramash, wreck
rel accident; collision
4 *syn* see COLLAPSE 2
crashing *adj syn* see UTTER
crass *adj syn* see COARSE 3
rel churlish, loutish
ant refined
crate *n syn* see JALOPY
crave *vb* **1** *syn* see BEG
2 *syn* see DESIRE 1
con contemn, despise, disdain, scorn
ant spurn
3 *syn* see LONG
idiom have a craving for
4 *syn* see DEMAND 2
craven *adj syn* see COWARDLY
craven *n syn* see COWARD
craving *n syn* see DESIRE 1
crawfish (out) *vb syn* see BACK DOWN
crawl *vb* **1** *syn* see CREEP 1
rel grovel; worm
2 *syn* see TEEM
‖3 *syn* see LAMBASTE 3
craze *vb syn* see MADDEN 1

craze *n syn* see FASHION 3
 rel enthusiasm, fever
crazed *adj syn* see INSANE 1
craziness *n syn* see FOOLISHNESS
crazy *adj* **1** *syn* see INSANE 1
 rel doting, gaga, moonstruck; beheaded,
 silly; erratic, possessed
 idiom as crazy as a loon, having a screw
 loose, having bats in one's belfry, not having
 all one's marbles (*or* buttons)
 ant sane
 2 *syn* see FOOLISH 2
 rel goofy, senseless
 idiom beyond the realm of reason, out of all
 reason
 con practical, reasonable, reasoned, sensible
 ant sane
||**crazy** *adv syn* see VERY 1
crazy house *n syn* see ASYLUM 3
cream *n* **1** *syn* see OINTMENT
 2 *syn* see BEST
 idiom (the) top cream
||**cream** *vb syn* see WHIP 2
||**crease** *n syn* see WRINKLE
create *vb* **1** *syn* see GENERATE 1
 idiom call into being
 2 *syn* see FOUND 2
 3 *syn* see COMPOSE 2
 rel conceive, formulate; imagine
creation *n syn* see UNIVERSE
creative *adj syn* see INVENTIVE
 rel causal, institutive, occasional; Prome-
 thean
 ant uncreative
creator *n syn* see FATHER 2
 rel brain(s), brainpower, mastermind
creature *n* **1** *syn* see BEAST
 2 *syn* see HUMAN
 3 *syn* see SYCOPHANT
credence *n syn* see BELIEF 1
 rel acceptance, accepting, admission, admitting; confidence, reliance, trust
 con skepticism; distrust, mistrust; disbelief,
 incredulity, unbelief
credentials *n pl* something presented or held
 by one as proof that he is what or who he
 claims to be <her academic *credentials* were
 excellent>
 syn certification, document(s), documentation, paper(s)
 rel voucher; accreditation, endorsement,
 sanction; character, recommendation, reference, testimonial
credible *adj* **1** *syn* see BELIEVABLE
 rel satisfactory, satisfying; solid, sound,
 straight, valid
 idiom to be believed
 con unsatisfactory; preposterous, ridiculous
 ant incredible
 2 *syn* see AUTHENTIC 1
 rel likely, probable; rational, reasonable;
 conclusive, determinative
 ant incredible
credit *n* **1** *syn* see BELIEF 1
 rel confidence, reliance, trust
 2 *syn* see INFLUENCE 1
 rel fame, renown, reputation, repute
 con disrepute, ignominy, obloquy, opprobrium
 ant discredit

3 one that enhances another <he is a *credit*
 to his family>
 syn asset
 rel honor
4 favorable notice or attention resulting
 from an action or achievement <took all the
 credit for the idea>
 syn acknowledgment, recognition
 rel attention, notice; distinction, fame,
 honor; glory, kudos
credit *vb* **1** *syn* see FEEL 3
 con disbelieve, pooh-pooh
 ant discredit
 2 *syn* see ASCRIBE
creditable *adj* **1** *syn* see BELIEVABLE
 ant discreditable
 2 *syn* see RESPECTABLE 1
 rel satisfactory; suitable
 ant discreditable
credo *n syn* see IDEOLOGY
credulous *adj* ready or inclined to believe
 especially on slight or insufficient evidence
 <deceiving the *credulous* young girls>
 syn unsuspecting, unsuspicious, unwary
 rel believing; accepting, unquestioning;
 trustful, trusting; green, inexperienced;
 naive, simple, unsophisticated; dupable,
 gullible
 con mistrustful, suspecting, suspicious;
 careful, wary; doubtful, doubting, questioning
 ant incredulous, skeptical
creed *n* **1** *syn* see RELIGION 1
 2 *syn* see RELIGION 2
 3 *syn* see IDEOLOGY
creek *n* ||**1** *syn* see INLET
 rel ria
 2 a natural stream of water normally smaller
 than and often tributary to a river <went
 wading in the *creek*>
 syn ||branch, brook, ||burn, ||crick, gill, race,
 ||rindle, ||rithe, rivulet, ||run, runnel, stream
 rel ||beck, brooklet, ||rigolet, rill, rillet, run-
 let, streamlet; freshet; ditch, watercourse;
 wadi
creep *vb* **1** to move along a surface in a prone
 or crouching position <a cat *creeping*
 through the grass>
 syn crawl, slide, snake
 rel glide, slither; sneak, steal, tiptoe; edge,
 inch; sniggle, wriggle
 2 *syn* see STEAL 3
 3 *syn* see SNEAK
crème de la crème *n syn* see ARISTOC-
 RACY
crepehanger *n syn* see PESSIMIST
crescendo *n syn* see APEX 2
crest *n* **1** *syn* see TOP 1
 rel cap
 2 *syn* see RIDGE 1
 3 *syn* see APEX 2
crest *vb syn* see SURMOUNT 3
crestfallen *adj syn* see DOWNCAST
 idiom ||in a funk
 ant elated
cretin *n syn* see FOOL 4
 rel zombie
crew *n syn* see GROUP 1
 rel aggregation, collection, congregation;
 gang, retinue, set

crib *n* **1** *syn* see BROTHEL
  2 *syn* see PONY
  rel plagiarism
‖**crib** *vb* *syn* see GRIPE
‖**crick** *n* *syn* see CREEK 2
crime *n* **1** a serious breach of the public law
  <armed robbery is a *crime*>
  syn misdeed, offense
  rel criminality, illegality, lawlessness; delict, delictum; breach, break, infringement, transgression, violation; wrong, wrongdoing; felony
  2 *syn* see EVIL 3
crimeless *adj* *syn* see INNOCENT 2
criminal *adj* *syn* see UNLAWFUL
criminal *n* one who has committed a usually serious offense <car thieves and other *criminals*>
  syn felon, lawbreaker, malefactor, offender
  rel scofflaw; transgressor, trespasser, wrongdoer; crook, ‖twicer; gangster, hood, mobster, racketeer, thug; fugitive, outlaw; convict, jailbird
criminate *vb* *syn* see ACCUSE
  ant exonerate
crimp *vb* **1** *syn* see CRUMPLE 1
  2 *syn* see RESTRAIN 1
crimp *n* *syn* see OBSTACLE
crimple *vb* *syn* see CRUMPLE 1
crimson *vb* *syn* see BLUSH
  ant blanch
cringe *vb* *syn* see FAWN
  rel blench, flinch, quail, recoil, wince; ‖croodle, crouch, shrink
  idiom bow and scrape, eat dirt
cringing *adj* *syn* see FAWNING
  rel obeisant, prostrate
  idiom bowing and scraping, eating dirt, eating humble pie, on one's hands and knees
crinkle *vb* *syn* see CRUMPLE 1
crinkle *n* *syn* see WRINKLE
  rel crimp
cripple *vb* **1** *syn* see MAIM
  rel lame
  2 *syn* see PARALYZE 1
  3 *syn* see WEAKEN 1
crisis *n* *syn* see JUNCTURE 2
crisp *adj* **1** *syn* see SHORT 6
  con flabby, flaccid, limp
  2 *syn* see INCISIVE
  rel piquing, provoking, stimulating
crisscross *vb* *syn* see INTERSECT
criterion *n* *syn* see STANDARD 3
  rel adjudgment, judgment
critic *n* one given to harsh or captious judgment <chronic *critics* of the administration>
  syn aristarch, carper, caviler, criticizer, faultfinder, knocker, momus, smellfungus, Zoilus
  rel Monday morning quarterback; nitpicker, quibbler; belittler, disparager; complainer; censurer; muckraker, mudslinger
  con backer, supporter, partisan; advocate, champion, protagonist
critic *adj* *syn* see CRITICAL 1

critical *adj* **1** exhibiting the spirit of one who looks for and points out faults and defects <constant *critical* comments about her attire>
  syn captious, carping, caviling, cavillous, censorious, critic, faultfinding, hypercritical, overcritical
  rel discerning, discriminating, penetrating; finicky, fussy, particular; belittling, demeaning, disparaging, humbling, lowering
  con cursory, shallow, superficial; encouraging, flattering, praising
  ant uncritical
  2 *syn* see ACUTE 6
  rel conclusive, decisive, determinative; consequential, important, momentous, significant, weighty
criticism *n* **1** a discourse that evaluates or analyzes something (as a work of art or literature) <read every *criticism* of the new play>
  syn comment, critique, notice, review, reviewal
  rel analysis, examination, study; commentary, observation; opinion; appraisal, assessment, estimate, rating
  2 an unfavorable observation or commentary <her recent theatrical offerings have met only with *criticism*>
  syn flak, knock, ‖pan, rap, swipe
  rel cavil, nit-picking, quibble; aspersion, censure, denunciation; blast; roast
  idiom bad press
  con blurb, puff; hype, plug, promo
  ant commendation
criticize *vb* to make adverse comments about (someone or something) openly, often publicly, and with varying severity <*criticized* his opponent's liberal views>
  syn blame, censure, condemn, cut up, denounce, denunciate, knock, pan, rap, reprehend, reprobate, skin; *compare* LAMBASTE 3, REPROVE, SCOLD 1
  rel blast, castigate, fulminate (against), fustigate, roast, scathe
  idiom find fault with, pull (*or* pick *or* tear) to pieces, take to task
  con approve, countenance, endorse, OK (*or* okay)
  ant praise
criticizer *n* *syn* CRITIC, aristarch, carper, caviler, faultfinder, knocker, momus, smellfungus, Zoilus
critique *n* *syn* see CRITICISM 1
‖**critter** *n* *syn* see BEAST
croak *vb* **1** *syn* see GRUMBLE 1
  rel complain, quarrel
  ‖**2** *syn* see DIE 1
‖**croaker** *n* *syn* see PHYSICIAN
croaking *adj* *syn* see HOARSE 1
croaky *adj* *syn* see HOARSE 1
crock *n* *syn* see NONSENSE 2
‖**crocked** *adj* *syn* see INTOXICATED 1
crone *n* *syn* see HAG 2
  rel frump, slattern, sloven
crony *n* *syn* see ASSOCIATE 3
  idiom bosom buddy
‖**crooch** *vb* *syn* see CROUCH
‖**croodle** *vb* *syn* see SNUGGLE
crook *vb* **1** *syn* see CURVE

---

syn synonym(s)   *rel* related word(s)
ant antonym(s)   *con* contrasted word(s)
idiom idiomatic equivalent(s)
‖ use limited; if in doubt, see a dictionary

‖2 *syn* see STEAL 1

‖3 *syn* see CHEAT

crooked *adj* 1 departing from a straight line or course <a *crooked* road>
syn bending, curving, devious, twisting; *compare* CURVED, WINDING
rel oblique; circuitous, indirect, roundabout; errant, meandering, rambling, serpentine, snaky, tortuous, winding; zigzag
con direct, undeviating
ant straight

2 deviating from rectitude <*crooked* police officers on the take>
syn corrupt, dishonest, snide; *compare* CORRUPT 2, VENAL 1
rel devious, indirect, shifty, underhand; double-dealing, fraudulent; deceitful, lying, untruthful; ruthless, unscrupulous
con aboveboard, forthright, straightforward; conscientious, honorable, just, proper, righteous, scrupulous, upright
ant honest, straight

crookedly *adv* *syn* see AWRY 1
ant straight

crop *n* *syn* see HARVEST 2

crop *vb* 1 *syn* see TOP 1
rel chop, hew, slash; detach, disengage
2 *syn* see MOW
3 *syn* see CUT 6
rel snip

cropping *n* *syn* see HARVEST 1

cross *n* 1 *syn* see TRIAL 1
idiom a cross to bear
2 *syn* see HYBRID

cross *vb* 1 *syn* see DENY 4
2 *syn* see BETRAY 2
idiom bite the hand that feeds one, stab in the back
3 *syn* see TRAVERSE 4
4 to cause (an animal or plant) to breed with one of a different kind <*crossing* a horse with an ass results in a mule>
syn crossbreed, cross-mate, hybridize, interbreed, intercross
rel mongrelize
5 *syn* see INTERSECT
idiom lie (or be) athwart

cross *adj* *syn* see IRASCIBLE
rel captious, carping, caviling, faultfinding
idiom cross as a bear

cross *prep* *syn* see ACROSS

crossbred *n* *syn* see HYBRID

crossbreed *vb* *syn* see CROSS 4

crossbreed *n* *syn* see HYBRID

crosscut *vb* *syn* see INTERSECT

cross-examination *n* a thorough, typically formal questioning for full information <*cross-examination* of a hostile witness>
syn grill, grilling, interrogation, third degree
rel debriefing; questioning

cross-grained *adj* 1 *syn* see CANTANKEROUS
2 *syn* see CONTRARY 3
rel difficult

crossing *adj* *syn* see TRANSVERSE

cross-mate *vb* *syn* see CROSS 4

crosspatch *n* *syn* see GROUCH

crossroad *n*, *usu* **crossroads** *pl but sing or pl in constr* *syn* see JUNCTURE 2

‖**cross talk** *n* *syn* see BANTER

crossways *adv* *syn* see ACROSS 1
rel transversely; askew, awry, crisscross
con lengthwise
ant longways

crosswise *adv* *syn* see ACROSS 1
con longways
ant lengthwise

crosswise *adj* *syn* see TRANSVERSE
ant lengthwise

crotchet *n* *syn* see CAPRICE
rel eccentricity, kink, kinkiness, quirk, twist
idiom bee in one's bonnet (*or* brain), flea in one's nose, kink in one's horn, maggot in one's brain

crotchety *adj* *syn* see CANTANKEROUS

crouch *vb* to stoop low with the limbs close to the body <*crouched* behind a rock and watched>
syn ‖crooch, huddle, hunch, scrooch (down); *compare* SQUAT
rel bend, bow, dip, ‖duck; hunker (down), ‖quat, squat, stoop, ‖swat; cower, cringe, flinch, quail, wince; grovel

crow *vb* *syn* see BOAST
rel cry, exult, jubilate

crowd *vb* 1 *syn* see PRESS 1
rel ram, shove
2 *syn* see PRESS 7
rel bunch, cluster

crowd *n* 1 a usually large group of people <a *crowd* gathered before the palace>
syn crush, drove, horde, multitude, press, push, squash, throng; *compare* MULTITUDE 1
rel army, host, legion; flock, gaggle, herd, swarm; mob, rabble, rout
2 *syn* see GATHERING 2
rel huddle, parley; troop; herd; rally
3 *syn* see MULTITUDE 1
4 *syn* see SET 5

crowded *adj* 1 *syn* see FULL 1
rel overcharged, overloaded
ant uncrowded
2 *syn* see CLOSE 4
ant uncrowded

crown *n* 1 *syn* see TOP 1
2 *syn* see WREATH
rel diadem, tiara
3 *syn* see APEX 2

crown *vb* 1 *syn* see SURMOUNT 3
2 *syn* see COVER 3
3 *syn* see CLIMAX

crown (with) *vb* *syn* see ENDOW 1

crucial *adj* *syn* see ACUTE 6
rel deciding, decisive, important; necessary, vital; clamorous, compelling, crying, imperative, insistent, pressing

crucible *n* *syn* see TRIAL 1

crucify *vb* *syn* see AFFLICT
rel bedevil, bother, browbeat
idiom kill by inches, nail to the cross, put on the rack

crud *n* a deposit or incrustation of something filthy, greasy, or sticky <machinery all covered with *crud*>
syn ‖cab, goo, gook, gunk; *compare* GOO 1
rel filth, muck, slime, sludge; debris, junk, rubbish, trash

‖**cruddle** *vb* *syn* see CURDLE

crude adj 1 syn see UNREFINED 3
  2 syn see COARSE 3
    rel backward, ignorant, unenlightened;
    boorish, cloddish, clodhopping, ill-bred,
    loutish, lowbred; savage; insensible
  3 syn see RUDE 1
    rel immature, unmatured; coarse, graceless
    con cultivated, cultured, refined; developed,
    matured, ripened
    ant consummate, finished
  4 syn see OBSCENE 2
    rel blue, risqué
    idiom rated X
  5 rough in plan or execution <*crude* imitations, completely lacking in the original
  artistry>
    syn coarse, inexpert, prentice; compare
    RUDE 1
    rel amateurish, unproficient, unskilled,
    untaught, untrained; raw, rough, rude,
    unfinished, unpolished; inadequate, ineffec-
    tive, inferior, poor
    con finished, perfected, polished
    ant expert

cruel adj syn see FIERCE 1
    rel atrocious, heinous, monstrous, outra-
    geous; bestial, bloodthirsty, brutish; heart-
    less, implacable, relentless; impiteous, un-
    pitying
    con compassionate, sympathetic, tender;
    clement, forbearing, lenient, merciful; hu-
    mane, kindly

‖**cruise** vb syn see GO 1

cruise n syn see VOYAGE
    rel sail

‖**cruiser** n syn see PROSTITUTE

crumb n syn see PARTICLE

crumble vb syn see DECAY
    rel mush, squash

crumbly adj syn see SHORT 6
    rel mush, squash

‖**crump** adj syn see SHORT 6

crumple vb 1 to press or twist into folds or
  wrinkles <*crumple* a piece of paper>
    syn crimp, crimple, crinkle, ‖crunkle, rim-
    ple, ruck (up), ‖ruckle, rumple, screw,
    scrunch, wrinkle
    rel crease, fold; buckle, cockle; wad
    ant smooth
  2 syn see GIVE 12

crunch vb syn see CHEW 1

crunchy adj syn see SHORT 6

‖**crunkle** vb syn see CRUMPLE 1

crusading adj syn see EVANGELICAL

crush vb 1 syn see PRESS 3
    rel ‖scruze, squeeze
  2 to reduce or be reduced to a pulpy or broken mass <*crushed* rose petals>
    syn becrush, bruise, mash, ‖mush (up),
    pulp, squash
    rel press, squeeze; contuse; batter, maim;
    beat, pound; dash, quash, ‖quat, smash;
    comminute, powder, pulverize, triturate
  3 syn see PULVERIZE 1
  4 syn see PRESS 1

  5 to bring to an end by destroying or defeating <the police *crushed* the rebellion>
    syn annihilate, extinguish, put down,
    quash, quell, quench, squash, suppress;
    compare SUPPRESS 2
    rel ‖quelch, repress, squelch, strangle; beat
    down, conquer, defeat, subdue, subjugate;
    ruin, wreck; abolish, demolish, destroy; blot
    out, obliterate
    idiom crush (or grind) under one's heel, ride
    down into the dust, roll (or trample) in the
    dust
  6 syn see CONQUER 1
    idiom bring one to his knees
  7 syn see PRESS 7

crush n 1 syn see CROWD 1
  2 syn see INFATUATION
    rel calf love, puppy love

‖**crust** n syn see EFFRONTERY

crust vb syn see CAKE 1

crusty adj 1 syn see BLUFF
    rel irritable, snappish, waspish; choleric,
    cranky, irascible, splenetic, testy; crabbed,
    dour, saturnine, surly
  2 syn see OBSCENE 2

crux n syn see SUBSTANCE 2

cry vb 1 syn see CALL 1
    rel bleat
  2 to show distress, grief, or pain by tears and
  usually incoherent utterances <the little girl
  cried when she fell down>
    syn blub, blubber, boohoo, ‖pipe, sob, wail,
    weep; compare BAWL 2, WHIMPER
    rel sniff, snivel, whimper, whine; break
    down, choke up; groan, moan, sigh; be-
    moan, bewail, keen, lament, mourn, sorrow;
    bawl, howl, squall, yowl
    idiom cry one's eyes (or heart) out, ‖pipe
    one's eye, shed tears
  3 syn see SHOUT 1
  4 syn see PUBLICIZE

cry n 1 syn see BATTLE CRY
    rel slogan
  2 syn see REPORT 1
  3 syn see FASHION 3
  4 syn see CALL 1
    rel screech, squawk; squeak; caw

cry down vb syn see DECRY 2
    ant cry up

crying adj 1 syn see PRESSING
    rel necessary, needed
  2 syn see OUTRAGEOUS 2

cry off vb syn see BACK DOWN

cry out vb syn see EXCLAIM

crypt n a subterranean chamber <a burial
  crypt>
    syn catacomb, undercroft, vault
    rel cell; chamber, compartment, room;
    cave, cavern, grotto

cryptanalyze vb syn see DECODE

cryptic adj being intentionally obscure and
  mysterious <the senator made some *cryptic*
  statements about intelligence operations>
    syn dark, Delphian, enigmatic, mystifying;
    compare OBSCURE 3
    rel equivocal, murky, obscure, opaque,
    tenebrous, unclear, uninformative, vague;
    incomprehensible, inexplicable, strange,
    unfathomable; abstruse, mysterious; eva-
    sive, secretive

---

syn synonym(s)   rel related word(s)
ant antonym(s)   con contrasted word(s)
idiom idiomatic equivalent(s)
‖ use limited; if in doubt, see a dictionary

crystal *adj syn* see CLEAR 4
  idiom clear as crystal, crystal clear
cry up *vb syn* see PRAISE 2
  idiom beat the drum for, praise to the skies
  ant cry down
cubby *n syn* see CUBBYHOLE
cubbyhole *n* an excessively small room or place <a cramped *cubbyhole* of an office>
  syn cubby, mousehole, pigeonhole
  rel recess; niche; cubicle
  idiom hole in the wall
‖**cubes** *n pl syn* see DICE
cuckoo *n syn* see CRACKPOT
cuckoo *adj syn* see INSANE 1
cuddle *vb* 1 *syn* see CARESS
  rel embrace, enfold, hold
  2 *syn* see SNUGGLE
cudgel *n* a short solid stick used as a weapon or an instrument of punishment <beat the prisoner with a *cudgel*>
  syn bat, baton, billy, billy club, bludgeon, club, knobkerrie, mace, nightstick, ‖shillelagh, spontoon, truncheon, war club
  rel birch, cane, ferule, hickory, paddle, rattan, rod, switch; blackjack; quarterstaff; bastinado
cue *n syn* see HINT 1
cuff *vb syn* see SLAP 1
cuff *n* a sharp blow typically delivered with the hand <gave him a good *cuff* in the face>
  syn box, buffet, ‖bust, chop, clout, haymaker, ‖paste, poke, punch, slap, smack, sock, spank, ‖spat, ‖swack; *compare* BLOW 1, HIT 1
  rel bat, blow, clip, wallop
cul-de-sac *n syn* see DEAD END
  rel stalemate
cull *vb* 1 *syn* see GLEAN
  rel accumulate, amass, collect, round up
  2 *syn* see CHOOSE 1
  rel discriminate
  idiom separate the sheep from the goats, separate the wheat from the chaff
‖**cull** *n syn* see FOOL 3
‖**cully** *n syn* see ASSOCIATE 3
culmen *n syn* see APEX 2
culminate *vb syn* see CLIMAX
culmination *n syn* see APEX 2
  rel extremity, limit, maximum
culpability *n syn* see BLAME
  con blamelessness, innocence
  ant inculpability
culpable *adj syn* see BLAMEWORTHY
  rel impeachable, indictable
  ant inculpable
cult *n* 1 *syn* see RELIGION 1
  2 *syn* see RELIGION 2
cultivable *adj syn* see ARABLE
  ant uncultivable
cultivatable *adj syn* see ARABLE
  ant uncultivatable
cultivate *vb* 1 *syn* see TILL
  rel crop, farm, manage
  2 *syn* see NURSE 2
  rel raise, rear; educate, instruct, teach, train; ameliorate, better, improve
  con disregard, ignore, neglect, slight
  3 *syn* see GROW 1
  rel develop, mature, ripen
cultivated *adj syn* see GENTEEL 1

rel courteous, polite
  ant uncultivated
cultivation *n syn* see CULTURE
culture *n* enlightenment and excellence of taste acquired by intellectual and aesthetic training <a man of *culture* is known by his reading>
  syn breeding, cultivation, polish, refinement
  rel education, enlightenment, erudition, learning; gentility, manners; discrimination, taste; savoir-faire, sophistication, urbanity; class, elegance
  con greenness, ignorance, inexperience, verdancy; crudeness, vulgarity
cultured *adj syn* see GENTEEL 1
  rel educated, enlightened, erudite, learned, literate; civilized
  ant uncultured
culverhouse *n syn* see DOVECOTE
cumber *vb syn* see BURDEN
cumbersome *adj syn* see UNWIELDY
  rel irksome, tiresome, wearisome
cumbrance *n syn* see ENCUMBRANCE
  rel burden, charge, pressure
cumbrous *adj syn* see UNWIELDY
  rel clogging, hampering, hindering, impeding
cumshaw *n syn* see GRATUITY
cumulate *vb syn* see ACCUMULATE
  rel obtain, secure
  ant dissipate
cumulation *n syn* see ACCUMULATION
  rel stockpile; snowball
cumulative *adj* increasing or produced by addition of like or similar things <the *cumulative* effect of several drugs>
  syn accumulative, additive, additory, chain, summative
  rel accumulated, amassed; augmenting, increasing, multiplying; advancing, heightening, intensifying, magnifying, snowballing
  con dispersed, dissipated, scattered
cunning *adj* 1 *syn* see CLEVER 4
  rel well-devised, well-laid, well-planned; crackerjack, masterful
  idiom too clever by half
  2 *syn* see SLY 2
  rel acute, keen, sharp; knowing, smart; wary
  idiom not to be caught with chaff
  con artless, naive, unsophisticated
cunning *n* 1 *syn* see ART 1
  rel deftness, dexterousness; adeptness, expertness; cleverness, ingeniousness, ingenuity
  2 skill in devising or using indirect or subtle methods <a woman able to maneuver people with great *cunning*>
  syn art, artfulness, artifice, cageyness, canniness, craft, craftiness, foxiness, slyness, wiliness
  rel savvy, sharpness, shrewdness; cleverness, ingeniousness, ingenuity; agility, facility, finesse, slickness; subtlety; insidiousness, shiftiness, trickiness
  3 *syn* see DECEIT 1
  idiom satanic cunning, the cunning of the serpent
cupidity *n* intense desire for possessions and wealth <the sight of so much money aroused his *cupidity*>

syn avarice, avariciousness, avidity, greed, rapacity

rel acquisitiveness, greediness, possessiveness, rapaciousness; eagerness, voracity; craving, desire; lust; infatuation, passion

cur *n* 1 *syn* see SNOT 1

rel riffraff

2 *syn* see CAD

curative *adj* restoring or tending to restore to a state of normalcy or health <a *curative* drug>

syn curing, healing, remedial, remedying, restorative, sanative, sanatory, vulnerary, wholesome

rel medicable, medicative, medicinal; corrective, therapeutic; invigorating, tonic; beneficial, helpful, salutary, wholesome

curb *vb* 1 *syn* see HAMPER

2 *syn* see DENY 2

rel repress, suppress

ant goad

3 *syn* see RESTRAIN 1

rel fetter, hamper, hog-tie, manacle, shackle

idiom hold in leash, keep a tight rein on

con unbridle, unleash

ant spur

curd *vb* *syn* see CURDLE

curdle *vb* to cause to become coagulated or thickened and often made sour <hot weather will *curdle* milk>

syn ‖clabber, ‖cruddle, curd, ‖lopper, turn

rel clot, coagulate, condense, thicken; ferment; go off, sour, spoil

cure *n* 1 *syn* see REMEDY 1

2 *syn* see REMEDY 2

cure *vb* to rectify an unhealthy or undesirable condition <aspirin *cured* his headache>

syn heal, remedy

rel doctor, medicate; restore; ameliorate, better, improve

cure-all *n* *syn* see PANACEA

cureless *adj* *syn* see HOPELESS 2

curing *adj* *syn* see CURATIVE

curio *n* *syn* see KNICKKNACK

curiosity *n* 1 *syn* see INTEREST 3

rel inquisitiveness, questioning

ant disinterest

2 something that arouses interest especially because of uncommon or exotic characteristics <an architectural *curiosity*>

syn conversation piece, oddity

rel exception, nonesuch, rarity; marvel, prodigy, wonder; anomaly; freak, monstrosity

idiom something to write home about

curious *adj* 1 *syn* see INQUISITIVE 1

rel searching; analytical; prurient

ant incurious

2 interested in what is not one's personal or proper concern <a *curious* old woman prying into her neighbors' affairs>

syn inquisitive, inquisitorial, inquisitory, ‖nibby, nosy, peery, prying, snoopy

rel interfering, intermeddling, meddling, tampering; examining, inspecting, scrutinizing; impertinent, intrusive, meddlesome

---

idiom consumed (*or* burning *or* eaten up) with curiosity, curious as a cat (*or* monkey)

con aloof, detached, disinterested, indifferent, unconcerned, uninterested; apathetic, impassive, phlegmatic, stolid

ant incurious

3 *syn* see STRANGE 4

curl *vb* *syn* see WIND 2

rel crook; roll; ringlet; kink

con straighten, unkink, unwind

ant uncurl

currency *n* *syn* see MONEY

current *adj* 1 *syn* see PRESENT

rel topical, up-to-date

con antiquated, antique, obsolete

2 *syn* see PREVAILING

rel accustomed, customary; a la mode, fashionable, modern, popular

ant antique

current *n* 1 *syn* see FLOW

2 *syn* see TENDENCY 1

curry *vb* *syn* see WHIP 2

curse *n* 1 a denunciation that conveys a wish or threat of evil <the dying man's *curse* against his family>

syn anathema, commination, imprecation, malediction, malison

rel execration, objurgation; damning, denunciation; blasphemy, profanation, profanity, sacrilege

ant blessing

2 *syn* see SWEARWORD

3 *syn* see PLAGUE 1

curse *vb* 1 *syn* see EXECRATE 1

rel blaspheme; blight; doom

idiom call down curses on the head of, call down evil on

ant bless

2 *syn* see SWEAR 3

idiom ‖curse up a storm

cursed *adj* 1 *syn* see DAMNED 2

rel hateful

2 *syn* see EXECRABLE 1

rel disgusting; odious

ant blessed

cursing *n* *syn* see BLASPHEMY 1

cursive *adj* *syn* see EASY 9

cursory *adj* *syn* see SUPERFICIAL 2

rel fast, hasty, hurried, quick, rapid, speedy, swift; brief, short; casual, desultory, haphazard, random

con careful, meticulous, scrupulous

ant painstaking

curt *adj* 1 *syn* see CONCISE

2 *syn* see BLUFF

rel imperious, peremptory

ant voluble

curtail *vb* 1 *syn* see SHORTEN

ant prolong, protract

2 *syn* see ABRIDGE 1

ant extend

curtains *n pl but sing in constr* *syn* see DEATH 1

curtilage *n* *syn* see COURT 1

curvaceous *adj* having a shapely figure marked by pronounced curves <*curvaceous* bikini-clad girls swarmed over the beach>

syn ‖built, curvesome, curvilinear, curvy, Junoesque, rounded, ‖stacked, well-developed; compare BUXOM, SHAPELY

---

syn synonym(s)   *rel* related word(s)

ant antonym(s)   *con* contrasted word(s)

idiom idiomatic equivalent(s)

‖ use limited; if in doubt, see a dictionary

rel shapeful, shapely, statuesque, well=proportioned; attractive, charming, pleasing
idiom ‖built (or stacked) like a brick out-house

curvation *n syn* see CURVE

curvature *n syn* see CURVE

curve *vb* to swerve or cause to swerve from a straight line or course <the road *curves* to the right>
syn bend, bow, crook, round; *compare* WIND 2
rel deflect, divert, turn; deviate, swerve, veer; coil, curl, spiral, twist, wind; incurve
ant straighten

curve *n* something (as a line or surface) that curves or is curved <a slight *curve* to her eyebrows>
syn arc, arch, bend, bow, curvation, curvature, round
rel incurvation, incurvature; inflection, rondure; circuit, circumference, compass

curved *adj* having or characterized by a curve or curves <a *curved* vault>
syn arced, arched, arciform, arrondi, bent, bowed, curvilinear, round, rounded; *compare* CROOKED 1
rel declinate; embowed, incurvate, in-curved; excurved; bending, twisted, twisting
ant straight

curvesome *adj syn* see CURVACEOUS

curvilinear *adj* 1 *syn* see CURVED
2 *syn* see CURVACEOUS

curving *adj syn* see CROOKED 1

curvy *adj syn* see CURVACEOUS

cushy *adj syn* see COMFORTABLE 2

cusp *n syn* see POINT 9

cuspidate *adj syn* see POINTED 1

cuss *n* 1 *syn* see SWEARWORD
2 *syn* see MAN 3

cuss *vb syn* see SWEAR 3
idiom ‖cuss up a blue streak

cussed *adj syn* see DAMNED 2

cussing *n syn* see BLASPHEMY 1

cussword *n syn* see SWEARWORD

custodian *n* one that guards, protects, or maintains (as property or records) <was the *custodian* of the manor for many years>
syn cerberus, claviger, ‖custodier, custos, guardian, keeper, warden, watchdog
rel curator, steward; castellan, governor; overseer, supervisor

‖**custodier** *n syn* see CUSTODIAN

custody *n* the act or duty of guarding and preserving <the government has *custody* of all state gifts>
syn care, guardianship, keeping, safekeeping, trust, ward
rel caretaking; charge, management, supervision; protection

custom *n* 1 *syn* see HABIT 1
rel precedent; ritual; mold; fixture, institution; prescription, rubric; canon, law, precept, rule
idiom matter of course
con departure, deviation, shift; exception; irregularity
2 *syn* see PATRONAGE 2

custom *adj syn* see CUSTOM-MADE

customarily *adv syn* see USUALLY 1
rel conventionally, traditionally; normally, ordinarily; routinely

idiom as a matter of course
con rarely; never
ant occasionally

customary *adj* 1 *syn* see USUAL 1
rel acknowledged, recognized, understood; standard; conventional, orthodox, traditional; prescriptive, regulation, stipulated
idiom being the customary (or usual) thing
con occasional; infrequent, inhabitual, sporadic, uncommon; irregular
ant uncustomary
2 *syn* see COMMON 4
rel household, popular; general, universal
ant uncustomary

custom–built *adj syn* see CUSTOM-MADE

customer *n* one that patronizes or uses the services of something (as a store or restaurant) <many *customers* in the shop>
syn client, patron
rel buyer, consumer, purchaser, shopper

customized *adj syn* see CUSTOM-MADE

custom–made *adj* made according to personal order and individual specifications <he always wore a *custom-made* suit>
syn custom, custom-built, customized, custom-tailored, made-to-order, tailor-made
ant mass-produced

custom–tailored *adj syn* see CUSTOM=MADE

custos *n syn* see CUSTODIAN

cut *vb* 1 to penetrate with or as if with a sharp edge <*cut* his hand on a broken bottle>
syn gash, incise, pierce, slash, slice, slit
rel cleave, dissever, sever, sunder; rend, rip, rive, tear; lacerate, wound
2 *syn* see SHORTEN
3 *syn* see REDUCE 2
4 *syn* see MOW
5 to penetrate and divide with an edged tool or instrument <*cut* the melon into slices>
syn carve, cleave, dissect, dissever, sever, slice, split, sunder
rel divide, part, separate; chop, dice, hash, mince, mow
idiom lay open
6 to reduce by severing parts <the barber *cut* his hair too short>
syn clip, crop, pare, prune, shave, shear, skive, trim
rel cut back, dock, lop, poll, pollard, shrub; amputate; curtail
7 to refuse social recognition especially by way of rebuke <his friends *cut* him after the scandal broke>
syn cold-shoulder, ostracize, snob, snub
rel disdain, ignore, rebuff, reject, slight, turn away; affront, insult, offend
idiom give the cold shoulder (to), show one his place, slam the door in one's face, slam the door on, slap one in the face, turn aside (or away) from, turn one's back (on or upon)
8 *syn* see DILUTE
9 *syn* see FELL 2
10 *syn* see OPERATE 2

cut *n* 1 *syn* see PART 1
2 *syn* see SHARE 1
3 *syn* see TRENCH
4 *syn* see TYPE

cut *adj syn* see INTOXICATED 1

cut back *vb* 1 *syn* see SHORTEN

2 *syn* see REDUCE 2
cut down *vb syn* see REDUCE 2
cut in *vb syn* see INTRUDE 1
cut off *vb* **1** *syn* see KILL 1
  2 *syn* see INTERCEPT
  3 *syn* see ISOLATE
  4 *syn* see DISINHERIT 1
cutoff *n syn* see SHORTCUT
cut out *vb* **1** *syn* see EXCISE
  2 *syn* see SUPPLANT 1
cutpurse *n syn* see PICKPOCKET
cutthroat *n syn* see ASSASSIN
cutting *adj syn* see INCISIVE
  rel piercing, probing
cut up *vb* **1** *syn* see CRITICIZE
  2 to behave in a boisterously comic or unruly
manner <children *cutting up* in front of
company>
  syn act up, carry on, horse, horseplay

rel caper, cavort, romp; clown; show off;
roughhouse; misbehave
  idiom cut a dido (*or* shine), cut up rough,
‖kick up a shindy, raise Cain (*or* Ned),
whoop it up
cutup *n syn* see ZANY 2
cycle *n* **1** a complete course of recurrent
operations or events <a 24-hour *cycle* of
medication>
  syn circle, round, wheel; *compare* SUCCES-
SION 2
  rel chain, sequel, sequence, series; course,
run; circuit, loop, ring
  2 *syn* see BICYCLE
cyclone *n syn* see TORNADO
cyclopean *adj syn* see HUGE
  ant lilliputian
cynical *adj syn* see SARDONIC
cyprian *n syn* see WANTON
czar *n syn* see MAGNATE

D

dab *vb syn* see SMEAR 1
‖**dab** *n syn* see EXPERT
dabbler *n syn* see AMATEUR 2
  con adept, artist, connoisseur; expert, master, professional
dabbling *adj syn* see AMATEURISH
  rel sciolistic, shallow, sophomoric, superficial
  con adept, capable, competent
‖**dabster** *n syn* see EXPERT
dad *n syn* see FATHER 1
dada *n syn* see FATHER 1
dad-blamed *adj* **1** *syn* see DAMNED 2
  2 *syn* see UTTER
dad-blasted *adj* **1** *syn* see DAMNED 2
  2 *syn* see UTTER
dad-burned *adj* **1** *syn* see DAMNED 2
  2 *syn* see UTTER
daddy *n syn* see FATHER 1
daedal *adj syn* see COMPLEX 2
daffy *adj* **1** *syn* see INSANE 1
  2 *syn* see FOOLISH 2
daft *adj syn* see INSANE 1

daily *adj* of each or every day <*daily* prayers
for the dead>
  syn diurnal, quotidian
  con nocturnal; alternate, intermittent, periodic, recurrent, spasmodic; erratic, fitful,
fluctuating, infrequent, irregular; occasional, sporadic
  ant nightly
dainty *n syn* see DELICACY
dainty *adj* **1** *syn* see CHOICE
  rel beautiful, bonny, fair, lovely, pretty;
delectable, delicious, delightful; airy, diaphanous, ethereal, light
  con coarse, vulgar
  ant gross
  2 *syn* see NICE 1
  rel acute, penetrative, perceptive
  con careless, neglectful, negligent, thoughtless
‖**daisy** *n syn* ‖DILLY, ‖corker, crackerjack,
dandy, humdinger, jim-dandy, knockout,
‖lalapalooza, ‖lulu, nifty
dale *n syn* see VALLEY
dally *vb* **1** *syn* see TRIFLE 1
  rel frolic, gambol, play, rollick, romp,
sport; caress, cosset, cuddle, dandle, fondle,
pet
  2 *syn* see DELAY 2
  con fleet, rush, scurry, skedaddle

---

syn synonym(s)   *rel* related word(s)
ant antonym(s)   *con* contrasted word(s)
idiom idiomatic equivalent(s)
‖ use limited; if in doubt, see a dictionary

ant hasten

dam vb syn see HINDER
rel repress, suppress
con air, express, utter, vent

damage n syn see INJURY 1
rel impairment, marring; deterioration, dilapidation, disrepair, ruining, wrecking; deleteriousness, disadvantage, drawback
con amelioration, betterment, improvement; benefit, profit; advantage, service, use
ant repair

damage vb syn see INJURE 1
rel demolish, destroy, raze, ruin, wreck; deteriorate, dilapidate; abuse, ill-treat, maltreat, mistreat, misuse, outrage
con ameliorate, amend, better, improve; mend
ant repair

damaged adj having been injured <damaged merchandise>
syn flawed, impaired, marred, spoiled
rel blemished, broken, imperfect, injured, unsound
con flawless, good, intact, unbroken, unhurt, unimpaired, uninjured, unmarred, whole; corrected, improved, rectified, repaired
ant undamaged

damaging adj syn see HARMFUL

dame n 1 syn see MATRIARCH
2 syn see BELDAM 1
3 syn see WOMAN 1

damn vb 1 syn see SENTENCE
rel castigate, discipline, penalize, punish; banish, cast out, expel
con deliver, ransom, rescue, redeem; reward
ant save
2 syn see EXECRATE 1
rel abominate; vituperate
3 syn see SWEAR 3

damn n syn see PARTICLE

damnable adj 1 syn see EXECRABLE 1
rel abhorrent, abominable, detestable, hateful, odious; damned
con admirable, commendable, estimable; laudable, praiseworthy
2 syn see DAMNED 2
3 syn see UTTER

damned adj 1 being doomed to eternal punishment <a damned soul>
syn condemned, doomed, lost
rel anathematized, cursed, reprobate; done for
idiom gone to blazes, hell bound
con delivered, ransomed, redeemed
ant saved
2 deserving censure or strong disapproval — often used as a generalized expression of annoyance <this damned door won't open>
syn blamed, blankety-blank, blasted, bleeding, blessed, blighted, blinding, ‖blinking, ‖blistering, ‖blooming, confounded, ‖consarned, cursed, cussed, dad-blamed, dad-blasted, dad-burned, damnable, dang, darn (or durn), dashed, doggone, dratted, execrable, goldarn, infernal, perishing, so-and-so
3 syn see UTTER

damned adv syn see VERY 1

damp adj slightly or relatively wet <her dress was still damp>
syn dampish, dank, moist, moisty, wettish
rel drenched, saturated, soaked, soaking; soggy, water-logged
con arid, dry

dampen vb syn see MUFFLE 2

dampish adj syn see DAMP

damsel n syn see GIRL 1

dance vb 1 to perform a rhythmic and patterned succession of steps usually to music <the band was good enough to dance to>
syn foot (it), hoof (it), prance, step, tread
rel shuffle, trip, truck
idiom ‖cut a rug, trip the light fantastic
2 syn see FLIT 2
rel quaver, quiver, shake, tremble, wobble

dancer n a professional performer of dances <dancers performing a ballet>
syn ballerina, ballet girl, coryphée, dancing girl, danseur, danseuse, figurant, figurante, hoofer
rel chorine, chorus boy, chorus girl, chorus man; danseur noble, premier danseur, premiere danseuse, prima ballerina

dancing girl n syn see DANCER

dandle vb syn see CARESS
rel disport, play, sport

dandy n 1 syn see FOP
con clod, lout, lump, oaf, slob, slouch
ant sloven
2 syn ‖DILLY, ‖corker, crackerjack, ‖daisy, humdinger, jim-dandy, ‖lalapalooza, ‖lulu, nifty, peach

‖dandy adj 1 syn see MARVELOUS 2
2 syn see EXCELLENT
rel grand, hunky-dory, keen, nifty, swell
idiom fine and dandy
con ‖bum, ‖crummy, grim, ‖lousy, ‖putrid, rotten
ant blah

dang adj 1 syn see DAMNED 2
2 syn see UTTER

danger n the state of being exposed to injury, pain, or loss <they are seeking a place where children can play without danger>
syn hazard, jeopardy, peril, risk
rel menace, precariousness, threat; emergency, exigency, pass; precipice
idiom dangerous ground, thin ice
con safety; exemption, immunity; defense, guard, protection, safeguard, shield
ant security

dangerous adj 1 attended by or involving the possibility of injury, pain, or loss <a dangerous crossing>
syn chancy, ‖dangersome, hairy, hazardous, jeopardous, parlous, perilous, risky, treacherous, unhealthy, unsound, wicked; compare GRAVE 3
rel insecure, precarious, uncertain, unsafe; chance, haphazard, hit-or-miss, random; critical, menacing, serious, threatening
idiom beset (or fraught) with danger, on a collision course
con certain, reliable; harmless, innocent
ant safe, secure
2 syn see GRAVE 3

‖dangersome adj syn see DANGEROUS 1

dangle vb syn see HANG 1

dank adj syn see DAMP

danseur n syn see DANCER

danseuse *n syn* see DANCER
dap *vb syn* see GLANCE 1
dapper *adj* trimly neat and tidy <a *dapper* dresser, always neat as a pin>
  syn bandbox, doggish, doggy, natty, sassy, sparkish, spiffy, spruce, sprucy, well-groomed; *compare* NEAT 2, STYLISH
  rel chichi; jaunty, rakish; showy
  con dowdy, drab, unstylish; disheveled, disordered, slipshod, sloppy, slovenly, unkempt, untidy; blowsy, dowdy, frowsy, shabby, slatternly
dappled *adj syn* see VARIEGATED
  con pure, smooth, spotless, unbroken, uniform
dare *vb syn* see FACE 3
  rel change, hazard, risk
  idiom take the bull by the horns
  con avoid, evade; flee, run
dare *n syn* see DEFIANCE 1
daredevil *adj syn* see ADVENTUROUS
  con timid, timorous; cautious, chary, circumspect, wary; discreet, judicious, prudent, sane, sensible
daring *adj syn* see ADVENTUROUS
dark *adj* **1** deficient in light <a *dark* room>
  syn caliginous, dim, dun, dusk, dusky, gloomy, lightless, murky, obscure, somber, tenebrous, unilluminated
  rel cloudy, dull, shadowy, shady; pitch-black, pitch-dark
  con bright, brilliant, luminous, radiant; enlightened, illuminated, illumined, lighted
  ant light
  2 *syn* see CRYPTIC
  rel abstruse, esoteric, hidden, occult, recondite; anagogic, cabalistic, darkling, mystic, mystical; complicated, intricate, knotty
  con clear, perspicuous; easy, facile, light, simple
  ant lucid
  3 of dark complexion <her *dark* good looks>
  syn bistered, black-a-vised, brunet, dark-skinned, dusky, swart, swarth, swarthy
  con blond, fair, light; ruddy, tawny
  ‖**4** *syn* see BLIND 1
darken *vb syn* see OBSCURE
  ant illuminate
dark-skinned *adj syn* see DARK 3
darling *n syn* see SWEETHEART 1
darling *adj* **1** *syn* see FAVORITE 1
  2 *syn* see DELIGHTFUL
darn (or **durn**) *adj* **1** *syn* see DAMNED 2
  2 *syn* see UTTER
dart *n syn* see SHAFT 2
dart *vb syn* see FLY 1
  rel hasten, hurry, precipitate, speed; run, scamper, scoot, scurry, sprint, spurt
  con dally, dawdle, delay, linger, tarry; lumber, plod, slog, trudge
dash *vb* **1** *syn* see RUSH 1
  rel run, scamper, scoot, scurry, sprint
  con dally, dawdle, delay, linger, tarry; lumber, plod, slog, trudge

  2 *syn* see RUN 1
  3 *syn* see BLAST 1
  4 *syn* see FRUSTRATE 1
dash *n* **1** *syn* see SPIRIT 5
  rel energy, force, might, power, strength; intensity, vehemence; impressiveness
  con apathy, dullness, languor, lethargy, listlessness, sluggishness, stagnation, torpor
  2 *syn* see HINT 1
  rel impress, impression, stamp
dashed *adj* **1** *syn* see DAMNED 2
  2 *syn* see UTTER
dashing *adj* **1** *syn* see LIVELY 1
  2 *syn* see STYLISH
  rel flashy, flaunting; dapper, jaunty, spiffy, spruce
  idiom cutting a fine figure
  con unfashionable, unstylish; modest, unostentatious, unpretentious
  ant drab
dastard *n syn* see COWARD
date *vb* to go or take on a date <he *dated* her several times that winter>
  syn see, take out
  rel accompany, escort; court, woo
  idiom go out with
date *n* **1** *syn* see ENGAGEMENT 3
  2 *syn* see ESCORT 1
dated *adj syn* see OLD-FASHIONED
  ant up-to-the-minute
dateless *adj syn* see ETERNAL 4
  ant ephemeral
daub *vb syn* see SMEAR 1
  rel spatter, speckle, spot; dapple, fleck, variegate
daunt *vb syn* see DISMAY 1
  rel browbeat, bully, cow, intimidate; baffle, foil, frustrate, thwart
  con arouse, awaken, rally, rouse, stir, waken; actuate, drive, impel, move; activate, energize, vitalize
  ant enhearten
dauntless *adj syn* see BRAVE 1
  rel indomitable, invincible, unconquerable
  con hesitant, reluctant
  ant poltroon
dauntlessness *n syn* see COURAGE
  ant poltroonery
dawdle *vb* **1** *syn* see IDLE
  2 *syn* see DELAY 2
  rel amble, saunter, stroll; stay, wait; toy, trifle; fritter, waste
  idiom fritter away time
  con arouse, rally, rouse, stir; hasten, hurry, speed
dawdler *n syn* see LAGGARD
dawn *n* **1** the first appearance of light in the morning <birds which sing at *dawn*>
  syn aurora, cockcrow, cockcrowing, dawning, daybreak, daylight, light, morn, morning, sunrise, sunup
  rel prime
  idiom break of day, crack of dawn, first blush (*or* flush) of day, first light, peep of day, the wee small hours
  2 *syn* see BEGINNING
  ant sunset
dawning *n syn* **1** *syn* see DAWN 1
  2 *syn* see BEGINNING
  ant sunset

---

syn synonym(s)   *rel* related word(s)
ant antonym(s)   *con* contrasted word(s)
idiom idiomatic equivalent(s)
‖ use limited; if in doubt, see a dictionary

day *n* 1 the time of light between one night and the next <waiting for *day* to dawn>
syn daylight, daytime
rel light, sunlight, sunshine
con dark, nighttime
ant night
2 *usu* **days** *pl syn see* PERIOD 2
daybreak *n syn see* DAWN 1
daydream *n syn see* FANCY 4
rel conceiving, fancying, imagination, imagining
con substantiality, tangibility; authenticity, truth, verity
daydreaming *adj syn see* DREAMY 1
daydreamy *adj syn see* DREAMY 1
daylight *n* 1 *syn see* DAWN 1
syn see DAY 1
dayspring *n syn see* BEGINNING
daystar *n syn see* SUN 1
daytime *n syn see* DAY 1
daze *vb* 1 to confuse with light <the bright sunlight *dazed* him>
syn bedazzle, blind, dazzle
rel overcome, overpower, overwhelm; dizzy
2 to dull or deaden the powers of the mind through some disturbing experience or influence <*dazed* by the news of the accident>
syn bedaze, bemuse, benumb, paralyze, petrify, stun, stupefy
rel bewilder, confound, disorder, distract, dumbfound, mystify; befuddle, confuse, fuddle, muddle; dazzle, dizzy; rock
con enhance, expand, heighten, sharpen; alert, arouse, waken
daze *n syn see* HAZE 2
dazzle *vb syn see* DAZE 1
dead *adj* 1 devoid of life <a *dead* person>
syn asleep, cold, deceased, defunct, departed, exanimate, extinct, inanimate, late, lifeless, spiritless, unanimated
rel bloodless, breathless; gone, reposing; inactive, inert; belowground, buried
idiom dead as a doornail, gone the way of all flesh, out of one's misery, pushing up daisies
con animate, animated, vital; being, existing; active, live
ant alive
2 *syn see* DEATHLY 1
rel insensible, insentient, numb, unfeeling, unresponsive; inanimate, unconscious
con feeling, responsive, sensitive, sentient; animate, animated, living, spirited, vivacious
ant alive
3 *syn see* NUMB 1
4 *syn see* OBSOLETE
ant living; viable
5 *syn see* EXTINCT 2
6 *syn see* DULL 7
rel bleak, blank
con glorious, resplendent
7 *syn see* UTTER
dead *adv syn see* DIRECTLY 1
deaden *vb* 1 to impair in vigor, force, activity, or sensation <the news *deadened* his distress>
syn benumb, blunt, desensitize, dull, mull, numb
rel anesthetize, paralyze, unnerve; stun, stupefy
con animate, vivify; energize, invigorate; activate, vitalize

ant enliven
2 *syn see* MUFFLE 2
dead end *n* a course which leads to nothing further <had reached a *dead end* in negotiations>
syn blind alley, cul-de-sac, impasse, pocket
rel corner, hole; deadlock, halt, standstill; bottleneck
deadened *adj* 1 *syn see* DEATHLY 1
2 *syn see* NUMB 1
‖**deader** *n syn see* CORPSE
deadfall *n syn see* PITFALL
deadliness *n syn see* FATALITY 1
deadlock *n syn see* DRAW 4
rel condition, posture, situation, state; dilemma, plight, predicament, quandary
con decision, determination, resolution, solution
deadly *adj* 1 causing or causative of death <a *deadly* disease>
syn deathly, fatal, lethal, mortal, mortiferous, pestilent, pestilential; *compare* PERNICIOUS
rel destroying, destructive; killing, slaying; internecine; baneful, noxious, pernicious; poisonous, toxic, virulent
con healthful, healthy, wholesome; advantageous, beneficial, restorative, sanative
2 *syn see* PERNICIOUS
con harmless, innocuous, inoffensive, unoffending
3 *syn see* DEATHLY 1
deadpan *adj syn see* EXPRESSIONLESS
dead to rights *adv syn see* RED-HANDED
deadweight *n syn see* LOAD 3
‖**deadwood** *n syn see* ADVANTAGE 3
deaf *adj syn see* OBSTINATE
deal *vb* 1 *syn see* DISTRIBUTE 1
rel partake, participate, share
con receive, take; detain, hold, hold back, keep, retain, withhold; appropriate, arrogate, confiscate
2 *syn see* GIVE 10
rel impart, mete, render
con annul, cancel, remove, rescind, revoke
deal (out) *vb syn see* ADMINISTER 2
rel dish, dish out, help, serve; offer, present, proffer, tender
con hold, hold back, keep, retain, withhold
deal (with) *vb syn see* TREAT 2
rel control, direct; clear, rid, unburden
con misconduct, misdirect, mishandle, mismanage; disregard, ignore, neglect; burden, cumber, encumber
deal *n* 1 *syn see* AGREEMENT 2
2 treatment received in a transaction from another <a fair *deal*>
syn shake
dealer *n syn see* MERCHANT
dealings *n pl syn see* COMMERCE 1
rel affairs, business, concerns, doings, matters, things; proceedings
deambulatory *adj syn see* ITINERANT
dean *n syn see* LEADER 1
dear *adj* 1 *syn see* FAVORITE 1
2 *syn see* LOVING
3 *syn see* COSTLY 1
con inexpensive, low, moderate, modest, nominal
ant cheap

dear *n syn* see SWEETHEART 1

dearth *n syn* see ABSENCE
  rel infrequency, rareness, scarcity, uncommonness; exiguousness, meagerness, scantiness, scantness; insufficiency, paucity
  con superfluity, surplus; lavishness, prodigality, profusion
  ant excess

death *n* **1** the end or the ending of life <*death* of a man><*death* of an enterprise>
  syn curtains, decease, defunction, demise, dissolution, grim reaper, (the) Pale Horse, passing, quietus, silence, sleep
  rel annihilation, ending, expiration, extinction, grave, termination
  idiom crossing the bar
  ant life
  2 *syn* see FATALITY 2

deathful *adj syn* see DEATHLY 1

deathless *adj syn* see IMMORTAL 1
  rel eternal; abiding, lasting, persisting

deathlike *adj* **1** *syn* see DEATHLY 1
  2 *syn* see GHASTLY 2

deathly *adj* **1** suggesting death (as in inertness or appearance) <fell in a *deathly* faint>
  syn corpselike, corpsy, dead, deadened, deadly, deathful, deathlike
  rel cadaverous, haggard, wasted; ghastly, grisly, gruesome, macabre; appalling, dreadful, horrible
  con healthy, hearty, robust; stout, sturdy; energetic, strenuous, vigorous
  2 *syn* see DEADLY 1

debacle *n* **1** *syn* see DEFEAT 1
  2 *syn* see COLLAPSE 2

debar *vb syn* see EXCLUDE
  rel forbid, interdict; block, hinder, impede, obstruct
  con accept, receive; allow, let, permit
  ant admit

debark *vb syn* see DISEMBARK

debase *vb* **1** to cause to become impaired in quality or character <vulgarly outrageous movies that *debase* the taste of the people>
  syn animalize, bastardize, bestialize, brutalize, canker, corrupt, debauch, demoralize, deprave, pervert, poison, rot, stain, vitiate, warp; *compare* ADULTERATE
  rel damage, harm, impair, injure, mar, spoil; contaminate, defile, dishonor, pollute, taint; commercialize
  con enhance, heighten; lift, raise; ameliorate, better, improve
  ant elevate; amend
  2 *syn* see HUMBLE
  rel cripple, debilitate, disable, enfeeble, sap, undermine, weaken
  con acclaim, laud, praise; refresh, rejuvenate, renew, restore
  3 *syn* see ADULTERATE
  rel damage, impair, worsen; corrupt, defile, spoil
  idiom play the devil (*or* the mischief) with
  con amend, upgrade

debased *adj* being lowered in quality or character <became *debased* in his greed for money>
  syn corrupted, debauched, depraved, perverted, vitiate, vitiated
  rel decadent, degenerate, degenerated, deteriorated; abandoned, dissolute, profligate, reprobate
  con ameliorated, bettered, improved; elevated, lifted, raised
  ant elevated

debatable *adj syn* see MOOT
  ant undebatable

debate *n* **1** *syn* see ARGUMENTATION
  rel controverting, rebutting, refuting
  2 *syn* see ATTENTION 1

debate *vb syn* see DISCUSS 1
  rel altercate, quarrel, wrangle; confute, controvert, disprove, rebut, refute; demonstrate, prove; contend, contest
  con agree, coincide, concur; affirm, aver, maintain, profess

debauch *vb* **1** *syn* see DEBASE 1
  rel decoy, inveigle, lure, seduce, tempt
  con amend, remedy; clean, cleanse, purge, purify; preserve, reclaim, save
  2 *syn* see SEDUCE 2

debauch *n syn* see ORGY 2

debauched *adj syn* see DEBASED
  rel lascivious, lecherous, lewd, libertine, libidinous, licentious, wanton
  con delivered, reclaimed, redeemed, rescued, saved; chaste, decent, pure; moral, virtuous; continent, temperate

debilitate *vb syn* see WEAKEN 1
  rel devitalize; attenuate, extenuate; harm, hurt, mar, spoil
  con energize, vitalize; fortify, reinforce, strengthen; refresh, rejuvenate, renew, restore; rally, rouse, stir
  ant invigorate

debility *n syn* see INFIRMITY 1

debris *n syn* see REFUSE
  rel dregs, dross, rubble

debt *n* **1** *syn* see EVIL 2
  2 *syn* see INDEBTEDNESS 1
  3 something (as money) that is owed <struggling to keep ahead of his *debts*>
  syn arrear(s), arrearage, due, indebtedness, liability; *compare* INDEBTEDNESS 1
  rel default, deficit, delinquency, nonpayment, outstandings; debit, demurrage
  con asset, credit; compensation, refund, reimbursement, remuneration

debunk *vb syn* see EXPOSE 4

debut *vb* to make one's formal entrance into society <she *debuted* on her 20th birthday>
  syn come out
  idiom make one's bow

decadence *n syn* see DETERIORATION 1
  rel regress, regression, regressiveness, retrogradation, retrograding, retrogression, retrogressiveness; debasement, degradation
  con advance, progress, progression; amelioration, bettering, betterment, improvement
  ant rise; flourishing

decadent *adj syn* see EFFETE 3

decamp *vb* **1** *syn* see GET OUT 1
  2 *syn* see ESCAPE 1
  rel exit, go, leave, quit, retire, withdraw; avoid, elude, evade, shun

con arrive, come

decapitate vb 1 syn see BEHEAD
2 syn see DESTROY 1

decay vb to undergo or to cause to undergo destructive changes <apples *decaying* in the basket>
syn break down, corrupt, crumble, decompose, disintegrate, molder, ||perish, putrefy, putresce, rot, spoil, taint, turn
rel deteriorate, debilitate, enfeeble, sap, undermine, weaken; contaminate, defile, pollute; dilapidate, ruin, wreck; curdle, ferment, sour, work; dry-rot
idiom go bad, go to pot, go to seed, go to wrack and ruin
con mature, ripen; refresh, renew, restore; activate, energize, vitalize; cleanse, purify; galvanize, quicken, stimulate, strengthen

decayed adj 1 syn see EFFETE 3
2 syn see BAD 5

decease n syn see DEATH 1

decease vb syn see DIE 1

deceased adj syn see DEAD 1

deceit n 1 the act or practice of imposing upon the credulity of others by dishonesty, fraud, or trickery <he was full of *deceit* in his business dealings>
syn cunning, dissemblance, dissimulation, duplicity, guile
rel chicane, chicanery, deception, double-dealing, fraud, trickery; artifice, craft; cheating, cozening, defrauding, entrapping, overreaching, trapping
con honesty, scrupulosity, scrupulousness, uprightness; candidness, candor, frankness, openness; forthrightness, straightforwardness
2 syn see IMPOSTURE

deceitful adj syn see DISHONEST 1
rel artful, crafty, cunning, foxy, guileful, insidious, sly, tricky, wily; clandestine, furtive, stealthy, underhand, underhanded; deceptive, delusive, delusory, misleading
con assuring, convincing, reassuring
ant trustworthy

deceive vb to lead astray or frustrate by underhandedness <advertising that *deceives* the public>
syn beguile, betray, ||bitch, bluff, ||bunk, cozen, delude, double-cross, four-flush, humbug, illude, juggle, mislead, mock, sell out, suck in, take in, two-time
rel cheat, defraud, do, overreach; circumvent, outwit; bamboozle, befool, dupe, gull, hoax, hoodwink, spoof, trick, victimize; throw off
idiom pull one's leg, pull the wool over one's eyes, put something over (or across), take for a ride, take into camp, throw off the scent (or track)
con correct, disabuse, rectify, unblind; acquaint, advise, apprise, inform
ant undeceive; enlighten

deceiving adj syn see MISLEADING
ant undeceiving; enlightening

decelerate vb syn see DELAY 1
ant accelerate

decency n syn see DECORUM 1
rel appropriateness, fitness, fittingness, suitability; ceremoniousness, conventionality, formality

con impropriety, indecorousness, unseemliness; inappropriateness, unfitness, unsuitability; discourteousness, impoliteness, rudeness
ant indecency

decent adj 1 syn see DECOROUS 1
con awkward, clumsy, gauche, inept, maladroit; discomfiting, disconcerting, embarrassing; crude, rough, rude, uncouth
2 syn see CHASTE
rel noble; good, right; rigid, strict; ascetic, austere, severe
con lewd; libertine, wanton; abandoned, dissolute, profligate, reprobate
ant indecent; obscene
3 syn see RESPECTABLE 5
4 better than mediocre but less than excellent <the accommodations were *decent*>
syn acceptable, adequate, all right, common, good, respectable, right, satisfactory, sufficient, tolerable, unexceptionable, unexceptional, unimpeachable, unobjectionable; compare RESPECTABLE 5, SUFFICIENT 1
rel average, fair, mediocre, middling
con imperfect, inadequate, unacceptable, unsatisfactory; excellent, fine, superior
5 syn see SUFFICIENT 1

decently adv syn see WELL 1

deception n 1 the act of deliberately deceiving <resort to falsehood and *deception* in avoiding the tax>
syn cheat, chicane, chicanery, dipsy-doodle, dirt, dishonesty, double-dealing, dupery, four-berie, fraud, hanky-panky, highbinding, indirection, sharp practice, subterfuge, ||suck-in, trickery
rel cunning, deceit, dissimulation, duplicity, guile; cheating, cozening, defrauding, overreaching; bamboozling, befooling, duping, gulling, hoaxing, hoodwinking; manipulation; ride, ||snow job
con candidness, frankness, openness; honesty, integrity, probity; artlessness, ingenuousness, naiveté
2 syn see IMPOSTURE
rel delusion, hallucination, illusion, mirage
3 syn see FALLACY 2

deceptive adj syn see MISLEADING
rel colorable, plausible, specious; apparent, illusory, ostensible, seeming
con authentic, bona fide, genuine, veritable; actual, real, true; dependable, reliable, trustworthy

deceptiveness n syn see FALLACY 2

decide vb to come or to cause to come to a conclusion <he *decided* how to solve the problem>
syn conclude, determine, figure, resolve, rule, settle
rel gather; adjudge, adjudicate, judge; conjecture, guess, surmise; establish, fix, set
idiom cast the die, make up one's mind, settle in one's mind
con falter, hesitate, vacillate, waver; fluctuate, oscillate; balk, demur, scruple, shy

decided adj 1 beyond any doubt or ambiguity <a *decided* advantage over her opponent>
syn assured, clear-cut, definite, pronounced

rel determined, resolved; certain, positive, sure; categorical, explicit, express, unequivocal; clear, obvious, runaway; unmistakable
con doubtful, dubious, problematic, uncertain; equivocal, obscure, vague
ant questionable

2 free from doubt or wavering <he had a *decided* manner>
syn bent, decisive, determined, intent, resolute, resolved, set, settled
rel certain, cocksure, positive, sure; iron-jawed; established, fixed; earnest, purposeful, serious; unfaltering, unhesitating, unwavering
con doubtful, dubious, irresolute, uncertain; faltering, hesitant, vacillating, wavering; undetermined, unresolved, unsettled, unsure
ant undecided

3 *syn* see POSITIVE 1

decidedness *n syn* see DECISION 2

decimate *vb* **1** *syn* see DESTROY 1
2 *syn* see SLAUGHTER 2

decipher *vb* **1** *syn* see DECODE
ant cipher, encipher
2 *syn* see SOLVE 2
rel paraphrase, translate; analyze, break down
idiom find the key of
con misconstrue, misinterpret, misunderstand; confuse, muddle; bewilder, confound, mystify, puzzle; jumble, mix, scramble

decision *n* **1** a position arrived at after consideration <the *decision* of the committee remains firm>
syn conclusion, determination, resolution, settlement
rel accord, agreement, understanding; accommodation, adjustment, arrangement; compromise, reconciliation; choice, preference, selection
con deadlock, draw, stalemate, standoff, tie
2 freedom from doubt or wavering <a man of unusual *decision*>
syn decidedness, determination, firmness, purposefulness, purposiveness, resoluteness, resolution, resolve
rel doggedness, obstinacy, obstinance, perseverance, persistence, stubbornness; earnestness, seriousness; backbone, fortitude, grit, pluck
con changeableness, indetermination, irresolution; uncertainty, unsureness; faltering, fluctuation, hesitation, vacillation, wavering
ant indecision

decisive *adj syn* see DECIDED 2
rel imperative, imperious, masterful, peremptory; assured, self-assured, self-confident; steadfast, unswerving, unwavering
con fluctuating, oscillating; hesitant, reluctant; doubtful, dubious, irresolute, uncertain, undecided
ant indecisive

deck *vb syn* see ADORN
rel apparel, array, attire, clothe, dress; accouter, appoint, furnish

con deface, disfigure; impair, mar, spoil; contort, deform, distort; dismantle, divest, strip

deck (out) *vb syn* see DRESS UP 1

declaim *vb syn* see ORATE

declamatory *adj syn* see RHETORICAL

declaration *n* the act of declaring, proclaiming, or publicly announcing <a *declaration* of war>
syn advertisement, announcement, broadcast, proclamation, promulgation, pronouncement, pronunciamento, publication
rel information, notice, notification; communication; disclosure, revelation; report, statement; acknowledgment, avowal
con concealment, hiding; denial, disaffirmation; recall, recantation, retraction, revocation

declare *vb* **1** to make known openly or publicly <*declared* his intention to run for the senate>
syn advertise, announce, annunciate, blaze (abroad), blazon, broadcast, bruit (about), disseminate, proclaim, promulgate, publish, sound, tout, vend
rel acquaint, advise, apprise, inform, notify; communicate, impart; pronounce; disclose, discover, divulge, reveal; report
idiom declare oneself, make public (*or* known)
con hold, hold back, keep back, reserve, withhold; recall, recant, retract, revoke
2 *syn* see ASSERT 1
rel air, broach, express, utter, vent, ventilate, voice; acknowledge, admit, own
idiom have one's say
con controvert; deny; repress, suppress; conceal, hide
3 *syn* see SAY 1
rel broach, express, voice
idiom speak one's piece

declare off *vb syn* see BACK DOWN

declass *vb syn* see DEGRADE 1
rel disbar, exclude, rule out; abash, discomfit, disconcert
con aggrandize, exalt, magnify

déclassé *adj syn* see INFERIOR 2

declension *n syn* see DETERIORATION 1
rel regression, regressiveness, retrogression, retrogressiveness; dilapidation, ruination
con ascension, ascent; rise, rising; advance, progress, progression; development, maturation

declination *n* **1** *syn* see DETERIORATION 1
2 *syn* see FAILURE 4

decline *vb* **1** *syn* see SET 12
ant ascend
2 *syn* see FAIL 1
rel backslide, lapse, relapse; slide; return, revert; recede, retrograde; abate, ebb, subside, wane
idiom go downhill, take a turn for the worse
con advance, progress; develop, mature; gain, recover
3 *syn* see DETERIORATE 1
4 to turn away by not accepting, receiving, or considering <he *declined* the invitation>
syn disapprove, dismiss, refuse, reject, reprobate, repudiate, spurn, turn down

---

syn synonym(s)   *rel* related word(s)
ant antonym(s)   *con* contrasted word(s)
idiom idiomatic equivalent(s)
‖ use limited; if in doubt, see a dictionary

rel balk, boggle, demur, jib, scruple, shy, stick, stickle; abstain, forbear, refrain; deny, gainsay; abjure, renounce; bypass
idiom send regrets
con receive, take; accede, acquiesce, assent, consent; choose, select; adopt, embrace, espouse
ant accept

decline *n* **1** *syn* see FAILURE 4
rel devitalization, weakening
con advancement, progress; recovery; development, maturation
2 *syn* see DETERIORATION 1
rel comedown, descent, drop, fall, falling off, slump; ebb, wane; backsliding, lapse, relapse
con development, evolution
3 a downward movement (as in price or value) <stocks suffered a *decline* in the market>
syn dip, downslide, downswing, downtrend, downturn, drop, falloff, sag, slide, slip, slump
rel lapse, loss, lowering; depression; decrease, drop-off, sell-off
con upswing, uptrend, upturn
4 *syn* see DESCENT 4

declivate *adj syn* see INCLINED 3
declivitous *adj syn* see INCLINED 3
declivity *n syn* see DESCENT 4
ant acclivity

decode *vb* to convert code into ordinary language <*decode* a message>
syn break, crack, cryptanalyze, decipher, decrypt
rel anagram; render, translate; ‖dope out, figure out, make out; resolve, solve, unfold, unravel, unriddle, work, work out; elucidate, explain, interpret
con cipher, codify, encipher; anagrammatize
ant code, encode, encrypt

decollate *vb syn* see BEHEAD
decolor *vb syn* see WHITEN 1
rel wash out; achromatize, fume, peroxide
con blacken; dye, imbue, stain, tinge, tint; paint, shade
ant color

decolorize *vb syn* see WHITEN 1
ant color

decompose *vb* **1** *syn* see ANALYZE
con combine, join, link, write; synthesize, unify; amalgamate, merge, mix
ant compound
2 *syn* see DECAY
rel deliquesce, liquefy, melt; break up, dissolve

decompound *vb syn* see ANALYZE
ant compound

decorate *vb syn* see ADORN
rel accouter, appoint, equip, furnish, outfit
con impair, injure, mar, spoil; blot, blotch, foul, mutilate, scar, uglify; dismantle, divest, strip

decorated *adj syn* see BEMEDALED
decoration *n syn* see HONOR 2
decorous *adj* **1** conforming to an accepted standard of propriety or good form <*decorous* behavior seems regrettably out of fashion>

syn au fait, becoming, befitting, Christian, civilized, comely, conforming, correct, decent, de rigueur, done, nice, proper, respectable, right, seemly
rel ceremonial, ceremonious, conventional, formal; dignified, elegant; appropriate, fit, fitting, meet, seasonable, suitable; prim, punctilious, rigid, stiff, stuffy
con blatant, clamorous, obstreperous, strident; aggressive, assertive, pushing, pushy; coarse, gross, vulgar; easy, fast, loose; improper, incorrect, unbecoming
ant indecorous
2 *syn* see GOOD 13

decorously *adv syn* see WELL 1
decorousness *n syn* see ORDER 7
rel ceremoniousness, conventionality, formality, solemnity; convenance, convention, form, usage
con inappropriateness, incorrectness; unfitness, unsuitability, unsuitableness; disorder, misbehavior, misconduct, misdeed, misdemeanor
ant indecorousness

decorticate *vb syn* see SKIN 2
rel bark; scalp; denude, divest

decorum *n* **1** socially acceptable behavior or accepted standards of this <they found his conduct quite lacking in *decorum*>
syn decency, dignity, etiquette, propriety, seemliness
rel convenance, convention, form, usage
con laxity, laxness, license, slackness; carelessness, heedlessness, inconsiderateness, mannerlessness; inappropriateness, incorrectness
ant indecorum
2 *syn* see ORDER 7
rel ceremoniousness, conventionality, formality, solemnity; convenance, convention, form, usage
con inappropriateness, incorrectness; unfitness, unsuitability, unsuitableness; disorder, misbehavior, misconduct, misdeed, misdemeanor
ant indecorum; license
3 *usu* **decorums** *syn* see MANNER 3

decoy *n* **1** *syn* see LURE 2
rel chicane, chicanery, deception, trickery; drawing card
con rebuff, repellence, repellency, repellent, repugnance, repulse, repulsion
2 a person used as a lure <used the detective as a *decoy* to catch the pushers>
syn blind, ‖bonnet, ‖booster, capper, shill, shillaber, stick
rel lugger, roper, steerer; come-on, front, plant, stall

decoy *vb syn* see LURE
rel deceive, delude, mislead; ensorcell, wile
con disgust, repel; sicken; offend, repulse, revolt

decrease *vb* to grow less especially gradually <his influence *decreased* as a new generation grew up>
syn abate, bate, close, diminish, drain (away), dwindle, lessen, peak (out), peter (out), rebate, recede, reduce, taper, taper off
rel abbreviate, abridge, clip, curtail, retrench, shorten, trim; contract, shrink; allay, alleviate, ease, lighten, mitigate; ebb, sub-

side; cut, cut back, cut down, lower; deduct, subtract

con augment, enlarge, multiply; elongate, extend, lengthen, prolong, protract; amplify, dilate, distend, expand, swell; accumulate, amass

ant increase

decree *n* **1 syn** see EDICT 1

2 syn see LAW 1

rel behest, bidding, injunction, order; charge, charging, direction, instruction; announcement, declaration, proclamation, promulgation, pronouncement

decree *vb* **syn** see DICTATE

rel compel, constrain, force, oblige; demand, require

decrepit *adj* **1 syn** see WEAK 1

rel haggard, wasted, worn; aged, old, superannuated; creaky, quavering, shaking, tottering

con strong; lusty; hale, healthy, hearty, robust, sound, well

ant sturdy

2 syn see SHABBY 1

rel damaged, impaired, injured, marred, spoiled; cast-off, ragged, used; slipshod, sloppy, unkempt

decrepitude *n* **syn** see INFIRMITY 1

ant vigor

decretum *n* **syn** see LAW 1

decry *vb* **1 syn** see DEPRECIATE 1

2 to indicate one's low opinion of something <*decrying* his opponent's character>

syn abuse, bad-mouth, belittle, cry down, depreciate, derogate, detract (from), diminish, discount, disparage, dispraise, downcry, ‖low-rate, minimize, oppobriate, put down, run down, take (from), take away, write off

rel deprecate, disapprove; censure, condemn, criticize, denounce, reprehend, reprobate; asperse, calumniate, defame, malign, traduce, vilify; discredit, disgrace

idiom bring into discredit, cast a slur upon, cast blame upon, dump on, throw stones at

con acclaim, eulogize, laud, praise; aggrandize, exalt, magnify; applaud, commend, compliment, recommend; endorse, sanction; approve, countenance, favor

ant extol, puff

decrypt *vb* **syn** see DECODE

decumbent *adj* **syn** see PRONE 4

decussate *vb* **syn** see INTERSECT

dedicate *vb* **syn** see DEVOTE 1

rel address, apply, direct, give, surrender; commit, confide, consign, entrust; allot, appropriate, assign, set (aside)

idiom give over to

dedition *n* **syn** see SURRENDER

deduce *vb* **syn** see INFER

rel cogitate; consider, deem, regard; conceive, fancy, imagine; assume, presume, presuppose; read (into)

idiom take to mean

deducible *adj* **syn** see DEDUCTIVE

deduct *vb* **1** to take away one quantity from another <*deduct* the cost from his bill>

syn discount, draw back, knock off, substract, subtract, take, take away, take off, take out

rel decrease, diminish, lessen, reduce; roll back

con cast, figure, sum, tot, total

ant add

2 syn see INFER

deduction *n* **1** an amount subtracted from a sum <*deductions* from gross income>

syn abatement, discount, rebate, reduction, subtraction

rel allowance, credit, cut; decrease, decrement, depreciation, diminution; charge-off, offtake, takeoff, write-off; dockage

con accession, accretion, augmentation, increase, increment, raise, rise; appreciation

ant addition

2 syn see INFERENCE 1

3 syn see INFERENCE 2

rel cogitation, deliberation, reasoning, reflection, speculation, thinking; consideration, contemplation; meditation, mulling, musing, pondering, rumination

deductive *adj* that can be deduced or developed from premises <*deductive* laws>

syn a priori, deducible, derivable, dogmatic, reasoned

rel illative, inferential, ratiocinative; conjectural, hypothetical, purported, putative, supposed, suppositious; academic, speculative, theoretical

con categorical, definite, explicit, express; instinctive, intuitive

deed *n* **1 syn** see ACTION 1

2 syn see FEAT 2

rel gaining, securing, winning; adventure, enterprise, quest; cause, crusade

idiom bold stroke

3 a written, signed, and usually sealed instrument that spells out some bargain, transfer, or contract <the *deed* to the property>

syn charter, conveyance

rel bargain, compact, contract, covenant, pact

deed *vb* **syn** see TRANSFER 4

deem *vb* **1 syn** see CONSIDER 3

rel conjecture, guess, surmise, suspect, ‖suspicion, understand; ‖allow, assume, believe, ‖calculate, daresay, divine, expect, presume, suppose

idiom hold to be true

2 syn see FEEL 3

idiom take for granted

de-emphasize *vb* **syn** see SOFT-PEDAL

deep *adj* **1** having great extension downward or inward <a *deep* well><a *deep* closet>

syn abysmal, profound; *compare* BOTTOM-LESS 2

con depthless, shallow, superficial, unprofound; flat, level, plain, plane

ant shallow

2 syn see INTENSIVE

3 syn see RECONDITE

rel complex, complicated, intricate; arcane, mysterious; concealed, hidden

con easy, facile, simple; apparent, clear, distinct, evident, manifest, obvious; lucid, perspicuous; depthless, shallow, superficial, unprofound

---

syn synonym(s)   **rel** related word(s)
ant antonym(s)   **con** contrasted word(s)
idiom idiomatic equivalent(s)
‖ use limited; if in doubt, see a dictionary

4 *syn* see SLY 2
rel shrewd; acute, keen, knowing, sharp; contriving, intriguing, plotting
con ingenuous, naive, simple, unsophisticated; aboveboard, forthright, straightforward

5 *syn* see INTENT
rel abstracted, concentrated; centered, fixed, focused, set
con distracted, diverted; detached, disinterested, indifferent, unconcerned, uninterested

deep *n* 1 *syn* see OCEAN

deep-dyed *adj syn* see INVETERATE 1

deepen *vb syn* see INTENSIFY

deepness *n* 1 *syn* see DEPTH 1
ant shallowness
2 *syn* see DEPTH 2

deep-rooted *adj syn* see INVETERATE 1

deep-seated *adj* 1 *syn* see INHERENT
2 *syn* see INVETERATE 1
rel constitutional, immanent, indwelling, ingrained, inherent, intrinsic; deep, profound; inner, internal, inward; implanted; infixed
con peripheral, shallow, superficial, surface; adventitious, casual, chance, incidental
ant skin-deep

‖**deep-six** *vb syn* see DISCARD

deep water *n syn* see PREDICAMENT

deface *vb* to mar the appearance of <*deface* the wall with graffiti>
syn disfashion, disfeature, disfigure
rel blemish, damage, harm, impair, injure, mar, spoil; contort, deform, distort, misshape; batter, mangle, mutilate; demolish, destroy; dilapidate, ruin, wreck
con mend, patch, repair; freshen, improve, refurbish, renew, restore; adorn, beautify, deck, decorate, embellish, ornament

defacer *n syn* see VANDAL

de facto *adv syn* see VERY 2

defalcation *n syn* see FAILURE 3
rel laxness, negligence, remissness, slackness; failing, fault
con discharge, effectuation, execution, fulfillment; completion, conclusion

defamation *n syn* see DETRACTION
ant puffery

defamatory *adj syn* see LIBELOUS

defame *vb syn* see MALIGN
rel belie, misrepresent
idiom cast a slur on, throw mud at
con applaud, commend, compliment; exalt, magnify; back, champion, support, uphold
ant laud; puff

default *n* 1 *syn* see FAILURE 1
rel deficiency, fault, imperfection, shortcoming; lapse, weakness; disregard, omission, overlooking, slight
2 *syn* see ABSENCE

defeasance *n syn* see DEFEAT 1

defeat *vb* 1 *syn* see CONQUER 1
rel bar, block, hinder, impede, obstruct; repress, suppress
idiom beat all hollow, get the better of, grind into the dust, ‖have by the short hairs
con capitulate, defer, give in, submit; back down, withdraw
2 to win a victory over <*defeated* his opponent in the race>

syn best, down, outdo, ‖pip, worst; *compare* CONQUER 1, WHIP 2
rel outfight, outgame; nose out
idiom get the better of

defeat *n* 1 an overthrow especially of an army in battle <the brigade suffered a *defeat*>
syn beating, debacle, defeasance, discomfiture, downcast, downthrow, drubbing, ‖dusting, licking, overthrow, rout, shellacking, thrashing, trouncing, vanquishment, warming
rel bafflement, check, foil, frustration; rebuff, repulse, reversal, reverse, setback; ‖cleaning, ‖cleanup, clobbering, lambasting
con conquest, triumph; gaining, securing, winning; ascendancy, supremacy
ant victory
2 *syn* see FAILURE 2

defeater *n syn* see VICTOR 1
ant defeated

defect *n* 1 *syn* see BLEMISH
rel failing, fault, foible, frailty; infirmity, weakness; deficiency, imperfection, shortcoming
con excellence, faultlessness, impeccability; merit, perfection, virtue
2 *syn* see ABSENCE
rel scantiness, scarceness, scarcity, shortage
con overage, overplus, superfluity, surplus, surplusage
ant excess

defect *vb* to desert a cause or party often in order to espouse another <he *defected* from the Communist party>
syn apostatize, desert, rat, renounce, repudiate, tergiversate, tergiverse, turn
rel abandon, forsake; back out, renege, withdraw; depart, go, leave, quit; reject, spurn
idiom change sides, go back on, go over, turn one's coat, walk (*or* run) out on
con adhere (to), cling (to), hang on, stick (to *or* with); cherish, cultivate, foster

defection *n* conscious abandonment of allegiance or duty <*defection* from family responsibilities in times of trouble>
syn apostasy, desertion, falseness, recreancy, tergiversation
rel alienation, disaffection, estrangement; disloyalty, faithlessness; abandonment, forsaking; divorce, parting, runout, separation, sundering; disownment, rejection, repudiation
idiom running out on, ‖taking a runout powder
con constancy, faithfulness, loyalty, resoluteness, staunchness, steadfastness; allegiance, fealty, fidelity; dependability, reliability, trustworthiness

defective *adj* 1 *syn* see FAULTY
rel broken, damaged, injured
con faultless, flawless, impeccable, unblemished, undamaged
ant defective
2 *syn* see DEFICIENT 1
rel corrupted, debased, vitiated; deranged, disordered, disturbed, unsettled; unhealthy, unsound
con entire, perfect, whole; complete, full, plenary; healthy, sound

ant intact; defectless

defector *n syn* see RENEGADE

defend *vb* **1** to keep safe (as from danger or against attack) <*defend* the country from aggression>
syn bulwark, cover, fend, guard, protect, safeguard, screen, secure, shield
rel avert, prevent; ward; oppose, resist, withstand; battle, contend, fight, war; conserve, preserve, save
idiom stand on the defensive, stave off from
con aggress, assail, assault, fall (on *or* upon); bombard, storm; beset, besiege, overrun; capitulate, cave, submit, yield
ant attack
2 *syn* see MAINTAIN 2
rel air, express, utter, vent, voice; account, explain, justify, rationalize; back, champion, support, uphold
idiom speak (*or* stand *or* stick) up for
con contradict, deny, gainsay, traverse; confute, controvert, disprove, rebut, refute

defendable *adj syn* see TENABLE 1
ant undefendable

defense *n* **1** means or method of defending <the skunk's powerful *defense* against attackers>
syn aegis, armament, armor, guard, protection, safeguard, security, shield, ward
rel arms, munitions, weaponry, weapons; fastness, fort, fortress, stronghold
con aggression, offense, offensive
ant attack
2 *syn* see APOLOGY 1
rel answer, rejoinder, reply, response, retort, return; exculpation, excuse, explanation, rationalization
con censure, condemnation, criticism, decrial, reprehension, reprobation, reproof; assault, attack, onset, onslaught

defenseless *adj syn* see HELPLESS 1

defensible *adj* **1** *syn* see TENABLE 1
ant indefensible
2 *syn* see JUSTIFIABLE
ant indefensible

defer *vb* to delay an action or proceeding <decided to *defer* voting until the next meeting>
syn adjourn, delay, hold off, hold over, hold up, intermit, lay over, postpone, prorogue, put off, put over, remit, shelve, stand over, stay, suspend, waive
rel detain, retard, slow; block, hinder, impede, obstruct; stall; extend, lengthen, prolong, obstruct
idiom hold up on, lay to one side, put on ice, set aside
con accelerate, hasten, hurry, speed; expedite, further, promote
ant advance

defer *vb syn* see YIELD 2
rel accede, acquiesce, agree, assent; accommodate, adapt, adjust, conform; cringe, fawn, truckle
con combat, fight, oppose, resist; object, remonstrate; balk, demur, stickle, strain

ant withstand

deference *n syn* see HONOR 1
rel acquiescence, compliance; submission, submissiveness
con insolence, irreverence; disesteem, disfavor; discourtesy, incivility, rudeness
ant disrespect

deferential *adj* **1** *syn* see RESPECTFUL
2 *syn* see INGRATIATING

defi *n syn* see DEFIANCE 1

defiance *n* **1** the act or an instance of defying <presented a *defiance* to his rival>
syn cartel, challenge, dare, defi, defy, stump
rel call, muster, summons; command, enjoinder, order
con capitulation, submission, surrender
2 disposition to resist or unwillingness to brook opposition <exhibited *defiance* toward his teacher>
syn contempt, contumacy, despite, recalcitrance, stubbornness
rel factiousness, insubordination, insurgency, rebelliousness; headstrongness, intractableness, unruliness; boldness, bravado, brazenness, impudence, insolence; audacity, effrontery, hardihood, temerity; contrariness, perversity
con acquiescence, compliance; amenableness, docility, obedience, tractableness; submissiveness

deficiency *n* **1** *syn* see FAILURE 3
rel absence, default, defect, want
con copiousness, plenty; great deal, heap, lot, much
2 *syn* see IMPERFECTION
rel dearth, defect, lack, privation, want; default, dereliction, miscarriage, neglect
ant excess

deficient *adj* **1** showing lack of something necessary <*deficient* in judgment>
syn defective, ‖half-assed, inadequate, incomplete, insufficient, lacking, uncomplete, wanting
rel faulty, flawed, imperfect, unsound; damaged, impaired, injured, marred; amiss, bad, unsatisfactory
idiom in want of
con complete, entire, intact, whole; acceptable, adequate, sufficient
2 *syn* see SHORT 3
rel infrequent, rare, uncommon
idiom found wanting
con excessive, extravagant, immoderate, inordinate; enough, satisfactory, sufficing
ant adequate, sufficient

deficit *n syn* see FAILURE 3
con copiousness, plenty; excess, surplus, surplusage

defile *vb* **1** *syn* see CONTAMINATE 1
rel desecrate, profane; befoul, dirty, foul, sully, tarnish
con consecrate, hallow
ant cleanse; purify
2 *syn* see RAPE
rel dishonor, shame, soil, sully
3 *syn* see TAINT 1

defiled *adj syn* see IMPURE

define *vb* **1** *syn* see PRESCRIBE 2
rel circumscribe, limit, mark (off), mark (out); designate; delineate, describe

---

syn synonym(s) *rel* related word(s)
ant antonym(s) *con* contrasted word(s)
idiom idiomatic equivalent(s)
‖ use limited; if in doubt, see a dictionary

con confound, confuse, mistake
2 *syn see* BORDER 1
3 *syn see* ETCH 2
rel explain, expound, interpret
definite *adj* **1** having distinct or certain limits <*definite* dimensions>
syn circumscribed, determinate, fixed, limited, narrow, precise, restricted
rel assigned, defined, prescribed; established, set; decided, determined, settled
con ambiguous, obscure, vague; unconditional, unlimited, unqualified, unrestricted; indeterminate, uncircumscribed; imprecise, loose, undefined
ant indefinite
2 *syn see* EXPLICIT
rel complete, full; downright, forthright; incisive
con doubtful, dubious, questionable; ambiguous
ant indefinite; equivocal
3 *syn see* POSITIVE 1
4 *syn see* DECIDED 1
ant uncertain
definitely *adv* **1** *syn see* EXPRESSLY 1
2 *syn see* EASILY 2
definiteness *n syn see* PRECISION
ant indefiniteness
definitive *adj* **1** *syn see* CONCLUSIVE
rel determining, settling; concluding, final, last, terminal, ultimate; closing, completing, ending, finishing, terminating; absolute, categorical
con inconclusive, indecisive; temporary, transitory
ant provisional, tentative
2 *syn see* EXPLICIT
rel actual, real
con doubtful, dubious, questionable; ambiguous
ant indefinitive
definitiveness *n syn see* PRECISION
ant indefinitiveness, indefinitude
definitude *n syn see* PRECISION
ant indefinitiveness, indefinitude
deflect *vb* **1** *syn see* TURN 6
rel disperse, swerve; hook, skew
2 *syn see* WARD 1
rel hold off, keep off
deflection *n* **1** *syn see* DEVIATION 1
rel bending, curving, twisting; departing, swerve, swerving, veer, veering
2 *syn see* TURN 2
deflorate *vb syn see* RAPE
deflower *vb* **1** *syn see* RAPE
2 *syn see* RAVAGE
deform *vb* to mar or spoil by or as if by twisting <a face *deformed* by bitterness>
syn contort, distort, misshape, torture, warp, wind
rel batter, cripple, maim, mangle, mutilate; deface, disfigure; damage, impair, injure, mar, spoil; blemish, flaw; screw (up), squinch
deformity *n* a physical blemish or disfigurement <the dwarf's humpback *deformity*>
syn distortion, malconformation, malformation, misshape
rel defacement, deformation, disfigurement; damage, impairment, injury; aberration, abnormality; irregularity, unnaturalness

defraud *vb syn see* CHEAT
rel bamboozle, hoax, trick; circumvent, foil, outwit; fleece, milk, stick; take in
idiom do out of, put over a fast one, take to the cleaner's
defrauder *n syn see* SWINDLER
deft *adj syn see* DEXTEROUS 1
rel agile, brisk, fleet; apt, prompt, quick, ready; adept, crack, crackerjack; ingenious, neat
con heavy-handed, unskillful; blundering, bungling, butterfingered; rigid, stiff, wooden
ant awkward, unhandy
deftness *n syn see* ADDRESS 1
rel agility, fleetness, nimbleness; assuredness, confidence
con incompetence, inefficiency; clumsiness, heavy-handedness, maladroitness
ant awkwardness
defunct *adj* **1** *syn see* DEAD 1
rel inactive, inert
ant alive; live
2 *syn see* EXTINCT 2
ant surviving
defunction *n syn see* DEATH 1
defy *vb syn see* FACE 3
rel deride, mock, ridicule; gibe, flout; scorn, scout, spurn; disregard, ignore
idiom fling (*or* throw) down the gauntlet, hurl defiance at
con blench, flinch, quail, shrink
ant recoil
defy *n syn see* DEFIANCE 1
dégagé *adj syn see* EASYGOING 3
ant mannered
degeneracy *n syn see* DETERIORATION 1
degenerate *adj* **1** *syn see* EFFETE 3
rel deteriorating, retrograde, retrogressive, worsening; failing, sinking
2 *syn see* VICIOUS 2
rel degraded, demeaned
con ethical, moral, virtuous; honorable, just, upright
ant regenerate
degenerate *vb syn see* DETERIORATE 1
rel corrupt, deprave, vitiate; backslide, lapse; return, revert
con improve, upgrade; lift, uplift
degeneration *n syn see* DETERIORATION 1
rel regression, regressiveness, retrogression, retrogressiveness; depreciation; corruption, depravation, depravedness, depravity, perversion
con regeneracy, regenerateness; progress, progression
ant regeneration
degradation *n syn see* DEMOTION
ant advancement; elevation
degrade *vb* **1** to lower in station, rank, or grade <*degraded* in rank for misconduct>
syn break, bump, bust, declass, demerit, demote, disgrade, disrate, downgrade, put down, reduce
rel abase, debase, humble, humiliate, lower; disbar, rule out
con advance, further; boost, lift, raise; enhance, heighten
ant elevate
2 *syn see* HUMBLE
rel belittle, decry, derogate, detract, disparage; diminish, lessen, reduce

con elevate, raise; acclaim, extol, laud, praise
ant uplift

degree *n* **1** a unitary component of a process, course, or order of classification <advanced by *degrees*>
syn grade, notch, rung, stage, step
2 relative size or character of the parts or components in a complex whole compared with other like things <the *degree* of difference between the two jobs> <his work demands a high *degree* of intelligence>
syn proportion, rate, ratio, scale
rel dimension; extent, magnitude, measure, size

dégringolade *n syn see* DETERIORATION 1

dehydrate *vb syn see* DRY 1
ant hydrate; rehydrate

deific *adj* **1** *syn see* DIVINE 1
2 *syn see* DIVINE 2

deification *n syn see* APOTHEOSIS 2

deign *vb syn see* STOOP 1

deject *vb syn see* DISCOURAGE 1
ant exhilarate; cheer

dejected *adj syn see* DOWNCAST
idiom down in the dumps (*or* mouth), in the dumps
ant animated

dejection *n syn see* SADNESS
rel despair, desperation
ant exhilaration

‖**dekko** *vb syn see* SEE 2

delay *vb* **1** to cause to be late or behind in movement or progress <was *delayed* by traffic>
syn bog (down), decelerate, detain, embog, hang up, mire, retard, set back, slacken, slow (up *or* down)
rel block, hinder, impede, obstruct; defer, hold over, hold up, intermit, postpone, put off, stay, suspend; arrest, check, interrupt
idiom hang fire
con accelerate, hasten, hurry, precipitate, quicken, speed; advance, forward, further, promote
ant expedite
2 to move or act slowly so that progress or work is retarded <their landlord kept *delaying* in making repairs>
syn dally, dawdle, dilly, dillydally, drag, lag, linger, loiter, mull, poke, procrastinate, put off, tarry, trail
rel hang back, idle, wait; drone; falter, hesitate, vacillate, waver
idiom take one's own sweet (*or* good) time
ant hasten, hurry
3 *syn see* DEFER

delectable *adj syn see* DELIGHTFUL
rel choice, dainty, delicate, exquisite, rare; palatable, sapid, savory, tasty, toothsome
con loathsome, offensive, repulsive, revolting
ant distasteful

delectate *vb syn see* PLEASE 2

delectation *n* **1** *syn see* PLEASURE 2

rel gratification, gratifying, regalement, regaling; enjoyment, relish
ant distaste
2 *syn see* ENJOYMENT 1

‖**deleerit** *adj syn see* INTOXICATED 1

delegate *n* a person standing in the place of another or others <was a *delegate* to the convention>
syn catchpole, deputy, representative, representative; *compare* AGENT 2
rel agent, factor, proxy; alternate, replacement, stand-in, substitute, surrogate; mouthpiece, spokesman; emissary, envoy

delegate *vb* to appoint as one's representative <*delegated* her to watch the children>
syn commission, depute, deputize
rel ascribe, assign, charge; appoint, designate, name; choose, pick, select

delete *vb syn see* ERASE
rel eliminate, exclude, rule out; omit

deleterious *adj syn see* HARMFUL
rel destroying, destructive; ruining, ruinous
con advantageous, profitable; healthful, healthy, salubrious, wholesome
ant salutary

deliberate *adj* **1** arrived at after due thought <a *deliberate* judgment>
syn advised, aforethought, considered, designed, premeditated, prepense, studied, studious, thought-out
rel planned, projected, schemed; calculated; careful, meticulous, scrupulous; foresighted, forethoughtful, provident, prudent
con chance, chancy, desultory, haphazard, happy-go-lucky, hit-or-miss, random; aimless, designless, purposeless; hasty, hurried; abrupt, impetuous, sudden; automatic, instinctive, spontaneous
ant casual
2 *syn see* VOLUNTARY
rel intended, meant, meditated, purposed; determined, purposeful; aware, cognizant, conscious
con careless, heedless, inadvertent, thoughtless; unintended, unpurposed
ant impulsive
3 *syn see* SLOW 2
rel calculating, cautious, chary, circumspect, wary; careful, heedful; collected, composed, cool, imperturbable
con hasty, headlong, impetuous, sudden
ant abrupt, precipitate

deliberate *vb* **1** *syn see* PONDER 2
2 *syn see* THINK 5
rel excogitate, study, weigh; argue, debate, discuss, talk over

deliberately *adv syn see* INTENTIONALLY

deliberation *n* **1** *syn see* ATTENTION 1
2 *syn see* THOUGHT 1
3 *syn see* CONFERENCE 1

delicacy *n* something special and delicious to eat <fresh fruit in the winter was once an uncommon *delicacy*>
syn bonne bouche, dainty, goody, kickshaw, morsel, tidbit (*or* titbit), treat
rel banquet, feast, regale; cosseting, indulgence, luxury
idiom choice bit, dish fit for a king

delicate *adj* **1** *syn see* CHOICE

---

syn synonym(s)	*rel* related word(s)
ant antonym(s)	*con* contrasted word(s)
idiom idiomatic equivalent(s)	
‖ use limited; if in doubt, see a dictionary	

rel delectable, delicious, delightful; balmy, gentle, lenient, mild, soft; aerial, airy, ethereal
con coarse, crude, vulgar
ant gross
2 *syn* see FINE 1
3 *syn* see NICE 1
rel perceptive, sensitive
con insensitive, undiscriminating, unperceptive
4 *syn* see FRAGILE 1
5 lacking in strength or substance <a *delicate* constitution>
syn flimsy, slight
rel feeble, fragile, frail, weak; sickly, unhealthy; decrepit, infirm
con stalwart, stout, strong, sturdy, tenacious, tough; hale, healthy, robust, sound, well, wholesome
6 *syn* see TACTFUL
rel adept, expert, masterly, proficient; discreet, foresighted, prudent; careful, heedful, cautious, wary
con impolitic; imprudent, indiscreet; awkward, clumsy, gauche, inept, maladroit; unskillful
7 marked by or requiring tact <a *delicate* situation>
syn precarious, sensitive, ticklish, touchy, tricky
rel uncertain, unpredictable; hair-trigger, volatile; sticky
delicatesse *n syn* see TACT
ant indelicacy
delicious *adj syn* see DELIGHTFUL
rel appetizing, palatable, sapid, savory, toothsome; choice, dainty, delicate, exquisite, rare
con banal, flat, inane, insipid, jejune, wishy=washy
delight *vb* **1** *syn* see EXULT
2 *syn* see PLEASE 2
rel amuse, divert, entertain; allure, attract, charm, enchant, fascinate; enrapture, entrance, transport
con aggrieve, distress, pain, trouble; afflict, try; grieve; bother, irk; bore
delight (in) *vb* **1** *syn* see ADMIRE 1
rel enjoy, like, savor; eat up, luxuriate (in)
con abhor, abominate, hate, loathe
2 *syn* see LOVE 1
delight *n syn* see PLEASURE 2
rel glee, hilarity, jollity, mirth; ecstasy, rapture, transport; contentment, satisfaction; relish
con abhorrence, detestation, hate, hatred; dislike, distaste; discontent, dissatisfaction
ant aversion; disappointment
delightful *adj* highly pleasing to the senses or to aesthetic taste <a *delightful* view>
syn adorable, ambrosial, darling, delectable, delicious, heavenly, luscious, lush, scrumptious, yummy
rel charming, enchanting, fascinating; alluring, attractive; beautiful, fair, lovely; ineffable; agreeable, gratifying, pleasant, pleasing; satisfying
con miserable, wretched; distasteful, obnoxious, repellent, repugnant; abhorrent, detestable, hateful, odious; boring, irksome, tedious; distressing, troubling

ant abominable, horrid
delimit *vb* **1** *syn* see DEMARCATE 1
rel decide
2 *syn* see LIMIT 2
delimitate *vb* **1** *syn* see DEMARCATE 1
2 *syn* see LIMIT 2
delineate *vb* **1** *syn* see REPRESENT 1
rel design, plan; evoke, paint
2 *syn* see ETCH 2
delineation *n* **1** *syn* see REPRESENTATION
rel design, plan; evocation, painting; account, story, version
2 *syn* see OUTLINE
delinquency *n* **1** *syn* see FAILURE 1
rel nonobservance; nonfulfillment; lapse, weakness
delinquent *adj syn* see NEGLIGENT
deliquesce *vb syn* see LIQUEFY
rel decay, decompose, disintegrate
con cake, harden, indurate, set, solidify
delirious *adj* **1** disordered in mind especially temporarily <*delirious* from the fever>
syn raving, wandering
rel deranged, disarranged, disordered, disturbed, unsettled; bewildered, confused, distracted; rambling; irrational, unreasonable; crazed, crazy, demented, insane, lunatic, mad, maniac
idiom out of one's head (*or* mind)
con rational, reasonable; sane, sensible; comatose, unconscious
2 *syn* see FURIOUS 2
rel overexcited, overwrought; ecstatic, rapturous, transported; delighted, enthused, thrilled
idiom all agog, beside oneself
con collected, composed, easy, relaxed; unexcited, unmoved, unstimulated
delirium *n* frenzied excitement or wild enthusiasm <in a *delirium* of patriotic feeling>
syn frenzy, furor
rel ardor, enthusiasm, fervor, passion, zeal; ecstasy, rapture, transport
con nonchalance, sangfroid; indifference, unconcern
ant apathy
deliver *vb* **1** *syn* see RESCUE
con immure, imprison, incarcerate, intern, jail; capture, catch, ensnare, entrap, snare, trap; condemn, damn, doom
2 *syn* see GIVE 3
rel relinquish, resign, surrender, yield
con keep, retain
3 *syn* see BEAR 5
4 *syn* see SAY 1
rel broach, express, vent, voice; communicate, impart
5 *syn* see GIVE 10
rel dispatch, send, transmit; fling, hurl, pitch, throw
delivery *n syn* see BIRTH 1
Delphian *adj* **1** *syn* see PROPHETIC
2 *syn* see CRYPTIC
delude *vb syn* see DECEIVE
idiom play tricks (*or* a trick) on
con enlighten, illume, illuminate, illustrate, light, lighten; elucidate, explain
deluding *adj syn* see MISLEADING
deluge *n syn* see FLOOD 2
rel flux; overrunning

deluge *vb* **1** to flow over so as to submerge or enclose <the lowlands were completely *deluged*>
syn drown, engulf, flood, inundate, overflow, overwhelm, submerge, swamp, whelm
rel overrun; flush, gush, pour, sluice, stream
2 *syn* see WET
con dehydrate, desiccate, dry, parch
3 to affect overwhelmingly as if by a deluge of water <he was *deluged* by telephone calls>
syn flood, overwhelm, swamp, whelm
rel overcome; oversupply; abound, teem

delusion *n* **1** something accepted as true that is actually false or unreal <people who suffer from *delusions* of persecution>
syn hallucination, ignis fatuus, illusion, mirage, phantasm
rel chicane, chicanery, deception, trickery; cheat, counterfeit, deceit, fake, fraud, humbug, imposture, sham; daydream, dream, fancy, fantasy, figment, vision; apparition, eidolon, ghost, phantom, shade
ant reality
2 *syn* see FALLACY 2
ant verity

delusive *adj syn* see MISLEADING
rel chimerical, fanciful, fantastic, imaginary, quixotic, visionary; apparent, illusory, ostensible, seeming
con authentic, bona fide, genuine, veritable; actual, real, true

delusory *adj syn* see MISLEADING

deluxe *adj syn* see LUXURIOUS 3
rel choice, dainty, delicate, elegant, exquisite, rare, recherché
con coarse, common, ordinary; inelegant

delve *vb* ‖**1** *syn* see DIG 1
rel gouge (out), hollow (out), quarry (out), scoop (out); burrow, tunnel; comb, ferret out, search, seek
2 *syn* see MINE

delve (into) *vb syn* see EXPLORE

delve *n syn* see HOLE 1

delving *n syn* see INQUIRY 1

demagogue *n* a leader who makes use of popular prejudices and false claims especially for political advantage <*demagogues* who endanger the orderly processes of democratic government>
syn rabble-rouser
rel fomenter, inciter, instigator; agitator, firebrand, hothead, incendiary, inflamer; troublemaker

demand *n* **1** *syn* see REQUIREMENT 1
2 *syn* see NEED 3

demand *vb* **1** to ask for something as or as if one's right or due <the physician *demanded* payment of his bill>
syn call, challenge, claim, exact, postulate, require, requisition, solicit
rel ask, request; bid, charge, command, direct, enjoin, order; cite, summon, summons; coerce, compel, constrain, force, oblige, necessitate

con cede, relinquish, resign, waive; allow, concede, grant; give, offer, tender
2 to have as a need or requirement <it *demands* considerable practice to master the piano>
syn ask, call (for), crave, necessitate, require, take
rel fail, lack, need, want
idiom need (or want), doing, stand in need of

demanding *adj syn* see ONEROUS
rel rigid, rigorous, severe, stern, strict, stringent; crying, imperative, importunate, instant, pressing, urgent
ant undemanding

demarcate *vb* **1** to mark the limits of <*demarcate* the boundary between two countries>
syn bound, delimit, delimitate, determine, limit, mark (out), measure
rel establish, fix, set; assign, define, prescribe; circumscribe, confine, restrict
2 *syn* see DISTINGUISH
rel insulate, isolate, seclude, segregate, sequester

demean *vb syn* see BEHAVE 1

demean *vb syn* see HUMBLE
rel belittle, decry, derogate, detract, disparage; contemn, despise, scorn
con elevate, enhance, heighten

demeanor *n syn* see BEARING 1
rel behavior, conduct

dement *n syn* see LUNATIC 1

demented *adj syn* see INSANE 1
rel delirious, frenzied, hysterical

demerit *n syn* see IMPERFECTION

demerit *vb syn* see DEGRADE 1

demeritorious *adj syn* see BLAMEWORTHY
ant meritorious

demesne *n syn* see FIELD

demigod *n syn* see SUPERMAN

demimondaine *n syn* see HARLOT 1

demimonde *n syn* see HARLOT 1

demirep *n syn* see HARLOT 1

demise *vb syn* see DIE 1

demise *n syn* see DEATH 1
rel annihilation, ending, expiration, extinction

demit *vb syn* see ABDICATE 1

demit *vb syn* see LOWER 3

demiurgic *adj syn* see INVENTIVE

‖**demob** *vb syn* see DISCHARGE 7
ant mobilize

demobilize *vb syn* see DISCHARGE 7
rel break up, disband, dispel, disperse, scatter; retire, withdraw
ant mobilize

democratic *adj* of or relating to a political system in which the supreme power is held and exercised by the people <a *democratic* government>
syn popular, self-governing, self-ruling
rel representative; libertarian
con totalitarian; absolute, arbitrary, autocratic, despotic; tyrannical, tyrannous; fascistic, nazi, patriarchal
ant authoritarian; undemocratic

démodé *adj syn* see OLD-FASHIONED
ant a la mode

demoded *adj syn* see OLD-FASHIONED

---

syn synonym(s)	*rel* related word(s)
ant antonym(s)	*con* contrasted word(s)
idiom idiomatic equivalent(s)	
‖ use limited; if in doubt, see a dictionary	

ant a la mode

demolish *vb syn* see DESTROY 1
rel dilapidate; crush, smash; break, burst, crack
con build, erect, frame, raise, rear
ant construct; rebuild
2 *syn* see TOTAL 3

demon *n syn* see DEVIL 2

demoniac *adj syn* see FIENDISH
rel crazed, crazy, insane, maniac; fired, inspired
con celestial, heavenly
ant angelic

demonian *adj syn* see FIENDISH
rel crazed, crazy, insane, maniac; fired, inspired
con celestial, heavenly
ant angelic

demonic *adj syn* see FIENDISH
rel crazed, crazy, insane, maniac; fired, inspired
con celestial, heavenly
ant angelic

demonstrate *vb* **1** *syn* see SHOW 2
rel display, exhibit, expose, flaunt, parade; explain, set forth
idiom go to show
con conceal, hide, secrete; camouflage, cloak, disguise, dissemble, mask
2 *syn* see PROVE 1
rel authenticate, validate
3 *syn* see ESTABLISH 6

demonstration *n syn* see EXHIBITION 1

demonstrative *adj* marked by display of feeling <was *demonstrative* in his welcome>
syn expansive, outgoing, unconstrained, unreserved, unrestrained
rel affectionate, loving; effusive, outpouring, profuse; candid, frank, open, outspoken, plain
con constrained, reserved, restrained, reticent, taciturn; bashful, shy; retiring, shrinking; introverted; aloof, detached, indifferent, unconcerned; chilly, cold, frigid, glacial, icy
ant undemonstrative

demoralize *vb* **1** *syn* see DEBASE 1
rel debilitate, undermine, weaken; damp, dampen
2 *syn* see DISCOURAGE 1
rel agitate, disturb, upset; disarrange, disorder, disorganize, unsettle; confuse, jumble, muddle, snarl; debilitate, undermine, weaken; unman, unnerve
con arrange, order, organize; energize, fortify, invigorate, strengthen

demote *vb syn* see DEGRADE 1
rel demean, lower
ant promote

demotion *n* the action or an instance of demoting <received a *demotion* from sergeant to corporal>
syn degradation, downgrading, reduction
rel debasement, humbling, humiliation; blackballing, disbarment, exclusion, suspension
con advancement, preferment, upgrading; aggrandizement; boost, elevation, lift, raise

demur *vb* to object or have scruples <he *demurred* at any horseplay>
syn balk, boggle, gag, jib, scruple, shy, stick, stickle, strain, stumble
rel falter, hesitate, vacillate, waver; combat, fight, oppose, resist; expostulate, object, protest, remonstrate; deprecate, disapprove
con accept, admit, receive, take; acquiesce, agree, assent, consent, subscribe, yes; concur; defer, relent, submit, succumb, yield
ant accede

demur *n* **1** *syn* see QUALM
rel faltering, hesitancy, hesitation; aversion, disinclination, loathness; expostulation, protest
con promptness, quickness, readiness
2 the act of objecting or taking exception <accepted without *demur*>
syn challenge, demurral, demurrer, difficulty, objection, protest, question, remonstrance, remonstration
rel reluctance, unwillingness; faltering, hesitancy, hesitation; deprecation, disapproval; protestation; difference, disagreement, dissent, variance
con acquiescence, agreement, assent, consent; concurrence; submission

demure *adj syn* see SHY 1
rel decent, decorous, nice, proper, seemly; prim; earnest, serious, solemn; close, reserved, reticent, silent
con impertinent, intrusive, meddlesome, obtrusive, officious; brash, forward, unbashful, unretiring

demurral *n syn* see DEMUR 2

demurrer *n syn* see DEMUR 2

den *n* **1** *syn* see LAIR 1
2 *syn* see HIDEOUT
3 *syn* see SINK 1

denaturant *n syn* see ADMIXTURE 1

denial *n* **1** refusal to satisfy a request or desire <*denial* of his visiting privileges>
syn disallowance, refusal, rejection
rel declination, nonacceptance
con allowing, conceding, grant, letting; leave, permission, sufferance
2 refusal to admit the truth <his *denial* that he took the money>
syn contradiction, gainsaying, negation
rel controversion, disproof, rebuttal, refutal, refutation; refusal, rejection, repudiation
con acknowledgment, avowal, confession; affirmation, assertion, confirmation
ant admission
3 *syn* see RENUNCIATION
rel abstaining, refraining
con indulgence, self-indulgence; overdoing, overindulgence

denigrate *vb syn* see MALIGN

denizen *n* **1** *syn* see INHABITANT
rel citizen, national, subject
2 *syn* see HABITUÉ 1

denominate *vb syn* see NAME 1

denomination *n* **1** *syn* see NAME 1
2 *syn* see RELIGION 2

denotative *adj syn* see INDICATIVE

denote *vb syn* see MEAN 2
rel insinuate; announce, argue, bespeak, prove

denotive *adj syn* see INDICATIVE

denounce *vb syn* see CRITICIZE

rel accuse, arraign, charge, impeach, incriminate, indict, tax; revile, vituperate; delate, inform
idiom cry harrow (*or* haro)
con panegyrize, praise
ant eulogize

de novo *adv syn* see OVER 7

dense *adj* 1 *syn* see CLOSE 4
rel heaped, massed, piled; crammed, crowded, jam-packed
con dispersed, dissipated, scattered; rare, thin; exiguous, meager, scant, scanty, spare
ant sparse; tenuous
2 *syn* see STUPID 1
rel obtuse; impassive, phlegmatic, stolid; lethargic, sluggish, torpid
ant subtle; bright

denticulate *adj syn* see SERRATE

denudate *vb syn* see STRIP 2

denude *vb* 1 *syn* see STRIP 1
2 *syn* see STRIP 2

denuded *adj syn* see OPEN 2

denunciate *vb syn* see CRITICIZE
rel delate, inform; menace, threaten
ant eulogize

deny *vb* 1 *syn* see DISCLAIM
rel abandon, desert, forsake
con adopt, embrace, espouse; recognize
ant acknowledge; admit
2 to refuse to grant <he was unwilling to *deny* the child's request>
syn disallow, keep back, refuse, withhold
idiom say no to, turn thumbs down on
con allow, concede, let, permit; afford, give
ant grant
3 to restrain (as oneself) from or forgo what is pleasant or satisfying <decided to *deny* himself a second piece of pie>
syn abstain, constrain, curb, hold back, refrain
rel eschew, forbear, forgo, sacrifice; inhibit, restrain; avoid, shun
con overdo, overindulge
ant indulge
4 to refuse to accept as true, valid, or worthy of consideration <*denying* the existence of witches>
syn contradict, contravene, cross, disaffirm, gainsay, impugn, negate, negative, traverse
rel decline, refuse, reject, repudiate; confute, controvert, disprove, rebut, refute; downface
con affirm, assert, aver; allow, grant; authenticate, corroborate, substantiate, validate, verify; avow, confess; claim, submit
ant concede; confirm

depart *vb* 1 *syn* see GO 2
rel set out, start, strike out, toddle
con linger, stay, tarry, wait; come; approach, near
ant arrive; abide, remain
2 *syn* see DIE 1
con exist, live, survive
3 *syn* see SWERVE 2

rel abandon, desert, forsake; reject, repudiate; cast, discard; differ, disagree, dissent, vary
4 *syn* see DIGRESS 2

departed *adj* 1 *syn* see DEAD 1
idiom called home, gone to a better land
2 *syn* see EXTINCT 2

departing *adj syn* see PARTING

departure *n* 1 the act of going, coming out, or leaving a place <the hasty *departure* of the refugees>
syn egress, egression, exit, exiting, exodus, offgoing, setting-out, withdrawal
rel going, leaving, quitting, retreat; decampment, flight; farewell, leave-taking
con coming, entering, ingress
ant arrival
2 *syn* see DEVIATION 1
rel rambling, straying, wandering

depend *vb syn* see HANG 1

depend (on *or* upon) *vb* 1 to rest or to be contingent upon something uncertain, variable, or indeterminable <our trip *depends* upon the weather>
syn hang (on *or* upon), hinge (on *or* upon), ‖pend, stand (on *or* upon), turn (on *or* upon)
rel base, bottom, found, ground, rest, stay
idiom hang in the balance
2 *syn* see RELY (on *or* upon)
rel incline, lean

dependable *adj* 1 *syn* see RELIABLE 1
rel assured, confident, sure; responsible; constant, faithful, loyal, staunch, steadfast, steady
idiom as good as one's word, to be counted on
con capricious, fickle, inconstant, mercurial, unstable; dishonest, lying, mendacious, untruthful
ant independable, undependable
2 *syn* see TRUE 9
3 *syn* see CERTAIN 3

dependence *n syn* see TRUST 1

dependent *adj* 1 determined or conditioned by another <a conclusion that is *dependent* on a premise>
syn conditional, contingent, relative, reliant
rel exposed, liable, open, subject, susceptible; iffy, provisional, provisory; uncertain; circumscribed, limited, restricted
con categorical, ultimate; boundless, eternal, illimitable, uncircumscribed; basal, basic, fundamental, primary, underived
ant absolute; infinite; original
2 *syn* see SUBORDINATE
rel counting, depending, reckoning, relying, trusting; accessory, ancillary, appurtenant; abased, debased, humbled
con principal; paramount, predominant, preponderant, preponderating, sovereign
ant independent

depict *vb syn* see REPRESENT 1
rel narrate, recite, recount, rehearse, relate; report, state; outline, sketch

depiction *n syn* see REPRESENTATION

deplete *vb* to bring to a low estate by depriving of something essential <an epidemic which *depletes* an army of manpower>
syn bankrupt, drain, draw, draw down, exhaust, impoverish, use up

---

syn synonym(s)   *rel* related word(s)
ant antonym(s)   *con* contrasted word(s)
idiom idiomatic equivalent(s)
‖ use limited; if in doubt, see a dictionary

rel cripple, debilitate, disable, enfeeble, sap, undermine, weaken; decrease, diminish, lessen, reduce; bleed, draw off, dry up, empty, milk; consume, expend, finish, spend, wash up
idiom dig into
con augment, enlarge, increase; bolster, fortify, strengthen; rebuild, repair, restore, revive
ant renew, replace

depleted *adj syn* see EFFETE 2
rel sapped, weakened
con augmented, enlarged, increased

deplorable *adj* of a kind to cause great distress <a *deplorable* loss of life>
syn afflictive, calamitous, dire, distressing, dolorous, grievous, heartbreaking, heart-rending, lamentable, mournful, regrettable, unfortunate, woeful
rel awful, dreadful, terrible; horrifying, intolerable, overwhelming, sickening, unbearable; miserable, wretched; disastrous
idiom as bad as bad can be, as bad as can be
con beneficial, helpful, salutary; advantageous, favorable, propitious

deplore *vb* 1 to manifest grief or sorrow for something <*deplore* the death of a close friend>
syn bemoan, bewail, grieve, lament, moan, weep
rel deprecate, disapprove; mourn, sorrow; cry, keen, wail
con boast, brag, crow, vaunt; rejoice
2 *syn* see REGRET

depone *vb syn* see TESTIFY 2

deport *vb* 1 *syn* see BEHAVE 1
2 *syn* see BANISH

deportation *n syn* see EXILE 1

deportment *n syn* see BEHAVIOR
2 *syn* see BEARING 1

depose *vb* 1 to remove from a throne or other high position <trying to *depose* the king in favor of his brother> <*deposed* industrial leaders>
syn dethrone, discrown, disenthrone, displace, disthrone, uncrown, unmake
rel overthrow, subvert, upset; chuck, dismiss, eject, oust, throw out
con inaugurate, induct, install, instate, invest; crown, enthrone, throne
2 *syn* see ASSERT 1
3 *syn* see TESTIFY 2

deposit *vb syn* see BANK
rel put by, store, stow

deposit *n syn* see SEDIMENT

depository *n syn* see DEPOT 2

depot *n* 1 *syn* see ARMORY
2 a place where something is deposited or stored <a gasoline *depot*>
syn arsenal, depository, magazine, repository, store, storehouse
rel storeroom, warehouse
3 *syn* see RAILROAD STATION
rel terminal, terminus

deprave *vb syn* see DEBASE 1
con elevate, ennoble, exalt, raise, uplift

depraved *adj* 1 *syn* see DEBASED
rel degenerate, infamous, vicious, villainous; degraded; twisted, warped
con scrupulous, upright

2 *syn* see VICIOUS 2

depravity *n syn* see VICE 1

deprecate *vb syn* see DISAPPROVE 1
rel bemoan, bewail, deplore, lament; derogate, detract
ant endorse

depreciate *vb* 1 to reduce the value of <*depreciate* the dollar>
syn cheapen, decry, devalorize, devaluate, devalue, downgrade, lower, mark down, soften, underprize, underrate, undervalue, write down, write off
rel depress; abate, decrease, diminish, dwindle, lessen, reduce; erode
con augment, increase; bloat, blow up, expand, inflate; amplify, magnify
ant appreciate
2 *syn* see DECRY 2
rel underestimate, underrate, undervalue; discountenance, disesteem, disfavor
con cherish, prize, treasure, value; comprehend, understand
ant appreciate

depreciation *n syn* see DETRACTION

depreciative *adj syn* see DEROGATORY
rel underestimating, underrating, undervaluing
ant appreciative

depreciatory *adj syn* see DEROGATORY
rel underestimating, underrating, undervaluing
ant appreciative

depredate *vb syn* see RAVAGE

depredator *n syn* see MARAUDER

depress *vb* 1 *syn* see LOWER 3
2 to lower in spirit or mood <the thought of all his debts *depressed* him>
syn oppress, press, sadden, weigh down
rel ail, distress, trouble; afflict, torment, try; contrist, deject, discourage, dishearten, dispirit; bother, disturb, perturb, upset
con delight, gladden, gratify, please, rejoice; excite, inspire, stimulate; brighten, cheer up, encourage, buoy, elevate
ant elate, exhilarate; cheer

depressant *adj syn* see GLOOMY 3

depressed *adj* 1 *syn* see DOWNCAST
rel lugubrious, melancholy
ant exhilarated; animated
2 *syn* see UNDERPRIVILEGED

depressing *adj* 1 *syn* see GLOOMY 3
con cheering, elevating, uplifting; exciting, inspiring
ant exhilarating
2 *syn* see SAD 2

depression *n* 1 *syn* see SADNESS
rel boredom, doldrums, ennui, tedium
con glee, hilarity, mirth
ant buoyancy; elation
2 a low spot <a *depression* in the land>
syn basin, concavity, dip, hollow, sag, sink, sinkage, sinkhole; *compare* NOTCH 1
rel cavity, hole, pocket, vacuity, vacuum, void; crater, pit; scoop
3 a period of lowered economic activity and extensive unemployment <indicators that warn of a coming *depression*>
syn recession, slump, stagnation
rel crash, decline, dislocation, drop; sag; paralysis; ||stagflation

con expansion; booming, development, growth; advancement, progress
ant boom

depressive *adj syn* see GLOOMY 3
deprivation *n syn* see PRIVATION 2
deprive *vb* **1** *syn* see STRIP 2
2 to prevent one from possessing <to *deprive* a person of his civil rights>
syn bereave, disinherit, dispossess, divest, lose, oust, rob; *compare* STRIP 2
rel dock; bare, denude, dismantle, strip
con furnish, give, supply; clothe, endow, equip, fit (out), invest, outfit
ant provide

deprived *adj syn* see UNDERPRIVILEGED
deprivement *n syn* see PRIVATION 2
depth *n* **1** the perpendicular extent or measurement downward from a surface <measured the *depth* of the river>
syn deepness, drop
rel profoundness, profundity; lowness; sounding; draft
con shallowness; altitude, elevation
2 the quality of being profound (as in insight) or full (as of knowledge) <her answer showed she had great *depth* in that subject>
syn abyss, deepness, profoundness, profundity
rel sense, wisdom, wiseness; brain, intellect, intelligence; keenness, sharpness
con shallowness, superficiality, unprofoundness; sciolism, smatter, smattering

depthless *adj syn* see SUPERFICIAL 2
depurate *vb syn* see PURIFY 1
depute *vb syn* see DELEGATE
deputize *vb syn* see DELEGATE
deputy *n* **1** *syn* see AGENT 2
rel substitute, surrogate; replacement
2 *syn* see DELEGATE

derange *vb* **1** *syn* see DISORDER 1
rel perturb; discommode, incommode, inconvenience
con compose, settle
ant arrange; adjust
2 *syn* see UPSET 5
3 *syn* see MADDEN 1

deranged *adj syn* see INSANE 1
rel disarranged, disordered, disturbed
derangement *n syn* see INSANITY 1
rel disarrangement, disorder; confusion; disturbance; unsoundness

derelict *adj* **1** given up especially by the owner or occupant <a *derelict* old home>
syn abandoned, deserted, desolate, forsaken, lorn, solitary, uncouth
rel dilapidated, dingy, faded, run-down, seedy, shabby, threadbare
con cherished, prized, treasured; attended, kept up, maintained
2 *syn* see NEGLIGENT
rel irresponsible, undependable, unreliable, untrustworthy
con dependable, reliable, responsible, trustworthy; careful, heedful, thoughtful
ant faithful

derelict *n* **1** *syn* see OUTCAST
2 *syn* see VAGABOND
dereliction *n syn* see FAILURE 1
rel abuse, misuse, outrage
ant faithfulness
deride *vb syn* see RIDICULE
rel banter, chaff, jolly, kid, rag, rib
de rigueur *adj syn* see DECOROUS 1
derision *n syn* see LAUGHINGSTOCK
derivable *adj syn* see DEDUCTIVE
derivate *adj syn* see SECONDARY 2
derivation *n syn* see SOURCE
derivational *adj syn* see SECONDARY 2
derivative *adj syn* see SECONDARY 2
ant underivative
derivative *n syn* see OUTGROWTH 2
derive *vb* **1** to reach (as a conclusion) as an end point of reasoning and observation <evidence from which he *derived* a startling new set of axioms>
syn educe, evolve, excogitate
rel conclude, deduce, gather, infer, judge; arrive (at), elicit, extract, reach; develop, elaborate, formulate, put (together), work out
2 *syn* see INFER
3 *syn* see TAKE 14
derive (from) *vb syn* see SPRING 1
derived *adj syn* see SECONDARY 2
dernier cri *n syn* see FASHION 3
dernier ressort *n syn* see RESOURCE 3
derogate *vb syn* see DECRY 2
rel decrease, lessen, reduce; discredit, disgrace
con enhance, heighten, intensify
derogatory *adj* designed or tending to belittle <*derogatory* comments about the actor's performance>
syn depreciative, depreciatory, detracting, disadvantageous, disparaging, dyslogistic, pejorative, slighting, uncomplimentary
rel belittling, decrying, minimizing; aspersing, calumnious, defamatory, maligning, vilifying; degrading, demeaning, humiliating; despiteful, malevolent, malicious, spiteful; contumelious, disdainful, scornful
con admiring, esteeming; acclaiming, laudatory, praising; appreciative
ant complimentary
derout *vb syn* see ROUT 1
derriere *n syn* see BUTTOCKS
descant *n* **1** *syn* see MELODY
2 *syn* see SONG 2
descant *vb syn* see DISCOURSE 1
descend *vb* **1** *syn* see FALL 1
ant rise
2 *syn* see STOOP 1
3 *syn* see DETERIORATE 1
descendant *n* **1** descendants *pl syn* see OFFSPRING
ant ancestors, ascendants
2 *syn* see OUTGROWTH 2
descent *n* **1** the act or process of passing from a higher to a lower level or state <a parachute *descent*><his slow *descent* to the gutter>
syn drop, fall
rel plummeting, plunging, sinking
con rise, upswing, upturn; advance, headway, progress, progression; betterment, improvement

---

syn synonym(s)   *rel* related word(s)
ant antonym(s)   *con* contrasted word(s)
idiom idiomatic equivalent(s)
‖ use limited; if in doubt, see a dictionary

ant ascent

2 *syn* see COMEDOWN

3 *syn* see ANCESTRY

4 an inclination downward <the steep *descent* of the mountain>
syn decline, declivity, dip, drop, fall
rel downgrade, grade, gradient, incline, slope; drop, drop-off
con acclivity, upgrade, uphill
ant ascent, rise

describe *vb* **1** *syn* see RELATE 1
rel communicate, impart; transmit; construe, elucidate, explain, explicate, expound; exemplify, illustrate; characterize, distinguish

2 *syn* see REPRESENT 1

description *n* **1** *syn* see REPRESENTATION

2 a descriptive statement <a fascinating *description* of his adventures>
syn narration, recital, recountal, recounting
rel anecdote, narrative, story, tale, yarn; account, chronicle, version; report, statement

3 *syn* see TYPE

descry *vb* **1** *syn* see SEE 1

2 *syn* see FIND 1
rel appreciate, comprehend, understand; realize

desecrate *vb syn* see RAVAGE

desecrated *adj syn* see IMPURE 3

desecration *n syn* see PROFANATION
ant consecration

desensitize *vb syn* see DEADEN 1
ant sensitize

desert *n syn* see WASTE 1

desert *n usu* **deserts** *pl syn* see DUE 1
rel chastening, chastisement, discipline, disciplining, punishment
idiom just deserts

desert *vb* **1** *syn* see ABANDON 1
rel depart, go, leave
con adhere, cohere
ant cleave (to), stick (to)

2 *syn* see DEFECT
rel abscond, decamp, escape, flee, fly
idiom go over the hill
con abide, remain, stay

deserted *adj syn* see DERELICT 1
rel empty, vacant; uninhabited, unoccupied; bare, barren

desertion *n syn* see DEFECTION
rel perfidiousness, perfidy, treacherousness, treachery

deserve *vb syn* see EARN 2
rel gain, get, win; demand
idiom have it coming

deserved *adj syn* see JUST 3
ant undeserved

deserving *n syn* see DUE 1

deserving *adj syn* see WORTHY 1
ant undeserving

desexualize *vb syn* see STERILIZE

desiccate *vb* **1** *syn* see DRY 1

2 to drain or be drained of emotional or intellectual vitality <this book is *desiccated* by undue concentration on statistics>
syn devitalize, dry up
rel deplete, drain, exhaust; divest; decay, fade, shrivel, wither, wizen
con brighten, enliven

desiderate *vb syn* see DESIRE 1

desight *n syn* see EYESORE

design *vb* **1** *syn* see INTEND 2

2 *syn* see PLAN 2
rel delineate, diagram; create, invent; construct, fashion, form, frame, produce; contrive
con accomplish, achieve, effect, execute, fulfill, perform

3 to work out the arrangement of the parts of <*design* an urban center>
syn arrange, lay out, map (out), plan, set out; *compare* PLAN 2
rel delineate, diagram, draft, outline, sketch

design *n* **1** *syn* see PLAN 1
rel delineation, diagram, draft, outline, sketch, tracing; creation, invention
con accomplishment, achievement, execution, fulfillment, performance

2 *syn* see INTENTION
rel conation, volition, will; deliberation, reflection, thinking, thought; intrigue, machination, plot
con accident, chance, fortuity, hap; impulse

3 *syn* see FIGURE 3

4 *syn* see MAKEUP 1

designate *vb* **1** *syn* see NAME 1

2 to declare a person one's choice <*designated* him to fill the position>
syn appoint, finger, make, name, nominate, tap
rel choose, elect, opt, pick, select, single; assign, delegate, depute; dictate
con disapprove, disfavor, object (to), oppose; disallow, reject, turn down

3 to set aside (as funds) for a specific use <*designated* the income to be used for charity>
syn allocate, earmark
rel specify; appropriate, reserve; stipulate; allot, apportion, mete (out)

designation *n syn* see NAME 1
rel identification, recognition; classification, pigeonhole, pigeonholing

designative *adj syn* see INDICATIVE

designed *adj syn* see DELIBERATE 1
rel decided, determined, resolved
con casual, chance, contingent, fluky, fortuitous, incidental; impulsive, spontaneous; natural, normal, regular, typical
ant accidental

designedly *adv syn* see INTENTIONALLY

designless *adj syn* see RANDOM

desire *n* **1** a longing for something that promises enjoyment or satisfaction <he had a strong *desire* for fame and fortune>
syn appetite, appetition, craving, itch, lust, passion, urge
rel hankering, hunger, hungering, longing, pining, thirst, thirsting, yearning; desideratum, desiderium; avarice, cupidity, greed, rapacity; concupiscence, eros
con abhorrence, repellency, repugnance, repulsion; aversion, disfavor, dislike
ant distaste

2 *syn* see LUST 2

desire *vb* **1** to have a longing for something <women who *desire* success>
syn ‖choose, covet, crave, desiderate, want, wish

rel hanker, hunger, long, pine, thirst, yearn; enjoy, fancy, like; aim, aspire, pant
idiom set one's eyes (*or* heart) upon
con abhor, abominate, detest, hate, loath; decline, refuse, reject, repudiate, spurn
2 *syn* see ASK 2

desired *adj syn* see TRUE 7

desirous *adj syn* see COVETOUS

desist *vb syn* see STOP 2
rel abstain, forbear; abandon, relinquish, resign, yield
idiom have done with
con continue; persevere
ant persist

desistance *n syn* see END 2

desk *n* a table, frame, or case with a sloping or horizontal surface especially for writing <sat meditating at her *desk*>
syn escritoire, secretaire, secretary, writing desk
rel lectern, reading desk

desolate *adj* **1** *syn* see DERELICT 1
rel empty, vacant; uninhabited, unoccupied
2 *syn* see INCONSOLABLE
3 *syn* see GLOOMY 3
rel bare, barren; destitute, poor, poverty-stricken; dark, murky

desolate *vb syn* see RAVAGE

despair *vb* to lose all hope or confidence <*despaired* of winning>
syn despond, give up
rel abandon, drop, relinquish, renounce, resign, surrender, yield
idiom lose heart (*or* courage *or* faith *or* hope)
con await, count (on), depend (on), hope, look (for); trust (in *or* to)
ant expect

despairing *adj syn* see DESPONDENT
rel atrabilious, melancholic, melancholy, cynical, misanthropic, pessimistic; depressed, oppressed, weighed down
con optimistic, roseate, rose-colored; assured, confident, sanguine, sure
ant hopeful

desperado *n syn* see OUTLAW
rel convict, criminal, lawbreaker

desperate *adj* **1** *syn* see DESPONDENT
rel foolhardy, rash, reckless, venturesome; headlong, precipitate; baffled, balked, circumvented, foiled, frustrated, outwitted, thwarted
con collected, composed, cool, nonchalant; assured, confident, sanguine, sure
2 *syn* see ACUTE 6
3 *syn* see INTENSE 1
4 *syn* see OUTRAGEOUS 2

despicable *adj* **1** *syn* see CONTEMPTIBLE
rel disgraceful, disreputable, ignominious, infamous, loathsome
con applaudable, commendable
ant laudable, praiseworthy
2 *syn* see BASE 3

despisable *adj syn* see CONTEMPTIBLE

despisal *n syn* see DESPITE 1

despise *vb* to regard as beneath one's notice and unworthy of consideration or interest <he had always *despised* the weak>
syn abhor, contemn, disdain, look down, scorn, scout
rel abominate, detest, execrate, hate, loathe; reject, repudiate, spurn; avoid, eschew, renounce, shun; disregard, ignore, overlook, slight, snub
idiom have no use for, look down one's nose at
con apprize, cherish, prize, treasure, value; admire, regard, respect
ant appreciate, esteem

despisement *n syn* see DESPITE 1

despite *n* **1** the feeling or attitude of despising <felt *despite* toward the lowly>
syn contempt, despisal, despisement, disdain, disparagement, scorn
rel disdainfulness, insolence, superciliousness; abhorrence, abomination, detestation, hate, hatred, loathing; rejection, repudiation, spurning; aversion, disfavor, dislike, distaste; cold shoulder, rebuff, slight, snub; disgust, loathing
con admiration, esteem, honor, regard, respect; attraction, liking
ant appreciation
2 *syn* see MALICE
rel contempt, disdain, scorn; abhorrence, abomination, detestation, hate, hatred, loathing
con admiration, esteem, respect; awe, fear, reverence
ant appreciation
3 *syn* see DEFIANCE 2
rel harm, hurt, injury
4 *syn* see AFFRONT
rel cut, discourtesy, incivility; rebuff, slight, snub

despite *prep syn* see AGAINST 4

despiteful *adj syn* see MALICIOUS

despitefulness *n syn* see MALICE

despoil *vb syn* see RAVAGE

despoiler *n* **1** *syn* see MARAUDER
2 *syn* see VANDAL

despond *vb* **1** *syn* see DESPAIR
rel droop, sag; languish
idiom reach the depths
con expect, hope, look
2 *syn* see MOPE 1

despondent *adj* having lost all or nearly all hope <*despondent* about his health>
syn despairing, desperate, desponding, forlorn, hopeless
rel grieving, mourning, sorrowful; dejected, depressed, melancholy, sad; disconsolate, dispirited, downcast, woebegone; discouraged, disheartened
con cheerful, glad, happy, joyful, joyous; buoyant, elastic, resilient, volatile; hopeful, optimistic
ant lighthearted

desponding *adj syn* see DESPONDENT

despot *n syn* see TYRANT

despotic *adj syn* see ABSOLUTE 4

despotism *n syn* see TYRANNY

despotize *vb syn* see TYRANNIZE

desquamate *vb syn* see SCALE 2

destine *vb syn* see PREDESTINE 1

destiny *n syn* see FATE

---

syn synonym(s)   *rel* related word(s)
ant antonym(s)   *con* contrasted word(s)
idiom idiomatic equivalent(s)
‖ use limited; if in doubt, see a dictionary

rel design, goal, intent, intention, objective

destitute *adj* 1 *syn* see DEVOID
rel deficient; bankrupt, bankrupted, depleted, drained, exhausted; divested, stripped
con complete, full, replete
2 *syn* see POOR 1
rel depleted, drained, exhausted
idiom on one's uppers, on the rocks
con comfortable, prosperous, well-fixed, well-off, well-to-do
ant opulent

destituteness *n syn* see POVERTY 1
rel absence, dearth, lack; adversity, misfortune
con competence, sufficiency
ant opulence

destitution *n syn* see POVERTY 1
rel absence, dearth, lack, privation, want; adversity, misfortune
con competence, sufficiency
ant opulence

destroy *vb* 1 to bring to ruin <the army *destroyed* the enemy village><his health was finally *destroyed* by drink>
syn annihilate, atomize, decapitate, decimate, demolish, destruct, discreate, dismantle, dissolve, dynamite, pull down, pulverize, quench, raze, rub out, ruin, ‖ruinate, shatter, shoot, smash, tear down, unbuild, undo, unframe, unmake, wrack, wreck; *compare* TOTAL 3
rel abolish, extinguish; devastate, pillage, ravage, sack, waste; eradicate, exterminate, extirpate, wipe; mangle, mutilate; rubble; doom
idiom blow to bits, bring to an end, dispose of, tear to shreds
con establish, found, institute, organize; fabricate, fashion, forge, form, make, manufacture, shape; conserve, preserve, protect, save
2 *syn* see KILL 1

destroyer *n* 1 *syn* see VANDAL
2 *syn* see DOWNFALL 2

destruct *vb syn* see DESTROY 1

destruction *n* 1 *syn* see DOWNFALL 2
2 *syn* see RUIN 3

destructive *adj* having the capability, property, or effect of destroying <a *destructive* windstorm> <his brother was a *destructive* influence in his life>
syn annihilative, ruinous, shattering, wrackful, wreckful
rel calamitous, deadly, disastrous, fatal, lethal, mortal; consumptive; internecine; baneful, deleterious, detrimental
con creative, formative; harmless, innocuous, inoffensive; helpful, improving
ant constructive

desuetude *n* 1 *syn* see END 2
2 *syn* see DISUSE

desultory *adj* 1 *syn* see FITFUL
rel erratic; shifting, vagrant, wavering
con constant, invariable, unchanging, unfailing
ant steady
2 *syn* see RANDOM
rel fitful, spasmodic; disorderly, unmethodical, unsystematic; capricious, fickle, inconstant, mercurial

con orderly, systematic
ant assiduous; methodical

detach *vb* to remove one thing from another with which it is in union or association <*detach* sheets from a loose-leaf book>
syn abstract, disassociate, disconnect, disengage, dissociate, uncouple, unfix
rel cut off, divorce, part, separate, sever, sunder; disjoin, disunite; disassemble, dismantle, dismember, dismount; disaffiliate
idiom take apart
con fasten, fix; bind, tie; combine, conjoin, unite
ant affix, attach

detached *adj* 1 *syn* see ALONE 1
rel separate, unconnected
con abutting, adjacent; connected, joined, linked
ant adjoining; attached
2 *syn* see INDIFFERENT 2
con anxious, concerned, solicitous; self≠centered, selfish
ant interested
3 *syn* see NEUTRAL
rel distant, remote, removed

detachment *n syn* see SEPARATION 1

detail *n syn* see POINT 1
con anatomy, framework, skeleton, structure; bulk, mass; design, plan

detail *vb syn* see SPECIFY 3

detailed *adj syn* see CIRCUMSTANTIAL
rel abundant, copious; exhausting, exhaustive, thoroughgoing

detailedly *adv syn* see THOROUGHLY 2

detain *vb* 1 *syn* see ARREST 2
rel buttonhole, hold, restrain
2 *syn* see KEEP 5
3 *syn* see DELAY 1
rel check, curb, inhibit, restrain

detect *vb syn* see FIND 1

detectable *adj syn* see PERCEPTIBLE

detection *n syn* see DISCOVERY

detective *n* one employed or engaged in detecting lawbreakers or in getting information that is not readily or publicly accessible <used *detectives* to locate the missing witness>
syn dick, ‖eye, gumshoe, hawkshaw, investigator, plainclothesman, Sherlock, Sherlock Holmes, sleuth, ‖tec; *compare* INFORMER, PRIVATE DETECTIVE
rel G-man; roper; shoofly; ‖nare

detention *n syn* see ARREST
rel imprisonment, incarceration, internment

deter *vb* 1 *syn* see DISSUADE
rel prevent; block, hinder, impede, obstruct; debar, shut out; frighten, scare; inhibit, restrain
con abet, incite, instigate; excite, provoke, stimulate; actuate, motivate
2 *syn* see PREVENT 2

deteriorate *vb* 1 to pass from a higher to a lower type or condition <the road quickly *deteriorated* into a bumpy path>
syn decline, degenerate, descend, disimprove, disintegrate, retrograde, rot, sink, worsen
rel crumble, decay, decompose; impair, mar, spoil; debilitate, undermine, weaken; depreciate, lessen

idiom be the worse for wear, go downhill, go to pot (*or* the dogs)
con better, improve; advance, progress; enhance, heighten
ant ameliorate
2 *syn* see FAIL 1

deterioration *n* 1 a falling from a higher to a lower level (as of quality or character) <the *deterioration* of business during the depression>
syn atrophy, decadence, declension, declination, decline, degeneracy, degeneration, dégringolade, devaluation, devolution, downfall, downgrade, ruin
rel impairment, spoiling; crumbling, decay, decaying, decomposition, disintegration, dissolution, dry rot, rotting; debasement, degradation; depreciation, lessening; dislocation, disruption
con betterment, help; enhancement, heightening, improvement
ant amelioration
2 *syn* see FAILURE 4
con convalescence, recovering, recuperation
ant improvement

determinable *adj syn* see TERMINABLE
determinant *n syn* see CAUSE 1
rel factor; authority, influence, weight
determinate *adj* 1 *syn* see INFLEXIBLE 3
2 *syn* see DEFINITE 1
ant indeterminate
determinate *vb syn* see IDENTIFY
determination *n* 1 *syn* see DECISION 1
2 *syn* see DECISION 2
ant indetermination
determine *vb* 1 *syn* see ESTABLISH 6
rel fix, set; settle
2 *syn* see PREDESTINE 1
3 *syn* see DEMARCATE 1
4 *syn* see DECIDE
rel bias, dispose, incline, predispose; actuate, drive, impel, move; induce, persuade
5 *syn* see CLOSE 3
6 *syn* see DISCOVER 3
determined *adj syn* see DECIDED 2
rel earnest, purposeful, serious; unfaltering, unhesitating, unwavering
con unresolved, unsettled; hesitant, hesitating, wavering
ant undetermined
detest *vb syn* see HATE
rel reject, repudiate, spurn
con love; appreciate, treasure, value
ant adore
detestable *adj syn* see HATEFUL 2
rel sorry; atrocious, heinous, monstrous, outrageous
ant adorable
detestation *n* 1 *syn* see ABOMINATION 2
rel antipathy, disgust
con affection, attachment, love; forbearance, indulgence, tolerance
ant adoration
2 *syn* see ABOMINATION 1
ant adoration

dethrone *vb syn* see DEPOSE 1
ant enthrone, throne
detonate *vb syn* see EXPLODE 1
detour *n* an indirect course often temporarily replacing part of a usual route <a *detour* around road construction> <took a *detour* to show him the lake>
syn roundabout, runaround
rel bypass
detour *vb syn* see SKIRT 2
detract (from) *vb syn* see DECRY 2
rel libel, slander; decrease, lessen, reduce
con enhance, heighten, intensify
detracting *adj* 1 *syn* see DEROGATORY
2 *syn* see LIBELOUS
detraction *n* the expression of damaging or malicious opinions <his persistent *detraction* of his rival's motives was wholly unfair>
syn backbiting, backstabbing, belittlement, calumny, character assassination, defamation, depreciation, disparagement, scandal, slander, sycophancy, tale
rel damage, harm, hurt, injury; injustice, wrong; aspersion, calumniation, libel, libeling, maligning, slandering, traducing, vilification
con enhancement, heightening, laudation, praise; approbation, approval
ant commendation
detractive *adj syn* see LIBELOUS
detractory *adj syn* see LIBELOUS
detriment *n syn* see DISADVANTAGE
rel damage, harm, hurt, injury, mischief; impairment, marring, spoiling
ant advantage, benefit
detrimental *adj syn* see HARMFUL
con aiding, helpful, helping; harmless
ant beneficial
2 *syn* see ADVERSE 2
de trop *adj syn* see SUPERFLUOUS
detruncate *vb syn* see TOP 1
deuced *adj syn* see UTTER
‖**deval** *vb syn* see STOP 3
devalorize *vb syn* see DEPRECIATE 1
devaluate *vb syn* see DEPRECIATE 1
devaluation *n syn* see DETERIORATION 1
devalue *vb syn* see DEPRECIATE 1
devast *vb syn* see RAVAGE
devastate *vb syn* see RAVAGE
devastation *n syn* see RUIN 3
‖**devel** *vb syn* see STRIKE 2
develop *vb* 1 *syn* see EXPAND 4
2 *syn* see UNFOLD 3
rel actualize, materialize, realize
3 *syn* see MATURE
rel dilate, expand; enroot, establish; flourish, prosper, thrive
con shrivel, wither, wizen
4 to come to have usually gradually <*develop* a taste for dry wine>
syn acquire, form
rel gain, get, obtain; achieve, attain, reach
5 *syn* see HAPPEN 1
development *n* progressive advance from a lower or simpler to a higher or more complex form <*development* of a seed into a plant><*development* of an industry>
syn evolution, evolvement, flowering, growth, progress, progression, unfolding, upgrowth

---

rel advance, advancement, ongoing
con decadence, declension, degeneration, deterioration, devolution
ant decline

deviant *adj* **1** *syn* see ABNORMAL 1
con normal; natural
2 *syn* see IRREGULAR 1

deviate *vb* **1** *syn* see SWERVE 2
2 *syn* see ERR
idiom deviate from the path of virtue

deviation *n* **1** departure from a course or procedure or from a norm or standard <no *deviation* from traditional methods was permitted>
syn aberration, deflection, departure, divergence, diversion, turning
rel alteration, change, modification, variation; breach, transgression, violation; anomaly, failing, fault; blunder, error, lapse
con accordance, agreement, conformance, conformity, correspondence
2 *syn* see TURN 2

deviative *adj* *syn* see ABNORMAL 1

device *n* **1** *syn* see TRICK 2
2 something (as a mechanical device) that performs a function or effects a desired end <invented many handy household *devices*>
syn contraption, contrivance; *compare* GADGET 1
rel appliance, implement, instrument, tool, utensil; apparatus, machine, mechanism; expedient, makeshift, resort, resource, shift; creation, invention; dingus, doohickey, hickey, thingumbob
3 *syn* see FIGURE 3
rel attribute, emblem, symbol, type; insignia, motto

deviceful *adj* *syn* see INVENTIVE

devil *n* **1** *often cap* the personal supreme spirit of evil and unrighteousness in Jewish and Christian theology
syn Apollyon, Beelzebub, ‖Cloot(s), ‖Clootie, diablo, fiend, Lord Harry, Lucifer, Old Gooseberry, Old Nick, Old Scratch, Satan, serpent
rel cacodemon; dybbuk
idiom Prince of Darkness
2 an extremely and malignantly wicked person <he was a *devil* who would stop at nothing to get what he wanted>
syn Archfiend, demon, fiend, Satan, succubus; *compare* SCAMP, VILLAIN 1
rel blackguard, caitiff, knave; scoundrel, villain; beast, brute
3 *syn* see SCAMP

‖**devil–devil** *n* *syn* see SPELL
‖**devil–dodger** *n* *syn* see CLERGYMAN
deviling *n* *syn* see IMP 1
devilish *adj* **1** *syn* see FIENDISH
rel iniquitous, nefarious, villainous; accursed, cursed, damnable, execrable; bad, evil, wicked
ant angelic
2 *syn* see SATANIC 1
devilkin *n* *syn* see IMP 1
devil–may–care *adj* *syn* see WILD 7
rel rash, reckless
con careful, heedful, responsible, thoughtful
devilment *n* *syn* see MISCHIEVOUSNESS
devilry *n* *syn* see MISCHIEVOUSNESS

‖**devil's–bones** *n pl* *syn* see DICE
deviltry *n* *syn* see MISCHIEVOUSNESS
devious *adj* **1** *syn* see OBSCURE 2
2 *syn* see CROOKED 1
rel deviating, digressing, diverting
ant straightforward
3 *syn* see ERRATIC 1
4 *syn* see ERRANT 2
rel artful, crafty, cunning, foxy, insidious, sly, tricky
5 *syn* see UNDERHAND
ant straightforward

devise *n* *syn* see LEGACY 1
devise *vb* **1** *syn* see PLAN 2
2 *syn* see CONTRIVE 2
rel create, discover; forge, form, shape; design
3 *syn* see PLOT
4 *syn* see WILL

devitalize *vb* *syn* see DESICCATE 2
rel deprive; eviscerate, weaken
ant vitalize

devoid *adj* showing a want or lack <a poem *devoid* of worth>
syn destitute, empty, innocent, void
rel bare, barren; lacking, wanting; deficient
con filled, full; furnished, provided, supplied
ant replete

devoir *n* **1** *syn* see OBLIGATION 2
2 *syn* see TASK 1

devolution *n* *syn* see DETERIORATION 1
rel regression, regressiveness, retrogression, retrogressiveness; receding, recession, retrogradation, retrograding
con development; progress, progression
ant evolution

devote *vb* **1** to set apart for a particular and often a better or higher use or end <a woman who *devotes* her life to helping others>
syn consecrate, dedicate, hallow
rel sanctify, vow; commit, confide, consign, entrust
idiom set apart
2 *syn* see GIVE 1
3 *syn* see ADDRESS 3
rel attempt, endeavor, strive, struggle, try; employ, use, utilize

devote (to) *vb* *syn* see HABITUATE 2
rel attach, wrap (up)

devoted *adj* *syn* see LOVING
rel constant, faithful, loyal, true; thoughtful; fervid, zealous

devotee *n* **1** *syn* see ADDICT
2 *syn* see AMATEUR 1

devotion *n* **1** *syn* see FIDELITY 1
rel enthusiasm, fervor, passion, zeal; affection, attachment, love; consecration, dedication, devotement
2 *syn* see LOVE 1

devour *vb* **1** *syn* see EAT 1
2 *syn* see EAT UP 1
idiom eat like a horse, eat one's head off
3 *syn* see CONSUME 1
4 *syn* see RAVAGE
rel demolish, destroy; ruin, wreck; dissipate, squander
5 to exhibit avid interest in or enjoyment of <the crowd *devoured* the lurid scene>

syn ‖eat up
rel delight (in), enjoy, rejoice (in), relish, revel (in); feast (on), gloat (over *or* on)
con avoid, eschew, shun

devout *adj* showing fervor in the practice of religion <a *devout* churchgoer>
syn godly, holy, pietistic, pious, prayerful, religious
rel ardent, fervent, fervid, zealous; adoring, revering, venerating, worshiping
con impious, irreligious, ungodly, unholy; irreverent; apostate, backsliding
ant undevout

dexter *adj syn* see FAVORABLE 5
ant sinister

dexterity *n* 1 *syn* see ADDRESS 1
rel adeptness, skillfulness; effortlessness, smoothness
con awkwardness, maladroitness
ant clumsiness
2 *syn* see ART 1

dexterous *adj* 1 ready and skilled in physical movements <a *dexterous* worker>
syn adroit, clever, deft, handy, neat-handed, nimble
rel agile; adept, expert, masterly, proficient, skilled, skillful; easy, effortless, facile, smooth
con awkward, gauche, inept, maladroit
ant clumsy
2 *syn* see CLEVER 4

dexterousness *n syn* see ADDRESS 1
ant clumsiness

dextrorotatory *adj* *syn* see RIGHT-HANDED
ant levorotatory

diablerie *n* 1 *syn* see MISCHIEVOUSNESS
2 *syn* see EVIL 3

diablo *n syn* see DEVIL 1

diabolic *adj* 1 *syn* see SATANIC 1
2 *syn* see FIENDISH
rel evil, ill, wicked
ant angelic

diabolism *n syn* see SATANISM

diabolonian *adj syn* see FIENDISH

diacritic *adj syn* see CHARACTERISTIC

diagnose *vb syn* see IDENTIFY

diagnostic *adj syn* see CHARACTERISTIC

diagnosticate *vb syn* see IDENTIFY

diagonal *adj* between horizontal and vertical in direction <cloth with a *diagonal* stripe>
syn bevel, beveled, bias, biased, slanted, slanting; *compare* INCLINED 3

diagonally *adv* in a line running across from corner to corner <decided to place the couch *diagonally* at the end of the room>
syn catercorner (*or* catty-corner *or* kitty-corner), cornerwise, slantingways, slant-ways, slantwise, ‖slaunchways
idiom on the bias
con parallelly, square, straight

‖**dial** *n syn* see FACE 1

dial *vb syn* see TUNE 3

dialect *n* 1 *syn* see LANGUAGE 1

2 a form of language that is not recognized as standard <the Doric *dialect* of ancient Greece>
syn argot, cant, jargon, lingo, patois, patter, slang, vernacular; *compare* TERMINOLOGY, VERNACULAR 3
rel localism, provincialism, regionalism

dialectic *n syn* see ARGUMENTATION

dialogue *n* 1 *syn* see CONVERSATION 1
2 *syn* see CONVERSATION 2

diametric *adj syn* see OPPOSITE

diapason *n* 1 *syn* see MELODY
2 *syn* see RANGE 5

diaphanous *adj syn* see FILMY

diarrhea *n* abnormally frequent intestinal evacuations with more or less fluid stools <they were taken with severe *diarrhea*>
syn ‖backdoor trots, dysentery, flux, Montezuma's revenge, ‖runs, scour(s), ‖squirts, summer complaint, ‖trots
idiom Montezuma's revenge, summer complaint

diatribe *n syn* see TIRADE

‖**dibs** *n pl* 1 *syn* see MONEY
2 *syn* see CLAIM 1

dice *n pl, sing* **die** a pair or set of small cubes marked on each face with from one to six spots and used in various games and in gambling by being shaken and thrown to come to rest at random <staked everything on a cast of the *dice*>
syn ‖African dominoes, bones, ‖cubes, ‖devil's-bones, ‖ivory, ‖tats

dice *vb syn* see DISCARD

dicey *adj syn* see UNCERTAIN 1

dichotomize *vb syn* see SEPARATE 1

dick *n* 1 *syn* see DETECTIVE

dicker *vb syn* see HAGGLE 2

dickey *adj syn* see WEAK 2

dictate *vb* to promulgate expressly something to be followed, observed, obeyed, or accepted <the commission *dictated* the policies to be followed>
syn decree, impose, lay down, ordain, prescribe, set
rel control, direct, manage; guide, lead; govern, rule; say, tell, utter; bid, charge, command, enjoin, instruct, order

dictate *n syn* see COMMAND 1

dictative *adj syn* see DICTATORIAL

dictator *n syn* see TYRANT

dictatorial *adj* imposing one's will or opinions on others <the chief was inclined to be *dictatorial* with his subordinates>
syn authoritarian, authoritative, dictative, doctrinaire, dogmatic, magisterial; *compare* TOTALITARIAN 1
rel bossy, domineering, imperative, imperious, masterful, peremptory; absolute, arbitrary, autocratic, despotic, tyrannical; arrogant, haughty, overbearing, proud; firm, stern
con amenable, biddable, docile, obedient, tractable; menial, obsequious, servile, slavish, subservient

dictatorship *n syn* see TYRANNY

diction *n syn* see WORDING

dictionary *n syn* see TERMINOLOGY

dictum *n syn* see MAXIM

‖**dicty** *adj syn* see SNOBBISH

---

syn synonym(s)   *rel* related word(s)
ant antonym(s)   *con* contrasted word(s)
idiom idiomatic equivalent(s)
‖ use limited; if in doubt, see a dictionary

didactic *adj* overburdened with instruction and the proprieties <his speech to the new freshmen was painfully *didactic*>
syn moral, moralizing, preachy, schoolmasterish, sermonic, sermonizing, teachy
rel advisory, exhortative, hortative; preceptive
ant undidactic

‖**didder** *vb syn* see SHAKE 1
diddle *vb* 1 *syn* see IDLE
2 *syn* see CHEAT
diddle–daddle *vb syn* see IDLE
diddler *n syn* see SWINDLER
dido *n* 1 *usu* didoes *pl syn* see PRANK
2 *syn* see KNICKKNACK
die *vb* 1 to pass from physical life <he *died* at an advanced age>
syn cash in, ‖check out, conk, ‖cop out, ‖croak, decease, demise, depart, drop, expire, go, ‖kick in, ‖kick off, pass, pass away, pass out, peg out, perish, pip, pop off, ‖snuff (out), succumb, ‖swelt
idiom be gathered to one's fathers, bite the dust (*or* ground), breathe one's last, cash in one's checks (*or* chips), give up the ghost, ‖kick the bucket, ‖kick up one's heels, meet one's end, shuffle off this mortal coil, ‖snuff it, turn up one's toes (to the daisies)
con be, exist, subsist; flourish, thrive
ant live
2 *syn* see PERISH 2
die (down *or* away) *vb syn* see ABATE 4
rel recede; disappear
con ascend, mount, rise
ant come up
die *n* 1 *see* DICE
‖2 *syn* see TOY 2
die–away *adj syn* see LANGUID
diehard *n* 1 an irreconcilable opponent of change <party *diehards* who would make no concessions>
syn bitter-ender, conservative, fundamentalist, old liner, praetorian, pullback, right, rightist, right wing, right-winger, standpat, standpatter, tory; *compare* REACTIONARY
rel mossback, old fogy, stick-in-the-mud; intransigent; true blue; right-center
con liberal, progressive, radical
2 *syn* see REACTIONARY
die–hard *adj syn* see CONSERVATIVE 1
differ *vb* 1 to be unlike or distinct in nature, form, or characteristics <the houses *differ* only in a few minor details>
syn disagree, vary
rel depart, deviate, diverge
con accord, conform, correspond
ant agree
2 to be of unlike or opposite opinion <men who *differ* on religious matters>
syn disaccord, disagree, discord, dissent, divide, vary
rel clash, conflict, jar; bicker, quarrel, squabble; argue, debate, dispute; oppose, protest (against)
idiom differ in opinion, hold opposite views
con coincide, concert, concur, harmonize; accord, conform, correspond
ant agree
difference *n* 1 *syn* see DISSIMILARITY
rel modification, variation

con equivalence, equivalency, sameness
ant resemblance
2 *syn* see DISCORD
rel clash, conflict
3 *syn* see VARIANCE 1
difference *vb syn* see KNOW 4
different *adj* 1 unlike in kind or character <could hardly be more *different*>
syn disparate, dissimilar, distant, divergent, diverse, other, otherwise, unalike, unequal, unlike, unsimilar, various
rel particular, single; distinctive, individual, peculiar; divers, sundry
con akin, analogous, comparable, like, parallel, similar, uniform; equal, equivalent, self-same
ant alike, identical, same
2 *syn* see DISTINCT 1
differential *adj syn* see DISCRIMINATORY
differentiate *vb syn* see KNOW 4
rel comprehend, understand
con confound, mistake
ant confuse
differently *adv syn* see OTHERWISE 1
difficile *adj syn* see HARD 6
difficult *adj syn* see HARD 6
rel problem, problematic
idiom easier said than done, no picnic, tough sledding
ant simple
difficultly *adv syn* see HARD 8
difficulty *n* 1 something obstructing one's course and demanding effort and endurance if one's end is to be attained <she encountered great *difficulties* on her way to success>
syn asperity, hardness, hardship, rigor, vicissitude
rel impediment, obstacle, obstruction, snag; dilemma, fix, jam, pickle, plight, predicament, quandary, scrape; emergency, exigency, pass, pinch, strait; bother, inconvenience, problem, trouble
idiom hard nut to crack, hard row to hoe, heavy sledding
2 *syn* see DEMUR 2
3 *syn* see QUARREL
diffident *adj syn* see SHY 1
rel blenching, flinching, shrinking; hesitant, reluctant
con assured, presumptuous, sanguine, sure; self-assured, self-confident, self-possessed, self-reliant; brazen, impudent, shameless
ant confident
difform *adj syn* see LOPSIDED
diffuse *adj syn* see WORDY
rel exuberant, lavish, profuse; casual, desultory, random; lax, loose, slack; lengthy, long
con concentrated; condensed
ant succinct
diffuse *vb* 1 *syn* see SPREAD 1
rel extend; expand
con compact, consolidate; center, centralize, focus
ant concentrate
2 *syn* see INTERFUSE 2
dig *vb* 1 to loosen and turn over or remove (as soil) with or as if with a spade <*dig* for potatoes> <*dug* through her drawer looking for the scarf>

syn ‖delve, excavate, grub, shovel, spade
rel quarry; enter, penetrate, pierce, probe; dig up, root, rootle, root out
2 to form by digging <*dig* a trench>
syn dig out, excavate, scoop, shovel, spade
3 *syn* see THRUST 2
‖4 *syn* see RESIDE 1
5 *syn* see POKE 1
‖6 *syn* see APPREHEND 1
7 *syn* see ENJOY 1
dig (into) *vb syn* see EXPLORE
dig *n* 1 *syn* see POKE 1
2 *syn* see SITE 3
digest *n syn* see COMPENDIUM 1
rel abridgment, synopsis
digest *vb* 1 *syn* see BEAR 10
2 *syn* see EPITOMIZE 1
digit *n syn* see NUMBER
dignification *n syn* see APOTHEOSIS 2
dignify *vb syn* see EXALT 1
con abase, debase
ant demean
dignitary *n syn* see NOTABLE 1
dignity *n* 1 *syn* see STATUS 2
2 *syn* see DECORUM 1
rel excellence, merit, perfection, virtue; ethicalness, ethics, morality, nobility, nobleness
con impropriety, indecency, indecorum, unseemliness
3 *syn* see ELEGANCE
rel augustness, grandeur, grandness, magnificence, majesty, nobility, nobleness; address, poise
dig out *vb* 1 *syn* see DIG 2
2 *syn* see RUMMAGE 1
digress *vb* 1 *syn* see SWERVE 2
2 to turn aside from the main subject of attention or course of argument <he *digressed* into too many side issues>
syn depart, divagate, diverge, excurse, ramble, stray, wander
rel drift, roam
idiom get off the subject, go off on a tangent
con advance, proceed, progress
digression *n* a departure from a subject or theme <a *digression* from the main point of the speech>
syn aside, discursion, divagation, excursion, excursus, parenthesis
rel episode, excurse, incident, underaction; deflection, deviation, divergence; departure; drifting, rambling, straying, wandering
‖**dike** (out *or* up) *vb syn* see DRESS UP 1
dilapidate *vb syn* see RUIN 2
rel crumble, decay, decompose, disintegrate; disregard, forget, ignore, neglect, overlook, slight
con mend, rebuild, repair; rejuvenate, renew, renovate, restore
dilapidated *adj syn* see SHABBY 1
rel damaged, impaired, injured, marred; crumbled, decayed
dilate *vb syn* see EXPAND 3
rel augment, enlarge, increase; extend, lengthen, prolong, protract; broaden, widen

con compress, condense, contract, shrink; attenuate
ant circumscribe; constrict
dilate (on or upon) *vb syn* see DISCOURSE 1
rel describe, narrate, recite, recount, rehearse, relate
con abbreviate, abridge, curtail, shorten
dilatory *adj syn* see SLOW 2
rel lax, neglectful, negligent, remiss, slack
con assiduous, busy, industrious, sedulous; prompt, quick, ready; hasty, impetuous, precipitate
ant diligent
dilemma *n syn* see PREDICAMENT
rel bewilderment, mystification, perplexity
idiom horns of a dilemma
dilettante *n* 1 *syn* see CONNOISSEUR
2 *syn* see AMATEUR 2
dilettante *adj syn* see AMATEURISH
dilettantish *adj syn* see AMATEURISH
dilettantist *adj syn* see AMATEURISH
diligent *adj syn* see ASSIDUOUS
rel persevering, persistent, persisting; unflagging
con deliberate, laggard, leisurely, slow; desultory
ant dilatory
dilly *adj syn* see FOOLISH 2
‖**dilly** *n* one that is remarkable or extraordinary of its kind <came up with a *dilly* of an idea to sell the product>
syn ‖corker, crackerjack, ‖daisy, dandy, ‖dinger, ‖doozer, humdinger, jim-dandy, knockout, ‖lalapalooza, ‖lulu, nifty, peach, ‖pip, pippin, ripper, ripsnorter, rouser
dilly *vb syn* see DELAY 2
dillydally *vb syn* see DELAY 2
dilute *vb* to make less strong or concentrated <*dilute* acid>
syn cut, thin, weaken
rel moderate, qualify, temper; deliquesce, liquefy; alter, modify
con enrich, fortify, richen, upgrade; condense, densify, evaporate, thicken
ant concentrate
dilute *adj* of relatively low strength or concentration <*dilute* acid>
syn diluted, thin, washy, watered-down, waterish, watery, weak
rel reduced; adulterated, sophisticated; impaired, impoverished, weakened
con condensed, densified, thickened
ant concentrated
diluted *adj syn* see DILUTE
ant concentrated
dim *adj* 1 *syn* see DARK 1
ant bright
2 *syn* see DULL 7
‖3 *syn* see DULL 9
4 *syn* see FAINT 2
con manifest, plain
ant distinct
dim *vb* 1 *syn* see OBSCURE
2 *syn* see DULL 5
3 *syn* see DULL 4
dime novel *n* a usually paperback melodramatic novel <read mostly *dime novels*>
syn dreadful, penny dreadful, shilling shocker, shocker, yellowback
rel bloodcurdler, chiller, ‖killer-diller; thriller; pulp

---

syn synonym(s)   *rel* related word(s)
ant antonym(s)   *con* contrasted word(s)
idiom idiomatic equivalent(s)
‖ use limited; if in doubt, see a dictionary

dimension n 1 usu **dimensions** pl syn see SIZE 1
2 usu **dimensions** pl syn see RANGE 2
dimensionality n syn see SIZE 1
diminish vb 1 syn see ABRIDGE 1
2 syn see DECREASE
rel ebb, subside, wane; moderate, temper; attenuate, extenuate
con aggravate, enhance, heighten, intensify
3 syn see DECRY 2
diminutive adj syn see TINY
‖**dimmet** n syn see EVENING 1
dimple vb syn see RIPPLE
‖**dimps** n syn see EVENING 1
‖**dimpsy** n syn see EVENING 1
dim-sighted adj syn see PURBLIND
dimwit n syn see DUNCE
dim-witted adj syn see RETARDED
con alert, keen
din n a welter of discordant sounds <the din of a machine shop>
syn babel, brouhaha, ‖chirm, clamor, hubbub, hullabaloo, jangle, music, pandemonium, racket, racketry, tintamarre, tumult, uproar; compare COMMOTION 4
rel blatancy, boisterousness, clamorousness, stridency; bedlam; clangor, clatter, rattle; clash, percussion; ‖row; noise, sound
con calm, lull, quietude, stillness; concord, consonance, harmony; melody, musicality, tunefulness
diner n syn see EATING HOUSE
‖**dinero** n syn see MONEY
ding vb 1 syn see STRIKE 2
2 syn see SURPASS 1
‖**ding** n syn see BLOW 1
ding-a-ling n syn see CRACKPOT
dingdong adv syn see HARD 3
dinge n syn see SADNESS
‖**dinger** n syn see ‖DILLY, ‖corker, crackerjack, ‖daisy, dandy, humdinger, jim-dandy, knockout, ‖lalapalooza, ‖lulu
dingus n syn see DOODAD
dingy adj syn see SHABBY 1
rel grimed, smirched, soiled, sullied, tarnished; dull; dusky, gloomy, murky
con bright, brilliant, luminous, shining; clean, cleanly
dining table n syn see TABLE 1
dinky adj syn see MINOR 2
‖**dinky-di** adj syn see FAITHFUL 1
dinner n a usually elaborate meal served to guests or a group often to mark an occasion or honor an individual <the annual club dinner>
syn banquet, feast, regale, spread
rel ‖blowout, festival, fete, junket; breakfast, collation, luncheon
dinner table n syn see TABLE 1
dinosauric adj syn see HUGE
‖**dinsome** adj syn see VOCIFEROUS
dint n syn see POWER 4
dip vb 1 to plunge or thrust momentarily or partially under the surface of a liquid <dip a dress in cleansing fluid>
syn douse, duck, dunk, immerse, souse, submerge, submerse
rel pitch, plunge
2 to lift a portion of by reaching below the surface with something shaped to hold liquid <dip drinking water from a spring>

syn bail, lade, ladle, scoop
rel dish, spoon; bucket (up or out), draw
‖3 syn see PAWN
4 syn see DUCK 2
5 syn see PLUMMET
6 syn see SET 12
7 syn see SWERVE 1
dip (into) vb syn see BROWSE
dip n 1 syn see DESCENT 4
2 syn see DECLINE 3
3 syn see DEPRESSION 2
‖4 syn see PICKPOCKET
diplomacy n syn see TACT
diplomatic adj syn see TACTFUL
rel bland, smooth; courteous, polite; astute, shrewd; artful, crafty, guileful, wily
ant undiplomatic
‖**dippy** adj syn see FOOLISH 2
‖**dipsy-doodle** n syn see DECEPTION 1
dire adj 1 syn see FEARFUL 3
2 syn see DEPLORABLE
rel depressing, oppressing
3 syn see OMINOUS
4 syn see PRESSING
5 syn see ACUTE 6
direct vb 1 syn see ADDRESS 6
2 to turn something toward its appointed or intended mark or goal <directed her eyes to the door>
syn address, aim, cast, head, incline, lay, level, point, present, set, train, turn, zero (in)
rel beam; divert; fasten, focus
3 syn see ADDRESS 3
rel fix, set, settle
con deflect, divert; deviate, digress, diverge, swerve
4 syn see GUIDE
ant misdirect
5 syn see GOVERN 3
6 syn see CONDUCT 3
7 syn see COMMAND
rel assign, define, prescribe
direct adj 1 being or passing in a straight line of descent from parent to offspring <direct ancestors>
syn lineal
2 admitting free or continuous passage <a direct route to the beach>
syn straight, straightforward, through, uninterrupted
rel linear; continuous, unbroken, undeviating, unswerving
con circuitous, roundabout
ant indirect
3 syn see FRANK
ant devious
4 marked by absence of an intervening agency, instrumentality, or influence <he had no direct knowledge of the crime>
syn firsthand, immediate, primary
rel contiguous, next, proximate
ant indirect
direct adv 1 syn see DIRECTLY 1
2 syn see VERBATIM
direction n 1 syn see VIEWPOINT 2
directive n 1 syn see EDICT 1
2 syn see MEMORANDUM 2
3 syn see MESSAGE 1
directly adv 1 without deviation of course <the turnpike runs directly east and west>

syn dead, direct, due, right, straight, straightly, undeviatingly
idiom as the crow flies, in a beeline
con circuitously, deviously, round about; discursively, ramblingly
ant indirectly
2 *syn* see VERBATIM
3 *syn* see IMMEDIATELY 1
4 *syn* see AWAY 3
5 *syn* see PRESENTLY 1
direful *adj* 1 *syn* see FEARFUL 3
2 *syn* see OMINOUS
dirt *n* 1 *syn* see EARTH 2
2 *syn* see DECEPTION 1
dirt poor *adj syn* see POOR 1
dirty *adj* 1 soiled or begrimed with dirt <wash those *dirty* hands>
syn black, dungy, filthy, foul, grimy, grubby, grungy, impure, mucky, murky, nasty, soily, sordid, squalid, unclean, uncleanly
rel contaminated, defiled, polluted, tainted; dreggy; draggled, draggletailed, draggly
idiom dirty as a pig
con immaculate, spotless; unsoiled, unspotted, unsullied
ant clean
2 *syn* see IMPURE 1
ant clean
3 *syn* see OBSCENE 2
4 *syn* see WILD 6
dirty *vb* 1 *syn* see SOIL 2
ant clean
2 *syn* see TAINT 1
idiom dirty one's hands
disability *n syn* see DISADVANTAGE
disable *vb* 1 *syn* see DISQUALIFY
2 *syn* see PARALYZE 1
3 *syn* see WEAKEN 1
rel harm, hurt, mar, spoil; batter, maim, mangle, mutilate; ruin, wreck
con restore, resuscitate, revive, revivify
ant rehabilitate
disabuse *vb* to set free from mistakes (as in reasoning or judgment) <he was *disabused* of the notion that he was indispensable to the company>
syn purge, undeceive, undelude
rel amend, correct, emend, rectify, redress; disillude, disillusion, unblind; enlighten, illuminate; free, liberate, release
idiom open one's eyes, prick the (*or* one's) bubble, puncture one's balloon, set (*or* put) right (*or* straight)
con deceive, delude, mislead; dupe, gull
disaccord *vb* 1 *syn* see CLASH 2
2 *syn* see DIFFER 2
ant accord
disaccord *n syn* see DISCORD
ant accord
disacknowledge *vb syn* see DISCLAIM
disadvantage *n* an unfavorable or prejudicial quality or circumstance <the machine has two serious *disadvantages*>
syn detriment, disability, drawback, handicap

rel bar, impediment, obstacle, obstruction; blocking, hamper, hindrance, imposition
con aid, assistance, help; service, usefulness, utility, value, worth
ant advantage
disadvantaged *adj syn* see UNDERPRIVILEGED
ant advantaged
disadvantageous *adj syn* see DEROGATORY
disadvise *vb syn* see DISSUADE
disaffect *vb syn* see ESTRANGE
rel agitate, discompose, disquiet, disturb, upset
ant win (over)
disaffection *n syn* see ESTRANGEMENT
disaffirm *vb syn* see DENY 4
disagree *vb* 1 *syn* see DIFFER 1
ant agree
2 *syn* see DIFFER 2
ant agree
disagreeable *adj* 1 *syn* see BAD 8
rel annoying, distressing, disturbing, woeful
ant agreeable
2 *syn* see IRRITABLE
ant agreeable
disallow *vb* 1 *syn* see DENY 2
con accede, acquiesce, assent
ant allow
2 *syn* see DISCLAIM
rel debar, exclude, shut out
ant allow
disallowance *n syn* see DENIAL 1
disappear *vb syn* see VANISH
rel go, leave
ant appear
disappoint *vb syn* see FRUSTRATE 1
disapprove *vb* 1 to feel or express an objection <*disapprove* of his actions>
syn deprecate, discommend, discountenance, disesteem, disfavor, frown, object
rel blame, censure, condemn, criticize, denounce, reprehend, reprobate; decry, depreciate, detract, disparage, dispraise; expostulate, remonstrate
idiom look askance at, make a wry face at, not go for, take a dim view of, take exception to
con applaud, commend, compliment, recommend; accredit, certify, endorse, sanction; approbate, countenance, favor
ant approve
2 *syn* see DECLINE 4
disarm *vb* 1 *syn* see PARALYZE 1
2 to influence favorably by persuasive words or acts <*disarmed* by her smile>
syn unarm, unsteel, win (over)
rel allure, attract, bewitch, captivate, charm, enchant, fascinate
con alert, caution, tip (off), warn
ant arm
disarming *adj syn* ingratiating, deferential, ingratiatory, insinuating, insinuative, saccharine, silken, silky
disarrange *vb syn* see DISORDER 1
rel mislay, misplace; displace, replace; overturn
ant arrange
disarray *n syn* see CONFUSION 3
con arrangement, marshaling

---

syn synonym(s)   *rel* related word(s)
ant antonym(s)   *con* contrasted word(s)
idiom idiomatic equivalent(s)
‖ use limited; if in doubt, see a dictionary

disarray vb syn see DISORDER 1
  ant array
disassemble vb syn see DISMOUNT
disassociate vb syn see DETACH
disaster n a sudden calamitous event bringing great damage, loss, or destruction <a flood *disaster* struck the valley>
  syn calamity, cataclysm, catastrophe, misadventure, tragedy, woe(s)
  rel accident, casualty, fatality, mishap; adversity, distress, misadventure, mischance, misfortune; rock(s)
disastrous adj syn see FATAL 2
  rel hapless, luckless, unfortunate; destructive
  con fortunate, happy, lucky, providential
disavow vb syn see DISCLAIM
  rel impugn, negate, negative
  con allow, concede, grant; assert, justify, maintain
  ant avow
disband vb to cease to exist as a unit <the dance group *disbanded* after a farewell concert>
  syn break up, disperse, dissolve
  rel dispel, dissipate, scatter; dichotomize, disjoin, disjoint, dissect, dissever, disunite, divide, divorce, part, separate, sever, sunder
  idiom go their several ways, part company
  con combine, concur, conjoin, cooperate, unite; assemble, collect, congregate, gather; call up, summon
  ant band
disbelief n syn see UNBELIEF
  rel atheism, deism; rejection, repudiation, spurning
  con credence, credit, faith
  ant belief
disbelieve vb to hold not to be true or real <*disbelieved* his professions of sincerity>
  syn discredit, unbelieve
  rel distrust, doubt, mistrust, question, suspect; eschew, reject, scorn, scout
  con accept, ‖buy, swallow
  ant believe
disbelieving adj syn see INCREDULOUS
disbodied adj syn see IMMATERIAL 1
disburden vb syn see UNLOAD
disburse vb 1 syn see SPEND 1
  2 syn see DISTRIBUTE 1
disbursement n syn see EXPENSE 1
discalceate adj syn see DISCALCED
discalced adj wearing only sandals on the feet <*discalced* monks>
  syn barefoot, discalceate
  con calced, shod
discard vb to get rid of <*discard* old clothes> <people who *discard* traditional values>
  syn abdicate, cashier, cast, chuck, ‖deep-six, ‖dice, ditch, dump, jettison, junk, lay aside, reject, scrap, shed, ‖shoot, shuck (off), slough, throw away, throw out, wash out
  rel abandon, desert, forsake; repudiate, spurn; dismiss, eject, oust
  idiom do away with, let go by the board
  con adopt, embrace, espouse, take on, take up; employ, use, utilize; hold, hold back, keep, retain; cherish, esteem, nurture
discarding n syn see DISPOSAL 2
discarnate adj syn see IMMATERIAL 1

discarnate adj syn see IMMATERIAL 1
discept vb syn see DISCUSS 1
discern vb 1 syn see SEE 1
  rel ascertain, discover; anticipate, apprehend, divine, foresee
  2 syn see KNOW 4
discernible adj syn see PERCEPTIBLE
  ant indiscernible
discerning adj syn see WISE 1
  ant undiscerning
discernment n syn see WIT 3
  rel intuition, reason; sagaciousness, sagacity
  con crassness, density, slowness; blindness
discharge vb 1 syn see UNLOAD
  2 syn see EXEMPT
  3 syn see SHOOT 1
  4 syn see FREE
  rel dismiss, eject, expel, oust; eliminate, exclude
  5 to give outlet to <the river *discharges* its waters into the bay>
  syn disembogue, emit, flow, give off, pour, void
  rel eject, exude, release
  6 syn see DISMISS 3
  rel displace, replace, supersede, supplant
  con hire; contract
  ant engage
  7 to release from service with the armed forces <*discharged* from the army with the rank of sergeant>
  syn ‖demob, demobilize, muster out, separate
  rel disenroll; deactivate, inactivate; bounce, cashier, dismiss, drop, fire, sack
  8 syn see CLEAR 5
  9 syn see ANNUL 4
discinct adj syn see NEGLIGENT
disciple n syn see FOLLOWER
  rel enthusiast, fanatic, zealot
disciplinary adj syn see PUNITIVE
discipline n 1 syn see PUNISHMENT
  2 syn see WILL 3
discipline vb 1 syn see PUNISH 1
  rel overcome, reduce, subdue, subjugate; bridle, check, curb, inhibit, restrain
  2 syn see TEACH
  rel guide, lead; conduct, control, direct, manage
disclaim vb to refuse to admit, accept, or approve <the senator *disclaimed* the comment attributed to him> <*disclaim* responsibility for a subordinate's mistake>
  syn deny, disacknowledge, disallow, disavow, disown, repudiate
  rel contradict, contravene, gainsay, traverse; refuse, reject, spurn; deprecate; belittle, disparage, minimize; abjure, forswear, recant, renounce, retract; challenge, criticize
  idiom turn one's back on, wash one's hands of
  con acknowledge, avow, own; accept, admit, receive, take
  ant claim
disclose vb 1 syn see OPEN 2
  2 syn see REVEAL 1
  rel acknowledge, admit, avow, confess, own
  idiom make public
  con conceal, hide; camouflage, cloak, disguise, dissemble, mask

discolor vb 1 syn see TAINT 1
2 syn see STAIN 1
discolor adj syn see VARIEGATED
discombobulate vb 1 syn see DISCOMPOSE 1
2 syn see CONFUSE 2
discomfit vb syn see EMBARRASS
rel annoy, bother, irk, vex; disturb, perturb, upset
discomfiture n 1 syn see DEFEAT 1
2 syn see COMEDOWN
3 syn see EMBARRASSMENT
rel agitation, disquiet, perturbation, upset; commotion; prickles
discomforting adj syn see UNCOMFORTABLE
ant comforting
discommend vb syn see DISAPPROVE 1
rel admonish; criticize, reprehend; censure
con approve, endorse, sanction
ant commend; recommend
discommode vb syn see INCONVENIENCE
rel flurry, fluster, perturb, upset; bother, irk, vex
discommoding adj syn see INCONVENIENT
discommodious adj syn see INCONVENIENT
discompose vb 1 to destroy or impair one's capacity for collected thought or decisive action <*discomposed* by the rudeness of his friend>
syn agitate, bother, discombobulate, dismay, disquiet, disturb, flurry, fluster, perturb, unhinge, unsettle, untune, upset; compare EMBARRASS
rel disagree; annoy, irk, vex; harass, harry, pester, plague, worry
con calm, quiet, settle, soothe, tranquilize; allay, alleviate, assuage; appease, conciliate, mollify, pacify, placate, propitiate
ant compose
2 syn see DISORDER 1
ant compose
discomposure n syn see EMBARRASSMENT
ant composure
disconcert vb syn see EMBARRASS
rel bewilder, nonplus, perplex, puzzle
disconcertion n syn see EMBARRASSMENT
disconcertment n syn see EMBARRASSMENT
disconfirm vb syn see DISPROVE 1
disconnect vb syn see DETACH
ant connect
disconnected adj syn see INCOHERENT 2
ant connected
disconsolate adj 1 syn see DOWNCAST
rel comfortless, inconsolable; sorrowful, woeful; doleful, melancholy; unhappy
ant cheerful
2 syn see INCONSOLABLE
3 syn see GLOOMY 3
ant cheerful, cheery
disconsonant adj syn see INCONSONANT 1
discontent adj syn see DISCONTENTED
ant content

discontented adj showing or expressing a sense of grievance or thwarted aspirations or desires <*discontented* with his position>
syn discontent, disgruntled, dissatisfied, malcontent, malcontented, uncontent, uncontented, ungratified
rel disquieted, disturbed, perturbed, restless, upset; displeased; unhappy
con satisfied; gratified, pleased; happy; elated, exultant, jubilant, triumphant
ant contented
discontinuance n syn see END 2
ant continuance, continuation
discontinuation n syn see END 2
ant continuance, continuation
discontinue vb syn see STOP 3
ant continue
discontinuity n syn see GAP 1
ant continuity
discontinuous adj syn see INCOHERENT 2
ant continuous
‖**disconvenience** n syn see INCONVENIENCE
ant convenience
‖**disconvenience** vb syn see INCONVENIENCE
ant convenience
discord n the state of those who disagree and lack harmony <a household full of turmoil and *discord*>
syn conflict, contention, difference, disaccord, disharmony, dispeace, dissension, dissent, dissidence, dissonance, disunion, disunity, division, inharmony, mischief, strife, unpeace, variance
rel discrepancy, incompatibility, incongruity, inconsistency, inconsonance, uncongeniality; animosity, antagonism, antipathy, enmity, hostility, rancor; polarization; collision
con accord, consonance; agreement, concordance, concurrence
ant concord, harmony
discord vb 1 syn see CLASH 2
ant concord, harmonize
2 syn see DIFFER 2
ant accord
discordant adj 1 syn see INHARMONIOUS 2
2 syn see INCONSONANT 1
con according, agreeing, congenial, harmonious, harmonizing
ant concordant
3 syn see ANTIPATHETIC 1
ant concordant
4 syn see DISSONANT 1
discotheque n syn see NIGHTCLUB
discount n syn see DEDUCTION 1
discount vb 1 syn see DEDUCT 1
con boost, hike, increase, mark up, raise
2 syn see NEGLECT
3 syn see DECRY 2
discountenance vb 1 syn see EMBARRASS
idiom put out of countenance
2 syn see DISAPPROVE 1
rel reproach, reprove
con encourage, favor
ant countenance
discourage vb 1 to weaken the stamina, interest, or zeal of <the long winter and lack of fuel *discouraged* the settlers>

---

syn synonym(s)   rel related word(s)
ant antonym(s)   con contrasted word(s)
idiom idiomatic equivalent(s)
‖ use limited; if in doubt, see a dictionary

syn chill, deject, demoralize, dishearten, disparage, dispirit

rel depress, weigh; afflict, try; damp, dampen, droop; distress, trouble; bother, irk, vex

idiom take the heart out of

con cheer, embolden, hearten, inspirit, nerve, steel

ant encourage

2 *syn* see DISSUADE

rel check, inhibit, restrain; prevent; frighten, scare

idiom lay a wet blanket on, throw cold water on

con advocate, countenance, favor; approve, back, endorse

ant encourage

discouraging *adj syn* see GLOOMY 3

rel deterring; hindering

ant encouraging

discourse *n* **1** *syn* see SPEECH 1

2 a systematic, serious, and often learned exposition of a subject or topic <his *discourses* during the seminar were long remembered>

syn disquisition, dissertation, memoir, monograph, monography, thesis, tractate, treatise

rel article, essay, paper; lecture, sermon; rhetoric, speech, talk

discourse *vb* **1** to express oneself especially formally and at length <*discourses* knowledgeably about the laws of nature>

syn descant, dilate (on *or* upon), discuss, dissert, dissertate, expatiate, sermonize

rel converse, speak, talk, voice; argue, dispute; harangue, lecture, orate, perorate; amplify, develop, elaborate, enlarge, expand; explain, expound; comment, commentate, remark

2 *syn* see ACT 1

discourteous *adj syn* see RUDE 6

con chivalrous, civil, courtly, gallant

ant courteous

discover *vb* **1** *syn* see EXPOSE 4

2 *syn* see REVEAL 1

rel advertise, proclaim, publish

con repress, suppress

3 to become or be made aware of something not previously known <*discover* a secret>

syn ascertain, catch on, determine, find out, hear, learn, see, tumble, unearth

rel descry, detect, encounter, espy, hit (on *or* upon), meet (with), spot; discern, note, observe, perceive

idiom get wise to

con miss, overlook; disregard, ignore

discovery *n* the gaining knowledge of or ascertaining the existence of something previously unknown or unrecognized <the *discovery* of a new chemical element>

syn detection, espial, find, strike, unearthing

rel disclosure, exposition, exposure, revelation, uncovering

discreate *vb syn* see DESTROY 1

discredit *vb* **1** *syn* see DISBELIEVE

ant credit

2 to deprive of credibility <he *discredited* the rumor immediately>

syn blow up, disprove, explode, puncture, shoot

rel expose, show up; destroy, ruin

idiom bring to naught, knock the bottom out of, not leave a leg to stand on

con accept, believe, credit

discredit *n syn* see DISGRACE

ant credit

discreditable *adj syn* see DISREPUTABLE 1

discreet *adj* **1** *syn* see CAUTIOUS

con foolhardy

ant indiscreet

2 *syn* see PLAIN 1

3 *syn* see CONSERVATIVE 2

discreetness *n syn* see PRUDENCE 1

ant indiscreetness

discrepancy *n syn* see DISSIMILARITY

discrepant *adj syn* see INCONSONANT 1

rel different, disparate, divergent, diverse; disagreeing, varying

con agreeing, conforming, corresponding, jibing, squaring, tallying; alike, identical, like, parallel, similar, uniform

discrepate *vb syn* see KNOW 4

discrete *adj syn* see DISTINCT 1

con blended, fused, merged, mingled

ant indiscrete

discretion *n syn* see PRUDENCE 1

rel moderation, restraint; gumption, judgment, sense, wisdom

con asininity, fatuousness, foolishness, simplicity; foolhardiness, rashness, recklessness

ant indiscretion

discretionary *adj syn* see OPTIONAL

discriminate *vb syn* see KNOW 4

rel note, perceive, remark; collate, compare, contrast

ant confound

discriminating *adj syn* see ECLECTIC 1

rel careful; judicious, prudent, wise

ant undiscriminating

discrimination *n syn* see WIT 3

rel judgment, sense

con crassness, density, slowness

discriminative *adj syn* see DISCRIMINATORY

ant undiscriminative

discriminatory *adj* applying or favoring discrimination in treatment <*discriminatory* employment practices against women>

syn discriminative

rel biased, inequitable, partial, partisan, prejudiced, prepossessed; unfair, unjust

con dispassionate, equal, equitable, fair, impartial, just, objective, unbiased, uncolored, unprejudiced

ant nondiscriminatory

discrown *vb syn* see DEPOSE 1

disculpate *vb syn* see EXCULPATE

ant inculpate

discumber *vb syn* see EXTRICATE 2

discursion *n syn* see DIGRESSION

discuss *vb* **1** to exchange views about something in order to arrive at the truth or to convince others <met to *discuss* community needs>

syn agitate, argue, canvass, debate, discept, dispute, ‖kick around, moot, pro-and-con, thrash out, toss (around)

rel deliberate, hash over, reason (out), talk over; consider, weigh
idiom consider pro and con, go into, reason the point
2 *syn* see DISCOURSE 1
rel elucidate, explicate, interpret

discussion *n syn* see CONFERENCE 1

disdain *n* **1** *syn* see DESPITE 1
rel antipathy, aversion; arrogance, haughtiness, insolence, superciliousness
con awe, fear, reverence
2 *syn* see PRIDE 3

disdain *vb syn* see DESPISE
con accept, receive, take; acknowledge, admit, own; esteem, respect
ant admire

disdainful *adj syn* see PROUD 1
rel rejecting, repudiating, spurning; contemning, despising, scorning, scouting; antipathetic, averse, unsympathetic
ant admiring; respectful

disdainfulness *n syn* see PRIDE 3

disease *n* **1** a kind or instance of impairment of a living being that interferes with normal bodily function <tuberculosis has become a controllable *disease*>
syn affection, ailment, complaint, condition, disorder, ill, infirmity, malady, sickness, syndrome; *compare* INFIRMITY 1, SICKNESS 1
rel bug, ‖epizootic, ‖misery, virus
2 *syn* see INFIRMITY 1
ant health

diseasedness *n syn* see SICKNESS 1

disedge *vb syn* see DULL 3

disembark *vb* to go ashore out of a ship <*disembark* at the next port>
syn debark, land
rel put in
con board, get on
ant embark

disembarrass *vb syn* see EXTRICATE 2
rel clear, rid, unburden
ant embarrass

disembodied *adj syn* see IMMATERIAL 1

disembogue *vb syn* see DISCHARGE 5

disembowel *vb syn* see EVISCERATE

disembroil *vb syn* see EXTRICATE 2
ant embroil

disemploy *vb syn* see DISMISS 3

disenable *vb syn* see DISQUALIFY

disenchanted *adj syn* see SOPHISTICATED 2

disencumber *vb syn* see EXTRICATE 2
rel alleviate, lighten, relieve
con depress, oppress, weigh
ant encumber

disenfranchise *vb syn* see DISFRANCHISE

disengage *vb* **1** *syn* see DETACH
rel free, liberate, release
con associate, connect, join, link, unite
ant engage
2 *syn* see LOOSE 3

disentangle *vb syn* see EXTRICATE 2
rel detach, disengage; part, separate, sever, sunder

---

con enmesh, involve
ant entangle, tangle

disenthrall *vb syn* see FREE

disenthrone *vb syn* see DEPOSE 1

disentranced *adj syn* see SOPHISTICATED 2

disentwine *vb syn* see EXTRICATE 2

disesteem *vb syn* see DISAPPROVE 1

disesteem *n syn* see DISGRACE
ant esteem

disfashion *vb syn* see DEFACE

disfavor *n* **1** *syn* see DISLIKE
rel distrust, mistrust
con approbation, approval; admiration, esteem, liking, regard, respect
ant favor
2 *syn* see DISGRACE

disfavor *vb syn* see DISAPPROVE 1
con accept, approbate, approve, countenance, go (for), hold (with)
ant favor

disfeature *vb syn* see DEFACE

disfigure *vb syn* see DEFACE
ant adorn

disfranchise *vb* to deprive of a legal right and especially of the right to vote <people subtly *disfranchised* by community apathy>
syn disenfranchise
rel deprive, take away
ant affranchise, enfranchise, franchise

disgorge *vb* **1** *syn* see VOMIT
2 *syn* see ERUPT 2

disgrace *n* the state of one who has lost esteem and good repute <retired in *disgrace* after the scandal became public>
syn contempt, discredit, disesteem, disfavor, dishonor, disrepute, ignominy, infamy, obloquy, odium, opprobrium, shame
rel abasement, debasement, debasing, degradation, humbling, humiliation; black eye, blot, brand, spot, stain, stigma
con admiration, regard; awe, fear, reverence; fame, glory, honor, renown, repute
ant esteem, respect

disgraceful *adj syn* see DISREPUTABLE 1
ant respectable; respectworthy

disgracious *adj syn* see RUDE 6
ant gracious

disgrade *vb syn* see DEGRADE 1

disgruntled *adj syn* see DISCONTENTED

disguise *vb* to alter so as to hide the true appearance or character of <*disguised* herself with a wig> <*disguised* his anger behind a false geniality>
syn camouflage, cloak, dissemble, dissimulate, dress up, mask
rel conceal, hide; obfuscate, obscure; belie, falsify, garble, misrepresent; affect, assume, counterfeit, feign, pretend, sham, simulate
con display, exhibit, expose, flaunt, parade, show; betray, disclose, discover, reveal

disguise *n* **1** *syn* see MASK 2
rel deception, delusion; speciousness
2 *syn* see PRETENSE 2

disguised *adj syn* see INTOXICATED 1

disguisement *n syn* see MASK 2

disgust *vb* to be offensive to the taste or sensibilities of <the sight of filth *disgusted* him>
syn nauseate, reluct, repel, repulse, revolt, sicken

---

syn synonym(s)   *rel* related word(s)
ant antonym(s)   *con* contrasted word(s)
idiom idiomatic equivalent(s)
‖ use limited; if in doubt, see a dictionary

rel offend, outrage
idiom make one sick, stick in one's craw (*or* crop *or* gizzard), turn one's stomach
con charm, entice, tempt; delight, gratify, please, rejoice, tickle

disgusted *adj syn* see FED UP

disgusting *adj syn* see OFFENSIVE

‖**dish** *vb syn* see CHAT 1

disharmonic *adj syn* see DISSONANT 1
ant harmonic, harmonious

disharmonious *adj syn* see DISSONANT 1
ant harmonic, harmonious

disharmonize *vb syn* see CLASH 2
ant harmonize

disharmony *n syn* see DISCORD
ant harmony

dishearten *vb syn* see DISCOURAGE 1
ant hearten

disheartening *adj syn* see GLOOMY 3
rel despondent, pessimistic
con encouraging, optimistic
ant heartening

disheveled *adj syn* see SLOVENLY 1

dishonest *adj* 1 unworthy of trust or belief <made a *dishonest* report on their progress>
syn deceitful, knavish, lying, mendacious, roguish, shifty, unhonest, untruthful
rel crooked, devious, furtive, oblique; faithless, false, perfidious, untrustworthy; cheating, cozening, ‖cronk, defrauding, double-dealing, fraudulent, swindling, two-faced; insidious, tricky
con conscientious, honorable, just, scrupulous, upright; aboveboard, forthright, straightforward; candid, fair, frank, open, plain; dependable, reliable, sure, trustworthy, trusty
ant honest
2 *syn* see CROOKED 2

dishonesty *n syn* see DECEPTION 1

dishonor *n syn* see DISGRACE
con reverence, veneration; authority, credit, influence, prestige, weight
ant honor

dishonorable *adj syn* see DISREPUTABLE 1
ant honorable

dish out *vb syn* see GIVE 3

dishy *adj syn* see BEAUTIFUL

disillusioned *adj syn* see SOPHISTICATED 2
con beguiled, deceived, deluded, misled

disimpassioned *adj syn* see COOL 2
ant heated, impassioned

disimprison *vb syn* see FREE
ant imprison

disimprove *vb syn* see DETERIORATE 1
ant improve

disinclination *n syn* see DISLIKE
ant inclination

disinclined *adj* lacking the will or desire to do something <*disinclined* to accept her story>
syn afraid, averse, backward, hesitant, indisposed, loath, reluctant, shy, uneager, unwilling, unwishful
rel antipathetic, unsympathetic; doubtful, dubious; opposing, resisting; balking, boggling, shying, sticking, stickling; objecting, protesting
con anxious, avid, eager, keen; disposed, predisposed, ready, willing

ant inclined

disingenuous *adj* lacking in candor and often giving a false appearance of simple frankness <had a *disingenuous* way of asking for advice when he really wanted help>
syn uncandid, unfrank
rel false, feigned, insincere, left-handed; artful, crafty, cunning, foxy, guileful, insidious, sly, tricky, wily; devious, indirect, oblique
con artless, naive, natural, simple, unsophisticated; candid, frank, open, plain; sincere, unfeigned; aboveboard, direct, straightforward
ant ingenuous

disinherit *vb* 1 to deprive (an heir apparent) of the right to inherit <the father *disinherited* his wayward son in his will>
syn cut off
rel disown, repudiate; dispossess
idiom cut off without a cent
2 *syn* see DEPRIVE 2

disinhume *vb syn* see EXHUME
ant inhume

disintegrate *vb* 1 *syn* see DECAY
rel deliquesce; disperse, dissipate, scatter
con articulate, concatenate; blend, coalesce, fuse, merge; associate, combine, conjoin, connect, join, link, unite
2 *syn* see DETERIORATE 1

disinter *vb syn* see EXHUME
ant inter

disinterest *n syn* see APATHY 2
ant interest

disinterested *adj* 1 *syn* see INDIFFERENT 2
rel negative, neutral
con concerned, curious; fervent, impassioned, passionate
ant interested
2 *syn* see NEUTRAL
rel fair, just, impartial, unbiased
con biased, prejudiced; involved
ant concerned

disject *vb syn* see STREW 1

disjoin *vb syn* see SEPARATE 1

disjoint *vb* 1 *syn* see SEPARATE 1
2 *syn* see DISORDER 1

disjointed *adj syn* see INCOHERENT 2

dislike *n* a state of mind or feeling marked by an inner avoidance of something usually felt as unpleasant or repugnant <a pronounced *dislike* for mathematics>
syn aversion, bad books, disfavor, disinclination, disliking, displeasure, disrelish, dissatisfaction, distaste, indisposition
rel detestation, hate, hatred; deprecation, disapproval; prejudice, scunner
idiom ‖a derry on
con affection, attachment, love; partiality, predilection, preference
ant liking

disliking *n syn* see DISLIKE
ant liking

dislimb *vb syn* see MAIM

dislimn *vb syn* see OBSCURE

dislocate *vb* 1 *syn* see DISORDER 1
2 *syn* see MOVE 4

disloyal *adj syn* see FAITHLESS
rel alienated, disaffected, estranged
ant loyal

disloyalty n 1 syn see INFIDELITY
   ant loyalty
   2 syn see TREACHERY
   ant loyalty
dismal adj syn see GLOOMY 3
   con animated, gay, lively; cheerful
dismals n pl, used with the syn see SADNESS
dismantle vb 1 syn see STRIP 2
   con appoint, equip, outfit
   2 syn see DESTROY 1
   3 syn see REVOKE 2
   4 syn see DISMOUNT
dismay n syn see FEAR 1
   con aplomb, assurance, confidence, self-
possession; mettle, resolution, spirit
dismay vb 1 to unnerve and check by arousing fear, apprehension, or aversion <*dismayed* by the task that lay ahead>
   syn appall, consternate, daunt, horrify,
shake
   rel bewilder, confound, dumbfound, mystify, nonplus, perplex, puzzle; abash, discomfit, disconcert, embarrass, faze, rattle;
discourage, dishearten; affright, alarm,
frighten, scare, terrify
   idiom set one back on one's heels, take
aback
   con assure, ensure, secure; excite, galvanize,
pique, provoke, quicken, stimulate
   2 syn see DISCOMPOSE 1
dismayed adj syn see AGHAST 2
   rel discomfited, disconcerted, fazed, rattled
   ant undismayed
dismember vb 1 syn see MAIM
   rel part, separate, sever, sunder
   2 syn see DISMOUNT
dismiss vb 1 syn see DIVORCE 2
   2 syn see DECLINE 4
   3 to let go from one's employ or service
<during the recession thousands of em-
ployees were *dismissed*>
   syn ax, boot (out), bounce, ‖can, cashier,
discharge, disemploy, drop, fire, kick out, let
out, sack, terminate, turn off
   rel depose, deselect, displace, furlough, lay
off, remove, retire, suspend, unseat; reject,
turn away; riff
   idiom give one the gate (*or* one's walking
papers), let go; give the ax (*or* the can) to
   con hire; contract, engage; get, obtain,
procure, secure
   ant employ
   4 syn see EJECT 1
   rel cast, discard, shed, slough
   idiom send one to Coventry
   5 to refuse to consider seriously <*dismisses*
the other performers as mere amateurs>
   syn kiss off, pooh-pooh
   rel deride, mock, rally, ridicule, taunt, twit;
flout, gibe, gird, jeer, scoff; contemn, despise, disdain, scorn, scout; reject
dismissive adj syn see PROUD 1
dismount vb to take down or apart from an
assembled position <*dismount* a revolver for
cleaning>

   syn disassemble, dismantle, dismember,
take down
   rel detach, disengage; disconnect, disjoin,
disunite, separate
   idiom take apart, take to pieces
   con assemble, construct, put together; combine, unite
disobedient adj refusing or neglecting to
obey <the *disobedient* child refused to come
in>
   syn naughty, obstreperous, unruly; *compare*
CONTRARY 3, NAUGHTY 1
   rel headstrong, recalcitrant, willful; contumacious, insubordinate, rebellious
   con amenable, biddable, docile, tractable;
decorous, good, well-behaved
   ant obedient
disoblige vb syn see INCONVENIENCE
   con accommodate, convenience, favor
   ant oblige
disorder n 1 syn see CONFUSION 3
   con orderliness; pattern, plan
   ant order
   2 breach of public order <the overthrow of
the government caused *disorder* in the coun-
try>
   syn anarchism, anarchy, distemper, misrule, riot
   rel anomie; agitation, commotion, convulsion, tumult, turbulence, turmoil, upheaval
   ant order
   3 syn see DISEASE 1
   4 syn see SICKNESS 1
disorder vb 1 to undo the fixed or proper
order of something <*disorder* the carefully
arranged contents of a drawer>
   syn derange, disarrange, disarray, discompose, disjoint, dislocate, disorganize, disrupt, distemper, disturb, jumble, ‖mam-
mock, mess (up), mix up, muddle, muss
(up), ‖mux, rummage, shuffle, tumble, unsettle, upset; *compare* CONFUSE 5
   rel ball up, embroil; dishevel, rumple
   idiom make hay of
   con arrange, marshal, methodize, organize,
systematize; align, array, line, line up, range;
adjust, fix, regulate
   ant order
   2 syn see UPSET 5
disordered adj 1 syn see INCOHERENT 2
   2 syn see INSANE 1
disorderly adj syn see TURBULENT 1
disorderly house n syn see BROTHEL
disorganize vb syn see DISORDER 1
   ant organize
disown vb syn see DISCLAIM
   ant own
disparage vb 1 syn see DECRY 2
   ant applaud
   2 syn see DISCOURAGE 1
disparagement n 1 syn see DETRACTION
   rel animadversion, aspersion, reflection,
stricture
   2 syn see DESPITE 1
disparaging adj syn see DEROGATORY
   rel underestimating, underrating, undervaluing
   con acclaiming, extolling, praising; exalting,
magnifying
disparate adj syn see DIFFERENT 1

---

syn synonym(s)	*rel* related word(s)
ant antonym(s)	*con* contrasted word(s)
idiom idiomatic equivalent(s)	
‖ use limited; if in doubt, see a dictionary	

rel discordant, discrepant, incompatible, inconsistent, inconsonant; distinct, separate
ant analogous, comparable

disparity *n* the state of being different (as in degree, rank, excellence, or number) <the *disparity* between the rich and the poor> <their stories showed significant *disparity*>
syn disproportion, imparity, inequality, unevenness
rel alterity, difference, dissemblance, dissimilarity, dissimilitude, distinction, divergence, divergency, otherness, unlikeness
con adequation, equality, equatability, equivalence, equivalency, sameness; correlation, correspondence, likeness; evenness
ant parity

dispassionate *adj* 1 *syn* see NEUTRAL
rel imperturbable, unflappable, unruffled
con fervent, vehement; intemperate
2 *syn* see FAIR 4
rel aloof, indifferent; frank, open; aboveboard, straightforward

dispatch *vb* 1 *syn* see SEND 1
rel hasten, quicken, speed
2 *syn* see KILL 1
3 *syn* see EAT UP 1

dispatch *n* 1 *syn* see HASTE 1
con dawdling, loitering, procrastination
ant delay
2 *syn* see ALACRITY
rel diligence, industriousness

dispeace *n* *syn* see DISCORD

dispel *vb* *syn* see SCATTER 1
rel dismiss, eject, expel, oust; crumble, disintegrate

dispensable *adj* capable of being dispensed with <many household gadgets are readily *dispensable*>
syn nonessential, unessential, unrequired
rel needless, unnecessary, unneeded; minor, trivial, unimportant
con essential, imperative, necessary, necessitous, required; vital
ant indispensable

dispensation *n* *syn* see FAVOR 4

dispense *vb* 1 *syn* see DISTRIBUTE 1
2 *syn* see GIVE 3
rel portion, prorate
3 *syn* see ADMINISTER 2
4 *syn* see HANDLE 2
5 *syn* see EXEMPT

disperse *vb* 1 *syn* see SCATTER 1
rel discharge, dismiss
con call, cite, convene, convoke, summon
ant assemble, congregate; collect
2 *syn* see DISTRIBUTE 1
3 *syn* see SPREAD 1
4 *syn* see DISBAND

dispirit *vb* *syn* see DISCOURAGE 1
idiom dampen (*or* lower) one's spirits
ant inspirit

dispirited *adj* *syn* see DOWNCAST
rel melancholy, sad
ant high-spirited, inspirited

dispiriting *adj* *syn* see GLOOMY 3
rel dejecting, distressing; oppressing
ant inspiriting

displace *vb* 1 *syn* see BANISH
2 *syn* see DEPOSE 1
3 *syn* see SUPPLANT 1

displaced person *n* *syn* see REFUGEE

displacement *n* *syn* see EXILE 1

display *vb* 1 *syn* see OPEN 2
rel demonstrate, evidence, evince, lay out, manifest, show
con camouflage, cloak, disguise, dissemble, mask; conceal, hide, secrete
2 *syn* see SHOW 4
3 *syn* see SHOW 1

display *n* 1 *syn* see EXHIBITION 1
2 a striking or spectacular exhibition <a parvenu's *display* of wealth>
syn array, fanfare, panoply, parade, pomp, shine, show
rel ostentation, ostentatiousness, pretension, pretentiousness, showiness; setout

displeasing *adj* *syn* see BAD 8
rel annoying, bothersome, irksome, vexing
con agreeable, gratifying, pleasant
ant pleasing

displeasure *n* *syn* see DISLIKE
rel anger; vexation
con delight, enjoyment
ant pleasure

disponible *adj* *syn* see AVAILABLE 1

disport *n* *syn* see PLAY 1
rel jollity, merriment

disport *vb* 1 *syn* see SHOW 4
2 *syn* see BEHAVE 1
3 *syn* see PLAY 1

disposal *n* 1 *syn* see ORDER 3
2 the act of ridding oneself of something <incinerators used for the *disposal* of trash>
syn discarding, disposition, dumping, jettison, junking, relegation, riddance, scrapping, throwing away
rel chucking, clearance; demolishing, demolition, destroying, destruction
con acquirement, acquisition; accumulation, collection, cumulation, deposit, hoard, trove

dispose *vb* 1 *syn* see INCLINE 3
ant indispose
2 *syn* see ORDER 1

disposed *adj* *syn* see WILLING 1
ant indisposed

disposition *n* 1 *syn* see DISPOSAL 2
rel control, controlling, direction, management
2 *syn* see ORDER 3
3 the complex of especially mental and emotional qualities that distinguish an individual <a man of irritable *disposition*>
syn character, complexion, humor, individualism, individuality, makeup, nature, personality, temper, temperament
rel mood, tone, vein; cast, stamp, tenor, type; being; identity
idiom frame of mind
4 *syn* see LEANING 2

dispossess *vb* *syn* see DEPRIVE 2
con provide, supply

dispossession *n* *syn* see PRIVATION 2

dispraise *vb* *syn* see DECRY 2
ant praise

disproportion *n* *syn* see DISPARITY

disproportional *adj* *syn* see LOPSIDED

disproportionate *adj* *syn* see LOPSIDED
ant proportionate

disprove *vb* 1 to show by presenting evidence that something is not true <the defendant's claims were *disproved* by the testimony>
syn break, confound, confute, controvert, disconfirm, evert, rebut, refute
rel contravene, impugn, negative, traverse; overthrow, overturn
con evidence, show; demonstrate, display, illustrate, manifest; argue, bespeak, tell
ant prove
2 *syn* see DISCREDIT 2

disputable *adj syn* see MOOT
disputation *n syn* see ARGUMENTATION
disputatious *adj syn* see CONTENTIOUS 2
dispute *vb* 1 *syn* see ARGUE 2
con give in, surrender
2 *syn* see DISCUSS 1
rel confute, controvert, disprove, rebut, refute
con allow, grant
ant concede
3 *syn* see QUESTION 2
4 *syn* see RESIST
dispute *n* 1 *syn* see ARGUMENT 2
rel conflict, discord, dissension, strife
2 *syn* see QUARREL
disqualified *adj syn* see UNFIT 2
ant qualified
disqualify *vb* to deprive of a power, right, or privilege <a conviction of perjury *disqualified* him from being a witness>
syn disable, disenable, incapacitate
rel bar, bate, debar, eliminate, except, exclude, rule out, suspend
con empower, enable
ant qualify
disquiet *vb syn* see DISCOMPOSE 1
rel distress, trouble
con calm, compose, lull, still
ant quiet, soothe, tranquilize
disquiet *n* 1 *syn* see CARE 2
ant quiet
2 *syn* see UNREST
ant quiet
disquietude *n* 1 *syn* see CARE 2
2 *syn* see UNREST
ant quietness, quietude
disquisition *n syn* see DISCOURSE 2
rel inquiry, investigation; argumentation, debate, disputation
disquisitive *adj syn* see INQUISITIVE 1
disrate *vb syn* see DEGRADE 1
disregard *vb syn* see NEGLECT
con attend, mind, tend, watch; note, notice, observe, remark
ant regard
disregard *n syn* see APATHY 2
rel forgetting, ignoring, neglecting, omission, omitting, overlooking, slighting
con consideration, thoughtfulness
disregardful *adj syn* see NEGLIGENT
ant regardful
disrelish *n syn* see DISLIKE
ant relish
disremember *vb syn* see FORGET 1

disreputable *adj* 1 not reputable or decent <was punished for his *disreputable* conduct>
syn discreditable, disgraceful, dishonorable, ignominious, inglorious, shabby, shady, shameful, shoddy, unrespectable
rel abject, mean, sordid; beggarly, cheap, contemptible, despicable, pitiable, scurvy, sorry
con admirable, creditable, estimable, honorable, respectable
ant reputable
2 *syn* see SHABBY 1
disrepute *n syn* see DISGRACE
ant repute
disrespect *n syn* see INSOLENCE
ant respect
disrespectful *adj syn* see RUDE 6
ant respectful
disrobe *vb* 1 *syn* see STRIP 1
2 *syn* see STRIP 2
disrupt *vb* 1 *syn* see OPEN 3
2 *syn* see DISORDER 1
dissatisfaction *n syn* see DISLIKE
ant satisfaction
dissatisfactory *adj syn* see BAD 1
ant satisfactory
dissatisfied *adj syn* see DISCONTENTED
rel annoyed, bothered, irked, vexed
con content, contented, gratified
ant satisfied
dissect *vb* 1 *syn* see SEPARATE 1
2 *syn* see CUT 5
rel penetrate, pierce, probe
3 *syn* see ANALYZE
dissection *n syn* see ANALYSIS 1
rel examination, inspection, review, scrutiny; criticism, critique
dissemblance *n syn* see DISSIMILARITY
ant resemblance, semblance
dissemblance *n syn* see DECEIT 1
dissemble *vb syn* see DISGUISE
con demonstrate, evidence, evince, manifest, show
dissembler *n syn* see HYPOCRITE
disseminate *vb* 1 *syn* see SPREAD 1
2 *syn* see DECLARE 1
3 *syn* see STREW 1
dissension *n syn* see DISCORD
rel altercation, bickering, quarrel, wrangle; argument, controversy, dispute
con amity, friendship, goodwill
ant accord; comity
dissent *vb syn* see DIFFER 2
rel balk, boggle, demur, shy, stickle
con accede, acquiesce, agree, subscribe
ant assent; concur
dissent *n* 1 *syn* see DISCORD
2 *syn* see HERESY
rel disagreement, nonagreement, nonconcurrence
dissenter *n syn* see HERETIC
dissert *vb syn* see DISCOURSE 1
dissertate *vb syn* see DISCOURSE 1
dissertation *n syn* see DISCOURSE 1
rel exposition; argumentation, disputation
dissever *vb syn* see SEPARATE 1
2 *syn* see CUT 5
dissidence *n* 1 *syn* see DISCORD
2 *syn* see HERESY

---

syn synonym(s)   *rel* related word(s)
ant antonym(s)   *con* contrasted word(s)
idiom idiomatic equivalent(s)
|| use limited; if in doubt, see a dictionary

dissident adj syn see HERETICAL

dissident n syn see HERETIC

dissimilar adj syn see DIFFERENT 1
rel antithetical, antonymous, contradictory, contrary, opposite
ant similar

dissimilarity n lack of agreement or correspondence or an instance of this <the *dissimilarities* in the cultures of the two countries>
syn alterity, difference, discrepancy, dissemblance, dissimilitude, distance, distinction, divarication, divergence, divergency, otherness, unlikeness
rel disparity, diversity; discordance, incongruity, inconsistency, inconsonance; discord, variance; severance; offset; margin
con affinity, analogy, likeness, resemblance, similitude; accordance, congruity, consistency, consonance; agreement, conformity, correspondence
ant similarity

dissimilitude n syn see DISSIMILARITY
ant similitude

dissimulate vb syn see DISGUISE

dissimulation n syn see DECEIT 1
rel camouflaging, cloaking, disguising, dissembling, masking; concealing, hiding, secreting; feigning, pretending, pretense, shamming; hypocrisy, pharisaism, sanctimony

dissimulator n syn see HYPOCRITE

dissipate vb 1 syn see SCATTER 1
rel crumble, disintegrate
ant accumulate; concentrate (as efforts, thoughts)
2 syn see WASTE 2
rel disappear, evanesce, evaporate, vanish
ant absorb (as time, attention)

dissipation n syn see ENTERTAINMENT

dissociate vb syn see DETACH
rel alienate, estrange
ant associate

dissolute adj syn see ABANDONED 2
rel lax, light, loose, slack, wanton, wayward; fast, raffish, rakish, wild

dissolution n 1 syn see SEPARATION 1
2 syn see DEATH 1

dissolve vb 1 syn see DESTROY 1
2 syn see ADJOURN 2
3 syn see ANNUL 4
4 syn see LIQUEFY
5 syn see SOLVE 2
6 syn see DISBAND

dissonance n syn see DISCORD

dissonant adj 1 marked by a mingling of discordant sounds <the two bands playing different pieces at the same time sounded *dissonant*>
syn cacophonic, cacophonous, discordant, disharmonic, disharmonious, immusical, inharmonic, inharmonious, rude, unharmonious, unmusical
rel grating, harsh, hoarse, jarring, raucous, rugged, strident
con blending, chiming, concerted, harmonic, symphonious; euphonious, harmonious, mellifluous, mellow, melodious, musical; agreeable, pleasing
ant consonant

2 syn see INCONSONANT 1

dissuade vb to turn one aside from a purpose, a project, or a plan <they tried to *dissuade* a friend from making a mistake>
syn deter, disadvise, discourage, divert
rel derail, throw off; advise, counsel; exhort, prick, urge
idiom talk out of
con get, induce, prevail; affect, influence, touch
ant persuade

distance n 1 an extent of areal or linear measure <he did not know the *distance* he had walked>
syn length, stretch
rel area, extent; ambit, compass, extension, orbit, purview, radius, range, reach, scope, sweep
2 the length of a literal or figurative course traversed or to be traversed <she had come a long *distance* from her pitiful beginnings>
syn way, ways
rel extent, size; piece, spell
3 syn see EXPANSE
4 syn see DISSIMILARITY

distance vb syn see OUTSTRIP 1

distant adj 1 not close in space, time, or relationship <traveling to a more *distant* place> <the *distant* days of the Pilgrim fathers> <a *distant* cousin>
syn far, faraway, far-flung, far-off, off-lying, outlying, remote, removed
rel apart, isolated, obscure, out-of-the-way, retired, secret; secluded, sequestered
idiom at a distance
con close, near, nearby, next, nigh; adjacent, adjoining, contiguous
2 syn see DIFFERENT 1
3 syn see UNSOCIABLE
rel arrogant, haughty, proud; modest, retiring, shy
con forward, presuming, ‖pushy, self-assertive

distaste n syn see DISLIKE
rel abhorrence, repugnance, repulsion, revulsion; antipathy, hostility
con relish, zest; appetite, desire; enjoyment
ant taste

distasteful adj 1 syn see UNPALATABLE 1
ant tasteful, tasty
2 syn see BITTER 2
rel obnoxious, repellent, repugnant, repulsive; abominable, detestable, hateful, odious
con agreeable, grateful, gratifying, pleasant, pleasing, welcome

distemper vb syn see DISORDER 1

distemper n syn see DISORDER 2

distend vb syn see EXPAND 3
rel augment, enlarge, increase; extend, lengthen
ant constrict

disthrone vb syn see DEPOSE 1

distill vb syn see DRIP

distinct adj 1 capable of being distinguished as differing <the novel has two related, but nevertheless *distinct*, plots>
syn different, discrete, diverse, separate, several, various
rel distinctive, individual, peculiar; particular, single, sole; especial, individual, special, specific; disparate, dissimilar, divergent

con identical, same, selfsame; corresponding, equivalent, like, similar
ant indistinguishable
2 *syn* see CLEAR 5
rel defined, prescribed; categorical, definite, explicit, express, specific; lucid, perspicuous; clear-cut, incisive, trenchant
con faint, obscure
ant indistinct; nebulous
distinction *n* 1 *syn* see DISSIMILARITY
con affinity, analogy, likeness, similarity, similitude
ant indistinction, resemblance
2 *syn* see EMINENCE 1
3 *syn* see HONOR 2
distinctive *adj syn* see CHARACTERISTIC
rel separate, single, unique; discrete, distinct, several
con common, familiar, ordinary, popular, vulgar; alike, analogous, comparable, identical, like, parallel; equal, equivalent, same
distinctively *adv syn* see ESPECIALLY 1
distinctiveness *n syn* see INDIVIDUALITY 3
distingué *adj syn* see GENTEEL 1
distinguish *vb* 1 *syn* see KNOW 4
rel divide, part; detach, disengage; demarcate, set off
con confuse, mistake
ant confound
2 *syn* see EXALT 1
3 *syn* see CHARACTERIZE 2
idiom set apart
4 *syn* see SEE 1
5 *syn* see IDENTIFY
distinguished *adj syn* see FAMOUS 2
rel courtly, dignified, grand, imposing, stately
ant undistinguished
distort *vb* 1 *syn* see MISREPRESENT
rel misconstrue, misinterpret; alter, change
2 *syn* see DEFORM
rel bend, curve, twist
distortion *n syn* see DEFORMITY
distract *vb* 1 *syn* see CONFUSE 2
2 *syn* see MADDEN 1
distracted *adj syn* see DISTRAUGHT
distraction *n* 1 *syn* see INSANITY 1
2 *syn* see ENTERTAINMENT
distrait *adj* 1 *syn* see ABSTRACTED
2 *syn* see DISTRAUGHT
distraught *adj* 1 agitated with doubt or mental conflict <*distraught* over the health of her child>
syn distracted, distrait, distressed, harassed, tormented, troubled, worried
rel agitated, concerned, discomposed, flustered, perturbed, upset; addled, confused, muddled; bewildered, nonplussed
idiom beside oneself
con composed, cool, imperturbable, nonchalant, unflappable, unruffled; calm, tranquil; unconcerned, undisturbed, unworried
ant collected
2 *syn* see INSANE 1

distress *n* the state of being in serious trouble or in mental or physical anguish <in great *distress* over the decision she had to make>
syn agony, dolor, misery, passion, suffering
rel affliction, cross, trial, tribulation, visitation; anguish, grief, heartbreak, sorrow, woe; exigency, pass, pinch, strait; difficulty, hardship, rigor, vicissitude; ache, pain, pang, throe, twinge
con comfort, comforting, consolation, solace, solacing; allaying, alleviation, assuagement, ease, relief, relieving; peace, security, tranquility
distress *vb* 1 *syn* see TRY 2
rel afflict, rack, torment, torture
con allay, alleviate, assuage, lighten, mitigate, relieve
2 to cause pain or suffering to <the death of his longtime friend *distressed* him deeply>
syn aggrieve, constrain, grieve, hurt, injure, pain
rel harass, strain, stress, try, trouble; depress, oppress, weigh
con comfort, console, solace; aid, assist, help
3 *syn* see TROUBLE 1
rel annoy, harry, pester, plague
distressed *adj syn* see DISTRAUGHT
distressing *adj syn* see DEPLORABLE
distribute *vb* 1 to give out, usually in shares, to each member of a group <*distributed* his possessions among his heirs>
syn deal, disburse, dispense, disperse, divide, ‖divvy, dole (out), lot (out), measure (out), partition
rel allocate, allot, apportion, assign, mete (out); parcel, portion, prorate, ration; administer, dribble; bestow, donate, give, present
con assemble, gather; accumulate, hoard
ant amass; collect
2 *syn* see SPREAD 1
distribution *n syn* see ORDER 3
district *n* 1 *syn* see QUARTER 2
2 *syn* see LOCALITY 1
rel division, region
distrust *vb* to have no trust or confidence in <he *distrusted* most politicians>
syn doubt, misdoubt, mistrust, suspect, ‖suspicion
rel disbelieve, discredit, unbelieve
con bank, count, depend, reckon, rely; commit, confide, consign, entrust
ant trust
distrustful *adj syn* see SUSPICIOUS 2
distrustfully *adv syn* see ASKANCE 2
disturb *vb* 1 *syn* see MOVE 4
2 *syn* see DISCOMPOSE 1
rel alarm, frighten, scare, terrify; bewilder, distract, perplex, puzzle; discommode, incommode, inconvenience, trouble
3 *syn* see DISORDER 1
rel displace, replace; move, remove, shift; interfere, intermeddle, meddle, tamper
con establish, fix, set, settle; adjust, regulate
disunify *vb syn* see ESTRANGE
disunion *n* 1 *syn* see SEPARATION 1
2 *syn* see DISCORD
disunite *vb* 1 *syn* see SEPARATE 1
2 *syn* see ESTRANGE

---

syn synonym(s)   *rel* related word(s)
ant antonym(s)   *con* contrasted word(s)
idiom idiomatic equivalent(s)
‖ use limited; if in doubt, see a dictionary

disunity *n syn* see DISCORD
disusage *n syn* see DISUSE
disuse *n* cessation of use, practice, or exercise
<to keep the mind from falling into *disuse*, one must exercise one's reading abilities>
<his muscles became atrophied from *disuse*>
  syn desuetude, disusage
  con appliance, application, employment, operation, play, usance; exercise
  ant use
disused *adj syn* see OBSOLETE
ditch *n syn* see TRENCH
ditch *vb* 1 *syn* see DISCARD
  ‖2 *syn* see HIDE
‖**dite** *n syn* see PARTICLE
dither *vb* 1 *syn* see SHAKE 1
  2 *syn* see HESITATE
  3 *syn* see CHAT 1
dither *n* 1 *syn* see JITTERS
  2 *syn* see COMMOTION 2
dithyrambic *adj syn* see IMPASSIONED
ditto *n syn* see REPRODUCTION
ditty *n syn* see SONG 2
diurnal *adj syn* see DAILY
  ant nocturnal
diuturnal *adj syn* see LASTING
divagate *vb syn* see DIGRESS 2
divagation *n syn* see DIGRESSION
divarication *n syn* see DISSIMILARITY
dive *vb syn* see PLUNGE 2
  rel bound, jump, leap, spring; impel, move
dive *n* a shabby or disreputable place for drinking or entertainment <got a schooner of beer at the *dive* down the street>
  syn barrelhouse, hangout, honky-tonk, joint
  rel dump, hole; bar, barroom, lounge, pothouse, pub, saloon, taproom, tavern
‖**diver** *n syn* see PICKPOCKET
diverge *vb* 1 *syn* see SWERVE 2
  rel differ, disagree, vary; divide, part, separate
  ant converge; conform
  2 *syn* see DIGRESS 2
divergence *n* 1 *syn* see DISSIMILARITY
  rel diversity, variety
  con accord, concord, consonance, harmony
  ant conformity; correspondence
  2 *syn* see DEVIATION 1
  rel division, parting, separation; differing, disagreeing, varying
  con agreement, coincidence, concurrence
  ant convergence
divergency *n syn* see DISSIMILARITY
divergent *adj* 1 *syn* see DIFFERENT 1
  rel antithetical, contradictory, contrary, opposite; aberrant, abnormal, atypical
  con alike, identical, parallel, same
  ant convergent
  2 *syn* see IRREGULAR 1
divers *adj syn* see SEVERAL 3
divers *pron, pl in constr syn* see SUNDRY
diverse *adj* 1 *syn* see DIFFERENT 1
  rel contrasted, contrasting, contrastive; contradictory, contrary, opposite
  con equal, equivalent, same
  ant identical, selfsame
  2 *syn* see DISTINCT 1
  idiom of every description

3 *syn* see MANIFOLD
diversely *adv syn* see OTHERWISE 1
diverseness *n syn* see VARIETY 1
diversiform *adj syn* see MANIFOLD
diversion *n* 1 *syn* see DEVIATION 1
  2 *syn* see PLAY 1
  3 *syn* see ENTERTAINMENT
  rel frivolity, levity
  4 *syn* see ENJOYMENT 1
diversity *n syn* see VARIETY 1
  rel difference, dissimilarity, distinction, divergence, divergency, unlikeness
  ant uniformity; identity
divert *vb* 1 *syn* see TURN 6
  rel swerve; alter, change, modify
  con fix, set, settle
  2 *syn* see DISSUADE
  rel abstract, detach, disengage
  3 *syn* see AMUSE
  rel delight, gladden, please, regale, tickle
divertissement *n syn* see ENTERTAINMENT
divest *vb* 1 *syn* see STRIP 2
  ant invest, vest; apparel, attire, clothe
  2 *syn* see DEPRIVE 2
  rel despoil, plunder, spoil
  ant invest, vest
divestiture *n syn* see PRIVATION 2
divide *vb* 1 *syn* see SEPARATE 1
  rel carve, chop, cut
  ant unite
  2 *syn* see DISTRIBUTE 1
  3 *syn* see APPORTION 2
  rel allocate, allot, assign
  4 *syn* see DIFFER 2
  rel part, separate
  con combine, concur, conjoin, cooperate
  ant unite
dividend *n syn* see REWARD
divine *n syn* see CLERGYMAN
divine *vb syn* see FORESEE
divine *adj* 1 of or relating to God or a god
<the *divine* will>
  syn deific, godly
  rel chthonian
  2 like or like that of God or a god <men who aspire to *divine* honors>
  syn deific, godlike
  rel extramundane, superhuman, superphysical, transmundane
  3 *syn* see MARVELOUS 1
division *n* 1 *syn* see PART 1
  2 *syn* see SEPARATION 1
  3 *syn* see DISCORD
divorce *n syn* see SEPARATION 1
divorce *vb* 1 *syn* see SEPARATE 1
  rel disaffect, wean
  2 to end a marriage by legal action <unable to agree, they decided to *divorce*><*divorced* his wife>
  syn dismiss, put away, unmarry
  rel break up, separate, split; annul, cancel
divorcement *n syn* see SEPARATION 1
divulge *vb syn* see REVEAL 1
  rel proclaim; gossip, tattle
‖**divvy** *vb* 1 *syn* see DISTRIBUTE 1
  2 *syn* see APPORTION 2
‖**dizzard** *n syn* see DUNCE
dizzy *adj* 1 *syn* see GIDDY 1
  rel asinine, fatuous, foolish; inane

2 affected by a sensation of being whirled about or around <the speed with which she dispatched her tasks made the onlookers *dizzy*>
syn giddy, light, light-headed, swimming, swimmy, vertiginous
rel reeling, whirling; bewildered, confounded, distracted, puzzled; addled, befuddled, confused, dazed, dazzled, fuddled, muddled
idiom with spots before one's eyes
3 *syn* see EXCESSIVE 1
dizzy *vb syn* see CONFUSE 2
do *vb* 1 *syn* see PERFORM 2
  2 *syn* see CLOSE 3
  3 *syn* see ACT 1
  4 *syn* see CHEAT
  idiom do out of, sell one a bill of goods
  5 *syn* see COOK 1
  6 *syn* see BEHAVE 1
  7 *syn* see SHIFT 5
  8 *syn* see HAPPEN 1
  9 *syn* see TRAVEL 2
  10 *syn* see SERVE 3
  11 *syn* see SERVE 5
‖**do** *n syn* see SUCCESS
doable *adj syn* see POSSIBLE 1
doc *n syn* see PHYSICIAN
docile *adj syn* see OBEDIENT
  rel adaptable, pliable, pliant
  con obstinate, self-willed, stubborn, willful
  ant indocile; ungovernable, unruly
‖**docious** *adj syn* see OBEDIENT
dock *n syn* see WHARF
docket *n syn* see PROGRAM 1
doctor *n syn* see PHYSICIAN
doctor *vb* 1 *syn* see TREAT 4
  2 *syn* see MEND 2
  3 *syn* see ADULTERATE
doctrinaire *adj syn* see DICTATORIAL
  rel bullheaded, dogged, mulish, obstinate, pertinacious, pigheaded, stiff-necked, stubborn
  ant undoctrinaire
doctrine *n* a principle accepted as valid and authoritative <the *doctrine* of evolution>
  syn canon, dogma, tenet
  rel instruction, teaching; axiom, basic, fundamental, principle
  idiom article of belief (*or* faith)
document *n* 1 something preserved and serving as evidence (as of an event, a situation, or the culture of a period) <ceramic and flint artifacts provide our only *document* of this ancient people>
  syn archive(s), monument, record
  rel evidence, testimony
  2 *usu* documents *pl syn* see CREDENTIALS
documentation *n syn* see CREDENTIALS
doddering *adj syn* see SENILE
doddery *adj syn* see SENILE
dodge *vb* 1 to avoid or evade by some maneuver or shift <*dodging* in and out among the crowd> <*dodged* his pursuer with ease>
  syn duck, fence, parry, shirk, sidestep

rel malinger; avoid, elude, escape, evade, skirt; slide, slip; short-circuit
  idiom fight shy of
  con banter, beard, brave, challenge, dare, defy, front, venture; confront, encounter, meet
  ant face
  2 *syn* see EQUIVOCATE 2
dodo *n syn* see DUNCE
‖**dods** *n pl syn* see SULK
‖**dodunk** *n syn* see DUNCE
doff *vb syn* see REMOVE 3
do for *vb syn* see HELP 1
dofunny *n syn* see DOODAD
dog *n* 1 a highly variable carnivorous domesticated mammal <many households have *dogs* as pets>
  syn bowwow, canine, hound, ‖pooch, tyke
  rel pup, puppy; cur, ‖feist, mongrel, mutt
  2 *syn* see SNOT
  3 *syn* see FRANKFURTER
  4 *syn* see JALOPY
dog *vb syn* see TAIL
Dogberry *n syn* see POLICEMAN
dogfall *n syn* see DRAW 4
dogfight *n syn* see BRAWL 2
dogged *adj* 1 *syn* see INFLEXIBLE 2
  2 *syn* see PERSISTENT 1
doggery *n syn* see RABBLE 2
doggish *adj syn* see DAPPER
doggone *adj* 1 *syn* see DAMNED 2
  2 *syn* see UTTER
doggy *adj syn* see DAPPER
dogma *n syn* see DOCTRINE
  rel belief, conviction, persuasion, view
dogmatic *adj* 1 *syn* see DICTATORIAL
  2 *syn* see DEDUCTIVE
dog nap *n syn* see NAP
dog's age *n syn* see AGE 2
‖**dogsbody** *n syn* see SLAVE 2
do in *vb* 1 *syn* see RUIN 1
  2 *syn* see MURDER 1
  3 *syn* see EXHAUST 4
doing *n syn* see ACTION 1
doit *n syn* see PARTICLE
doldrums *n pl* 1 *syn* see TEDIUM
  rel blues, dejection, depression, dumps, gloom; apathy, disinterest, indifference, listlessness
  con high spirits, spirits
  2 *syn* see ABEYANCE
  rel depression, retardation, slump, stagnation; inactivity
dole (out) *vb* 1 *syn* see ADMINISTER 2
  2 *syn* see DISTRIBUTE 1
‖**dole** *n* 1 *syn* see SORROW
  2 *syn* see MISFORTUNE
doleful *adj* 1 *syn* see DOWNCAST
  2 *syn* see WOEFUL 1
  3 *syn* see MELANCHOLY 2
  rel grieving, mourning, sorrowing; piteous, pitiful
  con blithe, blithesome, radiant, sparkling, sunny
  ant cheerful, cheery
dolefuls *n pl, used with the syn* see SADNESS
dolent *adj syn* see WOEFUL 1
dolesome *adj syn* see MELANCHOLY 2
dolittle *n syn* see SLUGGARD
‖**doll** *n syn* see WOMAN 1

---

syn synonym(s)   *rel* related word(s)
ant antonym(s)   *con* contrasted word(s)
idiom idiomatic equivalent(s)
‖ use limited; if in doubt, see a dictionary

dollar *n* a currency bill representing one hundred cents <had a single *dollar* left>
syn bill, ‖bone, ‖buck, ‖fish, ‖frogskin, ‖iron man, oner, rock, ‖skin, ‖smacker, ‖smackeroo

dollop *n syn* see DRAM 1

doll out *vb syn* see DRESS UP 1

doll up *vb syn* see DRESS UP 1

dolor *n syn* see DISTRESS
con blessedness, bliss, felicity, happiness
ant beatitude

dolorous *adj* 1 *syn* see DEPLORABLE
2 *syn* see WOEFUL 1
3 *syn* see MELANCHOLY 2

dolt *n syn* see DUNCE

dolthead *n syn* see DUNCE

doltish *adj syn* see STUPID 1

domain *n syn* see FIELD

‖**dome** *n syn* see HEAD 1

domestic *adj* 1 of or relating to the household or family <*domestic* chores required to maintain a home>
syn family, home, household
con civic, public; personal, private; business, occupational, professional
2 of, relating to, or carried on within an indicated or implied country <charts of *domestic* as well as foreign waters>
syn home, ‖inland, internal, intestine, municipal, national, native
ant foreign
3 *syn* see TAME

domesticate *vb* to adapt (an animal or plant) to life in intimate association with and to the advantage of man <the man who *domesticated* the first dog>
syn domesticize, domiciliate, master, tame
rel gentle, subdue; housebreak; break, bust, train

domesticated *adj syn* see TAME

domesticize *vb syn* see DOMESTICATE

domicile *n syn* see HABITATION 2

domicile *vb syn* see HARBOR 2

domiciliate *vb* 1 *syn* see HARBOR 2
2 *syn* see DOMESTICATE

dominance *n syn* see SUPREMACY

dominant *adj* 1 superior to all others in power, influence, or importance <the Sumerians were a *dominant* race of ancient times>
syn ascendant, master, overruling, overbalancing, overbearing, overweighing, paramount, predominant, predominate, preponderant, prevalent, regnant, sovereign
rel prevailing; preeminent, supreme, surpassing, transcendent; chief, first, foremost, leading, main, principal; governing, ruling
con collateral, dependent, secondary, subject, tributary; unimportant
ant subordinate
2 *syn* see CHIEF 2

dominate *vb* 1 *syn* see GOVERN 3
2 *syn* see RULE 2
3 *syn* see OVERLOOK 2

domination *n* 1 *syn* see SUPREMACY
2 *syn* see POWER 1

dominator *n syn* see LEADER 2

domineer *vb syn* see RULE 2

domineering *adj syn* see MASTERFUL 1
rel arrogant, insolent, lordly
con obsequious, servile, slavish; bootlicking, groveling, sycophantic, toadying

ant subservient; fawning

‖**dominie** *n syn* see CLERGYMAN

dominion *n* 1 *syn* see SUPREMACY
2 *syn* see FIELD
3 *syn* see OWNERSHIP

domino *n syn* see MASK 1

domitae naturae *adj syn* see TAME

don *vb* 1 to place on one's person (an article of clothing) <*donned* a raincoat for his trip>
syn assume, draw on, get on, huddle (on), put on, slip (on), throw
rel apparel, array, attire, clad, clothe, dress, enclothe, garb, garment, raiment
con cast, pull (off), remove, take off, throw off; unclothe, undress; disrobe
ant doff
2 to clothe or envelop oneself in <able to *don* a new personality at will>
syn assume, pull, put on, strike, take on
rel camouflage, color, disguise; belie, falsify, garble, misrepresent

donate *vb syn* see GIVE 1

donation *n* a gift of money or its equivalent to a charity, humanitarian cause, or public institution <sought *donations* for victims of the flood>
syn alms, benefaction, beneficence, charity, contribution, offering
rel aid, assistance, help, relief; philanthropy; bequest, endowment; appropriation, grant, subsidy, subvention; allowance, dole, pittance, ration

donator *n syn* see DONOR

done *adj* 1 *syn* see DECOROUS 1
2 *syn* see COMPLETE 4
3 *syn* see EFFETE 2
4 *syn* see THROUGH 4

done for *adj syn* see THROUGH 3

done in *adj syn* see EFFETE 2

‖**doney** *n syn* see GIRL FRIEND 1

‖**donicker** *n syn* see TOILET

Don Juan *n* 1 *syn* see GALLANT 2
2 *syn* see WOLF

donk *n syn* see DONKEY 1

donkey *n* 1 the domestic ass <the *donkey*, a typical pack animal>
syn ass, burro, donk, jackass, ‖moke, ‖neddy, ‖Rocky Mountain canary
rel ‖dickey, jack; hinny, mule; jennet, jenny, jenny ass
2 *syn* see FOOL 1

donkeyish *adj syn* see FOOLISH 2

donkey's years *n pl syn* see AGE 2

donkeywork *n syn* see WORK 2

donnybrook *n syn* see BRAWL 2

donor *n* one that gives something to another <a *donor* of funds to research foundations>
syn bestower, conferrer, donator, giver, presenter
rel contributor, subscriber

do–nothing *n syn* see SLUGGARD

‖**donsie** *adj syn* see UNWELL

doodad *n* something trivial which is hard to classify or whose name is unknown <wondered what the little round *doodad* was for>
syn business, dingus, dofunny, doohickey, gadget, gizmo, ‖hootenanny, jigger, rigamajig, thingum, thingumajig, thingumbob, thingummy; *compare* GADGET 1, WHAT≈DO-YOU-CALL-IT

doodle *n syn* see FOOL 1
||**doodle** *vb syn* see CHEAT
doodle *vb syn* see FIDDLE 2
doohickey *n syn* see DOODAD
doom *n syn* see FATE
    rel calamity, cataclysm, catastrophe, disaster, tragedy
doom *vb syn* see SENTENCE
doom (to) *vb syn* see PREDESTINE 1
doomed *adj syn* see DAMNED 1
doomful *adj syn* see OMINOUS
door *n* **1** an opening by which one can enter or leave a structure and especially a building <looked through the front *door*>
    syn doorway, entrance, entranceway, entry, entryway, portal
    2 a means or right of entering, approaching, or participating <viewed education as the *door* to success>
    syn access, adit, admission, admittance, entrance, entrée, entry, ingress, way
doormat *n syn* see WEAKLING
doorway *n syn* see DOOR 1
||**doozer** *n syn* ||DILLY, ||corker, ||daisy, dandy, ||dinger, humdinger, jim-dandy, ||lalapalooza, ||lulu, peach
dope *n* **1** *syn* see DRUG 2
    2 *syn* see DUNCE
dope (up) *vb syn* see ADULTERATE
doped *adj syn* see DRUGGED
dope out *vb* **1** *syn* see SOLVE 2
    2 *syn* see INFER
    3 *syn* see PLAN 2
dopey *adj syn* see LETHARGIC
do-re-mi *n syn* see MONEY
||**dorm** *vb syn* see DOZE
dormancy *n syn* see ABEYANCE
dormant *adj syn* see LATENT
    ant active
||**dort** *vb syn* see SULK
||**dorts** *n pl syn* see SULK
||**dorty** *adj syn* see SULLEN
||**doss** *n syn* see SLEEP 1
||**doss** *vb syn* see SLEEP
dot *n syn* see POINT 11
dot *vb* **1** *syn* see SPECKLE 1
    2 *syn* see SPOT 2
dot *n syn* see DOWRY
dotage *n* advanced age accompanied by a decline of mental poise and alertness <a doddering eighty-year-old entering his *dotage*>
    syn second childhood, senility; *compare* OLD AGE
    rel decrepitude, feebleness, infirmity; age, elderliness, senectitude
    con adolescence, youth; maturity
dote (on *or* upon) *vb syn* see ADORE 3
    rel enjoy, fancy, like
    idiom be sweet on
    ant loathe
||**doted** *adj syn* see SENILE
doting *adj* **1** *syn* see SENILE
    2 *syn* see LOVING
    rel asinine, fatuous, foolish, silly, simple

dottiness *n syn* see FOOLISHNESS
dotty *adj* **1** *syn* see INFATUATED
    2 *syn* see FOOLISH 2
double *adj* **1** *syn* see TWOFOLD 1
    2 *syn* see TWIN
    3 *syn* see TWOFOLD 2
    4 *syn* see INSINCERE
double *n* **1** *syn* see MATE 5
    2 *syn* see IMAGE 1
    3 *syn* see TURN 2
    rel departure, digression, divergence, swerving, veering
double *vb* **1** to make twice as great or as many <*doubled* the amount of his salary>
    syn dualize, dupe, duplicate
    rel replicate; amplify, augment, enlarge, increase, magnify; supplement
    con decrease, lessen, minimize
    ant halve
    2 to make of two thicknesses by turning or bending usually in the middle <he *doubled* the towel for better absorbency>
    syn fold
    rel pleat, plicate, turn over
    3 *syn* see ESCAPE 2
    4 *syn* see DUB
double-barreled *adj* **1** *syn* see TWOFOLD 2
    2 *syn* see TWOFOLD 1
double-cross *vb* **1** *syn* see DECEIVE
    2 *syn* see BETRAY 2
double-dealer *n syn* see SWINDLER
double-dealing *n syn* see DECEPTION 1
double-dealing *adj syn* see INSINCERE
double-distilled *adj syn* see UTTER
||**double-dog dare** *vb syn* see FACE 3
double-dome *n syn* see INTELLECTUAL 2
double-dyed *adj syn* see UTTER
double-edged *adj syn* see OBSCURE 3
double entendre *n syn* see AMBIGUITY
double-faced *adj* **1** *syn* see OBSCURE 3
    2 *syn* see INSINCERE
doublehearted *adj syn* see INSINCERE
double meaning *n syn* see AMBIGUITY
double-minded *adj* **1** *syn* see VACILLATING 2
    idiom of two minds
    2 *syn* see INSINCERE
doublet *n syn* see COUPLE
double-talk *n* **1** *syn* see NONSENSE 2
    2 *syn* see GOBBLEDYGOOK
double-tongued *adj syn* see INSINCERE
doubt *vb* **1** *syn* see QUESTION 2
    2 *syn* see DISTRUST
    con accredit, credit, trust; accept, believe, ||buy, swallow
doubt *n syn* see UNCERTAINTY
    rel dubiousness, questionableness; disbelief, incredulity, unbelief
    con dependence, faith, reliance, trust
    ant certitude; confidence
doubtable *adj syn* see DOUBTFUL 1
    ant undoubtable
doubter *n syn* see SKEPTIC
doubtful *adj* **1** not having or affording assurance of the certainty or soundness of something or someone <their chance of success is *doubtful*>
    syn ambiguous, borderline, clouded, doubtable, dubious, dubitable, equivocal, fishy, impugnable, indecisive, open, precarious, problematic, queasy, shady, shaky, suspect,

suspicious, uncertain, unclear, undecided, uneasy, unsettled, unstable, unsure; *compare* MOOT

rel question-begging; touch-and-go; chancy, insecure, questionable, speculative; hazy, obscure; unlikely; contingent, iffy

idiom at issue, in dispute, in doubt, in question

con decisive, open-and-shut, positive, sure; inarguable, incontestable, unarguable, undeniable, undoubted, unquestionable

ant indubitable

2 *syn* see MOOT

3 *syn* see IMPROBABLE 1

doubtfully *adv syn* see ASKANCE 2

doubtfulness *n syn* see UNCERTAINTY

doubting Thomas *n syn* see SKEPTIC

doubtless *adv* **1** *syn* see EASILY 2

2 *syn* see PRESUMABLY

doubtlessly *adv* **1** *syn* see WELL 7

ant doubtfully

2 *syn* see EASILY 2

dough *n syn* see MONEY

doughface *n syn* see MASK 1

‖**doughhead** *n syn* see DUNCE

doughty *adj syn* see BRAVE 1

doughy *adj syn* see PALE 1

do up *vb syn* see MEND 2

dour *adj* **1** *syn* see GRIM 2

rel rigid, rigorous, strict; implacable

2 *syn* see SULLEN

douse *n syn* see BLOW 1

douse *vb syn* see REMOVE 1

douse *vb* **1** *syn* see DIP 1

2 *syn* see WET

con bake, dehydrate, desiccate, dry, parch

3 *syn* see SPLASH

4 *syn* see EXTINGUISH 1

‖**dout** *vb syn* see EXTINGUISH 1

dove *n syn* see PACIFIST

ant hawk

dovecote *n* a small compartmented raised house or box for domestic pigeons <old countryseats with elaborate stone *dovecotes*>

syn columbary, culverhouse, dovehouse, pigeon house, pigeonry

rel aviary, birdhouse; perch, roost

dovehouse *n syn* see DOVECOTE

dover *n syn* see NAP

dovetail *vb syn* see AGREE 4

dowager *n syn* see MATRIARCH

dowd *n syn* see SLATTERN 1

dowdy *n syn* see SLATTERN 1

dowdy *adj* **1** *syn* see SLATTERNLY

con chic, fashionable, modish, stylish; flashy, garish, gaudy

ant smart

2 *syn* see TACKY 2

ant smart

3 *syn* see OLD-FASHIONED

dower *n syn* see DOWRY

dower *vb syn* see ENDOW 1

rel accouter, appoint, equip, furnish, outfit

‖**dowly** *adj syn* see OVERCAST

down *adv* **1** from a higher to a lower level <the land sloped *down* toward the sea>

syn downward, downwardly, downwards, netherwards

rel below, earthward, groundward; downgrade, downhill, downslope

con aloft, upward, upwardly, upwards

ant up

2 to completion <wash *down* the car>

syn completely, fully, through-and-through

idiom from top to bottom

3 *syn* see SERIOUSLY 1

down *adj* **1** *syn* see SLOW 3

2 *syn* see DOWNCAST

ant up

3 *syn* see SICK 1

4 *syn* see LOWER

ant up

5 *syn* see COMPLETE 4

down *n syn* see COMEDOWN

down *vb* **1** *syn* see SWALLOW 1

2 *syn* see DEFEAT 2

3 *syn* see FELL 1

4 *syn* see KILL 1

5 *syn* see OVERCOME 1

down *n* a soft fluffy material or covering <the *down* on a peach>

syn floss, flue, fluff, fur, fuzz, lint, pile

down–and–out *n syn* see PAUPER

down–at–heel *adj syn* see SHABBY 1

downcast *n syn* see DEFEAT 1

downcast *adj* low in spirits <felt *downcast* by the rejection>

syn bad, blue, cast down, chapfallen, crestfallen, dejected, depressed, disconsolate, dispirited, doleful, down, downhearted, down-in-the-mouth, downthrown, droopy, dull, heartsick, heartsore, hipped, low, low-spirited, mopey, soul-sick, spiritless, sunk, woebegone; *compare* SAD 1

rel discouraged, disheartened; oppressed, weighed down; distressed, troubled; despondent, forlorn; listless; broody, moody; gloomy, glum, morose

idiom in the depths

con cheerful, happy, joyous, lighthearted; excited, exhilarated, intoxicated; buoyed up, gladdened; encouraged, heartened; animated, gay, lively, sprightly, vivacious; delighted, pleased

ant elated

downcry *vb syn* see DECRY 2

downfall *n* **1** *syn* see DETERIORATION 1

rel comedown, descent, discomfiture, down

2 something that causes a downfall <drink was his *downfall*>

syn bane, destroyer, destruction, ruin, ruination, undoing

rel headache, problem, trouble

idiom road to ruin

con aid, help, support

downgrade *n syn* see DETERIORATION 1

ant upgrade

downgrade *vb* **1** *syn* see DEPRECIATE 1

ant upgrade

2 *syn* see DEGRADE 1

ant upgrade

downgrading *n syn* see DEMOTION

ant upgrading

downhearted *adj syn* see DOWNCAST

down–in–the–mouth *adj syn* see DOWNCAST

downright *adj* **1** *syn* see UTTER

2 being what is stated beyond any possibility of doubt <a *downright* lie>

syn flat, indubitable, unquestionable, up-and-down; *compare* POSITIVE 3 *rel* out-and-out, sure-enough; absolute, positive; certain, clear

downside–up *adj syn* see UPSIDE-DOWN 2

downslide *n syn* see DECLINE 3

downswing *n syn* see DECLINE 3

downthrow *n syn* see DEFEAT 1

downthrown *adj syn* see DOWNCAST

down–to–date *adj syn* see UP-TO-DATE

down–to–earth *adj syn* see REALISTIC

downtrend *n syn* see DECLINE 3

downtrodden *adj* oppressed by superior power <the *downtrodden* peasants>
  syn abject, underfoot
  rel oppressed, persecuted; abused, maltreated, mistreated

downturn *n syn* see DECLINE 3

downward *adv syn* see DOWN 1
  ant upward

downwardly *adv syn* see DOWN 1
  ant upward

downwards *adv syn* see DOWN 1
  ant upwards

‖**downy** *adj syn* see SLY 2

dowry *n* the money, goods, or estate that a woman brings to her husband in marriage <from a poor family, she came to her marriage with no *dowry*>
  syn dot, dower, marriage portion
  con bride-price, dowry, settlement

doxy *n* 1 a usually young woman who engages in promiscuous sexual intercourse <a *doxy* who frequented singles bars>
  syn ‖chippy, floozy, grisette, light-o'-love, nymph, nymphet, party girl, roundheel, tart, ‖tootsie; *compare* HARLOT 1, PROSTITUTE, WANTON
  rel groupie
  idiom woman of easy virtue
  ‖**2** *syn* see MISTRESS

doyen *n* 1 *syn* see LEADER 1
  2 *syn* see EXPERT

doze *vb* to sleep lightly <he was inclined to *doze* at his desk>
  syn ‖dorm, drowse, ‖sloom, slumber, ‖snoozle, ‖sog; *compare* NAP, SLEEP

doze (off) *vb* to fall into a light sleep <*dozed* off while sitting before the fire>
  syn drop off, drowse (off)
  idiom drift off

doze *n* a light sleep <was caught in a *doze* at her desk>
  syn drowse, ‖sloom, slumber; *compare* NAP, SLEEP 1

dozy *adj syn* see SLEEPY 1

DP *n syn* see REFUGEE

drab *n* 1 *syn* see HAG 2
  2 *syn* see SLATTERN 1
  3 *syn* see PROSTITUTE

drab *adj syn* 1 *syn* see DULL 8
  2 *syn* see COLORLESS 2
  rel bleak, desolate, dismal, dispiriting, dreary, dingy, faded
  con bright, brilliant, luminous

draconian *adj syn* see RIGID 3

draffy *adj syn* see WORTHLESS 1

draft *n* DRINK 3, drag, drain, drench, ‖peg, swig, swill

draft *vb* 1 to enroll in the armed forces by compulsion <*drafted* when he was barely eighteen>
  syn conscribe, conscript; *compare* CALL UP
  rel induct; enlist, enroll, muster (in *or* out); impress, press
  2 *syn* see SKETCH
  3 to formulate and produce <*drafting* plans to meet an emergency>
  syn draw up, formulate, frame, make, prepare
  rel concoct, contrive, devise, invent; fabricate, fashion, forge, form, manufacture, shape; plan, project; outline, sketch
  4 *syn* see DRAIN 1

drag *n* 1 *syn* see DRAW 1
  2 *syn* see DRINK 3
  ‖**3** *syn* see PULL 2
  ‖**4** *syn* see WAY 1
  5 *syn* see BORE

drag *vb* 1 *syn* see PULL 2
  con propel, push, shove, thrust; drive, impel, move
  2 *syn* see DELAY 2
  idiom drag one's feet (*or* heels)
  con hasten, hurry
  3 to hang down and be drawn behind <her dress *dragged* in the dust>
  syn draggle, trail, traipse
  rel droop, hang, sag

‖**drag down** *vb syn* see EARN 1

dragging *adj syn* see LONG 2

draggle *vb syn* see DRAG 3

draggle–tail *n syn* see SLATTERN 1

draggletailed *adj syn* see SLATTERNLY

dragoon *vb syn* see INTIMIDATE

drain *vb* 1 to draw off (liquid) by degrees <*drain* the water from the swimming pool>
  syn draft, draw, draw off, pump, siphon, tap
  rel milk; bleed; suck; empty, exhaust
  2 *syn* see TIRE 1
  3 *syn* see DEPLETE
  idiom bleed white

drain (away) *vb syn* see DECREASE

drain *n syn* see DRINK 3

drained *adj syn* see EFFETE 2

dram *n* 1 a small quantity of something (as alcoholic liquor) to drink <a *dram* of brandy helped to break his chill>
  syn ‖caulker, dollop, drop, jolt, nip, shot, slug, snifter, snort, snorter, spot, toothful, tot, ‖wet
  rel draft, drink, ‖peg, potation, pull, swig, swill; finger; jigger; dash; ‖splash; snack; quick one
  2 *syn* see PARTICLE

drama *n* dramatic art, literature, or affairs <was interested in *drama* during her college years>
  syn boards, footlights, (the) stage, theater
  rel show business

dramatic *adj* 1 of or relating to drama <made no objections to his son's *dramatic* ambitions>
  syn dramaturgic, histrionic, theatral, theatric, theatrical, thespian
  2 *syn* see THEATRICAL 2

---

syn synonym(s)   *rel* related word(s)
ant antonym(s)   *con* contrasted word(s)
idiom idiomatic equivalent(s)
‖ use limited; if in doubt, see a dictionary

ant undramatic
dramatist *n syn see* PLAYWRIGHT
dramatizer *n syn see* PLAYWRIGHT
dramaturge *n syn see* PLAYWRIGHT
dramaturgic *adj syn see* DRAMATIC 1
drape *vb* 1 *syn see* SWATHE
2 *syn see* SPRAWL 2
dratted *adj syn see* DAMNED 2
draw *vb* 1 *syn see* PULL 2
rel bring, fetch; educe, elicit, evoke, extract
con propel, push, shove, thrust; drive, impel, move
2 *syn see* DRAIN 1
3 *syn see* ATTRACT 1
4 *syn see* INDUCE 1
5 *syn see* TAKE 14
6 *syn see* INFER
7 *syn see* EXTEND 3
8 *syn see* DEPLETE
9 *syn see* EVISCERATE
draw *n* 1 a sucking pull on something (as a sipping straw or cigarette) <took a long *draw* on his pipe before answering>
syn drag, puff, pull
rel smoke; inhale
2 *syn see* ADVANTAGE 3
3 *syn see* ATTRACTION 1
4 an indecisive ending to a contest or competition <the prizefight ended in a *draw*>
syn deadlock, dogfall, stalemate, standoff, tie
rel dead heat, photo finish; standstill
con loss; win
draw back *vb syn see* DEDUCT 1
drawback *n syn see* DISADVANTAGE
rel evil, ill; inconvenience, trouble
con advantage, edge
draw down *vb* 1 *syn see* EARN 1
2 *syn see* DEPLETE
draw in *vb syn see* INDUCE 1
drawing *adj syn see* ATTRACTIVE 1
drawing power *n syn see* ATTRACTION 1
drawing room *n syn see* SALON 1
drawn *adj syn see* HAGGARD
con hale, robust
drawn–out *adj syn see* LONG 2
draw off *vb syn see* DRAIN 1
rel abstract; withdraw; move, remove, shift, transfer
draw on *vb* 1 *syn see* EFFECT 1
2 *syn see* INDUCE 1
3 *syn see* DON 1
draw out *vb syn see* EXTEND 3
draw up *vb* 1 *syn see* DRAFT 3
2 *syn see* STOP 4
dray horse *n syn see* SLAVE 2
dread *n syn see* FEAR 1
dreadful *adj syn see* FEARFUL 3
‖**dreadful** *adv syn see* VERY 1
dreadful *n syn see* DIME NOVEL
dreadfully *adv syn see* VERY 1
dream *n* 1 *syn see* FANCY 4
2 *syn see* PIPE DREAM
dream *vb syn see* LONG
dreamer *n* one whose conduct is guided more by ideals than practicalities <a *dreamer* proposing glorious plans impossible to make work>
syn castle-builder, idealist, ideologue, utopian, visionary

rel daydreamer, illusionist, lotus-eater, wishful thinker; Don Quixote; theorist
con pragmatist, realist; Babbitt, Philistine; pedant
dream up *vb syn see* CONTRIVE 2
dreamy *adj* 1 given to dreaming, reverie, or fancy <a *dreamy* and most impractical person>
syn astral, daydreaming, daydreamy, otherworldly, unworldly, visionary
rel fanciful, idealistic, romantic, whimsical
con down-to-earth, practical, pragmatic, realistic; actual, factual
2 *syn see* MARVELOUS 2
drear *adj syn see* GLOOMY 3
dreary *adj* 1 *syn see* GLOOMY 3
2 *syn see* DULL 9
dreck *n syn see* REFUSE
dreg *n, usu* **dregs** *pl* 1 *syn see* SEDIMENT
2 *syn see* RABBLE 2
‖**dreich** *adj syn see* LONG 2
drench *n syn see* DRINK 3
drench *vb* 1 *syn see* WET
rel dip, duck, dunk, immerse, submerge
2 *syn see* SOAK 1
3 *syn see* POUR 3
drenched *adj syn see* WET 1
dress *vb* 1 *syn see* CLOTHE
ant undress
2 *syn see* BANDAGE
3 to remove the entrails from <*dress* fish, fowl, or game>
syn clean, gut
rel butcher, slaughter
4 *syn see* TILL
rel fertilize, topdress
dress (up) *vb syn see* ADORN
dress *n* 1 *syn see* CLOTHES
2 *syn see* COSTUME
dress down *vb syn see* SCOLD 1
dress up *vb* 1 to attire in best or formal clothes <*dressed up* to go to the theater>
syn deck (out), ‖dike (out *or* up), doll out, doll up, ‖dude up, fix up, gussy up, prank, ‖prick (up), primp, prink (up), slick, smarten (up), smug, spiff, spruce (up), tog (out *or* up), ‖toggle, trick (off, out, *or* up)
rel prettify, pretty (up); apparel, array, attire, clad, clothe, dress, enclothe, garb, garment, raiment; overdress; preen; prim (up)
idiom dress fit to kill, dress to the nines, put on the dog
2 *syn see* DISGUISE
drib *vb syn see* DRIP
drib *n syn see* DROP 1
dribble *vb* 1 *syn see* DRIP
2 *syn see* DROOL 2
dribble (away) *vb syn see* WASTE 2
dribble *n syn see* PITTANCE
driblet *n* 1 *syn see* PITTANCE
2 *syn see* DROP 1
drift *n* 1 *syn see* FLOW
2 *syn see* PILE 1
rel array, batch, bunch, bundle, clump, cluster, clutch, group, lot, parcel, set
‖3 *syn see* DROVE 2
4 *syn see* TENDENCY 1
rel motion, movement, progress, progression; aim, intent, intention, purpose

5 syn see LEANING 2
6 syn see TENOR 1
   rel direction, line, set
drift *vb* **1** to become carried or floated along
<cakes of ice *drifting* along the stream>
   syn float, ride, wash
   rel dart, fly, sail, scud, shoot, skim; dance,
flicker, flit, flitter, flutter, hover
2 syn see SAUNTER
3 syn see WANDER 1
4 syn see SLIDE 6
5 syn see HEAP 1
drifter *n* **1 syn** see ROVER
2 syn see VAGABOND
driftwood *n* vagrant impoverished people
<the *driftwood* of skid row>
   syn flotsam, jetsam, wreckage
drill *vb* **1 syn** see PERFORATE
2 syn see EXERCISE 3
   rel accustom, habituate
drill *n syn* see EXERCISE 3
drilling *n syn* see EXERCISE 3
drink *vb* **1** to take in (potable liquid) <the
boys *drank* all the soda>
   syn imbibe, quaff, sip, sup (off *or* up), swallow, toss
   rel drain, gulp, guzzle, slosh, slurp, swig,
swill; wash down
   idiom wet one's whistle
2 to salute and wish honor and health to (a
person) by raising and then drinking from a
vessel <*drink* to the bride and groom>
   syn pledge, toast
   rel honor, salute; wet
3 to partake of alcoholic liquors especially
habitually or to excess <he *drinks* but does
not smoke>
   syn booze, guzzle, imbibe, liquor (up), ‖lush
(up), nip, soak, swig, swill, swizzle, tank up,
tipple, tope
   idiom bend the elbow, cheer the inner man,
drink like a fish, go on a binge, hit the bottle,
take a nip
drink *n* **1** liquid suitable for swallowing
<able to make palatable *drink* from seawa-
ter>
   syn beverage, drinkable, liquor, potable
   rel liquid; brew; potion
2 syn see LIQUOR 2
3 a portion of potable liquid <took a *drink*
from the cup>
   syn draft, drag, drain, drench, ‖peg, swig,
swill
   rel draw, pull; finger, jigger; libation
4 syn see OCEAN
drinkable *adj syn* see POTABLE
drinkable *n syn* see DRINK 1
drinkery *n syn* see BAR 5
drip *vb* to let fall drops of moisture or liquid
<trees *dripping* after the rain>
   syn distill, drib, dribble, drop, trickle, trill,
weep
   rel spatter, sprinkle, spurtle; gush, pour,
sluice, stream
‖**drip** *n* **1 syn** see NONSENSE 2

---

2 syn see DUNCE
dripping *adj syn* see WET 1
drippy *adj syn* see SENTIMENTAL
drive *vb* **1 syn** see MOVE 5
   rel coerce, compel, force; incite, instigate
   con check, curb, inhibit, restrain; guide,
lead, pilot, steer
2 syn see PUSH 1
3 to urge along (as cattle) <cowboys *driving*
the great herds north>
   syn ‖drove, herd, run
   rel shepherd; wrangle; egg, exhort, goad,
prick, prod, punch, sic, spur, urge
4 syn see THRUST 2
5 to operate and steer (a motor vehicle)
<*drive* a car>
   syn auto, charioteer, motor, pilot, tool,
wheel
   rel operate, run, work; guide, steer; roll;
chauffeur
6 syn see IMPRESS 3
7 syn see PLUNGE 2
8 syn see LABOR 1
drive *n* **1** a short trip in a vehicle <took a
drive around town>
   syn ride, spin, turn; *compare* TRIP 1
   rel whirl; joyride; excursion, outing
2 syn see DRIVEWAY
3 syn see ENTERPRISE 4
4 syn see VIGOR 2
   rel impetus, momentum, speed, velocity
drivel *vb* **1 syn** see DROOL 2
2 syn see BABBLE 2
3 syn see WASTE 2
drivel *n* **1 syn** see NONSENSE 2
2 syn see GIBBERISH 1
driveling *adj syn* see INSIPID 3
driver *n syn* see MOTORIST
driveway *n* a private road giving access from
a public way <the *driveway* to a house>
   syn ‖avenue, drive
   rel court, place, row, street
driving *adj syn* see ENERGETIC 2
drizzle *vb syn* see SPRINKLE 5
drogher *n syn* see BEARER 2
drôlerie *n syn* see JOKE 1
droll *adj syn* see LAUGHABLE
   rel absurd, preposterous
droll *n syn* see HUMORIST 2
drollery *n* **1 syn** see JOKE 1
2 syn see HUMOR 4
drollness *n syn* see HUMOR 4
drone *vb* **1 syn** see HUM
2 syn see IDLE
drony *adj syn* see LAZY
drool *vb* **1** to secrete or become filled with
saliva usually in anticipation of food
<mouths *drooled* as we waited for dinner>
   syn water
   idiom water at the mouth
2 to let saliva or some other substance flow
from the mouth <babies often *drool* uncon-
trollably>
   syn dribble, drivel, salivate, slabber, slaver,
slobber
3 syn see ENTHUSE 2
4 syn see BABBLE 2
drool *n syn* see NONSENSE 2
droop *vb* **1 syn** see SLOUCH
2 syn see LOWER 3

---

syn synonym(s)   *rel* related word(s)
ant antonym(s)   *con* contrasted word(s)
idiom idiomatic equivalent(s)
‖ use limited; if in doubt, see a dictionary

3 to become literally or figuratively limp through loss of vigor or freshness <he walked along, his shoulders *drooping* from exhaustion>
syn flag, sag, swag, wilt
rel drop, fall, sink, slump, subside; dangle; hang, loll, lop, sling, suspend; decline, deteriorate, ‖dwine, fade, fail, languish, weaken

droopy *adj syn* see DOWNCAST

drop *n* **1** the quantity of fluid that falls in one spherical mass <a *drop* of rain>
syn drib, driblet, droplet, globule, gobbet
rel dribble, drip, trickle
2 *syn* see PARTICLE
3 *syn* see DRAM
4 *syn* see DESCENT 4
5 *syn* see DESCENT 1
6 *syn* see DECLINE 3
7 *syn* see DEPTH 1

drop *vb* **1** *syn* see FALL 2
2 *syn* see FALL 1
ant mount
3 *syn* see PLUMMET
rel slide, slip
con rally, rebound; ascend, climb; soar
ant mount
4 *syn* see COLLAPSE 2
rel backslide, lapse, relapse
5 *syn* see DIE 1
6 *syn* see DRIP
7 *syn* see FELL 1
8 *syn* see QUIT 6
9 *syn* see CANCEL 2
10 *syn* see DISMISS 3
11 *syn* see LOSE 2
12 *syn* see LOSE 2

drop (in *or* by) *vb syn* see VISIT 2
drop (off) *vb syn* see SLIP 6
droplet *n syn* see DROP 1
drop off *vb syn* see DOZE (off)
dropsical *adj syn* see INFLATED
dropsied *adj syn* see INFLATED
drossy *adj syn* see WORTHLESS 1
droughty *adj syn* see DRY 1
‖**drouk** *vb syn* see SOAK 1
drove *n* **1** *syn* see CROWD 1
2 a group of domestic animals reared or handled as a unit <a *drove* of cattle>
syn ‖drift, flock, herd
rel drive; pack; school
‖**drove** *vb syn* see DRIVE 3
drown *vb* **1** *syn* see OVERWHELM 4
2 *syn* see DELUGE 1
3 *syn* see WET
drowse *vb syn* see DOZE
drowse (off) *vb syn* see DOZE (off)
drowse *n syn* see DOZE
drowsy *adj syn* see SLEEPY 1
rel lackadaisical, languid, languorous
con alert, vigilant, watchful; active, dynamic, live; energetic, lively, vivacious
drub *vb* **1** *syn* see BEAT 1
2 *syn* see LAMBASTE 3
3 *syn* see WHIP 2
drubbing *n syn* see DEFEAT 1
drudge *vb* to perform hard, menial, or monotonous work <*drudged* all day washing floors>
syn grind, grub, ‖muck, plod, slave, slog, toil

rel hammer, peg (away *or* at *or* on), plow, plug, pound (away); perform, work
idiom keep one's nose to the grindstone
con idle, laze, loaf, lounge; dally, dawdle, potter, putter; cheat, chisel

drudge *n* **1** *syn* see SLAVE 2
2 *syn* see WORK 1
3 *syn* see HACK 2

drudgery *n syn* see WORK 2
drudging *adj syn* see IRKSOME

drug *n* **1** a substance used by itself or in a mixture in the treatment or diagnosis of disease <a life-sustaining *drug*>
syn biologic, medicinal, pharmaceutic, pharmaceutical
rel cure, medicament, medication, medicine, physic, remedy, specific; simple
2 a narcotic substance or preparation <depended on *drugs* to make life bearable>
syn dope, ‖hop, narcotic, opiate

drugged *adj* being under the influence of a drug taken for nonmedical purposes <was *drugged* on LSD>
syn doped, high, hopped-up, spaced-out, stoned, tripped out, turned on, ‖wiped out, zonked
idiom on a trip
ant straight

druggist *n* one who deals in medicinal drugs
syn apothecary, ‖chemist, pharmacist
rel pharmacologist

drum *vb syn* see SOLICIT 1
drumfire *n syn* see BARRAGE
drumhead *adj syn* see SUMMARY 2
drum up *vb syn* see SOLICIT 1
drunk *adj syn* see INTOXICATED 1
rel drinking, drinky
idiom roaring drunk
con bone-dry, dry
ant sober

drunk *n* **1** *syn* see BINGE 1
2 *syn* see DRUNKARD

drunkard *n* one who drinks alcoholic liquors to excess <*drunkards* lurching homeward when the bar finally closes>
syn bibber, ‖bloat, ‖blotter, boozehound, boozer, drunk, fuddler, guzzler, inebriate, lush, ‖lusher, rumdum, rummy, ‖rumpot, ‖shicker, soak, soaker, sot, sponge, stiff, swillbowl, swiller, tippler, toper, tosspot
rel alcoholic, dipsomaniac; wino; drammer
idiom elbow bender (*or* crooker)
ant teetotaler

drunken *adj syn* see INTOXICATED 1
drunkery *n syn* see BAR 5
‖**druthers** *n syn* see CHOICE 1
dry *adj* **1** devoid of or deficient in moisture <preferred a *dry* climate>
syn arid, bone-dry, droughty, moistureless, sere, thirsty, unwatered, waterless
rel baked, dehydrated, desiccated, parched; bald, bare, barren; depleted, drained, exhausted, impoverished; juiceless, sapless, sapped
con drenched, dripping, saturated, soaked, soaking, sodden, sopping, soppy, soused, wringing-wet; damp, dank, humid, moist; exuberant, lush, luxuriant, prodigal, profuse
ant wet
2 *syn* see THIRSTY 1

3 marked by the absence of or abstention from alcoholic beverages <a *dry* party>
syn bone-dry, teetotal
ant wet
4 **syn** see IMPASSIVE 1
5 **syn** see ARID 2
6 **syn** see PLAIN 1
7 **syn** see SOUR 1
ant sweet
8 **syn** see HARSH 3
dry *vb* 1 to treat or affect so as to deprive of moisture <clothes *dried* in the wind>
syn dehydrate, desiccate, exsiccate, parch, sear
rel evaporate; anhydrate; deplete, drain, exhaust; shrivel, wither, wizen
con deluge, douse, drench, soak, sop, souse; damp, dampen, moisten
ant wet
2 **syn** see HARDEN 1
dryasdust *adj syn* see ARID 2
dry land *n syn* see EARTH 2
||**dry-shave** *vb syn* see CHEAT
dry up *vb* 1 *syn* see DESICCATE 2
2 **syn** see WITHER
3 **syn** see SHUT UP 1
dual *adj* 1 *syn* see TWOFOLD 1
2 **syn** see TWIN
dualistic *adj syn* see TWOFOLD 1
dualize *vb syn* see DOUBLE 1
dub *vb* 1 *syn* see NAME 1
2 **syn** see BOTCH
dub *vb* to provide (a motion-picture film) with a new sound track (as by substituting dialogue in a foreign language) <*dubbed* the Italian movie into English>
syn double
dubiety *n syn* see UNCERTAINTY
rel hesitancy; faltering, vacillation, wavering
con decidedness, decisiveness
ant decision
dubiosity *n syn* see UNCERTAINTY
rel addlement, confusion, muddlement; faltering, vacillation, wavering
con cocksureness, positiveness
ant decidedness
dubious *adj* 1 *syn* see MOOT
2 **syn** see DOUBTFUL 1
rel skeptical; mistrustful; disinclined, hesitant, reluctant
con dependable, tried, trustworthy, trusty; certain, positive, sure
ant cocksure; reliable
3 **syn** see IMPROBABLE 1
4 **syn** see UNRELIABLE 1
ant trustworthy
dubitable *adj syn* see DOUBTFUL 1
ant indubitable
dubitancy *n syn* see UNCERTAINTY
duce *n syn* see TYRANT
||**duck** *n syn* see ECCENTRIC
duck *vb* 1 *syn* see DIP 1
2 to lower (as the head or body) quickly <had to *duck* his head to get through the door>

syn dip, stoop
rel bend; bow
3 **syn** see DODGE 1
rel avert, prevent, ward
4 **syn** see ESCAPE 2
duck soup *n syn* see SNAP 1
duct *n syn* see CHANNEL 1
ductile *adj syn* see PLASTIC
rel responsive; submitting; fluid, liquid
con intractable, refractory; adamant, obdurate
ductus *n syn* see HANDWRITING
dud *n syn* see FAILURE 5
dude *n syn* see FOP
||**dude up** *vb syn* see DRESS UP 1
dudgeon *n syn* see OFFENSE 2
rel fury, ire, rage, wrath; humor, mood, temper
duds *n pl* 1 *syn* see CLOTHES
||2 *adj* see RAGS 1
due *adj* 1 *syn* see JUST 3
rel good, right; equitable, fair, just; coming, earned
con excessive, exorbitant, extravagant, immoderate, inordinate; deficient
ant undue
2 having reached the date at which payment is required <a note that would become *due* after eighteen months>
syn mature, payable
3 **syn** see UNPAID 2
due *n* 1 what one fairly has coming <the artist has finally been accorded her *due*>
syn comeuppance, desert(s), deserving, lumps, merit, right(s)
rel deservedness, dueness; entitlement; compensation, payment, recompense; recompensing, repayment, satisfaction; reprisal, retaliation, retribution, revenge, vengeance; guerdon, need, reward
idiom what is coming to one
2 **syn** see DEBT 3
due *adv syn* see DIRECTLY 1
duel *vb syn* see RESIST
due to *prep syn* see OVER 6
||**duff** *vb syn* see CHEAT
duff *n syn* see BUTTOCKS
duffer *n* ||1 *syn* see PEDDLER
2 **syn** see DUNCE
dulcet *adj* 1 *syn* see MELODIOUS 1
con grinding, rasping, scraping, scratching
ant grating
2 **syn** see SWEET 1
dull *adj* 1 *syn* see STUPID 1
ant sharp
2 **syn** see RETARDED
con advanced, precocious
3 **syn** see INSENSIBLE 1
4 **syn** see DOWNCAST
5 **syn** see COLORLESS 2
ant bright
6 lacking sharpness of edge or point <a knife with a *dull* blade>
syn blunt, obtuse
rel blunted, dulled, unsharpened
con honed, keen, razor-sharp, unblunted, whetted
ant sharp
7 lacking warmth, luster, or brilliance <a smooth *dull* finish>

---

syn synonym(s)   **rel** related word(s)
ant antonym(s)   **con** contrasted word(s)
idiom idiomatic equivalent(s)
|| use limited; if in doubt, see a dictionary

syn blind, dead, dim, flat, lackluster, lusterless, mat, muted

rel cold, dingy, drab, dun, leaden, somber; deadened, lifeless

con beaming, bright, brilliant, effulgent, fulgent, incandescent, lambent, lucent, lucid, luminous, lustrous, radiant, refulgent; burnished, polished, shiny

8 cloudy in color <a *dull* brown>

syn drab, muddy, murky, subfusc

rel blurry, cloudy, hazy; flat, lackluster, lifeless, lusterless; mousy

ant clear; rich

9 being so unvaried or uninteresting as to provoke boredom or tedium <any routine constantly repeated can become *dull*>

syn banausic, blah, ‖dim, dreary, humdrum, monotone, monotonous, pedestrian, plodding, poky, stodgy

rel boring, irksome, tedious, tiring, wearisome; brainless; exhausting, fagging, fatiguing

con animating, exciting, stimulating; gay, spritely

ant lively

10 *syn* see OVERCAST

11 *syn* see ARID 2

rel matter-of-fact, prosaic, prosy; bloodless

idiom dull as ditchwater

con exciting, stimulating

ant lively

dull *vb* **1** to make less clear, distinct, or bright <colors *dulled* by the sun>

syn dim, fade, muddy, pale, tarnish

rel discolor, wash out; blur

con brighten, freshen, intensify

2 *syn* see DEADEN 1

ant sharpen

3 to deprive of sharpness (as of edge or point) <*dull* a spade>

syn blunt, disedge, obtund, turn

idiom take the edge off

con edge, hone

ant sharpen

4 to impair one or more of the senses <age had *dulled* his hearing>

syn blear, blur, dim

rel debilitate, enfeeble, weaken; darken; retard, slow

ant sharpen

5 to make slow or obtuse <his mind had been *dulled* by drink>

syn blunt, hebetate, stupefy

rel becloud, befog, cloud, darken, dim; benumb, deaden, numb; retard, slow

con quicken, stimulate, whet

ant sharpen

dullard *n syn* see DUNCE

dullhead *n syn* see DUNCE

dullness *n syn* see LETHARGY 1

rel denseness, stupidity

con edge, incisiveness, keenness

ant sharpness

‖**dullsville** *n* **1** *syn* see BORE

rel burg, hick town, jerkwater town, mudhole, one-horse town, Podunk, tank town, whistle-stop

2 *syn* see TEDIUM

dumb *adj* **1** lacking the power to speak <deaf and *dumb* from birth>

syn inarticulate, mute, silent, speechless, unarticulate, voiceless; *compare* SILENT 2

ant articulate

2 *syn* see SILENT 2

rel incoherent, indistinct, maundering, tongue-tied

3 *syn* see SILENT 3

con speaking, talking; talkative, verbose

4 *syn* see STUPID 1

idiom dumb as an ox

dumb (up) *vb syn* see SHUT UP 2

dumbbell *n syn* see DUNCE

‖**dumb bunny** *n syn* see DUNCE

‖**dumb cluck** *n syn* see DUNCE

dumbfound *vb* **1** *syn* see SURPRISE 2

2 *syn* see STAGGER 5

dumbfounded *adj syn* see AGHAST 2

‖**dumbhead** *n syn* see DUNCE

dummkopf *n syn* see DUNCE

dummy *n* **1** *syn* see DUNCE

2 *syn* see STOOGE 1

dummy *adj syn* see ARTIFICIAL 2

‖**dummy (up)** *vb syn* see SHUT UP 2

dump *vb* **1** *syn* see DISCARD

‖**2** *syn* see BEAT 1

dump *n* **1** *syn* see ARMORY

2 *syn* see STY 1

dumping *n syn* see DISPOSAL 2

dumpling *n syn* see FATTY

dumps *n pl syn* see SADNESS

idiom low spirits

dumpy *adj syn* see STOCKY

rel formless, shapeless, unformed

dun *adj syn* see DARK 1

dun *vb syn* see WORRY 1

dunce *n* a dull-witted person <the traditional *dunce* in pointed cap>

syn beetlehead, blockhead, bonehead, boob, booby, ‖bufflehead, cabbagehead, chowderhead, chucklehead, chump, clod, clodpate, clodpoll, ‖cluck, dimwit, ‖dizzard, dodo, ‖dodunk, dolt, dolthead, dope, ‖doughhead, ‖drip, duffer, dullard, dullhead, dumbbell, ‖dumb bunny, ‖dumb cluck, ‖dumbhead, dummkopf, dummy, dunderhead, dunderpate, fathead, featherweight, goof, ‖goon, hammerhead, idiot, ignoramus, ironhead, knothead, knucklehead, lackwit, lame-brain, lunk, lunkhead, ‖moonraker, moron, muddlehead, mug, muggins, mutt, muttonhead, nitwit, noddy, noodle, numskull, oaf, pinhead, poke, prune, pumpkin head, put, ‖schnook, simp, simpleton, ‖spoon, squarehead, ‖stunpoll, ‖stupe, stupid, thickhead, thickskull, turnip, wantwit, woodenhead, zombie

rel lightweight; ass, donkey, fool, imbecile, jackass, jerk, nincompoop, ninny, ‖schmo, ‖schmuck; birdbrain, featherbrain, scatterbrain

idiom dumb ox, Simple Simon

con brain, highbrow, intellectual, thinker, wit; pundit, sage, savant, scholar, wise man; prodigy, wizard; genius, mastermind

duncical *adj syn* see STUPID 1

dunderhead *n syn* see DUNCE

dunderpate *n syn* see DUNCE

dundrearies *n pl syn* see SIDE-WHISKERS

dungeon *n* a close dark prison or vault commonly underground <the prisoners were kept in lightless *dungeons*>

syn oubliette
rel vault; black hole; cell; jail, prison
dungy *adj syn* see DIRTY 1
dunk *vb syn* see DIP 1
rel saturate, soak, sop
duo *n syn* see COUPLE
dupe *n syn* see FOOL 3
dupe *vb* to delude by underhand methods <the public is easily *duped* by extravagant claims in advertising>
syn bamboozle, befool, catch, chicane, con, dust, flimflam, fool, gull, hoax, hoodwink, hornswoggle, job, kid, pigeon, ‖rig, spoof, trick, victimize
rel beguile, betray, deceive, delude, double=cross, mislead; cheat, cozen, defraud, over-reach; baffle, circumvent, outwit
idiom pull one's leg, put something over (*or* across)
con enlighten, inform, wise (up)
dupe *vb syn* see DOUBLE 1
dupery *n syn* see DECEPTION 1
duple *adj syn* see TWOFOLD 1
duplex *adj syn* see TWOFOLD 1
duplicate *adj syn* see SAME 2
duplicate *n syn* see REPRODUCTION 1
rel analogue, counterpart, parallel
2 *syn* see MATE 5
duplicate *vb* **1** *syn* see DOUBLE 1
2 *syn* see COPY
duplicitous *adj syn* see UNDERHAND
duplicity *n syn* see DECEIT 1
rel faithlessness, perfidiousness, perfidy, treacherousness, treachery
durable *adj syn* see LASTING
rel stout, strong, tenacious
con feeble, fragile, frail, weak
duration *n syn* **1** *syn* see CONTINUATION 1
2 *syn* see RUN 2
3 *syn* see TERM 2
duress *n syn* see FORCE 4
during *prep* in the course of <*during* the disorder some men kept their heads>
syn amid, mid, midst, over, throughout
dusk *adj syn* see DARK 1
dusk *n syn* see EVENING 1
‖**dusk dark** *n syn* see EVENING 1
dusky *adj syn* see DARK 3
2 *syn* see DARK 1
3 *syn* see GLOOMY 3
4 *syn* see OBSCURE 3
dust *n* **1** *syn* see DUSTING
2 *syn* see QUARREL
‖**3** *syn* see REFUSE
dust *vb* **1** *syn* see SPRINKLE 1
2 *syn* see WHIP 2
3 *syn* see DUPE
idiom throw dust in one's eyes
‖**4** *syn* see HURRY 2

dusting *n* **1** a small quantity lightly applied to or sprinkled on <a *dusting* of sugar on the cake>
syn dust, powdering, sprinkling
‖**2** *syn* see DEFEAT 1
‖**dust off** *vb syn* see MURDER 1
dustup *n syn* see QUARREL
dusty *adj syn* see ARID 2
Dutch *n syn* see TROUBLE 3
duteous *adj syn* see RESPECTFUL
dutiful *adj syn* see RESPECTFUL
duty *n* **1** *syn* see OBLIGATION 2
rel accountability, amenability, answerability, liability
2 *syn* see FUNCTION 1
3 *syn* see LOAD 3
4 *syn* see TAX 1
5 *syn* see TASK 1
6 *syn* see USE 4
dwarf *n* a very small person <she was a tiny little thing, almost a *dwarf*>
syn homunculus, hop-o'-my-thumb, Lilliputian, manikin, midge, midget, peewee, pygmy, runt, Tom Thumb
rel half-pint, ‖ribe, ‖shrimp, wart; dwarfling; minimus
ant giant
dwarf *vb syn* see STUNT
dwarf *adj syn* see TINY
dwarfish *adj syn* see TINY
dwell *vb* **1** *syn* see RESIDE 1
2 *syn* see CONSIST 3
dweller *n syn* see INHABITANT
dwelling *n syn* see HABITATION 1
dwindle *vb* **1** *syn* see DECREASE
rel ebb, subside, wane; attenuate, extenuate, thin; moderate; disappear
2 *syn* see FAIL 3
‖**dwine** *vb syn* see FAIL 1
dyad *n syn* see COUPLE
dye *n syn* see COLOR 6
dyed-in-the-wool *adj syn* see INVETERATE 1
dyestuff *n syn* see COLOR 6
dying *adj syn* see MORIBUND
dynamic *adj* **1** *syn* see ACTIVE 1
rel activating, energizing, vitalizing
ant static
2 *syn* see VIGOROUS
rel forceful, forcible; intense, vehement, violent
con idle, inactive, passive
ant inert
dynamite *vb syn* see DESTROY 1
dynamo *n syn* see HUSTLER 2
dysentery *n syn* see DIARRHEA
dyslogistic *adj syn* see DEROGATORY
ant eulogistic
dyspathy *n syn* see ANTIPATHY 2
dyspeptic *adj syn* see ILL-TEMPERED
dysphoria *n syn* see SADNESS

---

syn synonym(s)   *rel* related word(s)
ant antonym(s)   *con* contrasted word(s)
idiom idiomatic equivalent(s)
‖ use limited; if in doubt, see a dictionary

E

each *adj syn* see ALL 2
  rel any, several, various; particular, respective, specific

each *adv syn* see APIECE
  idiom a shot, a throw, a whack

eager *adj* moved by a strong and urgent desire or interest <young executives *eager* to succeed>
  syn agog, anxious, appetent, ardent, athirst, avid, breathless, impatient, keen, raring, solicitous, thirsty
  rel enthusiastic, gung ho, heated, hot; ambitious, intent; acquisitive, covetous, craving, desirous, hankering, ‖honing, hungry, longing, pining, wishful, yearning; impatient, restive, restless
  idiom champing at the bit, ready and willing
  con aloof, disinterested, incurious, indifferent, unconcerned, uninterested; apathetic, detached, impassive, stolid
  ant listless

eagerness *n* a strong and urgent desire or interest <an *eagerness* to learn>
  syn ardor, enthusiasm, zing
  rel alacrity, avidity, keenness, quickness; ambition; gusto, ‖mustard, zest
  con lackadaisicality, languor, lethargy; aloofness, disinterest, apathy, deliberation, detachment, impassivity, stolidity
  ant listlessness

eagle eye *n syn* see EYE 3

eagle–eyed *adj syn* see SHARP-EYED

ear *n syn* see NOTICE 1

earlier *adv* 1 *syn* see BEFORE 2
  2 *syn* see HITHERTO 1
  3 *syn* see BEFORE 3

earliest *adj syn* see FIRST 2
  con final, terminal, ultimate
  ant latest

early *adv* 1 at or nearly at the beginning of a period, course, process, or series <it is much too *early* to guess the outcome>
  syn betimes, seasonably, soon, timely
  rel first
  2 in advance of the expected or usual time <these apples bear *early* and heavy>
  syn betimes, oversoon, prematurely
  rel beforehand
  idiom ahead of time, bright and early

early *adj* 1 of, relating to, or occurring near the beginning of a period of time, a development, or a series <*early* Renaissance><*early* art forms>
  syn primitive, primordial
  rel original, pristine; ancient, antediluvian, antiquated, primal, primeval; antecedent, preceding, prevenient, prior
  con conclusive, final, last, terminal, ultimate; eventual; intermediate, middle, midmost

  ant late
  2 occurring before the expected or usual time <an *early* death><an *early* peach>
  syn overearly, oversoon, premature, previous, ‖soon, untimely; *compare* PRECOCIOUS
  rel anticipative, anticipatory, precipitant, precocious; unanticipated, unexpected
  con slow, tardy; anticipated, expected
  ant late

earmark *vb syn* see DESIGNATE 3

earn *vb* 1 to receive as return for effort <*earn* a living wage>
  syn acquire, bring in, ‖drag down, draw down, gain, get, knock down, make, win
  rel attain, effect, obtain, procure, realize, receive, secure
  2 to be or make worthy of <his devotion to duty *earned* him a promotion>
  syn deserve, merit, rate
  rel bag, come by, harvest, net, reap, score

earnest *n syn* see EARNESTNESS
  rel attention, interest; enthusiasm, warmth, zeal
  ant jest, play

earnest *adj syn* see SERIOUS 1
  rel ardent, enthusiastic, passionate, pressing, warm, zealous; assiduous, busy, diligent, industrious, perseverant, sedulous; sincere, wholehearted, whole-souled
  con buoyant, effervescent, elastic, flippant, light
  ant frivolous

earnest *n syn* see PLEDGE 1

earnestly *adv* 1 *syn* see HARD 3
  rel seriously, soberly, solemnly, thoughtfully; zealously
  2 *syn* see SERIOUSLY 1

earnestness *n* a state of freedom from all jesting or trifling <he studied with great *earnestness*>
  syn earnest, intentness, serious-mindedness, seriousness
  rel doggedness, perseverance, persistence; decision, determination, firmness, purposefulness, resolve; absorption, attentiveness, concentration, engrossment; deliberation; gravity, sobriety
  con levity, lightness; shallowness, superficiality; carelessness, slackness
  ant frivolity

earnings *n pl syn* see PROFIT

earshot *n* the range within which something (as a voice) may be heard <the gossips were still within *earshot* of her>
  syn hearing, sound
  idiom carrying (or hearing) distance

earsplitting *adj syn* see LOUD 1
  rel penetrating, shrill

earth *n* 1 the entire area in which man lives and acts <expect the destruction of the *earth*>

syn globe, (the) planet, world

rel orb, sphere; cosmos, creation, macrocosm, universe, vale

2 areas of land as distinguished from sea and air <clayey *earth,* difficult to drain>

syn dirt, dry land, ground, land, soil, terra firma

rel clay, gravel, humus, loam, mud, sand; fill, subsoil; terrain, turf; clod

earthlike *adj syn* see EARTHY 1

earthly *adj* 1 of, relating to, or characteristic of this earth or man's life on earth <*earthly* pursuits>

syn earthy, mundane, sublunary, tellurian, telluric, terrene, terrestrial, uncelestial, worldly

rel carnal, corporeal, earthbound, physical; material, temporal; unspiritual

con celestial, empyreal, empyrean, heavenly; ideal, utopian; divine, spiritual

2 *syn* see PROBABLE

rel imaginable, potential

earthquake *n* a shaking or trembling of the earth that is volcanic or tectonic in origin <homes destroyed by *earthquakes*>

syn quake, ‖quaker, shake, shock, temblor (*or* tremblor), tremor

earthy *adj* 1 consisting of, resembling, or suggesting earth <a stale *earthy* smell>

syn earthlike, terrene, terrestrial

rel clayey, dusty, muddy, sandy

2 *syn* see EARTHLY 1

3 *syn* see MATERIALISTIC

4 *syn* see REALISTIC

ant impractical

ease *n* 1 *syn* see REST 1

rel idleness, inactivity, inertia, inertness, passivity, supinity; calmness, security

con labor, toil, travail; adversity, difficulty; burden, care, worry

2 *syn* see UNCONCERN

3 freedom from or mitigation of pain <medication brought him instant *ease*>

syn alleviation, easement, mitigation, relief

rel decrease, diminishment, moderation, reduction; calming, soothing

con discomfort, unrest; agony, pain

4 *syn* see READINESS 3

rel adroitness, artfulness, cleverness, deftness, effortlessness, expertise, expertness, fluency, knack, poise, skillfulness, smoothness; dispatch, efficiency

con awkwardness, clumsiness, maladroitness, stiffness, woodenness; constraint; inconvenience, pains; exertion

ant effort

5 *syn* see PROSPERITY 2

ease *vb* 1 *syn* see RELIEVE 1

rel deaden, dull; ameliorate, help

con afflict, torment

2 *syn* see LOOSE 5

rel disengage, free, release

con bind, restrain, tighten

3 to make less difficult <new laws that will *ease* voting requirements>

---

syn synonym(s)   *rel* related word(s)
ant antonym(s)   *con* contrasted word(s)
idiom idiomatic equivalent(s)
‖ use limited; if in doubt, see a dictionary

syn facilitate

rel aid, assist, better, help, improve; forward, further, promote, speed

idiom clear (*or* prepare) the way (for), grease the wheels, open the door (to *or* for)

con hinder, impede, retard

easeful *adj syn* see COMFORTABLE 2

easement *n syn* see EASE 3

rel allayment, appeasement, assuagement, mollification

ease off *vb* 1 *syn* see LOOSE 5

2 *syn* see ABATE 4

3 *syn* see RELAX 2

easily *adv* 1 without discomfort, difficulty, or reluctance <*easily* translated the document>

syn effortlessly, facilely, freely, lightly, readily, smoothly, well

rel competently, dexterously, efficiently, fluently, handily, simply

idiom hands down, slick as a whistle

con awkwardly, clumsily, ineptly, stiffly; arduously, wearily

ant laboriously

2 without question <this is *easily* the best course of action>

syn absolutely, definitely, doubtless, doubtlessly, positively, unequivocally, unquestionably

rel actually, assuredly, certainly, clearly, decidedly, indeed, really, truly, undoubtedly

idiom no doubt

con apparently, perhaps, probably, seemingly; doubtfully, equivocally, questionably

3 *syn* see WELL 7

easy *adj* 1 causing or involving little or no difficulty <an *easy* solution>

syn effortless, facile, light, royal, simple, smooth, untroublesome

rel apparent, clear, distinct, evident, manifest, obvious, plain; clear-cut, straightforward, uncomplicated, uncompounded, uninvolved

idiom easy as falling off a log, easy as pie, nothing to it

con arduous, difficult, troublesome; abstruse, complex, complicated, intricate, knotty

ant hard

2 *syn* see FORBEARING

rel compassionate, condoning, excusing, forgiving, pardoning, sympathetic; benign, kindly; lax, moderate, soft; humoring, mollycoddling, pampering, spoiling

con austere, exacting, rigid, severe, stern, strict, stringent

3 easily taken advantage of or imposed upon <he was *easy* prey to her wiles>

syn fleeceable, gullible, naive, susceptible

rel credulous, trusting, unmistrusting, unsuspicious; deceivable, deludable, dupable, exploitable; artless, dewy-eyed, green, simple, unsophisticated

con critical, cynical, disbelieving, mistrustful, scoffing, skeptical, suspicious, unbelieving

4 *syn* see FAST 7

5 *syn* see COMFORTABLE 2

rel secure

con discontented, dissatisfied; miserable

ant uncomfortable

6 *syn* see AMIABLE 1
rel familiar, gregarious, informal; courtly, diplomatic, pleasant, polite, sociable; smooth, suave, urbane
con brusque, curt, unfriendly, unpleasant; constrained, embarrassed, formal, restrained; discourteous, impolite, undiplomatic, ungracious; stiff, unsocial, withdrawn, wooden
ant ill at ease

7 *syn* see CALM 2
rel relaxed; lethargic, unambitious
con agitated, tense, troubled, uptight

8 *syn* see PROSPEROUS 3
rel successful, thriving
idiom in easy circumstances, on easy street
con straitened

9 marked by ready facility (as of expression) <an *easy* style of writing>
syn cursive, effortless, flowing, fluent, running, smooth
rel facile; graceful
con effortful, labored
ant difficult

easygoing *adj* **1** *syn* see CALM 2
con agitated, flurried, flustered, harassed; anxious, concerned, upset, worried
ant uptight

2 *syn* see LAZY
rel apathetic, careless, indifferent, unconcerned; unambitious
con active, ambitious, diligent, dynamic, energetic, industrious, live, vigorous

3 not constrained or bound by rigid standards <enjoyed the *easygoing* morality of a commune>
syn breezy, casual, ‖common, dégagé, hang-loose, informal, low-pressure, relaxed, ‖sonsy, unconstrained, unfussy, unreserved
rel affable, folksy; flexible, lax, moderate, offhand, off-handed, unaffected; carefree, devil-may-care, happy-go-lucky; outgiving; uninhibited
idiom free and easy
con ceremonious, decorous, formal, proper, stuffy; constrained, inflexible, inhibited, restrained, rigid, starchy, stiff

easy mark *n* **1** *syn* see FOOL 3

2 *syn* see SOFT TOUCH 1

‖**easy rider** *n* **1** *syn* see SYCOPHANT

2 *syn* see PIMP 1

easy street *n* *syn* see PROSPERITY 2

eat *vb* **1** to take in as food <they quickly *ate* a light breakfast>
syn consume, devour, feed (on), ingest, meal, partake (of), take; *compare* CONSUME 5
rel banquet, feast, gormandize; eat up, gobble (up *or* down), gorge (on), ‖mop (up), polish off, scoff; breakfast, dine, lunch, nosh, snack, sup; mouth, ‖muckamuck, nibble, pick
idiom break bread, get away with, have (*or* take) a bite, take nourishment, ‖put on the feed bag

2 *syn* see CONSUME 1

3 to consume gradually <the acid *ate* the surface of the copper>
syn bite, corrode, eat away, erode, gnaw, scour, wear (away)

rel nibble (away); consume, decompose, disintegrate, dissolve

eatable *adj* *syn* see EDIBLE

eat away *vb* *syn* see EAT 3

eating house *n* a cheap often small restaurant <grabbed a quick sandwich at a local *eating house*>
syn beanery, ‖buffet, café, ‖caff, coffee shop, cookshop, diner, ‖greasy spoon, ‖hashery, ‖hash house, lunch counter (*or* bar), luncheonette, lunchroom, lunch wagon (*or* cart), quick-lunch, sandwich shop, snack bar (*or* counter)
rel cafeteria, eatery, tearoom; trattoria

‖**eats** *n pl syn* see FOOD 1

eat up *vb* **1** to eat completely and without delay <*eat up* your dinner before it gets cold>
syn devour, dispatch, polish off
rel down, eat; bolt, gobble (up *or* down), gorge (on), ‖mop (up), wolf

2 *syn* see CONSUME 1

‖**3** *syn* see DEVOUR 5
rel luxuriate (in), riot (in), wallow (in)
idiom be beside oneself over, be thrilled to death by, smack one's lips over, take delight in

‖**4** *syn* see LOVE 1

ebb *vb* *syn* see ABATE 4
rel decline, peter (out); recede, retreat, retrograde
con ascend, increase, mount, rise; advance, progress
ant flow

ebbing *n* *syn* see FAILURE 4
rel declining, sinking

ebon *adj* *syn* see BLACK 1

ebony *adj* *syn* see BLACK 1

ebullience *n* lively or enthusiastic expression of thoughts or feelings <her bubbling *ebullience* was infectious>
syn buoyancy, effervescence, exuberance, exuberancy
rel animation, enthusiasm, gaiety, high-spiritedness, liveliness, vitality, vivaciousness, vivacity; agitation, excitement, exhilaration, ferment
con apathy, impassivity, languor, lethargy, listlessness, passivity, sluggishness, stolidity, torpidity, torpor; enervation, inactivity, inertia, lifelessness; disinterest, unconcern, uninterest

ebullient *adj* *syn* see EXUBERANT 1

eccentric *adj* **1** not having the same center <not concentric but *eccentric* circles>
syn off-center
rel uncentered; off-balance, unbalanced
con centered; balanced
ant concentric

2 *syn* see STRANGE 4
rel anomalous, irregular, unnatural; exceptionable, exceptional, quirky, quizzical; beheaded, ‖dippy, wacky; fantastic, grotesque
con customary, habitual; natural, normal, regular, typical

eccentric *n* one who deviates from established patterns especially in odd or whimsical ways <an *eccentric* who filled his house with statues of himself>

syn case, character, ||duck, oddball, oddity, original, quiz, ||spook, ||wack, zombie
rel bohemian, maverick, nonconformist, unconformist; dissenter, heretic; caution, coot, ||geezer; crackpot, crank, freak, kook, screwball
idiom queer duck (*or* potato)
con conformer, conformist, conventionalist, traditionalist; bore, bromide, dullard

ecclesiast *n syn see* CLERGYMAN

ecclesiastic *n syn see* CLERGYMAN

ecclesiastical *adj* of, relating to, or belonging to a church especially as an established institution <*ecclesiastical* law>
syn church, churchly, churchmanly, spiritual
rel apostolic, canonical, episcopal, episcopalian, evangelistic, theological; clerical, ministerial, papal, pastoral, patriarchal, pontifical, prelatial, priestly, rabbinical, sacerdotal; cathedralesque, churchlike, pantheonic, synagogal, synagogical, tabernacular, templelike
con lay, secular

ecdysiast *n syn see* STRIPTEASER

echelon *n syn see* LINE 5

echoic *adj syn see* ONOMATOPOEIC

éclat *n syn see* FAME 2
rel bang, brilliance, brilliancy, display, luster, noticeableness, prominence, remarkableness; distinction, standing; kudos
con oblivion, obscurity; contempt, derision, scorn

eclectic *adj* 1 selecting what appears to be the best from various doctrines, methods, or styles <an *eclectic* taste in music>
syn discriminating, select, selective
rel elective, selecting; choosing, choosy, discerning, fastidious, finicky, fussy, particular, picky
2 composed of elements drawn from various sources <an *eclectic* art incorporating romanticism and impressionism>
syn catholic
rel broad, comprehensive, inclusive; assorted, mingled, mixed; diverse, diversified, heterogeneous, multifarious, multiform, varied; derived, unoriginal
con distinctive, narrow; new, original

eclipse *vb syn see* OBSCURE

economical *adj syn see* SPARING
rel careful, forehanded, prudent; economizing, penny-wise; cheeseparing, close, mean, miserly, niggardly, penny-pinching, penurious, scrimping, skimping, spare, stingy
con generous, lavish, wasteful
ant extravagant

economic poison *n syn see* PESTICIDE

economize *vb* to avoid unnecessary waste or expense <*economize* on food by using leftovers>
syn save
rel conserve; scrimp, skimp
con dissipate, scatter, waste
ant squander, throw away

---

syn synonym(s)   *rel* related word(s)
ant antonym(s)   *con* contrasted word(s)
idiom idiomatic equivalent(s)
|| use limited; if in doubt, see a dictionary

---

economy *n* careful management of material resources <retired people often must learn to practice *economy*>
syn forehandedness, frugality, husbandry, providence, prudence, thrift, thriftiness
rel meanness, miserliness, niggardliness, parcity, parsimony, scrimping, skimping, stinginess; carefulness, discretion
con improvidence, lavishness, prodigality, squandering, thriftlessness, wastefulness
ant extravagance

ecstasy *n* intense exaltation of mind and feelings <was in *ecstasy* over flying>
syn heaven, rapture, rhapsody, seventh heaven, transport; *compare* EXHILARATION
rel beatitude, blessedness, bliss, blissfulness, felicity, gladness, happiness; delectation, delight, elation, joy, joyfulness, overjoyfulness, pleasure; enchantment, euphoria, intoxication, madness; exaltation, inspiration; paradise; afflatus, frenzy, fury
idiom cloud nine
con dejection, downheartedness, lowness, low-spiritedness, oppression; blues, dumps, melancholy
ant depression

ecumenical *adj syn see* UNIVERSAL 2
rel heaven-wide; all-comprehending, all-comprehensive, all-covering, all-including, all-pervading; comprehensive, general, inclusive
con diocesan, local, parochial, provincial; circumscribed, insular, limited, narrow, restricted

edacious *adj syn see* VORACIOUS

eddy *n* a swirling mass especially of water <dark *eddies* in the flooded stream>
syn maelstrom, vortex, whirl, whirlpool
rel gurge, surge, swirl, twirl, whirl; back current, back stream, countercurrent, counterflow, counterflux; backwash, backwater

eddy *vb syn see* SWIRL

edge *n* 1 *syn see* BORDER 1
rel end, extremity; ledge, side
con area, surface
2 a cutting quality <there was an *edge* to his voice as he answered>
syn incisiveness, keenness, sharpness
rel bite, cut, sting; knife-edge, razor-edge; acerbity, acidity, acridity, causticity; astringency, stringency; acuteness, penetration, shrillness, thinness
3 *syn see* VERGE 2
4 *syn see* ADVANTAGE 3
con bar, encumbrance, obstacle; disadvantage

edge *vb* 1 *syn see* SHARPEN
2 *syn see* BORDER 1
3 *syn see* SIDLE

edge in *vb syn see* INSINUATE 3

edgy *adj* 1 *syn see* TENSE 2
rel skittish; excitable, excited, high-strung, overstrung; irritable, touchy; impatient, restless
idiom on edge
con detached; peaceful, placid; patient
2 *syn see* EXCITABLE

edible *adj* suitable for use as food <*edible* plant products>
syn comestible, eatable, esculent

rel digestible; nourishing, nutritious, nutritive; palatable, savory, succulent, tasty, toothsome
ant inedible

edibles *n pl syn* see FOOD 1

edict *n* **1** a publicly proclaimed order or rule of conduct by a competent authority <a government *edict* regarding curfew enforcement>
syn decree, directive, ruling, ukase
rel instrument; order; manifesto, proclamation, pronouncement, pronunciamiento; bull
2 *syn* see LAW 1

edifice *n* a large, magnificent, or massive building <a marble *edifice* now used as a museum>
syn erection, pile, structure; *compare* BUILDING, HUT

edify *vb syn* see ILLUMINATE 2
rel better, enhance; elucidate; educate, instruct, teach
con debase, deprave

edition *n* the total number of copies of the same work printed during a stretch of time <the initial *edition* of 50,000 copies was exhausted in a month>
syn impression, printing, reissue, reprinting

educate *vb syn* see TEACH
rel cultivate, nurture; brief, explain, inform

education *n* **1** the act or process of educating <devoted herself to the *education* of illiterate adults>
syn instruction, schooling, teaching, training, tuition, tutelage
rel coaching, pedagogy, tutorage, tutoring, tutorship; direction, guidance
2 the product or result of being educated <obtained his *education* in local schools and in college>
syn erudition, knowledge, learning, scholarship, science
rel culture, edification, enlightenment, learnedness, literacy
con ignorance, illiteracy

educational *adj syn* see INFORMATIVE

educative *adj syn* see INFORMATIVE

educe *vb* **1** to draw out something hidden, latent, or reserved <*educed* important information from the witness>
syn elicit, evince, evoke, extort, extract, milk
rel drag, draw, draw out, pull, wrest, wring; gain, get, obtain, procure, secure; distill
con miss, overlook, pass over
2 *syn* see DERIVE 1
rel reason (out), think (out)

eerie *adj syn* see WEIRD 1
rel bizarre, fantastic, grotesque; arcane; crawly

efface *vb syn* see ERASE
rel eradicate, extirpate; eliminate, exclude, rule out

effect *n* **1** a condition or occurrence traceable to a cause <the *effect* of the medicine was dizziness>
syn aftereffect, aftermath, causatum, consequence, corollary, end product, event, eventuality, issue, outcome, precipitate, result, sequel, sequence, upshot

rel pursuance; development, fruit, outgrowth, ramification; denouement, repercussion; conclusion, end; side effect
con antecedent, determinant, occasion, reason; base, basis, foundation, ground, groundwork
ant cause

2 effects *pl syn* see POSSESSION 2

3 the force of impression of one thing on another <had a profound *effect* on our lives>
syn impact, imprint, influence, mark, repercussion
rel backlash, backwash; recoil, reflex, response; aftereffect, aftermath

effect *vb* **1** to induce to come into being <specific genes *effect* specific bodily characters>
syn bring about, cause, draw on, make, produce, secure
rel conceive, create, generate; bring on, induce; enact, render, turn out, yield
con impede, limit, restrict; repress, suppress
2 to carry to a successful conclusion <found a pass that allowed them to *effect* passage through the mountains>
syn bring off, carry out, carry through, effectuate; *compare* FULFILL 1, PERFORM 2
rel actualize, realize; achieve, procure
con fail, fall down
3 *syn* see ENFORCE

effective *adj* producing or capable of producing a result <an *effective* rebuke>
syn effectual, efficacious, efficient, virtuous
rel adequate, capable, competent; cogent, compelling, convincing, sound, telling, valid; able, active, dynamic; operative, useful; direct
con abortive, bootless, fruitless, futile, vain; empty, hollow, idle, nugatory, otiose, pointless; inoperative, useless, worthless
ant ineffective

effectiveness *n* **1** *syn* see POINT 3
rel forcefulness, potency, power, strength, verve, vigor
con impotence, weakness
ant ineffectiveness
2 *syn* see EFFICIENCY 1
3 *syn* see EFFICACY 1

effectual *adj syn* see EFFECTIVE
rel accomplishing, achieving, effecting, fulfilling; practicable, sound, useful, valid, workable; conclusive, decisive, determinative, influential; authoritative, potent, powerful, strong, toothy
con impotent, weak
ant ineffectual

effectuate *vb syn* see EFFECT 2

effeminate *adj* lacking manly strength and purpose <a young man with extravagant and *effeminate* mannerisms>
syn epicene, Miss-Nancyish, pansified, prissy, sissified, sissy, unmanly
rel chichi, old-maidish, overnice, precious; foppish, sappy, silken
ant manly, masculine

effervescence *n syn* see EBULLIENCE
rel bubbling, ebullition, fizzing, foaming
con deadness, flatness, staleness

effervescent *adj* **1** *syn* see EXUBERANT 1
2 *syn* see ELASTIC 2

rel animated, boiling, bubbly, excited, gay, lively, sparkling, sprightly, vivacious; gleeful, hilarious, jolly, mirthful
con lifeless, listless, subdued; earnest, sedate, serious, solemn

effete *adj* **1** *syn* see STERILE 1
2 having lost energy or drive <*effete*, weary, burned-out revolutionaries>
syn all in, bleary, ‖clapped-out, depleted, done, done in, drained, exhausted, far-gone, spent, used up, washed-out, worn-out
rel consumed; debilitated, enfeebled, fatigued
idiom on one's last legs, out on one's feet
con alive, lively, vigorous, vital
3 having lost character <a soft, *effete* society>
syn decadent, decayed, degenerate, overripe
rel decaying, declining; soft, weak; dissolute, immoral

efficacious *adj* *syn* see EFFECTIVE
rel active, operative, productive; influential, potent, powerful, puissant, strong
con abortive; impotent, powerless, useless, vain, weak
ant inefficacious

efficacy *n* **1** the power to produce an effect <*efficacy* of the drug>
syn capability, effectiveness, efficiency, potency
rel capableness, use; adequacy, capacity, sufficiency
con ineffectiveness, inefficiency; uselessness, worthlessness
ant inefficacy
2 *syn* see EFFICIENCY 1

efficiency *n* **1** the capacity to produce desired results with a minimum expenditure of energy, time, or resources <demands a high degree of *efficiency* on the job>
syn effectiveness, efficacy, performance
rel ability, address, adeptness, competence, expertise, know-how, proficiency, prowess, skill; capability, resourcefulness; productivity
con inadequacy, incompetence, ineffectiveness; unproductiveness
ant inefficiency
2 *syn* see EFFICACY 1

efficient *adj* *syn* see EFFECTIVE
rel able, capable, competent, fitted, qualified; adept, expert, masterly, proficient, skilled, skillful
con incapable, incompetent, inexpert, unadept, unproficient, unqualified, unsuitable; unproductive; ineffectual
ant inefficient

effloresce *vb* *syn* see BLOSSOM

effort *n* **1** the active use of energy in producing a result <thought the job wasn't worth the *effort*>
syn elbow grease, exertion, pains, trouble, while
rel labor, toil, travail, work; energy, force, might, power, puissance; attempt, endeavor, essay

idiom sweat of one's brow
con adroitness, facility, smoothness; do-nothingness, inaction, indolence, inertia, lackadaisicalness, languor, laziness
ant ease
2 *syn* see TASK 2

effortful *adj* *syn* see HARD 6

effortless *adj* **1** *syn* see EASY 1
rel adept, expert, masterly, proficient, ready, skilled, skillful
con laborious, toilsome, trying
ant painstaking
2 *syn* see EASY 9

effortlessly *adv* *syn* see EASILY 1
rel adeptly, adroitly, efficiently, expertly, proficiently, skillfully
con painstakingly
ant arduously, laboriously

effrontery *n* flagrant disregard of courtesy or propriety and an arrogant assumption of privilege <had the *effrontery* to insult her father>
syn brashness, brass, cheek, chutzpah, confidence, ‖crust, face, gall, nerve, presumption; *compare* INSOLENCE
rel audacity, hardihood, temerity; assurance, self-assurance, self-confidence; brazenness, impudence; impertinence, insolence
con courtesy, grace, propriety

effulgent *adj* *syn* see BRIGHT 1
rel vivid; glorious, resplendent, splendid
con dark, dusky, gloomy, murky

effusive *adj* unduly demonstrative <*effusive* assurances of undying love>
syn gushing, gushy, slobbering, slobbery, sloppy
rel expansive, fulsome, outpouring, profuse; demonstrative, unconstrained, unreserved, unrestrained; cloying, slushy; smarmy
con close, restrained, reticent, taciturn; bashful, modest, shy
ant reserved

egg (on) *vb* *syn* see URGE
rel agitate, excite, pique, stimulate; instigate; arouse, drive, rally, stir up, whip (on *or* up)
con arrest, bridle

egghead *n* *syn* see INTELLECTUAL 2

egocentric *adj* **1** concerned with the individual person rather than society <an *egocentric* approach to world problems>
syn individualist, individualistic
rel self-centered, selfish
2 concerned only with one's own activities or needs and usually tending to self-assertion or self-satisfaction <an *egocentric* man, lacking feeling for others>
syn egoistic, egomaniacal, egotistic, self-absorbed, self-centered, self-concerned, self-interested, self-involved, selfish, self-seeking, self-serving; *compare* POMPOUS 1
rel conceited, narcissistic, self-affected, self-applauding, self-conceited, self-concentered, self-indulgent, self-loving, stuck-up, vainglorious; megalomaniac
idiom wrapped up in oneself

egoism *n* **1** *syn* see EGOTISM 1
rel self-assurance, self-confidence, self-possession
ant altruism

---

syn synonym(s)   *rel* related word(s)
ant antonym(s)   *con* contrasted word(s)
idiom idiomatic equivalent(s)
‖ use limited; if in doubt, see a dictionary

2 *syn* see CONCEIT 2
rel self-satisfaction
con meekness, modesty
ant humility

egoistic *adj syn* see EGOCENTRIC 2
rel individualistic; self-satisfied, swell-headed
con humble, modest
ant altruistic

egomaniacal *adj syn* see EGOCENTRIC 2
rel self-exalting, self-glorifying, vainglorious

egotism *n* **1** an exaggerated sense of one's own importance <in believing that he was indispensable, he exhibited consummate *egotism*>
syn egoism, self-importance
rel conceit, conceitedness, narcissism, self=esteem, self-love, vainness; boastfulness, boasting, bragging, gasconade, gasconism, megalomania, vaunting
con humility, lowliness; bashfulness, diffidence, shyness; modesty
ant altruism
2 *syn* see CONCEIT 2
rel arrogance, superiority; contempt
con humbleness, self-effacement
ant humility

egotistic *adj syn* see EGOCENTRIC 2
rel boastful, cocky, inflated, pretentious, proud, puffed up, self-satisfied; conceited, stuck-up
idiom in love with oneself, stuck on oneself
con humble, modest; self-effacing, shy

egregious *adj* conspicuously bad or objectionable <an *egregious* mistake>
syn capital, flagrant, glaring, gross, rank
rel arrant, outright, stark; infamous, nefarious, notorious; atrocious, deplorable, heinous, monstrous, outrageous, preposterous
con measly, minor, petty, piddling, slender, slight, trifling, trivial

egress *n* **1** *syn* see DEPARTURE 1
rel emergence, emerging
con coming, entering; arrival
ant ingress
2 a place or means of going out <a gate providing *egress* from the pasture>
syn exit, outlet
rel opening, passage; escape
idiom way out
con entrance, entry, entryway
ant access, ingress

egression *n syn* see DEPARTURE 1
con entrance, entering
ant ingression

eidolon *n syn* see APPARITION

ejaculate *vb syn* see EXCLAIM
rel call (out), shout, vociferate, yell

eject *vb* **1** to drive or force (somebody) out <*eject* an intruder from one's home>
syn boot (out), chase, chuck, dismiss, evict, extrude, kick out, out, throw out; *compare* BANISH
rel displace, dispossess; drive off, rout, run off; debar, disbar, eliminate, exclude, rule out, shut out; bump, cashier, discharge, fire, sack; discard, shed; reject, repudiate, spurn
idiom give one his walking papers, send packing, show one the door

con accept, admit, install, receive; entertain, harbor, house, lodge, shelter
2 *syn* see ERUPT 1

elaborate *adj* **1** *syn* see COMPLEX 2
2 marked by complexity of detail or ornament <an *elaborate* coiffure>
syn complicated, fancy, intricate
rel detailed, highly-wrought; decorated, dressy, embellished, ornate; elegant; busy, overdone, overworked, overwrought
con common, ordinary, plain, unpolished; inartificial, inornate, natural
ant simple

elaborate *vb* **1** *syn* see EXPAND 4
rel comment, discuss, dwell (upon); clarify, explain, expound, interpret
2 *syn* see UNFOLD 3

élan *n syn* see SPIRIT 5
rel impetus

élan vital *n syn* see SOUL 1

elapse *vb syn* see PASS 3
rel flow, glide, pass (by), slide, slip (by); lapse, run out

elastic *adj* **1** able to withstand strain without being permanently affected or injured <a rubber band is *elastic*>
syn flexible, resilient, springy, stretch, stretchy, supple, whippy
rel ductile, malleable, pliable, pliant, plastic, rubberlike, rubbery; adaptable, moldable, stretchable, yielding; bouncy, limber, lithe
con brittle; inflexible, stiff, tense
ant rigid
2 able to recover quickly from depression and maintain high spirits <had an *elastic* optimistic nature>
syn airy, bouncy, buoyant, effervescent, expansive, resilient, volatile
rel animated, gay, lively, sprightly, vivacious; ebullient, high-spirited, mettlesome, soaring, spirited; adaptable, recuperative
con blue, dejected, depressed, gloomy, melancholy, sad; flaccid, limp

elate *vb* to elevate the spirits of <the phenomenal sales record *elated* him>
syn commove, excite, exhilarate, inspire, set up, spirit (up), stimulate
rel brighten, cheer, cheer up, encourage; delight, gladden, gratify, overjoy; buoy, elevate, exalt, uplift
con distress; oppress, weigh; weary
ant depress

elated *adj syn* see INTOXICATED 2
rel enchanted, enraptured, exalted, transported; delighted, ecstatic, euphoric, exultant, jubilant, overjoyed
idiom in heaven, in seventh heaven, on cloud nine
con blue, deflated, unhappy

elation *n* **1** the quality or state of being elated <felt great *elation* when he won the presidential nomination>
syn euphoria, exaltation, exhilaration
rel buoyancy; happiness, joy; excitement; rapture, transport
idiom stars in one's eyes
con blues, depression; distress, misery, sadness, unhappiness
ant deflation

2 *syn* see EUPHORIA 2
   ant depression
elbow *vb syn* see PUSH 2
elbowroom *n syn* see ROOM 3
   rel space
elder *n* 1 *syn* see SENIOR 2
   2 *syn* see OLDSTER
   3 *syn* see SUPERIOR
elderliness *n syn* see OLD AGE
elderly *adj syn* see AGED 1
   rel aging, declining
   con juvenile, young
   ant youthful
eldorado *n syn* see BONANZA
elect *adj syn* see SELECT 1
   rel choice, rare; hand-picked, singled out;
   designated, destined, ordained; delivered,
   redeemed, saved
   con refused, rejected, repudiated, spurned;
   disdained, scorned; damned, doomed, reprobate
elect *vb* 1 *syn* see CHOOSE 1
   rel decide, determine, resolve, settle; conclude, judge; accept, admit, receive
   con reject; dismiss, eject, expel, oust
   ant abjure
   2 to select by or as if by ballot <the board of
   directors *elected* a new chairman>
   syn ballot, vote (in)
   rel choose, designate, name, opt, pick, select, single; nominate; appoint
   3 *syn* see WILL
election *n syn* see CHOICE 1
elective *adj syn* see OPTIONAL
electrify *vb syn* see THRILL
   rel provoke; jar, stagger, stun
eleemosynary *adj syn* see CHARITABLE 1
   rel beneficent, generous, liberal, munificent,
   openhanded
   con close, parsimonious, tight
elegance *n* impressive beauty of form, appearance, or behavior <the sumptuous *elegance* of the furnishings>
   syn dignity, grace
   rel beauty, charm; cultivation, culture,
   polish, refinement, sophistication, style,
   taste, tastefulness; lushness, magnificence,
   ornateness, poshness, richness, splendor,
   sumptuousness
   con grotesqueness, ugliness; clumsiness,
   crudeness, roughness, rudeness; austerity,
   bareness, inornateness, severity
elegant *adj syn* see CHOICE
   rel august, grand, majestic, noble, stately;
   beautiful, graceful, handsome, lovely; cultivated, cultured, finished, polished, refined,
   tasteful; luxurious, opulent, sumptuous
   con coarse, rough, rude, uncouth; grotesque
element *n* 1 *syn* see ESSENTIAL 1
   2 one of the parts, substances, or principles
   that make up a compound or complex whole
   <analyzed the various *elements* of the
   problem>
   syn component, constituent, factor, ingredient; *compare* POINT 1

   rel fundamental, principle; item, member,
   part, particle, piece, portion; detail, particular; aspect, facet, feature, view
   con bulk, mass, volume; entirety, whole;
   sum, total, totality
   ant composite, compound
   3 **elements** *pl syn* see ALPHABET 2
   rel basics, basis, foundations, groundwork;
   outlines
   4 *syn* see POINT 1
   rel division, member, section, sector, segment
elemental *adj* 1 of, relating to, or being an
   ultimate and irreducible element <such
   elemental aspects of life as sex and nutri-
   tion>
   syn basic, elementary, essential, fundamental, primitive, substratal, underlying
   rel primary, prime, primordial; inherent,
   intrinsic, radical
   con secondary, subordinate; casual, incidental, trivial, unimportant
   2 *syn* see ELEMENTARY 1
   3 *syn* see INHERENT
elementary *adj* 1 of, relating to, or dealing
   with the simplest principles of something
   <can't handle the most *elementary* decision-
   making>
   syn basal, beginning, elemental, rudimental, rudimentary, simplest
   rel introductory, prefatory, preliminary;
   easy, simple; rude, unsubtle
   con complex, complicated, elaborate, intricate, labyrinthine; sophisticated
   ant advanced
   2 *syn* see ELEMENTAL 1
elephantine *adj* 1 *syn* see HUGE
   con slender, slight, slim, thin; dainty
   2 *syn* see PONDEROUS 2
   rel awkward, clumsy, graceless, maladroit,
   ungraceful
   con graceful, nimble, quick
elevate *vb* 1 *syn* see LIFT 1
   rel ensky, erect
   con cut (down), deflate, depress, scale
   (down)
   ant lower
   2 *syn* see ADVANCE 2
   rel boost; enhance, glorify, heighten
   con demote, downgrade, lower, reduce;
   abase, debase, degrade
elevated *adj* 1 being positioned above a
   surface <an *elevated* monorail>
   syn lifted, raised, upheaved, uplifted,
   upraised, uprisen
   rel high; aerial
   con ground-level, low, lowered, low-lying,
   unelevated
   ant sunken
   2 being on a high moral or intellectual plane
   <*elevated* ideas>
   syn high-minded, moral, noble
   rel ethical, honorable, righteous, upright,
   upstanding, virtuous
   con base, ignoble, mean; immoral, low,
   unethical; intolerable, unacceptable
   3 *syn* see GRAND 3
   4 being exceedingly dignified in form, tone,
   or style <an *elevated* prose style>
   syn eloquent, high, lofty

---

syn synonym(s)   *rel* related word(s)
ant antonym(s)   *con* contrasted word(s)
idiom idiomatic equivalent(s)
‖ use limited; if in doubt, see a dictionary

rel dignified, formal; grand, grandiloquent, grandiose, high-flown, majestic, stately, towering
con informal; lowly, unassuming

elevation *n* **1** *syn* see HEIGHT
rel acclivity, ascent; rise
con depression, descent; flatness, levelness
2 *syn* see ADVANCEMENT 1
rel advance, boost, raise; ennoblement, exaltation, glorification, lionization; apotheosis, deification, immortalization; magnification
con downgrading; depreciation, detraction, disparagement
ant degradation

elf *n* *syn* see FAIRY

elicit *vb* *syn* see EDUCE 1
rel bring, fetch
con eschew, forego; abandon

elide *vb* *syn* see NEGLECT

eligible *adj* qualified to be or worthy of being chosen <an *eligible* bachelor>
syn fit, suitable
rel acceptable, desirable, likely, preferable, seemly; capable, fitted, qualified, suited, worthy; marriageable, nubile; visitable
con undesirable; disqualified, unfit, unqualified, unsuitable, unworthy
ant ineligible

eliminate *vb* **1** *syn* see EXCLUDE
rel freeze out, shut out; dismiss, ‖dump, eject, evict, expel, oust; delete, erase, expunge
con accept, receive
2 *syn* see REMOVE 4
3 *syn* see PURGE 3

elite *n* **1** *syn* see BEST
rel elect, pink, select; ‖hoi polloi
idiom cream of the crop, crème de la crème, pick of the bunch
2 *syn* see ARISTOCRACY
rel drawing rooms; Four Hundred; beautiful people, jet set, smart set
idiom high society, horsey set
con hoi polloi, (the) masses, mob, peasantry, people, proletariat, rabble

elixir *n* *syn* see PANACEA
rel balm, cure, therapy, therapeutic

ell *n* *syn* see ANNEX

elocution *n* *syn* see ORATORY

elongate *vb* *syn* see EXTEND 3
rel drag (out); string
con contract, draw in; compress; curtail, retrench; shrink
ant abbreviate, shorten

elongate *adj* *syn* see LONG 1
rel lengthened
ant abbreviated, shortened

elongated *adj* *syn* see LONG 1
rel drawn (out), lengthened, prolonged, prolonged, protracted, stretched
con contracted, drawn (in), shrunken
ant shortened

elongation *n* *syn* see EXTENSION 1

elope *vb* to go away secretly usually with the intention of marrying <decided to *elope* rather than endure a big wedding>
syn run away
idiom go to Gretna Green

eloquence *n* discourse marked by force and persuasiveness suggesting strong feeling <read the poem with *eloquence*>
syn expression, expressiveness, expressivity, facundity
rel meaningfulness, persuasiveness; fervor, force, forcefulness, passion, power, spirit, vigor

eloquent *adj* **1** *syn* see VOCAL 3
rel forceful, potent, powerful; ardent, fervent, fervid, impassioned, passionate; glib, silver-tongued, voluble
con inarticulate, ineffective, weak
2 *syn* see EXPRESSIVE
rel graphic, indicative, revealing, suggestive, telling; affecting, impressive, moving, poignant, touching
3 *syn* see ELEVATED 4

else *adv* *syn* see OTHERWISE 2

else *adj* *syn* see ADDITIONAL

‖**elseways** *adv* *syn* see OTHERWISE 2

elsewise *adv* *syn* see OTHERWISE 2

elucidate *vb* *syn* see CLARIFY 2
rel exemplify; demonstrate, prove; annotate, spell out; enlighten
con confuse, darken

elude *vb* *syn* see ESCAPE 2
rel baffle, circumvent, foil, frustrate, outwit, thwart; flee, fly
idiom give the slip
con accost, face; chase, follow, pursue, tag, tail, trail

elusion *n* *syn* see ESCAPE 2

elusive *adj* not easily perceived, grasped, comprehended, pinned down, or isolated <inspiration need not be forever *elusive*> <they finally isolated the *elusive* virus that caused the disease>
syn elusory, evasive, intangible
rel evanescent, fleeting, fugitive; baffling, imponderable, incomprehensible, mysterious; insubstantial, phantom

elusory *adj* *syn* see ELUSIVE
rel nebulous, vague

elvish *adj* *syn* see PLAYFUL 1

elysium *n* *syn* see HEAVEN 2

emaciated *adj* being very lean through loss of flesh (as from hunger or disease) <*emaciated* bony hands clutched at him>
syn cadaverous, gaunt, skeletal, wasted
rel bony, lean, scrawny, skinny, wizened; starved, underfed, undernourished
idiom all skin and bones, thin as a rail
con fit, husky, solid, well-fed, well-nourished; chubby, plump, portly, rotund, stocky, stout; corpulent, obese
ant fleshy

emanate *vb* *syn* see SPRING 1
rel initiate; emit, exude, radiate

emancipate *vb* *syn* see FREE
ant enslave

emasculate *vb* *syn* see UNNERVE
rel debilitate, devitalize
con energize, vitalize

emasculate *adj* *syn* see WEAK 4

embark *vb* *syn* see BOARD 1

embark (on *or* upon) *vb* *syn* see BEGIN 1

embarrass *vb* to throw into a state of self-conscious distress <bawdy stories *embarrassed* her>

syn abash, confound, confuse, discomfit, disconcert, discountenance, faze, rattle; *compare* DISCOMPOSE 1

rel agitate, bother, discompose, flurry, fluster, perturb; nonplus; chagrin, distress, vex; queer

idiom put on the spot, put to the blush

con calm, relieve, soothe

embarrassing *adj syn see* INCONVENIENT

embarrassment *n* the quality, state, or condition of being embarrassed <felt great *embarrassment* when she fell down>

syn abashment, confusion, discomfiture, discomposure, disconcertion, disconcertment, unease, uneasiness

rel constraint, strain; agitation, discombobulation, perturbation; chagrin, distress, vexation; humiliation, mortification; difficulty, Queer Street

con assurance, calm, imperturbability, savoir faire

embed *vb syn see* ENTRENCH 1

embellish *vb* 1 *syn see* ADORN

rel apparel, array, ‖doll up, dress up, emblaze, embroider, enrich, furbish

con bare, denude, divest, strip

2 *syn see* EMBROIDER

embellishment *n syn see* EXAGGERATION

rel floridity, ostentation

embezzle *vb* to appropriate dishonestly and fraudulently to one's own use <*embezzled* a trust fund>

syn misappropriate, peculate

rel loot, pilfer, steal, thieve

embitter *vb syn see* EXACERBATE

rel bitter, sour

emblem *n* 1 *syn see* SYMBOL 1

2 *syn see* INSIGNIA

emblematize *vb syn see* REPRESENT 2

embodiment *n* a concrete or actual entity in which something (as an idea, principle, or type) is embodied <he is the *embodiment* of all our hopes>

syn incarnation, personification; *compare* APOTHEOSIS 1

rel manifestation; prosopopoeia; archetype; apotheosis, epitome, quintessence

embody *vb* 1 to make an abstraction concrete or perceptible often by representation in human or animal form <Dickens *embodied* hypocrisy in his Uriah Heep>

syn exteriorize, externalize, incarnate, manifest, materialize, objectify, personalize, personify, personize, substantiate; *compare* REPRESENT 2

rel actualize, hypostatize, realize, reify, symbolize, typify; demonstrate, evince, exemplify, exhibit, illustrate, show (forth)

ant disembody

2 to cause to become a body or part of another body <*embodied* a revenue provision in the new law>

syn combine, incorporate, integrate

rel absorb, amalgamate, assimilate, blend, consolidate, fuse, merge, unify

3 *syn see* INCLUDE

rel compose, consist (of), constitute

4 *syn see* REPRESENT 2

embog *vb syn see* DELAY 1

embolden *vb syn see* ENCOURAGE 1

rel impel; inspire; chance, hazard, venture

con deter, discourage

ant abash

embouchement *n syn see* MOUTH 5

embouchure *n syn see* MOUTH 5

embowel *vb syn see* EVISCERATE

embrace *vb* 1 to gather into one's arms usually as a gesture of affection <*embraced* his wife>

syn clasp, ‖clinch, clip, ‖coll, enfold, hug, press, squeeze

rel cling, grip, hold; encircle, entwine, envelop, enwind, fold, lock, twine, wrap; cuddle, fondle, nuzzle, snuggle; cradle, hold

idiom ‖go into a clinch

2 *syn see* ADOPT

rel accept, accommodate, admit, incorporate, receive, take (over), take in; seize (upon), welcome

con reject; abjure, deny, forswear, renounce

ant spurn

3 *syn see* INCLUDE

rel compose, cover, enclose, hold

embracement *n syn see* ESPOUSAL 4

embracing *n syn see* ESPOUSAL 4

embrangle *vb syn see* ENTANGLE 3

embroider *vb* to give an elaborate account of, often with florid language and fictitious details <*embroidered* the story of his adventures in the army>

syn color, embellish, exaggerate, fudge, magnify, overcharge, overdraw, overpaint, overstate, pad, stretch

rel aggrandize, amplify, build up, distend, elaborate, enhance, enlarge (upon), expand; dramatize, hyperbolize, overdo, overelaborate, overembellish, overemphasize, overestimate

idiom lay it on thick, stretch (*or* strain) the truth

con deemphasize, minimize, play (down), underestimate, understate

embroidering *n syn see* EXAGGERATION

embroil *vb syn see* INVOLVE 1

embroilment *n* 1 *syn see* QUARREL

2 *syn see* ENTANGLEMENT 1

embryo *n syn see* SEED 2

emend *vb syn see* CORRECT 1

rel alter, edit, emendate; polish, retouch

emerge *vb syn see* APPEAR 1

rel derive, originate, spring, stem; arise, materialize, rise; come (forth), come out, emanate, flow, issue (forth); proceed

idiom appear on the horizon, come on the scene, come out in the open, come to light, make its appearance

con disappear, fade, fade (out); evaporate; dissolve

emergency *n syn see* JUNCTURE 2

rel difficulty, extremity; clutch, fix, hole, pinch, push, squeeze, vicissitude; climax

idiom turn of events

emigrant *n* one that leaves one place to settle in another <a city teeming with *emigrants* from many lands>

---

syn synonym(s)   rel related word(s)

ant antonym(s)   con contrasted word(s)

idiom idiomatic equivalent(s)

‖ use limited; if in doubt, see a dictionary

syn immigrant, migrant
rel alien, displaced person, DP, émigré, evacuee, exile, expatriate, fugitive, refugee; migrator, migratory
con aborigine, native

emigrate *vb syn* see MIGRATE

émigré *n* **1** a person forced to immigrate usually for political reasons <a city filled with White Russian *émigrés*>
syn exile, expatriate, expellee
rel emigrant, immigrant; alien, displaced person, DP, evacuee, fugitive, refugee
2 *syn* see REFUGEE

eminence *n* **1** a condition, position, or state of great importance or superiority <the *eminence* of the presidency>
syn distinction, illustriousness, kudos, preeminence, prestige, prominence, prominency, renown
rel greatness, loftiness, prepotency, significance, superiority; authority, credit, dignity, importance, influence, power, weight; fame, famousness, glory, honor, reputation, repute
con insignificance, unimportance; obscurity
2 *syn* see NOTABLE 1
3 a natural elevation <the house stood on an *eminence* overlooking the river>
syn projection, prominence
rel peak, raise, rise, uprise; altitude, elevation; height; highness, loftiness
con cavity, depression, dip

eminency *n syn* see FORTE

eminent *adj syn* see FAMOUS 2
rel well-known; august, dominant, exalted, important, lofty, noble, preeminent; big league, big-name, big-time
con uncelebrated, unremarkable, unrenowned; common, lowly

eminently *adv syn* see VERY 1

emissary *n syn* see MESSENGER

emit *vb* **1** *syn* see DISCHARGE 5
2 to discharge something such as moisture, vapor, or fumes <a smokestack *emitting* effluents>
syn give off, give out, issue, release, throw off, vent
rel discharge, evacuate, expel; let out, loose, pass (off); pour (out), reek; drip, emanate, excrete, extrude, exude, ooze, secrete; exhale, expire

emolument *n syn* see WAGE
rel guerdon

emote *vb* to give expression to emotion especially on or as if on the stage <she *emotes*, postures, and harangues at the slightest provocation>
syn emotionalize
rel gush, sentimentalize; carry on, rage, rant, storm, take on

emotion *n syn* see FEELING 3
rel excitability, responsiveness, sensibility, sensitiveness, sensitivity, susceptibilities; sensation
con coldness, detachment, reserve, unfeelingness

emotionable *adj syn* see EMOTIONAL 1

emotional *adj* **1** dominated by, prone to, or moved by emotion <an irritable *emotional* woman who was easily upset by trivialities>
syn emotionable, feeling, sensitive, sentient

rel responsive, susceptible, susceptive; softhearted, sympathetic; ardent, fervent, passionate; rhapsodic, rhapsodical
con cold, detached, insensitive, reserved, taciturn, unfeeling
ant emotionless, unemotional
2 appealing to or arousing emotion <an *emotional* sermon>
syn affective, emotive, moving; *compare* MOVING 2
rel affecting, stirring, touching

emotionalize *vb syn* see EMOTE

emotionless *adj* **1** *syn* see COLD 2
rel nonemotional, undemonstrative; cool, dispassionate, distant, immovable, impassive, remote, reserved; heartless, unfeeling
con responsive, softhearted, sympathetic; ardent, fervent, passionate
ant emotional
2 *syn* see MATTER-OF-FACT 3

emotive *adj syn* see EMOTIONAL 2

empathy *n syn* see SYMPATHY 2
rel accord, affinity, communion, compatibility, concord, congeniality, fellow feeling, rapport, responsiveness, warmth; appreciation, comprehension, understanding
idiom community of interests
con animosity, animus, antagonism, antipathy, enmity

emphasis *n* force brought to bear on something to bring out what is important <the school's *emphasis* on discipline>
syn accent, accentuation, stress
rel attention; force, insistence; weight

emphasize *vb* to give emphasis to especially by displaying more or less prominently <the papers *emphasized* crime stories>
syn feature, italicize, play (up), stress, underline, underscore
rel accent, accentuate, charge, highlight, mark, pinpoint, point (up), punctuate, spotlight; assert, press
idiom bear down on (*or* upon)
con depreciate, minimize, play (down), shrug off, underrate, understate
ant de-emphasize

emphatic *adj* marked by, uttered with, or made prominent by stress or emphasis <made his point in an *emphatic* argument>
syn assertive, forceful, insistent, resounding
rel aggressive, energetic, insistive, vigorous; accented, accentuated, assertative, decided, emphasized, marked, pointed, stressed, underlined
con insipid, milk-and-water, unaggressive, unassertive, weak, wishy-washy; de-emphasized, played (down), understated
ant unemphatic

empirical *adj* originating in, relying on, or based on factual information, observation, or direct sense experience <an *empirical* basis for an ethical theory>
syn experient, experiential, experimental
rel observational; factual
con conjectural, speculative, unproved, unsubstantiated; ideal, imagined
ant theoretical

employ *vb* **1** *syn* see USE 2
rel avail, exert, practice, work; devote, engross, monopolize

2 to provide with a job that pays wages
<*employed* a new draftsman>
syn engage, hire, put on, take on
rel add, contract (for), procure,
retain, secure, sign (on *or* up)
employable *adj syn* see OPEN 5
employed *adj syn* see BUSY 1
employment *n* 1 *syn* see USE 1
rel purpose; disposition, exercise, exploita-
tion, handling, utilization
2 *syn* see EXERCISE 1
3 *syn* see WORK 1
rel assignment, mission; office, position,
post, situation; function
4 the act of employing for wages <handled
the *employment* of new workers>
syn engagement, engaging, hiring
rel enlistment, enrollment, recruitment,
signing on
empower *vb* 1 *syn* see INVEST 2
2 *syn* see AUTHORIZE 1
3 *syn* see ENABLE 2
rel endow, invest; authorize, charge, commission, entitle, entrust, license, privilege,
sanction
con debar, disallow, disbar, exclude, rule
out, shut out
emprise *n syn* see ADVENTURE
emptiness *n syn* see VACUITY 2
emptor *n syn* see PURCHASER
empty *adj* 1 lacking contents that could or
should be present <an *empty* apartment>
<the whole book is *empty* of meaning>
syn bare, clear, stark, vacant, vacuous, void
rel barren, blank; abandoned, deserted,
emptied, forsaken, godforsaken, unfilled,
unfurnished uninhabited, untenanted, va-
cated; destitute, devoid; depleted, drained,
exhausted
con complete, replete; filled, occupied,
packed, teeming
ant full
2 *syn* see VAIN 1
rel paltry, petty, trifling, trivial; banal, flat,
inane, ineffectual, insipid, jejune, vapid;
dumb, fatuous, foolish, ignorant, silly, simple
con meaningful, pregnant, significant; authentic, bona fide, genuine, veritable
3 *syn* see EXPRESSIONLESS
4 *syn* see DEVOID
empty *vb syn* see VACATE 2
empty–headed *adj* 1 *syn* see GIDDY 1
rel brainless, rattleheaded; ignorant, simple
2 *syn* see VACUOUS 2
3 *syn* see IGNORANT 1
empyreal *adj syn* see CELESTIAL
rel aerial, airy; extraterrestrial; divine, holy,
spiritual, sublime
ant terrestrial
empyrean *adj syn* see CELESTIAL
empyrean *n* 1 *syn* see HEAVEN 2
2 *syn* see SKY
emulate *vb syn* see RIVAL 2
rel challenge, outvie

emulation *n syn* see CONTEST 1
emulative *adj syn* see SLAVISH 3
emulous *adj syn* see AMBITIOUS 1
rel aiming, striving; agog, athirst; competitive, vying
con unambitious, unaspiring; detached,
disinterested, uninterested
enable *vb* 1 *syn* see AUTHORIZE 1
rel allow, let, permit; sanction
2 to render able often by giving power,
strength, or competence to <her education
enabled her to find an excellent job>
syn empower
rel allow, let, permit; condition, fit, prepare,
qualify, ready
con inhibit, preclude, prevent; disallow,
enjoin, forbid, prohibit
enact *vb* 1 to cause to be by legal and authoritative act <*enact* a law>
syn constitute, establish, make
rel bring about, institute; authorize, decree,
proclaim; accomplish, carry (through),
effect, effectuate, execute, legislate, pass, put
(through), ratify
con abolish, abrogate, annul, cancel, invalidate, nullify, rescind, revoke; overturn
ant repeal
2 *syn* see ACT 1
rel depict, portray, represent
enamored *adj* 1 moved by intense sexual
attraction <became more desperately *enamored* of the man every day>
syn mashed, smitten, soft (on), spoony
(over *or* on)
rel infatuated; crazy (over *or* about), mad
(about), nuts (about), silly (over *or* about),
wild (about); amorous, devoted, loving
idiom head over heels in love, stuck on,
sweet on
2 *syn* see INFATUATED
3 taking great pleasure in something <found
herself *enamored* of those huge English
teas>
syn bewitched, captivated, charmed, enchanted, entranced, fascinated
rel fond
encamp *vb syn* see CAMP
encampment *n syn* see CAMP 1
enceinte *adj syn* see PREGNANT 1
enchant *vb* 1 *syn* see BEWITCH 1
2 *syn* see ATTRACT 1
rel delight, enthrall, please, send, thrill;
mesmerize
idiom carry away, knock dead
con disillusion, dissatisfy, let down
ant disenchant
enchanted *adj syn* see ENAMORED 3
rel delighted, pleased; pixilated
ant disenchanted
enchanter *n syn* see MAGICIAN 1
enchanting *adj syn* see ATTRACTIVE 1
rel attractive, pleasing; delectable, delightful; beguiling, enthralling, entrancing, intriguing, witching; exciting, sirenic
con repellent
enchantment *n syn* see MAGIC 1
enchantress *n syn* see WITCH 1
enchiridion *n syn* see HANDBOOK
rel book, text
encincture *vb syn* see BELT 1

---

syn synonym(s)   **rel** related word(s)
ant antonym(s)   **con** contrasted word(s)
idiom idiomatic equivalent(s)
|| use limited; if in doubt, see a dictionary

encircle *vb syn* see SURROUND 1
  rel band, cincture, circuit, enring; halo, wreathe

enclose *vb* **1** to shut up or confine by or as if by barriers <a valley *enclosed* by mountains>
  syn cage, close in, coop, corral, envelop, fence, hedge, hem, immure, mew, mure, pen, shut in, wall
  rel bound, circumscribe, confine, contain, limit, restrict; circle, compass, encircle, encompass, surround; environ; enlock
  2 *syn* see ENFOLD 1

enclosure *n syn* see COURT 1

enclothe *vb syn* see CLOTHE

encomiastic *adj syn* see EULOGISTIC

encomium *n* a formal expression of praise <an unstinted *encomium* of a national hero>
  syn citation, eulogy, panegyric, salutation, tribute
  rel approval, kudos, laud, laudation, magnification, praise; acclaim, acclamation, applause, plaudits; accolade, commendation, compliment
  con abuse, invective, obloquy, vituperation; criticism, critique, faultfinding

encompass *vb* **1** *syn* see SURROUND 1
  rel bound, delimit
  2 *syn* see INCLUDE

encounter *vb* **1** *syn* see CONFRONT 1
  rel clash, collide, conflict
  2 *syn* see ENGAGE 5
  3 *syn* see MEET 6
  rel ‖bump (into), come (across), run (across), run (into)
  idiom cross the path of, fall in with, meet up with
  con miss, pass (by)
  4 *syn* see FIND 1

encounter *n* a sudden, hostile, and usually brief confrontation or dispute between factions or persons <a sharp courtroom *encounter* between opposing lawyers>
  syn brush, run-in, set-to, skirmish, velitation
  rel conflict, contest; scrap; fight, fray; battle; argument, contention, quarrel

encourage *vb* **1** to fill with courage or strength of purpose especially in preparation for a hard task <the teacher's praise *encouraged* the student to try harder>
  syn animate, cheer, chirk (up), embolden, enhearten, hearten, inspirit, nerve, ‖pearten (up), steel, strengthen; *compare* SUPPORT 5
  rel assure, reassure; boost, excite, galvanize, pique, provoke, quicken, stimulate; buck up, buoy (up), energize, fortify, invigorate, rally, stir
  idiom give a shot in the arm
  con deject, depress, discourage, dishearten, dispirit; affright, caution, frighten
  ant discourage
  2 to give the support of one's approval to <the government openly *encouraged* East-West détente>
  syn advocate, countenance, favor
  rel approve, back, endorse, go (for), sanction, subscribe (to); abet, assist, reinforce, support, sustain; incite, instigate; induce, prevail

idiom lend one's countenance to, lend one's favor (or support) to, smile upon
  con deter, dissuade, divert, hinder; inhibit, restrain; disapprove
  ant discourage
  3 *syn* see ADVANCE 1
  rel patronize, push, support; develop, improve, subsidize
  con weaken; check, retard, slow
  ant discourage

encouraging *adj syn* see HOPEFUL 2

encroach *vb syn* see TRESPASS 2
  rel barge (in), ‖bust (in), butt (in), chisel (in), horn (in), muscle (in), worm (in); interfere, interpose, intervene, meddle; overstep
  idiom foist oneself upon, stick one's nose in (or into)
  con ignore, let (alone), pass over; avoid

encrust (*or* **incrust**) *vb syn* see CAKE 1

encumber *vb syn* see BURDEN
  rel freight; discommode, incommode, inconvenience; fetter, hamper, handicap; block, impede, obstruct; oppress, overburden

encumbrance *n* something that impedes and makes action difficult <told his story simply without the *encumbrance* of unnecessary details>
  syn clog, cumbrance, hindrance, impedance, impediment
  rel disadvantage, handicap, load; difficulty, hardship, inconvenience
  con aid; catalyst, impetus, stimulus
  ant assist, assistance

encyclopedic *adj* embracing, comprehensively treating, or informed in a wide range of subjects <an *encyclopedic* article on world history>
  syn comprehensive, inclusive
  rel all-comprehensive, all-embracing, all-inclusive, complete; extensive, general; discursive

end *n* **1** *syn* see LIMIT 1
  rel borderline, tip; extreme, extremity
  con center, hub, middle
  2 ceasing of a course (as of action or activity) or the point at which something ceases <the *end* of the war>
  syn cease, cessation, close, closing, closure, conclusion, desistance, desuetude, discontinuance, discontinuation, ending, finish, period, stop, termination, terminus; *compare* FINALE
  rel consummation, culmination; expiration; coda, curtains, finale, finality, finis, terminal, windup
  idiom cutoff point, end of the line, stopping point
  con genesis, inception
  ant beginning
  3 *syn* see FINALE
  4 something residual <melted down candle *ends*>
  syn bit, fragment, scrap
  rel butt end, fag end, leaving, remainder, remnant, residue; part, particle, piece

end *vb syn* see CLOSE 3
  ant begin

endable *adj syn* see TERMINABLE

endanger *vb* to bring into peril (as of harm or disaster) <conspirators who were *endangering* the cause of freedom>
syn compromise, hazard, imperil, jeopard, jeopardize, jeopardy, menace, peril, risk
rel expose, lay (open); chance, venture
con guard, protect, shelter, shield; preserve, save

endeavor *vb syn* see TRY 5
rel determine, intend, purpose; address, apply, bid (for), drive (at), go (for); strain

endeavor *n syn* see ATTEMPT
rel exertion, push; labor, toil, travail, work

ended *adj syn* see COMPLETE 4

endemic *adj syn* see NATIVE 2
rel home-bred, native-born
con pandemic; extraneous, extrinsic
ant exotic

ending *n* 1 *syn* see END 2
ant beginning
2 *syn* see FINALE

endless *adj* 1 *syn* see LIMITLESS
2 *syn* see EVERLASTING 1
rel constant, continuous; deathless, immortal, undying; boundless, limitless, unbounded, unlimited; self-perpetuating
3 *syn* see CONTINUAL
rel overlong

endorse *vb syn* see APPROVE 2
rel attest, authenticate, pass (on *or* upon), vouch, witness; command, recommend; advocate, enable; champion, stand by, support, uphold
con deprecate, disapprove; anathematize, denounce

endorsement *n syn* see SANCTION

endow *vb* 1 to furnish or provide with a gift, talent, or good quality <poets *endowed* with genius>
syn crown (with), dower, endue
rel bestow, confer; accord, award, grant; empower, enable; enhance, enrich, heighten
con bare, denude, divest, strip; despoil, ravage, spoliate; deplete, drain, exhaust
2 to furnish, (as an institution) with a store of capital <*endowed* a hospital>
syn finance, fund, subsidize
rel found, organize; bequeath, contribute, donate, subscribe, support; award, grant, back, promote, sponsor; provide, supply
con beggar, impoverish, pauperize; drain, draw (on)

end product *n syn* see EFFECT 1

endue *vb syn* see ENDOW 1
rel clothe, invest, vest; accouter, equip, furnish, outfit

endurable *adj syn* see BEARABLE

endurance *n* 1 *syn* see CONTINUATION 1
2 *syn* see TOLERANCE 1

endure *vb* 1 *syn* see CONTINUE 1
rel bide, linger
con crumble, decay, disintegrate; collapse, fall
ant perish
2 *syn* see ACCEPT 2

stand, submit (to), suffer, undergo
con break, collapse, give in, resign
3 *syn* see BEAR 10

enduring *adj* 1 *syn* see LASTING
ant fleeting
2 *syn* see OLD 2
3 *syn* see SURE 2
rel durable, resolute, solid, sound, stable, staunch, sturdy, substantial
con capricious, changeable, fickle, inconstant, mercurial, unstable, variable

endways *adv syn* see LENGTHWISE

endwise *adv syn* see LENGTHWISE

enemy *n* an individual or group that is hostile toward another <the senator was blackmailed by a political *enemy*>
syn foe
rel adversary, antagonist, opponent; assailant, attacker, combatant, invader; competitor, contender, colleague, rival
con benefactor, friend, supporter; ally, collaborator, colleague, confederate, friendly; adherent, follower, partisan, upholder

energetic *adj* 1 *syn* see VIGOROUS
rel aggressive, emphatic, vibrant; indefatigable
con easygoing, faineant, idle, languorous, lethargic
2 disposed to or having a capacity for action <an *energetic* campaign worker>
syn active, driving, enterprising, lively
rel animated, breezy, brisk, fresh, kinetic, peppy, spirited, sprightly, spry, vivacious, zippy
idiom full of go (*or* life *or* pep *or* zip)
con apathetic, inert; lethargic, limp, listless, passive, phlegmatic, spiritless, spunkless
ant inactive

energetically *adv syn* see HARD 1
rel firmly, strenuously; busily, industriously, zealously
idiom at full tilt
con idly, lazily, lethargically, listlessly; slowly
ant unenergetically

energize *vb* 1 *syn* see VITALIZE
idiom put pep (*or* zip) into
con emasculate, enervate; debilitate, enfeeble
2 *syn* see STRENGTHEN 2
rel arm, empower, enable; build (up), sustain
con daunt

energy *n* 1 *syn* see POWER 4
rel activity, operativeness; forcefulness, mightiness, powerfulness
con impotence; decrepitude, feebleness, weakness; powerlessness
ant inertia
2 vigorous and effectual application and operation of power <work with *energy*>
syn birr, go, hardihood, ||moxie, pep, potency, tuck, vigor; *compare* VIGOR 2
rel application, effectiveness, efficacy; effort, spontaneousness; toughness
con kef, languor, lethargy, listlessness, sluggishness; ergophobia

enervate *vb syn* see UNNERVE

---

syn synonym(s)   *rel* related word(s)
ant antonym(s)   *con* contrasted word(s)
idiom idiomatic equivalent(s)
|| use limited; if in doubt, see a dictionary

rel debilitate, devitalize, disable; exhaust, fatigue, jade, tire, weary

con activate, energize, vitalize; galvanize, quicken, stimulate

enervated *adj syn* see LANGUID

rel debilitated, devitalized, enfeebled, undermined, weakened; exhausted, fatigued, run-down, tired, weary; decadent, degenerate, degenerated, deteriorated

con active, animated, energetic, lusty, strenuous, vigorous, vital; strong, sturdy, tenacious, tough

enfant terrible *n syn* see SCAMP

enfeeble *vb syn* see WEAKEN 1

rel devitalize, exhaust

con galvanize; harden, strengthen

ant fortify

enfold *vb* **1** to surround or cover closely <a heavy fog *enfolded* the ships>

syn enclose, enshroud, envelop, enwrap, invest, shroud, veil, wrap; *compare* SWATHE

rel cover, drape; encase, ensheathe; encircle, encompass, environ, gird, girdle, surround

2 *syn* see EMBRACE 1

enforce *vb* to put something into effect or operation <*enforce* a law>

syn effect, implement, invoke

rel accomplish, administer, carry (out or through), discharge, execute, fulfill, perform; compel, force, oblige

con disregard, forget, ignore, neglect; relax

enfranchise *vb* to admit to full political rights as a freeman or citizen <slaves were emancipated in 1863 but were not *enfranchised* until the Fifteenth Amendment went into effect in 1870>

syn affranchise, franchise

rel emancipate, free, liberate, release; deliver, extricate, rescue

con enslave, oppress, subject

ant disenfranchise, disfranchise

engage *vb* **1** to come into contact and interlock with <the teeth of one gear wheel *engaging* those of another>

syn intermesh, mesh

rel interact, interlace, interlock, interplay

con free, release

ant disengage

2 *syn* see PROMISE 1

rel commit; bind, tie; affiance, betroth, troth

3 *syn* see EMPLOY 1

con dismiss, eject, fire

ant discharge

4 to hold the attention of <the puzzle *engaged* him all evening>

syn busy, engross, immerse, occupy, soak

rel absorb, imbue, involve; arrest, captivate, enthrall, fascinate, grip; monopolize, preengage, preoccupy

5 to enter into contest or conflict with <ordered to seek out and *engage* the enemy fleet>

syn encounter, face, meet, take on

rel assault, attack, strike; battle, fight

idiom do battle with, join battle with

con elude, escape, evade

engaged *adj syn* **1** see BUSY 1

ant unengaged

2 pledged in marriage <the *engaged* couple made a charming pair>

syn affianced, betrothed, contracted, intended, plighted, ‖promised

rel committed, pledged

con free, uncommitted, unpledged

ant unengaged

3 *syn* see INTENT

engagement *n* **1** *syn* see PROMISE

2 the act or state of being engaged to be married <the couple recently announced their *engagement*>

syn betrothal, betrothing, betrothment, espousal, troth

rel pledge, plight, promise

ant disengagement

3 a promise to be in an agreed place at a specified time, usually for a particular purpose <had an *engagement* with him for nine that evening>

syn appointment, assignation, date, rendezvous, tryst

rel arrangement, invitation; interview; get-together, meeting, visit

4 *syn* see EMPLOYMENT 4

5 *syn* see BATTLE

engaging *adj syn* **1** see ATTRACTIVE 1

2 *syn* see SWEET 1

rel alluring, appealing, attractive, captivating, charming, enchanting, entrancing, fetching, fascinating, interesting, intriguing

con repellent, repelling, repulsive; unappealing, unattractive, uninteresting

ant loathsome

engaging *n syn* see EMPLOYMENT 4

engender *vb syn* see GENERATE 3

rel develop; excite, stimulate; arouse, quicken, rouse, stir

engineer *vb* to contrive or plan out usually with subtle skill or craft <*engineered* an agreement between the two rival governments>

syn finagle, machinate, maneuver, wangle; *compare* MANIPULATE 2

rel arrange, contrive, devise, mastermind, plan (out), set up; intrigue, plot, scheme; manage, manipulate, negotiate; put (over), put (through), swing

idiom pull strings (or wires)

engird *vb syn* see BELT 1

engirdle *vb syn* see BELT 1

englut *vb syn* see GULP

engrave *vb* **1** to cut into a surface usually with a graving tool in order to form an inscription or a pictorial illustration <*engraved* a banknote design on the copper plate>

syn etch, grave, incise

rel chase, enchase; carve; inscribe

2 to impress deeply <the incident was *engraved* in his memory>

syn etch, impress, imprint, inscribe

rel carve; fix; instill; print; embed, entrench, infix, ingrain, root

engross *vb* **1** *syn* see WRITE

rel enscroll, scroll; superscribe

2 *syn* see MONOPOLIZE

rel apply, fill, occupy, preoccupy; assimilate, take up; arrest, engage, grip, ‖hog, hold, immerse, involve; attract, captivate, enthrall

con bewilder, distract; disperse, dissipate, scatter

3 *syn* see ENGAGE 4

engrossed *adj syn* see INTENT
rel consumed, monopolized, occupied; submerged; assiduous, busy, diligent, industrious, sedulous
idiom caught up in, lost in, taken up with
con detached, disinterested, indifferent, unconcerned, uninterested

engrossing *adj* gripping the attention completely so as to exclude everything else <the *engrossing* nature of his task made the time pass quickly>
syn absorbing, consuming, monopolizing
rel all-consuming, controlling, gripping; interesting, intriguing; exciting, provoking, stimulating; obsessing, preoccupying
con boring, drab, dull, monotonous; unentertaining, unexciting, uninteresting

engulf *vb syn* see DELUGE 1

enhance *vb* **1** *syn* see INTENSIFY
rel elevate, lift, raise; enlarge (upon), exaggerate, strengthen; augment, build (up), increase; adorn, beautify, embellish, embroider
con belittle, deprecate, detract, minimize
2 *syn* see FLATTER

enhancement *n syn* see ACCOMPANIMENT 1
rel improvement, intensification

enhearten *vb syn* see ENCOURAGE 1

enigma *n syn* see MYSTERY
rel crux, knot, puzzler, sticker; bewilderment, perplexity, question, question mark
idiom hard nut to crack

enigmatic *adj syn* see CRYPTIC

enisle *vb syn* see ISOLATE

enjewel *vb syn* see BEJEWEL

enjoin *vb* **1** *syn* see COMMAND
rel decree, dictate, impose, prescribe, rule; adjure, advise, counsel; admonish, caution, forewarn
con acquiesce, agree, comply, conform, obey, submit, yield
2 *syn* see FORBID
rel deny, disallow

enjoy *vb* **1** to take pleasure in or receive satisfaction from <*enjoyed* the meal>
syn ‖dig, go, like, ‖mind, relish
rel cotton (to); take (to); appreciate, dote (on *or* upon), fancy, love; delight (in), drink (in), eat up, luxuriate (in), savor
con abhor, abominate, detest, hate, loathe; condemn, despise, scorn
2 *syn* see HAVE 1
rel fill, occupy, maintain; boast, command

enjoyableness *n syn* see AMENITY 1
rel attractiveness, pleasingness, pleasurableness; niceness

enjoyment *n* **1** an attitude, circumstance, or favorable response to a stimulus that tends to make one gratified or happy <gave himself up to vigorous *enjoyment* of his pipe>
syn delectation, diversion, pleasure, relish; *compare* PLEASURE 2

---

syn synonym(s)   *rel* related word(s)
ant antonym(s)   *con* contrasted word(s)
idiom idiomatic equivalent(s)
‖ use limited; if in doubt, see a dictionary

---

rel delight, joy; amusement, entertainment; indulgence, savor; recreation, relaxation; gratification, satisfaction
con abhorrence, antipathy, aversion; repugnance, repulsion
2 *syn* see PLEASURE 2

enkindle *vb syn* see LIGHT 1

enlarge *vb* **1** *syn* see INCREASE 1
rel add (to), embroider, exaggerate; grow, stretch, widen
con attenuate; abridge; compress
2 *syn* see EXPAND 4
3 *syn* see INCREASE 2

enlargement *n syn* see EXPANSION 2

enlighten *vb syn* see ILLUMINATE 2
rel direct, educate, guide, inform, instruct, school, teach, train; acquaint, advise, apprise, inform
con bewilder, confuse, mystify, perplex, puzzle; addle, fuddle, muddle

enlightening *adj* tending to dissipate ignorance or increase knowledge and awareness <an *enlightening* glimpse of government in action>
syn illuminant, illuminating, illuminative, illumining
rel broadening, edifying, educational, instructive; clarifying, elucidative, explanatory
con unedifying, uninstructive; confusing, obfuscatory, obscuring

enlist *vb syn* see ENTER 3

enliven *vb syn* see QUICKEN 1
rel refresh, rejuvenate, renew, restore; excite, galvanize, invigorate, jazz (up), pep (up), provoke, stimulate; amuse, cheer, divert, entertain, recreate; exhilarate, fire, inspire
idiom give (new) life to
con depress, oppress, weigh
ant subdue

en masse *adv syn* see ALTOGETHER 3

enmesh *vb syn* see ENTANGLE 3
rel drag (into), draw (in), hook, tangle; embarrass, implicate
idiom make party to
con disembarrass, disentangle
ant extricate

enmeshment *n syn* see ENTANGLEMENT 1

enmity *n* deep-seated dislike or ill will or a manifestation of such feeling <the country had experienced generations of racial *enmity*>
syn animosity, animus, antagonism, antipathy, hostility, rancor
rel uncordiality, unfriendliness; alienation, dead set, disaffection, estrangement; abhorrence, detestation, dislike, hate, hatred, loathing; aversion; bad blood, bitterness, daggers, gall, ill will, malevolence, malice, malignancy, malignity, spite, spleen
con amicability, cordiality, friendliness, neighborliness, comity, empathy, friendship, goodwill, sympathy, understanding
ant amity

ennoble *vb syn* see EXALT 1

ennui *n syn* see TEDIUM
rel blues, dejection, depression, dumps, melancholy, sadness; fatigue, languidness, languor, listlessness, spiritlessness, tiredness, weariness; satiety, surfeit

ennui *vb syn* see BORE
  con enliven, stimulate, vitalize
enormity *n* 1 the quality or state of being
abnormally, monstrously, or outrageously
evil <the utter *enormity* of the crime>
  syn atrociousness, atrocity, heinousness,
monstrousness
  rel grossness, outrage, outrageousness,
rankness; depravity; flagrancy
  con excusableness, remissibility, veniality;
bearableness, tolerability
  2 the quality or state of being huge <the
enormity of the task confounded him>
  syn enormousness, hugeness, immensity,
magnitude, tremendousness, vastness
  rel bigness, greatness, massiveness; grave-
ness, seriousness, weightiness
  con diminutiveness, minuteness, smallness,
tininess; triviality, unimportance
enormous *adj syn* see HUGE
  rel stupendous
  ant tiny
enormousness *n syn* see ENORMITY 2
  rel monstrousness, prodigiousness, stupen-
dousness
enough *adj syn* see SUFFICIENT 1
enough *adv* 1 in or to a degree or quantity
that satisfies some condition <unstable
enough to react with water>
  syn adequately, sufficiently
  rel abundantly, amply; acceptably, admissi-
bly, satisfactorily; commensurately, proportionately
  2 in a tolerable degree <she sang well
enough>
  syn averagely, fairly, moderately, passably,
rather, so-so, tolerably
  rel acceptably, decently, satisfactorily
enough *n* as much as is needed or wanted
<we have *enough* for all of our needs>
  syn adequacy, competence, sufficiency,
sufficient
  rel abundance, ampleness, plenty
  con inadequateness; deficiency, deficit, lack,
shortage, want; outage, ullage, wantage
  ant inadequacy, insufficiency
enounce *vb syn* see ENUNCIATE 1
enrage *vb syn* see ANGER 1
  idiom make one's blood boil, work up into a
passion
  ant placate
enrapture *vb syn* see TRANSPORT 2
  rel elate, gladden, gratify, please, rejoice;
allure, attract, captivate, charm, enchant,
enthrall, fascinate
enravish *vb syn* see TRANSPORT 2
enrich *vb* to make financially rich or richer
<*enriched* himself through speculation>
  syn richen
enrichment *n syn* see ACCOMPANIMENT 1
enroll *vb* 1 to take in (as a person) by entering identification in a list, catalog, or roll
<the school *enrolls* about 800 students>
  syn list, register
  rel enter, insert; catalog, inscribe, record;
enlist, line (up), recruit, sign (up); join, ma-
triculate
  con discard, omit, reject
  2 *syn* see LIST 3
  3 *syn* see ENTER 3

ensample *n* 1 *syn* see MODEL 2
  2 *syn* see EXAMPLE 3
ensanguined *adj syn* see BLOODY 1
ensconce *vb* 1 *syn* see HIDE
  2 to establish or place firmly, comfortably,
or snugly <was happily *ensconced* on the
sofa before the fire>
  syn install, settle
  rel establish, fix, locate, place, plant, seat,
set, situate, station
ensepulcher *vb syn* see ENTOMB 1
enshroud *vb syn* see ENFOLD 1
  rel cloak, conceal, curtain, hide
  con disclose, display, illustrate, open (up),
reveal, show, uncover, unveil
ensign *n syn* see FLAG
enslave *vb* to reduce to and hold in a state of
servitude <free peasants reduced to serfdom
or *enslaved*>
  syn enthrall, subjugate
  rel disenfranchise, disfranchise; subject;
oppress, shackle, yoke
  con affranchise, enfranchise; free, liberate
  ant emancipate
enslavement *n syn* see BONDAGE
ensnare *vb syn* see CATCH 3
  rel decoy, entice, inveigle, lure; hook, net,
snag; bag, capture
ensnarl *vb* 1 *syn* see ENTANGLE 1
  2 *syn* see ENTANGLE 3
ensorcell *vb syn* see BEWITCH 1
ensorcellment *n syn* see MAGIC 1
ensphere *vb syn* see BALL
ensue *vb syn* see FOLLOW 1
  rel derive, emanate, issue, proceed, stem;
attend, result
  idiom be subsequent (to), come next
  con antecede, forerun, preface
ensuing *adj* 1 *syn* see SUBSEQUENT 1
  2 *syn* see NEXT
ensure *vb* to make something certain or sure
<provisions *ensuring* that the rank and file
have a voice in union policy-making>
  syn assure, cinch, insure, secure
  rel certify, guarantee, warrant; arrange,
establish, provide, set out
enswathe *vb syn* see SWATHE
entangle *vb* 1 to twist or interweave so as to
make separation difficult <*entangled* the
yarn>
  syn ensnarl, intertangle, perplex, snarl,
tangle
  rel intertwine, interweave, ‖snirl, twist; ball
up
  2 *syn* see COMPLICATE
  3 to catch or hold as if in a net from which
escape is difficult <a firm hopelessly *entangled* in financial difficulties>
  syn embrangle, enmesh, ensnarl, trammel;
compare CATCH 3, INVOLVE 1
  rel burden, clog, fetter, hamper, impede;
bag, capture, catch, ensnare, entrap, snare,
trap; discomfit, embarrass, embroil
  con extricate, untangle; detach, disengage;
clear, free; disburden, unfetter
  ant disentangle
  4 *syn* see CATCH 3
entanglement *n* 1 the condition of being
deeply involved or closely linked often in an
embarrassing or compromising way <*entan-*

glements with underworld figures tarnished his reputation>
syn embroilment, enmeshment, involvement; *compare* WEB 2
rel ensnarement; affair, intrigue, liaison; association, contact
2 syn see WEB 2

enter *vb* **1** to come or go into some place or thing <he *entered* the room>
syn come (in), go in, ingress, penetrate
rel pierce, probe
idiom set foot in
con egress, exit, go out, leave; come out, emerge, sally; escape, flee
ant issue
2 to cause or permit to go in or into <*enter* synonyms in a thesaurus>
syn admit, introduce
rel inject, insert, intercalate, interpolate, put (in), set down; docket, inscribe, list, post, record, register; enroll
3 to make or become a member of <decided to *enter* the army>
syn enlist, enroll, join (up), muster, sign on, sign up
rel come (into), go (into)
idiom get oneself into, take up (*or* out) membership (in)
4 syn see BEGIN 1

enterprise *n* **1 syn** see ADVENTURE
rel attempt, effort, endeavor, striving, struggle; campaign, cause, project, pursuit, task, undertaking; deed
2 syn see PROJECT 2
rel speculation
3 a unit of economic or business organization or activity <an economy encouraging the expansion of small, privately owned *enterprises*>
syn business, company, concern, establishment, firm, house, outfit
rel interest; organization; corporation; industry
4 readiness to attempt or engage in what requires energy or daring <complained about his brother's lack of *enterprise*>
syn ambition, drive, get-up-and-go, initiative, push; *compare* VIGOR 2
rel ambitiousness, eagerness, energy, enthusiasm, ‖hustle, vigor; boldness, courage, daring, venturesomeness; inventiveness, self-reliance
con languor, lethargy; indolence, laziness, sloth; apathy, inertia

enterprising *adj* **1 syn** see ENERGETIC 2
rel aggressive, ambitious, busy, eager, hustling, pushing, up-and-coming; adventurous, venturesome
2 showing initiative, resolution, and determined effort (as in pursuing a course or a career) <an *enterprising* young woman likely to go far>
syn go-ahead, gumptious, up-and-coming
rel aggressive, pushing; diligent, hardworking, industrious, zealous; ambitious, aspiring, craving, hungry, itching, lusting, yearn-

ing; audacious, daring, dashing, venturesome
idiom on one's toes
ant unenterprising

entertain *vb* **1 syn** see HARBOR 2
rel invite; admit, receive; cherish, cultivate, foster; feed, nourish
con banish, eject, throw out; ignore, neglect
2 syn see AMUSE
rel delight, enliven, gladden, gratify, please, regale, revel

entertainment *n* something diverting, amusing, or entertaining <staged a floor show as *entertainment* for her guests>
syn amusement, dissipation, distraction, diversion, divertissement, recreation
rel disport, play, sport; enjoyment, gaiety, pleasure; relaxation, rest

enthrall *vb* **1 syn** see ENSLAVE
rel master, subdue
con emancipate
2 to hold spellbound <told mystery stories that *enthralled* his playmates>
syn catch up, fascinate, grip, hold, mesmerize, spellbind
rel absorb, engage, preoccupy; charm, enchant, engross, intrigue
con bore, ennui, weary

enthuse *vb* **1 syn** see THRILL
2 to show great enthusiasm <tourists *enthusing* over the medieval towns>
syn drool, rave, rhapsodize, rhapsody
con censure, criticize, belittle, depreciate, disparage, dispraise, knock, undervalue

enthusiasm *n* **1 syn** see PASSION 6
rel craze, fascination, infatuation, mania
con impassivity, phlegm, stolidity; aloofness, detachment, indifference, unconcern
ant apathy
2 syn see EAGERNESS
rel earnest, interest; ebullience, élan

enthusiast *n* a person who manifests extreme and often uncritical ardor, fervor, or devotion in an attachment <an increasing number of ecology *enthusiasts*>
syn bigot, bug, fanatic, fiend, freak, maniac, nut, zealot
rel addict, aficionado, buff, bum, devotee, fan, habitué, lover, votary; partisan, supporter; bear, extremist
con depreciator, detractor, disparager, knocker

enthusiastic *adj* filled with or marked by enthusiasm <was *enthusiastic* about golf>
syn ‖buggy, ‖bugs, gung ho, keen, nutty, warm, zealous
rel ardent, devoted, eager, fervent, hearty, spirited; ‖gaga, ‖gone (on), hopped-up; hipped, obsessed; passionate, vascular; rabid
con apathetic, detached, indifferent, reluctant, uninterested
ant unenthusiastic

entice *vb* **syn** see LURE
con alarm, fright, frighten (off), terrify
ant scare (off)

enticement *n* **syn** see LURE 2

enticing *adj* being extremely and often dangerously attractive <she looked at him with an *enticing* smile>
syn Circean, fetching, luring, tempting

---

rel attractive, beguiling, bewitching, enchanting, fascinating, intriguing, inviting, siren, witching; captivating; likable, pleasant, pleasing

entify *vb syn* see MATERIALIZE 2

entire *adj* **1** *syn* see WHOLE 3
rel all, gross; plenary
con incomplete, unfinished; limited, qualified
ant partial
2 *syn* see WHOLE 1
rel concatenated, integrated; compacted, consolidated, unified
con broken (up); faulty
ant impaired
3 *syn* see WHOLE 4

entirely *adv* **1** *syn* see WELL 3
2 *syn* see ONLY 1

entireness *n* **1** *syn* see ENTIRETY 1
con incompleteness
2 *syn* see INTEGRITY 2

entirety *n* **1** the state of being complete <the striking *entirety* and self-sufficiency of the feudal community>
syn allness, completeness, entireness, oneness, totality, wholeness
rel collectiveness, unity; integrity, plenitude; comprehensiveness, omneity, universality
con disunity, division, separateness; fragmentation, incompleteness
2 *syn* see WHOLE 1
rel collectivity, complex, everything
con component, detail, element, item, part
ant particular

entitle *vb* **1** *syn* see NAME 1
2 to furnish with proper authority or grounds for seeking or claiming something <this ticket *entitles* the bearer to free admission>
syn authorize, qualify
rel empower, license; allow, enable, let, permit

entity *n* **1** one that has real and independent existence <each *entity* of the series requires separate study>
syn being, existence, existent, individual, something, thing
rel body, object
2 *syn* see THING 5
3 *syn* see WHOLE 2

entomb *vb* **1** to deposit in or as if in a tomb <relics *entombed* in pyramids>
syn ensepulcher, sepulcher, sepulture, tomb; *compare* BURY 1
rel bury, inhume, inter, ‖plant; inurn; enshrine, shrine
con dig (up), disinhume, disinter, exhume, unbury
ant disentomb
2 *syn* see BURY 1

entombment *n syn* see BURIAL 2

entourage *n* one's attendants or subordinates <the queen's *entourage*>
syn following, retinue, suite, train
rel associates, attendants, courtiers, followers, retainers; hangers-on, sycophants, toadies

entrails *n pl* the internal organs of the body <some of the *entrails* are valued as food>

syn gut(s), innards, insides, internals, inwards, ‖pudding(s), stuffing, tripes, viscera
rel bowels, intestines; vitals; giblets, pluck, purtenance

entrammel *vb syn* see HAMPER
con assist, expedite, facilitate; extricate

entrance *n* **1** the act or fact of going in or coming in <awaited the *entrance* of the army into the city>
syn entry, ingress, ingression
rel arrival, coming, incoming, ingoing; penetration
con departure, egress, emergence, emerging, emigration, exit
ant egression, exiting
2 *syn* see DOOR 1
rel access, aperture, opening, threshold
ant exit
3 *syn* see DOOR 2
rel open door

entrance *vb syn* see TRANSPORT 2
rel gladden, please, rejoice; attract, bewitch, captivate, charm, enchant, fascinate; enthrall, hypnotize, spellbind
con disappoint, disgust, repel, repulse; bore

entranced *adj syn* see ENAMORED 3

entranceway *n syn* see DOOR 1

entrap *vb* **1** *syn* see CATCH 3
2 *syn* see LURE

entreat *vb syn* see BEG
rel blandish, coax, wheedle; pester, plague, press, urge

entreaty *n syn* see PRAYER

entrée *n syn* see DOOR 2
rel introduction; open door

entrench *vb* **1** to establish so solidly or strongly as to make dislodgment or change extremely difficult <prejudices *entrenched* for generations>
syn embed, fix, infix, ingrain, lodge, root
rel found, ground; implant; confirm, define, establish, settle, strengthen
con eliminate, eradicate, root out, uproot; banish, cast out, eject, expel; remove
ant dislodge
2 *syn* see TRESPASS 2
rel interfere, intervene
idiom break in upon, stick one's nose into

entrenched *adj syn* see INVETERATE 1

entrepreneur *n* **1** one who owns, launches, manages, and assumes the risks of an economic venture <theatrical *entrepreneurs* making fortunes from successful shows>
syn undertaker
rel organizer; backer, impresario; contractor; administrator, manager; producer; promoter
2 *syn* see GO-BETWEEN 2

entrust *vb* **1** to confer a trust upon <*entrusted* him with responsibility for completing the work>
syn charge, trust
rel confer, impose; delegate, relegate; allocate, allot, assign
2 *syn* see COMMIT 1
rel deliver, deposit, leave, trust; bank, count, depend, reckon, rely
idiom give in trust

entry *n* **1** *syn* see ENTRANCE 1
2 *syn* see DOOR 1

rel access, opening, threshold
con egress
ant exit
3 syn see DOOR 2
entryway n syn see DOOR 1
rel threshold
con egress
ant exit
entwine vb syn see WIND 2
rel entangle, entwist, interlace, interplait, intertwine, interweave; enmesh
con uncoil, undo, unravel, untwine, untwist, unwind, unwrap; straighten (out)
enumerate vb 1 syn see COUNT 1
2 to specify one after the other <*enumerated* the advantages of his position>
syn list, numerate, tick off
rel run (over), tell off; identify, mention, recite, recount, relate, specify
3 syn see ITEMIZE 1
enunciate vb 1 to make a definite or systematic statement of <was the first to *enunciate* the modern principle of inertia>
syn enounce, state
rel develop, formulate, outline, postulate; advance, lay down, submit; announce, declare, proclaim; affirm; show
idiom set forth
2 syn see ARTICULATE 2
rel express, intone, modulate, vocalize, voice
envelop vb 1 syn see ENFOLD 1
rel cloak, hide, mask
2 syn see SWATHE
3 syn see ENCLOSE 1
rel guard, protect, shield
envenom vb syn see EXACERBATE
envious adj maliciously grudging another's advantages <*envious* of her rival's charm>
syn envying, green-eyed, invidious, jealous
rel coveting, covetous, grasping, greedy; begrudging, grudging; appetent, desirous, longing, yearning; resentful, umbrageous
idiom green with envy
con benign, benignant; generous, kind; tolerant; unconcerned, uninterested
enviousness n syn see ENVY
environ vb syn see SURROUND 1
rel enclose, fence, go (around)
environment n surrounding or associated matters that influence or modify a course of development <the socioeconomic *environment* in Germany that produced Hitler>
syn ambience, ambient, atmosphere, climate, medium, milieu, mise-en-scène, surroundings
rel habitat; backdrop, background, context, setting; situation, status
environs n pl 1 an enclosing line or margin <several thousand businesses located within the *environs* of the city>
syn bound(s), boundary, compass, confine(s), limits, precinct(s), purlieus; compare LIMIT 1
rel fringes

2 the suburban areas or districts around a city or heavily populated area <a new system of parks for the national capital and its *environs*>
syn outskirt(s), purlieus, suburbs
rel locality, neighborhood, vicinity; surroundings
envisage vb syn see THINK 1
rel behold, grasp, look (upon), picture, regard, survey, view; externalize, materialize, objectify; foresee
idiom form a mental picture of, have a picture of, picture to oneself, view in the mind's eye
envision vb syn see THINK 1
rel call up, conjure up, summon up; picture, view; foresee
idiom have a mental picture of, picture to oneself, view in the mind's eye
envoy n 1 a representative with a rank between an ambassador and a minister resident who is accredited to a foreign government <the President received the *envoy* from Spain>
syn envoy extraordinary, minister plenipotentiary
rel ambassador, attaché, chargé d'affaires, consul, councillor, internuncio, legate, minister, nuncio; diplomat
2 syn see MESSENGER
envoy extraordinary n syn see ENVOY 1
envy n spiteful malice and resentment over another's advantage <his lavish life-style provoked *envy* among his colleagues>
syn enviousness, invidiousness, jealousy
rel covetousness; grudging; resentment
envy vb to experience envy <while she outwardly criticized her sister's looks, she secretly *envied* them>
syn begrudge, grudge
rel covet, crave, desire, hanker, long, want, yearn
idiom be green with envy
envying adj syn see ENVIOUS
enwrap vb 1 syn see SWATHE
2 syn see ENFOLD 1
rel enswathe, swaddle, swathe; sheathe
ephemeral adj syn see TRANSIENT
rel brief, short, temporary, unenduring; episodic
idiom here today and gone tomorrow
con endless, enduring, eternal, everlasting, lasting
ant perpetual
epicene adj syn see EFFEMINATE
epicure n one who takes great and fastidious pleasure in eating and drinking <was a real *epicure*, and his dinners were excellent>
syn bon vivant, gastronome, gastronomer, gastronomist, gourmand, gourmet
rel amateur, connoisseur, epicurean; glutton, ravener; high liver
epicurean adj syn see SENSUOUS
epidemic n the sudden widespread occurrence of something felt to resemble an epidemic disease <an *epidemic* of art forgeries>
syn outbreak, plague, rash; compare OUTBREAK 1
epigrammatic adj syn see PITHY
epilogue n 1 the final part that rounds out or completes the design of a nondramatic liter-

---

syn synonym(s)   rel related word(s)
ant antonym(s)   con contrasted word(s)
idiom idiomatic equivalent(s)
‖ use limited; if in doubt, see a dictionary

ary work <the author wrote an *epilogue* to his book explaining that some of his earlier impressions were wrong>
syn afterword
rel postlude; conclusion, ending
con prelude; foreword, introduction, preface
ant prologue
2 something that resembles an epilogue in rounding out or giving point to something else <an incident that can be regarded as an *epilogue* to the history of Roman Britain>
syn sequel
rel follow-up, postscript
ant prologue

episode *n syn* see OCCURRENCE

epistle *n syn* see LETTER 2
rel communication

epitaph *n* an inscription on a tombstone in memory of the one buried there
syn hic jacet

epitome *n* **1** *syn* see ABRIDGMENT
2 *syn* see SUMMARY
3 *syn* see APOTHEOSIS 1

epitomize *vb* **1** to make or give an epitome of <a report which *epitomizes* one of the most complex theories of all time>
syn condense, digest, inventory, nutshell, sum, summarize, summate, sum up, synopsize
rel boil down, capsulize; outline, tabulate
con elaborate, enlarge (on), expand
2 to serve as the typical representation or ideal expression of <he *epitomized* safe, dull conservatism>
syn exemplify, typify
rel embody, incarnate, incorporate, personify, represent, symbolize
3 *syn* see REPRESENT 2

epitomized *adj syn* see CONDENSED

epoch *n syn* see PERIOD 2
rel interval; term

epochal *adj* uniquely or highly significant <had to make an *epochal* decision: whether or not to declare war>
syn momentous
rel consequential, far-reaching, important; unmatched, unparalleled
con inconsequential, minor, petty, small-time, trivial, unimportant

equable *adj syn* see STEADY 2
rel methodical, orderly, regular, systematic; immutable, invariable, unchangeable; equal, equivalent, same
con variable; fitful, spasmodic
ant inequable, unequable

equal *adj* **1** *syn* see SAME 2
rel equable, even, uniform; alike, like; commensurate, corresponding, proportionate
idiom one and the same
con different, disparate, divergent, diverse, varied; unalike, unequable, uneven; irregular
ant unequal
2 *syn* see FAIR 4
idiom without distinction
con discriminating, discriminative, unfair
ant inequitable
3 *syn* see EVEN 3
4 *syn* see EVEN 4
5 *syn* see PROPORTIONAL

equal *n* one that is equal to another in status, achievement, value, meaning, or effect <he has no *equal* in common sense and honesty>
syn counterpart, equivalent, like, match; *compare* OPPOSITE NUMBER, PARALLEL
rel companion, fellow, mate, peer; alter ego, double, twin; competitor, rival; similar

equal *vb* **1** *syn* see AMOUNT 2
rel compare, parallel; accord, agree, square, tally; reach
idiom amount to the same thing
2 *syn* see EVEN 2
3 to make or produce something equal to (as in quality or value) <*equal* that if you can>
syn match, measure up, meet, rival, tie, touch
rel beat, top

equality *n syn* see EQUIVALENCE

equalize *vb* **1** to make equal in amount, degree, or status <*equalize* educational opportunities>
syn equate, even
rel balance, level, square
2 *syn* see EVEN 2

equally *adv* **1** *syn* see EVENLY 1
2 *syn* see EVENLY 2

equanimity *n* the characteristic quality of one who is self-possessed and not easily disturbed or perturbed <faced disaster with bland *equanimity*>
syn ataraxy, calmness, composure, coolness, imperturbability, phlegm, sangfroid, self-possession; *compare* CONFIDENCE 2
rel balance, equilibrium, equipoise, poise; aplomb, assurance, confidence, self-assurance; detachment; placidity, serenity, tranquillity
con alarm, anxiety, apprehension; excitability, nervousness; agitation, discomposure, disquiet, disturbance, perturbation

equatability *n syn* see EQUIVALENCE

equate *vb* **1** *syn* see EQUALIZE 1
2 to treat, represent, or regard as equal, equivalent, or comparable <*equated* retreat with cowardice>
syn assimilate, compare, liken, match, paragon, parallel
rel associate, relate, similize; consider, hold, regard, represent, treat

equidistant *adj syn* see MIDDLE 1

equilibrium *n syn* see BALANCE 1
rel stabilization, steadiness, steadying; counterbalance, counterpoise
con top-heaviness

equip *vb syn* see FURNISH 2
rel provide, supply; fit (out), rig (up *or* out), turn (out); gear, prepare, qualify

equipment *n* items needed for the performance of a task or useful in effecting an end <the *equipment* for the polar expedition included ships, instruments, sleds, dogs, and supplies>
syn accouterment(s), apparatus, gear, habiliments, machinery, material(s), matériel, outfit, paraphernalia, tackle, tackling
rel accessories, appurtenances, attachments, fittings, trappings; baggage, belonging(s), impedimenta, rig, things, traps; equipage, provisioning, provisions

equipoise *n syn* see BALANCE 1

rel counterbalance, counterpoise, counterweight

equitable *adj 1 syn* see FAIR 4
  rel level, stable; equivalent, identical, same
  idiom fair and square
  con discriminatory
  ant inequitable, unfair
  2 *syn* see EVEN 3

equity *n syn* see JUSTICE 1
  rel equitableness, justness
  con bias, discrimination, partiality, unfairness
  ant inequity

equivalence *n* the state or property of being equivalent or the result of making equivalent <the *equivalence* of paper money and coins>
  syn adequation, equality, equatability, equivalency, par, parity, sameness
  rel likeness; compatibility, correlation, correspondence; exchangeability, interchangeability
  con discrepancy, disparity, divergence, incompatibility, inequality, unlikeness
  ant difference

equivalency *n syn* see EQUIVALENCE

equivalent *adj 1 syn* see SAME 2
  rel commensurate, proportionate; convertible, correlative, corresponding, parallel, reciprocal, substitute
  con disparate, divergent, diverse, various; discordant, discrepant, incompatible, inconsonant
  ant different
  2 *syn* see LIKE

equivalent *n syn* see EQUAL
  rel obverse, reciprocal, substitute; parallel

equivocal *adj 1 syn* see OBSCURE 3
  rel hazy, indistinct; doubtful, dubious, questionable; indeterminate, multivocal
  idiom clear as mud
  con clear, distinct, understandable; categorical, explicit, unambiguous, univocal; certain, conclusive
  ant unequivocal
  2 characterized by a mixture of opposing feelings <an *equivocal* attitude toward the expensive proposal>
  syn ambivalent
  rel uncertain, undecided
  idiom having mixed (*or* divided) feelings
  con assured, certain, decided, sure
  3 *syn* see DOUBTFUL 1
  rel disreputable
  idiom open to question
  con credible

equivocality *n syn* see AMBIGUITY

equivocate *vb 1 syn* see LIE
  rel elude, escape, evade
  2 to avoid committing oneself by speaking evasively <he'd rather be brutally frank with them than *equivocate* on that issue>
  syn dodge, evade, hedge, pussyfoot, shuffle, sidestep, tergiversate, tergiverse, weasel; *compare* SKIRT 3
  rel cavil, prevaricate, quibble; fence, parry; avoid, elude, eschew

  idiom beat around (*or* about) the bush, beg the question, mince words

equivocating *adj syn* see EVASIVE 1
  rel deceptive, delusive, misleading

equivocation *n 1 syn* see AMBIGUITY
  rel hedging; coloring, distortion, misrepresentation; deceit, dissimulation, duplicity
  ant explicitness
  2 *syn* see FALLACY 2
  rel haggling, quibbling; fib, fibbing, lie, lying

equivoque *n syn* see AMBIGUITY

era *n syn* see PERIOD 2
  rel term; stage

eradicate *vb syn* see ANNIHILATE 2
  rel demolish, destroy, raze; liquidate, purge
  con establish, fix, set; implant, inculcate, instill; breed, engender, generate, propagate

erase *vb* to eliminate or neutralize with or as if with a stroke of the pen <time has *erased* their sad memories> <*erase* an error>
  syn annul, black (out), blot out, cancel, delete, efface, expunge, obliterate, wipe (out), x (out)
  rel disannul, negate, nullify; abolish, blank (out), cross (off *or* out), cut out, dele, eliminate, excise, extirpate, rub out, scrape, sponge (out), strike (out); neutralize; remove, take out, withdraw
  con impress, imprint, print, stamp; insert; reinstate, renew, restore

ere *prep syn* see BEFORE 1

erect *adj* standing up straight <the dog's *erect* ears pricked forward>
  syn arrect, raised, stand-up, straight-up, upright, upstanding
  rel erectile; elevated, lifted, upraised; perpendicular, standing, vertical
  con decumbent, flat, prostrate, recumbent; drooping, hanging, pendent

erect *vb 1 syn* see BUILD 1
  2 *syn* see MAKE 3
  rel compose, create; make up, run up
  con demolish, destroy, tear up, unbuild, wreck
  3 to fix in an upright position <*erected* a flagpole>
  syn put up, raise, rear, set up; *compare* BUILD 1
  rel elevate, heighten, hoist, lift, upraise, uprear; upend
  4 *syn* see EXALT 1
  idiom put on a pedestal
  ant abase
  5 to bring into existence as if by raising a building <*erect* social barriers along religious lines>
  syn build up, construct, establish, hammer (out), set up
  rel fabricate, fashion, forge, form, shape; bring about, effect
  con break down, tear down; liquidate, purge; dispose (of), eliminate, remove

erection *n syn* see EDIFICE

eremitic *adj syn* see ANTISOCIAL

ergo *adv syn* see THEREFORE

erode *vb 1 syn* see EAT 3
  rel crumble, decay, deteriorate, disintegrate; consume
  2 *syn* see ABRADE 1

---

syn synonym(s)   *rel* related word(s)
ant antonym(s)   *con* contrasted word(s)
idiom idiomatic equivalent(s)
|| use limited; if in doubt, see a dictionary

rel grate, rub (off *or* away), scrape (off *or* away)

erotic *adj* of, devoted to, affected by, or tending to arouse sexual love or desire <*erotic* art>
syn amative, amatory, amorous, aphrodisiac
rel ardent, fervent, fervid, impassioned, lovesome, passionate; earthy; carnal, epicurean, fleshly, voluptuous; bawdy, sexy, spicy; concupiscent, lecherous; lascivious, lewd, lickerish, prurient, salacious, sensual

eroticism *n syn* see LUST 2

err *vb* to depart from a standard (as of wisdom or morality) <the human tendency to *err*>
syn deviate, stray, wander
rel miscalculate; lapse, slip (up), stumble, trip; transgress, trespass; offend; sin
idiom go astray (*or* amiss *or* wrong), leave the straight and narrow

errable *adj syn* see FALLIBLE

errant *adj* 1 *syn* see ERRATIC 1
rel drifting, itinerant, meandering, rambling, ranging, roaming, roving, shifting, straying
con static, unmoving
2 deviating from an accepted pattern or standard <a parent scolding her *errant* child>
syn aberrant, devious, erring
rel deviating, straying, wandering; misbehaving, mischievous, naughty
idiom off the straight and narrow
3 *syn* see FALLIBLE
rel aberrant, erring; unreliable
con perfect, trustworthy
ant inerrant

erratic *adj* 1 moving about aimlessly or irregularly without a fixed course <an *erratic* breeze barely stirred the leaves of the tree>
syn devious, errant, stray, wandering
rel curving, meandering, roundabout, winding; shifting, undirected
con fixed, stable, unmoving; active, animated, brisk, lively, sprightly
ant static
2 *syn* see UNCERTAIN 1
rel doubtful, dubious
ant stable
3 *syn* see ARBITRARY 1
rel changeable, inconsistent, inconstant, unpredictable, variable; mercurial, unstable, volatile
con consistent, conventional, predictable, stable
4 *syn* see STRANGE 4
rel anomalous, irregular, unnatural
con natural, normal, regular, typical; customary, usual

erring *adj syn* see ERRANT 2

erroneous *adj* 1 *syn* see FALSE 1
rel amiss, askew, awry, off; defective; mistaken
idiom all off, all wrong, way off the mark
con right, true
ant accurate, correct
2 *syn* see MISTAKEN

erroneousness *n syn* see FALLACY 1
rel inaccurateness, mistakenness

con accuracy, accurateness, rightness
ant correctness

error *n* 1 an often unintentional deviation from truth or accuracy <made an *error* in adding the figures>
syn mistake, x
rel inaccuracy; miscalculation, miscomputation; oversight, slip
2 something (as an act, statement, or belief) that departs from what is or is generally held to be acceptable <spying on the opposing party proved to be a grave *error*>
syn blooper, blunder, boner, bull, bungle, ‖clanger, fluff, goof, lapse, miscue, misstep, mistake, rock, slip, slipup, trip; *compare* FAUX PAS
rel fault, misdoing, misjudgment, stumble; ‖boo-boo, botch, fumble, muff; howler, screamer; impropriety, indecorum
3 *syn* see FALLACY 1
rel misreading, misunderstanding; delusion, illusion

errorless *adj syn* see IMPECCABLE 1
con imprecise, inaccurate, incorrect, unexact, wrong

ersatz *adj syn* see ARTIFICIAL 2
rel factitious, synthetic; fake

ersatz *n syn* see IMITATION

erstwhile *adv syn* see BEFORE 2

erstwhile *adj syn* see FORMER 2

eruct *vb* 1 *syn* see BELCH 1
idiom bring up gas
2 *syn* see ERUPT 1

eructate *vb syn* see BELCH 1

erudite *adj syn* see LEARNED
rel lettered, well-read; studious
ant illiterate

eruditeness *n syn* see ERUDITION 2

erudition *n* 1 *syn* see EDUCATION 2
2 the quality or state of being erudite <a scholar of great cultivation and *erudition*>
syn eruditeness, learnedness, scholarliness, scholarship
rel cultivation, culture, education, intellectuality, literacy; bookishness, pedantry, studiousness
ant illiteracy

erupt *vb* 1 to give off or release (as something pent up) forcefully <the volcano *erupted* gouts of lava>
syn belch, disgorge, eject, eruct, expel, irrupt, spew
rel cast (out *or* up), hurl, throw off; boil, discharge, emit; jet, spout, spurt; extravasate
2 to break away or burst from limits or restraint <riots *erupted* in the ghetto>
syn break out, burst (forth), explode
rel detonate, touch off; go off

eruption *n* 1 *syn* see OUTBURST 1
2 *syn* see OUTBREAK 1

escalade *vb syn* see ASCEND 1
con clamber (down), climb (down); go (down)

escalate *vb* 1 *syn* see ASCEND 1
2 to increase in extent, volume, amount, number, intensity, or scope <a little war threatens to *escalate* into a huge, ugly one>
syn expand, grow
rel broaden, enlarge, heighten, increase, intensify, spread, widen

con decrease, limit, minimize; constrict, contract, narrow; collapse, shrink, shrivel
ant de-escalate

escapade *n* a usually adventurous action that runs counter to approved or conventional conduct <childish *escapades* on Halloween>
syn caper, lark, rollick; *compare* PRANK
rel antic, frolic, vagary; prank; fling, spree; mischief, roguery

escape *vb* **1** to run away especially from something that limits one's freedom and threatens one's well-being <trying to *escape* from prison>
syn abscond, break, ║bunk, decamp, flee, fly, scape
rel get away, make off, mosey, run away; bail out, ║ditch, double, duck out, flit, jump, skip; depart; disappear, vanish
idiom cut and run, cut loose, fly the coop, take it on the lam
con come back, return; abide, remain, stay; chase, follow, pursue, tag, trail
2 to get away or keep away from what one does not wish to incur, endure, or encounter <made every effort to *escape* suspicion>
syn avoid, balk, double, duck, elude, eschew, evade, shun, shy; *compare* SHAKE 5, SKIRT 3
rel burke, bypass, circumvent; dodge, shake, shun, skit; miss
idiom fight shy of, give the slip
con catch, contract, incur; abide, bear, brook, endure, stand, suffer, tolerate; dare, face, meet

escape *n* **1** the act or fact of escaping or having escaped physically <succeeded in making his *escape* from the prison>
syn breakout, escapement, escaping, flight, getaway, lam, ║scape, slip
rel departure; deliverance, liberation, release
con return; grasp, grip, hold, retention; imprisonment, incarceration
2 the act or fact of escaping or having escaped what one does not wish to incur, encounter, or endure <sought *escape* from responsibility>
syn avoidance, come-off, elusion, escaping, eschewal, evasion, runaround, shunning
rel bypassing, circumvention, dodging, ducking, sidestepping; elusiveness, evasiveness
con abidance, abiding, bearing, endurance, enduring, submission, submitting, toleration; facing

escapement *n syn see* ESCAPE 1

escaping *n syn see* ESCAPE 1
2 syn see ESCAPE 2

eschew *vb* **1 syn see** ESCAPE 2
idiom shy away from, steer clear of
con adopt, embrace, espouse
ant choose
2 syn see FORGO
rel abstain, refrain

idiom let well enough alone

eschewal *n syn see* ESCAPE 2
rel shirking; shying

escort *n* **1** a boy or man who goes on a date with a girl or woman <had her pick of *escorts* to the dance>
syn date
rel beau, boyfriend, fellow; cavalier, gallant, squire, vis-à-vis
2 a person who leads or directs another or others in a way or course (as through difficult terrain) <served as our *escort* when we drove through the desert>
syn guide
rel attendant, companion, guard

escort *vb* **1 syn see** ACCOMPANY
2 syn see GUIDE
rel bring; squire

escritoire *n syn see* DESK

esculent *adj syn see* EDIBLE

esoteric *adj syn see* RECONDITE

especial *adj* **1 syn see** SPECIAL 1
rel preeminent, supreme, surpassing; dominant, paramount, predominant, preponderant; exceptional, notable, singular, unusual
con unexceptional, usual
ant general
2 syn see EXPRESS 2

especially *adv* **1** in a special way <was *especially* good at math>
syn distinctively, particularly, special, specially, specifically
rel remarkably, unusually; exceptionally, markedly, peculiarly, singularly, uniquely; eminently, notably, preeminently, supremely
idiom before all else
2 syn see EXPRESSLY 2

espial *n syn see* DISCOVERY

espionage *n* systematic secret observation in order to accumulate information <agents engaged in industrial *espionage*>
syn spying
rel observation, reconnaissance, sleuthing, surveillance, watching

espousal *n* **1 syn see** ENGAGEMENT 2
2 often espousals *pl syn see* WEDDING
3 syn see MARRIAGE
rel mating; union
idiom getting hitched, taking on the ball and chain, tying the knot
con estrangement, separation
4 ready acceptance of or the taking up of a cause or belief <his wholehearted *espousal* of left-wing philosophies worried his family>
syn adoption, embracement, embracing
rel acceptance, approval; advocacy; aid, promotion, support
con denial, rejection; disapproval, dislike, distaste; antipathy, aversion, intolerance
ant repudiation

espouse *vb* **1 syn see** MARRY 1
2 syn see ADOPT
rel accept, approve; advocate, back, champion, support, uphold
con abandon, desert, forsake; deny, reject; disapprove, dislike
ant repudiate

esprit *n* **1 syn see** SPIRIT 5
rel acumen, acuteness, brains, brightness, cleverness, intelligence, mind, quick-witted-

---

syn synonym(s)   **rel** related word(s)
ant antonym(s)   **con** contrasted word(s)
idiom idiomatic equivalent(s)
║ use limited; if in doubt, see a dictionary

ness, sharpness, wit; courage, mettle, tenacity; fervor, passion

2 syn see MORALE

rel camaraderie, fellowship; devotion, loyalty; enthusiasm, fervor, passion

3 syn see WIT 5

esprit de corps *n syn* see MORALE

rel camaraderie, comradeship, fellowship; partisanship, partisanship; devotion, loyalty; enthusiasm, spirit

espy *vb* 1 *syn* see SEE 1

rel recognize, take in; sight, spot, spy; witness

idiom catch sight of, get a load of

2 syn see FIND 1

rel spy; make out; notice

essay *vb syn* see TRY 1

rel venture; labor, toil, travail, work

idiom give it a try (*or* fling *or* go), have at it, make a stab at, take a crack (*or* whack) at

essay *n* 1 *syn* see ATTEMPT

rel exertion; labor, toil, travail, work; go, venture

2 a relatively brief discourse written for others' reading or consideration <an *essay* on free will>

syn article, composition, paper, theme

rel discourse, discussion, explication, exposition, study; piece; tract, treatise; dissertation, thesis

essence *n* 1 a basic underlying or constituting entity, substance, or form <succeeds in conveying completely the cruel *essence* of loneliness>

syn being, essentia, essentiality, nature, texture

rel entity, form, substance

2 the most basic, significant, and indispensable element, attribute, quality, property, or aspect of a thing <the very *essence* of Machiavellianism is the belief that in politics there is neither good nor evil>

syn be-all and end-all, bottom, essentiality, marrow, pith, quintessence, quintessential, rock bottom, root, soul, stuff, substance, virtuality; *compare* BODY 3, CENTER 2, SUBSTANCE 2

rel timber; element, fiber, property; aspect, attribute, quality, spirit; inwardness, significance; crux, gist, kernel, nub, nubbin; distillate, distillation

essentia *n syn* see ESSENCE 1

essential *adj* 1 *syn* see INHERENT

con conditional, contingent, dependent

ant accidental

2 so important to the nature and essence of a thing as to be indispensable <the *essential* ingredient in this medicine is a new drug>

syn cardinal, constitutive, fundamental, vital

rel basal, basic, underlying; capital, chief, foremost, leading, main, principal; primal, primary, prime

con dependent, secondary, subordinate; accessory, auxiliary, contributory, subsidiary

3 syn see ELEMENTAL 1

4 urgently required <raw materials *essential* to industry>

syn imperative, indispensable, necessary, necessitous, prerequisite

rel needed, needful; required, requisite, wanted; right-hand; vital

con dispensable, unnecessary, unneeded, unrequired, unwanted

ant nonessential

essential *n* 1 something that forms part of the minimal body, character, or structure of a thing <prosperity is an *essential* of the good life>

syn basic, element, fundamental, part and parcel, rudiment

rel essence, stuff, substance; must, necessary, prerequisite, sine qua non

2 something necessary, required, or unavoidable <work was an *essential* to survival>

syn condition, must, necessity, precondition, prerequisite, requirement, requisite, sine qua non

idiom name of the game

essentiality *n* 1 *syn* see ESSENCE 1

2 syn see ESSENCE 2

essentially *adv* 1 in regard to the essential points <*essentially* the problem is this: he is unreliable>

syn au fond, basically, fundamentally, in essence

rel actually, really

idiom at bottom

2 syn see ALMOST 2

rel substantially, virtually

idiom in the main

establish *vb* 1 *syn* see SET 1

rel enroot, entrench, implant, inculcate, infix, instill, root; set down, set up; moor, rivet, secure; found, ground

con eradicate, exterminate, extirpate, uproot, wipe (out)

ant abrogate

2 syn see BASE

idiom lay the foundation for (*or* of)

3 syn see ENACT 1

rel formulate; authorize, decree, legislate, prescribe

ant repeal

4 syn see FOUND 2

rel endow, provide; originate; build

con disestablish; demolish, tear down

ant abolish

5 syn see ERECT 1

6 to make clear beyond a reasonable doubt <*established* an alibi for the time of the crime>

syn demonstrate, determine, make out, prove, show

rel authenticate, confirm, corroborate, document, substantiate, verify; attest; clarify

idiom afford (*or* offer) proof of

con discredit, expose, show up; confute, invalidate, parry, rebut, refute

ant disprove

established *adj syn* see FIRM 3

establishment *n* 1 *syn* see ENTERPRISE 3

rel workplace; institute, institution; foundation

2 *often cap* a group of influential leaders who represent an established order of society <the literary *establishment*>

syn Old Guard

rel conservative(s), diehard(s)

con liberal(s)

estate *n* **1** *syn* see ORDER 9
rel form, state
2 a class of people in a community distinguishable by social or political duties or privileges <a party platform appealing to people of every *estate*>
syn grade, rank
rel bracket, category; footing, level, order, standing; place, position, station; caste, class
3 an extensive landed property <spent the weekend at his country *estate*>
syn acres, land, manor, quinta
rel farm, ranch; plantation; villa

esteem *n syn* see REGARD 4
rel approval, liking; appreciation, valuation
ant abomination

esteem *vb* **1** *syn* see APPRECIATE 1
rel idolize, revere, worship
idiom hold dear, think the world of
ant despise
2 *syn* see ADMIRE 2
rel revere, venerate
idiom hold in esteem (*or* high regard)
con abhor
ant abominate

estimable *adj* **1** *syn* see WORTHY 1
2 *syn* see RESPECTABLE 1
rel admired, esteemed, respected
con disreputable, unworthy; bad
3 *syn* see HONORABLE 1

estimate *vb* **1** to judge something with respect to its worth <*estimated* the value of the jewels>
syn appraise, assay, assess, evaluate, rate, set (at), survey, valuate, value
rel adjudge, adjudicate, judge; ascertain, determine, discover; price, prize; decide, settle
2 *syn* see CALCULATE
rel cast, sum; count, enumerate
3 to fix some value (as size, distance, or composition) more or less accurately <*estimated* the rainfall at over six inches>
syn approximate, call, judge, place, put, reckon
rel round, round off; conjecture, guess, suppose, surmise; fancy, imagine; deduce, infer
con calculate, compute; measure

estimate *n* **1** the act of appraising or valuing the nature, character, quality, status, or worth of something <his influence as President is beyond *estimate*>
syn appraisal, appraisement, assessment, estimation, evaluation, valuation
rel calculation, measurement, reckoning; sizing up; projection
2 *syn* see ESTIMATION 1
idiom point of view

estimation *n* **1** the result of evaluating something <his *estimation* of the man's ability proved incorrect>
syn appraisal, appraisement, assessment, estimate, evaluation, judgment, stock

rel impression; opinion
2 *syn* see COMPUTATION
3 *syn* see ESTIMATE 1
4 *syn* see REGARD 4

estrange *vb* to cause one to break a bond or tie of affection or loyalty <her arrogance *estranged* her children and friends>
syn alien, alienate, disaffect, disunify, disunite, wean
rel break up, divide, divorce, part, separate, sever, split, sunder
idiom set at odds
con appease, conciliate, pacify, propitiate; associate, espouse, join, link, unite
ant reconcile

estrangement *n* the act of estranging or the condition of being estranged <a petty dispute resulted in total *estrangement*>
syn alienation, disaffection
rel division, divorce, schism; withdrawal
con appeasement, conciliation, propitiation
ant reconciliation

etceteras *n pl syn* see SUNDRIES

etch *vb* **1** *syn* see ENGRAVE 1
2 to set forth in a sharp, clear-cut manner with minute attention to detail <the most sharply *etched* character in the novel>
syn define, delineate
rel outline, set forth; depict, describe, picture, portray, represent
3 *syn* see ENGRAVE 2

eternal *adj* **1** *syn* see INFINITE 1
rel endless, interminable, unceasing, unending; lasting, permanent, perpetual; deathless, immortal, undying
con ephemeral, evanescent, momentary, passing, short-lived, temporary, transient
ant mortal
2 *syn* see EVERLASTING 1
rel deathless, undying
3 *syn* see CONTINUAL
con interrupted, sporadic
4 valid or existing unaltered at all times <right and wrong are *eternal* verities that cannot be changed>
syn ageless, dateless, intemporal, timeless
rel immemorial, lasting, perdurable, permanent, perpetual; immutable, inalterable, unalterable, unchangeable, unchanging
con alterable, changeable, changing, fluctuating, varying; debatable, questionable, suspect

eternalize *vb syn* see PERPETUATE
eternally *adv syn* see EVER 2
eternity *n* **1** a totality of infinite time <in *eternity* there is no change or passing away>
syn infinity, sempiternity
rel endlessness, infiniteness, infinitude, perpetuity, timelessness
con ephemerality, impermanence, transience; limitedness, restrictedness
ant finiteness
2 unending existence after death <belief in the *eternity* of our spiritual nature>
syn afterlife, everlastingness, eviternity, immortality, world-without-end
3 *syn* see AGE 2
idiom forever and a day, forever and ever

eternize *vb syn* see PERPETUATE
ethereal *adj syn* see AIRY 3

rel celestial, empyreal, empyrean, heavenly; vaporish, vaporlike, unsubstantial; filmy, gossamer; delicate, fragile, light
con heavy, thick
ant substantial

ethic *n* **1 ethics** *pl but usu sing in constr* the discipline dealing with what is good and bad and with moral duty and obligation <*ethics* has been called the science of the ideal of human character>
syn morals
2 a group of moral principles or set of values <the Christian *ethic*>
syn morality, morals, mores
3 ethics *pl* see the code of conduct or behavior governing an individual or a group (as the members of a profession) <medical *ethics*>
syn principles
rel moralities, morals, mores; criteria, standards
4 the complex of ideals, beliefs, or standards that characterizes or pervades a group, community, or people <the American work *ethic*>
syn ethos
rel belief, ideal, standard, value

ethical *adj syn* see MORAL 1
rel high-principled; elevated; upright, upstanding
con flagitious, iniquitous, nefarious; improper, indecent, indecorous, unbecoming, unseemly; immoral, low

ethnic *adj* **1** *syn* see HEATHEN
rel non-Christian, unchristian
2 of, relating to, or originating from the traits shared by members of a group as a product of their common heredity and cultural tradition <only a person thoroughly familiar with Yiddish can recognize the *ethnic* quality of the pun> <*ethnic* cookery>
syn racial
rel national; tribal

ethos *n syn* see ETHIC 4

etiquette *n* **1** *syn* see MANNER 5
2 *syn* see DECORUM 1
rel behavior, conduct, deportment, manners; amenities, civilities, formalities; convention, form, protocol
idiom social graces

eulogistic *adj* of, relating to, characterized by, or bestowing praise <the speaker made *eulogistic* remarks on the group's accomplishment>
syn encomiastic, laudative, laudatory, panegyrical, praiseful
rel approbatory, approving, commendatory, complimentary
con uncomplimentary; critical, disapproving, disparaging; abusive
ant dyslogistic

eulogize *vb syn* see PRAISE 2
rel applaud; belaud, bepraise
idiom praise to the skies, sing the praises of
ant vilify

eulogy *n syn* see ENCOMIUM
rel adulation, glorification
con calumny, slander
ant vilification

euphemism *n* an agreeable or inoffensive expression that is substituted for one that might offend or suggest unpleasantness <vandalism that goes under the *euphemism* of souvenir hunting>
syn nice Nelly, nice-nellyism
ant dysphemism

euphonic *adj syn* see MELODIOUS 1

euphonious *adj syn* see MELODIOUS 1

euphoria *n* **1** *syn* see ELATION 1
ant deflation, dysphoria
2 an often groundless or excessive feeling of well-being and happiness <drug-induced *euphoria*>
syn elation, exaltation, intoxication
rel ecstasy, frenzy; madness; glee
con anxiety, unease, uneasiness
ant depression

euphuistic *adj syn* see RHETORICAL
rel elaborate; colorful; verbose; elevated
con concise, simple, straightforward; lean

evacuee *n syn* see REFUGEE

evade *vb* **1** *syn* see ESCAPE 2
rel flee, fly, slip (away); foil, outwit, thwart
idiom keep (or know) one's distance
con accost, confront, dare, face
2 *syn* see EQUIVOCATE 1
rel bypass, circumvent, duck; parry, turn (aside)
idiom give (someone) the runaround
con confront, face; elucidate, explain

evaluate *vb syn* see ESTIMATE 1
rel appreciate; class, gauge, rank; criticize
2 *syn* see CLASS 2

evaluation *n* **1** *syn* see ESTIMATE 1
rel interpreting; judging, rating
2 *syn* see ESTIMATION 1
rel appreciation; interpretation; decision

evanesce *vb syn* see VANISH
rel disintegrate, dispel, disperse, dissipate, dissolve, scatter
idiom go up in smoke, vanish into thin air
con appear; coalesce
ant materialize

evanescent *adj syn* see TRANSIENT
rel temporary; flying; dissolving, fading, melting; disappearing, vanishing

evangelical *adj* characterized by or reflecting a missionary, reforming, or redeeming impulse or purpose <a mood of *evangelical* nationalism>
syn crusading, evangelistic
rel ardent, fervid, impassioned, militant, zealous; missionary, propagandizing, proselytizing

evangelist *n syn* see MISSIONARY

evangelistic *adj syn* see EVANGELICAL
rel missionary, reforming

evangelize *vb syn* see PREACH 1

evanish *vb syn* see VANISH
idiom pass out of the picture

evaporate *vb syn* see VANISH
rel escape, pass (away or off); weaken; vaporize
idiom go pouf

evasion *n syn* see ESCAPE 2
rel dodging, equivocating, equivocation, evading, excuse, subterfuge; haggling, quibbling; escapism
con confrontation, confronting; daring
ant facing

evasive *adj* **1** tending to evade or avoid confrontation <his answers were ambiguous and *evasive*>

syn equivocating, prevaricative, prevaricatory, shifty, shuffling
rel ambiguous, equivocal, unclear, vague; sliding, slippery, sly
con categorical, definite, explicit, unambiguous, univocal; candid, forthright
ant direct

2 *syn* see ELUSIVE

even *adj* 1 *syn* see LEVEL
con bent, crooked, curved, twisted
ant uneven

2 *syn* see STEADY 2
rel equal, identical, same; consistent, continual, continuous, undeviating, unvaried

3 giving no advantage to either side <an *even* exchange>
syn equal, equitable, fair
rel balanced, fair and square, square; honest, straightforward, unprejudiced
con inequitable, unequal, unfair
ant uneven

4 being nicely in balance <his chances for success or failure are *even*>
syn equal, even-up, fifty-fifty
rel balanced, comparable, proportionate
con disproportionate, unbalanced
ant uneven

5 being neither more nor less than the named or understood amount, extent, or number <an *even* mile>
syn exact, square
con approximate, imprecise, inaccurate

even *adv* 1 in a like manner <they can learn *even* as others do>
syn as well, exactly, expressly, just, precisely

2 at the very time <perhaps *even* now the moment has come to consider a retreat>
syn already

3 not this merely but also — used as an intensive to emphasize the identity or character of something <a huge, *even* monstrous animal>
syn indeed, nay, truly, verily, yea
rel absolutely, positively; quite, really

4 — used as an intensive to indicate an extreme, hypothetical, or unlikely case or instance <refused *even* to look at her> <*even* if this were so, it should not change our plans>
syn so much as
idiom even so much as

5 *syn* see YET 1

even *vb* 1 to make (as a surface) smooth, even, level, or flat <*even* the soil with a spade>
syn flatten, flush, lay, level, plane, smooth, smoothen
rel grade, roll; align; symmetrize; uniform; pancake
con rough, roughen

2 to make even or balanced in advantage <hoped to *even* the odds by training>
syn equal, equalize
rel balance, square

---

syn synonym(s)   *rel* related word(s)
ant antonym(s)   *con* contrasted word(s)
idiom idiomatic equivalent(s)
‖ use limited; if in doubt, see a dictionary

---

con unbalance, unequalize, upset; derange, disarrange

3 *syn* see EQUALIZE 1

evening *n* 1 the closing part of day and the early part of night <the last light of *evening*>
syn ‖dimmet, ‖dimps, ‖dimpsy, dusk, ‖dusk dark, eventide, gloaming, nightfall, owl=light, twilight
rel afternoon; sundown, sunset; duskiness, duskness
con sunrise; dawn
ant morning

2 a latter portion or a period of decline <in the *evening* of life>
syn sunset, twilight

3 a party taking place in the evening <their *evenings* were notable affairs>
syn soiree
rel reception; salon; party

evenly *adv* 1 in equal parts <a career divided *evenly* between stage and screen>
syn equally, fifty-fifty, squarely
rel commensurably, proportionately
con disproportionately, unequally
ant unevenly

2 in a just or fair manner <she was *evenly* polite to everyone>
syn equally, impartially
rel fairly, justly
con unfairly, unjustly

3 without variation or fluctuation <spread the paint *evenly*>
syn flatly, smooth, smoothly, uniformly
con irregularly, roughly
ant unevenly

event *n* 1 *syn* see OCCURRENCE
rel act, action, deed; achievement, exploit, feat; accident, chance, fortune

2 a matter worthy of remark <the trip was an *event* in their dull routine>
syn milepost, milestone, occasion
rel affair, landmark; delight, treat
idiom historic event
con insignificance, trifle, triviality

3 *syn* see EFFECT 1
rel offshoot, outgrowth; product, resultant, sequent
idiom end result

4 a postulated outcome, condition, or contingency <in the *event* of rain, we will not meet>
syn case, eventuality
rel chance, fortuity, hap, happenstance

5 any of the contests in a sports program <track-and-field *events*>
syn match, meet
rel competition, contest

6 *syn* see FACT 2

eventide *n* *syn* see EVENING 1

eventual *adj* *syn* see LAST
rel consequent, ensuing, inevitable, succeeding; ending, endmost
con antecedent, beginning, inceptive, initial, original

eventuality *n* 1 *syn* see EVENT 4
rel contingency, possibility

2 *syn* see EFFECT 1
con antecedent, beginning, root

eventually *adv* *syn* see YET 2
idiom in the long run

even–up *adj syn* see EVEN 4

ever *adv* **1** *syn* see ALWAYS 1
2 through all or an indefinite time <a name that will *ever* be respected>
syn always, eternally, evermore, forever, forevermore, in perpetuum
3 in each and every case <war and suffering have *ever* gone hand in hand>
syn invariably
rel consistently, regularly, usually
4 at any time or on any occasion <he is seldom if *ever* absent>
syn anytime, at all
5 in any way <nor was it *ever* important>
syn anyway, anywise, at all, once
6 — used as an intensive after an inverted verb-subject construction <is he *ever* proud of himself>
syn confoundedly, consumedly, excessively, extremely, immensely, inordinately, over, overfull, overly, overmuch, super, too, unduly
rel annoyingly, plaguey; grievously, mortally; consummately

ever and again *adv syn* see SOMETIMES
ever and anon *adv syn* see SOMETIMES
everlasting *adj* **1** lasting or enduring through all time <*everlasting* laws governing the physical universe>
syn amaranthine, ceaseless, endless, eternal, immortal, never-ending, unending, world-without-end; *compare* IMMORTAL 1
rel lasting, perdurable, permanent, perpetual; boundless, infinite, limitless, termless
con ephemeral, evanescent, momentary, short-lived, transitory
2 *syn* see CONTINUAL
con interrupted, off-and-on, periodic, sporadic

everlastingness *n syn* see ETERNITY 2
evermore *adv syn* see EVER 2
evert *vb syn* see DISPROVE 1
every *adj syn* see ALL 2
everybody *pron* every person <*everybody* must do what his conscience dictates>
syn all, everyman, everyone
idiom all and sundry
ant nobody
everyday *adj* **1** *syn* see COMMON 4
con distinctive, singular, unique; uncommon, unusual
ant exceptional
2 *syn* see PROSAIC 3
3 *syn* see ORDINARY 1
everyman *pron syn* see EVERYBODY
idiom the man in the street
everyone *pron syn* see EVERYBODY
ant no one
everyplace *adv syn* see EVERYWHERE 1
idiom all over the place
everything *pron* the whole amount <lost *everything* in the fire>
syn all
idiom all in all, the lot, the whole ball of wax, the whole bit (*or* shebang), the whole kit and kaboodle, the works
everywhere *adv* **1** in every place or in all places <poverty anywhere is a danger to peace and prosperity *everywhere*>

syn all over, all round (*or* all around), everyplace, far and near, far and wide, high and low, overall, throughout
idiom in all quarters, in every quarter
2 *syn* see WHEREVER

evict *vb syn* see EJECT 1
rel dislodge, dispossess, force (out), put out, shut out, turn out
idiom turn (*or* put) out bag and baggage, turn out of doors, turn out of house and home
con harbor, house, lodge, shelter

evidence *n* **1** *syn* see INDICATION 3
2 *syn* see TESTIMONY
evidence *vb syn* see SHOW 2
rel display, expose; attest, bespeak, betoken, confirm, indicate, prove, testify
evident *adj syn* see CLEAR 5
rel noticeable, prominent, pronounced
idiom as plain as the nose on one's face, plain as day
con inconspicuous; ambiguous, unapparent, unrecognizable; concealed, hidden
ant inevident

evidently *adv syn* see OSTENSIBLY
evil *n* **1** whatever is harmful, distressing, or disastrous <attempts to grasp the nature of *evil*>
syn ill
rel bad, badness, devilry, diablerie, diabolism, evilness, satanism, satanity, wickedness, wrong
con goodness, virtue
ant good
2 whatever is morally unacceptable <return good for *evil*>
syn debt, sin, wickedness, wrong
rel evildoing, misconduct, sinfulness, wrongdoing
con rectitude, righteousness, virtue
ant good
3 a particular thing (as an act) that is evil <choose the lesser of two *evils*>
syn crime, diablerie, iniquity, sin, tort, wrong, wrongdoing
rel badness, evilness, maleficence, vice, wickedness; misdeed, offense
evil *adj* **1** *syn* see WRONG 1
rel base, low, vile; flagitious, nefarious; baneful, pernicious; black, damnable, execrable
con high, noble; exemplary, salutary
ant good
2 *syn* see OFFENSIVE
rel distasteful, repellent; fetid, putrid, stinking
3 *syn* see MALICIOUS
rel angry, disagreeable, ugly, unpleasant, wrathful; harmful, hurtful, injurious, mischievous; destructive
4 *syn* see HARMFUL
rel calamitous, destructive, disastrous
con harmless, noninjurious
ant innocuous
5 reporting or predicting harm or misfortune <messengers bearing *evil* tidings>
syn bad, ill, unfavorable; *compare* OMINOUS
rel baleful, baneful, inauspicious; ill-boding, ill-omened, ominous

con auspicious, favorable
ant good
6 marked by misfortune or calamity <the family fell upon *evil* times>
syn bad, inauspicious
rel unfavorable, unfortunate, unlucky; difficult, hard, trying; calamitous, disastrous
con favorable; lucky; easy, prosperous; auspicious, halcyon, happy
ant good

evince *vb* **1** *syn* see SHOW 2
rel argue, attest, bespeak, betoken, confirm, indicate, prove; display, exhibit, expose, illustrate, signify
con repress, suppress; conceal, hide
2 *syn* see EDUCE 1
rel bring (about), cause; provoke, stimulate

eviscerate *vb* to take out the entrails of <*eviscerate* a turkey>
syn bowel, disembowel, draw, embowel, exenterate, gut, paunch

eviternity *n* *syn* see ETERNITY 2

evocative *adj* serving or tending to call something (as a mood) forth <conduct *evocative* of the utmost contempt>
syn evocatory, suggestive
rel meaningful, pregnant, weighty; arousing, moving, stimulating, stirring; causing, effecting, producing

evocatory *adj* *syn* see EVOCATIVE

evoke *vb* *syn* see EDUCE 1
rel excite, provoke, stimulate; arouse, awaken, rally, rouse, stir, waken; call forth, call up, conjure (up), raise, summon (forth or up)

evolution *n* *syn* see DEVELOPMENT
rel change, transformation

evolve *vb* **1** *syn* see DERIVE 1
rel get (at), obtain; advance
2 *syn* see UNFOLD 3
rel advance, progress; mature, open (up), ripen

evolvement *n* *syn* see DEVELOPMENT
rel metamorphosis, transformation

evulse *vb* *syn* see EXTRACT 1

exacerbate *vb* to cause to become increasingly bitter or severe <foolish words that only *exacerbated* the quarrel>
syn acerbate, embitter, envenom
rel annoy, exasperate, irritate, provoke; aggravate, heighten, intensify; inflame
idiom add fuel to the flame, fan the flames, feed the fire, pour oil on the fire
con appease, mollify, pacify, placate, quell; lessen, moderate
ant assuage

exact *vb* **1** *syn* see EXTORT 1
2 *syn* see LEVY
3 *syn* see DEMAND 1
rel coerce, compel, constrain, force, oblige; extort, extract, squeeze, wrest, wring

exact *adj* **1** *syn* see CORRECT 2
idiom on the money
2 *syn* see EVEN 5
ant imprecise, inexact

3 *syn* see SAME 1
4 *syn* see CAREFUL 2
5 *syn* see PRECISE 4

exacting *adj* *syn* see ONEROUS
rel rigid, rigorous, severe, stern, strict, stringent, finicky, fussy, particular; critical, hypercritical
con laissez-faire, lenient
ant unexacting

exactitude *n* *syn* see PRECISION

exactly *adv* **1** *syn* see JUST 1
rel ‖plumb, plunk; specifically
idiom on the dot (*or* nose), right on the nail
con about, around, more or less, roughly
ant approximately
2 *syn* see ALL 1
rel absolutely, expressly, positively; completely
3 as you say or state — used to express agreement or concurrence <"You are accusing me of lying?" he asked. "*Exactly*," she replied.>
syn precisely, yes
idiom quite so, (that's) for sure (*or* certain)
4 *syn* see EVEN 1

exactness *n* *syn* see PRECISION

exaggerate *vb* *syn* see EMBROIDER
rel hyperbolize, overcolor, romance, romanticize
idiom blow up out of (all) proportion, draw the long bow, make the eagle scream
ant understate

exaggeration *n* an overstepping of the bounds of truth <the passage shows the author's penchant for grotesque *exaggeration*>
syn coloring, embellishment, embroidering, hyperbole, overstatement
rel aggrandizement, amplification, enlargement; overcoloring, overdrawing, romance, stretching
idiom flight of fancy, tall talk
con minimizing, underestimation
ant understatement

exalt *vb* **1** to enhance the status of <propaganda that *exalts* nationalism to the level of religion>
syn aggrandize, dignify, distinguish, ennoble, erect, glorify, honor, magnify, pedestal, stellify, sublime, uprear
rel boost, build up, elevate, lift, promote, raise, upgrade, uplift; enhance, heighten, intensify; acclaim, enhalo, extol, laud, praise; apotheosize
con debase, degrade, demean, humble, humiliate; belittle, decry, depreciate, derogate, detract, disparage, downgrade, minimize
ant abase
2 *syn* see FIRE 2
rel pique, quicken, stimulate; deepen, enhance, sharpen; encourage, inspirit, spirit (up); uplift

exaltation *n* **1** *syn* see APOTHEOSIS 2
rel upgrading, uplifting; extolment, laudation, praise
con debasement, degradation, demeanment, humiliation; belittlement, depreciation, derogation, disparagement, downgrading
ant abasement

---

syn synonym(s)   *rel* related word(s)
ant antonym(s)   *con* contrasted word(s)
idiom idiomatic equivalent(s)
‖ use limited; if in doubt, see a dictionary

2 syn see ELATION 1

rel delectation, delight; bliss, joy, rapture

ant deflation

3 syn see EUPHORIA 2

ant depression

exalted *adj* **1** raised to or having high rank <moved in *exalted* circles> <Alexander was *exalted* to the papal throne in 1492>

syn astral, highest, highest-ranking, top=drawer, top-ranking

rel august, noble; eminent, illustrious, prominent; high, high-ranking; foremost, number one; first, leading, outstanding

con low, lowly, low-ranking, unimportant; minor; humble, plebeian

ant abject

2 syn see GRAND 3

ant abject

examination *n* a careful, detailed, and often formal study designed to uncover pertinent information <the doctor gave him a physical *examination*>

syn analysis, audit, check-over, checkup, inspection, perlustration, review, scan, scrutiny, survey, view

rel assay; breakdown, diagnosis, dissection; sifting, winnowing; canvass, catechization, inquiry, questioning, quizzing, testing

examine *vb* **1** *syn* see SCRUTINIZE 1

rel check (out), go (over), investigate, look (into); contemplate, look (at *or* over), observe

idiom give a going over, give the once-over, go over with a fine-toothed comb

2 syn see TRY 1

3 syn see ASK 1

rel cross-examine; grill; pump

idiom give the third degree to, put to the question

example *n* **1** *syn* see INSTANCE

2 syn see MODEL 2

idiom shining example

3 an instance that illustrates a rule or provides practice in its application <worked out his arithmetic *examples*>

syn ensample, illustration, problem

idiom case in point

exanimate *adj syn* see DEAD 1

exasperate *vb syn* see IRRITATE

rel agitate, work up

idiom try one's temper (*or* patience)

ant appease; mollify

exasperation *n* **1** *syn* see ANNOYANCE 2

rel irritation, vexation; displeasure; resentment

2 syn see ANNOYANCE 3

ex cathedra *adj syn* see OFFICIAL

excavate *vb* **1** *syn* see DIG 1

rel gouge (out), hollow (out), scoop (out), scrape (out), quarry (out)

2 syn see DIG 2

exceed *vb* **1** to go or be beyond a natural or set limit <the policeman *exceeded* his authority> <this task *exceeds* my powers>

syn outstep, overrun, overstep, surpass

rel outreach, overreach; dare, presume, venture

2 syn see SURPASS 1

exceedingly *adv syn* see VERY 1

excel *vb syn* see SURPASS 1

excellence *n* something that gives especial worth or value <the particular *excellence* of this cake is its lightness>

syn arete, excellency, merit, perfection, quality, virtue

rel value, worth; distinction, fineness, superiority; goodness, niceness, superbness; class

con blemish, defect, flaw; failing, foible, frailty, vice

ant fault

excellency *n syn* see EXCELLENCE

excellent *adj* meritoriously near the standard or model and eminently good of its kind <an *excellent* restaurant specializing in French cuisine>

syn A1, bang-up, banner, blue-ribbon, ||boss, bully, ||bunkum, capital, champion, classic, classical, ||dandy, famous, fine, first-class, first-rate, first-string, five-star, front=rank, Grade A, number one, par excellence, prime, quality, royal, skookum, ||slap-up, sovereign, stunning, superior, ||swingeing, top, top-notch, whiz-bang; *compare* MAR-VELOUS 2, SUPREME

rel high-class, high-grade, proper; ||rum; distinguished, exceptional, premium; brag, incomparable, magnificent, nobby, sensational, smart, superb, superlative, terrific, tip-top, unsurpassed

idiom all wool and a yard wide, beyond compare, out of this world

con mediocre; bad, inadequate, inferior, low, low-grade, low-quality, substandard; fourth-rate, second-class, second-rate; poor, shoddy, sorry, unsatisfactory, wretched; commonplace, mediocre, ordinary

ant execrable

except *vb* **1** *syn* see EXCLUDE

rel omit, pass over; exempt; reject

con incorporate, receive, work in

ant admit

2 syn see OBJECT 1

except *prep* with the exclusion or exception of <*except* Christmas, we had no long holiday>

syn apart from, aside from, bar, barring, bating, beside, besides, but, ||cep, except for, excluding, exclusive of, outside, outside of, save, saving

except *conj* **1** on any other condition than that <wouldn't go near that woman *except* I had to>

syn but, save, saving, unless, ||without

2 syn see ONLY

except for *prep syn* see EXCEPT

exceptionable *adj syn* see OBJECTIONABLE

con unimpeachable; exemplary

ant unexceptionable

exceptional *adj* **1** being out of the ordinary <an *exceptional* opportunity>

syn extraordinary, phenomenal, rare, remarkable, singular, uncommon, uncustomary, unimaginable, unique, unordinary, unthinkable, unusual, unwonted; *compare* STRANGE 4

rel infrequent, scarce; distinct, notable, noteworthy

con frequent; common, commonplace, familiar, ordinary, usual

ant unexceptional

2 *syn* see SUPERIOR 4
rel good; excellent, marvelous, outstanding, phenomenal, wonderful; extraordinary, singular, special
con common, ordinary, run-of-the-mill
ant average

exceptionally *adv syn* see VERY 1
rel especially, particularly; extraordinarily, unusually; marvelously, phenomenally, stupendously, wonderfully

excerpt *vb* to select (passages or details) as typical of a larger store <quotations *excerpted* from many authors>
syn extract
rel cull, glean; choose, pick, pick out, select, single; cite, quote

excess *n* 1 whatever exceeds a limit, measure, bound, or accustomed degree <the proper balance between sufficiency and *excess*>
syn fat, overabundance, overflow, overkill, overmuch, overplus, plethora, superfluity, surfeit, surplus, surplusage
rel overbalance, overspill; oversupply; profusion; superabundance
idiom enough and then some, enough and to spare, too much of a good thing
con insufficiency, lack, scarcity
ant deficiency; dearth
2 the amount or degree by which a thing or number exceeds another <an *excess* of 10 bushels over what was needed>
syn overage, overstock, oversupply, plus, surplus, surplusage
rel overproduction; overmeasure
ant deficit, shortfall
3 *often* **excesses** *pl* undue or immoderate personal indulgence especially in eating and drinking <*excess* at table is seldom healthful> <his *excesses* led to his failure in business>
syn immoderation, inordinateness, intemperance, overindulgence
rel extravagance, overdoing; indulgence, self-indulgence; immoderacy, immoderateness; dissipation, prodigality, saturnalia
con moderation; sobriety, temperateness; restraint, self-discipline, self-restraint
ant temperance

excess *adj syn* see SUPERFLUOUS
rel redundant; unessential

excessive *adj* 1 going beyond a normal or acceptable limit <spend an *excessive* amount on clothes>
syn dizzy, exorbitant, extravagant, extreme, immoderate, inordinate, sky-high, steep, stiff, stratospheric, supernatural, towering, unconscionable, undue, unmeasurable
rel boundless, limitless, unbounded; over, overboard, overmuch, overweening; super
idiom out of bounds
con exiguous, meager, narrow, scant, scanty, skimpy, sparse, tight
ant deficient
2 given to personal excesses <an *excessive* drinker, often drunk and never quite sober>

syn immoderate, inordinate, intemperate, overindulgent, unrestrained, untempered
rel extravagant; indulgent, self-indulgent; dissipated, prodigal
con conservative, moderate, sober, temperate
ant restrained

excessively *adv syn* see EVER 6

exchange *vb* 1 *syn* see TRADE 1
2 to give up, taking in return something else <*exchanged* his uniform for civilian clothes>
syn change, substitute, swap, switch, trade; *compare* TRADE 1
rel displace, replace
3 to give and receive reciprocally <*exchanged* a few words with her neighbor>
syn bandy, interchange
rel pay back, reciprocate
idiom give as much as one takes, give tit for tat, return the compliment

exchangeable *adj syn* see INTERCHANGEABLE

exchequer *n syn* see TREASURY 2

excise *vb* to remove by or as if by dissecting <*excise* a tumor> <*excised* some wordy passages>
syn cut out, exsect, extirpate, resect
rel amputate, cut off; elide, remove, strike out; eradicate, root out; delete, expurgate, exscind, slash

excitable *adj* easily excited <an *excitable* child who needs a firm hand>
syn agitable, alarmable, combustible, edgy, skittery, skittish, startlish, volatile
rel high-strung, mercurial, temperamental, unstable; touchy
idiom like a bundle of nerves, likely to go off at half cock, on edge, on the ragged edge
con calm, collected, cool, easy, easygoing, phlegmatic, placid, quiet
ant unexcitable

excite *vb* 1 *syn* see PROVOKE 4
rel agitate, discompose, disquiet, disturb, perturb, stir up; impassion; charge (up), energize, touch off, turn on
idiom set astir, set on fire, stir the blood
con allay, placate, soothe
ant quiet
2 *syn* see ELATE
rel move; fire
con depress, dishearten
3 *syn* see INTEREST

excited *adj syn* see INTOXICATED 2
rel animated, atwitter; agitated, charged (up), inflamed, pink; delighted, enthusiastic
idiom all fired up, all of a twitter, beside oneself
con apathetic, unmoved; deflated
ant unexcited

exciting *adj* absorbingly interesting <the most *exciting* day of her life> <an *exciting* personality>
syn exhilarant, exhilarating, exhilarative, eye-popping, inspiring, intoxicating, rousing, stimulating, stirring
rel interesting, intriguing; moving, provocative; heady, thrilling
con blah, dull, uninteresting, unintriguing; humdrum, monotonous, tedious
ant unexciting

---

syn synonym(s)   *rel* related word(s)
ant antonym(s)   *con* contrasted word(s)
idiom idiomatic equivalent(s)
‖ use limited; if in doubt, see a dictionary

exclaim vb to speak or utter suddenly and usually sharply, vehemently, or passionately <*exclaimed* in delight at the sight of the toy>

syn blat, blurt (out), bolt, cry out, ejaculate
rel burst (out); roar, snort

exclude vb to prevent the participation, consideration, or inclusion of <*excluded* that subject from discussion>

syn bar, bate, count out, debar, eliminate, except, rule out, suspend
rel ban; close out, estop, obviate, preclude, prevent, prohibit, ward (off); blackball, blacklist, ostracize; block; disbar; lock out, put out, shut out
idiom close (or shut) the door on
con comprehend, involve; embrace, take in
ant admit; include

excluding prep syn see EXCEPT

exclusionary adj syn see EXCLUSIVE 1

exclusive adj 1 having or exercising the power to limit or exclude <a tangle of *exclusive* laws>

syn exclusionary, exclusory
rel barring, debarring, excluding; limitative, limiting, restrictive; preclusive, prohibitive
con free, unlimited, unrestricted, unrestrictive
ant admissive

2 syn see SELECT 1
rel aristocratic, elite, preferred, privileged, tony; aloof, clannish, cliquey, cliquish; high-hat, snobbish, standoffish
con catholic, cosmopolitan, universal; common, familiar, ordinary, popular, vulgar
ant inclusive

3 syn see STYLISH
con tasteless; frumpy, unfashionable

4 syn see SOLE 4
rel individual, lone, only
con common, general, public

5 syn see WHOLE 5
con divided, partial

exclusive n syn see SCOOP

exclusively adv syn see ONLY 1
rel completely, wholly; particularly

exclusive of prep syn see EXCEPT

exclusory adj syn see EXCLUSIVE 1

excogitate vb 1 syn see CONSIDER 1

2 syn see DERIVE 1
rel contrive, invent, think (up); develop, think (out)

excoriate vb 1 syn see CHAFE 3

2 syn see LAMBASTE 3
idiom tear into

excorticate vb syn see SKIN 2

excrescence n syn see OUTGROWTH 1

excrescency n syn see OUTGROWTH 1

excruciate vb syn see AFFLICT
rel inflame, irritate; hurt, pain, wound; convulse
idiom prolong the agony

excruciating adj intensely or unbearably painful <his suffering was *excruciating*>

syn agonizing, harrowing, racking, tearing, tormenting, torturing, torturous
rel acute, extreme; piercing, sharp, shooting, stabbing; consuming, rending

exculpate vb to free from alleged fault or guilt <the court *exculpated* him after a thorough investigation>

syn absolve, acquit, clear, disculpate, exonerate, vindicate
rel explain, justify, rationalize; condone, excuse, forgive, pardon, remit; amnesty, free, let off
idiom clear the (or one's) record, wipe the slate clean
con blame, censure, denounce, reprehend, reprobate; incriminate; accuse, charge; arraign, indict; impeach; convict
ant inculpate

excurse vb syn see DIGRESS 2

excursion n 1 a trip not involving a prolonged or definite separation from one's usual abode or way of life <an afternoon *excursion* to the city>

syn jaunt, junket, outing, roundabout, sally
rel expedition, journey, trek, trip, safari; circuit, tour; one-way trip, pleasure trip, round trip; ||pasear, paseo, walk, ||walkabout

2 syn see DIGRESSION

excursus n syn see DIGRESSION

excusable adj 1 syn see VENIAL

2 syn see JUSTIFIABLE

excuse vb 1 to exact neither punishment nor redress for or from <she was much too ready to *excuse* her children's faults>

syn condone, forgive, pardon, remit
rel alibi, apologize (for), explain, justify, pretext, rationalize; absolve, acquit, clear, exculpate, exonerate, vindicate; extenuate, gloss (over), gloze, overwash, palliate, pass over, shrug off, whitewash, wink (at)
con blame, censure, criticize, reprehend, reprobate; castigate, chasten, chastise, correct, discipline; admonish, chide, rebuke, reprimand
ant punish

2 syn see EXEMPT

excuse n 1 a justifying explanation of a fault or defect <what's your *excuse* for being late>

syn alibi, plea, pretext, ||right; *compare* APOLOGY 1, 2
rel defense; explanation, justification, rationalization; reason

2 syn see APOLOGY 2

3 an inferior example of a specified kind <this heap is a sorry *excuse* for a car>

syn apology
rel makeshift, shift, stopgap, substitute
idiom a sorry specimen
con nonpareil, paragon; gem, jewel, treasure

exec n syn see EXECUTIVE

execrable adj 1 so odious as to be utterly detestable <an *execrable* crime>

syn accursed, cursed, damnable
rel atrocious, heinous, horrific, horrifying, monstrous; base, despicable, foul, low, vile; detestable, loathsome, nauseating, repulsive, revolting
idiom beneath (or below) contempt, not to be put up with (or endured)

2 syn see DAMNED 2

execrate vb 1 to denounce violently <*execrated* those responsible for the concentration camps>

syn anathematize, curse, damn, objurgate

rel censure, condemn, denounce, reprehend, reprobate, reprove; ban; revile; accurse, imprecate

con applaud, commend, compliment; acclaim, extol, laud, praise; admire

ant eulogize

2 *syn* see HATE

3 *syn* see SWEAR 3

execration *n syn* see BLASPHEMY 1

execute *vb* **1** *syn* see PERFORM 2

rel act; bring about, cause; carry out, complete, discharge, transact

2 *syn* see ADMINISTER 1

rel discharge, dispatch, transact; conduct, handle

3 *syn* see FULFILL 1

rel put through

4 *syn* see MURDER 1

rel eliminate, purge

idiom put to death

executive *n* one who holds an administrative or managerial position <a senior sales *executive*>

syn administrator, exec, manager, officer, official

rel businessman, businesswoman; entrepreneur; higher-up; director, leader, supervisor

exegesis *n syn* see EXPLANATION 1

exegetic *adj syn* see EXPLANATORY

exemplar *n syn* see MODEL 2

rel soul; exponent, illustration; prototype

exemplary *adj* **1** *syn* see GOOD 11

rel ideal, model; admirable, commendable, praiseworthy, worthy

con evil, corrupt; unworthy

2 *syn* see TYPICAL 1

exemplify *vb* **1** to use examples in order to clarify <a good teacher *exemplifies* each complex point>

syn illustrate, instance

rel clarify, clear up, spell out; cite, quote; enlighten, illuminate

2 *syn* see EPITOMIZE 2

rel demonstrate; illustrate

3 *syn* see REPRESENT 2

exempt *vb* to free from a liability or requirement <*exempt* a man from military service>

syn absolve, discharge, dispense, excuse, let off, privilege (from), relieve, spare

rel except; free

idiom give (one) exemption

exemption *n* freeing or the state of being free or freed from a charge or obligation to which others are subject <received a tax *exemption*>

syn immunity, impunity

rel exception; discharge, freedom, release

exenterate *vb syn* see EVISCERATE

exercise *n* **1** the act of bringing into play or realizing in action <one can usually avoid accidents by the *exercise* of foresight>

syn application, employment, exercising, exertion, operation, use; *compare* USE 1

con dereliction, disregard; neglect; carelessness, heedlessness, inattention, laxity

2 regular or repeated appropriate use of a faculty, power, or bodily organ <muscular atrophy from lack of *exercise*>

syn activity, exercising, exertion

rel action, movement; practice, use, workout

con inactiveness, inactivity; idleness, unemployment

3 something practiced or performed in order to develop, improve, or display a specific power or skill <spelling *exercises*>

syn drill, drilling, practice

4 a performance having a strongly marked secondary or ulterior aspect <his writing is an *exercise* in confusion>

syn lesson, study

exercise *vb* **1** *syn* see USE 2

idiom put into practice

2 *syn* see EXERT

3 to use repeatedly in order to master or strengthen <beginning swimmers *exercising* their new skill> <games that *exercise* the muscles>

syn drill, practice, rehearse

rel break in, condition, groom, prepare, train; cultivate, develop, foster, improve; fix, set

4 *syn* see ANNOY 1

exercising *n* **1** *syn* see EXERCISE 1

2 *syn* see EXERCISE 2

exert *vb* to bring to bear especially with sustained effort or lasting effect <*exerted* tremendous influence over his son's development>

syn exercise, ply, put out, throw, wield

rel apply, employ, use

idiom put forth

exertion *n* **1** *syn* see EXERCISE 1

2 *syn* see EFFORT 1

rel strain, striving, struggle

idiom hard (or long) pull

con ease, leisure, relaxation, repose, rest; inactivity, idleness

ant inertia

3 *syn* see EXERCISE 2

exfoliate *vb syn* see SCALE 2

exhale *vb* to let or force out of the lungs <*exhaled* a cloud of cigarette smoke>

syn breathe (out), expire, outbreathe

rel emit, let (out); blow

ant inhale, inspire

exhaust *vb* **1** *syn* see DEPLETE

rel dispel, disperse, dissipate, scatter; run out

idiom suck dry

con conserve, preserve, save; renew, restore

2 *syn* see CONSUME 1

3 *syn* see GO 4

4 to tire utterly <the 14-hour flight *exhausted* everyone>

syn see ‖BUGGER; *compare* TIRE 1

rel overdo, overdrive, overexert, overextend, overply, overwork; debilitate, enfeeble, weaken

idiom run one ragged, tire to death

con relax, rest, unlax

exhausted *adj syn* see EFFETE 2

rel run-down, worn, weakened; ‖beat, dog-tired, tired, ‖tucked up; limp; dead

idiom all done in (or for)

---

syn synonym(s)   *rel* related word(s)

ant antonym(s)   *con* contrasted word(s)

idiom idiomatic equivalent(s)

‖ use limited; if in doubt, see a dictionary

exhaustion *n syn* see FATIGUE
  rel collapse, prostration

exhaustive *adj* testing all possibilities or considering all the elements of <an *exhaustive* investigation was soon under way>
  syn complete, full-dress, thorough, thoroughgoing, whole-hog
  rel all-encompassing, all-out, comprehensive, full-blown, full-scale, out-and-out, profound, total; intensive, radical, sweeping
  con cursory; shallow; incomplete, partial; slipshod, unthorough
  ant superficial

exhaustively *adv* 1 *syn* see HARD 3
  con cursorily, superficially; incompletely, partially
  2 *syn* see THOROUGHLY 2

exhibit *vb* 1 *syn* see SHOW 2
  2 *syn* see LOOK 4
  3 *syn* see SHOW 4
  idiom parade one's wares, strut one's stuff

exhibit *n syn* see EXHIBITION 2

exhibition *n* 1 an act or instance of showing, evincing, or showing off <she gave an incredible *exhibition* of bad manners>
  syn demonstration, display, show, spectacle
  rel manifestation, sight
  2 a public display of objects of interest <a trade *exhibition*>
  syn exhibit, exposition, fair, show
  rel demonstration, display, offering, presentation, showing

exhibitive *adj syn* see INDICATIVE

exhilarant *adj syn* see EXCITING

exhilarate *vb syn* see ELATE
  rel animate, enliven, invigorate, vitalize; boost, buoy, exalt, inspirit, lift, pep (up), uplift; cheer, delight, gladden, ||send, thrill
  idiom send into ecstasies
  con deject, dishearten, dispirit, weigh down
  ant depress

exhilarated *adj syn* see INTOXICATED 2
  rel buoyed up, exalted, gladdened, pepped up, uplifted
  idiom in ecstasies, on cloud nine
  con blue, dispirited, down, low, unhappy, weighed down
  ant depressed

exhilarating *adj* 1 *syn* see EXCITING
  rel animating, animative, enlivening, inspiriting, invigorating, quickening, cheering, elevating, uplifting; breathtaking, electric
  con deflating, disheartening, dispiriting
  ant depressing
  2 *syn* see INVIGORATING

exhilaration *n syn* see ELATION 1 *compare* ECSTASY
  rel animation, enlivenment, firing, invigoration, quickening, stimulation, vitalization, vivification; electrification, excitation, excitement, galvanization; elevation, inspiration, uplift
  ant dejection

exhilarative *adj* 1 *syn* see EXCITING
  2 *syn* see INVIGORATING

exhort *vb syn* see URGE
  rel admonish, plead; call upon, insist; stimulate
  con block, deter, discourage, impede

exhumate *vb syn* see EXHUME

exhume *vb* to take out of a place of burial <the body was *exhumed* and burned>
  syn disinhume, disinter, exhumate, unbury, uncharnel
  rel dig up, disentomb, unearth; disembalm
  con bury, entomb, inter, ||plant
  ant inhume

exigency *n* 1 *syn* see JUNCTURE 2
  rel difficulty, hardship, rigor, vicissitude; dilemma, fix, jam, pickle, scrape; pressure, urgency
  2 *syn* see NEED 4
  rel demand, imperativeness, insistence, requirement; coercion, compulsion, constraint; duress, pressure, urgency
  idiom matter of life and death

exigent *adj* 1 *syn* see PRESSING
  rel acute; necessary; menacing, threatening
  2 *syn* see ONEROUS

exiguous *adj syn* see MEAGER 2
  rel diminutive, little, small, tiny; slender, slight, tenuous, thin; confined, limited, narrow, restricted, straitened
  ant ample

exile *n* 1 forced removal from one's native country <a deposed king living in *exile* in Rome>
  syn banishment, deportation, displacement, expulsion, ostracism, relegation
  rel exclusion; extradition; expatriation; diaspora, dispersion, migration, scattering
  con recall, restoration
  2 *syn* see ÉMIGRÉ
  rel nonperson, outcast, unperson
  idiom man without a country

exile *vb syn* see BANISH
  rel dispossess; evacuate; extradite; drive out
  idiom turn out of house and home
  con recall, restore

exist *vb* 1 *syn* see BE
  2 *syn* see CONSIST 1

existence *n* 1 the state or fact of having independent reality <customs that have recently come into *existence*>
  syn actuality, being
  rel life; presence; reality; perseity
  ant nonexistence
  2 *syn* see ENTITY 1
  rel essence; individuality

existent *adj* 1 *syn* see ACTUAL 1
  rel existing; present
  2 *syn* see EXTANT 1
  3 *syn* see PRESENT

existent *n syn* see ENTITY 1

existing *adj syn* see EXTANT 1

exit *n* 1 *syn* see DEPARTURE 1
  ant entry
  2 *syn* see EGRESS 2
  ant entrance, entry

exit *vb syn* see GO 2
  idiom make an (*or* one's) exit
  con arrive, come
  ant enter

exiting *n syn* see DEPARTURE 1
  ant entering

exodus *n syn* see DEPARTURE 1
  rel emigration, migration; flight
  con immigration; ingress
  ant influx

ex officio *adj syn* see OFFICIAL

exonerate *vb syn* see EXCULPATE
  rel disburden, free
  ant incriminate
exorbitant *adj syn* see EXCESSIVE 1
  rel overboard, overmuch; unwarranted;
outrageous, preposterous; exacting, extortionate
  idiom out of sight
  con equitable, fair, just; rational, reasonable
exordium *n syn* see INTRODUCTION
  rel preliminary
  con afterword, conclusion, epilogue, postscript
exotic *adj* 1 not native to the place where
found <*exotic* fish>
  syn foreign
  rel imported, introduced, naturalized; alien,
extrinsic, strange
  con aboriginal, autochthonous, endemic,
native; domestic, local
  ant indigenous
  2 excitingly or enticingly different or unusual <he was moved by her *exotic* beauty>
  syn romanesque, romantic, strange
  rel different, unusual; alluring, enticing,
fascinating, glamorous, mysterious
expand *vb* 1 *syn* see OPEN 4
  2 *syn* see INCREASE 1
  3 to increase or become increased in bulk,
volume, or size <water *expands* when
heated>
  syn amplify, dilate, distend, inflate, swell
  rel grow; bulk (up), enlarge, fill (out); bolster; mushroom; ‖plim, puff (up)
  con condense, decrease, deflate, shrink,
shrivel; ‖dwindle, lessen
  ant contract
  4 to express more fully and in greater detail
<*expanded* his notes into an essay>
  syn amplify, develop, elaborate, enlarge
  rel detail, explicate; augment; discourse,
expatiate
  con compress, condense, contract
  ant abridge
  5 *syn* see INCREASE 1
  6 *syn* see ESCALATE 2
  rel prolong, protract
  con de-escalate; circumscribe
  ant limit, restrict
expanse *n* a significantly large area or range
<a trackless *expanse* of moor>
  syn amplitude, breadth, distance, expansion, space, spread, stretch
  rel compass, extent, orbit, range, reach,
scope, sweep; area, domain, field, sphere,
territory; immensity, magnitude
expansion *n* 1 *syn* see EXPANSE
  2 the act or process of increasing in some
way <the recent *expansion* of science>
  syn enlargement, extension, spread
  con contraction, decrease, shrinking
expansive *adj* 1 *syn* see ELASTIC 2
  rel communicative, demonstrative, extroverted, gregarious, unconstrained, unreserved, unrestrained; effusive, gushy, lavish;
generous, liberal, openhanded

  con austere, severe, stern; reserved, reticent,
silent, taciturn
  2 *syn* see DEMONSTRATIVE
  ant withdrawn
  3 *syn* see COMMUNICATIVE
  4 *syn* see EXTENSIVE 1
  rel ample, large; big, great
  ant limited
expatiate *vb syn* see DISCOURSE 1
  rel narrate, recite, recount, rehearse, relate;
ramble
expatriate *vb syn* see BANISH
  ant repatriate
expatriate *n syn* see ÉMIGRÉ
  ant repatriate
expect *vb* 1 to anticipate in the mind <did
not *expect* him for dinner>
  syn await, count (on *or* upon), hope, look
  rel anticipate, apprehend, divine, foreknow,
foresee
  idiom bargain on (*or* for), look for
  ant despair (of)
  2 *syn* see UNDERSTAND 3
  rel feel, sense; presume, presuppose
expectancy *n* 1 the state of one who looks
forward to something <had an air of wistful
expectancy>
  syn anticipation, expectation
  rel presensation, presentiment
  2 *syn* see EXPECTATION 2
expectant *adj* 1 characterized by expectation
<an *expectant* crowd>
  syn anticipant, anticipative, anticipatory,
atiptoe, expecting
  rel open-eyed, openmouthed; hopeful;
eager; alert, watchful
  con apathetic, indifferent, uninterested;
unconcerned, unimpressed, unmoved
  2 *syn* see PREGNANT 1
  idiom anticipating a blessed event, waiting
for the stork
expectation *n* 1 *syn* see EXPECTANCY 1
  2 something that is expected <each had his
own dreams and *expectations*>
  syn expectancy
  rel design, hope, intention, motive, notion;
prospect
expecting *adj* 1 *syn* see EXPECTANT 1
  2 *syn* see PREGNANT 1
expediency *n* 1 *syn* see ORDER 11
  rel propitiousness; convenience
  2 *syn* see RESOURCE 3
  rel design, strategy, tactic; measure, step
  idiom card up one's sleeve, means to an end
expedient *adj* dictated by practical or prudential motives <decided it was not *expedient* to interfere yet>
  syn advisable, politic, prudent, tactical,
wise
  rel advantageous, beneficial, convenient,
practical, profitable, useful, utilitarian;
opportune, seasonable, timely, well-timed;
feasible, possible, practicable; appropriate,
fit, fitting, suitable; judicious
  con deleterious, detrimental; harmful, hurtful, injurious; fruitless, futile, vain; inappropriate, uncalled-for, unfitting, unsuitable;
impolite, imprudent, inadvisable, injudicious, unwise
  ant inexpedient

---

syn synonym(s)   *rel* related word(s)
ant antonym(s)   *con* contrasted word(s)
idiom idiomatic equivalent(s)

‖ use limited; if in doubt, see a dictionary

expedient *n syn* see RESOURCE 3
rel agency, instrument, instrumentality, means, medium

expedition *n* **1** *syn* see JOURNEY
rel campaign; entrada, exploration
2 *syn* see HASTE 1
rel alacrity, promptitude
con delay, retardation, slackening, slowing
ant procrastination
3 *syn* see ALACRITY
rel expeditiousness, speediness, swiftness; punctuality
con dawdling, delaying, faltering, hesitation

expeditious *adj syn* see FAST 3
rel effective, effectual, efficacious, efficient; prompt, ready
con ineffective, ineffectual, inefficacious, inefficient; dilatory, laggard, leisurely, slow
ant sluggish

expeditiously *adv syn* see FAST 2
rel effectively, efficaciously; punctually
con ineffectively; deliberately, dilatorily, leisurely, slowly
ant sluggishly

expeditiousness *n syn* see HASTE 1

expeditive *adj syn* see FAST 3

expel *vb* **1** *syn* see ERUPT 1
rel blow off, blow out, ejaculate, exhaust
2 *syn* see BANISH
rel drum out, read out; eliminate, turn out; ‖bounce
idiom give (one) the boot, give the bum's rush, give the old heave-ho, send to Coventry, throw out on one's ear
ant admit

expellee *n syn* see ÉMIGRÉ

expend *vb* **1** *syn* see SPEND 1
rel dispense, distribute; blow, exhaust, use up
idiom loose (*or* untie) the purse strings, open one's purse
con hoard, lay up, save
2 *syn* see GO 4

expenditure *n syn* see EXPENSE 1

expense *n* **1** something expended to secure a benefit or bring about a result <spared no *expense* in furnishing their home>
syn cost, disbursement, expenditure, outlay
2 a loss incurred in the course of gaining something <won the war at the *expense* of many lives>
syn cost, price, toll
rel decrement, forfeit, forfeiture, sacrifice; deprivation, loss

expensive *adj syn* see COSTLY 1
rel immoderate, uneconomical; big-ticket, high-priced
con economical, moderate; bargain, low-cost, low-priced, thrifty; cheap
ant inexpensive

experience *n syn* see ACQUAINTANCE 1
rel background; observation; know-how, practice, skill; savoir faire, sophistication; wisdom
ant inexperience

experience *vb* **1** to meet with directly (as through participation or observation) <*experience* pain> <trying to *experience* the problems of a different culture>
syn have, know, see, suffer, sustain, undergo

rel encounter, meet; accept, receive
2 *syn* see FEEL 2
rel behold, see, survey, view

experienced *adj* made skillful or wise through practice <an *experienced* sales executive>
syn old, old-time, practical, practiced, seasoned, skilled, versed, vet, veteran; *compare* PROFICIENT
rel broken in; accomplished, skillful; expert, qualified; old-line, wise
idiom having been around, knowing the score (*or* the ropes)
con apprentice, beginning, freshman, green, new, novice, raw, untested, untried
ant experienceless, inexperienced

experient *adj syn* see EMPIRICAL

experiential *adj syn* see EMPIRICAL

experiment *n* an operation or process carried out to resolve an uncertainty <*experiments* that added much to our understanding of nutritional needs>
syn experimentation, test, trial, trial and error, trial run
rel probe, research, search; examination, investigation; analysis, study

experiment *vb* to engage in experimentation <*experimenting* with regional solutions to urban problems>
syn experimentalize, experimentize, test (out), try (out), try on
rel investigate, probe, research, search; analyze, scrutinize, study, weigh
idiom play around with

experimental *adj* **1** *syn* see EMPIRICAL
2 of, relating to, or having the characteristics of experiment <*experimental* missile flights>
syn experimentative, test, trial
rel preliminary, preparatory; developmental; provisional, temporary, tentative
con tested, tried; permanent, proved; accepted, established, standard

experimentalize *vb syn* see EXPERIMENT

experimentation *n syn* see EXPERIMENT

experimentative *adj syn* see EXPERIMENTAL 2

experimentize *vb syn* see EXPERIMENT

expert *adj syn* see PROFICIENT
rel schooled, trained; adroit, deft, dexterous; pro, professional
con unpracticed; unschooled
ant amateur, inexpert

expert *n* one who has acquired special skill in or knowledge and mastery of something <a fingerprint *expert*>
syn adept, artist, artiste, authority, ‖dab, ‖dabster, doyen, master, master-hand, maven, passed master, past master, pro, professional, proficient, swell, virtuoso, whiz, wiz, wizard
rel ‖darb; specialist
con dabbler, dilettante, tyro; apprentice, novice, probationer
ant amateur

expertise *n* **1** *syn* see ABILITY 2
rel readiness; competence; skillfulness
2 *syn* see ART 1
rel quickness; cleverness, ingeniousness; finesse; savvy

expertism *n syn* see ABILITY 2

expertness *n syn* see ABILITY 2
  rel prowess; facility
expiate *vb* to make amends or give satisfaction for wrong done <*expiated* his crime with his life>
  syn atone
  rel amend, compensate (for), correct, rectify, redress, remedy
  idiom make up for, put right
expiative *adj syn* see PURGATIVE
expiatory *adj syn* see PURGATIVE
expire *vb* **1** *syn* see DIE 1
  idiom draw one's last breath; give up the breath of life
  con live, thrive
  2 see PASS 3
  3 *syn* see EXHALE
  ant inspire
explain *vb* **1** to make something comprehensible or more comprehensible <a commentary that *explains* the allegory>
  syn construe, explicate, expound, interpret, spell out; *compare* CLARIFY 2
  rel decipher, disentangle, undo, unravel, unriddle, unscramble, untangle; analyze, break down; clear up, resolve, solve
  idiom put into plain English
  con confound, confuse, puzzle
  ant obfuscate
  2 *syn* see CLARIFY 2
  3 to give the reason for or cause of <unable to *explain* his strange conduct>
  syn account, explain away, justify, rationalize
  rel condone, excuse; absolve, acquit, exculpate, exonerate, vindicate
explain away *vb syn* see EXPLAIN 3
explanation *n* **1** something that makes clear what is obscure <sought some *explanation* of the difficult passage>
  syn construal, construction, exegesis, explication, exposé, exposition, interpretation
  rel disentangling, unscrambling; enlightenment, illumination; definition, meaning; resolution, solution; demonstration, example, exemplification, illustration
  2 a statement of causes, grounds, or motives <refused an *explanation* for her act>
  syn account, justification, rationale, rationalization, reason
  rel grounds; motive
explanative *adj syn* see EXPLANATORY
explanatory *adj* serving to explain <*explanatory* notes in a book>
  syn exegetic, explanative, explicative, explicatory, expositional, expositive, expository, interpretive
  rel enlightening, illuminating; discursive; demonstrative, illustrative
  con baffling, bewildering, confusing, misleading, mystifying, puzzling
  ant obfuscatory
expletive *n syn* see SWEARWORD
explicate *vb syn* see EXPLAIN 1
  rel amplify, develop, dilate, enlarge (upon), expand, expatiate; demonstrate

  idiom dot the *i*'s (and cross the *t*'s)
explication *n syn* see EXPLANATION 1
  rel amplification, development, enlargement, expansion, expatiation
explicative *adj syn* see EXPLANATORY
  rel annotative, exemplificative, scholiastic
explicatory *adj syn* see EXPLANATORY
explicit *adj* characterized by full precise expression <gave the guard *explicit* orders about whom to admit>
  syn categorical, clean-cut, clear-cut, definite, definitive, express, specific, unambiguous
  rel certain, clear, distinct, lucid, perspicuous, plain, sure, understandable, unequivocal; accurate, correct, exact, precise
  con cryptic, dark, enigmatic, equivocal, obscure, unclear, vague; implicit, implied, inferred; imprecise, inaccurate, incorrect, inexact
  ant ambiguous
explicitly *adv syn* see EXPRESSLY 1
explode *vb* **1** to burst violently and noisily usually due to pressure within <the bomb *exploded*>
  syn blow up, burst, detonate, go off, mushroom
  rel blast, discharge
  idiom blow sky-high, blow to kingdom come
  con fail, fizzle, peter (out)
  2 *syn* see ERUPT 2
  rel flame (up), flare (up)
  idiom blow a fuse (*or* gasket)
  3 *syn* see DISCREDIT 2
  rel invalidate; deflate
  idiom shoot full of holes
exploit *n* **1** *syn* see ADVENTURE
  rel effort, job; maneuver
  2 *syn* see FEAT 2
  rel do, performance, stunt; blow, coup, stroke
  idiom bold stroke
exploit *vb* **1** *syn* see USE 2
  rel cultivate, work
  2 to take unfair advantage of <*exploits* his friend's good nature>
  syn abuse, impose (on *or* upon), use
  rel manipulate; bleed, fleece, skin, soak, stick
  3 *syn* see MANIPULATE 2
explore *vb* to search through or into <*explored* the possibilities of reaching an agreement>
  syn delve (into), dig (into), go (into), inquire (into), investigate, look (into), probe, prospect, sift
  rel burrow, mouse (out); quarry, search; examine, test, try; inquisite, question
  idiom nose around
explosion *n syn* see OUTBURST 1
exponent *n* one who actively promotes or backs something <an *exponent* of arbitration in labor disputes>
  syn advocate, champion, expounder, proponent, supporter
  rel backer, booster, partisan, promoter, protagonist; defender, upholder
  con antagonist, enemy; opposition
  ant opponent

---

syn synonym(s)   *rel* related word(s)
ant antonym(s)   *con* contrasted word(s)
idiom idiomatic equivalent(s)
‖ use limited; if in doubt, see a dictionary

expose *vb* **1** to make accessible to something detrimental or dangerous <he needlessly *exposed* his troops to enemy fire>
syn lay (open), subject, uncover
rel endanger, hazard, imperil, jeopard, jeopardize, jeopardy, peril, risk
idiom put (*or* leave) in harm's way
con cover, shelter; guard, protect
ant shield
2 *syn* see OPEN 2
rel unfold, unshroud
3 *syn* see SHOW 4
rel advertise, air, broadcast, publish
4 to reveal the faults, frailties, unsoundness, or pretensions of <the monograph *exposed* the theory as being pure myth>
syn debunk, discover, show up, uncloak, undress, unmask, unshroud
rel disclose, reveal, uncover
idiom lay bare
exposé *n syn* see EXPLANATION 1
exposed *adj* **1** *syn* see OPEN 2
rel apparent, evident, manifest; unconcealed, unhidden; revealed; visible
idiom laid bare
con covered, enveloped, sheathed
2 *syn* see LIABLE 2
rel likely; menaced, threatened
con defended, guarded, protected, safeguarded, shielded
exposition *n* **1** *syn* see EXPLANATION 1
rel presentation; discourse, discussion, disquisition, expounding; statement; delineation, enunciation
2 *syn* see EXHIBITION 2
rel display, production
expositional *adj syn* see EXPLANATORY
expositive *adj syn* see EXPLANATORY
rel depictive, descriptive, graphic; illuminative; delineative
expository *adj syn* see EXPLANATORY
rel disquisitional; critical
expostulate *vb syn* see OBJECT 1
rel combat, fight, oppose, resist; argue, debate, discuss, dispute
idiom raise one's voice against
exposure *n* the condition of being exposed to something detrimental <*exposure* to attack>
syn liability, openness, vulnerability, vulnerableness
rel susceptibility, susceptiveness, susceptivity; defenselessness, helplessness, unprotection; danger, jeopardy, peril, risk
con bulwark, cover, protection, safeguard, shelter, shield, shielding
expound *vb syn* see EXPLAIN 1
rel express, present, state; comment, discourse; clarify, delin- eate, describe, exemplify, illustrate
expounder *n syn* see EXPONENT
rel explainer, expositor
express *adj* **1** *syn* see EXPLICIT
rel expressed, uttered, voiced; out-and-out, unmistakable; unconditional, unqualified
con unexpressed, unsaid, unstated; ambiguous, equivocal; conditional, qualified
2 of a particular or exact sort <came for the *express* purpose of buying a car>
syn especial, set, special, specific
rel individual; definite, particular; explicit; intended, intentional, premeditated

ant vague
express *vb* **1** *syn* see WORD
2 to give expression to (as a thought, an opinion, or an emotion) <*expressed* his views freely>
syn air, give, put, state, vent, ventilate; *compare* SAY 1, WORD
rel broach, circulate, put about; disclose, tell; frame; enunciate, phrase; announce, declare, proclaim, pronounce; discharge, drain
con hint, insinuate, intimate, suggest
ant imply
3 *syn* see MEAN 2
rel communicate, convey, impart
4 *syn* see PRESS 3
expression *n* **1** an act, process, or instance of expressing in words <his anger found *expression* in a string of oaths>
syn statement, utterance, vent, voice
rel issue; manifestation, representation; observation, reflection
con hint, insinuation, intimation, suggestion
2 *syn* see PHRASE 2
rel word; verbalism; idiom; clause
3 one thing that calls to mind another often symbolically <sent flowers as an *expression* of sympathy>
syn gesture, indication, reminder, sign, token
rel embodiment, manifestation, representation, symbol; demonstration, show
4 *syn* see ELOQUENCE
rel graphicness, vividness
5 *syn* see LOOK 2
expressionless *adj* lacking expression <cold *expressionless* eyes>
syn blank, deadpan, empty, inexpressive, unexpressive, vacant
rel dull, lackluster, lusterless, vacuous; impassive, inscrutable, stolid, wooden; dead
con lustrous; responsive; alive, vital
ant expressive
expressive *adj* clearly conveying or manifesting something <a forceful and *expressive* word>
syn eloquent, facund, meaningful, pregnant, rich, sententious, significant
rel revealing, revelatory, suggestive; graphic, pictorial, vivid; alive, demonstrative, lively, responsive, senseful, spirited
con banal, commonplace, drab, dull, flat, jejune, inane, insipid, vacuous, vapid; impassive, indifferent; austere, severe, stern, stiff, wooden; blank, deadpan, empty, expressionless, vacant; dead
ant inexpressive, unexpressive
expressiveness *n syn* see ELOQUENCE
ant inexpressiveness
expressivity *n syn* see ELOQUENCE
expressly *adv* **1** in direct and unmistakable terms <his beliefs *expressly* repudiate the church's teachings>
syn categorically, definitely, explicitly, specifically
rel directly; unmistakably
con ambiguously, equivocally; conditionally; likely, possibly, probably

2 for the express purpose <programs designed *expressly* to serve immediate political objectives>
syn especially, in specie, specially, specifically
3 *syn* see EVEN 1

expropriate *vb syn* see APPROPRIATE 1
rel dispossess; take (away)

expulse *vb syn* see BANISH
rel ‖bounce; eject
con admit, receive

expulsion *n syn* see EXILE 1
rel driving out, forcing out; ejection, ousting; removal
idiom the boot, the old heave-ho

expunge *vb syn* see ERASE
rel discard, drop, exclude, omit; annihilate, eradicate

expurgate *vb* 1 *syn* see PURIFY 2
2 *syn* see CENSOR

expurgation *n syn* see PURIFICATION

expurgatorial *adj syn* see PURGATIVE

expurgatory *adj syn* see PURGATIVE

exquisite *adj* 1 *syn* see CHOICE
rel consummate, finished; faultless, flawless, impeccable
2 *syn* see IMPECCABLE 1
rel superb, superlative
con faulty, flawed, imperfect
3 *syn* see INTENSE 1
rel acute, extreme; consummate, transcending

exquisite *n syn* see FOP

exsect *vb syn* see EXCISE

exsiccate *vb syn* see DRY 1

extant *adj* 1 that is in existence <the most talented writer *extant*>
syn alive, around, existent, existing, living
con dead, defunct, destroyed, exterminated, extinct; departed, gone, lost
ant nonextant
2 *syn* see ACTUAL 1
rel current, immediate, present
con possible, potential
3 *syn* see PRESENT

extemporaneous *adj* composed, devised, or done at the moment rather than beforehand <made an *extemporaneous* speech after the dinner>
syn autoschediastic, extemporary, extempore, impromptu, improvised, offhand, spur-of-the-moment, unrehearsed, unstudied; *compare* UNINTENTIONAL
rel casual, informal; unprepared, unthought-out; impulsive, snap, spontaneous
idiom off the cuff, on the spur of the moment
con designed, planned, prepared, projected, schemed, thought-out; considered, deliberated, premeditated, studied

extemporary *adj syn* see EXTEMPORANEOUS

extempore *adj syn* see EXTEMPORANEOUS

extemporization *n syn* see IMPROVISATION

extemporize *vb syn* see IMPROVISE
rel dash off, knock off, toss off
idiom do offhand, play (it) by ear
con cook up, plan, prepare, think out

extend *vb* 1 *syn* see OPEN 4
con close, fold
2 *syn* see OFFER 1
rel allocate, allot; accord, advance, award, bestow, confer, grant; donate
idiom place at one's disposal
3 to make or become longer <*extended* her visit by a week>
syn draw, draw out, elongate, lengthen, prolong, prolongate, protract, spin (out), stretch
rel amplify, enlarge, expand, increase
con abridge; curtail
ant shorten
4 *syn* see INCREASE 1
5 *syn* see RUN 8
rel advance, proceed; continue
6 *syn* see RANGE 3
7 to reach a certain point <his education doesn't *extend* beyond elementary school>
syn go
rel reach, run; advance; attain

extended *adj* 1 *syn* see LONG 1
rel prolonged, protracted, spread out, stretched out (*or* forth)
ant contracted
2 *syn* see EXTENSIVE 1
rel far-flung, widespread
con narrow; inextensive
ant unextended

extension *n* 1 the act or state of extending or being extended <a one-month *extension* of the price freeze seems likely>
syn elongation, lengthening, production, prolongation, prolongment, protraction
rel continuation, continuing; drawing out, stretch, stretch-out
con abridgment, shortening; contraction, curtailment, shrinking
2 *syn* see EXPANSION 2
rel augmentation, increase; spreading out
con abridgment, curtailment; reduction
ant contraction
3 *syn* see RANGE 2
rel magnitude, size, spread; comprehensiveness
4 *syn* see ANNEX

extensity *n syn* see RANGE 2

extensive *adj* 1 widely ranging in scope or application <*extensive* privileges>
syn broad, expansive, extended, scopic, scopious, wide
rel comprehensive, general, inclusive; far-reaching, far-spreading, spacious, wide-ranging; all-encompassing, all-inclusive, blanket, boundless, indiscriminate, unrestricted, wholesale
con circumscribed, constricted, limited, narrow, restricted; unextended
2 *syn* see BIG 1
con little, small

extent *n* 1 *syn* see RANGE 2
rel domain, field, province, sphere
2 *syn* see SIZE 1
rel compass, extension, orbit, radius, reach, scope, sweep

---

syn synonym(s)   *rel* related word(s)
ant antonym(s)   *con* contrasted word(s)
idiom idiomatic equivalent(s)
‖ use limited; if in doubt, see a dictionary

3 *syn* see ORDER 4

extenuate *vb* 1 *syn* see THIN 1
rel mitigate; moderate, qualify, temper
con aggravate, enhance, heighten
2 *syn* see PALLIATE
rel explain, justify, rationalize; apologize
idiom put a gloss on (*or* upon *or* over), put a good face upon

exterior *adj syn* see OUTER
rel outermost, outmost
con inner, ingrained, inherent, intrinsic
ant interior

exteriorize *vb syn* see EMBODY 1
ant interiorize

exterminate *vb* 1 *syn* see ANNIHILATE 2
rel finish off; execute; kill (off)
idiom do away with, put an end to, put out of the way
2 *syn* see SLAUGHTER 3
idiom wipe off the face of the earth, wipe off the map

external *adj syn* see OUTER
rel out, outermost, outmost, peripheral
con ingrained, inherent, intrinsic
ant internal

externalize *vb syn* see EMBODY 1
ant internalize

extinct *adj* 1 *syn* see DEAD 1
2 that has died out altogether <an *extinct* civilization>
syn bygone, dead, defunct, departed, gone, lost, vanished
rel nonexistent; collapsed, fallen, overthrown; disappeared
idiom gone from the face of the earth
con existent, existing, living; active; contemporary, current
ant extant
3 *syn* see OBSOLETE
rel antiquated, archaic, old-fashioned
con modern; contemporary
ant current

extinguish *vb* 1 to cause to cease burning <firemen *extinguishing* the blaze>
syn douse, ||dout, out, put out, quench, ||squench
rel blow out, snuff out; smother
con fire, kindle, start; torch
ant ignite
2 *syn* see ANNIHILATE 2
rel erase, expunge, obliterate
3 *syn* see CRUSH 5
rel check; smother, stifle; snuff (out); choke (out), trample (down)
idiom put the lid (*or* the kibosh) on
con encourage, fire (up)
ant inflame

extinguishment *n syn* see REPRESSION 1

extirpate *vb* 1 *syn* see ANNIHILATE 2
rel efface, erase, expunge, demolish, destroy, raze; kill off
con breed, engender, generate, propagate
2 *syn* see EXCISE

extol *vb syn* see PRAISE 2
idiom beat the drum for, make much of
ant decry

extort *vb* 1 to obtain something by pressure or intimidation <racketeers *extorting* protection money>
syn exact, gouge, pinch, screw, shake down, squeeze, wrench, wrest, wring; *compare* CHEAT, FLEECE 1
rel demand; coerce, force; extract, get, obtain, secure; bleed, fleece, skin
idiom bleed one white, make one pay through the nose, put the screws to
2 *syn* see EDUCE 1

extra *adj syn* see SUPERFLUOUS
rel added, additional, supplemental, supplementary

extra *adv* to a degree or extent beyond the usual <she was *extra* smart>
syn extremely, rarely, ||uncommon, uncommonly, unusually
rel especially; particularly; considerably, markedly, noticeably
con barely, scarcely

extract *vb* 1 to draw out forcibly or with effort <*extract* a confession> <*extract* a tooth>
syn evulse, pull, tear, yank
rel pry; avulse
2 *syn* see EKE OUT 3
3 *syn* see GLEAN
4 *syn* see EDUCE 1
5 *syn* see EXCERPT
rel abridge, condense, shorten

extraction *n syn* see ANCESTRY

extraneous *adj* 1 *syn* see EXTRINSIC
rel accidental, adventitious, incidental
con constitutional, ingrained, inherent; germane, material, pertinent
2 *syn* see IRRELEVANT
rel incidental; unessential; unrelated; pointless; inappropriate
idiom beside the point
ant relevant

extraordinary *adj syn* see EXCEPTIONAL 1
rel amazing; stupendous, terrific, wonderful
idiom out of the ordinary
con customary, normal, regular, usual
ant ordinary

extravagance *n* 1 *syn* see LUXURY
2 the quality, state, fact, or an instance of being extravagant <by living simply and avoiding *extravagance* they saved enough for the trip>
syn extravagancy, lavishness, overdoing, prodigality, squander, unthrift, waste, wastefulness
rel improvidence, spendthriftness; excess, indulgence, overindulgence
con moderation, temperateness; care, forehandedness, frugality, austerity
ant economy

extravagancy *n syn* see EXTRAVAGANCE 2

extravagant *adj* 1 grossly exaggerated <*extravagant* accusations>
syn fantastic, preposterous, wild
rel unbalanced, unrestrained; absurd, foolish, ludicrous, nonsensical, ridiculous, silly; bizarre, crazy; exaggerated, implausible
con plausible, sensible; restrained
ant reasonable
2 *syn* see EXCESSIVE 1
rel exuberant, lavish, profuse; prodigal, profligate, wasteful
con economical, frugal, sparing
ant restrained

extreme *adj* **1** very great <the project demanded *extreme* secrecy>
syn deep, uttermost
2 *syn* see ARDENT 2
rel deep, moving
3 departing sharply from the traditional or usual <*extreme* political views>
syn extremist, fanatic, rabid, radical, revolutional, revolutionary, revolutionist, ultra, ultraist; *compare* OUTLANDISH 3
rel excessive; immoderate; desperate, drastic; extravagant, unreasonable; violent, wild
con conservative, moderate, restrained; reasonable, sensible
4 *syn* see EXCESSIVE 1
rel intolerable, unwarranted
5 most distant from a center <an *extreme* edge of the city>
syn farthest, furthermost, furthest, outermost, outmost, remotest, utmost, uttermost
extreme *n* **1** an extreme state or condition <an *extreme* of poverty>
syn extremity
rel excess, inordinancy
2 something situated at or marking one end or the other of a range <*extremes* of heat and cold>
syn extremity, limit
rel climax, consummation, culmination; ceiling, crest, crown, height; peak, pinnacle, summit, top; maximum, minimum; utmost, uttermost
extremely *adv* **1** *syn* see EVER 6
2 *syn* see VERY 1
3 *syn* see EXTRA
extremist *n syn* see RADICAL
extremist *adj syn* see EXTREME 3
extremity *n* **1** *syn* see EXTREME 2
rel acme, apex, apogee, vertex, zenith
2 *syn* see EXTREME 1
extricate *vb* **1** *syn* see KNOW 4
2 to free from an undesirable situation or condition <*extricate* himself from financial difficulties>
syn clear, clear away, discumber, disembarrass, disembroil, disencumber, disentangle, disentwine, unentangle, unscramble, untangle, untie, untwine
rel unravel; abstract, detach, disengage; disburden, disemburden; deliver, disinvolve, free, liberate, release, rescue; resolve
con embroil, entangle, tangle; clog, fetter, hog-tie, manacle, shackle, trammel; block, hamper, hinder, impede, obstruct
extrinsic *adj* not properly part of a thing <a point *extrinsic* to his basic thesis>
syn alien, extraneous, foreign
rel acquired, gained; exterior, external, outer, outside, outward
con native; inner, inside, interior, internal, inward; individual, personal
ant intrinsic
extrude *vb syn* see EJECT 1
exuberance *n syn* see EBULLIENCE
rel gayness; friskiness, life, liveliness, sprightliness, zest, zestfulness; abandon, ardor

exuberancy *n syn* see EBULLIENCE
exuberant *adj* **1** joyously unrestrained and enthusiastic <his warm *exuberant* personality>
syn brash, ebullient, effervescent, high=spirited, vivacious
rel gay, lively, spirited, sprightly, zestful; frolicsome; ardent, passionate
con constrained, inhibited, repressed, restrained, subdued; calm, impassive, quiet
ant austere
2 *syn* see PROFUSE
rel fecund, fertile, fruitful, prolific; rampant, rank; diffuse
con scant, scanty, spare
exude *vb* to flow slowly out <a sticky resin *exuded* from the bark>
syn bleed, ooze, percolate, ‖screeve, seep, ‖sew, ‖sicker, strain, sweat, transude, weep
rel emanate; discharge, emit; trickle
exult *vb* to rejoice especially with feelings or display of triumph or self-satisfaction <the players were *exulting* in their victory>
syn delight, glory, jubilate, triumph
rel rejoice; celebrate; boast, brag, crow, show off
con lament, mourn
ant bemoan
exultance *n syn* see EXULTATION
exultant *adj* manifesting proud elation <*exultant* over her successes>
syn cock-a-hoop, cock-a-whoop, exulting, jubilant, triumphal, triumphant
rel happy, joyous, overjoyed; delighting, rejoicing; elated, flushed
idiom in high feather
con depressed, mournful, unhappy
exultation *n* the act of exulting or the state of being exultant <the *exultation* of victory and the thrill of power>
syn exultance, jubilance, jubilation, triumph
rel delight, elation, satisfaction; celebration, rejoicing; gloating
exulting *adj syn* see EXULTANT
exuviate *vb syn* see SHED 2
eye *n* **1** an organ of sight <turned his *eyes* to the view>
syn lamp, ocular, oculus, ‖ogle, orb, peeper, winker
2 the faculty of seeing with or as if with the eyes <had a keen *eye* for details>
syn eyesight, seeing, sight, vision
3 very close watching or observation <kept an *eye* on him>
syn eagle eye, scrutiny, surveillance, tab, watch
4 *often* eyes *pl* a way of looking at something <in the *eyes* of the law, a man is innocent until proven guilty>
syn view, viewpoint; *compare* VIEWPOINT 2
rel attitude, position, thinking; conception, grasp; conclusion, judgment
5 *syn* see OPINION
6 *syn* see LOOP 1
7 *syn* see LOOP 2
‖8 *syn* see DETECTIVE
eye *vb* **1** to fix the eyes on <the child *eyed* the presents with delight>
syn consider, contemplate, gaze (upon), look (at *or* upon), view; *compare* LOOK 7

---

rel regard; stare (at)
2 to keep a close watch on <the detective *eyed* the suspect>
syn eyeball, scrutinize, watch; *compare* TAIL
rel stare (at); size up
idiom keep a close (*or* an eagle) eye on
3 *syn* see LOOK 7
eyeball *vb syn* see EYE 2
eye–catching *adj syn* see NOTICEABLE

eyeful *n syn* see BEAUTY
eyeless *adj syn* see BLIND 1
eye–popping *adj syn* see EXCITING
eyesight *n syn* see EYE 2
eyesore *n* something offensive to the sight <the old abandoned house was a neighborhood *eyesore*>
syn desight, fright, mess, monstrosity, sight
eyewash *n syn* see NONSENSE 2
eyewitness *n syn* see SPECTATOR

F

fable *n* 1 *syn* see FICTION
2 *syn* see ALLEGORY 2
fabric *n* 1 *syn* see BUILDING
2 *syn* see TEXTURE 2
fabricate *vb syn* see MAKE 3
rel turn out; create, formulate, invent; concoct, contrive, devise
fabrication *n syn* see FICTION
rel creation; deceit, fib; artifact, opus, product, production, work
fabulous *adj syn* see MYTHICAL
rel amazing, astonishing, astounding, incredible, marvelous, unbelievable, wonderful; exorbitant, extravagant, inordinate, outrageous, preposterous; monstrous, prodigious, stupendous
con believable, colorable, credible
facade *n syn* see MASK 2
face *n* 1 the front part of the head including the eyes, nose, mouth, cheeks, chin, and forehead <hid his *face* from the camera>
syn countenance, ‖dial, features, ‖kisser, ‖map, mug, ‖mush, muzzle, ‖pan, phiz, ‖puss, visage
rel lineaments, physiognomy
2 *syn* see LOOK 2
3 *syn* see APPEARANCE 2
4 *syn* see MASK 2
5 *syn* see EFFRONTERY
6 a distortion of the face usually as an expression of contempt or distaste <the old man made a *face* at the flat beer>
syn grimace, moue, mouth, mouthing, mow, mug
rel frown, glower, lower, pout, scowl
idiom wry face, wry mouth
con grin, simper, smile, smirk
7 *syn* see MAKEUP 3
8 *syn* see TOP 2
face *vb* 1 to have the face or front in a specified direction <the house *faces* toward the river>
syn front, look
rel border, meet
ant back
2 *syn* see MEET 6
rel watch; gaze, glare, stare; await, expect, look (for)

3 to confront with courage or boldness <ready to *face* her accusers>
syn ‖banter, beard, brave, challenge, dare, defy, ‖double-dog dare, front, outdare, outface, venture
rel confront, encounter, meet; oppose, resist, withstand; contend, fight
idiom brazen it out, face the music, face up to, take the bull by the horns
con elude, escape, eschew, evade, shun
ant avoid
4 *syn* see CONFRONT 1
5 *syn* see ACCOST 2
rel beard, brave, challenge, dare, defy
idiom stand up to
6 *syn* see ENGAGE 5
7 *syn* see SHEATHE
facet *n syn* see PHASE
rel face, front
facetious *adj syn* see WITTY
rel jesting, joking, quipping, wisecracking; blithe, jocund, jolly, jovial, merry; comic, comical, droll, funny, laughable, ludicrous
con grave, serious, sober, solemn, somber
ant lugubrious
facile *adj syn* see EASY 1
rel adroit, deft, dexterous; fluent, glib, voluble; cursory, shallow, superficial, uncritical
con awkward, clumsy, constrained, cumbersome, labored, maladroit; tongue-tied; deep, profound, thorough
ant arduous
facilely *adv syn* see EASILY 1
ant arduously
facilitate *vb syn* see EASE 3
facility *n* 1 *syn* see READINESS 3
rel skill, wit; aptitude, bent, leaning, propensity, turn; abandon, spontaneity, unconstraint; address, poise, tact; effortlessness, lightness, smoothness
con awkwardness, clumsiness, ineptness, maladroitness; rigidity, stiffness, woodenness; effort, exertion, pains
2 *syn* see AMENITY 2
rel accommodation, advantage, aid, fitting
con difficulty, hardship, inconvenience
facing *prep* 1 *syn* see AGAINST 1

con side by side
2 *syn* see BEFORE 2

facsimile *n syn* see REPRODUCTION
con archetype, model, original, pattern, prototype, standard

fact *n* 1 the quality of being actual <the realm of *fact* is distinct from fancy>
syn actuality, reality
rel authenticity, genuineness, truth
con fancy, fantasy, fiction
2 something that has actual existence <stubborn *facts* that cannot be confuted>
syn event, phenomenon
rel circumstance, detail, episode, particular; happening, incident, occurrence; observable
con contingency, eventuality, hope, possibility, potentiality, probability
ant illusion

faction *n syn* see COMBINATION 2
rel camp, offshoot, wing
idiom splinter group

factious *adj syn* see INSUBORDINATE
rel contending, fighting, warring; belligerent, contentious, quarrelsome; alienated, disaffected, estranged
con companionable, gregarious, social; acquiescent, compliant; faithful, loyal, true
ant cooperative

factitious *adj syn* see SYNTHETIC
rel affected, assumed, counterfeited, false, feigned, forced, pretended, sham, shammed, simulated
con authentic, bona fide, genuine, veritable; artless, naive, simple, spontaneous
ant natural

factor *n* 1 *syn* see ELEMENT 2
rel antecedent, cause, determinant; agency, agent, instrument, instrumentality, means
2 *syn* see AGENT 2
rel bailiff, majordomo, seneschal, steward; adjutant, aid, assistant, coadjutor, helper

factory *n* an establishment for the manufacturing of goods <a shoe *factory*>
syn manufactory, mill, plant, works

factual *adj syn* see ACTUAL 2
rel certain, undoubted, veritable; authentic, legitimate, unquestionable, valid
con erroneous, false, questionable, wrong
ant illusory

facultative *adj syn* see OPTIONAL

faculty *n* 1 *syn* see GIFT 2
rel instinct; property, quality; leaning, penchant, proclivity, propensity; predilection
con inability, incapability, incapacity, ineptness
2 *syn* see POWER 3

facund *adj syn* see EXPRESSIVE

facundity *n syn* see ELOQUENCE

fad *n syn* see FASHION 3
rel caprice, conceit, fancy, vagary, whim, whimsy
con custom, habit, practice, usage

fade *vb* 1 *syn* see FAIL 1
2 *syn* see DULL 1

3 *syn* see VANISH
rel deliquesce, dissolve, melt; abate, diminish, dwindle, ebb, lessen, moderate, wane; attenuate, rarefy, thin
idiom fade like a shadow
con intensify; eternalize, immortalize, perpetuate

faded *adj syn* see SHABBY 1
rel haggard, washed-out, wasted, worn; dim, murky; achromatic, colorless; ashen, pale, pallid, wan
con energetic, lusty, vigorous; colorful; vivid

fag *n syn* see CIGARETTE

fag *vb syn* see EXHAUST 4
con refresh, relax, rest, restore

‖**fag** *n syn* see HOMOSEXUAL

‖**faggot** *n syn* see HOMOSEXUAL

fail *vb* 1 to lose strength, power, vitality, or intensity <his health *failed* and he retired early>
syn decline, deteriorate, ‖dwine, fade, flag, languish, weaken
rel jade, sink, slip, waste (away), worsen
idiom go downhill, hit the skids
con better, improve, strengthen
2 to become used up <food *failed* before they got back to civilization>
syn give out, run out
rel dwindle, shrink, wane
3 to be or become inadequate or deficient <the spring gradually *failed* as the drought persisted>
syn dwindle, shrink, wane, waste (away), weaken
rel decrease, diminish, lessen; give out, run out; short
idiom be found wanting
con appreciate, gain, grow, increase, wax
4 to prove less than adequate or successful <the attack *failed*>
syn bomb, ‖flop, flummox, wash out
rel bankrupt, deplete, drain, exhaust, impoverish; bust out, flunk, ‖spin
idiom come to grief, fall flat (or short), go on the rocks, ‖lay an egg, ‖take the count
ant succeed
5 to be unable to meet financial engagements <the bank *failed*>
syn break, bust, crash, fold
rel gazette; close, end, finish, terminate
idiom be ruined, go bankrupt, go broke, go on the rocks, go to the wall, go under
con boom, prosper
6 *syn* see NEGLECT
idiom be found wanting, come (or fall) short of

failing *n syn* see FAULT 2
rel imperfection, shortcoming
idiom weak point

failing *adj syn* see SHORT 3

failure *n* 1 omission of performance of an action or task <the mechanic's *failure* to adjust the brakes>
syn default, delinquency, dereliction, neglect, oversight
rel laxity, negligence, remissness, slackness; indifference, unconcern
con accomplishment, achievement, discharge, effectuation, fulfillment

---

syn synonym(s)　　*rel* related word(s)
ant antonym(s)　　con contrasted word(s)
idiom idiomatic equivalent(s)
‖ use limited; if in doubt, see a dictionary

2 lack of satisfactory performance or effect <the *failure* of the candidate in the election>
syn defeat, insuccess, nonsuccess, unsuccess, unsuccessfulness
rel failing, fault, imperfection, shortcoming
idiom no go
ant success

3 the fact or state of being inadequate <the crop *failure* brought on a near famine>
syn defalcation, deficiency, deficit, inadequacy, insufficience, insufficiency, lack, scantiness, shortage, underage; *compare* ABSENCE, SCARCITY
rel inferiority, meagerness, poorness, skimpiness; dearth, paucity
con abundance, adequacy, sufficiency

4 a marked weakening <felt a gradual *failure* of physical strength>
syn declination, decline, deterioration, ebbing, waning
rel debilitation, enfeeblement, exhaustion, flagging, weakness
con improvement; invigoration, revitalization, strengthening

5 one that has failed <he is a *failure* in school because of inattention>
syn bomb, bummer, bust, dud, flop, lemon, loser
rel botch, fiasco, fizzle, hash, muddle, washout; has-been, might-have-been
ant success

fain *adj syn* see WILLING 1

faineant *n syn* see SLUGGARD

faineant *adj syn* see LAZY
rel apathetic, impassive, phlegmatic
con active, energetic, vigorous; busy, industrious

faint *adj* 1 *syn* see GENTLE 1
2 scarcely or imperfectly perceptible <he had only a *faint* idea of how he could help>
syn blear, bleary, dim, fuzzy, ill-defined, indistinct, obscure, shadowy, unclear, undefined, undetermined, undistinct, vague; *compare* OBSCURE 3
rel blurred, dusty, pale, wan, weak; hushed, inaudible, low, muffled, small, soft, stifled, thin
con bright, distinct, evident, obvious, patent, unmistakable; certain, sure
ant clear

faint *n* the act or condition of losing consciousness <was so frightened she fell into a *faint*>
syn blackout, coma, swoon, syncope
rel grayout, swim; dizziness, vertigo; knockout
idiom a dead faint

faint *vb* to lose consciousness <*fainted* at the sight of blood>
syn black out, ‖crap out, pass out, ‖swarf, ‖swelt, swoon
rel gray out
idiom faint dead away, fall in a faint, go out like a light, pass out cold

faintly *adv syn* see SOTTO VOCE

fair *adj* 1 *syn* see BEAUTIFUL 1
rel dainty, delicate, exquisite; charming, enchanting; chaste, pure
con ill-favored, ugly
ant foul

2 not stormy <a *fair* day>
syn clarion, clear, cloudless, fine, pleasant, rainless, sunny, sunshine, sunshining, sunshiny, unclouded, undarkened
rel calm, placid, tranquil, unthreatening; balmy, clement, mild, pretty
con overcast, stormy, threatening

3 of light complexion <*fair* people often sunburn badly>
syn blond, light
rel ruddy, tawny
con brunet, dark, swarthy

4 characterized by honesty, justice, and freedom from improper influence <a *fair* decision by the judge>
syn candid, dispassionate, equal, equitable, impartial, impersonal, indifferent, just, nondiscriminatory, nonpartisan, objective, square, unbiased, uncolored, undistinctive, unprejudiced, unprepossessed
rel detached, disinterested; balanced, rational, reasonable, sane; open-minded, straight
con biased, inequitable, partial, partisan, prejudiced, prepossessed, unjust
ant unfair

5 observing the rules <a *fair* fight>
syn clean, sportsmanlike, sportsmanly
rel decent, honest, lawful
con dirty, dishonest, fixed
ant unfair

6 *syn* see EVEN 3

7 *syn* see MEDIUM
rel common, ordinary
con choice, good, prime, right; bad, poor, wrong

fair *n syn* see EXHIBITION 2
rel carnival, festival

fair–haired *adj syn* see FAVORITE 1

fairish *adj syn* see MEDIUM

fairly *adv* 1 *syn* see ENOUGH 2
2 *syn* see SOMEWHAT 2

fairy *n* a benevolent mythical being <children who believe in *fairies*>
syn brownie, elf, fay, nisse, pixie, sprite
rel gremlin, imp, leprechaun, puck; dwarf, gnome, goblin, kobold
con ogre, troll

fairyland *n syn* see UTOPIA

faith *n* 1 *syn* see BELIEF 1
con dubiety, dubiosity, skepticism, uncertainty
2 *syn* see TRUST 1
con disbelief, incredulity, unbelief; apprehension, misgiving
3 *syn* see RELIGION 1
4 *syn* see RELIGION 1
rel doctrines, dogmas, tenets

faithful *adj* 1 firm in adherence to whatever one is bound to by duty or promise <a *faithful* public official, conscientious and above reproach>
syn allegiant, ardent, constant, ‖dinky-di, fast, liege, loyal, resolute, staunch, steadfast, steady, true
rel dependable, reliable, tried, trustworthy; affectionate, devoted, loving; dyed-in-the-wool
con disloyal, false, perfidious, traitorous, treacherous; fickle, inconstant, unstable
ant faithless

2 *syn* see TRUE 3
idiom at one with, on all fours with
3 *syn* see AUTHENTIC 1
faithfulness *n* **1** *syn* see ATTACHMENT 1
2 *syn* see FIDELITY 1
faithless *adj* not true to allegiance or duty
<a *faithless* husband>
syn disloyal, false, perfidious, recreant,
traitorous, treacherous, unfaithful, unloyal,
untrue
rel capricious, fickle, inconstant, unstable;
fluctuating, wavering; changeable, changeful
con constant, loyal, resolute, staunch,
steadfast, true
ant faithful
faithlessness *n* **1** *syn* see TREACHERY
2 *syn* see INFIDELITY
fake *vb* *syn* see ASSUME 4
fake *n* **1** *syn* see IMPOSTURE
2 *syn* see IMPOSTOR
fake *adj* **1** *syn* see COUNTERFEIT
rel fabricated, forged; concocted, framed,
invented
con bona fide, genuine
2 *syn* see FICTITIOUS 2
faker *n* *syn* see IMPOSTOR
rel cheat, cheater, cozener, defrauder, swindler
fall *vb* **1** to pass downward <fruit *falling* off a
tree> <the temperature *fell* sharply>
syn descend, drop, lower
rel decline, dip, plummet, sink; decrease,
diminish, lessen; dangle, drag, droop, trail
ant rise
2 to come down suddenly and involuntarily
<*fell* on the ice>
syn drop, go down, keel (over), pitch,
plunge, slump, topple, tumble
rel slip, sprawl, stumble, trip
idiom come a cropper, take a header, take a
spill
con ascend, climb
3 to suffer ruin, defeat, or failure <the city
fell after a long siege>
syn go down, go under, submit, succumb,
surrender
rel give up, yield
con endure, prevail, resist; conquer, triumph, vanquish, win
4 *syn* see ABATE 4
ant rise
5 *syn* see PLUMMET
fall (off *or* away) *vb* *syn* see SLIP 6
fall (on *or* upon) *vb* *syn* see ATTACK 1
fall *n* **1** *syn* see DESCENT 1
2 *syn* see DESCENT 4
3 *usu* falls *pl but sing or pl in constr syn* see
WATERFALL
fallacious *adj* **1** *syn* see ILLOGICAL
ant sound, valid
2 *syn* see MISLEADING
ant veritable
fallaciousness *n* *syn* see FALLACY 1
rel ambiguity, equivocation; deception,
deluding, misleading; faultiness, illogicality,
unreasonableness

---

syn synonym(s)   *rel* related word(s)
ant antonym(s)   *con* contrasted word(s)
idiom idiomatic equivalent(s)
‖ use limited; if in doubt, see a dictionary

ant soundness, validity
fallacy *n* **1** a false or erroneous idea <his
argument is based on a *fallacy*>
syn erroneousness, error, fallaciousness,
falsehood, falseness, falsity, untruth
rel misconception, misconstrual, misinterpretation, misunderstanding
con comprehension, grasp, understanding;
correctitude, correctness, truth
ant verity
2 unsound and misleading reasoning <the
fallacy of her theory is clearly evident>
syn casuistry, deception, deceptiveness,
delusion, equivocation, sophism, sophistry,
speciousness, spuriousness
rel elusion, evasion, inconsistency, quibble,
quibbling
fall back *vb* **1** *syn* see RETREAT 2
2 *syn* see RECEDE 1
fall flat *vb* *syn* see FAIL 4
fall guy *n* **1** *syn* see SCAPEGOAT
2 *syn* see FOOL 3
fallible *adj* liable or inclined to error <a
fallible rule>
syn errable, errant
rel careless, faulty, heedless
con careful, heedful; inerrable, inerrant,
unerring; exact, perfect, precise
ant infallible
falling-out *n* *syn* see QUARREL
falloff *n* *syn* see DECLINE 3
fall out *vb* **1** *syn* see HAPPEN 1
2 *syn* see QUARREL
fall to *vb* *syn* see PITCH IN 1
false *adj* **1** not in conformity with what is
true <the information turned out to be
false>
syn counterfactual, erroneous, inaccurate,
incorrect, specious, unsound, untrue, wrong;
compare ILLOGICAL
rel deceptive, delusive, delusory, distorted,
fallacious, misleading; deceitful, dishonest,
fraudulent, lying, mendacious, untruthful
idiom contrary to fact, off the mark
con accurate, correct, established, factual,
truthful, veracious, veridical
ant true
2 *syn* see MISLEADING
3 *syn* see FAITHLESS
rel apostate, backsliding, renegade;
crooked, devious; hollow
ant true
4 *syn* see COUNTERFEIT
rel apparent, ostensible, seeming
con bona fide, genuine
ant real
5 *syn* see ARTIFICIAL 2
false face *n* *syn* see MASK 1
false front *n* *syn* see MASK 2
falsehood *n* **1** *syn* see FALLACY 1
2 *syn* see LIE
rel fakery, feigning, pretense, sham; deceit,
dissimulation, fraud
ant truth
3 *syn* see MENDACITY
falseness *n* **1** *syn* see FALLACY 1
2 *syn* see INFIDELITY
3 *syn* see DEFECTION
falsifier *n* *syn* see LIAR
falsify *vb* **1** *syn* see LIE

2 syn see MISREPRESENT
 rel alter, change; cook, doctor; contort; contradict, contravene, deny, traverse

falsity *n* **1** syn see LIE
 2 syn see FALLACY 1
 rel bluff, fabrication, fake, sham; disingenuousness, hypocrisy, insincerity, uncandidness
 ant verity
 3 syn see INFIDELITY

falter *vb* **1** syn see TEETER
 2 syn see HESITATE
 rel blench, flinch, quail, recoil, shrink; quake, quaver, shake, shudder, tremble; tick over
 con persevere, persist; decide, determine, resolve

faltering *adj* syn see VACILLATING 2

fame *n* **1** syn see REPUTATION 2
 2 the state of being widely known for one's deeds <his *fame* was short-lived>
 syn celebrity, éclat, notoriety, renown, ‖rep, reputation, repute
 rel acclaim, acclamation, applause; acknowledgment, recognition; conspicuousness, prominence; distinction, eminence, glory, greatness, honor, illustriousness, note, preeminence
 con disgrace, dishonor, disrepute, ignominy, obloquy, odium, opprobrium, shame
 ant obscurity; infamy

famed *adj* syn see FAMOUS 2
 ant obscure; ill-famed

familiar *n* syn see FRIEND

familiar *adj* **1** closely associated <time and interests have made them *familiar*>
 syn chummy, close, confidential, intimate, thick
 rel amicable, friendly, neighborly; affable, boon, cordial, genial, gracious, sociable; comfortable, cozy, easy, snug; forward, fresh, impertinent, intrusive, obtrusive, officious
 con detached, disinterested, incurious, indifferent, remote, unconcerned; ceremonial, ceremonious, conventional, formal
 ant aloof
 2 syn see COMMON 4
 rel accustomed, habitual, wonted; commonplace, prosaic
 con new, newfangled, new-fashioned, novel; rare, strange, uncommon; chimerical, fantastic
 ant unfamiliar
 3 well-informed especially through study or experience <*familiar* with what is being taught in the schools>
 syn abreast, acquainted, au courant, au fait, conversant, informed, up, versant, versed
 rel aware, cognizant, conscious, mindful
 con unacquainted, unconversant, uninformed, unversed; insensible, unaware, unconscious, unmindful; ignorant, unenlightened, unknowing
 ant unfamiliar

familiarity *n* syn see ACQUAINTANCE 1
 rel awareness, cognition, comprehension, knowledge, understanding
 ant unfamiliarity

familiarize *vb* syn see ACCUSTOM

 rel acquaint, adapt, adjust, condition, naturalize, season

family *n* **1** a group of persons of or regarded as of common ancestry <traditionally all people belong to the *family* of Noah>
 syn clan, folk, house, kin, kindred, lineage, race, stock, tribe
 rel brood, dynasty, line, stirp, strain; issue, offspring, progeny
 idiom kith and kin, one's own flesh and blood
 2 a group of usually related persons living in one house and under one head <was the only child in her *family*>
 syn folks, house, household, ménage

family *adj* syn see DOMESTIC 1

family tree *n* syn see GENEALOGY

famished *adj* syn see HUNGRY

famous *adj* **1** syn see WELL-KNOWN
 2 widely known and honored for achievement <a *famous* physician>
 syn celebrated, celebrious, distinguished, eminent, famed, great, illustrious, notable, prestigious, prominent, redoubtable, renowned; *compare* WELL-KNOWN
 rel estimable, honorable, reputable, respectable, well-thought-of
 idiom held in esteem
 con humble, inconspicuous, undistinguished, unimportant, unknown
 ant obscure; infamous
 3 syn see EXCELLENT
 ant wretched

fan *n* **1** syn see ADDICT
 2 syn see AMATEUR 1

fan *vb* **1** syn see BLOW 1
 ‖**2** syn see SEARCH 2

fan (out) *vb* syn see OPEN 4

fanatic *adj* syn see EXTREME 3

fanatic *n* syn see ENTHUSIAST

fancied *adj* syn see IMAGINARY 1

fancier *n* syn see AMATEUR 1

fanciful *adj* **1** syn see IMAGINARY 1
 rel apocryphal, fabulous, fictitious, legendary, mythical; bizarre, fantastic, grotesque; absurd, preposterous; false, wrong
 con matter-of-fact, prosaic; truthful, veracious
 ant realistic
 2 syn see FICTITIOUS 1
 ant veridical

fancy *n* **1** syn see WILL 1
 2 syn see CAPRICE
 rel idea; irrationality, unreasonableness; contrariness, perverseness
 3 syn see IMAGINATION
 rel envisagement, envisioning, objectification
 idiom flight of fancy
 con awareness, experience, perception
 4 an idea or image present in the mind but having no concrete or objective reality <unable to tell fact from *fancy*>
 syn daydream, dream, fantasy (*or* phantasy), nightmare, phantasm, vision
 rel fable, fabrication, fiction, figment, invention; concept, conception, idea, notion; chimera, delusion, illusion; fata morgana, hallucination, mirage
 idiom figment of the imagination

con actuality, fact, reality

fancy *vb* **1** *syn* see LIKE
rel approve, endorse, sanction
idiom have a fancy (or hankering) for; have one's heart set on
con deprecate, disapprove; abhor, abominate, detest, dislike, hate, loathe
2 *syn* see THINK 1
con demonstrate, prove, test, try
fancy *adj syn* see ELABORATE 2
fancy–free *adj syn* see FREE 6
fancy house *n syn* see BROTHEL
fancy man *n* **1** *syn* see LOVER 1
2 *syn* see PIMP 1
fancy woman *n syn* see HARLOT 1
fanfare *n syn* see DISPLAY 2
fanny *n syn* see BUTTOCKS
fantastic *adj* **1** *syn* see FICTITIOUS 1
rel implausible, incredible, unbelievable; absurd, preposterous; irrational, unreasonable; deceptive, delusive, delusory, misleading
con common, commonplace, everyday, familiar, ordinary; customary, prevailing, universal, usual
2 conceived or made without reference to reality <their explanation was *fantastic*>
syn antic, bizarre, grotesque
rel adroit, clever, ingenious; eccentric, erratic, odd, queer, singular, strange; absurd, nonsensical, preposterous, ridiculous
con factual, solid, sound, valid, well≈grounded; plausible, reasonable
3 *syn* see FOOLISH 2
4 *syn* see MONSTROUS 1
5 *syn* see EXTRAVAGANT 1
fantasy (or **phantasy**) *n* **1** *syn* see IMAGINATION
rel conceiving, envisioning, fancying, imagining; externalizing, objectifying
2 *syn* see FANCY 4
rel caprice, freak, vagary, whim, whimsy; bizarrerie, grotesquerie
con actuality, fact, reality
3 *syn* see PIPE DREAM
far *adv syn* see WELL 8
far *adj syn* see DISTANT 1
idiom a long day's journey
ant near
far and away *adv* by a considerable margin <he was *far and away* the best man for the job>
syn by all odds, by a long shot, by far, by long odds, by odds, out and away
rel decidedly, definitely; doubtless, unconditionally, undoubtedly, unequivocally, unquestionably; absolutely, positively; just, quite, very
con barely; slightly; possibly
far and near *adv syn* see EVERYWHERE 1
far and wide *adv syn* see EVERYWHERE 1
faraway *adj* **1** *syn* see DISTANT 1
ant near-at-hand
2 *syn* see ABSTRACTED
rel disregardful, heedless, oblivious, stargazing, unheeding, unmindful

idiom off one's guard
farce *n syn* see MOCKERY 2
farceur *n syn* see ZANY 2
farcical *adj syn* see LAUGHABLE
rel absurd, extravagant, nonsensical, outrageous, preposterous
fare *vb* **1** *syn* see GO 1
rel advance, progress
idiom make headway
con stay, stop
2 *syn* see SHIFT 5
farewell *interj syn* see GOOD-BYE
farewell *n syn* see PARTING
farewell *adj syn* see PARTING
farfetched *adj syn* see FORCED
rel bizarre, fantastic, grotesque; eccentric, erratic, queer, strange
con accustomed, usual, wonted
far-flung *adj syn* see DISTANT 1
far-gone *adj syn* see EFFETE 2
farming *n syn* see AGRICULTURE
rel cultivation, tillage; agronomy, geoponics, hydroponics
far-off *adj syn* see DISTANT 1
idiom behind the farthest range
ant nearby
far-out *adj syn* see OUTLANDISH 3
farther *adv syn* see BEYOND 1
farther *adj syn* see ADDITIONAL
farthest *adj syn* see EXTREME 5
ant nearest
fascinate *vb* **1** *syn* see ENTHRALL 2
2 *syn* see ATTRACT 1
rel affect, impress, influence, strike, sway, touch; delight, gladden, please, rejoice; absorb, engage, engross, occupy, preoccupy
con disgust, horrify, repel; affront, insult, offend, outrage, shame
3 *syn* see INTEREST
fascinated *adj syn* see ENAMORED 3
fascinating *adj syn* see ATTRACTIVE 1
rel delectable, delightful; seducing
fascination *n syn* see CHARM 3
fashion *n* **1** *syn* see METHOD 1
rel custom, habit, practice, usage, wont
2 *syn* see VEIN 1
3 the prevailing or accepted custom <follow the *fashion*>
syn bandwagon, chic, craze, cry, dernier cri, fad, furore, mode, rage, style, thing, ton, trend, ||twig, vogue
rel drift, tendency; convention, form, usage
idiom the in thing, the last word, the latest thing
fashion *vb syn* see MAKE 3
rel contrive, devise; design, plan, plot; turn out
fashionable *adj syn* see STYLISH
rel current, popular, prevalent, up-to-the≈minute
idiom all the rage
ant unfashionable
fast *adj* **1** *syn* see SURE 1
rel fixed, held, inextricable, stuck, wedged
con insecure, loose, shaky, unstable
2 *syn* see FAITHFUL 1
3 moving, proceeding, or acting with great celerity <a *fast* horse>
syn breakneck, expeditious, expeditive, fleet, harefooted, hasty, posthaste, quick, raking, rapid, snappy, speedy, swift

---

syn synonym(s) *rel* related word(s)
ant antonym(s) *con* contrasted word(s)
idiom idiomatic equivalent(s)
|| use limited; if in doubt, see a dictionary

rel active, alert, brisk, keen, lively

idiom quick as lightning, quick as thought, swift as an arrow

con lethargic, logy, poky, sluggish, tardy, torpid; languid, languorous; deliberate, gradual

ant slow

4 persistent in adhering to something <a *fast* grip>

syn firm, fixed, secure, set, tenacious, tight; compare STABLE 4, SURE 1

idiom stuck fast

con insecure, loose, relaxed, unfirm, weak; free, unattached, unfixed

5 *syn* see WILD 7

6 *syn* see LICENTIOUS 2

7 sexually promiscuous—usually used of a woman <she's said to be *fast*>

syn easy, light, loose, ‖riggish, unchaste, wanton, whorish

rel careless, heedless, lax, slack; bawdy, indecent; lascivious, lecherous, lewd, libertine, licentious, lickerish, riotous

idiom no better than one should be, of easy virtue

con chaste, decent, decorous, modest, moral, pure, virtuous

fast *adv* **1** *syn* see HARD 7

2 in a rapid manner <run up the hill as *fast* as you know how>

syn apace, chop-chop, expeditiously, flat-out, fleetly, full tilt, hastily, lickety-split, posthaste, presto, promptly, pronto, quick, quickly, rapidly, soon, speedily, swift, swiftly

idiom by leaps and bounds, in a flash, in a twinkling, in nothing flat, in short order, like a bat out of hell, like a blue streak, like a flash, like a house afire, like a shot, like a streak, like greased lightning, like wildfire

con deliberately, leisurely; apathetically, lethargically, sluggishly

ant slow, slowly

fasten *vb* **1** to cause one thing to hold to another <*fasten* a feather to a hat>

syn affix, attach, fix, rivet

rel connect, join, link, unite; adhere, cleave, cling, cohere, stick

con divide, divorce, part, separate, sever, sunder; loose, loosen

ant unfasten

2 to fix in place or in a desired position <*fasten* the door>

syn anchor, catch, fix, moor, secure

rel bed, implant, infix, lodge, set, settle; embed, join, wedge; establish; bar, hitch, hook

idiom make fast (or secure or sure)

con loose, undo, unloose, unloosen

ant unfasten

3 to direct (as attention or hope) directly and steadily <*fastened* his whole mind on the problem>

syn concenter, concentrate, fix, fixate, focus, put, rivet

rel address, apply, devote, direct, train, turn

con falter, vacillate, waver

fastidious *adj syn* see NICE 1

rel demanding, exacting; captious, critical, hypercritical

con cursory, uncritical

fastigium *n syn* see TOP 1

fastness *n syn* see FORT

rel retreat, shelter; defense, guard, protection; adytum, sanctum

fat *adj* **1** *syn* see FATTY 1

2 having excess adipose tissue <a *fat* woman overflowing her chair>

syn corpulent, fleshy, gross, heavy, obese, overblown, overweight, porcine, portly, pursy, stout, upholstered, weighty; compare ROTUND 2

rel beefy, bulky, chunky, dumpy, full-bodied, heavyset, squat, stocky, stubby, thick, thickset; paunchy, potbellied; brawny, burly, husky

idiom broad in the beam, fat as a pig

con angular, gaunt, lank, lanky, rawboned, scrawny, skinny, spare; slender, slight, slim, thin

ant lean

3 *syn* see LARGE 1

rel broad, deep, wide

con narrow, skinny

4 *syn* see RESONANT

‖**5** *syn* see REMOTE 4

fat *n* **1** *syn* see FATTY 1

2 *syn* see EXCESS 1

fatal *adj* **1** *syn* see DEADLY 1

2 bringing on an adverse fate <to accept his word was a *fatal* mistake>

syn calamitous, cataclysmic, catastrophic, disastrous, fateful, ruinous

rel baneful, pernicious; baleful, malefic, maleficent, malign, sinister; ill-fated, ill-starred, unlucky

con advantageous, beneficial, profitable; auspicious, benign, favorable, propitious

fatal *n syn* see FATALITY 2

fatality *n* **1** the condition of causing death <the tuberculosis *fatality* remains high>

syn deadliness, lethality, mortality

rel malignancy, noxiousness, perniciousness, poisonousness, virulence

2 an instance of dying especially as the result of accident or disaster <two *fatalities* over the weekend>

syn casualty, death, fatal

‖**fat cat** *n syn* see NOTABLE 1

fate *n* whatever is destined or inevitably decreed for one <the *fate* of the bill has not been decided>

syn circumstance, destiny, doom, kismet, lot, moira, portion, weird

rel consequence, effect, issue, outcome, result, upshot; end, ending, termination; ineluctability, inescapableness, inevitability, inevitableness, unavoidability

con accident, chance, fortune, hazard, luck

fate *vb syn* see PREDESTINE 1

fateful *adj* **1** *syn* see OMINOUS

rel important, momentous, significant; conclusive, decisive, determinative; acute, critical, crucial

con inconclusive, insignificant, trivial, unimportant

2 *syn* see FATAL 2

fathead *n syn* see DUNCE

fatheaded *adj syn* see STUPID 1

father *n* **1** a male human parent <scarcely knew his *father*>

syn dad, dada, daddy, ‖governor, ‖old man, pa, ‖pap, papa, ‖pappy, ‖pater, pop, poppa; *compare* MOTHER 1

2 one that originates or institutes <the *father* of radiotelegraphy>

syn architect, author, creator, founder, generator, inventor, maker, originator, patriarch, sire

rel builder, encourager, motor, mover, organizer, prime mover, producer, promoter, promulgator, supporter; inaugurator, initiator, introducer

con disciple, follower

father *vb* **1** to be the male parent in reproduction <didn't know who *fathered* the child>

syn beget, breed, get, procreate, progenerate, sire

rel engender, generate, ingenerate; spawn

2 *syn see* GENERATE 1

fatherland *n syn see* COUNTRY

fatherless *adj syn see* ILLEGITIMATE 1

fathom *vb* **1** *syn see* SOUND

2 *syn see* KNOW 1

rel penetrate, pierce, probe; perceive, recognize; ‖dig, savvy

fathomable *adj syn see* UNDERSTANDABLE

fathomless *adj syn see* BOTTOMLESS 2

fatidic *adj syn see* PROPHETIC

fatigue *n* complete depletion of strength <suffering from *fatigue*>

syn exhaustion, lassitude, tiredness, weariness

rel enervation, ennui, languor, listlessness; debilitation, faintness, feebleness, weakness

con briskness, energy, liveliness, vigor, vitality; endurance, strength

fatigue *vb syn see* TIRE 1

rel deplete; exhaust, fag, tucker, wear out; debilitate, disable, weaken; annoy, bother, irk, vex

con refresh, rejuvenate, renew, restore; assuage, relieve

fatigued *adj syn see* TIRED 1

fatness *n syn see* OBESITY

‖**fatso** *n syn see* FATTY

fatty *adj* **1** containing fat especially in unusual amounts <a rather *fatty* steak>

syn adipose, fat

rel blubbery, lardy, suety

ant lean

2 having the qualities of fat <the constant frying left a *fatty* deposit on the kitchen woodwork>

syn greasy, oily, oleaginous, unctuous

fatty *n* a fat person <*fatties* trying to diet>

syn blimp, butterball, dumpling, ‖fatso, ‖tub

rel overweight; pudge, roly-poly, strapper; potbelly

idiom tons of fun

ant skinny

fatuous *adj syn see* SIMPLE 3

rel idiotic, imbecile, moronic; besotted, fond, infatuated, insensate; absurd, dumb, silly, stupid

con judicious, prudent, sage, sane, sapient, wise

ant sensible

faucet *n* a fixture for controlling the passage of fluid <turn off the *faucet*>

syn cock, gate, hydrant, petcock, spigot, stopcock, tap, valve

rel bung, spile

fault *n* **1** *syn see* IMPERFECTION

rel infirmity, weakness

con faultlessness, impeccability; meticulousness, preciseness, precision

2 imperfection in character or an ingrained moral weakness <he has few *faults*>

syn failing, foible, frailty, vice

rel infirmity, weakness; blemish, defect, flaw

con excellence, perfection, virtue; desirability, goodness, rightness

ant merit

3 *syn see* BLAME

rel accountability, answerability, liability, responsibility; crime, error, offense, sin, transgression

faultfinder *n* **1** *syn see* CRITIC

2 *syn see* GROUCH

faultfinding *adj syn see* CRITICAL 1

rel particular, pernickety; ultracritical

con appreciative, cherishing, prizing, valuing

faultily *adv syn see* AMISS 1

rel erroneously, fallaciously, inaccurately, mistakenly, unfairly

con correctly, right

faultless *adj* **1** *syn see* IMPECCABLE 1

rel entire, intact, perfect, whole; blameless

con defective, deficient, imprecise, inaccurate, inexact, uncorrect

ant faulty

2 *syn see* INNOCENT 2

faulty *adj* marked by a fault or defect <a *faulty* mechanism>

syn amiss, defective, flawed, imperfect, sick

rel imprecise, inaccurate, inexact, uncorrect; deficient, inadequate, incomplete; erroneous, fallacious, fallible, specious, wrong; blemished, damaged, defaced, disfigured, marred

con accurate, correct, exact, nice, precise, right; complete, entire, intact, perfect, whole; excellent, good; unflawed, unimpaired

ant faultless

faux pas *n* a breach of etiquette or of social convention <hustled him out of the room before he could commit another *faux pas*>

syn blooper, boner, ‖boo-boo, break, gaffe, impropriety, indecorum, solecism; *compare* ERROR 2

rel bungle, misstep, stumble; howler, screamer; indiscretion, misjudgment, oversight, pratfall

favor *n* **1** *syn see* REGARD 4

ant disfavor

2 *syn see* APPROBATION 1

con depreciation, derogation, disparagement

ant disfavor

3 *syn see* GIFT 1

rel aid, assistance, backing, encouragement, help, support

---

syn synonym(s)   *rel* related word(s)
ant antonym(s)   *con* contrasted word(s)
idiom idiomatic equivalent(s)
‖ use limited; if in doubt, see a dictionary

4 a special privilege <willing to grant a *favor* to a good friend>
syn courtesy, dispensation, indulgence, kindness, service
rel aid, assistance, cooperation, help

favor *vb* **1** *syn* see APPROVE 1
rel endorse, OK (*or* okay), sanction; appreciate, prize, value
idiom set great store by
con decry, depreciate, disparage
ant disfavor

2 *syn* see OBLIGE 2
rel humor, indulge, pamper
idiom do one a favor (*or* service), do right by
con baffle, circumvent, foil, frustrate, thwart

3 *syn* see ENCOURAGE 2
4 *syn* see RESEMBLE
con contradict, differ

favorable *adj* **1** expressing approval <a *favorable* recommendation>
syn approbative, approbatory, approving
rel benignant, kind, kindly; recommendatory, well-disposed; commendatory, complimentary, laudatory, praiseful
idiom in one's favor
con depreciative, disapprobatory, disapproving, disparaging, uncomplimentary; censorious, condemnatory, critical, fault-finding
ant unfavorable

2 *syn* see PLEASANT 1
3 *syn* see GOOD 1
rel healthful, salutary, wholesome
con disadvantageous, unpropitious; damaging, hampering
ant unfavorable

4 *syn* see TIMELY 1
5 indicative of a successful outcome <*favorable* conditions for opening a new business>
syn auspicious, benign, bright, dexter, fortunate, propitious, white
rel advantageous, beneficial, profitable; happy, lucky, promising, providential; cheering, encouraging, reassuring
idiom full of promise
con calamitous, cataclysmic, catastrophic, disastrous, fatal, fateful, ruinous; baleful, malefic, maleficent, malign, sinister; ill-fated, ill-starred, unlucky; inauspicious, unpromising, unpropitious
ant unfavorable

favorably *adv* *syn* see WELL 5
favored *adj* *syn* see FAVORITE 2
favoring *adj* *syn* see GOOD 1
favorite *adj* **1** accorded special treatment or attention <a *favorite* daughter>
syn beloved, blue-eyed, darling, dear, fair-haired, loved, pet, precious, white-haired, white-headed
rel admired, adored, esteemed, revered; cherished, prized, treasured
idiom dear as the apple of one's eye, dear to one's heart, held dear
con contemned, despised, disdained; abhorrent, detested, hated

2 constituting a favorite <*favorite* melodies>
syn favored, popular, preferred, well-liked
rel laudable, pleasant, praiseworthy; cherished, prized, treasured

con despised, detested, disliked, hated, unpopular; eschewed, rejected

fawn *vb* *syn* to act or behave with abjectness in the presence of a superior <*fawn* on the master>
syn apple-polish, bootlick, ‖brownnose, cotton, cower, cringe, grovel, honey (up), kowtow, slaver, toady, truckle
rel blandish, cajole, coax, wheedle; butter (up), flatter, make up (to); cater (to), pander (to); crawl; abase, debase, demean; bow, cave, defer, submit, yield; court, invite, woo
idiom be at one's beck and call, curry favor, dance attendance, kiss one's feet, lick one's shoes (*or* boots), make a doormat of oneself, ‖suck up to
con contemn, despise, disdain, scorn, scout; reject, repudiate, spurn; flout, gibe, jeer, scoff; deride, mock, ridicule, taunt
ant domineer

fawning *adj* characteristic of one that fawns <sent *fawning* greetings>
syn bootlicking, cowering, cringing, groveling, kowtowing, parasitic, sycophant, sycophantic, sycophantical, sycophantish, toadying, toadyish, truckling
rel flunkyish, obsequious, servile, slavish; subservient; compliant, deferential, humble, submissive, yielding; ingratiating; adulatory, flattering, mealy-mouthed; crawling, spineless; abject, ignoble, mean
con arrogant, disdainful, haughty, insolent, lordly, overbearing, proud, supercilious; contemptuous, insulting, scathing, scornful; authoritative, imperious, magisterial, masterful
ant domineering

fay *n* *syn* see FAIRY
faze *vb* *syn* see EMBARRASS
rel confound, dumbfound, mystify, nonplus, perplex, puzzle; confuse, muddle; appall, daunt, dismay, horrify; annoy, bother, irritate, vex
con calm, compose, quiet, relax, soothe; ease, relieve

fealty *n* *syn* see FIDELITY 1
rel faith, trueness, truth; dependability, reliability, trustworthiness; devotedness, support
con disloyalty, traitorousness, treacherousness
ant perfidy

fear *n* **1** agitation or dismay in the anticipation of or in the presence of danger <living in *fear* of what the future might hold>
syn alarm, cold feet, consternation, dismay, dread, fright, horror, panic, terror, trepidation, trepidity
rel apprehension, foreboding, misgiving, presentiment; angst, anxiety, concern, worry; agitation, discomposure, disquietude, perturbation; chickenheartedness, cowardice, cowardliness, faintheartedness, timidity, timorousness; funk, scare
idiom cold sweat
con boldness, bravery, courage, courageousness, dauntlessness, fortitude, gallantry, intrepidity, prowess, valiancy, valor
ant fearlessness

2 *syn* see REVERENCE 2

rel esteem, respect
con contempt, scorn

fearful *adj* **1** *syn* see AFRAID 1
rel agitated, alarmed, discomposed, disquieted, disturbed, perturbed
con audacious, bold, brave, courageous, dauntless, unafraid, valiant
ant unafraid
2 inspired or moved by fear <*fearful* of loud noises>
syn afraid, apprehensive; *compare* AFRAID 1
rel alarmed, disquieted, disturbed; aflutter, agitated, jittery, nervous, perturbed, uneasy; anxious, concerned, solicitous, worried
con assured, confident, sanguine, sure; collected, composed, cool, imperturbable, nonchalant, unflappable, unperturbed
ant unafraid
3 causing fear <a *fearful* sight>
syn appalling, awful, dire, direful, dreadful, formidable, frightful, horrible, horrific, redoubtable, shocking, terrible, terrific, tremendous
rel alarming, frightening, terrifying; ghastly, grim, grisly, gruesome, lurid, macabre; baleful, malign, sinister; overwhelming, sublime
con attractive, charming, delightful, enchanting, pleasant, pleasing
ant reassuring

fearless *adj syn* see BRAVE 1
rel assured, confident, sanguine, sure
con afraid, frightened, scared, terrified
ant fearful

feasible *adj syn* see POSSIBLE 1
rel practical; advantageous, beneficial, profitable; appropriate, fit, fitting, suitable
con impossible, impracticable, unachievable, unattainable, unworkable; ambitious, pretentious, utopian
ant infeasible, unfeasible

feast *n syn* see DINNER
rel entertainment, festivity; refreshment, repast; meal

feat *n* **1** *syn* see ADVENTURE
idiom bold stroke, deed of derring-do
2 a remarkable act or performance <Washington's *feat* of tossing a dollar across the river>
syn achievement, deed, exploit, tour de force
rel act, action; accomplishment, consummation, execution, performance; conquest, triumph, victory
3 *syn* see TRICK 3

feather *n syn* see TYPE
featherbrain *n syn* see SCATTERBRAIN
featherbrained *adj syn* see GIDDY 1
rel capricious, fickle, impulsive, whimsical; shallow, superficial, unprofound
featherhead *n syn* see SCATTERBRAIN
featherlight *adj syn* see LIGHT 1
featherweight *n syn* see DUNCE
featherweight *adj syn* see LIGHT 1

feature *n* **1** *syn* see QUALITY 1
2 *syn* see CHARACTERISTIC 1
rel article, detail, item, particular; component, constituent, element, factor, ingredient; individuality, particularity, peculiarity, speciality, specialty; attribute, property, quality
3 features *pl syn* see FACE 1

feature *vb* ‖**1** *syn* see RESEMBLE
2 *syn* see THINK 1
3 *syn* see EMPHASIZE

febrile *adj syn* see FEVERISH 1

feckless *adj* **1** having no real worth or purpose <after years of *feckless* negotiations>
syn fustian, good-for-nothing, meaningless, purposeless, unpurposed, useless, worthless
rel bootless, fruitless, futile, unavailing, vain; ineffective, ineffectual, inefficacious
con meaningful, purposeful, worthwhile; fruitful; effective, effectual, efficacious; consequential, important, momentous, significant, weighty
ant efficient, ‖feckful
2 *syn* see CARELESS 1
rel carefree, easygoing, happy-go-lucky, lackadaisical, nonchalant; remiss; irresponsible, undependable, unreliable, untrustworthy
con attentive, considerate, thoughtful; meticulous, punctilious, punctual, scrupulous; dependable, reliable, responsible, trustworthy
3 *syn* see IRRESPONSIBLE
ant ‖feckful

fecund *adj syn* see FERTILE
rel breeding, generating, propagating, reproducing
con infertile, sterile
ant barren

fecundity *n* **1** *syn* see FERTILITY
rel productiveness, productivity; exuberance, lavishness, lushness, luxuriance, prodigality, profuseness, profusion
con infertility, sterility, unproductiveness
ant barrenness, infecundity
2 *syn* see ELOQUENCE

federation *n syn* see ALLIANCE 2

fed up *adj* disgusted and completely out of patience <*fed up* with her bad behavior>
syn disgusted, sick, tired, weary
rel bored; glutted, sated, satiated, surfeited
idiom fed to the gills (or teeth), full up to here with, sick and tired of, sick (or tired) to death
con enchanted, enraptured, enthralled; delighted, excited, exhilarated, pleased, thrilled

fee *n syn* see WAGE
rel consideration; charge, cost, expense, price

‖**feeb** *n syn* see FOOL 4

feeble *adj* **1** *syn* see WEAK 1
rel emasculated, enervated, unmanned, unnerved; helpless; aged, doddering, senile; ailing, sapless
con hale, healthy, sound; lusty, strenuous; strong
ant robust
2 *syn* see TENUOUS 3

feebleminded *adj syn* see RETARDED

syn synonym(s)   *rel* related word(s)
ant antonym(s)   *con* contrasted word(s)
idiom idiomatic equivalent(s)
‖ use limited; if in doubt, see a dictionary

ant strong-minded
feebleness *n syn* see INFIRMITY 1
feed *vb syn* see GIVE 3
feed (on) *vb syn* see EAT 1
  idiom have (*or* take) a bite, ‖put on the feed bag (*or* nose bag)
feed *n* **1** *syn* see MEAL
  2 *syn* see FOOD 1
  rel banquet, feast, meal, repast
feel *vb* **1** *syn* see TOUCH 1
  rel manipulate, ply, wield; explore, sound; fumble, grope
  2 to have as an emotional response <*felt* pleasure in her company>
  syn experience, know, savor, taste
  rel apprehend; notice, observe, perceive; encounter, meet; endure, suffer, undergo
  idiom be aware (*or* conscious) of, be sensible of
  con disregard, ignore
  3 to view as right or true <we *feel* that he should retire soon>
  syn believe, consider, credit, deem, hold, sense, think; *compare* CONSIDER 3
  rel assume, presume, suppose, suspect; conclude, deduce, gather, infer, judge; conjecture, guess, surmise; esteem; repute
  idiom take (it) into one's head
  con challenge, distrust, doubt, misdoubt, mistrust, question
  4 *syn* see GROPE
feel (for) *vb syn* see COMPASSIONATE
feel *n* **1** *syn* see TOUCH 3
  2 *syn* see TOUCH 4
  3 *syn* see AIR 3
  con basis, essence, reality
feeler *n* an attempt to ascertain opinion <the letter was a *feeler* to see how they would react>
  syn trial balloon
  rel query, question; inquiry, probe, test; leader, leading question; sounding board; intimation, representation; prospectus; kiteflying
feeling *n* **1** *syn* see SENSATION 1
  rel action, behavior, reaction; responsiveness; palpability, palpableness, perceptibility, perceptibleness, tangibility, tangibleness
  con apathy, indifference, insensibility, numbness
  2 *syn* see TOUCH 4
  3 subjective response or reaction (as to a person or situation) <a *feeling* of sadness>
  syn affection, affectivity, emotion, passion, sentiment
  rel humor, mood, temper, vein; attitude, outlook; belief, opinion, view; concept, idea, impression, notion, thought
  4 *syn* see OPINION
  5 *syn* see AIR 3
  rel impress, impression, imprint
feeling *adj syn* see EMOTIONAL 1
  con numb, unmoved, unresponsive
  ant unfeeling
feel out *vb syn* see PROBE 2
feign *vb syn* see ASSUME 4
feigned *adj syn* see ARTIFICIAL 3
  rel counterfeit, false, sham
  con heartfelt, hearty, sincere, wholehearted, whole-souled

feint *n syn* see TRICK 1
  rel make-believe, pretense, pretension; befooling, hoax, hoodwinking; cheat, counterfeit, deceit, fake, humbug, imposture, sham; expedient, resort, shift
felicitate *vb syn* see CONGRATULATE
  rel commend, compliment, recommend; salute
  con comfort, console, solace; commiserate, condole (with); pity; gibe, jeer, scoff; deride, mock, ridicule, taunt; contemn
felicitous *adj syn* see FIT 1
  rel convincing, telling; opportune, pat, seasonable, timely, well-timed; apposite, apropos, germane, pertinent, relevant
  con awkward, clumsy, gauche, inept, maladroit; unfortunate, unhappy, unlucky
  ant infelicitous
feline *adj syn* see STEALTHY 2
fell *vb* **1** to force an opponent off his feet <*felled* the heckler with a single blow>
  syn bowl (down *or* over), bring down, down, drop, flatten, floor, ground, knock down, knock over, lay low, level, mow (down), prostrate, throw down, tumble
  rel shoot, shoot down
  idiom lay level with the ground
  con pick up, raise
  2 to bring down by cutting <*felled* the great oak by the driveway>
  syn chop, cut, hew
  rel flatten, level, raze; cleave, rive, split; sever, sunder; gash, hack, mangle, slash
fell *adj* **1** *syn* see FIERCE 1
  rel baleful, malefic, maleficent, malign, sinister; implacable, relentless, unrelenting; fearful, horrible, horrific, terrific
  con compassionate, sympathetic, tender; clement, forbearing, lenient, merciful; humane
  2 *syn* see GRAVE 3
fell *n syn* see HIDE
fellow *n* **1** *syn* see PARTNER
  2 *syn* see ACCOMPANIMENT 2
  3 *syn* see MATE 5
  4 *syn* see MAN 3
fellow feeling *n syn* see SYMPATHY 2
fellowship *n* **1** *syn* see COMPANY 1
  2 *syn* see ASSOCIATION 2
felo-de-se *n syn* see SUICIDE
felon *n syn* see CRIMINAL
female *n syn* see WOMAN 1
female *adj syn* see FEMININE
feminine *adj* of, relating to, or characterized by qualities considered typical of a woman <clothing for the career woman that manages to be both *feminine* and businesslike>
  syn female, muliebral, womanish, womanlike, womanly
  rel effeminate; ladylike
  con male, manlike, manly, masculine, virile; manful, mannish
femme fatale *n syn* see SIREN
fen *n syn* see SWAMP
fence *n syn* see BAR 2
fence *vb* **1** *syn* see ENCLOSE 1
  2 *syn* see DODGE 1
  rel feint, maneuver; baffle, foil, outwit
fend *vb* **1** *syn* see DEFEND 1
  2 *syn* see WARD 1

fend (off) *vb* to give a sharp check to <tried to *fend* off his attentions>
  syn hold off, keep off, rebuff, rebut, repel, repulse, stave off, ward (off)
  rel refuse, reject; snub, spurn; avert, avoid
  idiom hold (*or* keep) at bay, keep at a distance, keep at arm's length
  con allure, attract, captivate, charm, enchant, fascinate; embolden, hearten
feral *adj* 1 *syn see* BRUTISH
  rel barbaric, barbarous, ferocious, fierce, inhuman, savage, vicious
  con gentle, mild, tame
  2 *syn see* SAVAGE 1
ferine *adj syn see* BRUTISH
ferment *vb syn see* SEETHE 4
ferment *n* 1 *syn see* UNREST
  2 *syn see* COMMOTION 1
ferocious *adj* 1 *syn see* FIERCE 1
  rel rapacious, ravening, ravenous, voracious; implacable, relentless
  ant tender
  2 *syn see* SAVAGE
ferret out *vb syn see* SEEK 1
  rel elicit, extract; nose out, pry (out); penetrate, pierce, probe; chase, follow, pursue, trail; ascertain, determine, discover, learn
  con conceal, hide, screen, secrete; camouflage, disguise; cover (up), hush (up), suppress
  ant squirrel (away)
ferry *vb syn see* CARRY 1
fertile *adj* marked by abundant productivity <*fertile* soil><a *fertile* mind>
  syn childing, fecund, fruitful, productive, proliferant, prolific, rich, spawning
  rel bearing, producing, yielding; abundant, bountiful, copious, exuberant, generous, lush, luxuriant, plenteous, plentiful, teeming; creative, ingenious, inventive, pregnant, resourceful; exciting, galvanizing, provoking, quickening, stimulating
  con barren, impotent, unfruitful; dull, imitative, stupid, unproductive
  ant infertile, sterile
fertility *n* the quality or state of being fertile <insure the *fertility* of the soil>
  syn fecundity, fruitfulness, prolificacy
  rel abundance, copiousness, plentifulness; creativity, ingenuity, inventiveness, resourcefulness
  con barrenness, impotence, unfruitfulness
  ant infertility, sterility
fervent *adj syn see* IMPASSIONED
  rel devout, pious, religious; responsive, tender, warm, warmhearted; heartfelt, hearty, sincere, unfeigned, wholehearted, whole-souled; earnest, serious; eager, enthusiastic
  con apathetic, impassive, phlegmatic; aloof, detached, indifferent, unconcerned
fervid *adj* 1 *syn see* IMPASSIONED
  con collected, composed, cool, imperturbable, nonchalant
  ant gelid

  2 *syn see* FEVERISH 2
fervor *n syn see* PASSION 6
  rel devoutness, piety, piousness; earnestness, seriousness, solemnity; heartiness, sincerity, wholeheartedness; empressement, warmth
  con apathy, impassiveness, impassivity; aloofness, detachment, indifference, unconcern; languor, lethargy, torpor
fescennine *adj syn see* OBSCENE 2
fess (up) *vb syn see* ACKNOWLEDGE 1
fester *vb syn see* RANKLE
festive *adj syn see* MERRY
festivity *n syn see* MERRYMAKING
fetch *vb syn see* SELL 4
fetching *adj syn see* ENTICING
fetch up *vb* ‖1 *syn see* BRING UP 1
  2 *syn see* STOP 4
fetid *adj syn see* MALODOROUS 1
  rel loathsome, repugnant, repulsive, revolting
  con aromatic, balmy, odorous, redolent
  ant fragrant
fetish *n* 1 *syn see* CHARM 2
  2 irrational reverence or attachment <had a *fetish* for red hair>
  syn fixation, mania, obsession, thing
  rel preoccupation, prepossession; bias, partiality, predilection, prejudice; leaning, penchant, proclivity, propensity
  con antipathy, aversion, repugnance, repulsion; dislike, disrelish, distaste
fetter *n, usu fetters pl syn see* SHACKLE
fetter *vb syn see* HAMPER
  con disembarrass, disencumber, disentangle, extricate, untangle; detach, disengage
fettle *n syn see* ORDER 10
feud *n* 1 *syn see* VENDETTA
  2 *syn see* QUARREL
  rel argument; combat, contest
fevered *adj* 1 *syn see* FEVERISH 1
  ant afebrile
  2 *syn see* FEVERISH 2
feverish *adj* 1 abnormally heated by fever <the child's forehead felt *feverish*>
  syn febrile, fevered, fiery
  rel burning, flushed, hectic, hot, inflamed, pyretic
  ant afebrile
  2 marked by intense emotion or activity <a *feverish* imagination>
  syn burning, fervid, fevered, heated, hectic
  rel excited, high-strung, nervous, overwrought; frenzied, furious, passionate
  idiom keyed up
  con calm, composed, cool, serene, tranquil; apathetic, languid, lethargic, listless, phlegmatic
few *adj syn see* INFREQUENT
few *n* a small quantity or number <sold a *few* of the books>
  syn handful, scattering, smatch, smatter, smattering, spatter, spattering, sprinkling
  con abundance, many, multitude, numbers
fiat *n syn see* SANCTION
fib *n syn see* LIE
  rel equivocation, evasiveness; mendacity, untruthfulness
  idiom tall tale
fib *vb syn see* LIE

---

syn synonym(s)   *rel* related word(s)
ant antonym(s)   *con* contrasted word(s)
idiom idiomatic equivalent(s)
‖ use limited; if in doubt, see a dictionary

rel concoct, fabricate, make up, trump up
idiom draw the long bow, stretch the truth

fibber *n syn* see LIAR
fibbery *n syn* see MENDACITY
fiber *n syn* see TEXTURE 2
fibrous *adj syn* see MUSCULAR 1
fibster *n syn* see LIAR
fickle *adj syn* see INCONSTANT 1
rel unfaithful; undependable, unreliable
con stable, unchanging
ant constant, true
fiction *n* a story, account, explanation, or conception which is an invention of the human mind <his belief was based on a *fiction*>
syn fable, fabrication, figment
rel concoction, fantasy, invention; falsehood, lie, misrepresentation, untruth; anecdote, narrative, story, tale, yarn; fish story
con actuality, reality
ant fact
fictional *adj syn* see FICTITIOUS 1
fictitious *adj* 1 suggestive of fiction especially in lacking a sound factual basis <*fictitious* values in logic>
syn chimerical, fanciful, fantastic, fictional, fictive, illusory, imaginary, suppositious, suppositious, unreal
rel concocted, created, invented, made; fabricated, fashioned; cooked-up, false, made-up, trumped-up, untrue; romantic
con actual, real, true; authentic, genuine; factual, veritable; truthful, veracious, verisimilar
2 not genuine <the gigolo wooed the heiress with *fictitious* ardor>
syn fake, mock, sham, simulated; *compare* ARTIFICIAL 2
rel deceptive, delusive, delusory, misleading; dishonest, unreal, untrue; artificial, ersatz, factitious, synthetic
con authentic, bona fide, veritable; actual, honest, real, true
ant genuine
fictive *adj syn* see FICTITIOUS 1
fiddle *vb* 1 to handle something nervously or absently <always *fiddling* with his tie>
syn fidget, play, trifle, twiddle
rel feel, handle, touch
2 to work aimlessly, fruitlessly, or pointlessly <*fiddled* around with the engine for hours>
syn doodle, mess, mess around, potter, puddle, putter, tinker
rel dabble, fool, monkey
fiddle *n syn* see IMPOSTURE
fiddle-faddle *n syn* see NONSENSE 2
fiddlesticks *n pl syn* see NONSENSE 2
fidelity *n* 1 constancy to something to which one is bound by a pledge or duty <we must practice *fidelity* to our word>
syn allegiance, ardor, devotion, faithfulness, fealty, loyalty, piety
rel constancy, staunchness, steadfastness; dependability, reliability, trustworthiness
con disloyalty, falseness, falsity, perfidiousness, traitorousness, treacherousness, treachery; undependableness, unreliability, untrustworthiness
ant perfidy; faithlessness

2 *syn* see ATTACHMENT 1
ant infidelity

fidget *vb syn* see FIDDLE 1
fidgety *adj syn* see NERVOUS
field *n* a limited area of knowledge or endeavor to which pursuits, activities, and interests are confined <a lawyer eminent in her *field*>
syn bailiwick, champaign, demesne, domain, dominion, precinct, province, region, sphere, terrain, territory, walk
rel bounds, confines, limits; area, department; compass, orbit, purview, range, reach, scope, sweep
con terra incognita
fiend *n syn* see DEVIL 1
2 *syn* see DEVIL 2
3 *syn* see ENTHUSIAST
fiendish *adj* having or manifesting qualities associated with devils, demons, and fiends <inflicted *fiendish* tortures on his captive>
syn demoniac, demonian, demonic, devilish, diabolic, diabolonian, satanic, serpentine, unhallowed
rel hellish, infernal; baleful, malefic, maleficent, malign, sinister; malevolent, malicious, malignant; atrocious, heinous, monstrous, outrageous; barbarous, cruel, ferocious, inhuman, savage, vicious
con benign, benignant, kind, kindly; gentle, mild; compassionate, sympathetic, tender
fierce *adj* 1 displaying fury or malignity in looks or actions <*fierce* native tribes>
syn barbarous, cannibalic, cruel, fell, ferocious, grim, inhuman, inhumane, savage, truculent, wolfish
rel menacing, threatening; enraged, infuriated, maddened; aggressive, bellicose, belligerent, pugnacious; brutal, merciless, pitiless, ruthless, vicious; wild
con benign, benignant, gentle, kind, kindly; peaceful; subdued, submissive, tame
ant mild
2 *syn* see INTENSE 1
rel excessive, extreme, inordinate; penetrating, piercing; superlative, supreme, transcendent
con gentle, mild, subdued
fiercely *adv syn* see HARD 2
fiery *adj* 1 *syn* see BURNING 1
2 *syn* see HOT 1
ant frigid, icy
3 *syn* see FEVERISH 1
4 *syn* see SPIRITED 2
rel headlong, hotheaded, impetuous, madcap, precipitate; fervid, impassioned, perfervid; fierce, intense, vehement, violent; enthusiastic, excitable, impulsive, unrestrained; irascible, irritable
con deliberate, leisurely, slow; apathetic, dull, impassive, lethargic, phlegmatic, sluggish; enervated, listless, spiritless
5 *syn* see IMPASSIONED
ant icy
fifty-fifty *adv syn* see EVENLY 1
fifty-fifty *adj syn* see EVEN 4
fight *vb* 1 *syn* see CONTEND 1
rel strive, struggle; rowdy, scuffle, tussle; debate, dispute; altercate, bicker, quarrel, scrap, spat, squabble, tiff, wrangle

idiom ‖mix it, mix it up, put up a fight
con bow, capitulate, submit, succumb, yield
2 *syn* see RESIST
  con abide, bear, endure, suffer; advocate, back, champion, support, uphold; defend, guard, protect, shield
fight *n* **1** *syn* see BRAWL 2
2 *syn* see QUARREL
3 *syn* see ATTACK 2
fighter *n* *syn* see SOLDIER
fighting man *n* *syn* see SOLDIER
figment *n* *syn* see FICTION
  rel daydream, dream, fancy, nightmare; bubble, chimera, illusion; creation
figurant *n* *syn* see DANCER
figurante *n* *syn* see DANCER
figuration *n* **1** *syn* see OUTLINE
2 *syn* see ALLEGORY 1
figure *n* **1** *syn* see NUMBER
  rel character, symbol
2 *syn* see FORM 1
  rel delineation; appearance, build, frame, physique
3 a unit in a decorative composition (as in a fabric) <a rug with geometrical *figures* in blue and red>
  syn design, device, motif, motive, pattern
  rel decoration, embellishment, ornamentation
figure *vb* **1** *syn* see CALCULATE
2 *syn* see ADD 2
  rel count, enumerate, number
3 *syn* see DECIDE
figure out *vb* *syn* see SOLVE 2
  rel disentangle, unscramble, untangle; crack, decode
  con obfuscate, obscure; conceal, hide, screen
figuring *n* *syn* see COMPUTATION
filch *vb* *syn* see STEAL 1
filcher *n* *syn* see THIEF
file *n* *syn* see LINE 5
filius nullius *n* *syn* see BASTARD 1
filius populi *n* *syn* see BASTARD 1
fill *vb* **1** to make full in a way or to a degree that prevents further entry or passage <*fill* a cavity in a tooth>
  syn block, choke, clog, close, congest, obstruct, occlude, plug, stop, stopper
  rel bar, dam, jam; ‖bung, pug
  con clear, free
2 *syn* see LOAD 3
3 *syn* see SATISFY 5
4 *syn* see SATIATE
  rel overfeed, overfill, overstuff
fille de joie *n* *syn* see PROSTITUTE
fillet *n* *syn* see STRIP 1
fill in *vb* **1** *syn* see INTRODUCE 6
2 *syn* see INFORM 2
fill-in *n* *syn* see SUBSTITUTE 1
film *n* **1** *syn* see HAZE 1
2 *syn* see MOVIE
filmy *adj* characterized by fineness and delicacy of texture <*filmy* curtains>
  syn diaphanous, flimsy, gauzy, gossamer, sheer, tiffany, transparent

  rel dainty, delicate, fine
  con coarse, heavy, opaque, rough
filthy *adj* **1** *syn* see DIRTY 1
  rel disheveled, slipshod, sloppy, slovenly, unkempt; loathsome, offensive, repulsive, revolting, verminous; coarse, gross, obscene, ribald, vulgar
  con cleaned, cleansed; clean, cleanly; neat, shipshape, tidy, trig, trim
  ant immaculate, spick-and-span
2 *syn* see OBSCENE 2
filthy lucre *n* *syn* see MONEY
finagle *vb* *syn* see ENGINEER
final *adj* *syn* see LAST
  rel crowning, ending, finishing; conclusive, decisive, definitive, irrefutable, unanswerable, unappealable
  con earliest, maiden, original, primary; beginning, incipient, introductory; inaugural
  ant initial
finale *n* a final part or element (as of a sequence, series, or action) <the solution of the mystery forms the *finale* of the play>
  syn close, conclusion, end, ending, finish, windup; *compare* END 2
  rel climax, consummation, culmination; denouement, payoff; cessation, termination
  con beginning, genesis, initiation, rise, start; inception, origin, root, source
  ant prologue
finally *adv* *syn* see YET 2
  idiom at last, at length, at long last, in the long run, when all is said and done
finance *vb* **1** *syn* see CAPITALIZE
  idiom put up the money, raise the dough
2 *syn* see ENDOW 2
  rel back, bank, bankroll, grubstake, stake, underwrite; patronize, promote, sponsor, support
financial *adj* of or relating to finance <the *financial* interests of the country>
  syn fiscal, monetary, pecuniary, pocket
  rel business, commercial, economic
find *vb* **1** to come upon <they soon *found* what they needed>
  syn catch, descry, detect, encounter, espy, hit (on *or* upon), meet (with), spot, turn up
  rel discern, discover, note, sight; distinguish, identify, recognize; dig up, scare up
  idiom bring to light, come up with, fall in with, lay one's finger (on *or* upon), lay one's hand (on *or* upon)
  con miss, overlook, pass (over)
  ant lose
2 *syn* see GIVE 3
find *n* **1** one of unexpected worth or merit obtained or encountered more or less by chance <the young understudy proved to be a remarkable *find*>
  syn treasure, treasure trove
  rel boast, gem, jewel, pride
  idiom one in a thousand (*or* million)
2 *syn* see DISCOVERY
find out *vb* *syn* see DISCOVER 3
fine *n* a pecuniary penalty exacted by an authority <paid a *fine* of ten dollars>
  syn amercement, forfeit, mulct, penalty
  rel damages, reparation; punishment; assessment

---

syn synonym(s)   **rel** related word(s)
ant antonym(s)   **con** contrasted word(s)
idiom idiomatic equivalent(s)
‖ use limited; if in doubt, see a dictionary

fine vb syn see PENALIZE
 rel distrain, exact, levy, tax; confiscate, sequestrate

fine adj 1 marked by subtlety of perception or discrimination <I cannot follow these *fine* distinctions>
 syn delicate, finespun, hairline, hairsplitting, nice, refined, subtle
 rel abstruse, esoteric, recondite; cryptic, enigmatic, obscure; minute, petty, trifling
 con definite, explicit, express, specific; clear, lucid, perspicuous; broad, extensive, general, generic, indefinite, wide
 2 consisting of small particles <*fine* sand>
 syn impalpable, powdery, pulverized
 rel light, loose, porous
 ant coarse
 3 syn see EXCELLENT
 rel beautiful, splendid; enjoyable, pleasant
 idiom fine and dandy
 con miserable, wretched; atrocious, awful, objectionable, unpleasant
 4 syn see FAIR 2

finecomb vb syn see SCOUR 2

finery n dressy clothing <decked out in all her *finery*>
 syn best bib and tucker, bravery, frippery, full dress, ||glad rags, regalia, Sunday best, war paint
 rel apparel, clothes; foofaraw, frill, gewgaw, ornament, trimming
 con rags, tatters

finespun adj syn see FINE 1

finesse vb syn see MANIPULATE 2

fine–tooth–comb vb syn see SCOUR 2

finger vb 1 syn see TOUCH 1
 2 syn see DESIGNATE 2
 3 syn see IDENTIFY

finical adj syn see NICE 1
 con slipshod, sloppy, slovenly; blowsy, dowdy, frowzy, slatternly

finicking adj syn see NICE 1

finicky adj syn see NICE 1

finish vb 1 syn see CLOSE 3
 rel accomplish, achieve, effect, fulfill
 idiom have done with
 2 syn see GO 4
 3 syn see KILL 1
 4 syn see MURDER 1

finish n 1 syn see END 2
 2 syn see FINALE
 3 syn see ACQUIREMENT
 rel correctness, discrimination, propriety, refinement; elegance, grace, polish; cultivation, taste

finished adj 1 syn see COMPLETE 4
 2 syn see THROUGH 3
 3 syn see CONSUMMATE 1
 rel cultivated, cultured, refined; smooth, suave, urbane; elegant, exquisite; all-around, many-sided, versatile
 con imperfect, incomplete
 ant crude; unfinished

finish off vb syn see CLIMAX

finite adj having definite or definable limits or boundaries <a *finite* thickness>
 syn bound, bounded, limited
 rel confined, restricted; definable, defined, definite, determinate, fixed, terminable; exact, precise, specific

 con boundless, unbounded, unlimited; absolute, complete, total
 ant infinite

||fink n syn see INFORMER

fire n 1 a destructive burning <the house was destroyed by *fire*>
 syn conflagration, holocaust, inferno
 rel blaze, flame, flare, glare; burning, charring, scorching, searing
 idiom sea of flames, sheet of fire
 2 syn see PASSION 6
 rel animation, exhilaration, liveliness; dash, drive, energy, ginger, gusto, heartiness, pep, punch, snap, spirit, starch, verve, vigor, vim, zest, zing, zip
 con languor, lassitude, lethargy, listlessness, stupor, torpidity, torpor; apathy, impassivity, phlegm

fire vb 1 syn see LIGHT 1
 idiom set fire to, set on fire
 con extinguish, quench, smother
 2 to stimulate (as mental powers) to higher or more intense activity <a painting that *fired* the viewer's imagination>
 syn animate, exalt, inform, inspire; *compare* PROVOKE 4
 rel arouse, enliven, rouse, stir; electrify, excite; heighten, intensify; enthuse, thrill
 con appall, dismay; alarm, frighten, terrify
 ant daunt
 3 syn see DISMISS 3
 rel eject, expel, oust
 idiom give the pink slip, give the sack, strike off the rolls
 con engage; appoint, designate, elect, name
 ant hire
 4 syn see SHOOT 1
 5 syn see THROW 1
 6 to dry or harden by subjecting to heat <*fire* bricks>
 syn bake, burn, kiln

firebug n syn see INCENDIARY

fire–new adj syn see BRAND-NEW

firewater n syn see LIQUOR 2

firm adj 1 syn see FAST 4
 2 syn see STABLE 2
 3 having a texture or consistency that resists deformation by external force <*firm* flesh>
 syn hard, solid
 rel close, compact, dense, thick; inelastic, inflexible, rigid, stiff, unyielding; sturdy, substantial, tough
 con flaccid, flimsy, floppy, limp, loose, slack, sleazy, soft, squishy
 ant flabby
 4 that has been established and is not usually subject to change <a *firm* price>
 syn certain, fixed, set, settled, stated, stipulated
 rel established, going, prevailing; consistent, stable, steady, unwavering; definite, exact, explicit, specific, undeviating; flat
 con changeable, fluctuating, shaky, shifting, unsteady, variable
 5 syn see SURE 1
 6 syn see SURE 2

firm adv syn see HARD 7

firm n syn see ENTERPRISE 3

firmament n syn see SKY

firmly adv 1 syn see HARD 7

2 *syn* see HARD 9
firmness *n* 1 *syn* see STABILITY
2 *syn* see DECISION 2
first *adj* 1 being number one in a series <the *first* day of the week>
syn foremost, headmost, inaugural, initial, leading
con final, terminal, ultimate; interjacent, intermediary, intermediate, intervenient, intervening
ant last
2 preceding all others <succeeded at her *first* try>
syn earliest, initial, maiden, original, pioneer, primary, prime
rel early, pristine; primal, primogenial, primordial
con derivative, imitative, secondary
ant final
3 exceeding all others <he was the *first* statesman of his era>
syn arch, champion, chief, foremost, head, leading, premier, principal
rel eminent, highest, preeminent, primary, prime, supreme; dominant, paramount, predominant, sovereign; main, outstanding
con ancillary, auxiliary, secondary, subsidiary
ant subordinate
4 most rudimentary <had not the *first* chance of success>
syn least, slightest, smallest
rel measly, slight, slim, trifling, trivial
con considerable, goodly, significant, substantial, tolerable, worthwhile
first *adv* *syn* see FIRSTLY
first–class *adj* *syn* see EXCELLENT
idiom in a class by itself
con fair, indifferent, middling; unexceptional, unnoteworthy, unremarkable
firsthand *adj* *syn* see DIRECT 4
firstly *adv* as the first thing to be mentioned <*firstly*, we wish to consider the economic problem>
syn first, initially
rel incipiently, originally, primarily
idiom before all (*or* anything) else, first of all, first off, to begin with
con ultimately
ant finally, lastly
first off *adv* *syn* see AWAY 3
first–rate *adj* *syn* see EXCELLENT
con fair, indifferent, middling, poor; unexceptional, unnoteworthy, unremarkable
first–string *adj* *syn* see EXCELLENT
firth *n* *syn* see INLET
fiscal *adj* *syn* see FINANCIAL
fish *n* 1 *syn* see FOOL 3
‖2 *syn* see DOLLAR
fish *vb* *syn* see HINT 4
fishwife *n* *syn* see VIRAGO
fishy *adj* *syn* see DOUBTFUL 1
fissure *n* 1 *syn* see CRACK 3
rel abyss, chasm, gorge, ravine; breach, rent, rupture; gash, hole, opening

2 *syn* see BREACH 3
fist *n* *syn* see HANDWRITING
fisticuffs *n pl syn* see BOXING
fit *n* *syn* see ATTACK 3
fit *adj* 1 adapted to an end or use by nature or art <food *fit* for a king>
syn applicable, appropriate, apt, befitting, felicitous, fitting, happy, just, meet, proper, right, rightful, suitable; *compare* JUST 3
rel adapted, adjusted; congruous, consonant; decent, decorous; acceptable, adequate, tolerable
con improper, inadequate, inappropriate, unsuitable; false, wrong
ant unfit
2 *syn* see ELIGIBLE
rel able, competent
3 *syn* see GOOD 2
4 *syn* see HEALTHY 1
idiom fit as a fiddle
ant unfit
fit *vb* 1 *syn* see SUIT 4
2 *syn* see BELONG 1
3 *syn* see PREPARE 1
4 *syn* see ADAPT
fit (in) *vb* *syn* see AGREE 4
fitful *adj* lacking steadiness or regularity in course, movement, or succession <a *fitful* breeze>
syn catchy, desultory, on-again-off-again, spasmodic, sporadic, spotty
rel intermittent, interrupted, irregular, periodic, recurrent; haphazard, hit-or-miss, random; changeable, variable; capricious, inconstant, unstable
con equable, even, steady, uniform; methodical, orderly, regular, systematic
ant constant
fitly *adv* *syn* see WELL 1
fitness *n* 1 *syn* see ORDER 10
2 *syn* see ORDER 11
rel decency, decorum, harmony
ant unfitness
3 *syn* see USE 3
fit out *vb* *syn* see FURNISH 1
fitted *adj* *syn* see ASSORTED 2
fitting *adj* 1 *syn* see FIT 1
rel apposite, apropos, germane, pertinent, relevant, seemly; accordant, concordant, harmonious
2 *syn* see TRUE 7
fittingly *adv* 1 *syn* see WELL 1
2 *syn* see WELL 4
fivefold *adj* *syn* see QUINTUPLE
five–star *adj* *syn* see EXCELLENT
fix *vb* 1 *syn* see SET 1
rel stabilize, steady; decide, determine, rule; specify
con change, modify, vary
ant alter; abrogate
2 *syn* see ENTRENCH 1
rel inculcate, instill
con overthrow, overturn, subvert, upset
3 *syn* see FASTEN 1
4 *syn* see FASTEN 2
con dislodge, displace
5 *syn* see FASTEN 3
6 *syn* see PREPARE 1
7 *syn* see MEND 2
8 *syn* see ADJUST 2

---

syn synonym(s)   *rel* related word(s)
ant antonym(s)   *con* contrasted word(s)
idiom idiomatic equivalent(s)
‖ use limited; if in doubt, see a dictionary

rel mend, patch, rebuild, repair; amend, emend, revise
con disorganize, unsettle
9 *syn* see SOLVE 1
10 *syn* see STERILIZE
11 *syn* see BRIBE
fix *n syn* see PREDICAMENT
fixate *vb syn* see FASTEN 3
fixation *n syn* see FETISH 2
rel craze, fascination, infatuation
idiom bee in one's bonnet
fixed *adj* **1** *syn* see FAST 4
2 *syn* see IMMOVABLE 1
3 *syn* see DEFINITE 1
4 *syn* see INFLEXIBLE 3
5 *syn* see FIRM 4
con changing, variable, varying
6 *syn* see SURE 2
7 *syn* see WHOLE 5
con distracted, erratic, wandering
fixedly *adv syn* see HARD 7
rel stubbornly, tenaciously
fixture *n syn* see INSTITUTION
fix up *vb syn* see DRESS UP 1
fizz *vb syn* see HISS
fizzle *vb syn* see HISS
flabbergast *vb syn* see SURPRISE 2
rel overwhelm, shock
flabby *adj syn* see LIMP 1
rel soft, yielding; impotent, powerless; enervated, languid, listless; spiritless
con taut, tense, tight; strong, sturdy, tenacious, tough; gritty, plucky
ant firm
flaccid *adj syn* see LIMP 1
rel emasculated, enervated, unnerved; debilitated, enfeebled, sapped, weakened
con elastic, flexible, springy, supple; limber, lithe; energetic, lusty, nervous, vigorous
ant resilient
flag *n* a piece of fabric that is used as a symbol (as of a nation) or as a signaling device <we respect the *flag* of our fathers>
syn banderole, banner, bannerol, burgee, color, ensign, gonfalon, gonfanon, jack, oriflamme, pendant, pennant, pennon, standard, streamer
flag *vb syn* see SIGNAL
flag *vb* **1** *syn* see FAIL 1
2 *syn* see DROOP 3
rel abate, ebb, wane
flagellate *vb syn* see WHIP 1
flagitious *adj syn* see VICIOUS 2
rel criminal, scandalous, sinful, wicked; disgraceful, shameful; flagrant, glaring, gross
con good, upstanding, virtuous
flagrant *adj syn* see EGREGIOUS
rel bold, conspicuous, obvious, striking; heinous; flagitious, wicked; disgraceful, scandalous, shameful, shocking
con hidden, inconspicuous, obscure; excusable, unimportant
flagrante delicto *adv syn* see REDHANDED
flag-waver *n syn* see PATRIOTEER
flair *n syn* see GIFT 2
flak *n syn* see CRITICISM 2
flake (off) *vb syn* see SCALE 2
‖**flake out** *vb syn* see COLLAPSE 2

flam *n syn* see IMPOSTURE
flamboyant *adj* **1** *syn* see ORNATE
2 *syn* see SHOWY
flame *n* **1** *syn* see SWEETHEART 1
2 *syn* see GIRL FRIEND 2
3 *syn* see BOYFRIEND 2
flame *vb syn* see BLAZE
rel coruscate, glint; fire, ignite, kindle, light
flaming *adj* **1** *syn* see BURNING 1
2 *syn* see IMPASSIONED
flammable *adj syn* see COMBUSTIBLE 1
ant incombustible, nonflammable
flap *n syn* see COMMOTION 1
flapdoodle *n syn* see NONSENSE 2
flare *vb syn* see BLAZE
rel dart, shoot; flicker, flutter
idiom burst into flame
ant gutter out
flare (up) *vb syn* see ANGER 2
idiom ‖blow one's stack (or top or lid), fly into a passion, fly off the handle
con calm (down), cool (off or down), simmer down
flare *n syn* see OUTBREAK 1
flare-up *n syn* see OUTBURST 1
flaring *adj syn* see BURNING 1
flash *vb* **1** to shoot forth light (as in rays or sparks) <lightning *flashed* in the sky>
syn coruscate, glance, gleam, glimmer, glint, glisten, glitter, scintillate, shimmer, spangle, sparkle, twinkle
rel dart, shoot; blare, blaze, burn, flame, flare, glare, glow, incandesce; blink, flicker, spark; dazzle; beam, radiate, shine
2 *syn* see BLINK 2
3 *syn* see SHOW 4
flash *n* **1** a sudden brief light <saw a *flash* sweep across the sky>
syn coruscation, glance, gleam, glimmer, glint, glisten, glitter, quiver, scintillation, shimmer, sparkle, twinkle
rel blare, blaze, flame, flare, glare, glow; flicker; beam, ray
2 *syn* see INSTANT 1
idiom half a second (or shake), twinkling of an eye
flashy *adj syn* see GAUDY
rel flamboyant, florid, ornate; flashing, glittering, sparkling
con dowdy, slatternly; natural, simple, unaffected; chic, modish, smart
flat *adj* **1** *syn* see LEVEL
idiom flat as a billiard table (or pancake)
con rugged, scabrous, uneven; hilly, mountainous
2 *syn* see PRONE 4
3 *syn* see DOWNRIGHT 2
4 *syn* see COLORLESS 2
5 *syn* see INSIPID 3
rel dull, lifeless, flavorless, stale, tasteless
6 *syn* see UNPALATABLE 1
7 *syn* see POOR 1
8 *syn* see DULL 7
flat *n syn* see APARTMENT 1
‖**flatfoot** *n syn* see POLICEMAN
flatly *adv syn* see EVENLY 3
flat-out *adj syn* see UTTER
flat-out *adv syn* see FAST 2
flatten *vb* **1** *syn* see EVEN 1
2 *syn* see FELL 1

flatter *vb* to be becoming to <a neckline designed to *flatter* the stylishly stout>
syn become, enhance, suit
rel adorn, beautify, decorate, embellish, ornament; finish, perfect
idiom put in the best light
con deface, disfigure; distort; mar, spoil

flattery *n* flattering speech or attentions <*flattery* will get you nowhere>
syn adulation, blandishment, blarney, incense, oil, soft soap
rel compliments; laud, laudation, praise; cajolery, coaxing, wheedling; fulsomeness, unctuousness; bootlicking, fawning, ingratiation, obsequiousness, sycophancy, toadying, truckling
idiom honeyed words
con censure, condemnation, criticism, reprehension, reprobation; castigation, excoriation; aspersion, insult; contempt, disdain, scorn; belittling, depreciation, derogation, detraction, disparagement

flatulent *adj syn see* INFLATED
rel empty, hollow, vain; shallow, superficial
con weighty, cogent, compelling, convincing, telling; forceful, forcible, potent

flaunt *vb syn see* SHOW 4
rel boast, brag, gasconade, vaunt; disclose, discover, divulge, reveal; advertise, broadcast, declare, proclaim, publish; flourish, wave
idiom dangle before the (or one's) eyes
con camouflage, cloak, disguise, dissemble, mask; bury, conceal, hide, screen, secrete

flavor *n syn see* TASTE 3

flavorless *adj syn see* UNPALATABLE 1
ant flavorsome

flavorsome *adj syn see* PALATABLE
con flat, insipid, vapid, wishy-washy; bland, mild; displeasing, tasteless, unflavored, unpalatable, unpleasant, unsavory
ant flavorless

flaw *n syn see* BLEMISH
rel cleavage, rent, rip, riving, split, tear

flawed *adj* 1 *syn see* DAMAGED
ant flawless
2 *syn see* FAULTY
ant flawless

flawless *adj* 1 *syn see* WHOLE 1
ant flawed
2 *syn see* PERFECT 2
3 *syn see* IMPECCABLE 1
con defective, faulty, flawed, imperfect, unsound
4 *syn see* IDEAL 3

flaxen *adj syn see* BLOND 1

flay *vb syn see* LAMBASTE
rel assail, attack, beat; tongue-lash

fleckless *adj syn see* PERFECT 2

flection *n syn see* TURN 4

fledgling *n syn see* NOVICE

flee *vb* 1 *syn see* ESCAPE 1
rel avoid, elude, evade, shun
idiom take a (runout) powder
2 *syn see* RUN 2

fleece *vb* 1 to obtain something valuable from by improper means <a corrupt mayor who *fleeced* the town treasury>
syn bleed, milk, mulct, rook, stick, sweat; *compare* CHEAT, EXTORT 1
rel cheat, cozen, defraud, do, hustle, ‖rope (in), swindle, take; pluck
idiom sell one a bill of goods, take for a sucker, take to the cleaner's
2 *syn see* OVERCHARGE 1

fleeceable *adj syn see* EASY 3

fleecy *adj syn see* HAIRY 1

fleer *vb* 1 *syn see* SNEER 1
2 *syn see* SCOFF
rel grin, smile, smirk
idiom cast in one's teeth, curl one's lip at, laugh one out of court

fleet *vb* 1 *syn see* WHILE
rel dally, fritter, idle, potter, squander, waste
2 *syn see* FLY 4
idiom go like the wind (or lightning), make (good) time
3 *syn see* HURRY 2

fleet *adj syn see* FAST 3
rel agile, brisk, nimble, spry; alert, animated, lively, spirited, sprightly, vivacious

fleeting *adj syn see* TRANSIENT
con abiding, enduring, persistent
ant lasting

fleetly *adv syn see* FAST 2

flesh *n syn see* MANKIND

fleshiness *n syn see* OBESITY

fleshliness *n syn see* ANIMALITY

fleshly *adj* 1 *syn see* BODILY
2 *syn see* CARNAL 1
rel epicurean, luxurious, sensuous, sybaritic, voluptuous; lay, profane, secular, temporal
con divine, religious, spiritual; intellectual, mental, psychic

fleshy *adj syn see* FAT 2
ant emaciated

flexible *adj syn see* ELASTIC 1
rel amenable, docile, manageable, tractable; acquiescent, compliant
con brittle, crisp, fragile, frangible; firm, hard, rigid, stiff, unyielding, wooden; intractable, recalcitrant, refractory, ungovernable; callous, hardened, indurated
ant inflexible

flexuous *adj syn see* WINDING

flexure *n syn see* TURN 4

flibbertigibbet *n syn see* SCATTERBRAIN

flick *n syn see* MOVIE

flicker *vb* 1 *syn see* FLIT 2
2 *syn see* BLINK 2
rel fluctuate, oscillate, swing, vibrate, waver; blaze, flame, flare, glare; coruscate, glance, gleam, glint, glitter, sparkle; quiver, tremble

flier *n syn see* PILOT 2

flight *n syn see* ESCAPE 1

flightiness *n syn see* LIGHTNESS
rel capriciousness, fickleness, inconstancy, instability, mercurialness
con constancy, equableness, steadfastness
ant steadiness

flighty *adj syn see* GIDDY 1

---

syn synonym(s)   *rel* related word(s)
ant antonym(s)   *con* contrasted word(s)
idiom idiomatic equivalent(s)
‖ use limited; if in doubt, see a dictionary

rel changeable, inconstant, mercurial, unstable; buoyant, effervescent, volatile; gay, lively, sprightly; irresponsible
con constant, dependable, reliable, responsible, trustworthy; stable; sedate
ant steady

flimflam *n* **1** *syn* see IMPOSTURE
 2 *syn* see NONSENSE 2
flimflam *vb* **1** *syn* see DUPE
 2 *syn* see CHEAT
flimflammer *n syn* see SWINDLER
flimsy *adj* **1** *syn* see FILMY
 2 *syn* see IMPLAUSIBLE
 ant substantial
 3 *syn* see DELICATE 5
 4 *syn* see WEAK 1
 ant sturdy
 5 *syn* see LIMP 1
flinch *vb syn* see RECOIL
 rel avoid, elude, escape, eschew, evade, shun; retire, withdraw; recede, retreat
fling *vb* **1** *syn* see RUSH 1
 2 *syn* see THROW 1
 con catch, grab, receive
fling *n* a casual attempt <I'm willing to take a *fling* at almost any job>
 syn crack, go, pop, shot, slap, stab, ‖stagger, try, whack, whirl
 rel attempt, effort, essay, trial
 con best, limit, maximum
 ant utmost
 2 *syn* see SPREE 1
flip (through) *vb syn* see BROWSE
flippancy *n syn* see LIGHTNESS
 rel archness, pertness, sauciness; impishness, mischievousness, playfulness, roguishness, waggishness; cheekiness, cockiness, freshness
 con earnestness, gravity, soberness, solemnity
 ant seriousness
flirt *vb syn* see TRIFLE 1
 rel disport, play, sport; caress, fondle, pet
flirt *n* a woman who trifles amorously <a charming girl but an outrageous *flirt*>
 syn coquette, vamp
flit *vb syn* see HURRY 2
 2 to move briskly, irregularly, and usually intermittently <the hummingbird *flitted* from flower to flower>
 syn dance, flicker, flitter, flutter, hover
 rel dart, float, fly, scud, skim
 3 *syn* see FLY 4
flitter *vb syn* see FLIT 2
 rel quaver, quiver, teeter
float *vb* **1** *syn* see DRIFT 1
 2 *syn* see HANG 3
 3 *syn* see FLY 1
 rel drift, waft
floater *n syn* see VAGABOND
flock *n* **1** *syn* see MULTITUDE 1
 2 *syn* see DROVE 2
flog *vb syn* see WHIP 1
flood *n* **1** *syn* see FLOW
 2 a great or overwhelming flow of or as if of water <a *flood* of messages>
 syn cataclysm, cataract, deluge, flooding, inundation, niagara, overflow, pour, spate, torrent
 rel current, flow, stream, tide; excess, superfluity, surplus; outgushing, outpouring

con dribble, drip, dropping
 ant trickle
flood *vb* **1** *syn* see DELUGE 1
 2 *syn* see DELUGE 3
flooding *n syn* see FLOOD 2
floor *vb syn* see FELL 1
floozy *n syn* see DOXY 1
‖**flop** *vb* **1** *syn* see RETIRE 4
 2 *syn* see FAIL 4
 con come off, go over, succeed
flop *n syn* see FAILURE 5
floppy *adj syn* see LIMP 1
florid *adj* **1** *syn* see RHETORICAL
 2 *syn* see ORNATE
 rel ostentatious, pretentious, showy
 con bald, bare, barren; austere, unadorned
 3 *syn* see RUDDY
 ant pallid
florilegium *n syn* see ANTHOLOGY
floss *n syn* see DOWN
flotsam *n syn* see DRIFTWOOD
flounce *vb syn* see SASHAY
flounder *vb syn* see WALLOW 2
 rel strive, struggle; labor, toil, travail
flourish *vb syn* see SUCCEED 3
 rel bloom, blossom, flower; augment, increase, multiply; amplify, expand; develop, grow, wax
 con shrivel, wither; contract, shrink; abate, ebb, subside, wane
 ant languish
flourishing *adj* enjoying a vigorous growth <a *flourishing* economy>
 syn booming, prospering, prosperous, roaring, robust, thrifty, thriving; *compare* SUCCESSFUL
 rel vigorous; rampant, rank; exuberant, lush, luxuriant, profuse
 idiom going strong, in full swing
 con decadent, declining, deteriorating; failing; decreasing, dwindling
 ant languishing
flout *vb syn* see SCOFF
 rel disregard, slight; repudiate, spurn; insult; defy
 idiom thumb one's nose at
 con admire, esteem, regard, respect
 ant revere
flow *vb* **1** *syn* see POUR 2
 rel cascade, jet, spout, spurt; well; course, ripple, run
 2 *syn* see SPRING 1
 3 *syn* see TEEM
 4 *syn* see DISCHARGE 5
flow *n* something suggestive of running water <she expressed herself in a *flow* of words>
 syn current, drift, flood, flux, rush, spate, stream, tide
 rel progression, sequence, series, succession; continuance, continuation, continuity
flower *n* **1** the often showy part of a seed plant that bears reproductive organs <children picking *flowers* in the meadow>
 syn bloom, blossom, posy
 rel bud, floret; shoot, spray
 2 *syn* see BEST
 3 *syn* see ARISTOCRACY
flower *vb syn* see BLOSSOM
flowering *n syn* see DEVELOPMENT
 ant fading

flowery *adj syn* see RHETORICAL
  rel diffuse, prolix, redundant, verbose, wordy
  con compendious, concise, laconic, pithy, succinct, summary, terse
flowing *adj syn* see EASY 9
flub *vb syn* see BOTCH
fluctuant *adj* **1** *syn* see WEAK 2
  2 *syn* see UNCERTAIN 1
flue *n syn* see DOWN
fluent *adj* **1** *syn* see VOCAL 3
  rel loquacious, talkative; easy, effortless, facile, smooth; apt, prompt, quick, ready
  con stammering, stuttering; tongue-tied; dumb; fettered, hampered, trammeled
  2 *syn* see EASY 9
fluff *n* **1** *syn* see DOWN
  2 *syn* see ERROR 2
fluff *vb syn* see BOTCH
fluid *adj syn* see CHANGEABLE 1
fluky *adj syn* see ACCIDENTAL
flummadiddle *n syn* see NONSENSE 2
flummox *vb syn* see FAIL 4
flurry *n syn* see STIR 1
  rel confusion, excitement, turbulence, turmoil; haste, hurry
flurry *vb syn* see DISCOMPOSE 1
  rel bewilder, distract, perplex; excite, galvanize, provoke, quicken, stimulate
flush *n* **1** *syn* see BLOOM 3
  2 *syn* see BLOOM 2
flush *vb* **1** *syn* see BLUSH
  2 *syn* see EVEN 1
flush *adj* **1** *syn* see RICH 1
  2 *syn* see RUDDY
  3 *syn* see LEVEL
flushed *adj syn* see RUDDY
fluster *vb* **1** *syn* see DISCOMPOSE 1
  rel bewilder, confound, distract, mystify, nonplus, perplex, puzzle; addle, confuse, fuddle, muddle
  ant steady
  2 *syn* see CONFUSE 2
flutter *vb syn* see FLIT 2
  rel quaver, quiver, shake, tremble, wobble; beat, palpitate, pulsate, throb; fluctuate, oscillate, swing, vibrate; flap
flux *n* **1** *syn* see DIARRHEA
  2 *syn* see FLOW
flux *vb syn* see LIQUEFY
fly *vb* **1** to pass lightly or quickly over or above a surface <clouds *flying* across the sky>
  syn float, float, sail, scud, shoot, skim, skirr
  rel dance, flicker, flit, flitter, flutter, hover; arise, ascend, mount, rise, soar; glide, slide, slip
  2 *syn* see RUN 2
  rel hide; retreat, withdraw
  3 *syn* see ESCAPE 1
  4 to pass swiftly as if on wings <how time *flies* when we are happy>
  syn fleet, flit, sail, sweep, wing
  rel soar; hasten, hurry, speed; barrel, skim, whisk, whiz, zip; breeze, dart, dash, rush, tear

  idiom go like the wind (*or* lightning), outstrip the wind
  con dally, dawdle, dillydally, drift; lag, linger, loiter, trail; crawl, creep, poke
  ant drag
  5 *syn* see HURRY 2
fly–boy *n syn* see PILOT 2
fly–by–night *adj syn* see UNRELIABLE 1
flying colors *n pl syn* see SUCCESS
flyspeck *n syn* see POINT 11
foam *n* a mass of bubbles gathering in or on the surface of a liquid or something as insubstantial as such a mass <a *foam* of delicate lace at her throat>
  syn froth, lather, spume, suds, yeast
fob off *vb syn* see FOIST 3
focal point *n syn* see CENTER 2
focus *n syn* see CENTER 2
  idiom center of attraction (*or* interest), focus of attention
focus *vb* **1** *syn* see FASTEN 3
  2 *syn* see CONVERGE
  idiom come to a focus
foe *n syn* see ENEMY
  con associate, companion, comrade
  ant friend
fog *n syn* see HAZE 2
fog *vb* **1** *syn* see OBSCURE
  rel bewilder, distract, mystify, perplex, puzzle
  2 *syn* see CONFUSE 4
  rel addle, muddle
foggy *adj syn* see HAZY
  idiom in a fog
fogram *n syn* see FOGY
fogy *n* a person who is behind the times or overconservative <his father is an old *fogy*>
  syn antediluvian, fogram, fossil, fuddy=duddy, mid-Victorian, moldy fig, mossback, square, stick-in-the-mud
  rel conservative, diehard; back number
  idiom regular old fogy
  ant modern
fogyish *adj syn* see CONSERVATIVE 1
  ant up-to-the-minute
foible *n syn* see FAULT 2
  rel imperfection, shortcoming
foil *vb syn* see FRUSTRATE 1
  rel discomfit, disconcert, embarrass, faze, rattle; curb, restrain
foist *vb* **1** *syn* see INSINUATE 3
  2 *syn* see IMPOSE 4
  3 to pass or offer (something spurious) as genuine or worthy <his theory was far more reasonable than many *foisted* on the public>
  syn fob off, palm (on *or* upon), palm off, pass off, work off; *compare* IMPOSE 4
  rel beguile, deceive, delude, mislead; bamboozle, dupe, gull, hoax, hoodwink, trick; cheat, defraud, overreach, swindle; impose, inflict, wish
fold *n syn* see WRINKLE
fold *vb* **1** *syn* see DOUBLE 2
  2 *syn* see FAIL 5
fold up *vb* **1** *syn* see GIVE 12
  2 *syn* see RUIN 3
foliage *n* the leaves of plants <a tree with handsome *foliage*>
  syn leafage, umbrage, verdure
  rel greenness, herbage; growth, vegetation

---

syn synonym(s)   *rel* related word(s)
ant antonym(s)   *con* contrasted word(s)
idiom idiomatic equivalent(s)
‖ use limited; if in doubt, see a dictionary

folk *n* **1** *syn* see FAMILY 1
  2 folks *pl syn* see FAMILY 2
folklore *n syn* see LORE 2
follow *vb* **1** to come after in time <a juggling
  act *followed* the singer>
  syn ensue, succeed, supervene
  rel displace, replace, supersede, supplant;
  postdate
  con herald, lead, preface, usher (in); antedate, predate
  ant precede
  2 to go after or on the track of <*followed* the
  boys to their hiding place>
  syn chase, chivy, pursue, trail; *compare*
  TAIL
  rel trace, track; hunt, search, seek; dog,
  hound, tag; accompany, attend, convoy;
  ape, copy, imitate; exercise, practice
  con guide, lead, pilot, steer; elude, escape,
  evade; abandon, desert
  ant precede; forsake
  3 *syn* see OBEY
  4 *syn* see APPREHEND 1
follower *n* one who attaches himself to another <he is a born *follower*>
  syn adherent, cohort, disciple, henchman,
  partisan, satellite, sectary, sectator, supporter
  rel addict, devotee, freak, habitué, votary;
  admirer, fan, fancier; advocate; bootlicker,
  hanger-on, lickspittle, parasite, sycophant,
  toady
  ant leader
following *adj syn* see NEXT
following *n* **1** *syn* see ENTOURAGE
  2 the body of persons who attach themselves
  to another especially as disciples, patrons, or
  admirers <he has a strong *following* in this
  country>
  syn audience, clientage, clientele, public
following *prep syn* see AFTER 2
folly *n syn* see FOOLISHNESS
  rel fatuity, stupidity
  ant wisdom
foment *vb syn* see INCITE
  rel goad, spur; cultivate, foster, nurse, nurture
  con repress, suppress
  ant quell
fomenter *n syn* see INSTIGATOR
fond *adj* **1** *syn* see OPTIMISTIC
  2 *syn* see LOVING
  rel responsive, romantic, sentimental, sympathetic, tender, warm; indulgent
  idiom silly over
fondle *vb syn* see CARESS
  rel clasp, embrace, hug; nestle, snuggle
fondness *n* **1** *syn* see LOVE 1
  2 *syn* see APPETITE 3
  rel partiality, predilection; relish
  con disgust; hate
font name *n syn* see GIVEN NAME
food *n* **1** things that are edible <conserve a
  nation's supply of *food*>
  syn bread, ‖chow, comestibles, ‖eats, edibles, feed, foodstuff, grub, meat, ‖muck-
  amuck, nurture, provender, provisions,
  scoff, ‖tuck, viands, victuals, vivres
  2 material which feeds and supports the
  mind or spirit <*food* for thought>

syn aliment, nourishment, nutriment, pabulum, pap, sustenance
foodstuff *n syn* see FOOD 1
foofaraw *n syn* see COMMOTION 3
fool *n* **1** a person lacking in judgment or
  prudence <stop acting like a *fool*>
  syn ass, asshead, donkey, doodle, idiot,
  imbecile, jackass, jerk, madman, mooncalf,
  nincom, nincompoop, ninny, ninnyhammer,
  poop, ‖schmo, ‖schmuck, tomfool
  rel blockhead, dimwit, dope, dumbbell,
  dummy, nitwit, numskull, pinhead; birdbrain, featherbrain, featherhead, rattlebrain,
  scatterbrain; goose, silly
  2 a retainer formerly kept to provide casual
  entertainment <a king's *fool*>
  syn idiot, jester, motley
  rel buffoon, clown, comedian, comic, merry-andrew
  3 one who is victimized or made to appear
  foolish <she's nobody's *fool*>
  syn butt, chump, ‖come-on, ‖cull, dupe,
  easy mark, fall guy, fish, gudgeon, gull,
  mark, monkey, ‖mug, patsy, pigeon, sap,
  saphead, ‖schlemiel, simple, sucker, victim
  rel pushover; laughingstock; loser; instrument, tool
  4 one who is mentally deficient <a badly
  retarded child, little more than a *fool*>
  syn ament, cretin, ‖feeb, half-wit, idiot,
  imbecile, moron, natural, simpleton, softhead, underwit, zany
fool *vb* **1** *syn* see TRIFLE 1
  2 *syn* see MEDDLE
  3 *syn* see BANTER
  4 *syn* see DUPE
fool (around) *vb syn* see PHILANDER
fool (away) *vb syn* see WASTE 2
foolhardy *adj syn* see ADVENTUROUS
  rel headlong, impetuous, precipitate
  con calculating, cautious, circumspect;
  careful, prudent
  ant wary
fooling *n syn* see HORSEPLAY
foolish *adj* **1** *syn* see SIMPLE 3
  rel idiotic, imbecilic, moronic; daft, feeble-
  minded, half-witted; ‖half-assed, half=
  cocked; irrational
  con bright, clever, intelligent, quick-witted
  ant smart
  2 felt to be ridiculous because not exhibiting
  good or conventional sense <a *foolish* invest-
  ment>
  syn absurd, ‖balmy, cockamamie, crazy,
  daffy, ‖dilly, ‖dippy, donkeyish, dotty, fantastic, harebrained, idleheaded, insane,
  kooky, loony, loopy, lunatic, mad, nutty,
  ‖potty, preposterous, sappy, silly, tomfool,
  unearthly, wacky, zany
  rel laughable, ludicrous, ridiculous; half=
  baked, headless, jerky, nonsensical; offbeat,
  unacceptable, unconventional, unorthodox
  con judicious, sage, sapient; discreet, foresighted, prudent; canny, shrewd, slick
  ant sensible; wise
foolishness *n* the quality or state of being
  foolish <the *foolishness* of so many of her
  schemes>
  syn absurdity, craziness, dottiness, folly,
  inanity, insanity, lunacy, preposterousness,
  senselessness, silliness, witlessness

rel imprudence, indiscretion, injudiciousness, insensibility, unwiseness; irrationality, unreasonableness; impracticality; absurdness, ludicrousness, ridiculousness; bull, bunk, nonsense

con discretion, judiciousness, prudence, sensibility, wiseness; rationality, reasonableness; practicality; soundness, canniness, shrewdness

ant sense, wisdom

foot *n syn* see BOTTOM 3

foot *vb syn* see ADD 2

foot (it) *vb* **1** *syn* see DANCE 1
   2 *syn* see WALK 1

footing *n syn* see BASIS 1
   2 *syn* see STATUS 1
   3 *syn* see BASE 1
   4 *syn* see TERM 5

footlicker *n syn* see SYCOPHANT

footlights *n pl syn* see DRAMA

footprint *n* the mark or impression made by a foot <*footprints* in the sand>
   syn footstep, spoor, step, track, tract, vestige
   rel sign, trace; pug, pugmark

footslog *vb syn* see PLOD 1

footstep *n syn* see FOOTPRINT

footstone *n syn* see TOMBSTONE

foozle *vb syn* see BOTCH

fop *n* a man who is conspicuously fashionable or elegant in dress or appearance <felt contempt for the mincing overdressed *fop*>
   syn Beau Brummel, blood, buck, coxcomb, dandy, dude, exquisite, gallant, lounge lizard, macaroni, petit-maître, popinjay
   rel fashion plate, silk stocking; blade, cavalier, man-about-town, spark, sport, swell; ladies' man, lady-killer, masher
   idiom man of the world

for *prep* **1** *syn* see TO 5
   2 on the side of <I'm *for* Smith all the way>
   syn in favor of, pro, with
   con anti, contra
   ant against
   3 *syn* see AFTER 1

for *conj syn* see BECAUSE

forage *vb syn* see SCOUR 2

forager *n syn* see MARAUDER

foray *vb* **1** *syn* see INVADE 1
   2 *syn* see RAID 1

foray *n syn* see INVASION

forbear *vb* **1** *syn* see FORGO 1
   rel bridle, curb, inhibit, restrain; avoid, escape, evade, shun; cease, desist
   2 *syn* see REFRAIN 1
   rel bear, endure, suffer, tolerate

forbearance *n* **1** *syn* see PATIENCE
   rel restraint, temperance; endurance
   2 the quality of being forbearing <she is known for her *forbearance* with children>
   syn clemency, indulgence, lenience, leniency, mercifulness, tolerance, toleration; *compare* MERCY
   rel longanimity, long-suffering; patience; charity, grace, lenity, mercy

con firmness, inflexibility, rigidity, sternness, strictness; austerity, harshness, inexorability

ant vindictiveness

forbearing *adj* disinclined to be severe or rigorous <*forbearing* toward her husband's weaknesses>
   syn charitable, clement, easy, indulgent, lenient, merciful, tolerant
   rel gentle, mild; longanimous, long-suffering, patient; considerate, thoughtful
   con grim, implacable, merciless, relentless; impatient, nervous, restive; firm, inflexible, rigid, stern, strict; austere, harsh
   ant unrelenting

forbid *vb* to debar one from using, doing, or entering or something from being used, done, or entered <smoking is *forbidden* here> <security regulations *forbid* the entry of unauthorized persons>
   syn ban, enjoin, inhibit, interdict, outlaw, prohibit, taboo
   rel debar, exclude, rule out, shut out; estop, obviate, preclude, prevent; forestall; proscribe, veto; check, curb, halt, restrain, stop; bar, block, hinder, impede, obstruct
   con allow, let, suffer; authorize, license; approve, endorse, sanction; command, order; abide, bear, endure, tolerate
   ant permit; bid

forbiddance *n syn* see TABOO

forbidden *adj* not permitted or allowed <accepting bribes is *forbidden*>
   syn banned, prohibited, verboten
   ant permitted

force *n* **1** *syn* see POWER 4
   rel pressure, strain, stress, tension; headway, impetus, momentum, speed, velocity; vigor
   2 *syn* see POINT 3
   3 forces *pl syn* see TROOP 2
   4 the exercise of power in order to impose one's will on a person or to have one's will with a thing <move a huge boulder by main *force*>
   syn coercion, compulsion, constraint, duress, violence
   rel fierceness, intensity, vehemence; effort, exertions, pains, trouble
   con compliance, submission, yielding; impotence, powerlessness, weakness
   ant forcelessness

force *vb* **1** *syn* see RAPE
   2 to cause a person or thing to yield to pressure <hunger *forced* him to steal the food>
   syn coerce, compel, concuss, constrain, make, oblige, shotgun
   rel drive, impel, move; command, enjoin, order; demand, exact, require; press, pressure, sandbag; cause, occasion
   con blandish, cajole, coax, wheedle; get, induce, persuade, prevail; entice, inveigle, lure, seduce, tempt

force (on or upon) *vb syn* see INFLICT 2

‖**force** *n syn* see WATERFALL

forced *adj* produced or kept up through effort <a *forced* laugh>
   syn farfetched, labored, strained
   rel coerced, compelled, constrained; artificial, factitious; unnatural; inflexible, rigid, stiff, wooden; exhausting, fatiguing

---

syn synonym(s)   *rel* related word(s)
ant antonym(s)   *con* contrasted word(s)
idiom idiomatic equivalent(s)
‖ use limited; if in doubt, see a dictionary

con easy, effortless, smooth; impulsive, instinctive, spontaneous; artless, natural, normal, unaffected, unsophisticated
ant unforced

forceful *adj* **1** *syn* see POWERFUL 2
rel compelling, constraining; manful, virile; cogent, telling
con decrepit, frail, infirm
ant feeble
2 *syn* see EMPHATIC

forcefully *adv* *syn* see HARD 1

forceless *adj* *syn* see WEAK 4

forcible *adj* *syn* see POWERFUL 2
rel intense, vehement, violent; aggressive, assertive, militant, self-assertive; coercive

forcibly *adv* *syn* see HARD 1

forcing bed *n* *syn* see BREEDING GROUND

forcing house *n* *syn* see BREEDING GROUND

fore *adv* *syn* see BEFORE 1

forebear *n* *syn* see ANCESTOR 1

forebode *vb* *syn* see AUGUR 2

foreboding *n* *syn* see APPREHENSION 3
rel augury, foretoken, omen, portent, prognostic; forewarning, warning

forecast *vb* *syn* see FORETELL
rel conjecture, guess, surmise; conclude, gather, infer

forecast *n* *syn* see PREDICTION

forecaster *n* *syn* see PROPHET

foredestine *vb* *syn* see PREDESTINE 2

forefather *n* *syn* see ANCESTOR 1

forefeel *vb* *syn* see FORESEE

foregoer *n* *syn* see FORERUNNER 2

foregoing *adj* *syn* see PRECEDING
ant following

forehandedness *n* *syn* see ECONOMY

forehead *n* the part of the face above the eyes <his broad noble *forehead*>
syn brow, frons, front

foreign *adj* **1** *syn* see EXOTIC 1
ant native
2 *syn* see EXTRINSIC
rel incompatible, incongruous, inconsistent, inconsonant; distasteful, obnoxious, repellent, repugnant; accidental, adventitious
con applicable, apposite, apropos, material, pertinent, relevant; akin, alike, uniform
ant germane
3 *syn* see IRRELEVANT

foreigner *n* *syn* see STRANGER

foreknow *vb* *syn* see FORESEE
rel conclude, gather, infer

foreland *n* *syn* see PROMONTORY

foremost *adj* **1** *syn* see FIRST 1
2 *syn* see FIRST 3

forename *n* *syn* see GIVEN NAME

forenoon *n* *syn* see MORNING 2

forensic *adj* *syn* see ARGUMENTATION

foreordain *vb* **1** *syn* see PREDESTINE 1
2 *syn* see PREDESTINE 2

forerun *vb* **1** *syn* see PRECEDE 2
2 *syn* see ANNOUNCE 2

forerunner *n* **1** one that goes before and in some way announces the coming of another <a coma is often a *forerunner* of death>
syn harbinger, herald, outrider, precursor
rel anticipator; advertiser, announcer; advertisement, announcement, augury, foretoken, omen, portent, presage, prognostic; forewarning, warning; mark, sign, symptom, token; foreshadow

2 one belonging to an early developmental period of something contemporary or fully developed <the water-driven dynamo that was a *forerunner* of present-day giant atomic power plants>
syn ancestor, antecedent, antecessor, foregoer, precursor, predecessor, prototype
rel example, exemplar, model, pattern; pioneer; author, initiator, originator
con consequence, result; effect, event, issue, outgrowth; conclusion, consummation, culmination
ant end product

foresee *vb* to know or expect in advance that something will happen or come into existence or be made manifest <he had not *foreseen* his present problems>
syn anticipate, apprehend, divine, forefeel, foreknow, preknow, previse, prevision, see, visualize
rel forebode, forecast, foretell, predict, presage, prognosticate, prophesy; descry, discern, espy, perceive
idiom look for, look forward to

foreseer *n* *syn* see PROPHET

foreshadow *vb* **1** *syn* see ADUMBRATE 1
2 *syn* see AUGUR 2

foreshow *vb* **1** *syn* see AUGUR 2
2 *syn* see ANNOUNCE 2

foresight *n* *syn* see PRUDENCE
rel clairvoyance, discernment, perception
ant hindsight

forest *n* a heavily wooded area
syn timber, timberland, weald, wood(s), woodland
rel coppice, copse, grove, thicket; wildwood, woodlot
con field, meadow, plain, prairie

forestall *vb* **1** *syn* see PREVENT 2
con court, invite, woo; advance, forward, further, promote
2 *syn* see PREVENT 1

foretell *vb* to tell something before it happens through or as if through special knowledge or occult power <the prophet *foretold* the fall of the city>
syn adumbrate, augur, call, forecast, portend, predict, presage, prognosticate, prophesy, soothsay, vaticinate
rel anticipate, apprehend, divine, foreknow, foresee; announce, declare, proclaim; disclose, divulge, reveal; forewarn, warn; bode, forebode, foreshadow, foreshow, foretoken, promise; prefigure

foreteller *n* *syn* see PROPHET

foretelling *n* *syn* see PREDICTION

forethink *vb* *syn* see PREMEDITATE

forethought *n* *syn* see PRUDENCE 1
rel deliberation, premeditation; gumption, judgment, sense
ant rashness; impetuosity

foretime *n* *syn* see PAST

foretoken *n* something that serves as a sign of future happenings <they felt that her new job was a *foretoken* of good fortune>
syn augury, bodement, boding, omen, portent, presage, prognostic
rel badge, indication, mark, note, sign, symptom, token; forerunner, harbinger,

herald, precursor; forewarning, shadow, warning; intimation, promise; ostent; hint, inkling, suggestion

foretoken *vb syn* see AUGUR 2

forever *adv syn* see EVER 2

forevermore *adv syn* see EVER 2

forewarn *vb syn* see WARN 1

forewarning *n syn* see WARNING

foreword *n syn* see INTRODUCTION

forfeit *n syn* see FINE

forfeit *vb syn* see LOSE 1

forfend *vb syn* see PREVENT 2

forgather *vb syn* see GATHER 6

forge *vb syn* see MAKE 3
rel beat, pound, turn out; copy, imitate

forget *vb* 1 to lose the remembrance of <I soon *forgot* his name>
syn disremember, ‖misremember, unknow
rel misrecollect; blow up, fluff; unlearn
idiom clean forget, draw a blank
con recall, recollect
ant remember
2 *syn* see NEGLECT
con bethink, mind, recall, recollect
ant remember

forgetful *adj* tending to lose or let go from one's mind something once known or learned <she is growing *forgetful*>
syn oblivious, unmindful, unwitting
rel lax, neglectful, negligent, remiss, slack; careless, heedless, thoughtless; absent, absentminded, abstracted; bemused
con alert, alive, awake, aware, cognizant, conscious, sensible; attentive, considerate, thoughtful

forgetfulness *n syn* see OBLIVION

forgivable *adj syn* see VENIAL

forgive *vb syn* see EXCUSE 1
idiom forgive and forget

forgo *vb* to deny oneself something for the sake of an end <he vowed to *forgo* all luxuries until the debt was paid>
syn eschew, forbear, sacrifice
rel abandon, relinquish, surrender, waive; abdicate, renounce, resign; forsake, give up

fork (out) *vb syn* see SPEND 1

forlorn *adj* 1 dejected and saddened especially by reason of being alone <a *forlorn* lost child>
syn lonely, lonesome, lorn
rel abandoned, deserted, desolate, forgotten, forsaken; miserable, wretched; friendless, homeless; defenseless, helpless; depressed, oppressed, weighed down; alone, solitary
2 *syn* see DESPONDENT
rel cynical, pessimistic; fruitless, futile, vain
con hopeful, optimistic, roseate, rose-colored

form *n* 1 outward appearance of something as distinguished from the substance of which it is made <the carefully graded *form* of the curves>
syn cast, configuration, conformation, figure, shape

rel contour, outline, profile, silhouette; anatomy, framework, skeleton, structure; economy, organism, scheme, system
2 conduct regulated by an external control (as custom or a formal protocol of procedure) <observing the *forms* of polite society>
syn ceremonial, ceremony, formality, liturgy, rite, ritual
rel procedure, proceeding, process; custom, habit, practice, usage; canon, law, precept, regulation, rule; method, mode; decorum, etiquette, propriety
3 a fixed or accepted way of doing or sometimes of expressing something <good *form* in swimming>
syn convenance, convention, usage
rel fashion, manner, mode, style, way

form *vb* 1 *syn* see MAKE 3
rel devise; create, invent; turn out; design, plan, plot, project, scheme; establish, found, organize
con demolish, destroy, ruin, wreck
2 *syn* see DEVELOP 4
3 *syn* see CONSTITUTE 1

formal *adj* 1 *syn* see CEREMONIAL
rel methodical, orderly, regular, systematic; decorous, proper, seemly; prim, unbending; distant, reserved
ant informal
2 *syn* see NOMINAL

formality *n* 1 *syn* see FORM 2
rel convenance, convention
ant informality
2 *syn* see RITE 2

formation *n syn* see MAKEUP 1

former *adj* 1 *syn* see PRECEDING
con following, succeeding, supervening
ant latter
2 having been such at some previous time <*former* friends>
syn bygone, erstwhile, late, old, once, onetime, past, quondam, sometime, whilom
con current, present; future, prospective

formerly *adv syn* see BEFORE 2

formidable *adj* 1 *syn* see FEARFUL 3
ant comforting
2 *syn* see HARD 6
ant simple

formless *adj* having no definite or recognizable form <a *formless* fear>
syn amorphous, inchoate, shapeless, unformed, unshaped
rel chaotic, orderless, unordered, unorganized; indistinct, obscure, unclear, vague; indefinite, indeterminate, undefined; crude, raw, rough, rude
con distinct, formed; definite, explicit, express, specific; ordered, organized

formulate *vb* 1 *syn* see WORD
2 *syn* see CONTRIVE 2
3 *syn* see DRAFT 3

‖**fornent** *prep syn* see BESIDE 1

for real *adv syn* see SERIOUSLY 1

forsake *vb syn* see ABANDON 1
rel spurn; leave; abdicate, resign
ant return (to), revert (to)

forsaken *adj syn* see DERELICT 1

forswear *vb* 1 *syn* see ABJURE
2 *syn* see PERJURE

---

fort *n* a structure or place offering resistance to a hostile force <settlers fled to the *fort*>
syn citadel, fastness, fortress, redoubt, stronghold

forte *n* that in which one excels <writing is her strongest *forte*>
syn eminence, long suit, medium, métier, oyster, strong suit
rel ableness, effectiveness, efficiency; ability, competence; bag, thing
idiom cup of tea, dish of tea, strong point
con inadequacy, incapability, incompetence, inefficiency; greenness, rawness

forth *adv* **1** *syn* see AHEAD 2
2 *syn* see ALONG 1

forthcome *vb* *syn* see LOOM 2

forthcoming *adj* being soon to appear or take place <the *forthcoming* holidays>
syn approaching, coming, nearing, oncoming, upcoming
rel future; imminent, impending, pending; anticipated, awaited, expected
con distant, far-off, remote; bygone, former, gone, gone-by, past

forthright *adj* **1** *syn* see STRAIGHTFORWARD 2
con covert, secret, stealthy, surreptitious, underhand; deceitful, mendacious, untruthful
ant furtive
2 *syn* see FRANK

forthwith *adv* **1** *syn* see AWAY 3
2 *syn* see SHORT 1

fortify *vb* **1** *syn* see STRENGTHEN 2
rel arouse, rally, rouse, stir; refresh, renew, restore
con dilute, thin
ant enfeeble
2 *syn* see GIRD 3

fortitude *n* a quality of character combining courage and staying power <she bore up under all her problems with admirable *fortitude*>
syn backbone, grit, guts, intestinal fortitude, ‖moxie, nerve, sand, spunk; *compare* COURAGE
rel courage, mettle, pith, resoluteness, resolution, spirit, stick-to-itiveness, tenacity; boldness, bravery, courageousness, dauntlessness, fearlessness, intrepidity, valiancy, valor, valorousness; endurance, stamina, strength; constancy, determination, perseverance; bottom
con cowardliness, fearfulness, timidity, timorousness; faintheartedness, milksoppiness, weakness; cowardice, yellowness
ant pusillanimity

fortress *n* *syn* see FORT

fortuitous *adj* *syn* see ACCIDENTAL
con activated, actuated, motivated; projected, schemed
ant deliberate

fortuitously *adv* *syn* see INCIDENTALLY 1
ant deliberately

fortuity *n* *syn* see ACCIDENT 1
ant deliberation

fortunate *adj* **1** *syn* see FAVORABLE 5
ant disastrous
2 *syn* see LUCKY
ant unfortunate

fortunately *adv* *syn* see WELL 5

fortunateness *n* *syn* see LUCK 3
ant unfortunateness

fortune *n* **1** *syn* see CHANCE 2
rel destiny, doom, portion
con design, intent, intention
2 *syn* see LUCK 3
ant misfortune
3 *syn* see WEALTH 2
4 a very large amount of money <those furs must have cost a *fortune*>
syn ‖bomb, boodle, bundle, mint, packet, pile, pot, ‖roll, wad
idiom king's ransom, pretty penny, tidy sum

fortuneless *adj* *syn* see POOR 1

forty winks *n pl but sing or pl in constr* *syn* see NAP

forward *adj* **1** *syn* see PRESUMPTUOUS
2 *syn* see WISE 5
ant bashful
3 *syn* see PRECOCIOUS
con regressive, retrograde, retrogressive
ant backward

forward *adv* **1** *syn* see BEFORE 1
2 *syn* see AHEAD 2
ant backward
3 *syn* see ALONG 1

forward *vb* **1** *syn* see ADVANCE 1
rel back, champion, support, uphold
con baffle, circumvent, foil, frustrate, outwit, thwart
ant balk
2 *syn* see SEND 1

fossil *n* *syn* see FOGY

foster *vb* **1** *syn* see NURSE 2
rel back, champion, support, uphold; entertain, harbor, house, lodge, shelter; accommodate, assist, favor, help, oblige
con combat, fight, oppose, resist, withstand; curb, inhibit, restrain; ban, forbid, interdict, prohibit; abuse, disregard, neglect
2 *syn* see ADVANCE 1

foul *adj* **1** *syn* see OFFENSIVE
2 *syn* see DIRTY 1
rel fetid, malodorous, noisome, putrid, stinking; loathsome, offensive, repulsive, revolting
ant fair; undefiled
3 *syn* see OBSCENE 2

foul *vb* **1** *syn* see SOIL 2
rel contaminate, defile, pollute; desecrate, profane
2 *syn* see CONTAMINATE 2

foul play *n* *syn* see MURDER

foul up *vb* *syn* see CONFUSE 5

found *vb* **1** *syn* see BASE
rel support, sustain; erect, raise, rear
2 to set going or to bring into existence <*founded* a new school for graduate studies>
syn constitute, create, establish, institute, organize, set up, start
rel begin, commence, inaugurate, initiate; fashion, form
con close, conclude, end, finish, terminate; arrest, check, halt, stay, stop

foundation *n* **1** *syn* see BASIS 1
2 *syn* see BASIS 3
3 *syn* see BASE 1

foundational *adj syn* see FUNDAMENTAL 1
foundationless *adj syn* see BASELESS
founder *n syn* see FATHER 2
founder *vb syn* see SINK 1
fount *n syn* see SOURCE
fountain *n syn* see SOURCE
fountainhead *n syn* see SOURCE
four *n syn* see QUARTET
fourberie *n syn* see DECEPTION 1
four–flush *vb syn* see DECEIVE
foursome *n syn* see QUARTET
foursquare *adj syn* see SQUARE 1
fourth *n syn* see QUARTER 1
foxiness *n syn* see CUNNING 2
foxy *adj* **1** *syn* see SLY 2
  rel deceitful, dishonest
  con aboveboard, forthright, straightforward
  2 *syn* see BEAUTIFUL
foyer *n syn* see VESTIBULE
fracas *n* **1** *syn* see QUARREL
  2 *syn* see BRAWL 2
fractional *adj syn* see INCOMPLETE 1
fractious *adj* **1** *syn* see UNRULY 1
  ant orderly
  2 *syn* see IRRITABLE
  ant peaceable
fracturable *adj syn* see FRAGILE 1
fracture *n syn* see BREACH 3
fragile *adj* **1** easily broken <a *fragile* dish of the finest porcelain>
  syn breakable, delicate, fracturable, frail, frangible, shatterable, shattery
  rel brittle, crisp, crumbly, crunchy, friable, short
  con infrangible, unbreakable; elastic, flexible, resilient; stout, strong, sturdy, tenacious
  ant tough
  2 *syn* see WEAK 1
  ant durable
fragment *n* **1** *syn* see PARTICLE
  2 *syn* see END 4
fragment *vb syn* see SHATTER 1
fragmentary *adj syn* see INCOMPLETE 1
fragrance *n* a sweet or pleasant odor <the *fragrance* of flowers>
  syn aroma, balm, bouquet, incense, perfume, redolence, scent, spice
  rel odor, smell
  con fetidness, fetor, malodor, noisomeness, rancidness, rankness
  ant stench, stink
fragrant *adj syn* see SWEET 2
  rel delectable, delicious, delightful
  ant fetid
frail *adj* **1** *syn* see WEAK 1
  rel slender, slight, slim, tenuous, thin; petty, puny
  con hale, healthy, sound
  ant robust
  2 *syn* see FRAGILE 1
  con solid, substantial
frailty *n syn* see FAULT 2
frame *vb* **1** *syn* see CONTRIVE 2
  2 *syn* see DRAFT 3

3 *syn* see MAKE 3
framework *n syn* see STRUCTURE 3
franchise *n syn* see SUFFRAGE
franchise *vb syn* see ENFRANCHISE
frangible *adj syn* see FRAGILE 1
frank *adj* marked by free, forthright, and sincere expression <a *frank* answer>
  syn candid, direct, forthright, man-to-man, open, openhearted, plain, plainspoken, single, single-eyed, single-hearted, single= minded, straightforward, unconcealed, undisguised, undissembled, undissembling, unmannered, unreserved, unvarnished; *compare* COMMUNICATIVE, STRAIGHT- FORWARD 2
  rel ingenuous, naive, natural, simple, unsophisticated; bluff, blunt; heart-to-heart, sincere; honest, scrupulous, upright; dispassionate, fair, impartial, just, unbiased; barefaced, brazen, outspoken, uninhibited
  con reserved, reticent, secretive, silent, taciturn, uncommunicative; covert, furtive, secret, sneaking, underhand; deceitful, deceptive, dishonest, evasive, false, lying, mendacious, tricky, untruthful; insincere
  ant reticent
frank *n syn* see FRANKFURTER
frankfurter *n* a seasoned beef or beef and pork sausage <baked beans served with the obligatory *frankfurters*>
  syn dog, frank, hot dog, wiener, wienerwurst, ‖wienie
frantic *adj syn* see FURIOUS 2
frantically *adv syn* see HARD 2
fraternity *n syn* see ASSOCIATION 2
fraud *n* **1** *syn* see DECEPTION 1
  2 *syn* see IMPOSTURE
  rel bamboozlement, bamboozling, dupery, duping, hoodwinking
  3 *syn* see IMPOSTOR
fray *n* **1** *syn* see BRAWL 2
  rel contention, discord, dissension, strife
  2 *syn* see CLASH 2
frayed *adj syn* see RAGGED
frazzle *vb syn* see EXHAUST 4
frazzled *adj syn* see RAGGED
freak *n* **1** *syn* see CAPRICE
  2 one that is physically abnormal <pitiful *freaks* displayed in sideshows>
  syn abortion, lusus, miscreation, monster, monstrosity
  rel aberration, chimera, malconformation, malformation, misshape, mosaic, mutation, sport; abnormality, anomaly, curiosity, oddity; rara avis, rarity; androgyne, hermaphrodite
  idiom freak of nature
  3 *syn* see ENTHUSIAST
freakish *adj syn* see ARBITRARY 1
freckle *vb syn* see SPECKLE 1
free *adj* **1** not subject to the rule or control of another <a *free* country>
  syn autarchic, autarkic, autonomous, independent, separate, sovereign
  rel free-born, unenslaved; delivered, emancipated, enfranchised, freed, liberated, released; democratic, self-directing, self-governing, self-ruling; sui juris; individualistic, unregimented
  con coerced, compelled, constrained, forced, obliged; dependent, restricted, sub-

---

syn synonym(s)   *rel* related word(s)
ant antonym(s)   *con* contrasted word(s)
idiom idiomatic equivalent(s)
‖ use limited; if in doubt, see a dictionary

ject; inferior, subordinate, subservient;
captive, enslaved, enthralled, subjugated
ant bond

2 not bound, confined, or detained by force
<the prisoner was now *free*>
syn loose, unconfined, unrestrained
rel unbound, unchained, unfettered, un-
shackled, untied; clear, loose, scot-free;
emancipated, freed, liberated; independent
idiom at liberty, free as a bird, free as air,
free to come and go
con confined, restrained; impounded, imprisoned, incarcerated, interned, jailed;
bound, chained, fettered, shackled, tied

3 *syn* see LIBERAL 1
ant close

4 *syn* see OUTSPOKEN

5 not costing or charging anything <a *free*
public school>
syn chargeless, complimentary, costless,
gratis, gratuitous
rel unpaid, uncompensated, unremunerated
idiom for free, for love, for nothing, on the
cuff, on the house
con charged, paid; costly, dear, expensive,
high, high priced

6 not having the affections fixed on a particular object <she was happy to be *free* and in
no hurry to fall in love again>
syn fancy-free, heart-whole

free *vb* to relieve from constraint or restraint
<*free* an oppressed people>
syn discharge, disenthrall, disimprison,
emancipate, liberate, loose, loosen, manumit, redeem, release, ‖spring, unbind, unchain, unshackle
rel clear, detach, disencumber, disengage,
disentangle, extricate; deliver, ransom, redeem, rescue; affranchise, enfranchise
idiom cut loose
con fetter, hamper, hog-tie, manacle,
shackle, trammel; immure, imprison, incarcerate, intern, jail; circumscribe, confine,
limit, restrict; curb, inhibit, restrain; enslave,
enthrall, subjugate

freebooter *n* **1** *syn* see MARAUDER
2 *syn* see PIRATE

freedom *n* the power or condition of acting
without compulsion <*freedom* of the press>
syn liberty, license
rel exemption, immunity; prerogative,
privilege, right; compass, latitude, scope,
sweep
con coercion, compulsion, constraint; restraint
ant necessity

free-for-all *n* *syn* see BRAWL 2
free hand *n* *syn* see CARTE BLANCHE
freehanded *adj* *syn* see LIBERAL 1
freeloader *n* *syn* see PARASITE
freely *adv* EASILY 1, effortlessly, facilely,
lightly, readily, smoothly, well
free-minded *adj* *syn* see HAPPY-GO=
LUCKY
free-spoken *adj* *syn* see OUTSPOKEN
freezer *n* *syn* see JAIL
freezing *adj* *syn* see COLD 1
ant scorching
freight *n* *syn* see LOAD 1
frenetic *adj* *syn* see FURIOUS 2

frenzied *adj* *syn* see FURIOUS 2
frenziedly *adv* *syn* see HARD 2
frenzy *n* *syn* see DELIRIUM
frenzy *vb* *syn* see MADDEN 1
frequent *adj* *syn* see COMMON 4
ant infrequent, rare
frequent *vb* to go to or to be in often <he *frequents* the bar down the street>
syn affect, hang around, hang out, haunt,
resort
rel attend, go (to), visit; infest, overrun
con avoid, miss, sidestep
ant shun
frequenter *n* *syn* see HABITUÉ 1
frequently *adv* **1** *syn* see OFTEN
ant infrequently
2 *syn* see USUALLY 2
fresh *adj* **1** *syn* see NEW 1
rel gleaming, glistening, sparkling; striking,
vital, vivid; virginal, youthful; crude, green,
raw, uncouth; artless, naive, natural, unsophisticated
con hackneyed, shopworn, stereotyped,
threadbare, trite
ant stale
2 *syn* see ADDITIONAL
3 *syn* see INEXPERIENCED
4 *syn* see WISE 5
freshman *n* *syn* see NOVICE
freshness *n* *syn* see INEXPERIENCE
fret *vb* **1** *syn* see WORRY 3
rel chafe, fume; brood, mope
idiom eat one's heart out
2 *syn* see ANNOY 1
3 *syn* see CHAFE 3
4 *syn* see RIPPLE
fretful *adj* **1** *syn* see IRRITABLE
rel captious, carping, caviling, critical,
faultfinding; contrary, perverse
con forbearing, long-suffering, patient,
resigned; subdued, submissive, tame
2 *syn* see IMPATIENT 1
friable *adj* *syn* see SHORT 6
fribble *adj* *syn* see GIDDY 1
fribbling *adj* *syn* see GIDDY 1
fried *adj* *syn* see INTOXICATED 1
friend *n* a person with whom one is on good
and, usually, familiar terms <he is one of my
closest *friends*>
syn acquaintance, amigo, cater-cousin,
confidant, familiar, intimate, mate; *compare*
ASSOCIATE 3
rel alter ego, best friend, bosom friend; ally,
colleague, partner; nodding acquaintance
con enemy; adversary, antagonist, opponent; competitor, rival
ant foe
friendliness *n* *syn* see GOODWILL 1
rel affability, amiability, congeniality, cordiality, neighborliness, sociability
ant unfriendliness
friendly *adj* **1** *syn* see AMICABLE 1
rel close, familiar, intimate; affectionate,
devoted, loving
ant unfriendly; belligerent
2 *syn* see HARMONIOUS 3
3 *syn* see SYMPATHETIC 2
ant unfriendly
friendship *n* *syn* see GOODWILL 1

rel affinity, attraction; empathy; accord, concord, consonance, harmony; alliance, coalition, federation, fusion, league
con antagonism, antipathy, hostility, rancor; hate
ant animosity

fright *n* **1** *syn* see FEAR 1
  2 *syn* see EYESORE

fright *vb* *syn* see FRIGHTEN

frighten *vb* to strike or to fill with fear or dread <the puppy was *frightened* by the unfamiliar noises>
  syn affright, alarm, awe, fright, scare, ‖spook, startle, terrify, terrorize
  rel appall, astound, daunt, disconcert, dismay, faze, horrify, shock; demoralize, unman, unnerve; browbeat, bulldoze, cow, intimidate; agitate, discompose, disquiet, perturb, upset
  idiom curdle the blood, curl the hair, freeze the blood, frighten one out of one's wits, give one a scare, give one a turn, make one's blood run cold, make one's flesh creep, make one's hair stand on end, make one's teeth chatter, make one tremble, put one's heart in one's mouth, scare hell out of, scare one spitless, scare one stiff, scare the life out of, scare the pants off of, scare to death, strike terror into, take one's breath away
  con embolden, encourage, hearten, reassure

frightened *adj* *syn* see AFRAID 1
  idiom in a fright
  ant unfrightened

frightful *adj* *syn* see FEARFUL 3

frigid *adj* **1** *syn* see COLD 1
  2 *syn* see COLD 2
  3 free from or deficient in passion <claimed his wife was a *frigid* woman>
  syn cold, inhibited, passionless, undersexed, unresponsive
  idiom as cold as an iceberg
  con affectionate, demanding, loving
  ant ardent; amorous

frill *n* *syn* see LUXURY

fringe *n* *syn* see BORDER 1

fringe *n* *syn* see BORDER 1

frippery *n* *syn* see FINERY

frisk *vb* **1** *syn* see GAMBOL
  2 *syn* see SEARCH 2

frisky *adj* *syn* see PLAYFUL 1

fritter *vb* *syn* see WASTE 2

frivol away *vb* *syn* see WASTE 2

frivolity *n* *syn* see LIGHTNESS
  rel coquetting, dallying, flirting, toying, trifling; fun, game, jest, play, sport
  ant seriousness; staidness

frivolous *adj* *syn* see GIDDY 1
  rel shallow, superficial, unprofound; gay, light, playful
  ant serious

‖**frogskin** *n* *syn* see DOLLAR

frolic *vb* **1** *syn* see REVEL 1
  2 *syn* see GAMBOL

frolic *n* *syn* see PRANK

frolicsome *adj* **1** *syn* see ANTIC 2
  2 *syn* see PLAYFUL 1

from *prep* **1** *syn* see AFTER 1
  2 in the face of <protect them *from* exploitation>
  syn against

frondeur *n* *syn* see REBEL

frons *n* *syn* see FOREHEAD

front *n* **1** *syn* see FOREHEAD
  2 *syn* see MASK 2
  3 a person, group, or thing used to mask the identity or true character of a controlling agent <the export company was a *front* for illegal activities>
  syn blind
  rel disguise, facade, mask

front *vb* **1** *syn* see FACE 1
  2 *syn* see FACE 3
  3 *syn* see MEET 6
  4 *syn* see ACCOST 2

frontier *n* **1** a region between two countries <lived on the *frontier* between Mexico and the U.S.>
  syn border, borderland, march, marchland
  2 a rural region that forms the margin of settled or developed territory <settlers found living on the *frontier* was a hard life>
  syn backcountry, backland, ‖backveld, backwash, backwater, backwoods, ‖boondocks, ‖boonies, bush, hinterland, ‖outback, sticks, up-country
  idiom the back of beyond

frontier *adj* *syn* see BACK 1

fronting *prep* *syn* see AGAINST 1

front–rank *adj* *syn* see EXCELLENT

frore *adj* *syn* see COLD 1

frosty *adj* *syn* see COLD 1

froth *n* *syn* see FOAM
  rel flippancy, frivolity, levity, lightness

froward *adj* *syn* see CONTRARY 3

frown *vb* **1** to put on a dark or malignant countenance or aspect <he *frowned* at the naughty child>
  syn gloom, glower, lower, scowl
  rel glare; grimace; pout, sulk
  idiom look black, look daggers
  con grin, laugh
  ant smile
  2 *syn* see DISAPPROVE 1

frowsy *adj* **1** *syn* see SLATTERNLY
  rel lax, neglectful, negligent, remiss, slack
  ant trim; smart
  2 *syn* see MALODOROUS 1

frugal *adj* *syn* see SPARING
  rel careful, meticulous; discreet, prudent; conserving, preserving; cheeseparing, penny-pinching, scrimping, stinting
  ant wasteful

frugality *n* *syn* see ECONOMY

‖**fruit** *n* *syn* see HOMOSEXUAL

fruitage *n* *syn* see HARVEST 2

fruitful *adj* *syn* see FERTILE
  rel breeding, propagating, reproducing; abounding
  con abortive, bootless, futile, vain
  ant unfruitful; fruitless

fruitfulness *n* *syn* see FERTILITY

fruition *n* *syn* see PLEASURE 2
  rel actualization, materialization, realization; accomplishment, fulfillment; achievement, attainment

fruitless *adj syn* see FUTILE
  rel barren, infertile, sterile, unfruitful; foiled, frustrated, thwarted; infructuous, unprofitable
  con fecund, fertile, prolific
  ant fruitful

||**fruity** *adj syn* see INSANE 1
frumpish *adj syn* see TACKY 2
frumpy *adj syn* see TACKY 2
frustrate *vb* **1** to come between a person and his aim or desire or to defeat another's plan <my efforts are *frustrated* at every turn>
  syn baffle, balk, beat, bilk, buffalo, circumvent, dash, disappoint, foil, ruin, thwart; *compare* OUTWIT
  rel annul, cancel, counteract, negative, neutralize, nullify; anticipate, forestall; conquer, defeat, lick, overcome; forbid, inhibit, prohibit; obviate, preclude, prevent; bar, block, hinder, impede, obstruct; arrest, check, halt, interrupt
  idiom cut the ground from under one, dash one's hope, defeat expectation, throw a monkey wrench into the works, upset one's applecart
  con accomplish, achieve, bring about, effect, perform; advance, forward, further, promote; abet, foment, incite, instigate
  ant fulfill
  2 *syn* see NEUTRALIZE
frying pan *n* a pan with a handle used for frying food <some still prefer the sturdy cast-iron *frying pan*>
  syn skillet, spider
fuddle *vb syn* see CONFUSE 2
  ant clarify, clear
fuddler *n syn* see DRUNKARD
fuddy–duddy *n* **1** *syn* see FOGY
  2 *syn* see STUFFED SHIRT
  3 *syn* see FUSSBUDGET
fudge *vb syn* see EMBROIDER
fudge *n syn* see NONSENSE 2
fugacious *adj syn* see TRANSIENT
fugitive *adj syn* see TRANSIENT
fugitive *n syn* see REFUGEE
fulfill *vb* **1** to do what is required by the terms of so as to make effective <found themselves unable to *fulfill* their contract>
  syn complete, execute, implement, perform; *compare* EFFECT 2
  rel effect, effectuate; discharge
  2 *syn* see SATISFY 5
fulgent *adj syn* see BRIGHT 1
full *adj* **1** containing as much as is possible <the hamper is *full*>
  syn awash, big, block and block, brimful, brimming, bung-full, chockablock, chock=full, cram-full, crammed, crowded, jam-full, jammed, jam-packed, loaded, packed, ||packed out, replete, stuffed, ||trig
  rel abounding, teeming
  idiom full to bursting (*or* overflowing), ready to burst
  con blank, vacant, void; bare, barren
  ant empty
  2 *syn* see CIRCUMSTANTIAL
  ant incomplete
  3 *syn* see WHOLE 2
  con denuded, dismantled, divested, stripped
  4 *syn* see SATIATED

full–blooded *adj* **1** *syn* see PUREBRED
  2 *syn* see RUDDY
full–blown *adj* **1** *syn* see MATURE 1
  2 *syn* see TOTAL 5
full–bodied *adj syn* see STRONG 3
full–bosomed *adj syn* see BUXOM
full dress *n syn* see FINERY
full–dress *adj syn* see EXHAUSTIVE
full–fledged *adj syn* see MATURE 1
full–grown *adj syn* see MATURE 1
full–mouthed *adj syn* see LOUD 1
fullness *n syn* see BREADTH 2
full–out *adj syn* see TOTAL 5
full–scale *adj syn* see TOTAL 5
full tilt *adv syn* see FAST 2
fully *adv* **1** *syn* see DOWN 2
  2 *syn* see WELL 3
fulsome *adj* too obviously extravagant or ingratiating to be accepted as genuine or sincere <offering sickeningly *fulsome* praise>
  syn oily, oleaginous, slick, smarmy, soapy, unctuous, unctuous
  rel canting, holier-than-thou, hypocritical, pecksniffian, pharisaical, sanctimonious; bland, glib, honey-mouthed, honey=tongued, ingratiating, mealy-mouthed, oily-tongued, smooth, smooth-tongued, suave; buttery, flattering, wheedling; excessive, extravagant, exuberant, lavish, profuse; cloying, satiating, sating; bombastic, grandiloquent, magniloquent
  con earnest, genuine, heartfelt, hearty, sincere, true, truthful, unfeigned, wholehearted, whole-souled
fumble *vb* **1** *syn* see GROPE
  2 *syn* see BOTCH
  rel flounder, stumble
  3 *syn* see MUMBLE
fume *n syn* see SNIT
fume *vb syn* see ANGER 2
fun *vb syn* see BANTER
fun *n* **1** action or speech intended to amuse or arouse laughter <you know he only said it in *fun*>
  syn game, jest, joke, play, sport
  rel amusement, diversion, entertainment, recreation; blitheness, jocundity, joviality, merriment; glee, hilarity, jollity, mirth; mischief, teasing
  con soberness, thoughtfulness
  ant earnestness, seriousness
  2 *syn* see PLAY 1
function *n* **1** the acts or operations expected of a person or thing <fulfill one's *function* as a mother>
  syn business, duty, office, province, role
  rel affair, concern; job, task, work
  2 *syn* see USE 4
  3 *syn* see POWER 3
  rel action, behavior, operation
function *vb* **1** *syn* see ACT 4
  2 *syn* see ACT 5
  3 to operate in the proper or expected manner <finally succeeded in getting the motor to *function*>
  syn act, go, run, work
  rel do, operate, perform
functional *adj syn* see PRACTICAL 2
functioning *adj syn* see ACTIVE 1

fund *n syn* see SUPPLY
fund *vb syn* see ENDOW 2
fundament *n syn* see BUTTOCKS
fundamental *adj* **1** forming or affecting the groundwork, roots, or lowest part of something <the *fundamental* rules of poetry>
syn basal, basic, bottom, foundational, meat-and-potatoes, primary, radical, underlying
rel primal, prime, primordial; elemental, elementary
con incidental
2 *syn* see ELEMENTAL 1
3 *syn* see ESSENTIAL 2
rel indispensable, necessary, needful, requisite; dominant, paramount
fundamental *n* **1** *syn* see PRINCIPLE 1
rel component, constituent, element, factor
2 *syn* see ESSENTIAL 1
3 *usu* **fundamentals** *pl syn* see ALPHABET 2
fundamentalist *n syn* see DIEHARD 1
fundamentally *adv syn* see ESSENTIALLY 1
ant superficially
funeral director *n syn* see MORTICIAN
funereal *adj syn* see GLOOMY 3
rel grave, solemn
con animated, gay, lively, sprightly, vivacious; blithe, jocund, jolly, jovial, merry
ant festive
fungible *adj syn* see INTERCHANGEABLE
funk *vb syn* see SMELL 3
funk *n syn* see COWARD
funker *n syn* see COWARD
funky *adj syn* see MALODOROUS 1
funnel *vb syn* see CONDUCT 4
funniness *n syn* see HUMOR 4
funny *adj syn* see LAUGHABLE
rel antic, bizarre, fantastic, grotesque
idiom too funny for words
con doleful, dolorous, lugubrious, melancholy, plaintive
ant unfunny
‖**funny farm** *n syn* see ASYLUM 3
funnyman *n syn* see HUMORIST 2
fur *n* **1** *syn* see HIDE
2 *syn* see DOWN
furbish *vb syn* see POLISH 1
furious *adj* **1** *syn* see WILD 6
2 marked by uncontrollable excitement often under the stress of a powerful emotion <in a state of *furious* activity>
syn corybantic, delirious, frantic, frenetic, frenzied, mad, rabid, wild
rel excited, provoked, stimulated; enthusiastic, fanatic; desperate, feverish, hasty, impetuous; fierce, intense, vehement, violent; excessive, extravagant, extreme, inordinate; enraged, incensed, infuriated, maddened; hysterical, irrational, unreasonable; bewildered, distracted, upset; crazed, demented, insane, mad, maniac
con calm, composed, peaceful, placid, quiet, serene, subdued, tranquil; apathetic, impassive, imperturbable, inexcitable
3 *syn* see INTENSE 1

furiously *adv syn* see HARD 2
furl *vb syn* see ROLL 3
furnish *vb* **1** to supply one with what is needed (as for daily living or a particular activity) <*furnished* him the papers for his application>
syn accouter, appoint, arm, equip, fit out, gear, outfit, rig, turn out
rel dower, endow, endue; apparel, array, clothe; mount; give, provide, supply
con denude, dismantle, divest, strip; despoil, spoliate; relieve (of), take away
2 *syn* see GIVE 3
furor *n syn* see DELIRIUM
furore *n* **1** *syn* see STIR 1
2 *syn* see FASHION 3
3 *syn* see COMMOTION 3
furrow *n syn* see WRINKLE
rel channel, groove, rut
further *adv* **1** *syn* see BEYOND 1
2 *syn* see AGAIN 4
further *adj syn* see ADDITIONAL
further *vb syn* see ADVANCE 1
rel engender, generate, propagate
con bar, block, impede, obstruct; forestall, prevent
ant hinder; retard
furthermore *adv syn* see ALSO 2
furthermost *adj syn* see EXTREME 5
furthest *adj syn* see EXTREME 5
furtive *adj* **1** *syn* see SECRET 1
rel artful, crafty, cunning, foxy, guileful, insidious, scheming, shifty, sly, sneaky, tricky, wily; calculating, cautious, circumspect; cloaked, disguised, masked
con brash, impudent, presumptuous
ant forthright; barefaced, brazen
2 *syn* see STEALTHY 1
ant open
furtively *adv syn* see SECRETLY
ant openly
furuncle *n syn* see ABSCESS
fury *n syn* see ANGER
rel passion; furor; acerbity, acrimony, asperity
fuse *vb* **1** *syn* see LIQUEFY
2 *syn* see MIX 1
rel compact, consolidate, unify
fusillade *n syn* see BARRAGE
fusion *n syn* see MIXTURE
fuss *n* **1** *syn* see STIR 1
rel fluster, perturbation; bother, flap, stew; racket, rumpus; haste, hurry, speed
2 *syn* see COMMOTION 3
3 *syn* see QUARREL
fuss *vb* **1** *syn* see WORRY 3
idiom fret and fume
2 *syn* see COMPLAIN
3 *syn* see GRIPE
4 *syn* see NAG
fussbudget *n* one who becomes upset over trifles <he is the biggest *fussbudget* I know, always going into a tizzy over nothing>
syn fuddy-duddy, fusser, fusspot, granny, old lady, old maid
rel perfectionist, precisionist, stickler
fusser *n syn* see FUSSBUDGET
fusspot *n syn* see FUSSBUDGET
fussy *adj* **1** *syn* see BUSTLING
2 *syn* see CAREFUL 2

---

syn synonym(s)   *rel* related word(s)
ant antonym(s)   *con* contrasted word(s)
idiom idiomatic equivalent(s)
‖ use limited; if in doubt, see a dictionary

3 syn see NICE 1
   rel fretful, irritable, querulous

fustian *n syn* see BOMBAST

fustian *adj syn* see FECKLESS 1

fusty *adj* **1 syn** see MALODOROUS 1
   rel close, moldy; dirty, filthy, squalid; disheveled, slipshod, sloppy, slovenly, unkempt
   2 syn see OLD-FASHIONED

futile *adj* barren of results <efforts to convince him were *futile*>
   syn abortive, bootless, fruitless, ineffective, ineffectual, unavailable, unavailing, unprevailing, unproductive, useless, vain
   rel empty, hollow, idle, nugatory, otiose; inadequate, inefficacious, inefficient, insufficient; unsatisfactory, unsuccessful
   idiom in vain, no dice, of no avail, to no effect
   con effectual, efficacious, fruitful; advantageous, beneficial, profitable
   ant effective

future *n* time that is to come <you must try to do better in the *future*>
   syn aftertime, afterward, by-and-by, hereafter, offing, to-be; *compare* PRESENT
   idiom time to come
   ant past

fuzz *n* **1 syn** see DOWN
   ‖**2 syn** see POLICEMAN

fuzzy *adj syn* see FAINT 2

G

gab *vb syn* see CHAT 1

gab *n syn* see CHATTER

gabber *n syn* see CHATTERBOX

gabble *vb* **1 syn** see GIBBER
   2 syn see BABBLE 2
   3 syn see CHAT 1

gabble *n syn* see CHATTER

gabby *adj syn* see TALKATIVE

gad *vb syn* see WANDER 1

gadget *n* **1** a usually small and often novel mechanical or electronic device or contrivance <a new kitchen *gadget* for separating egg whites>
   syn concern, gimmick, gizmo, jigger, widget; *compare* DEVICE 2, DOODAD, WHAT=
DO-YOU-CALL-IT
   rel apparatus, appliance, contraption, tool, utensil
   2 syn see DOODAD

gaffe *n syn* see FAUX PAS

gaffer *n* a man of advanced years <doddering *gaffers* on the park benches>
   syn graybeard, patriarch; *compare* BELDAM 1, OLDSTER
   rel duffer, geezer, grandfather, old boy, veteran

gag *vb* **1 syn** see RETCH
   2 syn see DEMUR

gag *n syn* see JOKE 1
   rel ruse, trick, wile

gaiety *n* **1 syn** see MERRYMAKING
   2 syn see MIRTH
   rel cheerfulness, gladness, happiness; geniality, pleasantness, winsomeness; animation, conviviality, entertainment, exhilaration, liveliness, merrymaking, radiance, spiritedness, vivacity
   con blues, cheerlessness, dismalness, dreariness, gloom, grief, infelicity, joylessness, misery, moodiness, moroseness, pensiveness, solemnity, somberness, sorrow, sullenness, uncheerfulness, wistfulness, woe

gain *n syn* see PROFIT
   rel cut, rake-off, share, take, winnings; ice
   ant loss

gain *vb* **1** to arrive at a goal, point, or end <*gained* success in the theater>
   syn accomplish, achieve, attain, rack up, reach, realize, score, win
   rel complete, consummate, fulfill, perfect, produce; succeed
   con falter, flop, flounder, flunk, lose
   2 syn see IMPROVE 3
   rel invigorate, renew, strengthen; cure, heal, remedy
   3 syn see EARN 1
   4 syn see GET 1
   ant lose
   5 syn see CLEAR 6
   ant lose

gainful *adj syn* see ADVANTAGEOUS 1
   rel fat, fruitful, generous, lush, productive, rich; satisfying, substantial

gainsay *vb syn* see DENY 4
   rel combat, fight, oppose, resist, withstand
   ant admit

gainsaying *n syn* see DENIAL 2
   ant admission; admitting

gait *n syn* see SPEED 2

gal *n* **1 syn** see GIRL 1
   2 syn see GIRL FRIEND 1
   3 syn see WOMAN 1

gall *n syn* see EFFRONTERY
   rel arrogance, conceit, haughtiness, loftiness, lordliness, overbearance, pomposity, pride, priggishness, self-importance, smugness
   con bashfulness, humbleness, humility, lowliness, modesty, shyness
   ant meekness

gall *vb* **1 syn** see ABRADE 1
   rel bark, burn, fray, frazzle, grate, graze, scrape, scratch, scuff, skin
   2 syn see CHAFE 3
   rel distress, pain; cut, score, wound
   3 syn see ANNOY 1

4 syn see IRRITATE
rel chide, disturb, harass, harry, torment, worry; bedevil, bother, needle, trouble
gallant n **1** syn see FOP
2 an individual who is amorously attracted to the opposite sex <his fiancee accused him of being a trifling *gallant*>
syn amorist, Casanova, Don Juan, lothario, paramour, Romeo
rel dirty old man, lecher, libertine, rake, satyr; admirer, adorer, beau, date, escort, lover, sparker, suitor, swain, wooer
idiom gay blade
gallant adj syn see COURTLY
rel suave, urbane; attentive, considerate, thoughtful
con heedless, inattentive, indifferent, thoughtless, unconcerned
ant ungallant
2 syn see BRAVE 1
ant dastardly
gallantry n **1** syn see COURTESY 1
rel deference, duty, homage, honor; reverence, suavity, urbanity; address, poise, savoir faire, tact
con boorishness, churlishness, clownishness, loutishness; discourteousness
ant discourtesy
2 syn see HEROISM
rel bravery, dauntlessness; mettle, resolution, spirit
ant dastardliness
gallery n syn see MUSEUM
galley slave n syn see SLAVE 2
gallimaufry n syn see MISCELLANY 1
galling adj syn see BITTER 2
gallivant vb syn see WANDER 1
gallows n pl syn see SUSPENDERS
‖**galluptious** adj syn see MARVELOUS 2
‖**galluses** n pl syn see SUSPENDERS
galoot n syn see MAN 3
galumph vb syn see LUMBER
galvanize vb syn see PROVOKE 4
rel activate, energize, vitalize
gambit n syn see TRICK 1
rel design, plan, plot
gamble vb **1** to engage in a game of chance for something of value <swore he would never *gamble* for high stakes again>
syn bet, game, lay, play, put (on), set, stake, wager
rel chance, hazard, lot, risk, speculate, venture
idiom buck the odds, take a flyer (on), try one's luck
2 to take a chance on something <*gambled* on the train being late>
syn chance, hazard, risk, venture; compare VENTURE 1
rel brave, challenge, dare, defy, face; endanger, imperil, jeopardize
idiom go it blind, take a chance (or one's chances), tempt fortune, trust to luck
gambol vb to leap or tumble about playfully <young lambs *gamboling* in the meadow>

syn caper, cavort, frisk, frolic, rollick, romp
rel lark, revel, roister; bound, leap, spring
idiom kick up one's heels, let off steam
game n **1** syn see FUN 1
con business, duty, labor, study, toil
2 games pl syn see ATHLETICS
3 animals under pursuit <hunting big *game* is a risky and expensive sport>
syn chase, prey, quarry
rel kill, ravin, victim
game vb syn see GAMBLE 1
game adj syn see BRAVE 1
game plan n syn see PLAN 1
gamesome adj syn see PLAYFUL 1
gamin n syn see URCHIN
gamine n syn see TOMBOY
gammer n syn see BELDAM 1
gamut n syn see RANGE 5
gamy adj syn see MALODOROUS 1
‖**gander** n syn see PEEP
gangling adj being tall, thin, and usually loose-jointed <a *gangling* high-school boy>
syn gangly, lanky, rangy, spindling, spindly
rel bony, gaunt, lank, lean, scrawny, skinny, spare, tall, thin
con low, low-set, low-statured, short, squat, stocky, sturdy, thickset
gangly adj syn see GANGLING
‖**gangrel** n syn see VAGABOND
gap n **1** an open space in a barrier <the sheep got through a *gap* in the fence>
syn breach, break, discontinuity, hole, opening
rel fracture, rupture; chink, cleavage, cleft, crack, crevice, fissure, slit, slot; division, interspace, interval, separation; aperture, cranny, orifice
2 syn see RAVINE
3 a period of discontinuity <a *gap* of an hour between speakers>
syn breach, break, hiatus, interim, interruption, interval, lacuna; compare PAUSE
rel caesura, intermission, lull, pause, respite, rest
gape vb **1** syn see GAZE 1
2 syn see LOOK 7
3 syn see YAWN
gaping adj syn see CAVERNOUS 1
garb vb syn see CLOTHE
garbage n syn see REFUSE
rel dregs, rubble; filth, sewage, slop
garble vb syn see MISREPRESENT
rel becloud, conceal, hide, obfuscate, obscure
garden house n syn see SUMMERHOUSE
gargantuan adj syn see HUGE
ant lilliputian
garish adj syn see GAUDY
rel overdone, overwrought
con dark, dim, dreary, dull, dusky, murky; quiet, unpretentious
ant somber
garland n **1** syn see WREATH
2 syn see ANTHOLOGY
garment vb syn see CLOTHE
garner vb **1** syn see REAP
2 syn see GLEAN
3 syn see ACCUMULATE
rel gather, glean, harvest, reap; hoard, store
con disseminate, spread

---

syn synonym(s)   rel related word(s)
ant antonym(s)   con contrasted word(s)
idiom idiomatic equivalent(s)
‖ use limited; if in doubt, see a dictionary

garnish vb syn see ADORN
garrulous adj syn see TALKATIVE
  rel blabbing, prattling, prolix, verbose, windy, wordy
  con concise; terse; blunt, brusque, curt
  ant taciturn
‖**gas** n syn see NONSENSE 2
‖**gas** vb syn see CHAT 1
‖**gasbag** n syn see BRAGGART
gasconade vb syn see BOAST
gash vb syn see CUT 1
  rel carve, split; injure, wound; furrow, mark, notch; lance, nip
gasp vb syn see PANT 1
‖**gasper** n syn see CIGARETTE
gastronome n syn see EPICURE
  rel aesthete, connoisseur, dilettante
gastronomer n syn see EPICURE
gastronomist n syn see EPICURE
gate n syn see FAUCET
gather vb 1 syn see GROUP 1
  rel choose, cull, pick, select; accumulate, amass
  idiom separate the wheat from the chaff (or the sheep from the goats)
  con dispel, disperse, dissipate
  ant scatter
  2 syn see REAP
  rel cull, pick, pluck; heap, mass, pile, stack
  3 syn see GLEAN
  4 syn see INFER
  rel catch, fathom, follow, grasp, take in
  idiom put two and two together
  5 syn see UNDERSTAND 3
  6 to bring or come together <a crowd *gathered* to watch the fight>
  syn assemble, cluster, congregate, congress, forgather, muster, raise, rendezvous; *compare* GROUP 1
  rel aggregate, troop; affiliate, ally, associate, league; encounter, meet
  con break up, disband, disperse, part, separate; disintegrate, disorganize, dissolve
  ant scatter
  7 syn see LOOM 2
gathering n 1 syn see CONCOURSE
  2 a number of individuals come or brought together <a *gathering* in the town park>
  syn aggregation, assemblage, assembly, collection, company, congeries, congregation, crowd, group, muster, ruck; *compare* GROUP 1
  rel bunch, crew, crush, flock, gang, horde, mass, press, rout, swarm, turnout
  3 syn see HARVEST 1
gauche adj syn see AWKWARD 2
  rel crude, green, unpolished
  con bland, smooth, suave, urbane
  ant adroit
gaudy adj cheaply or vulgarly showy <*gaudy* sideshow posters>
  syn blatant, brazen, chintzy, flashy, garish, glaring, loud, meretricious, tawdry, tinsel
  rel obtrusive, ostentatious, pretentious, showy; tasteless; coarse, crude, gross, vulgar; brummagem, fake, phony, sham
  con restrained, tasteful, unobtrusive; factual, illuminating, informative
  ant quiet
gauge n syn see STANDARD 3

gauge vb syn see MEASURE 2
gaum n syn see OAF 2
gaunt adj 1 syn see LEAN
  2 syn see EMACIATED
  ant bloated
‖**gaup** (or **gawp**) vb 1 syn see LOOK 7
  2 syn see GAZE 1
gauzy adj syn see FILMY
gawk vb syn see GAZE 1
gawk n syn see OAF 2
gawky adj syn see CLUMSY 1
gay adj 1 syn see MERRY
  2 syn see LIVELY 1
  rel frolicsome, playful, sportive
  con earnest, sedate, serious, solemn, somber, staid; quiet, silent, still
  ant grave, sober
  3 syn see COLORFUL
  4 syn see WILD 7
  5 syn see HOMOSEXUAL
  6 syn see PRESUMPTUOUS
gaze vb 1 to look long and usually attentively <*gazed* out the window>
  syn bore, gape, ‖gaup (or gawp), gawk, glare, gloat, goggle, peer, stare; *compare* LOOK 7
  rel look, see, watch; peek, peep; contemplate, inspect, observe, scrutinize, survey; admire, ogle, regard
  con glance, skim, skim
  2 syn see LOOK 7
gaze (upon) vb syn see EYE 1
gazebo n syn see SUMMERHOUSE
gear n syn see EQUIPMENT
  rel accessories, adjuncts, appendages, appurtenances; belongings, effects, means, possessions
gear vb syn see FURNISH 1
‖**gee** n syn see MAN 3
‖**gee** vb syn see AGREE 4
Gehenna n syn see HELL
gel vb syn see COAGULATE
gelastic adj syn see LAUGHABLE
gelate vb syn see COAGULATE
gelatinize vb syn see COAGULATE
geld vb syn see STERILIZE
gelid adj syn see COLD 1
  con ardent, burning, fervent, scorching, sweltering, torrid
  ant fervid
‖**gelt** n syn see MONEY
gem vb syn see BEJEWEL
‖**gendarme** n syn see POLICEMAN
genealogy n an account often in chart form recording a line of ancestors <decided to prepare a *genealogy* of his family>
  syn ‖begats, family tree, pedigree, stemma
general adj 1 conforming to what is expected in the ordinary course of events <the *general* problems of everyday life>
  syn common, commonplace, matter-of-course, natural, normal, prevalent, regular, run-of-the-mill, typic, typical, usual
  rel everyday, popular; familiar, universal; habitual, humdrum, routine, uneventful
  con abnormal, extraordinary, irregular, novel, strange, unexpected, unforeseeable, unusual

2 belonging or relating to the whole <a *general* change in the weather>
syn common, generic, universal
rel natural, normal, regular, typical; broad, inclusive, wide
con individual, particular, special; characteristic, distinctive, peculiar
3 **syn** *see* ALL-AROUND 2
4 **syn** *see* PUBLIC 4

generally *adv* 1 in a reasonably inclusive manner <the forest was *generally* coniferous>
syn chiefly, largely, mainly, mostly, overall, predominantly, primarily, principally
rel about, approximately, practically, roughly, roundly
con altogether, totally, wholly
2 **syn** *see* ALTOGETHER 3
3 **syn** *see* USUALLY 2

generate *vb* 1 to bring into existence <*generate* new business>
syn create, father, hatch, make, originate, parent, procreate, produce, sire, spawn
rel bring about, effect, impose, occasion; introduce; cause; found, inaugurate, institute, set up; develop, induce, whip (up)
idiom bring to pass, give birth to, give rise to
con demolish, destroy, extinguish, ruin; degenerate, deteriorate, impair, worsen
2 **syn** *see* PROCREATE 2
3 to be the cause or source of something immaterial <actions that *generated* a good deal of suspicion>
syn breed, cause, engender, get up, hatch, induce, muster (up), occasion, produce, provoke, work up
rel accomplish, achieve, perform
idiom give birth to, give rise to

generator *n* **syn** *see* FATHER 2

generic *adj* **syn** *see* GENERAL 2
ant specific

generous *adj* 1 marked by a noble or for-bearing spirit <*generous* toward the weakness of others>
syn benevolent, big, chivalrous, considerate, greathearted, lofty, magnanimous
rel altruistic, charitable, kindhearted, kindly, thoughtful, ungrudging, unselfish; fair, honest; long-suffering, tolerant; helpful, willing
con base, ignoble, mean, self-centered, selfish; grim, hard, harsh, intolerant
ant ungenerous
2 **syn** *see* LIBERAL 1
ant stingy
3 **syn** *see* PLENTIFUL
rel lavish; luxuriant; affluent, wealthy
con scant, scanty, sparse

generously *adv* **syn** *see* WELL 2

genesis *n* **syn** *see* BEGINNING
rel provenance, provenience
con cessation, conclusion, culmination, end, finish, termination

genial *adj* 1 **syn** *see* GRACIOUS 1

rel amicable, friendly, neighborly; blithe, cheerful, jocund, jolly, jovial, merry
con discourteous, rude, uncivil, ungracious; crabbed, morose, sullen; ironic, sarcastic, sardonic, satiric
ant caustic (*remarks, comments*); saturnine (*manner, disposition, aspect*)
2 **syn** *see* GENTLE 2

geniality *n* **syn** *see* AMENITY 1

genitalia *n pl* the external components of the reproductive system <nude bathers were reminded of the local ordinance prohibiting public exposure of the *genitalia*>
syn genitals, parts, private parts, privates, privities, privy parts, pudendum (*usu* pudenda *pl*), secrets

genitals *n pl* **syn** *see* GENITALIA

genius *n* **syn** *see* GIFT 2
rel creativity, ingenuity, inventiveness, originality; astuteness, brains, grasp, intellect, intelligence, understanding

gent *n* **syn** *see* MAN 3

genteel *adj* 1 having characteristics or qualities befitting the upper classes <in those days croquet was a very *genteel* sport> <his manner was perfectly *genteel*>
syn cultivated, cultured, distingué, polished, refined, urbane, well-bred
rel elegant, fashionable, graceful, stylish; chivalrous, gentlemanly, knightly, ladylike, noble; mannerly, well-mannered
con coarse, common, crude, ill-bred, rough, rude, uncouth, uncultured, unpolished, vulgar
ant ungenteel
2 **syn** *see* CIVIL 2
rel well-behaved; aristocratic, cultured
con crude, discourteous, inconsiderate, rough, rude
3 involving or excessively preoccupied with the airs and forms of middle-class or upper-class proprieties <a shy *genteel* girl terrified of blundering socially>
syn affected, la-di-da, ||lardy-dardy, mincing, pretentious, stilted, too-too; *compare* PRECIOUS 4, PRIM 1
rel artificial, formal, highfalutin
con cultured, genuine, honest, refined; gracious, polished; gentlemanly, ladylike
4 **syn** *see* PRIM 1
rel narrow; intolerant, uncharitable; confined, insular, parochial, provincial
idiom nasty nice
con charitable, tolerant, understanding; broad-minded, easy, relaxed

gentile *adj* **syn** *see* HEATHEN

gentility *n* **syn** *see* ARISTOCRACY

gentle *adj* 1 free from all harshness, roughness, or intensity <a *gentle* summer breeze>
syn balmy, bland, faint, lenient, mild, smooth, soft
rel delicate, mellow, tender; hushed, low, soothing; calm, halcyon, peaceful, placid, quiet, serene, tranquil
con coarse, harsh, rough; exquisite, fierce, intense, savage, vehement, violent; forceful, forcible, powerful
2 having a pleasant easygoing nature <a *gentle* person in everything she does>
syn affable, amiable, genial

---

rel kind, pleasant, pleasing, tender; agreeable, benign, mild; compassionate, kindly, softhearted, sympathetic, warmhearted

con belligerent, cantankerous, contentious, ill-natured, petty, quarrelsome; aggressive, demanding, overbearing

ant harsh, stern

gentleman *n* **1** a person of good or noble birth <the contributions of the country *gentleman* to social stability>
syn ‖aristo, aristocrat, blue blood, patrician
rel Brahmin; chevalier; nob, swell
con churl, clown, lout
ant boor
2 *syn* see MAN 3

gentleman friend *n syn* see BOYFRIEND 1

gentlewoman *n syn* see WOMAN 1

gentry *n syn* see ARISTOCRACY

genuine *adj* **1** *syn* see AUTHENTIC 2
con artificial, ersatz, factitious; counterfeited, sham, simulated; sophisticated
ant fraudulent
2 *syn* see ACTUAL 2
con uncommon, unordinary, unusual; alleged, apocryphal, apparent, fabulous, fictitious, mythical
3 free from hypocrisy or pretense <a *genuine* love for his fellowman>
syn heart-whole, honest, real, sincere, true, undesigning, undissembled, unfeigned;
compare NATURAL 5, SINCERE 1
rel reliable, trustworthy, unaffected, unimpeachable, veritable
con affected, hypocritical
ant insincere

genuinely *adv syn* see VERY 2

germ *n syn* see SEED 2

germane *adj syn* see RELEVANT
con incompatible, incongruous, inconsonant
ant foreign

gest *n syn* see ADVENTURE

gestapo *adj syn* see TERRORISTIC

gestation *n syn* see PREGNANCY

gesture *n syn* see EXPRESSION 3

gesture *vb syn* see SIGNAL

get *vb* **1** to come into possession of <hoped to *get* a fortune from his invention>
syn acquire, annex, chalk up, compass, gain, have, land, obtain, pick up, procure, pull, secure, win
rel educe, elicit, evoke, extort, extract, ‖promote; accept, receive; clutch, grab, grasp, take; accomplish, achieve, effect; capture, carry; draw
idiom come by
con abnegate, eschew, forbear, forgo, give up, sacrifice; abandon, forsake, renounce
2 *syn* see EARN 1
3 *syn* see BECOME 1
rel achieve, attain, effect, realize
idiom get to be, turn out to be
4 *syn* see CONTRACT 1
5 *syn* see FATHER 1
6 *syn* see PREPARE 1
rel arrange, order, right; adjust, coordinate, organize
7 *syn* see CATCH 1
8 *syn* see AFFECT
rel bend, bias, dispose, predispose, prompt

con benumb, deaden, numb; blunt, dull, harden
9 *syn* see NONPLUS 1
rel bother, distress, disturb, perturb, upset; discomfit, disconcert, embarrass
10 *syn* see IRRITATE
idiom try one's temper
con calm, compose, cool, lull, soothe, subdue
11 *syn* see LEARN 1
idiom get into one's head
12 *syn* see MEMORIZE
13 *syn* see INDUCE 1
rel provoke; beg, coax, press, pressure, urge
14 *syn* see REACH 4
15 *syn* see COME 1

get along *vb* **1** *syn* see ADVANCE 5
rel depart, go
con recede, regress, retreat, retrogress, reverse, revert
2 *syn* see SHIFT 5
rel flourish, prosper, succeed, thrive

get away *vb syn* see GO 2

getaway *n syn* see ESCAPE 1

get back *vb syn* see RECOVER 1

get by *vb syn* see SHIFT 5

get in *vb syn* see COME 1

get off *vb* **1** *syn* see GO 2
rel advance, progress
2 *syn* see BEGIN 1

get on *vb* **1** *syn* see DON 1
2 *syn* see ADVANCE 5
3 *syn* see SHIFT 5

get out *vb* **1** to go away quickly, immediately, and often secretly <had to *get out* before the police arrived>
syn begone, bug off, buzz off, clear out, decamp, hightail, kite, scram, skedaddle, skiddoo, take off, ‖vamoose
rel depart, duck (out), egress, exit, go, leave, split
idiom beat it, be off, make tracks, take a powder, take a runout powder
con abide, remain, reside, stay
2 to become known <we can't let this story *get out*>
syn break, come out, leak, out, transpire
3 *syn* see PUBLISH 2

gettable *adj syn* see AVAILABLE 1

get up *vb* **1** *syn* see ROLL OUT
2 *syn* see RISE 1
3 *syn* see GENERATE 3

getup *n* **1** *syn* see COSTUME
2 *syn* see VIGOR 2

get-up-and-go *n* **1** *syn* see VIGOR 2
2 *syn* see ENTERPRISE 4

gewgaw *n syn* see KNICKKNACK

ghastly *adj* **1** disturbingly frightening or repellent in appearance or aspect <the *ghastly* sight of burned and rotting bodies>
syn grim, grisly, gruesome, hideous, horrible, horrid, horrifying, lurid, macabre, terrible, terrifying
rel appalling, awful, dreadful, frightening, frightful, shocking; disgustful, disgusting, nauseant, nauseating, sickening
con appealing, attractive, charming, pleasant, touching; acceptable, bearable; trivial, unimportant

2 resembling or suggestive of a ghost <a *ghastly* form slightly visible through the fog>
syn cadaverous, corpselike, deathlike, ghostlike, ghostly, shadowy, spectral
rel ashen, livid, lurid, pale; uncanny, weird; gruesome, haggard, macabre; dim, faint, weak; charnel, mortuary, sepulchral

ghost *n syn* see APPARITION
rel demon, devil

ghost *vb syn* see GHOSTWRITE

ghostlike *adj syn* see GHASTLY 2

ghostly *adj syn* see GHASTLY 2

ghostwrite *vb* to write for and in the name of another <a *ghostwritten* autobiography>
syn ghost, spook

GI *n syn* see SOLDIER

giant *n* something of monstrous size, appearance, or power <a *giant* of a tractor>
syn behemoth, leviathan, mammoth, monster, whale
rel cyclops, polypheme

giant *adj syn* see HUGE
rel gross, hulking
con paltry, petty, puny, trifling, trivial
ant dwarf

gibber *vb* to utter or speak rapidly, inarticulately, and usually unintelligibly <a *gibbering* idiot>
syn babble, chatter, gabble, jabber
rel blather, drivel, prate, prattle, yammer; stammer, stutter; mumble, mutter; mow
idiom run off at the mouth
con articulate, enunciate, pronounce

gibberish *n* **1** unintelligible or meaningless talk <the *gibberish* of an imbecile>
syn babble, drivel, Greek, jabber, jabberwocky, nonsense, skimble-skamble; *compare* GIBBERISH 3
rel blather, bunkum, claptrap, twaddle; blabber, gabble, palaver, prattle
2 *syn* see GOBBLEDYGOOK
3 speech or actions that are esoteric in nature and suggest the magical, strange, or unknown <the shaman's strange *gibberish*>
syn abracadabra, hocus-pocus, mumbo jumbo, mummery
rel magic, sorcery, thaumaturgy

gibbet *vb syn* see HANG 2

gibble-gabble *n syn* see CHATTER

gibe *vb syn* see SCOFF
rel rail, rally, revile, scold, twit

giddy *adj* **1** having a lightheartedly silly nature <tried to teach a bunch of *giddy* Girl Scouts how to make a fire>
syn bird-witted, dizzy, empty-headed, featherbrained, flighty, fribble, fribbling, frivolous, harebrained, hoity-toity, light, light-headed, rattlebrained, scatterbrained, silly, skittish, volage, yeasty
rel capricious, fickle, impulsive, whimsical; brainless, exuberant, thoughtless, witless
idiom giddy as a goose
con earnest, pensive, sedate, serious, sober, solemn, staid, thoughtful

syn synonym(s) *rel* related word(s)
ant antonym(s) *con* contrasted word(s)
idiom idiomatic equivalent(s)
‖ use limited; if in doubt, see a dictionary

2 *syn* see DIZZY 2
rel bemused, flustered
idiom going around in circles, like a chicken with its head cut off, seeing double

gift *n* **1** something freely given by one person to another for his benefit or pleasure <the watch was a graduation *gift*>
syn benevolence, boon, ‖compliment, favor, largess, present
rel alms, benefaction, contribution, donation; award, bestowal, grant, presentation; legacy; offering, reward, tip; remembrance, souvenir, token
2 a natural or special facility or capableness <has a *gift* for electronics>
syn aptness, bent, bump, faculty, flair, genius, head, knack, nose, set, talent, turn; *compare* LEANING 2
rel ability, aptitude, capability; accomplishment, acquirement, attainment; instinct, numen, power; forte, leaning, propensity, specialty
con awkwardness, clumsiness, maladroitness

gigantean *adj syn* see HUGE

gigantesque *adj syn* see HUGE

gigantic *adj syn* see HUGE
rel hulking, stupendous
con paltry, petty, puny, trifling, trivial

giggle *vb syn* see LAUGH

gill *n syn* see CREEK 2

gimcrack *n syn* see KNICKKNACK

gimmick *n* **1** *syn* see GADGET 1
2 *syn* see TRICK 1
rel cheat, counterfeit, deceit, dodge, fake, humbug, imposture; fun, game, jest, method, sport

gimp *n syn* see SPIRIT 5

gingerly *adj syn* see CAUTIOUS

gingery *adj syn* see SPIRITED
con lethargic, listless, poky, slow; dead, dull, flat, insipid, stuffy; dreary; blasé, lackadaisical, nonchalant

gin mill *n syn* see BAR 5

gird *vb* **1** *syn* see BELT 1
ant ungird
2 *syn* see SURROUND 1
rel wrap, wreathe
3 to prepare oneself for action <*girded* himself for the coming trial>
syn brace, fortify, prepare, ready, steel, strengthen
rel bolster, buttress, support, sustain; harden, reinforce, shore (up); invigorate; dispose, prepare
idiom gird one's loins, whet the knife

gird *vb syn* see SCOFF

girdle *n syn* see BELT 1

girdle *vb* **1** *syn* see BELT 1
2 *syn* see SURROUND 1

girl *n* **1** a young unmarried female person <hired a *girl* to babysit>
syn ‖bird, damsel, gal, lass, lassie, maid, maiden, miss, missy, ‖quail, ‖quiff, wench
rel hoyden, tomboy; deb, debutante, subdeb, subdebutante; bobby-soxer; schoolgirl; gamine
‖**2** *syn* see WOMAN 1
3 *syn* see MAID 2
4 *syn* see GIRL FRIEND 1

girl Friday *n syn* see RIGHT-HAND MAN

girl friend *n* **1** a woman who is a man's usual or preferred companion <took his *girl friend* out every weekend>
syn best girl, ‖chick, ‖doney, gal, girl, lady friend, lass, mouse, popsy

2 a woman who shares with a man a strong and usually equal sexually oriented mutual attraction <his wife caught him with his *girl friend*>
syn ‖baby, beloved, flame, honey, inamorata, ladylove, steady, sweetheart, sweetie, truelove

3 *syn* see MISTRESS

gist *n syn* see SUBSTANCE 2
rel sap, soul, spirit; subject, theme, topic; bearing, drift, tenor

give *vb* **1** to provide gratuitously <*gave* their labor to rebuild the burned church>
syn bestow, devote, donate, give away, hand out, present; *compare* CONTRIBUTE 1
rel accord, award, confer, grant, hand; afford, contribute, furnish, provide; aid, assist, benefact, help
con decline, refuse; withhold; lease, sell

2 to provide by or as if by formal action <he was *given* a diploma>
syn accord, award, confer, grant; *compare* GRANT 1
rel bestow, hand over, present; allocate, appropriate, assign
con decline, refuse; withhold

3 to put into the possession of another usually for use or consumption <*gave* the dog a drink of water>
syn deliver, dish out, dispense, feed, find, furnish, hand, hand over, provide, supply, transfer, turn over
rel administer, commit, offer; deal, disburse, disperse, distribute, divide, dole (out), lot (out); afford, lend
con have, hold, hold back, keep, keep back, reserve, retain, withhold

4 *syn* see OFFER 1
rel bestow, confer, render; administer, dispense, issue

5 *syn* see EXPRESS 2

6 *syn* see ALLOT

7 to furnish as a result or product <6 + 6 *gives* 12>
syn produce, yield
rel be, equal, make; afford, furnish, offer, supply

8 *syn* see SPEND 1

9 *syn* see SELL 2

10 to bestow or dispense by some action <*gave* him a punch in the nose>
syn administer, deal, deliver, inflict, strike
rel bestow, dispense; fetch

11 *syn* see ADDRESS 1

12 to fail in response to physical stress <the bridge *gave* under the heavy load>
syn bend, break, cave, collapse, crumple, fold up, go, yield
rel fail, relax, relent, slacken, weaken
idiom cave in, give way

13 *syn* see HAPPEN 1

give away *vb* **1** *syn* see GIVE 1

2 *syn* see REVEAL 1

give back *vb* **1** *syn* see RETREAT 2

---

rel back out, backtrack, backwater; crumble, fail, falter, weaken
2 *syn* see RESTORE 5

given *adj syn* see APT 1

given name *n* the name that precedes one's surname <arguing over the baby's *given name*>
syn baptismal name, Christian name, font name, forename, personal name, prename
rel first name, middle name; appellation, appellative, compellation, denomination, style; praenomen; epithet, label, tag

give off *vb* **1** *syn* see EMIT 2
2 *syn* see DISCHARGE 5

give out *vb* **1** *syn* see EMIT 2
2 *syn* see COLLAPSE 2
3 *syn* see FAIL 2

give over *vb syn* see STOP 3

giver *n syn* see DONOR

give up *vb* **1** *syn* see RELINQUISH
2 *syn* see DESPAIR

gizmo *n* **1** *syn* see DOODAD
2 *syn* see GADGET

glabrous *adj syn* see HAIRLESS
rel beardless, shaven, smooth-shaven
con bristled, bristly, hairy, hirsute, stubbled, stubbly

glacial *adj* **1** *syn* see COLD 1
2 *syn* see COLD 2
rel aloof, distant, remote, reserved, standoffish, withdrawn; exclusive, inaccessible, seclusive, unapproachable
con affable, gregarious, sociable

glad *adj* **1** characterized by or expressing the mood of one who is pleased or delighted <she was *glad* to be on vacation>
syn happy, joyful, joyous, lighthearted
rel delighted, gratified, pleased, rejoiced, tickled; blithe, exhilarated, jocund, jolly, jovial, merry; gleeful, hilarious, mirthful
idiom filled with (or full of) delight
con blue, dejected, depressed, downcast, melancholy; despondent, dispirited, heavyhearted, sadhearted, unhappy; forlorn, joyless, sorrowful, woeful
ant sad

2 full of brightness and cheerfulness <a *glad* spring morning>
syn bright, cheerful, cheery, radiant
rel beaming, sparkling; beautiful, genial, pleasant
con dark, dim, dull, gloomy, somber

gladden *vb syn* see PLEASE 2
rel comfort, console, solace; animate, enliven, exhilarate, invigorate, liven, quicken, vivify
con depress, oppress, weigh; discourage, dishearten, dispirit; damp, dampen; bother, irk
ant sadden

gladiatorial *adj syn* see BELLIGERENT

‖glad rags *n pl syn* see FINERY

glamorous *adj syn* see ATTRACTIVE 1

glamour *n syn* see CHARM 3

glance *vb* **1** to strike a surface obliquely so as to go off at an angle <the bullet *glanced* off the stone wall>
syn carom, dap, graze, ricochet, skim, skip
rel brush, kiss, scrape, shave, slant; contact, hit, strike, touch; bounce, careen, rebound

con center, focus
2 *syn* see BRUSH
3 *syn* see FLASH 1
glance (at *or* over) *vb syn* see BROWSE
glance *n* **1** *syn* see FLASH 1
   2 *syn* see PEEP
glance *vb syn* see POLISH 1
glare *vb* **1** *syn* see BLAZE
   rel dazzle, flash, gleam, glisten, glitter
   2 *syn* see GAZE 1
   rel frown, glower, lower, scowl
glaring *adj* **1** *syn* see EGREGIOUS
   rel conspicuous, noticeable, outstanding;
   excessive, extreme, inordinate; obtrusive
   ant unnoticeable
   2 *syn* see GAUDY
   rel cheap, coarse, crude, gross
   con elegant, tasteful
glass *n syn* see MIRROR 1
glass *vb syn* see REFLECT 1
∥**glasshouse** *n syn* see GREENHOUSE
glassy *adj syn* see SLEEK
glaze *vb syn* see POLISH 1
glaze *n syn* see LUSTER
gleam *n syn* see FLASH 1
gleam *vb* **1** *syn* see SHINE 1
   2 *syn* see FLASH 1
   rel burn
gleaming *adj syn* see LUSTROUS 1
glean *vb* to gather by effort and usually bit by
   bit <evidence *gleaned* from various testimo-
   nies>
   syn cull, extract, garner, gather, pick up
   rel sift, winnow; ascertain, conclude, deduce, learn
   con amass, heap, pile
glee *n syn* see MIRTH
   rel delectation, delight, enjoyment, joy,
   pleasure; blitheness; joyousness
   ant gloom
gleeful *adj syn* see MERRY
glen *n syn* see VALLEY
glib *adj* characterized by very fluent often
   superficial address toward others <*glib*
   chatter>
   syn silver-tongued, vocative, voluble, well-
   hung; *compare* TALKATIVE
   rel articulate, eloquent, facile, fluent, vocal
   con inarticulate, unfluent
glide *vb* **1** *syn* see SLIDE 1
   rel float, fly, sail, scud, shoot, skim
   2 *syn* see STEAL 3
   3 *syn* see SNEAK
glimmer *vb syn* see FLASH 1
glimmer *n syn* see FLASH 1
glimpse *n syn* see PEEP
glint *vb syn* see FLASH 1
glint *n* **1** *syn* see FLASH 1
   2 *syn* see LUSTER
glissade *n syn* see SLIDE 1
   rel float, fly, sail, scud, shoot, skim
glisten *vb syn* see FLASH 1
glisten *n syn* see FLASH 1
glistening *adj syn* see LUSTROUS 1
glitter *vb* **1** *syn* see FLASH 1

2 *syn* see SPANGLE 1
glitter *n syn* see FLASH 1
gloaming *n syn* see EVENING 1
gloat *vb syn* see GAZE 1
   con begrudge, covet, envy, grudge
global *adj* **1** *syn* see UNIVERSAL 2
   ant parochial
   2 *syn* see ALL-ROUND 2
   rel all-inclusive, blanket, catholic, grand,
   universal
globe *n* **1** *syn* see BALL
   2 *syn* see EARTH 1
globule *n syn* see DROP 1
gloom *vb* **1** *syn* see FROWN 1
   rel brood, mope
   con smile; bubble, effervesce, enthuse, sparkle
   2 *syn* see OBSCURE
gloom *n syn* see SADNESS
   con hilarity, jollity, mirth; gaiety, gladness
   ant glee
gloomy *adj* **1** *syn* see DARK 1
   rel bleak, dismal, dreary
   ant brilliant
   2 *syn* see SULLEN
   rel cheerless, dejected, depressed, downcast, joyless, melancholy, oppressed, solemn, unhappy, weary
   con glad, happy, joyful, joyous, lighthearted; blithe, jocund, jovial, merry
   ant cheerful
   3 causing or marked by gloom <the *gloomy*
   atmosphere of the dungeon>
   syn acheronian, acherontic, black, bleak,
   cheerless, cold, depressant, depressing,
   depressive, desolate, disconsolate, discouraging, disheartening, dismal, dispiriting,
   drear, dreary, dusky, funereal, joyless, lugubrious, morne, mournful, sad, somber, tenebrific, unhappy, woebegone
   rel despondent, mirthless, pessimistic;
   melancholy, mournful, sad; drab, dull,
   muzzy
   con bright, cheerful, happy; cheering, emboldening, encouraging, heartening, optimistic
   ant gloomless
glorification *n syn* see APOTHEOSIS 2
glorify *vb* **1** *syn* see PRAISE 2
   2 *syn* see EXALT 1
glorious *adj* **1** *syn* see SPLENDID 2
   rel brilliant, effulgent, lustrous, radiant;
   imposing, impressive; majestic, noble; ravishing, stunning; beautiful
   ant inglorious
   2 *syn* see MARVELOUS 2
glory *vb syn* see EXULT
gloss *n syn* see LUSTER
   rel glossiness, silkiness, sleekness, slickness;
   burnish
gloss *vb syn* see POLISH 1
gloss (over) *vb syn* see PALLIATE
   rel account, explain, justify, rationalize;
   belie, falsify, miscolor, misrepresent
gloss *vb syn* see ANNOTATE
glossy *adj* **1** *syn* see LUSTROUS 1
   2 *syn* see SLEEK
glow *vb* **1** *syn* see BLAZE
   rel burn; ignite, kindle, light
   2 *syn* see BLUSH

---

syn synonym(s)   *rel* related word(s)
ant antonym(s)   *con* contrasted word(s)
idiom idiomatic equivalent(s)
∥ use limited; if in doubt, see a dictionary

glow n syn see BLOOM 3
glower vb syn see FROWN 1
  rel stare; look, watch
glowing adj 1 syn see RUDDY
  2 syn see IMPASSIONED
  rel enthusiastic; avid, desirous, eager, fierce, keen; burning, heated
gloze (over) vb syn see PALLIATE
  rel account, explain, justify, rationalize; belie, falsify, miscolor, misrepresent
gluey adj syn see STICKY 1
glum adj syn see SULLEN
  rel close-lipped, silent, taciturn, tight-lipped; depressed, oppressed, weighed down
  con glad, happy, joyful, joyous, light-hearted
  ant cheerful
glut vb syn see SATIATE
  rel cram, feast, stuff
  idiom make a pig of (oneself)
  con scant, skimp
  ant stint
glutted adj syn see SATIATED
gluttonous adj syn see VORACIOUS
  rel hoggish, piggish; indulgent, intemperate
  con sober, temperate; ascetic, austere; sparing
  ant abstemious
gnaw vb 1 syn see WORRY 1
  rel haunt, irritate, rankle
  2 syn see EAT 3
  rel abrade, fret; consume, crumble
gnome n syn see MAXIM
gnostic adj syn see WISE 1
go vb 1 syn see move on a course <they were glad to be *going* toward home>
  syn ‖cruise, fare, hie, journey, pass, proceed, ‖process, push on, repair, travel, wend
  rel advance; approach, near
  idiom gain ground, get over the ground, make one's way
  ant stop
  2 to move out of and away from where one is <it's time to go now>
  syn ‖blow, depart, exit, get away, get off, leave, ‖mog, move, pop off, pull out, push off, quit, retire, run along, shove off, take off, withdraw
  rel abscond, decamp, escape, flee, fly, hightail
  idiom take a powder
  con abide, remain, stay; arrive
  ant come
  3 syn see RUN 8
  4 to be brought to or toward an end <his money will soon be *gone*>
  syn consume, exhaust, expend, finish, run through, spend, use up, wash up
  rel deplete, devour, dissipate, fritter (away); overspend, squander, waste
  con conserve, preserve, save
  5 syn see DIE 1
  6 syn see PASS 2
  7 syn see GIVE 12
  8 syn see HAPPEN 1
  9 syn see BECOME 1
  10 syn see RANGE 3
  11 syn see SUCCEED 3
  12 syn see SUCCEED 2
  13 syn see RESORT 2

  14 syn see FUNCTION 3
  15 syn see EXTEND 7
  16 syn see AGREE 4
  17 syn see BELONG 1
  18 syn see BEAR 10
  19 syn see ENJOY 1
go (for) vb syn see APPROVE 1
go (into) vb syn see EXPLORE
go (together or with) vb syn see SUIT 4
go n 1 syn see OCCURRENCE
  2 syn see VIGOR 2
  3 syn see ENERGY 2
  4 syn see FLING 1
  5 syn see SPELL 1
  6 syn see SIEGE
  7 syn see SUCCESS
goad n syn see STIMULUS
  rel compulsion, drive, impulsion; desire, lust, passion, urge, zeal
  ant curb
goad vb syn see URGE
  rel impel, move; coerce, compel, force; instigate
go-ahead adj syn see ENTERPRISING 2
goal n 1 syn see AMBITION 2
  2 syn see USE 4
goat n syn see SCAPEGOAT
goatish adj syn see LUSTFUL 2
gob n 1 syn see LUMP 1
  2 usu **gobs** pl syn see SCAD
gob n syn see MOUTH 1
gobbet n syn see DROP 1
gobble vb syn see GULP
gobbledygook n wordy unintelligible language <the *gobbledygook* of bureaucrats>
  syn double-talk, gibberish
  rel double Dutch, Greek, jabberwocky; ‖bull, bunkum, claptrap, drivel, garbage, malarkey, nonsense, poppycock, twaddle
go-between n 1 syn see MARRIAGE BROKER
  2 an intermediate agent between individuals or groups <served as a *go-between* in the labor dispute>
  syn broker, entrepreneur, interagent, interceder, intercessor, intermediary, intermediate, intermediator, mediator, middleman
  rel agent, attorney, deputy, factor, proxy; emissary, envoy, messenger; delegate, representative; arbitrator, negotiator
godless adj syn see IRRELIGIOUS
  rel agnostic, atheistic, infidel
  ant godly
godlike adj syn see DIVINE 2
godly adj 1 syn see DIVINE 1
  2 syn see SAINTLY
  3 syn see DEVOUT
  ant godless
go down vb 1 syn see FALL 2
  rel droop, sag, sink; cave (in), collapse, crumple, fold
  2 syn see SET 12
  3 syn see SINK 1
  4 syn see FALL 3
  5 syn see HAPPEN 1
God's acre n syn see CEMETERY
godsend n syn see GOOD 1
go-getter n syn see HUSTLER 1
goggle vb 1 syn see LOOK 7
  2 syn see GAZE 1

go in *vb syn* see ENTER 1

Golconda *n syn* see BONANZA

goldarn *adj* 1 *syn* see DAMNED 2
    2 *syn* see UTTER

goldbrick *n syn* see SLACKER

goldbrick *vb syn* see IDLE

golden *adj* 1 *syn* see BLOND 1
    2 *syn* see MELLIFLUOUS

golden–ager *n syn* see OLDSTER

gold mine *n syn* see BONANZA

golem *n syn* see ROBOT 2

gone *adj* 1 *syn* see EXTINCT 2
    2 *syn* see ABSENT 1
    3 *syn* see LOST 2
    4 *syn* see PREGNANT 1

gonfalon *n syn* see FLAG

gonfanon *n syn* see FLAG

goo *n* 1 a sticky substance <slipped on a patch of greasy *goo* on the walk>
    syn gook, goop, gumbo, gunk, muck; *compare* CRUD
    rel dope
    2 *syn* see CRUD

good *adj* 1 having a helpful or auspicious character <a *good* wind>
    syn advantageous, benefic, beneficial, brave, favorable, favoring, helpful, propitious, toward, useful
    rel convenient, suitable; desirable, needed; appropriate, proper, right
    con disadvantageous, unfavorable; damaging, hampering, harmful; unwanted
    ant ill

    2 adapted to the end in view <they doubted that the fruit was *good* to eat>
    syn appropriate, convenient, fit, meet, proper, suitable, useful
    rel all right, apt, becoming, conformable, congruous, fitting, seemly
    con inadequate, inappropriate, undesirable, unfit, unsuitable, useless
    3 *syn* see WHOLE 1
    con blemished, damaged, defective, flawed, impaired, imperfect, unsound
    ant bad
    4 *syn* see ADVANTAGEOUS 1
    5 *syn* see PLEASANT 1
    6 *syn* see HEALTHFUL
    7 *syn* see CLEVER 5
    8 *syn* see CONSIDERABLE 2
    9 *syn* see WELL-FOUNDED
    10 *syn* see DECENT 4
    11 conforming to a high standard of morality or virtue <if you can't be *good*, be careful>
    syn blameless, exemplary, guiltless, inculpable, innocent, irreprehensible, irreproachable, lily-white, pure, righteous, unblamable, virtuous
    rel incorrupt, sound, uncorrupted, untainted
    con blameworthy, impure, unrighteous; evil, iniquitous, reprobate, sinful
    ant bad
    12 *syn* see CHARITABLE 1

    13 behaving in an acceptable or desirable manner <a *good* child>
    syn decorous, well-behaved
    rel polite, proper; considerate, kindly, thoughtful
    con ill-behaved, indecorous, naughty; careless, heedless, inconsiderate, mischievous, thoughtless
    ant bad
    14 *syn* see SKILLFUL 2
    ant bad
    15 *syn* see ABLE

good *n* 1 something that is desirable or beneficial <it's an ill wind that blows no *good*>
    syn advantage, benediction, benefit, blessing, boon, godsend
    con bane, harm, misfortune; detriment, jinx
    ant evil, ill
    2 *syn* see RIGHT 1
    3 *syn* see WELFARE
    4 **goods** *pl syn* see POSSESSION 2
    5 **goods** *pl syn* see MERCHANDISE

good–bye *interj* — used as a conventional expression of good wishes at parting <the party was over; the time had come to say *good-bye*>
    syn adieu, by, bye-bye, ‖cheerio, farewell, so long, ‖toodle-oo
    rel good day, good evening, good morning, good night
    idiom be good, be seeing you, fare you well, keep in touch, see you (later)
    con hello, how do, howdy, hullo

good–bye *n syn* see PARTING

good–bye *adj syn* see PARTING

good faith *n* a state of mind characterizing one free from fraud, deceit, or misconduct <determined to act in *good faith*>
    syn bona fides, sincereness, sincerity, uberrima fides
    rel decency, decorum, propriety, seemliness; ethicality, morality, virtuousness

good–fellowship *n syn* see CAMARADERIE

good–for–nothing *n syn* see WASTREL 1

good–for–nothing *adj* 1 *syn* see FECKLESS 1
    2 *syn* see WORTHLESS 1
    ant precious

good–hearted *adj syn* see KIND

good–humored *adj syn* see AMIABLE 1
    rel buoyant, cheerful, cheery, genial, smiling
    ant ill-humored

good–looking *adj syn* see BEAUTIFUL
    ant ill-looking

good–natured *adj syn* see AMIABLE 1
    rel altruistic, benevolent, charitable; acquiescent, compliant
    con choleric, cranky, cross, irascible, splenetic, touchy; crabbed, gloomy, glum, morose, splenetic
    ant contrary; ill-natured

goodness *n* the quality or state of being morally excellent <that eternal *goodness* that burns away evil>
    syn morality, probity, rectitude, righteousness, rightness, uprightness, virtue
    rel honesty, honor, integrity; grace, merit, quality, superiority
    ant badness, evil

---

syn synonym(s)   *rel* related word(s)
ant antonym(s)   *con* contrasted word(s)
idiom idiomatic equivalent(s)
‖ use limited; if in doubt, see a dictionary

good sense *n syn* see SENSE 6
good–tasting *adj syn* see PALATABLE
good–tempered *adj syn* see AMIABLE 1
con crabbed, surly; snappish, touchy; irascible
ant bad-tempered, ill-tempered
goodwill *n* **1** benevolent interest or concern <trying to promote interracial *goodwill*>
syn amity, benevolence, comity, friendliness, friendship, kindliness
rel altruism, charity, favor, generosity, helpfulness, kindness, rapport, sympathy, tolerance
con animus, disfavor, enmity, hatred, intolerance, malevolence
ant animosity, ill will
2 *syn* see ALACRITY
goody *n syn* see DELICACY
goody–goody *n syn* see PRUDE
gooey *adj* **1** *syn* see STICKY 1
2 *syn* see SENTIMENTAL
goof *n* **1** *syn* see DUNCE
2 *syn* see ERROR 2
‖**goof** (off) *vb syn* see IDLE
goof (up) *vb syn* see BOTCH
go off *vb syn* see EXPLODE 1
gook *n* **1** *syn* see GOO
2 *syn* see CRUD
3 *syn* see NONSENSE 2
go on *vb* **1** *syn* see PERSEVERE
2 *syn* see BEHAVE 1
‖**goon** *n syn* see DUNCE
goop *n syn* see GOO 1
goose egg *n syn* see ZERO 1
goosey *adj* **1** *syn* see STUPID 1
2 *syn* see NERVOUS
go over *vb syn* see SUCCEED 2
gordian *adj syn* see COMPLEX 2
gore *n syn* see BLOOD 1
gorge *n syn* see RAVINE
gorge *vb syn* see SATIATE
rel bolt, devour, gobble, guzzle, raven, wolf; overeat, overindulge, stuff
idiom eat like a horse, eat one out of house and home
gorged *adj syn* see SATIATED
gorgeous *adj* **1** *syn* see SPLENDID 2
rel elegant, luxurious, opulent, plush, sumptuous; flamboyant, garish, gaudy, ostentatious, pretentious, showy; beautiful, colorful
2 *syn* see GRAND 2
‖**gorilla** *n syn* see THUG 1
gory *adj syn* see BLOODY 1
gospel *n syn* see VERACITY 2
gossamer *adj syn* see FILMY
gossip *n* **1** a person who habitually retails private, scandalous, or sensational and often inaccurate information <her life ruined by a vicious old *gossip*>
syn carrytale, circulator, clack, gossiper, gossipmonger, ‖long tongue, mumblenews, newsmonger, quidnunc, rumorer, rumormonger, scandalizer, scandalmonger, sieve, tabby, talebearer, telltale; *compare* BUSYBODY, INFORMER
2 *syn* see REPORT 1
rel account, chronicle, conversation, story, tale; babble, banter, chatter, prate
gossip *vb* to disclose something, often of questionable veracity, that is better kept to

oneself <*gossiped* about his neighbor's business>
syn blab, noise (about *or* abroad), rumor, talk, tattle
rel babble, chat, chatter, prate, prattle; hint, imply, insinuate, suggest
idiom dish the dirt, spill the beans, tell idle tales, tell tales out of school
gossiper *n syn* see GOSSIP 1
gossipmonger *n syn* see GOSSIP 1
Gothic *adj syn* see BARBARIAN 1
rel brutal, coarse, crude
gouge *vb syn* see EXTORT 1
rel cheat, con, swindle; overcharge
go under *vb* **1** *syn* see FALL 3
2 *syn* see SINK 1
gourmand *n syn* see EPICURE
gourmet *n syn* see EPICURE
govern *vb* **1** to exercise sovereign authority <a dictator may *govern* in a thoroughly enlightened manner>
syn overrule, reign, rule, sway
rel captain, command, head; administer, conduct, control, direct, manage, master; regulate, supervise
2 *syn* see ADMINISTER 1
3 to exercise a decisive role in influencing the actions and conduct of <parents who *govern* their children wisely>
syn control, direct, dominate, handle, manage
rel directionalize, guide, lead, shepherd, steer; boss, oversee, supervise
idiom be at the helm (*or* wheel), be in the driver's seat, hold the reins
‖**governor** *n syn* see FATHER 1
grab *vb syn* see SEIZE 2
grabble *vb syn* see GROPE
grabby *adj syn* see COVETOUS
grace *n* **1** a short prayer either asking a blessing before or giving thanks after a meal <taught each child a *grace* of his own>
syn benediction, blessing, thanks, thanksgiving
rel invocation, petition
2 *syn* see MERCY
rel compassionateness, responsiveness, tenderness; forbearance, indulgence, leniency; goodness
3 *syn* see ELEGANCE
graceless *adj* **1** *syn* see BARBARIC 1
2 *syn* see INFELICITOUS
ant graceful
gracious *adj* **1** marked by kindly courtesy <her *gracious* attitude toward those around her>
syn affable, congenial, cordial, genial, sociable, ‖sonsy
rel amiable, complaisant, easy, obliging; benign, benignant, kind, kindly; chivalrous, courteous, courtly; approachable, bonhomous, clubby, forthcoming, forthgoing, outgoing
con boorish, churlish; blunt, brusque, crabbed, crusty, curt, gruff, short, sullen, surly
ant ungracious
2 *syn* see COURTLY
rel mannered, starchy
gradation *n* the difference or variation between two things that are nearly alike <the

gradations were too small to be seen with the unaided eye>
syn nuance, shade
rel difference, distinction, divergence; change, modification, variation

grade *n* 1 *syn* see DEGREE 1
2 *syn* see ESTATE 2
3 *syn* see CLASS 1
4 *syn* see QUALITY 3
5 *syn* see SLOPE

grade *vb syn* see CLASS 2
rel arrange, order; assort, sort

Grade A *adj syn* see EXCELLENT

gradient *n syn* see SLOPE

gradual *adj* proceeding slowly usually by minute or imperceptible steps or degrees <his health showed *gradual* improvement>
syn piecemeal, step-by-step
rel deliberate, dilatory, lagging, poky, sluggish
con acute, sharp, sudden
ant abrupt

gradually *adv* by small degrees or amounts <*gradually* he learned the new job>
syn bit by bit, little by little, piecemeal
idiom a little at a time, by degrees
con quickly, rapidly, speedily; at once, immediately, suddenly

grain *n syn* see PARTICLE

grainy *adj syn* see COARSE 1

grammar *n syn* see ALPHABET 2

grand *adj* 1 large and impressive in size, scope, extent, or conception <the platform provided a *grand* view of the canyon>
syn august, baronial, grandiose, imposing, lordly, magnific, magnificent, majestic, noble, princely, royal, stately; *compare* HUGE
rel monumental, prodigious, stupendous, tremendous; towering; gorgeous, splendid, sublime; superb
con measly, paltry, petty, puny, trifling, trivial
2 marked by great magnificence, display, and usually ceremony or formality <delighted to attend the *grand* presidential fete>
syn gorgeous, impressive, lavish, luxurious, splendid, sumptuous
rel magnificent, majestic; flashy, garish, gaudy, ornate, ostentatious, showy
con crude, meretricious, obtrusive, vulgar; flimsy, tawdry
3 noble in character or spirit <a *grand* outlook on life>
syn elevated, exalted, lofty, noble, superb
rel magnificent, splendid
con average, common, commonplace, ordinary; base, lowly, mean, poor

grandam *n syn* see BELDAM 1

grande dame *n syn* see MATRIARCH

grandiloquent *adj syn* see RHETORICAL

grandiose *adj* 1 *syn* see GRAND 1
rel ostentatious, pretentious, showy; cosmic, overwhelming, unfathomable, vast
2 *syn* see AMBITIOUS 2

---

syn synonym(s)   *rel* related word(s)
ant antonym(s)   *con* contrasted word(s)
idiom idiomatic equivalent(s)
‖ use limited; if in doubt, see a dictionary

granny *n syn* see FUSSBUDGET

grant *vb* 1 to give as a favor or right <*granted* him an extension of payments>
syn accord, award, concede, vouchsafe
rel bestow, confer, donate, give, present; allow, permit; cede, relinquish, yield
con decline, refuse, turn down
2 *syn* see ACKNOWLEDGE 1
con differ, disagree, dissent; challenge, dispute, object, protest
3 *syn* see GIVE 2

grant *n syn* see APPROPRIATION
rel gift; assistance, benefaction, contribution, donation; alms, charity, dole, handout

granular *adj syn* see COARSE 1

grapevine *n syn* see REPORT 1

graph *n syn* see CHART 1
rel diagram, outline, sketch

graphic *adj* 1 giving a clear visual impression especially in words <gave a *graphic* description of the whole incident>
syn photographic, pictorial, picturesque, vivid
rel clear, lucid, perspicuous; clear-cut, incisive; cogent, compelling, convincing, telling; definite, explicit, precise, realistic, striking, visual
con confused, hazy, indistinct, obscure
2 *syn* see PICTORIAL 1

grapple *n syn* see HOLD

grapple *vb* 1 *syn* see SEIZE 2
2 *syn* see WRESTLE

grasp *vb* 1 *syn* see TAKE 4
2 *syn* see APPREHEND 1
rel envisage, fathom, perceive
3 *syn* see KNOW 1

grasp *n syn* see HOLD

graspable *adj syn* see UNDERSTANDABLE
ant ungraspable

grasping *adj syn* see COVETOUS
rel extorting, extortionate

grass *n syn* see MARIJUANA

grate *vb* 1 *syn* see SCRAPE 1
rel abrade, bark, chafe, fray, gall, scuff, skin
2 *syn* see IRRITATE

grateful *adj* 1 feeling or expressing gratitude <was *grateful* for the gift>
syn obliged, thankful
rel appreciative, beholden; gratified, pleased
idiom filled with gratitude
ant ungrateful
2 *syn* see PLEASANT 1
rel comforting, consoling, solacing; refreshing, rejuvenating, renewing, restorative, restoring; delectable, delicious, delightful
ant obnoxious

gratefulness *n syn* see AMENITY 1

gratify *vb* 1 *syn* see PLEASE 2
rel appease, baby, cater (to), coddle, favor, humor, indulge, pamper
con bother, irk; aggravate, exasperate, irritate, nettle, rile; agitate, disturb, perturb, upset
2 *syn* see SATISFY 3
3 *syn* see INDULGE 1
idiom do one proud

gratifying *adj syn* see PLEASANT 1
rel contenting, satisfying; delighting, gladdening, regaling, rejoicing

con invidious, obnoxious; offensive, revolting

grating *adj syn* see HARSH 3

gratis *adj syn* see FREE 5

gratuitous *adj* **1** *syn* see FREE 5
rel voluntary, willing
2 *syn* see SUPEREROGATORY
3 *syn* see BASELESS
rel indefensible, reasonless, unsupportable

gratuity *n* something given over and above what is due, generally in return for or expectation of good service <he found that an occasional *gratuity* smoothed his path>
syn cumshaw, lagniappe, largess, ‖palm grease, ‖palm oil, ‖perk(s), perquisite, pourboire, tip
rel alms, benefaction, contribution, donation; offering, reward

grave *vb* **1** *syn* see ENGRAVE 1
2 *syn* see IMPRESS 3

grave *n* a place of interment <his *grave* is in the church burial ground>
syn burial, ‖pit, sepulcher, sepulture, tomb
rel catacomb, crypt, vault; mausoleum; ossuary; cinerarium
idiom final resting place

grave *adj* **1** *syn* see SERIOUS 2
2 *syn* see SERIOUS 1
rel heavy, ponderous; grim, sad, saturnine; awful, dreadful, horrible, terrible
con flippant, light, light-minded
ant gay
3 involving marked risk of impairment or destruction <a *grave* illness>
syn dangerous, fell, grievous, major, serious, ugly; *compare* DANGEROUS 1
rel deadly, destructive, dire, fatal, killing, murderous; frightening, ghastly, terrible; afflictive, severe
con paltry, petty, trivial; harmless, innocuous; temporary, transitory

gravely *adv syn* see SERIOUSLY 2

grave marker *n syn* see TOMBSTONE

gravestone *n syn* see TOMBSTONE

graveyard *n syn* see CEMETERY

gravid *adj syn* see PREGNANT 1

gravidity *n syn* see PREGNANCY

graybeard *n syn* see GAFFER

gray matter *n syn* see MIND 1

graze *vb* **1** *syn* see BRUSH
2 *syn* see GLANCE 1
3 *syn* see ABRADE 1
rel harm, hurt, injure; bruise, contuse, wound

greasy *adj* **1** *syn* see FATTY 2
2 *syn* see SLICK 1

‖**greasy spoon** *n syn* see EATING HOUSE

great *adj* **1** *syn* see LARGE 1
con measly, paltry, petty, puny, trifling, trivial
ant little
2 *syn* see FAMOUS 2
rel superlative, supreme, surpassing, transcendent

great deal *n syn* see MUCH

greater *adj* **1** *syn* see BEST
2 *syn* see SUPERIOR 1

great gun *n syn* see NOTABLE 1

greathearted *adj* **1** *syn* see BRAVE 1
2 *syn* see GENEROUS 1

greatly *adv syn* see VERY 1

greatness *n syn* see SIZE 2

greed *n syn* see CUPIDITY
rel gluttonousness, gluttony, rapaciousness, ravenousness, voraciousness

greedy *adj syn* see COVETOUS
con bounteous, bountiful, generous, liberal, munificent, openhanded; exuberant, lavish, prodigal, profuse

Greek *n syn* see GIBBERISH 1

green *adj* **1** *syn* see YOUNG 1
2 *syn* see INEXPERIENCED
con grown-up, ripe, mature, matured; educated, instructed; trained; proficient, skilled, skillful
ant experienced

green *n syn* see COMMON 2

‖**greenbacks** *n pl syn* see MONEY

green-eyed *adj syn* see ENVIOUS

greenhorn *n syn* see RUSTIC

greenhouse *n* a glass-enclosed structure for the cultivation and protection of tender plants <a small window *greenhouse* full of bloom>
syn conservatory, ‖glasshouse
rel coolhouse, hotbed, hothouse

greenness *n* **1** *syn* see YOUTH 1
2 *syn* see INEXPERIENCE

greet *vb syn* see ADDRESS 7

greeting *n* the ceremonial words or acts of one who meets, welcomes, or formally addresses another <after the *greeting* the chairman called the roll>
syn salutation, salute
rel address, hail, hello, welcome
con farewell, good-bye
ant valediction

gregarious *adj syn* see SOCIAL 2

grief *n syn* see SORROW
rel bemoaning, bewailing, deploring, lamenting
con comfort, comforting, consolation, solace, solacing
ant joy

grievance *n syn* see INJUSTICE 2
rel hardship, rigor; affliction, cross, trial, tribulation

grieve *vb* **1** *syn* see DISTRESS 2
2 to feel or express deep distress <*grieved* at the loss of so many lives>
syn mourn, sorrow
rel bear, endure, suffer; bemoan, bewail, deplore, lament; cry, keen, wail, weep
ant rejoice
3 *syn* see DEPLORE 1

grievous *adj* **1** *syn* see ONEROUS
2 *syn* see BITTER 2
3 *syn* see GRAVE 3
4 *syn* see DEPLORABLE

‖**grifter** *n syn* see SWINDLER

grill *n syn* see CROSS-EXAMINATION

grilling *n syn* see CROSS-EXAMINATION

grim *adj* **1** *syn* see FIERCE 1
rel foreboding, ominous
2 forbidding in action or appearance <had a *grim* and determined expression on his face>
syn austere, bleak, dour, hard, harsh, severe, stringent
rel cold, forbidding, ‖off-putting; fixed, rigid, set; determined, firm, stern

con calm, mellow, mild, soft, warm; attractive, beautiful, pleasing
ant pleasant

3 being extremely obdurate or firm in action or purpose <fought with *grim* determination>
syn implacable, ironfisted, merciless, mortal, relentless, ruthless, unappeasable, unflinching, unrelenting, unyielding
rel adamant, inexorable, inflexible, obdurate, resolute, stubborn, unforgiving, vindictive; certain, inevitable; determined, dogged
con considerate, gentle, mild; clement, forbearing, indulgent
ant lenient

4 *syn* see GHASTLY 1
rel loathsome, offensive, repugnant, repulsive, revolting

grimace *n syn* see FACE 6
grimace *vb* to distort one's face by way of expressing a feeling <*grimaced* with pain>
syn mop, mouth, mow, mug, ‖mump
rel contort, deform, distort, misshape
idiom make a face (*or* mouth), make a wry face (*or* mouth), pull a face, screw up one's face

grime *vb syn* see SOIL 2
grim reaper *n syn* see DEATH 1
grimy *adj syn* see DIRTY 1
grin *vb syn* see SMILE
con frown, gloom
ant grimace

grind *vb syn* see DRUDGE
grind *n* **1** *syn* see WORK 2
2 *syn* see ROUTINE
grip *vb* **1** *syn* see TAKE 4
2 *syn* see ENTHRALL 2
grip *n syn* see HOLD
rel coercion, constraint, duress, restraint
gripe *vb* to complain emphatically and often petulantly <students *griping* about the cafeteria food>
syn ‖beef, ‖bellyache, ‖bitch, bleat, ‖blow off, crab, ‖crib, fuss, kvetch, squawk, yammer, yawp (*or* yaup); *compare* COMPLAIN
rel brawl, kick, take on; croak, grouch, grouse, grumble, murmur, mutter
con applaud, approve, cheer; rejoice; accept, bear, endure, tolerate

gripe *n* **1** *syn* see HOLD
2 *usu* gripes *pl syn* see STOMACHACHE
griper *n syn* see GROUCH
grisette *n syn* see DOXY 1
grisly *adj syn* see GHASTLY 1
rel eerie, uncanny, weird
grit *n syn* see FORTITUDE
con faltering, hesitation, vacillation, wavering
ant faintheartedness

grobian *n syn* see BOOR 2
grog *n syn* see LIQUOR 2
‖groggery *n syn* see BAR 5
‖grogshop *n syn* see BAR 5
groove *n syn* see ROUTINE

groovy *adj syn* see MARVELOUS 2
grope *vb* to reach out or about blindly (as in testing or searching) <*groped* along the wall in search of a door>
syn feel, fumble, grabble
rel poke, pry, root; examine, explore, search

gross *adj* **1** *syn* see EGREGIOUS
rel excessive, exorbitant, extreme, immoderate, inordinate
con paltry, trifling, trivial
ant petty

2 *syn* see UTTER
3 *syn* see FAT 2
4 *syn* see WHOLE 4
ant net
5 *syn* see MATERIAL 1
6 *syn* see COARSE 3
7 *syn* see OBSCENE 2
rel animal, carnal, fleshy, sensual; loathsome, offensive, repulsive, revolting; improper, unrefined
con decent, decorous, proper, refined

gross *n syn* see WHOLE 1
grotesque *adj syn* see FANTASTIC 2
rel baroque, flamboyant, rococo; eerie, uncanny, weird; extravagant, extreme; comic, comical, droll, ludicrous

grotto *n syn* see CAVE
grouch *n* an habitually irritable or complaining person <it's hard to live with a *grouch*>
syn ‖bellyacher, complainer, crab, crabber, crank, crosspatch, faultfinder, griper, grouser, growler, grumbler, grump, kicker, malcontent, sorehead, sourpuss
con optimist, Pollyanna

grouch *vb syn* see GRUMBLE 1
ground *n* **1** *syn* see BASIS 1
2 *syn* see BASE 1
3 *syn* see REASON 3
rel evidence, testimony; antecedent, cause, determinant; demonstration, test, trial
4 grounds *pl syn* see SEDIMENT
5 *syn* see EARTH 2
ground *vb* **1** *syn* see FELL 1
2 *syn* see BASE
rel buttress, support, sustain
grounded *adj syn* see AGROUND
groundless *adj syn* see BASELESS
ant well-founded, well-grounded
groundwork *n* **1** *syn* see BASIS 1
2 *syn* see BASE 1
group *n* **1** a usually comparatively small assemblage of individuals <people gathered in *groups* about the hall>
syn assembly, band, bevy, bunch, cluster, covey, crew, party; *compare* COMPANY 4, GATHERING
rel circle, clique, coterie, set
con crowd, crush, horde, mob, press, rout, throng

2 *syn* see GATHERING 2
3 an assemblage of things constituting a unit <a *group* of houses behind the church>
syn array, batch, battery, body, bunch, bundle, clot, clump, cluster, clutch, lot, parcel, passel, platoon, set, sort, suite
rel assemblage, collection, mess, shooting match
4 *syn* see SET 5
5 *syn* see SYNDICATE

---

syn synonym(s)   *rel* related word(s)
ant antonym(s)   *con* contrasted word(s)
idiom idiomatic equivalent(s)
‖ use limited; if in doubt, see a dictionary

6 *syn* see CLASS 1

group *vb* **1** to make into or bring together in a group <*grouped* the children according to age>
syn assemble, cluster, collect, gather, round up; *compare* GATHER 6
rel adjust, arrange, harmonize, organize, systematize; allocate, dispose, distribute, place; bunch, crowd, huddle
idiom bring together, get together
con disband, disperse, scatter, separate
2 *syn* see ASSORT

‖**group grope** *n syn* see ORGY 2

grouping *n syn* see CLASS 1

grouse *vb syn* see GRUMBLE 1

grouser *n syn* see GROUCH

grovel *vb syn* see FAWN
idiom lick the dust (*or* one's boots)

groveler *n syn* see SYCOPHANT

groveling *adj syn* see FAWNING

grow *vb* **1** to cause (something living) to exist or flourish <*grew* a crop of wheat>
syn breed, cultivate, produce, propagate, raise
rel care (for), foster, nurse, nurture, rear, tend
2 *syn* see MATURE
3 *syn* see ESCALATE 2
4 *syn* see BECOME 1

growl *vb syn* see RUMBLE

growler *n syn* see GROUCH

grown *adj* **1** *syn* see MATURE 1
2 *syn* see OVERGROWN

grown-up *adj syn* see MATURE 1
ant childish; callow

growth *n syn* see DEVELOPMENT

grow up *vb syn* see MATURE

grub *vb* **1** *syn* see DIG 1
rel burrow, poke, root
2 *syn* see SCOUR 2
3 *syn* see DRUDGE

grub *n* **1** *syn* see HACK 2
2 *syn* see FOOD 1

grubber *n syn* see HACK 2

grubby *adj syn* see DIRTY 1
ant immaculate

grubstake *vb syn* see CAPITALIZE

grudge *vb syn* see ENVY
rel deny; refuse

grudge *n syn* see MALICE
rel grievance, injury, injustice

gruesome *adj syn* see GHASTLY 1
rel appalling, daunting; horrendous, horrific; baleful, sinister

gruff *adj* **1** *syn* see BLUFF
rel crabbed, dour, morose, saturnine, sullen, surly; boorish, churlish; fierce, truculent
con bland, smooth, suave, urbane; fulsome, oily, slick, soapy, unctuous
2 *syn* see HOARSE 1

grumble *vb* **1** to complain in a low harsh voice and often in a surly manner <workers *grumbling* about the low wages>
syn croak, grouch, grouse, ‖grunt, murmur, mutter, scold; *compare* COMPLAIN
rel ‖beef, ‖bellyache, ‖bitch, brawl, crab, fuss, gripe, holler, squawk, whine; groan, moan; complain, kick
con applaud, cheer; rejoice
2 *syn* see RUMBLE

grumbler *n syn* see GROUCH

grump *n* **1** grumps *pl syn* see SULK
2 *syn* see GROUCH

grump *vb syn* see SULK

Grundy *n syn* see PRUDE

grungy *adj syn* see DIRTY 1

‖**grunt** *vb syn* see GRUMBLE 1

guarantee *n* **1** an assurance for the fulfillment of a condition <gave him a *guarantee* that the work would be done according to specifications>
syn bail, bond, guaranty, security, surety, warranty; *compare* PLEDGE 1
rel earnest, pledge, promise, token, undertaking, word; oath, vow
2 *syn* see WORD 8

guarantee *vb syn* see WARRANT 2

guarantor *n syn* see SPONSOR

guaranty *n syn* see GUARANTEE 1
rel bargain, contract

guaranty *vb syn* see WARRANT 2

guard *n* **1** *syn* see DEFENSE 1
2 a person or group on sentinel duty <posted six *guards* around the diamond necklace><turned out the *guard*>
syn lookout, picket, sentinel, sentry, ward, watch, watchman
rel guardian, jailer, keeper, turnkey, warden, warder; patrolman; outguard, patrol

guard *vb syn* see DEFEND 1
rel attend, mind, tend, watch; accompany, chaperon, conduct, convoy, escort

guarded *adj* **1** *syn* see ULTERIOR
2 *syn* see CAUTIOUS
ant unguarded

guardian *n syn* see CUSTODIAN

guardianship *n syn* see CUSTODY

guardroom *n syn* see JAIL

gudgeon *n syn* see FOOL 3

guerdon *n syn* see REWARD

guerdon *vb syn* see PAY 1

guerrilla *n syn* see PARTISAN 2

guess *vb* **1** *syn* see CONJECTURE
rel reason, speculate; deduce; estimate, reckon
idiom venture a guess
2 *syn* see PREDICT 2

guest *n* **1** *syn* see VISITOR 1
2 guests *pl syn* see COMPANY 1

guff *n* **1** *syn* see NONSENSE 2
2 *syn* see BACK TALK

guffaw *vb syn* see LAUGH

guide *vb* to put or lead on a course or into the way to be followed <*guided* them safely through the minefields>
syn conduct, direct, escort, lead, pilot, route, see, shepherd, show, steer
rel accompany, chaperon, convoy; control, manage; contrive, engineer, maneuver
idiom see one on one's way
con bewilder, distract, mystify, perplex, puzzle; beguile, deceive, delude, mislead
ant misguide

guide *n* **1** *syn* see LEADER 1
2 *syn* see ESCORT 2
rel conductor, director, leader, pilot
3 *syn* see HANDBOOK

guidebook *n syn* see HANDBOOK

guild *n syn* see ASSOCIATION 2

guile *n syn* see DECEIT 1

ant ingenuousness; candor

guileful *adj* **1** *syn* see SLY 2
  ant guileless
  2 *syn* see UNDERHAND
guileless *adj* *syn* see NATURAL 5
  ant guileful
guillotine *vb* *syn* see BEHEAD
guilt *n* *syn* see BLAME
  rel crime, offense, sin; responsibility
  ant innocence; guiltlessness
guiltless *adj* **1** *syn* see GOOD 11
  2 *syn* see INNOCENT 2
  ant guilty
guilty *adj* *syn* see BLAMEWORTHY
  rel accountable, answerable, responsible;
  impeached, incriminated, indicted
  ant innocent; guiltless
guise *n* **1** *syn* see COSTUME
  2 *syn* see APPEARANCE 2
  3 *syn* see MASK 2
gulch *n* *syn* see RAVINE
gulf *n* **1** *syn* see INLET
  2 a hollow place of vast width and depth <a
  gulf extending deep into the earth>
  syn abysm, abyss, chasm
  rel cave, cavity, hollow; crevasse, gulch,
  ravine; pit, shaft, well
gull *vb* *syn* see DUPE
gull *n* *syn* see FOOL 3
gullible *adj* *syn* see EASY 3
  ant astute
gulp *vb* to swallow hurriedly or greedily or in
  one swallow <*gulped* his lunch and ran off>
  syn bolt, cram, englut, gobble, guzzle, ingurgitate, slop, slosh, wolf
  rel devour, glut, stuff
  con nibble, pick
gum (up) *vb* *syn* see BOTCH
gumbo *n* *syn* see GOO 1
gummy *adj* *syn* see STICKY 1
gumption *n* *syn* see SENSE 6
  rel astuteness, perspicaciousness, perspicacity, sagaciousness, sagacity, shrewdness
gumptious *adj* *syn* see ENTERPRISING 2
gumshoe *n* **1** *syn* see DETECTIVE
  2 *syn* see POLICEMAN

gumshoe *vb* *syn* see SNEAK
gun *n* *syn* see ASSASSIN
gung ho *adj* *syn* see ENTHUSIASTIC
gunk *n* **1** *syn* see GOO 1
  2 *syn* see CRUD
gunman *n* *syn* see ASSASSIN
‖**gunsel** *n* *syn* see ASSASSIN
gunslinger *n* *syn* see ASSASSIN
gurge *vb* *syn* see SWIRL
gurgle *vb* *syn* see SLOSH 1
gush *vb* *syn* see POUR 2
  rel flood, flush; emanate, issue, spring
gushing *adj* *syn* see EFFUSIVE
gushy *adj* *syn* see EFFUSIVE
gussy up *vb* *syn* see DRESS UP 1
gust *n* *syn* see OUTBURST 1
gusto *n* *syn* see TASTE 4
  rel delectation, delight, enjoyment, pleasure; ardor, enthusiasm, fervor, passion, zeal
gusty *adj* *syn* see WINDY 1
‖**gusty** *adj* *syn* see PALATABLE
gut *n* **1** *usu* **guts** *pl* *syn* see ENTRAILS
  ‖**2** *syn* see ABDOMEN
  3 **guts** *pl* *syn* see COURAGE
  4 **guts** *pl* *syn* see FORTITUDE
gut *vb* **1** *syn* see EVISCERATE
  2 *syn* see DRESS 3
gut *adj* *syn* see INNER 2
gutless *adj* *syn* see COWARDLY
  ant ‖gutsy
‖**gutsy** *adj* *syn* see BRAVE 1
guy *n* *syn* see MAN 3
guzzle *vb* **1** *syn* see DRINK 3
  2 *syn* see GULP
guzzler *n* *syn* see DRUNKARD
gyp *n* **1** *syn* see SWINDLER
  2 *syn* see IMPOSTURE
gyp *vb* *syn* see CHEAT
gypper *n* *syn* see SWINDLER
gyrate *vb* **1** *syn* see TURN 1
  2 *syn* see SPIN 1
gyration *n* *syn* see REVOLUTION 1
gyre *vb* **1** *syn* see TURN 1
  2 *syn* see SPIN 1
gyre *n* *syn* see REVOLUTION 1
gyve *n*, *usu* **gyves** *pl* *syn* see SHACKLE

H

habiliment *n* **1** **habiliments** *pl* *syn* see EQUIP-
MENT
  2 *usu* **habiliments** *pl* *syn* see CLOTHES

habit *n* **1** a mode of behaving or doing fixed
by constant repetition <it was his *habit* to
rise early>
  syn consuetude, custom, habitude, manner,

practice, praxis, trick, usage, use, way, wont
  rel bent, disposition, inclination, proclivity,
tendency, turn; convention, fashion, form,
mode, pattern, style; addiction; groove, rote,
routine, rut, set
  2 *syn* see PHYSIQUE
  rel carcass; framework; contour, outline
habitable *adj* *syn* see LIVABLE 1
  ant unhabitable, uninhabitable
habitant *n* *syn* see INHABITANT
habitat *n* the physical environment natural
to a kind of being <the watery *habitat* of the
eel>

---

syn synonym(s)   *rel* related word(s)
ant antonym(s)   *con* contrasted word(s)
idiom idiomatic equivalent(s)
‖ use limited; if in doubt, see a dictionary

syn haunt, home, locality, range, site, stamping ground

rel environment, locale, surroundings, territory

habitation *n* **1** the act of inhabiting or the state of being inhabited <places suitable for *habitation*>

syn inhabitancy, inhabitation, occupancy, occupation, residence, settlement

rel colonization, domiciliation, peopling; sojourning

2 the place where one lives <*habitations* unfit for human occupancy>

syn abode, commoracy, domicile, dwelling, home, house, residence, residency

rel apartment, flat, tenement; housing, lodging, lodgment, quarters; haunt, haven, homeplace, homestead, place, seat; ‖digs, nest, nook, ‖pad, ‖roost; astre, fireside, hearth, hearthside, hearthstone, roof, rooftree

idiom roof over one's head, where one hangs one's hat

habitual *adj* **1** *syn* see USUAL 1

rel constant, established, ingrained, inveterate, persistent, steady

con infrequent, irregular, sporadic, uncommon

ant occasional

2 acting by force of habit <*habitual* smokers who blue the air>

syn accustomed, chronic, confirmed, habituated

rel continual, inveterate, persistent, regular, steady; automatic, instinctive, involuntary; addicted; customary, wonted

con conscious, deliberate, premeditative, purposive, witting

habitually *adv* *syn* see USUALLY 1

ant occasionally

habituate *vb* **1** *syn* see ACCUSTOM

2 to make acceptable or desirable (as to oneself) through use <*habituate* oneself to poverty>

syn addict, adjust, confirm (in), devote (to), take (to)

rel bear, endure, inure, support, tolerate; condition, familiarize, season

con balk (at), object (to), resist

habituated *adj* *syn* see HABITUAL 2

habitude *n* *syn* see HABIT 1

rel attitude, position, stand; condition, situation, state

con humor, mood, temper; caprice, freak, vagary, whim

habitué *n* **1** one who frequents a place <an *habitué* of libraries>

syn denizen, frequenter, haunter

rel customer, devotee, patron, sojourner; employer, user

2 *syn* see ADDICT

habitus *n* *syn* see PHYSIQUE

hack *vb* to cut with repeated crude or ruthless blows <*hack* a path through the jungle>

syn hackle, haggle, slash

rel gash, mangle; chop, cut, fell, hew

hack *n* **1** *syn* see TAXICAB

2 one who surrenders intellectual or personal integrity for an assured reward (as a regular income) <party *hacks* and hangers-on>

syn drudge, grub, grubber, hireling, mercenary, slavey

rel grind, lackey, servant, slave; machine, plodder; potboiler

hack *adj* **1** *syn* see INFERIOR 2

rel commonplace, dull, ordinary, trite, usual; inconsequential, petty, trivial

con individual, original, uncommon, unusual

2 *syn* see TRITE

rel antiquated, old, outmoded, outworn

con lively; unfamiliar

hackle *vb* *syn* see HACK

hackneyed *adj* *syn* see TRITE

rel antediluvian, antiquated, archaic, obsolete, outmoded, out-of-date; conventional, everyday, quotidian, stock; moth-eaten

ant unhackneyed

Hadean *adj* *syn* see INFERNAL 1

rel gloomy, murky, stygian

hades *n* *syn* see HELL

hag *n* **1** *syn* see WITCH 1

2 an ugly or evil-looking old woman <a pitiful homeless *hag*>

syn ‖bag, ‖bat, beldam, biddy, crone, drab, trot, witch

rel gammer, grandam; ‖battle-ax, fishwife, gorgon, harpy, harridan, shrew, slattern, virago, vixen

haggard *adj* thin and contracted by or as if by fatigue or inner distress <*haggard* from their long vigil>

syn careworn, drawn, pinched, worn

rel angular, gaunt, lank, lean, scraggy, scrawny, skinny, spare; ashen, faded, pale, pallid, wan; exhausted, fagged, fatigued, tired, wearied, worn-down

con energetic, lusty, strenuous, vigorous; easy, relaxed

haggle *vb* **1** *syn* see HACK

2 to argue as to terms <*haggle* over prices>

syn bargain, chaffer, dicker, higgle, huckster, palter

rel barter, deal, horse-trade, trade; bicker, cavil, dispute, quibble, squabble, stickle, wrangle

hagridden *adj* *syn* see OBSESSED

hagride *vb* *syn* see WORRY 1

hail *n* *syn* see BARRAGE

hail *vb* **1** *syn* see ADDRESS 7

rel hallo, hallow, holler, shout

2 *syn* see COMMEND 2

con belittle, deprecate, disparage, downgrade; berate, censure, condemn, libel, rap; dismiss, reject

hail (from) *vb* *syn* see ORIGINATE 5

hair *n* a minute distance, degree, or margin <won the election by a *hair*>

syn ace, hairbreadth, whisker; *compare* HINT 2

rel bit, fraction, jot, mite, particle, trace, trifle

hairbreadth *n* *syn* see HAIR

haircutter *n* *syn* see BARBER

hairless *adj* lacking hair <he had a shining *hairless* head>

syn bald, glabrous, smooth

rel baldish; shaved, shaven, shorn, tonsured

ant hairy

hairline *adj* *syn* see FINE 1

hairsplitting *adj syn* see FINE 1
hair-trigger *adj syn* see INSTANTANEOUS
hairy *adj* 1 covered with or as if with hair <wore a *hairy* overcoat>
    syn fleecy, hirsute, pileous, pilose, whiskered, woolly
    rel bristly, bushy, downy, fluffy, fuzzy, lanate, nappy, pubescent, rough, shaggy, tomentose, tufted, unshorn, villous
    con bald, barefaced, beardless, glabrous, shaved, shaven, shorn, smooth
    ant hairless
  2 *syn* see DANGEROUS 1
  3 *syn* see ROUGH 1
halcyon *adj syn* see CALM 1
    con blustery, fevered, furious, raging, rough, stormy, tempestuous, troubled, tumultuous, wild
hale *adj syn* see HEALTHY 1
    rel husky, stout, strapping
    idiom hale and hearty
    ant infirm
haleness *n syn* see HEALTH
‖**half-assed** *adj syn* see DEFICIENT 1
half-blind *adj syn* see PURBLIND
half blood *n syn* see HYBRID
    ant full blood
half-breed *n syn* see HYBRID
    ant full blood
halfhearted *adj syn* see TEPID 1
‖**half-seas over** *adj syn* see INTOXICATED 1
halfway *adj syn* see MIDDLE 1
half-wit *n syn* see FOOL 4
half-witted *adj syn* see RETARDED
hall *n syn* see PASSAGE 4
hallo *vb syn* see CALL 1
hallow *vb syn* see BLESS 1
  2 *syn* see DEVOTE 1
    con defile, desecrate, pollute, profane
hallowed *adj syn* see HOLY 1
hallucination *n syn* see DELUSION 1
    rel apparition, fata morgana, phantom, wraith
hallway *n syn* see PASSAGE 4
halt *vb syn* see LIMP 1
halt *vb* 1 *syn* see STOP 4
    ant proceed
  2 *syn* see STOP 3
  3 *syn* see ARREST 1
  4 *syn* see HESITATE
  5 *syn* see CLOSE 2
halting *adj* 1 *syn* see AWKWARD 2
  2 *syn* see VACILLATING 2
ham-handed *adj syn* see AWKWARD 2
hammer *vb* 1 to strike or shape with or as if with a hammer <brass *hammered* into bowls and trays>
    syn beat, malleate, pound
    rel elaborate, fashion, form, shape
  2 *syn* see BEAT 1
  3 *syn* see IMPRESS 3
  ‖4 *syn* see STAMMER 1
hammer (out) *vb syn* see ERECT 5
hammerhead *n syn* see DUNCE

hammerheaded *adj syn* see STUPID 1
hamper *vb* to impede in moving, progressing, or acting freely <the long dress *hampered* her escape>
    syn clog, curb, entrammel, fetter, hobble, hog-tie, leash, shackle, tie, tie up, trammel; *compare* HINDER, RESTRAIN 1
    rel cumber, encumber, handicap, hinder, impede, lumber, obstruct; baffle, balk, bar, block, foil, frustrate, thwart; restrain, restrict, retard; discomfit, embarrass; check, inconvenience, inhibit
    idiom tie one's hands
    con free, liberate, loose, release, unfetter, unleash, unshackle
    ant aid, facilitate
hamper *n syn* see OBSTACLE 1
hams *n pl syn* see BUTTOCKS
hand *n* 1 *syn* see SIDE 1
  2 *syn* see PHASE
  3 *syn* see HANDWRITING
  4 *syn* see HELP 1
  5 *syn* see WORKER
  6 *syn* see TOUCH 6
hand *vb* 1 *syn* see GIVE 3
  2 *syn* see PASS 9
handbill *n syn* see POSTER
handbook *n* a concise reference book <a *handbook* of wild flowers>
    syn Baedeker, compendium, enchiridion, guide, guidebook, manual, vade mecum
    con cyclopedia, encyclopedia
hand down *vb* to convey in succession <a skill *handed down* from father to son>
    syn bequeath, hand on, pass (on), transmit
    con get, obtain, receive
handful *n syn* see FEW
handicap *n* 1 *syn* see DISADVANTAGE
    rel burden, encumbrance, load; embarrassment
    ant asset
  2 *syn* see ADVANTAGE 3
handicraft *n syn* see TRADE 1
hand in *vb syn* see SUBMIT 2
handkerchief *n* a small usually square piece of cloth used especially for blowing the nose <carry a pocket *handkerchief*>
    syn hankie, kerchief, ‖wipe, ‖wiper
‖**handle** *n* 1 *syn* see NAME 1
  2 *syn* see NICKNAME
handle *vb* 1 *syn* see TOUCH 1
    rel test, try; manipulate
  2 to deal with or manage usually with dexterity or efficiency <*handles* his tools with great skill>
    syn dispense, maneuver, manipulate, ply, swing, wield
    rel direct, guide, manage, operate, run, work; brandish, flourish, shake, wave; aim, lay, level, point
  3 *syn* see OPERATE 3
  4 *syn* see TREAT 2
    rel conduct, control, direct, manage
  5 *syn* see GOVERN 3
  6 *syn* see USE 2
handling *n syn* see OVERSIGHT 1
handmaid *n syn* see MAID 2
hand on *vb syn* see HAND DOWN
hand out *vb syn* see GIVE 1
hand over *vb* 1 *syn* see RELINQUISH

---

syn synonym(s)   *rel* related word(s)
ant antonym(s)   *con* contrasted word(s)
idiom idiomatic equivalent(s)
‖ use limited; if in doubt, see a dictionary

2 *syn* see GIVE 3

3 *syn* see COMMIT 1

hand running *adv syn* see TOGETHER 2

handsome *adj* 1 *syn* see LIBERAL 1
con economical, frugal, sparing; scrimpy, skimpy

2 *syn* see BEAUTIFUL
rel august, majestic, noble, stately; chic, dashing, fashionable, modish, smart, stylish
con inelegant, unsightly
ant unhandsome

handwriting *n* writing in which the letters are formed by a hand-guided implement (as a pen) <legible *handwriting*>
syn calligraphy, chirography, ductus, fist, hand, penmanship, script
rel longhand

handy *adj* 1 *syn* see CONVENIENT 2
idiom at one's hand (*or* elbow), ready to hand
ant unhandy

2 *syn* see PRACTICAL 2
rel adaptable, advantageous, beneficial, wieldy
con clumsy, cumbersome, cumbrous, unwieldy
ant unhandy

3 *syn* see DEXTEROUS 1

hang *vb* 1 to place or be placed so as to be supported at one point or side usually at the top <*hang* the washing on the line>
syn dangle, depend, sling, suspend
rel attach, hook; fix, pin, tack (up); adhere, cling, stick

2 to put to death by suspending by the neck <was *hanged* for stealing a sheep>
syn gibbet, noose, scrag, string (up), turn off
rel execute, lynch
idiom bring to the gallows, hang by the neck, make dance on air (*or* nothing)

3 to remain poised or stationary as if suspended in midair <clouds *hanging* in the west>
syn float, hover, poise

4 to project outward or incline downward <children *hanging* out the windows to watch a parade>
syn beetle, bend (over), jut, lean (over), overhang
rel drape, droop, loll, lop, sag, trail

hang (on *or* upon) *vb syn* see DEPEND (on *or* upon) 1

hang *n* the special method of doing, using, or dealing with something <can't get the *hang* of this gadget>
syn knack, swing, trick
rel art, craft, skill

hang around *vb syn* see FREQUENT

hanger–on *n syn* see PARASITE
rel bystander, follower, spectator, sycophant

hanging *adj syn* see SUSPENDED

hand–loose *adj syn* see EASYGOING 3

hang on *vb syn* see PERSEVERE

hang out *vb* 1 *syn* see RESIDE 1

2 *syn* see FREQUENT

hangout *n* 1 *syn* see RESORT 2

2 *syn* see DIVE

hang up *vb syn* see DELAY 1

hanker *vb syn* see LONG
rel covet, desire, wish

hankie *n syn* see HANDKERCHIEF

hanky–panky *n syn* see DECEPTION 1

hap *n syn* see ACCIDENT 1
rel destiny, fate, lot, portion

hap *vb syn* see HAPPEN 1

hap *vb syn* see BUNDLE UP

haphazard *adj syn* see RANDOM
rel accidental; careless, helter-skelter, slipshod; unorganized, unsystematic
con deliberate, designed, intentional, voluntary, willful
ant planned

haphazard *adv syn* see ABOUT 4
rel accidentally, aimlessly, carelessly, casually, promiscuously

haphazardly *adv syn* see ABOUT 4
rel accidentally, aimlessly, carelessly, casually, promiscuously

hapless *adj syn* see UNLUCKY
rel infelicitous; miserable, woeful, wretched

happen *vb* 1 to take place or come about <the incident *happened* at midnight>
syn befall, betide, break, chance, come, come off, develop, do, fall out, give, go, go down, hap, occur, pass, rise, transpire
rel go off, turn out
idiom come to pass

2 to come by chance <he unexpectedly *happened* on a new method>
syn bump, chance, hit, light, luck, meet, stumble, tumble
rel befall

happening *n syn* see OCCURRENCE

happify *vb syn* see PLEASE 2

happily *adv syn* see WELL 5

happiness *n* a state of well-being or pleasurable satisfaction <felt *happiness* at her husband's success>
syn beatitude, blessedness, bliss, blissfulness
rel content, contentedness, satisfaction; cheer, cheerfulness, felicity, gladness; gaiety, jollity, joy; delectation, delight, enjoyment, pleasure
con discontent, dissatisfaction, vexation; cheerlessness, despair, desperation, despondency, hopelessness; distress, misery, wretchedness
ant unhappiness

happy *adj* 1 *syn* see LUCKY
rel accidental, casual, fortuitous, incidental; opportune, seasonable, timely
ant unhappy

2 *syn* see FIT 1
rel effective, effectual, efficacious, efficient; cogent, convincing, telling; pat, seasonable, well-timed; correct, nice, right
ant unhappy

3 *syn* see GLAD 1
rel content, contented, satisfied
ant unhappy; disconsolate

happy–go–lucky *adj* disposed to accept cheerfully whatever happens <enjoyed a *happy-go-lucky* existence without needlessly worrying>
syn carefree, free-minded, insouciant, lighthearted, lightsome; *compare* COOL 2
rel casual, easy, easygoing; blithe, careless, cheerful, feckless, heedless, lackadaisical;

debonair, nonchalant, unconcerned; devil‑may‑care, reckless
con careful, cautious, circumspect, discreet, guarded, prudent
happy hunting ground *n syn* see HEAVEN 2

hara–kiri *n syn* see SUICIDE
harangue *n syn* see TIRADE
harangue *vb syn* see ORATE
harass *vb* 1 *syn* see RAID 1
2 *syn* see WORRY 1
rel badger, bait, bullyrag, chivy, devil, heckle, hector, hound, ride
idiom give a bad (*or* hard) time
3 *syn* see TRY 2
harassed *adj syn* see DISTRAUGHT
harasser *n syn* see BULLY 1
harassment *n syn* see ANNOYANCE 1
rel aggravation, disturbance, exasperation, irritation, perturbation
harbinger *n syn* see FORERUNNER 1
harbinger *vb syn* see ANNOUNCE 2
harbor *n* 1 *syn* see SHELTER 1
2 *syn* see INLET
3 a place where seacraft may ride secure <a small craft retreated to the safety of the *harbor*>
syn anchorage, ‖chuck, harborage, haven, port, riding, road(s), roadstead
harbor *vb* 1 to provide with shelter or a refuge <*harbored* the refugees in our homes>
syn chamber, haven, house, roof, shelter, shield
rel cherish, foster, nurse, nurture; conceal, hide, secrete; guard, protect, safeguard, screen
idiom give shelter (*or* asylum) to
con eject, evict, expel, oust; banish, deport, exile; eliminate, exclude, shut out
2 to provide with a usually temporary place to live <the miners were *harbored* in camps>
syn accommodate, bestow, billet, board, bunk, domicile, domiciliate, entertain, house, hut, lodge, put up, quarter, room, roost
rel cabin, camp, encamp
harborage *n syn* see SHELTER 1
2 *syn* see REFUGE 1
3 *syn* see HARBOR 3
hard *adj* 1 *syn* see FIRM 2
rel compacted, compressed, concentrated, consolidated, packed; callous, hardened, indurate, indurated, set; adamantine, flinty, granitic, iron, ironhard
con fluid, liquid; flabby, limp; ductile, malleable, plastic, pliable, pliant; elastic, flexible, limber, resilient, supple
ant soft
2 *syn* see SPIRITUOUS
ant soft
3 *syn* see REALISTIC
4 *syn* see INSENSIBLE 5
5 *syn* see INTENSIVE
6 demanding great toil and effort <a *hard* but rewarding task>

syn arduous, difficile, difficult, effortful, formidable, heavy, knotty, labored, laborious, operose, rough, rugged, serious, severe, slavish, sticky, strenuous, terrible, toilful, toilsome, tough, uphill
rel burdensome, exacting, onerous; complex, complicated, intricate, involved, scabrous; backbreaking, distressing, exhausting, fatiguing, grinding, tiring, wearing, wearisome, wearying; bothersome, demanding, irksome, rocky, straining, troublesome, trying; merciless, unsparing
con effortless, facile, light, simple, smooth
ant easy
7 *syn* see ACTUAL 2
8 *syn* see GRIM 1
9 *syn* see SEVERE 3

hard *adv* 1 with great or utmost force <hit the nail *hard*>
syn energetically, forcefully, forcibly, hardly, might and main, mightily, powerfully, strongly, vigorously
rel actively, animatedly, briskly, snappily, spiritedly, sprightly, vivaciously; earnestly, intensely, keenly, seriously, urgently, wholeheartedly
idiom with all one's might
con faintly, feebly, nervelessly, softly, strengthlessly, unenergetically, weakly
ant easily, easy
2 in a violent manner <the wind blew *hard* all the next day>
syn fiercely, frantically, frenziedly, furiously, hardly, madly, stormily, tumultuously, turbulently, violently, wildly
rel boisterously, exuberantly, rowdily, uproariously; angrily, brutally, ferociously, savagely, viciously
idiom like a house afire, like fury, like mad
con gently, mildly, softly
3 with intentness and determination <made up her mind to study *hard*>
syn assiduously, dingdong, earnestly, exhaustively, intensely, intensively, painstakingly, thoroughly, unremittingly
rel conscientiously, meticulously, punctiliously
con carelessly, casually, desultorily, fitfully, haphazardly
4 in a fixed and intensive manner <stared *hard* at the offender>
syn closely, intently, searchingly, sharply
con casually, cursorily, idly, offhand
5 in such manner as to cause hardship, difficulty, or defeat <things will go *hard* with him if he doesn't reform>
syn badly, hardly, harshly, painfully, rigorously, roughly, severely; *compare* AMISS 2
rel cruelly; relentlessly; meanly, shabbily, unfairly
con comfortably, pleasantly, smoothly; acceptably, satisfactorily, satisfyingly
ant easily, easy
6 with great or excessive resentment or grief <don't take your setback so *hard*>
syn bitterly, hardly, keenly, rancorously, resentfully, sorely
con casually, lightly, nonchalantly, offhandedly
7 in a firm manner <hold on *hard*>

---

syn synonym(s) *rel* related word(s)
ant antonym(s) *con* contrasted word(s)
idiom idiomatic equivalent(s)
‖ use limited; if in doubt, see a dictionary

syn fast, firm, firmly, fixedly, solidly, steadfastly, tight, tightly
con easily, easy, loose, loosely, slackly
8 with difficulty <breathing *hard* after the climb>
syn arduously, burdensomely, difficultly, hardly, laboriously, onerously, toilsomely
rel exhaustingly, gruelingly, painfully, tiredly; awkwardly, cumbersomely, cumbrously, inconveniently, ponderously, unhandily, unwieldily
con effortlessly, evenly, handily, readily, smoothly
ant easily, easy
9 to the point of hardness <the pond is frozen *hard*>
syn firmly, hardly, solid, solidly
10 *syn* see CLOSE

hard–boiled *adj* **1** *syn* see UNFEELING 2
rel coarse, crude, rough; seasoned, sophisticated, worldly-wise
idiom not born yesterday
con artless, guileless, naive, simple-hearted, unsophisticated; kindly, mild, soft
2 *syn* see REALISTIC

harden *vb* **1** to make or become physically hard or solid <this substance *hardens* immediately on exposure to air>
syn cake, concrete, congeal, dry, indurate, set, solidify
rel compact, consolidate, densify, firm, stiffen; anneal, caseharden, temper; calcify, fossilize, lithify, ossify, petrify
con deliquesce, dissolve, fuse, liquefy, melt
ant soften
2 to make proof against hardship, strain, or exposure <frontier life *hardened* most men quickly to rough conditions>
syn acclimate, acclimatize, climatize, season, toughen
rel accustom, habituate, indurate, inure; accommodate, adapt, adjust, conform
con emasculate, enervate; debilitate, devitalize, enfeeble, sap, undermine, weaken
ant soften

hardened *adj syn* see UNFEELING 2
hardfisted *adj syn* see STINGY
ant openhanded
hardhanded *adj syn* see STINGY
ant openhanded
hardheaded *adj* **1** *syn* see OBSTINATE
2 *syn* see REALISTIC
hardhearted *adj syn* see UNFEELING 2
hardihood *n* **1** *syn* see TEMERITY
rel boldness, intrepidity; brazenness, cockiness; fortitude, grit, guts, pluck, sand
ant cowardice; timidity
2 *syn* see INSOLENCE
3 *syn* see ENERGY 1
hardiness *n syn* see TEMERITY
ant cowardice; timidity
hard–line *adj syn* see TOUGH 3
hardly *adv* **1** *syn* see HARD 1
2 *syn* see HARD 2
3 *syn* see HARD 5
4 *syn* see HARD 6
5 *syn* see HARD 8
6 *syn* see JUST 2
7 *syn* see HARD 9
hardly ever *adv syn* see SELDOM

hardness *n syn* see DIFFICULTY 1
ant easiness
hardpan *n syn* see BASE 1
hardscrabble *adj syn* see BARREN 2
hard–shell *adj syn* see INVETERATE 1
hardship *n syn* see DIFFICULTY 1
rel adversity, mischance, misfortune; danger, hazard, peril; affliction, trial, tribulation; drudgery, toil, travail; discomfort, distress
con comfort, ease
hardy *adj syn* see TOUGH 4
ant tender
harebrain *n* **1** *syn* see SCATTERBRAIN
2 *syn* see CRACKPOT
harebrained *adj* **1** *syn* see GIDDY 1
2 *syn* see FOOLISH 2
harefooted *adj syn* see FAST 3
hark *vb syn* see LISTEN
rel mark, mind, note, notice, remark
idiom be all ears, not miss a trick
harlequin *n syn* see CLOWN 3
harlot *n* **1** a woman who engages in unlawful or socially unacceptable sexual intercourse often for material gain <ply the trade of a *harlot*>
syn blowen, courtesan, demimondaine, demirep, fancy woman, hetaera, kept woman, paphian, whore; *compare* DOXY, MISTRESS, PROSTITUTE, WANTON
2 *syn* see PROSTITUTE
harlotry *n syn* see PROSTITUTION
harm *n syn* see INJURY 1
rel deleteriousness; banefulness, noxiousness, perniciousness; mischance, misfortune, misuse; impairment, marring
con aid, help; accommodation, benefaction; charity, favor, service
ant benefit
harm *vb syn* see INJURE 1
rel abuse, ill-use, maltreat, mistreat, misuse, molest; dilapidate, ruin; discommode, incommode, inconvenience; sabotage, sap, undermine
idiom do violence to
con ameliorate, better, improve; avail, profit
ant benefit
harmful *adj* inflicting or capable of inflicting injury <a *harmful* drug>
syn bad, damaging, deleterious, detrimental, evil, hurtful, ill, injurious, mischievous, nocent, nocuous, prejudicial, prejudicious
rel baleful, baneful, malefic, malign, malignant; noisome, noxious, pernicious, toxic; insalubrious, unhealthful, unhealthy, unwholesome; dangerous, hazardous, risky, unsafe
con innocuous, inoffensive, nontoxic; beneficent, beneficial, benign, benignant, favorable, helpful, salutary, useful; safe, unhazardous
ant harmless
harmless *adj* not having hurtful or injurious qualities <*harmless* pastimes>
syn innocent, innocuous, innoxious, inobnoxious, inoffensive, unoffending, unoffensive; *compare* SAFE 3
rel guiltless; nontoxic, painless, safe
con baneful, dangerous, malignant, noxious, pernicious, toxic, virulent; damaging,

destructive, detrimental, hurtful, injurious; deadly, fell, ruinous; improper, unsuitable, wrong
ant harmful

harmonic *adj syn* see HARMONIOUS 1

harmonious *adj* **1** musically concordant <a *harmonious* morning chorus of birds>
syn blending, chiming, consonant, harmonic, musical, symphonic, symphonious
rel canorous, dulcet, euphonious, mellifluous, mellisonant, melodious, musical, silvery, sonorous, sweet, tuneful; chordal, contrapuntal, counterpointed, polyphonic
idiom in concert, in tune
con clashing, discordant, dissonant, grating, harsh, jangling, jarring, raucous, shrill, strident, tuneless, unmusical, untuneful; atonal
ant disharmonious, inharmonious, unharmonious

2 having the parts agreeably related <a building with *harmonious* proportions>
syn accordant, concordant, congruous; *compare* CONSONANT 1
rel agreeable, pleasing, satisfying; concinnate, symmetrical
con clashing, incongruous, unsymmetrical; askew, distorted, skewed
ant inharmonious, unharmonious

3 marked by accord in sentiment or action <a *harmonious* effort to reach a practicable agreement>
syn amicable, amical, congenial, friendly
rel coactive, collaborative, cooperative; empathetic, empathic, simpatico, sympathetic; calm, irenic, pacific, peaceful
idiom of one accord
con incompatible, uncongenial, uncooperative, unfriendly, unsympathetic; belligerent, contentious, pugnacious
ant disharmonious, inharmonious, unharmonious

harmonize *vb* **1** *syn* see AGREE 3
rel cooperate, match, unite
con differ, disagree
ant clash; conflict

2 *syn* see AGREE 4
ant differ (from)

3 to bring into consonance or accord <*harmonize* the factions of a political party>
syn accommodate, attune, conform, coordinate, integrate, proportion, reconcile, reconciliate, tune
rel adapt, adjust, correlate; coapt, relate
con alienate, disrupt, estrange
ant disharmonize

4 to combine or adapt so as to achieve a desired effect <*harmonize* the elements of a story>
syn arrange, blend, integrate, orchestrate, symphonize, synthesize, unify
rel coordinate, correlate

harmonizing *n syn* see RECONCILIATION

harmony *n* **1** musical agreement of sounds <singing in *harmony*>
syn accord, chorus, concert, concord, consonance, tune

rel mellifluousness, melodiousness, melody, musicality, sonority, tunefulness; diapason, polyphony
con cacophony, discord, discordance, discordancy, dissonance, harshness, inharmoniousness, jangle, stridency, tunelessness, unharmoniousness, unmusicalness, untunefulness; atonality
ant disharmony, inharmony

2 the effect produced when different things come together without clashing or disagreement <goals that are in *harmony* with our capabilities>
syn accord, agreement, chime, concord, concordance, consonance, tune; *compare* CONSISTENCY
rel conformance, conformity, correspondence; articulation, coaptation, compatibility, congruity; concatenation, concurrence, integration, oneness, togetherness, unity
con disagreement, discord, disparity, dissidence, disunity, variance
ant conflict

3 the state of persons who are in full and perfect agreement <friends who live in *harmony*>
syn concord, rapport, unity
rel affinity, empathy, fellow-feeling, kinship; peace, tranquillity
idiom meeting of minds
con contention, dissension, strife
ant discord

4 *syn* see SYMMETRY
rel concinnity, consonance; dignity, elegance, grace; integrity, unity
con asymmetry, discordance, discordancy, imbalance
ant inharmony

harness *vb syn* see HITCH 2

‖**harness bull** (*or* **cop**) *n syn* see POLICEMAN

harpy *n syn* see VIRAGO

harrier *n syn* see BULLY 1

harrow *vb syn* see AFFLICT
rel fret, irritate, pester; badger, bait, bedevil, devil, heckle, hector, needle, tantalize, tease

harrowing *adj syn* see EXCRUCIATING

harry *vb* **1** *syn* see RAVAGE

2 *syn* see RAID 1

3 *syn* see WORRY 1
rel disturb, irk, perturb, upset; badger, irritate

harsh *adj* **1** *syn* see ROUGH 1
rel coarse, granular, loose; bristly, scraggly, scratchy, shaggy, stubbly
con glossy, satiny, silken, silky, sleek, slick, velvety

2 *syn* see ACRID
rel acerb, acerbic, biting, burning, mordant; pungent, tangy; dry, sour, tart
con mild, smooth, sweet, velvety

3 disagreeable to the ear <many birds have *harsh* cries>
syn dry, grating, hoarse, jarring, rasping, raucous, rough, rugged, rusty, squawky, strident, stridulent, stridulous
rel discordant, dissonant, immelodious, ineuphonious, inharmonious, unmelodious, unmusical; grinding, jangling, scraping;

---

syn synonym(s) *rel* related word(s)
ant antonym(s) *con* contrasted word(s)
idiom idiomatic equivalent(s)
‖ use limited; if in doubt, see a dictionary

blaring, brassy; ear-piercing, piercing, shrill, squeaky

con euphonious, harmonious, mellow, melodic, melodious, musical, sonorous, sweet; low, soft; agreeable, pleasing

4 *syn see* UNCOMFORTABLE

5 *syn see* GRIM 2

6 *syn see* SEVERE 3

ant mild

harshly *adv syn see* HARD 5

con considerately; gently, lightly, well; famously

ant smoothly

haruspex *n syn see* PROPHET

harvest *n* **1** the act, process, or occasion of gathering a crop <the time of *harvest*>

syn cropping, gathering, harvesting, ingathering, reaping

rel garnering, storing

con planting, seedtime, sowing

2 the gathered produce of land <a bountiful *harvest* saved the settlers>

syn crop, fruitage

rel yield; bearing, vintage

harvest *vb syn see* REAP

rel assemble, collect; accumulate, amass, bin, store (up), stow (away); cache, hide, hoard, squirrel, stash

harvesting *n syn see* HARVEST 1

hash *vb syn see* CHOP 2

hash *n* **1** *syn see* MISCELLANY 1

2 *syn see* CLUTTER 2

3 *syn see* MESS 3

‖**hashery** *n syn see* EATING HOUSE

‖**hash house** *n syn see* EATING HOUSE

hassle *n* **1** *syn see* QUARREL

2 *syn see* COMMOTION 4

3 *syn see* ATTEMPT

hassle *vb* **1** *syn see* ARGUE 2

rel cavil; brawl, fight, spar, struggle

2 *syn see* WORRY 1

haste *n* **1** rapidity of motion or action <we finished our job with great *haste*>

syn celerity, dispatch, expedition, expeditiousness, hurry, hustle, rustle, speed, speediness, swiftness

rel fastness, fleetness, quickness, rapidity; pace, velocity; dash, drive

con languidness, languor, leisureliness, reluctance, slowness, lethargy, sluggishness, torpor

ant deliberateness, deliberation

2 rash or headlong action <oversights due to *haste*>

syn hastiness, hurriedness, precipitance, precipitancy, precipitateness, precipitation, rush

rel impetuosity, impetuousness, impulsiveness

con care, carefulness, circumspection, hastelessness, unhurriedness

ant deliberateness, deliberation

haste *vb syn see* HURRY 2

hasten *vb syn see* SPEED 3

2 *syn see* HURRY 2

hastily *adv syn see* FAST 2

rel agilely, nimbly; impetuously, impulsively, unpremeditatedly; carelessly, recklessly, thoughtlessly; precipitately, prematurely, suddenly

con carefully, designedly, studiedly, thoughtfully; gradually, leisurely, slowly, sluggishly

ant deliberately

hastiness *n syn see* WASTE 2

hasty *adj* **1** *syn see* FAST 3

rel agile, brisk, nimble; hurried, quickened

con dilatory, laggard, leisured, leisurely

2 *syn see* PRECIPITATE 1

ant deliberate

3 *syn see* RASH 1

rel devil-may-care, slambang, slapdash

hatch *vb* **1** *syn see* GENERATE 3

2 *syn see* GENERATE 1

hatch (up) *vb syn see* CONTRIVE 2

hatchet man *n syn see* ASSASSIN

hate *n* **1** *syn see* ABOMINATION 2

rel animosity, animus, antipathy, hostility, ill will, rancor; disgust, scorn, spite

con affection; toleration; adoration, veneration

ant love

2 *syn see* ABOMINATION 1

rel bother, grievance, gripe, irritant, nuisance, ‖pain, trouble

ant delight

hate *vb* to feel extreme enmity or dislike <Cain *hated* his brother> <*hate* to meet strangers>

syn abhor, abominate, detest, execrate, loathe

rel contemn, despise, disdain, dislike, scorn; deprecate, disapprove; resent

con cherish, enjoy, fancy, like, relish, favor, prefer, prize; esteem, respect, revere; dote; idolize, worship

ant love

hateable *adj syn see* HATEFUL 2

ant lovable

hateful *adj* **1** *syn see* MALICIOUS

rel acrimonious, ill-natured; bitter, resentful; mean

con benevolent, charitable, cordial, genial, good-humored, good-natured, kind, kindly, pleasant

2 deserving of or arousing hate <found herself in a *hateful* situation>

syn abhorrent, abominable, detestable, hateable, horrid, odious

rel distasteful, distressing, obnoxious, repellent, repulsive; contemptible, despicable, execrable, opprobrious, reprehensible; scurvy; foul, infamous, vile; accursed, blasphemous, damnable, unspeakable

con compatible, congenial, consonant; alluring, appealing, attractive, charming, enchanting; agreeable, delectable, delightful, likable, pleasant, pleasing

ant lovable; sympathetic

hatred *n syn see* ABOMINATION 2

rel antipathy, dislike; animosity, enmity, hostility, rancor

con affability, benevolence, benignity, charitableness, cordiality

ant admiration

haughtiness *n syn see* PRIDE 3

ant lowliness

haughty *adj syn see* PROUD 1

rel aloof, detached, distant, indifferent, reserved; egotistic; contemptuous, scornful *con* humble; obsequious, servile, subservient

ant lowly

haul *vb* **1** *syn* see PULL 2
rel move, remove, shift; boost, elevate, hoist, lift, raise

haul *n* *syn* see LOAD 1

haul up *vb* *syn* see STOP 4

haunches *n pl* *syn* see BUTTOCKS

haunt *vb* *syn* see FREQUENT

haunt *n* **1** *syn* see RESORT 2

2 *syn* see HABITAT

3 *syn* see APPARITION

haunter *n* *syn* see HABITUÉ 1

hauteur *n* *syn* see PRIDE 3

ant lowliness

haut monde *n* *syn* see ARISTOCRACY

have *vb* **1** to keep, control, or experience as one's own <can't *have* your cake and eat it too>
syn enjoy, hold, own, possess, retain
idiom be possessed of, have in hand
con lack, need, want

2 *syn* see INCLUDE
rel admit, compose, comprise

3 *syn* see BEAR 3

4 *syn* see GET 1

5 *syn* see EXPERIENCE 1

6 *syn* see LET 2

7 *syn* see KNOW 1

8 *syn* see OUTWIT

9 *syn* see BRIBE

10 *syn* see MUST 2

haven *n* **1** *syn* see HARBOR 3

2 *syn* see SHELTER 1

haven *vb* *syn* see HARBOR 1

haversack *n* *syn* see BACKPACK

havoc *n* *syn* see RUIN 3
rel calamity, cataclysm, catastrophe; despoiling, pillaging, ravaging; vandalism

havoc *vb* *syn* see RAVAGE

hawk *vb* *syn* see PEDDLE 2

hawker *n* *syn* see PEDDLER

hawk-eyed *adj* *syn* see SHARP-EYED

hawkshaw *n* *syn* see DETECTIVE

haymaker *n* *syn* see CUFF

hayseed *n* *syn* see RUSTIC
ant city slicker, slicker

hazard *n* **1** *syn* see CHANCE 2

2 *syn* see DANGER

hazard *vb* **1** *syn* see VENTURE 1

2 *syn* see GAMBLE 1

3 *syn* see ENDANGER

hazardous *adj* *syn* see DANGEROUS 1
ant safe; unhazardous

haze *vb* *syn* see OBSCURE

haze *n* **1** an atmospheric condition that is characterized by the presence of fine particulate material in the air and that deprives the air of its transparency <*haze* obscured the distant hills>
syn brume, film, mist, smaze
rel cloud, ||drisk, fog, murk, ||smeech, smog, smoke, vapor; cloudiness, mistiness, murkiness, smokiness

2 a state of mental vagueness or obtuseness <lived in a *haze* of pleasant memories>
syn befuddlement, daze, fog, ||maze, muddledness, muddleheadedness, muddlement
rel dream, reverie, stupor, trance; absentmindedness, abstraction, bemusement, preoccupation, woolgathering
con alertness, attentiveness, awareness

hazy *adj* obscured or made dim by or as if by haze <had only a *hazy* idea of where they were>
syn cloudy, foggy, misty, mushy, vague, vaporous, vapory
rel blurred, clouded, dim, indefinite, indistinct, murky, nebulous, obscure; bemused, dreamy, tranced, stuporous; dazed, ||mazed, muzzy

he *n* *syn* see MAN 3

head *n* **1** the upper division of the body that contains the brain, the chief sense organs, and the mouth <put your hat on your *head*>
syn ||bean, ||belfry, ||chump, ||coco, ||coconut, ||conk, ||dome, headpiece, noddle, noggin, noodle, ||nut, ||pallet, pate, poll, sconce
rel brainpan, cranium, crown, scalp

2 *syn* see MIND 1

3 *syn* see GIFT 2

4 *syn* see LEADER 2
con subordinate; aide, assistant, helper

5 *syn* see PROMONTORY

6 *syn* see TOILET

7 *syn* see HEADLINE

8 *syn* see SUBJECT 2

head *adj* *syn* see FIRST 3

head *vb* **1** *syn* see BEHEAD

2 *syn* see DIRECT 2

3 to commence to go in an indicated direction <the cowboys *headed* for town>
syn bear, light out, make, set out, strike out, take off
rel go, proceed, start
idiom make a beeline for

4 *syn* see SPRING 1

heading *n* *syn* see HEADLINE

headland *n* *syn* see PROMONTORY

headline *n* a word or group of words usually in large type introducing and summarizing a newspaper story <*headlines* that screamed the news of the president's death>
syn head, heading
rel banner, banner head, bannerline, scarehead, screamer, spreadhead

headlong *adj* *syn* see PRECIPITATE 1
rel daredevil, daring, foolhardy, rash, reckless

headman *n* *syn* see LEADER 2

headmost *adj* *syn* see FIRST 1

headpiece *n* *syn* see HEAD 1

headshaker *n* *syn* see SKEPTIC

head start *n* *syn* see ADVANTAGE 3

headstone *n* *syn* see TOMBSTONE

headstrong *adj* *syn* see OBSTINATE
con subdued; tame; amenable, biddable, docile, meek, obedient, tractable

headway *n* **1** *syn* see ADVANCE 2

heady *adj* *syn* see SHREWD

heal *vb* *syn* see CURE

healing *adj* *syn* see CURATIVE

health *n* the state of being sound in body or mind <the patient was nursed back to *health*>

---

syn synonym(s) *rel* related word(s)
ant antonym(s) *con* contrasted word(s)
idiom idiomatic equivalent(s)
|| use limited; if in doubt, see a dictionary

syn haleness, healthiness, soundness, wholeness

rel stamina, vitality, well-being; euphoria

con debility, decrepitude, feebleness; ill health, illness, sickliness

ant disease, infirmity

healthful *adj* conducive or beneficial to the health or soundness of body or mind <regular exercise is a *healthful* practice>

syn good, healthy, hygienic, salubrious, salutary, salutiferous, wholesome

rel advantageous, beneficial, profitable, useful; corrective, curative, remedial; aiding, alleviative, helpful, mitigative, restorative, sanative

con insalubrious, unhealthy, unhygienic, unwholesome; damaging, deleterious, detrimental, harmful, injurious, mischievous, pernicious

ant unhealthful

healthiness *n syn* see HEALTH

ant unhealthiness

healthy *adj* **1** enjoying or manifesting health <a *healthy* baby>

syn ‖bunkum, fit, hale, right, sane, sound, well, well-conditioned, well-liking, whole, wholesome

rel hearty, iron, lusty, robust, thriving, vigorous; rugged, stalwart, strong, sturdy, tough; agile, chipper, spry; blooming, rosy, thriving

idiom fit as a fiddle, in (top) condition, in fine fettle, in shape, in trim, sound as a dollar, up to snuff

con decrepit, delicate, feeble, fragile, frail, weak; infirm, ‖poorly, sickly

ant unhealthy

2 *syn* see HEALTHFUL

ant unhealthful

3 *syn* see SAFE 3

heap *n* **1** *syn* see PILE 1

rel congeries, gathering

2 *syn* see MUCH

3 *syn* see SCAD

4 *syn* see JALOPY

heap *vb* **1** to throw or collect in a pile <*heap* up leaves for a bonfire>

syn bank, cock, drift, hill, mound, pile, stack

rel cord, ‖dess, rick, shock; bunch, clump, lumber, ‖lump, mass; deposit, dump; accumulate, amass, assemble, collect, gather, group

con broadcast, disperse, distribute, scatter, separate, spread, strew

2 *syn* see LOAD 3

hear *vb* **1** *syn* see LISTEN

idiom get wind of

2 *syn* see DISCOVER 3

hearing *n* **1** *syn* see EARSHOT

2 an opportunity to be heard <they finally obtained a *hearing* on their complaints>

syn audience, audition

rel conference, interview, meeting, parley; test, tryout; discussion, negotiation

hearken *vb syn* see LISTEN

hearsay *n syn* see REPORT 1

heart *n* **1** the seat or center of secret thoughts and emotions <in his *heart* he knew he was seriously in the wrong>

syn bosom, breast, soul

idiom bottom of the heart, cockles of the heart

2 *syn* see COURAGE

3 *syn* see TASTE 4

4 *syn* see CENTER 2

5 *syn* see CENTER 3

heartache *n syn* see SORROW

idiom aching heart, heavy heart

heartbreak *n* **1** *syn* see SORROW

rel agony, bale, torment

idiom bleeding heart

heartbreaking *adj syn* see DEPLORABLE

hearten *vb syn* see ENCOURAGE 1

rel energize, enliven; arouse, rally, rouse, stir

con damp, dampen; weigh

ant dishearten

heartfelt *adj syn* see SINCERE 1

rel bona fide, genuine, honest, true, unfeigned; deep, profound

con hypocritical, insincere; false, pretended

heartless *adj syn* see UNFEELING 2

heartrending *adj syn* see DEPLORABLE

heart–searching *n syn* see INTROSPECTION

heartsick *adj syn* see DOWNCAST

heartsore *adj syn* see DOWNCAST

heartthrob *n syn* see SWEETHEART 1

heart–whole *adj* **1** *syn* see FREE 6

2 *syn* see GENUINE 3

hearty *adj syn* see SINCERE 1

rel responsive, warm, warmhearted; deep, profound; exuberant, profuse

con cold, dispassionate, emotionless

ant hollow

‖**heat** *n syn* see POLICEMAN

heated *adj* **1** *syn* see HOT 1

ant chilled

2 *syn* see FEVERISH 2

3 *syn* see ANGRY

heathen *adj* of or relating to people who do not acknowledge the God of the Bible <ancient *heathen* sacrificial rites>

syn ethnic, gentile, infidel, infidelic, pagan, profane

rel heathenish, paganish

heave *vb* **1** *syn* see THROW 1

2 *syn* see TOSS 2

3 *syn* see PANT 1

4 *syn* see RETCH

‖**5** *syn* see VOMIT

heaven *n* **1** *usu* **heavens** *pl syn* see SKY

2 an abode of blissful spiritual life after death <the religious conceptions of *heaven* and hell>

syn Abraham's bosom, bliss, Canaan, Civitas Dei, elysium, empyrean, happy hunting ground, kingdom come, New Jerusalem, nirvana, paradise, Zion

rel afterworld, eternity, glory, hereafter, promised land; everlastingness, immortality

idiom Beulah Land (*or* Land of Beulah), City of God, Kingdom of God, Kingdom of Heaven

con earth, world; Gehenna, hades, inferno, netherworld, perdition, pit, Sheol, Tartarus, Tophet, underworld

ant hell

3 *syn* see UTOPIA

4 *syn* see ECSTASY

heavenly *adj* 1 *syn* see CELESTIAL
con hadean, Tartarean
ant hellish
2 *syn* see DELIGHTFUL

heavy *adj* 1 having great or relatively great weight <a *heavy* load>
syn hefty, massive, ponderous, weighty; *compare* UNWIELDY
rel awkward, bulky, clumsy, lumbering, lumbersome; unhandy, unmanageable, unwieldy; cumbersome, cumbrous
con airy, buoyant, weightless; handy, manageable, wieldy
ant light
2 *syn* see FAT 2
3 *syn* see SERIOUS 2
4 *syn* see RECONDITE
5 *syn* see PREGNANT 1
6 *syn* see LETHARGIC
7 *syn* see OVERCAST
8 *syn* see HARD 6
9 *syn* see RICH 3

heavy *n syn* see NOTABLE 1

heavy–footed *adj* *syn* see PONDEROUS 2

heavy–handed *adj* 1 *syn* see AWKWARD 2
2 *syn* see PONDEROUS 2

heavyhearted *adj syn* see SAD 1
ant lighthearted

heavyheartedness *n syn* see SADNESS
ant lightheartedness

heavyset *adj syn* see STOCKY

heavyweight *n syn* see NOTABLE 1
con lightweight

hebetate *vb syn* see DULL 5

hebetude *n syn* see LETHARGY 1

hebetudinous *adj syn* see LETHARGIC

heckle *vb* 1 *syn* see BAIT 2
rel plague, worry; discomfit, disconcert, embarrass, faze, rattle; tease, torment
2 *syn* see MOLEST

hectic *adj syn* see FEVERISH 2

hector *n syn* see BULLY 1

hector *vb* 1 *syn* see INTIMIDATE
2 *syn* see BAIT 2

hedge *vb* 1 *syn* see EQUIVOCATE 2
2 *syn* see ENCLOSE 1

hedonist *n* one given to the zealous pursuit of pleasure <lead the life of a *hedonist*>
syn carpet knight, pleasuremonger, sybarite
rel bon vivant, man-about-town; epicure, epicurean, gourmand, gourmet; debauchee, libertine, rake; sensualist, voluptuary; pleasure-seeker
ant ascetic

hedonistic *adj syn* see SYBARITIC
con austere, self-denying, self-disciplined, self-restricted
ant ascetic

heebie–jeebies *n pl syn* see JITTERS

heed *vb syn* see LISTEN
rel mark, mind, note; observe, see, watch
idiom give (or pay) heed to

heed *n* 1 *syn* see NOTICE 1

rel awareness, interest, mindfulness; audience, hearing
2 *syn* see ATTENTION 1
rel concern, interest
con inattention, unconcern
3 *syn* see CARE 4

heedful *adj* 1 *syn* see ATTENTIVE 1
ant heedless, unheeding
2 *syn* see MINDFUL 2
ant heedless, unheeding
3 *syn* see CAREFUL 2

heedfully *adv syn* see WELL 2
ant heedlessly, unheeding

heedfulness *n syn* see CARE 4
ant heedlessness

heedless *adj syn* see CARELESS 1
ant heedful, heeding

heedlessness *n syn* see APATHY 2
ant heedfulness

hee–haw *vb syn* see LAUGH

heel *n* 1 *syn* see REMAINDER
2 *syn* see VILLAIN 1

heel *vb syn* see SLANT 1

hefty *adj* 1 *syn* see HEAVY 1
2 *syn* see HUSKY 1
3 *syn* see BIG 1

height *n* the distance a thing rises above the level on which it stands <the *height* of a building>
syn altitude, elevation
rel highness, loftiness, rise, tallness, stature
con lowness, profundity
ant depth

heighten *vb* 1 *syn* see INCREASE 1
2 *syn* see INCREASE 2
rel elevate, lift, raise; better, improve; enlarge, increase
con diminish, lessen, shrink
3 *syn* see INTENSIFY

heinie (or hiney) *n syn* see BUTTOCKS

heinous *adj syn* see OUTRAGEOUS 2
con paltry, petty, trifling, trivial
ant venial

heinousness *n syn* see ENORMITY 1

heir *n* one who inherits <died without *heirs*>
syn heritor, inheritor

‖**heist** *vb syn* see STEAL 1

hell *n* a place or state of the dead or of the damned <went to *hell* for his sins>
syn abyss, barathrum, blazes, Gehenna, hades, inferno, netherworld, Pandemonium, perdition, pit, Sheol, Tophet
rel limbo, Styx, Tartarus
idiom the hot place, infernal regions, place of torment
ant heaven

hell *vb syn* see REVEL 1

hell–fired *adj syn* see UTTER

hellish *adj syn* see INFERNAL 2

helotry *n syn* see BONDAGE

help *n* 1 an act or instance of giving what will benefit or assist <the stranded travelers received *help* from passersby>
syn aid, assist, assistance, comfort, hand, lift, relief, secours, succor, support
rel benefit, cooperation, service
ant hindrance
2 something that is beneficial <the rain was a real *help* to late crops>
syn aid, support

---

syn synonym(s)   *rel* related word(s)
ant antonym(s)   *con* contrasted word(s)
idiom idiomatic equivalent(s)
‖ use limited; if in doubt, see a dictionary

rel benefit, use

3 *syn* see HELPER

help *vb* 1 to give assistance or support <*help* the children with their lessons>
syn abet, aid, assist, benefact, do for, help out, stead
rel back, bolster, boost, champion, second, support, uphold; avail, benefit, profit; advance, facilitate, forward, further, promote, serve; befriend, succor
idiom give a lift, lend a hand (*or* a helping hand), stand back of (*or* behind)
con bar, block, impede, obstruct, oppose; baffle, balk, foil, frustrate, thwart; discomfit, embarrass; damage, harm, hurt, injure
ant hinder

2 *syn* see IMPROVE 1
rel alleviate, mitigate, palliate, relieve
con harm, impair, worsen

helper *n* one that helps <was made boss and assigned a dozen *helpers*>
syn aid, ancilla, assistant, attendant, help, striker
rel helpmate, helpmeet; auxiliary, deputy, subordinate; associate, follower; employee, laborer, servant, worker
idiom helping hand, right-hand man

helpful *adj* 1 of service or assistance <*helpful* suggestions>
syn aidant, aiding, assistive, serviceable
rel beneficial, effective, profitable, salutary, usable; constructive, practical, useful
con timeserving, uncooperative, unreliable; impractical, ineffectual
ant unhelpful

2 *syn* see GOOD 1

helpless *adj* 1 lacking protection or support <*helpless* nestlings>
syn defenseless, unprotected
rel abandoned, desolate, forlorn, forsaken, friendless; feeble, weak

2 *syn* see POWERLESS

helplessly *adv syn* see WILLY-NILLY

help out *vb syn* see HELP 1

helter-skelter *adv* 1 *syn* see PELL-MELL

2 *syn* see ABOUT 4

hem *n syn* see BORDER 1

hem *vb* 1 *syn* see BORDER

2 *syn* see ENCLOSE 1

3 *syn* see SURROUND 1

hence *adv* 1 *syn* see AWAY 1

2 *syn* see THEREFORE

henceforth *adv* from this time forward <made up his mind to keep out of trouble *henceforth*>
syn henceforward, hereafter; *compare* THENCEFORTH
idiom from now on

henceforward *adv syn* see HENCEFORTH

henchman *n syn* see FOLLOWER
rel attendant; lackey, minion, stooge

henpeck *vb syn* see NAG

hep *adj syn* see WISE 4

herald *n syn* see FORERUNNER 1
rel courier, crier, messenger

herald *vb* 1 *syn* see ANNOUNCE 2

2 *syn* see TOUT

Herculean *adj syn* see HUGE

herd *n syn* see DROVE 2

herd *vb syn* see DRIVE 3

here *adv syn* see HITHERTO 2

hereafter *adv syn* see HENCEFORTH

hereafter *n* 1 *syn* see FUTURE

2 an existence or place of existence after this life <buried pots and tools with the dead for use in the *hereafter*>
syn afterlife, afterworld, beyond, otherworld
idiom great beyond (*or* hereafter), life after death, next world (*or* life), world beyond the grave, world to come
con here and now

here and there *adv syn* see SOMETIMES

heresy *n* defection from a dominant belief or ideology <the *heresy* of the flat-earth theory>
syn dissent, dissidence, heterodoxy, misbelief, nonconformism, nonconformity, schism, unorthodoxy
rel impiety, infidelity; apostasy, defection, revisionism; error, fallacy

heretic *n* one who is not orthodox in his beliefs <a *heretic* in religion>
syn dissenter, dissident, misbeliever, nonconformist, schismatic, schismatist, sectary, separatist
rel apostate, defector, iconoclast, recreant, recusant, renegade; infidel, unbeliever; deviationist, revisionist
ant orthodox

heretical *adj* of, relating to, or characterized by heresy <*heretical* beliefs>
syn dissident, heterodox, nonconformist, schismatic, sectarian, unorthodox
rel apostate, infidel, miscreant, revisionist; differing, disagreeing, dissentient, dissenting, dissentive, misbelieving, unbelieving
con conventional, established; agreeing, conforming, conformist
ant orthodox

heretofore *adv syn* see BEFORE 2

heritage *n* 1 something that one receives or is entitled to receive by succession (as from a parent) <the *heritage* of freedom>
syn birthright, heritance, inheritance, legacy, patrimony

2 *syn* see TRADITION 1

heritance *n syn* see HERITAGE 1

heritor *n syn* see HEIR

hermaphrodite *adj syn* see BISEXUAL

hermaphroditic *adj syn* see BISEXUAL

hermetic *adj* 1 *syn* see RECONDITE

2 *syn* see SECLUDED

hermit *n syn* see RECLUSE

heroic *adj* 1 *syn* see BRAVE 1
ant pusillanimous

2 *syn* see HUGE

heroism *n* conspicuous courage or bravery <received an award for *heroism*>
syn gallantry, prowess, valiance, valiancy, valor, valorousness
rel boldness, bravery, courage, doughtiness, fearlessness, intrepidity, spirit; chivalry, nobility
con cowardice, spiritlessness, timidity, timorousness, weakness
ant pusillanimity

hesitancy *n syn* see HESITATION

hesitant *adj* 1 *syn* see DISINCLINED
con resolute, staunch, steadfast

2 *syn* see VACILLATING 2

hesitate *vb* to show irresolution or uncertainty <*hesitate* to buy a new car just now>
syn dither, falter, halt, shilly-shally, stagger, vacillate, waver, whiffle, wiggle-waggle
rel balk, boggle, demur, scruple, stick, stickle; fluctuate, oscillate, swing; dawdle, delay, dillydally, hang back, procrastinate, stall, temporize; pause

hesitating *adj syn* see VACILLATING 2

hesitation *n* the act or action of hesitating <several persons volunteered without *hesitation*>
syn hesitancy, indecision, indecisiveness, irresolution, shilly-shally, to-and-fro, vacillation, wavering
rel doubt, dubiety, dubiosity, mistrust, uncertainty; averseness, indisposition, reluctance
con alacrity, eagerness; courage, mettle, resolution, spirit, tenacity; aplomb, assurance, confidence

hetaera *n syn* see HARLOT 1

heteroclite *adj syn* see ABNORMAL 1

heterodox *adj syn* see HERETICAL
ant orthodox

heterodoxy *n syn* see HERESY
ant orthodoxy

heterogeneous *adj syn* see MISCELLANEOUS
ant homogeneous

hew *vb syn* see FELL 2

hex *vb syn* see BEWITCH 1

hex *n* **1** *syn* see JINX
2 *syn* see WITCH 1

hiatus *n syn* see GAP 3

hic jacet *n syn* see EPITAPH

hick *n syn* see RUSTIC

hick town *n syn* see BURG

hidden *adj syn* see ULTERIOR
ant open

hide *vb* to withdraw or withhold from sight or observation <they *hid* their loot in a cave>
syn bury, ‖bush up, cache, conceal, cover, ‖ditch, ensconce, occult, plant, screen, secrete, stash
rel mantle, mask, obscure, shade, shield; entomb, inter; cloak, curtain, shroud, veil; harbor, lodge, seclude, shelter
con bare, disclose, discover, display, exhibit, expose, reveal, show; uncover, unmask, unveil, unwrap; flaunt, parade, show off

hide *n* an animal skin <tanned *hides* for shoe leather>
syn fell, fur, jacket, pelt, skin

hide *vb syn* see WHIP 1

hideaway *n syn* see HIDEOUT

hidebound *adj syn* see ILLIBERAL

hideous *adj* **1** *syn* see UGLY 2
ant lovely
2 *syn* see OFFENSIVE
3 *syn* see GHASTLY 1

hideout *n* a place of retreat or concealment <a gangsters' *hideout*>

---

syn synonym(s)   *rel* related word(s)
ant antonym(s)   *con* contrasted word(s)
idiom idiomatic equivalent(s)
‖ use limited; if in doubt, see a dictionary

syn den, hideaway, lair
rel covert, haven, hermitage, refuge, retreat, sanctuary, shelter; robbers' roost

hie *vb syn* see GO 1

hierarch *n syn* see LEADER 2

hieratic *adj syn* see SACERDOTAL

higgle *vb syn* see HAGGLE 2

higgler *n syn* see PEDDLER

high *adj* **1** having a relatively great upward extension <a *high* building>
syn altitudinous, tall; *compare* LOFTY 6
rel aerial, eminent, lofty, soaring, towering; big, gigantic, grand, large, prominent
idiom tall (or high) as a steeple
con little, short, squat
ant low
2 *syn* see COSTLY 1
ant low
3 *syn* see MALODOROUS 1
4 *syn* see ELEVATED 4
5 *syn* see ACUTE 4
6 *syn* see DRUGGED

high and low *adv syn* see EVERYWHERE 1

high-and-mighty *adj syn* see PROUD 1

highball *vb syn* see HURRY 2

highbinding *n syn* see DECEPTION 1

highbrow *n syn* see INTELLECTUAL 2

highbrow *adj syn* see INTELLECTUAL 2

highbrowed *adj syn* see INTELLECTUAL 2
ant lowbrow, low-browed

higher *adj syn* see SUPERIOR 1

higher-up *n syn* see SUPERIOR

highest *adj syn* see TOP 1
ant lowest

2 *syn* see EXALTED 1

highest-ranking *adj syn* see EXALTED 1

highfalutin *adj syn* see RHETORICAL
con down-to-earth, matter-of-fact

highfalutin *n syn* see BOMBAST

high-flown *adj syn* see RHETORICAL

high-handed *adj syn* see MASTERFUL 1

high hat *n syn* see SNOB

high-hat *adj syn* see SNOBBISH

high-hearted *adj syn* see SPIRITED 2

high jinks *n pl* **1** *syn* see HORSEPLAY
2 *syn* see REVELRY 2

highly *adv syn* see VERY 1

high-minded *adj syn* see ELEVATED 2
ant low-minded

high-muck-a-muck *n syn* see NOTABLE 1

high-principled *adj syn* see HONORABLE 1

high roller *n syn* see SPENDTHRIFT

high sign *n* **1** *syn* see SIGN 1
2 a private usually covert signal, warning, or cue <I gave him the *high sign* when I saw the police approaching>
syn ‖office
rel tip, tip-off, wink; nod; alarm, SOS, warning

high-sounding *adj syn* see PRETENTIOUS 3

high-spirited *adj syn* see SPIRITED 2
rel jolly, lighthearted, merry, mirthful
ant low-spirited
2 *syn* see EXUBERANT 1

high-strung *adj* **1** *syn* see TENSE 3
2 *syn* see NERVOUS

hightail *vb syn* see GET OUT 1

highway *n syn* see WAY 1

high yellow *n syn* see MULATTO

hike *vb* **1** *syn* see RAISE 9

2 to travel about or through on foot <*hiked* through the woods>
syn tramp, tromp
rel footslog; stroll, walk; ramble, rove, wander; explore

hike *n* **1** *syn* see TRAMP 3
2 *syn* see RISE 3

hilarity *n* *syn* see MIRTH

hill *n* *syn* see PILE 1

hill *vb* *syn* see HEAP 1

hillbilly *n* *syn* see RUSTIC

hillman *n* *syn* see RUSTIC

hind *adj* *syn* see POSTERIOR 2

hind end *n* *syn* see BUTTOCKS

hinder *vb* to put obstacles in the way of <their cause was *hindered* by the excesses of overzealous supporters>
syn bar, block, brake, dam, impede, obstruct, overslaugh; *compare* HAMPER
rel arrest, check, interrupt, retard; clog, entrammel, fetter, hamper, hog-tie, manacle, shackle, trammel; curb, deter, hamstring, inhibit, restrain, tie (down); embog, mire; burden, handicap, lumber; baffle, balk, frustrate, thwart
idiom bog down
con abet, advance, aid, assist, ease, encourage, facilitate, forward, promote; accelerate, hasten, quicken, speed
ant further, help

hinder *adj* *syn* see POSTERIOR 2
ant fore, front

‖**hinder** *n* *syn* see BUTTOCKS

hindmost *adj* *syn* see POSTERIOR 2
con foremost, headmost
2 *syn* see LAST

hindrance *n* *syn* see ENCUMBRANCE
ant help

hinge (on *or* upon) *vb* *syn* see DEPEND (on *or* upon) 1

hint *n* **1** a slight or indirect pointing out of something and especially of the way to an end <give me a *hint* on how you would deal with the matter>
syn clue, cue, indication, inkling, intimation, notion, suggestion, telltale, wind
rel innuendo, insinuation; inspiration, prompting; aiming, direction, pointing; key, pointer, tip; advice, assistance
con command, directive, instruction, order
2 a very small amount or admixture <add a *hint* of garlic to the salad>
syn breath, cast, dash, intimation, lick, shade, shadow, smack, smatch, smell, soupçon, spice, sprinkling, strain, streak, suggestion, suspicion, taste, tincture, tinge, touch, trace, trifle, twang, vein, whiff, whisper, wink; *compare* HAIR
rel adumbration, taint, vestige; particle, scintilla
con abundance, heap, lot
ant oodles
3 *syn* see ASSOCIATION 4

hint *vb* **1** *syn* see SUGGEST 1
2 *syn* see POINT 2
3 *syn* see ADUMBRATE 1
4 to seek to obtain by sly or indirect means <kept *hinting* for an invitation to the party>
syn angle, fish
rel beg, coax, plead; importune, press; seek, solicit

con ask (for), demand, insist (on *or* upon)

hinterland *n* *syn* see FRONTIER 2

hipped *adj* **1** *syn* see DOWNCAST
2 *syn* see OBSESSED

hire *n* *syn* see WAGE

hire *vb* **1** to take or engage something or grant the use of something for a stipulated price or rate <*hire* a conveyance>
syn charter, lease, let, rent
rel contract (for), engage; sublease, sublet, subrent
2 *syn* see EMPLOY 2
ant fire

hired girl *n* *syn* see MAID 2

hireling *n* *syn* see HACK 2

hiring *n* *syn* see EMPLOYMENT 4

hirsute *adj* *syn* see HAIRY 1
ant hairless

hiss *vb* to make a sibilant sound <he thought he heard a snake *hiss*>
syn buzz, fizz, fizzle, sibilate, sizz, sizzle, swish, wheeze, whish, whisper, whiz, whoosh

hiss *n* *syn* see RASPBERRY

history *n* **1** *syn* see ACCOUNT 7
2 a chronological record of events <a *history* of the American Revolution>
syn annals, chronicle
rel account, recital, relation, report; diary, journal, memoir; epic, saga, tale

histrionic *adj* *syn* see DRAMATIC 1

hit *vb* **1** *syn* see STRIKE 2
rel buffet, pound, stroke
idiom give one a clip
2 *syn* see OCCUR 2
3 *syn* see HAPPEN 2

hit (on *or* upon) *vb* *syn* see FIND 1

hit *n* **1** a stroke delivered with a part of the body or an instrument <gave the disobedient boy a *hit* on the head with her ruler>
syn ‖conk, knock, lick, rap, swat, swipe, wipe; *compare* BLOW 1, CUFF
2 *syn* see SMASH 6
3 *syn* see MURDER

hitch *vb* **1** *syn* see LIMP 1
2 to attach as a means of motive power <*hitched* the team to a wagon>
syn couple, harness, yoke
idiom make fast
con free, release, unfasten; uncouple, unharness, unyoke
ant unhitch
‖**3** *syn* see MARRY 2
4 *syn* see HITCHHIKE

hitchhike *vb* to travel by securing free rides <*hitchhiked* to California>
syn hitch, thumb
idiom bum (*or* hook) a ride

hitherto *adv* **1** up to this particular point or time <imposed order upon what was *hitherto* haphazard>
syn as yet, earlier, so far, thus far, yet
rel before, formerly, heretofore, once, previously
idiom up to now (*or* then)
2 to this place <the appointed delegate shall come *hitherto*>
syn here

hit man *n* *syn* see ASSASSIN

hit-or-miss *adj* *syn* see RANDOM

hive *vb syn* see ACCUMULATE
hoard *n* 1 *syn* see ACCUMULATION
  2 *syn* see RESERVE
hoard *vb* to store up beyond one's present or reasonable need <*hoarding* sugar during war>
  syn squirrel, stash; *compare* ACCUMULATE, SAVE 4
  rel ‖sock away; garner, lay by, lay up
  idiom take all one can lay one's hands on
  con consume, use up; blow, dissipate, tool (away), fritter, frivol away, prodigalize, throw away, trifle (away), waste
hoarse *adj* 1 rough or dry in sound <developed a *hoarse* cough>
  syn croaking, croaky, gruff, husky
  rel coarse, dry, guttural, thick
  2 *syn* see HARSH 3
  con honeyed, mellifluent, mellifluous, smooth
hoary *adj syn* see ANCIENT 1
hoax *vb syn* see DUPE
hoax *n syn* see IMPOSTURE
hobble *vb* 1 *syn* see LIMP 1
  2 *syn* see HAMPER
hobo *n syn* see VAGABOND
hoboism *n syn* see VAGRANCY
hock *vb syn* see PAWN
hocus-pocus *n syn* see GIBBERISH 3
‖hodge *n syn* see RUSTIC
hodgepodge *n syn* see MISCELLANY 1
hogback *n syn* see RIDGE 1
hogshead *n syn* see CASK
hog-tie *vb syn* see HAMPER
hogwash *n syn* see NONSENSE 2
hoi polloi *n syn* see RABBLE 2
hoist *vb syn* see LIFT 1
hoity-toity *adj syn* see GIDDY 1
hokum *n syn* see NONSENSE 2
hold *vb* 1 *syn* see KEEP 5
  2 *syn* see ENTHRALL 2
  3 *syn* see HAVE 1
  4 *syn* see CONTAIN 2
  5 *syn* see FEEL 3
hold (with) *vb syn* see APPROVE 1
hold *n* the act or manner of grasping or holding <lost his *hold* on the side of the boat>
  syn clamp, clasp, clench, clinch, clutch, grapple, grasp, grip, gripe, tenure
  rel handclasp, handhold; purchase
hold back *vb* 1 *syn* see RESTRAIN 1
  2 *syn* see KEEP 5
  3 *syn* see DENY 3
hold down *vb syn* see RESTRAIN 1
holder *n syn* see OWNER
hold in *vb syn* see RESTRAIN 1
hold off *vb* 1 *syn* see FEND (off)
  2 *syn* see DEFER
hold out *vb syn* see OFFER 1
hold over *vb syn* see DEFER
hold up *vb syn* see DEFER
hole *n* 1 *syn* see APERTURE
  2 *syn* see GAP 1
  3 a space within the substance of a body or mass <buried their trash in a *hole* in the ground>
  syn cavity, hollow, vacuity, void
  rel gap, hiatus, lacuna; cranny, interstice, niche; fissure, rent, rift; vacancy, vacuum
  4 *syn* see HOVEL
  5 *syn* see PREDICAMENT
hole *vb syn* see OPEN 3
hole-and-corner *adj syn* see SECRET 1
holiday *n syn* see VACATION
holiness *n* a state of spiritual soundness and unimpaired virtue <the *holiness* of the saints>
  syn saintliness, sanctity
  rel blessedness, divineness, divinity, sacredness; consecration, devotion, devoutness, piety, piousness, spirituality
holler *vb syn* see CALL 1
hollo *vb syn* see CALL 1
hollow *adj* 1 having a muffled or reverberating quality <had a deep *hollow* gloomy voice>
  syn cavernous, reverberant, sepulchral
  rel echoing, resonant, resounding, reverberating, sounding
  con dead, dull, flat, toneless
  2 *syn* see VAIN 1
hollow *n* 1 *syn* see DEPRESSION 2
  2 *syn* see HOLE 3
holocaust *n syn* see FIRE 1
holy *adj* 1 dedicated to the service of or set apart by religion <pilgrimages to *holy* places>
  syn blessed, consecrated, hallowed, sacred, sanctified, unprofane; *compare* SACRED 2
  rel adored, glorified, revered, reverenced, venerated, worshiped; divine, religious, spiritual
  2 *syn* see SAINTLY
  ant unholy
  3 *syn* see DEVOUT
‖Holy Joe *n syn* see CLERGYMAN
holy place *n syn* see SHRINE
Holy Writ *n syn* see BIBLE
homage *n syn* see HONOR 1
home *n* 1 *syn* see HABITATION 2
  2 *syn* see HABITAT
  3 *syn* see COUNTRY
home *adj* 1 *syn* see DOMESTIC 1
  2 *syn* see DOMESTIC 2
homeland *n syn* see COUNTRY
homely *adj* 1 *syn* see PLAIN 1
  rel commonplace, familiar, intimate
  2 *syn* see PLAIN 5
  idiom homely as a mud (or hedge) fence, homely enough to sour milk
  ant comely
homicidal *adj syn* see MURDEROUS
homicide *n* 1 *syn* see MURDERER
  2 *syn* see MURDER
homilize *vb syn* see PREACH 1
hominine *adj syn* see HUMAN
hominoid *n syn* see ANTHROPOID
‖homo *n syn* see HOMOSEXUAL
homoerotic *adj syn* see HOMOSEXUAL
homophile *adj syn* see HOMOSEXUAL
Homo sapiens *n syn* see MANKIND
homosexual *adj* relating to or exhibiting sexual desire toward a member of one's own sex <*homosexual* acts between consenting adults>
  syn gay, homoerotic, homophile, inverted, ‖queer, uranian

---

syn synonym(s) *rel* related word(s)
ant antonym(s) *con* contrasted word(s)
idiom idiomatic equivalent(s)
‖ use limited; if in doubt, see a dictionary

rel androgynous, bisexual, epicene; transvestite; lesbian, sapphic; camp, effeminate; ||swishy

homosexual *n* one who is inclined to or practices homosexuality <a bar frequented by *homosexuals*>
syn ||fag, ||faggot, ||fruit, ||homo, invert, ||queer, uranian, uranist
rel transvestite; ||fairy, ||nance, ||nancy, ||pansy, ||queen, ||swish; ||dyke, lesbian, sapphist; pederast, sodomite

homunculus *n syn* see DWARF
honcho *n syn* see LEADER 2
hone *vb syn* see SHARPEN
honed *adj syn* see SHARP 1
honest *adj* 1 *syn* see GENUINE 3
rel reliable, unaffected, unimpeachable
2 *syn* see UPRIGHT 2
rel candid, forthright, frank, open, plain; dispassionate, objective; truthful, veracious
ant dishonest

honestness *n syn* see HONESTY
ant dishonesty

honesty *n* uprightness as evidenced in character and actions <he was generally known as a person of scrupulous *honesty*>
syn honestness, honor, honorableness, incorruption, integrity
rel conscientiousness, justness, probity, scrupulousness, uprightness; dependability, reliability, trustworthiness; goodness, morality, rectitude, virtue
con deceitfulness, mendaciousness, mendacity, untruthfulness; deceit, duplicity, guile
ant dishonesty

honey *n* 1 *syn* see SWEETHEART 1
2 *syn* see GIRL FRIEND 2
honey *vb syn* see SUGARCOAT 1
honey (up) *vb syn* see FAWN
honeybunch *n syn* see SWEETHEART 1
honeyed *adj syn* see MELLIFLUOUS
honky-tonk *n syn* see DIVE
honor *n* 1 respect or esteem shown one as his due or claimed by one as a right <received the *honor* due his rank>
syn deference, homage, obeisance, reverence
rel admiration, esteem; adoration, adulation, devotion, veneration, worship; acknowledgment, compliment, recognition, regard, respect
con contempt, despite, disdain, scorn; disregard, neglect, slighting
ant dishonor
2 an evidence or symbol of distinction <received many *honors* for her devoted public service>
syn accolade, award, badge, bays, decoration, distinction, kudos, laurels
rel deference, esteem, respect; admiration, approval
3 *syn* see HONESTY
con disgrace, ignominy, shame
ant dishonor, dishonorableness

honor *vb syn* see EXALT 1
ant dishonor

honorable *adj* 1 deserving of or entitled to honor (as because of rank, achievements, or service) <medicine is an *honorable* profession>
syn estimable, high-principled, noble, sterling, worthy; *compare* VENERABLE 1
rel august, illustrious, reverend, venerable, worshipful
ant dishonorable
2 *syn* see UPRIGHT 2
ant dishonorable

honorableness *n syn* see HONESTY
ant dishonor, dishonorableness

||**hooch** *n* 1 *syn* see LIQUOR 2
2 *syn* see MOONSHINE 2
||**hood** *n syn* see THUG 1
hoodlum *n syn* see THUG 1
hoodoo *n syn* see JINX
hoodwink *vb syn* see DUPE
hooey *n syn* see NONSENSE 2
hoof *vb syn* see WALK 1
hoof (it) *vb syn* see DANCE 1
hoofer *n syn* see DANCER
hook *vb syn* see STEAL 1
||**hooker** *n syn* see PROSTITUTE
hookshop *n syn* see BROTHEL
hookup *n syn* see ASSOCIATION 1
hooligan *n syn* see THUG 1
||**hoosegow** *n syn* see JAIL
hoosier *n syn* see RUSTIC
hoot *n* 1 *syn* see RASPBERRY
2 *syn* see PARTICLE
||**hootenanny** *n syn* see DOODAD
hop *vb* 1 *syn* see SKIP 1
2 *syn* see JUMP 1
||**hop** *n syn* see DRUG 2
hope *n syn* see EXPECT 1
hope *n syn* see TRUST 1
hopeful *adj* 1 full of hope or inclined to hope <the candidate was *hopeful* of winning>
syn hoping; *compare* CONFIDENT 1, EXPECTANT 1, OPTIMISTIC
rel anticipative, assured, satisfied, secure; cheerful, content, easy, undisturbed; fond, optimistic, Pollyannaish, rose-colored, sanguine, upbeat
con doubtful, insecure, pessimistic, uncertain; discouraged, disheartened, gloomy, glum
ant hopeless
2 exhibiting qualities that inspire hope <a *hopeful* prospect for improvement>
syn couleur de rose, encouraging, likely, promiseful, promising, roseate, rose-colored, rosy
rel advantageous, auspicious, propitious; bright, cheering, cheery, golden, halcyon, happy, sunny; budding, up-and-coming
con discouraging, disheartening, dismal, dreary, gloomy, pessimistic
ant hopeless

hopeful *n syn* see CANDIDATE
hopeless *adj* 1 *syn* see DESPONDENT
rel gloomy, glum, morose
con cheerful; assured, confident, optimistic, sanguine, sure
ant hopeful
2 offering no prospect of change for the better <his case was *hopeless* and beyond all human aid>
syn cureless, immedicable, impossible, incurable, insanable, irremediable, irreparable, uncorrectable, uncurable, unrecoverable
rel insoluble; incorrigible, irredeemable

idiom beyond hope (*or* remedy *or* repair), beyond human aid
con correctable, curable, medicable, remediable, reparable
ant hopeful

hoper *n syn see* OPTIMIST
hoping *adj syn see* HOPEFUL 1
hop-o'-my-thumb *n syn see* DWARF
hopped-up *adj syn see* DRUGGED
hopping *adj syn see* BUSTLING
horde *n syn see* CROWD 1
horizon *n syn see* KEN
horn in *vb* 1 *syn see* MEDDLE
  2 *syn see* INTRUDE 1
‖**horning** *n syn see* SHIVAREE
hornswoggle *vb syn see* DUPE
horrible *adj* 1 *syn see* GHASTLY 1
  rel abhorrent, abominable, detestable, hateful; loathsome, obnoxious, offensive, repulsive, revolting
  con gratifying, pleasing, soothing
  2 *syn see* FEARFUL 3
  3 *syn see* OFFENSIVE
horrid *adj* 1 *syn see* GHASTLY 1
  2 *syn see* HATEFUL 2
  3 *syn see* OFFENSIVE
horrific *adj syn see* FEARFUL 3
horrify *vb syn see* DISMAY 1
horrifying *adj syn see* GHASTLY 1
horror *n* 1 *syn see* FEAR 1
  rel distress, pain, shock, throe, wrench
  2 *syn see* ABOMINATION 2
hors d'oeuvre *n syn see* APPETIZER
horse *n syn see* SAWHORSE
horse *vb syn see* CUT UP 2
‖**horsefeathers** *n pl syn see* NONSENSE 2
horse opera *n syn see* WESTERN
horseplay *n* rough or boisterous play <their friendly *horseplay* almost ended in tragedy>
  syn fooling, high jinks, roughhouse, roughhousing, rowdiness, skylarking
  rel buffoonery, clowning
horseplay *vb syn see* CUT UP 2
horse sense *n syn see* SENSE 6
hospice *n syn see* HOTEL
hospitable *adj syn see* SOCIAL
  ant inhospitable
host *n syn see* MULTITUDE 1
hostage *n syn see* PLEDGE
  rel guaranty, security, surety
hostel *n syn see* HOTEL
hostelry *n syn see* HOTEL
hostile *adj* 1 marked by lack of friendliness or by opposition <takes a *hostile* view of a tax increase><*hostile* tribes>
  syn ill, inimical, inimical, unfriendly
  rel argumentative, competitive, contrary, dim, disaffected, disapproving, opposed, opposite, unfavorable; dour, sour; bellicose, belligerent, contentious, pugnacious; militant, warlike
  con amicable, benign, friendly
  ant unhostile
  2 *syn see* BITTER 3
hostility *n syn see* ENMITY

hot *adj* 1 marked by a notable amount of heat <a *hot* day>
  syn ardent, baking, blistering, boiling, broiling, burning, fiery, heated, red-hot, scalding, scorching, sizzling, sultry, sweltering, sweltry, torrid, white-hot
  rel febrile, fevered, feverish, feverous, hectic; summery, tropic, tropical; mild, warm
  idiom hot as a firecracker (*or* furnace), hot as an oven, hot as hell
  con chilly, cool, frigid, icy
  ant cold
  2 *syn see* LUSTFUL 2
  3 *syn see* MARVELOUS 2
  4 *syn see* CONTRABAND
hot air *n syn see* NONSENSE 2
hotbed *n syn see* BREEDING GROUND
hot-blooded *adj syn see* IMPASSIONED
  con callous, hard, unfeeling
  ant cold-blooded
hotchpotch *n syn see* MISCELLANY 1
hot dog *n syn see* FRANKFURTER
hotel *n* an establishment for the lodging and entertainment especially of transients <spent their vacation at a resort *hotel*>
  syn auberge, caravansary, hospice, hostel, hostelry, inn, lodge, public house, roadhouse, tavern
  rel boardinghouse, lodging house, pension, rooming house, spa; boatel, motel, motor inn; ‖fleabag, ‖flophouse
hotfoot *adv syn see* PELL-MELL
hotfoot *vb syn see* HURRY 1
hotheaded *adj syn see* RASH 1
  ant cool
hothouse *n syn see* BREEDING GROUND
hot spot *n syn see* NIGHTCLUB
hot-tempered *adj* 1 *syn see* ILL-TEMPERED
  2 *syn see* IRASCIBLE
hot water *n* 1 *syn see* PREDICAMENT
  2 *syn see* TROUBLE 3
hound *n* 1 *syn see* DOG 1
  2 *syn see* ADDICT
hound *vb syn see* BAIT 2
house *n* 1 *syn see* HABITATION 2
  2 *syn see* FAMILY 2
  3 *syn see* FAMILY 1
  4 *syn see* ENTERPRISE 3
house *vb* 1 *syn see* HARBOR 1
  2 *syn see* HARBOR 2
housebreak *vb* to commit an act of breaking open and entering with a felonious purpose the dwelling of another by day or night <was arrested again in September for *housebreaking*>
  syn break in; *compare* BURGLARIZE, ROB 1
  rel knock over, rob; ransack, rifle
  idiom break and enter
household *n syn see* FAMILY 2
household *adj syn see* DOMESTIC 1
housemaid *n syn see* MAID 2
houseman *n syn see* BOUNCER 1
house of God *syn see* HOUSE OF WORSHIP
house of prayer *syn see* HOUSE OF WORSHIP
house of worship a building for religious exercises <there are many *houses of worship* in this city>
  syn church, house of God, house of prayer, tabernacle, temple

---

syn synonym(s) **rel** related word(s)
ant antonym(s) **con** contrasted word(s)
idiom idiomatic equivalent(s)
‖ use limited; if in doubt, see a dictionary

rel abbey, basilica, bethel, cathedral, chantry, chapel, conventicle, ‖fane, ‖kirk, masjid, meetinghouse, minster, mosque, oratory, pagoda, sanctuary, shrine, stupa, synagogue
idiom the Lord's house

house trailer *n syn* see TRAILER

housing *n syn* see SHELTER 2

hovel *n* a small wretched dwelling place <migrants forced to live in *hovels*>
syn burrow, hole; *compare* HUT
rel hut, hutch, shack, shanty; pigpen, pigsty, sty

hover *vb* **1** *syn* see FLIT 2
2 *syn* see HANG 3

howbeit *adv syn* see HOWEVER

howbeit *conj syn* see THOUGH

however *conj syn* see ONLY

however *adv* in spite of that <I accept your decision; I cannot, *however*, approve of it>
syn after all, howbeit, nevertheless, nonetheless, notwithstanding, per contra, still, still and all, though, withal, yet
idiom all the same, be that as it may, for all that, on the other hand

howl *vb* **1** to utter or emit a loud sustained doleful sound or outcry <the dogs *howled* through the night>
syn bay, quest, ululate, wail
rel bark, growl, yelp; blubber, cry, keen, weep, whimper; bawl, squall, yowl
2 *syn* see YELL 2
3 *syn* see BAWL 2

howl *n syn* see RIOT 2

hoyden *n syn* see TOMBOY

hub *n syn* see CENTER 2

hubbub *n* **1** *syn* see DIN
2 *syn* see COMMOTION 4

‖**hubby** *n syn* see HUSBAND

hubristic *adj syn* see PROUD 1

huckster *n syn* see PEDDLER

huckster *vb* **1** *syn* see HAGGLE 2
2 *syn* see PEDDLE 2

huddle *vb* **1** *syn* see CROUCH
2 *syn* see CONFER 2

huddle (on) *vb syn* see DON 1

huddle *n syn* see CONFUSION 3

hue *n syn* see COLOR 1

huff *vb* **1** *syn* see PANT 1
2 *syn* see IRRITATE

huff *n syn* see OFFENSE 2

huffy *adj* **1** *syn* see PROUD 1
2 *syn* see IRRITABLE

hug *vb syn* see EMBRACE 1

huge *adj* exceedingly or excessively large <*huge* corporations> <ate a *huge* dinner>
syn Antaean, behemothic, Brobdingnagian, Bunyanesque, colossal, cyclopean, dinosauric, elephantine, enormous, gargantuan, giant, gigantean, gigantesque, gigantic, Herculean, heroic, immense, jumbo, leviathan, lusty, mammoth, massive, massy, mastodonic, mighty, monster, monstrous, monumental, mountainous, planetary, prodigious, pythonic, ‖swapping, Titan, titanic, tremendous, unfathomed, untold, vast, walloping, whacking, whaling, whopping; *compare* GRAND 1
rel bulky, extensive, great, immeasurable, magnificent, towering; outsize, oversize
con diminutive, little, miniature, minute, petite, small, teeny, tiny, wee, weeny

hugely *adv syn* see VERY 1

hugeness *n syn* see ENORMITY 2

hugger–mugger *n* **1** *syn* see SECRECY
2 *syn* see CLUTTER 2

hugger–mugger *adv syn* see SECRETLY

hugger–mugger *adj syn* see SECRET 1

hugger–muggery *n syn* see SECRECY

hull *n* an outer covering of a fruit or seed <peanut *hulls*>
syn case, husk, pod, shell, shuck, skin, ‖slough
rel chaff; bark, peel, rind

hull *vb syn* see SHUCK

hullabaloo *n syn* see DIN

hum *vb* to make a low prolonged sound <the wind *hummed* in the chimney>
syn bombinate, ‖bum, bumble, buzz, drone, ‖sowf, strum, thrum
rel moan, murmur, purr, vibrate, whisper
con howl, roar, shriek

human *adj* of, relating to, or characteristic of mankind <problems of *human* relationships>
syn hominine, mortal
rel anthropological, ethnologic, ethological; anthropoid, hominid, hominoid
con angelic, divine, superhuman; animal, brute, subhuman

human *n* a member of the human race <every *human* has a right to live>
syn being, body, ‖character, creature, individual, life, man, mortal, party, person, personage, soul, wight; *compare* MAN 3, MANKIND

humane *adj syn* see CHARITABLE 1
rel chickenhearted, compassionate, kindhearted, soft-hearted; benevolent, gentle, kind, kindly, mild
ant inhuman, inhumane

humanitarian *adj syn* see CHARITABLE 1

humanity *n syn* see MANKIND

humankind *n syn* see MANKIND

humanoid *adj syn* see ANTHROPOID

humble *adj* **1** lacking all signs of pride, aggressiveness, or self-assertiveness <accepted her success with *humble* appreciation>
syn lowly, meek, modest, unassuming
rel simple, unobtrusive, unostentatious, unpretentious; acquiescent, compliant, resigned; quiet, subdued, submissive
con ostentatious, pretentious, showy; vain, vainglorious; arrogant, disdainful, haughty, lordly, overbearing, proud, toplofty
ant conceited
2 *syn* see IGNOBLE 1

humble *vb* to make lower in status, prestige, or esteem <his devotion to duty *humbled* his critics>
syn abase, bemean, cast down, debase, degrade, demean, humiliate, lower, sink
rel chagrin, mortify; abash, discomfit, embarrass
idiom bring low, take down a peg or two
con aggrandize, exalt, magnify

humbug *n* **1** *syn* see IMPOSTURE
2 *syn* see IMPOSTOR
3 *syn* see NONSENSE 2

humbug *vb syn* see DECEIVE

humdinger *n syn* ‖DILLY, ‖corker, crackerjack, ‖daisy, dandy, jim-dandy, ‖lulu, nifty, peach, ‖pip

humdrum *adj syn* see DULL 9
humdrum *n syn* see MONOTONY
humid *adj* containing or characterized by an uncomfortable amount of atmospheric warmth and moisture <a *humid* climate>
 syn mucky, muggy, soggy, sticky, sultry; *compare* STIFLING 1, STUFFY 1
 rel clammy, dank, sodden; close, oppressive, stuffy; sweltering
 con arid, dry; cool, crisp, fresh
humiliate *vb syn* see HUMBLE
humming *adj syn* see BUSTLING
humor *n* **1** *syn* see DISPOSITION 3
 2 *syn* see MOOD 1
 3 *syn* see CAPRICE
 4 that quality or element which appeals to a sense of the ludicrous or incongruous <see the *humor* in a situation>
 syn comedy, comicality, comicalness, drollery, drollness, funniness, humorousness, wittiness
 rel jocosity, jocularity, jocundity, jocundness; flippancy, levity, lightness; banter, chaffing, jesting, joking, kidding
 con earnestness, seriousness, solemnity; depth, profundity
 5 something that is or is designed to be humorous <his heavy *humor* fell flat>
 syn wit
 rel banter, chitchat, pleasantry, repartee
 6 *syn* see WIT 5
 ant humorlessness
humor *vb* **1** *syn* see INDULGE 1
 2 *syn* see BABY
humorist *n* **1** *syn* see WAG 1
 2 a person noted for or specializing in humor <a writer best known as a *humorist*>
 syn comedian, comic, funnyman, jester, joker, jokester, quipster, wag, wit
 rel buffoon, card, clown, cutup, gagman, gagster, jokesmith, merry-andrew, prankster, punster, zany; banterer, kidder
humorous *adj syn* see WITTY
humorousness *n syn* see HUMOR 4
humorsome *adj syn* see MOODY
‖**hump** *vb syn* see CARRY 1
hunch *vb syn* see CROUCH
hunch *n syn* see LUMP 1
hunger *vb syn* see LONG
hungry *adj* feeling distressed from lack of food <a group of *hungry* children>
 syn famished, ‖peckish, ravenous, starved, starving
 rel rapacious, voracious
 con full, glutted, gorged, sated, satiated
 ant surfeited
hunk *n syn* see LUMP 1
hunker (down) *vb syn* see SQUAT
hunkers *n pl syn* see BUTTOCKS
hunks *n pl but sing or pl in constr syn* see MISER
hunky–dory *adj syn* see MARVELOUS 2
Hunnic *adj syn* see BARBARIAN 1
Hunnish *adj syn* see BARBARIAN 1
hunt *vb* **1** to search for or pursue (game or prey) for the purpose of capturing or killing

<hunted deer in bow-and-arrow season only>
 syn chase, run
 rel dog, ferret, hawk, hound; course, drive, stalk, start, still-hunt, track; capture, kill, snare; gun, shoot
 idiom go hunting
 2 *syn* see SEEK 1
hunt (down *or* out *or* up) *vb syn* see RUMMAGE 3
hunting *n* the act or practice of seeking and taking wild and especially game animals <lived by *hunting* and fishing>
 syn chase, venery
 rel angling, coursing, falconry, fishing, gunning, hawking, shooting
hurdle *n syn* see OBSTACLE
hurdle *vb* **1** *syn* see CLEAR 8
 2 *syn* see JUMP 1
 3 *syn* see OVERCOME 1
hurl *vb syn* see THROW 1
hurly–burly *n syn* see COMMOTION 4
hurrah *n* **1** *syn* see PASSION 6
 2 *syn* see COMMOTION 3
 3 *syn* see ARGUMENT 2
hurricane *n* a violent rotating storm or system of winds originating in the tropics and often moving into temperate latitudes <the *hurricane* struck the coast today>
 syn tropical cyclone, tropical storm, typhoon, ‖willy-willy; *compare* TORNADO, WHIRLWIND 1
 rel williwaw
hurried *adj syn* see PRECIPITATE 1
 ant unhurried
hurriedness *n syn* see HASTE 2
hurry *vb* **1** *syn* see SPEED 3
 2 to proceed or move with dispatch <*hurry* home after school>
 syn barrel, barrelhouse, beeline, bucket, bullet, bustle, ‖dust, fleet, flit, fly, haste, hasten, highball, hotfoot, hustle, ‖nip, pelt, rock, rocket, run, rush, scoot, scour, ‖skeet, skin, smoke, speed, stave, ‖tatter, whirl, whish, whisk, whiz, zip; *compare* RUSH 1
 rel jog, peg, skip, trot; bowl (along), breeze; dig in; post
 idiom get a move on, go (*or* move) like lightning, make tracks, step on it, step on the gas
 con creep, dally, dawdle, drag, lag, linger, loiter, poke, saunter, stroll
hurry *n syn* see HASTE 1
hurry–scurry *adv syn* see PELL-MELL
hurt *vb* **1** *syn* see INJURE 1
 rel abuse, afflict, mistreat, misuse
 ant benefit
 2 *syn* see INJURE 3
 3 *syn* see DISTRESS 2
 4 to experience or be the seat of sharp physical distress <my arm still *hurts*>
 syn ache, pain, ‖suffer; *compare* SMART
hurt *n syn* see INJURY 1
hurtful *adj* **1** *syn* see HARMFUL
 con harmless, innocuous
 2 *syn* see PAINFUL 1
hurting *adj syn* see PAINFUL 1
husband *n* the male partner in a marriage <neglected his responsibilities as a *husband*>
 syn ‖hubby, lord, man, ‖master, mister, Mr., ‖old man

---

syn synonym(s) *rel* related word(s)
ant antonym(s) *con* contrasted word(s)
idiom idiomatic equivalent(s)
‖ use limited; if in doubt, see a dictionary

rel consort, helpmate, helpmeet, mate, other half, spouse; benedict, bridegroom

husbanding *n syn* see CONSERVATION 1
ant squandering

husbandry *n* **1** *syn* see ECONOMY
2 *syn* see AGRICULTURE

hush *vb syn* see SILENCE

hush (up) *vb syn* see SUPPRESS 3

hush *adj syn* see STILL 3

hush *n* **1** *syn* see QUIET 1
2 *syn* see SECRECY

hushed *adj* **1** *syn* see CALM 1
2 *syn* see PRIVATE 2

hushful *adj syn* see STILL 3

hush–hush *adj syn* see SECRET 1

hush–hush *n syn* see SECRECY

husk *n syn* see HULL

husk *vb syn* see SHUCK

husky *adj syn* see HOARSE 1

husky *adj* **1** big and muscular <a *husky* man carried in the trunks>
syn beefy, burly, hefty
rel brawny, muscular, well-built; stalwart, stout, strapping, strong, sturdy; Herculean, mighty, powerful; Bunyanesque, gigantic
con delicate, fragile, frail; puny, scrawny, slight; elfin; mousey
2 *syn* see LARGE 1

hussy *n* **1** *syn* see WANTON
2 *syn* see MINX

hustle *vb* **1** *syn* see PUSH 2
2 *syn* see HURRY 2

hustle *n syn* see HASTE 1

hustler *n* **1** an alert enterprising individual <he's a *hustler*, eager to get ahead in the world>
syn dynamo, go-getter, live wire, peeler, rustler, self-starter
rel humdinger, hummer; new broom; doer, powerhouse
idiom busy bee
con dawdler, idler; slow coach, slowpoke, stick-in-the-mud
2 *syn* see PROSTITUTE

hustling *adj syn* see BUSTLING

hut *n* a small, simply constructed dwelling often for temporary or intermittent occupancy <the shepherds lived in *huts* in the summer>
syn box, cabin ‖caboose, camp, cot, cottage, lodge, shack, shanty; *compare* BUILDING, EDIFICE, HOVEL
rel bungalow, cabana, chalet, crib, dacha, hooch (*or* hootch), hovel, hutch, lean-to, shed, summer house

hut *vb syn* see HARBOR 2

Hyblaean *adj syn* see MELLIFLUOUS

hybrid *n* an offspring produced by parents of different strains, breeds, varieties, species, or genera <the mule is a *hybrid* of the ass and the horse>
syn bastard, cross, crossbred, crossbreed, half blood, half-breed, mongrel, mule
rel incross, incrossbred, outcross; combina-

tion, composite, mixture
con pureblood, purebred, thoroughbred

hybridize *vb syn* see CROSS 4

hydrant *n syn* see FAUCET

‖**hydro** *n syn* see SPA 1

hydroponics *n* the growing of plants in nutrient solution and without soil <tomatoes grown by *hydroponics*>
syn aquiculture, nutriculture
idiom soilless agriculture

hygienic *adj syn* see HEALTHFUL
ant unhygienic

hymeneal *adj syn* see MATRIMONIAL

hymn *n syn* see SONG 2

hymn *vb* **1** *syn* see PRAISE 2
2 *syn* see SING

hypaethral *adj syn* see OUTDOOR

hype *n syn* see PUBLICITY

hype *vb syn* see PUBLICIZE

hyperbole *n syn* see EXAGGERATION
con depreciation, minimization, understatement
ant litotes

hypercritical *adj syn* see CRITICAL 1

hypercriticize *vb syn* see QUIBBLE 1

hypnotic *adj syn* see SOPORIFIC 1

hypocorism *n syn* see NICKNAME

hypocrisy *n* the pretense or affectation of having virtues, principles, or beliefs that one does not actually have <political *hypocrisy*>
syn cant, hypocriticalness, pecksniffery, pharisaicalness, pharisaism, sanctimoniousness, sanctimony, sham, Tartuffery, Tartuffism
rel pietism, religiosity; casuistry, glibness, insincerity, self-righteousness, unctuousness; charlatanry, humbug, quackery
con candidness, fairness, openness; honesty, probity, truthfulness
ant sincerity

hypocrite *n* one who affects virtues, qualities, or attitudes he does not have <don't be a *hypocrite* — if you don't approve, say so>
syn dissembler, dissimulator, lip server, pharisee, Tartufe, whited sepulcher
rel pietist; actor, attitudinizer, bluffer, charlatan, faker, four-flusher, fraud, humbug, impostor, masquerader, phony, poser, poseur, pretender, quack, sham

hypocritical *adj* **1** characterized by hypocrisy <*hypocritical* compliments>
syn canting, pecksniffian, pharisaic, pharisaical, sanctimonious, self-righteous
rel goody-goody, holier-than-thou, moralistic, pietistic, religiose; casuistic; affected, insincere; bland, glib, mealymouthed, oily, smooth, smooth-spoken, smooth-tongued, unctuous
con honest, open, straightforward
ant sincere
2 *syn* see INSINCERE

hypocriticalness *n syn* see HYPOCRISY
ant sincerity

hypostatize *vb syn* see MATERIALIZE 2

hypothesis *n syn* see THEORY 1

hypothetical *adj* **1** *syn* see SUPPOSED 1
rel doubtful, problematic
2 *syn* see ABSTRACT 1

I

icky *adj syn* see OFFENSIVE

iconographic *adj syn* see PICTORIAL 1

icy *adj* **1** *syn* see COLD 1
ant fiery
2 *syn* see COLD 2
ant fiery

idea *n* what exists in the mind as a representation (as of something comprehended) or as a formulation (as of a plan) <that's not my *idea* of a good time>
syn apprehension, conceit, concept, conception, image, impression, intellection, notion, perception, thought
rel assumption, belief, conclusion, conviction, estimation, feeling, inclination, judgment, opinion, persuasion, presumption, reaction, reflection, sentiment, view; conjecture, guess, hypothesis, speculation, supposition, surmise, suspicion, theory; caprice, fancy, fantasy, vagary, whim, whimsy; brainstorm, inspiration

ideal *adj* **1** *syn* see ABSTRACT 1
ant actual
2 *syn* see CONCEPTUAL
3 constituting a standard (as of perfection or excellence) <the *ideal* man of letters>
syn flawless, indefectible, model
rel archetypal, archetypical, prototypal, prototypical
con average, normal, representative, typical
4 *syn* see PERFECT 3
5 *syn* see TYPICAL 1

ideal *n* **1** *syn* see MODEL 2
2 *syn* see PARAGON

idealist *n syn* see DREAMER

idealist *adj syn* see IDEALISTIC

idealistic *adj* characterized by idealism <made an *idealistic* speech on human rights>
syn idealist, utopian, visionary
rel impractical, poetical, quixotic, romantic, starry, starry-eyed, unrealistic
con empirical, matter-of-fact, practical, pragmatic, rational, realistic
ant unidealistic

ideational *adj syn* see CONCEPTUAL

identic *adj syn* see SAME 2
ant nonidentical

identical *adj* **1** *syn* see SAME 1
2 *syn* see SAME 2
ant nonidentical

identicalness *n syn* see IDENTITY 1

identification *n syn* see RECOGNITION 1

identify *vb* to establish the identity of <the culprit was *identified* by his fingerprints>
syn determinate, diagnose, diagnosticate, distinguish, finger, pinpoint, place, recognize, spot
rel find; determine, establish, make out, pick out, select, separate (out)

identity *n* **1** the quality of being the same in all that constitutes the objective reality of separate things <the *identity* of the two texts is exact>
syn identicalness, oneness, sameness, self-sameness
rel agreement, likeness, resemblance, semblance, similarity, similitude; correspondence, equality, equivalence; uniformity
con dissimilarity, dissimilitude, unlikeness, unsimilarity
ant nonidentity
2 *syn* see INDIVIDUALITY 4

ideologue *n syn* see DREAMER

ideology *n* an overall view of or attitude toward life <an *ideology* based on tolerance>
syn credo, creed, weltanschauung
rel outlook, philosophy, view

idiom *n syn* see LANGUAGE 1

idiosyncratic *adj* **1** *syn* see CHARACTERISTIC
2 *syn* see STRANGE 4

idiot *n* **1** *syn* see FOOL 1
2 *syn* see FOOL 2
3 *syn* see FOOL 4
4 *syn* see DUNCE

‖**idiot box** *n syn* see TELEVISION

idle *adj* **1** *syn* see VAIN 1
2 *syn* see VACANT 4
3 *syn* see INACTIVE
ant busy

idle *vb* to spend time in idleness <people *idling* in the park>
syn ‖brogue, bum, dawdle, diddle, diddle-daddle, drone, goldbrick, ‖goof (off), ‖lallygag, laze, lazy, loaf, loiter, loll, lounge
rel relax, repose, rest; amble, linger, mooch, mosey, saunter, stroll, tarry; hang around, sit around, sit back, sit by
idiom dog it, kill time, lie around, mark time

idleheaded *adj syn* see FOOLISH 2

idleness *n syn* see SLOTH 1

idler *n syn* see SLUGGARD

idolatry *n syn* see ADORATION

idolization *n syn* see ADORATION

idolize *vb syn* see ADORE 3
idiom worship the ground one walks on

iffy *adj syn* see UNCERTAIN 1

ignis fatuus *n syn* see DELUSION 1

ignitable *adj syn* see COMBUSTIBLE 1

ignite *vb syn* see LIGHT 1

ignited *adj syn* see BURNING 1

ignoble *adj* **1** belonging to or characteristic of socially or economically inferior classes <a person of *ignoble* antecedents>

---

syn synonym(s)　　*rel* related word(s)
ant antonym(s)　　*con* contrasted word(s)
idiom idiomatic equivalent(s)

‖ use limited; if in doubt, see a dictionary

syn base, baseborn, humble, low, lowborn, lowly, mean, plebeian, unennobled, unwashed

rel coarse, common, homely, inferior, inglorious, modest, ordinary, peasant, plain, poor, popular, simple, vulgar

con highborn, highbred, wellborn, wellbred; eminent, high, lofty, proud, superior

ant noble

2 *syn* see BASE 3

ant noble

ignominious *adj syn* see DISREPUTABLE 1

ignominy *n syn* see DISGRACE

rel contempt, despite, disdain, scorn; chagrin, mortification

con glory, honor; esteem, respect

ignoramus *n syn* see DUNCE

ignorance *n* **1** the state of being unlearned <the blight of *ignorance*>

syn benightedness, illiteracy

rel callowness, greenness, inexperience, naiveté, rawness, simpleness, simplicity, uncouthness, uncultivation, unsophistication; empty-headedness, unintelligence, witlessness; know-nothingism, philistinism

con education, enlightenment, erudition, learning, literacy

2 the state of being unaware or uninformed <*ignorance* of the law>

syn innocence, inscience, nescience, unacquaintance, unacquaintedness, unawareness, unfamiliarity, unknowingness

con acquaintance, acquaintanceship, experience; awareness, familiarity, knowledgeableness

ignorant *adj* **1** lacking knowledge or education <an *ignorant* boy with no taste for school>

syn benighted, empty-headed, illiterate, know-nothing, rude, uneducated, uninstructed, unlettered, unschooled, untaught, untutored

rel lowbrow, uncultured, unintellectual; callow, green, inexperienced; crude, gross, raw, uncouth; ingenuous, naive, simple, unsophisticated

con educated, erudite, learned, literate

2 lacking information on or awareness of something <was *ignorant* of the circumstances surrounding the affair>

syn incognizant, inconversant, oblivious, unacquainted, unaware, unfamiliar, uninformed, uninstructed, unknowing, unwitting

idiom in the dark

con aware, conscious, conversant, informed, knowing, knowledgeable

3 *syn* see BACKWARD 5

ignore *vb syn* see NEGLECT

rel avoid, evade

ilk *n syn* see TYPE

ill *adj* **1** *syn* see EVIL 5

ant good

2 *syn* see HARMFUL

3 *syn* see SICK 1

4 *syn* see RUDE 6

5 *syn* see HOSTILE 1

ill *n* **1** *syn* see EVIL 1

ant benefit

2 *syn* see DISEASE 1

ill–adapted *adj syn* see UNFIT 1

ill–advised *adj* **1** *syn* see RASH 1

2 *syn* see INADVISABLE

ant well-advised

3 *syn* see UNWISE

ant well-advised

illation *n* **1** *syn* see INFERENCE 1

2 *syn* see INFERENCE 2

ill–behaved *adj syn* see NAUGHTY 1

ill–boding *adj syn* see OMINOUS

ill–bred *adj* **1** *syn* see BOORISH

ant well-bred

2 *syn* see RUDE 6

ant well-bred, well-mannered

ill–chosen *adj syn* see INFELICITOUS

ill–defined *adj syn* see FAINT 2

ant well-defined

illegal *adj syn* see UNLAWFUL

rel banned, forbidden, interdicted, prohibited, proscribed, outlawed, unauthorized, unlicensed, unwarranted; felonious; contraband, hot; actionable, irregular

con authorized, lawful, licensed, licit, permitted, regular, right

ant legal

illegality *n* the quality or state of being illegal <the *illegality* of an act>

syn illegitimacy, illicitness, unlawfulness

rel badness, impropriety, wrongness

con lawfulness, legitimacy, licitness; propriety

ant legality

illegible *adj* incapable of being read or deciphered <an *illegible* signature>

syn indecipherable, undecipherable, unreadable

rel faint, indistinct, obscure, unclear

ant legible, readable

illegitimacy *n* **1** the state or condition of being born out of wedlock <he accepted the fact of his *illegitimacy*>

syn bastardy, illegitimateness, supposititiousness

rel bar sinister

ant legitimacy, legitimateness

2 *syn* see ILLEGALITY

ant legitimacy, legitimateness

illegitimate *adj* **1** not recognized by law as lawful offspring <an *illegitimate* child>

syn baseborn, bastard, fatherless, misbegotten, natural, spurious, supposititious, unfathered

rel birthless; adulterine

ant legitimate

2 *syn* see UNLAWFUL

ant legitimate

illegitimate *n syn* see BASTARD 1

ant legitimate

illegitimateness *n syn* see ILLEGITIMACY 1

ant legitimacy, legitimateness

ill–famed *adj syn* see INFAMOUS 1

ill–fated *adj syn* see UNLUCKY

ill–favored *adj* **1** *syn* see UGLY 2

ant well-favored

2 *syn* see OBJECTIONABLE

ill–flavored *adj syn* see UNPALATABLE 1

ill–humored *adj syn* see ILL-TEMPERED

ant good-humored, good-natured

illiberal *adj* unwilling or unable to grasp the point of view of others <had the *illiberal* outlook of an old-time schoolmaster>

syn bigoted, brassbound, hidebound, intolerant, narrow, narrow-minded, small≠
minded, unenlarged
rel biased, jaundiced, one-sided, opinionated, partial, partisan, prejudiced; grudging,
little, mean, paltry, petty, small, uncharitable, ungenerous; insular, parochial, provincial; rigid, rigorous, stringent
con broad-minded, open-minded, tolerant,
unbigoted; advanced, progressive, radical
ant liberal

illicit *adj syn* see UNLAWFUL
ant licit

illicitness *n syn* see ILLEGALITY

illimitable *adj syn* see INFINITE 1
rel endless, interminable
ant limitable; limited

illiteracy *n syn* see IGNORANCE 1

illiterate *adj syn* see IGNORANT 1

illiterate *n* one who cannot read or write
<the training of adult *illiterates*>
syn analphabet
rel functional illiterate, semiliterate, sublit-
erate
ant literate

ill-judged *adj syn* see UNWISE

ill-kempt *adj syn* see SLOVENLY 1

ill-looking *adj syn* see UGLY 2
ant good-looking, ‖well-looked

ill-mannered *adj syn* see RUDE 6
ant well-bred, well-mannered

ill-natured *adj syn* see ILL-TEMPERED
ant good-humored, good-natured

illness *n syn* see SICKNESS 1
ant health

illogical *adj* contrary to or devoid of logic
<came to an *illogical* conclusion from the
facts presented>
syn fallacious, invalid, irrational, mad,
nonrational, reasonless, sophistic, unreasonable, unreasoned; *compare* FALSE 1
rel inconsistent; specious; unscientific,
unsound; absurd, meaningless, senseless
idiom without rhyme or reason
con rational, reasonable, sensible; plausible,
sane, sound, valid
ant logical

ill-omened *adj syn* see OMINOUS
ant auspicious

ill-seasoned *adj syn* see UNSEASONABLE 1
ant seasonable

ill-starred *adj syn* see UNLUCKY
rel bodeful, fateful, foreboding, ominous,
portentous; baleful, malefic, malign, sinister;
unfavorable, unpromising, unpropitious

ill-suited *adj syn* see UNFIT 1

ill-tempered *adj* having a bad temper <an
ill-tempered old man>
syn bad-tempered, dyspeptic, hot-tempered, ill-humored, ill-natured, ‖rusty, tempersome
rel crabbed, surly; fractious, huffy, irritable,
peevish, petulant, querulous, snappish, sour,
waspish; shrewish, vixenish

con calm, easy, placid, serene, tranquil;
amiable, complaisant, considerate, good≠
natured, kindly, obliging, tolerant
ant good-tempered, sweet-tempered, well≠
tempered

ill-timed *adj* **1** *syn* see UNSEASONABLE 1
ant seasonable
2 *syn* see IMPROPER 1

ill-treat *vb syn* see ABUSE 4
rel aggrieve, harass, harry, molest
con befriend, relieve, succor; countenance,
encourage, favor, patronize

illude *vb syn* see DECEIVE

illume *vb* **1** *syn* see ILLUMINATE 1
2 *syn* see ILLUMINATE 2

illuminant *adj syn* see ENLIGHTENING

illuminate *vb* **1** to supply with physical light
<a room dimly *illuminated* by firelight>
syn illume, illumine, light, lighten
rel brighten; irradiate; floodlight, highlight,
spotlight; fire, ignite, kindle
con blur, cloud, darken, dim, dull, obscure,
pale
2 to supply with spiritual or intellectual light
<the worth of a truly *illuminating* book>
syn edify, enlighten, illume, illumine, improve, irradiate, uplift
rel better, improve; ennoble, exalt, refine;
finish, mature, perfect, polish
con becloud, cloud, darken, obfuscate,
obscure, overshadow, shadow
3 *syn* see CLARIFY 2
rel construe, define, dramatize, expound,
express, gloss, interpret
idiom shed light on (*or* upon)
con baffle, confound, confuse, mystify,
pose, puzzle, stump

illuminati *n pl syn* see INTELLIGENTSIA

illuminating *adj syn* see ENLIGHTENING

illuminative *adj syn* see ENLIGHTENING

illumine *vb* **1** *syn* see ILLUMINATE 1
2 *syn* see ILLUMINATE 2

illumining *adj syn* see ENLIGHTENING

ill-use *vb syn* see ABUSE 4
con befriend, relieve, succor; countenance,
encourage, favor, patronize

illusion *n* **1** *syn* see DELUSION 1
rel invention; bubble, chimera, dream, will≠
o'-the-wisp; appearance, seeming, semblance
2 *syn* see PIPE DREAM

illusionist *n syn* see MAGICIAN 2

illusive *adj syn* see APPARENT 2

illusory *adj* **1** *syn* see FICTITIOUS 1
ant factual
2 *syn* see APPARENT 2
rel chimerical, fanciful, fantastic, imaginary, unreal, visionary; deceptive, delusive,
delusory, misleading
con actual, real, veritable; authentic, true,
valid
ant factual

illustrate *vb* **1** *syn* see CLARIFY 2
rel display, exhibit, expose, show; disclose,
discover, reveal
con cloak, conceal, enshroud, mask, screen,
shroud, veil
2 *syn* see EXEMPLIFY 1
rel elucidate, explain, expound, interpret;
demonstrate, manifest, show; enliven, vivify

---

syn synonym(s)   *rel* related word(s)
ant antonym(s)   *con* contrasted word(s)
idiom idiomatic equivalent(s)
‖ use limited; if in doubt, see a dictionary

3 *syn* see REPRESENT 2
4 *syn* see SHOW 2

illustration *n* 1 *syn* see EXAMPLE 3
2 *syn* see INSTANCE

illustrational *adj syn* see PICTORIAL 1

illustrative *adj syn* see PICTORIAL 1

illustratory *adj syn* see PICTORIAL 1

illustrious *adj syn* see FAMOUS 2
rel glorious, resplendent, splendid, sublime; conspicuous, lofty, outstanding, signal, striking
con abject, inglorious, mean; disgraceful, dishonorable, ignoble, ignominious, shameful
ant infamous

illustriousness *n syn* see EMINENCE 1
ant infamy

ill will *n syn* see MALICE
rel hostility, rancor, venom
ant goodwill

image *n* 1 one strikingly like another especially in appearance or manner <she was the *image* of her mother>
syn double, picture, portrait, ringer, simulacrum, spit, spitting image
rel counterpart, equal, equivalent, match
idiom chip off the old block, dead ringer, speaking likeness, spit and image
2 *syn* see IDEA

image *vb* 1 *syn* see REPRESENT 1
2 *syn* see THINK 1
3 *syn* see REFLECT 1

imaginable *adj syn* see THINKABLE 2
ant unimaginable

imaginary *adj* 1 having no real existence but existing in imagination <elves are *imaginary* beings>
syn fancied, fanciful, imagined, notional, shadowy
rel imaginative; abstract, hypothetical, ideal, visionary; apparitional, chimerical, fantastic, figmental, hallucinatory, illusory; phantasmal, phantasmic, quixotic, spectral; unreal, unsubstantial
con genuine, true, valid
ant actual, real
2 *syn* see FICTITIOUS 1
ant actual, real

imagination *n* the power or function of the mind by which mental images are formed or the exercise of that power <children have great *imagination*>
syn fancy, fantasy (*or* phantasy), imaginativeness
rel creativity, inspiration, invention, inventiveness, visualization
con literalness, matter-of-factness, prosaism, unimaginativeness

imaginativeness *n syn* see IMAGINATION
ant unimaginativeness

imagine *vb* 1 *syn* see THINK 1
2 *syn* see UNDERSTAND 3

imagined *adj syn* see IMAGINARY 1
con known, recognized, seen

imbecile *adj syn* see RETARDED

imbecile *n* 1 *syn* see FOOL 4
2 *syn* see FOOL 1

imbibe *vb* 1 *syn* see ABSORB 1
2 *syn* see DRINK 1
3 *syn* see DRINK 3

imbricate *vb syn* see OVERLAP

imbroglio *n syn* see QUARREL

imbrued *adj syn* see BLOODY 1

imbue *vb syn* see INFUSE 1

imitate *vb* 1 *syn* see COPY
2 *syn* see MIMIC

imitation *adj syn* see ARTIFICIAL 2
ant real

imitation *n* something made or produced as an often inferior likeness of something else <usually wore *imitations* of her costly jewels>
syn copy, ersatz, simulacrum
rel counterfeit, fake, forgery, phony, sham, simulation; counterpart, duplicate, replica, reproduction; likeness, semblance
ant original

imitative *adj* 1 *syn* see ONOMATOPOEIC
2 *syn* see SLAVISH 3

immaculate *adj* 1 *syn* see CHASTE 1
ant maculate
2 *syn* see IMPECCABLE 1
3 *syn* see CLEAN 1

immalleable *adj syn* see STIFF 1
ant malleable

immaterial *adj* 1 not composed of matter <*immaterial* forces>
syn asomatous, bodiless, disbodied, discarnate, disembodied, incorporeal, insubstantial, metaphysical, nonmaterial, nonphysical, spiritual, unbodied, ‖uncorporal, unembodied, unfleshly, unmaterial, unphysical, unsubstantial
rel impalpable, imponderable; psychic, subjective; aerial, airy, ethereal; insensible, unearthly, unworldly; supernatural; celestial, heavenly; apparitional, ghostly, shadowy
con bodily, corporeal, fleshly, incarnate; material, objective, palpable, physical, substantial; mundane, terrestrial, worldly
ant material
2 *syn* see IRRELEVANT
ant material

immature *adj* 1 *syn* see YOUNG 1
rel precocious, premature
ant mature
2 *syn* see CHILDISH
ant mature

immeasurable *adj* 1 *syn* see INCALCULABLE 1
2 *syn* see LIMITLESS

immediacy *n syn* see PROXIMITY

immediate *adj* 1 *syn* see DIRECT 4
ant distant (*of relatives*)
2 *syn* see INSTANTANEOUS
3 *syn* see CLOSE 6

immediately *adv* 1 in direct connection without intermediary <*immediately* in front of the viewers>
syn contiguously, directly
2 *syn* see AWAY 3
rel anon, shortly, soon
idiom right now

immedicable *adj syn* see HOPELESS 2
ant medicable

immense *adj syn* see HUGE

immensely *adv syn* see EVER 6

immensity *n syn* see ENORMITY 2

immerse *vb* 1 *syn* see DIP 1

rel saturate, soak
2 syn see BAPTIZE
3 syn see ENGAGE 4
immersed *adj syn* see INTENT
immigrant *n syn* see EMIGRANT
imminent *adj* **1** about to take place <their departure is *imminent*>
  syn impending, proximate
  rel approaching, coming, nearing, upcoming; brewing, gathering; pending; likely, possible, probable; ineluctable, inescapable, inevasible, inevitable, unavoidable, unescapable
  idiom in prospect, in store, in the cards, in the offing, in the wind, in view
  con distant, far-off, remote
2 menacingly near <a thunderstorm was *imminent*>
  syn lowering (*or* louring), lowery (*or* loury), menacing, overhanging, threatening
  rel alarming, ominous, sinister; brewing, gathering; minatory
immingle *vb syn* see MIX 1
immix *vb syn* see MIX 1
immixture *n syn* see MIXTURE
immobile *adj* **1** *syn* see IMMOVABLE 1
  ant mobile, movable
2 syn see STATIC
immobilize *vb syn* see PARALYZE 1
immoderate *adj* **1** *syn* see EXCESSIVE 1
  ant moderate
2 syn see EXCESSIVE 2
  ant moderate
immoderation *n syn* see EXCESS 3
  ant moderation
immolate *vb syn* see SACRIFICE 1
immoral *adj* **1** *syn* see IMPURE 1
  ant moral
2 syn see WRONG 1
  ant moral
immorality *n syn* see VICE 1
  ant morality
immortal *adj* **1** not subject to death <the *immortal* gods>
  syn deathless, undying; *compare* EVERLASTING 1
  rel endless, enduring, imperishable, indestructible, perpetual, sempiternal, timeless
  con ephemeral, evanescent, fleeting, fugitive, passing, short-lived, transient, transitory
  ant mortal
2 syn see EVERLASTING 1
immortality *n syn* see ETERNITY 2
  ant mortality
immortalize *vb syn* see PERPETUATE
immotile *adj syn* see IMMOVABLE 1
  ant motile
immotive *adj syn* see IMMOVABLE 1
immovable *adj* **1** incapable of moving or being moved <an *immovable* rock>
  syn fixed, immobile, immotile, immotive, irremovable, ‖sitfast, steadfast, unmovable
  rel adamant, fast, rooted, stable, stationary, stuck, unmoving, unyielding

con portable, removable, transferable, transportable
  ant movable
2 syn see INFLEXIBLE 3
immunity *n syn* see EXEMPTION
  ant susceptibility
immure *vb* **1** *syn* see ENCLOSE 1
2 syn see IMPRISON
immusical *adj syn* see DISSONANT 1
  ant musical
immutable *adj syn* see INFLEXIBLE 3
  ant mutable
imp *n* **1** a small demon, devil, or wicked spirit <the *imps* of hell>
  syn deviling, devilkin
  rel elf, gnome, goblin, gremlin, ‖hob, hobgoblin, kobold, ouph, pixie, puck, sprite, troll
2 syn see URCHIN
impact *n* **1** a forcible or enforced contact between two or more things <a crater formed by the *impact* of a meteorite>
  syn appulse, blow, bump, clash, collision, concussion, crash, impingement, jar, jolt, jounce, percussion, shock, smash, wallop
  rel brunt; buffet, hit, pound, punch, rap, slap, smiting, strike, stroke; bounce, quake, quiver, rock, shake, tremble, tremor; encounter, meeting
2 syn see EFFECT 3
impair *vb syn* see INJURE 1
  rel sap, undermine, weaken
  con ameliorate, better
  ant improve; repair
impaired *adj syn* see DAMAGED
impale *vb* to pierce or fix with or as if with something pointed <an insect *impaled* on a pin>
  syn lance, skewer, skiver, spear, spike, spit, transfix, transpierce
  rel perforate, pierce, prick, punch, puncture, stab
impalpable *adj* **1** *syn* see IMPERCEPTIBLE
  ant palpable
2 syn see FINE 2
imparity *n syn* see DISPARITY
  ant parity
impart *vb syn* see COMMUNICATE 1
impartial *adj syn* see FAIR 4
  ant partial
impartially *adv syn* see EVENLY 2
impassable *adj* **1** not allowing passage <an *impassable* barrier>
  syn impenetrable, impermeable, impervious, imperviable, impervious, unpierceable
  con penetrable, permeable, pervious
  ant passable
2 syn see INSUPERABLE
impasse *n* **1** *syn* see DEAD END
2 syn see PREDICAMENT
impassible *adj syn* see INSENSIBLE 5
  rel cold, emotionless, passionless, unemotional, unfeeling; inert, unresponsive
  ant passible
impassioned *adj* actuated by or showing intense feeling <*impassioned* oratory>
  syn ardent, blazing, burning, dithyrambic, fervent, fervid, fiery, flaming, glowing, hot-blooded, overheated, passionate, perfervid, red-hot, torrid, white-hot

---

syn synonym(s)   *rel* related word(s)
ant antonym(s)   *con* contrasted word(s)
idiom idiomatic equivalent(s)
‖ use limited; if in doubt, see a dictionary

rel feverish, fierce, furious, intense, vehement, violent; deep, profound, warm, zealous; gushing, gushy, maudlin, melodramatic, mushy, overemotional, romantic, sentimental

con cold, cool, dispassionate, frigid, icy, unemotional; objective

ant unimpassioned

impassive *adj* **1** unresponsive to what might normally excite interest or emotion <*impassive* endurance of pain>

syn apathetic, dry, matter-of-fact, phlegmatic, stoic, stolid

rel calm, cold, cool; collected, composed, dispassionate, emotionless, imperturbable, inexcitable, unexcitable, unflappable; inexpressive, reserved, reticent, taciturn, unemotional, unexpressive; bovine, passionless, placid, spiritless, unconcerned, wooden; callous, hardened, indurated, insensible; cold-blooded, coldhearted, heartless

con compassionate, sympathetic, tender, warm, warmhearted

ant responsive

2 *syn* see INSUSCEPTIBLE

impassivity *n syn* see APATHY 1

impatient *adj* **1** lacking power to endure hardship, distress, or opposition <married to an *impatient* self-centered man>

syn chafing, fretful, unpatient

rel abrupt, hasty, headlong, impetuous; anxious, edgy, itchy, nervous; irascible, irritable

idiom all of a stew

con enduring, forbearing, tolerant; self-controlled, Spartan, stoic

ant patient

2 *syn* see INTOLERANT 1

rel demanding, harsh

3 *syn* see EAGER

ant patient

impeach *vb syn* see ACCUSE

impeccable *adj* **1** absolutely correct and beyond criticism <*impeccable* manners>

syn errorless, exquisite, faultless, flawless, immaculate, irreproachable

rel accurate, clean, correct, exact, nice, perfect, precise, right; infallible, unerring

con defective, deficient, faulty; blameworthy, censurable, criticizable, culpable; cursory, shallow, superficial, uncritical

ant peccant

2 *syn* see PERFECT 2

impecunious *adj syn* see POOR 1

ant affluent; flush

impecuniousness *n syn* see POVERTY 1

ant affluence; flushness

impedance *n syn* see ENCUMBRANCE

impede *vb syn* see HINDER

rel discomfit, disconcert, embarrass, faze, rattle

ant aid, assist

impediment *n* **1** *syn* see ENCUMBRANCE

ant aid, assistance

2 *syn* see OBSTACLE

impel *vb syn* see MOVE 5

rel compel, constrain, force; foment, incite, instigate; goad, spur; inspire, motivate

con check, curb, inhibit

ant restrain

impend *vb syn* see LOOM 2

impending *adj syn* see IMMINENT 1

impenetrable *adj* **1** *syn* see IMPASSABLE 1

rel firm, solid, substantial

ant penetrable

2 *syn* see INCOMPREHENSIBLE 1

ant penetrable

3 *syn* see MYSTERIOUS

impenetrate *vb syn* see PERMEATE

impenitent *adj syn* see REMORSELESS

ant penitent

imperative *adj* **1** *syn* see MASTERFUL 1

rel bidding, commanding, ordering; harsh, stern

con begging, entreating, imploring; lenient, mild, soft

2 *syn* see PRESSING

rel acute, critical, crucial

3 *syn* see ESSENTIAL 4

rel basic, fundamental; claimed, demanded, exacted

4 *syn* see MANDATORY

imperceptible *adj* incapable of being apprehended by the senses or intellect <*imperceptible* changes in temperature>

syn impalpable, imponderable, inappreciable, indiscernible, insensible, intangible, invisible, unapparent, unappreciable, undiscernible, unobservable, unperceivable

rel faint, inconspicuous, indistinct, indistinguishable, insignificant, obscure, undistinguishable, unnoticeable, vague; ephemeral, evanescent, fugitive, momentary; slight, trivial

con apparent, appreciable, discernible, observable, palpable, ponderable, sensible, visible

ant perceivable, perceptible

imperceptive *adj* lacking perception or insight <*imperceptive* criticism that misses the point of the play>

syn impercipient, unperceiving, unperceptive

rel unappreciative, undiscerning, unobservant; cursory, shallow, slapdash, superficial

con astute, discerning, discriminating, judicious, perspicacious; delicate, nice, refined, sensitive, subtle

ant perceiving, perceptive, percipient

impercipient *adj syn* see IMPERCEPTIVE

ant perceiving, perceptive, percipient

imperfect *adj syn* see FAULTY

ant perfect

imperfection *n* an instance of failure to reach a standard of excellence or perfection <watch for *imperfections* in the cloth>

syn deficiency, demerit, fault, shortcoming, sin

rel blemish, defect, flaw; failing, foible, frailty

ant perfection

imperial *adj syn* see MASTERFUL 1

imperil *vb syn* see ENDANGER

imperious *adj* **1** *syn* see MASTERFUL 1

rel heavy-handed, oppressive, strict, stringent; absolute, arbitrary

con considerate, easy, gentle, kindly

2 *syn* see MANDATORY

imperishable *adj syn* see INDESTRUCTIBLE

impermanent *adj syn* see TRANSIENT

ant permanent
impermeable *adj syn see* IMPASSABLE 1
  ant permeable
impersonal *adj* 1 *syn see* NEUTRAL
  2 *syn see* FAIR 4
  3 *syn see* MATTER-OF-FACT 3
impersonate *vb syn see* ACT 1
impersonator *n syn see* ACTOR 1
impertinence *n syn see* INSOLENCE
impertinent *adj* 1 *syn see* IRRELEVANT
  ant pertinent
  2 going beyond what is proper or acceptable
in thrusting oneself into the affairs of others
<*impertinent* interference with her sister's
family>
  syn busy, intrusive, meddlesome, ‖nebby,
obtrusive, officious, polypragmatic
  rel arrogant, bold, brash, brazen, fresh,
impudent, pert, presumptuous, saucy; inquisitive, interfering, meddling, nosy, prying; offensive, rude
  con decent, decorous, proper, seemly; reserved, reticent, silent; apposite, germane,
pertinent, relevant
  3 *syn see* RUDE 6
  4 *syn see* INSOLENT 2
imperturbation *n syn see* EQUANIMITY
imperturbable *adj syn see* COOL 2
  rel complacent, self-satisfied, smug; unaffected, unmoved, untouched
  con discomfited, disconcerted, fazed, rattled; irascible, splenetic, testy
  ant choleric; touchy
imperviable *adj syn see* IMPASSABLE 1
impervious *adj syn see* IMPASSABLE 1
  ant pervious
impetuous *adj syn see* PRECIPITATE 1
  rel spontaneous; restive; ardent, fervid,
impassioned, passionate
  con equable, even, steady; advised, considered, deliberate, planned, premeditated
impetuously *adv syn see* PELL-MELL
impetus *n syn see* STIMULUS
impignorate *vb syn see* PAWN
impingement *n syn see* IMPACT 1
impious *adj* 1 lacking reverence for holy or
sacred matters <made *impious* remarks
about the church>
  syn irreverent, irreverential, profane, ungodly, unhallowed, unholy
  rel godless, iconoclastic, irreligious, sacrilegious, scandalous, undevout
  con devout, godly, religious, spiritual
  ant pious
  2 lacking due respect (as toward one's parents) <an *impious* son>
  syn unduteous, undutiful
  rel disobedient, froward, unfaithful, wayward; contrary, perverse, wrongheaded
  con duteous, dutiful
impish *adj syn see* PLAYFUL 1
  rel arch, pert, saucy; flippant, fresh, giddy;
casual, devil-may-care, free and easy, offhand
impishness *n syn see* MISCHIEVOUSNESS

implacable *adj syn see* GRIM 3
  con peaceable, tractable; kindly, tolerant
  ant placable
implant *vb* to introduce into the mind <*implanted* worthy ideals in their children>
  syn inculcate, infix, inseminate, instill
  rel imbue, infuse, ingrain, inoculate, leaven,
root; impenetrate, impregnate, penetrate,
permeate, pervade, saturate; inspire
implausible *adj* not plausible or readily
believable <an *implausible* explanation>
  syn flimsy, improbable, inconceivable,
incredible, thick, thin, unbelievable, unconceivable, unconvincing, unsubstantial, weak;
compare TENUOUS 3
  rel doubtful, dubious, fishy; problematic,
puzzling, suspect
  idiom a bit thick
  con meaty, pithy; solid, sound, substantial;
believable, conceivable, credible; likely,
probable
  ant plausible
implement *n* a usually relatively simple
device for performing a mechanical or manual operation <spades, hoes, and other
gardener's *implements*>
  syn instrument, tool, utensil
  rel apparatus, appliance; contrivance, device; contraption, gadget
implement *vb* 1 *syn see* FULFILL 1
  2 *syn see* ENFORCE
  rel actualize, materialize, realize
implemental *adj syn see* INSTRUMENTAL
impliable *adj syn see* STIFF 1
  ant pliable
implicate *vb syn see* INVOLVE 1
  rel affect, concern; incriminate
  con absolve, acquit, exculpate, exonerate
implicated *adj syn see* INTERESTED
implication *n syn see* ASSOCIATION 4
implicit *adj* 1 *syn see* TACIT 1
  idiom taken for granted
  ant explicit
  2 being such in essential character <our
implicit freedom is better than your nominal
liberty>
  syn constructive, practical, virtual
  rel absolute, complete, unqualified, wholehearted; genuine, real
  ant spelled out
implied *adj syn see* TACIT 1
imploration *n syn see* PRAYER
implore *vb syn see* BEG
imply *vb* 1 *syn see* POINT 2
  2 *syn see* SUGGEST 1
  con state; express; affirm, assert, declare
impolite *adj syn see* RUDE 6
  ant polite
impolitic *adj* 1 *syn see* UNWISE
  ant politic
  2 *syn see* INADVISABLE
  ant politic
  3 *syn see* TACTLESS
imponderable *adj syn see* IMPERCEPTIBLE
  ant appreciable, ponderable
imponderous *adj syn see* LIGHT 1
  ant ponderous
import *vb* 1 *syn see* MEAN 2
  2 *syn see* MATTER
import *n* 1 *syn see* MEANING 1

---

syn synonym(s)   *rel* related word(s)
ant antonym(s)   *con* contrasted word(s)
idiom idiomatic equivalent(s)
‖ use limited; if in doubt, see a dictionary

rel construction, interpretation

2 *syn* see IMPORTANCE

rel value, worth; design, intent, object, objective, purpose; emphasis, stress

importance *n* the quality or state of being of notable worth or influence <persons of national and worldwide *importance*>

syn consequence, import, magnitude, moment, momentousness, pith, significance, ||signification, weight, weightiness

rel conspicuousness; distinction, eminence, mark, prominence, salience; notability, note, noteworthiness, reputation, standing; substance, value, worth, worthiness; gravity, seriousness

con inconsequence, insignificance, paltriness, pettiness, triviality

ant unimportance

important *adj* **1** marked by or indicative of notable worth or consequence <an *important* discovery> <his manner was grave and *important*>

syn big, consequential, considerable, material, meaningful, momentous, significant, substantial, weighty

rel conspicuous, distinctive, exceptional, impressive, marked, memorable, notable, noteworthy, noticeable, outstanding, prominent, remarkable, salient, unusual; essential, valuable, worthwhile; worthy; effective, potent, powerful, telling; big-time, first-class, first-rate, front-page, top-notch; distinguished, eminent, famous, noted

con inconsiderable, little, minor, paltry, petty, slight, trivial

ant unimportant

2 *syn* see POMPOUS 1

importunate *adj* *syn* see PRESSING

rel persevering, persistent; dogged, pertinacious

importune *vb* *syn* see BEG

impose *vb* **1** *syn* see DICTATE

rel charge, command, enjoin, order; demand, exact, require; compel, constrain, oblige

2 *syn* see LEVY

3 *syn* see INFLICT 2

4 to force another to accept <*imposed* all the dirty jobs on her sister>

syn foist, wish; *compare* FOIST 3, INFLICT 2

rel burden, lade, saddle; fob, fob off, palm off

idiom take advantage of

5 to take usually unwarranted advantage <did not wish to *impose* by turning up unannounced>

syn infringe, intrude, obtrude, presume

rel encroach, trespass

idiom make free, take liberties

impose (on *or* upon) *vb* *syn* see EXPLOIT 2

imposing *adj* **1** *syn* see GRAND 1

rel impressive, moving; imperial, regal

ant unimposing

2 *syn* see PRETENTIOUS 3

impossible *adj* **1** not capable of being realized or attained <*impossible* goals>

syn impracticable, impractical, infeasible, irrealizable, unattainable, unfeasible, unrealizable, unworkable

rel absurd, inexecutable, unobtainable, unreasonable, unthinkable

idiom out of the question

con attainable, feasible, realizable; practicable, practical, rational, reasonable

ant possible

2 *syn* see HOPELESS 2

impost *n* *syn* see TAX 1

impostor *n* one who passes himself off as something or someone he is not <the presumed heir was discovered to be an *impostor*>

syn fake, faker, fraud, humbug, phony, pretender; *compare* CHARLATAN

rel imitator, mimic; beguiler, deceiver, misleader; cheat, pettifogger, shyster, trickster; hypocrite; charlatan, mountebank, quack; bluffer, dissembler, four-flusher, shammer

idiom wolf in sheep's clothing

imposture *n* the act, practice, or an instance of imposing on another by use of an assumed character or name <his claims were based on *imposture*>

syn cheat, counterfeit, deceit, deception, fake, flam, flimflam, fraud, gyp, hoax, humbug, mare's nest, phony, put-on, ||rig, sell, sham, spoof, swindle

rel copy, imitation; fabrication, forgery; artifice, feint, gambit, maneuver, ploy, ruse, sleight, stratagem, trick, wile; make-believe, pretense, pretension

impotent *adj* **1** *syn* see POWERLESS

rel crippled, disabled, enfeebled

con able, capable, competent

ant potent

2 *syn* see WEAK 4

con forceful, powerful, puissant, strenuous, vigorous

ant potent

3 *syn* see STERILE 1

impoverish *vb* **1** *syn* see DEPLETE

ant enrich

2 *syn* see RUIN 3

impoverished *adj* *syn* see POOR 1

impoverishment *n* *syn* see POVERTY 1

impracticable *adj* **1** *syn* see IMPOSSIBLE 1

ant feasible, practicable

2 incapable of being successfully used or turned to account <a route through the mountains that is *impracticable* in winter>

syn impractical, nonfunctional, unfunctional, unserviceable, unusable, unworkable, useless

rel disadvantageous, unacceptable, undesirable, unsatisfactory; awkward, inconvenient, troublesome

con functional, practical, serviceable, usable, useful, workable

ant practicable

impractical *adj* **1** incapable of dealing prudently with practical matters <a very *impractical* person whose checkbook never balanced>

syn ivory-tower, ivory-towered, ivory-towerish, nonrealistic, unpractical, unrealistic, viewy

rel idealistic, otherworldly, quixotic, romantic, starry-eyed, visionary

con commonsensible, commonsensical, realistic, sensible, worldly-wise

ant practical

2 *syn* see IMPRACTICABLE 2
ant practical
3 *syn* see IMPOSSIBLE 1

imprecate *vb syn* see SWEAR 3

imprecation *n* **1** *syn* see BLASPHEMY 1
2 *syn* see PRAYER
3 *syn* see CURSE 1
con blessing

impregnable *adj syn* see INVINCIBLE 1
rel safe, secure; defended, guarded, protected, safeguarded, shielded
con exposed, open, susceptible

impregnate *vb* **1** *syn* see PERMEATE
rel inoculate, leaven
2 *syn* see SOAK 1

impress *vb* **1** *syn* see ENGRAVE 2
2 *syn* see AFFECT
rel enthuse, electrify, thrill; excite, galvanize, pique, provoke, stimulate
idiom make (or leave) one's mark
3 to fix in the mind or memory by emphasis or repetition <the speaker *impressed* his principal thesis upon his audience>
syn drive, grave, hammer, pound, stamp
rel establish, fix, set
idiom drive home to one, fix in one's mind, get into one's head

impress *n syn* see IMPRESSION 1

impressible *adj syn* see SENTIENT 3

impression *n* **1** the perceptible trace or traces left by pressure <the *impression* made by a die>
syn impress, imprint, indentation, print, stamp
rel dent, dint, hollow; trace, track, vestige; mark, sign
2 *syn* see IDEA
3 *syn* see EDITION

impressionable *adj syn* see SENTIENT 3
rel affectable, influenceable

impressive *adj* **1** *syn* see MOVING 2
rel august, grand, imposing, majestic, noble; splendid, superb; arresting, notable, striking
ant unimpressive
2 *syn* see GRAND 2

imprint *vb syn* see ENGRAVE 2

imprint *n* **1** *syn* see IMPRESSION 1
2 *syn* see EFFECT 3

imprison *vb* to shut up closely so that escape is impossible or unlikely <the offender was quickly sentenced and *imprisoned*>
syn bastille, confine, constrain, immure, incarcerate, intern, jail, jug, ‖prison, ‖quod
rel circumscribe, limit, restrict; check, curb, restrain
idiom put under lock and key
con free, liberate, release

improbable *adj* **1** not likely to be true or to occur <the immediate success of their plan is *improbable*>
syn doubtful, dubious, questionable, unlikely
ant probable
2 *syn* see IMPLAUSIBLE

impromptu *n syn* see IMPROVISATION

impromptu *adj syn* see EXTEMPORANEOUS
rel prompt, quick

improper *adj* **1** unsuited to the circumstances or the occasion <wore quite *improper* dress for such a formal reception>
syn ill-timed, inadmissible, inappropriate, inapt, inept, intempestive, malapropos, unapt, unbecoming, unbefitting, uncomely, undue, unfitting, unseasonable, unseemly, unsuitable, untimely
rel infelicitous, unhappy; inapplicable, inapposite; fresh, impertinent, sassy; crude, gauche, tactless
idiom out of place, out of season
con apposite, appropriate, apropos, apt, becoming, befitting, felicitous, fitting, germane, happy, opportune, pat, pertinent, seasonable, suitable, timely, well-timed
ant proper
2 *syn* see INDECOROUS
rel informal, unceremonious, unconventional
con correct, right
ant proper

impropriety *n* **1** the quality or state of being improper (as in social behavior) <was shocked by the *impropriety* of their actions>
syn incorrectness, indecorousness, indecorum, inelegance, unbecomingness, unmeetness, unseemliness, untowardness
rel inadmissibility, objectionableness, unacceptableness
con becomingness, decency, decorousness, decorum, meetness
ant propriety, seemliness
2 *syn* see FAUX PAS; compare ERROR 2
3 *syn* see BARBARISM

improve *vb* **1** to make more acceptable or bring nearer to some standard <studied hard to *improve* her chances of success>
syn ameliorate, amend, better, help, meliorate
rel cultivate, develop, perfect; correct, emend, rectify, reform, remedy; edit, revise; enhance, enrich, refine, rub up, upgrade
con diminish, downgrade, lessen, lower
2 *syn* see ILLUMINATE 2
3 to grow or become better (as in health or well-being) <the invalid is steadily *improving*>
syn ameliorate, convalesce, gain, look up, mend, perk (up), recuperate
rel advance, better, progress; recover; rally, revive, strengthen
idiom gain ground, make progress
con decline, deteriorate, fail, flag, languish, run down, sink, weaken

improvident *adj* not foreseeing or providing for the future <an *improvident* way of life>
syn thriftless, unthrift, unthrifty
rel careless, heedless, imprudent; extravagant, prodigal, profligate, spendthrift; lavish, profuse, reckless; uneconomical, wasteful
con careful, economical, frugal, parsimonious, prudent, saving, sparing
ant provident, thrifty

improvisate *vb syn* see IMPROVISE

---

syn synonym(s)   *rel* related word(s)
ant antonym(s)   *con* contrasted word(s)
idiom idiomatic equivalent(s)
‖ use limited; if in doubt, see a dictionary

improvisation *n* something that is improvised <the pianist played several clever *improvisations*>
syn autoschediasm, extemporization, impromptu

improvise *vb* to perform or provide on the spur of the moment <*improvise* an excuse for being late>
syn ad-lib, extemporize, improvisate
rel concoct, contrive, devise, invent

improvised *adj syn* see EXTEMPORANEOUS

imprudent *adj* **1** *syn* see UNWISE
ant prudent
2 *syn* see INADVISABLE
ant prudent

impudence *n syn* see INSOLENCE

impudent *adj* **1** *syn* see WISE 5
2 *syn* see INSOLENT 2
3 *syn* see SHAMELESS

impugn *vb syn* see DENY 4
rel assail, attack
idiom call in (*or* into) question (*or* doubt), throw doubt on
con back, support, uphold
ant advocate; authenticate

impugnable *adj syn* see DOUBTFUL 1

impulse *n syn* see STIMULUS
rel excitant; lust, passion, urge; actuation, drive, impulsion

impulsive *adj syn* see SPONTANEOUS
rel abrupt, hasty, headlong, impetuous, precipitate, sudden
con considered, designed, premeditated; calculating, cautious, circumspect
ant deliberate

impulsiveness *n syn* see ABANDON 2

impunity *n syn* see EXEMPTION

impure *adj* **1** morally or mentally unclean <*impure* thoughts>
syn dirty, immoral, unchaste, unclean, uncleanly
rel belowstairs, carnal, immodest, indecent, indecorous, lascivious, lewd, lustful, prurient, scarlet, sensual; filthy, vile
con chaste, clean, cleanly, decent, decorous, immaculate, modest, virtuous; moral
ant pure
2 *syn* see DIRTY 1
3 made unfit for ceremonial purposes <altars overturned and sacred vessels made *impure* by the touch of profane hands>
syn common, defiled, desecrated, polluted, profaned, unclean
rel unhallowed, unholy
con clean, consecrated, undefiled
ant pure
4 *syn* see UNREFINED 3

impute *vb syn* see ASCRIBE
rel accuse, indict; adduce; hint, insinuate, intimate

in *adj syn* see STYLISH

in *n syn* see PULL 2

inability *n* lack of sufficient power, resources, or capacity to perform <suffered from an *inability* to make quick decisions>
syn inadequacy, incapability, incapacity, incompetence, ineffectiveness, ineffectualness, inefficacy
rel inadeptness, inaptitude, inaptness, inefficiency, ineptitude, ineptness

con adequacy, capability, capacity; competence, efficiency
ant ability

inaccessible *adj* not capable of being achieved <an *inaccessible* goal>
syn inapproachable, unapproachable, unattainable, un-come-at-able, ungetatable, unobtainable, unreachable
rel distant, far, faraway, far-off, out-of-the-way, remote
ant accessible

inaccurate *adj syn* see FALSE 1
con right, true
ant accurate

inaction *n* lack of action or activity <the delay was due to the committee's *inaction*>
syn inactiveness, inactivity
rel drift, idleness, indolence, inertness, lethargy, quiescence, slackness, slothfulness, torpidity
con activeness, activity

inactive *adj* not characterized by or engaged in usual or normal activity <forced by illness to lead an *inactive* life>
syn asleep, idle, inert, passive, quiet, sleepy
rel abeyant, dormant, inoperative, latent, quiescent; do-nothing, indolent, lethargic, lymphatic, slack, slothful, sluggish, torpid; motionless, sedentary, static; disengaged, jobless, unemployed, unoccupied, unworking; ossified
con busy, employed, engaged, occupied; energetic, strenuous, vigorous; animated, brisk, lively
ant active

inactiveness *n syn* see INACTION

inactivity *n syn* see INACTION
ant activity

in addition *adv syn* see AGAIN 4

inadept *adj syn* see UNSKILLFUL 1
ant adept

inadequacy *n* **1** *syn* see INABILITY
2 *syn* see FAILURE 3
ant adequacy

inadequate *adj* **1** *syn* see DEFICIENT 1
ant adequate
2 *syn* see SHORT 3
ant adequate
3 *syn* see MEAGER
ant adequate
4 *syn* see WEAK 4
ant adequate

inadmissible *adj* **1** *syn* see IMPROPER 1
2 *syn* see OBJECTIONABLE
ant admissible

in advance *adv syn* see BEFORE 1

in advance of *prep* **1** *syn* see BEFORE 1
2 *syn* see UNTIL

inadvertent *adj* **1** *syn* see CARELESS 1
ant advertent
2 *syn* see UNINTENTIONAL

inadvisable *adj* not likely to have a satisfactory outcome <it seemed *inadvisable* to go any farther because of threatening weather>
syn ill-advised, impolitic, imprudent, inexpedient, unadvisable, unexpedient
rel careless, inappropriate, incautious, rash, undesirable, unsensible; foolish, indiscreet, pointless, unwise; foolhardy, harebrained
con expedient, judicious, politic, prudent, sensible, wise

ant advisable

in all *adv syn see* ALTOGETHER 2

in all probability *adv syn see* PRESUMABLY

inalterable *adj syn see* INFLEXIBLE 3
ant alterable

inamorata *n* **1** *syn see* GIRL FRIEND 2
2 *syn see* MISTRESS

inamorato *n syn see* BOYFRIEND 2

in and out *adv syn see* THOROUGHLY 2

inane *adj syn see* INSIPID 3
rel asinine, fatuous, foolish, silly; idle, vain; blank, empty, hollow
con expressive, meaningful, pregnant, significant, weighty
ant deep, profound

inanimate *adj* **1** *syn see* INSENSATE 1
ant animate
2 *syn see* DEAD 1
ant animate; living

inanity *n syn see* FOOLISHNESS

inapplicable *adj syn see* IRRELEVANT
ant applicable

inapposite *adj syn see* IRRELEVANT
ant apposite

inappreciable *adj* **1** *syn see* IMPERCEPTIBLE
ant appreciable
2 *syn see* MEAGER

inapproachable *adj syn see* INACCESSIBLE
ant approachable

inappropriate *adj* **1** *syn see* UNFIT 1
rel indecorous, unseemly; inconsonant
con felicitous, fitting, happy, meet, proper; fit, suitable
ant appropriate
2 *syn see* IMPROPER 1

inapt *adj* **1** *syn see* UNFIT 1
rel awkward, clumsy, gauche, maladroit; banal, flat, insipid, jejune
con apposite, germane, pertinent, relevant
ant apt
2 *syn see* IMPROPER 1
ant apt
3 *syn see* UNSKILLFUL 1
ant adept

inarguable *adj syn see* POSITIVE 3
ant arguable

inarticulate *adj* **1** *syn see* DUMB 1
ant articulate
2 *syn see* TACIT 1
3 failing to give or incapable of giving clear or effective verbal expression to one's ideas or feelings <made some *inarticulate* explanation for being late> <was completely *inarticulate* when it came to expressing affection>
syn incoherent, maundering, tongue-tied, unvocal
rel faltering, halting, hesitating, mumbling, stammered, stammering; blurred, indistinct
con facile, glib, smooth
ant articulate

inartificial *adj syn see* NATURAL 5
ant artificial

inasmuch as *conj syn see* BECAUSE

inattentive *adj* not paying proper attention <an *inattentive* pupil dozing at his desk>
syn inobservant, unheeding, unnoticing, unobservant, unobserving, unperceiving, unwatchful
rel distracted, distrait, distraught; careless, heedless, thoughtless, undiscerning, unmindful, unthinking; bored, ennuyé
ant attentive; observant

inaugural *adj syn see* FIRST 1

inaugural *n syn see* INITIATION

inaugurate *vb* **1** *syn see* INITIATE 3
2 *syn see* BEGIN 1
3 *syn see* INTRODUCE 3

inauguration *n syn see* INITIATION

inauspicious *adj* **1** *syn see* OMINOUS
ant auspicious
2 *syn see* EVIL 6

in between *prep syn see* BETWEEN 2

inborn *adj* **1** *syn see* INNATE 1
ant acquired
2 *syn see* INHERENT

inbred *adj syn see* INHERENT

in brief *adv syn see* BRIEFLY

incalculable *adj* **1** being great beyond calculation <*incalculable* damage>
syn immeasurable, inestimable, measureless, uncountable, unmeasurable, unmeasured, unreckonable
rel countless, innumerable, unnumbered, untold; boundless, enormous, infinite, limitless, vast
con minimal, slight, trivial
ant infinitesimal
2 *syn see* UNCERTAIN 1
ant calculable

in camera *adv syn see* SECRETLY

incandescent *adj syn see* BRIGHT 1

incantation *n* **1** *syn see* SPELL
2 *syn see* MAGIC 1

incapability *n syn see* INABILITY
ant capability

incapable *adj* **1** *syn see* UNFIT 2
ant capable
2 *syn see* INEFFICIENT 2
ant capable

incapacitate *vb* **1** *syn see* PARALYZE 1
2 *syn see* DISQUALIFY
ant capacitate

incapacity *n syn see* INABILITY
ant capacity

incarcerate *vb syn see* IMPRISON

incarnadine *vb syn see* REDDEN 1

incarnate *vb syn see* EMBODY 1

incarnation *n syn see* EMBODIMENT

incautious *adj* **1** lacking in caution <made an *incautious* prediction>
syn unalert, unguarded, unvigilant, unwary, unwatchful; *compare* CARELESS 1
rel imprudent, indiscreet, injudicious; bold, brash, impetuous, rash, reckless; neglectful, negligent, regardless, thoughtless, unmindful; hasty
idiom caught napping, off one's guard
con careful, circumspect, judicious, wary, watchful; discreet, judicious, prudent; sensible, thoughtful, wise
ant cautious
2 *syn see* RASH 1
ant cautious

---

syn synonym(s)   *rel* related word(s)
ant antonym(s)   *con* contrasted word(s)
idiom idiomatic equivalent(s)
‖ use limited; if in doubt, see a dictionary

3 *syn* see IRRESPONSIBLE

incendiary *n* a person who deliberately and unlawfully sets fire to a building or other property <a fire set by an *incendiary*>
syn arsonist, firebug, torch
rel pyromaniac

incendiary *adj syn* see INFLAMMATORY

incense *n* **1** *syn* see FRAGRANCE
2 *syn* see FLATTERY

incense *vb syn* see ANGER 1
ant placate

incentive *n syn* see STIMULUS

inception *n syn* see SOURCE
con closing, completion, conclusion
ant termination

inceptive *adj syn* see INITIAL 1
ant terminal

incertitude *n syn* see UNCERTAINTY
ant certitude

incessant *adj syn* see CONTINUAL
ant intermittent

inchoate *adj* **1** *syn* see FORMLESS
2 *syn* see INCOHERENT 2

incident *n syn* see OCCURRENCE

incident *adj* **1** *syn* see CONCOMITANT
ant essential, fundamental
2 *syn* see RELATED

incidental *adj syn* see ACCIDENTAL
ant essential

incidentally *adv* **1** by chance <in this discussion grave questions were brought up *incidentally*>
syn accidentally, casually, fortuitously
ant deliberately
2 by way of interjection or digression <another leading industry, *incidentally*, has quadrupled its business in four years>
syn by the bye, by the way, in passing, obiter, parenthetically
idiom in the bygoing

incipient *adj syn* see INITIAL 1

incise *vb* **1** *syn* see CUT 1
2 *syn* see ENGRAVE 1

incisive *adj* having, manifesting, or suggesting a keen alertness of mind <a man well known for his *incisive* wit>
syn biting, clear-cut, crisp, cutting, ingoing, penetrating, trenchant
rel acute, drilling, keen, sharp; acerb, acerbic, caustic, mordant, scathing, slashing, tart; concise, laconic, succinct, terse
con diffuse, prolix, verbose, wordy; feeble, limp, pithless, sapless
ant unincisive

incisiveness *n syn* see EDGE 2

incitation *n syn* see STIMULUS

incite *vb* to aid or promote the activity or development of <*incite* a riot>
syn abet, foment, instigate, provoke, raise, set, set on, stir (up), whip (up)
rel forward, further, promote, stimulate; set off, trigger; agitate, solicit; encourage, motivate, motive; excite, inflame, rouse
con check, curb, discourage, inhibit, restrain; calm, quiet, subdue

incitement *n syn* see STIMULUS
ant restraint; inhibition

inciter *n syn* see INSTIGATOR

incivil *adj syn* see RUDE 6
ant civil

inclement *adj syn* see SEVERE 3
ant clement

inclination *n* **1** *syn* see LEANING 2
ant disinclination
2 *syn* see WILL 1
ant disinclination
3 *syn* see APPETITE 3
ant disinclination
4 *syn* see SLOPE

incline *vb* **1** *syn* see TEND 1
2 *syn* see SLANT 1
rel deflect, turn
3 to have an attitude toward or to influence one to take an attitude <*inclined* to believe the story> <his argument *inclined* me to share his view>
syn bend, bias, dispose, predispose; *compare* PREJUDICE 2, TEND 1
rel affect, influence, prompt, sway; drive, impel, induce, move, persuade
ant disincline, indispose
4 *syn* see DIRECT 1

incline *n syn* see SLOPE

inclined *adj* **1** *syn* see WILLING 1
ant disinclined
2 *syn* see APT 1
ant disinclined
3 sloping from the horizontal or perpendicular <cars running on an *inclined* track>
syn declivate, declivitous, inclining, leaning, oblique, pitched, pitching, sloped, sloping, tilted, tilting, tipped; *compare* DIAGONAL
rel dipping, grading, graded, raked

inclining *n syn* see LEANING 2

inclining *adj syn* see INCLINED 3

include *vb* to possess as an integral part of a whole <the park *includes* a zoo and a botanical garden>
syn comprehend, contain, embody, embrace, encompass, have, involve, subsume, take in
rel comprise, cover, encircle, enclose, hold; number; admit, receive
con leave out, omit; preclude, reject; debar; eliminate, rule out
ant exclude

inclusive *adj* **1** *syn* see ALL-AROUND 2
2 *syn* see ENCYCLOPEDIC

incogitable *adj syn* see INCREDIBLE 1
ant cogitable

incogitant *adj syn* see RASH 1

incognizable *adj syn* see INCOMPREHENSIBLE 1
ant cognizable

incognizant *adj syn* see IGNORANT 2
ant cognizant

incoherent *adj* **1** *syn* see LOOSE 3
2 lacking cohesion or continuity <an *incoherent* presentation>
syn disconnected, discontinuous, disjointed, disordered, inchoate, incohesive, muddled, unconnected, uncontinuous, unorganized
rel discordant, incompatible, incongruous, inconsistent, inconsonant, inharmonious
con ordered, orderly; connected; organized, planned, plotted
ant coherent
3 *syn* see INARTICULATE 3

incohesive *adj syn* see INCOHERENT 2

ant cohesive

incombustible *adj syn* see NONCOMBUSTI-BLE

ant combustible

income *n syn* see REVENUE

incommode *vb syn* see INCONVENIENCE
rel block, hinder, impede, obstruct; annoy, bother, irk, vex
con favor, oblige; humor, indulge; gratify, please
ant accommodate

incommodious *adj* **1** *syn* see INCONVE-NIENT
ant commodious
2 *syn* see CRAMPED
ant commodious

incommunicable *adj* **1** *syn* see UNUTTER-ABLE
ant communicable
2 *syn* see RESERVED 1
ant communicable, communicative

incomparable *adj syn* see SUPREME
rel matchless
con common, commonplace, ordinary; indifferent, mediocre, medium, middling
ant average

incompatible *adj syn* see INCONSONANT 1
rel adverse, antagonistic, counter; antipathetic; antipodal, antipodean, antithetical, contradictory, contrary, opposite; irreconcilable, unadaptable, unconformable
ant compatible
2 *syn* see IRRECONCILABLE
ant compatible

incompetence *n syn* see INABILITY

incompetent *adj* **1** *syn* see UNFIT 2
ant competent
2 *syn* see INEFFICIENT 2
ant competent

incomplete *adj* **1** lacking a part or parts <an *incomplete* text of a speech>
syn fractional, fragmentary, part, partial
rel broken, deficient, incoherent, lacking, short, wanting; bitty, composite, scrappy
con intact, undamaged, whole
ant complete
2 *syn* see DEFICIENT 1
ant complete

incompliant *adj* **1** *syn* see OBSTINATE
ant compliant
2 *syn* see STIFF 1

incomprehensible *adj* **1** lying above or beyond the reach of the human mind <the *incomprehensible* universe>
syn impenetrable, incognizable, uncomprehensible, unfathomable, ungraspable, unintelligible, unknowable
rel inscrutable, mysterious, mystifying, unsearchable; cryptic, enigmatic, obscure, unclear; imperceptible, indistinguishable
con cognizable, fathomable, graspable, intelligible, knowable; clear, lucid, plain, simple, straightforward; rational, reasonable
ant comprehensible, understandable
2 *syn* see INCONCEIVABLE 1

ant comprehensible, graspable

inconceivable *adj* **1** impossible to comprehend in the absence of actual experience or knowledge <color is *inconceivable* to those born blind>
syn incomprehensible, unimaginable, unknowable, ununderstandable
idiom beyond one's grasp
con comprehensible, imaginable, knowable, understandable
ant conceivable
2 *syn* see INCREDIBLE 1
ant conceivable
3 *syn* see IMPLAUSIBLE
con believable, convincing, credible, plausible
ant conceivable

inconclusive *adj* leading to no conclusion or definite result <the report was *inconclusive*>
syn indecisive
rel open, uncertain, undecided, unsettled; incomplete, unfinished
con clarifying, illuminating; decisive
ant conclusive

incondite *adj syn* see RUDE 6

inconformable *adj syn* see IRRECONCIL-ABLE
ant conformable

incongruent *adj syn* see INCONSONANT 1
ant congruent, congruous

incongruous *adj syn* see INCONSONANT 1
rel alien, extraneous, foreign; bizarre, fantastic, grotesque
idiom out of place
con appropriate, fit, fitting, meet, seemly, suitable
ant congruent, congruous

inconnu *n syn* see STRANGER

inconquerable *adj* **1** *syn* see INVINCIBLE 1
2 *syn* see INSUPERABLE

inconscient *adj syn* see ABSTRACTED
ant conscient, conscious

inconscious *adj syn* see INSENSIBLE 2
ant conscious

inconsequent *adj syn* see PETTY 2

inconsequential *adj syn* see PETTY 2
ant consequential

inconsiderable *adj* **1** *syn* see LITTLE 3
ant considerable
2 *syn* see MEAGER
ant considerable
3 *syn* see PETTY 2
ant considerable

inconsiderate *adj* **1** *syn* see RASH 1
ant considerate
2 *syn* see SHORT 5
ant considerate

inconsistent *adj* **1** *syn* see INCONSTANT 1
ant consistent
2 *syn* see INCONSONANT 1
ant consistent
3 *syn* see IRRECONCILABLE
ant consistent

inconsolable *adj* incapable of being consoled <she was *inconsolable* over the loss of her child>
syn desolate, disconsolate, unconsolable
rel comfortless, dejected, forlorn, heartsick
ant consolable

inconsonant *adj* **1** not in agreement with one another or not agreeable one to the other

syn synonym(s)   *rel* related word(s)
ant antonym(s)   *con* contrasted word(s)
idiom idiomatic equivalent(s)
‖ use limited; if in doubt, see a dictionary

syn conflicting, disconsonant, discordant, discrepant, dissonant, incompatible, incongruent, incongruous, inconsistent, unmixable

rel ill-matched, ill-suited, mismated, uncongenial; inappropriate, unsuitable

con accordant, compatible, congenial, congruous, consistent

ant consonant

2 syn see INHARMONIOUS 2

ant consonant

inconspicuous *adj* not readily noticeable <occupied an *inconspicuous* position>

syn obscure, unconspicuous, unemphatic, unnoticeable

rel indistinct, insignificant, unnoticeable, unobtrusive, vague

con eye-catching, showy, striking; distinct, noticeable

ant conspicuous, prominent

inconstant *adj* **1** lacking firmness or steadiness (as in purpose or devotion) <depended too much on an *inconstant* friend>

syn capricious, changeable, fickle, inconsistent, lubricious, mercurial, temperamental, ticklish, uncertain, unstable, variable, volatile; *compare* CHANGEABLE 1, MUTABLE 2, UNCERTAIN 1

rel changeful, mutable, protean, unsettled, unsteady; elusive, erratic, vacillating, vagrant, wavering, wayward; irresolute, shifty, shilly-shally; undependable, unreliable; disloyal, faithless, false, perfidious, traitorous, treacherous, untrue; frivolous, light, light-minded

con dependable, reliable, trustworthy, trusty; faithful, loyal, resolute, staunch, steadfast, true

ant constant

2 syn see MUTABLE 2

ant constant

incontestable *adj syn* see POSITIVE 3

ant contestable

incontinent *adj syn* see LICENTIOUS 2

ant continent

incontinently *adv syn* see PELL-MELL

incontrovertible *adj syn* see POSITIVE 3

ant controvertible

inconvenience *n* the quality or state of being inconvenient <hated the *inconvenience* of not having a telephone>

syn bother, bothersomeness, ‖disconvenience, troublesomeness

rel aggravation, annoyance, exasperation, trial; fuss, pother, stew

ant convenience

inconvenience *vb* to subject to disturbance or discomfort <was not seriously *inconvenienced* by the bad weather>

syn discommode, ‖disconvenience, disoblige, incommode, put about, put out, trouble

rel discompose, disturb; interfere, intermeddle, meddle; aggravate, exasperate, try

idiom put to trouble

ant convenience

inconvenient *adj* not conducive to physical, mental, or social ease and comfort <he came at an *inconvenient* time>

syn awkward, discommoding, discommodious, embarrassing, incommodious

rel bothersome, pestiferous, troublesome; inexpedient; detrimental, disadvantageous, prejudicial

con appropriate, becoming, fitting, suitable; acceptable, bearable, tolerable; advantageous, desirable, helpful

ant convenient

inconversable *adj syn* see SILENT 3

ant conversable

inconversant *adj syn* see IGNORANT 2

ant conversant

incorporate *vb* **1** *syn* see ABSORB 1

2 syn see EMBODY 2

incorporeal *adj syn* see IMMATERIAL 1

ant corporeal

incorrect *adj syn* see FALSE 1

ant correct

incorrectly *adv syn* see AMISS 1

ant correctly

incorrectness *n syn* see IMPROPRIETY 1

ant correctitude, correctness

incorruptible *adj syn* see INDESTRUCTIBLE

ant corruptible

incorruption *n syn* see HONESTY

ant corruption

increase *vb* **1** to make greater or more numerous <*increase* crops by good cultural practices>

syn aggrandize, augment, beef (up), boost, build, compound, enlarge, expand, extend, heighten, magnify, manifold, multiply, plus, push

rel aggravate, enhance, intensify; amplify, dilate, distend, inflate, swell; elongate, lengthen, prolong, protract; reinforce, strengthen

con abate, abbreviate, condense, contract; depreciate, diminish, lessen, lower, reduce; curtail, shorten, shrink; minimize

ant decrease

2 to become greater or more numerous <his wealth *increased* over the years>

syn augment, build, burgeon, enlarge, expand, heighten, mount, multiply, rise, run up, snowball, upsurge, wax

rel dilate, distend, inflate, intensify, lengthen, strengthen, swell; pullulate, swarm, teem

con abate, condense, contract, diminish, lessen, lower, reduce, shorten, shrink; die off, die (out), end, terminate

ant decrease

3 syn see RAISE 9

increase *n* **1** *syn* see ADDITION

ant decrease

2 syn see RISE 3

increate *adj syn* see SELF-EXISTENT

ant created

incredible *adj* **1** too extraordinary or improbable to admit of belief <an *incredible* story of privations overcome>

syn incogitable, inconceivable, insupposable, unbelievable, unimaginable, unthinkable

rel absurd, outlandish, preposterous, ridiculous; impossible, untenable

idiom beyond belief, out of the question

con acceptable, believable, conceivable, likely, plausible, reasonable
ant credible
2 *syn* see IMPLAUSIBLE
ant credible

incredulity *n syn* see UNBELIEF
con gullibility, naiveté
ant credulity, credulousness

incredulous *adj* unwilling to admit or accept what is offered as true <his explanation met an *incredulous* response from his listeners>
syn aporetic, disbelieving, questioning, quizzical, show-me, skeptical, unbelieving
rel hesitant, suspicious, uncertain, wary; distrustful, distrusting, mistrustful; doubting, dubious, unconvinced, unsatisfied
con trustful, trusting; unsuspecting, unsuspicious, unwary; gullible, naive
ant credulous

increment *n syn* see ADDITION

incriminate *vb syn* see ACCUSE
rel implicate, involve
ant exonerate

incrustate *vb syn* see CAKE 1

inculcate *vb syn* see IMPLANT
rel educate, instruct, teach; communicate, impart

inculpable *adj* **1** *syn* see GOOD
ant culpable
2 *syn* see INNOCENT 2
ant culpable

inculpate *vb syn* see ACCUSE
ant exculpate

incult *adj syn* see COARSE 3

incur *vb* to bring (something usually unpleasant) upon oneself <he foolishly *incurred* debts beyond his ability to pay>
syn contract
rel acquire, get; bring on, induce
idiom bring down on (or upon)
con avoid, elude, escape, eschew, evade, shun; discharge, pay, settle

incurable *adj syn* see HOPELESS 2
ant curable

incurious *adj syn* see INDIFFERENT 2
rel absent, absentminded, abstracted, distraught, preoccupied
con nosy, prying, snoopy; impertinent, intrusive, meddlesome; observant, observing
ant curious, inquisitive

incursion *n syn* see INVASION

indebted *adj* owing gratitude or recognition (as for a favor or service rendered) <was *indebted* to the book for most of her information>
syn beholden, obligated, obliged
rel duty-bound, honor-bound

indebtedness *n* **1** a state of owing something <unable to escape from *indebtedness*>
syn arrearage, debt, liability, obligation; *compare* DEBT 3
rel delinquency, nonpayment; bankruptcy, failure, insolvency
con discharge, liquidation, satisfaction; exoneration, freeing, release

2 *syn* see DEBT 3

indecent *adj* **1** *syn* see INDECOROUS
ant decent
2 *syn* see OBSCENE 2
ant decent

indecipherable *adj syn* see ILLEGIBLE
ant decipherable

indecision *n syn* see HESITATION
ant decision, decisiveness

indecisive *adj* **1** *syn* see INCONCLUSIVE
ant decisive
2 *syn* see DOUBTFUL 1
con certain, incontrovertible, undebatable, unequivocal
ant decisive
3 *syn* see VACILLATING 2
rel undecided, unsettled
idiom of two minds
con decided, determined, firm, positive, resolved, settled, unfaltering, unhesitant, unhesitating, unwavering
ant decisive

indecisiveness *n syn* see HESITATION
ant indecision, indecisiveness

indecorous *adj* not conforming with accepted standards of propriety or good taste <they regarded argument in public as *indecorous*>
syn improper, indecent, indelicate, malodorous, ridiculous, rough, unbecoming, undecorous, ungodly, unseemly, untoward
rel inappropriate, incorrect, unbefitting, unfit, unfitting; immodest, inelegant, undignified; coarse, gross, loose, offensive, shameful, tasteless, vulgar; discourteous, ill-mannered, impolite, rude, uncivil; irregular, unlawful
idiom in bad form
con becoming, courteous, decent, nice, proper, seemly; conventional, formal
ant decorous

indecorousness *n syn* see IMPROPRIETY 1
ant decorousness

indecorum *n* **1** *syn* see FAUX PAS
2 *syn* see IMPROPRIETY 1
ant decorum

indeed *adv* **1** *syn* see WELL 7
2 *syn* see EVEN 3

indefatigable *adj* capable of prolonged and arduous effort <a teacher who has *indefatigable* patience with slow learners>
syn inexhaustible, tireless, unflagging, untiring, unweariable, unwearying, weariless
rel assiduous, diligent, painstaking, sedulous; determined, dogged, patient, persevering, persistent, pertinacious, relentless, steadfast, stubborn, tenacious, unfaltering, unflinching, unrelenting, unwavering; energetic, strenuous, studious
con dawdling, dilatory, laggard, lagging, procrastinating; fainéant, indolent, lackadaisical, lazy, slothful, sluggish
ant fatigable

indefectible *adj* **1** *syn* see PERFECT 2
2 *syn* see IDEAL 3

indefensible *adj syn* see INEXCUSABLE
ant defensible

indefinable *adj syn* see UNUTTERABLE
ant definable

---

syn synonym(s)   *rel* related word(s)
ant antonym(s)   *con* contrasted word(s)
idiom idiomatic equivalent(s)
‖ use limited; if in doubt, see a dictionary

indefinite *adj* 1 having no exact limits <a region with *indefinite* boundaries>
syn indeterminate, indistinct, inexact, undeterminable
rel unclear, undefined, unfixed, unspecific; broad, loose, wide; general, obscure, vague
con exact, measured; known
ant definite
2 *syn* see LIMITLESS
ant definite

indelible *adj* that cannot be removed or erased <made an *indelible* impression on his hearers>
syn ineffaceable, ineradicable, inerasable, inexpungible, inextirpable, uneradicable, unerasable
rel indestructible, undestroyable; enduring, permanent
con effaceable, eradicable, erasable, removable; ephemeral, evanescent, passing, temporary, transitory
ant delible

indelicate *adj syn* see INDECOROUS
rel callow, crude, rude, uncouth; lewd, wanton
con chaste, modest, pure
ant delicate

indemnification *n syn* see REPARATION
indemnify *vb syn* see COMPENSATE 3
indemnity *n syn* see REPARATION
indentation *n* 1 *syn* see NOTCH 1
2 *syn* see IMPRESSION 1
indenture *n syn* see NOTCH 1
indentured *adj syn* see BOUND 2
independent *adj* 1 *syn* see FREE 1
2 *syn* see SELF-SUFFICIENT
ant dependent
independently *adv syn* see APART 1
idiom on one's own
indescribable *adj syn* see UNUTTERABLE
ant describable
indestructible *adj* incapable of being destroyed <*indestructible* idealism>
syn imperishable, incorruptible, inexterminable, inextinguishable, inextirpable, irrefragable, irrefrangible, quenchless, undestroyable, unperishable
rel changeless, immutable, unalterable, unchangeable; deathless, immortal, perpetual, undying; durable, enduring, lasting, permanent; indelible, ineradicable; unextinguishable, unquenchable
con alterable, changeable, corruptible, impermanent, temporary, transient, unlasting; mortal, temporal; evanescent
ant destroyable, destructible, perishable
indeterminate *adj syn* see INDEFINITE 1
ant determinate
index *n syn* see INDICATION 3
Indian sign *n syn* see JINX
indicate *vb syn* see POINT 2
2 to give evidence of or serve as ground for a valid or reasonable inference <several polls *indicate* a landslide for the incumbent>
syn announce, argue, attest, bespeak, betoken, testify, witness
rel denote, import, mean, signify; demonstrate, prove; evidence, evince, manifest, show; display, exhibit, express, illustrate; connote, hint, imply, suggest

3 *syn* see SHOW 5
indication *n* 1 *syn* see HINT 1
2 *syn* see EXPRESSION 3
3 something that is an outward manifestation of something else <such *indications* of prosperity as second cars and color TVs>
syn evidence, index, indicia, mark, sign, significant, symptom, token; *compare* SYMBOL 1, TESTIMONY
rel expression, manifestation; hint, suggestion; proof; prefiguration; type
indicative *adj* serving to indicate <the roar of the crowd was *indicative* of its approval>
syn denotative, denotive, designative, exhibitive, indicatory, indicial, significative
rel characteristic, demonstrative, evidential, evincive, expressive, suggestive, symbolic, symptomatic, testatory
indicatory *adj syn* see INDICATIVE
indicia *n pl syn* see INDICATION 3
indicial *adj syn* see INDICATIVE
indict *vb syn* see ACCUSE
indifference *n syn* see APATHY 2
indifferent *adj* 1 *syn* see FAIR 4
2 marked by a lack of interest or concern <was *indifferent* to suffering and poverty>
syn aloof, by-the-way, casual, detached, disinterested, incurious, numb, pococurante, remote, unconcerned, uncurious, uninterested, withdrawn; *compare* UNSOCIABLE
rel apathetic, impassive, insensible; dispassionate; careless, heedless, negligent, regardless, uncaring, unmindful; inattentive, unobserving
con attentive, considerate, heedful, interested, mindful, regardful, sympathetic
ant concerned
3 *syn* see COLD 2
4 *syn* see MEDIUM
indigence *n syn* see POVERTY 1
ant affluence, opulence
indigency *n syn* see POVERTY 1
ant affluence, opulence
indigenous *adj* 1 *syn* see NATIVE 2
con alien, extraneous, foreign
ant exotic; naturalized
2 *syn* see INNATE 1
indigent *adj syn* see POOR 1
ant affluent, opulent
indignant *adj syn* see ANGRY
ant gratified
indignation *n syn* see ANGER
ant gratification
indignity *n syn* see AFFRONT
rel grievance, injury, injustice, wrong
indirect *adj* 1 deviating from a direct line or straightforward course <made *indirect* inquiries about the new neighbor>
syn circuitous, circular, collateral, oblique, roundabout
rel circumlocutory, crooked, devious; meandering, serpentine, sinuous, tortuous, twisting, winding; errant, vagrant, wandering
ant direct; forthright, straightforward
2 *syn* see UNDERHAND
ant straight
indirection *n syn* see DECEPTION 1
indiscernible *adj syn* see IMPERCEPTIBLE
ant discernible, distinguishable

indiscreet *adj syn* see UNWISE
  ant discreet

indiscriminate *adj* **1** including all or nearly all within the range of choice, operation, or effectiveness <her charity was *indiscriminate* but generous>
  syn indiscriminating, indiscriminative, sweeping, undiscriminated, undiscriminating, undistinguishing, wholesale
  rel assorted, heterogeneous, miscellaneous, promiscuous; shallow, superficial, uncritical; broad, extensive, wide
  con discretionary, discriminative; choosy, picky; critical, perfectionist
  ant selective; discriminate, discriminated
  2 *syn* see RANDOM
  3 *syn* see MISCELLANEOUS

indiscriminating *adj syn* see INDISCRIMINATE
  ant discriminating

indiscriminative *adj syn* see INDISCRIMINATE
  ant discriminative

indispensable *adj syn* see ESSENTIAL 4
  rel cardinal, fundamental
  ant dispensable

indisposed *adj* **1** *syn* see UNWELL
  2 *syn* see DISINCLINED
  rel antagonistic, antipathetic, hostile, inimical
  con amicable, neighborly; responsive, sympathetic
  ant disposed

indisposition *n* **1** *syn* see DISLIKE
  2 *syn* see SICKNESS 1

indisputable *adj* **1** *syn* see POSITIVE 3
  ant disputable
  2 *syn* see REAL 3

indistinct *adj* **1** *syn* see INDEFINITE 1
  ant distinct
  2 *syn* see FAINT 2
  ant distinct

indistinguishable *adj syn* see SAME 2
  ant distinguishable

indite *vb syn* see WRITE

individual *adj* **1** *syn* see PERSONAL 1
  ant common, popular
  2 *syn* see SPECIAL 1
  rel separate, single, sole
  con generic, universal
  ant general
  3 *syn* see CHARACTERISTIC
  ant common
  4 *syn* see SEVERAL 1

individual *n* **1** *syn* see ENTITY 1
  2 *syn* see THING 5
  3 *syn* see HUMAN

individualism *n* **1** *syn* see DISPOSITION 3
  2 *syn* see INDIVIDUALITY 3

individualist *adj syn* see EGOCENTRIC 1

individualistic *adj syn* see EGOCENTRIC 1

individuality *n* **1** *syn* see DISPOSITION 3
  2 *syn* see UNITY 1
  3 distinctive character <a person of marked *individuality*>

---

  syn distinctiveness, individualism, particularity, singularity
  rel character, personality
  4 individual identity <a teacher who respects children's *individualities*>
  syn identity, ipseity, personality, seity, selfdom, selfhood, selfness, singularity
  rel independence, separateness, uniqueness; difference, dissimilarity, unlikeness
  con likeness, resemblance, similarity

individualize *vb syn* see CHARACTERIZE 2

individually *adv syn* see APART 1

individuate *vb syn* see CHARACTERIZE 2

indocile *adj syn* see UNRULY 1
  ant docile

indolence *n syn* see SLOTH 1
  ant industry

indolent *adj syn* see LAZY
  con active, diligent, energetic, vigorous
  ant industrious

indomitable *adj* **1** *syn* see INVINCIBLE 1
  ant domitable
  2 *syn* see INSUPERABLE
  rel dogged, pertinacious, stubborn; resolute, staunch, steadfast
  ant domitable
  3 *syn* see UNRULY 1

indoors *adv* in or into a building <stayed *indoors* during the storm>
  syn inside, within, withindoors, withinside
  con outdoors, outside, without, withoutdoors
  ant outdoors

indubitable *adj* **1** *syn* see POSITIVE 3
  ant dubitable, questionable
  2 *syn* see AUTHENTIC 2
  ant doubtful, dubious
  3 *syn* see DOWNRIGHT 2

induce *vb* **1** to move another to do or agree to something <*induced* him to give up smoking for the sake of his health>
  syn argue (into), bring around, convince, draw, draw in, draw on, get, oversway, persuade, prevail (on or upon), procure, prompt, talk (into), win (over)
  rel influence, sway; abet, incite, lead; actuate, impel, move; activate, motivate
  con check, curb, hold back, restrain
  2 *syn* see GENERATE 3

inducible *adj syn* see INDUCTIVE

induct *vb syn* see INITIATE 3

induction *n syn* see INITIATION

inductive *adj* derived or derivable by reasoning from a part to a whole, from particulars to generals, or from the individual to the universal <used an *inductive* approach to the problem>
  syn a posteriori, inducible
  rel Baconian, epagogic
  2 *syn* see PRELIMINARY

indulge *vb* **1** to give free rein to (as curiosity or a desire) <*indulged* their taste for gourmet foods>
  syn cater (to), gratify, humor
  rel favor, oblige, satisfy; delight, please, regale
  idiom give rein to
  con bridle, check, constrain, curb, restrain
  2 *syn* see BABY
  3 *syn* see WALLOW 3

---

syn synonym(s)   *rel* related word(s)
ant antonym(s)   *con* contrasted word(s)
idiom idiomatic equivalent(s)
‖ use limited; if in doubt, see a dictionary

indulgence n 1 syn see FORBEARANCE 2
  rel benignancy, benignity, benignness, kindliness, kindness; gentleness, mildness
  con rigor, severity, sternness; rigidity, rigorousness; harshness
  ant strictness
  2 syn see FAVOR 4
indulgent adj syn see FORBEARING
  rel cosseting, pampering, permissive; condoning, excusing, forgiving, pardoning; benign, benignant, kind, kindly
  con severe, stern; harsh, rigorous, stringent
  ant strict
indurate vb syn see HARDEN 1
industrious adj syn see ASSIDUOUS
  rel active, busy, live, dynamic; persevering, persistent
  con idle, inactive; lethargic, sluggish
  ant indolent, slothful; unindustrious
industry n syn see BUSINESS 4
indwell vb syn see BELONG 3
indweller n syn see INHABITANT
indwelling adj syn see INHERENT
inebriant n syn see LIQUOR 2
inebriate n syn see DRUNKARD
inebriated adj syn see INTOXICATED 1
inebrious adj syn see INTOXICATED 1
inedible adj not fit for food <an *inedible* plant>
  syn inesculent, uneatable
  rel indigestible, unwholesome; insipid, unappetizing; baneful, noxious, poisonous
  con eatable, esculent; digestible, wholesome; appetizing, savory, tasty; harmless, innocuous, innoxious, nonpoisonous
  ant edible
ineffable adj syn see UNUTTERABLE
  rel celestial, empyreal, empyrean, heavenly; ethereal; divine, holy, sacred, spiritual; abstract, ideal, transcendent, transcendental
  con expressible; utterable
ineffaceable adj syn see INDELIBLE
ineffective adj 1 syn see FUTILE
  ant effective
  2 syn see WEAK 4
  3 not producing or not capable of producing a required result <*ineffective* remedies>
  syn inefficacious, inefficient
  rel inadequate, incompetent, inferior; useless, worthless
  con active, effectual, efficacious; esteemed, valuable
  ant effective
ineffectiveness n syn see INABILITY
  ant effectiveness
ineffectual adj 1 syn see FUTILE
  ant effectual
  2 syn see INEFFECTIVE 3
  ant effectual
  3 syn see WEAK 4
  4 syn see LITTLE 2
ineffectualness n syn see INABILITY
  ant effectualness
inefficacious adj syn see INEFFECTIVE 3
  ant efficacious
inefficacy n syn see INABILITY
  ant efficacy
inefficient adj 1 syn see INEFFECTIVE 3
  ant efficient
  2 incapable of the proper performance of duties <*inefficient* workmen>

  syn incapable, incompetent, inept, inexpert, unexpert, unskilled, unskillful, unworkmanlike
  rel careless, slipshod, slovenly; unfitted, unprepared, unqualified, untrained; unskilled, unskillful
  con able, adept, capable, competent, expert, proficient, qualified, skilled, skillful, workmanlike
  ant efficient
inelaborate adj syn see PLAIN 1
  ant elaborate
inelastic adj syn see STIFF 1
  ant elastic
inelegance n syn see IMPROPRIETY 1
  ant elegance
inelegant adj syn see COARSE 3
ineligible adj syn see UNFIT 2
  ant eligible
ineluctable adj syn see INEVITABLE
  con doubtful, dubious, questionable; likely, possible, probable
ineludible adj syn see INEVITABLE
inenarrable adj syn see UNUTTERABLE
inept adj 1 syn see IMPROPER 1
  ant apt
  2 syn see INFELICITOUS
  ant apropos, apt
  3 syn see AWKWARD 2
  ant apt; adept
  4 syn see UNSKILLFUL 1
  ant able
  5 syn see INEFFICIENT 2
  ant competent, efficient
inequable adj syn see INEQUITABLE
  ant equable
inequality n 1 the quality of being uneven <hampered by the *inequality* of the ground>
  syn asperity, irregularity, roughness, unevenness
  rel cragginess, jaggedness, ruggedness, rugosity
  con equality, evenness, levelness, smoothness
  2 syn see DISPARITY
  ant equality
inequitable adj not fair or just <an *inequitable* tax burden>
  syn inequable, unequitable, unfair, unjust, unrighteous
  rel undeserved, undue, unmerited; bad, wrong, wrongful; arbitrary, high-handed, oppressive
  con fair, just
  ant equitable
inequitableness n syn see INJUSTICE 1
  ant equitableness
inequity n syn see INJUSTICE 1
  ant equity
ineradicable adj syn see INDELIBLE
  ant eradicable
inerasable adj syn see INDELIBLE
  ant erasable
inerrable adj syn see INFALLIBLE 1
  ant errable
inerrant adj syn see INFALLIBLE 1
  rel accurate, correct, exact, precise; dependable, reliable, trustworthy
  ant errant
inert adj syn see INACTIVE

rel impotent, powerless; apathetic, impassive, phlegmatic, stolid; dead, inanimate, lifeless
con animated, awake; alert, vigilant, watchful; live, operative
ant animated; dynamic

inerudite *adj syn* see UNSCHOLARLY
ant erudite, learned

inescapable *adj syn* see INEVITABLE
ant escapable

inescapably *adv syn* see WILLY-NILLY

inesculent *adj syn* see INEDIBLE
ant esculent

in essence *adv* 1 *syn* see ESSENTIALLY 1
2 *syn* see VIRTUALLY

inessential *adj syn* see UNNECESSARY
ant crucial, essential

inestimable *adj* 1 *syn* see INCALCULABLE 1
2 *syn* see PRECIOUS 1

inevasible *adj syn* see INEVITABLE

inevitable *adj* incapable of being avoided or escaped <the effect of the scandal on the election was *inevitable*>
syn certain, ineluctable, ineludible, inescapable, inevasible, necessary, returnless, unavoidable, unescapable, unevadable
rel ineliminable, sure, unpreventable; decided, settled; destined, foreordained; inexorable, inflexible
idiom as sure to follow as night follows day, in the cards
con eludible, escapable, evadable
ant avoidable, evitable

inevitably *adv syn* see WILLY-NILLY

inexact *adj syn* see INDEFINITE 1
ant exact

inexcusable *adj* being without excuse or justification <an *inexcusable* blunder>
syn indefensible, inexpiable, unforgivable, unjustifiable, unpardonable, untenable
rel blamable, blameworthy, censurable, criticizable; impermissible, unallowable, unpermissible; intolerable, reprehensible
con allowable, blameless, defensible, forgivable, justifiable, pardonable, venial
ant excusable

inexhaustible *adj syn* see INDEFATIGABLE

inexorable *adj syn* see INFLEXIBLE 2
rel resolute; immobile, immovable
con compassionate, responsive, sympathetic, tender; clement, forbearing, indulgent, lenient

inexpedient *adj syn* see INADVISABLE
ant expedient

inexpensive *adj syn* see CHEAP 1
ant expensive

inexperience *n* lack or serious deficiency of practical wisdom <his failure was due to his *inexperience*>
syn callowness, freshness, greenness, rawness
rel ignorance, naiveté; amateurishness; unfamiliarity; unsophistication, verdancy
con grasp, understanding; polish, sophistication; skill, training

ant experience

inexperienced *adj* lacking knowledge, skill, or practice based on direct observation and participation <hired *inexperienced* help>
syn callow, fresh, green, inexpert, raw, rude, unconversant, unexperienced, unfleshed, unpracticed, unseasoned, untried, unversed, young
rel ignorant, immature, inept, naive; prentice, unacquainted, unfamiliar, unskilled, untrained
con expert, old, practiced, seasoned, skilled, versed, veteran
ant experienced

inexpert *adj* 1 *syn* see INEXPERIENCED
ant expert
2 *syn* see UNSKILLFUL 1
ant expert
3 *syn* see INEFFICIENT 2
ant expert
4 *syn* see CRUDE 5

inexpiable *adj syn* see INEXCUSABLE
ant expiable

inexplainable *adj syn* see INEXPLICABLE
ant explainable, explicable

inexplicable *adj* not capable of being explained or accounted for <an *inexplicable* discrepancy in the accounts>
syn inexplainable, unaccountable, unexplainable; *compare* MYSTERIOUS
rel indecipherable, indescribable, inscrutable, undefinable, unfathomable, unsolvable; mysterious, odd, peculiar, strange
con clear, obvious, plain; comprehensible, graspable, intelligible
ant explainable, explicable

inexpressible *adj syn* see UNUTTERABLE
ant expressible

inexpressive *adj syn* see EXPRESSIONLESS
ant expressive

inexpugnable *adj syn* see INVINCIBLE 1
rel irresistible, unopposable
con assailable, attackable
ant expugnable

inexpungible *adj syn* see INDELIBLE

inexterminable *adj syn* see INDESTRUCTIBLE

inextinguishable *adj syn* see INDESTRUCTIBLE
ant extinguishable

inextirpable *adj* 1 *syn* see INDESTRUCTIBLE
2 *syn* see INDELIBLE

inextricable *adj syn* see INSOLUBLE
ant extricable

infallible *adj* 1 incapable of being in error <an *infallible* ear for pitch in music>
syn inerrable, inerrant, sure, unerring
rel faultless, flawless, impeccable, undeceivable; correct, exact, perfect
con deceivable, faulty, unsure; doubtful, dubious, questionable
ant fallible
2 not liable to mislead, deceive, or disappoint <an *infallible* remedy>
syn certain, sure, surefire, unfailing
rel effective, efficacious, efficient; handy, helpful, useful; acceptable, agreeable, satisfying; satisfactory

---

syn synonym(s)   **rel** related word(s)
ant antonym(s)   **con** contrasted word(s)
idiom idiomatic equivalent(s)
‖ use limited; if in doubt, see a dictionary

con doubtful, questionable, uncertain, unsure; useless, worthless; unacceptable, unsatisfying; unsatisfactory
ant fallible

infamous *adj* **1** having an extremely and deservedly bad reputation <one of the most *infamous* of the dictator's henchmen>
syn ill-famed, notorious, opprobrious
rel abominable, atrocious, evil, hateful, heinous, iniquitous, odious, scandalous, vile, villainous; contemptible, despicable, scurvy, sorry
con distinguished, eminent, esteemed, honored, illustrious, notable, prestigious, reputable
2 *syn* see VICIOUS 2
rel disgraceful, disreputable, ignominious, shameful
con glorious, splendid, sublime
ant illustrious

infamy *n* *syn* see DISGRACE
rel notoriety, notoriousness

infancy *n* **1** early childhood <the helplessness of *infancy*>
syn babyhood, infanthood
rel childhood, immaturity, juvenility, nonage
con adulthood, maturity, old age, senescence
2 the state or period of being under the age established by law for the attainment of full civil rights <his heirs were still in *infancy*>
syn minority, nonage
rel immaturity, juniority, juvenility
con adulthood, adultness, maturity, seniority
ant majority

infant *n* *syn* see BABY 1

infant *adj* *syn* see YOUNG 1

infanthood *n* *syn* see INFANCY 1

infantile *adj* *syn* see CHILDISH
ant adult

infantine *adj* *syn* see CHILDISH
ant adult

infatuate *adj* *syn* see INFATUATED

infatuated *adj* possessed with or marked by a strong attachment or foolish or unreasoning love or desire <*infatuated* with a woman he can't have>
syn besotted, dotty, enamored, infatuate
rel bewitched, captivated, enraptured, obsessed; foolish, silly
con detached, dispassionate, objective, undazzled, unprepossessed

infatuation *n* a strong and unreasoning but transitory attachment <went through a series of *infatuations* before she settled down>
syn béguin, crush, ‖pash, passion
rel ardor, craze, devotion, fascination, obsession, rage

in favor of *prep* *syn* see FOR 1

infeasible *adj* *syn* see IMPOSSIBLE 1
ant feasible

infectious *adj* **1** capable of causing infection <viruses and other *infectious* agents>
syn infective
rel mephitic, miasmic, noxious, pestilent, pestilential, poisonous, toxic, virulent
con healthful, hygienic, salutary, wholesome

2 transmissible by infection <*infectious* diseases>
syn catching, communicable, contagious
3 easily communicated or diffused <her enthusiasm was *infectious*>
syn catching, contagious, taking
rel irresistible, sympathetic

infective *adj* *syn* see INFECTIOUS 1

infecund *adj* *syn* see STERILE 1
ant fecund

infelicitous *adj* marked by a lack of appropriateness and grace of expression <made a very *infelicitous* remark>
syn awkward, graceless, ill-chosen, inept, unfortunate, unhappy
rel inappropriate, inapropos, inapt, malapropos, unapt; deplorable, gauche, regrettable
con fortunate, graceful, happy
ant felicitous

infer *vb* to arrive at by reasoning from evidence or from premises <we *inferred* from his questions that he was a stranger in the vicinity>
syn collect, conclude, deduce, deduct, derive, ‖dope out, draw, gather, judge, make, make out; *compare* CONJECTURE
rel induce; conjecture, glean, guess, reckon, speculate, surmise, think; ascertain, construe, interpret, reason, understand
idiom come to (or draw or reach) a conclusion; read between the lines

inference *n* **1** the deriving of a conclusion by reasoning <the answer was obtainable by *inference*>
syn deduction, illation, judgment, ratiocination
rel conjecture, guessing, reckoning, supposition, surmise
2 a determination arrived at by reasoning <a wrong *inference* based on incomplete evidence>
syn conclusion, deduction, illation, judgment, ratiocination, sequitur
rel assumption, conjecture, guess, presumption, reckoning, supposition, surmise

inferior *adj* **1** being or regarded as being below the level of another thing <the *inferior* latitudes of the northern hemisphere>
syn lesser, low, lower, nether, subjacent, under
rel junior, minor, secondary, subaltern, subordinate
con greater, higher, over, overlying
ant superior
2 of little or less importance, value, or merit <sold *inferior* goods at high prices>
syn common, déclassé, hack, low-grade, mean, poor, second-class, second-drawer, second-rate; *compare* CHEAP 2
rel average, fair, indifferent, mediocre, middling, ordinary; bad, base, paltry, punk, shoddy, sleazy, sorry, tawdry, tin-pot, wretched; good-for-nothing, lousy, ‖no-account, no-good, unworthy, valueless, worthless
con choice, excellent, first-class, first-rate, high-grade, prime
ant superior

inferior *n* one lower than another (as in station or worth) <a man inclined to be disdainful of his social *inferiors*>
syn poor relation, scrub, secondary, subaltern, subordinate, underling, understrapper
rel attendant, auxiliary, deputy; retainer, satrap, subject, vassal; hanger-on, heeler, henchman, hireling, minion, satellite, sycophant; adherent, disciple, follower
con chief, head, leader, master, principal
ant superior

infernal *adj* **1** of or relating to a nether world of the dead <the *infernal* regions>
syn chthonian, chthonic, Hadean, plutonian, plutonic, sulphurous, Tartarean
con celestial, elysian, Hesperidean, paradisaic, paradisal, paradisiacal
ant supernal
2 resembling or appropriate to hell or its inhabitants <an *infernal* glow in the sky>
syn avernal, cimmerian, hellish, pandemoniac, plutonian, plutonic, stygian
rel demoniac, devilish, diabolic, fiendish; sulphurous
ant celestial, heavenly
3 *syn* see DAMNED 2
4 *syn* see UTTER

inferno *n* **1** *syn* see HELL
2 *syn* see FIRE 1

inferred *adj syn* see TACIT 1

infertile *adj* **1** *syn* see STERILE 1
rel depleted, drained, exhausted, impoverished
con breeding, generating, propagating, reproducing
ant fertile
2 *syn* see BARREN 2
ant fertile

infest *vb* **1** to spread or swarm over in a troublesome manner <lawns *infested* with weeds>
syn beset, overrun, overspread, overswarm
rel abound, crawl, swarm, teem; annoy, harass, harry, pester, plague, worry
2 to live in or on as a parasite <a dog *infested* by fleas>
syn parasite, parasitize

infidel *adj syn* see HEATHEN

infidelic *adj syn* see HEATHEN

infidelity *n* betrayal of a moral obligation <a leader guilty of *infidelity* to the responsibilities he had accepted>
syn disloyalty, faithlessness, falseness, falsity, perfidiousness, perfidy, unfaithfulness; *compare* TREACHERY
rel fickleness, inconstancy; treacherousness, treachery, treason
idiom bad faith
con devotion, faithfulness, fealty; constancy, loyalty, steadfastness
ant fidelity

infiltrate *vb syn* see INSINUATE 3

infinite *adj* **1** being without known limits <the idea of an *infinite* universe>
syn eternal, illimitable, perdurable, sempiternal, supertemporal

rel everlasting, perpetual
con bounded, circumscribed, limited, restricted
ant finite
2 *syn* see LIMITLESS
ant finite

infinity *n syn* see ETERNITY 1

infirm *adj syn* see WEAK 1
ant hale

infirmity *n* **1** the quality or state of being enfeebled and weakened in health <suffering from old age and attendant physical *infirmity*>
syn debility, decrepitude, disease, feebleness, infirmness, malaise, sickliness, unhealthiness; *compare* DISEASE 1, SICKNESS 1
rel debilitation, decay, enfeeblement, failing, frailty, weakening, weakness; diseasedness, unwellness; illness, indisposition, sickness, unhealth
ant haleness
2 *syn* see DISEASE 1
3 *syn* see SICKNESS 1

infirmness *n syn* see INFIRMITY 1

infix *vb* **1** *syn* see ENTRENCH 1
2 *syn* see IMPLANT

inflame *vb* **1** *syn* see LIGHT 1
ant extinguish
2 *syn* see IRRITATE

inflammable *adj syn* see COMBUSTIBLE 1
ant nonflammable, noninflammable

inflammatory *adj* exciting or tending to excite anger, animosity, or disorder <*inflammatory* speeches designed to spark rebellion>
syn incendiary
rel exciting, incitive, instigative, provocative; revolutionary, seditionary, seditious
con calming, moderating, soothing, temperate

inflate *vb syn* see EXPAND 3
ant deflate

inflated *adj* swollen with or as if with something insubstantial <had an *inflated* idea of his own importance>
syn dropsical, dropsied, flatulent, overblown, tumescent, tumid, turgid, windy
rel aureate, bombastic, flowery, grandiloquent, magniloquent, rhetorical; ostentatious, pretentious, showy; fustian, ranting, rhapsodical; diffuse, prolix, verbose, wordy
con compendious, concise, laconic, pithy, succinct, summary, terse

inflatus *n syn* see INSPIRATION

inflection *n* a particular manner of employing the sounds of the voice in speech <questions end on a rising *inflection*>
syn accent, intonation, tone
rel articulation, enunciation, pronunciation; timbre, tonality
idiom tone of voice

inflexible *adj* **1** *syn* see STIFF 1
rel immobile, immovable
con elastic, resilient, springy, supple; ductile, malleable, pliable, pliant; fluid, liquid
ant flexible
2 rigidly firm in will or purpose <a person of *inflexible* resolution>
syn adamant, adamantine, brassbound, dogged, inexorable, iron, obdurate, relent-

---

syn synonym(s) *rel* related word(s)
ant antonym(s) *con* contrasted word(s)
idiom idiomatic equivalent(s)
‖ use limited; if in doubt, see a dictionary

less, rigid, rockbound, rock-ribbed, single-minded, steadfast, stubborn, unbendable, unbending, uncompliant, uncompromising, unswayable, unyielding; *compare* STIFF 1
rel intractable, obstinate; indomitable, invincible, unconquerable; grim, hard, implacable, unrelenting; dyed-in-the-wool, fixed, set, ‖sot
con agreeable, amenable, compliant, docile, pliant, responsive, swayable, yielding; mild, open
ant flexible
3 incapable of changing or being changed <*inflexible* rules>
syn constant, determinate, fixed, immovable, immutable, inalterable, invariable, ironclad, unalterable, unchangeable, unmodifiable, unmovable
rel strict; rigorous; established, set, settled; changeless, unchanging
con adaptable, adjustable, alterable, changeable, mutable, variable
ant flexible
4 *syn* see TOUGH 3
inflict *vb* **1** *syn* see GIVE 10
2 to cause one to endure (something damaging or painful) <*inflict* retribution>
syn force (on *or* upon), impose, visit, wreak, wreck; *compare* IMPOSE 4
rel expose, subject
idiom lay open to, put on the spot
con guard, protect, shelter, shield
inflow *n* *syn* see INFLUX
ant outflow, outflux
influence *n* **1** power exerted over the minds or behavior of others <a person of great *influence* in national politics>
syn authority, credit, prestige, weight; *compare* PULL 2
rel command, domination, dominion, mastery; ascendancy, dominance, eminence, predominance, consequence, importance, moment; ‖drag, in, pull
2 *syn* see PULL 2
3 *syn* see EFFECT 3
influence *vb* **1** *syn* see AFFECT
2 *syn* see PREJUDICE 2
influenceable *adj* *syn* see RECEPTIVE 1
influx *n* a flowing in <anticipated an *influx* of immigrants>
syn inflow, influxion, inpour, inpouring, inrush
rel accession, augmentation, increase; illapse
con outpour, outpouring, outrush; efflux, effluxion, exodus
ant outflow, outflux
influxion *n* *syn* see INFLUX
ant effluxion
inform *vb* **1** *syn* see FIRE 2
rel imbue, infuse, leaven, permeate; enlighten, illuminate; endow, endue
2 to make aware or cognizant of something <was kept *informed* of developments>
syn acquaint, advise, apprise, clue (*or* clew), fill in, notify, post, tell, warn, wise (up)
rel educate, enlighten, instruct, teach; familiarize; caution, forewarn
idiom keep posted
3 to give information about someone especially as an informer <his suspicions

aroused, he *informed* on his neighbor to the police>
syn ‖nark, peach, ‖pimp, rat, ‖sing, snitch, squeak, squeal, ‖stool; *compare* TALK 6
rel blab, tattle, tell; betray, give away, turn in
informal *adj* **1** conducted or carried out without rigidly prescribed procedure <carried on an *informal* investigation>
syn irregular, unceremonious, unofficial
rel casual, spontaneous; unauthorized; unconventional; private, special
con authorized, ceremonious, conventional, official, regular
ant formal
2 *syn* see EASYGOING 3
rel familiar, natural, simple
con affected, mannered, prim, rigid, stiff, stilted
ant formal
information *n* **1** *syn* see KNOWLEDGE 2
2 *syn* see NEWS
informational *adj* *syn* see INFORMATIVE
informative *adj* imparting information <gave an *informative* talk>
syn educational, educative, informational, informatory, instructional, instructive
rel edifying, elucidative, enlightening, explanatory, illuminating
ant uninformative
informatory *adj* *syn* see INFORMATIVE
informed *adj* *syn* see FAMILIAR 3
ant uninformed
informer *n* one who informs against another <his arrest was brought about by an *informer*>
syn betrayer, ‖canary, ‖fink, ‖nark, ‖pimp, snitch, squawker, ‖squeaker, squealer, stool, stoolie, stool pigeon, talebearer, tattler, tattletale, tipster; *compare* BUSYBODY, DETECTIVE, GOSSIP 1, SPY
infra *adv* **1** *syn* see BELOW 2
ant above, supra
2 *syn* see AFTER
infract *vb* *syn* see VIOLATE 1
infraction *n* *syn* see BREACH 1
rel crime, offense, sin; error, faux pas, lapse, slip
infrastructure *n* **1** *syn* see BASE 1
ant superstructure
2 *syn* see BASIS 1
infrequent *adj* appearing, happening, or met with so seldom as to attract attention <held only *infrequent* press conferences>
syn few, occasional, rare, scarce, seldom, semioccasional, sporadic, uncommon, unfrequent
rel isolated, scattered; meager, scant, scanty, sparse; exceptional, limited, unusual, odd, spasmodic, stray
idiom few and far between
con abundant, common, numerous, regular; ordinary, routine
ant frequent
infrequently *adv* **1** *syn* see SELDOM
ant frequently
2 *syn* see OCCASIONALLY
ant frequently
infringe *vb* **1** *syn* see TRESPASS 2
2 *syn* see VIOLATE 1

3 *syn* see IMPOSE 5

infringement *n syn* see BREACH 1

infuriate *vb syn* see ANGER 1

infuse *vb* **1** to introduce one thing into another so as to change or affect it <a teacher who *infused* her pupils with the desire to learn>
  syn imbue, ingrain, inoculate, invest, leaven, steep, suffuse
  rel animate, fire, inform, inspire; implant, inculcate, instill; impregnate, permeate, pervade, saturate; indoctrinate
  2 *syn* see INTERFUSE 2

ingather *vb syn* see REAP

ingathering *n syn* see HARVEST 1

ingeminate *vb syn* see REPEAT

ingenerate *adj syn* see INHERENT

ingenious *adj* **1** *syn* see INVENTIVE
  2 *syn* see CLEVER 4

ingenuous *adj syn* see NATURAL 5
  con covert, furtive, stealthy, surreptitious, underhand; artful, crafty, foxy, guileful, insidious, sly, tricky, wily
  ant disingenuous

ingest *vb syn* see EAT 1

inglorious *adj syn* see DISREPUTABLE 1
  ant glorious

ingoing *adj syn* see INCISIVE

ingot *n syn* see BAR 1

ingrain *vb* **1** *syn* see ENTRENCH 1
  rel engrave, etch, grave, incise
  2 *syn* see INFUSE 1

ingrained *adj syn* see INHERENT
  rel chronic, confirmed, deep-rooted, inveterate
  con exterior, external, outer, outside, outward

ingratiating *adj* intended or designed to gain favor <an *ingratiating* smile>
  syn deferential, disarming, ingratiatory, insinuating, insinuative, saccharine, silken, silky
  rel adulatory; fawning, sycophantic

ingratiatory *adj syn* see INGRATIATING

ingredient *n syn* see ELEMENT 2

ingress *n* **1** *syn* see ENTRANCE 1
  ant egress
  2 *syn* see DOOR 2
  ant egress

ingress *vb syn* see ENTER 1
  ant egress

ingression *n syn* see ENTRANCE 1
  ant egression

in-group *n syn* see CLIQUE
  ant outgroup

ingurgitate *vb syn* see GULP

inhabit *vb* to dwell in as a place of settled residence <islands *inhabited* by Polynesians>
  syn occupy, people, populate, tenant
  rel settle; abide, dwell, live

inhabitable *adj syn* see LIVABLE 1
  ant uninhabitable

inhabitancy *n syn* see HABITATION 1

inhabitant *n* one that occupies a particular place regularly <*inhabitants* of large cities>

  syn denizen, dweller, habitant, indweller, liver, occupant, resident, ‖residenter, resider
  rel aborigine, autochthon, indigene, native

inhabitation *n syn* see HABITATION 1

inhale *vb* to draw (as air) into the lungs <*inhaling* smoke>
  syn breathe (in), inspire
  ant exhale, expire

inharmonic *adj syn* see DISSONANT 1
  ant harmonic

inharmonious *adj* **1** *syn* see DISSONANT 1
  ant harmonious
  2 lacking harmony especially in sentiment <the committee meeting was singularly *inharmonious*>
  syn discordant, inconsonant, uncongenial, unharmonious
  rel antagonistic, cat-and-dog, conflicting, conflictive, differing, disagreeing, incompatible, incongruous, quarrelsome
  con concordant, congenial, consonant; amiable, compatible; collaborative
  ant harmonious

inharmony *n syn* see DISCORD
  ant harmony

inhaust *vb syn* see ABSORB 1

inhere *vb* **1** *syn* see CONSIST 1
  2 *syn* see BELONG 3

inherent *adj* being a part, element, or quality of a thing's inmost being <*inherent* rights of every citizen>
  syn born, built-in, congenital, connate, constitutional, deep-seated, elemental, essential, inborn, inbred, indwelling, ingenerate, ingrained, innate, intimate, intrinsic
  rel inner, internal, inward, resident; basic, elementary, immanent, integral; characteristic, distinctive, individual, peculiar; natural, normal, regular, typical; bred-in-the-bone
  con shallow, superficial; accidental, fortuitous, incidental; alien, extraneous, extrinsic, foreign
  ant adventitious

inheritance *n* **1** *syn* see HERITAGE 1
  2 *syn* see LEGACY 1

inherited *adj syn* see INNATE 1

inheritor *n syn* see HEIR

inhibit *vb* **1** *syn* see FORBID
  rel avert, ward
  ant allow
  2 *syn* see RESTRAIN 1
  ant activate; animate

inhibited *adj syn* see FRIGID 3
  ant uninhibited

inhuman *adj syn* see FIERCE 1
  rel malicious, malign, malignant; implacable, relentless, unrelenting; devilish, diabolical, fiendish
  con altruistic, benevolent, charitable, eleemosynary, humanitarian, philanthropic; compassionate, tender
  ant humane

inhumane *adj syn* see FIERCE 1
  ant humane

inhumation *n syn* see BURIAL 2
  ant exhumation

inhume *vb syn* see BURY 1
  ant disinhume, exhume

inimicable *adj syn* see HOSTILE 1

---

syn synonym(s)   *rel* related word(s)
ant antonym(s)   *con* contrasted word(s)
idiom idiomatic equivalent(s)
‖ use limited; if in doubt, see a dictionary

inimical *adj syn* see HOSTILE 1

iniquitous *adj syn* see WRONG 1

iniquity *n syn* see EVIL 3

initial *adj* **1** marking a commencement or constituting a start <*initial* symptoms of the disease>
syn beginning, inceptive, incipient, initiative, initiatory, introductory, nascent
rel basic, elementary, first, fundamental; embryonic, germinal; early, infant; antecedent; earliest, introductory, primary
con closing; concluding, conclusive; terminal, terminative; last, ultimate
ant final
2 *syn* see FIRST 2
3 *syn* see FIRST 1
ant final

initially *adv* **1** in the beginning <*initially* we were confused but soon enough we fully understood>
syn originally, primarily, primitively
rel first, firstly, incipiently
idiom at first, at the first go-off, from the word go
con lastly, ultimately
ant finally
2 *syn* see FIRSTLY

initiate *vb* **1** *syn* see BEGIN 1
ant terminate
2 *syn* see INTRODUCE 3
3 to put through the formalities for becoming a member or official <the club *initiated* four new members>
syn inaugurate, induct, install, instate, invest
rel institute; admit, enter, introduce, take in

initiation *n* the process or an instance of being formally introduced into an office or made a member of an organization <a fraternity *initiation*>
syn inaugural, inauguration, induction, installation, investiture
rel baptism; institution, introduction

initiative *adj syn* see INITIAL 1

initiative *n syn* see ENTERPRISE 4

initiatory *adj syn* see INITIAL 1

injudicious *adj syn* see UNWISE
ant judicious

injunction *n syn* see COMMAND 1

injure *vb* **1** to deplete the soundness, strength, effectiveness, or perfection of something <*injured* her prestige by making rash statements>
syn blemish, damage, harm, hurt, impair, mar, prejudice, spoil, tarnish, vitiate
rel disserve; disadvantage; endamage, weaken; blight, queer; foul up, louse up; contort, deface, deform, disfigure, distort; bespatter, foul, smirch; disable, incapacitate
con assist, help, succor; better, enhance, improve; benefit; strengthen
ant aid
2 *syn* see DISTRESS 2
idiom do dirt to
3 to inflict bodily hurt on <was *injured* in an auto accident>
syn hurt, wound
rel damage, harm; afflict, torment, torture; batter, cripple, maim, mangle, mutilate
idiom draw blood

injurious *adj syn* see HARMFUL

injury *n* **1** an act or the result of inflicting something that causes loss or pain <we cannot forgive his *injury* of the painting> <his falsehood caused grave *injury* to his brother's reputation>
syn damage, harm, hurt, mischief, outrage, ruin
rel agony, discomfiture, distress, misery, suffering; pain, pang; detriment, disservice, loss; bad, evil, ill
2 *syn* see INJUSTICE 2

injustice *n* **1** absence of justice <preached against *injustice*>
syn inequitableness, inequity, unfairness, unjustness, wrong
rel crime, malfeasance, malpractice, villainy, wrongdoing; favoritism, inequality, partiality, partisanship
con equity, fairness, right
ant justice, justness
2 an act or instance of unjustness <pointed out various *injustices* in the law> <you do him an *injustice* when you call him lazy>
syn grievance, injury, wrong
rel damage, harm, hurt, mischief, outrage, ruin; breach, infraction, infringement, tort, transgression, trespass, violation

ink *vb syn* see SIGN 1

inkling *n syn* see HINT 1

inky *adj syn* see BLACK 1

‖**inland** *adj syn* see DOMESTIC 1
ant foreign

inlet *n* a recess in the shores of a body of water <*inlets* of lakes and rivers>
syn arm, bay, bayou, bight, cove, ‖creek, firth, gulf, harbor, ‖loch, ‖lough, slough

inn *n syn* see HOTEL

innards *n pl syn* see ENTRAILS

innate *adj* **1** existing in or belonging to an individual inherently <*innate* vigor>
syn congenital, connate, connatural, inborn, indigenous, inherited, native, natural, unacquired
rel constitutional, deep-seated, essential, ingrained, inherent, intrinsic; hereditary; normal, regular, standard, typical
con accidental, adventitious, fortuitous, incidental; affected, assumed, feigned, simulated; cultivated, fostered, nurtured
ant acquired
2 *syn* see INHERENT

inner *adj* **1** situated further in <the *inner* layers were less worn>
syn ‖innermore, inside, interior, internal, intestine, inward
rel central, focal, middle, nuclear; close, familiar, intimate; constitutional, essential, inherent, intrinsic
con exterior, external, outside, outward
ant outer
2 arising from one's inmost self <*inner* thoughts and feelings>
syn gut, interior, internal, intimate, visceral, viscerous
rel individual, personal, private; concealed, hidden, secret
con exterior, outer; open, public

‖**innermore** *adj syn* see INNER 1

innervate *vb syn* see PROVOKE 4

innerve *vb syn* see PROVOKE 4
innholder *n syn* see SALOONKEEPER
innkeeper *n syn* see SALOONKEEPER
innocence *n syn* see IGNORANCE 2
innocent *adj* 1 *syn* see GOOD 11
  rel unstained, unsullied, white, white=
  handed
  2 free from legal guilt or fault <the defendant was found *innocent*>
  syn blameless, clean, crimeless, faultless,
  guiltless, inculpable, unguilty
  idiom in the clear
  ant guilty
  3 *syn* see LAWFUL
  4 *syn* see DEVOID
  5 *syn* see NATURAL 5
  6 *syn* see HARMLESS
  con harmful, injurious, mischievous
innocuous *adj* 1 *syn* see HARMLESS
  con harmful, injurious; evil; troublesome
  ant pernicious
  2 *syn* see INSIPID 3
innominate *adj syn* see ANONYMOUS
innovation *n syn* see CHANGE 2
  rel deviation, introduction, wrinkle
innovational *adj syn* see INVENTIVE
innovative *adj syn* see INVENTIVE
innovator *n* one who introduces something
  new <an *innovator* of bold ideas in the field
  of computers>
  syn introducer, inventor, original, originator
  rel author, creator, maker, producer; architect, builder, developer
innovatory *adj syn* see INVENTIVE
innoxious *adj syn* see HARMLESS
  ant noxious
innuendo *n syn* see INSINUATION
innumerable *adj* too many to be counted
  <received *innumerable* requests for help>
  syn countless, innumerous, numberless,
  uncountable, uncounted, unnumberable,
  unnumbered, untold
  ant numberable, numerable
innumerous *adj syn* see INNUMERABLE
inobnoxious *adj syn* see HARMLESS
  ant obnoxious
inobservant *adj syn* see INATTENTIVE
  ant observant
inobtrusive *adj syn* see QUIET 4
  ant obtrusive
inoculate *vb syn* see INFUSE 1
  rel admit, enter, introduce
inodorous *adj syn* see ODORLESS
  ant odorous; smelly
inoffensive *adj syn* see HARMLESS
  con loathsome, repulsive, revolting; distasteful, obnoxious, repellent, repugnant
  ant offensive
inopportune *adj syn* see UNSEASONABLE 1
  ant opportune
inordinate *adj* 1 *syn* see EXCESSIVE 1
  rel irrational, unreasonable; gratuitous,
  supererogatory, uncalled-for, wanton; extra,
  superfluous, surplus

  con moderate, temperate; checked, curbed,
  inhibited, restrained
  2 *syn* see EXCESSIVE 2
inordinately *adv syn* see EVER 6
inordinateness *n syn* see EXCESS 3
in passing *adv syn* see INCIDENTALLY 2
in perpetuum *adv syn* see EVER 2
inpour *n syn* see INFLUX
  ant outpour, outpouring
inpouring *n syn* see INFLUX
  ant outpour, outpouring
inquest *n syn* see INQUIRY 1
inquietude *n syn* see UNREST
  rel anxiety, uneasiness
  ant quiet, quietness, quietude
inquire *vb syn* see ASK 1
  rel investigate, probe, search; scrutinize,
  study
inquire (into) *vb syn* see EXPLORE
inquiring *adj syn* see INQUISITIVE 1
inquiry *n* 1 the act or an instance of seeking
  truth, information, or knowledge about
  something <an exhaustive *inquiry* revealed
  no evidence of a conspiracy>
  syn delving, inquest, inquisition, investigation, probe, probing, quest, research
  rel catechizing, interrogation, questioning;
  audit, check, examination, inspection, scrutiny; hearing; inquirendo
  2 a request for information <addressed his
  inquiry to the personnel director>
  syn interrogation, interrogatory, query,
  question, questioning
inquisition *n syn* see INQUIRY 1
inquisitive *adj* 1 given to examination or
  investigation <an *inquisitive* child who was
  interested in everything around her>
  syn curious, disquisitive, inquiring, investigative, questioning
  rel nosy, prying, snoopy
  con indifferent, unconcerned, uninquisitive,
  uninterested
  ant incurious
  2 *syn* see CURIOUS 2
  ant incurious, uninquiring
inquisitorial *adj syn* see CURIOUS 2
inquisitory *adj syn* see CURIOUS 2
in re *prep syn* see APROPOS
in respect to *prep syn* see APROPOS
in reverse *adv syn* see ABOUT 6
inroad *n syn* see INVASION
inroad *vb syn* see INVADE 1
inrush *n syn* see INFLUX
  ant outrush
insalubrious *adj syn* see UNWHOLESOME 1
  ant salubrious, salutary
insalutary *adj syn* see UNWHOLESOME 1
  ant salubrious, salutary
insanable *adj syn* see HOPELESS 2
ins and outs *n pl* characteristic peculiarities
  or technicalities <soon learned the *ins and
  outs* of his job>
  syn minutiae, ropes
  rel details, incidentals, particulars; ramifi-
  cations; oddities, peculiarities, quirks
insane *adj* 1 being afflicted by or manifesting
  unsoundness of mind or an inability to control one's rational processes <adjudged
  insane after a period of observation>
  syn bananas, ∥batty, bedlamite, ∥bonkers,
  brainsick, ∥buggy, ∥bughouse, ∥bugs, crack-

---

syn synonym(s)   *rel* related word(s)
ant antonym(s)   *con* contrasted word(s)
idiom idiomatic equivalent(s)
∥ use limited; if in doubt, see a dictionary

brained, cracked, ‖crackers, ‖cracky, ‖cranky, crazed, crazy, cuckoo, daffy, daft, demented, deranged, disordered, distraught, fruity, ‖loco, loony, lunatic, mad, maniac, ‖mental, mindless, non compos mentis, nuts, nutsy, nutty, reasonless, screwy, teched, unbalanced, unsane, unsound, wacky, witless, wrong
rel irrational, unreasonable; bewildered, distracted; dotty, eccentric, off, rocky, strange, touched; ‖dippy
idiom around the bend, crazy as a coot, not all there, not right in one's head, ‖off one's dot, off one's nut (*or* rocker), ‖off one's onion, out of (*or* off) one's head, out of one's mind, touched in the head
con judicious, sapient, sensible, wise; rational, reasonable; balanced; logical, subtle; healthy, sound; clear, lucid
ant sane
2 *syn* see FOOLISH 2
rel fanciful, fantastic, imaginary, visionary; impractical, unrealistic
con feasible, possible, sane, practicable, usable; rational, reasonable, sane, sensible; practical, realistic

insaneness *n syn* see INSANITY 1
ant saneness, sanity

insanity *n* 1 grave disorder of mind that impairs one's capacity to function safely or normally in society <his *insanity* required confinement in a mental institution>
syn aberration, alienation, derangement, distraction, insaneness, lunacy, madness, psychopathy, unbalance
rel acromania; delirium, frenzy, hysteria; delusion, hallucination, illusion; irrationality, unreasonableness; dotage
con judiciousness, sageness, sensibility, wiseness; rationality, reasonableness; healthiness, soundness, wholesomeness
ant saneness, sanity
2 *syn* see FOOLISHNESS
rel asininity, fatuousness, stupidity; impracticality

insatiable *adj* incapable of being satisfied or appeased <an *insatiable* lust for glory>
syn insatiate, quenchless, unappeasable, unquenchable, unsatiate, unsatisfiable
rel unsatiated, unsatisfied; demanding, exigent, importunate, insistent, urgent; clamorous, crying, pressing, yearning
con appeasable, quenchable, satisfiable; satiate, satiated, satisfied; controlled, curbed, restrained
ant satiable

insatiably *adv syn* see VERY 1

insatiate *adj syn* see INSATIABLE
ant satiate, satiated

inscience *n syn* see IGNORANCE 2

inscribe *vb* 1 *syn* see WRITE
rel engrave, enscroll
2 *syn* see LIST 3
3 *syn* see ENGRAVE 2

inscrutable *adj syn* see MYSTERIOUS

insecure *adj* 1 not confident or sure <feels very *insecure* about his future>
syn unassured, unconfident, unsure
rel hesitant, questioning, uncertain
idiom in suspense, up in the air

con assured, confident, self-assured, self≈ confident, sure
ant secure
2 *syn* see WEAK 2
ant secure

inseminate *vb syn* see IMPLANT

insensate *adj* 1 lacking animate awareness or sensation <would often talk to stones and other *insensate* objects>
syn inanimate, insensible, insentient, senseless, unfeeling
rel exanimate, unanimated; anesthetic, insensitive
con aware, cognizant, conscious; feeling, sensible, sentient
ant sensate
2 *syn* see SIMPLE 3
3 *syn* see INSENSIBLE 5

insensibility *n syn* see APATHY 1
ant sensibility

insensible *adj* 1 *syn* see INSENSATE 1
ant sensible
2 deprived of consciousness <knocked *insensible* by a sudden punch>
syn cold, comatose, inconscious, senseless, unconscious
idiom out cold
3 *syn* see NUMB 1
4 *syn* see IMPERCEPTIBLE
ant sensible
5 devoid or insusceptible of emotion or passion <*insensible* to love or compassion>
syn anesthetic, bloodless, dull, hard, impassible, insensate, insensitive, rocky
rel blunt, obtuse; apathetic, impassive, phlegmatic, stoic, stolid; callous, hardened, indurated, pachydermatous, thick-skinned; absorbed, engrossed, intent, rapt
con alert, alive, awake, aware, cognizant, conscious; affected, impressed, influenced, touched
ant sensible

insensitive *adj* 1 *syn* see INSENSIBLE 5
rel aloof, incurious, indifferent, unconcerned
con compassionate, responsive, tender
ant sensitive
2 *syn* see NUMB 1
ant sensitive
3 *syn* see INSUSCEPTIBLE
ant sensitive

insentient *adj* 1 *syn* see INSENSATE 1
ant sentient
2 *syn* see INSUSCEPTIBLE

insert *vb syn* see INTRODUCE 6
rel interlope, intrude, obtrude; implant, inculcate, instill; admit, enter
con detach, disengage
ant abstract, extract

in short *adv syn* see BRIEFLY 1

inside *n* 1 *syn* see INTERIOR
ant outside
2 **insides** *pl syn* see ENTRAILS

inside *adj* 1 *syn* see INNER 1
ant outside
2 *syn* see PRIVATE 2

inside *adv syn* see INDOORS
ant outside

inside out *adv syn* see THOROUGHLY 2

insidious *adj syn* see SLY 2

rel perfidious, treacherous; dangerous, perilous; gradual, subtle

insight *n* 1 *syn* see SAGACITY
2 *syn* see INTUITION

insighted *adj syn* see WISE 1

insightful *adj syn* see WISE 1
rel discriminating, penetrating; inseeing

insignia *n* a distinguishing mark of authority, office, or honor <wore a coronet with the strawberry leaf *insignia* of his ducal rank>
syn badge, emblem
rel decoration; regalia

insignificancy *n syn* see NONENTITY

insignificant *adj* 1 *syn* see SENSELESS 5
ant significant
2 *syn* see MINOR 2
3 *syn* see LITTLE 3
ant significant

insincere *adj* not being or expressing what one appears to be or express <an *insincere* person who could not be trusted>
syn ambidextrous, double, double-dealing, double-faced, doublehearted, double-minded, double-tongued, hypocritical, left-handed, mala fide
rel deceitful, dishonest, lying, mendacious, untruthful; shifty, slippery, tricky
con candid, frank, open, plain; direct, forthright, straight, straightforward
ant sincere

insinuate *vb* 1 *syn* see INTRODUCE 6
2 *syn* see SUGGEST 1
rel ascribe, impute
con affirm, assert, aver, avouch, avow, declare, profess; air, broach, express, state, voice
3 to introduce (as oneself) by stealthy, smooth, or artful means <*insinuated* himself into the confidence of others>
syn edge in, foist, infiltrate, work in, worm
rel insert, intercalate, interject, interpolate, interpose, introduce

insinuating *adj syn* see INGRATIATING

insinuation *n* a stealthy or indirect hinting or suggestion <*insinuations* about her opponent's probity>
syn innuendo, insinuendo
rel hint, hinting, implication, implying, intimation, suggestion; animadversion, aspersion, reflection; ascription, imputation

insinuative *adj syn* see INGRATIATING

insinuendo *n syn* see INSINUATION

insipid *adj* 1 *syn* see UNPALATABLE 1
rel bland, mild
con appetizing, flavorable, tasty
ant sapid, savory
2 *syn* see ARID 2
rel commonplace, ordinary, plain; mundane, prosaic, unimaginative
3 devoid of qualities that make for spirit and character <an *insipid* little story of teenage puppy love>
syn banal, bland, driveling, flat, inane, innocuous, jejune, milk-and-water, namby-

pamby, sapless, swashy, vapid, waterish, watery, wishy-washy
rel slight, tenuous, thin; feeble, weak; subdued, tame; mild, soft; pointless
con piquant, poignant, pungent, racy, spicy; fiery, gingery, high-spirited, mettlesome, peppery, spirited, spunky; exciting, piquing, provocative, provoking
ant sapid

insistent *adj* 1 *syn* see PERSISTENT 1
2 *syn* see EMPHATIC
rel persevering, persistent, pressing; obtrusive
3 *syn* see PRESSING

insociable *adj syn* see UNSOCIABLE
ant sociable

insolate *vb syn* see SUN

insolence *n* the quality, state, or an instance of being insulting or grossly lacking in respect <court-martialed because of *insolence* to an officer>
syn boldness, disrespect, hardihood, impertinence, impudence, insolency, insolentness; *compare* EFFRONTERY
rel brazenness; presumption; arrogance; rudeness; contempt
con deference; correctness, decency, decorum, decorousness, properness, seemliness
ant respect, respectfulness

insolency *n syn* see INSOLENCE
ant respect, respectfulness

insolent *adj* 1 *syn* see PROUD 1
rel imperative, peremptory; dictatorial, magisterial
ant deferential
2 exhibiting boldness or effrontery <an *insolent* child with no respect or regard for anyone>
syn audacious, bold, ‖boldacious, brazen, contumelious, impertinent, impudent, procacious, saucy
rel arrogant, disdainful, overbearing; discourteous, impolite, rude, uncivil, ungracious
con humble, lowly, meek, modest, unassertive; civil, courteous, polite
ant deferential

insolentness *n syn* see INSOLENCE
ant respect, respectfulness

insoluble *adj* admitting of no solution <seemingly *insoluble* problems faced the city council>
syn inextricable, insolvable, irresolvable, irresolvable, unsoluble, unsolvable
rel inexplicable, unexplainable; inconceivable, unaccountable; mysterious
con answerable, explicable, understandable; resolvable; clear, plain, straightforward
ant soluble, solvable

insolvable *adj syn* see INSOLUBLE
ant soluble, solvable

insomnia *n* prolonged inability to obtain adequate sleep <sleeping pills failed to relieve his *insomnia*>
syn insomnolence, sleeplessness
rel restlessness, wakefulness; stress, tension

insomnolence *n syn* see INSOMNIA

insorb *vb syn* see ABSORB 1

insouciance *n syn* see APATHY 2

insouciant *adj syn* see HAPPY-GO-LUCKY

---

syn synonym(s)   *rel* related word(s)
ant antonym(s)   *con* contrasted word(s)
idiom idiomatic equivalent(s)
‖ use limited; if in doubt, see a dictionary

inspect *vb syn* see SCRUTINIZE 1
rel notice, observe; catechize, inquire, interrogate, question; review

inspection *n syn* see EXAMINATION
rel inquest, inquiry, inquisition, investigation, probe, research; oversight, supervision, surveillance

inspiration *n* a divine or seemingly divine imparting of knowledge or power <*inspiration* is the only plausible explanation for his exquisite work>
syn afflation, afflatus, inflatus
rel animus, genius, muse, vision; enlightenment, illumination; brainstorm, brain wave

inspire *vb* **1** *syn* see INHALE
ant expire
2 *syn* see FIRE 2
rel quicken, stimulate; infect, infuse; endow, endue
3 *syn* see ELATE
4 *syn* see AFFECT

inspiring *adj syn* see EXCITING
ant uninspiring

inspirit *vb syn* see ENCOURAGE 1
rel exalt, fire, inform, inspire
ant dispirit

in spite of *prep syn* see AGAINST 4

instability *n* the state or quality of not being firm or fixed <the *instability* of the economy>
syn precariousness, shakiness, unfixedness, unsettledness, unstability, unstableness, unsteadfastness, unsteadiness
rel undependability, unreliability; inconstancy, insecurity
con firmness, soundness, stoutness, sturdiness; fixity, solidity
ant stability, stableness

install *vb* **1** *syn* see INITIATE 3
2 *syn* see ENSCONCE 2

installation *n syn* see INITIATION

instance *n* an individual that clearly belongs to an indicated class <their rescue was an *instance* of great courage>
syn case, case history, example, illustration, representative, sample, sampling, specimen
rel ground, proof, reason; detail, item, particular; exponent

instance *vb syn* see EXEMPLIFY 1
2 *syn* see MENTION
rel exemplify, illustrate

instant *n* **1** an infinitesimal space of time <came not an *instant* too soon>
syn breathing, crack, flash, ‖jiff, jiffy, minute, moment, second, shake, split second, ‖tick, trice, twinkle, twinkling, wink
2 *syn* see POINT 7
3 *syn* see OCCASION 5

instant *adj* **1** *syn* see PRESSING
2 *syn* see PRESENT
3 *syn* see INSTANTANEOUS

instantaneous *adj* done, occurring, or acting without any perceptible duration of time <*instantaneous* answers to tough questions>
syn hair-trigger, immediate, instant; *compare* QUICK 2
rel spontaneous; fast, quick, rapid; momentary, transitory
con late, tardy; slow, sluggish

instanter *adv syn* see AWAY 3

instantly *adv syn* see AWAY 3
idiom in a flash, on a dime, on the spot

instate *vb syn* see INITIATE 3

instead *adv* as an alternative to something expressed or implied <longed *instead* for a quiet country life>
syn alternately, alternatively, in lieu, rather

insteep *vb syn* see SOAK 1

instigate *vb syn* see INCITE
rel activate, actuate; hint, insinuate, suggest; plan, plot, scheme; goad, urge; fire, inflame

instigation *n syn* see STIMULUS

instigator *n* one that goads or urges forward <the *instigator* of the riot>
syn agitator, fomenter, inciter, mover
rel firebrand, incendiary, inflamer, rabble-rouser

instill *vb syn* see IMPLANT

instinctive *adj* **1** prompted by natural instinct or propensity <was quite unable to control her *instinctive* fear of snakes>
syn instinctual, intuitive, visceral
rel congenital, inborn, innate; ingrained, inherent, intrinsic; natural
ant reasoned
2 *syn* see SPONTANEOUS
rel natural, normal, regular, typical
ant intentional

instinctual *adj syn* see INSTINCTIVE 1

institute *vb* **1** *syn* see FOUND 2
ant abrogate
2 *syn* see INTRODUCE 3

institute *n syn* see LAW 1

institution *n* something or someone well established in a customary relationship <he's been in the office so long that he has become an *institution*>
syn fixture
rel custom, habit; establishment, rite

instruct *vb* **1** *syn* see TEACH
rel acquaint, apprise, inform; engineer, guide, lead, pilot, steer
2 *syn* see COMMAND
rel assign, define, prescribe

instruction *n syn* see EDUCATION 1

instructional *adj syn* see INFORMATIVE

instructive *adj syn* see INFORMATIVE
rel didactic, moralistic, moralizing

instrument *n* **1** *syn* see MEAN 2
2 *syn* see IMPLEMENT
rel equipment, gear, machinery, paraphernalia, tackle

instrumental *adj* serving as a means, agent, or tool <was *instrumental* in organizing the strike>
syn implemental, ministerial
rel conducive, helpful; serviceable, useful

instrumentality *n syn* see MEAN 2
rel energy, force, might, power

instrumentation *n syn* see MEAN 2

insubordinate *adj* unwilling to submit to authority <*insubordinate* soldiers are court-martialed>
syn contumacious, factious, insurgent, mutinous, rebellious, seditious
rel intractable, recalcitrant, refractory; ungovernable, unruly; indocile, uncompliant, uncomplying; disaffected, dissentious
con amenable, biddable, docile, obedient, tractable; subdued, submissive, tame

ant subordinate

insubstantial *adj* **1** *syn* see IMMATERIAL 1
ant substantial

2 *syn* see WEAK 1
ant substantial

3 *syn* see TENUOUS 3
ant substantial

insuccess *n* *syn* see FAILURE 2
ant success, successfulness

insufferable *adj* incapable of being endured <that man is an *insufferable* bore>
syn insupportable, intolerable, unbearable, unbrookable, unendurable, unsufferable, unsupportable
rel distressing, painful; unacceptable
ant supportable

insufficience *n* **1** *syn* see FAILURE 3
ant sufficiency

2 *syn* see SCARCITY
ant sufficiency

insufficiency *n* **1** *syn* see FAILURE 3
ant sufficiency

2 *syn* see SCARCITY
ant sufficiency

insufficient *adj* **1** *syn* see DEFICIENT 1
ant sufficient

2 *syn* see SHORT 3
ant sufficient

insular *adj* having the narrow and limited outlook characteristic of geographic isolation <the *insular* thinking of peasant communities>
syn local, ‖parish-pump, parochial, provincial, sectarian, small-town
rel regional, sectional; insulated, isolated, secluded; circumscribed, confined, limited, restricted; illiberal, narrow, narrow-minded
con broad-minded, liberal; cosmopolitan, metropolitan, urban

insulate *vb* *syn* see ISOLATE

insult *vb* *syn* see OFFEND 3
rel abase, debase, degrade, humble, humiliate; fleer, flout, gibe, gird, jeer, scoff, sneer; deride, mock, ridicule, taunt; rump
con admire, esteem, respect
ant honor

insult *n* *syn* see AFFRONT
rel abuse, invective, obloquy, vituperation; disgrace, ignominy, opprobrium, shame; disdainfulness, insolence, superciliousness; contempt, disdain, scorn; unpleasantry
con deference, homage, honor, obeisance, reverence

insuperable *adj* incapable of being surmounted, overcome, or passed over <they met with *insuperable* difficulties>
syn impassable, inconquerable, indomitable, insurmountable, invincible, unconquerable, unsurmountable
rel unachievable, unattainable; unsurpassable; impenetrable, impregnable, invulnerable
con surmountable; achievable, negotiable
ant superable

insupportable *adj* *syn* see INSUFFERABLE

ant bearable, supportable

insupposable *adj* *syn* see INCREDIBLE 1
ant supposable

insuppressible *adj* *syn* see IRREPRESSIBLE
ant suppressible

insuppressive *adj* *syn* see IRREPRESSIBLE

insure *vb* *syn* see ENSURE
rel guard, protect, safeguard, shield

insurgent *n* *syn* see REBEL

insurgent *adj* *syn* see INSUBORDINATE

insurmountable *adj* *syn* see INSUPERABLE
ant surmountable

insurrect *vb* *syn* see REVOLT 1

insurrectionist *n* *syn* see REBEL

insusceptible *adj* incapable of being moved, affected, or impressed <*insusceptible* to flattery>
syn impassive, insensitive, insentient, unimpressible, unimpressionable, unresponsive, unsusceptible
con impressible, impressionable, responsive, sensitive, sentient
ant susceptible

intact *adj* **1** *syn* see WHOLE 1
ant defective

2 *syn* see VIRGIN 1
ant deflowered

intangible *adj* **1** *syn* see IMPERCEPTIBLE
rel rare, tenuous, thin; slender, slight; aerial, aeriform, airy, ethereal; eluding, elusive, evading, evasive; touchless
ant tangible

2 *syn* see ELUSIVE

integer *n* *syn* see NUMBER

integral *adj* *syn* see WHOLE 3

integral *n* *syn* see WHOLE 2

integrate *n* *syn* see WHOLE 2

integrate *vb* **1** *syn* see HARMONIZE 4

2 *syn* see HARMONIZE 3

3 to join together systematically <an economic system that successfully *integrates* private gain with public responsibility>
syn articulate, concatenate
rel combine, conjoin, link, unite; compact, concentrate, consolidate, unify; blend, coalesce, fuse, merge; organize, systematize
con disperse, dissipate, scatter; analyze, break down, resolve
ant disintegrate

4 *syn* see UNIFY 1

5 *syn* see EMBODY 2

integrative *adj* tending to integrate <*integrative* forces in a fragmented society>
syn centralizing, centripetal, compacting, concentrating, consolidating, unifying
ant disintegrative

integrity *n* **1** *syn* see HONESTY
rel forthrightness, straightforwardness

2 the quality or state of being complete or undivided <trying to maintain the *integrity* of the empire>
syn completeness, entireness, perfection, wholeness
rel soundness, stability; absoluteness, purity, simplicity

intellect *n* **1** *syn* see REASON 5
rel comprehension; intuition

2 a person with great intellectual powers <one of the great *intellects* of his time>
syn brain, intellectual, intelligence

---

syn synonym(s)	*rel* related word(s)	
ant antonym(s)	*con* contrasted word(s)	
idiom idiomatic equivalent(s)		
‖ use limited; if in doubt, see a dictionary		

rel genius; egghead; pundit; thinker

intellection *n syn* see IDEA

intellective *adj syn* see MENTAL 1

intellectual *adj* **1** *syn* see MENTAL 1
con animal, fleshly, sensual
ant carnal
2 devoted to or engaged in the creative use of the intellect <the play appealed to the *intellectual* members of the audience>
syn cerebral, highbrow, highbrowed, intellectualistic

intellectual *n* **1** *syn* see INTELLECT 2
2 a person who possesses or has pretensions of strong intellectual interest or superiority <accused of being an *intellectual* and a snob>
syn Brahmin, double-dome, egghead, highbrow
3 intellectuals *pl syn* see INTELLIGENTSIA

intellectualistic *adj syn* see INTELLECTUAL 2

intelligence *n* **1** the ability to learn and to cope <what he lacked in education, he made up in *intelligence*>
syn brain(s), brainpower, mentality, mother wit, sense, wit
rel acumen, discernment, insight, judgment; perspicacity, sagacity, wisdom
2 *syn* see INTELLECT 2
3 *syn* see NEWS

intelligent *adj* **1** *syn* see RATIONAL
con irrational, unreasonable
ant unintelligent
2 mentally keen or quick <quite *intelligent* for his age>
syn alert, brainy, bright, brilliant, clever, knowing, knowledgeable, quick-witted, ready-witted, sharp, smart; *compare* WISE 4
rel astute, perspicacious, sagacious, shrewd; acute, keen; adroit, cunning, ingenious
con foolish, idiotic, imbecilic, moronic; crass, dense, dull, dumb, slow, stupid
ant unintelligent

intelligentsia *n* a class of articulate persons devoted to intellectual, cultural, and social matters <the *intelligentsia* posed a threat to the new regime>
syn clerisy, illuminati, intellectuals, literati
rel avant-garde, vanguard

intelligible *adj syn* see UNDERSTANDABLE
ant unintelligible

intemperance *n syn* see EXCESS 3
rel drunkenness, insobriety; debauchery
ant temperance

intemperate *adj* **1** *syn* see EXCESSIVE 2
rel bibacious, bibulous, crapulous, drunken; gluttonous
ant temperate, tempered
2 *syn* see SEVERE 3
ant temperate

intempestive *adj syn* see IMPROPER 1

intemporal *adj syn* see ETERNAL 4
ant temporal

intend *vb* **1** *syn* see MEAN 2
2 to have in mind as a purpose <*intended* to read the book>
syn aim, contemplate, design, mean, ||mind, plan, propose, purpose
rel attempt, endeavor, essay, strive, try; plot, scheme; assign, designate, destine

idiom figure on, have in mind to, look forward to

intendance *n syn* see OVERSIGHT 1

intended *adj syn* see ENGAGED 2

intended *n syn* see BETROTHED

intendment *n* **1** *syn* see INTENTION
2 *syn* see MEANING 1

intensate *vb syn* see INTENSIFY

intense *adj* **1** extreme in degree, power, or effect <*intense* hatred>
syn concentrated, desperate, exquisite, fierce, furious, terrible, vehement, vicious, violent
rel aggravated, enhanced, heightened, intensified; accentuated, emphasized, stressed
ant subdued
2 *syn* see INTENSIVE
3 *syn* see ARDENT 2
ant slight

intensely *adv* **1** *syn* see HARD 3
rel fiercely, furiously, vehemently, viciously, violently
2 *syn* see SERIOUSLY 2

intensify *vb* to increase markedly in measure or degree <both companies *intensified* their efforts to win the contract> <the pain *intensified* sharply>
syn aggravate, deepen, enhance, heighten, intensate, magnify, mount, redouble, rise, rouse
rel accent, accentuate, emphasize, stress; aggrandize, exalt; sharpen
con moderate, qualify; alleviate, ease, lighten, relieve; decrease, diminish, lessen, reduce
ant abate; allay, mitigate; temper

intensive *adj* highly concentrated <an *intensive* study of the causes of the war>
syn blood-and-guts, deep, hard, intense, profound
con casual, shallow, superficial

intensively *adv syn* see HARD 3

intent *n* **1** *syn* see INTENTION
rel conation, volition, will
con chance, fortune, hap, hazard, luck
ant accident
2 *syn* see MEANING 1

intent *adj* **1** having one's mind or attention deeply fixed <the student was too *intent* on his work to hear the phone>
syn absorbed, deep, engaged, engrossed, immersed, preoccupied, rapt, wrapped, wrapped up
rel attending, attentive, minding, watching; concentrated, riveted
con absent, absent-minded, abstracted, bemused, faraway, preoccupied; daydreaming, napping, oblivious
ant distracted
2 *syn* see DECIDED 2

intention *n* what one purposes to accomplish or do <her *intention* was to finish by noon>
syn animus, design, intendment, intent, meaning, plan, purpose; *compare* AMBITION 2
rel project, scheme; desire, hope, wish

intentional *adj syn* see VOLUNTARY
rel intended, meant, proposed, purposed; advised, considered, designed, designful, premeditated, studied

con accidental, casual, fortuitous; careless, heedless, inadvertent, thoughtless
ant unintentional

intentionally *adv* with intention <hurt her *intentionally*>
syn ‖apurpose, deliberately, designedly, on purpose, prepensely, purposedly, purposely, purposively
ant unintentionally

intentive *adj syn see* ATTENTIVE 1

intently *adv syn see* HARD 4

intentness *n syn see* EARNESTNESS

inter *vb syn see* BURY 1
ant disinter

interact *vb* to act upon one another <humor and pathos *interacted* to make a moving drama>
syn coact, interplay, interreact
rel collaborate, cooperate; combine, join, merge, unite

interagent *n syn see* GO-BETWEEN 2

interblend *vb syn see* MIX 1

interbreed *vb syn see* CROSS 4

intercalate *vb syn see* INTRODUCE 6

intercede *vb syn see* INTERPOSE 2

interceder *n syn see* GO-BETWEEN 2

intercept *vb* to stop, seize, or interrupt in progress or course <*intercept* a forward pass>
syn block, catch, cut off
rel grab, seize, take; check, curb
con fumble, miss; loose, release

intercessor *n syn see* GO-BETWEEN 2

interchange *vb syn see* EXCHANGE 3
rel reverse, transpose

interchangeable *adj* permitting mutual substitution <*interchangeable* parts>
syn commutable, exchangeable, fungible, interconvertible, substitutable
rel changeable, convertible; reciprocal, reciprocative

interchurch *adj syn see* NONSECTARIAN

intercommunication *n* 1 *syn see* COMMUNICATION 3
2 *syn see* CONTACT 2

intercomparable *adj syn see* LIKE

interconnect *vb syn see* INTERJOIN

interconvertible *adj syn see* INTERCHANGEABLE

intercourse *n* 1 *syn see* COMMERCE 2
2 *syn see* COMMUNICATION 3
3 *syn see* CONTACT 2

intercreedal *adj syn see* NONSECTARIAN

intercross *vb* 1 *syn see* INTERSECT
2 *syn see* CROSS 4

interdenominational *adj syn see* NONSECTARIAN

interdict *vb syn see* FORBID
ant sanction

interdiction *n syn see* TABOO
ant sanction

interest *n* 1 participation in advantage, profit, and responsibility <he owned a half *interest* in a furniture store>
syn claim, share, stake

---

syn synonym(s)   *rel* related word(s)
ant antonym(s)   *con* contrasted word(s)
idiom idiomatic equivalent(s)
‖ use limited; if in doubt, see a dictionary

---

2 *syn see* WELFARE
3 readiness to be concerned with or moved by something <had an *interest* in art>
syn concern, curiosity, interestedness, regard
rel enthusiasm, excitement, passion; attention, care, concernment; absorption, engrossment
con apathy, indifference, unconcern
ant disinterest

interest *vb* to engage the attention and interest of <his appeal failed to *interest* his listeners>
syn appeal, attract, excite, fascinate, intrigue
rel arouse, tantalize, titillate; lure, pull, snare, tempt; pique
ant bore

interested *adj* having a share or concern in some affair <all *interested* parties met for the reading of the will>
syn affected, concerned, implicated, involved
rel biased, partial, partisan, prejudiced
con aloof, incurious, indifferent, unconcerned; apathetic, bored, ennuyé
ant detached, disinterested

interestedness *n syn see* INTEREST 3

interfere *vb* 1 *syn see* INTERPOSE 2
rel bar, block, hinder, impede, obstruct
2 *syn see* MEDDLE
rel discommode, incommode, inconvenience, trouble; baffle, balk, foil, frustrate, thwart

interflow *vb syn see* MIX 1

interfuse *vb* 1 *syn see* MIX 1
2 to cause to pass into or through <*interfused* illuminating anecdotes with the informative text>
syn diffuse, infuse, interlard, intersow, intersperse, intersprinkle
rel impenetrate, impregnate, interpenetrate, penetrate, pervade, saturate
3 *syn see* PERMEATE

interfusion *n syn see* MIXTURE

interim *n syn see* GAP 3

interim *adj syn see* TEMPORARY

interior *adj* 1 *syn see* INNER 1
con extraneous, extrinsic, foreign
ant exterior
2 *syn see* INNER 2

interior *n* the internal or inner part <the *interior* of the house>
syn inside, inward(s), within
rel center, heart; belly, bosom; innards, internals
ant exterior, outside

interject *vb syn see* INTRODUCE 6

interjoin *vb* to join mutually <*interjoined* several stations into a new system>
syn anastomose, interconnect, interlink, intertie
rel interdigitate, interlace, interlock, interrelate
con disunite, part, separate, sunder
ant disjoin

interknit *vb syn see* INTERWEAVE

interlace *vb syn see* INTERWEAVE

interlard *vb syn see* INTERFUSE 2

interlink *vb syn see* INTERJOIN

interlope vb 1 syn see INTRUDE
  2 syn see MEDDLE

interlude n an intervening or interruptive period or space <an *interlude* of happiness in a tragic story> <woodland broken by *interludes* of meadow>
  syn break, intermission, interregnum, interval, parenthesis
  rel breather, lull, pause, respite, rest; episode, idyll; meantime, meanwhile, spell; entr'acte

intermeddle vb syn see MEDDLE
  rel encroach, entrench, invade, trespass

intermeddler n syn see BUSYBODY

intermediary adj syn see MIDDLE 2

intermediary n 1 syn see GO-BETWEEN 2
  2 syn see MEAN 2

intermediate vb syn see INTERPOSE 2

intermediate adj 1 syn see MIDDLE 2
  2 syn see MEDIUM

intermediate n syn see GO-BETWEEN 2

intermediator n syn see GO-BETWEEN 2

interment n syn see BURIAL 2
  ant disinterment

intermesh vb syn see ENGAGE 1

interminable adj syn see CONTINUAL
  rel eternal, infinite; lasting, permanent
  con intermittent, periodic; discontinued, stopped; closed, completed, ended, finished, terminated

intermingle vb syn see MIX 1

intermission n 1 syn see ABEYANCE
  2 syn see INTERLUDE

intermit vb syn see DEFER
  rel arrest, check, interrupt
  con continue, persist, iterate, reiterate, repeat

intermittent adj occurring or appearing in interrupted sequence <they predict *intermittent* rain throughout the day>
  syn alternate, isochronal, isochronous, periodic, periodical, recurrent, recurring
  rel cyclic, cyclical, iterant, iterative, metrical, rhythmic, rhythmical, seasonal, serial; arrested, checked, interrupted; fitful, spasmodic; infrequent, occasional, sporadic; discontinuing, discontinuous
  con constant, perpetual; everlasting, interminable
  ant continual, continuous; incessant, unceasing

intermix vb syn see MIX 1

intermixture n syn see MIXTURE

intermutual adj syn see COMMON 1

intern vb syn see IMPRISON

internal adj 1 syn see INNER 1
  ant external
  2 syn see INNER 2
  3 syn see DOMESTIC 2
  ant external

internals n pl syn see ENTRAILS

internuncio n syn see MESSENGER

interpenetrate vb syn see PERMEATE

interplay n syn see INTERACT

interpolate vb syn see INTRODUCE 6
  rel admit, enter; interlope, intrude; add, annex, append, superadd
  con cancel, delete, erase, expunge

interpose vb 1 syn see INTRODUCE 6
  rel cast, throw, toss; push, shove, thrust

  2 to come between disagreeing elements <forced to *interpose* when the argument grew heated>
  syn intercede, interfere, intermediate, intervene, mediate, step in
  rel butt in, interlope, intrude, obtrude; intermeddle, meddle; arbitrate, moderate, negotiate

interpret vb 1 syn see EXPLAIN 1
  rel exemplify, illustrate; annotate, gloss; comment, commentate
  con contort, deform, distort; garble, misrepresent; misconstrue, misinterpret
  2 syn see REPRESENT 1

interpretation n 1 syn see EXPLANATION 1
  2 manner of artistic presentation in performance or adaptation or an instance of this <*interpretation* involves a re-creative effort by the performer>
  syn reading, rendering, rendition, version

interpretive adj syn see EXPLANATORY

interreact vb syn see INTERACT

interregnum n syn see INTERLUDE

interrogate vb syn see ASK 1

interrogation n 1 syn see CROSS-EXAMINATION
  2 syn see INQUIRY 2

interrogatory n syn see INQUIRY 2

interrupt vb 1 syn see ARREST 1
  rel defer, intermit, postpone, suspend
  2 to ask questions or make remarks while another is speaking <a chatterbox who habitually *interrupts* everyone>
  syn break in, chime in, chip in
  rel cut in, put in
  idiom break in on (or upon)

interruption n 1 syn see GAP 3
  rel rent, rift, rupture, split
  2 syn see ABEYANCE

intersect vb to divide by passing through or across <parallel lines can never *intersect*>
  syn crisscross, cross, crosscut, decussate, intercross
  rel traverse; bisect

intersow vb syn see INTERFUSE 2

intersperse vb syn see INTERFUSE 2

intersprinkle vb syn see INTERFUSE 2

intertangle vb syn see ENTANGLE 1

intertie n syn see INTERJOIN

intertrude vb syn see INTRUDE 1

intertwine vb syn see INTERWEAVE

intertwist vb syn see INTERWEAVE

interval n 1 syn see PAUSE
  2 syn see INTERLUDE
  3 syn see GAP 3

intervene vb syn see INTERPOSE 2
  rel divide, part, separate, sever

intervolve vb syn see INTERWEAVE

interweave vb to blend or unite intimately <joy and melancholy are often closely *interwoven*>
  syn interknit, interlace, intertwine, intertwist, intervolve, interwind, interwork, interweathe, inweave
  rel associate, join, link; blend, fuse, mix

interwind vb syn see INTERWEAVE

interwork vb syn see INTERWEAVE

interweathe vb syn see INTERWEAVE

intestinal fortitude n syn see FORTITUDE

intestine adj 1 syn see DOMESTIC 2

2 *syn* see INNER 1
intimacy *n syn* see ACQUAINTANCE 1
intimate *vb syn* see SUGGEST 1
rel attest, bespeak, betoken, indicate
con air, express, utter, vent, voice; affirm,
assert, aver, avouch, declare, profess
intimate *adj* **1** *syn* see INHERENT
2 *syn* see INNER 2
3 *syn* see FAMILIAR 1
rel nearest, next; affectionate, devoted,
fond, loving; privy, secret
con distant, remote
4 having or marked by a warm personal
relation <*intimate* friends for many
years><an *intimate* friendship>
syn ‖buddy-buddy, chummy, cozy, pally,
‖palsy-walsy
idiom thick as thieves
intimate *n syn* see FRIEND
rel associate, companion, comrade, crony
con outsider, stranger
intimation *n* **1** *syn* see HINT 1
2 *syn* see HINT 2
intimidate *vb* to frighten or coerce into
submission or obedience <refused to be
intimidated by the manager>
syn bludgeon, bluster, ‖bounce, browbeat,
bulldoze, bully, bullyrag, cow, dragoon,
hector, ‖ruffle, strong-arm, terrorize
rel alarm, disquiet, frighten, scare, terrify;
badger, bait, chivy, hound, ride; coerce,
compel, constrain, force, oblige; ‖ruffianize
con blandish, cajole, coax, wheedle; induce,
persuade, prevail
intimidator *n syn* see BULLY 1
into *prep syn* see TO 1
intolerable *adj syn* see INSUFFERABLE
ant tolerable
intolerant *adj* **1** unwilling or unable to endure with composure <he was inclined to be
very *intolerant* of interruption>
syn impatient, unforbearing, unindulgent
rel contemptuous, disdainful; fractious,
irritable, snappish, waspish; indignant, irate,
outraged, stuffy, upset, worked up
con forbearing, indulgent, long-suffering,
patient; resigned, uncomplaining
ant tolerant
2 *syn* see ILLIBERAL
rel inflexible, obdurate; antipathetic, averse,
unsympathetic
con forbearing, indulgent, lenient
ant tolerant
intonation *n syn* see INFLECTION
in toto *adv syn* see ALL 1
intoxicant *n syn* see LIQUOR 2
intoxicated *adj* **1** significantly under the
influence of alcoholic liquor <some people
become *intoxicated* more easily than others>
syn alcoholized, ‖bagged, blind, ‖blotto,
‖boiled, ‖bombed, ‖boozed, ‖boozy, ‖buffy,
buzzed, ‖canned, ‖capernoited, cockeyed,
crocked, cut, ‖deleerit, disguised, drunk,
drunken, fried, ‖half-seas over, inebriated,
inebrious, ‖jagged, ‖juiced, ‖lit, ‖lit up,
‖loaded, looped, ‖lushed, muddled, ‖oiled,

‖organized, ‖pickled, ‖pie-eyed, ‖piped,
‖pipped, ‖pissed, pixilated, ‖plastered, polluted, ‖potted, rum-dum, ‖screwy, ‖shick,
shicker, ‖shot, slewed, slopped, sloppy,
smashed, soshed, sozzled, ‖spiflicated,
squiffed, ‖stewed, stiff, ‖stinking, ‖stinko,
stoned, ‖swacked, tanked, ‖tiddly, tight,
unsober, wet, zonked
rel befuddled, bemused, besotted, dazed,
dopey, fuddled, loopy, maudlin, sodden,
soppy, sotted, tipsy
idiom disguised with drink, full as a tick, in
drink (*or* liquor), in one's cups, in the bag,
stewed to the gills, the worse for drink, three
sheets in (*or* to) the wind, under the table,
under the weather, with drink taken
con abstemious, abstinent, moderate, temperate
ant sober
2 profoundly and usually pleasantly moved
<*intoxicated* with the beauty of the scene>
syn elated, excited, exhilarated, turned-on
rel affected, concerned, interested, moved;
galvanized, piqued, quickened, stimulated
con disinterested, unconcerned; depressed,
disheartened, distressed, saddened
intoxicating *adj syn* see EXCITING
intoxication *n syn* see EUPHORIA 2
intractable *adj* **1** *syn* see UNRULY 1
ant tractable
2 *syn* see OBSTINATE
ant tractable
intransigent *adj syn* see OBSTINATE
intrepid *adj syn* see BRAVE 1
ant craven
intricate *adj* **1** *syn* see COMPLEX 2
rel arduous, difficult, hard
2 *syn* see ELABORATE 2
intrigue *vb* **1** *syn* see INTEREST
2 *syn* see PLOT
intrigue *n* **1** *syn* see PLOT 2
2 *syn* see AMOUR 2
intrinsic *adj syn* see INHERENT
con added, annexed, appended, superadded
ant extrinsic
intrinsically *adv syn* see PER SE
introduce *vb* **1** *syn* see ENTER 2
rel inaugurate, induct, install; bring forward
2 *syn* see BROACH
3 to bring into practice or use <*introduce*
reforms in the welfare system>
syn inaugurate, initiate, institute, launch,
originate, set up, usher in
rel establish, found, organize; innovate,
invent; unveil; pioneer
4 to cause to know each other personally
<planned to *introduce* her to his mother>
syn acquaint, present, ‖quaint
5 *syn* see PRECEDE 3
6 to put among or between others <*introduced* several new lines of dialogue>
syn fill in, insert, insinuate, intercalate,
interject, interpolate, interpose, throw in
rel inlay, inlet, inset; inject, instill; work in
con eject, evict, oust; eliminate, exclude
ant abstract; withdraw
introducer *n syn* see INNOVATOR
introduction *n* something that serves as a
preliminary or antecedent <the crisis could
be the *introduction* to a general war>

---

syn synonym(s)   *rel* related word(s)
ant antonym(s)   *con* contrasted word(s)
idiom idiomatic equivalent(s)
‖ use limited; if in doubt, see a dictionary

syn exordium, foreword, overture, preamble, preface, prelude, prelusion, proem, prolegomenon, prologue

introductory *adj* 1 *syn* see PRELIMINARY
ant closing, concluding
2 *syn* see INITIAL 1

introspection *n* the examination of one's own thought and feeling <a man much given to *introspection*>
syn heart-searching, self-contemplation, self-examination, self-observation, self-questioning, self-reflection, self-scrutiny, self-searching, soul-searching
rel contemplation, meditation, reflection; self-analysis
ant extrospection

intrude *vb* 1 to thrust or force in without permission, welcome, or fitness <constantly *intruded* himself into his sister's affairs>
syn butt in, chisel (in), cut in, horn in, intertrude, obtrude
rel encroach, entrench, infringe, invade, muscle, trespass; insinuate, intercalate, interject, interpolate, interpose, introduce; interfere, intervene; intermeddle, meddle; bother, disturb, pester
con retire, stand off, withdraw
2 *syn* see IMPOSE 5

intrusive *adj syn* see IMPERTINENT 2
rel butting in, intruding, obtruding
con bashful, coy, diffident, modest, retiring, shy
ant unintrusive

intuition *n* immediate apprehension or cognition <skeptical of the traditional woman's *intuition*>
syn anschauung, insight, intuitiveness
rel second sight, sixth sense
ant ratiocination

intuitive *adj syn* see INSTINCTIVE 1
rel direct, immediate, presentative
ant ratiocinative

intuitiveness *n syn* see INTUITION

inumbrate *vb* see SHADE

inundate *vb syn* see DELUGE 1

inundation *n syn* see FLOOD 2

inurbane *adj syn* see RUDE 6
ant urbane

inure *vb syn* see ACCUSTOM
rel discipline, train

inutile *adj syn* see WORTHLESS 1
ant utile

invade *vb* 1 to enter for conquest or plunder <the Danes *invaded* England>
syn foray, inroad, overrun, overswarm, raid
rel loot, pillage, plunder, ravage
2 *syn* see TRESPASS 2
rel impenetrate, interpenetrate, permeate, pervade

invalid *adj* 1 *syn* see ILLOGICAL
ant valid
2 *syn* see NULL

invalidate *vb syn* see ABOLISH 1
rel counteract, counterbalance, negative, neutralize, offset; discredit
ant validate

invaluable *adj syn* see PRECIOUS 1
ant worthless

invariable *adj* 1 *syn* see INFLEXIBLE 3
ant variable

2 *syn* see SAME 3
ant variable, varying

invariably *adv* 1 *syn* see ALWAYS 1
2 *syn* see EVER 3

invasion *n* a hostile entrance into the territory of another <Hitler's *invasion* of Poland>
syn foray, incursion, inroad, irruption, raid
rel aggression, attack, offense, offensive; breach, infraction, infringement, transgression, trespass, violation; encroachment, entrenchment

invective *adj syn* see ABUSIVE
rel censorious, condemnatory, damnatory, denunciatory, reproachful

invective *n syn* see ABUSE
rel diatribe, jeremiad, philippic, tirade

inveigh (against) *vb syn* see OBJECT 1

inveigle *vb syn* see LURE

inveiglement *n syn* see LURE 2

invent *vb syn* see CONTRIVE 2
rel conceive, envision, imagine; create, mint, produce, turn out; inaugurate, initiate

invention *n* a product of creative imagination <his most famous *invention* is the electric light bulb>
syn brainchild, coinage, contrivance
rel concoction, contraption, innovation, novelty; creation, opus, original

inventive *adj* adept or prolific at producing new things and ideas <had a very *inventive* turn of mind> <she was an *inventive* genius>
syn creative, demiurgic, deviceful, ingenious, innovational, innovative, innovatory, original, originative
rel fertile, fruitful, productive, teeming; causative, constructive, formative
con sterile, uncreative, unproductive
ant uninventive

inventor *n* 1 *syn* see INNOVATOR
2 *syn* see FATHER 2

inventory *n* 1 *syn* see SUPPLY
2 *syn* see RESERVE

inventory *vb* 1 to make an itemized report or record of <will *inventory* all office supplies>
syn catalog, itemize, tally
rel list, record, register; enumerate, tabulate
idiom take account (*or* stock) of
2 *syn* see ITEMIZE 1
3 *syn* see EPITOMIZE 1

inveracity *n syn* see LIE
ant veracity

inverse *vb syn* see REVERSE 1

inversion *n syn* see REVERSAL 1

invert *vb syn* see REVERSE 1
rel flip, turn down, turn over

invert *n syn* see HOMOSEXUAL

invertebrate *n syn* see WEAKLING

invertebrate *adj syn* see WEAK 4
rel disorganized, structureless

inverted *adj* 1 *syn* see UPSIDE-DOWN 1
2 *syn* see HOMOSEXUAL

invest *vb* 1 *syn* see INITIATE 3
rel endow, endue; consecrate, honor
ant divest, strip
2 to make a formal grant of power or authority <the Constitution *invests* the Congress with taxation powers>
syn authorize, empower, vest

rel bequeath, endow
con hold back, keep back, reserve, withhold
ant divest
3 *syn* see ENFOLD 1
4 *syn* see BESIEGE
5 *syn* see INFUSE 1
investigate *vb syn* see EXPLORE
rel muckrake, poke, pry
investigation *n syn* see INQUIRY 1
rel observation, observing; sounding, survey, surveying
investigative *adj syn* see INQUISITIVE 1
investigator *n syn* see DETECTIVE
investiture *n syn* see INITIATION
inveterate *adj* 1 firmly established or having something firmly established <the *inveterate* tendency to overlook the obvious>
syn bred-in-the-bone, confirmed, deep-dyed, deep-rooted, deep-seated, dyed-in-the-wool, entrenched, hard-shell, irradicable, settled, sworn
rel accustomed, addicted, chronic, habituated; customary, habitual, usual; hardened, indurated; established, fixed, set; inbred, innate; abiding, enduring, persistent, persisting
2 *syn* see OLD 2
invidious *adj* 1 *syn* see LIBELOUS
2 *syn* see ENVIOUS
rel bitter; hateful
3 *syn* see REPUGNANT 1
rel abominable, detestable, hateful, odious
con agreeable, grateful, gratifying, pleasant, pleasing
invidiousness *n syn* see ENVY
invigorate *vb syn* see STRENGTHEN 2
rel refresh, rejuvenate, renew, restore; rally, rouse, stir; activate, animate, stimulate, vitalize, vitaminize
ant debilitate
invigorating *adj* having an enlivening effect <an *invigorating* discussion>
syn animating, bracing, exhilarating, exhilarative, quickening, stimulating, stimulative, tonic, vitalizing
rel brisk, lively; fascinating, interesting
con anesthetic, numbing, somniferous
ant deadening
invincible *adj* 1 incapable of being conquered <the team proved to be *invincible*>
syn impregnable, inconquerable, indomitable, inexpugnable, invulnerable, unassailable, unbeatable, unconquerable, undefeatable
rel inviolable, untouchable; unattackable
con conquerable, subduable, surmountable, vanquishable
ant vincible
2 *syn* see INSUPERABLE
ant vincible
inviolable *adj syn* see SACRED 3
rel consecrated, hallowed; blessed, divine, holy; chaste, pure
ant violable
inviolate *adj syn* see SACRED 3

rel intact, perfect; faultless, flawless
con desecrated, profaned; defiled, polluted
invisible *adj syn* see IMPERCEPTIBLE
rel hidden, unseeable
ant visible
invitation *n syn* see PROPOSAL
invite *vb* to request the presence or participation of <*invited* guests to dinner> <*invited* the major nations to confer>
syn ask, bid
rel call, call in, summon; court, solicit, woo; entice, inveigle, lure, tempt
invoice *n syn* see BILL 1
invoke *vb* 1 *syn* see BEG
2 *syn* see ENFORCE
involuntary *adj syn* see SPONTANEOUS
rel unintended, unintentional, unwitting
ant voluntary
involve *vb* 1 to bring a person or thing into circumstances or a situation from which extrication is difficult <nations *involved* in war>
syn embroil, implicate, mire, tangle; compare ENTANGLE 3
rel catch up; draw (into)
2 *syn* see INCLUDE
involved *adj* 1 *syn* see COMPLEX 2
rel confused, muddled
con easy, facile, simple
2 *syn* see INTERESTED
rel enmeshed, entangled
ant uninvolved
involvement *n syn* see ENTANGLEMENT 1
invulnerable *adj syn* see INVINCIBLE 1
ant vulnerable
inward *adj syn* see INNER 1
con alien, extraneous, extrinsic, foreign
ant outward
inward *n* 1 *often* inwards *pl syn* see INTERIOR
2 inwards *pl syn* see ENTRAILS
inwardness *n syn* see ACQUAINTANCE 1
inweave *vb syn* see INTERWEAVE
iota *n syn* see PARTICLE
ipseity *n syn* see INDIVIDUALITY 4
irascible *adj* easily aroused to anger <an *irascible* fellow and hard to get along with>
syn choleric, cranky, cross, hot-tempered, ireful, passionate, peppery, quick-tempered, ratty, ‖stomachy, temperish, testy, tetchy, touchy; compare CANTANKEROUS, IRRITABLE
rel fractious, huffy, irritable, peevish, petulant, querulous, snappish, waspish; impatient, jittery, jumpy, nervous, restive; bristly, crabbed, surly
con amiable, complaisant, good-natured, obliging; calm, quiet, relaxed; long-suffering, patient, tolerant
irate *adj syn* see ANGRY
ire *n syn* see ANGER
ire *vb syn* see ANGER 1
ireful *adj syn* see ANGRY
2 *syn* see IRASCIBLE
irenic *adj syn* see PACIFIC
ant acrimonious
irk *vb* 1 *syn* see ANNOY 1
rel discommode, incommode, inconvenience, trouble
2 *syn* see TRY 2

---

syn synonym(s) *rel* related word(s)
ant antonym(s) *con* contrasted word(s)
idiom idiomatic equivalent(s)
‖ use limited; if in doubt, see a dictionary

irking n syn see ANNOYANCE 1

irksome adj tending to cause boredom or tedium <an *irksome* task>
syn boresome, boring, drudging, tedious, tiresome, tiring
rel dull, stupid; exhausting, fagging, fatiguing, wearisome
con exciting, inspiring, provocative, stimulative, stirring
ant absorbing, engrossing

iron n, usu **irons** pl syn see SHACKLE 1

iron adj syn see INFLEXIBLE 2

ironbound adj syn see ROUGH 1

ironclad adj syn see INFLEXIBLE 3

ironfisted adj 1 syn see STINGY
2 syn see GRIM 3

ironhanded adj syn see RIGID 3

ironhead n syn see DUNCE

ironhearted adj syn see UNFEELING 2
ant softhearted

ironic adj syn see SARDONIC
rel biting, cutting, incisive, trenchant; caustic, mordant, scathing

∥**iron man** n syn see DOLLAR

irradiate vb syn see ILLUMINATE 2

irradicable adj syn see INVETERATE 1

irrational adj syn see ILLOGICAL
rel crazy, demented, insane
con logical, reasonable, sensible
ant rational

irrealizable adj syn see IMPOSSIBLE 1
ant realizable

irrebuttable adj syn see POSITIVE 3
ant rebuttable

irreclaimable adj syn see IRRECOVERABLE
ant reclaimable

irreconcilable adj incapable of being made consistent <the two versions of the story are completely *irreconcilable*>
syn incompatible, inconformable, inconsistent
rel discordant, discrepant, dissonant, inaccordant, incongruent, incongruous, inharmonious
ant reconcilable

irrecoverable adj not capable of being recovered, regained, remedied, or rectified <suffered an *irrecoverable* loss in the fire>
syn irreclaimable, irredeemable, irremediable, irreparable, irretrievable
ant recoverable

irredeemable adj syn see IRRECOVERABLE
ant redeemable

irreflective adj syn see CARELESS 1
ant reflective

irrefragable adj syn see INDESTRUCTIBLE

irrefrangible adj syn see INDESTRUCTIBLE

irrefutable adj syn see POSITIVE 3
ant refutable

irregular adj 1 not according with or explainable by law, rule, or custom <unusual problems require *irregular* solutions>
syn abnormal, anomalous, deviant, divergent, off-key, unnatural, unregular
rel aberrant, atypical; exceptional, odd, peculiar, queer, singular, strange, unique
con natural, normal, typical; accustomed, customary, habitual, usual, wonted
ant regular

2 syn see INFORMAL 1
3 syn see LOPSIDED
ant regular
4 syn see RANDOM
rel occasional, sporadic; erratic, fitful, spasmodic; inconstant, uneven, unsteady
5 syn see SPOTTY 1

irregular n syn see PARTISAN 2

irregularity n syn see INEQUALITY 1
ant regularity

irregularly adv syn see OCCASIONALLY
ant regularly

irrelative adj syn see IRRELEVANT
ant relative

irrelevant adj not applicable or pertinent <age should be *irrelevant* to employability>
syn extraneous, foreign, immaterial, impertinent, inapplicable, inapposite, irrelative
rel inconsequential, insignificant, unimportant
idiom beside the point, neither here nor there, out of the question
con applicable, appurtenant, germane, material, pertinent, significant
ant relevant

irreligious adj lacking religious emotions, doctrines, or practices <an *irreligious* person but not openly hostile to organized religion>
syn godless, nonreligious, unreligious
rel indevout, undevout; ungodly, unholy, unsanctimonious; blasphemous, impious, profane, sacrilegious; amoral, unmoral
con devout, pious
ant religious

irremediable adj 1 syn see IRRECOVERABLE
ant remediable
2 syn see HOPELESS 2

irremovable adj syn see IMMOVABLE 1
ant removable

irreparable adj 1 syn see IRRECOVERABLE
ant reparable
2 syn see HOPELESS 2

irreprehensible adj syn see GOOD 11
ant reprehensible

irrepressible adj impossible to repress, restrain, or control <an *irrepressible* joy over his brother's good fortune>
syn insuppressible, insuppressive, irrestrainable, uncontainable, uncontrollable, unrestrainable
rel bubbling over, effervescent, enthusiastic, rhapsodic
ant repressible

irreproachable adj 1 syn see GOOD 11
2 syn see IMPECCABLE 1

irresoluble adj syn see INSOLUBLE
ant resoluble

irresolute adj syn see VACILLATING 2
ant resolute

irresolution n syn see HESITATION
ant resolution

irresolvable adj syn see INSOLUBLE
ant resolvable

irresponsible adj lacking in responsibility <*irresponsible* behavior>
syn carefree, careless, feckless, incautious, reckless, uncareful, wild
rel undependable, unreliable, untrustworthy; unaccountable, unanswerable

con careful, cautious, discreet, heedful; dependable, reliable, trustworthy
ant responsible

irrestrainable *adj syn* see IRREPRESSIBLE
ant restrainable

irretrievable *adj syn* see IRRECOVERABLE
ant retrievable

irreverent *adj syn* see IMPIOUS 1
ant reverent

irreverential *adj syn* see IMPIOUS 1
ant reverential

irreversible *adj syn* see IRREVOCABLE
ant reversible

irrevocable *adj* incapable of being recalled or revoked <an *irrevocable* decision of the Supreme Court>
syn irreversible, nonreversible, unrepealable
rel constant, established, fixed; immutable, unchangeable, unmodifiable
con repealable, reversible; alterable, changeable, modifiable
ant revocable

irritable *adj* easily exasperated <the miserable weather made us all *irritable*>
syn disagreeable, fractious, fretful, huffy, peevish, pettish, petulant, ‖pindling, prickish, prickly, querulent, querulential, querulous, raspish, raspy, snappish, snappy, twitty, waspish, waspy, whiny; *compare* CANTANKEROUS, IRASCIBLE
rel cranky, cross, testy, touchy; choleric, irascible, splenetic
con amiable, complaisant, good-natured, obliging; affable, cordial, genial, gracious, sociable
ant easygoing

irritant *n syn* see ANNOYANCE 3

irritate *vb* to excite to angry annoyance <his rude interruptions really *irritated* her>
syn aggravate, burn (up), exasperate, gall, get, grate, huff, inflame, nettle, peeve, pique, provoke, put out, rile, roil; *compare* ANNOY 1
rel abrade, bother, ‖bug, chafe, exercise, fret, irk, ruffle, try, vex; anger, enrage, incense, infuriate, madden; affront, offend
con appease, conciliate, mollify, pacify, placate, propitiate; delight, gladden, gratify, please

irrupt *vb syn* see ERUPT 1

irruption *n syn* see INVASION

Ishmael *n syn* see OUTCAST

Ishmaelite *n syn* see OUTCAST

island *vb syn* see ISOLATE

isochronal *adj syn* see INTERMITTENT

isochronous *adj syn* see INTERMITTENT

isolate *vb* to set apart from others <the jury was *isolated* for several days>
syn close off, cut off, enisle, insulate, island, segregate, separate, sequester
rel quarantine; block (off); abstract, detach, disengage, remove; divide, part, sever, sunder
con associate, connect, join, link, unite

isolate *adj syn* see ALONE 1

isolated *adj syn* see ALONE 1
rel retired, secluded, withdrawn; abandoned, deserted, forsaken, stranded

isolation *n syn* see SOLITUDE

issue *n* 1 *syn* see OFFSPRING
2 *syn* see EFFECT 1
3 *syn* see PROBLEM 2
rel matter; subject, topic

issue *vb* 1 *syn* see SPRING 1
2 *syn* see EMIT 1
3 *syn* see PUBLISH 2

italicize *vb syn* see EMPHASIZE

itch *n* 1 *syn* see DESIRE 1
2 *syn* see LUST 2

itch *vb syn* see LONG

itchy *adj syn* see COVETOUS

item *adv syn* see ALSO 2

item *n syn* see POINT 1
rel component, piece; incidental, minutia

itemize *vb* 1 to set down in detail or by particulars <*itemize* deductions on a tax form>
syn enumerate, inventory, list, particularize, specialize, specify; *compare* SPECIFY 3
rel circumstantiate, document; count, number; cite, instance, mention; spell out
ant summarize
2 *syn* see INVENTORY

itemized *adj syn* see CIRCUMSTANTIAL
ant summarized

iterate *vb syn* see REPEAT

itinerant *adj* traveling from place to place <*itinerant* preachers>
syn ambulant, ambulatory, deambulatory, itinerate, nomadic, perambulant, perambulatory, peripatetic, roving, vagabond, vagrant, wandering, wayfaring
rel rambling, ranging, roaming; moving, shifting

itinerate *adj syn* see ITINERANT

itsy–bitsy *adj syn* see TINY

itty–bitty *adj syn* see TINY

‖**ivory** *n often* **ivories** *pl syn* see DICE

ivory–tower *adj syn* see IMPRACTICAL 1
ant down-to-earth

ivory–towered *adj syn* see IMPRACTICAL 1

ivory–towerish *adj syn* see IMPRACTICAL

---

syn synonym(s)   *rel* related word(s)
ant antonym(s)   *con* contrasted word(s)
idiom idiomatic equivalent(s)
‖ use limited; if in doubt, see a dictionary

J

jab *vb syn* see POKE 1
jab *n* **1** *syn* see POKE 1
  2 *syn* see PRICK 1
jabber *vb syn* see GIBBER
jabber *n* **1** *syn* see GIBBERISH 1
  2 *syn* see CHATTER
jabberer *n syn* see CHATTERBOX
jabberwocky *n syn* see GIBBERISH 1
jack *n* **1** *syn* see MARINER
  2 *syn* see FLAG
  ‖**3** *syn* see MONEY
jack (up) *vb syn* see RAISE 9
jackass *n* **1** *syn* see DONKEY 1
  2 *syn* see FOOL 1
jacket *n syn* see HIDE
jackleg *adj syn* see AMATEURISH
jackleg lawyer *n syn* see PETTIFOGGER
jackpot *n syn* see POT 3
jack-tar *n syn* see MARINER
jade *n* **1** *syn* see WANTON
  2 *syn* see MINX
jade *vb* **1** *syn* see TIRE 1
  rel cloy, pall, sate, satiate, surfeit; emasculate, enervate, unman, unnerve; depress, oppress, weigh
  con rejuvenate, renew, restore
  ant refresh
  2 *syn* see SATIATE
jaded *adj* **1** *syn* see TIRED 1
  ant refreshed
  2 *syn* see SATIATED
‖**jag** *n syn* see PRICK 1
jag *n syn* see BINGE 1
‖**jag** *vb syn* see CARRY 1
jagged *adj syn* see ROUGH 1
‖**jagged** *adj syn* see INTOXICATED 1
jail *n* a building or institution for the confinement of persons held in lawful custody <sent to *jail* for perjury>
  syn bastille, ‖big house, bridewell, ‖brig, ‖bucket, ‖caboose, ‖calaboose, ‖can, ‖carcel, chokey, ‖clink, ‖college, cooler, coop, freezer, guardroom, ‖hoosegow, jug, keep, lockup, pen, penitentiary, ‖pokey, prison, reformatory, rock pile, skookum-house, slammer, ‖stir, stockade
  idiom house of correction
jail *vb syn* see IMPRISON
  ant release
jailbird *n syn* see CONVICT
jake *n syn* see RUSTIC
jakes *n pl* but sing or pl in constr *syn* see PRIVY 1
jalopy *n* a dilapidated old automobile <bought a *jalopy* for $50>
  syn clunker, crate, dog, heap, junker, wreck
jam *vb* **1** *syn* see PRESS 1
  rel tamp, wad
  2 *syn* see CRAM 1
  3 *syn* see PRESS 7
jam *n syn* see PREDICAMENT

jam *n* a rich spread prepared by boiling fruit and sugar until the mixture thickens <enjoyed his mother's tasty berry *jams*>
  syn confiture, conserve, preserve
  rel jelly, marmalade
jam-full *adj syn* see FULL 1
jammed *adj syn* see FULL 1
jam-pack *vb syn* see CRAM 1
jam-packed *adj syn* see FULL 1
jangle *vb syn* see CLASH 2
jangle *n syn* see DIN
jape *n syn* see JOKE 1
jar *vb* **1** *syn* see CLASH 2
  2 *syn* see SHAKE 2
jar *n syn* see IMPACT 1
  rel fluctuation, sway, vibration; agitation, disturbance, upset
jargon *n* **1** *syn* see TERMINOLOGY
  2 *syn* see DIALECT 2
  rel idiom, speech; abracadabra, gibberish
jarring *adj syn* see HARSH 3
  ant soothing
jaundiced *adj syn* see BIASED 2
jaunt *n syn* see EXCURSION 1
‖**jaw** *n syn* see BACK TALK
jaw *vb* **1** *syn* see SCOLD 1
  2 *syn* see CHAT 1
jay *n syn* see RUSTIC
jazz *n syn* see NONSENSE 2
jealous *adj* **1** intolerant of rivalry or unfaithfulness <her husband was *jealous* of her flirting with other men>
  syn possessive, possessory
  rel covetous, demanding; grasping, grudging; envious, green-eyed, invidious; mistrustful, suspicious; doubting, questioning
  con tolerant, trusting, understanding
  2 *syn* see ENVIOUS
  3 *syn* see SUSPICIOUS 2
jealousy *n syn* see ENVY
jeer *vb syn* see SCOFF
  con fawn, toady, truckle; approve, endorse, OK, sanction
jejune *adj syn* see INSIPID 3
  rel slight, slim, tenuous, thin; arid, dry
jell *vb syn* see COAGULATE
  rel stiffen, thicken; cohere, stick
jellify *vb syn* see COAGULATE
jelly *vb syn* see COAGULATE
jellyfish *n syn* see WEAKLING
jeopard *vb syn* see ENDANGER
jeopardize *vb syn* see ENDANGER
jeopardous *adj syn* see DANGEROUS 1
jeopardy *n syn* see DANGER
  rel exposure; liability, openness, sensitiveness, susceptibility; accident, chance, hap
  ant safety
jeopardy *vb syn* see ENDANGER
jeremiad *n syn* see TIRADE
jerk *vb* to act on with or make a sudden sharp quick movement <*jerked* to one side> <*jerk* a root from the ground>

syn lug, lurch, snap, twitch, vellicate, yank
rel drag, pull; fling, sling, throw; toss;
wrench, wrest, wring

jerk *n* 1 *syn* see FOOL 1
jerkwater town *n syn* see BURG
jerry–build *vb syn* see THROW UP 1
jest *n* 1 *syn* see JOKE 1
rel banter, chaff, jolly; derision, ridicule,
twit
2 *syn* see FUN 1
con gravity, seriousness, soberness
ant earnest
3 *syn* see LAUGHINGSTOCK
jest *vb* 1 *syn* see SCOFF
2 *syn* see BANTER
jestee *n syn* see LAUGHINGSTOCK
jester *n* 1 *syn* see FOOL 2
2 *syn* see HUMORIST 2
jet *adj syn* see BLACK 1
jet *vb syn* see SQUIRT
jetsam *n syn* see DRIFTWOOD
jet set *n syn* see SMART SET
jettison *n syn* see DISPOSAL 2
jettison *vb syn* see DISCARD
ant salvage
jetty *n syn* see WHARF
jetty *adj syn* see BLACK 1
jewel *n syn* see PARAGON
jewel *vb syn* see BEJEWEL
jezebel *n syn* see WANTON
jib *vb syn* see DEMUR
jibe *vb syn* see AGREE 4
∥jiff *n syn* see INSTANT 1
jiffy *n syn* see INSTANT 1
jig *n syn* see TRICK 1
jigger *n* 1 *syn* see DOODAD
2 *syn* see GADGET 1
∥jiggery–pokery *n syn* see NONSENSE 2
jiggle *vb syn* see SHAKE 3
jillion *n syn* see SCAD
jim–dandy *n syn* see ∥DILLY
jimjams *n syn* see JITTERS
jimmies *n syn* see JITTERS
jimmy *vb syn* see PRY
jingle *vb* to make a repeated sharp light
ringing sound <the coins *jingled* in his
pocket>
syn chink, chinkle, clink, tingle, tinkle
rel clack, clatter, rattle
jinx *n* something that is felt or meant to bring
bad luck <her continual bad luck seemed
due to a *jinx*>
syn hex, hoodoo, Indian sign, voodoo,
whammy
rel charm, enchantment, spell; curse, evil
eye
jitters *n pl* a sense of panic or extreme nervousness <got the *jitters* whenever he
thought of the money he had lost>
syn ∥all-overs, dither, heebie-jeebies, ∥jim-
jams, ∥jimmies, jumps, shakes, shivers,
whim-whams, willies
jittery *adj syn* see NERVOUS
∥jive *vb syn* see BANTER
job *n* 1 *syn* see TASK 1

rel affair, concern, matter, thing
2 a regular remunerative employment <held
two *jobs* to make ends meet>
syn appointment, berth, billet, connection,
office, place, position, post, situation, spot;
compare WORK 1
rel assignment, engagement, posting; calling, employment, occupation, pursuit; profession, trade, vocation; niche, opening, slot
3 *syn* see WORK 1
4 *syn* see TASK 2
job *vb syn* see DUPE
jobless *adj syn* see UNEMPLOYED
jockey *vb syn* see MANIPULATE 2
jocose *adj syn* see WITTY
rel playful, roguish, sportive, waggish,
whimsical; comic, comical, droll, laughable,
ludicrous; blithe, jocund, jolly, jovial
con demure, earnest, grave, sedate, serious,
sober, solemn, staid
ant lugubrious
jocular *adj syn* see WITTY
rel jolly, jovial, merry; playful, sportive;
comic, comical, droll, laughable, ludicrous
con earnest, grave, serious, sober, solemn
jocularity *n syn* see MIRTH
jocund *adj syn* see MERRY
rel mischievous, playful, sportive
con dour, gloomy, glum, morose, saturnine,
sullen; grave, sedate, serious, solemn, somber, staid
jocundity *n syn* see MIRTH
jog *vb syn* see POKE 1
rel agitate, shake
joggle *vb syn* see SHAKE 3
john *n syn* see TOILET
John Law *n syn* see POLICEMAN
johnny *n syn* see TOILET
join *vb* 1 to bring or come together into some
manner of union <the couple were *joined* in
marriage soon thereafter>
syn associate, bracket, coadunate, coagment, coalesce, combine, compound, concrete, conjoin, conjugate, connect, couple,
link, marry, one, relate, unite, wed, yoke
rel agree, concur, cooperate; articulate,
concatenate, integrate; affix, attach, fasten;
knit, weave; bind, tie, tie up
con separate, sever, sunder; detach, disengage; disembarrass, disentangle, untangle
ant disjoin, part
2 *syn* see ADJOIN
join (up) *vb syn* see ENTER 3
joining *n syn* see JOINT 1
joint *n* 1 a place where two or more things are
united <the leak was found at a *joint* in the
pipeline>
syn connection, coupling, joining, junction,
juncture, seam, union
rel crux, link, tie; interconnection; abut-
ment, articulation, suture; concourse, confluence, meeting
2 *syn* see DIVE
joint *adj syn* see COMMON 1
jointly *adv syn* see TOGETHER 3
joke *n* 1 a remark, story, or action intended
to evoke laughter <had a good memory for
jokes>
syn crack, drôlerie, drollery, gag, jape, jest,
quip, sally, waggery, wisecrack, witticism,
∥yak

---

syn synonym(s)   *rel* related word(s)
ant antonym(s)   *con* contrasted word(s)
idiom idiomatic equivalent(s)
∥ use limited; if in doubt, see a dictionary

rel antic, caper, dido, monkeyshine, prank; bijouterie, bon mot; burlesque, caricature, parody, quiz, rib; badinage, persiflage, raillery; facetiousness, humorousness, jocoseness, jocularity, wittiness; humor, repartee, sarcasm, wit
2 syn see FUN 1
3 syn see LAUGHINGSTOCK
joke *vb syn* see BANTER
joker *n* **1 syn** see WAG 1
2 syn see HUMORIST 2
3 syn see ZANY 2
jokester *n* **1 syn** see HUMORIST 2
2 syn see ZANY 2
jollity *n* **1 syn** see MIRTH
rel blitheness; disport, frolic, gambol, play, rollick, romp, sport
con earnestness, gravity, sedateness, seriousness, solemnity, staidness
ant somberness
2 syn see MERRYMAKING
jolly *adj syn* see MERRY
rel frolicsome, mischievous, playful, roguish, sportive, waggish
con earnest, grave, sedate, serious, solemn, staid; doleful, dolorous, lugubrious, rueful
ant somber
jolly *vb syn* see BANTER
rel blandish, cajole
jolt *vb syn* see SHOCK 2
jolt *n* **1 syn** see IMPACT 1
2 syn see DRAM
jongleur *n syn* see BARD 1
josh *vb syn* see BANTER
joskin *n syn* see RUSTIC
jostle *vb syn* see PUSH 2
jot *n syn* see PARTICLE
jounce *n syn* see IMPACT 1
journal *n* a publication that appears at regular intervals <a monthly scientific *journal*>
syn magazine, newspaper, organ, periodical, review
journey *n* passing or a passage from one place to another <at that time it was a four day *journey* from Boston to New York> <she was tired though their *journey* was barely begun>
syn expedition, peregrination(s), travel(s), trek, trip; *compare* TRIP 1
rel excursion, jaunt, junket, sally, tour; cruise, voyage; pilgrimage, progress, safari
journey *vb syn* see GO 1
jovial *adj syn* see MERRY
rel facetious, humorous, jocose, jocular; affable, genial, sociable; amiable, good-natured; bantering, chaffing, jollying, joshing
con dour, gloomy, glum, morose, saturnine, sullen; grave, sedate, serious, solemn, staid
joviality *n syn* see MIRTH
joy *n syn* see PLEASURE 2
rel ecstasy, rapture, transport
ant sorrow; misery
joyance *n syn* see PLEASURE 2
joyful *adj syn* see GLAD 1
rel buoyant, effervescent, expansive
con despairing, desperate, despondent, forlorn, hopeless; depressed, oppressed, weighed down
ant joyless

joy girl *n syn* see PROSTITUTE
joyhouse *n syn* see BROTHEL
joy-juice *n syn* see LIQUOR 2
joyless *adj* **1 syn** see SAD 1
2 syn see GLOOMY 3
joyous *adj syn* see GLAD 1
rel ecstatic, rapturous, transported
con doleful, dolorous, melancholy; miserable, wretched
ant lugubrious
jubilance *n syn* see EXULTATION
jubilant *adj syn* see EXULTANT
jubilate *vb syn* see EXULT
jubilation *n syn* see EXULTATION
judge *n* **1** a person who impartially decides unsettled questions or controversial issues <the *judge* declared the ruling invalid>
syn arbiter, arbitrator, referee, umpire
rel intermediary, mediator, negotiator; conciliator, peacemaker, reconciler
2 an official entrusted with administration of laws <the *judge* gave the defendant a suspended sentence>
syn beak, court, justice, magistrate
judge *vb* **1** to decide something in dispute or controversy upon its merits and upon evidence <the committee will *judge* the truth of the testimony>
syn adjudge, adjudicate, arbitrate, referee, umpire
rel decide, determine, rule, settle
2 syn see INFER
rel demonstrate, prove, show; check, test, try
3 syn see ESTIMATE 3
judgmatic *adj syn* see WISE 2
judgment *n* **1 syn** see INFERENCE 1
rel decision, determination, ruling; belief, conviction, opinion, persuasion, view
2 syn see INFERENCE 2
3 syn see ESTIMATION 1
4 syn see SENSE 6
rel astuteness, perspicacity, sagacity, shrewdness; acumen, discernment, insight, penetration
judicious *adj syn* see WISE 2
rel rational, reasonable; dispassionate, equitable, fair, objective
con irrational, thoughtless, unreasonable; ill-considered
ant injudicious; asinine
jug *n syn* see JAIL
jug *vb syn* see IMPRISON
juggle *vb syn* see DECEIVE
juice *n syn* see LIQUOR 2
juiced *adj syn* see INTOXICATED 1
juicy *adj syn* see SUCCULENT
juju *n syn* see CHARM 2
jumble *vb* **1 syn** see CONFUSE 5
2 syn see DISORDER 1
jumble *n* **1 syn** see CLUTTER 2
2 syn see MISCELLANY 1
jumbo *adj syn* see HUGE
jump *vb* **1** to move suddenly through space by or as if by muscular action <*jumped* across the open trench>
syn bounce, bound, hop, hurdle, leap, lop, saltate, spring, vault
2 syn see START 1
3 syn see RAISE 9

jump (in *or* into) *vb syn* see PITCH IN 1
jump (off) *vb syn* see BEGIN 1
jumps *n pl syn* see JITTERS
jumpy *adj syn* see NERVOUS
  idiom on pins and needles
junction *n* **1** *syn* see CONCOURSE
  2 *syn* see JOINT 1
juncture *n* **1** *syn* see JOINT 1
  2 a critical or crucial time or state of affairs
  <was at a *juncture* where he had to make a
  decision>
  syn contingency, crisis, crossroad(s), emergency, exigency, pass, pinch, strait, turning
  point, zero hour
  rel condition, posture, situation, state,
  status; plight, predicament, quandary
  3 *syn* see POINT 7
jungle *n* **1** *syn* see CLUTTER 2
  2 *syn* see MAZE 1
junk *n syn* see REFUSE
junk *vb syn* see DISCARD
junker *n syn* see JALOPY
junket *n syn* see EXCURSION 1
junking *n syn* see DISPOSAL 2
Junoesque *adj syn* see CURVACEOUS
jurisdiction *n syn* see POWER 1
  rel bounds, confines, limits; compass,
  range, reach, scope; bailiwick, domain, field,
  province, sphere, territory
just *adj* **1** *syn* see WELL-FOUNDED
  2 *syn* see TRUE 3
  3 being what is called for by circumstances
  or accepted standards <punishments once
  considered fair and *just* are now held to be
  cruel, excessive, and unreasonable>
  syn appropriate, condign, deserved, due,
  merited, requisite, rhadamanthine, right,
  rightful, suitable; *compare* FIT 1
  rel fit, fitting, meet, proper
  con farfetched, irrelevant, remote, unconnected; improper, inapplicable, inapposite,
  inappropriate; abusive, cruel, harsh
  ant unjust
  4 *syn* see UPRIGHT 2
  rel rigid, strict; dependable, reliable, tried,
  trustworthy
  5 *syn* see FAIR 4
  rel aloof; condign, due, rightful
  ant unjust
  6 *syn* see FIT 1
just *adv* **1** as stated or indicated without
  deviation <*just* six inches long>
  syn accurately, bang, exactly, precisely,
  right, sharp, ‖smack-dab, spang, square,
  squarely
  rel definitely, directly, expressly, unmistakably
  con almost, nearly; approximately, impre-

cisely, inaccurately, inexactly, loosely
  2 by a very small margin <*just* enough food
  for one meal>
  syn barely, hardly, scarce, scarcely
  rel almost, approximately, nearly
  con copiously, fully, generously, lavishly,
  unstintedly, unstintingly
  3 no more than <*just* a note to remind you>
  syn but, merely, only, simply
  idiom nothing but
  4 *syn* see ALL 1
  5 *syn* see EVEN 1
just about *adv syn* see NEARLY
justice *n* **1** the action, practice, or obligation
  of awarding each his just due <his *justice*
  was stern but absolutely fair>
  syn equity
  rel evenness, fairness, impartiality
  con foul play, inequity, unjustness; bias,
  leaning, one-sidedness, partiality
  ant injustice
  2 *syn* see JUDGE 2
justifiable *adj* capable of being justified
  <thought her absence was not *justifiable*>
  syn condonable, defensible, excusable,
  tenable, vindicable, warrantable
  rel admissible, allowable, legitimate, reasonable; forgivable, pardonable, remissible
  ant unjustifiable
justification *n* **1** *syn* see EXPLANATION 2
  2 *syn* see APOLOGY 1
justified *adj syn* see WELL-FOUNDED
  ant unjustified
justify *vb* **1** *syn* see MAINTAIN 2
  rel demonstrate, prove; back, support,
  uphold
  con confute, disprove, refute
  2 *syn* see CONFIRM 2
  3 *syn* see EXPLAIN 3
  rel extenuate, gloss, gloze, palliate, whitewash
  con accuse, arraign, incriminate, indict;
  blame, condemn, denounce
  4 to constitute sufficient grounds <thought
  the storm warning *justified* his leaving
  early>
  syn warrant
  rel allow, permit; approve, authorize, sanction
justly *adv syn* see WELL 1
jut *vb* **1** *syn* see BULGE
  rel elongate, extend, lengthen
  2 *syn* see HANG 4
jut *n syn* see PROJECTION 1
juvenile *adj syn* see YOUNG 1
  ant adult
juvenile *n syn* see CHILD 1
juvenility *n syn* see YOUTH 1
juxtaposed *adj syn* see ADJACENT 3

---

syn synonym(s)   *rel* related word(s)
ant antonym(s)   *con* contrasted word(s)
idiom idiomatic equivalent(s)
‖ use limited; if in doubt, see a dictionary

K

‖**kale** *n syn* see MONEY

keck *vb syn* see RETCH

keel (over) *vb syn* see FALL 2

keen *adj* **1** see SHARP 1
2 *syn* see ENTHUSIASTIC
3 *syn* see EAGER
rel fervent, fervid, perfervid; fierce, intense, vehement; fired
con apathetic, impassive, phlegmatic, stolid; languid, listless
4 *syn* see SHARP 4
5 *syn* see ACUTE 3
con dull, obtuse
6 *syn* see LIVELY 1
‖**7** *syn* see MARVELOUS 2

keenly *adv syn* see HARD 6

keenness *n* **1** *syn* see EDGE 2
2 *syn* see WIT 3

keep *vb* **1** *syn* see OBEY
ant neglect
2 to notice or honor a day, occasion, or deed <*keep* the Sabbath by refraining from work>
syn celebrate, commemorate, observe, solemnize
rel regard, respect; bless, consecrate, sanctify; honor, laud, praise
idiom keep the faith
con disregard, forget, ignore, neglect, omit, overlook, slight; contravene, infringe, transgress, violate
ant break
3 *syn* see STOCK
4 *syn* see RESTRAIN 1
ant release
5 to hold in one's possession or under one's control <*kept* all the money for himself>
syn detain, hold, hold back, keep back, keep out, reserve, retain, withhold
rel conserve, preserve, save; enjoy, have, own, possess; conduct, control, direct, manage
con cast, discard, junk; refuse, reject, repudiate, spurn; abandon, resign, surrender, yield
ant relinquish
6 *syn* see REFRAIN 1
7 *syn* see CONDUCT 3

keep *n* **1** *syn* see LIVING
2 *syn* see JAIL

keep back *vb* **1** *syn* see KEEP 5
2 *syn* see DENY 2

keeper *n syn* see CUSTODIAN

keeping *n* **1** *syn* see CUSTODY
2 *syn* see PRESERVATION 1

keep off *vb syn* see FEND (off)

keep out *vb syn* see KEEP 5

keepsake *n syn* see REMEMBRANCE 3

keep up *vb syn* see MAINTAIN 1

keg *n syn* see CASK

‖**keister** *n syn* see BUTTOCKS

kelter *n syn* see REFUSE

ken *n* the extent of one's recognition, comprehension, perception, understanding, or knowledge <abstractions that are beyond the *ken* of small children>
syn horizon, purview, range, reach
rel comprehension, grasp, perception, understanding

kept woman *n syn* see HARLOT 1

kerchief *n* **1** a square of cloth used as a head covering or scarf <wore a *kerchief* around his neck>
syn babushka, bandanna
2 *syn* see HANDKERCHIEF

kernel *n syn* see SUBSTANCE 2

key *n syn* see PASSPORT

kibitzer *n syn* see BUSYBODY

kick *vb* **1** *syn* see OBJECT 1
rel combat, fight, oppose, resist, withstand; anathematize, condemn, curse, damn, execrate
idiom put up a fight (against)
2 *syn* see COMPLAIN

kick *n syn* see THRILL

‖**kick around** *vb syn* see DISCUSS 1

kick back *vb syn* see BACKFIRE

kicker *n syn* see GROUCH

‖**kick in** *vb* **1** *syn* see CONTRIBUTE 1
2 *syn* see DIE 1

kick off *vb* **1** *syn* see BEGIN 1
‖**2** *syn* see DIE 1

kick out *vb* **1** *syn* see DISMISS 3
2 *syn* see EJECT 1

kickshaw *n syn* see DELICACY

kid *n syn* see CHILD 1

kid *vb* **1** *syn* see DUPE
2 *syn* see BANTER

kidnap *vb* to carry off a person surreptitiously for an illegal purpose <an ex-convict *kidnapped* the child for ransom>
syn abduct, ‖snatch, spirit (away)
rel shanghai, waylay; coax, decoy, entice, inveigh, lure, seduce
idiom make off with
con deliver, ransom, redeem, rescue; bring (back), give back, restore, return

kidney *n syn* see TYPE

kid stuff *n syn* see SNAP 1

kill *vb* **1** to deprive of life <found it hard to *kill* animals>
syn carry off, cut off, destroy, dispatch, down, finish, lay low, put away, scrag, slay, take off; *compare* MURDER 1
rel butcher, choke, drown, massacre, poison, shoot, slaughter, suffocate; knife, sacrifice, stifle; annihilate, exterminate, ruin
idiom do (or make) away with, do for, put out of the way, put (or do) to death, put to sleep, take one's life
2 *syn* see VETO

killer *n syn* see MURDERER

killing *n syn* see MURDER

kiln *vb syn* see FIRE 6

kilter *n syn* see ORDER 10

kin *n* 1 *syn* see FAMILY 1
2 the members of one's immediate or extended family <all our *kin* gathered to celebrate great grandma's birthday>
syn cousinage, cousinhood, kinfolk, kinsmen
3 *syn* see RELATIVE

kind *n syn* see TYPE

kind *adj* showing or having a gentle considerate nature <mother was a *kind* person, always willing to help others>
syn benign, benignant, good-hearted, kindly
rel altruistic, benevolent, charitable, eleemosynary, humane, humanitarian, openhearted, philanthropic, propitious; compassionate, kindhearted, responsive, sympathetic, tender, warm, warmhearted; clement, forbearing, indulgent, lenient, merciful, tolerant; affable, amiable, cordial, genial, good-humored, good-natured, goodtempered, sweet-tempered; complaisant, obliging; gentle, good
con cruel, fell, fierce, inhuman, savage; hard, harsh, rough; grim, implacable, merciless, unrelenting
ant unkind

kindhearted *adj syn* see TENDER

kindle *vb* 1 *syn* see LIGHT 1
rel blaze, flame, flare, glow; excite, provoke, stimulate; arouse, foment, incite, instigate, rouse, stir
ant smother
2 *syn* see STIR 1
ant stifle

kindless *adj syn* see ANTIPATHETIC 2

kindliness *n syn* see GOODWILL 1
ant unkindliness

kindly *adj syn* see KIND
rel gracious, sociable; friendly, neighborly; attentive, considerate, thoughtful
con malevolent, malicious, malign, spiteful
ant unkindly; acrid (*of temper, attitudes, comments*)

kindly *adv syn* see WELL 2

kindness *n syn* see FAVOR 4

kindred *n syn* see FAMILY 1

kindred *adj syn* see RELATED
ant alien

kinfolk *n pl syn* see KIN 2

king *n syn* see MAGNATE

kingdom come *n syn* see HEAVEN 2

kinglike *adj syn* see KINGLY

kingly *adj* of, relating to, or befitting a king <a *kingly* entourage>
syn kinglike, majestic, monarchal, monarchical, regal, royal, sovereign
rel imperious, lordly, masterful, powerful, puissant; imperial, princely, queenly

kinky *adj syn* see OUTLANDISH 3

kinsman *n* 1 *syn* see RELATIVE

2 **kinsmen** *pl syn* see KIN 2

kinswoman *n syn* see RELATIVE

kismet *n syn* see FATE

kiss *vb* 1 to touch with the lips especially as a sign of affection <*kissed* his mother good night>
syn buss, lip, osculate, peck, smack, smooch, ‖smoodge, ‖smouch
2 *syn* see BRUSH

‖**kisser** *n syn* see FACE 1

kiss off *vb syn* see DISMISS 5

kite *vb syn* see GET OUT 1

kittenish *adj syn* see PLAYFUL 1

kitty *n syn* see POT 3

klutz *n syn* see OAF 2

knack *n* 1 *syn* see GIFT 2
rel quickness, readiness
ant ineptitude
2 *syn* see ABILITY 2
3 *syn* see HANG

knapsack *n syn* see BACKPACK

knave *n syn* see VILLIAN 1

knavish *adj syn* see DISHONEST

knell *vb syn* see RING

knickknack *n* a small or trivial ornamental article <a collection of pretty *knickknacks* was displayed on the mantel>
syn bauble, bibelot, curio, dido, gewgaw, gimcrack, novelty, objet d'art, pretty-pretty, rattletrap(s), toy, trifle, trinket, whatnot, whigmaleerie
rel souvenir; bric-a-brac, virtu; miniature; kickshaw, notion; trumpery

knifelike *adj syn* see SHARP 8
ant dull

knobkerrie *n syn* see CUDGEL

knock *vb* 1 *syn* see TAP 1
2 *syn* see CRITICIZE
ant boost

knock *n* 1 *syn* see HIT 1
2 *syn* see CRITICISM 2

knock about *vb syn* see MANHANDLE

knock down *vb* 1 *syn* see FELL 1
2 *syn* see EARN 1

knock-down-and-drag-out *n* 1 *syn* see BRAWL
2 *syn* see QUARREL

knocker *n syn* see CRITIC

knock off *vb* 1 *syn* see STOP 3
2 *syn* see DEDUCT 1
3 *syn* see MURDER 1
‖4 *syn* see ROB 1

knock out *vb syn* see EXHAUST 4

knockout *n* 1 *syn* see ‖DILLY
2 *syn* see BEAUTY

knock over *vb* 1 *syn* see FELL 1
2 *syn* see OVERTURN 1
3 *syn* see OVERWHELM 4
4 *syn* see ROB 1

knot *n* 1 *syn* see BOND 3
2 *syn* see BUMP 2
3 *syn* see MAZE 1

knothead *n syn* see DUNCE

knotty *adj* 1 *syn* see COMPLEX 2
2 *syn* see HARD 6

know *vb* 1 to possess an intellectual hold of <*knows* several languages>
syn appreciate, apprehend, cognize, comprehend, fathom, grasp, have, understand
rel apperceive; differentiate, discern, discriminate, distinguish, realize

---

syn synonym(s)　　*rel* related word(s)
ant antonym(s)　　*con* contrasted word(s)
idiom idiomatic equivalent(s)
‖ use limited; if in doubt, see a dictionary

idiom have at one's fingertips, see through
2 *syn* see EXPERIENCE 1
3 *syn* see FEEL 2
4 to recognize the differences between <*know* right from wrong>
syn difference, differentiate, discern, discrepate, discriminate, distinguish, extricate, separate, sever, severalize
con confound, mingle, mix
ant confuse, mix up
5 *syn* see RECOGNIZE 1
knowable *adj syn* see UNDERSTANDABLE
ant unknowable
know-how *n* **1** *syn* see ABILITY 2
2 *syn* see ART 1
knowing *adj* **1** *syn* see INTELLIGENT 2
rel vigilant, watchful; discerning, observant, perceptive
con blunt, obtuse
2 *syn* see WISE 1
3 *syn* see WISE 4
4 *syn* see AWARE
5 *syn* see SOPHISTICATED 2
know-it-all *n* *syn* see SMART ALECK

knowledge *n* **1** *syn* see EDUCATION 2
ant ignorance
2 the body of things known about or in science <made major contributions to scientific *knowledge*>
syn information, lore, science, wisdom
rel advice, intelligence, news; data, evidence, facts, input
knowledgeable *adj* **1** *syn* see INTELLIGENT 2
2 *syn* see WISE 1
know-nothing *adj syn* see IGNORANT 1
know-nothing *n* *syn* see DUNCE
knuckle *vb syn* see YIELD 2
knucklehead *n* *syn* see DUNCE
knuckle under *vb syn* see YIELD 2
kook *n* *syn* see CRACKPOT
kooky *adj syn* see FOOLISH 2
kowtow *vb syn* see FAWN
kowtowing *adj syn* see FAWNING
kudize *vb syn* see COMMEND 2
kudo *n* *syn* see COMPLIMENT 1
kudos *n* **1** *syn* see EMINENCE 1
2 *syn* see HONOR 2
kvetch *vb syn* see GRIPE

L

laager *vb syn* see CAMP
label *n* *syn* see TICKET 1
rel mark, marker
labor *n* **1** *syn* see WORK 2
rel endeavor, struggle
con ease, leisure, relaxation, repose, rest; amusement, diversion, entertainment, recreation; idleness, inactivity, inertia, inertness, passiveness
2 the physical activities involved in parturition <first *labors* are sometimes difficult>
syn birth pang(s), childbearing, childbirth, travail
labor *vb* **1** to exert one's powers of mind or body especially with painful or strenuous effort <*labored* all day to make a living>
syn drive, moil, strain, strive, toil, tug, work
idiom break one's neck
con idle, laze, loaf, lounge; goof (off), shirk, dawdle, poke, putter
‖**2** *syn* see TILL
labored *adj* **1** *syn* see HARD 6
2 *syn* see FORCED
rel heavy, ponderous, weighty; awkward, clumsy, inept, maladroit
laborer *n* *syn* see WORKER

laborious *adj syn* see HARD 6
ant easy, effortless
laboriously *adv syn* see HARD 8
ant easily, effortlessly
labyrinth *n* *syn* see MAZE 1
labyrinthine *adj syn* see COMPLEX 2
lacerated *adj* having jagged cuts or breaks <the *lacerated* area was badly swollen>
syn mangled, rent, torn
rel gashed, mutilated, ripped, slashed; jagged, ragged, saw-toothed, scalloped, scored; serrated
lachrymose *adj syn* see TEARFUL
lack *vb* to be without something and especially something essential or greatly needed <the building *lacks* a fire escape>
syn need, require, want
con enjoy, have, hold, own, possess
lack *n* **1** *syn* see ABSENCE
2 *syn* see FAILURE 3
lackadaisical *adj syn* see LANGUID
rel incurious, indifferent, unconcerned; faineant, indolent, lazy, slothful; idle, passive; emasculated; romantic, sentimental
con energetic, lusty, strenuous, vigorous; active, dynamic, live

lacking *adj* **1** *syn* see ABSENT 1
2 *syn* see DEFICIENT 1
lacking *prep syn* see WITHOUT 2
lackluster *adj* **1** *syn* see DULL 7
2 *syn* see COLORLESS 2
rel dead, leaden, rusty, tarnished
con lustrous
lackwit *n syn* see DUNCE
laconic *adj syn* see CONCISE
rel brusque
con garrulous, glib, loquacious, talkative
ant verbose, wordy
laconically *adv syn* see BRIEFLY
lacuna *n syn* see GAP 3
lad *n syn* see BOY 1
laddie *n syn* see BOY 1
lade *vb* **1** *syn* see BURDEN
2 *syn* see DIP 2
la–di–da *adj* **1** *syn* see PRECIOUS 4
2 *syn* see GENTEEL 3
ladies' man *n syn* see WOLF
lading *n syn* see LOAD 1
ladle *vb syn* see DIP 2
lady *n* **1** *syn* see WOMAN 1
2 *syn* see WIFE
lady friend *n syn* see GIRL FRIEND 1
lady–killer *n syn* see WOLF
ladylove *n syn* see GIRL FRIEND 2
lag *vb syn* see DELAY 2
rel retard, slacken, slow; stay
lag *adj syn* see LAST
‖**lag** *vb syn* see BANISH
‖**lag** *n syn* see CONVICT
laggard *adj syn* see SLOW 2
rel dawdling, delaying, loitering, procrastinating; comatose, lethargic, sluggish; apathetic, impassive, phlegmatic
con alert, vigilant, watchful, wide-awake; expeditious, fast, fleet, speedy
ant prompt, quick
laggard *n* one that delays unnecessarily or falls behind <no room for *laggards* on the expedition>
syn dawdler, lingerer, loiterer, slow coach, slowpoke, straggler
rel lazybones, loafer
con dynamo, go-ahead, go-getter, hustler, live wire, rustler; eager beaver
lagniappe *n syn* see GRATUITY
lair *n* **1** a resting or living place of a wild animal <photographed the wolf at the entrance to his *lair*>
syn burrow, couch, den, lodge
2 *syn* see HIDEOUT
‖**lalapalooza** *n syn* see ‖DILLY, ‖corker, crackerjack, ‖daisy, dandy, humdinger, jim=dandy, ‖lulu, peach, ‖pip
‖**lallygag** *vb syn* see IDLE
lam *vb syn* see BEAT 1
lam *n syn* see ESCAPE 1
lambaste *vb* **1** *syn* see BEAT 1
2 *syn* see WHIP 2
3 to assail with withering oral or written denunciation <the senator has been publicly *lambasted* for taking bribes>

syn blister, castigate, ‖crawl, drub, excoriate, flay, lash (into), roast, scarify, scathe, scorch, score, scourge, slam, slap, slash, ‖slate; *compare* CRITICIZE, REPROVE, SCOLD 1
rel censure, criticize, denounce, pan; berate, scold, tongue-lash; assail, attack, squabash
idiom burn one's ears, ‖crawl all over, give (one) a roasting, pin one's ears back, rake (one) over the coals, read the riot act, rip into
con applaud, extol, praise; approve, countenance, endorse
lambent *adj syn* see BRIGHT 1
lame–brain *n syn* see DUNCE
lament *vb syn* see DEPLORE 1
ant exult; rejoice
lamentable *adj syn* see DEPLORABLE
2 *syn* see MELANCHOLY 2
lamia *n syn* see WITCH 1
lamp *n syn* see EYE 1
lampoonery *n syn* see SATIRE
lampooning *adj syn* see SATIRIC
lance *vb syn* see IMPALE
land *n* **1** *syn* see EARTH 2
2 *syn* see COUNTRY
3 *syn* see ESTATE 3
land *vb* **1** *syn* see DISEMBARK
2 *syn* see ALIGHT
3 *syn* see GET 1
‖**lang syne** *n syn* see PAST
language *n* **1** a body or system of words and phrases used by a large community or by a people, a nation, or a group of nations <the English and French *languages*>
syn dialect, idiom, speech, tongue, vernacular
rel argot, cant, jargon, lingo, patois, slang
2 *syn* see TERMINOLOGY
languid *adj* lacking in vim or energy <doing the job in a slow and *languid* manner>
syn die-away, enervated, lackadaisical, languishing, languorous, limp, listless, spiritless
rel comatose, lethargic, sluggish, torpid; apathetic, impassive, phlegmatic; inactive, inert, supine
con alert, awake, ‖fly, keen, lively, wide=awake
ant vivacious; chipper
languish *vb syn* see FAIL 1
ant flourish
languishing *adj syn* see LANGUID
rel debilitated, enfeebled, weakened; faineant, indolent; longing, pining, yearning
con hale, healthy, robust, sound; energetic, lusty, vigorous
ant flourishing, thriving; unaffected
languor *n syn* see LETHARGY 1
rel exhaustion, fatigue, weariness; blues, depression, dumps; doldrums, ennui, tedium
con celerity, legerity; gusto, zest
ant alacrity
languorous *adj syn* see LANGUID
rel dilatory, laggard, leisurely, slow; faineant, indolent, slothful; passive; lax, loose, relaxed, slack; indulged, pampered
ant vigorous; strenuous (*of times, seasons*)
lank *adj syn* see LEAN
rel attenuated, extenuated

---

syn synonym(s)   *rel* related word(s)
ant antonym(s)   *con* contrasted word(s)
idiom idiomatic equivalent(s)
‖ use limited; if in doubt, see a dictionary

con chubby
  ant burly
lanky *adj* **1** *syn* see GANGLING
  2 *syn* see LEAN
lap *vb* *syn* see OVERLAP
lap *vb* **1** *syn* see SLOSH 1
  2 *syn* see BATHE 2
lapse *n* **1** *syn* see ERROR 2
  rel crime, offense, sin, vice; failing, foible,
  frailty; breach, transgression, trespass, violation
  2 a temporary deviation or fall especially
  from a higher to a lower state <a *lapse*
  into nonproductiveness> <ashamed of his
  lapse from grace>
  syn backsliding, relapse
  rel decadence, declension, decline, degeneration, deterioration, devolution; recession,
  retrogradation; regression, retrogression
  con advance, progress; development, maturation; amendment; betterment, improvement
lapse *vb* to fall from a better or higher state
  into a lower or poorer one <*lapsed* into his
  old vulgar ways>
  syn backslide, recidivate, relapse
  rel return, revert; slide, slip; decline, degenerate, deteriorate; subside; descend; recede,
  retrograde; apostatize
  con advance, progress; develop, mature;
  amend, mend; better, improve
larcener *n* *syn* see THIEF
larcenist *n* *syn* see THIEF
larcenous *adj* prone to committing larceny
  <*larcenous* employees were robbing the
  company blind>
  syn sticky-fingered, thieving, thievish
  rel burglarious; light-fingered
larceny *n* *syn* see THEFT
‖**lardy–dardy** *adj* *syn* see GENTEEL 3
lares and penates *n pl syn* see POSSESSION
  2
large *adj* **1** above the average of its kind in
  magnitude <a *large* increase in the tax rate>
  syn big, bull, fat, great, husky, oversize
  rel colossal, enormous, gigantic, huge,
  immense, mammoth, vast, voluminous;
  monstrous, monumental, prodigious, stupendous, tremendous; excessive, exorbitant,
  extravagant, extreme, immoderate, inordinate
  con diminutive, little, minute, tiny, wee;
  slender, slight, slim, thin
  ant small
  2 *syn* see BIG 1
largely *adv* *syn* see GENERALLY 1
largeness *n* *syn* see SIZE 2
large–scale *adj* *syn* see BIG 1
largess *n* **1** *syn* see GIFT 1
  2 *syn* see GRATUITY
largest *adj* *syn* see BEST
lark *n* **1** *syn* see ESCAPADE
  2 *syn* see PRANK
larkish *adj* *syn* see PLAYFUL 1
‖**larrup** *vb* **1** *syn* see WHIP 1
  2 *syn* see WHIP 2
‖**larruping** *adv* *syn* see VERY 1
lascivious *adj* **1** *syn* see LICENTIOUS 2
  rel coarse, gross, obscene
  2 *syn* see LUSTFUL 2

lash *vb* **1** *syn* see RUSH 1
  2 *syn* see POUR 3
  3 *syn* see WHIP 1
  4 *syn* see WAG
  5 *syn* see SCOLD 1
lash (into) *vb* *syn* see LAMBASTE 3
lashings *n pl syn* see MUCH
lass *n* **1** *syn* see GIRL 1
  2 *syn* see GIRL FRIEND 1
lassie *n* *syn* see GIRL 1
lassitude *n* **1** *syn* see FATIGUE
  2 *syn* see APATHY 2
  3 *syn* see LETHARGY 1
  rel doldrums, ennui, tedium; blues, depression, dumps; impotence, powerlessness
  con energy, force, might, power, strength
  ant vigor
last *vb* *syn* see CONTINUE 1
last *adj* following all relevant others (as in
  time, order, or importance) <he was the *last*
  one in line>
  syn closing, concluding, eventual, final,
  hindmost, lag, latest, latter, rearmost, terminal, terminating, ultimate
  rel bottommost, end, extreme, furthest,
  outermost, remotest, utmost, uttermost
  con beginning, inaugural, initial, introductory, original, primary, prime
  ant first
lasting *adj* existing or continuing for so long
  a time as to seem fixed or established <his
  reading made a *lasting* impression on him>
  syn diuturnal, durable, enduring, perdurable, perduring, permanent, stable; *compare*
  OLD 2
  rel abiding, continuing, persisting; endless,
  everlasting, unceasing; continual, continuous, incessant, perennial, unremitting; eternal, sempiternal; indelible, indissoluble,
  inexhaustible, inexpungible, inexpungible
  con ephemeral, evanescent, fugitive, momentary, passing, short-lived, transient,
  transitory
  ant fleeting
last word *n* *syn* see APOTHEOSIS 1
late *adj* **1** *syn* see TARDY
  con opportune, seasonable, well-timed
  ant early; prompt, punctual
  2 *syn* see DEAD 1
  3 *syn* see FORMER 2
  4 *syn* see MODERN 1
lated *adj* *syn* see TARDY
lately *adv* *syn* see NEW
latency *n* *syn* see ABEYANCE
latent *adj* not now manifest or showing signs
  of existence or activity <a *latent* infection>
  syn abeyant, dormant, lurking, potential,
  prepatent, quiescent
  rel concealed, hidden; idle, inactive, inert;
  immature, unmatured, unripe
  con active, dynamic, live, operative; activated, energized, vitalized
  ant patent
later *adj* *syn* see SUBSEQUENT 1
later *adv* *syn* see AFTER
  ant earlier
laterally *adv* *syn* see SIDEWAYS 1
latest *adj* *syn* see LAST
  ant earliest
lather *n* **1** *syn* see FOAM

2 *syn* see COMMOTION 4

3 *syn* see COMMOTION 2

lather *vb syn* see WHIP 1

latitude *n syn* see ROOM 3

latrine *n syn* see TOILET

latter *adj syn* see LAST
  ant former

latterly *adv syn* see AFTER

laud *vb syn* see PRAISE 2
  rel adore, revere, reverence, venerate, worship; admire; flatter
  con blame, condemn; anathematize, curse, damn, execrate, objurgate
  ant revile

laudable *adj syn* see WORTHY 1
  ant illaudable

laudative *adj syn* see EULOGISTIC

laudatory *adj syn* see EULOGISTIC

laugh *vb* to show mirth, joy, or scorn with a smile and a usually explosive sound <*laughed* at all the funny things that happened>
  syn chortle, chuckle, giggle, guffaw, heehaw, snicker, ‖sniggle, tehee, titter
  rel cachinnate, cackle, crow, roar, whoop; beam, grin, simper, smile, smirk

laughable *adj* provoking laughter or mirth <the *laughable* antics of the clowns>
  syn comic, comical, droll, farcical, funny, gelastic, ludicrous, ridiculous, risible
  rel amusing, diverting, entertaining, rich; facetious, humorous, jocose, jocular, witty; derisive, derisory, mocking
  con grave, serious, solemn; boring, irksome, tedious, tiresome, wearisome; affecting, impressive, moving, pathetic, poignant, touching

laughingstock *n* an object of ridicule <totally unaware that he was the *laughingstock* of the entire office>
  syn butt, derision, jest, jestee, joke, mock, mockery, pilgarlic, sport
  rel gazingstock; mark, target

launch *vb* 1 *syn* see THROW 1

2 *syn* see BEGIN 1

3 *syn* see INTRODUCE 3

laurels *n pl syn* see HONOR 2

lavatory *n syn* see TOILET

lave *vb syn* see BATHE 2

lavish *adj* 1 *syn* see PROFUSE
  con scant, scanty; economical, frugal, thrifty; discreet, provident, prudent; miserly, niggardly, parsimonious, penurious, stingy
  ant sparing

2 *syn* see GRAND 2

lavishness *n syn* see EXTRAVAGANCE 2
  ant sparingness

law *n* 1 a principle governing conduct, action, or procedure <found it hard to live by outdated *laws*>
  syn assize, canon, decree, decretum, edict, institute, ordinance, precept, prescript, prescription, regulation, rule, statute
  rel command, dictate, mandate

2 *syn* see PRINCIPLE 1
  rel exigency, necessity
  ant chance

lawbreaker *n syn* see CRIMINAL

lawcourt *n syn* see COURT 2

lawful *adj* being in accordance with law <obtained *lawful* custody of the child>
  syn innocent, legal, legitimate, licit
  rel condign, due, rightful; allowable, permissible; justifiable, warrantable; bona fide
  idiom of right
  con flagitious, iniquitous, nefarious; improper, unjustifiable, wrong; criminal, guilty, peccant; illegitimate, illicit
  ant lawless, unlawful

lawless *adj syn* see UNLAWFUL
  ant lawful

lawlessness *n syn* see ANARCHY 1
  rel conflict, contention, difference, discord, dissension, strife, variance

lawsuit *n syn* see SUIT 1

lawyer *n* a person authorized to practice law in the courts or to serve clients in the capacity of legal agent or adviser <took the problem to his family *lawyer*>
  syn attorney, attorney-at-law; *compare* PETTIFOGGER
  rel advocate, ‖barrister, counsel, counselor, ‖mouthpiece, pleader, ‖solicitor; jurisconsult, jurisprudent, jurist; legist

lax *vb syn* see LOOSE 1

lax *adj* 1 *syn* see LOOSE 1
  con firm, hard, solid; elastic, resilient, springy
  ant rigid

2 *syn* see NEGLIGENT
  rel forgetful, oblivious, unmindful
  con austere, severe, stern; rigid, rigorous; conscientious, honest, scrupulous, upright
  ant strict, stringent

lay *vb* 1 *syn* see SET 1

2 *syn* see GAMBLE 1

3 *syn* see EVEN 1

4 *syn* see ASCRIBE

5 *syn* see DIRECT 2

6 *syn* see SET 5

7 *syn* see ADDUCE

lay (for) *vb syn* see SURPRISE 1

lay (open) *vb syn* see EXPOSE 1

lay *n* 1 *syn* see MELODY

2 *syn* see SONG 2

lay *adj syn* see PROFANE 1
  con professional

lay aside *vb* 1 *syn* see DISCARD

2 *syn* see SAVE 4

lay away *vb* 1 *syn* see SAVE 4

2 *syn* see BURY 1

lay by *vb syn* see SAVE 4

lay down *vb* 1 *syn* see RELINQUISH

2 *syn* see PRESCRIBE 2

3 *syn* see DICTATE

layer *n syn* see BOOKMAKER

lay in *vb syn* see SAVE 4

lay low *vb* 1 *syn* see FELL 1

2 *syn* see KILL 1

lay off *vb syn* see REST 3

lay out *vb* 1 *syn* see DESIGN 3

2 *syn* see SPEND 1

lay over *vb syn* see DEFER

lay up *vb* 1 *syn* see ACCUMULATE

---

syn synonym(s)   *rel* related word(s)
ant antonym(s)   *con* contrasted word(s)
idiom idiomatic equivalent(s)
‖ use limited; if in doubt, see a dictionary

2 *syn* see SAVE 4

laze *vb syn* see IDLE
con drudge, grind, labor, toil, travail, work

laze *n syn* see SLOTH 1

laziness *n syn* see SLOTH 1
ant industriousness

lazy *adj* not easily aroused to action or activity <the hot humid weather made them *lazy*>
syn drony, easygoing, faineant, indolent, slothful, slowgoing, work-shy
rel idle, inactive, inert, passive, supine, trifling; comatose, lethargic, sluggish, torpid; lackadaisical, languid, languorous, listless, unenergetic, unindustrious; lax, neglectful, negligent, remiss, shiftless, slack
con diligent, hardworking; brisk, chipper, energetic, vigorous; active, animated, lively, spry, vivacious; prompt, quick, ready
ant industrious

lazy *vb syn* see IDLE

lazybones *n syn* see SLUGGARD

lead *vb* 1 *syn* see GUIDE
rel get, induce, persuade, prevail
con drive, impel; coerce, compel, constrain, force, oblige
ant follow
2 *syn* see PRECEDE 3
3 *syn* see CONVERT 1

lead *n syn* see LEADER 1

leader *n* 1 one that takes the lead or initiative <each group selected its own *leader* for the tour>
syn ‖bell cow, bellwether, dean, doyen, guide, lead, pilot
rel pacemaker, pacesetter; forerunner, harbinger, herald, precursor; conductor, director, rector
con adherent, dependent, hanger-on, henchman, satellite
ant follower
2 a person in whom resides authority or ruling power <the company had only one *leader*>
syn boss, chief, chieftain, cock, dominator, head, headman, hierarch, honcho, master
rel captain, commander, general; director, principal, superintendent, superior; foreman, manager, straw boss
con inferior, subaltern, subordinate, underling, understrapper
3 *syn* see NOTABLE 1

leading *adj* 1 *syn* see FIRST 1
2 *syn* see FIRST 3
ant subordinate
3 *syn* see WELL-KNOWN

lead off *vb syn* see BEGIN 1

lead on *vb* 1 *syn* see LURE
2 *syn* see TRIFLE 2

leaf (through) *vb syn* see BROWSE

leafage *n syn* see FOLIAGE

league *n* 1 *syn* see ALLIANCE 2
2 *syn* see ASSOCIATION 2
3 *syn* see CLASS 1
4 a group of sports clubs or teams that play one another competitively <the new baseball *league*>
syn association, circuit, conference, loop, wheel
rel division

league *vb syn* see UNITE 2

leak *vb syn* see GET OUT 2

lean *vb* 1 *syn* see SLANT 1
rel bend, curve; deflect, divert, sheer, turn
2 *syn* see TEND 1

lean (over) *vb syn* see HANG 4

lean *n syn* see SLOPE

lean *adj* thin because of absence of superfluous flesh <a *lean* working horse>
syn angular, bony, gaunt, lank, lanky, meager, rawboned, scraggy, scrawny, skinny, spare; *compare* THIN 1
rel slender, slight, slim, spare-set, stringy, thin; cadaverous, haggard, pinched, wasted, worn; wizened
con brawny, burly, husky, muscular, sinewy; stalwart, stout, strong, sturdy; corpulent, fat, fatty, flabby, obese, plump, portly, rotund
ant fleshy

leaning *n* 1 *syn* see SLOPE
2 an attraction to a particular activity, thing, or end <a strong *leaning* toward liberal views>
syn bent, bias, disposition, drift, inclination, inclining, lurch, partiality, penchant, predilection, predisposition, proclivity, propensity, sentiment, tendency; *compare* GIFT 2, PREJUDICE
rel favor, favoritism, odds
con avoidance, evasion, shunning; disdaining, scorning, scouting, spurning; disinterest, dislike, distaste

leaning *adj syn* see INCLINED 3

leap *vb* 1 *syn* see JUMP 1
rel arise, ascend, mount, rise, soar
con drop, fall, sink, slump
2 *syn* see CLEAR 8

learn *vb* 1 to acquire knowledge of or skill in by study and experience <*learn* a trade>
syn get, master, pick up
rel con, peruse, study
idiom make oneself master of
2 *syn* see MEMORIZE
3 *syn* see DISCOVER 3

learned *adj* possessing or manifesting unusually wide and deep knowledge <a most *learned* scholar in his field>
syn erudite, scholarly, scholastic
rel cultivated, cultured; academic, bookish, pedantic, professorial; abstruse, esoteric, polymath, recondite
con ignorant, illiterate, uneducated, unlearned, unlettered, untutored

learnedness *n syn* see ERUDITION 2

learning *n syn* see EDUCATION 2

lease *vb syn* see HIRE 1

leash *vb syn* see HAMPER

least *adj syn* see FIRST 4

leave *vb* 1 *syn* see WILL
rel commit, confide, consign, entrust; allot, apportion, assign
2 *syn* see LET 2
3 *syn* see GO 2
4 *syn* see QUIT 6
5 *syn* see RELINQUISH

leave *n* 1 *syn* see PERMISSION
rel assent
con refusal, rejection; forbiddance, interdiction, prohibition

2 *syn* see VACATION
leaven *vb syn* see INFUSE 1
rel moderate, qualify, temper; enliven, quicken, vivify
leave off *vb syn* see STOP 3
leave-taking *n syn* see PARTING
leaving *n, usu* **leavings** *pl syn* see REMAINDER
rel fragments, pieces, portions; discards, junk, scrap
lecherous *adj syn* see LICENTIOUS 2
lecture *n syn* see SPEECH 2
lecture *vb syn* see TALK 7
ledger *n syn* see TOMBSTONE
leech *n syn* see PARASITE
leer *vb syn* see SNEER 1
lees *n pl syn* see SEDIMENT
leeway *n syn* see ROOM 3
left-handed *adj syn* see INSINCERE 1
legacy *n* **1** a gift by will especially of money or personal property <received a *legacy* of $5,000 from her late uncle>
syn bequest, devise, inheritance
2 *syn* see HERITAGE 1
legal *adj syn* see LAWFUL
ant illegal
legal tender *n syn* see MONEY
legate *vb syn* see WILL
legend *n* **1** *syn* see MYTH 1
2 *syn* see CAPTION
3 *syn* see LORE 2
legendary *adj syn* see MYTHICAL
legerdemain *n syn* see MAGIC 2
legion *n syn* see MULTITUDE 1
legion *adj syn* see MANY
legitimate *adj* **1** *syn* see LAWFUL
rel cogent, sound, valid; acknowledged, recognized; customary, usual; natural, normal, regular, typical
ant illegitimate
2 *syn* see TRUE 8
ant arbitrary
leisure *n syn* see REST 1
con drudgery, grind, labor
ant toil
leisurely *adj syn* see SLOW 2
rel lax, relaxed, slack; delayed, retarded, slackened; comfortable, easy, restful
con fast, hasty, quick, rapid, speedy; headlong, impetuous, precipitate
ant hurried; abrupt
leitmotiv *n* a dominant recurring thematic element or feature (as in a work of art) <the *leitmotiv* of man against nature often appears in his paintings>
syn motif
rel motive, theme
lemon *n syn* see FAILURE 5
lend *vb* to give into another's keeping for temporary use on condition that the borrower return the same or its equivalent <I do not have another copy of the book to give, but I can *lend* you mine>
syn advance, loan
rel lease-lend, lend-lease; allow, furnish, give; accommodate, oblige

length *n* **1** *syn* see DISTANCE 1
2 *syn* see RANGE 2
lengthen *vb syn* see EXTEND 3
ant shorten; abbreviate
lengthening *n syn* see EXTENSION 1
ant shortening
lengthways *adv syn* see LENGTHWISE
ant widthways, widthwise
lengthwise *adv* in the direction of the length <the students folded their papers *lengthwise*>
syn endways, endwise, lengthways, longitudinally, longways, longwise
con latitudinally, widthways; broadside, broadway, broadwise
ant widthways, widthwise
lengthy *adj* **1** *syn* see LONG 2
ant short
2 *syn* see LONG 1
lenience *n syn* see FORBEARANCE 2
leniency *n syn* see FORBEARANCE 2
lenient *adj* **1** *syn* see GENTLE 1
ant caustic
2 *syn* see FORBEARING
rel condoning, excusing, forgiving, pardoning; benign, benignant; compassionate, tender; humoring, indulging, pampering, mollycoddling, spoiling
con rigid, rigorous, stringent; austere, severe
ant stern; exacting
3 *syn* see AMIABLE 1
lenity *n syn* see MERCY
rel tenderness; benevolence, charitableness, humaneness
con rigidity, rigorousness, strictness, stringency; austerity, sternness
ant severity
leper *n syn* see OUTCAST
lessen *vb* **1** *syn* see ABRIDGE 1
rel amputate, clip, crop, truncate
2 *syn* see DECREASE
rel attenuate, dilute, thin, weaken
lesser *adj* **1** *syn* see INFERIOR 1
2 *syn* see MINOR 1
lesson *n syn* see EXERCISE 4
lesson *vb syn* see REPROVE
let *vb* **1** *syn* see HIRE 1
2 to neither forbid nor prevent <*let* the boy go to the movies>
syn allow, have, leave, permit, suffer
rel accredit, approve, certify, endorse, sanction; authorize, commission, license; concede, grant
con ban, enjoin, forbid, inhibit, interdict, prohibit; bar, block, hinder, impede, obstruct; circumvent, foil, frustrate, thwart
let down *vb syn* see LOWER 3
lethal *adj syn* see DEADLY 1
con renewing, restorative, restoring
lethality *n syn* see FATALITY 1
lethargic *adj* deficient in alertness or activity <became *lethargic* after taking the drug>
syn comatose, dopey, heavy, hebetudinous, sluggish, slumberous, stupid, torpid
rel dormant, idle, inactive, inert, passive, supine; apathetic, impassive, phlegmatic, spiritless, stolid; lackadaisical, languid, languorous, listless; dilatory, laggard, slow

---

syn synonym(s)   *rel* related word(s)
ant antonym(s)   *con* contrasted word(s)
idiom idiomatic equivalent(s)
‖ use limited; if in doubt, see a dictionary

con alert, aware, responsive; apt, prompt, quick, ready; brisk, gingery, peppery, spirited
ant energetic

lethargy *n* **1** physical and mental inertness <disgusted, he sank into a state of *lethargy*>
syn coma, dullness, hebetude, languor, lassitude, sleep, slumber, stupor, torpidity, torpidness, torpor
rel comatoseness, sluggishness; indolence, laziness, sloth, slothfulness; idleness, inactivity, inertia, inertness, passiveness, supineness; apathy, impassivity, inanition, phlegm
con aptness, promptness, quickness, readiness; alertness, quick-wittedness
ant vigor
2 *syn* see APATHY 2

lethe *n* *syn* see OBLIVION

let off *vb* *syn* see EXEMPT

let on *vb* **1** *syn* see ACKNOWLEDGE 1
2 *syn* see REVEAL 1

let out *vb* ‖ **1** *syn* see REVEAL 1
2 *syn* see DISMISS 3

letter *n* **1** letters *pl syn* see ALPHABET 1
2 a direct or personal written or printed message addressed to a person or organization <wrote several *letters* to her friends>
syn epistle, missive, note
rel dispatch, memorandum, message, report

‖**lettuce** *n* *syn* see MONEY

let up *vb* *syn* see ABATE 4

levee *n* **1** *syn* see WHARF
2 *syn* see RED-LIGHT DISTRICT

level *vb* **1** *syn* see EVEN 1
2 *syn* see DIRECT 2
3 *syn* see FELL 1

level *adj* having a surface without bends, curves, or irregularities <looked for a *level* spot to land the plane>
syn even, flat, flush, planate, plane, smooth
rel akin, alike, identical, like, parallel, similar, uniform; aligned; regular; equal, equivalent, same
con bumpy, irregular, lumpy, uneven; unaligned, unparallel; changing, varying; fluctuating, rolling, swaying, undulating; coarse, rough

lever *vb* *syn* see PRY

leviathan *n* *syn* see GIANT

leviathan *adj* *syn* see HUGE

levity *n* *syn* see LIGHTNESS
rel absurdity, folly, foolishness, silliness
con collection, quietude, sobriety
ant gravity

levy *n* *syn* see TAX 1

levy *vb* to determine and require satisfaction of (as a tax or obligation) <several broadbased taxes were *levied*>
syn assess, exact, impose, put (on *or* upon)
rel extort, wrest, wring; charge, lay (on *or* upon), place, set
con remit; abate, diminish, lessen

lewd *adj* *syn* see LICENTIOUS 2
rel coarse, gross, obscene; improper, indecent, indelicate
con modest, proper, self-restrained; temperate
ant chaste

lexicon *n* **1** *syn* see VOCABULARY 1
2 *syn* see TERMINOLOGY

liability *n* **1** *syn* see DEBT 3
ant asset
2 *syn* see INDEBTEDNESS 1
3 *syn* see EXPOSURE

liable *adj* **1** *syn* see RESPONSIBLE
rel bound, tied
con exempt, immune; free, independent
2 being likely to be affected by some usually adverse contingency or action <without the heat shield he was *liable* to be burned>
syn exposed, obnoxious, open, prone, sensitive, subject, susceptible
rel assailable, penetrable, vulnerable; attackable, beatable, conquerable, vincible
ant unliable
3 *syn* see APT 1
ant unliable

liaison *n* *syn* see AMOUR 2

liar *n* one that tells lies <he is a compulsive *liar*>
syn Ananias, falsifier, fibber, fibster, perjurer, prevaricator, storyteller

libel *vb* *syn* see MALIGN
rel burlesque, caricature, travesty

libelous *adj* injurious to reputation <the campaign degenerated into an exchange of *libelous* statements>
syn backbiting, calumnious, defamatory, detracting, detractive, detractory, invidious, maligning, scandalous, slanderous, traducing, vilifying
rel depreciative, depreciatory, derogative, disparaging, pejorative; contumelious, debasing, malevolent, vituperative
con adulating, adulatory, applauding, commendatory, eulogistic, eulogizing, laudatory, praising

liberal *adj* **1** marked by generosity and openhandedness <a *liberal* allowance for his son>
syn bounteous, bountiful, free, freehanded, generous, handsome, munificent, openhanded, unsparing
rel exuberant, lavish, prodigal, profuse; benevolent, charitable, eleemosynary, philanthropic
con closefisted, miserly, niggardly, parsimonious, penurious, stingy, tight, tightfisted; meager, scanty
ant close
2 *syn* see PLENTIFUL
3 not bound by authoritarianism, orthodoxy, or traditional forms <modern young people usually have a *liberal* attitude toward sex>
syn advanced, broad, broad-minded, progressive, radical, tolerant, wide
rel forbearing, indulgent, lenient
con rigid, rigorous, strict, stringent; dictatorial, doctrinaire, dogmatic, oracular; conservative, reactionary
ant authoritarian

liberate *vb* *syn* see FREE
rel detach, unhook; untangle; disembarrass
con bind, tie; ensnare, entrap, snare, trap; constrain, restrain, restrict

libertine *adj* *syn* see LICENTIOUS 2
con ethical; continent, sober, temperate
ant straitlaced

liberty *n* *syn* see FREEDOM

rel autonomy, independence; delivery, emancipation, enfranchisement, liberation
con circumscription, confinement, limitation, restriction
ant restraint

libidinous *adj* **1** *syn* see LICENTIOUS 2
rel coarse, gross, obscene
2 *syn* see LUSTFUL 2

library *n* a place in which literary, musical, artistic, or reference materials (as books or films) are kept for use but not for sale <planned to study all evening in the *library*>
syn archive(s), athenaeum
rel reading room

license *n* *syn* see FREEDOM
rel laxity, looseness, relaxation, slackness
con duty, obligation; decency, propriety; continence, sobriety, temperance
ant decorum

license *vb* *syn* see AUTHORIZE 1
rel allow, let, permit, suffer; certify, sanction
con check, curb, restrain
ant ban

licentious *adj* **1** *syn* see ABANDONED 2
2 disregarding sexual restraints <a coarse *licentious* man>
syn fast, incontinent, lascivious, lecherous, lewd, libertine, libidinous, lustful, randy, salacious, satyric
rel animal, carnal, fleshly, oversexed, sensual; abandoned, dissolute, profligate, reprobate; corrupt, debauched, depraved, scabrous; amoral, immoral, unmoral; lax, loose, relaxed
con chaste, decent, pure; moral, virtuous; rigid, strict; ascetic, austere, severe
ant continent

licit *adj* *syn* see LAWFUL
rel approved, sanctioned; authorized, licensed
con banned, forbidden, inhibited, interdicted, prohibited
ant illicit

lick *vb* **1** *syn* see WHIP 2
2 *syn* see OVERCOME 1

lick *n* **1** *syn* see HINT 2
2 *syn* see HIT 1

lickerish *adj* *syn* see LUSTFUL 2
lickerishness *n* *syn* see LUST 2
lickety–split *adv* *syn* see FAST 2
licking *n* *syn* see DEFEAT 1
lickspit *n* *syn* see SYCOPHANT
lickspittle *n* *syn* see SYCOPHANT
lie *vb* **1** *syn* see REST 1
2 *syn* see CONSIST 1

lie *vb* to be untruthful directly or indirectly <*lying* under oath is a crime>
syn equivocate, falsify, fib, palter, prevaricate
rel beguile, deceive, delude, misguide, misinform, misinstruct, mislead; distort, exaggerate, misstate

lie *n* a statement or declaration that is not true <was sued for printing *lies* about the candidate>

---

syn ‖bouncer, canard, cock-and-bull story, falsehood, falsity, fib, inveracity, misrepresentation, misstatement, prevarication, ‖rapper, story, tale, taradiddle, untruism, untruth
rel deceitfulness, dishonesty, distortion, fraudulence, inaccuracy, mendacity; fable, flam, myth; falsification, forgery, libel, perjury; fish story, song and dance
con veracity, verisimilitude, verity
ant truth

lie by *vb* *syn* see REST 3
lied *n* *syn* see SONG 2
lie down *vb* *syn* see REST 1
liege *adj* *syn* see FAITHFUL 1
lieutenant *n* *syn* see ASSISTANT 2
life *n* **1** *syn* see BIOGRAPHY
2 *syn* see HUMAN
3 *syn* see SPIRIT 5

lifeless *adj* **1** *syn* see DEAD 1
ant living
2 *syn* see COLORLESS 2
ant lifeful

lifelong *adj* *syn* see OLD 2
lifework *n* *syn* see MISSION
lift *vb* **1** to remove from a lower to a higher place or position <*lifted* the sack to his shoulder>
syn elevate, hoist, pick up, raise, rear, take up, uphold, uplift, upraise, uprear
rel arise, ascend, levitate, mount, rise, rocket, soar, surge, tower; aggrandize, exalt, magnify
con decrease, diminish, lessen, reduce; abase, debase, degrade, demean, humble, humiliate; depress, oppress, weigh
ant lower
2 *syn* see REVOKE 2
ant invoke
3 *syn* see STEAL 1
4 *syn* see RISE 4

lift *n* **1** *syn* see THEFT
2 *syn* see HELP 1

lifted *adj* *syn* see ELEVATED 1
ligament *n* *syn* see BOND 3
ligature *n* *syn* see BOND 3
light *n* *syn* see DAWN 1
light *adj* *syn* see FAIR 3
light *vb* **1** to cause something to start burning <*lighted* the fuse on the dynamite>
syn enkindle, fire, ignite, inflame, kindle
con douse, ‖dout, put out, quench, snuff; damp (down), smother, stamp (out)
ant extinguish
2 *syn* see ILLUMINATE 1

light *adj* **1** having little weight <the package was *light*>
syn featherlight, featherweight, imponderous, lightweight, unheavy, weightless
rel inconsequential, trifling, trivial; little, petty, small; flimsy, meager, slender, slight
idiom light as a feather
con bulky, burdensome, cumbersome, huge, massive, overweight, ponderous, portly, unwieldy, weighty
ant heavy
2 *syn* see EASY 1
ant arduous
3 *syn* see FAST 7
4 *syn* see GIDDY 1

---

syn synonym(s)   *rel* related word(s)
ant antonym(s)   *con* contrasted word(s)
idiom idiomatic equivalent(s)
‖ use limited; if in doubt, see a dictionary

5 *syn* see LITTLE 3
6 *syn* see DIZZY 2
light *vb* 1 *syn* see ALIGHT
2 *syn* see HAPPEN 2
lighted *adj syn* see BURNING 1
ant unlighted, unlit
lighten *vb syn* see ILLUMINATE 1
ant darken
lighten *vb syn* see RELIEVE 1
rel attenuate, dilute, extenuate, thin
con depress, oppress, weigh
light-headed *adj* 1 *syn* see GIDDY 1
2 *syn* see DIZZY 2
lighthearted *adj* 1 *syn* see HAPPY-GO≈
LUCKY
ant heavyhearted
2 *syn* see GLAD 1
rel buoyant, effervescent, expansive, resilient, volatile; high-spirited, spirited; gay, lively, sprightly, vivacious
con gloomy, glum, morose, sullen
ant despondent
3 *syn* see MERRY
ant heavyhearted
lighthouse *n* a building equipped to guide sea navigators by means of a powerful light <rowed out to the *lighthouse*>
syn beacon, pharos
rel direction, guidance
lightless *adj syn* see DARK 1
ant bright, ‖lightful
lightly *adv syn* see EASILY 1
light-mindedness *n syn* see LIGHTNESS
lightness *n* gaiety or indifference where seriousness and attention are called for <a crisis that allowed no room for *lightness*>
syn flightiness, flippancy, frivolity, levity, light-mindedness, volatility
rel buoyancy, effervescence, elasticity, expansiveness, resiliency; gaiety, liveliness, vivacity; cheerfulness, lightheartedness
con earnestness, gravity, sedateness, soberness, somberness, staidness
ant seriousness
light-o'-love *n syn* see DOXY 1
light out *vb syn* see HEAD 3
lightsome *adj* 1 *syn* see CHEERFUL 1
2 *syn* see HAPPY-GO-LUCKY
lightweight *adj syn* see LIGHT 1
like *vb* 1 *syn* see ENJOY 1
rel choose, elect, prefer, select; admire, esteem, regard, respect; approve, endorse; appreciate, comprehend, understand
ant dislike
2 *syn* see WILL
like *adj* being so similar as to appear to be the same or nearly the same (as in appearance, character, or quantity) <shirts of *like* design>
syn agnate, akin, alike, analogous, comparable, consonant, corresponding, equivalent, intercomparable, parallel, similar, such, suchlike, undifferenced, undifferentiated, uniform; *compare* SAME 2
rel equal, equivalent, identical, same, selfsame; allied, cognate, close, related, resembling; coextensive, commensurate
idiom of that ilk, on the order of
con different, disparate, divergent, diverse, various; dissimilar, distinct; discordant, discrepant, inconsistent, inconsonant

ant unlike
like *n syn* see EQUAL
likely *adj* 1 *syn* see PROBABLE
con problematic; certain, inevitable, necessary
ant unlikely
2 *syn* see APT 1
ant unlikely
3 *syn* see HOPEFUL 2
likely *adv syn* see PRESUMABLY
liken *vb syn* see EQUATE 2
likeness *n* agreement or correspondence in details (as of appearance, structure, or quality) <the remarkable *likeness* of the two cousins>
syn affinity, alikeness, analogy, comparison, resemblance, semblance, similarity, simile, similitude
rel equality, equivalence, identicalness, identity, sameness; agreement, conformity, correspondence; analogousness, comparableness, parallelism, uniformity
con difference, dissimilarity, distinction, divergence, divergency; disaffinity, opposition
ant unlikeness
likewise *adv* 1 *syn* see ALSO 1
2 *syn* see ALSO 2
liking *n* 1 *syn* see APPETITE 3
ant disliking
2 *syn* see WILL 1
lilliputian *adj syn* TINY, diminutive, minute, teensy, teensy-weensy, teenty, teeny, teeny-weeny, wee, weeny
ant Brobdingnagian
lilliputian *n syn* see DWARF
lily-livered *adj syn* see COWARDLY
lily-white *adj syn* see GOOD 11
limb *n* 1 a member of a woody plant that is an outgrowth from a main stem or from one of its divisions <hung the swing from a tree's *limb*>
syn bough, branch
rel shoot, spray, sprig, switch, twig; arm
2 *syn* see SCAMP
limber *adj syn* see SUPPLE 3
rel plastic, pliable, pliant; elastic, flexible, resilient, springy
con inflexible, rigid, stark, stiff, tense, wooden
limit *n* 1 a material or immaterial point beyond which something does not or cannot extend <there seemed no *limit* to the problems they faced>
syn bound, confine(s), end, limitation, term; *compare* ENVIRONS 1
rel circumscription, confinement, restriction, termination; border, brim, brink, edge, margin, rim, verge
2 **limits** *pl syn* see ENVIRONS 1
3 *syn* see EXTREME 2
limit *vb* 1 *syn* see DEMARCATE 1
2 to prescribe or serve as a restricting boundary <*limited* the naughty child to the house for three days> <ignorance that *limits* spiritual growth>
syn bar, circumscribe, confine, delimit, delimitate, prelimit, restrict
rel constrict, contract, lessen, narrow, pinch; check, curb, hinder, inhibit, restrain; appoint, assign, define, prescribe, set

con enlarge, expand, extend, increase, widen; develop, grow
ant broaden

limitation *n* **1** *syn* see LIMIT 1
2 *syn* see RESTRICTION 1

limited *adj* **1** *syn* see DEFINITE 1
rel inexhaustive, inextensive
con boundless, infinite
ant unlimited
2 *syn* see FINITE
3 *syn* see QUALIFIED 2
4 *syn* see LITTLE 2

limitless *adj* having no limits <the *limitless* black of deep space>
syn boundless, endless, immeasurable, indefinite, infinite, measureless, unbounded, unlimited, unmeasured
rel bottomless, countless, incalculable, incomprehensible, inexhaustible, innumerable, undrainable, unfathomable, vast, wasteless
con bound, bounded, finite, fixed, limited, measurable; comprehensible, fathomable; confined, restricted
ant limited

limn *vb* *syn* see REPRESENT 1

limp *vb* **1** to walk lamely <*limped* across the floor after his fall>
syn halt, hitch, hobble
rel toddle, totter, waddle; falter, stagger, stumble, wobble
2 *syn* see STUMBLE 6

limp *adj* **1** deficient in firmness of texture, substance, or structure <plants going *limp* from lack of water>
syn flabby, flaccid, flimsy, floppy, sleazy
rel lax, loose, relaxed, slack; limber, supple
con inflexible, rigid, stark, stiff, tense, wooden; firm, hard, solid; brittle, crisp
2 *syn* see LANGUID

limpid *adj* *syn* see TRANSPARENT 1

limpidity *n* *syn* see CLARITY

line *n* **1** *syn* see WAY 2
2 *syn* see COURSE 3
3 *syn* see WORK 1
‖**4** *syn* see SPIEL
5 a series of things arranged in continuous or uniform order <a *line* of cars waiting at the light>
syn echelon, file, queue, rank, row, string, tier
rel column, progression, succession, train; sequence, series
6 *syn* see OUTLINE
7 *syn* see MERCHANDISE

line *vb* **1** to arrange in a line or lines <*lined* the bottles along the shelf>
syn align, allineate, line up, range
rel arrange, array, marshal, order, ordinate
con derange, disarrange, disorder, disturb; disperse, dissipate, scatter
2 *syn* see ADJOIN

lineage *n* **1** *syn* see ANCESTRY
2 *syn* see FAMILY 1

lineal *adj* *syn* see DIRECT 1

lineament *n* *syn* see OUTLINE

lineation *n* *syn* see OUTLINE

line up *vb* *syn* see LINE 1

linger *vb* **1** *syn* see STAY 2
2 *syn* see DELAY 2
3 *syn* see SAUNTER

lingerer *n* *syn* see LAGGARD

lingo *n* *syn* see DIALECT 2

link *n* *syn* see BOND 3

link *vb* *syn* see JOIN 1

lint *n* *syn* see DOWN

lion *n* *syn* see NOTABLE 1

lionhearted *adj* *syn* see BRAVE 1

‖**lip** *n* *syn* see BACK TALK

lip *vb* **1** *syn* see KISS 1
2 *syn* see BATHE 2

lip server *n* *syn* see HYPOCRITE

liquefy *vb* to convert or to become converted to a liquid state <*liquefy* a block of ice by heating>
syn deliquesce, dissolve, flux, fuse, liquesce, melt, run, thaw
rel soften; thin
con clot, coagulate, congeal; harden; set; gel, jellify, jelly; condense, inspissate, thicken
ant solidify

liquesce *vb* *syn* see LIQUEFY

liquid *adj* *syn* see MELLIFLUOUS

liquidate *vb* **1** *syn* see CLEAR 5
2 *syn* see PURGE 3
3 *syn* see MURDER 1

liquor *n* **1** *syn* see DRINK 1
2 an intoxicating beverage usually distilled after being fermented <belted down a slug of *liquor*>
syn alcohol, aqua vitae, booze, ‖budge, drink, firewater, grog, ‖hooch, inebriant, intoxicant, ‖joy-juice, ‖juice, ‖lush, ‖sauce, spirit(s), ‖strunt, tipple
idiom Demon Rum, the bottle

liquor (up) *vb* *syn* see DRINK 3

lissome *adj* *syn* see SUPPLE 3

list *n* a series of items (as names) written down or printed especially as a memorandum or record <all the people on the *list* were present>
syn catalog, register, roll, roll call, roster, schedule
rel checklist, handlist; index; inventory

list *vb* **1** *syn* see ENUMERATE 2
2 *syn* see ITEMIZE 1
3 to enter in a list <his name was not *listed* in the telephone book>
syn book, catalog, enroll, inscribe
rel file, index, note, post, schedule, tabulate; record, register, roster
4 *syn* see ENROLL 1

list *vb* *syn* see SLANT 1

listen *vb* to perceive by ear usually with careful or responsive attention <now hear me; *listen* to my words>
syn attend, hark, hear, hearken, heed
idiom give a hearing to, give ear to, hang upon the lips (*or* words) of, keep one's ears open, lend one's (*or* an) ear, pick up one's ears, strain one's ears

listless *adj* *syn* see LANGUID
rel careless, heedless, thoughtless

---

syn synonym(s)   *rel* related word(s)
ant antonym(s)   *con* contrasted word(s)
idiom idiomatic equivalent(s)
‖ use limited; if in doubt, see a dictionary

con agog, anxious, avid, keen; alert, vigilant, watchful; energetic, lusty, vigorous; prompt, quick, ready
ant eager

listlessness *n syn* see APATHY 2

‖**lit** *adj syn* see INTOXICATED 1

literal *adj syn* see VERBATIM

literally *adv syn* see VERBATIM

literati *n pl syn* see INTELLIGENTSIA

literatim *adv syn* see VERBATIM

lithe *adj syn* see SUPPLE 3
rel slender, slight, slim, thin; lean, spare
con awkward, clumsy, gauche, inept, maladroit; inflexible, stiff, tense, wooden

lithesome *adj syn* see SUPPLE 3

litigious *adj syn* see CONTENTIOUS 2

litter *n* 1 *syn* see REFUSE
2 *syn* see CLUTTER 2

little *adj* 1 *syn* see SMALL 1
ant big
2 contemptibly limited <men with *little* minds picking at flaws in a great leader>
syn borné, ineffectual, limited, mean, narrow, paltry, set, small
rel bigoted, hidebound, illiberal, narrow-minded, provincial; contemptible; niggard, niggardly, self-centered, selfish
ant great
3 lacking importance <the nagging *little* details of a job>
syn casual, inconsiderable, insignificant, light, minor, minute, petty, ‖potty, shoestring, small, small-beer, trivial, unimportant; *compare* PETTY 2
rel fortuitous; incidental; collateral, secondary, subordinate, subsidiary
con consequential, meaningful, significant, substantial, weighty; basal, basic, essential, foundational, fundamental
ant important

little *adv syn* see SELDOM
ant much

little by little *adv syn* see GRADUALLY

‖**little woman** *n syn* see WIFE

‖**lit up** *adj syn* see INTOXICATED 1

liturgy *n* 1 *syn* see FORM 2
2 *syn* see RITE 2

livable *adj* 1 suitable for living <a very *livable* apartment>
syn habitable, inhabitable, lodgeable, occupiable, tenantable
rel cozy, homelike, homey, snug; acceptable, bearable, tolerable
ant unlivable
2 *syn* see BEARABLE

live *vb* 1 *syn* see BE
2 *syn* see RESIDE 1

live *adj syn* see ACTIVE 1
rel effective, effectual, efficacious, efficient
ant inactive, inert; dormant (*as a volcano*); defunct (*as an institution, journal*)

livelihood *n syn* see LIVING
rel art, craft, handicraft, profession, trade; emolument, fee, pay, salary, stipend, wage

lively *adj* 1 keenly alive and brisk <always thought of as a *lively* teacher>
syn alert, animate, animated, bright, ‖cant, ‖canty, chipper, ‖chirk, dashing, gay, keen, peart, peppy, pert, rousing, spirited, spirity, sprightful, sprightly, unpedantic, vivacious; *compare* CHEERFUL 1

rel agile, brisk, nimble, spry; buoyant, effervescent, elastic, expansive, resilient, volatile; blithe, cock-a-hoop, jocund, jolly, merry; gleeful, hilarious, mirthful; chirping, chirpy, chirrupy
con lethargic, sluggish, torpid; lackadaisical, languid, languorous, listless; apathetic, impassive, phlegmatic, stolid; boring, irksome, tedious
ant dull, unlively
2 *syn* see AGILE
idiom full of pep
3 *syn* see ENERGETIC 2
4 *syn* see BUSTLING
ant unanimated

liven *vb syn* see QUICKEN 1

liver *n syn* see INHABITANT

live wire *n syn* see HUSTLER 1

livid *adj* 1 *syn* see PALE 1
rel grisly; dusky, gloomy, murky
con bright, brilliant, effulgent, lucent, luminous, lustrous, radiant
2 *syn* see SENSATIONAL 2

living *adj* 1 having or showing life <the *living* things of a locality>
syn alive, animate, animated, vital, zoetic
rel being, existing, subsisting; active, dynamic, live, operative
con dead, deceased, defunct, demised, departed, gone, inanimate
ant lifeless
2 *syn* see EXTANT 1

living *n* supplies or resources needed to live <kept trying to earn a *living* the honest way>
syn alimenation, alimony, bread, bread and butter, keep, livelihood, maintenance, salt, subsistence, support, sustenance
rel sustainment, sustentation

load *n* 1 something which is carried, conveyed, or transported from one place to another <a *load* of grain just arrived>
syn burden, cargo, freight, haul, lading, payload
rel bale, pack, parcel; shipment
2 something heavy <could not lift the *load*>
syn weight
3 a burdensome or laborious responsibility <considered taking care of the children a heavy *load*>
syn burden, charge, deadweight, duty, millstone, onus, task, tax, weight
rel care, liability, obligation, responsibility; drag, drain, pressure
idiom millstone around one's neck
con breeze, child's play, cinch, duck soup, picnic, ‖pipe, pushover, snap
ant sinecure
4 *usu* **loads** *pl syn* see SCAD

load *vb* 1 *syn* see BURDEN
rel bear, carry, convey, transport
ant unload
2 *syn* see ADULTERATE
3 to make full or overfull <a basket *loaded* with fresh fruit>
syn charge, choke, fill, heap, pack, pile; *compare* CRAM 1
rel glut, gorge, surfeit; flood, oversupply, swamp

loaded *adj* 1 *syn* see FULL 1

‖2 *syn* see INTOXICATED 1
loaf *vb syn* see IDLE
  con labor, toil, travail, work
loafer *n syn* see SLUGGARD
loan *vb syn* see LEND
loan shark *n* one who lends money to individuals at exorbitant rates of interest <got involved with *loan sharks*>
  syn Shylock, usurer
  rel lender, loaner, moneylender; shark
loath *adj syn* see DISINCLINED
  ant anxious
loathe *vb syn* see HATE
  rel decline, refuse, reject, repudiate, spurn
  con covet, crave, desire, want, wish
  ant tolerate
loathing *n syn* see ABOMINATION 2
  ant tolerance
loathsome *adj syn* see OFFENSIVE
  rel hateful, invidious, obnoxious
  con bearable, endurable, sufferable, supportable; engaging, inviting; alluring, bewitching, charming, enchanting, fascinating
  ant tolerable
lobby *n syn* see VESTIBULE
lobster *n syn* see OAF 2
local *adj syn* see INSULAR
  ant cosmopolitan
locale *n syn* see SCENE 3
  rel area, district, neighborhood, vicinage, vicinity
locality *n* 1 a more or less definitely circumscribed place or region <searched for the child in the *locality* of the waterfront>
  syn area, district, neighborhood, vicinage, vicinity
  rel belt, region, tract, zone; section, sector; bailiwick, domain, field, province, sphere, territory
  idiom neck of the woods
  2 *syn* see HABITAT
located *adj syn* see SITUATED
location *n syn* see PLACE 1
‖**loch** *n syn* see INLET
lockup *n syn* see JAIL
‖**loco** *adj syn* see INSANE 1
locum tenens *n syn* see SUBSTITUTE 1
locus *n syn* see PLACE 1
locution *n syn* see PHRASE 2
lodge *vb* 1 *syn* see HARBOR 2
  rel accept, admit, receive, take; accommodate, contain, hold
  2 *syn* see ENTRENCH 1
lodge *n* 1 *syn* see HUT
  2 *syn* see HOTEL
  3 *syn* see LAIR 1
lodgeable *adj syn* see LIVABLE 1
lodging *n* 1 *syn* see ACCOMMODATIONS
  2 usu lodgings pl *syn* see APARTMENT 1
lodgment *n syn* see ACCOMMODATIONS
loftiest *adj syn* see TOP 1
loftiness *n syn* see PRIDE 3
lofty *adj* 1 *syn* see PROUD 1
  2 *syn* see AMBITIOUS 2
  3 *syn* see GRAND 3

4 *syn* see GENEROUS 1
5 *syn* see ELEVATED 4
6 extending or rising high in the air so as to have great or imposing height <a *lofty* monument to human aspiration>
  syn aerial, airy, skyscraping, soaring, spiring, topless, towering, towery; *compare* HIGH 1
  rel elevated, lifted, raised; aggrandized, exalted, magnified; august, imposing, majestic, stately
  con humble, low, modest
logical *adj* 1 *syn* see RATIONAL
  ant illogical
  2 having or showing skill in thinking or reasoning <a *logical* argument>
  syn analytic, analytical, ratiocinative, subtle
  rel cogent, compelling, convincing, sound, telling, valid; clear, lucid, perspicuous; rational, reasonable; discriminating
  con instinctive, intuitive; irrational, unreasonable; casuistical, sophistical
  ant illogical
logo *n syn* see MARK 7
logotype *n syn* see MARK 7
loiter *vb* 1 *syn* see DELAY 2
  2 *syn* see IDLE
loiterer *n syn* see LAGGARD
loll *vb* 1 *syn* see SLOUCH
  2 *syn* see IDLE
‖**lollop** *vb syn* see SLOUCH
lone *adj* 1 having no company <a *lone* figure walking through the snow>
  syn alone, lonely, lonesome, solitary
  rel single, sole, unique; abandoned, deserted, forsaken; isolated, secluded
  con attended, chaperoned, companioned, convoyed, escorted
  ant accompanied
  2 *syn* see ONLY 2
  3 *syn* see SINGLE 1
lonely *adj* 1 *syn* see LONE 1
  2 *syn* see FORLORN 1
loneness *n syn* see SOLITUDE
lonesome *adj* 1 *syn* see LONE 1
  2 *syn* see FORLORN 1
  3 *syn* see OBSCURE 2
long *adj* 1 having considerable extension in space or time <a *long* road> <it has been a *long* time since we have seen you>
  syn elongate, elongated, extended, lengthy
  rel extensive, longish, outstretched
  con brief, curtailed
  ant short
  2 unduly extended <went through many *long* days of misery>
  syn dragging, drawn-out, ‖dreich, lengthy, long-drawn-out, longsome, overlong, prolonged, protracted
  rel diffuse, diffusive, long-winded, prolix; flatulent, verbose, wordy
  con ephemeral, evanescent, fleeting, fugacious, fugitive, impermanent, passing, short-lived, transient, transitory; abbreviated, abridged, curtailed, shortened
  ant brief
long *n syn* see AGE 2
long *vb* to desire urgently <*long* for peace>
  syn ache, crave, dream, hanker, hunger, itch, lust, pine, sigh, suspire, thirst, yearn, yen

---

syn synonym(s)   *rel* related word(s)
ant antonym(s)   *con* contrasted word(s)
idiom idiomatic equivalent(s)
‖ use limited; if in doubt, see a dictionary

rel aim, aspire, want; miss

idiom have an appetite (*or* a longing) for

con abhor, detest, dread, fear, loathe

longanimity *n syn* see PATIENCE

||**long green** *n syn* see MONEY

longitudinally *adv syn* see LENGTHWISE

ant horizontally

long-lasting *adj syn* see OLD 2

ant ephemeral

long-lived *adj syn* see OLD 2

ant short-lived

longsome *adj syn* see LONG 2

long-suffering *n syn* see PATIENCE

rel subduedness; humility, lowliness, meekness

con impatience, uneasiness; irksomeness, tediousness, wearisomeness; boredom, ennui, tedium

long suit *n syn* see FORTE

rel specialism, specialization, specialty

longtimer *n syn* see VETERAN

con apprentice, neophyte, novice; newcomer, rookie, tenderfoot

||**long tongue** *n syn* see GOSSIP 1

longways *adv syn* see LENGTHWISE

long-winded *adj syn* see WORDY

rel extended, lasting, lengthy, long, long-drawn-out, prolonged, protracted

con brief, close, compact

longwise *adv syn* see LENGTHWISE

||**loo** *n syn* see TOILET

looby *n syn* see OAF 2

look *vb* 1 to make sure or take care (that something is or is not done) <*look* that you accuse no one unjustly>

syn mind, see, watch

rel attend, heed, tend; note, notice, observe; beware

2 *syn* see SEE 2

rel note, notice, observe, spot

idiom get a load of, take a gander at

3 *syn* see EXPECT 1

rel divine, forecast, foretell

ant despair (of)

4 to make apparent by the expression of the eyes or countenance <*looked* her annoyance at this interruption>

syn exhibit, show; *compare* SHOW 1

rel display, express, indicate, manifest

5 *syn* see SEEM

idiom strike one as

6 *syn* see FACE 1

7 to gaze in wonder or surprise <you should have seen them *look*>

syn eye, gape, ||gaup (*or* gawp), gaze, goggle, ogle, rubberneck, stare; *compare* GAZE 1

rel gawk; glare, gloat, glower; peer

8 *syn* see TEND 1

look (at *or* upon) *vb syn* see EYE 1

look (into) *vb syn* see EXPLORE

look *n* 1 the directing of one's eyes in order to see <he wanted one last *look* before departing>

syn sight, view

rel glance, glimpse, peek, peep, squint; cast, slant; eye, ||gander, ||look-see, regard; eyeful, gaze, stare, survey

2 facial aspect especially as indicative of mood or feeling <you should have seen the *look* on her face>

syn cast, countenance, expression, face, visage

rel mug, physiognomy, ||puss

3 *syn* see APPEARANCE 1

look down *vb* 1 *syn* see OVERLOOK 2

2 *syn* see DESPISE

3 *syn* see STARE DOWN

looker *n syn* see BEAUTY

looker-on *n syn* see SPECTATOR

look in *vb syn* see VISIT 2

look-in *n syn* see OPPORTUNITY

looking glass *n syn* see MIRROR 1

look out *vb syn* see BEWARE

lookout *n* 1 *syn* see GUARD 2

2 an elevated place affording a wide view for observation <guards posted at a *lookout* to watch for enemy troops entering the valley>

syn observatory, outlook, overlook

rel watchtower; crow's nest; cupola, widow's walk; fire tower

3 a careful looking or watching <kept a constant *lookout* for new developments>

syn surveillance, tout, vigil, vigilance, watch, watch and ward

rel observance, observation

4 *syn* see VISTA

5 *syn* see BUSINESS 8

look up *vb* 1 *syn* see IMPROVE 3

2 *syn* see VISIT 2

loom *vb* 1 *syn* see APPEAR 1

2 to take shape as an impending occurrence <an international economic crisis *looms* ahead>

syn brew, forthcome, gather, impend

rel approach, come on, make up, near

con disappear, fade, pass, vanish; die (down *or* away), diminish, dwindle, wane; recede, retreat, withdraw

3 to appear in an impressively great or exaggerated form <the power of the enemy *loomed* in the soldiers' imagination>

syn bulk, stand out

rel lower, rear, threaten, tower

con die (down *or* away), diminish, dwindle, wane

loon *n syn* see LUNATIC 1

loony *adj* 1 *syn* see FOOLISH 2

2 *syn* see INSANE 1

loony *n syn* see LUNATIC 1

loony bin *n syn* see ASYLUM 3

loop *n* 1 a curving or doubling of a line so as to form a closed or partly open curve <the transit makes a *loop* around town>

syn eye, ring

rel circlet, circuit, circumference, hoop, wreath; curve

2 a circular or curved piece used often to form a fastening or a handle <one of his belt *loops* is broken>

syn eye, ring, staple

rel hook

3 *syn* see LEAGUE 4

loop *vb syn* see SURROUND 1

rel arc, arch, bend, coil, curve

looped *adj syn* see INTOXICATED 1

loopy *adj syn* see FOOLISH 2

loose *adj* 1 not tightly bound, held, restrained, or stretched <*loose* rope>

syn lax, relaxed, slack
rel detached, free; flabby, flaccid, limp; desultory, negligent, remiss
con rigid, rigorous, stringent, taut, tense; exact, precise; bound, checked, curbed, inhibited, restrained, tied
ant strict; tight

2 *syn* see FREE 2
rel clear; disconnected, unattached, unconnected, undone, unfastened
con fast

3 not dense, close, or compact in structure <*loose* soil>
syn incoherent, nonadhesive
rel disconnected, disjointed, separate, unconnected
con compressed, condensed, contracted; concentrated, crammed, crowded, localized; close, compact, dense, thick

4 *syn* see FAST 7
rel capricious, extravagant, free, inconstant, reckless, unrestrained

loose *vb* 1 *syn* see FREE
2 *syn* see TAKE OUT (on)
3 to set free from a fastened or fixed condition <*loose* a knot>
syn disengage, unbind, undo, unfasten, unfix, unloose, unloosen
rel unbandage, unbar, unbolt, unbuckle, unbutton, unchain, unclasp, unglue, unhitch, unhook, unlace, unlash, unlatch, unlock, unpin, unscrew, unsnap, unstick, unstrap, untie
con bind, engage, fasten, fix, secure
4 *syn* see SHOOT 1
5 to make less rigid or tight <exercise *loosed* his muscles>
syn ease, ease off, lax, loosen, relax, slack, slacken, untighten
rel abate, alleviate, bate, lessen, let up, mitigate
con anchor, cement, clamp, clinch, fasten, knit, secure, set, tauten
ant tighten

loose-lipped *adj* *syn* see TALKATIVE
ant closemouthed

loosen *vb* 1 *syn* see LOOSE 5
ant tighten
2 *syn* see FREE

loosen up *vb* *syn* see RELAX 2
ant tighten (up)

loose-tongued *adj* *syn* see TALKATIVE
ant closemouthed

loot *n* 1 *syn* see SPOIL
rel lift, pillage, seizure
2 *syn* see MONEY

loot *vb* *syn* see ROB 1

looter *n* *syn* see MARAUDER

lop *vb* 1 *syn* see SLOUCH
2 *syn* see JUMP 1

lope *vb* *syn* see SKIP 1
rel run, sprint; romp, trip

‖**lopper** *vb* *syn* see CURDLE

lopsided *adj* lacking in balance, symmetry, or proportion <the arrangement of the furniture was *lopsided*>

syn asymmetric, difform, disproportional, disproportionate, irregular, nonsymmetrical, off-balance, overbalanced, proportionless, unbalanced, unequal, uneven, unproportionate, unsymmetrical
rel cockeyed, crooked, top-heavy, unsteady
con balanced, even, regular, symmetrical

loquacious *adj* *syn* see TALKATIVE
rel jabbering, overtalkative; prolix, verbose, wordy
con breviloquent, concise, succinct, taciturn, terse; abrupt, brusque, curt

lord *n* *syn* see HUSBAND

lord *vb* to affect an air of superiority and authority <nouveau riche love to *lord* it>
syn cock, peacock, pontificate, swagger, swank, swell
rel affect, pretend, put on; boss, order (about *or* around), overawe, overbear; tyrannize
idiom put on airs

Lord Harry *n* *syn* see DEVIL 1

lordly *adj* 1 *syn* see GRAND 1
2 *syn* see PROUD 1
rel egotistic, puffed; affected, snobbish, swollen; authoritarian, dictatorial, magisterial
con humble; abject, mean; subdued, submissive

lore *n* 1 *syn* see KNOWLEDGE 2
2 a body of traditions relating to a person, institution, or place <the Scottish Highlands are rich in local *lore*>
syn folklore, legend, myth, mythology, mythos, tradition
rel custom, folkway, traditionalism; fable, old wives' tale, saga, superstition, tale

Lorelei *n* *syn* see SIREN

lorn *adj* 1 *syn* see DERELICT 1
2 *syn* see FORLORN 1

lose *vb* 1 to suffer deprivation of <lost all his savings in a poor investment>
syn drop, forfeit, sacrifice
rel mislay, misplace, miss; give up, relinquish, surrender, yield
con cash in, profit; clear, make, realize, take in; obtain, win
ant gain
2 to fail to win, gain, or obtain <lost every contest she entered>
syn drop, lose out
rel decline, fall, succumb, yield
ant win
3 *syn* see DEPRIVE 2
4 *syn* see SHAKE 5
5 *syn* see RID

lose out *vb* *syn* see LOSE 2

loser *n* 1 *syn* see FAILURE 5
rel also-ran, underdog
ant winner
2 *syn* see CONVICT

losing *n* *syn* see LOSS 1

loss *n* 1 the action of having something go out of one's control or possession <took precautions against *loss* or theft of his property>
syn losing, mislaying, misplacement, misplacing; *compare* PRIVATION 2
rel forfeit, forfeiture, sacrifice; bereavement, deprivation, deprivement, dispossession, divestiture, divestment, privation

syn synonym(s)　　*rel* related word(s)
ant antonym(s)　　*con* contrasted word(s)
idiom idiomatic equivalent(s)
‖ use limited; if in doubt, see a dictionary

2 *syn* see PRIVATION 2

3 *syn* see RUIN 3

lost *adj* 1 *syn* see DAMNED 1

rel incorrigible, irreclaimable, irredeemable, irreformable, unconverted, unregenerate; graceless

2 no longer possessed <earned his *lost* reputation by his outrageous behavior>

syn gone, missing

rel absent, lacking; past; irrecoverable, irretrievable, irrevocable

con cherished, protected, treasured

3 *syn* see EXTINCT 2

4 *syn* see ABSTRACTED

rel absorbed; daydreamy, musing, unconscious

lot *n* 1 *syn* see SHARE 1

2 *syn* see FATE

rel decree, fortune; foreordination, predestination, predetermination

3 a measured portion of land having fixed boundaries <building *lots*>

syn parcel, plat, plot, tract

rel clearing, field, patch; part, plottage; block, frontage, real estate

4 *syn* see GROUP 3

rel aggregate, aggregation, conglomerate, conglomeration

5 *syn* see SET 5

6 *syn* see TYPE

7 *syn* see MUCH

lot *vb syn* see ALLOT

‖**lot** (on *or* upon) *vb syn* see RELY (on *or* upon)

lot (out) *vb syn* see DISTRIBUTE 1

lothario *n syn* see GALLANT 2

loud *adj* 1 marked by intensity or volume of sound <a *loud* blast on a trumpet>

syn blaring, earsplitting, full-mouthed, piercing, roaring, stentorian, stentorious, stentorophonic

rel booming, deafening, ear-piercing, fulminating, pealing, ringing, thunderous; resonant, resounding, sonorous; harsh, hoarse, raucous, stertorous, strident

con dulcet, gentle, mellifluous, mellow, quiet, smooth

ant low, soft

2 *syn* see GAUDY

rel brassy, vulgar; obnoxious, offensive; obtrusive

loudmouthed *adj syn* see VOCIFEROUS

‖**lough** *n syn* see INLET

lounge *vb syn* see IDLE

rel drift, vegetate; dally, slack; lie, lie down, recline

lounge *n syn* see BAR 5

lounge car *n syn* see PARLOR CAR

lounge lizard *n* 1 *syn* see FOP

2 *syn* see PARASITE

louse *n syn* see SNOT 1

louse up *vb syn* see BOTCH

lout *n syn* see OAF 2

rel boor, bumpkin, churl, clodhopper, hayseed, hick, peasant, rube, rustic, yokel; dolt

lout *vb syn* see RIDICULE

loutish *adj syn* see BOORISH

rel awkward, bungling, clumsy, inept, maladroit, rusty; callow, crude, gauche, raw, rough, uncouth

lovable *adj* gifted with traits and qualities that attract affection <a *lovable* child>

syn adorable, lovesome

rel admirable, agreeable, attractive, desirable, genial, likable, pleasing, winning, winsome; alluring, appealing, bewitching, captivating, charming, enchanting, engaging, enthralling, entrancing, fetching, ravishing, seductive

con dislikable, displeasing, distasteful, unattractive, unlikable, unpleasing; odious, offensive; abhorrent, abominable, obnoxious, repellent; contemptible, despicable, detestable

ant hateful; unlovable

love *n* 1 the feeling which animates a person who is genuinely fond of someone or something <a mother's *love* for her child>

syn affection, attachment, devotion, fondness

rel like(s), liking, regard; adoration, idolatry, piety, worship; allegiance, fealty, fidelity, loyalty; emotion, sentiment; crush, infatuation, passion, yearning; ardency, ardor, enthusiasm, fervor, zeal

con antipathy, aversion; animosity, animus, enmity, hostility, rancor; abhorrence, detestation, hatred

ant hate

2 the affection and tenderness felt by lovers <the ability to distinguish between *love* and lust was the mark of her maturity>

syn amorousness, amour, passion

rel crush, infatuation; desire, lust, yearning; ardency, ardor, fervor

idiom (the) tender passion

3 *syn* see LOVE AFFAIR

4 *syn* see SWEETHEART 1

love *vb* 1 to like or desire actively <she *loves* her material possessions all too dearly>

syn adore, delight (in), ‖eat up

rel appreciate, cherish, prize, treasure, value; dote (on *or* upon), fancy

idiom hold dear

con abjure, give up, reject, relinquish

2 to feel a lover's passion, devotion, or tenderness for <in spite of all their misfortunes, they continued to *love* each other devotedly>

syn adore, affection, worship

rel deify, exalt, idolize, revere, venerate; cherish, dote (on *or* upon); admire, fancy, like

con avoid, disregard, ignore, neglect, overlook, shun, slight

3 *syn* see CARESS

love affair *n* a romantic attachment or episode between lovers <saddened by the end of a summer *love affair*>

syn affair, amour, love, romance

rel flirtation, intrigue; triangle, ménage à trois

love child *n syn* see BASTARD 1

loved *adj syn* see FAVORITE 1

love letter *n* a letter expressing a lover's affection <she had never received a *love letter*>

syn billet-doux, mash note

rel valentine

loveling *n syn* see SWEETHEART 1

lovely *adj syn* see BEAUTIFUL
 rel alluring, bewitching, captivating, charming, enchanting, engaging, entrancing, lovesome; delectable, delightful; dainty, delicate, exquisite, rare; graceful
 ant hideous; unlovely

lovely *n syn* see BEAUTY

lover *n* **1** a man who is a woman's regular partner in nonmarital sexual activity
 syn boyfriend, fancy man, man, master, paramour
 rel cavalier servente, sugar daddy
 2 *syn* see BOYFRIEND 2
 3 *syn* see ADDICT
 4 *syn* see MISTRESS

lovesome *adj* **1** *syn* see LOVABLE
 2 *syn* see LOVING

lovey-dovey *adj syn* see SENTIMENTAL

loving *adj* feeling or expressing love <his *loving* son unfailingly waited upon him during his last years>
 syn affectionate, dear, devoted, doting, fond, lovesome
 rel adoring, attached, benevolent, cordial, kind, tender, warmhearted; attentive, caring, considerate, solicitous; amatory, amorous, erotic; enamored, infatuated; ardent, fervent, impassioned, passionate; faithful; bound up
 con aloof, detached, indifferent, unconcerned; chilly, cold, frigid
 ant unloving

low *adj* ‖**1** *syn* see SHORT 2
 rel squatty; unelevated
 2 *syn* see INFERIOR 1
 3 *syn* see POOR 1
 4 *syn* see IGNOBLE 1
 rel lowbred, rude
 5 *syn* see BASE 3
 rel scrubby, scruffy; miserable, woebegone, woeful
 con decent, decorous, proper, seemly; ethical, moral, noble; high, lofty
 6 *syn* see COARSE 3
 7 *syn* see UNWELL
 rel declining, weak; dizzy, faint, feverish
 8 *syn* see DOWNCAST
 9 of lesser degree, size, or amount than average or ordinary <the energy crisis resulted in *lower* speed limits for all vehicles>
 syn subaverage, subnormal
 rel fallen, reduced; brief, short; mediocre, moderate; atypical
 10 *syn* see CHEAP 1
 rel economical; moderate, nominal; cut, cut-rate, marked down, slashed
 con elevated, enhanced, increased, raised

lowborn *adj syn* see IGNOBLE 1
 ant highborn

lowbred *adj syn* see BOORISH
 ant highbred

low-cost *adj syn* see CHEAP 1

low-down *adj syn* see BASE 3

lower *vb syn* see FROWN 1
 rel peer, stare; intimidate, menace, threaten

lower *adj syn* see INFERIOR 1
 ant higher

lower *vb* **1** *syn* see FALL 1
 ant rise
 2 *syn* see DEPRECIATE 1
 rel demote; de-escalate, deflate
 con raise
 3 to cause or allow to descend <*lowered* the landing gear of the aircraft>
 syn couch, demit, depress, droop, let down, sink
 rel detrude, submerge; debase, reduce
 con elevate, hoist, lift, pull up, raise
 4 *syn* see REDUCE 2
 ant raise
 5 *syn* see HUMBLE
 ant elevate

lowering (*or* **louring**) *adj* **1** *syn* see IMMINENT 2
 rel frowning, gloomy, sullen; black, dark; foreboding, impending, portentous
 2 *syn* see OVERCAST

lowermost *adj syn* see BOTTOMMOST
 ant uppermost

lowery (*or* **loury**) *adj syn* see IMMINENT 2

lowest *adj syn* see BOTTOMMOST
 ant highest

low-grade *adj syn* see INFERIOR 2

low-key *adj syn* see SUBDUED 2

low-keyed *adj syn* see SUBDUED 2

lowlife *n* **1** *syn* see WRETCH 1
 2 *syn* see VILLAIN 1

lowly *adj* **1** *syn* see HUMBLE 1
 rel retiring, withdrawing; deferential, obeisant, reverential; obsequious, servile
 ant haughty
 2 *syn* see IGNOBLE 1
 3 *syn* see PROSAIC 3

low-pressure *adj syn* see EASYGOING 3
 ant high-pressure

low-priced *adj syn* see CHEAP 1

‖**low-rate** *vb syn* see DECRY 2

low-set *adj syn* see SHORT 2

low-spirited *adj syn* see DOWNCAST
 ant high-spirited

low-statured *adj syn* see SHORT 2

loyal *adj syn* see FAITHFUL 1
 con faithless; alienated, disaffected, estranged; contumacious, factious, insubordinate, mutinous, rebellious, seditious
 ant disloyal

loyalist *n syn* see PATRIOT 1

loyalty *n* **1** *syn* see FIDELITY 1
 rel trueness, truth
 ant disloyalty
 2 *syn* see ATTACHMENT 1

lubber *n syn* see OAF 2

lubberland *n syn* see UTOPIA

lubberly *adj syn* see BOORISH

‖**lubricate** *vb syn* see BRIBE

lubricious *adj* **1** *syn* see INCONSTANT 1
 2 *syn* see SLICK 1

lucent *adj* **1** *syn* see BRIGHT 1
 2 *syn* see CLEAR 4

lucid *adj* **1** *syn* see BRIGHT 1
 2 *syn* see SANE 2
 3 *syn* see UNDERSTANDABLE
 4 *syn* see CLEAR 4
 con dusky, gloomy, murky; muddy, turbid

lucidity *n* **1** *syn* see CLARITY

---

syn synonym(s)   *rel* related word(s)
ant antonym(s)   *con* contrasted word(s)
idiom idiomatic equivalent(s)
‖ use limited; if in doubt, see a dictionary

rel comprehensibility, intelligibility, understandability; distinctness, explicitness
ant ambiguity
2 *syn see* WIT 2
Lucifer *n syn see* DEVIL 1
luck *n* **1** *syn see* CHANCE 2
rel break, occasion, opportunity
2 *syn see* ACCIDENT 1
3 success dependent on chance <he had all the *luck* in the world and was greatly envied by every one of his associates>
syn fortunateness, fortune, luckiness
rel advantage, break, fluke, godsend, opportunity, windfall; weal; hap, kismet
ant ill-fortune
4 *syn see* CHARM 2
luck *vb syn see* HAPPEN 2
luckiness *n syn see* LUCK 3
luckless *adj syn see* UNLUCKY
rel miserable, wretched
ant lucky
lucky *adj* having a favorable outcome or an unforeseen or unpredictable success <he can only be described as *lucky*, as his success and fame are unearned>
syn fortunate, happy, providential, ‖sonsy, well
rel auspicious, benign, favorable, propitious; advantageous, beneficial, profitable; felicitous
idiom in luck
con baleful, malefic, maleficent, malign, sinister
ant luckless, unlucky
lucrative *adj syn see* ADVANTAGEOUS 1
lucre *n* **1** *syn see* PROFIT
2 *syn see* MONEY
luculent *adj syn see* CLEAR 4
ludicrous *adj syn see* LAUGHABLE
rel absurd, foolish, preposterous, silly; antic, bizarre, fantastic, grotesque
con doleful, dolorous, lugubrious, melancholy
lug *vb* **1** *syn see* PULL 2
2 *syn see* CARRY 1
3 *syn see* JERK
‖**lug** *n syn see* OAF 2
lugs *n pl syn see* POSE 2
lugubrious *adj* **1** *syn see* MELANCHOLY 2
rel depressing, oppressing, oppressive; dour, glum, morose, saturnine, sullen
con blithe, jocund, jolly, jovial, merry; cheerful, glad, joyful
ant facetious
2 *syn see* GLOOMY 3
lukewarm *adj* **1** *syn see* TEPID 1
2 *syn see* TEPID 2
rel irresolute, irresolved, uncommitted, unresolved; hesitant, indecisive, uncertain, undecided; cool; wishy-washy
ant icy; boiling
lull *vb* **1** *syn see* CALM
rel moderate, qualify, temper
ant agitate
2 *syn see* ABATE 4
lull *n* **1** *syn see* QUIET 1
2 *syn see* PAUSE
rel abeyance, quiescence
lullaby *n* a song to quiet children or lull them to sleep <sang a *lullaby* to the baby every night>

syn berceuse, cradlesong
‖**lulu** *n syn see* ‖DILLY
lumber *vb* to tread heavily or clumsily <the tired old man slowly *lumbered* home>
syn barge, clump, galumph, stumble, stump
rel plod, trudge; shamble, slog
lumber *vb syn see* BURDEN
lumbering *adj* **1** *syn see* CLUMSY 1
rel cumbersome, cumbrous, ponderous; hulking, hulky
2 *syn see* AWKWARD 2
luminary *n* **1** *syn see* CELEBRITY 2
rel leading light
2 *syn see* NOTABLE 1
luminous *adj* **1** *syn see* BRIGHT 1
2 *syn see* CLEAR 4
3 *syn see* UNDERSTANDABLE
lummox *n syn see* OAF 2
lump *n* **1** a compact mass of indefinite size and shape <dropped a large *lump* of butter into the steaming chowder>
syn chunk, clod, clump, gob, hunch, hunk, nugget, wad
rel particle, piece, portion; batch, bunch, ‖swad; bit, chip, crumb, morsel, scrap; wedge; block, bulk
2 *syn see* MUCH
3 *syn see* BUMP 2
rel bulge, protuberance, swelling
4 *syn see* OAF 2
5 lumps *pl syn see* DUE 1
lump *vb syn see* BEAR 10
lumpish *adj* **1** *syn see* BOORISH
2 *syn see* CLUMSY 1
lumpkin *n syn see* OAF 2
lumpy *adj syn see* RUDE 1
lunacy *n* **1** *syn see* INSANITY 1
rel absurdity, folly, foolery, foolishness; asininity, fatuity, inanity, ineptitude, stupidity
2 *syn see* FOOLISHNESS
lunatic *adj* **1** *syn see* INSANE 1
2 *syn see* FOOLISH 2
lunatic *n* **1** a person who is insane or of unsound mind <Bedlam was a famous old English asylum for *lunatics*>
syn bedlamite, dement, loon, loony, madling, madman, maniac, non compos, nut, Tom o' Bedlam
rel demoniac, energumen; raver; neuropath, neurotic, paranoid, psycho, psychoneurotic
2 *syn see* CRACKPOT
lunch counter (*or* bar) *n syn see* EATING HOUSE
luncheonette *n syn see* EATING HOUSE
lunchroom *n syn see* EATING HOUSE
lunch wagon (*or* cart) *n syn see* EATING HOUSE
lunge *vb syn see* PLUNGE 2
lunk *n syn see* DUNCE
lunkhead *n syn see* DUNCE
lupanar *n syn see* BROTHEL
lurch *n syn see* LEANING 2
lurch *vb* **1** *syn see* SEESAW
2 to move forward unsteadily while swaying from side to side <the sodden drunk *lurched* uncertainly toward the door>
syn careen, stagger, ‖stoit, ‖stoiter, ‖stot, sway, swing, weave, wobble; *compare* TEETER

rel reel, rock, roll, swag, toss, totter, whirl; bob; wave, waver
con march, stride
3 *syn* see TEETER
rel pitch, plunge
4 *syn* see JERK
5 *syn* see WALLOW 2
6 *syn* see STUMBLE 3

lure *n* **1** *syn* see ATTRACTION 1
2 something that leads an individual into a place or situation from which escape is difficult <used her charm as a *lure* to trap the unsuspecting youth>
syn allurement, bait, come-on, decoy, enticement, inveiglement, seducement, siren song, ∥stale, temptation, trap
rel appeal, attraction, incentive, inducement; con game, gimmick, suck-in, trick; ambush, blind, camouflage, delusion, fake, illusion
con caution, caveat, warning

lure *vb* to draw from a usual, desirable, or proper course or situation into one felt as unusual, undesirable, or wrong <the promise of money *lured* him away from his steady job>
syn allure, bait, decoy, entice, entrap, inveigle, lead on, seduce, tempt, toll, train
rel bag, capture, catch, draw in, ensnare, rope, snare, suck in; attract, beguile, bewitch, captivate, charm, enchant, fascinate, invite; draw, draw on; blandish, cajole, wheedle
idiom bait the hook, give the come-on
con drive (away *or* off), rebuff, repulse
ant repel

lurid *adj* **1** *syn* see PALE 1
2 *syn* see GHASTLY 1
rel ashen, ashy, livid, pale, pallid, wan; baleful, malefic, maleficent, malign, sinister
3 *syn* see SENSATIONAL 2

luring *adj syn* see ENTICING
ant repellent, repelling

lurk *vb syn* see SNEAK

lurking *adj syn* see LATENT

luscious *adj* **1** *syn* see DELIGHTFUL
rel appetizing, flavorsome, nectarious, palatable, piquant; choice, distinctive, exquisite, rare, rich
ant austere
2 *syn* see LUXURIOUS 3
3 *syn* see SENSUOUS
4 *syn* see ORNATE

lush *adj* **1** *syn* see PROFUSE
rel luxurious, sumptuous
2 *syn* see DELIGHTFUL
3 *syn* see SENSUOUS
4 *syn* see LUXURIOUS 3

lush *n* ∥**1** *syn* see LIQUOR 2
2 *syn* see DRUNKARD

lush (up) *vb syn* see DRINK 3

∥**lushed** *adj syn* see INTOXICATED 1

∥**lusher** *n syn* see DRUNKARD

lust *n* **1** *syn* see DESIRE 1
rel coveting, yearning, yen

2 sexual appetency <they mistakenly thought that *lust* was lasting love>
syn aphrodisia, concupiscence, desire, eroticism, itch, lickerishness, lustfulness, passion, prurience, pruriency
rel nymphomania, priapism, satyriasis, satyrism; excitement, heat, hunger, libido, rut; fervor; carnality, lasciviousness, lecherousness, lechery, lubricity, salacity

lust *vb syn* see LONG
rel desire, wish

luster *n* the quality or condition of shining by reflected light <the satiny *luster* of fine pearls>
syn glaze, glint, gloss, polish, sheen, shine
rel iridescence, opalescence; brilliance, brilliancy, effulgence; luminosity, radiance, refulgence; afterglow, gleam, glow; candescence, incandescence

lusterless *adj* **1** *syn* see DULL 7
ant lustrous
2 *syn* see COLORLESS 2

lustful *adj* **1** *syn* see LICENTIOUS 2
2 sexually excited <*lustful* old man>
syn concupiscent, goatish, hot, lascivious, libidinous, lickerish, passionate, prurient, ruttish, rutty, satyric
rel burning, hot-blooded, itching; lecherous, salacious

lustfulness *n syn* see LUST 2

lustral *adj syn* see PURGATIVE

lustrate *vb syn* see PURIFY 2

lustration *n syn* see PURIFICATION

lustratory *adj syn* see PURGATIVE

lustrous *adj* **1** having a high gloss or shine <a *lustrous* star sapphire>
syn burnished, gleaming, glistening, glossy, polished, sheeny, shining, shiny
rel gleamy, glimmering, glinting, sparkling; radiant
con dull, flat, lackluster, mat
ant lusterless
2 *syn* see BRIGHT 1
rel glorious, resplendent, splendid

lusty *adj* **1** *syn* see VIGOROUS
rel hale, healthy
ant effete
2 *syn* see STRONG 3
3 *syn* see HUGE

lusus *n syn* see FREAK 2

luxuriant *adj* **1** *syn* see PROFUSE
rel fecund, fertile, fruitful, prolific; rampant, rank
con barren, infertile, sterile, unfruitful
2 *syn* see LUXURIOUS 3

luxuriate *vb syn* see WALLOW 3
rel overindulge, overdo; eat up, enjoy, feast, love, riot

luxurious *adj* **1** *syn* see SENSUOUS
rel self-indulging, self-pampering; languishing, languorous
con self-abnegating, self-denying; austere, severe, stern
ant ascetic
2 *syn* see GRAND 2
rel imposing, majestic, stately
3 ostentatiously rich or magnificent <the robber barons built *luxurious* homes which rivaled the palaces of Europe>

---

syn synonym(s)   *rel* related word(s)
ant antonym(s)   *con* contrasted word(s)
idiom idiomatic equivalent(s)
∥ use limited; if in doubt, see a dictionary

syn Capuan, deluxe, luscious, lush, luxuriant, opulent, palace, palatial, plush, plushy,
sumptuous, upholstered
rel extravagant, grandiose, ostentatious,
posh, pretentious, showy; awful, grand,
imposing, magnificent, majestic, stately;
Lucullan; elaborate, fancy; costly, expensive, precious
con economical, frugal, sparing, thrifty;
exiguous, meager, scant, scanty, scrimpy,
skimpy, spare
luxury *n* something adding to pleasure but
not absolutely necessary <the poor cannot
even afford the essentials, let alone occa-

sional *luxuries*>
syn amenity, extravagance, frill, luxus,
superfluity
rel comfort; embellishment, redundancy,
self-indulgence; dainty, delicacy
con basics, essential(s), fundamental(s)

luxus *n syn* see LUXURY
lying *adj syn* see DISHONEST
rel false, wrong; deceptive, delusive, delusory, misleading
lying–in *n syn* see CONFINEMENT 2
lyncean *adj syn* see SHARP-EYED
lynx–eyed *adj syn* see SHARP-EYED

M

ma *n syn* see MOTHER 1
macabre *adj syn* see GHASTLY 1
rel deadly, deathlike, deathly; ghostlike,
ghostly
macaroni *n syn* see FOP
mace *n syn* see CUDGEL
‖**mace** *n syn* see SWINDLER
‖**mace** *vb syn* see CHEAT
machinate *vb* 1 *syn* see ENGINEER
2 *syn* see PLOT
machination *n syn* see PLOT 2
machine *n* 1 *syn* see CAR
2 *syn* see ROBOT 2
machinery *n syn* see EQUIPMENT
rel agency, agent, channel, instrument,
instrumentality, means, medium, organ,
vehicle; contraption, contrivance, device,
gadget; appliance, implement, instrument,
tool, utensil
‖**mack** *n syn* see PIMP 1
macquereau *n syn* see PIMP 1
macrocosm *n syn* see UNIVERSE
ant microcosm
macrocosmos *n syn* see UNIVERSE
ant microcosm
mad *adj* 1 *syn* see INSANE 1
rel delirious, frantic, frenetic, furious, rabid,
wild
2 *syn* see FOOLISH 2
3 *syn* see ILLOGICAL
4 *syn* see ANGRY
rel sore, worked up; affronted, offended,
outraged
5 *syn* see FURIOUS 2
mad *vb syn* see ANGER 1
mad *n syn* see ANGER
mad–brained *adj syn* see RASH 1
madcap *adj syn* see RASH 1
madden *vb* 1 to make insane <prolonged
solitary confinement had *maddened* the
prisoners>
syn craze, derange, distract, frenzy, unbalance, unhinge
rel shatter; possess
idiom drive insane (*or* mad *or* crazy)

2 *syn* see ANGER 1
con allay, assuage, mitigate, relieve
made–to–order *adj* *syn* see CUSTOM⸗
MADE
madhouse *n syn* see ASYLUM 3
madid *adj syn* see WET 1
madling *n syn* see LUNATIC 1
madly *adv syn* see HARD 2
rel foolishly, insanely, irrationally; hastily,
rashly
madman *n* 1 *syn* see LUNATIC 1
2 *syn* see FOOL 1
madness *n syn* see INSANITY 1
maelstrom *n syn* see EDDY
rel commotion, confusion, fury, storm,
turmoil
mafia *n syn* see CLIQUE
magazine *n* 1 *syn* see DEPOT 2
rel cache, lumber room
2 *syn* see ARMORY
3 *syn* see JOURNAL
rel publication; digest, gazette; annual,
bimonthly, biweekly, daily, monthly, quar-
terly, semiweekly, weekly
mage *n syn* see MAGICIAN 1
maggot *n syn* see CAPRICE
magian *n syn* see MAGICIAN 1
magian *adj syn* see MAGIC
magic *n* 1 the use of means (as charms or
spells) believed to have supernatural power
over natural forces <the practice of *magic*>
syn bewitchment, conjuring, conjury, enchantment, ensorcellment, incantation,
magicking, necromancy, sorcery, thaumaturgy, witchcraft, witchery, witching, wizardry
rel abracadabra, alchemy, augury, charm,
divining, exorcism, fortune-telling, mumbo
jumbo, occultism, soothsaying, sortilege,
voodooism; devilry, deviltry, diablerie,
diabolism, satanism; wicca
2 the art of producing mysterious effects by
illusion and sleight of hand <the club presented a program of clever *magic* to raise
funds>

syn conjuring, legerdemain

idiom sleight of hand

magic *adj* having seemingly supernatural qualities or powers <modern medicine has developed a host of *magic* drugs>

syn magian, magical, mystic, necromantic, sorcerous, thaumaturgic, witchy, wizardly

rel extraordinary, marvelous, prodigious, remarkable, stupendous, unbelievable, unprecedented

magical *adj syn* see MAGIC

magician *n* **1** one who practices magical arts <a *magician* cast a spell over the child>

syn archimage, charmer, conjurer, enchanter, mage, magian, magus, necromancer, sorcerer, voodoo, voodooist, warlock, wizard; *compare* WITCH 1

rel augurer, brujo, diviner, exorciser, exorcist, invocator, thaumaturge, thaumaturgist; medicine man, shaman; prophet, seer, soothsayer; fortune-teller, medium; diabolist, satanist

2 one who practices tricks of illusion and sleight of hand <a *magician* performed tricks for the children at the party>

syn conjurer, illusionist, trickster

magicking *n syn* see MAGIC 1

magisterial *adj* **1** *syn* see DICTATORIAL

rel disdainful, insolent, lordly, supercilious

2 *syn* see MASTERFUL 1

3 *syn* see POMPOUS 1

magistrate *n syn* see JUDGE 2

magnanimous *adj syn* see GENEROUS 1

rel altruistic, liberal, unselfish; great, highminded, knightly, noble, nobleminded, princely

con measly, paltry, petty, picayune, picayunish

magnate *n* a businessman of exceptional wealth, influence, or power <the oil and steel *magnates* who controlled whole nations>

syn baron, czar, king, merchant prince, mogul, prince, tycoon

rel figure, name, personage; ‖biggie, big gun, big-timer; ‖big wheel, fat cat, lion, nabob; plutocrat

idiom captain of industry

magnetic *adj syn* see ATTRACTIVE 1

rel arresting, irresistible; charismatic

con repellent, repugnant, repulsive

magnetism *n syn* see CHARM 3

magnetize *vb syn* see ATTRACT 1

magnific *adj syn* see GRAND 1

magnificent *adj* **1** *syn* see GRAND 1

rel glorious, resplendent, splendid, sublime, superb; luxurious, opulent, sumptuous

con abject, ignoble, mean, sordid; humble, lowly, meek; paltry

ant modest

2 *syn* see SPLENDID 2

3 *syn* see SUPERB 3

magnify *vb* **1** *syn* see PRAISE 2

2 *syn* see EXALT 1

rel augment, enlarge, increase; amplify, dilate, distend, expand, inflate, swell

3 *syn* see INCREASE 1

ant minify

4 *syn* see INTENSIFY

5 *syn* see OVERPLAY 2

6 *syn* see EMBROIDER

magniloquent *adj syn* see RHETORICAL

magnitude *n* **1** *syn* see ENORMITY 2

2 *syn* see SIZE 1

3 *syn* see SIZE 2

4 *syn* see ORDER 4

5 *syn* see IMPORTANCE

magnum opus *n syn* see MASTERPIECE 1

magpie *n syn* see CHATTERBOX

magus *n syn* see MAGICIAN 1

mahogany *n syn* see TABLE 1

maid *n* **1** *syn* see GIRL 1

2 a woman hired to do housework <in addition to her other duties the *maid* was expected to care for the baby>

syn biddy, girl, handmaid, hired girl, housemaid, maidservant

rel au pair girl; chambermaid, nursemaid, parlormaid; handmaiden; domestic, factotum, ‖muchacha, servant

idiom maid of all work

maiden *n syn* see GIRL 1

maiden *adj* **1** *syn* see VIRGIN 1

rel husbandless; old-maidish, spinsterish, spinsterly

2 *syn* see FIRST 2

maidenhead *n syn* see VIRGINITY

maidenhood *n syn* see VIRGINITY

maiden lady *n syn* see SPINSTER

maidservant *n syn* see MAID 2

maim *vb* to wound so severely as to deprive of the use of or to cause loss of a limb or member <an arm hanging useless, *maimed* in an auto accident>

syn cripple, dislimb, dismember, mayhem, mutilate; *compare* PARALYZE 1

rel disable, disfigure, hamstring; batter, break, ‖bung up, mangle, massacre, maul

con rehabilitate, restore, salvage; cure, fix, heal, mend, remedy, repair

main *n syn* see OCEAN

main *adj syn* see CHIEF 2

rel foremost, head, leading, paramount; cardinal, controlling, essential, fundamental, vital; prevailing

‖**main** *adv syn* see VERY 1

‖**mainline** *vb syn* see SHOOT UP 2

mainly *adv syn* see GENERALLY 1

mainstay *n* a chief reliance <the *mainstay* of the organization held things together>

syn backbone, pillar, sinew(s)

rel brace, buttress, crutch, maintainer, prop, staff, standby, stay, support, supporter, sustainer, upholder

maintain *vb* **1** to keep in a state of repair, efficiency, or validity <he followed a careful regimen to *maintain* his good health>

syn keep up, preserve, save, sustain; *compare* SAVE 3

rel husband, manage; care (for), cultivate; guard, protect

con disregard, ignore, neglect, omit, overlook, slight

2 to uphold as true, right, proper, or acceptable often in the face of challenge or indiffer-

---

ence <I *maintain* that his actions were justified by the circumstances>
syn argue, assert, claim, contend, defend,
justify, vindicate, warrant
rel affirm, aver, avouch, avow, declare,
profess, protest; emphasize, insist, persist,
stress; correct, rectify, right
con contradict, deny, gainsay, traverse;
challenge, query, question
3 *syn* see SUPPORT 3

maintenance *n syn* see LIVING

majestic *adj* 1 *syn* see GRAND 1
rel courtly, dignified; ceremonious; imperial
2 *syn* see KINGLY

major *adj* 1 *syn* see CHIEF 2
rel better, greater, higher, superior
2 *syn* see BIG 1
3 *syn* see GRAVE 3

make *vb* 1 *syn* see EFFECT 1
rel initiate, originate, start
2 *syn* see GENERATE 1
rel brew
3 to bring something into being by forming,
shaping, combining, or altering materials
<*made* a dress from odd bits of material>
syn assemble, build, construct, erect, fabricate, fashion, forge, form, frame, manufacture, mold, produce, put together, shape;
compare BUILD 1
4 *syn* see DRAFT 3
5 *syn* see CONSTITUTE 1
6 *syn* see PREPARE 1
7 *syn* see DESIGNATE 2
8 *syn* see ENACT 1
9 *syn* see INFER
10 *syn* see EARN 1
rel harvest, reap
11 *syn* see CLEAR 6
12 *syn* see FORCE 2
13 *syn* see HEAD 3
rel break (for)
‖14 *syn* see MEDDLE
15 *syn* see RUN 8

make-believe *n syn* see PRETENSE 2

make off *vb syn* see RUN 2
rel depart, go, leave, quit, retire, withdraw;
abscond, decamp, escape

make out *vb* 1 *syn* see APPREHEND 1
2 *syn* see ESTABLISH 6
3 *syn* see INFER
‖4 *syn* see SHIFT 5
5 *syn* see SUCCEED 3

make over *vb syn* see TRANSFER 4

make-peace *n syn* see PEACEMAKER

maker *n syn* see FATHER 2
rel executor, operator; manufacturer

makeshift *n syn* see RESOURCE 3

makeshift *adj* serving as a temporary expedient <forced to make *makeshift* plans>
syn provisional, rough-and-ready, rough-
and-tumble, stopgap

make up *vb* 1 *syn* see CONTRIVE 2
2 *syn* see MIX 1
3 *syn* see PREPARE 1
4 *syn* see CONSTITUTE 1
5 *syn* see COMPENSATE 1

make up (to) *vb syn* see ADDRESS 8

makeup *n* 1 the way in which parts or con-
stituents are related in an organized whole
<the complex *makeup* of the eye>

syn architecture, composition, constitution,
construction, design, formation
rel arrangement, ordering, organization,
plan, setup; form, shape, style
2 *syn* see DISPOSITION 3
rel cast, fiber, grain, mold, stamp, stripe,
vein; constitution, frame
3 cosmetics used to color and beautify the
face or body <with *makeup* on, she didn't
look bad>
syn face, maquillage, paint, war paint
rel powder; blackface, grease paint

maladroit *adj* 1 *syn* see AWKWARD 2
rel blundering, floundering, stumbling,
ungraceful; left-handed, unskilled
con deft, dexterous, handy; clever, cunning,
ingenious
ant adroit
2 *syn* see TACTLESS

malady *n syn* see DISEASE 1

mala fide *adj syn* see INSINCERE
ant bona fide

malaise *n syn* see INFIRMITY 1

malapert *adj syn* see SAUCY 1

malapert *n syn* see MINX

malapropos *adj* 1 *syn* see IMPROPER 1
ant apropos
2 *syn* see UNSEASONABLE 1

malarkey *n syn* see NONSENSE 2

malconformation *n syn* see DEFORMITY

malcontent *n* 1 *syn* see GROUCH
2 *syn* see REBEL

malcontent *adj syn* see DISCONTENTED
rel alienated, disaffected, estranged; disobedient, ungovernable, unruly; restless; contumacious, factious, insubordinate, mutinous,
rebellious, seditious

malcontented *adj syn* see DISCONTENTED

male *adj syn* see VIRILE 2
rel macho

male *n syn* see MAN 3

malediction *n syn* see CURSE 1
ant benediction

malefactor *n syn* see CRIMINAL
rel blackguard, knave, miscreant, rascal,
rogue, scoundrel; evildoer, sinner, wrongdoer

malefic *adj syn* see SINISTER
ant benefic

maleficent *adj syn* see SINISTER
ant beneficent

maleness *n syn* see VIRILITY
rel machismo, macho

malevolence *n syn* see MALICE
rel antagonism, hostility; abhorrence,
abomination, detestation
ant benevolence

malevolent *adj syn* see MALICIOUS
rel baleful, malefic, maleficent, sinister
con benign, benignant, kind, kindly
ant benevolent

malformation *n syn* see DEFORMITY

malice *n* a desiring or wishing pain, injury,
or distress to another <they sought to ruin
his reputation out of pure *malice*>
syn despite, despitefulness, grudge, ill will,
malevolence, maliciousness, malignancy,
malignity, spite, spitefulness, spleen
rel bane, poison, venom; bile; animosity,
animus, antipathy, down, enmity; hate,

hatefulness, hatred, invidiousness, meanness; bitterness, resentment, umbrage
con benevolence, benignancy, benignity, charity, kindliness, kindness

malicious *adj* having, showing, or indicative of intense often vicious ill will <the helpless victim of *malicious* rumors>
syn bitchy, catty, despiteful, evil, hateful, malevolent, malign, malignant, nasty, rancorous, spiteful, spitish, vicious, wicked
rel poisonous, poison-pen, venomous, virulent; baneful, deleterious, detrimental, noxious, pernicious; envious, green, green-eyed, jealous; mean, petty
con benevolent, charitable, friendly, kind, kindly; considerate, thoughtful

maliciousness *n syn* see MALICE

malign *adj* **1** *syn* see SINISTER
rel baneful, deleterious, detrimental, injurious, noxious, pernicious
con auspicious, favorable, propitious; fortunate, happy, lucky, providential
ant benign
2 *syn* see MALICIOUS
rel antagonistic, antipathetic, hostile, inimical
con benignant, kind, kindly
ant benign

malign *vb* to speak evil of for the purpose of injuring and without regard for the truth <the candidates increasingly *maligned* each other as the campaign degenerated>
syn asperse, befoul, bespatter, blacken, calumniate, defame, denigrate, libel, ‖scandal, scandalize, slander, slur, smear, spatter, tear down, traduce, vilify, villainize
rel decry, depreciate, derogate, detract, disparage; opprobriate, revile, vituperate; backbite, besmirch, defile, pollute, smirch, soil, stain, sully, taint, tarnish
idiom blow upon, cast aspersion(s) on (or upon)
con acclaim, applaud, eulogize, extol, laud, praise; defend, justify, maintain, vindicate

malignancy *n syn* see MALICE

malignant *adj syn* see MALICIOUS
rel devilish, diabolical, fiendish
con altruistic, benevolent, charitable, humane
ant benignant

maligning *adj syn* see LIBELOUS

malignity *n syn* see MALICE
rel revengefulness, vengefulness, vindictiveness
ant benignity

malison *n syn* see CURSE 1
ant benison

‖**malkin** *n syn* see SLATTERN 1

malleable *adj syn* see PLASTIC
rel governable, manageable; transformable
con intractable, recalcitrant, ungovernable, unmanageable, unruly
ant refractory

malleate *vb syn* see HAMMER 1

malodorous *adj* **1** having an unpleasant smell <*malodorous* cheeses>

syn fetid, frowsy, funky, fusty, gamy, high, mephitic, musty, nidorous, noisome, olid, putrid, rancid, rank, reeking, reeky, ‖smellful, smelly, stale, stenchful, stenchy, stinking, stinky, strong, whiffy; *compare* ODOROUS
rel bad, foul, nauseating, offensive, vile; decayed, decomposed, fuggy, off, rotten, spoiled, tainted; nasty, noxious, pestilential, poisonous, polluted
con clean, deodorized, fresh
ant fragrant, sweet
2 *syn* see INDECOROUS

maltreat *vb syn* see ABUSE 4

‖**mam** *n syn* see MOTHER 1

mama (*or* **mamma**) *n syn* see MOTHER 1

‖**mammock** *vb syn* see DISORDER 1

mammoth *n syn* see GIANT

mammoth *adj syn* see HUGE

mammy *n syn* see MOTHER 1

mamzer (*or* **momzer** *or* **momser**) *n syn* see BASTARD 1

man *n* **1** *syn* see HUMAN
2 *syn* see MANKIND
3 a male human being <just an average *man* trying to get by>
syn ‖bloke, boy, buck, ‖cat, chap, cuss, fellow, galoot, ‖gee, gent, gentleman, guy, he, male, ‖mun, skate, snap, ‖stirra; *compare* HUMAN
4 *syn* see HUSBAND
5 *syn* see LOVER 1
6 *syn* see POLICEMAN

manage *vb* **1** *syn* see CONDUCT 3
rel superintend; guide
2 *syn* see GOVERN 3
3 *syn* see SHIFT 5
rel bring about, carry out, contrive, effect, execute; accomplish, achieve, succeed
idiom sink or swim on one's own
con collapse, fail, fall down; give up, poop (out)

management *n syn* see OVERSIGHT 1

manager *n syn* see EXECUTIVE
rel handler, impresario; producer

man–at–arms *n syn* see SOLDIER

mancipium *n syn* see SLAVE 1

mandarin *n syn* see BUREAUCRAT

mandate *n syn* see COMMAND 1
rel decree, fiat, imperative; authority, authorization

mandatory *adj* containing or constituting a command <*mandatory* entrance examinations>
syn compulsatory, compulsory, imperative, imperious, obligatory, required
rel essential, indispensable, irremissible, necessary, needful, requisite; binding, commanding, compelling, de rigueur; forced, involuntary
con discretionary, elective, voluntary
ant optional

maneuver *n* **1** *syn* see MEASURE 7
2 *syn* see TRICK 1
rel contrivance, device; intrigue, machination, manipulation, plot; demarche, movement, plan; finesse, subterfuge

maneuver *vb* **1** *syn* see ENGINEER
rel navigate; finesse; design
2 *syn* see HANDLE 2

---

syn synonym(s)   *rel* related word(s)
ant antonym(s)   *con* contrasted word(s)
idiom idiomatic equivalent(s)
‖ use limited; if in doubt, see a dictionary

rel navigate

3 *syn* see MANIPULATE 2

man Friday *n syn* see RIGHT-HAND MAN

manful *adj syn* see BRAVE 1

manfulness *n syn* see VIRILITY
rel machismo, macho

mangle *vb syn* see BATTER 1
rel damage, impair, injure, mar; deface,
disfigure; contort, deform, distort; butcher,
hack

mangled *adj syn* see LACERATED

mangy *adj syn* see SHABBY 1

manhandle *vb* to treat roughly <riot police
manhandled innocent bystanders>
syn knock about, mishandle, rough (up),
roughhouse, slap around
rel abuse, maltreat, mistreat; batter, ‖bung
up, mangle, maul

mania *n syn* see FETISH 2
rel craze, enthusiasm, fancy, fascination,
infatuation, passion; compulsion, fixed idea,
hang-up, idée fixe

maniac *adj syn* see INSANE 1
rel berserk, delirious, frantic, frenetic, frenzied, furious, rabid, raging, ranting, violent,
wild

maniac *n* 1 *syn* see LUNATIC 1
2 *syn* see ENTHUSIAST

manifest *adj syn* see CLEAR 5
rel disclosed, divulged, revealed, told; evidenced, evinced, shown; noticeable, prominent
con implicit; obscure

manifest *vb* 1 *syn* see EMBODY 1
2 *syn* see SHOW 2
rel display, expose; express, utter, vent,
voice
con adumbrate, shadow
ant suggest

manifold *adj* comprehending or uniting
various features <a *manifold* operation>
syn diverse, diversiform, multifarious, multifold, multiplex, multivarious
rel multiphase, polymorphic, polymor-
phous
con homogeneous, pure, uniform; plain,
simple, straightforward, uncomplex, uncomplicated

manifold *vb syn* see INCREASE 1

manikin *n syn* see DWARF

manipulate *vb* 1 *syn* see HANDLE 2
2 to control or play upon by artful, unfair, or
insidious means <the sycophant cleverly
manipulated his master>
syn beguile, exploit, finesse, jockey, maneuver, play; *compare* ENGINEER
rel machinate, use; conduct, control, direct,
engineer, manage

mankind *n* the human race <all *mankind*
will benefit from this new discovery>
syn flesh, Homo sapiens, humanity, humankind, man, mortality; *compare* HUMAN

manlike *adj* 1 *syn* see ANTHROPOID
2 *syn* see VIRILE 2
rel macho

manliness *n syn* see VIRILITY
rel machismo, macho

manly *adj* 1 *syn* see VIRILE 2
rel macho
2 *syn* see BRAVE 1

man-made *adj syn* see SYNTHETIC

manner *n* 1 *syn* see HABIT 1
2 *syn* see METHOD 1
rel custom, habit, habitude, practice, usage,
use, wont; form, style
3 *syn* see STYLE 4
4 *syn* see VEIN 1
rel form, turn; affectation, affectedness,
mannerism; idiosyncrasy, peculiarity
5 **manners** *pl* habitual conduct or deportment in social intercourse evaluated according to some conventional standard of politeness or civility <a person with impeccable
manners>
syn amenities, civilities, decorum(s), etiquette, mores, proprieties
rel formalities, protocol; elegancies; bearing, behavior, demeanor, deportment, mien,
p's and q's; mannerliness
idiom conduct becoming a gentleman
con mannerlessness, unmannerliness

mannered *adj syn* see SELF-CONSCIOUS

mannerism *n syn* see POSE 2
rel eccentricity, idiosyncrasy; oddness,
peculiarity, queerness, singularity

mannerless *adj syn* see RUDE 6
ant mannerly

mannerly *adj syn* see CIVIL 2
ant mannerless, unmannerly

manor *n* 1 *syn* see MANSION
2 *syn* see ESTATE 3

mansion *n* a large imposing residence <the
governor's *mansion*>
syn castle, chateau, manor, villa
rel estate, hall, house

manslaughter *n syn* see MURDER

manslayer *n syn* see MURDERER

mantic *adj syn* see PROPHETIC

mantle *vb syn* see BLUSH

man-to-man *adj syn* see FRANK

manual *n syn* see HANDBOOK
rel abecedarium, hornbook, primer; text,
textbook

manufactory *n syn* see FACTORY

manufacture *vb syn* see MAKE 3

manumit *vb syn* see FREE
ant enslave

many *adj* consisting of a goodly but indefinite number <*many* lives were lost in the
flood>
syn legion, multifarious, multitudinal,
multitudinous, numerous, populous, ‖sev-
eral, sundry, various, voluminous
rel divers, manifold, multiple, multiplicate,
multiplied, myriad; abounding, abundant,
bounteous, bountiful, copious, plentiful
con meager, scant, scanty, sparse; only, sole
ant few

many *pron syn* see SUNDRY

many-sided *adj* 1 *syn* see MULTILATERAL
2 *syn* see VERSATILE

map *n* 1 *syn* see CHART 1
rel picture, portrayal; delineation, design,
diagram, draft, outline, sketch, tracing
‖2 *syn* see FACE 1

map (out) *vb syn* see DESIGN 3

maquillage *n syn* see MAKEUP 3

mar *vb syn* see INJURE 1
rel bruise, scar, scratch, warp; ruin, wreck

con adorn, beautify, decorate, embellish; mend, patch, repair; amend, correct, emend, rectify, reform, revise

maraud vb syn see RAID 1

marauder n one who raids in search of plunder <*marauders* sacked village after village>
syn bandit, brigand, bummer, cateran, depredator, despoiler, forager, freebooter, looter, pillager, plunderer, raider, ravager, ravisher, sacker, spoiler, spoliator
rel buccaneer, desperado, pirate; wrecker

marblehearted adj syn see UNFEELING 2
ant softhearted

marbles n pl syn see WIT 2

march n syn see FRONTIER 1
rel boundary, periphery; territory; outlands, provinces

march vb syn see ADJOIN
rel fringe, hem, rim, skirt; extend; parallel

march vb 1 syn see AGREE 4
2 syn see STRIDE 1
3 syn see ADVANCE 5

march n syn see ADVANCE 2

marchland n syn see FRONTIER 1

mare's nest n syn see IMPOSTURE
rel babel, clamor, din, hubbub, hullabaloo, racket, uproar

margin n 1 syn see BORDER 1
rel frame, trimming; shore; side
2 syn see ROOM 3
3 syn see MINIMUM

margin vb syn see BORDER 1
rel abut, connect, join, line, neighbor, touch

marijuana n the dried leaves and flowering tops of the pistillate hemp plant sometimes smoked for their intoxicating effect <*marijuana* was smoked by several students at the party>
syn boo, cannabis, grass, ‖Mary Jane, moocah, pot, ‖tea, weed
rel joint, reefer; hash, hashish

marine adj 1 of or relating to the sea <*marine* biology>
syn maritime, oceanic, thalassic
rel hydrographic, oceanographic; abyssal, bathyal, bathybic, bathysmal, benthic, dipsey, neritic, pelagic; aquatic, fluvial, fluviatile, lacustrine
2 of or relating to the navigation of the sea <*marine* charts and maps>
syn maritime, nautical, navigational
rel naval; seamanlike, seamanly; deep-sea, oceangoing, seafaring, seagoing

mariner n one engaged in sailing or handling a ship <the tanker crew was made up mostly of experienced *mariners*>
syn jack, jack-tar, sailor, sailorman, salt, seaman, tar, tarpaulin
rel bluejacket, gob, rating, ‖swab, ‖swabbie; ‖lascar, ‖limey; old salt, sea dog, shellback

marital adj syn see MATRIMONIAL

maritime adj 1 syn see MARINE 2
2 syn see MARINE 1

mark n 1 syn see AMBITION 2
2 syn see TARGET 1

3 syn see USE 4
4 syn see FOOL 3
5 syn see INDICATION 3
rel attribute, emblem, symbol, type; character, property, quality
6 syn see QUALITY 1
7 a device (as a word) pointing distinctly to the origin or ownership of merchandise to which it is applied and legally reserved to the exclusive use of the owner <the company was brought to court for illegally using the *mark* of its rival>
syn brand, brand name, logo, logotype, trademark
rel label, stamp
8 syn see CHARACTER 1
9 syn see NOTICE 1
10 syn see EFFECT 3

mark vb 1 syn see CHOOSE 1
2 syn see SHOW 5
3 syn see SHOW 2
4 syn see CHARACTERIZE 1
rel bespeak, betoken, denote, signify
idiom set apart
5 syn see SEE 1
rel record, register; attend, heed, regard

mark (out) vb syn see DEMARCATE 1
rel lay off, mark off; chart, lay out, map

mark down vb 1 syn see REDUCE 2
ant mark up
2 syn see DEPRECIATE 1

marked adj syn see NOTICEABLE
rel distinguished, noted; considerable

market n syn see STORE 4

market vb 1 syn see SELL 3
rel wholesale
2 syn see SELL 2

marketable adj capable of being sold <*marketable* commodities>
syn merchandisable, merchantable, salable, sellable, trafficable, vendible
rel commercial; profitable, selling; fit, good, sound, wholesome
con unmerchantable, unsalable
ant unmarketable

‖**maroon** vb syn see CAMP

marred adj syn see DAMAGED
rel banged-up, battered, bruised, mutilated; ruined, wrecked
ant unmarred

marriage n 1 the state of being united to a person of the opposite sex as husband or wife <*marriage* was not in the plans of this couple>
syn conjugality, connubiality, matrimony, wedlock
rel match, union
2 syn see WEDDING

marriage broker n one who arranges marriages <the old widow served as the town's *marriage broker*>
syn go-between, matchmaker
rel shadchan

marriage portion n syn see DOWRY

married adj syn see MATRIMONIAL

marrow n syn see ESSENCE 2
rel core, heart, kernel, meat

marrowy adj syn see PITHY

marry vb 1 to take as spouse <he *married* her for her money>

syn synonym(s)   rel related word(s)
ant antonym(s)   con contrasted word(s)
idiom idiomatic equivalent(s)
‖ use limited; if in doubt, see a dictionary

syn catch, espouse, wed

rel wive

idiom get hitched, get married, tie the knot

con annul, divorce, separate

2 to join in wedlock <the minister *married* all three daughters in one ceremony>

syn ‖hitch, mate, splice, tie, wed

idiom tie the knot, unite in marriage

3 *syn* see JOIN 1

marsh *n syn* see SWAMP

marshal *vb* **1** *syn* see ORDER 1

rel distribute, space; escort, guide, shepherd, usher

2 *syn* see MOBILIZE 3

marshland *n syn* see SWAMP

martial *adj* belonging to, engaged in, or appropriate to the affairs of war <the reviewing officer saw the company standing in *martial* array>

syn military, warlike

rel bellicose, belligerent, combative, pugnacious; aggressive, militant; high-spirited, mettlesome, spirited

con civil, civilian; irenic, pacific, peaceable, peaceful

ant unmartial

martyr *vb syn* see AFFLICT

martyrize *vb syn* see AFFLICT

marvel *n syn* see WONDER 1

marveling *n syn* see WONDER 2

rel surprise

marvelous *adj* **1** causing or exciting wonder <the way in which he could bring together opposing forces was truly *marvelous*>

syn amazing, astonishing, astounding, miraculous, prodigious, spectacular, staggering, strange, stupendous, surprising, wonderful, wondrous

rel awe-inspiring, awesome, awful, awing; incomprehensible, inconceivable, incredible, unimaginable; fabulous, phenomenal, supernatural; exceptional, extraordinary; bewildering, confounding, striking, stunning

con commonplace, ordinary, routine; blah, unexciting, uninteresting

2 superior or outstanding of its kind <had a *marvelous* weekend>

syn ‖cool, ‖dandy, divine, dreamy, ‖galluptious, glorious, groovy, hot, hunky-dory, ‖keen, ‖neat, nifty, peachy, ripping, sensational, super, swell, terrific, wonderful; *compare* EXCELLENT, SUPERIOR 4, SUPREME

rel agreeable, enjoyable, pleasant, pleasurable; rewarding, satisfying

con dreary, dull, humdrum, monotonous, tedious; inferior, low-grade, mean, poor, punk

‖Mary Jane *n syn* see MARIJUANA

mascot *n syn* see CHARM 2

masculine *adj syn* see VIRILE 2

ant effeminate, unmasculine

rel macho

masculinity *n syn* see VIRILITY

rel machismo, machoism

mash *n syn* see CLUTTER 2

mash *vb* **1** *syn* see CRUSH 2

‖**2** *syn* see PRESS 1

mashed *adj syn* see ENAMORED 1

masher *n syn* see WOLF

mash note *n syn* see LOVE LETTER

mask *n* **1** a cover or partial cover for the face that has openings for the eyes and is used especially for disguise <on Halloween he wore a pirate's *mask*>

syn domino, doughface, false face, visor, vizard

rel disguise, masquerade; veil

2 an outward appearance that seeks to obscure an underlying true character <he was able to maintain a *mask* of dignity and tranquillity in his time of anxiety>

syn cloak, color, coloring, cover, disguise, disguisement, facade, face, false front, front, guise, masquerade, muffler, pretense, pretext, put-on, semblance, show, veil, veneer, window dressing; *compare* APPEARANCE 2

rel affectation, air, pose, posture; fakery, sham; dissembling, dissimulation, seeming, simulation; appearance, aspect

mask *vb syn* see DISGUISE

rel screen, secrete, veil; blur; defend, guard, protect, safeguard, shield

masquerade *n syn* see MASK 2

masquerade *vb syn* see POSE 4

mass *n* **1** *syn* see BODY 4

2 *syn* see PILE 1

3 *syn* see BULK 1

rel aggregate, aggregation, conglomerate, conglomeration; sum, whole

4 *syn* see BODY 3

5 *syn* see MUCH

6 *usu* **masses** *pl syn* see RABBLE 2

massacre *vb syn* see SLAUGHTER 3

massacre *n* the act or an instance of killing a considerable number of human beings under circumstances of atrocity or cruelty <the *massacre* of the Indians by the soldiers and settlers>

syn bloodbath, bloodshed, butchery, carnage, slaughter

rel blood purge, decimation, genocide, pogrom; internecion; assassination, killing, murder, slaying

massive *adj* **1** *syn* see HEAVY 1

rel hulking, hulky, massy

2 *syn* see HUGE

3 *syn* see MONSTROUS 1

massy *adj syn* see HUGE

master *n* **1** *syn* see EXPERT

rel maestro, savant; genius, mastermind; guru, swami

2 *syn* see LEADER 2

rel overlord, overman, overseer

3 *syn* see VICTOR 1

‖**4** *syn* see HUSBAND

5 *syn* see LOVER 1

master *vb* **1** *syn* see OVERCOME 1

2 *syn* see DOMESTICATE

rel dominate, govern, predominate, rule

3 *syn* see CONQUER 1

4 *syn* see LEARN 1

master *adj* **1** *syn* see DOMINANT 1

2 *syn* see PROFICIENT

masterdom *n syn* see SUPREMACY

masterful *adj* **1** disposed to exercise or flaunt dictatorial authority in a way to override any protestation <the royal favorite was pompous and *masterful* when dealing with subordinates>

syn bossy, domineering, high-handed, imperative, imperial, imperious, magisterial, overbearing, peremptory

rel absolute, arbitrary, authoritarian, authoritative, dictative, dictatorial, doctrinaire, dogmatic; autocratic, despotic, tyrannical; high-and-mighty, self-willed

con humble, modest, unpretentious; indecisive, irresolute; submissive, yielding; feeble, weak

2 *syn* see PROFICIENT

rel adroit, deft, dexterous; preeminent, superlative, supreme, transcendent

master–hand *n syn* see EXPERT

masterly *adj syn* see PROFICIENT

rel preeminent, superlative, supreme, transcendent

masterpiece *n* **1** something done or made with extraordinary skill or brilliance <his latest work is unquestionably a *masterpiece*>

syn chef d'oeuvre, classic, magnum opus, masterwork, tour de force

rel objet d'art, masterstroke

con botch, disaster, fiasco

2 *syn* see SHOWPIECE

mastership *n syn* see ABILITY 2

masterwork *n syn* see MASTERPIECE 1

mastery *n* **1** *syn* see POWER 1

2 *syn* see ABILITY 2

masticate *vb syn* see CHEW 1

rel bruise, crush, macerate, mash, pulp, pulpify, smash, squash

mastodonic *adj syn* see HUGE

mat *adj syn* see DULL 7

matador *n syn* see BULLFIGHTER

match *n* **1** *syn* see OPPONENT

2 *syn* see EQUAL

rel analogue, parallel

3 *syn* see MATE 5

4 *syn* see PARALLEL

5 *syn* see EVENT 5

rel bout, engagement, game

match *vb* **1** *syn* see OPPOSE 1

2 *syn* see EQUATE 2

3 *syn* see AMOUNT 2

rel complement, supplement

4 *syn* see EQUAL 3

rel compare, stack up

idiom hold a candle to

matched *adj syn* see ASSORTED 2

rel balanced, equated, evened, similar; coordinated, harmonized; coupled, joined, mated, paired, yoked

ant unmatched

matchless *adj syn* see ALONE 3

ant matchable

matchmaker *n syn* see MARRIAGE BROKER

mate *n* **1** *syn* see PARTNER

2 *syn* see ACCOMPANIMENT 2

3 *syn* see FRIEND

rel bedmate, classmate, co-mate, helpmate, playmate, roommate, schoolmate, teammate

4 *syn* see SPOUSE

rel match, parti

5 one of a pair matched in one or more qualities <the *mate* of a shoe>

syn companion, coordinate, double, duplicate, fellow, match, reciprocal, twin

rel alter ego, complement, sosie; compeer, equal, equivalent, peer

mate *vb syn* see MARRY 2

rel breed, crossbreed, pair; generate, procreate

‖**mater** *n syn* see MOTHER 1

material *adj* **1** of or belonging to actuality <for him the *material* world is the only world>

syn corporeal, gross, objective, phenomenal, physical, sensible, substantial, tangible

rel actual, real, true; appreciable, palpable, perceptible; earthly, worldly; animal, carnal, fleshly, sensual

con impalpable, imperceptible, intangible, unsubstantial; spiritual

ant immaterial, nonmaterial

2 *syn* see IMPORTANT 1

ant immaterial

3 *syn* see RELEVANT

rel consequential, important, momentous, significant; cardinal, essential, fundamental, vital

ant immaterial

material *n* **1** *syn* see THING 5

rel component, constituent, element, ingredient; apparatus, equipment, machinery

2 *usu* **materials** *pl syn* see EQUIPMENT

materialistic *adj* of or relating to a preoccupation with or stress upon material rather than intellectual or spiritual things <*materialistic* values characterize the modern age>

syn banausic, earthy, mundane, sensual, temporal, worldly

rel carnal, profane; earthly, terrestrial, secular, unspiritual

con intellectual, mental; spiritual, unfleshly, unworldly; heavenly

materiality *n syn* see ACTUALITY 2

materialize *vb* **1** *syn* see EMBODY 1

rel appear, emerge, loom, show; issue, rise, spring

2 to convert mentally into something concrete <with the help of graphs and figures abstract ideas can be *materialized*>

syn entify, hypostatize, reify

rel actualize, pragmatize, realize; corporealize; symbolize, typify

matériel *n syn* see EQUIPMENT

matriarch *n* a dignified, usually elderly woman of some rank or authority <the local *matriarchs* controlled the town's social functions>

syn dame, dowager, grande dame, matron

rel materfamilias, mother

matrimonial *adj* of, relating to, or characteristic of marriage <the *matrimonial* bond between husband and wife>

syn conjugal, connubial, hymeneal, marital, married, nuptial, spousal, wedded

rel bridal, epithalamic

matrimony *n syn* see MARRIAGE 1

matron *n syn* see MATRIARCH

matter *n* **1** *syn* see SUBJECT 2

2 *syn* see AFFAIR 1

rel complication, grievance, to-do, worry; circumstance, predicament

---

syn synonym(s)   *rel* related word(s)
ant antonym(s)   *con* contrasted word(s)
idiom idiomatic equivalent(s)
‖ use limited; if in doubt, see a dictionary

3 *syn* see SUBSTANCE 2

4 *syn* see THING 5

5 *syn* see ORDER 4

matter *vb* to be of importance <being your own self is what really *matters*>
syn count, import, mean, signify, weigh
idiom carry weight

matter-of-course *adj syn* see GENERAL 1

matter-of-fact *adj* **1** see REALISTIC
rel objective, sound

2 *syn* see PROSAIC 1

3 involving no display of emotion <the *matter-of-fact* reading of the judge masked his inner anguish>
syn cold, cold-blooded, emotionless, impersonal, unimpassioned
rel unaffected, unsentimental; prosaic
con emotional, impassioned, personal
ant impassive 1

4 *syn* see IMPASSIVE 1

maturate *vb syn* see MATURE

mature *adj* **1** having attained the normal peak of natural growth and development <*mature* plants ready to bear fruit>
syn adult, full-blown, full-fledged, full-grown, grown, grown-up, matured, ripe, ripened
rel developed, ready
idiom of age
con childish, childlike; boyish, green, juvenile, maiden, puerile, youthful
ant immature

2 *syn* see DUE 2

3 *syn* see UNPAID 2

mature *vb* to become fully developed or ripe <she *matured* as an actress after several years of summer stock>
syn age, develop, grow, grow up, maturate, mellow, ‖ripe, ripen
rel blossom, flower; advance, progress, round; season; decline, deteriorate, olden, wane
idiom come of age

matured *adj syn* see MATURE 1
rel completed, finished; advised, considered, deliberate, designed, premeditated, studied
con callow, crude, green, raw, rough, rude, uncouth
ant premature, unmatured

2 *syn* see RIPE 3

maudlin *adj syn* see SENTIMENTAL
rel addled, befuddled, confused, fuddled, muddled; silly

maul *n syn* see BRAWL 2

maul *vb syn* see BATTER 1
rel flagellate, flail, lash, whip; bang, bash, buffet, pound; abuse, maltreat, manhandle, molest, rough (up)

maunder *vb syn* see WANDER 1

maundering *adj syn* see INARTICULATE 3

maven *n syn* see EXPERT

maverick *n syn* see BOHEMIAN

mawkish *adj syn* see SENTIMENTAL
rel banal, flat; cloying, nauseating, sickening

maxim *n* a general truth or fundamental principle usually expressed sententiously <Francis Bacon is noted for his fondness for *maxims*>
syn aphorism, apothegm, axiom, brocard, dictum, gnome, moral, rule, truism
rel commonplace, motto, platitude; law, precept, prescript; theorem; proverb
idiom rule of thumb

maximal *adj syn* see MAXIMUM
ant minimal

maximize *vb syn* see OVERPLAY 2
ant minimize

maximum *adj* greatest in quantity or highest in degree attainable or attained <apply *maximum* pressure above the point of injury>
syn maximal, outside, top, topmost, utmost; *compare* SUPREME
rel greatest, highest, largest
con least, lowest, slightest, smallest
ant minimum

maybe *adv syn* see PERHAPS

mayhem *vb syn* see MAIM

maze *n* **1** something intricately or confusingly elaborate or complicated <the landscape soon became a *maze* of superhighways>
syn jungle, knot, labyrinth, mesh, mizmaze, morass, skein, snarl, tangle, web
rel fog, haze; gordian knot; conglomeration, hodgepodge, miscellany, mishmash

‖**2** *syn* see HAZE 2

‖**mazuma** *n syn* see MONEY

MD *n syn* see PHYSICIAN

meager *adj* **1** *syn* see LEAN

2 being smaller than what is normal, necessary, or desirable <the remains of dinner provided only a *meager* meal that evening>
syn exiguous, poor, scant, scanty, scrimp, scrimpy, skimp, skimpy, spare, sparse; *compare* SHORT 3
rel deficient, inadequate, insufficient; inappreciable, inconsiderable, slight; bare, mere, minimum; miserable, shabby
con adequate, enough, sufficient; appreciable, considerable; copious, plentiful
ant ample

meal *n* the portion of food taken at one time to satisfy appetite <the noonday dinner was the big *meal* of the day in those times>
syn ‖chow, feed, ‖nosh, refection, repast
rel feast, ‖nosh-up, spread; refreshment, regalement; collation, snack; fare, grub, meat, mess, victuals; board, table

meal *vb syn* see EAT 1

mean *adj* **1** *syn* see IGNOBLE 1
ant wellborn

2 *syn* see INFERIOR 2

3 *syn* see LITTLE 2

4 *syn* see CONTEMPTIBLE

5 *syn* see CHEAP 2

6 *syn* see STINGY

7 *syn* see TROUBLESOME
rel difficult, formidable, rough, rugged, tough

8 *syn* see UNWELL

mean *vb* **1** *syn* see INTEND 2
rel desire, want, wish

2 to convey (as an idea) to the mind <your answer *means* nothing to me>
syn add up (to), connote, denote, express, import, signify, spell
rel designate, name; attest, betoken, indicate; hint, imply, intimate, suggest

3 *syn* see MATTER

mean *n* **1** *syn* see AVERAGE

2 *usu* **means** *sing or pl in constr* one by which work is accomplished or an end effected <careful planning is a major *means* of improving output> <use any *means* to secure peace>

syn agency, agent, channel, instrument, instrumentality, instrumentation, intermediary, medium, ministry, organ, vehicle

rel fashion, manner, method, mode, system, way; apparatus, equipment, machinery, paraphernalia

3 **means** *pl* one's total property including real property and intangibles <people of moderate *means* are feeling the effects of inflation worse>

syn assets, capital, resources, wealth

rel finances, fortune, funds, moneybags, pocket, purse; ‖bundle, nest egg, pile, reserves, savings; estate, holdings, possessions; intangibles

mean *adj* **1** *syn* see MIDDLE 2

2 *syn* see MEDIUM

meander *vb* **1** *syn* see WANDER 1

rel snake, turn, twist, wind

meanderer *n* *syn* see ROVER

meandering *adj* *syn* see WINDING

meandrous *adj* *syn* see WINDING

meaning *n* **1** the idea that something conveys to the mind <critics have endlessly debated the *meaning* of the poem>

syn acceptation, import, intendment, intent, message, purport, sense, significance, significancy, signification, sum and substance, understanding; *compare* SUBSTANCE 2, TENOR 1

rel drift, effect, essence, tenor; force, point, value; hint, implication, intimation, suggestion; connotation, definition, denotation

2 *syn* see INTENTION

meaningful *adj* **1** *syn* see EXPRESSIVE

ant meaningless

2 *syn* see IMPORTANT 1

meaningless *adj* **1** *syn* see SENSELESS 5

rel blank, empty, vacant

ant meaningful

2 *syn* see FECKLESS 1

measly *adj* *syn* see PETTY 2

measure *n* **1** *syn* see RATION

2 *syn* see TEMPERANCE 1

3 *syn* see SIZE 1

4 *syn* see MELODY

5 *syn* see RHYTHM

6 *syn* see STANDARD 3

7 an action planned or taken toward the accomplishment of a purpose <developed a new set of safety *measures*>

syn maneuver, move, procedure, proceeding, step

rel effort, project, proposal, proposition; expedient, makeshift, resort, resource, shift, stopgap

measure *vb* **1** *syn* see DEMARCATE 1

2 to ascertain the quantity, mass, extent, or degree of in terms of a standard unit or fixed amount <*measure* the depth of the water>

syn gauge, scale

rel size, size up; calculate, compute, estimate, figure, reckon

measure (out) *vb* *syn* see DISTRIBUTE 1

measureless *adj* **1** *syn* see INCALCULABLE 1

ant measurable

2 *syn* see LIMITLESS

ant measurable

measure up *vb* *syn* see EQUAL 3

meat *n* **1** *syn* see FOOD 1

2 *syn* see SUBSTANCE 2

meat-and-potatoes *adj* *syn* see FUNDAMENTAL 1

meathead *n* *syn* see OAF 2

meaty *adj* *syn* see PITHY

mechanical *adj* *syn* see PERFUNCTORY

meddle *vb* to concern oneself with officiously, impertinently, or indiscreetly <continually *meddling* in other people's affairs>

syn busybody, butt in, fool, horn in, interfere, interlope, intermeddle, ‖make, mess around, monkey (with), tamper (with)

rel intervene, intrude, invade, obtrude; pry, snoop, trespass

idiom put (or shove or stick) one's oar in, stick one's nose into

con disregard, ignore, neglect, omit, overlook, slight; avoid, eschew, shun

meddler *n* *syn* see BUSYBODY

meddlesome *adj* *syn* see IMPERTINENT 2

Meddlesome Mattie *n* *syn* see BUSYBODY

medial *adj* **1** *syn* see MIDDLE 1

2 *syn* see MIDDLE 2

3 *syn* see MEDIUM

median *n* *syn* see AVERAGE

rel center, middle

median *adj* **1** *syn* see MIDDLE 1

2 *syn* see MIDDLE 2

mediate *vb* *syn* see INTERPOSE 2

mediator *n* **1** *syn* see GO-BETWEEN 2

rel arbitrator, judge; conciliator, peacemaker; negotiator, troubleshooter

2 *syn* see MODERATOR

medical *n* *syn* see PHYSICIAN

medicament *n* *syn* see REMEDY 1

medicant *n* *syn* see REMEDY 1

medication *n* *syn* see REMEDY 1

medicinal *adj* *syn* see DRUG 1

medicine *n* *syn* see REMEDY 1

mediciner *n* *syn* see PHYSICIAN

medico *n* *syn* see PHYSICIAN

mediocre *adj* *syn* see MEDIUM

rel bad, inferior, poor; common, commonplace, ordinary, unexceptional

idiom no great shakes, nothing to write home about

meditate *vb* *syn* see PONDER 2

meditative *adj* **1** *syn* see THOUGHTFUL 1

rel musing, ruminant; wistful

2 *syn* see PENSIVE 2

medium *adj* midway between the extremes of a scale, measurement, or evaluation <bought a suit of *medium* quality>

syn average, fair, fairish, indifferent, intermediate, mean, medial, mediocre, middling, moderate, run-of-mine, run-of-the-mill, so-so

---

syn synonym(s)   *rel* related word(s)
ant antonym(s)   *con* contrasted word(s)
idiom idiomatic equivalent(s)

‖ use limited; if in doubt, see a dictionary

rel median, par; passable, tolerable; neutral; popular, vulgar; normal, standard
idiom fair to middling
con inferior, low-grade, poor; excellent, first-class, high-grade, prime, superior
medium *n* **1** *syn* see MEAN 2
rel intermediate, intermediation
2 *syn* see ENVIRONMENT
3 *syn* see FORTE
medley *n* *syn* see MISCELLANY 1
‖**meech** *vb* *syn* see SNEAK
meed *n* **1** *syn* see REWARD
rel recompensing, satisfaction
2 *syn* see RATION
rel desert, due, merit
meek *adj* *syn* see HUMBLE 1
rel gentle, mild; tame; forbearing, lenient, tolerant; long-suffering, patient
con high-spirited, mettlesome, spirited, spunky; contumacious, insubordinate, rebellious
ant arrogant
meet *vb* **1** *syn* see HAPPEN 2
2 *syn* see CONFRONT 1
3 *syn* see ENGAGE 5
rel brave, oppose
4 *syn* see EQUAL 3
5 *syn* see SATISFY 5
rel approach, equal, match, rival, tie, touch
6 to come together face-to-face or as if face-to-face <the two leaders agreed to *meet* in a series of summit talks>
syn close, encounter, face, front; *compare* CONFRONT 1
rel accost, greet, salute; bump, clash, collide, cross; grapple, tussle, wrestle; experience, suffer, sustain, undergo
con elude, escape, evade, shun
ant avoid
7 *syn* see CONVERGE 1
8 *syn* see CONVENE 1
meet (with) *vb* *syn* see FIND 1
meet *n* *syn* see EVENT 5
2 *syn* see CONTEST 2
meet *adj* **1** *syn* see FIT 1
rel accommodated, conformed, reconciled; good, right; equitable, fair, just
ant unmeet
2 *syn* see GOOD 2
ant unmeet
meeting *n* **1** *syn* see CONTEST 2
2 *syn* see CONCOURSE
3 *syn* see TALK 4
rel congress, moot
meetness *n* *syn* see ORDER 11
ant unmeetness
megacosm *n* *syn* see UNIVERSE
ant microcosm
megrim *n* *syn* see CAPRICE
rel impulse, urge
melancholic *adj* *syn* see SAD 2
melancholy *n* *syn* see SADNESS
rel miserableness, misery, wretchedness; despair, desperation; boredom, ennui, tedium
con hopefulness, optimism
ant exhilaration
melancholy *adj* **1** *syn* see SAD 1
2 expressing or suggesting sorrow or mourning <the gloomy day led him to a *melancholy* train of thought>

syn doleful, dolesome, dolorous, lamentable, lugubrious, moanful, mournful, plaintive, rueful, sighful, sorrowful, wailful, woeful; *compare* SAD 1, SAD 2
rel pensive, reflective, thoughtful; discomposing, disquieting, disturbing, perturbing; dismal, dreary, funereal, gloomy, lachrymose, somber, sombrous
con cheerful, glad, happy, joyful, joyous, lighthearted; gay, lively, vivacious
3 *syn* see SAD 2
mélange *n* *syn* see MISCELLANY 1
meld *vb* *syn* see MIX 1
melding *n* *syn* see UNIFICATION
melee *n* **1** *syn* see CLASH 2
rel dogfight, scuffle
2 *syn* see BRAWL 2
3 *syn* see MISCELLANY 1
meliorate *vb* *syn* see IMPROVE 1
melisma *n* *syn* see MELODY
mellay *n* **1** *syn* see BRAWL 2
2 *syn* see CLASH 2
mellifluent *adj* *syn* see MELLIFLUOUS
mellifluous *adj* having a smooth rich flow <his *mellifluous* voice held his audience in a trance>
syn golden, honeyed, Hyblaean, liquid, mellifluent, mellow; *compare* MELODIOUS 1
rel accordant, canorous, euphonic, euphonious, harmonious, mellisonant, silvery; golden-tongued, silver-tongued; dulcet, sweet; resonant, sonorous
con blatant, boisterous, clamorous, obstreperous, strident, vociferous; discordant, grating, harsh
mellisonant *adj* *syn* see MELODIOUS 1
mellow *adj* **1** *syn* see RIPE 3
2 *syn* see MELLIFLUOUS
mellow *vb* *syn* see MATURE 1
melodia *n* *syn* see MELODY
melodic *adj* **1** *syn* see MELODIOUS 2
2 *syn* see MELODIOUS 1
melodious *adj* **1** pleasing to the ear <*melodious* sounds of the forest>
syn dulcet, euphonic, euphonious, mellisonant, melodic, sweet, tuneful; *compare* MELLIFLUOUS
rel canorous, harmonious
con discordant, grating, harsh
ant unmelodious
2 containing, constituting, or characterized by melody <her voice shows marked improvement and a new richly *melodious* quality>
syn melodic, musical, songful, tuned, tuneful
rel cantabile, lyric, melic
melody *n* a rhythmic succession of single tones organized as an aesthetic whole <took out his flute and played a simple *melody*>
syn air, descant, diapason, lay, measure, melisma, melodia, strain, tune, warble; *compare* SONG 2
rel song; bel canto, canto, vocalise; lyrics
melt *vb* **1** *syn* see LIQUEFY
rel heat, warm
con coagulate, harden, set
ant freeze; solidify
2 *syn* see BURN 3
rel perspire, sweat

member *n syn* see PART 1

memento *n* 1 *syn* see REMEMBRANCE 3
  2 *syn* see VESTIGE 1

memo *n* 1 *syn* see NOTE 2
  2 *syn* see MEMORANDUM 2

memoir *n* 1 *syn* see BIOGRAPHY
  rel anecdote; memory, recollection, remembrance, reminiscence
  2 *syn* see DISCOURSE 2

memoirist *n syn* see BIOGRAPHER

memorable *adj syn* see NOTEWORTHY
  rel momentous, remembrable; deathless, unfadable, unforgettable
  ant unmemorable

memorandum *n* 1 *syn* see NOTE 2
  2 a communication that contains directive, advisory, or informative matter <the *memorandum* announced the holiday schedule>
  syn directive, memo, notice
  rel announcement, dispatch, minute; epistle, letter, missive, note; reminder, tickler; message; diary

memorial *adj* serving to preserve remembrance <a *memorial* plaque>
  syn commemorative, commemoratory
  rel celebrative, consecrative, dedicatory, enshrining

memorial *n* 1 *syn* see REMEMBRANCE 3
  2 *syn* see MONUMENT 2

memorialize *vb* 1 *syn* see ADDRESS 4
  2 to record or honor the memory of by or as if by a monument <the new library *memorializes* the late President>
  syn commemorate, monument, monumentalize
  rel etch, grave, impress, imprint; jog, nudge, remind
  idiom bring to mind, fix in the (*or* one's) mind (*or* memory), impress on one's mind, treasure in one's heart
  con forget, neglect, overlook

memorial park *n syn* see CEMETERY

memorize *vb* to commit to memory <the actors hadn't even *memorized* their lines>
  syn con, get, learn
  rel study
  idiom get (*or* learn) by heart, get (*or* learn) word for word
  con forget

memory *n* 1 the power or process of reproducing or recalling what has been learned <blessed with a good *memory*>
  syn recollection, remembrance, reminiscence
  rel reflection, retrospection; retention, retentiveness; mind, recall; mind's eye; awareness, cognizance, consciousness
  con forgetfulness, obliviousness, unmindfulness; lethe, oblivion
  2 a particular act of recalling <her *memory* of her wedding day remains vivid>
  syn anamnesis, recall, recollection, remembrance, reminiscence
  rel memento, souvenir

menace *vb* 1 *syn* see THREATEN

  rel alarm, frighten, scare; endanger, torment; loom, lower
  2 *syn* see ENDANGER

menacing *adj syn* see IMMINENT 2

ménage *n syn* see FAMILY 2
  rel ménage à trois

mend *vb* 1 *syn* see CORRECT 1
  2 to put into good shape or working order again <*mends* garments in her spare time>
  syn doctor, do up, fix, overhaul, patch, rebuild, recondition, reconstruct, repair, revamp, ‖right, ‖rightle, vamp
  rel condition, ready, service; refurbish, rejuvenate, renew, renovate, restore; correct, emend, rectify, redress, reform; heal
  3 *syn* see IMPROVE 3

mendacious *adj syn* see DISHONEST
  rel false, wrong; erroneous, fallacious, spurious; equivocating, fibbing, paltering, prevaricating
  ant veracious

mendaciousness *n syn* see MENDACITY
  ant veraciousness, veracity

mendacity *n* the practice or an instance of lying <he was ultimately caught by his own outrageous *mendacity*>
  syn falsehood, fibbery, mendaciousness, truthlessness, untruthfulness, unveracity
  rel boggling, caviling, dodging, equivocation, hedging, quibbling, shifting, sidestepping
  ant veraciousness, veracity

mendicancy *n* the practice or act of begging <the city passed an ordinance against *mendicancy*>
  syn beggary, bumming, cadging, mendicity, mooching, panhandling
  rel sponging

mendicity *n syn* see MENDICANCY

menial *adj syn* see SUBSERVIENT 2

mental *adj* 1 of or relating to the mind <the *mental* aspects of the problem>
  syn cerebral, intellective, intellectual, psychic, psychical, psychological
  rel immaterial, inner, spiritual; telepathic; intelligent, rational, reasoning, thinking; ideological
  con bodily, corporal, corporeal, physical, somatic; perceptive; sensual, sensuous
  ‖**2** *syn* see INSANE 1

mentality *n syn* see INTELLIGENCE 1

mention *vb* to refer to someone or something in a clear unmistakable manner <several donors were *mentioned* in the article>
  syn cite, instance, name, specify
  rel denominate, designate; detail; advert, allude, refer; quote
  idiom make mention of
  con disregard, ignore, neglect, overlook, pass by, pass over, slight

menu *n* a list of the dishes that may be ordered (as at a restaurant) or that are to be served (as at a banquet) <hoped to find something tasty on the *menu*><he saved the elaborate *menu* as a souvenir of the awards banquet>
  syn card, carte du jour
  idiom bill of fare

Mephistophelian *adj syn* see SATANIC 1

mephitic *adj* 1 *syn* see MALODOROUS 1

---

syn synonym(s)	*rel* related word(s)
ant antonym(s)	*con* contrasted word(s)
idiom idiomatic equivalent(s)	
‖ use limited; if in doubt, see a dictionary	

2 *syn* see POISONOUS

mercenary *n syn* see HACK 2

mercenary *adj syn* see CORRUPT 2
ant unmercenary

merchandisable *adj syn* see MARKETABLE
ant unmerchantable, unsalable

merchandise *n* the products that are bought and sold in business <*merchandise* of inferior quality>
syn commodities, goods, line, vendible(s), wares
rel effects; job lot, stock; staples

merchandise *vb syn* see SELL 3
rel advertise, publicize

merchandiser *n syn* see MERCHANT

merchant *n* a buyer and seller of commodities for profit <a *merchant* of dry goods>
syn businessman, dealer, merchandiser, trader, tradesman, trafficker
rel jobber, retailer, wholesaler

merchantable *adj syn* see MARKETABLE
ant unmerchantable, unsalable

merchant prince *n syn* see MAGNATE

merciful *adj syn* see FORBEARING
rel compassionate, pitiful, softhearted; benign, kind, kindly; condoning, forgiving, pardoning
ant merciless, unmerciful

mercifulness *n syn* see FORBEARANCE 2
rel commiseration, pity, ruth
con severeness, severity, sternness
ant mercilessness, unmercifulness

merciless *adj* 1 *syn* see PITILESS
ant merciful
2 *syn* see GRIM 3
rel compassionless, cutthroat, pitiless; gratuitous, uncalled-for, wanton
con charitable, lenient, tolerant; easy, easygoing
ant merciful

mercurial *adj syn* see INCONSTANT 1
rel buoyant, effervescent, elastic, expansive, resilient; mobile, movable; adroit, clever, cunning, ingenious
ant saturnine

mercy *n* a show of or a disposition to show kindness or compassion <the *mercy* of the Lord knows all seasons>
syn caritas, charity, clemency, grace, lenity; *compare* FORBEARANCE 2
rel commiseration, compassion, pity, ruth; benevolence, benignancy, benignity, kindliness, kindness; generosity, goodwill
con reprisal, retaliation, retribution, revenge, vengeance; castigation, chastening, chastisement, punishment

mere *adj syn* see VERY 4

merely *adv syn* see JUST 3

meretricious *adj syn* see GAUDY
rel deceptive, delusive, delusory, misleading, spurious; insincere

meretrix *n syn* see PROSTITUTE

merge *vb syn* see MIX 1

mergence *n syn* see UNIFICATION

merger *n* 1 *syn* see CONSOLIDATION 2
2 *syn* see UNIFICATION

merging *n syn* see UNIFICATION

meridian *n syn* see APEX 2

merit *n* 1 *syn* see EXCELLENCE
ant fault

2 *syn* see QUALITY 2
3 *syn* see DUE 1
rel gaining(s), winning(s)

merit *vb syn* see EARN 2
rel award, reward; recompense, repay, requite; entitle, justify, warrant

meritable *adj syn* see WORTHY 1
ant meritless

merited *adj syn* see JUST 3
rel entitled, justified, warranted
ant unmerited

meritorious *adj syn* see WORTHY 1

merriment *n* 1 *syn* see MIRTH
2 *syn* see MERRYMAKING

merry *adj* indicative of or marked by high spirits or lightheartedness <the *merry* life of the town folk was a joy to see>
syn blithe, blithesome, boon, festive, gay, gleeful, jocund, jolly, jovial, lighthearted, mirthful, riant
rel animated, lively, sprightly, vivacious; cheerful, glad, happy, joyful, joyous; hilarious, mad, unconstrained, wild
con gloomy, glum, melancholy; grave, sober, somber; earnest, sedate, serious, staid

merry–andrew *n syn* see CLOWN 3

merrymaking *n* gay or festive activity <a night of *merrymaking*>
syn festivity, gaiety, jollity, merriment, revel, reveling, revelment, revelry, whoopee
rel enjoyment, indulgence, pleasure, self-indulgence

mesh *n* 1 *usu* meshes *pl syn* see WEB 2
2 *syn* see MAZE 1
rel net, network

mesh *vb syn* see ENGAGE 1

meshuggaas *n syn* see NONSENSE 2

mesmeric *adj syn* see ATTRACTIVE 1

mesmerize *vb syn* see ENTHRALL 1
rel entrance, hypnotize

mess *n* ‖1 *syn* see MUCH
2 *syn* see EYESORE
3 a confused or disordered state, condition, or situation <upon becoming president, he proceeded to make a *mess* of the government>
syn botch, botchery, hash, mess-up, mix-up, muddle, mull, muss, shambles; *compare* MISCELLANY 1
rel confusion, disorder; wreck, wreckage
idiom kettle of fish

mess *vb* 1 *syn* see BOTCH
rel confuse, disorder, jumble
idiom make a mess of
2 *syn* see FIDDLE 2

mess (up) *vb syn* see DISORDER
rel damage, mar, ruin, spoil; ‖muck, mucker, muff

message *n* 1 something (as information) conveyed by writing, speech, or signals <left a *message* before he went out>
syn communication, directive, word
rel communiqué, dispatch, report; memo, memorandum; epistle, letter, missive, note
2 *syn* see MEANING 1

mess around *vb* 1 *syn* see FIDDLE 2
2 *syn* see MEDDLE
3 *syn* see PHILANDER

messenger *n* one who bears a message or does an errand <blamed the *messenger* for the bad news he brought>

syn bearer, carrier, courier, emissary, envoy, internuncio

rel herald; go-between, intermediary, mediator; dispatcher, post

mess–up *n syn* see MESS 3

messy *adj* 1 *syn* see SLOVENLY 1

rel dirty, grimy, grubby

con clean

ant neat

2 *syn* see SLIPSHOD 3

metagrobolize *vb syn* see PUZZLE

metamorphize *vb syn* see TRANSFORM

metamorphose *vb syn* see TRANSFORM

rel age, develop, mature, ripen

metanoia *n syn* see CONVERSION 1

metaphor *n syn* see ANALOGY 2

rel comparison, trope; allegory, personification

idiom figure of speech

metaphysical *adj* 1 *syn* see IMMATERIAL 1

rel supernatural, transcendent, transcendental

2 *syn* see SUPERNATURAL 1

mete (out) *vb* 1 *syn* see ADMINISTER 2

rel measure

2 *syn* see ALLOT

meter *n syn* see RHYTHM

method *n* 1 the means or procedures used in attaining an end <he claimed that his ends justified his *methods*>

syn fashion, manner, mode, modus, system, technique, way, wise

rel design, plan, schema, scheme; form, style; course, line; modus operandi, practice, procedure, process, routine; wrinkle

2 *syn* see ORDER 8

methodic *adj syn* see ORDERLY 1

ant desultory, unmethodical

methodical *adj syn* see ORDERLY 1

rel methodized, organized, systematized; analytical, logical; careful, meticulous, scrupulous

con casual, hit-or-miss, random; confused, jumbled

ant desultory, unmethodical

methodize *vb syn* see ORDER 1

rel establish, fix, set, settle

meticulous *adj syn* see CAREFUL 2

rel fastidious, pernickety, picky; cautious, strict, thorough; microscopic

métier *n* 1 *syn* see TRADE 1

2 *syn* see FORTE

metropolitan *adj syn* see COSMOPOLITAN 1

mettle *n syn* see COURAGE

mettlesome *adj syn* see SPIRITED 2

rel edgy, excitable, high-strung, skittish, startlish

mew *vb syn* see ENCLOSE 1

Mickey Mouse *adj syn* see PETTY 2

mid *adj* 1 *syn* see MIDDLE 2

2 *syn* see MIDDLE 1

mid *prep* 1 *syn* see AMID 1

2 *syn* see AMONG 1

3 *syn* see DURING

middle *adj* 1 equally distant from the extremes <the *middle* finger>

syn center, centermost, equidistant, halfway, medial, median, mid, middlemost, midmost

2 being at neither extreme <paid a *middle* price for it>

syn center, central, intermediary, intermediate, mean, medial, median, mid

middle *n syn* see CENTER 1

middlebrow *n syn* see PHILISTINE

middleman *n syn* see GO-BETWEEN 2

middlemost *adj syn* see MIDDLE 1

middle-of-the-road *adj syn* see MODERATE 4

middle-rate *adj syn* see MEDIUM

middle-road *adj syn* see MODERATE 4

middling *adj syn* see MEDIUM

rel inferior, poor, second-rate

midge *n syn* see DWARF

midget *n syn* see DWARF

midget *adj syn* see TINY

midmost *adj syn* see MIDDLE 1

midpoint *n syn* see CENTER 1

midst *n syn* see CENTER 1

midst *prep* 1 *syn* see AMID 1

2 *syn* see AMONG 1

3 *syn* see DURING

mid–Victorian *n syn* see FOGY

rel bluenose, goody-goody, Mrs. Grundy, prig, prude, puritan; Victorian

mien *n* 1 *syn* see BEARING 1

rel expression, manner, mannerism

2 *syn* see APPEARANCE 2

miff *n* 1 *syn* see OFFENSE 2

rel conniption, fit

2 *syn* see QUARREL

might *n* 1 *syn* see POWER 1

2 *syn* see POWER 4

rel energeticness, lustiness, strenuousness, vigor, vigorousness; forcefulness, forcibleness, powerfulness

3 *syn* see ABILITY 1

4 *syn* see MUSCLE 1

might and main *adv syn* see HARD 1

mightily *adv* 1 *syn* see HARD 1

rel arduously, laboriously, strenuously, toilsomely

2 *syn* see VERY 1

mighty *adj* 1 *syn* see POWERFUL 2

2 *syn* see STRONG 1

3 *syn* see HUGE

rel eminent, illustrious, renowned; august, grand, imposing, impressive, moving

mighty *adv syn* see VERY 1

migrant *adj syn* see MIGRATORY

migrant *n syn* see EMIGRANT

rel in-migrant, out-migrant; drifter, mover, nomad, traveler, wanderer

migrate *vb* to move from one country, place, or locality to another <his father had *migrated* to the Far West years before>

syn emigrate, transmigrate

rel immigrate, in-migrate, out-migrate, remigrate; drift, trek; nomadize, range, roam, rove, wander

migrative *adj syn* see MIGRATORY

ant nonmigratory

migratorial *adj syn* see MIGRATORY

ant nonmigratory

migratory *adj* moving habitually or occasionally from one region or climate to another <the study of *migratory* birds>

---

syn synonym(s)   *rel* related word(s)
ant antonym(s)   *con* contrasted word(s)
idiom idiomatic equivalent(s)
‖ use limited; if in doubt, see a dictionary

syn migrant, migrative, migratorial, mobile, transmigratory
rel errant, nomad, nomadic, ranging, roving, wandering
ant nonmigratory

mild *adj* **1** *syn* see GENTLE 1
rel choice, dainty, delicate, exquisite; moderate, temperate; benign, benignant
con intense, severe, sharp, vehement
ant fierce, harsh
2 *syn* see AMIABLE 1
rel docile, meek; subdued, submissive; deferential, obeisant, subservient

milepost *n syn* see EVENT 2
milestone *n syn* see EVENT 2
milieu *n syn* see ENVIRONMENT
militant *adj* **1** *syn* see BELLIGERENT
rel martial, military
2 *syn* see AGGRESSIVE
rel chauvinistic, jingoistic, militaristic, warmongering; soldierlike, soldierly
ant unmilitary

military *n syn* see TROOP 2
militate *vb syn* see WEIGH 3
milk *n syn* **1** *syn* see FLEECE 1
rel exact, exploit, extort; drain, empty, exhaust, pump, suck, wring
2 *syn* see EDUCE 1

milk-and-water *adj syn* see INSIPID 3
milk-livered *adj syn* see COWARDLY
milksop *n syn* see WEAKLING
rel effeminate; coward
milk-warm *adj syn* see TEPID 1
mill *n syn* see FACTORY
million *n syn* see SCAD
millstone *n syn* see LOAD 3
Milquetoast *n syn* see WEAKLING
mime *n syn* see ACTOR 1
mimic *n syn* see ACTOR 1
mimic *vb* to copy or exaggerate (as manner or gestures) often by way of mockery <*mimicked* her halting speech>
syn ape, burlesque, imitate, mock, parody, take off, travesty
rel hit off, mime, mum; act, do, enact, impersonate, perform, personate, play; copycat; pantomime

mimicry *n* the art or practice of closely imitating another in speech, gestures, or manners <engaged in *mimicry* of café society>
syn apery
rel imitation, mimesis, mimetism; mock, mockery, caricature, parody

miminy-piminy *adj syn* see NICE 1
mince *vb* **1** *syn* see CHOP 2
2 *syn* see SASHAY
mincing *adj syn* see GENTEEL 3
rel dainty, delicate, fastidious, finical, finicking, finicky, fussy, nice, particular, pernickety, persnickety, squeamish

‖**mincy** *adj syn* see NICE 1
mind *n* **1** the element or complex of elements in an individual that feels, perceives, thinks, wills, and reasons <sad to see such a *mind* dulled by drink and drugs>
syn brain, gray matter, head, ‖upper story, ‖upperworks, wit
rel brainpower, intellect, intelligence; consciousness, mentality; faculty, function, power

2 *syn* see WILL 1
rel disposition, temper, temperament
con aversion, disinclination, indisposition
3 *syn* see WIT 2
4 *syn* see OPINION
5 *syn* see MOOD 1
‖**6** *syn* see NOTICE 1

mind *vb* ‖**1** *syn* see REMEMBER
‖**2** *syn* see ENJOY 1
3 *syn* see SEE 1
‖**4** *syn* see INTEND 2
5 *syn* see OBEY
6 *syn* see LOOK 1
7 *syn* see BEWARE
8 *syn* see TEND 2
rel oversee, superintend, supervise; discipline, govern
con forget, slight
9 *syn* see CONSIDER 1

minded *adj syn* see WILLING 1
rel contemplating, intending, planning, purposing
mindful *adj* **1** *syn* see AWARE
ant unmindful
2 inclined to be aware <*mindful* of the ever-changing social scene>
syn heedful, observant, observative, observing, regardful, thoughtful
rel attentive, conscientious; aware, cognizant, conscious, conversant, sensible; alert, vigilant, watchful
con heedless, inattentive
ant mindless, unmindful

mindless *adj* **1** *syn* see SIMPLE 3
2 *syn* see INSANE 1
mine *n syn* see BONANZA
rel lode, quarry, vein; spring, well, wellspring
mine *vb* to dig into for the purpose of obtaining items of use or value <*mined* manuscripts looking for undiscovered masterpieces>
syn delve, quarry
rel burrow, drill, excavate, sap, scoop; work
mingle *vb* **1** *syn* see MIX 1
2 *syn* see SOCIALIZE
mingle-mangle *n syn* see MISCELLANY 1
mingy *adj syn* see STINGY
miniature *n syn* see MODEL 1
miniature *adj syn* see TINY
rel small-scale, subminiature
con large-scale
minify *vb syn* see ABRIDGE 1
rel dwarf, miniaturize, shrink
minikin *n syn* see TINY
minim *n syn* see PARTICLE
minimal *adj* constituting the least possible <*minimal* differences of opinion>
syn minimum
rel littlest, lowest, slightest, smallest; basal, basic, essential, fundamental
con maximum, topmost, utmost; greatest, highest, largest, most
ant maximal
minimize *vb syn* see DECRY 2
rel dwarf, reduce
ant magnify, maximize
minimum *n* the least quantity assignable, admissible, or possible <testing the use of a *minimum* of security at the prison>

syn margin
rel dab, hair, iota, jot, modicum, particle, pittance, smidgen, speck, whit
con abundance, bushel(s), gob(s), ‖lashings, load(s), lot(s), mass(es), much, oodles, profusion, scads, slather(s), ton(s), world(s)
ant maximum

minimum *adj syn see* MINIMAL
ant maximum

minion *n syn see* SYCOPHANT

minister (to) *vb* to attend to the wants and comforts of someone <*minister* to the sick and dying>
syn care (for), mother, nurse, serve, wait (on)
rel cure, heal, remedy; doctor, treat; pander

ministerial *adj syn see* INSTRUMENTAL

minister plenipotentiary *n syn see* ENVOY 1

ministry *n syn see* MEAN 2

minor *adj* 1 *syn see* LITTLE 3
rel dependent; inferior, piddling, trifling; junior, lower
con meaningful, significant
ant major
2 lower in standing or reputation than others of the same class <a *minor* poet of the late eighteenth century>
syn bush, bush-league, dinky, insignificant, lesser, minor-league, secondary, small, small-fry, small-time
rel average, fair, indifferent, mediocre, medium, middling, second-rate, undistinguished, unnoticeable; trivial, unimportant
con chief, foremost, leading, principal
ant major

minor *n syn see* INFANT 2

minority *n syn see* INFANCY 2
ant majority

minor-league *adj syn see* MINOR 2

minstrel *n syn see* BARD 1
rel balladist, singer, wait

mint *n syn see* FORTUNE 4

mint *adj syn see* BRAND-NEW
rel intact, original, perfect, unmarred

minus *prep syn see* WITHOUT 2
ant plus

minute *n syn see* INSTANT 1

minute *adj* 1 *syn see* TINY
2 *syn see* LITTLE 3
3 *syn see* CIRCUMSTANTIAL
rel careful, meticulous, punctilious, scrupulous
con abstract; general, universal; comprehending, comprehensive, embracing, embracive, including, inclusive

minutely *adj syn see* CONTINUAL

minutia *n, usu* **minutiae** *pl* 1 *syn see* INS AND OUTS
2 *syn see* TRIVIA

minx *n* a pert girl <her rivals called her a brazen *minx*>
syn hussy, jade, malapert, saucebox, slut, snip

rel broad, brat, upstart; baggage, chippy, drab, floozy, strumpet, tart, trollop, trull

miracle *n syn see* WONDER 1

miraculous *adj* 1 *syn see* SUPERNATURAL 1
2 *syn see* MARVELOUS 1
con natural, normal

mirage *n syn see* DELUSION 1

mire *n syn see* SWAMP
rel muck

mire *vb* 1 *syn see* DELAY 1
rel bemire, sink; adhere, cleave, cling, cohere, stick; enmesh, ensnare, entangle, entrap, involve, snare, trap
2 *syn see* INVOLVE 1

mirror *n* 1 a polished or smooth surface (as of glass) that forms images by reflection <spent hours looking at herself in the *mirror*>
syn glass, looking glass, ‖seeing glass
rel cheval glass, pier glass, reflector, speculum
2 *syn see* MODEL 2

mirror *vb* 1 *syn see* REFLECT 1
2 *syn see* REPRESENT 2

mirth *n* a mood or temper characterized by joy and high spirits and usually manifested in laughter and merrymaking <a man of contentment, but seldom of *mirth*>
syn glee, hilarity, jocularity, jocundity, jollity, joviality, merriment
rel cheer, cheerfulness, joyfulness, lightheartedness; gladness, happiness; frivolity, levity
con blues, dejection, depression, dumps, gloom, sadness; boredom, ennui, tedium; anguish, misery, woe; infelicity, wretchedness
ant melancholy

mirthful *adj syn see* MERRY
ant mirthless

miry *adj syn see* MUDDY 1

misadventure *n* 1 *syn see* DISASTER
2 *syn see* ACCIDENT 2
rel blunder, boner, bull, error, faux pas, howler, lapse, slip

misanthropic *adj syn see* ANTISOCIAL
rel misogynic
con altruistic, benevolent, charitable, humane, humanitarian
ant philanthropic

misapply *vb syn see* ABUSE 2
rel misappropriate, misdirect, mismanage

misapprehend *vb* 1 *syn see* MISUNDERSTAND 1
ant apprehend
2 *syn see* MISUNDERSTAND 2
ant apprehend

misappropriate *vb syn see* EMBEZZLE

misbegotten *adj syn see* ILLEGITIMATE 1

misbehaving *adj syn see* NAUGHTY 1
ant well-behaved

misbehavior *n syn see* MISCONDUCT

misbelief *n syn see* HERESY

misbeliever *n syn see* HERETIC

miscalculate *vb* to calculate wrongly <*miscalculate* the distance> <he seriously *miscalculated* the effect of his remark>
syn misestimate, misjudge, misreckon
rel discount, disregard, overlook; misconstrue, misinterpret, misunderstand; overesti-

---

syn synonym(s)	*rel* related word(s)
ant antonym(s)	*con* contrasted word(s)
idiom idiomatic equivalent(s)	
‖ use limited; if in doubt, see a dictionary	

mate, overprize, overrate, overvalue; underestimate, underprize, underrate, undervalue

miscarry vb to go wrong or amiss <her plans *miscarried* almost from the start>
syn misfire, miss
rel abort; fail, flop
idiom fall through, miss fire, miss the mark
con come off, prevail, succeed

miscellaneous adj consisting of diverse things or members <gathered together a *miscellaneous* lot of books for sale>
syn assorted, chowchow, conglomerate, heterogeneous, indiscriminate, mixed, motley, multifarious, promiscuous, unassorted, unsorted, varied
rel different, disparate, divergent, diverse, various; divers, many, sundry; odd; commingled, jumbled, mingled, scrambled
con akin, alike, identical, like, parallel, similar, uniform

miscellany n 1 an unorganized mixture of various dissimilar items or elements <sold a *miscellany* of old household effects>
syn assortment, brew, chowchow, colluvies, gallimaufry, hash, hodgepodge, hotchpotch, jumble, medley, mélange, melee, minglemangle, mishmash, mixed bag, motley, odds and ends, olio, olla podrida, omnium-gatherum, pasticcio, pastiche, patchwork, porridge, potpourri, rumble-bumble, salad, salmagundi, smorgasbord, stew
rel mess, muddle; accumulation, aggregation, congeries, conglomeration, cumulation; combination, mix, mixture
2 *syn* see ANTHOLOGY

mischance n 1 *syn* see MISFORTUNE
2 *syn* see ACCIDENT 2

mischief n 1 *syn* see INJURY 1
rel difficulty, hardship, trouble
2 *syn* see SCAMP
3 *syn* see MISCHIEVOUSNESS
4 *syn* see DISCORD

‖**mischiefful** adj *syn* see PLAYFUL 1

mischief-maker n *syn* see TROUBLEMAKER

mischievous adj 1 *syn* see HARMFUL 1
rel dangerous, hazardous, perilous, precarious, risky
2 *syn* see NAUGHTY 1
rel annoying, bothering, bothersome, irking, irksome, vexatious, vexing
3 *syn* see PLAYFUL 1
rel arch, foxy, insidious, sly, tricky

mischievousness n action or conduct that annoys or irritates without causing or meaning serious harm <a wag who was forever engaging in *mischievousness*>
syn devilment, devilry, deviltry, diablerie, impishness, mischief, roguery, roguishness, sportiveness, waggery, waggishness
rel doggery, odiousness, offensiveness; evil, harm, hurt, injury; annoying, pestering, teasing

miscolor vb *syn* see MISREPRESENT

miscomprehend vb *syn* see MISUNDERSTAND 1

misconceive vb *syn* see MISUNDERSTAND 2

misconduct n improper behavior <was charged with *misconduct*>

syn misbehavior, misdoing, wrongdoing
rel impropriety; malfeasance, malversation, misfeasance

misconstrue vb *syn* see MISUNDERSTAND 2

miscreant adj *syn* see VICIOUS 2

miscreant n *syn* see VILLAIN 1

miscreation n *syn* see FREAK 2
rel deformation, deformity

miscue n *syn* see ERROR 2

misdate n *syn* see ANACHRONISM 1

misdating n *syn* see ANACHRONISM 1

misdeed n *syn* see CRIME 1

misdeem vb 1 *syn* see MISJUDGE 2
2 *syn* see MISTAKE 1

misdoing n *syn* see MISCONDUCT

misdoubt vb *syn* see DISTRUST
rel apprehend, dread, fear

mise-en-scène n 1 *syn* see SCENE 1
2 *syn* see SCENE 3
3 *syn* see ENVIRONMENT

misemploy vb *syn* see ABUSE 2

miser n a mean grasping person <an old *miser* who loved only his bank account>
syn cheapskate, cheeseparer, chuff, hunks, moneygrubber, muckworm, nabal, niggard, ‖nipcheese, penny pincher, piker, scrooge, skin, skinflint, stiff, tightwad
rel glutton, hog, pig

miserable adj *syn* see WOEFUL 1
rel despairing, despondent, forlorn, hopeless; piteous, pitiable, pitiful; melancholy
con cheerful, glad, happy, joyful, joyous, lighthearted

miserly adj *syn* see STINGY
rel avaricious, covetous, grasping, greedy; abject, ignoble, sordid
con bountious, generous; altruistic, benevolent, charitable

misery n 1 a state of suffering and want that is the result of poverty or conditions beyond one's control <the poor learn to live with *misery*> <the utter *misery* in which the flood victims survived>
syn unhappiness, woe, wretchedness
rel agony, anguish; despondency, grief, sorrow; desolation, squalor
con beatitude, blessedness, bliss, felicity, happiness; content, ease, satisfaction
2 *syn* see DISTRESS
rel adversity, misfortune; dejection, depression, melancholy, sadness
ant blessedness
‖**3** *syn* see PAIN 1

misesteem vb *syn* see MISJUDGE 2

misestimate vb *syn* see MISCALCULATE

misfire vb *syn* see MISCARRY

misfortunate adj *syn* see UNLUCKY
ant fortunate

misfortune n adverse fortune or an instance of this <her hopes and dreams soon ended in *misfortune*> <unable to grasp why he had been struck by such a *misfortune*>
syn adversity, contretemps, ‖dole, mischance, mishap, tragedy, ‖unluck
rel calamity, cataclysm, catastrophe, disaster; accident, casualty; affliction, cross, trial, tribulation, visitation
con break, chance, luck, opportunity
ant fortune

misgiving *n syn* see APPREHENSION 3
  rel doubt, fear, qualm, suspicion; distrust, mistrust
misguided *adj syn* see MISTAKEN
mishandle *vb* 1 *syn* see MANHANDLE
  2 *syn* see ABUSE 2
mishap *n* 1 *syn* see MISFORTUNE
  2 *syn* see ACCIDENT 2
mishmash *n* 1 *syn* see MISCELLANY 1
  2 *syn* see CLUTTER 2
misidentify *vb syn* see MISTAKE 1
misimprove *vb syn* see ABUSE 2
misinterpret *vb syn* see MISUNDERSTAND
  1
misjudge *vb* 1 *syn* see MISCALCULATE
  2 to have a mistaken opinion of <her first impression led her to *misjudge* the girl>
  syn misdeem, misesteem, mistake
  rel misapprehend, miscomprehend, misconceive, misconstrue, misinterpret, misunderstand
  con catch on (to), penetrate, tumble (to), wise (up)
misknow *vb syn* see MISUNDERSTAND 1
mislaying *n syn* see LOSS 1
mislead *vb syn* see DECEIVE
  rel lie, misguide, misinform; entice, inveigle, lure, seduce, tempt
misleading *adj* having an appearance or character that leads one astray or into error <the president made several *misleading* statements to the people>
  syn beguiling, deceiving, deceptive, deluding, delusive, delusory, fallacious, false
  rel casuistical, sophistical, specious; wrong; bewildering, confounding, distracting, perplexing, puzzling; deceitful, inaccurate
  con clarifying, elucidative, explanatory, illuminating
‖**mismannered** *adj syn* see RUDE 6
mismatch *n syn* see CLASH 2
misorder *n syn* see CONFUSION 3
misplacement *n syn* see LOSS 1
misplacing *n syn* see LOSS 1
misread *vb syn* see MISUNDERSTAND 2
misreckon *vb syn* see MISCALCULATE
‖**misremember** *vb syn* see FORGET 1
misrepresent *vb* to give a false, imperfect, or misleading representation of <the summary totally *misrepresents* the facts of the case>
  syn belie, color, confuse, distort, falsify, garble, miscolor, misstate, pervert, twist, warp, wrench, wrest
  rel dress, embellish, embroider, gild, gloss, varnish; camouflage, cloak, disguise, dissemble, mask; counterfeit, feign, simulate; equivocate, lie, palter, prevaricate, weasel
  idiom give a false coloring, put a false construction (or appearance) on
misrepresentation *n syn* see LIE
misrule *n syn* see DISORDER 2
miss *vb* 1 *syn* see NEGLECT
  2 *syn* see MISUNDERSTAND 1
  3 *syn* see MISCARRY
‖**miss** *n syn* see ABSENCE

miss *n syn* see GIRL 1
misshape *vb syn* see DEFORM
misshape *n syn* see DEFORMITY
missing *adj* 1 *syn* see ABSENT 1
  2 *syn* see LOST 2
mission *n* a continuing task or responsibility that one is destined or fitted to do or specially called upon to undertake <his *mission* in life was to serve humanity>
  syn calling, lifework, vocation
  rel goal, purpose; business, profession, trade
missionary *n* one who attempts to convert others to a specific way of life, set of ideas, or course of action <served as a *missionary* for the feminist cause>
  syn apostle, colporteur, evangelist, missioner, propagandist
  rel revivalist; promoter
missioner *n syn* see MISSIONARY
missish *adj syn* see PRIM 1
missive *n syn* see LETTER 2
Miss-Nancyish *adj syn* see EFFEMINATE
misstate *vb syn* see MISREPRESENT
misstatement *n syn* see LIE
misstep *n syn* see ERROR 2
‖**missus** *n syn* see WIFE
missy *n syn* see GIRL 1
mist *n syn* see HAZE 1
mist *vb syn* see OBSCURE
mistake *vb* 1 to take one thing to be another <he *mistakes* sarcasm for wit>
  syn confound, confuse, misdeem, misidentify, mix, mix up
  rel misconceive, misknow; addle, jumble, muddle, tumble
  con discern, distinguish, grasp, perceive; differentiate, separate
  ant recognize
  2 *syn* see MISUNDERSTAND 2
  3 *syn* see MISJUDGE 2
mistake *n* 1 *syn* see ERROR 2
  rel confounding, confusion, mistaking; inadvertence; disregarding, neglect, neglecting, omission, omitting, slight, slighting
  2 *syn* see ERROR 1
mistaken *adj* acting, thinking, or judging in a manner at variance with truth or the facts <he is *mistaken* in his evaluation of the crisis>
  syn erroneous, misguided, wrong
  rel confounded, confused; deceived, deluded, misinformed
  idiom all wet, off base, off the track
  con accurate, correct, right, unerring; exact, precise
mister *n syn* see HUSBAND
mistimed *adj syn* see UNSEASONABLE 1
  ant well-timed
mistiming *n syn* see ANACHRONISM 1
mistreat *vb syn* see ABUSE 4
mistress *n* a woman who is a man's regular partner in nonmarital sexual activity <gave up his *mistress* when he married>
  syn ‖doxy, girl friend, inamorata, lover, paramour, woman; *compare* HARLOT 1
  rel bedmate; concubine; kept woman; dulcinea
mistrust *n syn* see UNCERTAINTY
  rel apprehension, foreboding, misgiving, presentiment

---

syn synonym(s)   *rel* related word(s)
ant antonym(s)   *con* contrasted word(s)
idiom idiomatic equivalent(s)
‖ use limited; if in doubt, see a dictionary

con dependence, faith, reliance
ant assurance, trust

mistrust *vb* **1** *syn* see DISTRUST
rel anticipate, apprehend, foresee; alarm, frighten, scare; appall, dismay
ant trust
2 *syn* see QUESTION 2

mistrustful *adj syn* see SUSPICIOUS 2
ant trustful, trusting

mistrustfully *adv syn* see ASKANCE 2
ant trustfully, trustingly

misty *adj syn* see HAZY

misunderstand *vb* **1** to fail to understand <he *misunderstood* the full meaning of the novel>
syn misapprehend, miscomprehend, misknow, miss
rel misconceive, misconstrue, misinterpret, misread, mistake
con apprehend, conceive, know, realize; fathom, follow, grasp, seize, take in
ant comprehend, understand
2 to interpret incorrectly <*misunderstood* the instructions>
syn misapprehend, misconceive, misconstrue, misinterpret, misread, mistake
rel misexplain, mistranslate; miscomprehend, misknow
con fathom, follow, take in
ant understand

misuse *vb* **1** *syn* see ABUSE 2
2 *syn* see ABUSE 4

mite *n syn* see PARTICLE

mitigate *vb syn* see RELIEVE 1
rel extenuate, palliate
con aggravate, enhance, heighten; augment, increase
ant intensify

mitigation *n syn* see EASE 3

mix *vb* **1** to combine or be combined into a more or less uniform whole <*mixed* the ingredients to make a thick sauce>
syn admix, amalgamate, blend, comingle, commingle, commix, compound, fuse, immingle, immix, interblend, interflow, interfuse, intermingle, intermix, make up, meld, merge, mingle
rel associate, combine, conjoin, inosculate, join, link, unite; braid, lump, work in; coalesce; blunge
con divide, part, separate, sever, sunder
2 *syn* see MISTAKE 1

mix *n syn* see MIXTURE

mixed *adj syn* see MISCELLANEOUS
rel amalgamated, blended, fused, merged, mingled

mixed bag *n syn* see MISCELLANY 1

mixologist *n syn* see BARTENDER

mixture *n* a product formed by the combination of two or more things <the tea is actually a *mixture* of several varieties>
syn admixture, alloy, amalgam, amalgamation, blend, commixture, composite, compost, compound, fusion, immixture, interfusion, intermixture, mix, mix-up
rel brew, concoction, confection, mélange

mix up *vb* **1** *syn* see CONFUSE 2
ant straighten (out)
2 *syn* see CONFUSE 5
3 *syn* see MISTAKE 1

4 *syn* see DISORDER 1
ant straighten (out *or* up)

mix-up *n* **1** *syn* see MESS 3
2 *syn* see MIXTURE

mizmaze *n syn* see MAZE 1

mizzle *vb syn* see SPRINKLE 5

mizzle *vb syn* see CONFUSE 2

moan *vb syn* see DEPLORE 1

moanful *adj syn* see MELANCHOLY 2

mob *n* **1** *syn* see RABBLE
2 a large disorderly crowd of people usually bent on riotous or destructive action <the *mob* screamed for a lynching>
syn rabble, rout
rel posse; crowd, crush, horde, press, push, throng; herd, swarm
3 *syn* see CLIQUE

mob *vb syn* see SCOLD 1

mobile *adj* **1** *syn* see MOVABLE
rel fluid, liquid; protean; capricious, fickle, inconstant, mercurial
con immutable, invariable, unchangeable
ant immobile
2 *syn* see CHANGEABLE 1
ant immobile, stable
3 *syn* see VERSATILE
4 *syn* see MIGRATORY

mobile home *n syn* see TRAILER

mobilize *vb* **1** to put into movement or circulation <an increase in prices *mobilizes* the whole cycle of inflation>
syn actuate, circulate, set off
rel activate, impel, propel
idiom set in motion
con inactivate, slow (down *or* up)
ant immobilize
2 *syn* see MOVE 5
3 to assemble (as resources) and make ready for use or action <the president tried to *mobilize* support for the new proposal>
syn marshal, muster, organize, rally

mobocracy *n syn* see ANARCHY 1

mock *vb* **1** *syn* see RIDICULE
rel buffoon, burlesque, caricature, parody, travesty
2 *syn* see DECEIVE
3 *syn* see MIMIC
rel affect, assume, counterfeit, feign, simulate

mock *n* **1** *syn* see LAUGHINGSTOCK
2 *syn* see MOCKERY 2

mock *adj* **1** *syn* see ARTIFICIAL 2
rel pseudo, quasi, so-called
2 *syn* see FICTITIOUS 2
rel bogus, phony

mockery *n* **1** *syn* see LAUGHINGSTOCK
2 an insincere, contemptible, or impertinent imitation of something worthwhile <arbitrary methods that make a *mockery* of justice>
syn burlesque, caricature, farce, mock, sham, travesty
rel derision, ridicule, sport; parody, satire, take-off; joke, laughingstock

mode *n* **1** *syn* see VEIN 1
2 *syn* see METHOD 1
3 *syn* see STATE 1

mode *n syn* see FASHION 3

model *n* **1** a miniature representation of something <a *model* of the dam that was accurate down to the last detail>

syn miniature, pocket edition
rel copy, mock-up, replica, reproduction; dummy, effigy

2 something set or held before one for guidance or imitation <Samuel Johnson's literary style is often used as a *model* for writers seeking precision and clarity>
syn archetype, beau ideal, ensample, example, exemplar, ideal, mirror, paradigm, pattern, standard; *compare* PARAGON
rel apotheosis, nonesuch, nonpareil, paragon; emblem, symbol, type; embodiment, epitome, quintessence; criterion, gauge, touchstone

model *adj* **1** *syn* see IDEAL 3
rel commendable, exemplary
2 *syn* see PERFECT 3
3 *syn* see TYPICAL 1

moderate *adj* **1** *syn* see SOBER 3
2 not excessive in degree, amount, or intensity <the new proposals were met with only *moderate* enthusiasm> <the snowfall is expected to be no more than *moderate*>
syn modest, reasonable, temperate
rel bland, gentle, mild, soft; inconsequential, inconsiderable, slight, small; paltry, piddling, trifling, trivial
con excessive, extreme, inordinate, intemperate, radical, unreasonable
ant immoderate
3 *syn* see MEDIUM
rel constant, equable, even, steady
4 avoiding extreme political or social measures <party policy became increasingly *moderate*>
syn middle-of-the-road, middle-road, soft≈ shell
con conservative, right, tory; left, radical, red; extremist, fanatical, ultra
5 *syn* see CONSERVATIVE 2

moderate *vb* **1** to modify as to avoid an extreme or keep within bounds <actors *moderate* their voices and gestures to fit the size of the theater>
syn modulate, restrain, temper
rel abate, decrease, diminish, lessen, reduce; alleviate, cushion, lighten, mitigate, mollify, relieve, slacken, slow; constrain, control, qualify; chasten, cool, subdue, tone (down)
con aggravate, enhance, heighten, intensify; augment, increase
2 *syn* see ABATE 4

moderately *adv* **1** *syn* see ENOUGH 2
2 *syn* see SOMEWHAT 2
ant extremely, immoderately

moderateness *n syn* see TEMPERANCE 1
ant immoderateness, immoderation

moderation *n syn* see TEMPERANCE 1
ant immoderateness, immoderation

moderator *n* one who arbitrates <the labor dispute was finally referred to a *moderator*>
syn arbitrator, mediator
rel arbiter, judge; conciliator, negotiator, peacemaker

modern *adj* **1** having taken place, existed, or developed in times close to the present <*modern* concepts of engineering made the bridge possible>
syn late, recent
rel contemporary, present-day; latter
con antiquated, old-fashioned, old hat, outdated, outmoded, outworn
ant old-time
2 *syn* see NEW 1
rel coincident, concomitant, concurrent, contemporaneous, contemporary; current, prevailing, prevalent
ant ancient, antique

modernistic *adj syn* see NEW 1
rel futuristic
ant antiquated

modernize *vb syn* see RENEW 1

modest *adj* **1** *syn* see HUMBLE 1
rel moderate, temperate; retiring, withdrawing; unboastful; unpresuming, unpresumptuous, unpretending
con barefaced, brazen, impudent, shameless
ant ambitious
2 *syn* see SHY 1
rel reticent, silent; nice, proper, seemly
3 *syn* see CHASTE
rel priggish, prim, prissy, prudish, puritanical, straitlaced, stuffy
con improper, indecent, indecorous, indelicate, unseemly
ant immodest
4 *syn* see MODERATE 2
5 *syn* see PLAIN 1

modicum *n syn* see PARTICLE

modification *n syn* see CHANGE 1
rel conversion, metamorphosis, transformation, transmogrification; qualification, tempering

modified *adj syn* see QUALIFIED 2

modify *vb syn* see CHANGE 1
rel modulate, restrain, temper; qualify

modish *adj syn* see STYLISH
rel voguish

modulate *vb syn* see MODERATE 1

modus *n syn* see METHOD 1

‖**mog** *vb syn* see GO 2

mogul *n syn* see MAGNATE

moiety *n syn* see PART 1

moil *vb* **1** *syn* see LABOR 1
‖**2** *syn* see SEETHE 4

moil *n* **1** *syn* see WORK 2
2 *syn* see COMMOTION 4

moira *n syn* see FATE

moist *adj* **1** *syn* see DAMP
2 *syn* see SENTIMENTAL

moistureless *adj syn* see DRY 1
ant moist

moisty *adj syn* see DAMP

‖**moke** *n syn* see DONKEY 1

mold *n syn* see TYPE

mold *vb syn* see MAKE 3

moldable *adj syn* see PLASTIC

molder *vb syn* see DECAY

moldy *adj syn* see OLD-FASHIONED

moldy fig *n syn* see FOGY

mole *n syn* see BIRTHMARK 1

molecule *n syn* see PARTICLE

molest *vb* to annoy or disturb with hostile intent or injurious effect <he was specifically warned by the court not to *molest* his former wife>

---

syn bait, heckle, persecute, torment
rel annoy, badger, bother, irk, pester; pother, tease; bedevil, beset, devil, trouble; harass, harry, vex

moll *n syn see* PROSTITUTE

mollify *vb* **1** *syn see* PACIFY
rel lighten; temper; abate, decrease, lessen, reduce
ant exasperate
2 *syn see* RELIEVE 1

‖**molly** *n syn see* WEAKLING

mollycoddle *n syn see* WEAKLING
rel ‖mollycot

mollycoddle *vb syn see* BABY
ant neglect; abuse

molt *vb syn see* SHED 2

mom *n syn see* MOTHER 1

‖**momble** *vb syn see* CONFUSE 2

moment *n* **1** *syn see* INSTANT 1
ant eternity
2 *syn see* POINT 7
3 *syn see* OCCASION 5
4 *syn see* IMPORTANCE
rel advantage, avail, profit, use

momentaneous *adj syn see* TRANSIENT

momentary *adj syn see* TRANSIENT
rel brief, quick, short; impulsive
ant agelong

momentous *adj* **1** *syn see* IMPORTANT 1
ant trivial
2 *syn see* EPOCHAL

momentousness *n syn see* IMPORTANCE
ant triviality

mommy *n syn see* MOTHER 1

momus *n syn see* CRITIC

monarch *adj syn see* KINGLY

monarchial *adj syn see* KINGLY

monarchical *adj syn see* KINGLY

mondaine *adj syn see* SOPHISTICATED 2

monetary *adj syn see* FINANCIAL
rel numismatic

money *n* something (as pieces of stamped metal or paper certificates) customarily and legally used as a medium of exchange <the only thing that he liked about his job was the *money*>
syn ‖blunt, ‖brass, ‖bread, ‖cabbage, cash, ‖chink, ‖chips, ‖coin, currency, ‖dibs, dinero, ‖do-re-mi, dough, filthy lucre, ‖gelt, ‖greenbacks, ‖jack, ‖kale, legal tender, ‖lettuce, ‖long green, loot, lucre, ‖mazuma, ‖moolah, ‖mopus, needful, ‖ooftish, pelf, rhino, rocks, ‖scratch, ‖shekels, ‖smash, stuff, ‖stumpy, ‖sugar, swag, ‖wampum
rel bankroll, capital, coinage, finances, funds, mammon, resources, riches, treasure, wealth, wherewithal; boodle, hay; ‖stiff

moneyed *adj syn see* RICH 1
ant penniless, unmoneyed

moneygrubber *n syn see* MISER

moneymaking *adj syn see* ADVANTAGEOUS 1

monger *n syn see* PEDDLER

monger *vb syn see* PEDDLE 2

mongerer *n syn see* PEDDLER

mongrel *n syn see* HYBRID

‖**moniker** *n* **1** *syn see* NAME 1
2 *syn see* NICKNAME

monish *vb syn see* REPROVE

monition *n syn see* WARNING

monitorial *adj syn see* MONITORY

monitory *adj* giving a warning <the parents wrote their son a *monitory* letter>
syn admonishing, admonitory, cautionary, cautioning, monitorial, warning
rel advisory, counseling; critical, expostulatory, remonstrant; exhortatory, hortatory; moralistic, moralizing, preachy

monkey *n* **1** *syn see* FOOL 3
2 *syn see* URCHIN

monkey *adj syn see* SMALL 1

monkey (with) *vb syn see* MEDDLE

monkeyshine *n usu* **monkeyshines** *pl*
syn see PRANK

monocratic *adj syn see* ABSOLUTE 4
con democratic

monogram *n* a sign of identity usually formed of the combined initials of a name <everything he owned had his *monogram* on it>
syn cipher
rel device, initials; John Hancock, signature

monograph *n syn see* DISCOURSE 2

monography *n syn see* DISCOURSE 2

monopolize *vb* to take up completely <he would attempt to *monopolize* every conversation>
syn absorb, consume, engross, sew up
rel corner, hog; devour; have, hold, own, possess; employ, use, utilize; control, manage
con contribute, participate, share

monopolizing *adj syn see* ENGROSSING

monopoly *n* exclusive possession <neither party has a *monopoly* on morality>
syn corner
rel cartel, consortium, pool, syndicate, trust; copyright; ownership, possessorship, proprietorship

monotone *n syn see* MONOTONY

monotone *adj syn see* DULL 9

monotonous *adj syn see* DULL 9
rel samely, uniform, unvaried; repetitious; jog-trot, singsong
con changing, varying; fresh, new, novel; absorbing, engrossing, interesting

monotonousness *n syn see* MONOTONY

monotony *n* a tedious sameness or reiteration <the *monotony* of his job finally got to him>
syn humdrum, monotone, monotonousness
rel boredom, ennui, tedium; dryness, flatness, uniformity
con variability, variation; diversification, diversity, multifariousness, variety

monster *n* **1** *syn see* FREAK 2
rel demon, devil, fiend, hellhound; bandersnatch
2 *syn see* GIANT

monster *adj syn see* HUGE

monstrosity *n* **1** *syn see* FREAK 2
2 *syn see* EYESORE

monstrous *adj* **1** extremely impressive <the traditional burial ceremonies turned into a *monstrous* spectacle>
syn cracking, fantastic, massive, monumental, mortal, prodigious, stupendous, towering, tremendous
rel grandiose, impressive, magnificent, showy, splendid, superb; colossal, enormous, huge, immense, mammoth, vast

con mean, petty, picayune, poky, small-time
2 *syn* see HUGE
3 *syn* see OUTRAGEOUS 2
rel glaring, rank; fateful, ominous, portentous; flagitious, infamous
‖**monstrous** *adv syn* see VERY 1
monstrousness *n syn* see ENORMITY 1
Montezuma's revenge *n syn* see DIARRHEA
monument *n* **1** *syn* see DOCUMENT 1
2 a lasting evidence or reminder of someone or something notable <the whole body of students who learned from him form his *monument*>
syn memorial, testimonial
rel memento, tribute
3 *syn* see TOMBSTONE
monument *vb syn* see MEMORIALIZE 2
monumental *adj* **1** *syn* see HUGE
2 *syn* see MONSTROUS 1
3 *syn* see TOWERING 4
monumentalize *vb syn* see MEMORIALIZE 2
moocah *n syn* see MARIJUANA
mooch *vb syn* see WANDER 1
moocher *n syn* see BEGGAR 1
mooching *n syn* see MENDICANCY
mood *n* **1** a state of mind in which an emotion or set of emotions gains ascendancy <a melancholy *mood* induced by the sight of ancient ruins>
syn humor, mind, strain, temper, tone, vein
rel character, disposition, individuality, personality, temperament; soul, spirit; affection, emotion, feeling, response
2 *syn* see TEMPER 1
3 *syn* see AIR 3
moody *adj* subject to moods <a *moody* person whose behavior was erratic and whose actions were unpredictable>
syn humorsome, temperamental
rel capricious, fickle, inconstant, mercurial, unstable, whimsical; broody
con calm, dispassionate, stable, steady, unexcitable; bovine, impassive, stolid
‖**moolah** *n syn* see MONEY
mooncalf *n syn* see FOOL 1
‖**moonraker** *n syn* see DUNCE
moonshine *n* **1** *syn* see NONSENSE 2
2 illegally distilled liquor <his death was caused by bad *moonshine*>
syn bathtub gin, ‖blockade, bootleg, ‖busthead, ‖hooch, mountain dew, white lightning
rel homebrew; ‖bug juice, grappa, ‖jake, smoke, squareface
moor *vb syn* see FASTEN 2
moot *vb* **1** *syn* see BROACH
2 *syn* see DISCUSS 1
moot *adj* open to question <it is a *moot* point whether he would have been tried and convicted>
syn arguable, debatable, disputable, doubtful, dubious, mootable, problematic, questionable, uncertain; *compare* DOUBTFUL 1

rel controversial, suspect; unsettled
con confirmed, established, settled; inarguable, indisputable, undebatable, unproblematic, unquestionable; certain, sure
mooting *n syn* see ARGUMENTATION
mootable *adj syn* see MOOT
mop *vb syn* see GRIMACE
mop *n syn* see GRIMACE
mop (up) *vb syn* see WHIP 2
mope *vb* **1** to become listless or dejected <*moped* for several days after the divorce>
syn brood, despond
rel ache, grieve, grump, pout, sulk
2 *syn* see SAUNTER
mopes *n pl syn* see SADNESS
mopey *adj syn* see DOWNCAST
moppet *n syn* see CHILD 1
‖**mopus** *n syn* see MONEY
moral *adj* **1** conforming to a standard of what is right and good <*moral* goodness may be distinguished from intellectual goodness>
syn ethical, moralistic, noble, principled, righteous, right-minded, virtuous
rel good, right; conscientious, honest, honorable, just, scrupulous, upright; chaste, decent, modest, pure
con amoral, nonmoral, unmoral
ant immoral
2 *syn* see DIDACTIC
3 *syn* see ELEVATED 2
moral *n syn* see MAXIM
morale *n* a sense of common purpose or a degree of dedication to a common task regarded as characteristic of or dominant in a group <*morale* was high among the troops>
syn esprit, esprit de corps
rel drive, spirit, vigor; assurance, confidence, self-confidence, self-possession
con enervation; aimlessness, purposelessness; egoism, egotism, self-centeredness
moralistic *adj syn* see MORAL 1
rel didactic
morality *n* **1** *syn* see GOODNESS
rel godliness, saintliness
2 *syn* see ETHIC 1
moralize *vb* to make moral reflections usually in an officious or tiresome manner <people avoided him as he was always *moralizing*>
syn preach, preachify, sermonize
rel lecture, pontificate
moralizing *adj syn* see DIDACTIC
morally *adv syn* see VIRTUALLY
morals *n pl* **1** *syn* see ETHIC 1
2 *syn* see ETHIC 2
rel conduct, habits, standards
morass *n* **1** *syn* see SWAMP
2 *syn* see MAZE 1
rel dunghill
moratorium *n syn* see SUSPENSION 2
morbid *adj* abnormally susceptible to or characterized by gloomy or unwholesome feelings <his *morbid* poetry is the product of his lifelong frustrations>
syn morose, sick, sickly
rel gloomy, melancholic; psychotic; dark, moody, saturnine, sullen
con healthy, sound, well, wholesome; solid, stable, stolid, sturdy
mordacious *adj syn* see CAUSTIC 1

---

syn synonym(s)   *rel* related word(s)
ant antonym(s)   *con* contrasted word(s)
idiom idiomatic equivalent(s)
‖ use limited; if in doubt, see a dictionary

mordancy *n syn* see ACRIMONY
rel incisiveness, pungency, trenchancy; acidity, acridity, causticity, mordacity

mordant *adj syn* see CAUSTIC 1

more *adj syn* see ADDITIONAL

more *adv syn* see ALSO 2
2 to a greater or higher degree <were *more* evenly matched>
syn better

more or less *adv* 1 *syn* see SOMEWHAT 2
2 *syn* see NEARLY

moreover *adv syn* see ALSO 2

mores *n pl* 1 *syn* see ETHIC 2
2 *syn* see MANNER 5

morgue *n syn* see PRIDE 3

moribund *adj* approaching death or a final end <found lying *moribund* in her bed> <with its mills shut down the city's economy was *moribund*>
syn dying
rel expiring, fading, going; decadent, deteriorating, regressing
idiom at death's door, on one's last legs, with one foot in the grave
con booming, flourishing, prospering, thriving; lively, viable

morn *n* 1 *syn* see DAWN 1
2 *syn* see MORNING 2

morne *adj syn* see GLOOMY 3

morning *n* 1 *syn* see DAWN 1
con sundown, sunset
2 the time before noon <it rained most of the *morning*>
syn forenoon, morn
con afternoon, evening; day, night

moron *n* 1 *syn* see FOOL 4
2 *syn* see DUNCE

moronic *adj syn* see RETARDED

morose *adj* 1 *syn* see SULLEN
rel choleric, cranky, irascible, splenetic, testy; irritable, waspish; brusque, gruff
con jocund, jolly, jovial, merry
ant blithe
2 *syn* see MORBID

morsel *n* 1 a small piece or quantity of food <tossed a *morsel* of meat to the dog>
syn bit, bite, mouthful
rel taste; tidbit; crumb, ort, scrap
2 *syn* see SNACK
3 *syn* see DELICACY

mort *n syn* see CORPSE

‖**mortacious** *adv syn* see VERY 1

mortal *adj* 1 *syn* see DEADLY 1
rel implacable, relentless, unrelenting
2 *syn* see GRIM 3
3 *syn* see MONSTROUS 1
4 *syn* see HUMAN
rel finite, temporal; frail, weak
5 *syn* see PROBABLE

mortal *n syn* see HUMAN

mortality *n* 1 *syn* see FATALITY 1
2 *syn* see MANKIND

mortally *adv syn* see VERY 1

mortgage *vb syn* see PAWN

mortician *n* one whose business is to prepare the dead for burial and to arrange and manage funerals <*morticians* must be certified>
syn funeral director, undertaker
rel embalmer

mortiferous *adj syn* see DEADLY 1

mortified *adj* 1 *syn* see SEVERE 1
2 *syn* see ASHAMED
rel annoyed, harassed, harried, worried

mortuary *adj syn* see SEPULCHRAL 1

mosey *vb syn* see SAUNTER

‖**moss** *n syn* see SWAMP

mossback *n* 1 *syn* see RUSTIC
2 *syn* see FOGY

most *adj syn* see BEST
rel greatest, highest, maximum, utmost, uttermost

most *adv syn* see VERY 1

most *adv syn* see NEARLY

mostly *adv syn* see GENERALLY 1
idiom for the most part

mote *n syn* see POINT 11

moth–eaten *adj* 1 *syn* see SHABBY 1
2 *syn* see OLD-FASHIONED

mother *n* 1 a female human parent <the *mother* of seven children>
syn ma, ‖mam, mama (*or* mamma), mammy, ‖mater, mom, mommy, ‖mum, mummy, ‖old lady, ‖old woman; *compare* FATHER 1
2 *syn* see SOURCE

mother *vb syn* see MINISTER (to)

mother country *n syn* see COUNTRY

motherland *n syn* see COUNTRY

mother–naked *adj syn* see NUDE 2

mother wit *n syn* see INTELLIGENCE 1

motif *n* 1 *syn* see LEITMOTIV
2 *syn* see SUBJECT 2
3 *syn* see FIGURE 3

motion *n* 1 the act or an instance of moving <the *motion* of the planets>
syn move, movement, stir, stirring
rel agitation, fluctuation, oscillation, sway, swing, wavering; locomotion
con inertia, inertness, passivity
2 an impulse or inclination of the mind or will <a *motion* of the will toward what appears good>
syn movement
rel goad, impulse, incentive, inducement, motive, spring, spur
con inertia, stagnation, vegetation

motion *vb syn* see SIGNAL

motionless *adj* being without motion <stood *motionless* so that he would remain undiscovered>
syn still, stock-still, stone-still
rel stagnant, static, stationary, unmoving; fixed, immobile, immotile, immotive, immovable, irremovable, ‖sitfast, steadfast, unmovable
con active, changing, mobile, moving

motion picture *n syn* see MOVIE

motivate *vb syn* see PROVOKE 4

motivation *n syn* see STIMULUS

motive *n* 1 the object influencing a choice or prompting an action <trying to discover what was his *motive* in killing the girl>
syn cause, consideration, reason, spring; *compare* STIMULUS
rel antecedent, determinant; emotion, feeling, passion; aim, end, intent, intention, purpose
2 *syn* see FIGURE 3
3 *syn* see SUBJECT 2

motley *adj* 1 *syn* see VARIEGATED

2 *syn* see MISCELLANEOUS
rel discrepant, incompatible, incongruous, uncongenial

motley *n* 1 *syn* see FOOL 2
2 *syn* see MISCELLANY 1

motor *n syn* see CAR

motor *vb* 1 *syn* see RIDE 1
2 *syn* see DRIVE 5

motorcar *n syn* see CAR

motor home *n syn* see TRAILER

motorist *n* a person who travels by automobile <the roads were crowded with *motorists* going to work>
syn autoist, automobilist, driver, operator

mottle *vb syn* see SPLOTCH

motto *n syn* see BATTLE CRY
rel byword, catchphrase, catchword, shibboleth, slogan, watchword, word

moue *n syn* see FACE 6

mound *vb syn* see HEAP 1

mound *n syn* see PILE 1

mount *n syn* see MOUNTAIN 1

mount *vb* 1 *syn* see INCREASE 2
2 *syn* see ASCEND 1
con descend, fall, lower
ant drop
3 *syn* see RISE 4
ant drop
4 *syn* see INTENSIFY
5 to get on (something) as a means of conveyance <*mount* a horse>
syn back, bestride
rel seat, settle
ant dismount
||6 *syn* see TESTIFY 2
7 *syn* see STAGE

mountain *n* 1 a relatively steep and high elevation of land <why are *mountains* in New England considered no more than hills in Colorado>
syn alp, mount, peak
rel butte, mesa; bald, dome; hill; bluff; volcano; sierra
con bottom, bottomland, dale, dell, vale, valley
2 *syn* see PILE 1
3 *syn* see MUCH
4 *syn* see OBSTACLE

mountain dew *n syn* see MOONSHINE 2

mountaineer *n syn* see RUSTIC

mountainous *adj syn* see HUGE

mountebank *n* 1 *syn* see CHARLATAN
2 *syn* see SWINDLER

mourn *vb syn* see GRIEVE 2
con delight, gladden, please, rejoice

mournful *adj* 1 *syn* see SAD 1
2 *syn* see SAD 2
3 *syn* see MELANCHOLY 2
4 *syn* see DEPLORABLE

mournfulness *n syn* see SADNESS

mouse *n* 1 *syn* see GIRL FRIEND 1
2 *syn* see BLACK EYE 1

mouse *vb* 1 *syn* see SNOOP
2 *syn* see STEAL 3

mousehole *n syn* see CUBBYHOLE

mousetrap *n syn* see PITFALL

mouth *n* 1 the opening through which food passes into the body of an animal <the *mouth* in vertebrates is one of the features of the face>
syn ||bazoo, gob, ||mush, ||row, ||trap, ||yap
rel mug, muzzle
2 *syn* see FACE 6
3 *syn* see SPOKESMAN
4 *syn* see BACK TALK
5 the place where a tributary enters a larger stream or body of water <the *mouth* of the Mississippi river is in the Gulf of Mexico>
syn embouchement, embouchure
rel estuary; delta

mouth *vb* 1 *syn* see ORATE
2 *syn* see BOAST
3 *syn* see REVEAL 1
4 *syn* see GRIMACE

mouthful *n syn* see MORSEL 1

mouthing *n syn* see FACE 6

mouthpiece *n syn* see SPOKESMAN

mouth–watering *adj syn* see PALATABLE

||**mouthy** *adj* 1 *syn* see TALKATIVE
2 *syn* see RHETORICAL

movable *adj* capable of moving or of being moved <a device with a *movable* attachment>
syn mobile, moving, unstable, unsteadfast, unsteady
rel remotive, removable; motile; changeable, changeful, mutable, variable; roving
con immobile, immotile, immotive, irremovable, steadfast; established, fixed, set, settled; stagnant, static, unmoving

movables *n pl syn* see POSSESSION 2

move *vb* 1 *syn* see GO 2
2 *syn* see ADVANCE 5
3 *syn* see BE
4 to change or cause to change from one place to another <he *moved* quickly down the staircase> <*move* the chair across the room>
syn dislocate, disturb, remove, shift, ship, transfer
rel displace, replace, supersede, supplant; bear, carry, convey, transmit, transport
5 to set or keep in motion or action <the mechanism that *moves* the locomotive>
syn actuate, drive, impel, mobilize, propel
rel activate, motivate
con bring up, draw up, fetch up, halt, haul up, pull up, stop
6 *syn* see PROVOKE 4
7 *syn* see AFFECT
rel induce, persuade, prevail
8 *syn* see CONVERT 1
9 *syn* see BEHAVE 1

move *n* 1 *syn* see MEASURE 7
2 *syn* see MOTION 2
rel alteration, change, modification, variation

movement *n* 1 *syn* see MOTION 1
rel act, action, deed; activity, dynamism, liveness, operation, operativeness
2 *syn* see MOTION 2

mover *n syn* see INSTIGATOR

movie *n* a representation (as of a story) by means of motion pictures <tired old *movies* that appear on TV>

syn cine, ‖cinema, film, flick, motion picture, moving picture, photoplay, picture, picture show, show
rel cinematics, cinematography

moving *adj* 1 *syn* see MOVABLE
2 having the power to excite deep and usually somber emotion <made a *moving* appeal for help for the orphaned children>
syn affecting, impressive, poignant, touching; *compare* EMOTIONAL 2
rel eloquent, expressive, facund, meaningful, pregnant, sententious, significant; arousing, awakening, rallying, rousing, stirring; exciting, provoking, quickening, stimulating; breathless, gripping
con unaffecting, unimpressive, untouching; casual, cold, formal
ant unmoving
3 *syn* see EMOTIONAL 2
moving picture *n syn* see MOVIE
mow *n syn* see PILE 1
mow *vb* to cut down standing grass or grain with a tool or a machine <*mowed* the lawn every week>
syn clip, crop, cut
rel reap; pare, trim
mow (down) *vb syn* see FELL 1
mow *n syn* see FACE 6
mow *vb syn* see GRIMACE
moxie *n* 1 *syn* see ENERGY 2
  2 *syn* see COURAGE
  3 *syn* see FORTITUDE
‖**mozo** *n syn* see WORKER
Mr. *n syn* see HUSBAND
Mrs. *n syn* see WIFE
Mrs. Grundy *n syn* see PRUDE
much *adv* 1 *syn* see VERY 1
  2 *syn* see OFTEN
  3 *syn* see NEARLY
much *n* a great quantity, amount, extent, or degree <learned *much* worth remembering from his experiences in the army>
syn barrel, great deal, heap, lashings, lot, lump, mass, ‖mess, mountain, multiplicity, pack, peck, ‖pile, plenty, ‖power, ‖sight; *compare* MULTITUDE 1, SCAD
rel excess, overage, oversupply, plethora, superfluity
idiom all kinds of
con bit, crumb, modicum, trifle; deficiency, inadequacy, insufficiency, undersupply
ant little
‖**much** *vb syn* see BABY
much as *conj syn* see THOUGH
muck *n* 1 *syn* see SLIME
  2 *syn* see REFUSE
  3 *syn* see GOO 1
muck *vb* 1 *syn* see SOIL 2
  ‖2 *syn* see BOTCH
  ‖3 *syn* see COMPLICATE
  4 *syn* see DRUDGE
  ‖5 *syn* see SAUNTER
‖**muckamuck** *n syn* see FOOD 1
muckamuck *n syn* see NOTABLE 1
mucker *vb syn* see BOTCH
mucker *n* 1 *syn* see BOOR
  2 *syn* see WRETCH 1
  3 *syn* see TOUGH
mucking *adj syn* see DAMNED 2
muckworm *n syn* see MISER

mucky *adj* 1 *syn* see DIRTY 1
  2 *syn* see MURKY 3
  3 *syn* see HUMID
‖**mucky** *vb syn* see SOIL 2
mucronate *adj syn* see POINTED 1
mud *vb syn* see ROIL 1
muddle *vb* 1 *syn* see ROIL 1
  2 *syn* see MUMBLE
  3 *syn* see CONFUSE 2
  4 *syn* see DISORDER 1
  5 *syn* see CONFUSE 5
  6 *syn* see COMPLICATE
  7 *syn* see STUMBLE 6
muddle (away) *vb syn* see WASTE 2
muddle *n* 1 *syn* see CONFUSION 3
  2 *syn* see MESS 3
  3 *syn* see CLUTTER 2
muddled *adj* 1 *syn* see INCOHERENT 2
  2 *syn* see INTOXICATED 1
muddledness *n syn* see HAZE 2
muddlehead *n syn* see DUNCE
muddleheadedness *n syn* see HAZE 2
muddlement *n syn* see HAZE 2
muddle through *vb syn* see SHIFT 5
muddy *adj* 1 having a great deal of mud <playing in the wet field, he got his shoes all *muddy*>
syn bemired, ‖claggy, ‖clarty, miry, oozy
rel black, dirty, dungy, filthy, foul, grubby, impure, nasty, soily, sordid, squalid, unclean, uncleanly; bedraggled, draggled
con clean, cleanly, immaculate, spotless, taintless, unsoiled, unsullied
ant mudless
  2 *syn* see TURBID
rel gloomy, murky; addled, confused, muddled
  3 *syn* see DULL 8
muddy *vb* 1 *syn* see SOIL 2
  2 *syn* see ROIL 1
  3 *syn* see DULL 1
  4 *syn* see CONFUSE 4
rel conceal, hide, screen
con illuminate, illumine, light, lighten
mudhole *n* 1 *syn* see POTHOLE
  2 *syn* see BURG
muff *vb syn* see BOTCH
muffle *vb* 1 *syn* see BUNDLE UP
rel cover, envelop, overspread, shroud, veil
2 to dull the sound of <closed the door to *muffle* the outside noises>
syn dampen, deaden, mute, stifle
rel mellow, soften, soft-pedal, subdue, tone (down); smother
con amplify, enhance, heighten, magnify, reinforce, strengthen
  3 *syn* see SUPPRESS 2
muffler *n syn* see MASK 2
mug *n* 1 *syn* see FACE 1
  2 *syn* see FACE 6
  3 *syn* see DUNCE
  ‖4 *syn* see FOOL 3
  5 *syn* see TOUGH
mug *vb syn* see GRIMACE
‖**mug** (up) *vb syn* see CRAM 4
muggins *n syn* see DUNCE
muggy *adj syn* see HUMID
rel damp, dampish, moist, moisty, wettish
con dry
mughouse *n syn* see ALEHOUSE

mug-up *n syn* see SNACK
mugwump *n syn* see NOTABLE 1
mulatto *n* a person of mixed Caucasian and Negro ancestry <the special conflicts faced by *mulattoes* with both whites and blacks>
  syn high yellow
  rel mulatta, mulattress; octoroon, quadroon; sambo, zambo; mustee; half-breed
mulct *n syn* see FINE
mulct *vb* **1** *syn* see PENALIZE
  rel claim, demand, exact, require
  2 *syn* see FLEECE 1
mule *n syn* see HYBRID
muleheaded *adj syn* see OBSTINATE
muley *adj syn* see OBSTINATE
muliebral *adj syn* see FEMININE
mulish *adj syn* see OBSTINATE
  rel ungovernable, unruly; fixed, set
mull *n syn* see MESS 3
mull *vb* **1** *syn* see DEADEN 1
  2 *syn* see CONFUSE 1
  3 *syn* see DELAY 1
mull (over) *vb syn* see PONDER 2
mulligrubs *n pl syn* see SULK
  rel blues, dejection, depression, (the) dismals, dumps, gloom, heavyheartedness, melancholy, mournfulness, sadness, unhappiness
‖**mullock** *n* **1** *syn* see REFUSE
  2 *syn* see CONFUSION 3
multeity *n syn* see VARIETY 1
multicolor *adj syn* see VARIEGATED
  ant monotone
multicolored *adj syn* see VARIEGATED
  ant monotone
multifarious *adj* **1** *syn* see MANY
  2 *syn* see MANIFOLD
  3 *syn* see MISCELLANEOUS
multifariousness *n syn* see VARIETY 1
multifold *adj syn* see MANIFOLD
multiform *adj syn* see MANIFOLD
  ant uniform
multiformity *n syn* see VARIETY 1
  ant uniformity
multihued *adj syn* see VARIEGATED
  ant monotone
multilateral *adj* having many sides <*multilateral* figures>
  syn many-sided
  ant one-sided, unilateral
multiloquent *adj syn* see TALKATIVE
multiloquious *adj syn* see TALKATIVE
multiplex *adj syn* see MANIFOLD
multiplicity *n* **1** *syn* see VARIETY 1
  ant unity
  2 *syn* see MUCH
multiply *vb* **1** *syn* see INCREASE 1
  2 *syn* see INCREASE 2
  3 *syn* see PROCREATE 1
multitude *n* **1** a very large number of individuals or things <that child always asks a *multitude* of questions>
  syn army, cloud, crowd, flock, host, legion, rout, scores; *compare* CROWD 1, MUCH, SCAD

  rel numbers, oodles, quantities
  con few, handful, scattering, smatter, smattering, sprinkling
  ant none
  2 *syn* see CROWD 1
multitudinal *adj syn* see MANY
  rel countless, innumerable, innumerous, numberless, uncountable, uncounted, unnumberable, unnumbered, untold
multitudinous *adj syn* see MANY
  rel countless, innumerable, innumerous, numberless, uncountable, uncounted, unnumberable, unnumbered, untold
multivarious *adj syn* see MANIFOLD
multivocal *adj syn* see VOCIFEROUS
mum *adj syn* see SILENT 2
‖**mum** *n syn* see MOTHER 1
mumble *vb* to utter with a low inarticulate voice <embarrassed, he *mumbled* an apology>
  syn ‖chunter, fumble, muddle, ‖mump, murmur, mutter, swallow
  rel maunder; limp, shuffle, stumble; ‖hammer, stammer, ‖stut, stutter; speak, talk, utter, verbalize, vocalize, voice
  idiom speak with mush in one's mouth
  con speak out, speak up; clamor, cry out, shout, vociferate
mumble *n syn* see MURMUR 1
mumblenews *n pl but sing or pl in constr syn* see GOSSIP 1
mumbo jumbo *n syn* see GIBBERISH 3
‖**mumchance** *adj syn* see SILENT 2
mummer *n syn* see ACTOR 1
mummery *n syn* see GIBBERISH 3
mummify *vb syn* see WITHER
mummy *n syn* see MOTHER 1
mummy *n syn* see WITHER
‖**mump** *vb* **1** *syn* see MUMBLE
  2 *syn* see GRIMACE
  3 *syn* see SULK
‖**mump** *vb syn* see CHEAT
mumpish *adj syn* see SULLEN
mumps *n pl syn* see SULK
‖**mun** *vb syn* see MUST 2
‖**mun** *n syn* see MAN 3
munch *vb syn* see CHEW 1
mundane *adj* **1** *syn* see EARTHLY 1
  rel profane, secular, temporal
  ant eternal
  2 *syn* see MATERIALISTIC
  rel animal, carnal, fleshly
  3 *syn* see PROSAIC 3
municipal *adj* **1** *syn* see DOMESTIC 2
  2 *syn* see URBAN
munificent *adj syn* see LIBERAL 1
  con close, mean, niggard, ungiving
murder *n* the crime of killing a person <a *murder* occurred during a gang shoot-out>
  syn blood, ‖bump-off, foul play, hit, homicide, killing
murder *vb* **1** to kill (a human being) unlawfully and with premeditated malice <planned a safe way to *murder* his rival>
  syn assassinate, ‖bump off, cool, do in, ‖dust off, execute, finish, knock off, liquidate, put away, rub out, scrag, slay; *compare* KILL 1
  rel asphyxiate, behead, decapitate, electrocute, garrote, guillotine, hang, lynch, smother, strangle

idiom take for a ride
2 *syn* see ANNIHILATE 2

murderer *n* one who kills a human being <a *murderer* who wouldn't hesitate to kill in cold blood>
syn homicide, killer, manslayer, slayer;
compare ASSASSIN
rel butcher, slaughterer

murdering *adj syn* see MURDEROUS

murderous *adj* characterized by or of a kind to cause murder or bloodshed <made a *murderous* assault on his former friend>
syn bloodthirsty, bloody, homicidal, murdering, sanguinary, sanguine, sanguineous
rel deadly; destructive, devastating, ruinous
con harmless, innocuous, trivial

mure *vb syn* see ENCLOSE 1

murk *vb* 1 *syn* see OBSCURE 1
2 *syn* see SOIL 2

murky *adj* 1 *syn* see DARK 1
rel glooming, glowering, lowering
con bright, brilliant, effulgent, radiant
2 *syn* see OBSCURE 3
3 having visible material in suspension <a *murky* liquid>
syn cloudy, mucky
rel muddy, roily, turbid
con clear, limpid, lucent, translucent, transparent; clean, fresh, pure, unpolluted
4 *syn* see DULL 8
5 *syn* see DIRTY 1

murmur *n* 1 a low indistinct but often continuous sound (as of voices) <could hear the *murmur* of the audience throughout the entire performance>
syn mumble, mutter, rumor, susurration, undertone, whisper
rel murmuration; buzz, drone, hum, purr; brool
2 *syn* see REPORT 1

murmur *vb* 1 *syn* see GRUMBLE 1
2 *syn* see COMPLAIN
3 *syn* see MUMBLE

muscle *n* 1 muscular strength <loading cargo calls for real *muscle*>
syn beef, brawn, might, sinew, thew
rel power, strength
con impotence
2 *syn* see POWER 4

muscle-bound *adj syn* see STIFF 4

muscular *adj* 1 marked by good well-developed musculature <his arms were lean but *muscular*>
syn fibrous, ropy, sinewy, stringy, wiry
rel flexible, elastic, resilient, springy, supple
con flabby, flaccid, flimsy, floppy, limp, sleazy; feeble, weak
2 strong and powerful in build or action <a *muscular* lad who could wield an ax like a man>
syn athletic, brawny, sinewy; *compare* STRONG 1
rel stalwart, stout, strong, sturdy; well-built, well-knit, well-set; beefy, burly, husky, Herculean, mighty, powerful
con faint, fragile, frail; delicate, feeble, weak; ‖pindling, puny, slight

muse *vb syn* see PONDER 1
rel excogitate, study

muse *n syn* see REVERIE

muse *n syn* see POET

museum *n* a room, building, or locale where a collection of objects is put on exhibition <an art *museum* with a famous collection of jade>
syn gallery
rel salon; picture gallery, pinacotheka

‖**mush** *n* 1 *syn* see MOUTH 1
2 *syn* see FACE 1

‖**mush** (up) *vb syn* see CRUSH 2

mushroom *vb syn* see EXPLODE 1

mushy *adj* 1 *syn* see SOFT 6
2 *syn* see HAZY
3 *syn* see SENTIMENTAL

music *n syn* see DIN

musical *adj* 1 *syn* see HARMONIOUS 1
ant unmusical; musicless
2 *syn* see MELODIOUS 2
ant unmusical; musicless

musician *n* one skilled in music <the one playing the sax is a real *musician*>
syn musicianer, ‖musicker, musico, virtuoso
rel performer, player

musicianer *n syn* see MUSICIAN

‖**musicker** *n syn* see MUSICIAN

musico *n syn* see MUSICIAN

muskeg *n syn* see SWAMP

muss *n* ‖1 *syn* see BRAWL 2
2 *syn* see MESS 3

muss (up) *vb syn* see DISORDER 1
rel dishevel, rumple, wrinkle

mussy *adj syn* see SLOVENLY 1

must *verbal auxiliary* 1 *syn* see WANT 3
2 — used to indicate requirement by immediate or future need or purpose <we *must* hurry if we want to catch the bus>
syn have, ‖mun, need
rel ought, should want
idiom have got to, must needs

must *n* 1 *syn* see OBLIGATION 2
2 *syn* see ESSENTIAL 2

muster *vb* 1 *syn* see ENTER 3
2 *syn* see MOBILIZE 3
3 *syn* see GATHER 5

muster (up) *vb syn* see GENERATE 3

muster *n* 1 *syn* see GATHERING 2
2 *syn* see ROSTER 1

muster out *vb syn* see DISCHARGE 7
ant call up, draft

muster roll *n syn* see ROSTER 1

musty *adj* 1 *syn* see MALODOROUS 1
rel dirty, filthy, squalid
2 *syn* see TRITE

mutable *adj* 1 *syn* see CHANGEABLE 1
rel fluctuating, swaying, swinging, wavering; fickle, inconstant, unstable
con equable, even, steady, uniform; durable, lasting, permanent, stable
ant immutable
2 liable to change or to be changed <a flexible and perhaps too *mutable* policy>
syn changeable, inconstant, shifty, slippery, uncertain, unstable, unsteady, variable;
compare CHANGEABLE 1, INCONSTANT 1
rel changeful, protean, unsettled; capricious, fickle, inconsistent, lubricious, mercurial, temperamental, ticklish, volatile; fluctuating, shilly-shally, vacillating, wavering
con constant, established, fixed, immovable, inalterable, invariable, set, unalterable, unchangeable, unmodifiable, unmovable

ant immutable

mutate *vb* **1** *syn* see TRANSFORM
  2 *syn* see CHANGE 1

mutation *n* **1** *syn* see CHANGE 1
  2 *syn* see CHANGE 2

mute *adj* **1** *syn* see DUMB 1
  2 *syn* see SILENT 1
  con articulate, eloquent, fluent, glib, vocal,
  voluble

mute *vb* *syn* see MUFFLE 2

muted *adj* *syn* see DULL 7

mutedly *adv* *syn* see SOTTO VOCE

mutilate *vb* **1** *syn* see MAIM
  rel damage, hurt, injure, mar, spoil; deface
  2 *syn* see STERILIZE

mutineer *n* *syn* see REBEL

mutinous *adj* *syn* see INSUBORDINATE
  rel alienated, disaffected

mutiny *vb* *syn* see REVOLT 1

mutt *n* *syn* see DUNCE

mutter *vb* **1** *syn* see MUMBLE
  2 *syn* see GRUMBLE 1
  rel repine, wail

mutter *n* *syn* see MURMUR 1

muttonchops *n pl* *syn* see SIDE-WHISKERS

muttonhead *n* *syn* see DUNCE

mutual *adj* *syn* see COMMON 1
  rel partaken, participated; associated, connected, related, united

mutually *adv* *syn* see TOGETHER 3

||**mux** *vb* *syn* see DISORDER 1

muzzle *n* *syn* see FACE 1

myopic *adj* affected by a condition in which
  the visual images come to a focus in front of
  the retina of the eye resulting especially in
  defective vision of distant objects <so *myopic* that he used glasses even to read>
  syn nearsighted, shortsighted
  rel presbyopic; astigmatic
  ant farsighted, hyperopic, longsighted

myriad-minded *adj* *syn* see VERSATILE

mysterial *adj* *syn* see MYSTERIOUS

mysterious *adj* being beyond one's powers
  to discover, understand, or explain <he had
  a *mysterious* sense of humor, laughing when
  other people did not>
  syn arcane, cabalistic, impenetrable, inscrutable, mysterial, mystic, numinous, unaccountable, unexaminable, unguessed, unknowable;   *compare*   INEXPLICABLE,
  STRANGE 4
  rel impenetrable, incognizable, incomprehensible, uncomprehensible, ungraspable,
  unintelligible, unknowable; abstruse, esoteric, occult, recondite; ambiguous, cryptic,

enigmatic, equivocal, obscure
  con explainable, explicable; apprehensible,
  comprehendible, comprehensible, fathomable, graspable, intelligible, knowable, lucid,
  scrutable; candid, frank, honest, straightforward
  ant unmysterious

mystery *n* something which baffles or per-
  plexes <the *mystery* of her disappearance
  has never been solved>
  syn Chinese puzzle, closed book, conundrum, enigma, mystification, puzzle, puzzlement, riddle, why
  rel poser, problem, stumper; perplexity;
  brainteaser, brain twister
  con open book

mystic *adj* **1** *syn* see MYSTICAL 1
  rel imaginary, visionary; quixotic
  2 *syn* see MYSTERIOUS
  3 *syn* see MAGIC

mystical *adj* **1** having a spiritual meaning or
  reality that is neither apparent to the senses
  nor obvious to the intelligence <the Church
  is the *mystical* body of Christ>
  syn anagogic, mystic, telestic
  rel abysmal, deep, profound; absolute,
  categorical, ultimate; divine, holy, sacred,
  spiritual; miraculous, supernatural, supranatural
  2 *syn* see SECRET 1

mystification *n* *syn* see MYSTERY

mystifying *adj* *syn* see CRYPTIC

myth *n* **1** a traditional story of ostensibly
  historical content whose origins have been lost
  <the various Greek *myths* that have come
  down to us>
  syn legend, mythos, mythus; *compare* AL-
  LEGORY 2
  rel saga; fable, fabrication, fiction, figment;
  creation, invention
  2 *syn* see ALLEGORY 2
  3 *syn* see LORE 2

mythical *adj* lacking factual basis or historical validity <a *mythical* account attributes
  the founding of the city to Noah>
  syn fabulous, legendary, mythological
  rel fictional, fictitious, fictive, imaginary,
  supposititious, unreal; fanciful, fantastic,
  visionary; created, invented
  con actual, real, true; authentic, genuine,
  veritable; truthful, veracious, verisimilar
  ant historical

mythological *adj* *syn* see MYTHICAL

mythology *n* *syn* see LORE 2

mythos *n* **1** *syn* see MYTH 1
  2 *syn* see LORE 2

mythus *n* *syn* see MYTH 1

N

nab vb 1 syn see ARREST 2
  2 syn see SEIZE 2
  3 syn see STEAL 1
‖**nab** n 1 syn see POLICEMAN
  2 syn see ARREST
nabal n syn see MISER
nabob n syn see NOTABLE 1
nada n syn see NOTHINGNESS
nadir n syn see BOTTOM 3
  con acme, climax, culmination; peak, summit
  ant apex, zenith
nag vb to find fault incessantly <stop *nagging* her over nothing>
  syn carp (at), fuss, henpeck, peck (at)
  rel annoy, harass, harry, pester, plague, tease, worry; bother, irk, vex; badger, bait, chivy, heckle, hector, hound, ride; egg, goad, needle, prod, urge
  idiom give a bad (*or* hard) time, pick at (*or* on), take it out on
  con commend, compliment, praise; acclaim, applaud, hail
nail vb 1 syn see CATCH 1
  ‖2 syn see SEIZE 2
  ‖3 syn see STEAL 1
  ‖4 syn see STRIKE 2
naive adj 1 syn see NATURAL 5
  rel fresh, original
  ant sophisticated
  2 syn see EASY 3
naked adj 1 syn see BARE 1
  2 syn see NUDE 2
  3 syn see OPEN 2
  rel disclosed, discovered, revealed; evident, manifest, obvious, palpable; colorless, uncolored; pure, sheer, simple
namby–pamby adj 1 syn see INSIPID 3
  2 syn see CHARACTERLESS
namby–pamby n syn see WEAKLING
name n 1 the word or combination of words by which something is called and by means of which it can be distinguished or identified <the *name* always given to the eldest son> <what is the *name* of that bird?>
  syn appellation, appellative, cognomen, compellation, call, denomination, designation, ‖handle, ‖moniker, nomen, rubric, style, title
  rel baptismal name, Christian name, font name, forename, personal name, prename; byname, byword, hypocorism, nickname, pet name, sobriquet; epithet, label, tag; alias, incognito, nom de guerre, nom de plume, pen name, pseudonym
  2 syn see REPUTATION 2
  3 syn see CELEBRITY 2
name vb 1 to give a name to <*named* the child for his grandfather>
  syn baptize, call, christen, denominate, designate, dub, entitle, style, term, title
  rel label, tag, ticket; nickname

  idiom give a handle, pin a moniker on
  2 syn see DESIGNATE 2
  rel advertise, announce, declare, publish
  3 syn see MENTION
  rel identify, recognize
nameable adj syn see NOTEWORTHY
nameless adj 1 syn see OBSCURE 5
  2 syn see ANONYMOUS
  ant named
namely adv that is to say <understandably his wife disapproves of his bad habits, *namely* gambling and drinking>
  syn scilicet, to wit, videlicet
  rel especially, expressly, particularly, specially, specifically
nana n syn see NURSEMAID
‖**nanny** n syn see NURSEMAID
nap n a short sleep <generally took an hour's *nap* after lunch>
  syn catnap, dog nap, ‖dover, forty winks, siesta, snooze; *compare* DOZE, SLEEP 1
  rel dogsleep; break, interlude, intermission, let up, pause, respite, rest
nap vb to sleep briefly <*napped* for an hour after lunch>
  syn catnap, ‖caulk (off), siesta, snooze; *compare* DOZE, SLEEP
  rel drowse; relax, rest, unlax
  idiom catch a wink of sleep, catch forty winks, take a nap (*or* siesta *or* snooze)
narcissism n syn see CONCEIT 2
narcissistic adj syn see VAIN 3
narcotic n 1 syn see DRUG 2
  2 syn see ANODYNE 2
narcotic adj syn see SOPORIFIC 1
‖**nark** n syn see INFORMER
‖**nark** vb syn see INFORM 3
narrate vb syn see RELATE 2
  rel descant, dilate, discourse, expatiate
narration n 1 syn see DESCRIPTION 2
  2 syn see STORY 2
narrative n 1 syn see STORY 2
  2 syn see ACCOUNT 7
narrow adj 1 syn see DEFINITE 1
  2 syn see LITTLE 2
  3 syn see ILLIBERAL
  rel inexorable, inflexible, obdurate
  con forbearing, indulgent, lenient, tolerant
  ant broad
  ‖4 syn see STINGY
narrow vb syn see CONSTRICT 2
narrow–fisted adj syn see STINGY
  ant openhanded
narrowhearted adj syn see STINGY
  ant openhearted
narrow–minded adj syn see ILLIBERAL
  ant broad-minded
nascent adj syn see INITIAL 1
nasty adj 1 syn see DIRTY 1
  rel coarse, gross, obscene, ribald, vulgar; improper, indecent, indecorous, indelicate, unseemly

2 *syn* see OFFENSIVE

3 *syn* see OBSCENE 2

4 *syn* see MALICIOUS

nates *n pl syn* see BUTTOCKS

national *adj* 1 *syn* see PUBLIC 1

2 *syn* see DOMESTIC 2

national *n syn* see CITIZEN 2

native *adj* 1 *syn* see INNATE 1

2 belonging to a locality by birth or origin <a *native* tradition> <delighted with the tasty *native* fruits>

syn aboriginal, autochthonous, endemic, indigenous

rel domestic, local

con adopted, introduced, naturalized

ant alien, foreign, nonnative

3 *syn* see DOMESTIC 2

4 *syn* see WILD 1

5 *syn* see UNREFINED 3

Nativity *n syn* see CHRISTMAS

||**natter** *vb syn* see CHAT 1

natty *adj syn* see DAPPER

natural *adj* 1 *syn* see ILLEGITIMATE 1

2 *syn* see INNATE 1

ant abnormal, unnatural

3 *syn* see GENERAL 1

4 *syn* see WILD 1

5 free from pretension or calculation <he spoke in a perfectly *natural* manner>

syn artless, guileless, inartificial, ingenuous, innocent, naive, simple, simplehearted, unaffected, unartful, unartificial, unschooled, unsophisticated, unstudied, untutored, unworldly; *compare* GENUINE 3

rel impulsive, instinctive, spontaneous; easy, unlabored, constitutional, ingrained, inherent; folksy, homespun, unpretentious, ignorant, primitive, undesigning; unconstrained, unembarrassed; candid, frank, open, plain; sincere, unfeigned; provincial, rustic

con ceremonial, ceremonious, conventional, formal; ostentatious, pretentious, showy; assumed, contrived, counterfeited, feigned, pretended; artful, sophisticated, studied

ant affected; artificial, unnatural

natural *n syn* see FOOL 4

natural child *n syn* see BASTARD 1

naturalness *n syn* see UNCONSTRAINT

ant unnaturalness

nature *n* 1 *syn* see TYPE

rel anatomy, framework, structure; conformation, figure, shape

2 *syn* see ESSENCE 1

3 *syn* see DISPOSITION 3

4 *syn* see UNIVERSE

naught (*or* **nought**) *n* 1 *syn* see NOTHING 1

2 *syn* see ZERO

naughty *adj* 1 guilty of misbehavior <a *naughty* boy who teased the cat and upset the milk>

syn bad, ill-behaved, misbehaving, mischievous, paw; *compare* DISOBEDIENT

rel contrary, froward, perverse, wayward; headstrong, intractable, recalcitrant, refractory, ungovernable, unruly, willful; disor-

derly, rowdy, ruffianly; evil, indecorous, wicked

con decorous, good, well-behaved; amenable, docile, obedient, tractable; amiable, complaisant, good-natured, obliging; polite, proper; considerate, kindly, thoughtful

2 *syn* see DISOBEDIENT

nausea *n* a stomach distress with an urge to vomit <overcome with *nausea* as the boat continued to pitch and wallow>

syn qualmishness, queasiness, squeamishness

nauseate *vb syn* see DISGUST

nauseated *adj* affected with nausea <was *nauseated* after taking the drug>

syn nauseous, squeamish; *compare* SQUEAMISH 1

rel choking, gagging; heaving; barfing, upchucking, vomiting

idiom ready (*or* about) to lose one's cookies

nauseating *adj syn* see OFFENSIVE

ant appetizing

nauseous *adj syn* see NAUSEATED

nautical *adj syn* see MARINE 2

navigable *adj syn* see PASSABLE

ant unnavigable

navigational *adj syn* see MARINE 2

nawob *n syn* see NOTABLE 1

nay *adv* 1 *syn* see NO

2 *syn* see EVEN 3

naze *n syn* see PROMONTORY

neanderthal *adj syn* see OLD-FASHIONED

near *adv* 1 *syn* see CLOSE

ant far

2 *syn* see ABOUT 5

near *prep* 1 *syn* see ABOUT 1

2 not far distant from <kept the boy *near* him>

syn ||aside, beside, by, nearby, nigh, round

idiom close to, hard by, within earshot, within reach, within sight

near *adj* 1 *syn* see CLOSE 6

ant far

2 *syn* see COMPARATIVE

near *vb syn* see APPROACH 1

rel equal, match, rival, touch

con alter, change, modify, vary; differ

||**nearabout** *adv syn* see NEARLY

near–at–hand *adj* 1 *syn* see NEIGHBORING

2 *syn* see CLOSE 6

3 *syn* see CONVENIENT 2

near–at–hand *adv syn* see ABOUT 5

nearby *adv* 1 *syn* see CLOSE

2 *syn* see ABOUT 5

nearby *prep* 1 *syn* see NEAR 2

2 *syn* see ABOUT 1

nearby *adj* 1 *syn* see CLOSE 6

2 *syn* see NEIGHBORING

3 *syn* see CONVENIENT 2

nearing *adj syn* see FORTHCOMING

nearly *adv* very close to <our work is *nearly* done for today>

syn about, all but, almost, approximately, as good as, just about, more or less, most, much, ||nearabout, nigh, practically, roughly, round, roundly, say, some, somewhere, well-nigh

rel virtually

idiom as near as never mind(s), in effect, in essence, in substance, in the main, nigh on

---

syn synonym(s)   *rel* related word(s)

ant antonym(s)   *con* contrasted word(s)

idiom idiomatic equivalent(s)

|| use limited; if in doubt, see a dictionary

(or onto or upon), to all (practical) intents and purposes

nearsighted adj syn see MYOPIC

neat adj **1** syn see STRAIGHT 3
2 manifesting care and orderliness <always kept a *neat* house>
syn chipper, orderly, prim, shipshape, snug, spick-and-span, tidy, trig, trim, uncluttered, well-groomed; *compare* DAPPER
rel clean, immaculate, spotless; dainty, fastidious, finicky, nice; methodical, regular, systematic; accurate, correct, exact, precise
idiom in good order, neat as a pin (or bandbox), neat as can be, neat as wax
con disheveled, disordered, slipshod, sloppy, slovenly, unkempt, untidy; dirty, filthy, foul, nasty; lax, negligent, remiss, slack
ant disorderly, messy
||3 *syn* see MARVELOUS 2

neat-handed adj syn see DEXTEROUS 1

neb n syn see BILL 1

nebbish n syn see WEAKLING

||**nebby** adj syn see IMPERTINENT 2

||**necessary** n syn see PRIVY 1

necessary adj **1** syn see ESSENTIAL 4
rel compelling, compulsory, constraining, mandatory, obligatory; important, momentous, significant; cardinal, fundamental
con insignificant, unessential, unimportant
ant unnecessary
2 syn see INEVITABLE
rel inerrable, inerrant, infallible, unerring

necessitate vb syn see DEMAND 2

necessitous adj **1** syn see POOR 1
rel depleted, drained, exhausted
2 syn see ESSENTIAL 4

necessity n **1** syn see NEED 4
rel coercion, compulsion, constraint, duress, obligation; indispensableness, needfulness, requisiteness
2 syn see OCCASION 3
3 syn see ESSENTIAL 2

neck vb syn see BEHEAD

necrology n syn see OBITUARY

necromancer n syn see MAGICIAN 1

necromancy n syn see MAGIC 1

necromantic adj syn see MAGIC

necropolis n syn see CEMETERY

necropsy n syn see AUTOPSY

||**neddy** n syn see DONKEY 1

need n **1** syn see OBLIGATION 2
2 syn see REQUIREMENT 1
3 opportunity or requirement to employ <found little *need* for his rifle>
syn demand, occasion, use
rel call, claim, exaction
4 a pressing lack of something essential <he is in *need* of food>
syn exigency, necessity
rel deficiency, deficit, lack, shortage, want
con adequacy, enough, sufficiency
5 syn see POVERTY 1

need vb **1** syn see LACK
rel claim, demand, exact; hanker, hunger, long, pine, thirst, yearn; covet, crave, desire, wish
2 syn see MUST 2

needed adj syn see NEEDFUL
ant unneeded

needful adj necessary for supply or relief <provided them with everything *needful*>
syn needed, required, requisite
rel essential, imperative, indispensable, necessary; lacked, wanted; cardinal, fundamental, vital
con excess, redundant, superfluous; nonessential, unessential; uncalled-for, unnecessary, unneeded
ant needless

needful n syn see MONEY

neediness n syn see POVERTY 1

needle vb syn see WORRY 1

needless adj syn see UNNECESSARY
ant needful

needy adj syn see POOR 1

ne'er adv syn see NEVER

ne'er-do-well n syn see WASTREL 1

nefarious adj syn see VICIOUS 2
rel atrocious, heinous, monstrous, outrageous; flagrant, glaring, gross, rank
ant exemplary

negate vb **1** syn see DENY 4
ant affirm
2 syn see ABOLISH 1
3 syn see NEUTRALIZE

negation n syn see DENIAL 1
ant affirmation

negative adj syn see ADVERSE 2

negative vb **1** syn see VETO
2 syn see DENY 4
ant affirm
3 syn see NEUTRALIZE
rel abrogate, invalidate, nullify

neglect vb to pass over without giving due attention <*neglected* his family for the sake of his mistress>
syn blink (at or away), discount, disregard, elide, fail, forget, ignore, miss, omit, overleap, overlook, overpass, pass, pass by, pass over, pretermit, slight, slough over, slur (over)
rel brush (off or aside), disdain, dismiss, reject, scant, scorn, shrug away, shrug off
idiom pay no attention to, pay no heed (or mind), think little of
con appreciate, prize, treasure, value; cultivate, foster, nurse, nurture
ant cherish

neglect n syn see FAILURE 1

neglected adj not properly or sufficiently attended to or cared for <the whole property had a *neglected* appearance>
syn run-down, uncared-for, untended
rel disregarded, ignored, overlooked, slighted, unheeded
con prized, treasured; fostered, tended; guarded, supervised, watched
ant cherished

neglectful adj syn see NEGLIGENT
ant attentive

negligent adj failing to give proper attention or care <*negligent* in taking care of the children> <a *negligent* man, prone to forgetfulness>
syn behindhand, careless, delinquent, derelict, discinct, disregardful, lax, neglectful, regardless, remiss, slack
rel heedless, inadvertent, inattentive, inconsiderate, thoughtless, unheedful, unthink-

ing; incurious, indifferent, unconcerned; slipshod, slovenly

con rigid, rigorous, strict; attentive, considerate, heedful, thoughtful; careful, exact, fussy, meticulous, punctilious, punctual, scrupulous

ant attentive

negligible *adj syn* see REMOTE 4
    ant significant

negotiable *adj syn* see PASSABLE
    ant nonnegotiable

negotiate *vb* **1** to bring about by mutual agreement <*negotiate* a treaty>

syn arrange, concert, settle

rel adjust, compose, transact; agree, bargain, contract, covenant

con break off, intermit, interrupt, suspend; differ, disagree, dissent

    2 *syn* see CLEAR 8

neigh *vb* to make the cry typical of a horse <the frightened horse *neighed* and stamped>

syn nicker, whicker, ‖whinner, whinny

neighbor *n syn* see LOCALITY 1

neighborhood *n* **1** *syn* see LOCALITY 1
    2 *syn* see ORDER 4

neighboring *adj* not distant <the need for understanding between *neighboring* countries>

syn adjacent, close-at-hand, close-by, contiguous, near-at-hand, nearby; *compare* CLOSE 6

rel abutting, adjoining, bordering, conterminous, touching; close, near

con distant, far, faraway, far-off, remote, removed; parted, separated

neighborly *adj syn* see AMICABLE

rel cooperative, gregarious, hospitable, social; cordial, gracious, sociable

ant unneighborly; ill-disposed

neonate *n syn* see BABY 1

neophyte *n syn* see NOVICE

neoteric *adj syn* see NEW 1

nepenthe *n syn* see ANODYNE 2

ne plus ultra *n syn* see APEX 2

nerve *n* **1** *syn* see FORTITUDE
    2 *syn* see TEMERITY
    3 *syn* see EFFRONTERY

nerve *vb syn* see ENCOURAGE 1

nerve center *n syn* see CENTER 2

nervous *adj* easily upset or irritated <a *nervous* fretful woman>

syn fidgety, goosey, high-strung, jittery, jumpy, nervy, spooky, twittery, unrestful

rel agitated, edgy, excitable, skittish, volatile; fretful, irritable, querulous, snappish, waspish

con calm, placid, serene, steady, tranquil; collected, composed, cool, imperturbable, inexcitable, poised, unflappable, unruffled

ant nerveless

nervous breakdown *n* an emotional disorder often characterized by depression, tenseness, irritability, headache, and susceptibility to fatigue <worked and worried himself into a *nervous breakdown*>

syn breakdown, collapse, crack-up, nervous prostration

rel neurasthenia; prostration

nervous prostration *n syn* see NERVOUS BREAKDOWN

nervy *adj* **1** *syn* see WISE 5
    2 *syn* see NERVOUS

rel excitable, fidgety, jerky, tense, twitchy

idiom tied up in knots

con composed, easy, relaxed

ant phlegmatic

    3 *syn* see TENSE 2

nescience *n syn* see IGNORANCE 2

nest egg *n syn* see RESERVE

nestle *vb syn* see SNUGGLE

net *vb syn* see CLEAR 6

nether *adj syn* see INFERIOR 1

nethermost *adj syn* see BOTTOMMOST
    ant uppermost

netherwards *adv syn* see DOWN 1
    ant upwards

netherworld *n syn* see HELL

nettle *vb syn* see IRRITATE

rel agitate, discompose, disturb, perturb, upset

nettlesome *adj syn* see THORNY

neuter *vb syn* see STERILIZE

neutral *adj* not experiencing or generating a strong emotional commitment or response <made a *neutral* response to his challenge>

syn abstract, colorless, detached, disinterested, dispassionate, impersonal, poker=faced, unpassioned

rel clinical, collected, composed, cool, nonchalant; calm, easy, relaxed; aloof, indifferent

con intemperate, loaded; fervent, impassioned, passionate, vehement

neutralize *vb* to make inoperative or ineffective usually by means of an opposite force, influence, or effect <attacked by the kind of propaganda that is difficult to *neutralize*>

syn annul, cancel (out), counteract, countercheck, frustrate, negate, negative, redress

rel balance, compensate, counterbalance, counterpoise, countervail, offset; abrogate, invalidate, nullify; conquer, defeat, overcome, subdue; override, overrule

con activate, animate, dynamize, vitalize

never *adv* not at any time <they had *never* seen him before>

syn ne'er

idiom never in all one's born days, never in one's life, never in the world, never on earth

con constantly, continuously, ever, invariably, perpetually

ant always

never-ending *adj syn* see EVERLASTING 1
    ant ended; transitory

never-failing *adj syn* see SURE 2

nevertheless *adv syn* see HOWEVER

nevus *n syn* see BIRTHMARK 1

new *adj* **1** recently come into existence or use or a particular state or relation <*new* styles that flatter stout figures>

syn fresh, modern, modernistic, neoteric, newfangled, new-fashioned, new-sprung, novel, recent

rel first-hand, independent, primary

con dated, outdated, outmoded, out-of-date; shabby, worn; hackneyed, old hat, trite

---

syn synonym(s)   **rel** related word(s)
ant antonym(s)   **con** contrasted word(s)
idiom idiomatic equivalent(s)
‖ use limited; if in doubt, see a dictionary

ant old

2 *syn see* UNFAMILIAR 1

3 *syn see* ADDITIONAL

4 *syn see* REFRESHED

new *adv* within recent time <the scent of new mown grass>
syn afresh, anew, lately, newly, of late, recently
con aforetime, before, earlier, formerly; heretofore, hitherto
ant once

newborn *n syn see* BABY 1

newcomer *n syn see* NOVICE

newfangled *adj syn see* NEW 1
ant oldfangled

new–fashioned *adj syn see* NEW 1
ant old-fashioned

New Jerusalem *n syn see* HEAVEN 2

newly *adv syn see* NEW

news *n pl but sing in constr* a report of events or conditions not previously known <her friend gave her the bad *news*>
syn advice, information, intelligence, speerings, tidings, word
rel announcement, report; dope, lowdown, ‖poop; gossip, rumor, tattle

newsmonger *n syn see* GOSSIP 1

newspaper *n syn see* JOURNAL

new–sprung *adj syn see* NEW 1

next *adj* being the one that comes immediately after another <the *next* day>
syn coming, ensuing, following; *compare* CONSECUTIVE
rel proximate

next *adv syn see* AFTER

next *prep syn see* AFTER 2

next to *prep syn see* BESIDE 1

nexus *n syn see* BOND 3

niagara *n syn see* FLOOD 2

nib *n syn see* BILL 1

‖**nibby** *adj syn see* CURIOUS 2

nice *adj* **1** having or displaying exacting standards <too *nice* about his food to like camp cooking>
syn ‖choicy, choosy, clerkish, dainty, delicate, fastidious, finical, finicking, finicky, fussy, miminy-piminy, ‖mincy, niminy-piminy, old-maidish, old-womanish, particular, pernickety, persnickety, picksome, picky, precious, squeamish, squeamy
rel discerning, discriminating, penetrating; overparticular, queasy; careful, meticulous, punctilious, scrupulous; judicious, sage, sapient, wise
con coarse, gross, vulgar; callow, crude, green, raw, uncouth; lax, neglectful, negligent, remiss, slack; careless, sloppy, slovenly

2 *syn see* FINE 1

3 *syn see* PLEASANT 1

4 *syn see* CORRECT 2
rel rigid, strict, stringent; exquisite, rare
con haphazard, happy-go-lucky, hit-or-miss, random; careless, heedless, inadvertent

5 *syn see* DECOROUS 1

nicely *adv syn see* WELL 1

nice Nelly *n* **1** *syn see* PRUDE

2 *syn see* EUPHEMISM

nice–nellyism *n syn see* EUPHEMISM

n'che *n syn see* NOOK

nick *n syn see* NOTCH 1

‖**nick** *vb syn see* STEAL 1

nicker *vb syn see* NEIGH

nickname *n* a descriptive or familiar name that is used instead of or in addition to one's proper name <because he was a redhead his friends gave him the *nickname* "Red">
syn byname, byword, ‖handle, hypocorism, ‖moniker, sobriquet
rel first name, middle name; appellation, appellative, compellation, denomination, style; epithet, label, tag

nictate *vb syn see* WINK

nictitate *vb syn see* WINK

nidorous *adj syn see* MALODOROUS 1

nifty *adj syn see* MARVELOUS 2

nifty *n syn see* ‖DILLY

niggard *n syn see* MISER

niggard *adj syn see* STINGY

niggardly *adj syn see* STINGY
ant bounteous, bountiful

niggling *adj syn see* PETTY 2

nigh *adv* **1** *syn see* CLOSE

2 *syn see* NEARLY

nigh *adj syn see* CLOSE 6

nigh *prep syn see* NEAR 2

2 *syn see* ABOUT 1

nigh *vb syn see* APPROACH 1

night *n* the time from dusk to dawn <stayed up all *night*>
syn nighttide, nighttime
con day, daytime

night *adj syn see* NIGHTLY

night and day *adv syn see* TOGETHER 2

nightclub *n* a restaurant serving liquor and providing entertainment <Las Vegas *nightclubs*>
syn bistro, cabaret, café, discotheque, hot spot, nightery, night spot, nitery, supper club, watering hole, watering place

nightery *n syn see* NIGHTCLUB

nightfall *n syn see* EVENING 1

nightly *adj* of, relating to, or associated with the night <*nightly* noises>
syn night, nocturnal
con daily, diurnal; matutinal, morning; evening, twilight, vespertine

nightmare *n syn see* FANCY 4

night spot *n syn see* NIGHTCLUB

nightstick *n syn see* CUDGEL

nighttide *n syn see* NIGHT

nighttime *n syn see* NIGHT

nightwalker *n syn see* PROSTITUTE

nihility *n syn see* NOTHINGNESS

nil *n syn see* NOTHING 1

nim *vb syn see* STEAL 1

nimble *adj* **1** *syn see* AGILE
rel light, lightsome; alert, vigilant, watchful, wide-awake

2 *syn see* DEXTEROUS 1

nimble–witted *adj syn see* WISE 4
ant slow-witted

niminy–piminy *adj syn see* NICE 1

nimmer *n syn see* THIEF

nincom *n syn see* FOOL 1

nincompoop *n syn see* FOOL 1

ninny *n syn see* FOOL 1

ninnyhammer *n syn see* FOOL 1

nip *vb* **1** *syn see* BLAST 1
rel arrest, check; press, squeeze; balk, frustrate, thwart

2 *syn* see STEAL 1

‖**3** *syn* see HURRY 2

nip *n syn* see DRAM

nip *vb syn* see DRINK 3

‖**nipcheese** *n syn* see MISER

nipper *n syn* see CHILD 1

nipping *adj syn* see COLD 1

nippy *adj syn* see COLD 1

nirvana *n syn* see HEAVEN 2

nisse *n syn* see FAIRY

‖**nit** *adv syn* see NO

nitery *n syn* see NIGHTCLUB

nitwit *n syn* see DUNCE

nitwitted *adj syn* see SIMPLE 3

‖**nix** *n syn* see NOTHING 1

‖**nix** *adv syn* see NO

‖**nix** *vb syn* see VETO

no *adv* — used as a function word to express negation, dissent, denial, or refusal <*no*, you can't come with me>

syn nay, ‖nit, ‖nix, ‖nope

idiom by no manner of means, by no means, in no case, no dice, not at any price, not for love or money, not for the life of me, not for the world, nothing doing, not on your life, no way, on no account, on no condition, under no circumstances

ant yes

‖**no-account** *adj syn* see WORTHLESS 1

Noachian *adj syn* see ANCIENT 1

noble *adj* 1 *syn* see GRAND 1

rel eminent, illustrious

con beggarly, contemptible, despicable, scurvy, sorry

ant cheap, ignoble, unnoble

2 *syn* see ELEVATED 2

ant base

3 *syn* see HONORABLE 1

ant ignoble

4 *syn* see MORAL 1

nobody *pron syn* see NO ONE

ant everybody; somebody

nobody *n syn* see NONENTITY

ant somebody

nocent *adj syn* see HARMFUL

ant innocent

nocturnal *adj syn* see NIGHTLY

con daily, diurnal

nocuous *adj syn* see HARMFUL

ant innocuous

nodding *adj syn* see SLEEPY 1

noddle *n syn* see HEAD 1

noddy *n syn* see DUNCE

noel *n syn* see CHRISTMAS

noggin *n syn* see HEAD 1

no-good *adj syn* see WORTHLESS 1

no-good *n* 1 *syn* see WASTREL 1

2 *syn* see WRETCH 1

noise *n syn* see SOUND 1

rel babel, clamor, din, hubbub, pandemonium, racket, uproar

con quiet, silence, stillness

noise (about *or* abroad) *vb syn* see GOSSIP

noiseful *adj syn* see NOISY

ant noiseless, silent

noiseless *adj syn* see STILL 3

con boisterous, clamorous, strident, vociferous

ant noiseful, noisy

noiselessness *n syn* see SILENCE 1

ant noisiness

noisome *adj* 1 *syn* see UNWHOLESOME 1

ant wholesome

2 *syn* see MALODOROUS 1

rel dirty, filthy, squalid; loathsome, revolting

ant balmy

3 *syn* see OFFENSIVE

noisy *adj* making noise <the *noisiest* car you ever heard>

syn clangorous, clattery, noiseful, rackety, sonorous, uproarious

rel blatant, boisterous, clamorous, obstreperous, strepitous, strident, vociferous; tumultuous, turbulent

con quiet, silent, still, stilly

ant noiseless

nomadic *adj syn* see ITINERANT

no man *pron syn* see NO ONE

ant everybody, everyman

nom de guerre *n syn* see PSEUDONYM

nomen *n syn* see NAME 1

nominal *adj* being something in name or form only <the *nominal* head of his party>

syn formal, so-called, titular

rel apparent, ostensible, seeming; alleged, pretended, professed

idiom in name only

con genuine, real, true

ant actual

nominate *vb syn* see DESIGNATE 2

rel intend, mean, propose, purpose; offer, present, proffer, tender

nonadhesive *adj syn* see LOOSE 3

nonage *n syn* see INFANCY 1

ant age

nonchalant *adj syn* see COOL 2

rel cheerful, glad, lighthearted; easy, effortless, light, smooth

con anxious, careful, concerned, solicitous, worried

noncombustible *adj* incapable of being burned <*noncombustible* material was used whenever possible>

syn apyrous, incombustible, nonflammable, noninflammable, uninflammable

rel fireproof, fire-resistant, fire-resistive, fire-retardant, flameproof

con flammable, inflammable

ant combustible

noncommittal *adj syn* see RESERVED 1

noncompos *n syn* see LUNATIC 1

non compos mentis *adj syn* see INSANE 1

nonconformism *n syn* see HERESY

ant conformism

nonconformist *n* 1 *syn* see HERETIC

ant conformist

2 *syn* see BOHEMIAN

ant conformist

nonconformist *adj syn* see HERETICAL

nonconformity *n syn* see HERESY

ant conformity

noncreative *adj syn* see UNORIGINAL

ant creative

nondiscriminatory *adj syn* see FAIR 4

syn synonym(s)   *rel* related word(s)
ant antonym(s)   *con* contrasted word(s)
idiom idiomatic equivalent(s)
‖ use limited; if in doubt, see a dictionary

ant discriminatory

none *pron syn* see NO ONE

nonentity *n* an utterly insignificant person <tired of dealing with subordinates and *nonentities*>
syn cipher, insignificancy, nobody, nothing, nullity, rushlight, whiffet, whippersnapper, whipster, zero, zilch
rel lightweight, obscurity, sad sack, small beer, small fry
idiom blank space in the rear rank, man in the street, no great shakes

nonesuch *n syn* see PARAGON
idiom one in a million

nonessential *adj syn* see DISPENSABLE
ant essential

nonetheless *adv syn* see HOWEVER

nonexistence *n syn* see NOTHINGNESS
ant existence; reality

nonflammable *adj syn* see NONCOMBUSTIBLE
ant flammable, inflammable

nonfunctional *adj syn* see IMPRACTICABLE 2
ant functional

noninflammable *adj syn* see NONCOMBUSTIBLE
ant flammable, inflammable

nonliterate *adj syn* see PRIMITIVE 6

nonmaterial *adj syn* see IMMATERIAL 1
ant material

nonobligatory *adj syn* see OPTIONAL
ant obligatory

no–nonsense *adj syn* see SERIOUS 1

nonpareil *n syn* see PARAGON

nonpartisan *adj syn* see FAIR 4
ant partisan

nonphysical *adj syn* see IMMATERIAL 1
ant physical

non–placet *vb syn* see VETO

nonplus *vb* 1 to cause to be at a total loss as to how to act or decide <was totally *nonplussed* by the economic problems>
syn beat, buffalo, get, stick, stump; *compare* PUZZLE
rel baffle, frustrate, stymie, thwart; confound, perplex, mystify; dumbfound; overcome, throw; paralyze; confuse, flurry, fluster, muddle, rattle
idiom put (*or* drive) to one's wit's end, put up a tree (*or* stump), throw on one's beam end
2 *syn* see STAGGER 5
rel faze, rattle; baffle, balk, frustrate

nonprofessional *n syn* see AMATEUR 2
ant professional

nonrational *adj syn* see ILLOGICAL
ant rational

nonrealistic *adj syn* see IMPRACTICAL 1
ant realistic

nonreligious *adj syn* see IRRELIGIOUS
rel lay, profane, secular, temporal
ant religious

nonresistant *adj syn* see PASSIVE 2
ant resistant, resisting

nonresisting *adj syn* see PASSIVE 2
ant resistant, resisting

nonreversible *adj syn* see IRREVOCABLE
ant reversible

nonsectarian *adj* not affiliated with or restricted to a particular religious group <the problems facing *nonsectarian* colleges>
syn interchurch, intercreedal, interdenominational, undenominational, unsectarian
con denominational
ant sectarian

nonsense *n* 1 *syn* see GIBBERISH 1
2 something uttered or proposed that seems senseless or absurd <his theories are mere *nonsense*>
syn ‖applesauce, balderdash, ‖baloney, bilge, ‖blague, blah, blather, blatherskite, bosh, ‖bull, ‖bunk, bunkum, bushwa, claptrap, ‖cobblers, ‖cock, ‖codswallop, ‖crap, crock, double-talk, ‖drip, drivel, drool, eyewash, fiddle-faddle, fiddlesticks, flapdoodle, flimflam, flummadiddle, fudge, ‖gas, gook, guff, hogwash, hokum, hooey, ‖horsefeathers, hot air, humbug, jazz, ‖jiggery-pokery, malarkey, meshuggaas, moonshine, piffle, pishposh, poppycock, punk, rot, rubbish, slipslop, tomfoolery, tommyrot, tosh, trash, trumpery, twaddle, whangdoodle, windbaggery
idiom stuff and nonsense

nonsuccess *n syn* see FAILURE 2
ant success, successfulness

nonsymmetrical *adj syn* see LOPSIDED
ant symmetrical

nonviolent *adj syn* see PACIFIC
ant violent

noodle *n* 1 *syn* see DUNCE
2 *syn* see HEAD 1

nook *n* a secluded or sheltered place <resting in a shady *nook*>
syn byplace, cranny, niche
rel alcove, recess; cubbyhole, hole

noon *n syn* see APEX 2

no one *pron* no person <*no one* will be allowed to leave early>
syn nobody, no man, none
idiom never a one, nobody on earth, nobody under the sun, not a blessed soul, not a soul
con all, everyman; many, some
ant everybody, everyone

noontide *n syn* see APEX 2

noose *vb syn* see HANG 2

‖**nope** *adv syn* see NO
ant ‖yep, ‖yup

norm *n syn* see AVERAGE

normal *adj* 1 *syn* see SANE 2
2 *syn* see GENERAL 1

nose *n* 1 the prominent part of the human face that bears the nostrils and covers the nasal passage <had a large *nose*>
syn beak, ‖beezer, ‖boko, ‖conk, pecker, proboscis, ‖schnozzle, smeller, ‖sneezer, ‖snitch, snoot, snout
2 *syn* see BUSYBODY
3 *syn* see GIFT 2

nose *vb* 1 *syn* see SMELL 1
2 *syn* see SNOOP

nose-dive *vb syn* see PLUMMET

nosegay *n syn* see BOUQUET 1

nosey Parker *n syn* see BUSYBODY

nosh *vb* ‖1 *syn* see MEAL
2 *syn* see SNACK

Nostradamus *n syn* see PROPHET

nostrum *n syn* see PANACEA

nosy adj syn see CURIOUS 2
notability n 1 syn see NOTABLE 1
  2 syn see CELEBRITY 2
notable adj 1 syn see NOTEWORTHY
  2 syn see FAMOUS 2
notable n 1 a person of consequence or prominence <*notables* of Congress and the diplomatic corps>
  syn big, big boy, ‖big bug, big cheese, ‖big chief, ‖biggie, big gun, ‖big noise, big shot, big-timer, ‖big wheel, bigwig, character, chief, dignitary, eminence, ‖fat cat, great gun, heavy, heavyweight, high-muck-a‑muck, leader, lion, luminary, muckamuck, mugwump, nabob, nawab, notability, personage, personality, pooh-bah, pot, somebody, VIP
  rel figure; baron, czar, king, magnate, mogul, prince; light, star; power
  idiom big-time operator, his nibs, Mr. Big
  con cipher, nobody, nonentity; functionary, underling
  2 syn see CELEBRITY 2
notably adv syn see VERY 1
notandum n syn see NOTE 2
notation n syn see NOTE 2
notch n 1 a usually V-shaped depression in an edge or surface <a *notch* in the table>
  syn indentation, indenture, nick; compare DEPRESSION 2
  rel cut, gash, incision, score, scratch; cleft, gap, nock
  2 syn see DEGREE 1
note vb syn see SEE 1
note n 1 syn see CALL 1
  2 a written reminder <made a *note* to return the call>
  syn chit, memo, memorandum, notandum, notation
  3 syn see REMARK 2
  rel reminder
  4 syn see LETTER 2
  5 syn see NOTICE 1
noted adj syn see WELL-KNOWN
  ant unnoted
note-perfect adj syn see PERFECT 2
noteworthy adj having a quality that attracts one's attention <a *noteworthy* event>
  syn ‖bodacious, memorable, nameable, notable, observable, red-letter, rubric
  rel conspicuous, noticeable, outstanding, prominent, remarkable; evident, manifest, patent; exceptional, extraordinary
  con blah, common, commonplace, inconsequential, insignificant, ordinary, quotidian, unimportant, unremarkable
  ant unnoteworthy
nothing n 1 something that does not exist <his hopes were based on *nothing*>
  syn naught (or nought), nil, ‖nix, wind
  idiom nothing at all, nothing whatever
  con something
  2 syn see ZERO 1
  3 syn see NONENTITY
  idiom (the) little end of nothing whittled down to a point

nothing adj syn see WORTHLESS 1
nothingness n the quality or state of being nothing <the house was blown into *nothingness* by the force of the explosion>
  syn nada, nihility, nonexistence, nullity, vacuity
  rel emptiness; vacuum, void
  con concreteness, solidity, substantiality; materiality, reality
  ant somethingness
notice n 1 a noting of or concerning oneself with something <take *notice* of the gathering clouds>
  syn attention, cognizance, ear, heed, mark, ‖mind, note, observance, observation, regard, remark
  rel care, concern, consideration, thought; apprehension, grasp, understanding
  con disinterest, disregard, indifference, unconcern; carelessness, heedlessness, unmindfulness; insouciance, negligence, recklessness
  2 syn see MEMORANDUM 2
  3 syn see CRITICISM 2
notice vb syn see SEE 1
  rel acknowledge, recognize; advert, allude, refer
  con disregard, ignore, neglect, overlook, slight
noticeable adj attracting or compelling notice or attention <they both showed a *noticeable* aversion to his company>
  syn arresting, arrestive, conspicuous, eye‑catching, marked, outstanding, pointed, prominent, remarkable, salient, sensational, signal, striking
  rel notable, noteworthy; evident, manifest, obvious, palpable, patent; spectacular
  con obscure, vague; concealed, hidden, shrouded; insignificant, undistinguished
  ant unnoticeable
notify vb syn see INFORM 2
  rel announce, broadcast, declare, proclaim, promulgate, publish; disclose, discover, divulge, reveal
notion n 1 syn see IDEA
  2 syn see CAPRICE
  3 syn see HINT 1
notional adj 1 syn see CONCEPTUAL
  2 syn see IMAGINARY 1
  ant real
notoriety n syn see FAME 2
  rel ballyhoo, promotion, propaganda, publicity
notorious adj 1 syn see WELL-KNOWN
  2 syn see INFAMOUS 1
notwithstanding prep syn see AGAINST 4
notwithstanding adv syn see HOWEVER
nourish vb 1 syn see NURSE 1
  2 syn see NURSE 2
nourishing adj syn see NUTRITIOUS
  ant unnourishing
nourishment n syn see FOOD 2
  rel keep, living, maintenance, support
nouveau riche n syn see UPSTART
novel adj syn see NEW 1
  rel different, odd, peculiar, singular, special, strange, uncommon, unfamiliar, unique, unusual
  con customary, habitual, usual; common, familiar, ordinary

---

syn synonym(s)　　rel related word(s)
ant antonym(s)　　con contrasted word(s)
idiom idiomatic equivalent(s)
‖ use limited; if in doubt, see a dictionary

novelty *n* **1** *syn* see CHANGE 2
  con old story
  2 *syn* see KNICKKNACK
novice *n* one who is just entering a field in which he has no previous experience <a *novice* in the theater —had never even had a walk-on role>
  syn apprentice, beginner, boot, colt, fledgling, freshman, neophyte, newcomer, novitiate, prentice, punk, recruit, rookie, tenderfoot, tyro
  rel amateur; cub; postulant, probationer; greenhorn, greeny; learner, student, trainee, undergraduate
  con expert, pro, professional
  ant doyen, old hand, old-timer, veteran
novitiate *n syn* see NOVICE
now *adv* **1** *syn* see TODAY
  ant then
  2 *syn* see AWAY 3
now *conj syn* see BECAUSE
now *n syn* see PRESENT
nowadays *adv syn* see TODAY
now and again *adv syn* see SOMETIMES
now and then *adv syn* see SOMETIMES
noxious *adj syn* see UNWHOLESOME 1
  ant wholesome; sanitary
  2 *syn* see PERNICIOUS
  rel fetid, noisome, putrid, stinking
  ant innocuous, innoxious
nuance *n syn* see GRADATION
  rel dash, soupçon, suggestion, suspicion, tinge, touch; nicety, refinement, subtlety
nub *n syn* see SUBSTANCE 2
nubbin *n syn* see SUBSTANCE 2
nubilous *adj* **1** *syn* see OVERCAST
  2 *syn* see OBSCURE 3
nucleus *n syn* see SEED 2
nude *adj* **1** *syn* see BARE 1
  con covered
  2 not wearing any clothes <all the boys liked to swim *nude*>
  syn au naturel, buff-bare, mother-naked, naked, raw, stark, ‖starkers, stark-naked, stripped, unclad, undressed
  rel peeled, uncovered; dishabille, garmentless, unattired, unrobed
  idiom ‖buck naked, in a state of nature, in one's birthday suit, in one's skin, in the altogether, in the buff, in the raw, stripped to the buff, without a stitch on, without a stitch to one's name
  con attired, robed; decent; covered
  ant clad, clothed, dressed
nudge *vb syn* see POKE 1
nudnick *n syn* see PEST 2
nugatory *adj syn* see VAIN 1
nugget *n syn* see LUMP 1
nuisance *n* **1** *syn* see PEST 2
  2 *syn* see ANNOYANCE 3
null *adj* having no legal or binding force or validity <a *null* ballot>
  syn bad, invalid, null and void, void
  rel ineffective, ineffectual, inefficacious, useless, worthless
  con acceptable, good, valid
null and void *adj syn* see NULL
nullify *vb syn* see ABOLISH 1
  rel counteract, neutralize; compensate, counterbalance, countervail, offset; confine, limit, restrict

nullity *n* **1** *syn* see NOTHINGNESS
  2 *syn* see NONENTITY
numb *adj* **1** devoid of sensation or feeling <my arm is *numb*>
  syn anesthetized, asleep, benumbed, dead, deadened, insensible, insensitive, numbed, senseless, unfeeling
  rel insensate, insentient, stupefied; comatose, unconscious
  con alert; aware, conscious; sensitive
  2 *syn* see INDIFFERENT 2
numb *vb syn* see DEADEN 1
  rel chill, freeze, frost
numbed *adj syn* see NUMB 1
number *n* a character by which an arithmetical value is designated <you must add the *numbers* of the first column>
  syn chiffer, cipher, digit, figure, integer, numeral, whole number
number *vb* **1** *syn* see COUNT 1
  2 *syn* see AMOUNT 1
numberless *adj syn* see INNUMERABLE
  ant numberable
number one *adj* **1** *syn* see CHIEF 2
  2 *syn* see EXCELLENT
numeral *n syn* see NUMBER
numerate *vb* **1** *syn* see ENUMERATE 2
  2 *syn* see COUNT 1
numerous *adj syn* see MANY
  rel big, great, large
numinous *adj* **1** *syn* see SUPERNATURAL 1
  2 *syn* see SACRED 2
  3 *syn* see SPIRITUAL 4
  4 *syn* see MYSTERIOUS
numskull *n syn* see DUNCE
numskulled *adj syn* see STUPID 1
nuptial *adj syn* see MATRIMONIAL
nuptial *n*, *usu* **nuptials** *pl syn* see WEDDING
nurse *n syn* see NURSEMAID
nurse *vb* **1** to feed from the breast <decided to *nurse* her baby>
  syn breast-feed, nourish, suckle
  rel bottle-feed
  2 to promote the growth, development, or progress of <*nursed* the flame into a blaze>
  syn cherish, cultivate, foster, nourish, nursle, nurture
  rel feed; advance, forward, further, promote; humor, indulge, pamper
  con check, hold back, retard, slow
  3 *syn* see MINISTER (to)
nursemaid *n* one who is regularly employed to look after children <the *nursemaid* had three children in her charge>
  syn ‖amah, ‖ayah, nana, ‖nanny, nurse, nurserymaid
  rel babysitter, ‖minder, sitter; chaperon; governess
nurserymaid *n syn* see NURSEMAID
nursle *vb syn* see NURSE 2
nurture *n syn* see FOOD 1
nurture *vb syn* see NURSE 2
  rel bring up, raise, rear; discipline, educate, school, train; back, bolster, support, sustain, uphold
  con disregard, ignore, neglect, overlook, pass over, slight
nut *n* **1** *syn* see PROBLEM 2
  2 *syn* see HEAD 1
  3 *syn* see CRACKPOT

4 *syn* see LUNATIC 1

5 *syn* see ENTHUSIAST

‖**nuthouse** *n syn* see ASYLUM 3

nutriculture *n syn* see HYDROPONICS

nutrient *adj syn* see NUTRITIOUS

nutriment *n syn* see FOOD 2
rel bread, bread and butter, keep, livelihood, living, maintenance, subsistence, support

nutrimental *adj syn* see NUTRITIOUS

nutritional *adj syn* see NUTRITIVE 1

nutritious *adj* promoting growth and repairing natural waste <*nutritious* food>
syn nourishing, nutrient, nutrimental, nutritive
rel good, healthful, salubrious, salutary, wholesome; balanced

con indigestible; bad, insalubrious, unhealthful, unwholesome
ant innutritious

nutritive *adj* **1** relating to or concerned with nutrition <*nutritive* organs of the body>
syn alimentary, alimentative, nutritional
rel digestive, metabolic; constructive, creative, formative, productive
2 *syn* see NUTRITIOUS

nuts *adj syn* see INSANE 1

nutshell *vb syn* see EPITOMIZE 1

nutsy *adj syn* see INSANE 1

nutty *adj* **1** *syn* see ENTHUSIASTIC
2 *syn* see INSANE 1
3 *syn* see FOOLISH 2

nuzzle *vb syn* see SNUGGLE

nymph *n syn* see DOXY 1

nymphet *n syn* see DOXY 1

O

oaf *n* **1** *syn* see DUNCE
2 a big clumsy, usually slow-witted person <an *oaf* who bumped into everything he passed>
syn bohunk, ‖gaum, gawk, klutz, lobster, looby, lout, lubber, ‖lug, lummox, lump, lumpkin, meathead, palooka, schlepp (*or* schlepper), slouch
rel ‖baboon, beast, bruiser, brute, bull, gorilla, hulk, missing link, ox; clod, clown, dub, galoot, slob; blunderbuss, blunderer, blunderhead

oar *vb syn* see ROW

oater *n syn* see WESTERN

oath *n syn* see SWEARWORD

obdurate *adj* **1** *syn* see UNFEELING 2
con tender
2 *syn* see INFLEXIBLE 2
rel mulish, stiff-necked; immovable
con relenting, submitting

obedient *adj* submissive to the will, guidance, or control of another <children should always be *obedient* to their parents>

syn amenable, biddable, docile, ‖docious, tractable
rel acquiescent, compliant, sheeplike, submissive, yielding; duteous, dutiful, loyal; law-abiding; obeisant, subservient
con insubordinate, rebellious; contrary, froward, perverse, wayward, willful; headstrong, intractable, recalcitrant, refractory, uncontrollable, ungovernable, unruly
ant contumacious, disobedient

obeisance *n syn* see HONOR 1
rel allegiance, fealty, loyalty

obeisant *adj syn* see SUBSERVIENT 2

obese *adj syn* see FAT 2
ant skinny

obesity *n* a condition characterized by excessive bodily fat <could barely walk because of his *obesity*>
syn adiposity, corpulence, fatness, fleshiness
rel chubbiness, chunkiness, embonpoint, grossness, plumpness, portliness, pudginess, rotundity, stockiness, stoutness, tubbiness
con lankiness, leanness, scrawniness, slenderness, slimness
ant skinniness

obey *vb* to act or behave in conformity with (as an order) or in duty to (as a parent) <*obey* a superior's order>

---

syn synonym(s)   *rel* related word(s)
ant antonym(s)   *con* contrasted word(s)
idiom idiomatic equivalent(s)
‖ use limited; if in doubt, see a dictionary

syn comply, conform, follow, keep, mind, observe

rel bow, defer, submit, yield; accede, acquiesce, agree, assent; fulfill, satisfy; carry out; heed, regard

idiom abide by

con break, disregard, transgress, violate; command, order

ant disobey

obfuscate *vb syn* see OBSCURE

ant clarify

obit *n syn* see OBITUARY

obiter *adv syn* see INCIDENTALLY 2

obiter dictum *n syn* see REMARK 2

obituary *n* a notice of a person's death usually with a short biographical account <always read the *obituaries* in the paper>

syn necrology, obit

object *n* 1 *syn* see THING 3

rel doodad; gadget

2 *syn* see THING 5

3 *syn* see BODY 4

4 *syn* see VIEW 6

5 *syn* see USE 4

object *vb* 1 to oppose by arguing against <*objecting* because the evidence was unclear>

syn except, expostulate, inveigh (against), kick, protest, remonstrate

rel balk, boggle, demur, dissent, jib, stickle; complain; criticize; challenge; spurn; rail, rant, rave, storm

con accede, agree, assent, consent; accredit, approve, sanction

ant acquiesce

2 *syn* see DISAPPROVE 1

objectify *vb syn* see EMBODY 1

objection *n syn* see DEMUR 2

objectionable *adj* arousing or likely to arouse objection <the language in that movie is *objectionable*>

syn exceptionable, ill-favored, inadmissible, unacceptable, undesirable, unwanted, unwelcome

rel abhorrent, loathsome, offensive, repellent, repugnant, repulsive, revolting; disagreeable, distasteful, invidious, obnoxious, unpleasant; unfit, unsuitable; censurable, reprehensible

con acceptable, agreeable, gratifying, pleasant, pleasing, welcome

ant unobjectionable

objective *adj* 1 *syn* see MATERIAL 1

rel external, outer, outside, outward

ant subjective

2 *syn* see FAIR 4

ant subjective

objective *n* 1 *syn* see AMBITION 2

2 *syn* see USE 4

objectless *adj syn* see RANDOM

objet d'art *n syn* see KNICKKNACK

objurgate *vb syn* see EXECRATE 1

rel castigate, censure

obligated *adj syn* see INDEBTED

obligation *n* 1 *syn* see OCCASION 3

2 something one is bound to do or forbear <it is our *obligation* to obey the law>

syn charge, commitment, committal, devoir, duty, must, need, ought, ‖right

rel compulsion, constraint, restraint; burden, requirement, responsibility; business, part, place

con choice, discretion, free will, option; decision, determination, pleasure, will

3 *syn* see INDEBTEDNESS 1

obligatory *adj syn* see MANDATORY

ant nonobligatory

oblige *vb* 1 *syn* see FORCE 2

2 to do a service or courtesy <you will *oblige* me greatly if you will get there on time>

syn accommodate, convenience, favor

rel gratify, please; avail, benefit, profit; aid, assist, contribute, help

con bother, discommode, incommode, inconvenience, trouble

ant disoblige

obliged *adj* 1 *syn* see GRATEFUL 1

2 *syn* see INDEBTED

obliging *adj syn* see AMIABLE 1

ant disobliging

oblique *adj* 1 *syn* see INCLINED 3

2 *syn* see INDIRECT 1

ant straight

obliquely *adv syn* see ASIDE 1

ant straight

obliterate *vb syn* see ERASE

oblivion *n* a state of forgetting or the fact of having forgotten <the *oblivion* of sleep>

syn forgetfulness, lethe, obliviousness

rel nirvana; insensibleness

con alertness, awareness, consciousness; memory, recall, recalling, recollection, remembrance

oblivious *adj* 1 *syn* see FORGETFUL

rel absorbed, unaware, unconscious

idiom turned off

2 *syn* see IGNORANT 2

obliviousness *n syn* see OBLIVION

obloquy *n* 1 *syn* see ABUSE

2 *syn* see ANIMADVERSION

3 *syn* see DISGRACE

obnoxious *adj* 1 *syn* see LIABLE 2

ant unobnoxious

2 *syn* see REPUGNANT 1

con congenial, likable, simpatico

ant grateful; unobnoxious

obnubilate *vb syn* see OBSCURE

obscene *adj* 1 *syn* see OFFENSIVE

2 marked by the use of words regarded as taboo in polite usage <knew all the *obscene* expressions for the genitalia>

syn barnyard, coarse, crude, crusty, dirty, fescennine, filthy, foul, gross, indecent, nasty, paw, profane, rank, raunchy, ‖raw, rocky, scatological, scurrilous, smutty, vulgar; *compare* RISQUÉ

rel bawdy, ribald, smoking-room; impure, lascivious, lewd, warm; lurid, pornographic, salacious, scabrous, sultry; earthy, rich; unprintable; foulmouthed

con acceptable, proper, tolerable; appropriate, fit, suitable; clean, decent, decorous, seemly

obscure *adj* 1 *syn* see DARK 1

rel clouded, cloudy, fuliginous; shadowy, shady, umbrageous

con clear, lucid; bright, brilliant, luminous

2 withdrawn from the main centers of human activity <was exiled to an *obscure* Siberian village>

syn devious, lonesome, out-of-the-way, remote, removed, retired, secret

rel distant, far, far-off; close, hidden, odd, secluded, sequestered, solitary; blind; inaccessible

idiom back of beyond, off the beaten track (*or* path), in the boondocks (*or* sticks)

con central; urban; populous

3 not readily understood or grasped <an *obscure* textual reference>

syn ambiguous, amphibological, double-edged, double-faced, dusky, equivocal, murky, nubilous, opaque, sibylline, tenebrous, uncertain, unclear, unexplicit, unintelligible, vague; *compare* CRYPTIC, FAINT 2

rel difficult, incomprehensible, inexplicable, puzzling, unfathomable; illegible; abstruse, Delphian, enigmatic, esoteric, inscrutable, mysterious, mystic, mystical; inconclusive, indecisive, indefinite

con definite, explicit, obvious; clear, express, unambiguous, unequivocal

ant lucid

4 *syn* see INCONSPICUOUS

rel humble, lowly, minor, unimportant

5 lacking the prominence, showiness, or worth by which attention might be attracted <an *obscure* Roman poet>

syn nameless, uncelebrated, unfamed, unheard-of, unknown, unnoted, unrenowned

rel inconspicuous; minor, undistinguished, unimportant

con celebrated, distinguished, named, notable, noted, noteworthy, renowned, well-known

ant famed, famous

6 *syn* see FAINT 2

ant clear

obscure *vb* to make dark, dim, or indistinct <fog *obscured* our view>

syn adumbrate, becloud, bedim, befog, cloud, darken, dim, dislimn, eclipse, fog, gloom, haze, mist, murk, obfuscate, obnubilate, overcast, overcloud, overshadow, shadow

rel blear, blur, fuzz; blind, conceal, dim out, hide, screen, shade, shroud; bemask, camouflage, cloak, cover, disguise, mask, veil; belie, falsify, misrepresent

con brighten, light (up), lighten; clarify, enlighten; elucidate, exemplify, explain

ant illuminate, illumine

obscured *adj syn* see ULTERIOR

obsequious *adj syn* see SUBSERVIENT 2

rel deferential; parasitic, sycophantic, toadying

con self-assertive

observable *adj* **1** *syn* see PERCEPTIBLE

ant unobservable

2 *syn* see NOTEWORTHY

observance *n* **1** *syn* see RITE 2

2 *syn* see NOTICE 1

ant nonobservance, unobservance

observant *adj* **1** *syn* see ATTENTIVE 1

rel awake

ant unobservant

2 *syn* see MINDFUL 2

observation *n* **1** *syn* see NOTICE 1

2 *syn* see REMARK 2

observative *adj syn* see MINDFUL 2

observatory *n syn* see LOOKOUT 2

observe *vb* **1** *syn* see OBEY

2 *syn* see KEEP 2

rel revere, reverence, venerate

ant break, violate

3 *syn* see SEE 1

4 *syn* see REMARK 2

observer *n syn* see SPECTATOR

observing *adj syn* see MINDFUL 2

ant unobserving

obsessed *adj* preoccupied intensely or abnormally <*obsessed* with cleanliness>

syn hagridden, hipped, queer

rel bewitched, dominated, gripped, held, possessed, prepossessed; bedeviled, beset, dogged, harassed, haunted, plagued, troubled; overcome

idiom have on the brain

con detached, unconcerned, uninterested; indifferent, neutral; cool, easygoing

obsession *n syn* see FETISH 2

obsolesce *vb syn* see OUTDATE

obsolete *adj* no longer active or in use <*obsolete* social customs>

syn dead, disused, extinct, outmoded, outworn, passé, superseded; *compare* ANCIENT 1

rel old-fashioned, old hat, old-time, old-timey, out-of-date, unfashionable; dusty, fusty, moldy, moth-eaten, musty, stale, timeworn

idiom behind the times

con contemporary, modern, new-fashioned, up-to-date, up-to-the-minute; novel, original, unique

ant current

obsolete *vb syn* see OUTDATE

obstacle *n* something that seriously hampers action or progress <lack of education is an *obstacle* to advancement>

syn bar, Chinese wall, crimp, hamper, hurdle, impediment, mountain, obstruction, rub, snag, stumbling block, traverse

rel clog, encumbrance, handicap, hindrance; bump, difficulty, hardship, vicissitude; catch, hitch; disincentive

con aid, assist, assistance, help

ant advantage

obstinate *adj* unwilling to submit (as to reason or control) <he had an *obstinate* determination to live as he pleased>

syn bullheaded, closed-minded, deaf, hardheaded, headstrong, incompliant, intractable, intransigent, muleheaded, muley, mulish, pertinacious, perverse, pervicacious, pigheaded, refractory, self-willed, ‖sot, stiff, stiff-necked, stubborn, tough, unpliable, unpliant, unyielding, willful, wrongheaded; *compare* UNRULY 1

rel resistant, unsubmissive, withstanding; contrary, crabbed, recalcitrant, renitent; inexorable, inflexible, obdurate; opinionated; resolute, staunch, steadfast, unbudging

con acquiescent, complaisant, compliant; submissive, yielding; agreeable, cooperative, willing

syn synonym(s)   *rel* related word(s)
ant antonym(s)   *con* contrasted word(s)
idiom idiomatic equivalent(s)
‖ use limited; if in doubt, see a dictionary

ant pliable, pliant

obstipated *adj syn* see CONSTIPATED

obstreperous *adj* 1 *syn* see VOCIFEROUS
2 *syn* see DISOBEDIENT

obstruct *vb* 1 *syn* see FILL 1
2 *syn* see HINDER
3 *syn* see SCREEN 3

obstruction *n syn* see OBSTACLE

obtain *vb syn* see GET 1

obtainable *adj* 1 *syn* see AVAILABLE 1
rel derivable
2 *syn* see PURCHASABLE 1

obtrude *vb* 1 *syn* see IMPOSE 5
2 *syn* see INTRUDE 1

obtrusive *adj syn* see IMPERTINENT 2
ant unobtrusive

obtund *vb syn* see DULL 3

obtuse *adj syn* see DULL 6

obviate *vb syn* see PREVENT 2
rel anticipate; interfere; interpose, intervene

obvious *adj syn* see CLEAR 5
ant abstruse, obscure; unobvious

occasion *n* 1 *syn* see OPPORTUNITY
2 *syn* see CAUSE 1
3 something that provides a reason for something else <there is no *occasion* for alarm>
syn call, cause, necessity, obligation
rel basis, foundation, ground, warrant; justification, right; excuse
4 *syn* see OCCURRENCE
5 a particular point of time at which something takes place <we always spoke, but on that *occasion* we didn't>
syn instant, moment, time, while
idiom point in time
6 *syn* see NEED 3
7 **occasions** *pl syn* see BUSINESS 8
8 *syn* see EVENT 2

occasion *vb syn* see GENERATE 3

occasional *adj syn* see INFREQUENT
rel incidental; casual, random
con accustomed, habitual, usual; constant, continual, continuous
ant customary

occasionally *adv* on a few occasions <*occasionally* she'll walk instead of drive>
syn infrequently, irregularly, on occasion, sporadically, uncommonly; *compare* SOMETIMES
rel off and on, once or twice
idiom every now and then, from time to time, ‖once in a way, once in a while
con continually, continuously, frequently; commonly, customarily, habitually, often; hardly ever, rarely, scarcely, seldom; never
ant constantly

occlude *vb syn* see FILL 1

occult *vb syn* see HIDE

occult *adj syn* see RECONDITE
rel arcane, mysterious; cabalistic, mystical, supernatural; eerie, unearthly, weird

occupancy *n syn* see HABITATION 1

occupant *n syn* see INHABITANT

occupation *n* 1 *syn* see WORK 1
2 *syn* see HABITATION 1

occupiable *adj syn* see LIVABLE 1

occupied *adj syn* see BUSY 1
ant unoccupied

occupy *vb* 1 *syn* see ENGAGE 4
2 *syn* see INHABIT

occur *vb* 1 *syn* see HAPPEN 1
2 to enter one's mind <it just *occurred* to me: she can't drive>
syn hit, strike
idiom come into one's head, come to mind, cross one's mind, flash across one's mind, go through one's head

occurrence *n* something that happens or takes place <the chance encounter turned out to be a fortunate *occurrence*>
syn circumstance, episode, event, go, happening, incident, occasion, thing
rel contingency, emergency, exigency, juncture, pass; condition, situation, state; adventure, experience

ocean *n* the body of water that covers nearly three-fourths of the earth <pulled the downed pilot from the *ocean*>
syn blue, brine, ‖briny, deep, drink, main, sea

oceanic *adj syn* see MARINE 1

ochlocracy *n syn* see ANARCHY 1

ocular *adj* 1 *syn* see VISUAL 2
2 *syn* see VISUAL 1

ocular *n syn* see EYE 1

oculus *n syn* see EYE 1

odd *adj* 1 being without a corresponding mate <had only an *odd* glove; the other was lost>
syn unmatched, unpaired
rel lone, only, single
con matched, paired
2 *syn* see ACCIDENTAL
3 *syn* see STRANGE 4

oddball *n syn* see ECCENTRIC

oddball *adj syn* see STRANGE 4

oddity *n* 1 *syn* see ECCENTRIC
2 *syn* see CURIOSITY 2

oddments *n pl syn* see SUNDRIES

odds *n pl syn* see ADVANTAGE 3

odds and ends *n pl* 1 *syn* see SUNDRIES
2 *syn* see MISCELLANY 1

odiferous *adj syn* see ODOROUS

odious *adj syn* see HATEFUL 2

odium *n* 1 *syn* see DISGRACE
rel hate, hatred
ant honor
2 *syn* see STIGMA

odor *n syn* see SMELL 1

odoriferous *adj syn* see ODOROUS

odorize *vb syn* see SCENT 2

odorless *adj* having no odor <*odorless* castor oil>
syn inodorous, scentless, smell-less
rel deodorant, deodorizing; unscented
con scented, smelly
ant odorous

odorous *adj* having or emitting an odor <*odorous* chemicals are often malodorous>
syn odiferous, odoriferous, scented; *compare* MALODOROUS 1, SWEET 2
rel redolent, reeking, smelling, smelly; heady, pungent, strong; olfactive, olfactory
ant inodorous, odorless, scentless

o'er *prep syn* see OVER 1

oeuvre *n* a substantial body of work constituting the lifework of a writer, composer, or artist <one of the more popular operas in the Mozart *oeuvre*>
syn corpus, opera omnia

rel output

off *adv syn* see AWAY 2

off *adj* **1** *syn* see REMOTE 4

2 *syn* see SLOW 3

offal *n syn* see REFUSE

off–balance *adj syn* see LOPSIDED

off–center *adj syn* see ECCENTRIC 1

off–color *adj* **1** *syn* see UNWELL

2 *syn* see RISQUÉ

offend *vb* **1** *syn* see TRESPASS 1

2 *syn* see VIOLATE 1

3 to cause hurt feelings or deep resentment <*offended* her by his cruel remark>

syn affront, insult, outrage

rel aggrieve, hurt, sting, wound; exasperate, gall, irritate, nettle; excite, provoke; appall, horrify, scandalize, shock; disoblige, displease, distress, disturb, miff, pique, upset

idiom hurt one's feelings, ruffle one's feathers, step (*or* tread) on one's toes

con delight, gratify, please, tickle; captivate, charm, enchant; please

offender *n syn* see CRIMINAL

offense *n* **1** *syn* see ATTACK 1

2 an emotional response to a slight or indignity <he is so sensitive that he takes *offense* at the slightest criticism>

syn dudgeon, huff, miff, pique, resentment, ‖snuff, umbrage

rel affront, indignity, insult; anger, indignation; displeasure; catfit, conniption, fit, tantrum; pet, tizzy; explosion, flare-up, outburst, scene

con delight, pleasure

3 *syn* see CRIME 1

offensive *adj* utterly unpleasant or distasteful to the senses or sensibilities <the *offensive* odor of garbage> <her arrogant assurance was more than a little *offensive*>

syn atrocious, disgusting, evil, foul, hideous, horrible, horrid, icky, loathsome, nasty, nauseating, noisome, obscene, repellent, repugnant, repulsive, revolting, sickening, ungrateful, unwholesome, vile

rel abhorrent, bad, disagreeable, objectionable, uncongenial, unpleasant; abominable, detestable, fulsome, odious; rank; appalling, awful, beastly, dreadful, frightful, ghastly, grim, grisly, gruesome, lurid, shocking, terrible; unappetizing, unpalatable, unsavory

con agreeable, appealing, attractive, pleasant, pleasing; favorable, unobjectionable, welcome; appetizing, palatable, savory; divine

ant inoffensive, unoffensive

offensive *n syn* see ATTACK 1

offer *vb* **1** to put something before another for acceptance or consideration <he was soon *offered* another job>

syn extend, give, hold out, pose, present, proffer, tender

rel display, exhibit, show

con accept, receive, take; decline, refuse, reject

2 *syn* see ADDUCE

3 *syn* see TRY 5

4 *syn* see SHOW 1

offering *n* **1** *syn* see VICTIM 1

2 *syn* see DONATION

offgoing *n syn* see DEPARTURE 1

offhand *adj syn* see EXTEMPORANEOUS

office *n* **1** *syn* see JOB 2

2 *syn* see FUNCTION 1

‖3 *syn* see PRIVY 1

‖4 *syn* see HIGH SIGN 2

officer *n* **1** *syn* see POLICEMAN

2 *syn* see EXECUTIVE

official *n syn* see EXECUTIVE

official *adj* derived from the proper office, officer, or authority <the mayor's office issued an *official* statement>

syn authoritative, ex cathedra, ex officio

rel approved, authorized, certified, cleared, endorsed, OK'd, sanctioned; canonical, cathedral

ant officious (*in diplomatic use*), unofficial

officially *adv syn* see OSTENSIBLY

officiate *vb syn* see ACT 4

officious *adj syn* see IMPERTINENT 2

offing *n syn* see FUTURE

offish *adj* **1** *syn* see UNSOCIABLE

2 *syn* see UNWELL

off–key *adj syn* see IRREGULAR 1

off–load *vb syn* see UNLOAD

off–lying *adj syn* see DISTANT 1

offscouring *n syn* see OUTCAST

offset *vb syn* see COMPENSATE 1

rel check, stop

offshoot *n syn* see OUTGROWTH 2

offspring *n pl* those who follow in direct parental line <a mother of numerous *offspring*>

syn ‖begats, brood, children, descendants, issue, posterity, progeniture, progeny, scions, seed

rel hatch, swarm; produce, spawn, young

con antecedents, ascendants, forebears, forefathers, progenitors

ant ancestors

offstage *adj or adv syn* see BACKSTAGE

ant onstage

‖off–the–peg *adj syn* see READY–MADE

off–the–rack *adj syn* see READY–MADE

off–the–shelf *adj syn* see READY–MADE

of late *adv syn* see NEW

oft *adv syn* see OFTEN

often *adv* many times <we called *often* but still could not reach you>

syn again and again, frequently, much, oft, oftentimes, ofttimes, over and over, repeatedly, time and again

idiom a number of times, many a time, many times over, time and time again

con infrequently, rarely; now and then, occasionally

ant seldom

oftentimes *adv syn* see OFTEN

ofttimes *adv syn* see OFTEN

ogle *vb syn* see LOOK 7

‖ogle *n syn* see EYE 1

ogress *n syn* see VIRAGO

oil *n syn* see FLATTERY

‖oiled *adj syn* see INTOXICATED 1

oily *adj* **1** *syn* see FATTY 2

---

2 *syn* see FULSOME

ointment *n* a semisolid medicinal or cosmetic preparation for application to the skin <put *ointment* on the burned skin>
syn balm, cerate, chrism, cream, salve, unction, unguent
rel embrocation, liniment; demulcent, emollient; lotion; dressing

OK (*or* okay) *adv syn* see YES 1

OK (*or* okay) *vb syn* see APPROVE 2

OK (*or* okay) *n syn* see APPROBATION

‖**okeydoke** *adv syn* see YES 1

old *adj* 1 *syn* see ANCIENT 1
con contemporary, current, recent; advanced
ant new
2 of long standing <the ending of such an *old* friendship was tragic>
syn continuing, enduring, inveterate, lifelong, long-lasting, long-lived, perennial; *compare* LASTING
rel constant, perpetual, staying; established, firm, solid, steady
con newfound, recent; brief, short-lived; casual, temporary, transitory, weak
ant new
3 *syn* see OLD-FASHIONED
rel primitive; traditional
con newish
ant modern, new
4 *syn* see AGED 1
idiom along in years, getting on
con juvenile, young
ant youthful
5 *syn* see EXPERIENCED
con young
ant new
6 *syn* see FORMER 2

old age *n* the final stage of the normal life span <spent his *old age* in a nursing home>
syn age, caducity, elderliness, senectitude, senescence, years; *compare* DOTAGE
rel decrepitude, feebleness; infirmity
idiom advanced years, declining years, winter of life
ant youth

olden *adj* 1 *syn* see ANCIENT 1
2 *syn* see AGED 1

oldest profession *n syn* see PROSTITUTION

oldfangled *adj syn* see OLD-FASHIONED
ant newfangled

old-fashioned *adj* typical of an earlier time and often replaced by something more modern or more fashionable <*old-fashioned* high-buttoned shoes>
syn antiquated, antique, archaic, belated, bygone, dated, démodé, demoded, dowdy, fusty, moldy, moth-eaten, neanderthal, old, oldfangled, old hat, old-time, old-timey, outdated, outmoded, out-of-date, passé, rococo, unmodern, vintage
rel aged, ancient; discarded, disused, obsolete; outworn, unfashionable; crusty, fogyish, fuddy-duddy, fusty, moss-backed, moss-grown, mossy, stodgy; Victorian; old-line
con modernistic, modish, newfangled, stylish, ‖trendy; current, recent, timely; new-fashioned, up-to-date, up-to-the-minute
ant contemporary; modern

Old Gooseberry *n syn* see DEVIL 1

Old Guard *n syn* see ESTABLISHMENT 2

old hand *n syn* see VETERAN

old hat *adj* 1 *syn* see OLD-FASHIONED
2 *syn* see TRITE

old lady *n* ‖1 *syn* see WIFE
‖2 *syn* see MOTHER 1
3 *syn* see FUSSBUDGET

old-line *adj syn* see CONSERVATIVE 1

old liner *n syn* see DIEHARD 1

old maid *n* 1 *syn* see SPINSTER
2 *syn* see FUSSBUDGET

old-maidish *adj syn* see NICE 1

‖**old man** *n* 1 *syn* see HUSBAND
2 *syn* see FATHER 1

Old Nick *n syn* see DEVIL 1

Old Scratch *n syn* see DEVIL 1

oldster *n* a person of advanced years <an *oldster* long retired from the business world>
syn ancient, elder, golden-ager, old-timer, senior, senior citizen; *compare* BELDAM 1, GAFFER
ant youngster, youth

old-time *adj* 1 *syn* see OLD-FASHIONED
2 *syn* see EXPERIENCED

old-timer *n* 1 *syn* see VETERAN
2 *syn* see OLDSTER

old-timey *adj syn* see OLD-FASHIONED

‖**old woman** *n* 1 *syn* see WIFE
2 *syn* see MOTHER 1

old-womanish *adj syn* see NICE 1

oleaginous *adj* 1 *syn* see FATTY 2
2 *syn* see FULSOME

olid *adj syn* see MALODOROUS 1

olio *n syn* see MISCELLANY 1

olla podrida *n syn* see MISCELLANY 1

omen *n syn* see FORETOKEN

omen *vb syn* see AUGUR 2

ominous *adj* indicative of future misfortune or calamity <dark *ominous* clouds preceded the storm>
syn apocalyptic, baleful, baneful, dire, direful, doomful, fateful, ill-boding, ill-omened, inauspicious, threatening, unlucky, unpropitious; *compare* EVIL 5, SINISTER
rel portentous; malefic, maleficent, malign, sinister; comminatory, forbidding, grim, lowering, menacing; hostile, inhospitable, unfriendly
con auspicious, benign, favorable, promising, propitious; beneficial

omission *n* something omitted or missing <several *omissions* in the list>
syn blank, chasm, overlook, oversight, preterition, pretermission, skip
rel inadvertence, inadvertency, lapse, slip; break, gap, hiatus, lacuna
con inclusion; accession, addition, augmentation, increase, reinforcement; superaddition

omit *vb syn* see NEGLECT

omitted *adj syn* see ABSENT 1
ant included

omnibus *n syn* see ANTHOLOGY

omnipotent *adj* having virtually unlimited authority or influence <an *omnipotent* leader>
syn all-powerful, almighty
rel divine, godlike; unlimited, unrestricted
con impotent, powerless; limited, restricted

omnipresent *adj* present at all places at all times <*omnipresent* God>
syn allover, ubiquitous, universal
rel boundless, endless, immeasurable, infinite, limitless, unending
con bounded, finite, limited, restricted; cramped, straitened; narrow, strait

omnium-gatherum *n syn* see MISCELLANY 1

on *prep* **1** *syn* see OVER 4
2 *syn* see OVER 3

on *adv syn* see ALONG 1

on-again-off-again *adj syn* see FITFUL

onanism *n syn* see SELF-GRATIFICATION

onanistic *adj syn* see SYBARITIC

once *adv* **1** *syn* see EVER 5
2 *syn* see BEFORE 2

once *adj syn* see FORMER 2

once and again *adv syn* see SOMETIMES

once more *adv syn* see OVER 3

oncoming *adj syn* see FORTHCOMING

on-dit *n syn* see REPORT 1

one *adj syn* see SINGLE 2

one *n syn* see DOLLAR

one *vb syn* see JOIN 1

one by one *adv syn* see APART 1

one-horse town *n syn* see BURG

oneness *n* **1** *syn* see UNITY 1
ant multiplicity
2 *syn* see UNIQUENESS
3 *syn* see ENTIRETY 1
4 *syn* see IDENTITY 1

onerous *adj* imposing great hardship or strain <found the care of his old mother an *onerous* task>
syn burdensome, demanding, exacting, exigent, grievous, oppressive, superincumbent, taxing, tough, trying, weighty
rel arduous, difficult, hard, laborious; heavy, hefty, ponderous; cumbersome, unruly, unwieldy; driving, heavy-handed
con easy, effortless; facile, light, simple, smooth, unexacting, untaxing

onerously *adv syn* see HARD 8

one-sided *adj syn* see BIASED 2
rel lopsided, weighted
con many-sided

one-sidedness *n syn* see PREJUDICE
con manysidedness

onetime *adj syn* see FORMER 2

onfall *n syn* see ATTACK 1

ongoing *n syn* see ADVANCE 2
rel development, growth

onlooker *n syn* see SPECTATOR

only *adj* **1** *syn* see ALONE 3
2 being one or more of which there exist no others <the *only* survivors of the wreck>
syn alone, lone, singular, sole, solitary, solo, unexampled, unique, unrepeatable
rel incomparable, inimitable, matchless, peerless, transcendent, unequaled, unparalleled, unrivaled; companionless, separate, unaccompanied, unattended, uncompanied, uncompanioned
con divers, many, multifarious, numerous, sundry, various

3 *syn* see SINGLE 2

only *adv* **1** to the exclusion of any alternative or competitor <he will confess *only* to you>
syn alone, but, entirely, exclusively, solely
2 *syn* see JUST 3

only *conj* in spite of which <it looks delicious, *only* I'm not hungry>
syn but, except, however, save, yet

on occasion *adv syn* see OCCASIONALLY

on offer *adj syn* see PURCHASABLE 1

onomatopoeic *adj* formed in imitation of a natural sound <*buzz* is an *onomatopoeic* word to describe the sound of bees>
syn echoic, imitative, onomatopoetic
rel emulative, simulative; mimetic, mimic, mimical

onomatopoetic *adj syn* see ONOMATOPOEIC

on purpose *adv syn* see INTENTIONALLY

onset *n* **1** *syn* see ATTACK 1
2 *syn* see BEGINNING

onslaught *n syn* see ATTACK 1

on the whole *adv syn* see ALTOGETHER 3

onus *n* **1** *syn* see LOAD 3
2 *syn* see BLAME
3 *syn* see STIGMA

onward *adv* **1** *syn* see AHEAD 2
2 *syn* see ALONG 1

onyx *adj syn* see BLACK 1

oodles *n pl but sometimes sing in constr syn* see SCAD

‖**ooftish** *n syn* see MONEY

‖**oofy** *adj syn* see RICH 1

ooid *adj syn* see OVAL

oomph *n syn* see SPIRIT 5

ooze *vb syn* see EXUDE

oozy *adj syn* see MUDDY 1

opaque *adj syn* see OBSCURE 3
ant transparent, transpicuous

ope *vb syn* see OPEN 1

open *adj* **1** not closed or obstructed <escaped through the *open* gate>
syn patent, unclosed, unobstructed
rel agape, dehiscent, gaping, patulous, ringent, wide, yawning; ajar; unbarred, unbolted, unfastened, unlocked, unsealed; clear, unimpeded
con blocked, obstructed; constricted, cramped, narrow, strait
ant closed, shut
2 lacking a cover or covering <an *open* wound that continued to ooze blood> <his chest *open* to the sun>
syn bare, denuded, exposed, naked, peeled, stripped, uncovered
3 *syn* see LIABLE 2
ant closed
4 not restricted to a particular group or situation <favored *open* enrollment in the schools>
syn accessible, open-door, public, unrestricted
rel attainable, available, obtainable, reachable, securable
idiom to be had, within reach
con limited, restricted; inaccessible, private
ant closed
5 available for use or consideration or decision <there are only two courses *open* to us>
syn accessible, employable, operative, practicable, usable

---

syn synonym(s)   *rel* related word(s)
ant antonym(s)   *con* contrasted word(s)
idiom idiomatic equivalent(s)
‖ use limited; if in doubt, see a dictionary

rel appropriate, fit, proper, suitable; acceptable, agreeable, pleasing
idiom within reach
con inaccessible, inoperative, unusable
ant closed
6 *syn* see DOUBTFUL 1
7 *syn* see FRANK
ant closed; clandestine

open *vb* 1 to change from a closed to an open condition <*open* the window>
syn ope, unblock, unclose, undo, unshut, unstop
rel clear, free, release; bare, disclose, expose, reveal
idiom lay open, swing open, throw open
con block, occlude, stop
ant close, shut

2 to make physically or mentally visible <dawn *opened* a surprising scene to his startled eyes>
syn disclose, display, expose, reveal, unclothe, uncover, unveil
rel adumbrate, hint, shadow, suggest
idiom bring to light, bring to (*or* into) view, lay bare, make plain, show forth
con cloak, conceal, hide, screen, secrete, shroud

3 to make an opening in <decided to *open* a can of beans>
syn breach, disrupt, hole, rupture
rel break, broach, tap, undo; cut, gash, slash, perforate, pierce
idiom lay open
con occlude, shut; fasten, secure
ant close

4 to spread out <the eagle slowly *opened* its mighty wings>
syn expand, extend, fan (out), outspread, outstretch, spread, unfold
rel billow, dilate, distend, swell; cover, mantle, overspread
con collect, concentrate, contract, gather (in)
ant close

5 *syn* see BEGIN 1
ant close

6 *syn* see CONVENE 1

open *n syn* see OUTDOORS

open air *n syn* see OUTDOORS

open–air *adj syn* see OUTDOOR
con indoor, inside; enclosed

open–and–shut *adj syn* see CLEAR 5

open–door *adj syn* see OPEN 4

open–eyed *adj syn* see WATCHFUL

openhanded *adj* 1 *syn* see LIBERAL 1
ant closefisted, tightfisted
2 *syn* see CLEAR 5

openhearted *adj syn* see FRANK

opening *n* 1 *syn* see BEGINNING
ant closing
2 *syn* see APERTURE
3 *syn* see GAP 1
4 *syn* see OPPORTUNITY

opening gun *n syn* see BEGINNING

openmouthed *adj syn* see VOCIFEROUS

openness *n syn* see EXPOSURE

open sesame *n syn* see PASSPORT

open up *vb syn* see OPERATE 2

opera omnia *n syn* see OEUVRE

operate *vb* 1 *syn* see ACT 5

2 to perform surgery <*operated* on him to remove a brain tumor>
syn cut, open up

3 to cause to function <knew how to *operate* earth-moving equipment>
syn handle, run, use, work
rel play; manage, maneuver; drive, pilot, steer; ply, wield
idiom make go
4 *syn* see CONDUCT 3

operation *n* 1 *syn* see EXERCISE 1
2 *syn* see USE 1

operative *adj* 1 *syn* see ACTIVE 1
ant inoperative
2 *syn* see OPEN 5

operative *n* 1 *syn* see WORKER
2 *syn* see PRIVATE DETECTIVE

operator *n syn* see MOTORIST

operose *adj* 1 *syn* see HARD 6
2 *syn* see ASSIDUOUS

opiate *adj syn* see SOPORIFIC 1

opiate *n* 1 *syn* see DRUG 2
2 *syn* see ANODYNE 2

opine *vb* to form or express an opinion <he *opined* that the story was true>
syn ‖opinion, opinionate
rel accept, believe, consider, hold, judge, regard, think, view; speculate
con deny, disclaim, disown, reject, repudiate; disbelieve, discredit, doubt

opinion *n* an idea or judgment held as true or valid <seek an expert *opinion* on the authenticity of the painting>
syn belief, conviction, eye, feeling, mind, persuasion, sentiment, view
rel attitude, impression, notion, think, thought; conclusion, estimate, estimation, judgment, reaction; assumption, conjecture, speculation, supposition, theory
idiom point of view
con disbelief, discredit, doubt, unbelief; distrust, mistrust, questioning, skepticism

‖**opinion** *vb syn* see OPINE

opinionate *vb syn* see OPINE

opponent *n* one who expresses or manifests opposition <her *opponent* in the debate>
syn adversary, antagonist, anti, con, match, opposer, oppugnant
rel enemy, foe; competitor, rival; assailant, combatant; counteragent
con ally, colleague, comrade, confederate, partner; advocate, champion
ant exponent, pro, proponent

opportune *adj syn* see TIMELY 1
rel appropriate, felicitous, happy
ant inopportune

opportunity *n* a state of affairs or combination of circumstances favorable to some end <all he asked was an *opportunity* to show what he could do>
syn break, chance, look-in, occasion, opening, shot, show, squeak, time
rel room, space; leisure, liberty; relief, spell, turn; juncture, pass; dog's chance, hope, prayer

oppose *vb* 1 to place over against something to provide resistance or counterbalance <*oppose* one military force with another>
syn counter, match, pit, play (off), vie
rel array, confront, face

idiom set over against
  2 *syn* see RESIST
opposed *adj syn* see ADVERSE 1
opposer *n syn* see OPPONENT
opposing *adj syn* see ADVERSE 1
opposite *n* something that is exactly opposed
or contrary <virtue and vice are *opposites*>
  syn antipode, antipole, antithesis, contra,
contradictory, contrary, converse, counter,
counterpole, reverse
  rel contrast, counterpoint, foil; contrapositive, inverse, obverse; antonym
  idiom the other extreme, the other side of
the coin
  con analogon, analogue, counterpart, like,
parallel, similar; equal, equivalent; correlate,
correlative; carbon copy, duplicate, replica
  ant same
opposite *adj* being so far apart as to be or to
seem irreconcilable <held *opposite* views on
the solution of the problem>
  syn antipodal, antipodean, antithetical,
contradictory, contrary, converse, counter,
diametric, polar, reverse
  rel contrasting; contrapositive, inverse,
obverse; antonymous; different, dissimilar,
divergent, opposed, unalike, unlike, unsimilar; independent, separate, unconnected,
unrelated
  con alike, analogous, equivalent, like, parallel, similar; equal; correlative
  ant same
opposite *prep syn* see TO 6
oppositely *adv syn* see AGAIN 5
opposite number *n* one holding an equivalent or parallel position <the Secretary of
State and his *opposite number*, the Foreign
Minister>
  syn coordinate, counterpart, vis-à-vis; *compare* EQUAL
  rel complement, cousin, equal, equivalent,
like, match, tally
opposition *n syn* see ANTAGONISM 2
oppressure *n syn* see ANTAGONISM 2
oppress *vb* 1 *syn* see WRONG
  rel harass, harry; afflict, torment, torture;
conquer, overcome, overthrow, subjugate
  2 *syn* see DEPRESS 2
  rel burden, distress, trouble
oppressive *adj* 1 *syn* see ONEROUS
  ant unoppressive
  2 *syn* see GLOOMY 3
oppressor *n syn* see TYRANT
opprobriate *vb syn* see DECRY 2
opprobrious *adj* 1 *syn* see ABUSIVE
  2 *syn* see INFAMOUS 1
opprobrium *n syn* see DISGRACE
  rel abuse, scurrility, vituperation
  con credit, prestige
oppugn *vb syn* see CONTEND 1
oppugnant *adj syn* see ADVERSE 1
oppugnant *n syn* see OPPONENT
opt (for) *vb syn* see CHOOSE 1
optate *vb syn* see CHOOSE 1
optic *adj syn* see VISUAL 1

optical *adj syn* see VISUAL 1
optimacy *n syn* see ARISTOCRACY
optimism *n* an inclination to put the most
favorable construction on actions and events
or to anticipate the best possible outcome
<was a practitioner of *optimism* in his every-
day life>
  syn Pollyannaism, rose-colored spectacles,
sanguineness, sanguinity
  rel brightness, buoyancy, happiness; idealism, positivism
  con hopelessness; despair, gloom, melancholy; malism; defeatism, fatalism, cynicism
  ant pessimism
optimist *n* one given to optimism <was a
jaunty *optimist*>
  syn hoper, Pollyanna
  rel dreamer, idealist, positivist
  con defeatist, fatalist, cynic, doubter, skeptic
  ant pessimist
optimistic *adj* anticipating only the best to
happen and minimizing all other possibilities <was *optimistic* about book sales that
year>
  syn fond, Pollyannaish, sanguine, upbeat;
compare HOPEFUL 1
  rel bright, cheerful, merry, sunny; hopeful,
hoping; assured, confident
  idiom feeling on top of the world, looking
on the bright side, riding (*or* sitting) on
cloud nine
  con cynical; doubtful, uncertain
  ant pessimistic
option *n syn* see CHOICE 1
  rel prerogative, privilege, right
optional *adj* not compulsory <attendance at
the meeting is *optional*>
  syn discretionary, elective, facultative, nonobligatory
  rel free, voluntary; alternative
  con demanded, imperative; enforced, involuntary; essential, necessary
  ant compulsory, mandatory, obligatory,
required
opulent *adj* 1 *syn* see RICH 1
  rel lavish, prodigal, profuse; extravagant,
ostentatious, pretentious, showy; plush,
swank
  con modest, simple, unpretentious
  2 *syn* see LUXURIOUS 3
  3 *syn* see PROFUSE
oracle *n syn* see REVELATION
oracular *adj syn* see PROPHETIC
oral *adj* 1 *syn* see VOCAL 1
  2 expressed or transmitted vocally <stories
of folk heroes kept alive in *oral* tradition>
  syn spoken, traditional, unwritten, verbal,
word-of-mouth
  rel narrated, recounted, related, told
  con chronicled, recorded, written, written
down
orate *vb* to talk in a declamatory, grandiloquent, or impassioned manner <*orated* to
the crowd about the flag and patriotism>
  syn bloviate, declaim, harangue, mouth,
perorate, rant, rave, soapbox
  rel elocute; bombast, rodomontade, sermonize, speechify; blah-blah
oratorical *adj syn* see RHETORICAL

---

syn synonym(s) *rel* related word(s)
ant antonym(s) *con* contrasted word(s)
idiom idiomatic equivalent(s)
|| use limited; if in doubt, see a dictionary

oratory *n* the art of speaking in public eloquently and effectively <a politician who was a master at *oratory*>
syn elocution, rhetoric, speechcraft

orb *n* **1** *syn* see BALL
2 *syn* see EYE 1

orbit *n* *syn* see RANGE 2

orchestra *n* a usually large group of musicians who perform together <a string *orchestra* played at the reception>
syn band, philharmonic, symphony
rel combo, ensemble

orchestrate *vb* *syn* see HARMONIZE 4

orchidaceous *adj* *syn* see SHOWY

orchids *n pl* *syn* see COMPLIMENT 1

ordain *vb* **1** *syn* see CONDUCT 3
2 *syn* see DICTATE

ordeal *n* *syn* see TRIAL 1

order *n* **1** *syn* see ASSOCIATION 2
2 *syn* see TYPE
rel bracket, branch, pigeonhole, set; estate, grade, rank, status
3 sequential occurrence in space or time <changed the *order* of the books on the shelf>
syn arrangement, disposal, disposition, distribution, ordering, sequence
rel array, arrayal, collocation; allocation, allotment, apportionment, arrayment, proration
con disarrangement, disordering; chaos, confusion, disorder, mix-up, muddle
4 general or approximate size or amount <a loss on the *order* of seven million dollars>
syn extent, magnitude, matter, neighborhood, range, tune, vicinity
rel approach, approximation, closeness, nearness, proximity
5 manner of being arranged in space or of occurring in time <tell everything in the *order* in which it happened>
syn consecution, procession, sequence, succession
rel consecutiveness, following, successiveness; chain, progression, series, train
6 *syn* see SUCCESSION 2
7 orderly conduct <about to call the meeting to *order* when the interruption occurred>
syn correctitude, correctness, decorousness, decorum, orderliness, properness, propriety, seemliness
rel goodness, niceness, rightness; fitness, suitability; integrity, probity, rectitude, uprightness
con impropriety, indecorousness, indecorum, unseemliness
ant disorder
8 orderly arrangement or disposition <troubled by the lack of *order* in their daily lives>
syn method, orderliness, pattern, plan, system
con anarchy, chaos, confusion, muddle, ‖snafu
ant disorder
9 state with respect to quality, functioning, or status <the equipment was in very poor *order*>
syn case, condition, estate, repair, shape
rel fettle, fitness, kilter, trim
10 a state of soundness <had her car put in *order* for spring>

syn condition, fettle, fitness, kilter, repair, shape, trim
rel adjustment, amendment, correction, gear, rectification
idiom working order
con disrepair
11 the state of being appropriate to or required by the circumstances <that remark is definitely out of *order*>
syn appositeness, appropriateness, aptness, expediency, fitness, meetness, propriety, rightness, suitability, suitableness
rel opportuneness, seasonableness, timeliness; auspiciousness, favorableness; felicity, grace
con inappropriateness, unfitness, unsuitability, unsuitableness
12 *syn* see COMMAND 1
rel authorization, permission

order *vb* **1** to bring about an orderly disposition of individuals, units, or elements <*ordered* his affairs in preparation for marriage>
syn arrange, array, dispose, marshal, methodize, organize, systematize
rel adjust, fix, regulate, right; align, line, line up, range; classify, codify, hierarchize; regiment, routine, routinize; streamline
idiom put (or set) in order, put in shape, put (or set) to rights, reduce to order, whip into shape (or order)
ant disorder
2 *syn* see COMMAND

ordering *n* *syn* see ORDER 3

orderliness *n* **1** *syn* see ORDER 7
ant disorderliness
2 *syn* see ORDER 8
ant disorderliness

orderly *adj* **1** following a set arrangement, design, or pattern <work out an *orderly* procedure and stick to it> <an *orderly* row of houses surrounded the village green>
syn methodic, methodical, regular, systematic
rel accurate, correct, exact, precise; alike, uniform; businesslike; conventional, formal
idiom in apple-pie order
con haphazard, irregular, unmethodical, unsystematic; careless, casual, free and easy
ant chaotic, disorderly
2 *syn* see NEAT 2
rel picked up
ant disordered; disorderly

order up *vb* *syn* see CALL UP

ordinance *n* *syn* see LAW 1

ordinarily *adv* *syn* see USUALLY 2

ordinary *adj* **1** of the customary or common type encountered in the normal course of events <*ordinary* traffic had been stopped to let the marchers pass>
syn everyday, plain, plain Jane, quotidian, routine, unremarkable, usual, workaday
rel commonplace, natural, normal, regular; customary, familiar, frequent
con infrequent, rare, uncommon; accidental, casual, chance, fortuitous
ant extraordinary
2 *syn* see COMMON 6

organ *n* **1** *syn* see MEAN 2
2 *syn* see JOURNAL

organize *vb* **1** *syn* see FOUND 2
  rel construct, put together
  2 *syn* see ORDER 1
  rel coordinate, integrate
  3 *syn* see MOBILIZE 3
‖**organized** *adj* *syn* see INTOXICATED 1
orgulous *adj* *syn* see PROUD 1
orgy *n* **1** *syn* see BINGE 1
  2 an act or occasion of excessive indulgence
  in sex <the infamous *orgies* of ancient
  Rome>
  syn bacchanal, bacchanalia, debauch,
  ‖group grope, party, saturnalia
  3 *syn* see SPREE 1
orifice *n* *syn* see APERTURE
oriflamme *n* *syn* see FLAG
origin *n* **1** *syn* see ANCESTRY
  rel maternity, parentage, paternity
  2 *syn* see SOURCE
original *n* **1** a first form from which copies or
  reproductions can be produced <students
  copying the da Vinci *original*>
  syn archetype, protoplast, prototype
  rel forerunner, mother, precursor; model,
  pattern; precedent
  con dummy, imitation, simulacrum; counterfeit, fake, forgery
  ant copy, reproduction
  2 *syn* see INNOVATOR
  3 *syn* see ECCENTRIC
original *adj* **1** *syn* see FIRST 2
  rel archetypal, prototypal
  2 *syn* see PRIMARY 5
  3 *syn* see INVENTIVE
  con banal, trite; derivative, initative
  ant unoriginal
originally *adv* *syn* see INITIALLY 1
originate *vb* **1** *syn* see GENERATE 1
  2 *syn* see INTRODUCE 3
  3 *syn* see SPRING 1
  4 *syn* see BEGIN 2
  5 to have one's origin or home base in <he
  originates from Ohio>
  syn come (from), hail (from)
  rel derive (from), spring (from), stem (from)
originative *adj* *syn* see INVENTIVE
  ant unoriginative
originator *n* **1** *syn* see FATHER 2
  2 *syn* see INNOVATOR
orison *n* *syn* see PRAYER
ornament *vb* *syn* see ADORN
  rel enrich; embroider
ornate *adj* elaborately and often preten-
  tiously decorated or designed <a very *ornate*
  room—all marble, gilt, and brocade>
  syn baroque, flamboyant, florid, luscious,
  rich, rococo
  rel elaborate, high-wrought, resplendent;
  labored, overdone, overelaborated, overem-
  bellished, overworked, overwrought; luxuriant, luxurious, opulent, sumptuous; aureate,
  gilded
  con natural, plain, quiet, simple; severe,
  unembellished, unornamented, unostentatious, unpretentious; restrained, subdued

ant austere; chaste
ornery *adj* ‖**1** *syn* see CHEAP 2
  2 *syn* see CANTANKEROUS
  3 *syn* see CONTRARY 3
orotund *adj* **1** *syn* see RESONANT
  rel loud, stentorian
  2 *syn* see RHETORICAL
orphan *adj* deprived by death of one and
  usually both parents <seeking homes for the
  countless *orphan* children from the disaster
  area>
  syn orphaned, parentless, unparented
  rel alone, solitary; abandoned, cast-off,
  forsaken, lost; disregarded, ignored, neglected, slighted
orphaned *adj* *syn* see ORPHAN
orphic *adj* *syn* see RECONDITE
orthodox *adj* **1** conforming to doctrines or
  practices that are held to be right or true by
  an authority, standard, or tradition <those
  who still hold an *orthodox* view about evolu-
  tion>
  syn accepted, authoritative, canonical,
  received, sanctioned, sound
  rel acknowledged, admitted, approved;
  customary, official, recognized, standard,
  traditional; correct, proper, right
  con heretical, heterodox, unauthoritative,
  uncanonical
  ant unorthodox
  2 *syn* see CONVENTIONAL 1
  3 *syn* see CONSERVATIVE 1
  ant unorthodox
oscillate *vb* *syn* see SWING 2
osculate *vb* *syn* see KISS 2
ostend *vb* *syn* see SHOW 2
ostensible *adj* **1** *syn* see APPARENT 2
  2 *syn* see ALLEGED
ostensibly *adv* to all outward appearances
  <*ostensibly* it was a business trip but actually
  it was all pleasure>
  syn apparently, evidently, officially, outwardly, professedly, seemingly
  rel externally, superficially; sensibly
  idiom on the face of it, on the surface, to the
  eye
  con genuinely, really, truly; au fond, basically
ostentatious *adj* *syn* see SHOWY
  ant unostentatious
ostracism *n* *syn* see EXILE 1
ostracize *vb* **1** *syn* see BANISH
  con accept, entertain, receive, welcome;
  harbor, haven, refuge, shelter
  2 *syn* see CUT 7
other *adj* **1** *syn* see DIFFERENT 1
  2 *syn* see ADDITIONAL
‖**othergates** *adv* *syn* see OTHERWISE 1
other half *n* *syn* see RABBLE 2
otherness *n* *syn* see DISSIMILARITY
‖**otherways** *adv* *syn* see OTHERWISE 2
‖**otherwhile** *adv* *syn* see SOMETIMES
otherwise *adv* **1** in a different way or manner
  <he could not act *otherwise*>
  syn differently, diversely, ‖othergates, variously
  ant likewise
  2 under different conditions <might *other-*
  wise have left>
  syn else, ‖elseways, elsewise, ‖otherways

---

syn synonym(s)   *rel* related word(s)
ant antonym(s)   *con* contrasted word(s)
idiom idiomatic equivalent(s)
‖ use limited; if in doubt, see a dictionary

otherwise adj syn see DIFFERENT 1

otherworld n syn see HEREAFTER 2

otherworldly adj 1 of or relating to a world other than the actual world <believed in the existence of *otherworldly* phenomena>
syn transcendental, transmundane
rel exterrestrial, extramundane, extraterrestrial; unearthly, unworldly
2 syn see DREAMY 3

otiose adj syn see VAIN 1
rel purposeless, useless; inexcusable; superfluous, supernumerary, surplus

oubliette n syn see DUNGEON

ought vb syn see WANT 3

ought n syn see OBLIGATION 2

ounce n syn see PARTICLE

oust vb 1 syn see DEPRIVE 2
2 syn see BANISH

out adv syn see OUTDOORS

out vb 1 syn see EJECT 1
2 syn see EXTINGUISH 1
3 syn see GET OUT 2

out n syn see SHOWING 1

out and away adv syn see FAR AND AWAY

out–and–out adj syn see UTTER

outback n syn see FRONTIER 2

outbalance vb syn see OUTWEIGH 1

outbloom vb syn see BLOSSOM

outbreak n 1 a sudden or violent beginning of activity <an *outbreak* of new housing starts>
syn burst, eruption, flare, outburst; *compare* EPIDEMIC
rel beginning, commencement, dawn, onset, outset
2 syn see EPIDEMIC

outbreathe vb syn see EXHALE

outburst n 1 a violent expression of emotion <an *outburst* of anger>
syn access, burst, eruption, explosion, flareup, gust, sally
rel scene, storm, tantrum; frenzy, rapture transport(s)
2 syn see OUTBREAK 1

outcast n one who is cast out by society <a political *outcast*>
syn castaway, derelict, Ishmael, Ishmaelite, leper, offscouring, pariah, untouchable
rel hobo, tramp, vagabond, vagrant; displaced person; exile, expatriate; reprobate
con big name, bigwig, celebrity, lion, luminary, name, notable, personage, somebody

outcome n syn see EFFECT 1

outcomer n syn see STRANGER

out–country adj syn see RURAL

outcrier n syn see PEDDLER

outcry n syn see COMMOTION 1

outdare vb syn see FACE 3

outdate vb to make obsolete or out-of-date <the automobile *outdated* the horse and buggy>
syn antiquate, obsolesce, obsolete, outmode, superannuate
rel age, date, fossilize; replace, supersede

outdated adj syn see OLD-FASHIONED 1
ant up-to-the-minute

outdistance vb syn see OUTSTRIP 1

outdo vb 1 syn see SURPASS 1
idiom out-Herod Herod, steal (*or* get) a march on

2 syn see DEFEAT 2

outdoor adj taking place, done, or existing in the open air <an *outdoor* restaurant>
syn alfresco, hypaethral, open-air, out-of-door, outside
ant indoor, inside

outdoors adv in or into the open air <went *outdoors* for some fresh air>
syn out, out of doors, outside, without, withoutdoors
ant indoors, inside, withindoors

outdoors n pl but sing in constr the space where air is unconfined <every night he let the dog run in the *outdoors*>
syn open, open air, out-of-doors, outside, without
idiom God's good (*or* green) earth

outer adj being or located outside something <the sheep's thick *outer* coat of wool>
syn exterior, external, outside, outward, over
rel extraneous, extrinsic, superficial, surface; outlying, remote
con inside, interior, internal, inward
ant inner

outermost adj syn see EXTREME 5
ant inmost, innermost

outface vb syn see FACE 3

outfit n 1 syn see EQUIPMENT
2 syn see COSTUME
3 syn see COMPANY 4
4 syn see ENTERPRISE 3

outfit vb syn see FURNISH 1

outfox vb syn see OUTWIT

outgeneral vb syn see OUTWIT
rel outfight, outflank, outgame
idiom steal a march

outgo vb syn see SURPASS 1

outgoing adj syn see DEMONSTRATIVE
ant aloof

outgrowth n 1 a projecting part of an organism <a warty *outgrowth* on the skin>
syn excrescence, excrescency, process, processus
rel enlargement, prolongation, swelling; offshoot, shoot
2 something that develops or grows directly out of something else <the new TV series was an *outgrowth* of a popular movie>
syn by-product, derivative, descendant, offshoot, spin-off
rel branch, member; child, offspring, product; aftereffect, consequence, effect, issue, outcome, result
con origin, root, source; antecedent, cause, determinant

outhouse n syn see PRIVY 1

outing n syn see EXCURSION 1

outjockey vb syn see OUTWIT

outland adj syn see RURAL

outlander n syn see STRANGER

outlandish adj 1 syn see BARBARIC 1
rel foreign, strange
2 syn see STRANGE 4
rel monstrous; outré
con commonplace, everyday
3 marked by sharp departure from the traditional or usual <men who wear beads, earrings, and other *outlandish* ornaments>
syn far-out, kinky, outré, ultra; *compare* EXTREME 3

rel bizarre, extravagant, outrageous, wild; unconventional, unorthodox

con conservative, conventional; compliant, conformable; moderate

4 *syn* see BACK 1

outlast *vb syn* see OUTLIVE

outlaw *n* a criminal of the American Western frontier <*outlaws* held up stagecoaches>

syn badman, ‖bandido, bandit, desperado

rel gunman, gunslinger

idiom bad guy

outlaw *vb syn* see FORBID

outlay *vb syn* see SPEND 1

outlay *n syn* see EXPENSE 1

outlet *n* **1** *syn* see APERTURE

2 *syn* see EGRESS 2

rel escape; release

3 *syn* see STORE 4

outline *n* the line that gives form or shape to a body or a figure <saw only a dark *outline* of the house through the gloom>

syn contour, delineation, figuration, line, lineament, lineation, profile, silhouette

rel configuration, conformation, figure, form, shape; skyline

con bulk, hulk, mass

outline *vb* **1** *syn* see BORDER 1

2 *syn* see SKETCH

outlive *vb* to remain in existence longer than <the committee has *outlived* its usefulness>

syn outlast, outwear, survive

rel outstand, outstay

outlook *n* **1** *syn* see LOOKOUT 2

2 *syn* see VISTA

3 *syn* see VIEW 4

4 *syn* see VIEWPOINT 2

outlying *adj syn* see DISTANT 1

outmaneuver *vb syn* see OUTWIT

idiom steal a march (on)

outmatch *vb syn* see SURPASS 1

outmode *vb syn* see OUTDATE

outmoded *adj* **1** *syn* see OLD-FASHIONED

2 *syn* see OBSOLETE

3 *syn* see TACKY 2

outmost *adj syn* see EXTREME 5

ant inmost, innermost

out-of-date *adj* **1** *syn* see OLD-FASHIONED

ant up-to-date

2 *syn* see TACKY 2

out-of-door *adj syn* see OUTDOOR

out-of-doors *n pl but sing in constr syn* see OUTDOORS

out of doors *adv syn* see OUTDOORS

out-of-the-way *adj syn* see OBSCURE 2

outpace *vb syn* see OUTSTRIP 1

outplace *vb syn* see REPLACE 3

output *n* the amount of something produced <an annual *output* of 3,000,000 units>

syn outturn, product, production, turnout, yield

rel gain, get, profit, take; crop, harvest

con input; raw material

outrage *n syn* see INJURY 1

outrage *vb* **1** *syn* see RAPE

2 *syn* see ABUSE 2

3 *syn* see WRONG

4 *syn* see OFFEND 3

outrageous *adj* **1** exceeding the limits of what is normal or tolerable <*outrageous* prices that threaten our way of life>

syn barbarous, unchristian, uncivilized, unconscionable, ungodly, unholy, wicked

rel abominable, awful, beastly, dreadful, ghastly, horrible, horrid, impossible, intolerable, terrible, unreasonable; scandalous, shocking

con normal, reasonable, tolerable; acceptable, bearable, endurable, supportable

2 enormously or flagrantly bad or horrible <*outrageous* treatment of prisoners>

syn atrocious, crying, desperate, heinous, monstrous, scandalous, shocking

rel enormous, flagrant, gross; egregious, nefarious, notorious, villainous

con condonable, excusable, forgivable, pardonable, defensible, justifiable; legitimate, reasonable; comprehensible, plausible, understandable

outrank *vb syn* see PRECEDE 1

outré *adj syn* see OUTLANDISH 3

outreach *vb syn* see OUTWIT

outrecuidance *n syn* see CONCEIT 2

outrider *n syn* see FORERUNNER 1

outright *adj* **1** *syn* see UTTER

2 *syn* see WHOLE 4

outrun *vb syn* see OUTSTRIP 1

outset *n syn* see BEGINNING

outshine *vb syn* see SURPASS 1

outside *n syn* see OUTDOORS

outside *adj* **1** *syn* see OUTER

rel alien, foreign

ant inside

2 *syn* see OUTDOOR

3 *syn* see MAXIMUM

4 *syn* see REMOTE 4

outside *adv syn* see OUTDOORS

outside *prep* **1** *syn* see BEYOND 1

2 *syn* see EXCEPT

outside of *prep syn* see EXCEPT

outsider *n syn* see STRANGER

con insider

outskirt *n usu* **outskirts** *pl syn* see ENVIRONS 2

outslick *vb syn* see OUTWIT

outsmart *vb syn* see OUTWIT

outspeed *vb syn* see OUTSTRIP 1

outspoken *adj* speaking without fear or reserve <quite *outspoken* in her views on mandatory retirement>

syn free, free-spoken, round, vocal

rel candid, direct, forthright, frank, open, plain, plainspoken, straightforward, unreticent; bluff, blunt; explicit, point-blank, unequivocal; strident

con reserved, restrained, reticent; private, retiring, shrinking; unassertive

outspread *vb syn* see OPEN 4

ant folded (of wings or a fan)

outstanding *adj* **1** *syn* see UNPAID 2

2 *syn* see NOTICEABLE

3 *syn* see CHIEF 2

4 *syn* see SUPERB 3

outstare *vb syn* see STARE DOWN

outstart *n syn* see BEGINNING

outstep *vb syn* see EXCEED 1

---

outstretch *vb syn* see OPEN 4
outstrip *vb* **1** to go faster than <could *outstrip* even the fastest horse>
syn distance, outdistance, outpace, outrun, outspeed
rel outfly, outsoar, outwing; outfoot, outrace, outride; outsail; outtravel; lose, shake off
con follow, trail; drag, hang back, lag
2 *syn* see SURPASS 1
outsweepings *n pl syn* see REFUSE
outthink *vb syn* see OUTWIT
outthrust *n syn* see PROJECTION 1
outtire *vb syn* see EXHAUST 4
outturn *n syn* see OUTPUT
outward *adj syn* see OUTER
ant inward
outwardly *adv syn* see OSTENSIBLY
ant inwardly
outwear *vb* **1** *syn* see EXHAUST 4
2 *syn* see OUTLIVE
rel endure, hold up
outweigh *vb* **1** to exceed in weight, value, or importance <her brother *outweighed* her by nearly fifty pounds> <the facts *outweigh* his argument>
syn outbalance, overbalance, overweigh, overweight
rel overbear
2 *syn* see COMPENSATE 1
outweighing *adj syn* see DOMINANT 1
outwit *vb* to defeat or get the better of by superior cleverness or ingenuity <*outwitted* the enemy by taking a different route>
syn have, outfox, outgeneral, outjockey, outmaneuver, outreach, outslick, outsmart, outthink, overreach, undo; *compare* FRUSTRATE 1
rel bamboozle, befool, dupe, gull, hoax, hoodwink, outtrick, outtrump, trick; outdo; outguess
outworn *adj syn* see OBSOLETE
oval *adj* having the shape of a longitudinal section of an egg <an *oval* pond>
syn ooid, ovate, oviform, ovoid
rel ovaloid; ellipsoidal, elliptic
ovate *adj syn* see OVAL
over *adv* **1** from one point to another across intervening space <sailed *over* to the island>
syn across, athwart, beyond, transversely
2 *syn* see AWAY 2
3 *syn* see EVER 6
4 at a higher point <the plane was directly *over*>
syn above, aloft, overhead
idiom on high
ant under
5 at or to an end <it's all *over* between them>
syn by, through
6 *syn* see THROUGH 1
7 yet another time <do the work *over*>
syn afresh, again, anew, de novo, once more
idiom over again
over *prep* **1** at a higher level <clouds hung *over* the town>
syn above, o'er
ant under
2 *syn* see ACROSS
3 with respect to <children squabbling *over* toys>

syn about, on, upon, with
4 so as to make contact with <hit him *over* the head>
syn on, upon
5 *syn* see DURING
6 as the result of <quarreled *over* money matters>
syn because of, due to, owing to, through
over *adj* **1** *syn* see SUPERIOR 1
ant under
2 *syn* see OUTER
over *vb syn* see CLEAR 8
overabounding *adj syn* see SUPERABUNDANT
overabundance *n syn* see EXCESS 1
overabundant *adj syn* see SUPERABUNDANT
overact *vb* to exaggerate in acting especially on the stage or screen <was criticized for *overacting* the part>
syn overplay
rel ham, mug; declaim, rant, spout
idiom chew the scenery
ant underact, underplay
over against *prep* **1** *syn* see AGAINST 1
2 *syn* see VERSUS 2
overage *n syn* see EXCESS 2
ant shortage, underage
overall *adv* **1** *syn* see EVERYWHERE 1
2 *syn* see GENERALLY 1
overall *adj syn* see ALL-AROUND 2
over and above *prep syn* see BESIDES 1
over and over *adv syn* see OFTEN
overbalance *vb syn* see OUTWEIGH 1
overbalanced *adj syn* see LOPSIDED
overbalancing *adj syn* see DOMINANT 1
overbearing *adj* **1** *syn* see MASTERFUL 1
2 *syn* see DOMINANT 1
3 *syn* see PROUD 1
rel absolute, autocratic, despotic, tyrannical
con passive, unassertive; acquiescent, compliant, unresisting
ant subservient
overblown *adj* **1** *syn* see FAT 2
2 *syn* see INFLATED
3 *syn* see RHETORICAL
4 *syn* see PRETENTIOUS 3
overbold *adj syn* see SHAMELESS
overbrim *vb syn* see OVERFLOW 2
overburden *vb syn* see OVERLOAD
overcast *vb* **1** *syn* see OBSCURE
2 *syn* see COVER 3
overcast *adj* clouded over <a gray *overcast* March day>
syn cloudy, ‖dowly, dull, heavy, lowering (*or* louring), nubilous, overclouded
rel brooding, dirty, oppressive, sullen
ant clear, cloudless
overcharge *vb* **1** to charge excessively for service or goods <a clip joint well known for *overcharging* customers>
syn clip, fleece, skin, soak, stick
ant undercharge
2 *syn* see OVERLOAD
3 *syn* see EMBROIDER
overcloud *vb syn* see OBSCURE
overclouded *adj syn* see OVERCAST
overcome *vb* **1** to get the better of <*overcome* a bad habit>
syn conquer, down, hurdle, lick, master, surmount, throw; *compare* CONQUER 2

rel beat, defeat; outlive, prevail
con adopt, embrace, take up; indulge
2 *syn* see CONQUER 2
3 *syn* see OVERWHELM 4
4 *syn* see WIN 1
overconfident *adj syn* see PRESUMPTUOUS
overcritical *adj syn* see CRITICAL 1
overdo *vb* to make excessive use or application of <he has *overdone* that joke to the point that it is no longer funny>
syn overplay, overuse, overwork
idiom go overboard, go to extremes, run into the ground
overdoing *n syn* see EXTRAVAGANCE 2
overdraw *vb syn* see EMBROIDER
overdue *adj* 1 *syn* see UNPAID 2
2 *syn* see TARDY
ant early
overearly *adv syn* see EARLY 2
overemphasize *vb syn* see OVERPLAY 2
ant underemphasize
overesteem *vb syn* see OVERVALUE
overestimate *vb syn* see OVERVALUE
ant underestimate
overfill *vb syn* see OVERFLOW 2
overflow *vb* 1 *syn* see DELUGE 1
2 to flow over the brim <the river *overflowed* its banks>
syn overbrim, overfill, overrun, run over, spill, well over
rel brim, cascade, slop, slosh
con drop, recede, withdraw
overflow *n* 1 *syn* see FLOOD 2
2 *syn* see EXCESS 1
overflowing *adj* 1 *syn* see ALIVE 5
2 *syn* see SUPERABUNDANT
overfull *adv syn* see EVER 6
overgrown *adj* covered with growth or herbage <a vacant lot *overgrown* with weeds>
syn grown, rank
rel braky, brambly, brushy, copsy, jungly, thicketed, thickety; dense, overrun, thick; lush
‖ **overhand** *n syn* see ADVANTAGE 3
overhang *vb* 1 *syn* see BULGE
2 *syn* see HANG 4
overhanging *adj syn* see IMMINENT 2
overhaul *vb* 1 *syn* see MEND 2
2 *syn* see CATCH 7
overhead *adv syn* see OVER 4
ant underfoot
overheated *adj syn* see IMPASSIONED
overindulgence *n syn* see EXCESS 3
overindulgent *adj syn* see EXCESSIVE 2
overkill *n syn* see EXCESS 1
overlade *vb syn* see OVERLOAD
overlap *vb* to extend over and cover a part of <each course of shingles should *overlap* the preceding course by several inches>
syn imbricate, lap, overlie, override, ride, shingle
overlay *vb syn* see COVER 3
overleap *vb* 1 *syn* see CLEAR 8
2 *syn* see NEGLECT
overlie *vb syn* see OVERLAP

overload *vb* to load to excess <*overload* a ship>
syn overburden, overcharge, overlade, overtax, overweigh, overweight
con lighten
overlong *adj syn* see LONG 2
overlook *vb* 1 *syn* see SURVEY 3
2 to rise above and afford a view of <the tower *overlooks* the city>
syn dominate, look down, overtop, tower (above *or* over)
rel oversee
3 *syn* see NEGLECT
4 *syn* see SUPERVISE
overlook *n* 1 *syn* see OMISSION
2 *syn* see LOOKOUT 2
overly *adv syn* see EVER 6
overlying *adj syn* see SUPERIOR 1
ant underlying
overmuch *n syn* see EXCESS 1
overmuch *adv syn* see EVER 6
overnice *adj syn* see PRECIOUS 4
overpaint *vb syn* see EMBROIDER
overpass *vb syn* see NEGLECT
overpeopled *adj syn* see OVERPOPULATED
ant underpeopled
overplay *vb* 1 *syn* see OVERACT
ant underact, underplay
2 to give undue attention or emphasis to <*overplaying* the trivial at the expense of the significant>
syn magnify, maximize, overemphasize, overstress
rel accent, accentuate, point up; dramatize, exaggerate, hyperbolize, overdraw, overstate, stretch; overvalue
idiom lay it on thick
con downgrade, downplay; minimize
3 *syn* see OVERDO
overplus *n syn* see EXCESS 1
overpopulated *adj* populated too densely <*overpopulated* cities>
syn overpeopled
rel congested, dense, overcrowded
con empty, vacant, void; unpopulated
ant underpopulated
overpower *vb* 1 *syn* see CONQUER 2
2 *syn* see OVERWHELM 4
overpress *vb syn* see PRESSURE
overprize *vb syn* see OVERVALUE
ant underprize, undervalue
overrate *vb syn* see OVERVALUE
ant underrate
overreach *vb* 1 *syn* see CHEAT
2 *syn* see OUTWIT
overreckon *vb syn* see OVERVALUE
overrefined *adj syn* see PRECIOUS 4
override *vb syn* see OVERLAP
overriding *adj syn* see CENTRAL 1
rel primary, principal
overripe *adj syn* see EFFETE 3
overrule *vb syn* see GOVERN 1
overruling *adj syn* see CENTRAL 1
overrun *vb* 1 *syn* see WHIP 2
2 *syn* see INVADE 1
3 *syn* see INFEST 1
4 *syn* see EXCEED 1
5 *syn* see OVERFLOW 2
oversea *adj syn* see OVERSEAS
overseas *adv* beyond or across the sea <served *overseas* for two years>

---

syn synonym(s)   *rel* related word(s)
ant antonym(s)   *con* contrasted word(s)
idiom idiomatic equivalent(s)
‖ use limited; if in doubt, see a dictionary

syn abroad
con stateside
overseas *adj* situated, originating in, or relating to lands overseas <attempting to tap the potential of *overseas* markets>
syn oversea, transmarine, ultramarine
rel alien, exotic, foreign, strange
con domestic, home; stateside
oversee *vb* **1** *syn* see SURVEY 3
2 *syn* see SUPERVISE
overset *vb* **1** *syn* see OVERTURN 1
2 *syn* see OVERTHROW 2
overshadow *vb* *syn* see OBSCURE
oversight *n* **1** the function or duty of watching or guarding for the sake of proper direction or control <had *oversight* of the children as they played>
syn care, charge, conduct, handling, intendance, management, running, superintendence, superintendency, supervision
rel custody, guard, guardianship; keeping, maintenance; surveillance; aegis, tutelage; cice- ronage; chaperonage; check, control
2 *syn* see FAILURE 1
3 *syn* see OMISSION
oversize *adj* *syn* see LARGE 1
ant undersized
overslaugh *vb* *syn* see HINDER
oversoon *adj* *syn* see EARLY 2
oversoon *adv* *syn* see EARLY 2
overspread *vb* **1** *syn* see COVER 3
2 *syn* see INFEST 1
overstate *vb* *syn* see EMBROIDER
ant understate
overstatement *n* *syn* see EXAGGERATION
ant understatement
overstep *vb* *syn* see EXCEED 1
rel infringe, transgress, trespass
overstock *n* *syn* see EXCESS 1
ant understock
overstress *vb* *syn* see OVERPLAY 2
oversupply *n* *syn* see EXCESS 2
ant undersupply
overswarm *vb* **1** *syn* see INFEST 1
2 *syn* see INVADE 1
oversway *vb* *syn* see INDUCE 1
overtake *vb* *syn* see CATCH 7
overtax *vb* *syn* see OVERLOAD
overthrow *vb* **1** *syn* see OVERTURN 1
2 to cause the downfall of <*overthrow* the government>
syn overset, overturn, topple, tumble, unhorse; *compare* CONQUER 1
rel depose, dethrone, oust, remove, unseat; liquidate, purge; conquer, defeat, destroy, ruin
con create, establish, found, set up
overthrow *n* *syn* see DEFEAT 1
overtone *n* *syn* see ASSOCIATION 4
overtop *vb* *syn* see OVERLOOK 2
overture *n* **1** action intended to attract favorable attention <made friendly *overtures* to the new member of the class>
syn advance, approach
rel bid, proposal, proposition, tender
2 *syn* see INTRODUCTION

overturn *vb* **1** to turn from an upright or level position <the embarrassed boy backed into the table and *overturned* a lamp>
syn knock over, overset, overthrow, tip (over), topple, turn over, upset
rel capsize, keel (over *or* up), upend, upturn; prostrate; down; roll (over)
con erect, right, set up, straighten (up)
2 *syn* see OVERTHROW 2
overturn *n* *syn* see SHAKE-UP
overuse *vb* *syn* see OVERDO
ant underuse
overvalue *vb* to set too high a value on <inclined to *overvalue* his own charm>
syn overesteem, overestimate, overprize, overrate, overreckon
rel cherish, prize, treasure; adore, idolize, worship
con belittle, depreciate
ant underprize, undervalue
overweening *adj* *syn* see PRESUMPTUOUS
overweigh *vb* **1** *syn* see OUTWEIGH 1
2 *syn* see OVERLOAD
overweighing *adj* *syn* see DOMINANT 1
overweight *vb* **1** *syn* see OUTWEIGH 1
2 *syn* see OVERLOAD
overweight *adj* *syn* see FAT 2
ant underweight
overwhelm *vb* **1** *syn* see DELUGE 1
2 *syn* see DELUGE 3
3 *syn* see WHIP 2
4 to subject to the grip of something overpowering and usually distressing or damaging <*overwhelmed* by the death of his only child> <human wants that tend to *overwhelm* environmental realities>
syn drown, knock over, overcome, overpower, prostrate, whelm
rel demoralize, devastate, dumbfound, shatter; floor, sink; disturb, upset; destroy, ruin, wreck; downgrade, lower, subordinate
overwhelmed *adj* *syn* see AGHAST 2
overwhelming *adj* *syn* see TOWERING 4
overwork *vb* *syn* see OVERDO
oviform *adj* *syn* see OVAL
ovoid *adj* *syn* see OVAL
owing *adj* *syn* see UNPAID 2
owing to *prep* *syn* see OVER 6
owl–light *n* *syn* see EVENING 1
own *vb* **1** *syn* see HAVE 1
2 *syn* see ACKNOWLEDGE 1
con deny, disclaim
ant disown, repudiate
owner *n* one that has the legal or rightful title <*owner* of the shop>
syn holder, possessor, proprietor
rel lord, master
con lessee, renter, tenant; squatter; interloper, intruder, trespasser
ownership *n* lawful claim or title <would soon have *ownership* of the house>
syn dominion, possession, possessorship, property, proprietary, proprietorship
rel hand
own up *vb* *syn* see ACKNOWLEDGE 1
oyster *n* *syn* see FORTE

P

pa n 1 syn see FATHER 1
pablum n syn see PAP 2
pabulum n syn see FOOD 2
pace n 1 syn see TEMPO
 2 syn see SPEED 2
 3 syn see ROUTINE
pace vb 1 syn see WALK 1
 2 syn see PRECEDE 2
pacific adj affording or promoting peace <a *pacific* policy>
 syn irenic, nonviolent, pacificatory, pacifist, peaceable, peaceful
 rel appeasing, conciliating, conciliatory, pacifying, propitiating, propitiatory; dovelike, gentle, inoffensive
 con belligerent, combative, contentious, pugnacious, quarrelsome; unpeaceable, unpeaceful; hawkish, violent, warlike
 ant bellicose, unpacific
pacificator n syn see PEACEMAKER
pacificatory adj syn see PACIFIC
pacificist n syn see PACIFIST
 idiom man of peace
pacifist n one who opposes war or violence as a means of settling disputes <*pacifists* mounted a campaign against the war>
 syn dove, pacificist
 rel satyagrahi; ‖conchie, conscientious objector; peacemonger
 con belligerent, combatant; chauvinist, hawk, jingo, jingoist, warmonger
 ant bellicist
pacifist adj syn see PACIFIC
 ant combative
pacify vb to allay anger or agitation <saw his mounting rage and tried to *pacify* him>
 syn appease, assuage, conciliate, mollify, placate, propitiate, sweeten
 rel dulcify, soften; allay, alleviate, mitigate, relieve; moderate, qualify, smooth (over), temper
 idiom pour balm into, pour oil on (the) troubled waters
 con arouse, stir (up)
 ant anger
pack n 1 syn see BACKPACK
 2 see MUCH
pack vb 1 syn see STOW
 2 see LOAD 3
 3 syn see CARRY 1
packed adj syn see FULL 1
 idiom packed like sardines (or herrings)
‖**packed out** adj syn see FULL 1
packet n syn see FORTUNE 4
packman n syn see PEDDLER
packsack n syn see BACKPACK

pact n 1 syn see CONTRACT
 rel settlement
 2 syn see TREATY
‖**pad** n syn see PROTECTION 2
pad vb syn see EMBROIDER
paddle vb syn see ROW
‖**paddy** n syn see POLICEMAN
pagan adj syn see HEATHEN
pageant n syn see PRETENSE 2
pagoda n syn see SUMMERHOUSE
pain n 1 a bodily sensation that causes acute discomfort or suffering <suffering from chest *pains*>
 syn ache, ‖misery, pang, stitch, throe, twinge
 rel discomfort, distress, hurt, suffering; agony, torment, torture
 2 pains pl syn see EFFORT 1
 rel assiduousness, diligence, industry, sedulousness
pain vb 1 syn see HURT 4
 rel agonize, convulse, crucify, excruciate, harrow, lacerate
 2 syn see DISTRESS 2
 rel afflict; distress, upset; wound; anguish
 idiom ‖hit one where one lives
 3 syn see TRY 2
painful adj 1 causing, marked by, or affected with pain <a *painful* wound>
 syn aching, afflictive, algetic, hurtful, hurting, sore
 rel raw; acute, piercing, sharp, shooting, stabbing, stinging; agonizing, excruciating, harrowing, racking, tormenting, torturous
 ant painless, unpainful
 2 syn see BITTER 2
 rel unappetizing, unsavory
 ant painless
painfully adv syn see HARD 5
 ant painlessly
pain-killer n syn see ANODYNE 1
painstaking adj syn see CAREFUL 2
painstakingly adv syn see HARD 3
 rel carefully, meticulously; lovingly
paint n syn see MAKEUP 3
pair n syn see COUPLE
paired adj syn see TWIN
pal n syn see ASSOCIATE 3
palace adj syn see LUXURIOUS 3
palace car n syn see PARLOR CAR
palatable adj agreeable or pleasant especially to the sense of taste <a *palatable* meal>
 syn aperitive, appetizing, flavorsome, good‑tasting, ‖gusty, mouth-watering, relishing, sapid, saporous, savorous, savorsome, savory, tasteful, tasty, toothsome, toothy
 rel delectable, delicious, delightful, luscious, scrumptious, yummy; tempting; saporific
 con bad-tasting, disagreeable, distasteful, ill-flavored, unappetizing

ant unpalatable

palate n syn see TASTE 4
palatial adj syn see LUXURIOUS 3
  rel noble, regal; monumental; impressive; rich, splendid
palaver n 1 syn see CONFERENCE 2
  rel dialogue, discussion; parley
  2 syn see CHATTER
  rel gas, guff, hot air
  3 syn see TERMINOLOGY
  4 syn see BUSINESS 8
palaverous adj syn see WORDY
pale adj 1 deficient in color or in intensity of color <a *pale* face>
  syn ashen, ashy, blanched, colorless, complexionless, doughy, livid, lurid, pallid, paly, wan, waxen
  rel sallow, sick, sickly; gray, pasty, pasty-faced, waxlike; white, whitened; deathlike, ghastly
  con flushed, ruddy; bright, colorful, florid
  2 being weak and thin in substance or in vital qualities <a *pale*, inadequate foreign policy>
  syn anemic, bloodless, pallid, waterish, watery
  rel inane, insipid, jejune, wishy-washy; insubstantial, unsubstantial; ineffective, ineffectual; faint, feeble, weak
  con strong, substantial; effective, effectual; bright, colorful
  ant brilliant
pale vb syn see DULL 1
Pale Horse n, used with the syn see DEATH 1
palinode vb syn see ABJURE
pall vb 1 syn see BORE
  2 syn see SATIATE
  rel disgust, weary
‖**pallet** n syn see HEAD 1
palliate vb to give a speciously fine appearance to what is erroneous, base, or evil <did not try to conceal or *palliate* his errors>
  syn blanch (over), extenuate, gloss (over), gloze (over), prettify, sugarcoat, varnish, veneer, white, whiten, whitewash
  rel alleviate, lighten, mitigate; condone, excuse; moderate, qualify, soften, temper; camouflage, cloak, conceal, cover up, disguise, dissemble, mask; hush (up)
  idiom paper over the cracks, put a good face on (or upon)
pallid adj 1 syn see PALE 1
  2 syn see PALE 2
pally adj syn see INTIMATE 4
palm (on or upon) vb syn see FOIST 3
‖**palm grease** n syn see GRATUITY
palm off vb syn see FOIST 3
‖**palm oil** n syn see GRATUITY
palooka n syn see OAF 2
palpable adj 1 syn see TANGIBLE 1
  2 syn see PERCEPTIBLE
  rel apparent, ostensible, seeming; believable, colorable, credible, plausible
  3 syn see CLEAR 3
  rel certain, positive, sure; arresting, noticeable, remarkable, striking
  con doubtful, dubious, problematic, questionable
  ant impalpable

palpate vb syn see TOUCH 1
palpation n syn see TOUCH 2
palpitate vb syn see PULSATE
  rel pitter-patter
‖**palsy-walsy** adj syn see INTIMATE 4
palter vb 1 syn see LIE
  rel evade, fence
  idiom play false, play fast and loose
  2 syn see HAGGLE 2
paltry adj 1 syn see CHEAP 2
  rel beggarly, shabby; pitiful
  2 syn see LITTLE 2
  rel base, low, low-down, vile
  3 syn see PETTY 2
  rel insignificant, unimportant
paly adj syn see PALE 1
pamper vb syn see BABY
  rel regale, tickle; caress, dandle, fondle, pet; overindulge
‖**pan** n 1 syn see FACE 1
  2 syn see CRITICISM 2
pan vb syn see CRITICIZE
panacea n a remedy for all ills or difficulties <bicycles are not a *panacea* for the traffic problem>
  syn catholicon, cure-all, elixir, nostrum
  rel relief; remedy
  idiom universal (or sovereign) remedy
pandect n syn see COMPENDIUM 1
pandemoniac adj syn see INFERNAL 2
pandemonium n 1 cap Pandemonium syn see HELL
  2 syn see SINK 1
  3 syn see DIN
pander n syn see PIMP 1
panegyric n syn see ENCOMIUM
panegyrical adj syn see EULOGISTIC
panegyrize vb syn see PRAISE 2
pang n syn see PAIN 1
  rel prick, stab, ‖stang
‖**pang** vb syn see CRAM 1
panhandler n syn see BEGGAR 1
panhandling n syn see MENDICANCY
panic n 1 syn see FEAR 1
  rel frenzy, hysteria; stampede
  con composure, equanimity, sangfroid, self-possession
  ‖2 syn see RIOT 1
‖**pank** vb syn see PANT 1
panoply n syn see DISPLAY 2
panorama n syn see RANGE 2
pan out vb syn see SUCCEED 2
pansified adj syn see EFFEMINATE
pant vb 1 to breathe quickly, spasmodically, or in a labored manner <was *panting* after running up the stairs>
  syn blow, gasp, heave, huff, ‖pank, ‖pegh, puff
  rel gulp; wheeze; wind; chuff
  idiom be out of breath
  2 syn see AIM 2
  rel hunger, long, pine, thirst; desire, want, wish
  idiom be consumed with desire (for)
pantywaist n syn see WEAKLING
pantywaist adj syn see CHARACTERLESS
pap n 1 syn see FOOD 2
  2 something (as reading matter) lacking in solid value or substance <the sentimental *pap* that he offered his readers>

syn pablum, rubbish, slop
rel garbage, trash
‖**pap** *n syn* see FATHER 1
papa *n syn* see FATHER 1
paper *n* **1** *syn* see ESSAY 2
 2 *usu* **papers** *pl syn* see CREDENTIALS
paphian *n syn* see HARLOT 1
pappy *adj syn* see SOFT 6
‖**pappy** *n syn* see FATHER 1
par *n* **1** *syn* see EQUIVALENCE
 2 *syn* see AVERAGE
 rel standard
parable *n syn* see ALLEGORY 2
 rel comparison, similitude
parachronism *n syn* see ANACHRONISM 1
parade *n syn* see DISPLAY 2
 rel exhibition
parade *vb syn* see SHOW 4
 rel disclose, divulge, reveal; advertise, declare, proclaim, publish; boast, brag, gasconade
 idiom parade one's wares
 con camouflage, cloak, disguise, dissemble, mask
paradigm *n syn* see MODEL 2
paradigmatic *adj syn* see TYPICAL 1
paradise *n* **1** *syn* see HEAVEN 2
 idiom the next world (*or* life)
 2 *syn* see UTOPIA
paragon *n* an individual of unequaled excellence often serving as a model <she is a *paragon* of a caring physician>
 syn ideal, jewel, nonesuch, nonpareil, phoenix; *compare* MODEL 2
 rel apotheosis, epitome, last word, quintessence, ultimate; archetype, beau ideal, exemplar, pattern; ‖beaut, beauty, crackerjack, gem, love, lovely, peach, trump; champ, champion; cream, pick, tops
paragon *vb syn* see EQUATE 2
parallel *adj syn* see LIKE
 ant nonparallel, unparallel
parallel *n* one that corresponds to or closely resembles another <we seek in vain a *parallel* for this situation>
 syn analogue, correlate, correspondent, counterpart, countertype, match; *compare* COUNTERPART 1, EQUAL
 rel equivalent; double, duplicate, duplication
parallel *vb* **1** *syn* see EQUATE 2
 2 to place (something) so as to be parallel with another <machines that combed and *paralleled* the fibers>
 syn collimate, collocate, parallelize
 rel align, line up
parallelize *vb syn* see PARALLEL 2
paralyze *vb* **1** to render completely powerless, ineffective, or inert <a general strike that *paralyzed* the nation>
 syn cripple, disable, disarm, immobilize, incapacitate, prostrate; *compare* MAIM, WEAKEN 1
 rel deaden, enfeeble, weaken; close, shut (down); freeze; demolish, destroy, knock out

idiom bring to a grinding halt, tie hand and foot
 2 *syn* see DAZE 2
 rel appall, daunt, dismay, horrify; cripple, disable, enfeeble, weaken; astound, flabbergast, nonplus
 con animate, enliven, pep (up), stimulate
 ant galvanize
paramount *adj syn* see DOMINANT 1
 rel capital, headmost; commanding, controlling; cardinal, crowning
paramour *n* **1** *syn* see GALLANT 2
 2 *syn* see LOVER 1
 3 *syn* see MISTRESS
parapet *n syn* see BULWARK
paraphernalia *n pl but sometimes sing in constr syn* see EQUIPMENT 1
paraphrase *n syn* see VERSION 1
paraphrase *vb* to express or interpret something (as a text or passage) in other words <*paraphrased* the complicated document>
 syn rephrase, restate, reword, translate (into)
 rel summarize; transcribe
 con quote, reproduce
parasite *n* a person who is supported or seeks support from another without making an adequate return <lived as a *parasite* in his father's house>
 syn barnacle, bloodsucker, freeloader, hanger-on, leech, lounge lizard, ‖spiv, sponge, sponger, sucker; *compare* SYCOPHANT
 rel dependent; smell-feast; deadbeat, idler, laze
parasite *vb syn* see INFEST 2
parasitic *adj syn* see FAWNING
 rel freeloading, leechlike, sponging
parasitize *vb syn* see INFEST 2
parboil *vb syn* see BOIL 2
parcel *n* **1** *syn* see PART 1
 2 *syn* see LOT 3
 3 *syn* see GROUP 3
parcel *vb syn* see APPORTION 1
 rel allocate, allot, assign; deal, disburse, disperse; dole (out), lot (out)
parch *vb syn* see DRY 1
‖**pard** *n syn* see PARTNER
pardon *n* a remission of penalty or punishment <the governor granted the prisoner a *pardon*>
 syn absolution, amnesty
 rel acquittal, exculpation, exoneration, indemnification, indemnity; forgiveness, remission; justification, vindication
 con conviction; condemnation
 ant punishment
pardon *vb syn* see EXCUSE 1
 rel justify; accept, tolerate; free, liberate, release
 idiom let bygones be bygones, wipe the slate clean
 con amerce, fine, mulct, penalize
 ant punish
pardonable *adj syn* see VENIAL
 ant unpardonable
pare *vb* **1** *syn* see CUT 6
 rel flay, scalp, skin, strip
 2 *syn* see REDUCE 2
parent *vb syn* see GENERATE 1

parenthesis *n* 1 *syn* see DIGRESSION
  2 *syn* see INTERLUDE
parenthetically *adv* *syn* see INCIDENTALLY 2
parentless *adj* *syn* see ORPHAN
  ant parented
par excellence *adj* *syn* see EXCELLENT
pariah *n* *syn* see OUTCAST
  rel déclassé
‖**parish–pump** *adj* *syn* see INSULAR
parity *n* *syn* see EQUIVALENCE
  rel analogy, parallelism, similitude; approximation, closeness, nearness
  ant disparity, imparity
parlance *n* *syn* see WORDING
parley *vb* 1 *syn* see SPEAK 3
  2 *syn* see CONFER 2
parley *n* 1 *syn* see TALK 4
  rel rap session
  2 *syn* see CONVERSATION 1
parlor car *n* a railroad passenger car equipped with individual revolving and reclining chairs and providing the services of an attendant
  syn chair car, club car, lounge car, palace car, tavern car
parlor house *n* *syn* see BROTHEL
  idiom flesh factory
parlous *adj* *syn* see DANGEROUS 1
parlous *adv* *syn* see VERY 1
Parnassian *n* *syn* see POET
parochial *adj* *syn* see INSULAR
  rel prejudiced; bigoted
  con unprejudiced; uncircumscribed, unlimited; cosmic, universal
  ant catholic
parody *n* *syn* see CARICATURE 2
  rel spoof, spoofery, rib, ridicule
parody *vb* *syn* see MIMIC
paronomasia *n* *syn* see PUN
parous *adj* *syn* see PREGNANT 1
parry *vb* 1 *syn* see DODGE 1
  rel preclude, prevent; anticipate, forestall
  2 *syn* see WARD 1
parsimonious *adj* *syn* see STINGY
  idiom penny-wise and pound-foolish
  ant prodigal
parson *n* *syn* see CLERGYMAN
part *n* 1 something less than the whole to which it belongs <a *part* of the road was paved>
  syn cut, division, member, moiety, parcel, piece, portion, section, segment
  rel component, constituent, element, ingredient; detail, fraction, fragment; bit, chip, scrap
  con aggregate, total; combination, complex; entirety, entity, totality, unity
  ant whole
  2 **parts** *pl syn* see GENITALIA
  3 *syn* see RATION
  4 *syn* see SHARE 1
  rel chunk
  5 *syn* see SIDE 4
part *vb* *syn* see SEPARATE 1
  ant unite
part *adj* *syn* see INCOMPLETE 1
partage *n* *syn* see SHARE 1
partake *vb* *syn* see SHARE 2
  rel accept, receive, take
  idiom take part in
partake (of) *vb* 1 *syn* see EAT 1
  2 *syn* see AMOUNT 2
  idiom bear resemblance (to)
partaker *n* *syn* see PARTICIPANT
part and parcel *n* *syn* see ESSENTIAL 1
partial *adj* 1 *syn* see BIASED 2
  ant impartial
  2 *syn* see INCOMPLETE 1
  rel halfway
  ant whole
partiality *n* 1 *syn* see PREJUDICE
  2 *syn* see LEANING 2
participant *n* one that takes part in something <were *participants* in the uprising>
  syn actor, partaker, participator, party, sharer
  rel aide, assistant, helper; colleague, confrere, fellow, partner
  con bystander, looker-on, nonparticipant, observer, onlooker, spectator, watcher
participate *vb* *syn* see SHARE 2
  rel enter (into), join (in)
  idiom be a party to, be in on, be (*or* get) in the act, have to do with
  con observe, watch; retire, withdraw
participator *n* *syn* see PARTICIPANT
particle *n* a tiny or insignificant amount, part, or piece <not a *particle* of sense>
  syn ace, atom, bit, crumb, damn, ‖dite, doit, dram, drop, fragment, grain, hoot, iota, jot, minim, mite, modicum, molecule, ounce, ray, ‖rissom, scrap, scruple, shred, smidgen, smitch, snap, speck, spot, syllable, tittle, whit, whoop
  rel morsel; snip; dribbet, dribble; dot
parti–color *n* *syn* see VARIEGATED
parti–colored *adj* *syn* see VARIEGATED
  ant unicolor, unicolorous
particular *adj* 1 *syn* see SINGLE 2
  ant general
  2 *syn* see CIRCUMSTANTIAL
  rel careful, meticulous, punctilious, scrupulous
  3 *syn* see SPECIAL 1
  rel appropriate; distinct; singular
  ant universal
  4 *syn* see SEVERAL 1
  5 *syn* see NICE 1
particular *n* *syn* see POINT 1
  rel speciality, specific
  con entirety
  ant universal
particularity *n* *syn* see INDIVIDUALITY 3
particularize *vb* 1 *syn* see SPECIFY 3
  idiom draw it fine
  2 *syn* see ITEMIZE 1
particularized *adj* *syn* see CIRCUMSTANTIAL
  ant generalized
particularly *adv* *syn* see ESPECIALLY 1
parting *n* a mutual separation of two or more persons <saddened by their approaching *parting*>
  syn adieu, congé, farewell, good-bye, leave‐taking
  rel separation; departure
  con joining, meeting; return
  ant reunion

parting *adj* given, taken, or performed during leave-taking <remembered his father's *parting* advice>
　syn departing, farewell, good-bye, valedictory
　rel final, last
partisan *n* **1** *syn* see FOLLOWER
　rel backer, champion, upholder; die-hard, stalwart
　con adversary, antagonist, opponent
　2 an irregular soldier who operates behind enemy lines <a train blown up by *partisans*>
　syn guerrilla, irregular, patriot
partisan *adj* *syn* see BIASED 2
　rel denominational, factional, sectarian; blind, devoted, die-hard, fanatic, unreasoning
　con impartial, indifferent, unbiased, unprejudiced
　ant nonpartisan
partition *n* *syn* see SEPARATION 1
partition *vb* *syn* see DISTRIBUTE 1
partner *n* one that is associated in any action with another <*partners* in crime>
　syn associate, cohort, confrere, consociate, copartner, fellow, mate, ‖pard
　rel assistant, helper, sidekick; bedfellow, buddy, chum, companion, comrade, crony, pal
partnership *n* *syn* see ASSOCIATION 1
　rel consociation, fellowship
parturient *adj* *syn* see PREGNANT 1
parturition *n* *syn* see BIRTH 1
party *n* **1** *syn* see COMBINATION 2
　rel alliance, union; side
　2 *syn* see PARTICIPANT
　3 *syn* see HUMAN
　4 *syn* see GROUP 1
　5 *syn* see COMPANY 4
　6 *syn* see ORGY 2
party girl *n* **1** *syn* see DOXY 1
　2 *syn* see PROSTITUTE
parvenu *n* *syn* see UPSTART
　idiom codfish aristocrat, pig in clover
‖**pash** *vb* *syn* see SHATTER 1
‖**pash** *n* *syn* see INFATUATION
pass *vb* **1** *syn* see GO 1
　rel jog, ‖mog
　2 *syn* see DIE 1
　idiom pass on to the Great Beyond
　con linger
　3 to move or come to a termination or end <as time *passes*, the pain too will *pass*>
　syn see ELAPSE
　rel slip (by); roll (on); fade (away), peter (out); cease, close, discontinue, end, stop, terminate
　con continue; linger
　4 *syn* see HAPPEN 1
　idiom come to pass
　5 *syn* see SURPASS 1
　idiom leave way behind, shoot ahead of
　6 *syn* see SPEND 3
　7 *syn* see NEGLECT
　8 *syn* see PROMISE 1

　9 to transfer by hand from one person to another <*pass* the salt>
　syn buck, hand, reach, ‖shoot
　rel give; fork (over)
pass (as or for) *vb* *syn* see POSE 4
pass (on) *vb* *syn* see HAND DOWN
pass (over) *vb* *syn* see TRAVEL 2
pass *n* *syn* see JUNCTURE 2
passable *adj* capable of being passed, crossed, or traveled <*passable* roads>
　syn navigable, negotiable, travelable
　rel open, unblocked; ‖motorable; accessible, attainable, reachable
　con blocked, closed; unnavigable; inaccessible, unattainable, unreachable
　ant impassable
passably *adv* *syn* see ENOUGH 2
passage *n* **1** movement or transference from one place or point to another <air *passage* from New York to London> <the *passage* of current through a wire>
　syn transit, travel
　rel traject, trajet, traverse, traversing; transfer, transference, transmission, transmittal, transmittance
　2 *syn* see TRANSITION
　3 *syn* see WAY 2
　4 a typically long narrow way connecting parts of a building <the office building contained endless *passages*>
　syn corridor, couloir, hall, hallway, passageway
　rel areaway
passageway *n* *syn* see PASSAGE 3
pass away *vb* **1** *syn* see DIE 1
　2 *syn* see PASS 3
pass by *vb* *syn* see NEGLECT
passé *adj* **1** *syn* see OBSOLETE
　2 *syn* see OLD-FASHIONED
　ant a la mode
passed master *n* *syn* see EXPERT
passel *n* *syn* see GROUP 3
passing *n* *syn* see DEATH 1
passing *adj* *syn* see TRANSIENT
　con lingering
passion *n* **1** *syn* see DISTRESS
　2 *syn* see DESIRE 1
　rel coveting; aiming, aspiring, panting
　3 *syn* see FEELING 3
　ant dispassion
　4 *syn* see TEMPER 4
　rel outbreak, outburst
　5 *syn* see LOVE 2
　rel heartthrob
　6 intense, high-wrought emotion that compels to action <the *passion* of an evangelist>
　syn ardor, calenture, enthusiasm, fervor, fire, hurrah, zeal
　rel dedication, devotion; eagerness, lust; lyricism; ecstasy, rapture, transport; fury, rage
　7 *syn* see LUST 2
　rel amorousness; sensuality, sensuousness
　8 *syn* see INFATUATION
passionate *adj* **1** *syn* see IRASCIBLE
　2 *syn* see IMPASSIONED
　rel excited, quickened, stimulated; high-powered, high-pressure, steamed up; headlong, impetuous, precipitate
　ant dispassionate

---

syn synonym(s)　　*rel* related word(s)
ant antonym(s)　　*con* contrasted word(s)
idiom idiomatic equivalent(s)
‖ use limited; if in doubt, see a dictionary

3 *syn* see LUSTFUL 2
rel steamy, sultry
ant passionless
passionless *adj syn* see FRIGID 3
rel detached, impassive, unsusceptible;
unaffected, unmoved; apathetic, indifferent,
uncaring, unconcerned, unfeeling; cold‑
blooded, coldhearted, frozen, heartless
ant passionate, passionful
passive *adj 1 syn* see INACTIVE
rel apathetic, impassive, phlegmatic, stolid
ant active
2 receiving or enduring without resistance
<a *passive* acceptance of her fate>
syn acquiescent, nonresistant, nonresisting,
resigned, submissive, unresistant, unresist‑
ing, yielding
rel bearing, enduring, patient; compliant,
docile, tractable; nonviolent
con resistant, resisting, unresigned, unsub‑
missive, unyielding
pass off *vb 1 syn* see FOIST 3
2 *syn* see POSE 4
pass on *vb syn* see COMMUNICATE 1
pass out *vb 1 syn* see FAINT
2 *syn* see DIE 1
pass over *vb syn* see NEGLECT
passport *n* a means of entry into a desirable
group, society, or condition of life <her skill
at sports was a *passport* to fame and for‑
tune>
syn key, open sesame, password, ticket
password *n 1* a word or phrase that must be
spoken by a person before he may pass a
guard <give the *password* before entering the
fort>
syn countersign, watchword, word
rel tessera
2 *syn* see PASSPORT
3 something (as a short phrase) used as a
sign of recognition among members of the
same society, class, or group <a fraternity
that has secret handshakes and *passwords*>
syn watchword, word
past *adj 1 syn* see PRECEDING
2 *syn* see FORMER 2
rel bypast, gone-by, late, previous
ant present
past *prep 1 syn* see BEYOND 1
rel by
ant before
2 *syn* see BEYOND 2
past *n* former time <reminisced about the
past>
syn foretime, ‖lang syne, yesterday, yester‑
year, yore; *compare* PRESENT
rel antiquity
idiom bygone days (or times), days gone by,
the good old days
con here and now; tomorrow
ant present; future
paste *vb syn* see BEAT 1
idiom give one a pasting
‖**paste** *n syn* see CUFF
pasticcio *n syn* see MISCELLANY 1
pastiche *n syn* see MISCELLANY 1
past master *n syn* see EXPERT
pastoral *adj syn* see RURAL
rel agrarian
patch *vb syn* see MEND 2

patchwork *n syn* see MISCELLANY 1
patchy *adj syn* see SPOTTY 1
pate *n syn* see HEAD 1
patent *adj 1 syn* see OPEN 1
2 *syn* see CLEAR 5
rel prominent; flagrant, glaring, gross, rank
idiom patently obvious
con impalpable, imperceptible, insensible;
concealed, hidden, secreted
ant latent
‖**pater** *n syn* see FATHER 1
path *n 1 syn* see TRAIL
2 *syn* see WAY 1
3 *syn* see WAY 2
pathetic *adj syn* see PITIFUL 1
pathos *n* a quality that moves one to pity and
sorrow <the *pathos* of the play was rarely
offset by moments of comedy>
syn poignance, poignancy
rel bathos
pathway *n syn* see TRAIL
patience *n* the power or capacity to endure
without complaint something difficult or
disagreeable <it took a lot of *patience* to put
up with him>
syn forbearance, longanimity, long-suffer‑
ing, patientness, resignation, uncomplain‑
ingness
rel composure, cool, equanimity, imper‑
turbability, self-control; endurance, suffer‑
ance, suffering, tolerance, toleration; nonre‑
sistance, passiveness, passivity, submission,
submissiveness
con fretfulness; restiveness, restlessness;
hastiness; rebellion, resistance
ant impatience
patientness *n syn* see PATIENCE
patois *n 1 syn* see VERNACULAR 3
2 *syn* see DIALECT 2
patriarch *n 1 syn* see FATHER 2
2 *syn* see GAFFER
patriarchal *adj syn* see VENERABLE 1
patrician *n syn* see GENTLEMAN 1
ant plebeian
patriciate *n syn* see ARISTOCRACY
ant plebs
patrimony *n syn* see HERITAGE 1
patriot *n 1* a person who loves his country
and supports its interests <*patriots* who
asked what they could do for their country>
syn loyalist
rel nationalist
ant traitor
2 *syn* see PATRIOTEER
3 *syn* see PARTISAN 2
patrioteer *n* one who is ostentatiously and
chauvinistically patriotic <bloodthirsty
patrioteers immersed in political witch‑
hunts>
syn flag-waver, patriot, superpatriot
rel jingo, jingoist
patrolman *n syn* see POLICEMAN
patron *n 1 syn* see PATRON SAINT
2 *syn* see SPONSOR
ant client; protégé
3 *syn* see CUSTOMER
patronage *n 1 syn* see BACKING
rel benefaction, guardianship, protection;
subsidy

2 commercial transactions of customers and patrons <developed a large *patronage* by offering fair prices and courteous service>
syn business, custom, trade, traffic
rel clientage, clientele
3 the power to make appointments to government jobs on a basis other than merit alone <ousted his enemies from office and used *patronage* to support his policies>
syn pork-barreling
rel cronyism

patron saint *n* a saint to whose protection and intercession a person, society, church, or place is dedicated <Saint Christopher is the *patron saint* of travelers>
syn avowry, patron
rel titular; guardian angel

patsy *n* 1 *syn* see SCAPEGOAT
2 *syn* see FOOL 3

patter *vb syn* see CHAT 1

patter *n* 1 *syn* see DIALECT 2

pattern *n* 1 *syn* see MODEL 2
rel original
2 *syn* see FIGURE 3
rel patterning
3 *syn* see ORDER 8
rel arrangement, constellation

paucity *n syn* see SCARCITY
rel fewness

Paul Pry *n syn* see BUSYBODY

paunch *n* 1 *syn* see ABDOMEN
2 *syn* see POTBELLY

paunch *vb syn* see EVISCERATE

pauper *n* a person having no financial resources except those derived from charity <beggar, down-and-out
rel have-not, indigent; ‖casual; almsman, lazarus
con have, millionaire, plutocrat

pauper *vb syn* see RUIN 3

pauperism *n syn* see POVERTY 1

pauperize *vb syn* see RUIN 3

pausation *n syn* see PAUSE

pause *n* a temporary cessation of activity or of an activity <a *pause* in the conversation>
syn comma, interval, lull, pausation; *compare* BREAK 4, GAP 3
rel caesura, hush, lapse, letup, suspension; interlude, intermission; recess, respite; wait; break, gap, interruption; cessation, ‖deval
con continuation, progression

paw *vb syn* see TOUCH 1

paw *adj* 1 *syn* see NAUGHTY 1
2 *syn* see OBSCENE 2

pawn *n syn* see PLEDGE 1

pawn *vb* to give or deposit as security for the payment of a loan or debt or for the fulfillment of an obligation <had to *pawn* all her jewels>
syn ‖dip, hock, impignorate, mortgage, pledge, ‖pop, ‖spout
ant redeem

pawn *n syn* see TOOL 2

pay *vb* 1 to discharge an obligation to usually with money <*paid* the doctor for his services>

syn compensate, guerdon, remunerate
rel indemnify, recompense, satisfy; cough (up), plunk down, pony (up), pungle (up), remit, render, tender; pay off
2 *syn* see CLEAR 5
3 *syn* see SPEND 1
4 *syn* see COMPENSATE 3
idiom make up for
5 *syn* see YIELD 5

pay *n syn* see WAGE

payable *adj* 1 *syn* see DUE 2
ant unpayable
2 *syn* see UNPAID 2

pay envelope *n syn* see WAGE

paying *adj syn* see ADVANTAGEOUS 1
rel productive; sound; solvent

payload *n syn* see LOAD 1

pay up *vb syn* see CLEAR 5

PDQ *adv syn* see AWAY 3

peaceable *adj syn* see PACIFIC
rel amicable, friendly, neighborly; amiable, complaisant
ant acrimonious; contentious; warlike

peaceful *adj syn* see PACIFIC
rel collected, composed, cool, unruffled; constant, equable, steady
con agitated, discomposed, disquieted, disturbed, perturbed, upset

peacemaker *n* one that makes or seeks to make peace <a president who was remembered as a great *peacemaker*>
syn make-peace, pacificator
rel arbitrator, mediator, negotiator; placater; appeaser, peacemonger; peacekeeper
con chauvinist, jingo, jingoist, militarist, war dog, warmonger; peacebreaker

peace officer *n syn* see POLICEMAN

peach *n syn* ‖DILLY, crackerjack, ‖daisy, dandy, humdinger, jim-dandy, ‖lalapalooza, ‖lulu, nifty, ‖pip
rel pearl

peach *vb syn* see INFORM 3

peachy *adj syn* see MARVELOUS 2

peacock *vb syn* see LORD

peacockish *adj syn* see SHOWY

peacocky *adj syn* see SHOWY

peak *n* 1 *syn* see VISOR 1
2 *syn* see TOP 1
3 *syn* see MOUNTAIN 1
4 *syn* see APEX 2

peak (out) *vb syn* see DECREASE

peaked *adj syn* see POINTED 1

peaked *adj syn* see SICKLY 2

‖peaking *adj syn* see SICKLY 2

peaky *adj syn* see POINTED 1

peaky *adj syn* see SICKLY 2

peal *vb syn* see RING

peanut *adj syn* see PETTY 2

‖peart *adj syn* see LIVELY 1

‖pearten (up) *vb syn* see ENCOURAGE 1

peasant *n syn* see RUSTIC

peck *n syn* see MUCH

peck *vb* 1 to strike at or pick up with the beak <a hen *pecking* the scattered grain from the ground>
syn beak, pick
2 *syn* see KISS 1

peck (at) *vb syn* see NAG

pecker *n* 1 *syn* see BILL 1
2 *syn* see NOSE 1

---

syn synonym(s)   *rel* related word(s)
ant antonym(s)   *con* contrasted word(s)
idiom idiomatic equivalent(s)
‖ use limited; if in doubt, see a dictionary

‖**peckish** *adj syn* see HUNGRY
pecksniffery *n syn* see HYPOCRISY
pecksniffian *adj syn* see HYPOCRITICAL
peculate *vb syn* see EMBEZZLE
peculiar *adj* 1 *syn* see CHARACTERISTIC
  rel unique
  2 *syn* see STRANGE 4
  rel uncustomary
  con normal
peculiarity *n syn* see QUALITY 1
pecuniary *adj syn* see FINANCIAL
pedantic *adj* too narrowly concerned with
scholarly matters <intellectual life that was
pedantic rather than broad and humane>
  syn academic, bookish, book-learned,
booky, quodlibetic, scholastic
  rel erudite, learned; didactic, donnish,
inkhorn, schoolish, schoolteacherish; arid,
dry, dryasdust, dull
  ant unpedantic
peddle *vb* 1 *syn* see PUSH 6
  2 to sell or offer for sale from place to place
<*peddled* fish from a pushcart>
  syn hawk, huckster, monger, vend
  rel sell; push
peddler *n* one who travels about with merchandise to sell <*peddlers* were once common in rural areas>
  syn ‖arab, cheap-jack (*or* cheap-john),
‖duffer, hawker, higgler, huckster, monger,
mongerer, outcrier, packman, piepoudre,
roadman, vendor
  rel colporteur, costermonger; pusher
peddling *adj syn* see PETTY 2
pedestal *vb syn* see EXALT 1
pedestrian *adj syn* see DULL 9
  rel commonplace, platitudinous, truistic;
banal, inane, jejune, wishy-washy; heavy
pedigree *n* 1 *syn* see GENEALOGY
  2 *syn* see ANCESTRY
pedigree *adj syn* see PUREBRED
pedigreed *adj syn* see PUREBRED
peek (in *or* out) *vb syn* see PEEP
peek *n syn* see PEEP
peel *vb* 1 *syn* see SKIN 2
  2 *syn* see SCALE 2
peeled *adj syn* see OPEN 2
peeler *n* 1 *syn* see STRIPTEASER
  2 *syn* see HUSTLER
‖**peeler** *n syn* see POLICEMAN
peep *vb syn* see CHIRP
  rel pip
peep *vb* to peer through or as if through a
hole or crevice <*peeped* cautiously under the
bed>
  syn peek (in *or* out)
  rel glance; look; peer, stare
  idiom take a peep (*or* peek)
peep *n* a brief and sometimes furtive look
<take a *peep* at the new neighbors>
  syn ‖looker, glance, glimpse, peek
  rel look-over, look-see; oeillade, ogle; stare
peeper *n* 1 *syn* see PEEPING TOM
  2 *syn* see EYE 1
peeping tom *n* a pruriently prying person <a
peeping tom spying on the couple>
  syn peeper, voyeur
  rel prowler, snoop, snooper
  idiom porch climber, window (*or* transom)
peeper

‖**peepy** *adj syn* see SLEEPY 1
peer *vb syn* see GAZE 1
  rel eye, rubberneck; pry, snoop
peerless *adj syn* see ALONE 3
  rel dominant, paramount, predominant,
sovereign
peery *adj syn* see CURIOUS 2
peeve *vb syn* see IRRITATE
  rel disturb; miff
  idiom make one hot under the collar
peevish *adj syn* see IRRITABLE
  rel captious, carping, caviling, critical,
faultfinding
  idiom being in a peeve
peewee *n syn* see DWARF
peewee *adj syn* see TINY
‖**peg** *n syn* see DRINK 3
‖**pegh** *vb syn* see PANT 1
peg out *vb* 1 *syn* see COLLAPSE 2
  2 *syn* see DIE 1
pejorative *adj syn* see DEROGATORY
  con acclaiming, extolling, lauding, praising;
aggrandizing, exalting, magnifying
pelf *n* 1 *syn* see MONEY
  ‖2 *syn* see REFUSE
pell-mell *adv* in or as if in confused haste
<barged in *pell-mell* without thinking>
  syn helter-skelter, hotfoot, hurry-scurry,
impetuously, incontinently
  rel hurriedly; indiscreetly; carelessly, heedlessly, rashly, thoughtlessly
  idiom on the spur of the moment
pell-mell *n syn* see CONFUSION 3
pell-mell *vb syn* see STAMPEDE 2
pellucid *adj* 1 *syn* see TRANSPARENT 1
  rel sheer
  con muddy, roily, turbid
  2 *syn* see CLEAR 4
pelt *n syn* see HIDE
pelt *vb* 1 *syn* see BEAT 1
  2 *syn* see HURRY 2
pen *vb syn* see ENCLOSE 1
  ant unpen
pen *n syn* see JAIL
penalize *vb* to inflict a penalty on <*penalize* a
delinquent taxpayer with a stiff fine>
  syn amerce, fine, mulct
  rel castigate, chasten, chastise, correct,
discipline, punish; condemn; judge
penalty *n syn* see FINE
penance *n syn* see PENITENCE
penchant *n syn* see LEANING 2
‖**pend** *vb syn* see DEPEND (on *or* upon) 1
pendant *n* 1 *syn* see FLAG
  2 *syn* see COUNTERPART 1
pendent *adj* 1 *syn* see SUSPENDED
  2 *syn* see PENDING
pending *adj* not yet settled or decided <a
claim still *pending*>
  syn pendent, undecided, undetermined,
unsettled
  idiom hanging in the balance, in suspense,
up in the air
  con decided, determined, settled
  ant closed
pendulant *adj syn* see SUSPENDED
pendulate *vb syn* see SWING 2
pendulous *adj* 1 *syn* see SUSPENDED
  2 *syn* see VACILLATING 2
penetrable *adj syn* see PERMEABLE

ant impenetrable

penetrate *vb* 1 *syn* see ENTER 1
rel encroach, invade, trespass
2 to enter or go through by or as if by overcoming resistance <the icy wind *penetrated* the heavy parka>
syn pierce
rel bore, perforate, prick, puncture; jab, knife, stab; drill, drive
3 *syn* see PERMEATE
rel insert, insinuate, interpolate, introduce
penetrating *adj* 1 *syn* see INCISIVE
rel penetrant, penetrative
2 *syn* see SHARP 4
penetration *n* *syn* see WIT 3
rel penetrativeness
penetrative *adj* *syn* see SHARP 4
penitence *n* regret for sin or wrongdoing <responded to true *penitence* with forgiveness>
syn attrition, compunction, contriteness, contrition, penance, penitency, remorse, remorsefulness, repentance, rue, ruth
rel qualm, scruple; self-accusation, self-castigation, self-punishment, self-reproach, self-reproof; anguish, distress, grief, regret, sadness, sorrow; debasement, degradation, humbling, humiliation
con adamancy, inexorableness, obduracy, obdurateness, stubbornness
penitency *n* *syn* see PENITENCE
penitent *adj* *syn* see REMORSEFUL
penitential *adj* *syn* see REMORSEFUL
penitentiary *n* *syn* see JAIL
idiom correctional institution
penmanship *n* *syn* see HANDWRITING
pennant *n* *syn* see FLAG
pennilessness *n* *syn* see POVERTY 1
pennon *n* *syn* see FLAG
penny dreadful *n* *syn* see DIME NOVEL
penny pincher *n* *syn* see MISER
penny–pinching *adj* *syn* see STINGY
penny–wise *adj* *syn* see STINGY
pennyworth *n* *syn* see BARGAIN
pensile *adj* *syn* see SUSPENDED
pension (off) *vb* *syn* see RETIRE 2
pensive *adj* 1 *syn* see THOUGHTFUL 1
rel musing, ruminating
2 being musingly sad and thoughtful <gazed out the window with a *pensive* expression on her face>
syn meditative, ‖pensy, wistful
rel absorbed, abstracted, contemplative, musing, preoccupied, thoughtful, withdrawn; blue, melancholy, sad, saddened
con alert, aware, interested, outgoing
‖**pensy** *adj* 1 *syn* see PENSIVE 2
2 *syn* see THOUGHTFUL 1
3 *syn* see SQUEAMISH 2
penumbra *n* *syn* see SHADE 1
penurious *adj* 1 *syn* see POOR 1
2 *syn* see STINGY
penury *n* *syn* see POVERTY 1
ant luxury
peon *n* *syn* see SLAVE 2

peonage *n* *syn* see BONDAGE
people *n* 1 *syn* see SOCIETY 3
2 *syn* see COMMONALTY
people *vb* *syn* see INHABIT
pep *n* 1 *syn* see ENERGY 2
2 *syn* see VIGOR 2
pepper *vb* *syn* see SPECKLE 3
peppery *adj* 1 *syn* see PUNGENT
2 *syn* see IRASCIBLE
3 *syn* see SPIRITED 2
rel pepperish; alert, keen, lively, peppy
peppy *adj* *syn* see LIVELY 1
per *prep* *syn* see VIA 2
‖**per** *adv* *syn* see APIECE
perambulant *adj* *syn* see ITINERANT
perambulate *vb* *syn* see TRAVERSE 5
‖**perambulator** *n* *syn* see BABY CARRIAGE
perambulatory *adj* *syn* see ITINERANT
per capita *adv* *syn* see APIECE
per caput *adv* *syn* see APIECE
perceive *vb* *syn* see SEE 1
rel ascertain, identify, realize, recognize; grasp, seize, take; apprehend
perceptible *adj* apprehensible as real or existent <a *perceptible* change in attitude>
syn appreciable, detectable, discernible, observable, palpable, sensible, tangible; *compare* TANGIBLE 1
rel distinguishable, recognizable; cognizable, understandable; clear, lucid, perspicuous; conspicuous, noticeable, signal
con impalpable, indiscernible, intangible, invisible, unappreciable, undetectable, undiscernible, unnoticeable, unobservable
ant imperceptible
perception *n* *syn* see IDEA
perceptive *adj* 1 *syn* see ACUTE 3
rel responsive
ant imperceptive, unperceptive
2 *syn* see WISE 1
rel prehensile, prehensive, prehensorial
ant imperceptive, unperceptive
perch *vb* *syn* see ALIGHT
perchance *adv* *syn* see PERHAPS
percipience *n* *syn* see WIT 3
percolate *vb* 1 *syn* see PERMEATE
2 *syn* see EXUDE
per contra *adv* *syn* see HOWEVER
percussion *n* *syn* see IMPACT 1
rel percussiveness
perdition *n* *syn* see HELL
perdurable *adj* 1 *syn* see LASTING
ant fleeting
2 *syn* see INFINITE 1
perdure *vb* *syn* see CONTINUE 1
perduring *adj* *syn* see LASTING
ant fleeting
peregrination *n*, *usu* **peregrinations** *pl* *syn* see JOURNEY
peremptory *adj* *syn* see MASTERFUL 1
rel certain, positive; decided, decisive; absolute, fixed, uncompromising; obstinate
perennial *adj* *syn* see OLD 2
rel durable, perdurable
perfect *adj* 1 *syn* see WHOLE 1
ant imperfect
2 being entirely without flaw and meeting supreme standards of excellence <a ballerina whose technique was *perfect*>

---

syn synonym(s) *rel* related word(s)
ant antonym(s) *con* contrasted word(s)
idiom idiomatic equivalent(s)
‖ use limited; if in doubt, see a dictionary

syn absolute, flawless, fleckless, impeccable, indefectible, note-perfect, unflawed; *compare* CONSUMMATE 1

rel excellent; consummate; expert, finished, masterful, masterly

con defective, faulty, flawed; deficient, inadequate, wanting; unfinished, unpolished; unsound

ant imperfect

3 precisely appropriate or right <found the *perfect* gift for him>

syn ideal, model, very

rel needed, required, requisite; appropriate, fit, proper, right, suitable; exact, express, precise

idiom being just the thing

con foolish, inappropriate, undesirable, unsuitable

4 *syn* see PURE 2

5 *syn* see WHOLE 3

rel consummate

6 *syn* see UTTER

perfect *vb syn* see POLISH 2

perfected *adj syn* see CONSUMMATE 1

ant unperfected

perfectibilian *n syn* see PERFECTIONIST

perfectibilist *n syn* see PERFECTIONIST

perfection *n* **1** *syn* see INTEGRITY 2

2 *syn* see EXCELLENCE

ant imperfection

perfectionist *n* one that demands or works to achieve perfection <a *perfectionist* who rehearsed one scene fifty times>

syn perfectibilian, perfectibilist, perfectist

rel precisian, precisionist, stickler

perfectist *n syn* see PERFECTIONIST

perfectly *adv syn* see WELL 3

perfervid *adj syn* see IMPASSIONED

rel enhanced, heightened, intensified

perfidious *adj syn* see FAITHLESS

rel mercenary, venal; alienated, disaffected, estranged; deceitful, dishonest

perfidiousness *n* **1** *syn* see INFIDELITY

2 *syn* see TREACHERY

perfidy *n* **1** *syn* see TREACHERY

rel foul play

idiom Judas' kiss

ant fealty

2 *syn* see INFIDELITY

rel betrayal, sellout

perforate *vb* to pierce through so as to leave a hole <*perforate* a sheet of postage stamps>

syn bore, drill, prick, ‖pritch, punch, puncture

rel pit; probe; drive, penetrate, pierce

perforce *adv syn* see WILLY-NILLY

perform *vb* **1** *syn* see FULFILL 1

2 to carry something (as a process) to a successful conclusion <*perform* a surgical procedure>

syn achieve, do, execute; *compare* EFFECT 2

rel accomplish, bring off; complete, end, finish, wind up

idiom carry to completion (*or* a successful conclusion), do to a turn, do up brown

3 *syn* see ACT 1

4 *syn* see ACT 5

performance *n syn* see EFFICIENCY 1

performer *n syn* see ACTOR 1

perfume *n syn* see FRAGRANCE

perfume *vb syn* see SCENT 2

perfumed *adj syn* see SWEET 2

perfumy *adj syn* see SWEET 2

perfunctory *adj* characterized by routine and often done merely as a duty <gave her his usual *perfunctory* nod>

syn automatic, mechanical

rel cursory, superficial; involuntary, unaware; routine, usual; standard, stock; cool, impersonal, indifferent; wooden; unconcerned, uninterested

con cordial, friendly, genial, hearty, warm

pergola *n syn* see ARBOR

perhaps *adv* conceivably but not certainly so <*perhaps* this is true, but I think it's debatable>

syn maybe, perchance, possibly

rel conceivably, feasibly, imaginably

idiom as it may be, as the case may be, for all one knows

con certainly, definitely, doubtlessly, surely, undoubtedly, unquestionably

perhaps *n syn* see THEORY 2

periapt *n syn* see CHARM 2

peril *n syn* see DANGER

rel exposure, liability, openness, subjection; endangerment

idiom cause for alarm, rocks (*or* breakers) ahead

peril *vb syn* see ENDANGER

perilous *adj syn* see DANGEROUS 1

rel shaky, tottery, unstable, unsteady; delicate, ticklish, touchy

perimeter *n* **1** *syn* see CIRCUMFERENCE

2 *syn* see BORDER 1

period *n* **1** *syn* see END 2

2 an extent of time set off or typified by someone or something <the Victorian *period*><a *period* of expansion>

syn age, day(s), epoch, time

rel on-again-off-again

periodic *adj syn* see INTERMITTENT

periodical *adj syn* see INTERMITTENT

periodical *n syn* see JOURNAL

peripatetic *adj syn* see ITINERANT

periphery *n* **1** *syn* see CIRCUMFERENCE

2 *syn* see BORDER 1

periphrase *n syn* see VERBIAGE 1

periphrasis *n syn* see VERBIAGE 1

perish *vb* **1** *syn* see DIE 1

ant survive

2 to suffer spiritual or moral death <nations *perishing* for lack of true leaders>

syn die

rel decline; collapse, go under; expire, succumb; disappear, vanish; cease, end

con flourish, prosper, thrive

ant endure

‖**3** *syn* see DECAY

perishing *adj syn* see DAMNED 2

perjure *vb* to make a false swearer of oneself by violating one's oath to tell the truth <a *perjured* witness>

syn forswear

rel equivocate; deceive, delude, mislead, trick; lie, prevaricate

idiom commit perjury, lie under oath, swear falsely

perjurer *n syn* see LIAR

perk (up) *vb syn* see IMPROVE 3

‖**perk** *n, usu* **perks** *pl syn see* GRATUITY

perlustrate *vb syn see* SCRUTINIZE 1

perlustration *n syn see* EXAMINATION

permanent *adj syn see* LASTING
  rel imperishable, invariable
  ant temporary

permeable *adj* capable of being permeated especially by fluids <a *permeable* membrane>
  syn penetrable, pervious, porose, porous
  rel passable
  con impassable, impenetrable, impervious
  ant impermeable

permeate *vb* to pass or cause to pass through every part of a thing <air *permeated* with cigar smoke>
  syn charge, compenetrate, impenetrate, impregnate, interfuse, interpenetrate, penetrate, percolate, pervade, saturate, transfuse
  rel invade; imbrue, imbue, infiltrate, infuse, ingrain; diffuse, suffuse; drench, soak, steep; fill

permissible *adj* that may be permitted <a *permissible* error>
  syn admissible, allowable
  rel unforbidden, unprohibited; allowed, permitted, tolerated; approved, authorized, endorsed, sanctioned; acceptable, bearable, tolerable
  con banned, forbidden, disallowed, prohibited, unpermitted, verboten; unacceptable, unbearable
  ant impermissible

permission *n* a sanctioning to act or do something that is granted by one in authority <received *permission* to leave work early>
  syn allowance, authorization, consent, leave, permit, sanction, sufferance
  rel acceptance, acquiescence; approbation, approval; endorsement
  ant prohibition

permit *vb syn see* LET 2
  rel tolerate
  idiom give one his head
  ant forbid, prohibit

permit *n syn see* PERMISSION

permutation *n syn see* CHANGE 2
  rel alteration, modification

pernicious *adj* exceedingly harmful or destructive <*pernicious* gossip>
  syn baneful, deadly, noxious, pestiferous, pestilent, pestilential; *compare* DEADLY 1
  rel damaging, deleterious, detrimental, harmful, hurtful; baleful, malefic, maleficent, malign, sinister; miasmatic, miasmic, poisonous, toxic, venomous; malignant, swart, virulent; destructive, devastating, ruinous; fatal, killing, lethal, mortal
  con harmless, uninjurious; nonmalignant, nonpoisonous, nontoxic
  ant innocuous

pernickety *adj syn see* NICE 1

perorate *vb syn see* ORATE

perpend *vb syn see* CONSIDER 1

perpendicular *adj syn see* VERTICAL
  rel stand-up, straight
  ant horizontal

perpendicularity *n syn see* VERTICALITY
  rel erectness, uprightness
  ant horizontality

perpetrate *vb syn see* COMMIT 2
  rel effect; inflict, wreak
  idiom ‖up and do

perpetual *adj syn see* CONTINUAL
  ant ephemeral, transient

perpetually *adv syn see* ALWAYS 1

perpetuate *vb* to make perpetual or cause to last indefinitely <*perpetuate* his memory for future generations>
  syn eternalize, eternize, immortalize
  rel bolster, conserve, keep, maintain, preserve, secure, support, sustain
  con annihilate, blot out, erase, expunge
  ant obliterate

perplex *vb* 1 *syn see* PUZZLE
  rel discompose, perturb; balk, thwart; astonish, astound, surprise
  idiom put (or drive) to one's wit's end
  2 *syn see* COMPLICATE
  3 *syn see* ENTANGLE 1

perquisite *n* 1 *syn see* GRATUITY
  2 *syn see* RIGHT 2

per se *adv* by, of, or in itself or oneself or themselves <not opposed to the death penalty *per se*>
  syn as such, intrinsically
  rel alone, independently, solely

persecute *vb* 1 *syn see* WRONG
  rel dragoon, rack, torment, torture
  con back, champion, support, uphold
  2 *syn see* MOLEST
  rel worry; hound, ride
  con humor, indulge, pamper; accommodate, favor, oblige

perseverant *adj syn see* PERSISTENT 1

perseverative *adj syn see* PERSISTENT 1

persevere *vb* to continue in a state, enterprise, or undertaking in spite of counter influences, opposition, or discouragement <*persevered* in her unpopular economic policy>
  syn carry on, go on, hang on, persist
  rel continue, get on, press (on), proceed
  idiom hang in there, hang tough, keep at it, keep driving, never say die, stick (*or* tough) it out
  con falter, hesitate, vacillate, waver; renounce, surrender, yield
  ant give up

persevering *adj syn see* PERSISTENT 1

persiflage *n syn see* BANTER

persist *vb* 1 *syn see* PERSEVERE
  con cease, discontinue, quit, stop
  ant desist
  2 *syn see* CONTINUE 1
  rel go on; linger; obtain, prevail
  ant desist

persistence *n* 1 *syn see* CONTINUATION 1
  2 *syn see* RUN 2
  rel course

persistent *adj* 1 continuing in a course of action without regard to discouragement, opposition, or previous failure <a *persistent* suitor>

---

syn synonym(s)   *rel* related word(s)
ant antonym(s)   *con* contrasted word(s)
idiom idiomatic equivalent(s)
‖ use limited; if in doubt, see a dictionary

syn dogged, insistent, perseverant, perseverative, persevering, persisting, persistive
rel determined, steadfast, tenacious, unshakable; relentless, unremitting
con malleable, pliant, tractable, yielding; infirm, invertebrate, spineless; vacillating, wavery, wobbling
2 *syn* see PRIMITIVE 3

persisting *adj syn* see PERSISTENT 1
persistive *adj syn* see PERSISTENT 1
persnickety *adj syn* see NICE 1
person *n syn* see HUMAN
rel chap, ‖cookie, coot, fellow, galoot, guy, specimen, stick

personage *n* **1** *syn* see NOTABLE 1
2 *syn* see HUMAN

personal *adj* **1** of, relating to, or affecting a particular person <owed his *personal* allegiance to his wife>
syn individual
rel particular, peculiar, special
con general, universal; common, joint, mutual, shared; commonplace, everyday, ordinary
2 *syn* see PRIVATE 1

personal effects *n pl* privately owned items (as clothing and toilet articles) normally worn or carried on the person <packed his *personal effects* in a small bag>
syn ‖plunder, stuff, things, traps, tricks
rel belongings, goods, possessions
idiom personal belongings

personality *n* **1** *syn* see INDIVIDUALITY 4
2 *syn* see DISPOSITION 3
3 *syn* see NOTABLE 1

personalize *vb* **1** *syn* see EMBODY 1
rel anthropomorphize
2 *syn* see REPRESENT 2

personal name *n syn* see GIVEN NAME
personate *vb* **1** *syn* see ACT 2
2 *syn* see REPRESENT 2

personification *n syn* see EMBODIMENT
personify *vb* **1** *syn* see EMBODY 1
rel reincarnate
2 *syn* see REPRESENT 2

personize *vb syn* see EMBODY 1
perspective *n syn* see VISTA
perspicacious *adj syn* see SHREWD
rel quick-sighted, sharp-sighted, sharp-witted

perspicacity *n syn* see WIT 3
perspicuity *n syn* see CLARITY
rel intelligibility; explicitness

perspicuous *adj syn* see CLEAR 4
perspiring *adj syn* see SWEATY
perspiry *adj syn* see SWEATY
persuadable *adj syn* see RECEPTIVE 1
ant unpersuadable

persuade *vb* **1** *syn* see INDUCE 1
rel affect, impress, touch; reason; convert
con discourage, hinder, prevent
ant dissuade
2 *syn* see CONVERT 1
3 *syn* see ASSURE 2
ant dissuade

persuasible *adj syn* see RECEPTIVE 1
ant unpersuasible

persuasion *n* **1** *syn* see OPINION
rel bias, partiality, predilection, prejudice, prepossession

2 *syn* see RELIGION 1
3 *syn* see RELIGION 2
rel affiliation; order
4 *syn* see TYPE

pert *adj* **1** *syn* see SAUCY 1
rel bold, daring; audacious, brazen
con shy
ant coy
2 *syn* see WISE 5
rel disrespectful, rude
3 *syn* see LIVELY 1

pertain *vb* **1** *syn* see BELONG 2
2 *syn* see BEAR (on *or* upon)
rel associate, combine, connect, join
idiom be pertinent (*or* relevant) to

pertinacious *adj syn* see OBSTINATE
rel fixed, unshakable; dogged, tenacious

pertinent *adj syn* see RELEVANT
rel pertaining
ant impertinent

perturb *vb syn* see DISCOMPOSE 1
rel trouble; unsettle
ant compose

pervade *vb syn* see PERMEATE
idiom spread through and through

perverse *adj syn* see VICIOUS 2
2 *syn* see OBSTINATE
rel cranky, irritable, unreasonable
3 *syn* see CONTRARY 3

pervert *vb* **1** *syn* see DEBASE 1
rel abuse, maltreat, mistreat, misuse, outrage; ruin
2 *syn* see ABUSE 2
rel ill-treat
3 *syn* see MISREPRESENT

perverted *adj syn* see DEBASED
rel defiled, polluted, tainted; contorted, distorted, warped; abused, misused, outraged

pervicacious *adj syn* see OBSTINATE
pervious *adj syn* see PERMEABLE
ant impervious

pesky *adj syn* see TROUBLESOME
pesky *adv syn* see VERY 1
pessimist *n* one who emphasizes adverse aspects or conditions and expects the worst <*pessimists* predicting another depression>
syn calamity howler, Cassandra, crepe-hanger, worrywart
rel fussbudget; Job's comforter; defeatist; killjoy; cynic, misanthrope
con positivist; idealist; Pollyanna
ant optimist

pest *n* **1** *syn* see ANNOYANCE 3
rel bane, trouble, vexation, worry
idiom pain in the neck, pea in the shoe, thorn in the flesh
2 one who pesters or annoys <a little *pest* who constantly asked questions>
syn nudnick, nuisance, pesterer
rel badgerer, heckler, tormentor
idiom pain in the neck

pester *vb syn* see WORRY 1
rel ride
idiom drive (one) crazy, drive (one) up the wall, pester to death

pester *n syn* see ANNOYANCE 3
pesterer *n syn* see PEST 2
‖**pesterment** *n syn* see ANNOYANCE 3

pesticide *n* a chemical agent used to destroy pests <the need to control indiscriminate use of *pesticides*>
  syn biocide, economic poison
  rel bactericide, fungicide, germicide, insecticide, microbicide, rodenticide, vermicide
pestiferous *adj syn see* PERNICIOUS
pestilence *n syn see* PLAGUE 1
pestilent *adj* **1** *syn see* DEADLY 1
  2 *syn see* PERNICIOUS
pestilential *adj* **1** *syn see* DEADLY 1
  2 *syn see* PERNICIOUS
pet *adj syn see* FAVORITE 1
pet *vb syn see* CARESS
  rel embrace, hug
pet *vb syn see* SULK
petcock *n syn see* FAUCET
peter (out) *vb syn see* DECREASE
Peter Funk *n syn see* SWINDLER
petite *adj syn see* SMALL 1
  rel diminutive, dwarf, lilliputian, miniature, wee
petition *n syn see* PRAYER
  rel request
petition *vb* to make an earnest, formal, and often written request <*petitioned* for a hearing before the labor board>
  syn appeal, sue (for *or* to)
  rel ask, request; beg, beseech, entreat, implore, plead, pray, supplicate
  con claim, demand, exact, press (for)
petitioner *n syn see* SUPPLIANT
petit-maître *n syn see* FOP
petrify *vb syn see* DAZE 2
  rel alarm, frighten, startle, terrify; appall, dismay, horrify; numb
  idiom turn to stone
pettifogger *n* an unscrupulous lawyer <done out of his rights by a slick *pettifogger*>
  syn jackleg lawyer, shyster; *compare* LAWYER
  rel ambulance chaser, Philadelphia lawyer; ‖bush lawyer
pettifogging *adj syn see* PETTY 2
pettish *adj syn see* IRRITABLE
petty *adj* **1** *syn see* LITTLE 3
  2 being often contemptibly insignificant or unimportant <*petty* quarrels and intrigues>
  syn inconsequent, inconsequential, inconsiderable, measly, Mickey Mouse, niggling, paltry, peanut, peddling, pettifogging, picayune, picayunish, piddling, piffling, pimping, puny, small, trifling, trivial, unconsequential, unconsidered, ungenerous, unvital; *compare* LITTLE 3
  rel negligible, unimportant; hair-drawn, hairsplitting; impertinent, irrelevant
  con consequential, considerable; big, gross; significant, vital
  ant important, momentous
petulant *adj syn see* IRRITABLE
  rel grouchy, sulky
phantasm *n* **1** *syn see* DELUSION 1
  rel fabrication, fiction, invention

  2 *syn see* APPARITION
  3 *syn see* FANCY 4
phantom *n syn see* APPARITION
pharisaic *adj syn see* HYPOCRITICAL
pharisaical *adj syn see* HYPOCRITICAL
pharisaicalness *n syn see* HYPOCRISY
pharisaism *n syn see* HYPOCRISY
pharisee *n syn see* HYPOCRITE
pharmaceutic *n syn see* DRUG 1
pharmaceutical *n syn see* DRUG 1
pharmacist *n syn see* DRUGGIST
pharmacon *n syn see* REMEDY 1
pharos *n syn see* LIGHTHOUSE
phase *n* one of the possible ways of viewing or being presented to view <the moral *phase* of the problem>
  syn angle, aspect, facet, hand, side
  rel condition, situation, state; position, posture, view, viewpoint; appearance, look, semblance; color, complexion
phenomenal *adj* **1** *syn see* MATERIAL 1
  con ontic
  ant noumenal
  2 *syn see* EXCEPTIONAL 1
phenomenon *n* **1** *syn see* FACT 2
  rel experience; actuality, reality
  2 *syn see* WONDER 1
  rel abnormality; anomaly, paradox; peculiarity, singularity, uniqueness, unusualness
philander *n syn see* WOLF
  idiom ‖skirt chaser
philander *vb* to have many love affairs <his reputation for *philandering* with married women>
  syn fool (around), mess around, play (around), wolf, womanize
  rel dally, flirt, trifle; chase, pursue; ‖tomcat (around)
  idiom ‖chase skirts, play Don Juan, play the femmes
philanderer *n syn see* WOLF
philanthropic *adj syn see* CHARITABLE 1
  rel bighearted, freehearted, greathearted, kindhearted, largehearted, openhearted; contributing, donating, freehanded, giving, magnanimous; civic-minded, public-spirited
  ant misanthropic
philharmonic *n syn see* ORCHESTRA
philippic *n syn see* TIRADE
philistine *n* a crass, prosaic, often priggish individual guided by material rather than artistic or intellectual values <*philistines* who opposed everything new and creative in art>
  syn Babbitt, boeotian, boob, middlebrow
  rel bourgeois; capitalist; materialist; boor, clown, lout, vulgarian
  ant aesthete
phiz *n syn see* FACE 1
phlegm *n* **1** *syn see* APATHY 1
  2 *syn see* EQUANIMITY
  rel nonchalance, unconcern
phlegmatic *adj syn see* IMPASSIVE 1
  rel calm, undemonstrative; aloof, incurious, indifferent, unconcerned; lethargic, sluggish
phoebus *n syn see* SUN 1
phoenix *n syn see* PARAGON
phonate *vb syn see* ARTICULATE 2
phone *vb syn see* TELEPHONE
phony *adj syn see* COUNTERFEIT

---

syn synonym(s)   **rel** related word(s)
ant antonym(s)   **con** contrasted word(s)
idiom idiomatic equivalent(s)
‖ use limited; if in doubt, see a dictionary

phony n 1 syn see IMPOSTURE
2 syn see IMPOSTOR

photo vb syn see PHOTOGRAPH
idiom take a photo (of)

photog n syn see PHOTOGRAPHER

photograph vb to use a camera to make a picture, image, or likeness of <*photographed* the whole family>
syn photo, shoot
rel cinematize, ‖cinematograph, cinemize, film, filmize, picture; snap, snapshot, snapshot; mug
idiom capture on film, take a picture (or photograph)

photographer n one who takes photographs <a newspaper *photographer*>
syn cameraman, camerist, photog, photographist, photoist
rel snapshooter, ‖snapshotter; shutterbug; paparazzo; photojournalist

photographic adj syn see GRAPHIC 1
rel accurate, detailed, exact

photographist n syn see PHOTOGRAPHER

photoist n syn see PHOTOGRAPHER

photoplay n syn see MOVIE

phrase n 1 syn see WORDING
rel styling
2 a group of words which, taken together, express a notion and may constitute part of a sentence <an adverbial *phrase*><a trite *phrase*>
syn expression, locution
rel phrasing; idiom; catchword, slogan
3 syn see CATCHWORD

phrase vb syn see WORD

phraseology n syn see WORDING
idiom choice of words

phrasing n syn see WORDING

phthisis n syn see TUBERCULOSIS

phylactery n syn see CHARM 2

physic n syn see REMEDY 1

physical adj 1 syn see MATERIAL 1
rel natural; elemental, elementary
ant spiritual
2 syn see BODILY
rel visceral; lusty; brute
ant mental

physician n a doctor of medicine <the shortage of *physicians* in rural areas>
syn ‖croaker, doc, doctor, MD, medical, mediciner, medico, ‖sawbones
rel medic; general practitioner; practitioner; surgeon; specialist
idiom medical doctor, medical man

physique n bodily makeup or type <a muscular *physique*>
syn build, constitution, habit, habitus
rel anatomy, structure; configuration, shape; body, figure, form, frame

picaroon n syn see PIRATE

picayune adj syn see PETTY 2

picayunish adj syn see PETTY 2

pick vb 1 syn see CHOOSE 1
idiom pick and choose
ant reject
2 syn see PECK 1

pick n syn see BEST

pick adj syn see SELECT 1

picked adj syn see SELECT 1

picket n syn see GUARD 2

pickle n syn see PREDICAMENT
idiom pretty pickle, ‖sticky wicket, tight spot

‖pickled adj syn see INTOXICATED 1

pick out vb syn see CHOOSE 1

pickpocket n one who steals from pockets <his wallet was lifted by a *pickpocket*>
syn ‖cannon, cutpurse, ‖dip, ‖diver, purse cutter, ‖wire
rel ‖ganef, thief; ‖mobsman, ‖swell-mobsman
idiom ‖pocket prowler

picksome adj syn see NICE 1

pick up vb 1 syn see LIFT 1
2 syn see GLEAN
3 syn see GET 1
4 syn see LEARN 1
5 syn see ARREST 2
rel book
idiom ‖take (someone) downtown
6 syn see RESUME 2
idiom pick up the thread again

pickup n syn see ARREST
rel booking

picky adj syn see NICE 1

picnic n syn see SNAP 1

pictorial adj 1 consisting of or relating to pictures <a collection of *pictorial* materials>
syn graphic, iconographic, illustrational, illustrative, illustratory, pictoric
rel photographic, pictographic
2 syn see GRAPHIC 1

pictoric adj syn see PICTORIAL 1

picture n 1 syn see REPRESENTATION
2 syn see IMAGE 1
3 syn see MOVIE

picture vb syn see REPRESENT 1
rel draw

picture show n syn see MOVIE

picturesque adj syn see GRAPHIC 1

piddling adj syn see PETTY 2

pie n syn see SNAP 1

piece n 1 syn see PART 1
2 syn see SNACK

pièce de résistance n syn see SHOWPIECE

piecemeal adv syn see GRADUALLY

piecemeal adj syn see GRADUAL

‖pie-eyed adj syn see INTOXICATED 1

piepoudre n syn see PEDDLER

pier n 1 syn see WHARF
rel pierage, wharfage
2 syn see PILLAR 1

pierce vb 1 syn see CUT 1
rel penetrate, perforate
2 syn see PENETRATE 2
rel run through

piercing adj 1 syn see SHARP 8
2 syn see LOUD 1
3 syn see ACUTE 4

pietistic adj syn see DEVOUT
rel reverencing, reverential

piety n syn see FIDELITY 1
rel docility, obedience; fervor, passion, zeal; holiness, sanctity

piffle n syn see NONSENSE 2

piffling adj syn see PETTY 2

‖pig n 1 syn see WANTON
2 syn see POLICEMAN

pigeon n syn see FOOL 3

pigeon vb syn see DUPE

pigeonhole *n* 1 *syn* see CUBBYHOLE
  2 *syn* see CLASS 1
  rel niche, slot

pigeonhole *vb syn* see ASSORT
  rel identify, label, name; place, rank, rate;
  catalog; break down, subdivide

pigeon house *n syn* see DOVECOTE

pigeonry *n syn* see DOVECOTE

pigheaded *adj syn* see OBSTINATE
  idiom not to be moved (*or* budged)

pigment *n syn* see COLOR 6

pigpen *n syn* see STY 1

pigsty *n syn* see STY 1

piked *adj syn* see POINTED 1

piker *n syn* see VAGABOND

piker *n syn* see MISER

pilaster *n syn* see PILLAR 1

pile *n* 1 a quantity of things heaped or
  stacked together <a *pile* of dirty clothes>
  syn bank, ‖bing, cock, drift, heap, hill,
  mass, mound, mountain, mow, pyramid,
  rick, ‖rickle, ‖ruck, shock, stack, stockpile,
  windrow
  rel barrow, pyre, tumulus; ‖dess, haycock,
  hayrick, haystack; accumulation, aggregate,
  aggregation, amassment, assemblage, collection, conglomeration, glomeration, hoard,
  jumble
  2 *syn* see MUCH
  3 *syn* see EDIFICE
  4 *syn* see FORTUNE 4
  idiom a pile of money

pile *vb* 1 *syn* see HEAP 1
  2 *syn* see LOAD 3

pile (in) *vb syn* see RETIRE 4

pile (out) *vb syn* see ROLL OUT
  idiom ‖get the lead out, shake a leg, ‖shake it
  out

pile *n syn* see DOWN

pileous *adj syn* see HAIRY 1
  con bare; pileless

pile up *vb syn* see SHIPWRECK 1

pileup *n syn* see CRASH 3

pilfer *vb syn* see STEAL 1

pilferer *n syn* see THIEF

pilgarlic *n syn* see LAUGHINGSTOCK

‖**pill** *n* 1 *syn* see CIGARETTE
  2 *syn* see BORE

pillage *vb* 1 *syn* see RAVAGE
  rel encroach, invade, trespass; appropriate,
  arrogate, confiscate, usurp
  idiom lay waste
  2 *syn* see STEAL 1

pillager *n syn* see MARAUDER

pillar *n* 1 a firm upright support for a superstructure <stone *pillars* supported the ceil-
  ing>
  syn column, pier, pilaster
  rel prop; pedestal; post
  2 *syn* see MAINSTAY

pilose *adj syn* see HAIRY 1

pilot *n* 1 *syn* see LEADER 1
  2 one who flies or is qualified to fly an air-
  plane <jet *pilots*>
  syn airman, aviator, birdman, flier, fly-boy

rel aerialist

pilot *vb* 1 *syn* see GUIDE
  2 *syn* see DRIVE 5

pimp *n* 1 a man who solicits for a prostitute,
  lives off her earnings, and often lives with
  her <after dark, the *pimp* appeared on the
  street seeking clients for his girls>
  syn bully, ‖cadet, ‖easy rider, fancy man,
  ‖mack, macquereau, pander
  rel procurer; white slaver
  ‖**2** *syn* see INFORMER

‖**pimp** *vb syn* see INFORM 3

pimping *adj syn* see PETTY 2

pimple *n syn* see ABSCESS
  rel ‖plouk

pimple *vb syn* see SPOT 2

pin *n syn* see BROOCH

pinch *vb* 1 *syn* see EXTORT 1
  2 *syn* see STEAL 1
  3 *syn* see ARREST 2
  4 *syn* see SCRIMP

pinch *n* 1 *syn* see JUNCTURE 2
  2 *syn* see THEFT
  3 *syn* see ARREST

pinchbeck *adj syn* see COUNTERFEIT

pinched *adj syn* see HAGGARD
  con stalwart, stout, strong, sturdy; healthy,
  robust

pinch hitter *n syn* see SUBSTITUTE 1

pinching *adj syn* see STINGY

pinchpenny *adj syn* see STINGY

‖**pindling** *adj syn* see IRRITABLE

pine *vb syn* see LONG
  rel brood, fret, mope; grieve, mourn; agonize

pinhead *n syn* see DUNCE

pinhead *adj syn* see STUPID 1

pinheaded *adj syn* see STUPID 1

pink *n syn* see BLUSH

pinken *vb syn* see BLUSH

Pinkerton *n syn* see PRIVATE DETECTIVE

pin money *n syn* see POCKET MONEY

pinnacle *n syn* see APEX 2

pinpoint *vb syn* see IDENTIFY

pint-size *adj syn* see TINY

pioneer *adj syn* see FIRST 2
  rel pilot

pious *adj syn* see DEVOUT
  rel priestlike, priestly
  ant impious

pip *vb* ‖**1** *syn* see DEFEAT 2
  2 *syn* see DIE 1

‖**pip** *n syn* ‖DILLY, ‖corker, crackerjack,
  daisy, dandy, humdinger, jim-dandy,
  ‖lalapalooza, ‖lulu, nifty

pipe *n* 1 *syn* see CASK
  ‖**2** *syn* see PIPE DREAM
  3 *syn* see SNAP 1

pipe *vb* ‖**1** *syn* see CRY 2
  2 *syn* see CONDUCT 4

‖**piped** *adj syn* see INTOXICATED 1

pipe down *vb syn* see SHUT UP 2

pipe dream *n* an illusory or fantastic plan or
  hope <*pipe dreams* of universal peace>
  syn bubble, chimera, dream, fantasy (*or*
  phantasy), illusion, ‖pipe, rainbow
  rel expectation, hope, prospect

pipeline *n* a person through whom information is transmitted <she was his news *pipeline* from the mayor's office>

---

syn synonym(s)   *rel* related word(s)
ant antonym(s)   *con* contrasted word(s)
idiom idiomatic equivalent(s)
‖ use limited; if in doubt, see a dictionary

syn channel, conduit
rel grapevine; origin, source, wellspring; supplier; connection, contact

piping *adj syn* see ACUTE 4

‖**pipped** *adj syn* see INTOXICATED 1

pippin *n syn* ‖DILLY, ‖corker, crackerjack, dandy, ‖dinger, ‖doozer, humdinger, jim= dandy, ‖lalapalooza, ‖pip

piquant *adj syn* see PUNGENT
rel high-flavored, well-flavored; appetizing, sparkling
con inane, jejune
ant banal

pique *n syn* see OFFENSE 2
rel annoyance, irk, irking, vexation; exasperation, irritation, provocation

pique *vb* 1 *syn* see IRRITATE
2 *syn* see PROVOKE 4
rel prick, punch; ignite
3 *syn* see PRIDE

pirate *n* a robber on the high seas <little boys dreaming of sailing as *pirates*>
syn buccaneer, corsair, freebooter, picaroon, rover, sea dog, sea robber, sea rover, sea wolf
rel viking; privateer; looter, marauder, pillager, plunderer, raider

‖**pirl** *vb syn* see SPIN 1

‖**piroot** *vb syn* see SNOOP

pirouette *vb syn* see SPIN 1

pishposh *n syn* see NONSENSE 2

‖**piss away** *vb syn* see WASTE 2

‖**pissed** *adj* 1 *syn* see ANGRY
2 *syn* see INTOXICATED 1

‖**pissed off** *adj syn* see ANGRY

pit *n* ‖1 *syn* see GRAVE
2 *syn* see HELL

pit *vb syn* see OPPOSE 1

pitch *vb* 1 *syn* see THROW 1
rel hoist, raise; move
2 *syn* see THROW 2
‖3 *syn* see PLANT 1
4 *syn* see FALL 2
idiom take a pitch
5 *syn* see PLUNGE 2
rel drop, fall, sink
6 *syn* see TOSS 2
7 *syn* see SEESAW

pitch *n syn* see SPIEL
rel persuasion

pitch–black *adj syn* see BLACK 1

pitch–dark *adj syn* see BLACK 1

pitched *adj syn* see INCLINED 3

pitch in *vb* 1 to set about doing something energetically <had a lot to do and decided to *pitch in*>
syn buckle (down), fall to, jump (in *or* into), set to, wade (in *or* into)
rel attack, tackle; launch, tee off; begin, commence, start (off *or* out *or* up)
idiom fall to it, fall to work, get busy (*or* cracking), get down to it, get going, get (*or* have) with it, go to it, hop (*or* jump) to it
con dally, dawdle, procrastinate, stall; vacillate
2 *syn* see CONTRIBUTE 1

pitching *adj syn* see INCLINED 3

pitchy *adj syn* see BLACK 1

piteous *adj syn* see PITIFUL 1

rel beseeching, entreating, imploring, supplicating; doleful, dolorous, melancholy, plaintive; ruined

pitfall *n* a hidden or obscure source of danger, error, or harm <*pitfalls* that trap the unwary investigator>
syn booby trap, deadfall, mousetrap, springe, trapfall
rel danger, hazard, peril, risk; cobweb, entanglement, mesh(es), toil(s), web; bait, lure, snare, trap

pith *n* 1 *syn* see ESSENCE 2
rel center, focus, nucleus; meaning, meaningfulness
2 *syn* see SUBSTANCE 2
idiom the long and (the) short
3 *syn* see CENTER 3
rel fulcrum; hub
4 *syn* see IMPORTANCE

pithy *adj* being rich in meaning and tersely cogent in expression <a *pithy* summary>
syn compact, epigrammatic, marrowy, meaty; *compare* CONCISE
rel brief, concise, lean, short, short and sweet, succinct; crisp, curt, terse; effective, forceful; meaningful, significant, substantial
idiom brief and to the point, down to brass tacks, right to the point
con flatulent, inflated, tumid, turgid; prolix, verbose, wordy
ant diffuse

pitiable *adj* 1 *syn* see PITIFUL 1
2 *syn* see CONTEMPTIBLE
rel miserable, wretched; deplorable, lamentable

pitiful *adj* 1 arousing or deserving pity <*pitiful* refugees driven from their homes>
syn commiserable, pathetic, piteous, pitiable, poor, rueful
rel affecting, moving, touching; miserable, woeful, wretched; heartrending
2 *syn* see CONTEMPTIBLE

pitiless *adj* devoid of or unmoved by pity <a *pitiless* concentration camp guard>
syn merciless, unmerciful, unpitying; *compare* UNFEELING 2
rel coldhearted, hardhearted, heartless, ironhearted, marblehearted, stony, stonyhearted, uncompassionate, unfeeling; barbarous, brutal, cruel, cutthroat, inhumane, savage
idiom lacking bowels of compassion, without an ounce of pity
con compassionate, humane, sympathetic; clement, merciful; tender, warmhearted
ant pitying

pittance *n* a small, often barely sufficient amount or allowance <a *pittance* of an education> <worked for a mere *pittance*>
syn dribble, driblet, ‖scrimption
rel bit, mite, scrap, smidgen, trace; inadequacy, insufficiency
idiom a drop in the bucket, cheeseparings and candle ends
con abundance, opulence, plenty, wealth

pity *n* sympathetic feeling for one suffering, distressed, or unhappy <felt the deepest *pity* for the prisoners>
syn commiseration, compassion, rue, ruth, sympathy

rel dejection, distress, melancholy, sadness, sorrow; charity, clemency, lenity, mercy
con contempt, disdain, disgust, scorn

pity *vb syn* see COMPASSIONATE

pivot *vb syn* see TURN 6

pivotal *adj syn* see CENTRAL 1
rel essential, vital; momentous; capital, principal

pixie *n* 1 *syn* see FAIRY
2 *syn* see SCAMP

pixie *adj syn* see PLAYFUL 1

pixieish *adj syn* see PLAYFUL 1

pixilated *adj* 1 *syn* see PLAYFUL 1
2 *syn* see INTOXICATED 1

placard *n syn* see POSTER

placard *vb syn* see POST

placate *vb syn* see PACIFY
rel comfort; tranquilize
idiom lay the dust
con anger, incense, infuriate, madden; excite, pique, provoke, stimulate
ant enrage

place *n* 1 the portion of space occupied by or chosen for something <the *place* where we'll meet>
syn location, locus, point, position, site, situation, spot, station, where
rel district, locality, vicinity; area, region, tract, zone; field, province, territory
2 *syn* see STATUS 1
3 *syn* see JOB 2

place *vb* 1 *syn* see SET 1
2 *syn* see ESTIMATE 3
3 *syn* see IDENTIFY
rel know, tell; nail, peg
idiom put one's finger on

placed *adj syn* see SITUATED
ant displaced

placid *adj* 1 *syn* see CALM 1
rel irenic, peaceful, serene, unagitated, unstirring
ant roiled
2 *syn* see CALM 2
rel detached, inexcitable, unmoved
con fidgety, jittery, jumpy, skittery; agitated
ant choleric

plague *n* 1 an epidemic disease causing a high mortality rate <smallpox finally ceased to be a *plague* in those nations>
syn curse, pestilence, scourge
rel infestation, invasion; affliction, disease; epidemic; ravage
2 *syn* see ANNOYANCE 3
rel bane, curse
3 *syn* see EPIDEMIC

plague *vb syn* see WORRY 1
rel chafe, gall; badger, bait, hassle, hector, hound, ride; afflict, torment

plain *adj* 1 free from all ostentation or superficial embellishment <just give the *plain* facts>
syn discreet, dry, homely, inelaborate, modest, simple, unadorned, unbeautified, undecorated, unelaborate, unembellished,

unembroidered, ungarnished, unornamented, unostentatious, unpretentious
rel muted, restrained; austere, bald, bare, severe, spartan, stark, unluxurious; homespun
con adorned, beautified, elaborate, embellished, embroidered, exaggerated; high≈flown, ostentatious, pretentious; flamboyant, rococo
ant rich
2 *syn* see STRAIGHT 3
3 *syn* see CLEAR 5
rel broad, unmistakable; legible
ant abstruse
4 *syn* see FRANK
rel unfeigned; abrupt
idiom plain and open
5 lacking allure without being positively ugly <a *plain* woman, drably dressed>
syn homely, unalluring, unattractive, unbeauteous, unbeautiful, uncomely, unhandsome, unpretty
rel plain-featured; inelegant; ordinary, plain Jane, unremarkable; ill-favored
idiom not much for looks, not much to look at, short on looks
con alluring, attractive, beautiful, comely, handsome; elegant; striking; knockout, sensational
6 *syn* see ORDINARY 1

plainclothesman *n syn* see DETECTIVE

plain dealing *adj syn* see STRAIGHTFORWARD 2

plain Jane *adj syn* see ORDINARY 1

plainness *n syn* see CLARITY
ant abstruseness

plainspoken *adj syn* see FRANK

plaintive *adj syn* see MELANCHOLY 2
rel deploring, lamenting, wailing; piteous, pitiful; sad, saddening

plan *n* 1 a method devised for making or doing something or attaining an end <each company had a *plan* for increasing profits>
syn blueprint, design, game plan, project, scheme, strategy
rel conception, idea, notion; ground plan, projection, projet; intent, intention, platform, purpose; means, method, way
idiom course (or plan) of action
2 *syn* see INTENTION
rel policy
3 *syn* see ORDER 8

plan *vb* 1 *syn* see DESIGN 3
2 to formulate a plan for arranging, realizing, or achieving something <*planned* next year's program>
syn arrange, blueprint, cast, chart, design, devise, ‖dope out, project; *compare* DESIGN 3
rel contemplate, meditate; cut out, draft, outline, sketch; figure (out), think (out); formulate, work out; organize
3 *syn* see INTEND 2
idiom be planning (or counting) on, have all intentions of, have every intention of

planate *n syn* see LEVEL

plane *vb syn* see EVEN 1

plane *adj syn* see LEVEL

planet *n, used with the syn* see EARTH 1

planetary *adj* 1 *syn* see HUGE

---

syn synonym(s)   *rel* related word(s)
ant antonym(s)   *con* contrasted word(s)
idiom idiomatic equivalent(s)
‖ use limited; if in doubt, see a dictionary

2 *syn* see UNIVERSAL 2

plangent *adj syn* see RESONANT

plant *vb* **1** to put or set into the ground for growth <*plant* corn>
syn ‖pitch, put in, seed, sow
rel drill; broadcast, dust, scatter; seed down
con crop, gather, harvest, reap
2 *syn* see HIDE
3 *syn* see BURY 1

plant *n syn* see FACTORY

plash *vb syn* see SPLASH

plaster *vb syn* see SMEAR 1

‖**plastered** *adj syn* see INTOXICATED 1

plastic *adj* susceptible of being modified in form or nature <the *plastic* quality of modeling clay>
syn adaptable, ductile, malleable, moldable, pliable, pliant, supple
rel elastic, flexible, resilient, supple, workable; impressionable, influenceable, suggestible, susceptible; amenable, bending, giving, tractable, yielding
con inflexible, rigid, stiff; accepted, customary, prevailing, set, standard, wonted

plat *n syn* see LOT 3

plateau *n* a usually extensive level land area raised sharply above adjacent land on at least one side <the *plateaus* of central Bolivia>
syn table, tableland, upland
rel mesa
con dale, glen, vale, valley; bottom, bottomland, lowland

platitude *n syn* see COMMONPLACE
rel inanity, insipidity, vapidity; mawkishness, sentimentality

platoon *n syn* see GROUP 3

plaudit *n, usu* **plaudits** *pl syn* see APPLAUSE
rel kudos

plausibility *n syn* see VERISIMILITUDE

plausible *adj syn* see BELIEVABLE
rel likely, possible, probable; presumable
con impossible, improbable, unlikely
ant implausible

play *n* **1** activity engaged in for amusement <children need periods of work and *play*>
syn disport, diversion, fun, recreation, sport
rel amusement, entertainment; frolic, gambol, romp; delectation, delight, enjoyment, pleasure
con business, duty, obligation; labor; drudgery
ant work
2 *syn* see FUN 1
rel sportiveness
ant earnest
3 *syn* see TRICK 1
4 *syn* see USE 1
5 *syn* see ROOM 3

play *vb* **1** to engage in an activity for amusement or recreation <*played* outside for hours>
syn disport, recreate, sport
rel amuse, divert, engage, entertain; frolic, gambol, rollick, romp
con labor, toil, travail; drudge, fag, slave
ant work
2 *syn* see FIDDLE 1
3 *syn* see TREAT 2
4 *syn* see MANIPULATE 2

5 *syn* see ACT 1
6 *syn* see GAMBLE 1

play (around) *vb syn* see PHILANDER

play (down) *vb syn* see SOFT-PEDAL
rel restrain; mute, soften
ant play (up)

play (off) *vb syn* see OPPOSE 1

play (up) *vb syn* see EMPHASIZE
idiom make a (big) production of
ant play (down)

playact *vb syn* see ACT 1

playactor *n syn* see ACTOR 1

player *n syn* see ACTOR 1

playful *adj* **1** given to or characterized by play, jests, or tricks <in a *playful* mood>
syn antic, coltish, elvish, frisky, frolicsome, gamesome, impish, kittenish, larkish, ‖mischiefful, mischievous, pixie, pixieish, pixilated, prankful, prankish, pranky, puckish, roguish, sportive, waggish, wicked
rel gay, lighthearted, whimsical; dashing, larking, lively, sprightly; blithe, jocund, jolly, jovial, merry; gleeful, hilarious, mirthful
idiom as playful as a kitten (*or* colt), feeling one's oats
con grim, stern, stolid; grave, serious
2 *syn* see ANTIC 2

‖**play–pretty** *n syn* see TOY 2

plaything *n syn* see TOY 2

playwright *n* one who writes plays <a famous Broadway *playwright*>
syn dramatist, dramatizer, dramaturge
rel librettist; scenarist

plaza *n syn* see COMMON 2

plea *n* **1** *syn* see EXCUSE 1
rel extenuation, mitigation, palliation; apology; out; vindication
2 *syn* see PRAYER
rel overture; call, cry
idiom solemn entreaty (*or* plea)

plead *vb syn* see BEG

pleasance *n syn* see AMENITY 1

pleasant *adj* **1** highly acceptable to the mind or senses <a *pleasant* personality><a *pleasant* respite>
syn agreeable, congenial, favorable, good, grateful, gratifying, nice, pleasing, pleasurable, pleasureful, welcome
rel cheerful, cheering, cheery, glad, joyful, joyous; alluring, attractive, charming, pretty; convivial, engaging
con displeasing, distasteful; harsh; obnoxious, repellent, repelling, repugnant, repulsive
ant unpleasant
2 *syn* see FAIR 2

pleasantness *n syn* see AMENITY 1
rel goodness, niceness
ant unpleasantness

please *vb* **1** *syn* see WILL
2 to give or be a source of pleasure to <her work *pleased* him>
syn arride, delectate, delight, gladden, gratify, happify, pleasure
rel content, satisfy, suit; amuse, tickle, titillate; regale, rejoice; overjoy
con vex; annoy; anger
ant displease
3 *syn* see SUIT 6

pleasing *adj syn* see PLEASANT 1
rel satisfactory, suitable; enchanting, winning; adorable, darling, delightful
ant displeasing, repellent

pleasurable *adj syn* see PLEASANT 1
ant unpleasurable

pleasure *n* **1** *syn* see WILL 1
2 the agreeable emotion accompanying the expectation, acquisition, or possession of something good or desirable <the *pleasures* and pains of growing up>
syn delectation, delight, enjoyment, fruition, joy, joyance; *compare* ENJOYMENT 1
rel bliss, felicity, happiness; kick, thrill
con vexation; annoyance; anger; affliction, distress, sorrow, trouble
ant displeasure
3 *syn* see ENJOYMENT 1
ant displeasure

pleasure *vb syn* see PLEASE 2

pleasure dome *n syn* see RESORT 3

pleasureful *adj syn* see PLEASANT 1

pleasuremonger *n syn* see HEDONIST

pleb *n* **plebs** *pl syn* see COMMONALTY

plebeian *adj syn* see IGNOBLE 1
ant patrician

plebeians *n pl syn* see COMMONALTY
ant patricians

plebs *n* **plebes** *pl syn* see COMMONALTY
rel peasantry, peasants
ant patricians, patriciate

pledge *n* something given or held as a sign of another's good faith or intentions <the new school is the *pledge* given by the community to its children>
syn earnest, pawn, security, token, warrant; *compare* GUARANTEE 1, PROMISE
rel bail, bond, guarantee, guaranty, surety, warranty; promise, word; oath, vow
2 *syn* see WORD 8

pledge *vb* **1** *syn* see PAWN
2 *syn* see DRINK 2
3 *syn* see PROMISE 1
rel bind, tie; commit, confide, consign, entrust
idiom give (*or* make) a solemn pledge, pledge one's honor
4 *syn* see VOW

plenteous *adj syn* see PLENTIFUL
rel full, hearty; fruitful, galore, prolific; luxurious, opulent, sumptuous; lavish, prodigal, profuse, profusive; rampant, rife

plentiful *adj* being more than sufficient without being excessive <a *plentiful* harvest>
syn abundant, ample, bounteous, bountiful, copious, generous, liberal, plenteous, plenty
rel enough, sufficient; fulsome, rich, unstinted; excessive, extravagant, overabundant, overflowing, superabundant; abounding, bumper, bursting, swarming, swimming, teeming
con deficient, exiguous, meager, skimpy; inadequate, insufficient
ant scant, scanty

plenty *n syn* see MUCH
rel abundance, cornucopia

plenty *adj syn* see PLENTIFUL

pleonasm *n syn* see VERBIAGE 1

plethora *n syn* see EXCESS 1
rel much, plenty; many; deluge, flood

pliable *adj syn* see PLASTIC
rel manipulable, manipulatable
con unadaptable, unflexible, unmalleable, unpliant
ant unpliable

pliant *adj syn* see PLASTIC
rel spongy
ant unpliant

plica *n syn* see WRINKLE

plight *vb syn* see VOW
idiom plight one's honor

plight *n syn* see PROMISE

plight *n syn* see PREDICAMENT
rel quandary

plighted *adj syn* see ENGAGED 2

plink *vb syn* see TINKLE 1

plod *vb* **1** to walk laboriously and heavily <slowly *plodded* across the sodden field>
syn footslog, ‖plodge, plunther, slog, slop, stodge, toil, ‖trash, trudge; *compare* TRAMP 1
rel tramp, trample, tromp; stamp, stomp, stump; flounder, wallow
2 *syn* see DRUDGE
idiom plug away at it

plodding *adj syn* see DULL 9

‖plodge *vb syn* see PLOD 1

plot *n* **1** *syn* see LOT 3
2 a secret plan for accomplishing a usually evil or unlawful end <an assassination *plot*>
syn cabal, conspiracy, covin, intrigue, machination, practice, scheme
rel design, plan; connivance, conniving; collusion, complicity; contraption, contrivance, device; artifice, maneuver, ruse, stratagem, trick

plot *vb* to work out a plan especially for something unlawful or wrong <*plotted* the overthrow of the government>
syn cogitate, ‖collogue, collude, connive, conspire, contrive, devise, intrigue, machinate, scheme (out)
rel lay; brew, concoct, cook (up), hatch, set up; finagle, maneuver

plow *vb* to cut into and work the surface of (soil) <*plow* a field>
syn break, plow up, turn, turn over
rel cultivate, till; fallow; ‖backset; furrow, list, ridge, trench; harrow, rake

plow up *vb syn* see PLOW
rel plow out

ploy *n syn* see TRICK 1

pluck *n syn* see COURAGE

‖plucked *adj syn* see BRAVE 1

plucky *adj syn* see BRAVE 1
idiom full of pluck (*or* spunk)
con feeble, weak
ant pluckless

plug *n syn* see PUFF 3

plug *vb* **1** *syn* see FILL 1
rel pack; cork
2 *syn* see PROMOTE 3

plugging *n syn* see WORK 2

plug-ugly *n syn* see TOUGH

---

syn synonym(s)   *rel* related word(s)
ant antonym(s)   *con* contrasted word(s)
idiom idiomatic equivalent(s)
‖ use limited; if in doubt, see a dictionary

plum *n syn* see REWARD
  rel catch, find
‖**plumb** *adv syn* see WELL 3
plumb *vb syn* see SOUND
plumb *adj syn* see VERTICAL
plumbless *adj syn* see BOTTOMLESS 2
  con plumbable
‖**plumb-line** *n syn* see SOUND
plumbness *n syn* see VERTICALITY
plume *vb syn* see PRIDE
plummet *vb* to decrease suddenly and
  sharply in financial value or price <the stock
  plummeted 60 points when the story broke>
  syn dip, drop, fall, nose-dive, plunge, skid,
  tumble
  rel decline, decrease, descend, sink; dump;
  precipitate; collapse, crash
  idiom take a sudden downturn (*or* downtrend)
  con increase; rise; shoot up
  ant skyrocket, soar
plummetless *adj syn* see BOTTOMLESS 2
plump *adj syn* see ROTUND 2
  rel fleshy, portly
  idiom plump as a partridge
  ant skinny
plumpish *adj syn* see ROTUND 2
  idiom like a butterball
plumpy *adj syn* see ROTUND 2
plunder *vb syn* see ROB 1
plunder *n* 1 *syn* see SPOIL
  ‖2 *syn* see PERSONAL EFFECTS
plunderage *n syn* see SPOIL
plunderer *n syn* see MARAUDER
plunge *vb* 1 *syn* see THRUST 1
  2 to thrust or cast oneself or something into
  or as if into deep water <*plunged* into the
  crowd>
  syn burst, dive, drive, lunge, pitch,
  ‖splunge; *compare* RUSH 1
  rel dip, immerse, submerge; plump, plunk;
  propel, push, shove, thrust; boil, charge,
  fling, rush, tear
  idiom plunge headlong
  con ease, glide, slide, slip
  3 *syn* see FALL 2
  idiom take a plunge
  4 *syn* see PLUMMET
  idiom drop like a rock, take a downward
  plunge
plunther *vb syn* see PLOD 1
plus *n syn* see EXCESS 2
plus *vb syn* see INCREASE 1
plush *adj syn* see LUXURIOUS 3
  idiom fit for the gods
plushy *adj syn* see LUXURIOUS 3
plutonian *adj* 1 *syn* see INFERNAL 1
  2 *syn* see INFERNAL 2
plutonic *adj* 1 *syn* see INFERNAL 1
  2 *syn* see INFERNAL 2
ply *vb* 1 *syn* see HANDLE 2
  rel exercise; function
  2 *syn* see EXERT
pneuma *n syn* see SOUL 1
pneumatic *adj syn* see AIRY 1
pocket *n syn* see DEAD END
pocket *vb* 1 *syn* see STEAL 1
  2 *syn* see ACCEPT 2
pocket *adj* 1 *syn* see TINY
  2 *syn* see CONDENSED

3 *syn* see FINANCIAL
pocket edition *n syn* see MODEL 1
pocket money *n* money for small personal
  expenses or incidentals <he had spent all his
  pocket money on candy and snacks>
  syn pin money, spending money
  rel petty cash; change, small change
  con fortune, resources; income
pocket-size *adj syn* see TINY
pococurante *adj syn* see INDIFFERENT 2
pod *n* 1 *syn* see HULL
  2 *syn* see POTBELLY
podex *n syn* see BUTTOCKS
podgy *adj syn* see ROTUND 2
Podunk *n syn* see BURG
poem *n* a particular example of metrical
  writing <recited a *poem* by Robert Frost>
  syn poesy, poetry, rhyme, rune, verse
poesy *n* 1 *syn* see POEM
  2 *syn* see POETRY 1
poet *n* a writer of verse <a *poet* to stir men's
  souls>
  syn bard, muse, Parnassian
  rel jongleur, rhapsodist, trouvère, trouveur;
  balladeer, elegist, idyllist, lyricist, lyrist,
  odist, satirist, sonneteer, sonnetist
poetaster *n* a writer of mediocre or inferior
  verse <*poetasters* who churn out tasteless
  verse>
  syn balladmonger, bardlet, bardling, poeticule, poetling, rhymer, rhymester, verseman, versemonger, verser, versesmith, versificator, versifier
poeticule *n syn* see POETASTER
poetling *n syn* see POETASTER
poetry *n* 1 metrical language or writing
  <studied the *poetry* of Milton>
  syn poesy, rhyme, song, verse
  2 *syn* see POEM
poignance *n syn* see PATHOS
poignancy *n syn* see PATHOS
poignant *adj* 1 *syn* see PUNGENT
  ant dull
  2 *syn* see MOVING 2
  rel agitating, disturbing, perturbing
point *n* 1 one unitary part of a whole made up
  of two or more parts <listened to each *point*
  of his opponent's argument>
  syn article, detail, element, item, particular,
  thing; *compare* ELEMENT 2
  rel characteristic, feature, trait; constituent,
  material, part; circumstantial, circumstanti-
  ality
  con aggregate, sum, total, whole
  2 *syn* see CHARACTERISTIC 1
  3 the quality of an utterance that arouses
  interest and produces an effect <a book that
  lacks *point*>
  syn cogency, effectiveness, force, punch,
  validity, validness
  rel appositeness, convincement, significance, suggestiveness; appeal, attraction,
  charm, fascination, interest
  4 *syn* see SUBJECT 2
  5 *syn* see TIP
  6 *syn* see PLACE 1
  7 a particular limited and often critical interval of time <at that *point* he was inter-
  rupted>
  syn instant, juncture, moment

rel brink, threshold, verge
idiom point in time
8 *syn* see VERGE 2
9 a sharp or slender and tapering terminal part <the *point* of a sword>
syn apex, cusp, tip
rel awn, barb, jag, nib, prong, snag, spike, tag, tine
10 *syn* see PROMONTORY
11 a tiny mark or spot <saw a distant *point* of light>
syn dot, flyspeck, mote, speck
rel bit, fleck, iota, minim, mite, particle, scrap, tittle, trace
point *vb* **1** *syn* see PUNCTUATE
2 to tend to show something as probable <all signs *point* to an economic recovery>
syn hint, imply, indicate, suggest; *compare* SUGGEST 1
idiom lead one to expect, make (*or* give) promise of, offer a good prospect of
3 *syn* see DIRECT 2
point (out) *vb* *syn* see REFER 3
point (to) *vb* *syn* see TESTIFY 1
pointed *adj* **1** tapering to a thin tip <a *pointed* rock>
syn acicular, aciculate, acuminate, acuminous, acute, cuspidate, mucronate, peaked, peaky, piked, pointy, sharp
con dull, rounded
ant blunt
2 *syn* see NOTICEABLE
pointer *n* *syn* see TIP
pointful *adj* *syn* see RELEVANT
pointless *adj* *syn* see SENSELESS 5
‖**pointsman** *n* *syn* see POLICEMAN
pointy *adj* *syn* see POINTED 1
poise *vb* **1** *syn* see STABILIZE
rel back, support, uphold
con agitate, disturb, upset; overthrow, overturn, subvert
2 *syn* see HANG 3
poise *n* **1** *syn* see BALANCE 1
2 *syn* see TACT
rel aplomb, assurance, confidence, self‑possession; calmness, serenity, tranquillity; dignity, elegance, grace
poised *adj* *syn* see CALM 2
poison *n* something that harms, interferes with, or destroys the activity, progress, or welfare of something else <the negative publicity was *poison* for her political ambitions>
syn bane, contagion, venom, virus
rel adulteration, contamination, corruption, sophistication
con catholicon, elixir, panacea
ant antidote
poison *vb* *syn* see DEBASE 1
poison *adj* *syn* see POISONOUS
poisonous *adj* having the properties or effect of poison <*poisonous* propaganda>
syn mephitic, poison, toxic, toxicant, venomous, virulent
rel miasmal, miasmatic, miasmic, pestilent, pestilential; deadly, fatal, lethal, mortal;

baneful, deleterious, detrimental, nocuous, noxious, pernicious
con corrective, countervailing, emendatory, healing, remedial
ant antidotal
‖**poke** *n* *syn* see BAG 1
poke *vb* **1** to thrust something into so as to stir up, urge on, or attract attention <he *poked* the man in front of him to get his attention>
syn dig, jab, jog, nudge, prod, punch
rel push, shove, thrust; arouse, awaken, rouse, stir; excite, galvanize, provoke, quicken, stimulate
2 *syn* see SNOOP
3 *syn* see DELAY 2
4 *syn* see BULGE
poke *n* **1** a quick thrust with or as if with the hand <gave him a *poke* in the ribs with my finger>
syn dig, jab, punch, stab
rel bunt, butt; boost, push, shove
2 *syn* see CUFF
3 *syn* see DUNCE
poker‑faced *adj* **1** *syn* see SERIOUS 1
2 *syn* see NEUTRAL
‖**pokey** *n* *syn* see JAIL
poky *adj* *syn* see DULL 9
polar *adj* *syn* see OPPOSITE
polemical *adj* *syn* see CONTENTIOUS 2
polestar *n* *syn* see CENTER 2
police *n* *syn* see POLICEMAN
‖**police constable** *n* *syn* see POLICEMAN
policeman *n* a member of a police force <ask the *policeman* for directions>
syn ‖bluebottle, bluecoat, ‖bobby, ‖bull, ‖constable, cop, ‖copper, Dogberry, flat‑foot, ‖fuzz, ‖gendarme, gumshoe, ‖harness bull (*or* cop), ‖heat, John Law, man, ‖nab, officer, ‖paddy, patrolman, peace officer, ‖peeler, ‖pig, ‖pointsman, police, ‖police constable, police officer, ‖rozzer, ‖trap
police officer *n* *syn* see POLICEMAN
policy *n* *syn* see COURSE 3
polish *vb* **1** to make smooth or glossy usually by friction <*polished* the silver>
syn buff, burnish, furbish, glance, glaze, gloss, rub, shine
rel brighten, scour, scrub
con roughen
2 to give an elegant finish to <attended classes to *polish* his manners>
syn perfect, refine, round, sleek, slick, smooth
rel better, improve, mend; brush up, furbish, touch up; mature, perfect
polish *n* **1** *syn* see LUSTER
2 *syn* see CULTURE
polished *adj* **1** *syn* see LUSTROUS 1
2 *syn* see SLEEK
3 *syn* see GENTEEL 1
polish off *vb* **1** *syn* see CONSUME 5
2 *syn* see EAT UP 1
polite *adj* *syn* see CIVIL 2
rel attentive, considerate, thoughtful
ant impolite
politic *adj* **1** *syn* see EXPEDIENT
rel astute, perspicacious, sagacious, shrewd
2 *syn* see TACTFUL
rel judicious, wise

---

syn synonym(s)   *rel* related word(s)
ant antonym(s)   *con* contrasted word(s)
idiom idiomatic equivalent(s)
‖ use limited; if in doubt, see a dictionary

polity n syn see COURSE 3

poll n syn see HEAD 1

pollard vb syn see TOP 1

polloi n syn see RABBLE 2

pollute vb 1 syn see CONTAMINATE 1
2 syn see CONTAMINATE 2

polluted adj 1 syn see IMPURE 3
2 syn see INTOXICATED 1

Pollyanna n syn see OPTIMIST
rel daydreamer, wishful thinker

Pollyannaish adj syn see OPTIMISTIC

Pollyannaism n syn see OPTIMISM

‖**polly-fox** vb syn see SKIRT 3

poltroon n syn see COWARD

poltroon adj syn see COWARDLY

poltroonish adj syn see COWARDLY

polyandrium n syn see CEMETERY

polychromatic adj syn see VARIEGATED

polychrome adj syn see VARIEGATED

polypragmatic adj syn see IMPERTINENT 2

polypragmatist n syn see BUSYBODY

pomp n syn see DISPLAY 2
rel ceremonial, ceremony, form, formality, liturgy, ritual

pom-pom girl n syn see PROSTITUTE

pompous adj 1 characterized by or exhibiting self-importance <a *pompous* old fool>
syn arrogant, bloated, important, magisterial, pontifical, puffy, self-important, stuffy, wiggy; compare EGOCENTRIC 2, PROUD 1
rel conceited, narcissistic, self-conceited, stuck-up, vain, vainglorious; affected, highfalutin, hoity-toity, pretentious; presumptuous, self-centered, selfish; flaunting, flossy, ostentatious
con natural, unaffected, unpretentious; humble, meek, plain, simple; modest, unassuming
2 syn see RHETORICAL

ponder vb 1 syn see CONSIDER 1
rel appraise, evaluate
2 to consider or examine attentively or deliberately <*ponder* the best way to do it>
syn ‖chaw, deliberate, meditate, mull (over), muse, revolve, roll, ruminate, turn over
rel cogitate, reason, reflect, speculate, think; brood, debate, dwell

pondering adj syn see THOUGHTFUL 1

ponderous adj 1 syn see HEAVY 1
rel substantial; burdensome, onerous, oppressive
2 lacking all lightness and grace <a *ponderous* prose style>
syn elephantine, heavy-footed, heavy-handed, uninspired
rel dreary, dry, dull, humdrum, lifeless, monotonous, pedestrian, plodding, stodgy, stuffy; arid, barren; flat, insipid, savorless, vapid; buckram, cardboard, muscle-bound, stiff, stilted, wooden
con sparkling, vivid; easy, natural, relaxed, supple, unlabored
3 syn see UNWIELDY

pontifical adj syn see POMPOUS 1

pontificate vb syn see LORD

pony n a literal translation of a foreign language text used especially surreptitiously by students in rendering a lesson <had his *pony* hidden in his lap>
syn crib, trot

‖**pooch** n syn see DOG 1

pooh n syn see RASPBERRY

pooh-bah n syn see NOTABLE 1

pooh-pooh n syn see RASPBERRY

pooh-pooh vb syn see DISMISS 5

pool n a small body of standing liquid <saw the *pool* of blood on the floor>
syn puddle

pool n 1 syn see POT 3
2 syn see SYNDICATE

poop n syn see FOOL 1

‖**poop** vb syn see EXHAUST

poor adj 1 lacking money or material possessions <they were so *poor* that the children had no winter coats>
syn beggared, broke, destitute, dirt poor, flat, fortuneless, impecunious, impoverished, indigent, low, necessitous, needy, penurious, poverty-stricken, stone-broke, stony, strapped, unprosperous
rel distressed, embarrassed, pinched, reduced, straitened; bankrupt, bankrupted, insolvent; hardscrabble; moneyless, penceless, penniless, unmoneyed; beggarly, down-and-out, pauperized; underprivileged
idiom down to one's bottom dollar, flat broke, hard up, in need, in penury, in rags, in want, on one's beam-ends, on one's uppers, out at elbows, out of pocket, poor as a church mouse, unable to keep the wolf from the door, unable to make ends meet
con affluent, comfortable, moneyed, ‖oofy, opulent, pecunious, prosperous, wealthy, well-fixed, well-heeled, well-off, well-to-do
ant rich
2 syn see MEAGER 2
3 syn see PITIFUL 1
4 syn see CHEAP 2
5 syn see INFERIOR 2
6 syn see BAD 1

poorly adj syn see UNWELL

poorness n syn see POVERTY 1

poor relation n syn see INFERIOR

poor-spirited adj syn see COWARDLY

pop vb 1 syn see STRIKE 2
‖2 syn see PAWN

pop n syn see FLING 1

pop n syn see FATHER 1

pop (in) vb syn see VISIT 2

popinjay n syn see FOP

pop off vb 1 syn see GO 2
2 syn see DIE 1

poppa n syn see FATHER 1

popping adj syn see BUSTLING

poppycock n syn see NONSENSE 2

popsy n syn see GIRL FRIEND 1

populace n syn see COMMONALTY

popular adj 1 syn see PUBLIC 4
2 syn see DEMOCRATIC
3 syn see CHEAP 1
4 syn see PREVAILING
5 syn see FAVORITE 2
ant unpopular
6 syn see WELL-KNOWN
ant unpopular

populate vb syn see INHABIT

populous adj syn see MANY

porcine adj syn see FAT 2

pork-barreling n syn see PATRONAGE 3

porky adj syn see FATTY 2

porose *adj syn* see PERMEABLE

porous *adj syn* see PERMEABLE

porridge *n syn* see MISCELLANY 1

port *n* 1 *syn* see HARBOR 3
2 *syn* see SHELTER 1

port *n syn* see BEARING 1

portable *adj* capable of being carried or moved about <a *portable* TV>
syn carriageable, portative, transportable
rel convenient, handy, manageable, wieldy
con fixed, stationary

portal *n syn* see DOOR 1

portative *adj syn* see PORTABLE

portend *vb* 1 *syn* see AUGUR 2
2 *syn* see FORETELL

portent *n* 1 *syn* see FORETOKEN
2 *syn* see WONDER 1

porter *n syn* see BEARER 2

portion *n* 1 *syn* see SHARE 1
2 *syn* see FATE
3 *syn* see PART 1
4 *syn* see RATION

portion *vb syn* see APPORTION 2

portion (out) *vb syn* see ADMINISTER 2

portly *adj syn* see FAT 2

portrait *n syn* see IMAGE 1

portraiture *n syn* see REPRESENTATION

portray *vb syn* see REPRESENT 1
rel photograph; copy, duplicate, reproduce

portrayal *n syn* see REPRESENTATION

pose *vb* 1 *syn* see OFFER 1
2 *syn* see PROPOSE 1
rel ask, query, question; confound, puzzle; baffle
3 to assume a particular physical posture <they *posed* for a family portrait>
syn posture, sit
rel peacock, strut
4 to assume an artificial or pretended attitude or character usually to deceive or impress <*posed* as a salesman>
syn attitudinize, masquerade, pass (as or for), pass off, posture; *compare* ACT 1
rel fake, feign, pretend, sham; profess, purport; grandstand, show off

pose *n* 1 *syn* see POSTURE 1
2 an adopted way of speaking or acting <his reticence is just a *pose*>
syn affectation, air(s), lugs, mannerism, prettyism
rel dog, prettiness; fake, pretense, pretension

pose *vb syn* see OFFER 1

pose *vb syn* see PUZZLE

posh *adj syn* see STYLISH

posit *vb syn* see PRESUPPOSE

posit *n syn* see ASSUMPTION 2

position *n* 1 a firmly held point of view or way of regarding something <took a conservative *position* on educational issues>
syn attitude, color, stance, stand; *compare* SIDE 4
rel belief, judgment, opinion, view; angle, slant, standpoint, viewpoint
2 *syn* see PLACE 1

3 *syn* see STATUS 1
4 *syn* see STATUS 2
5 *syn* see JOB 2

positioned *adj syn* see SITUATED

positive *adj* 1 expressed clearly and usually peremptorily <her answer was a *positive* no>
syn categorical, decided, definite, unequivocal
rel clear, unmistakable; decisive, emphatic, energetic, firm, forceful, forcible; explicit, express, specific, unambiguous
con irresolute, uncertain, undecided, unsure
2 *syn* see SURE 5
ant doubtful
3 not subject to being disputed or called in question <gave *positive* proof that he had been there>
syn certain, inarguable, incontestable, incontrovertible, indisputable, indubitable, irrebuttable, irrefutable, sure, uncontestable, uncontrovertible, undeniable, undisputable, undoubtable, unequivocal, unquestionable; *compare* DOWNRIGHT 2
rel assured, clear, decisive
con contestable, controvertible, debatable, disputable, doubtful, dubious, inconclusive, questionable, unconvincing
4 *syn* see UTTER
5 *syn* see ACTUAL 2
6 capable of being constructively applied <*positive* proposals for improving the city>
syn affirmative
rel practical, reasonable, sound
con impractical, unsound, unusable
ant negative
7 *syn* see RIGHT-HANDED

positively *adv syn* see EASILY 2

posture *n syn* see POSTURE 1

possess *vb* 1 *syn* see HAVE 1
2 *syn* see BEAR 3

possessed *adj syn* see CALM 2

possession *n* 1 *syn* see OWNERSHIP
2 **possessions** *pl* things one owns usually excluding real property and intangibles <lost all their *possessions* in the fire>
syn belongings, chattels, effects, goods, lares and penates, movables, things
rel appointments, fixtures, furnishings, furniture; accessories, appurtenances, baggage, ‖duds, duffle, equipment, impedimenta, paraphernalia, trappings, tricks; havings; tangibles

possessive *adj syn* see JEALOUS 1

possessor *n syn* see OWNER

possessorship *n syn* see OWNERSHIP

possessory *adj syn* see JEALOUS 1

possibilities *n pl syn* see POTENTIAL

possible *adj* 1 capable of being realized <a cure is still *possible*>
syn doable, feasible, practicable, viable, workable
rel advisable, expedient; achievable, attainable, available
con futile, hopeless, impracticable
ant impossible
2 *syn* see PROBABLE
rel dormant, latent, potential
3 *syn* see POTENTIAL 1

possibly *adv syn* see PERHAPS

post *vb* to affix to a usual place (as a wall) for public notices <*posted* the notice on the bulletin board>
syn placard, poster

post *vb syn* see INFORM 2

post *n syn* see JOB 2

post *n syn* see STATION

‖**post** *n syn* see AUTOPSY

poster *n* a notice or announcement for posting in a public place <nailed the *poster* to the side of the building>
syn affiche, bill, handbill, placard
rel advertisement, announcement, banner, broadside, notice, sign; billboard, signboard

poster *vb syn* see POST

posterior *adj* 1 *syn* see SUBSEQUENT 1
2 situated at or toward the back <the *posterior* part of the animal>
syn after, back, hind, hinder, hindmost, rear, retral
con fore, front
ant anterior

posterior *n* 1 *syn* see BACK 1
2 *syn* see BUTTOCKS

posterity *n syn* see OFFSPRING
ant ancestry

posthaste *adv syn* see FAST 2

posthaste *adj syn* see FAST 3

posthumous *adj* occurring after one's death <*posthumous* fame>
syn postmortal, postmortem, post-obit, post-obituary
rel delayed, late, retarded
con opportune, seasonable, timely
ant antemortem

postliminary *adj syn* see SUBSEQUENT 1

postmortal *adj syn* see POSTHUMOUS

postmortem *adj syn* see POSTHUMOUS
ant antemortem

postmortem *n syn* see AUTOPSY

postmortem examination *n syn* see AUTOPSY

post-obit *adj syn* see POSTHUMOUS

post-obituary *adj syn* see POSTHUMOUS

postpone *vb syn* see DEFER

posture *n* 1 the position or bearing of the body <erect *posture*>
syn attitude, carriage, pose, positure, stance
rel bearing, deportment, mien
2 *syn* see STATE 1
rel promptness, quickness, readiness

posture *vb* 1 *syn* see POSE 3
2 *syn* see POSE 4

posy *n* 1 *syn* see FLOWER 1
2 *syn* see BOUQUET 1
3 *syn* see ANTHOLOGY

pot *n* 1 *syn* see FORTUNE 4
2 *syn* see BET
3 the total of the bets at stake at one time <lost track of how much was in the *pot*>
syn jackpot, kitty, pool
4 *syn* see POTSHOT
‖5 *syn* see POTBELLY
6 *syn* see NOTABLE 1
7 *syn* see MARIJUANA

‖8 *syn* see TOILET

potable *adj* suitable for drinking <*potable* water>
syn drinkable
rel clean, fresh, pure, uncontaminated, unpolluted
con dirty, foul, impure, polluted, unclean
ant impotable

potable *n syn* see DRINK 1

potbelly *n* an enlarged, swollen, or protruding abdomen <he had the biggest *potbelly* we had ever seen>
syn bay window, corporation, paunch, pod, ‖pot

potency *n* 1 *syn* see POWER 4
ant impotence
2 *syn* see EFFICACY 1
3 *syn* see ENERGY 2
ant impotence

potent *adj* 1 *syn* see POWERFUL 2
ant impotent
2 *syn* see STRONG 3
3 able to copulate <a *potent* male>
syn virile
ant impotent

potential *adj* 1 existing in possibility <a *potential* site for the new factory>
syn possible
rel conceivable, imaginable, likely, plausible, probable, thinkable
idiom within the realm (*or* range) of possibility
con existent, extant; doubtful, impossible, questionable; impracticable, unsuitable
ant actual
2 *syn* see LATENT

potential *n* something that can develop or become actual <industrial *potential*>
syn possibilities, potentiality
ant actuality, reality

potentiality *n syn* see POTENTIAL
ant actuality

pother *n* 1 *syn* see COMMOTION 4
2 *syn* see STIR 1
3 *syn* see ANNOYANCE 2
4 *syn* see COMMOTION 2

pother *vb syn* see WORRY 3

pothole *n* a hole, depression, or rut in a road surface <*potholes* all over that stretch of highway>
syn chuckhole, mudhole

pothouse *n syn* see BAR 5

potpourri *n syn* see MISCELLANY 1

potshot *n* a critical remark made in a random or sporadic manner <took a few *potshots* at his neighbor's argument>
syn pot, shy, sideswipe
rel cut, crack, dig; gibe, jeer; aspersion, criticism, insult

potted *adj* 1 *syn* see CONDENSED
‖2 *syn* see INTOXICATED 1

potter *vb syn* see FIDDLE 2

potter (away) *vb syn* see WASTE 2

potter's field *n syn* see CEMETERY

potty *adj* ‖1 *syn* see LITTLE 3
‖2 *syn* see FOOLISH 2
3 *syn* see SNOBBISH

‖**potty** *n syn* see TOILET

pouch *n syn* see BAG 1

pouch *vb syn* see BULGE

pouf n syn see QUILT

poule n syn see PROSTITUTE

poultice n a soft, usually heated, and sometimes medicated mass spread on cloth and applied to sores or other lesions <slapped a mustard *poultice* over the boil>
syn cataplasm
rel plaster; compress; dressing

pound vb 1 syn see HAMMER 1
2 syn see BEAT 1
3 syn see IMPRESS 3

pound n syn see BLOW 1

pour vb 1 syn see DISCHARGE 5
2 to send forth or come forth abundantly <medical supplies *poured* into the stricken area>
syn flow, gush, roll, sluice, stream, surge
rel issue, proceed, spring; course, rill, run, rush, swarm; cascade, cataract; deluge, flood, inundate
3 to rain heavily <it *poured* for two solid days>
syn drench, lash, teem
rel beat; deluge, flood, stream
idiom come down in buckets (or torrents), rain cats and dogs

pour n syn see FLOOD 2

pourboire n syn see GRATUITY

pout vb 1 syn see SULK
2 syn see BULGE

pouts n pl syn see SULK

poverty n 1 the state of one with insufficient resources <repeated crop failures had reduced the farmers to *poverty*>
syn beggary, borasca, destituteness, destitution, impecuniousness, impoverishment, indigence, indigency, need, neediness, pauperism, pennilessness, penury, poorness, privation, unprosperousness, want
rel exigency, necessity; juncture, pass, pinch, strait; difficulty, distress, embarrassment; hardship, suffering; mendicancy
idiom hand-to-mouth existence, straitened circumstances
con affluence, comfort, luxury, opulence, prosperity, richness, wealth
ant riches
2 syn see SCARCITY

poverty–stricken adj syn see POOR 1

powder vb 1 syn see SPRINKLE 1
2 syn see PULVERIZE 1

powdering n syn see DUSTING

powdery adj syn see FINE 2

power n 1 the right or prerogative of determining, ruling, or governing or the exercise of that right or prerogative <party in *power*>
syn authority, command, control, domination, jurisdiction, mastery, might, strings, sway
rel birthright, prerogative, privilege, right; direction, management; ascendancy, dominance, dominion, masterdom, sovereignty, supremacy; superiority; influence, prestige, weight; force, strength
con forcelessness, impotence, weakness

ant impuissance, powerlessness
‖ 2 see MUCH
3 the ability of a living being to perform in a given way or a capacity for a particular kind of performance <the *power* to think clearly>
syn faculty, function
rel ability, capability, capacity; aptitude, bent, turn; endowment, gift, talent
con inability, incapability, incapacity; inaptness, ineptitude
4 the ability to exert effort for a purpose <raised the productive *power* of the nation>
syn arm, beef, dint, energy, force, might, muscle, potency, puissance, sinew, steam, strength, strong arm, vigor, virtue
rel ability, capability, capacity; effectiveness, dynamism, powder, voltage; dynamis, potentiality; competence, qualification
con inability, incapability, incapacity; ineffectiveness; incompetence

powerful adj 1 syn see STRONG 1
2 having or manifesting power to effect great or striking results <a *powerful* leader>
syn forceful, forcible, mighty, potent, puissant
rel able, capable, competent; effective, effectual, efficacious, efficient; dynamic, energetic, strenuous, vigorous; convincing, great, invincible; authoritative, dominant, influential, weighty
con faulty, feeble, flawed; impotent, inadequate, incompetent, weak
ant powerless

powerfully adv syn see HARD 1

powerless adj unable to effect one's purpose, intention, or end <*powerless* to leave>
syn helpless, impotent
rel inactive, inert, passive, supine; decrepit, feeble, infirm, weak; incapable, incompetent, ineffective, unfit
con effective, effectual, efficient; able, capable, competent; potent, puissant
ant powerful

powwow n syn see TALK 4

powwow vb syn see CONFER 2

‖ **prabble** n syn see QUARREL

practic adj syn see REALISTIC

practicable adj 1 syn see POSSIBLE 1
ant impracticable
2 syn see PRACTICAL 2
3 syn see OPEN 5
ant impracticable

practical adj 1 syn see IMPLICIT 2
2 capable of being turned to use or account <a *practical* knowledge of auto mechanics>
syn functional, handy, practicable, serviceable, useful, utile
con abstract, academic, theoretical
ant impractical, unpractical
3 syn see REALISTIC
ant impractical, unpractical
4 syn see EXPERIENCED

practically adv 1 syn see VIRTUALLY
2 syn see ALMOST 2
3 syn see NEARLY

practice vb syn see EXERCISE 3
rel execute, fulfill, perform; follow, pursue; iterate, repeat

practice n 1 syn see HABIT 1
rel procedure, proceeding, process; method, mode, system

---

syn synonym(s) *rel* related word(s)
ant antonym(s) *con* contrasted word(s)
idiom idiomatic equivalent(s)
‖ use limited; if in doubt, see a dictionary

3 *syn* see EXERCISE 3
rel use, usefulness, utility; convenance, convention, form, usage
ant theory; precept

practiced *adj syn* see EXPERIENCED
ant unpracticed

praetorian *adj syn* see CORRUPT 2

praetorian *n syn* see DIEHARD 1

pragmatic *n syn* see BUSYBODY

pragmatic *adj syn* see REALISTIC

pragmatical *adj syn* see REALISTIC

pragmatist *n syn* see BUSYBODY

praisable *adj syn* see WORTHY 1

praise *vb* 1 *syn* see COMMEND 1
ant censure, criticize
2 to glorify and exalt expecially in song or writing <*praised* God for all his blessings>
syn bless, celebrate, cry up, eulogize, extol, glorify, hymn, laud, magnify, panegyrize, psalm, psalmody, resound
rel aggrandize, dignify, distinguish, ennoble, erect, exalt, honor, sublime, uprear; enhance, heighten, intensify; apotheosize; proclaim
idiom sing the praises of
con asperse, calumniate, defame, libel, malign, traduce, vilify; belittle, decry, depreciate, derogate, detract (from), discount, disparage, minimize, opprobriate; censure, criticize, denounce, reprehend, reprobate; abuse, reproach, revile
ant dispraise; blame

praiseful *adj syn* see EULOGISTIC

praiseworthy *adj syn* see WORTHY 1
ant despicable

‖**pram** *n syn* see BABY CARRIAGE

prance *vb* 1 *syn* see SASHAY
2 *syn* see DANCE 1

‖**prang** *vb syn* see BUMP 1

‖**prang** *n syn* see CRASH 3

prank *n* a mischievous or roguish act <he was always playing *pranks* on his sister>
syn antic, caper, dido(es), frolic, lark, monkeyshine(s), ‖rig, shenanigan, shine(s), ‖skite, tomfoolery, trick, wheeze; *compare* ESCAPADE, TRICK 1
rel fooling, high jinks, horseplay, roughhouse, roughhousing, rowdiness, skylarking; gambol, play, rollick, sport; frivolity, levity, lightness; caprice, conceit, fancy, freak, vagary, whim, whimsy

prank *vb* 1 *syn* see ADORN
2 *syn* see DRESS UP 1

prankful *adj syn* see PLAYFUL 1

prankish *adj syn* see PLAYFUL 1

pranky *adj syn* see PLAYFUL 1

‖**prat** *n syn* see TRICK 1

prate *vb* 1 *syn* see CHAT 1
2 *syn* see BOAST
3 *syn* see BABBLE 2

prate *n syn* see CHATTER

prater *n syn* see CHATTERBOX

prattle *vb* 1 *syn* see CHAT 1
2 *syn* see BABBLE 2

prattle *n syn* see CHATTER

prattler *n syn* see CHATTERBOX

praxis *n syn* see HABIT 1

pray *vb syn* see BEG

prayer *n* an earnest and usually a formal request for something <the *prayer* in a bill in

equity is the part that specifies the kind of relief sought>
syn appeal, application, entreaty, imploration, imprecation, orison, petition, plea, suit, supplication
rel begging, beseeching, imploring, pleading; adoration, worship
con claim, demand, exaction

prayer *n syn* see SUPPLIANT

prayerful *adj syn* see DEVOUT

preach *vb* 1 to discourse publicly on a religious subject <*preached* at Sunday services>
syn evangelize, homilize, sermonize
rel minister, mission, missionary; prophesy; address, lecture, speak, talk
2 *syn* see MORALIZE

preach *n syn* see SERMON

preacher *n syn* see CLERGYMAN

preachify *vb syn* see MORALIZE

preaching *n syn* see SERMON

preachment *n syn* see SERMON

preachy *adj syn* see DIDACTIC

preamble *n syn* see INTRODUCTION

precarious *adj* 1 *syn* see DOUBTFUL 1
2 *syn* see DELICATE 7

precariousness *n syn* see INSTABILITY

precaution *n syn* see PRUDENCE 1

precede *vb* 1 to go before in rank, dignity, or importance <the small countries at the conference were *preceded* by the large wealthy ones> <those who still feel that age should *precede* beauty>
syn outrank, rank
2 to go before in time <all-out war was *preceded* by many small raids>
syn antecede, antedate, forerun, pace, predate
rel announce, foreshadow, harbinger, herald, presage
con ensue, supervene
ant follow, succeed
3 to cause to be preceded <*preceded* her address with a welcome to the visitors>
syn introduce, lead, preface, usher
ant follow

precedence *n syn* see PRIORITY

precedency *n syn* see PRIORITY

precedent *adj syn* see PRECEDING

precedently *adv syn* see BEFORE 1

preceding *adj* being before especially in time or in arrangement <the *preceding* day>
syn antecedent, anterior, foregoing, former, past, precedent, previous, prior
rel other; preexistent; precursive, precursory; erstwhile, heretofore, hitherto
con coming, ensuing, next, sequent, sequential, subsequent, successive
ant following, succeeding

preceding *prep syn* see BEFORE 1

precept *n syn* see LAW 1
rel axiom, fundamental, principle; doctrine, dogma, tenet; behest, bidding, injunction
ant practice; counsel

précieux *adj syn* see PRECIOUS 4

precinct *n* 1 *syn* see QUARTER 2
2 *syn* see FIELD
3 *precincts pl syn* see ENVIRONS 1

precious *adj* 1 of such great value that a suitable price is hard to estimate <a *precious* twelfth century painting>

syn costly, inestimable, invaluable, priceless, valuable; compare COSTLY 1

rel choice, exquisite, rare, recherché; treasurable; rich; prizable

idiom of price

con base, common, mean, paltry, poor, rubbishy, shabby, trashy; contemptible, despicable, miserable; claptrap, gimcrack, trumpery

ant cheap; worthless

2 syn see FAVORITE 1

3 syn see NICE 1

4 excessively refined <too *precious* to mingle with the common people>

syn affected, alembicated, chichi, la-di-da, overnice, overrefined, précieux; compare GENTEEL 3

rel ostentatious, pretentious, showy; artful, sophisticated, studied

con artless, ingenuous, naive, natural, simple, unaffected, unartful, unschooled, unsophisticated, unstudied, untutored; down-to-earth, matter-of-fact, practical, pragmatic, rational

precipitance n syn see HASTE 2
precipitancy n syn see HASTE 2
precipitant adj syn see PRECIPITATE 1
precipitate n 1 syn see SEDIMENT
    2 syn see EFFECT 1
precipitate adj 1 characterized by impetuous or unexpected haste <beat a *precipitate* retreat>

syn abrupt, hasty, headlong, hurried, impetuous, precipitant, precipitous, rushing, subitaneous, sudden

rel breakneck, headstrong, hotheaded, impatient, impulsive, madcap, refractory, uncontrolled, willful; unanticipated, unexpected, unforeseen, unlooked-for; overhasty

con leisurely, slow, unhurried

ant deliberate

2 syn see STEEP 1

precipitateness n syn see HASTE 2
precipitation n 1 syn see HASTE 2
    2 syn see SEDIMENT
precipitous adj 1 syn see PRECIPITATE 1
    2 syn see STEEP 1
précis n syn see COMPENDIUM 1
precise adj 1 syn see DEFINITE 1
    2 syn see CORRECT 2

rel rigid, stringent

con careless, heedless; lax, slack

ant imprecise; loose

3 syn see PRIM 1

4 distinguished from every other <arrived just at the *precise* moment when he was needed>

syn exact, very

rel specific; individual; particular

con general, inexact, nonspecific

ant imprecise

precisely adv 1 syn see JUST 1

idiom on the button

ant imprecisely; approximately

2 syn see EVEN 1

3 syn see EXACTLY 3

preciseness n syn see PRECISION
    ant impreciseness
precisian n syn see PURIST
precision n the quality or character of what is precise <the *precision* involved in close-tolerance machining>

syn accuracy, correctness, definiteness, definitiveness, definitude, exactitude, exactness, preciseness

rel care, carefulness; attention, heed

con inaccuracy, incorrectness, indefiniteness, inexactness; obscurity, unclearness, vagueness; unreliability, untrustworthiness

ant imprecision

precisionist n syn see PURIST
precludes vb syn see PREVENT 2

rel cease, discontinue, quit, stop

precocious adj exceptionally early in development <a *precocious* child, smart beyond her years>

syn advanced, forward; compare EARLY 2

rel ahead, early, overearly, oversoon, premature, previous, ‖soon; developed, mature

con backward, undeveloped; dull, slow, slow-witted, sluggish

ant retarded

precogitate vb syn see PREMEDITATE
preconception n an attitude, belief, or impression formed beforehand <had a lot of *preconceptions* about a man she'd never met>

syn prejudgment, prepossession; compare PREJUDICE

rel illusion; delusion

idiom preconceived notion (or idea or opinion)

precondition n syn see ESSENTIAL 2
precursor n 1 syn see FORERUNNER 1
    2 syn see FORERUNNER 2
predacious adj syn see RAPACIOUS 1
predate vb syn see PRECEDE 2
predative adj syn see RAPACIOUS 1
predatorial adj syn see RAPACIOUS 1
predatory adj syn see RAPACIOUS 1
predecessor n syn see FORERUNNER 2
predestinate vb syn see PREDESTINE 2
predestine vb 1 to fix the future of in advance <his treasured scribblings were *predestined* to light a kitchen fire>

syn destine, determine, doom (to), fate, foreordain, predetermine, preform, preordain

rel predecide; prejudge; preestablish

2 to determine by or as if by divine decree or eternal purpose <some believe that God *predestines* individuals to eternal life or to eternal damnation>

syn fordestine, foreordain, predestinate, predetermine, preordain

predetermine vb 1 syn see PREDESTINE 2
    2 syn see PREMEDITATE
    3 syn see PREDESTINE 1
predicament n a difficult, perplexing, or trying situation <was in a *predicament*, trying to decide whether or not to take the job>

syn box, corner, deep water, dilemma, fix, hole, hot water, impasse, jam, pickle, plight, quagmire, scrape, soup, spot

---

syn synonym(s)   rel related word(s)
ant antonym(s)   con contrasted word(s)
idiom idiomatic equivalent(s)
‖ use limited; if in doubt, see a dictionary

rel emergency, exigency, juncture, pass, pinch, strait; asperity, difficulty, hardness, hardship, rigor, vicissitude; Dutch, trouble; condition, posture, situation, state
idiom ‖in a bind

predicate *vb* **1** *syn* see ASSERT 1
2 *syn* see BASE

predict *vb* **1** *syn* see FORETELL
2 to conjecture correctly <*predicted* the turn of the market months in advance>
syn call, guess
rel conjecture, presume, suppose, surmise, think; conclude, gather, infer, judge
idiom hazard a conjecture (*or* guess)

prediction *n* something that is predicted <the *prediction* was for a good outcome>
syn cast, forecast, foretelling, prevision, prognosis, prognostication, prophecy, weird
rel conjecture, guess, surmising

predictor *n* *syn* see PROPHET

predilection *n* *syn* see LEANING 2

predispose *vb* *syn* see INCLINE 3
rel impress, strike, sway
con disaffect, disincline, disinterest, indispose

predisposed *adj* *syn* see WILLING 1
ant indisposed

predisposition *n* *syn* see LEANING 2
ant indisposition

predominant *adj* **1** *syn* see DOMINANT 1
ant subordinate
2 *syn* see CHIEF 2

predominantly *adv* *syn* see GENERALLY 1

predominate *adj* *syn* see DOMINANT 1

predominate *vb* *syn* see RULE 2

preeminence *n* **1** *syn* see SUPREMACY
2 *syn* see EMINENCE 1

preeminent *adj* **1** *syn* see SUPREME
2 *syn* see CHIEF 2

preempt *vb* **1** *syn* see APPROPRIATE 1
2 *syn* see ARROGATE 1

preen *vb* *syn* see PRIDE

preengage *vb* **1** *syn* see RESERVE 2
2 *syn* see PREPOSSESS 1

preface *n* *syn* see INTRODUCTION

preface *vb* *syn* see PRECEDE 3

prefatial *adj* *syn* see PRELIMINARY

prefatorial *adj* *syn* see PRELIMINARY

prefatory *adj* *syn* see PRELIMINARY

prefer *vb* **1** *syn* see ADVANCE 2
2 *syn* see CHOOSE 1
3 *syn* see PROPOSE 1

preferable *adj* *syn* see BETTER 2

preference *n* **1** *syn* see CHOICE 1
rel partiality, predilection, prepossession
2 *syn* see ADVANCEMENT 1

preferment *n* *syn* see ADVANCEMENT 1

preferred *adj* *syn* see FAVORITE 1

prefigurate *vb* *syn* see ADUMBRATE 1

prefigure *vb* *syn* see ADUMBRATE 1

preform *vb* *syn* see PREDESTINE 1

pregnance *n* *syn* see PREGNANCY

pregnancy *n* the condition of containing unborn young within the body <she was in the last trimester of her *pregnancy*>
syn gestation, gravidity, pregnance, situation

pregnant *adj* **1** containing unborn young within the body <she was *pregnant* with her second child>

syn big, childing, enceinte, expectant, expecting, gone, gravid, heavy, parous, parturient
idiom in an interesting condition, in the family way, with child (*or* young)
con barren, infertile; delivered; postpartum
2 *syn* see EXPRESSIVE
rel consequential, important, momentous, significant, weighty

prehend *vb* *syn* see CATCH 1

prehensile *adj* *syn* see COVETOUS

preindicate *vb* *syn* see ANNOUNCE 2

prejudgment *n* *syn* see PRECONCEPTION

prejudice *n* the inclination to take a stand (as in a conflict) usually without just grounds or sufficient information <could not review his competitor's work without *prejudice*>
syn bias, one-sidedness, partiality; *compare* LEANING 2, PRECONCEPTION
rel partisanship
idiom jaundiced eye
con detachment, dispassion, impartiality, indifference, neutrality
ant objectivity

prejudice *vb* **1** *syn* see INJURE 1
2 to cause to have opinions formed without due knowledge or examination <*prejudice* a man against his neighbor by innuendo>
syn bias, influence, prepossess; *compare* INCLINE 3, SLANT 3
rel bend, dispose, incline, predispose; angle, skew, slant; prejudge

prejudiced *adj* *syn* see BIASED 2
ant unprejudiced; disinterested

prejudicial *adj* **1** *syn* see HARMFUL
2 *syn* see DISCRIMINATORY

prejudicious *adj* *syn* see HARMFUL

prekindergarten *n* *syn* see CHILDISH

preknow *vb* *syn* see FORESEE

prelation *n* *syn* see ADVANCEMENT 1

prelect *vb* *syn* see TALK 7

‖prelim *adj* *syn* see PRELIMINARY

preliminary *adj* serving to make ready the way for something that follows <held a *preliminary* discussion to set up the agenda of the conference>
syn inductive, introductory, prefatial, prefatorial, prefatory, ‖prelim, preludial, prelusive, preparative, preparatory, proemial
rel primal, primary; elemental, elementary; basic, fundamental; fitting, preparing, readying
ant postliminary

prelimit *vb* *syn* see LIMIT 2

preliterate *adj* *syn* see PRIMITIVE 6

prelude *n* *syn* see INTRODUCTION

preludial *adj* *syn* see PRELIMINARY

prelusion *n* *syn* see INTRODUCTION

prelusive *adj* *syn* see PRELIMINARY

premature *adj* *syn* see EARLY 2

prematurely *adv* *syn* see EARLY 2

premeditate *vb* to think on and revolve in the mind beforehand <carefully *premeditating* each step of his plan of campaign>
syn forethink, precogitate, predetermine
rel prearrange, preplan, set up; predecide; prepare

premeditated *adj* *syn* see DELIBERATE 1
ant unpremeditated; spontaneous

premier *adj syn* see FIRST 3
premise *n syn* see ASSUMPTION 2
premise *vb syn* see PRESUPPOSE
premium *n syn* see REWARD
premium *adj syn* see SUPERIOR 4
premonition *n syn* see APPREHENSION 3
prename *n syn* see GIVEN NAME
prenotion *n syn* see APPREHENSION 3
prentice *n syn* see NOVICE
prentice *adj syn* see CRUDE 5
preoccupied *adj* 1 *syn* see INTENT
  2 *syn* see ABSTRACTED
  rel absorbed; forgetful
  ant unpreoccupied
preoccupy *vb syn* see PREPOSSESS 1
preordain *vb* 1 *syn* see PREDESTINE 1
  2 *syn* see PREDESTINE 2
preparative *adj syn* see PRELIMINARY
preparatory *adj syn* see PRELIMINARY
prepare *vb* 1 to make ready in advance usually for a particular use or disposition <*prepared* rooms for the expected guests>
  syn fit, fix, get, make, make up, ready
  rel furnish, provide, supply; dower, endow,
endue; equip, outfit; dispose, incline, predispose; prime
  idiom set the stage (for)
  ant unprepare
  2 *syn* see DRAFT 3
  3 *syn* see GIRD 3
prepared *adj syn* see READY 1
  ant unprepared
prepatent *adj syn* see LATENT
prepense *adj syn* see DELIBERATE 1
prepensely *adv syn* see INTENTIONALLY
preponderance *n syn* see SUPREMACY
preponderancy *n syn* see SUPREMACY
preponderant *adj syn* see DOMINANT 1
preponderate *vb syn* see RULE 2
preponderation *n syn* see SUPREMACY
prepossess *vb* 1 to influence or affect
strongly beforehand <was *prepossessed* with
the notion of his own superiority>
  syn preengage, preoccupy
  rel busy, engage, engross, immerse, occupy,
soak; absorb, imbue, involve
  2 *syn* see PREJUDICE 2
prepossessed *adj syn* see BIASED 2
  ant unprepossessed
prepossessing *adj syn* see ATTRACTIVE 1
prepossession *n syn* see PRECONCEPTION
preposterous *adj* 1 *syn* see FOOLISH 2
  rel irrational, unreasonable
  2 *syn* see EXTRAVAGANT 1
preposterousness *n syn* see FOOLISHNESS
prepotence *n syn* see SUPREMACY
prepotency *n syn* see SUPREMACY
prerequisite *n syn* see ESSENTIAL 2
prerequisite *adj syn* see ESSENTIAL 4
prerogative *n syn* see RIGHT 2
  rel exemption, immunity
presage *n* 1 *syn* see FORETOKEN
  2 *syn* see APPREHENSION 3
presage *vb* 1 *syn* see AUGUR 2
  rel bespeak, indicate

  2 *syn* see ANNOUNCE 2
  3 *syn* see FORETELL
prescribe *vb* 1 *syn* see DICTATE
  2 to fix arbitrarily or authoritatively for the
sake of order or of a clear understanding
<the Constitution *prescribes* the conditions
under which it may be amended>
  syn assign, define, lay down
  rel establish, fix, set, settle; decide, determine; choose, pick out, select
prescript *n syn* see LAW 1
prescription *n syn* see LAW 1
presence *n syn* see BEARING 1
  rel appearance, aspect, look, seeming
present *n syn* see GIFT 1
present *vb* 1 *syn* see INTRODUCE 4
  2 *syn* see GIVE 1
  3 *syn* see OFFER 1
  4 *syn* see ADDUCE
  5 *syn* see DIRECT 2
present *adj* now existing or in progress <the
present state of the economy seems to be
shaky from all reports>
  syn contemporary, current, existent, extant,
instant, present-day, todayish
  rel contemporaneous, modern; newfash-
ioned, up-to-date, up-to-the-minute
  con bygone, erstwhile, late, old, once, onetime, quondam, sometime, whilom
  ant past
present *n* the present time <the course covers U.S. history from 1900 to the *present*>
  syn now, today; *compare* FUTURE, PAST
  idiom here and now, this day and age
  ant past; future
presentable *adj syn* see RESPECTABLE 5
present–day *adj syn* see PRESENT
presenter *n syn* see DONOR
presentiment *n syn* see APPREHENSION 3
  rel discomposing, discomposure, disquietude, disturbance, perturbation
presently *adv* 1 without undue time lapse
<the results will be evident *presently*>
  syn anon, by and by, directly, shortly, soon
  2 *syn* see TODAY
presentment *n syn* see REPRESENTATION
preserval *n syn* see CONSERVATION 1
preservation *n* 1 the act of preserving or the
state of being preserved <the *preservation* of
peace in the world>
  syn conservation, keeping, safekeeping,
salvation, saving, sustentation
  rel defense, guard, protection, safeguard;
shield; care, guardianship, ward
  2 *syn* see CONSERVATION 1
preserve *vb* 1 *syn* see SAVE 3
  2 *syn* see MAINTAIN 1
preserve *n syn* see JAM
preside *vb* to occupy the place of authority
(as in an assembly) <the chief justice *presides*
over the supreme court> <the *presiding*
elders of the church>
  syn chair
  rel carry on, conduct, control, direct, keep,
manage, operate, ordain, run; administer,
handle, head, oversee, supervise
press *n syn* see CROWD 1
press *vb* 1 to act upon through steady pushing or thrusting force exerted in contact
<*pressed* her nose against the window>

---

syn synonym(s)   *rel* related word(s)
ant antonym(s)   *con* contrasted word(s)
idiom idiomatic equivalent(s)
‖ use limited; if in doubt, see a dictionary

syn bear, compress, constrain, crowd, crush, jam, ‖mash, push, ‖squab, squash, squeeze, squish, squush
rel propel, shove, thrust; drive, impel, move
2 *syn* see DEPRESS 2
3 to squeeze out the juice or contents of <*press* grapes>
syn crush, express
rel compress, squeeze
4 *syn* see PUSH 2
5 *syn* see PRESSURE
6 *syn* see EMBRACE 1
7 to crowd closely against or around someone or something <hundreds *pressed* around the performer after the show>
syn cram, crowd, crush, jam, squash, squeeze; *compare* CRAM 1
rel pack, ram, stuff, tamp; mass, pile; assemble, collect, congregate, gather
8 to force or push one's way (as through a crowd or against obstruction) <had to *press* through the traffic to get to the other side of town>
syn bear, squeeze
rel force, push, shove
press-agent *vb syn* see PUBLICIZE
press-agentry *n syn* see PUBLICITY
pressing *adj* demanding or claiming especially immediate attention <he was barely able to pay his most *pressing* debts>
syn burning, clamant, clamorous, crying, dire, exigent, imperative, importunate, insistent, instant, urgent
rel direct, immediate; claiming, demanding, exacting, requiring; compelling, constraining, forcing, obliging; acute, critical, crucial
pressure *n syn* see STRESS 1
pressure *vb* to insist upon unduly <*pressured* him into making the wrong move>
syn overpress, press, push
rel drive, impel, push
prestige *n* **1** *syn* see STATUS 2
2 *syn* see INFLUENCE 1
rel power, sway
3 *syn* see EMINENCE 1
prestigious *adj syn* see FAMOUS 2
presto *adv syn* see FAST 2
presumably *adv* by reasonable assumption <*presumably* the best qualified for the job should get it>
syn assumably, doubtless, likely, presumptively, probably
rel indubitably, surely, undoubtedly, unquestionably
presume *vb* **1** *syn* see CONJECTURE
2 *syn* see PRESUPPOSE
3 *syn* see IMPOSE 5
presuming *adj syn* see PRESUMPTUOUS
ant unassuming, unpresuming
presumption *n* **1** *syn* see EFFRONTERY
2 *syn* see PRESUPPOSITION 1
3 *syn* see ASSUMPTION 2
presumptively *adv syn* see PRESUMABLY
presumptuous *adj* marked by or based on bold and excessive self-confidence <in such company his demand for attention was utterly *presumptuous*>
syn brash, brassbound, confident, forward, gay, overconfident, overweening, presuming, pushful, pushing, ‖pushy, self-asserting, self-assertive, uppish, uppity

rel pretentious, self-assured, self-conceited; lofty, pompous, supercilious; complacent, self-satisfied, smug; inexcusable, outrageous
idiom too big for one's britches
con deferential, dutiful, respectful, submissive; appropriate, proper
presuppose *vb* to take something for granted or as true or existent especially as a basis for action or reasoning <a lecturer who talks above the heads of his listeners *presupposes* too extensive a knowledge on their part>
syn assume, posit, postulate, premise, presume
rel conjecture, guess, surmise; deduce, infer, judge; believe, expect, gather, imagine, reckon, suppose, suspect, take, think, understand; preconceive
presupposition *n* **1** an act of presupposing <going on her *presupposition* that they would succeed>
syn assumption, presumption
rel conjecture, guess, surmise; deduction, inference, judgment; belief, conviction, opinion, view
2 *syn* see ASSUMPTION 2
pretend *vb* **1** *syn* see ASSUME 4
rel beguile, deceive, delude, mislead; profess, purport
idiom make believe
2 *syn* see CONJECTURE
pretended *adj syn* see ALLEGED
pretender *n syn* see IMPOSTOR
pretense *n* **1** *syn* see CLAIM 1
2 the offering of something false as real or true <there is too much *pretense* in his piety>
syn charade, disguise, make-believe, pageant, pretension, pretentiousness
rel deceit, deception, fake, fraud, humbug, imposture, sham; affectation, air, mannerism, pose
con sincereness; reality, soundness, substantiality, validity; fairness, honesty
ant sincerity
3 *syn* see MASK 2
pretension *n* **1** *syn* see CLAIM 1
2 *syn* see AMBITION 1
3 *syn* see PRETENSE 2
pretentious *adj* **1** *syn* see SHOWY
ant unpretentious
2 *syn* see GENTEEL 3
ant unpretentious
3 flamboyant, turgid, or bombastic in manner or content <a *pretentious* literary style>
syn arty, arty-crafty, big, high-sounding, imposing, overblown
rel affected, feigned, put-on; pompier; aureate, bombastic, euphuistic, flowery, grandiloquent, magniloquent, rhetorical; inflated, tumid, turgid
con heartfelt, hearty, sincere, unfeigned, wholehearted, whole-souled; artless, genuine, natural, simple, unaffected
ant unpretentious
4 *syn* see AMBITIOUS 2
pretentiousness *n syn* see PRETENSE 2
ant unpretentiousness
preterition *n syn* see OMISSION
pretermission *n syn* see OMISSION
pretermit *vb syn* see NEGLECT

preternatural *adj* **1** *syn* see SUPERNATU-
RAL 1
   rel anomalous, unnatural; nonnatural
   2 *syn* see ABNORMAL 1
   ant natural
pretext *n* **1** *syn* see EXCUSE 1
   2 *syn* see MASK 2
prettify *vb* *syn* see PALLIATE
pretty *adj* **1** *syn* see SKILLFUL 1
   2 *syn* see BEAUTIFUL
   rel darling, ducky; cunning, cute
   ant unpretty
pretty *adv* *syn* see SOMEWHAT 2
   idiom pretty much
‖**pretty** *n* *syn* see TOY 2
prettyism *n* *syn* see POSE 2
pretty–pretty *n* *syn* see KNICKKNACK
preux *adj* *syn* see COURTLY
prevail *vb* **1** *syn* see CONQUER 2
   2 *syn* see WIN 1
   3 *syn* see RULE 2
prevail (on *or* upon) *vb* *syn* see INDUCE 1
   rel affect, impress
prevailing *adj* general (as in circulation,
acceptance, or use) in a given place or at a
given time <the *prevailing* point of view
among farmers>
   syn current, popular, prevalent, rampant,
regnant, rife, ruling, widespread
   rel dominant, predominant, preponderant;
common, familiar, ordinary; general, universal
   con exceptional, uncommon, unusual
prevalent *adj* **1** *syn* see DOMINANT 1
   2 *syn* see PREVAILING
   3 *syn* see GENERAL 1
   rel accustomed, customary, wonted
prevaricate *vb* *syn* see LIE
   rel belie, garble, misrepresent
prevarication *n* *syn* see LIE
prevaricative *adj* *syn* see EVASIVE 1
prevaricator *n* *syn* see LIAR
prevaricatory *adj* *syn* see EVASIVE 1
prevent *vb* to be or get ahead of or to deal
with beforehand <many problems are *prevented* easily if one plans wisely>
   syn anticipate, forestall
   rel baffle, balk, foil, frustrate, thwart; arrest, check, interrupt
   2 to stop from advancing or occurring <take
steps to *prevent* war> <measures designed to
prevent the spread of disease>
   syn avert, deter, forestall, forfend, obviate,
preclude, rule out, stave off, ward
   rel bar, block, dam, hinder, impede, obstruct; debar, shut out; forbid, inhibit, interdict, prohibit
   con allow, leave, let, suffer
   ant permit
previous *adj* **1** *syn* see PRECEDING
   subsequent; consequent
   2 *syn* see EARLY 2
previous *adv* *syn* see BEFORE 1
previously *adv* *syn* see BEFORE 2
   ant subsequently; consequently

previousness *n* *syn* see PRIORITY
previse *vb* *syn* see FORESEE
prevision *n* *syn* see PREDICTION
prevision *vb* *syn* see FORESEE
prey *n* **1** *syn* see GAME 3
   2 *syn* see VICTIM 2
‖**pribble** *n* *syn* see QUARREL
price *n* **1** the quantity of one thing that is
exchanged or demanded in barter or sale for
another <what is the *price* of this book>
   syn charge, cost, price tag, rate, tab, tariff
   2 *syn* see EXPENSE 2
priceless *adj* *syn* see PRECIOUS 1
   rel cherished, prized, treasured, valued
   idiom without price
price tag *n* *syn* see PRICE 1
prick *n* **1** a mark or shallow hole made by or
as if by a pointed tool <a needle *prick* in his
arm>
   syn jab, ‖jag, puncture, stab
   rel prickle; hole
   ‖**2** *syn* see SNOT 1
prick *vb* **1** *syn* see PERFORATE
   rel enter; cut, slash, slit
   2 *syn* see URGE
   rel excite, pique, stimulate
‖**prick** (up) *vb* *syn* see DRESS UP 1
prickish *adj* *syn* see IRRITABLE
prickly *adj* **1** *syn* see THORNY
   rel annoying, bothersome
   2 *syn* see IRRITABLE
pride *n* **1** *syn* see CONCEIT 2
   rel bighead, cockiness, overconfidence, self≠
assurance
   idiom overweening pride
   ant humility
   2 a reasonable or justifiable sense of one's
worth or position <inhumane treatment in
prison caused him to lose his *pride*>
   syn amour propre, self-esteem, self-regard,
self-respect
   rel dignity, face, pridefulness, self-confidence, self-trust
   con humiliation, mortification; shamefaced-
ness
   ant shame
   3 proud or disdainful behavior or actions
<her snobbishness and overbearing *pride*
were offensive>
   syn arrogance, disdain, disdainfulness,
haughtiness, hauteur, loftiness, morgue,
superbity, superciliousness
   rel condescension, snobbishness; contempt,
scorn; insolence; smugness; pretentiousness
   idiom haughty airs
   con humbleness, modesty, unpretentiousness
   ant humility
   4 *syn* see BEST
   idiom pride of the herd
pride *vb* to congratulate (oneself) for something one is, has, or has done or achieved
<he *prides* himself on his ancestry>
   syn pique, plume, preen
   rel boast, brag, crow, gasconade, vaunt;
congratulate, felicitate
   ant efface
‖**pridy** *adj* *syn* see PROUD 1
prier (*or* **pryer**) *n* *syn* see BUSYBODY
priestal *adj* *syn* see SACERDOTAL

---

syn synonym(s)   *rel* related word(s)
ant antonym(s)   *con* contrasted word(s)
idiom idiomatic equivalent(s)
‖ use limited; if in doubt, see a dictionary

priestish *adj syn* see SACERDOTAL
priestlike *adj syn* see SACERDOTAL
priestly *adj syn* see SACERDOTAL
‖**prig** *vb syn* see STEAL 1
prig *n syn* see THIEF
prig *n syn* see PRUDE
prig *adj syn* see PRIM 1
priggish *adj* 1 *syn* see COMPLACENT
  rel self-righteous; self-esteeming, self-loving
  2 *syn* see PRIM 1
prim *adj* 1 excessively concerned with what one regards as proper or right <a *prim* woman, easily shocked by vulgar language>
  syn bluenosed, genteel, missish, precise, prig, priggish, prissy, proper, prudish, puritanical, straitlaced, stuffy, tight-laced, Victorian; *compare* GENTEEL 3
  rel correct, nice, precise; decorous; rigid, stiff, wooden; ceremonial, ceremonious, conventional, formal, straight
  idiom prim and proper
  con lax, loose, slack; easy, easygoing, free
  2 *syn* see NEAT 2
prima facie *adj syn* see SELF-EVIDENT
primarily *adv* 1 *syn* see GENERALLY 1
  2 *syn* see INITIALLY 1
primary *adj* 1 *syn* see FIRST 2
  2 *syn* see PRIMITIVE 4
  3 *syn* see FUNDAMENTAL 1
  4 *syn* see DIRECT 4
  5 not based on or derived from something else <the *primary* studies in nuclear physics>
  syn original, prime, primitive, underivative, underived
  rel first, firsthand; basic, foundational, fundamental, principal, underlying
  con derivate, derivational, derivative, derived; borrowed, secondhand
  ant secondary
prime *n* 1 *syn* see MORNING 1
  2 *syn* see YOUTH 1
  3 *syn* see BEST
prime *adj* 1 *syn* see FIRST 2
  2 *syn* see EXCELLENT
  3 *syn* see PRIMARY 5
prime *vb syn* see PROVOKE 4
primeval *adj syn* see PRIMITIVE 4
primevous *adj syn* see PRIMITIVE 4
primitial *adj syn* see PRIMITIVE 4
primitive *adj* 1 *syn* see PRIMARY 5
  2 *syn* see EARLY 1
  3 closely approximating an early ancestral type <the opossums are *primitive* mammals>
  syn archaic, persistent, undeveloped, unevolved
  ant advanced
  4 of or relating to earlier ages of the world or of human history <archaeology is concerned especially with the study of *primitive* man>
  syn primary, primeval, primevous, primitial
  ant unprimitive
  5 *syn* see ELEMENTAL 1
  6 characterized by a lack of written language, simple technology, and a relatively simple social organization
  syn nonliterate, preliterate
  rel barbarian, uncivilized, uncultivated
  con advanced, civilized, cultivated

primitively *adv syn* see INITIALLY 1
primogenitor *n syn* see ANCESTOR 1
primordial *adj* 1 *syn* see EARLY 1
  2 *syn* see FIRST
primp *vb syn* see DRESS UP 1
primrose *n syn* see BEST
prince *n syn* see MAGNATE
princely *adj syn* see GRAND 1
principal *adj* 1 *syn* see CHIEF 2
  2 *syn* see FIRST 3
principally *adv syn* see GENERALLY 1
principium *n syn* see PRINCIPLE 1
principle *n* 1 a comprehensive and fundamental rule, doctrine, or assumption <the *principle* of free speech>
  syn axiom, fundamental, law, principium, theorem
  rel basis, foundation, ground; canon, precept, rule; convention, form, usage
  2 **principles** *pl syn* see ETHIC 3
  3 **principles** *pl syn* see ALPHABET 2
principled *adj syn* see MORAL 1
  ant unprincipled
‖**prink** *vb syn* see SASHAY
prink (up) *vb syn* see DRESS UP 1
print *n* 1 *syn* see IMPRESSION 1
  2 printed state or form <to see his name in *print*>
  syn black and white, writing
printing *n syn* see EDITION
prior *adj syn* see PRECEDING
  rel ahead, before, forward
  con after, behind
priority *n* the act, the fact, or the right of preceding another <the right to inherit a title is dependent mainly on *priority* of birth>
  syn antecedence, precedence, precedency, previousness
  rel arrangement, order, ordering; ascendancy, supremacy; preeminence, transcendence
prior to *prep* 1 *syn* see BEFORE 1
  2 *syn* see UNTIL
prison *n syn* see JAIL
‖**prison** *vb syn* see IMPRISON
prison bird *n syn* see CONVICT
prissy *adj* 1 *syn* see PRIM 1
  rel fastidious, finicky, squeamish
  2 *syn* see EFFEMINATE
‖**pritch** *vb syn* see PERFORATE
private *adj* 1 belonging to or concerning an individual person, company, or interest <*private* property>
  syn personal, privy
  rel intimate
  con common, general, shared
  ant public
  2 known only to a select few <the group had *private* information about the strike>
  syn closet, confidential, hushed, inside
  rel secret; discreet; concealed, hidden
  con common, general, open
  ant public
private detective *n* a person concerned with the maintenance of lawful conduct or the investigation of crime either as a regular employee of a private interest (as a hotel) or as a contractor for fees <retained a *private* detective to report on his wife's associates>

syn operative, Pinkerton, ‖private eye, ‖shamus; *compare* DETECTIVE

‖**private eye** *n syn* see PRIVATE DETECTIVE
privately *adv syn* see SECRETLY
private parts *n pl syn* see GENITALIA
privates *n pl syn* see GENITALIA
privation *n* 1 *syn* see ABSENCE
  2 the state of one deprived of something previously or normally possessed <suffered great *privation* during the famine>
  syn deprivation, deprivement, dispossession, divestiture, loss; *compare* LOSS 1
  rel distress, misery, suffering; losing, mislaying, misplacement, misplacing
  3 *syn* see POVERTY 1
privilege *n syn* see RIGHT 2
  rel allowance, concession; boon, favor
privilege (from) *vb syn* see EXEMPT
privities *n pl syn* see GENITALIA
privy *adj* 1 *syn* see PRIVATE 1
  2 *syn* see ULTERIOR
privy *n* 1 an outdoor toilet <in less settled areas, *privies* often take the place of indoor plumbing>
  syn backhouse, ‖biffy, ‖closet, jakes, ‖necessary, ‖office, outhouse
  2 *syn* see TOILET
privy parts *n pl syn* see GENITALIA
prize *n* 1 *syn* see REWARD
  2 *syn* see BEST
prize *vb syn* see APPRECIATE 1
prize *n syn* see SPOIL
prize *vb syn* see PRY
prizefighting *n syn* see BOXING
pro *prep syn* see FOR 2
  ant anti, con
pro *n syn* see EXPERT
pro-and-con *vb syn* see DISCUSS 1
probable *adj* being such as may become true or actual <seems to be a *probable* candidate>
  syn conceivable, earthly, likely, mortal, possible
  rel believable, colorable, credible, plausible; rational, reasonable; apparent, illusory, ostensible, seeming
  con doubtful, dubious, questionable, unlikely
  ant improbable, unprobable
probably *adv syn* see PRESUMABLY
  ant improbably
probe *n syn* see INQUIRY 1
probe *vb* 1 *syn* see EXPLORE
  2 to try to find out (as by discreet questioning) the views or intentions of <*probed* the neighbors on the subject of political reform>
  syn feel out, sound (out)
  rel ask, catechize, examine, inquire, interrogate, query, quiz
  idiom feel the pulse, launch a trial balloon, put out a feeler, see how the land lies, see which way the wind blows, test the water(s)
  3 *syn* see SCOUT
probing *n syn* see INQUIRY 1

probity *n syn* see GOODNESS
problem *n* 1 *syn* see EXAMPLE 3
  2 something requiring thought and skill to arrive at a proper conclusion or decision <what to do now is a *problem*>
  syn issue, nut, question
  rel enigma, mystery, puzzle; bugaboo, bugbear; count, point
  idiom a hard nut to crack
problematic *adj* 1 *syn* see DOUBTFUL 1
  ant unproblematic
  2 *syn* see MOOT
  ant unproblematic
proboscis *n syn* see NOSE 1
procacious *adj* 1 *syn* see INSOLENT 2
  2 *syn* see WISE 5
procedure *n* 1 *syn* see COURSE 3
  2 *syn* see MEASURE 7
  3 *syn* see PROCESS 1
proceed *vb* 1 *syn* see SPRING 1
  2 *syn* see GO 1
  3 *syn* see ADVANCE 5
  ant recede
proceeding *n* 1 *syn* see MEASURE 7
  2 *syn* see PROCESS 1
proceeds *n pl syn* see PROFIT
process *n* 1 the series of actions, operations, or motions involved in the accomplishment of an end <the *process* of making sugar from sugarcane>
  syn procedure, proceeding
  rel fashion, manner, method, mode, modus, system, technique, way, wise; routine; operation
  2 *syn* see OUTGROWTH 1
‖**process** *vb syn* see GO 1
procession *n syn* see ORDER 5
processus *n syn* see OUTGROWTH 1
proclaim *vb* 1 *syn* see DECLARE 1
  rel utter, vent, ventilate, voice
  2 *syn* see SHOW 2
proclamation *n syn* see DECLARATION
proclivity *n syn* see LEANING 2
procrastinate *vb syn* see DELAY 2
  rel defer, postpone, stay, suspend; prolong, protract
procreate *vb* 1 to produce offspring <*procreate* children>
  syn bear, beget, breed, generate, multiply, produce, propagate, reproduce
  rel mother; engender; hatch, spawn; proliferate
  idiom give birth to, multiply the earth
  2 *syn* see GENERATE 1
  3 *syn* see FATHER 1
procumbent *adj syn* see PRONE 4
procurable *adj syn* see AVAILABLE 1
procure *vb* 1 *syn* see GET 1
  2 *syn* see INDUCE 1
prod *vb* 1 *syn* see POKE 1
  2 *syn* see URGE
  rel instigate; excite, pique, provoke, stimulate
prodigal *adj syn* see PROFUSE
  ant parsimonious; frugal
prodigal *n syn* see SPENDTHRIFT
prodigality *n syn* see EXTRAVAGANCE 2
  ant parsimoniousness
prodigalize *vb syn* see WASTE 2
prodigious *adj* 1 *syn* see MARVELOUS 1

---

syn synonym(s)   *rel* related word(s)
ant antonym(s)   *con* contrasted word(s)
idiom idiomatic equivalent(s)
‖ use limited; if in doubt, see a dictionary

2 *syn* see MONSTROUS 1

3 *syn* see HUGE

prodigy *n syn* see WONDER 1

produce *vb* 1 *syn* see PROCREATE 1

2 *syn* see STAGE

3 *syn* see EFFECT 1

4 *syn* see GENERATE 1

5 *syn* see GENERATE 3

6 *syn* see MAKE 3

7 *syn* see BEAR 9

8 *syn* see GIVE 7

9 *syn* see GROW 1

produce *n syn* see PRODUCT 1

product *n* 1 something produced by physical labor or intellectual effort <the literary *products* of the Age of Reason>

syn produce, production

rel handiwork; consequence, effect, off-shoot, outcome, outgrowth, result; fruit, harvest

2 *syn* see OUTPUT

production *n* 1 *syn* see PRODUCT 1

2 *syn* see EXTENSION 1

3 *syn* see OUTPUT

productive *adj syn* see FERTILE

ant unproductive

proem *n syn* see INTRODUCTION

proemial *adj syn* see PRELIMINARY

profanation *n* a violation or misuse of something normally held sacred <the *profanation* of a religious ritual>

syn blasphemy, desecration, sacrilege, violation

rel contamination, defilement, pollution; corruption, debasement, perversion, vitiation; transgression, trespass

con glorification, hallowing, sanctification

ant purification; consecration

profane *adj* 1 not concerned with religion or religious purposes <he was speaking of *profane* history, not the history found in the Bible>

syn lay, secular, temporal, unsacred

rel earthly, mundane, terrestrial, worldly

con consecrated, hallowed, holy, sanctified; divine, religious, spiritual

ant sacred

2 *syn* see HEATHEN

3 *syn* see IMPIOUS 1

4 *syn* see SACRILEGIOUS

5 *syn* see OBSCENE 2

profaned *adj syn* see IMPURE 3

ant unprofaned

profanity *n syn* see BLASPHEMY 1

profess *vb syn* see ASSERT 1

professed *adj syn* see ALLEGED

professedly *adv syn* see OSTENSIBLY

profession *n syn* see TRADE 1

professional *n syn* see EXPERT

ant amateur

proffer *vb syn* see OFFER 1

proffer *n syn* see PROPOSAL

proficiency *n syn* see ADVANCE 2

proficient *adj* having or manifesting the knowledge, skill, and experience needed for success in a particular field or endeavor <a *proficient* glider pilot>

syn adept, crack, crackerjack, expert, master, masterful, masterly, skilled, skillful; *compare* EXPERIENCED, SKILLFUL 2

rel checked-out, drilled, exercised, practiced; effective, effectual, efficient; able, capable, competent, qualified; accomplished, consummate, finished

con ignorant, untaught, untrained; inexperienced; unskilled

ant incompetent

proficient *n syn* see EXPERT

profile *n syn* see OUTLINE

profit *n* the excess of returns over expenditure in a transaction or a series of transactions <his *profits* from the business venture were rewarding>

syn earnings, gain, lucre, proceeds, return

rel cleaning, cleanup, killing; receipt(s); output, outturn, product, production, turnout, yield

con cost, expenditure, expense, outgo

ant loss

profit *vb syn* see BENEFIT

ant lose

profitable *adj syn* see ADVANTAGEOUS 1

ant profitless, unprofitable

profligate *adj syn* see ABANDONED 2

profligate *n* 1 *syn* see WASTREL 1

2 *syn* see SPENDTHRIFT

profound *adj* 1 *syn* see RECONDITE

2 *syn* see DEEP 1

3 *syn* see INTENSIVE

profoundness *n syn* see DEPTH 2

profundity *n syn* see DEPTH 2

profuse *adj* proffered in or characterized by great abundance <*profuse* apologies> <a *profuse* flow of blood>

syn exuberant, lavish, lush, luxuriant, opulent, prodigal, profusive, riotous

rel abundant, copious; abounding, swarming, teeming; excessive, extravagant, immoderate; bounteous, bountiful, generous, liberal, munificent, openhanded

con exiguous, meager, scrimpy, skimpy, slight, small, sparse

ant scant, scanty

profusive *adj syn* see PROFUSE

progenerate *vb syn* see FATHER 1

progenitor *n syn* see ANCESTOR 1

progeniture *n syn* see OFFSPRING

progeny *n syn* see OFFSPRING

prognosis *n syn* see PREDICTION

prognostic *n syn* see FORETOKEN

prognosticate *vb syn* see FORETELL

prognostication *n syn* see PREDICTION

prognosticator *n syn* see PROPHET

program *n* 1 a formulated plan listing things to be done or to take place especially in chronological order <the *program* of a concert>

syn agenda, calendar, card, docket, programma, schedule, sked, timetable

rel bill; slate; plan

idiom order of the day

2 *syn* see COURSE 3

programma *n syn* see PROGRAM 1

progress *n* 1 *syn* see ADVANCE 2

ant regression, retrogression

2 a movement onward (as in time or space) <the *progress* of a disease> <they made slow *progress* toward their destination>

syn advance, course, progression

rel passage

3 *syn* see DEVELOPMENT

progress *vb* **1** *syn* see ADVANCE 5
  ant retrogress

progression *n* **1** *syn* see PROGRESS 2
  2 *syn* see SUCCESSION 2
  3 *syn* see DEVELOPMENT
  ant regression, retrogression

progressive *adj* *syn* see LIBERAL 3
  ant reactionary

prohibit *vb* *syn* see FORBID
  ant permit

prohibited *adj* *syn* see FORBIDDEN
  ant permit

prohibition *n* *syn* see TABOO
  ant permission

project *n* **1** *syn* see PLAN 1
  2 something (as a business operation) that one engages in or attempts <large-scale *projects* involving large sums of money>
  syn enterprise, undertaking
  rel affair, business, concern, matter, proposition, thing; adventure, emprise, exploit, feat, gest, venture

project *vb* **1** *syn* see PLAN 2
  rel intend, propose, purpose; delineate, diagram
  2 *syn* see THINK 1
  ‖ **3** *syn* see WANDER 1
  4 *syn* see BULGE
  rel extend, lengthen, prolong

projection *n* **1** something which extends beyond a level or a normal outer surface <buttresses are *projections* which serve to support a wall>
  syn bulge, jut, outthrust, protrusion, protuberance
  rel bump, bunch, swelling; extension, prolongation; hook, knob, point, spine, spur
  ant depression
  2 *syn* see EMINENCE 3

prolegomenon *n* *syn* see INTRODUCTION

proletariat *n* *syn* see RABBLE 2

proliferant *adj* *syn* see FERTILE

prolific *adj* *syn* see FERTILE
  rel abounding, swarming; breeding, generating, propagating, reproducing, reproductive
  ant barren, unfruitful

prolificacy *n* *syn* see FERTILITY
  ant barrenness, unfruitfulness

prolix *adj* *syn* see WORDY
  rel irksome, tedious, tiresome, wearisome; prolonged, protracted

prolixity *n* *syn* see VERBOSITY

prolixness *n* *syn* see VERBOSITY

prologue *n* *syn* see INTRODUCTION
  ant epilogue

prolong *vb* *syn* see EXTEND 3
  rel continue, endure, last, persist
  con abbreviate, retrench, shorten
  ant curtail

prolongate *vb* *syn* see EXTEND 3

prolongation *n* *syn* see EXTENSION 1

prolonged *adj* *syn* see LONG 2
  ant curtailed

prolongment *n* *syn* see EXTENSION 1

prominence *n* **1** *syn* see EMINENCE 1
  2 *syn* see EMINENCE 3

prominency *n* *syn* see EMINENCE 1

prominent *adj* **1** *syn* see NOTICEABLE
  ant inconspicuous
  2 *syn* see FAMOUS 2
  3 *syn* see WELL-KNOWN

promiscuous *adj* **1** *syn* see MISCELLANEOUS
  2 *syn* see RANDOM

promise *vb* **1** to give one's word to do, bring about, or provide <*promised* to render all possible assistance to the flood victims>
  syn engage, pass, pledge, undertake; *compare* VOW
  rel accede, agree, assent, consent; bargain, compact, contract; covenant, plight, swear, vow; assure, ensure, insure; guarantee
  idiom give (*or* make) a promise, pass one's word
  2 *syn* see AUGUR 2

promise *n* a declaration that one will do or refrain from doing something specified <never gave a *promise* that he did not intend to keep>
  syn engagement, plight, word; *compare* PLEDGE 1, WORD 8
  rel earnest, guarantee, pawn, pledge, security, token; covenant, swear, vow; assurance, warrant
  idiom word of honor

‖ **promised** *adj* *syn* see ENGAGED 2

promised land *n* *syn* see UTOPIA

promiseful *adj* *syn* see HOPEFUL 2

promising *adj* *syn* see HOPEFUL 2
  ant unpromising

promontory *n* a high point of land or rock projecting into a body of water beyond the line of coast <stood on the *promontory* watching boats come in with the tide>
  syn beak, bill, cape, foreland, head, headland, naze, point

promote *vb* **1** *syn* see ADVANCE 2
  con break, bust, declass, degrade, demerit, disgrade, disrate, downgrade, reduce
  ant bump, demote
  2 *syn* see ADVANCE 1
  3 to encourage public acceptance of (as a policy or merchandise) through publicity <official attempts to *promote* energy conservation> <television helped *promote* the new smaller cars>
  syn advertise, boost, plug, push; *compare* PUBLICIZE
  rel ballyhoo, propagandize; build up, cry, hype, press-agent, publicize, puff; communicate, impart
  idiom make much of
  con belittle, decry, depreciate, discredit, knock, run down
  ant disparage

promotion *n* **1** *syn* see ADVANCEMENT 1
  ant demotion
  2 *syn* see PUBLICITY
  rel advertisement

prompt *vb* **1** *syn* see INDUCE 1
  2 *syn* see URGE

prompt *adj* **1** *syn* see QUICK 2
  rel alert, vigilant, watchful, wide-awake; expeditious, speedy, swift

---

syn synonym(s)	*rel* related word(s)
ant antonym(s)	*con* contrasted word(s)
idiom idiomatic equivalent(s)	
‖ use limited; if in doubt, see a dictionary	

con lax, remiss, slack; dilatory
2 syn see PUNCTUAL 2
promptitude *n syn* see ALACRITY
promptly *adv syn* see FAST 2
promulgate *vb syn* see DECLARE 1
promulgation *n syn* see DECLARATION
prone *adj* **1 syn** see WILLING 1
2 syn see LIABLE 2
3 syn see APT 1
4 lying down <lying *prone* on the floor>
  syn decumbent, flat, procumbent, prostrate, reclining, recumbent
  rel resupine; supine; level
  con arrect, raised, stand-up, straight-up, upright, upstanding
  ant erect
pronounce *vb syn* see ARTICULATE 2
pronounced *adj syn* see DECIDED 1
pronouncement *n syn* see DECLARATION
||**pronto** *adv syn* see FAST 2
pronunciamento *n syn* see DECLARATION
proof *n* **1 syn** see REASON 3
2 syn see TESTIMONY
prop *n syn* see SUPPORT 3
prop *vb* **1 syn** see SUPPORT 4
2 syn see SUPPORT 5
propagandist *n syn* see MISSIONARY
propagate *vb* **1 syn** see PROCREATE 1
2 syn see GROW 1
3 syn see SPREAD 1
propel *vb* **1 syn** see PUSH 1
2 syn see MOVE 5
3 syn see URGE
propellant *n syn* see STIMULUS
propensity *n syn* see LEANING 2
  ant antipathy
proper *adj* **1 syn** see FIT 1
  ant improper
2 syn see TRUE 7
  ant improper
3 syn see DECOROUS 1
  ant improper
4 syn see ABLE
5 syn see GOOD 2
  ant improper
6 syn see CHARACTERISTIC
||**7 syn** see UTTER
8 syn see CORRECT 2
9 syn see PRIM 1
properly *adv* **1 syn** see WELL 4
  ant improperly
2 syn see WELL 1
  idiom by rights
  ant improperly
properness *n syn* see ORDER 7
  ant improperness
property *n* **1 syn** see QUALITY 1
2 syn see WEALTH 2
3 syn see OWNERSHIP
prophecy *n* **1 syn** see REVELATION
2 syn see PREDICTION
prophesier *n syn* see PROPHET
prophesy *vb syn* see FORETELL
prophet *n* one who predicts events or developments <there have been many *prophets* foretelling the end of the world>
  syn augur, auspex, forecaster, foreseer, foreteller, haruspex, Nostradamus, predictor, prognosticator, prophesier, seer, soothsayer

prophetic *adj* of, relating to, or characteristic of a prophet or prophecy <the old woman seemed to have *prophetic* powers>
  syn apocalyptic, Delphian, fatidic, mantic, oracular, prophetical, sibylline, vatic, vaticinal
  rel revelatory; interpretive; mysterious, mystic, strange, unexplainable
  ant unprophetic
prophetical *adj syn* see PROPHETIC
propinquity *n syn* see PROXIMITY
propitiate *vb syn* see PACIFY
  rel adapt, adjust, conform, reconcile; content, satisfy; intercede, mediate
propitiatory *adj syn* see PURGATIVE
propitious *adj* **1 syn** see FAVORABLE 5
  ant unpropitious; adverse
2 syn see TIMELY 1
  ant unpropitious
3 syn see GOOD 1
  ant unpropitious; adverse
||**propone** *vb syn* see PROPOSE 1
proponent *n syn* see EXPONENT
  ant opponent
proportion *n* **1 syn** see DEGREE 2
2 syn see SYMMETRY
  ant disproportion
3 syn see SIZE 1
proportion *vb syn* see HARMONIZE 3
proportional *adj* being in proportion <a starting salary *proportional* to her experience>
  syn commensurable, commensurate, equal, symmetrical
  rel correlative, corresponding, reciprocal; contingent, dependent, relative
  con asymmetrical, disproportionate, irregular, lopsided, nonsymmetrical, off-balance, overbalanced, unbalanced, unequal, uneven, unsymmetrical
  ant disproportional
proportionless *adj syn* see LOPSIDED
proposal *n* something which is proposed to another for consideration <his *proposal* for a new busing plan>
  syn invitation, proffer, proposition, suggestion
  rel motion; recommendation; idea, plan, project; outline, scheme
propose *vb* **1** to set before the mind for consideration <she *proposed* Mr. Smith for secretary of the club>
  syn pose, prefer, ||propone, proposition, propound, put, suggest
  rel move (for); offer, present, submit, tender; ask, request, solicit
  idiom put forth (*or* forward)
  ant withdraw
2 syn see INTEND 2
proposition *n syn* see PROPOSAL
proposition *vb syn* see PROPOSE 1
propound *vb syn* see PROPOSE 1
proprietary *n syn* see OWNERSHIP
proprietor *n syn* see OWNER
proprietorship *n syn* see OWNERSHIP
propriety *n* **1 syn** see ORDER 11
2 syn see DECORUM 1
  ant impropriety
3 syn see ORDER 7
  ant impropriety

4 **proprieties** *pl syn* see MANNER 5
prorate *vb syn* see APPORTION 2
prorogate *vb syn* see ADJOURN 2
prorogue *vb* 1 *syn* see DEFER
2 *syn* see ADJOURN 2
prosaic *adj* 1 belonging to or characteristic of prose as distinguished from poetry <his poetry is far more fanciful than his *prosaic* writings>
syn matter-of-fact, prose, prosing, prosy
rel actual, factual; literal
con figurative, metaphorical, symbolic; fanciful, florid, flowery, ornate
ant poetic
2 *syn* see COLORLESS 2
3 belonging to or suitable to the everyday world <the *prosaic* business of day-to-day housekeeping>
syn commonplace, everyday, lowly, mundane, workaday, workday
rel practicable, practical; boring, irksome, tedious
4 *syn* see COMMON 6
prosaicism *n syn* see COMMONPLACE
prosaism *n syn* see COMMONPLACE
proscribe *vb syn* see SENTENCE
proscription *n syn* see TABOO
prose *n syn* see CHAT 2
prose *adj syn* see PROSAIC 1
prosing *adj syn* see PROSAIC 1
prospect *n syn* see VISTA
prospect *vb syn* see EXPLORE
prosper *vb syn* see SUCCEED 3
rel augment, increase, multiply; bear, produce, turn out, yield
prospering *adj syn* see FLOURISHING
prosperity *n* 1 *syn* see SUCCESS
2 a state of good fortune and especially of financial success <his wise investments finally brought him a life of *prosperity*>
syn abundance, ease, easy street, prosperousness, thriving, well-being
rel affluence, riches, wealth
idiom bed of roses, comfortable (or easy) circumstances, life of ease, the good life
con misery, suffering; distress, embarrassment, indigence, poverty, straits
ant adversity
3 *syn* see WELFARE
4 a state of high general economic activity marked by relatively full employment <a war economy often generates *prosperity*>
syn boom, prosperousness
rel expansion; growth; inflation
con recession, slump, stagnation; bust
ant depression
prosperous *adj* 1 *syn* see TIMELY 1
rel appropriate, convenient, desirable; felicitous, fortunate, happy, lucky
con ill-seasoned, ill-timed, inauspicious, inopportune, unpropitious, unseasonable, untimely
ant unprosperous
2 *syn* see SUCCESSFUL
3 enjoying or marked by economic well-being <in *prosperous* circumstances>

syn comfortable, easy, ‖snug, substantial, well, well-fixed, well-heeled, well-off, well-to-do
rel affluent, opulent, rich, wealthy; halcyon
idiom comfortably off, comfortably situated, in (the) clover, in good case
con impecunious, necessitous, needy, poor; failing, unfortunate, unsuccessful
ant unprosperous
4 *syn* see FLOURISHING
rel lusty, strong
con decrepit, feeble, spindling, weak
prosperously *adv syn* see WELL 5
ant unprosperously
prosperousness *n* 1 *syn* see PROSPERITY 2
ant unprosperousness
2 *syn* see PROSPERITY 4
prostitute *vb syn* see ABUSE 2
rel corrupt, debase, debauch, deprave, vitiate
prostitute *n* a woman who engages in promiscuous sexual intercourse especially for money <streets haunted by *prostitutes*>
syn bawd, ‖callet, call girl, camp follower, cocotte, ‖cruiser, drab, fille de joie, harlot, ‖hooker, hustler, ‖joy girl, meretrix, moll, nightwalker, party girl, pom-pom girl, poule, quean, sporting girl, street girl, streetwalker, ‖tomato, whore; *compare* DOXY, HARLOT 1, WANTON
rel bar girl, B-girl, pickup; V-girl, victory girl; cocodette
idiom lady of pleasure, lady of the evening, woman of the street (or streets), woman of the town
prostitution *n* the act or practice of engaging in promiscuous sexual intercourse especially for money <the problem of *prostitution* around military installations>
syn harlotry, oldest profession, (the) social evil, streetwalking, whoredom
prostrate *adj syn* see PRONE 4
prostrate *vb* 1 *syn* see FELL 1
2 *syn* see PARALYZE 1
3 *syn* see OVERWHELM 4
4 *syn* see EXHAUST 4
prosy *adj* 1 *syn* see PROSAIC 1
2 *syn* see COLORLESS 2
protean *adj syn* see CHANGEABLE 1
protect *vb syn* see DEFEND 1
rel conserve, preserve, save; harbor, shelter
protection *n* 1 *syn* see DEFENSE 1
2 money paid under threat of depredation <offered *protection* to keep his store from being vandalized>
syn ‖pad
rel extortion, shakedown, squeeze; graft; bribe, payola
pro tem *adj syn* see TEMPORARY
pro tempore *adj syn* see TEMPORARY
protest *n syn* see DEMUR 2
protest *vb* 1 *syn* see ASSERT 1
2 *syn* see OBJECT 1
rel demonstrate; combat, fight, oppose, resist
ant agree
protoplast *n syn* see ORIGINAL 1
prototypal *adj syn* see TYPICAL 1
prototype *n* 1 *syn* see ORIGINAL 1
2 *syn* see FORERUNNER 2

---

syn synonym(s)   *rel* related word(s)
ant antonym(s)   *con* contrasted word(s)
idiom idiomatic equivalent(s)
‖ use limited; if in doubt, see a dictionary

prototypical adj syn see TYPICAL 1
protract vb syn see EXTEND 3
 ant curtail
protracted adj syn see LONG 2
 ant curtailed
protraction n syn see EXTENSION 1
 rel dallying, dawdling, delay, lag; stay, suspension
 ant curtailment
protrude vb syn see BULGE
protrusion n syn see PROJECTION 1
protuberance n syn see PROJECTION 1
protuberate vb syn see BULGE
proud adj 1 showing or feeling superiority toward others <a woman who was too *proud* to do her share of menial tasks>
 syn arrogant, cavalier, disdainful, dismissive, haughty, high-and-mighty, hubristic, huffy, insolent, lofty, lordly, orgulous, overbearing, ‖pridy, proudhearted, supercilious, superior, toploftical, toplofty; *compare* POMPOUS 1, VAIN 3
 rel contemptuous, scornful; misproud; ostentatious, pretentious; bloated, important, pompous, self-important, stuffy, wiggy; conceited, narcissistic, self-conceited, stuck-up, vain, vainglorious; domineering, high-handed, imperious, masterful
 con lowly, meek, modest, unassuming; chagrined, mortified
 ant humble
 2 syn see SPLENDID 2
proudhearted adj syn see PROUD 1
prove vb 1 to establish a point by appropriate objective means <gathered evidence that *proved* the need for better controls>
 syn demonstrate, test, try
 rel confirm, corroborate, substantiate, verify; argue, attest, bespeak, betoken, indicate
 ant disprove; refute
 2 syn see TRY 1
 3 syn see ESTABLISH 6
provenance n syn see SOURCE
provender n syn see FOOD 1
provenience n syn see SOURCE
prove out vb syn see SUCCEED 2
proverb n syn see SAYING
provide vb syn see GIVE 3
provide (for) vb syn see SUPPORT 3
providence n 1 syn see ECONOMY
 ant improvidence
 2 syn see PRUDENCE 1
 ant improvidence
provident adj syn see SPARING
 ant improvident
providential adj syn see LUCKY
 rel benignant, kind, kindly
province n 1 syn see FUNCTION 1
 rel calling, pursuit, work
 2 syn see FIELD
provincial n syn see RUSTIC
provincial adj 1 syn see RURAL
 2 syn see INSULAR
 rel bigoted, hidebound
 con cosmic, universal; progressive
 ant catholic
provision n syn see CONDITION 1
provisional adj 1 syn see CONDITIONAL 1
 rel temporary; contingent, dependent

 ant definitive
 2 syn see MAKESHIFT
provisionary adj syn see CONDITIONAL 1
provisions n pl syn see FOOD 1
proviso n syn see CONDITION 1
provisory adj syn see CONDITIONAL 1
provocation n syn see ANNOYANCE 1
provocative n syn see STIMULUS
provoke vb 1 syn see IRRITATE
 rel insult, outrage
 ant gratify
 2 syn see ANNOY 1
 rel anger, incense, madden
 3 syn see INCITE
 rel perturb, upset
 4 to lead one into doing or feeling or to produce by so leading a person <was *provoked* into finding a solution to the problem> <this foolish answer *provoked* an outburst of rage>
 syn excite, galvanize, innervate, innerve, motivate, move, pique, prime, quicken, rouse, ‖roust, stimulate, suscitate; *compare* FIRE 2, STIR 1
 rel arouse, awaken, bestir, build up, challenge, kindle, rally, stir, wake, waken, whet; animate, exalt, fire, inform, inspire; electrify, enthuse, thrill; titillate, titivate
 idiom bring (one) to one's feet
 con calm, relax, soothe
 5 syn see GENERATE 3
provoking n syn see ANNOYANCE 1
prowess n 1 syn see HEROISM
 2 syn see ADDRESS 1
proximate adj 1 syn see CLOSE 6
 2 syn see IMMINENT 1
 3 syn see RUDE 3
 ant exact
proximity n the quality or state of being near <the two houses are in close *proximity*>
 syn appropinquity, contiguity, contiguousness, immediacy, propinquity
 rel togetherness, closeness, nearness; adjacency, juxtaposition
 con farness, remoteness
 ant distance
proxy n syn see AGENT 2
prude n a person who is excessively or priggishly attentive to propriety or decorum <in that narrow atmosphere she hardened into a rigid, inhibited, censorious person—a thorough *prude*>
 syn bluenose, comstock, goody-goody, Grundy, Mrs. Grundy, nice Nelly, prig, puritan, ‖wowser
 rel spoilsport, stick-in-the-mud, wet blanket; fuddy-duddy, old fogy, stuffed shirt; fussbudget, old maid
 con freethinker, latitudinarian, libertarian
prudence n 1 a quality in a person that allows him to choose the sensible course <displayed *prudence* in setting up his business>
 syn canniness, caution, discreetness, discretion, foresight, forethought, precaution, providence; *compare* WIT 3
 rel acumen, astuticy, astuteness, clearsightedness, discrimination, keenness, penetration, percipience, perspicacity, shrewdness, wit; insight, sagaciousness, sagacity, sageness, sapience, wisdom; advisableness, expediency; calculation, circumspection

con indiscretion, unreasonableness, unwiseness
ant imprudence
2 *syn* see ECONOMY

prudent *adj* **1** *syn* see WISE 2
ant imprudent
2 *syn* see EXPEDIENT

prudish *adj syn* see PRIM 1
rel strict; austere, severe, stern

prune *n syn* see DUNCE

prune *vb syn* see CUT 6
rel brash, lop; thin; eliminate, exclude

prurience *n syn* see LUST 2

pruriency *n syn* see LUST 2

prurient *adj syn* see LUSTFUL 2
rel bawdy, erotic, lewd; sensual

pry *vb syn* see SNOOP
idiom nose into

pry *vb* to raise, move, or pull apart with or as if with a pry <*pry* up a floorboard>
syn jimmy, lever, prize
rel elevate, heave, lift, pick up, raise, rear, take up, uphold, uplift, upraise, uprear; turn, twist; disengage, disjoin, divide, separate

prying *adj syn* see CURIOUS 2
rel obtrusive, officious

psalm *vb syn* see PRAISE 2

psalmody *vb syn* see PRAISE 2

pseudo *adj syn* see COUNTERFEIT
rel wrong

pseudonym *n* a fictitious or assumed name <used a *pseudonym* in many of his adventures>
syn alias, anonym, nom de guerre
rel ananym; nom de plume, pen name; stage name; incognito

psychal *adj syn* see PSYCHIC 1

psyche *n syn* see SOUL 1

psychic *adj* **1** sensitive to nonphysical forces and influences <because he foretold many things correctly, people regarded him as *psychic*>
syn psychal, psychical, supersensible, supersensory
rel telepathic; spiritual; impressible, impressionable, responsive, sensible, sensile, sensitive, sentient, susceptible, susceptive
2 *syn* see MENTAL 1

psychical *adj syn* **1** see PSYCHIC 1
2 *syn* see MENTAL 1

psychological *adj syn* see MENTAL 1

psychopathy *n syn* see INSANITY 1

pub *n syn* see BAR 5

puberty *n syn* see YOUTH 1

pubescence *n syn* see YOUTH 1

public *adj* **1** of, relating to, or affecting the people as an organized community <*public* affairs>
syn civic, civil, national
rel government, governmental; community; state; municipal, urban
2 *syn* see OPEN 4
rel common, general, universal
con private
3 *syn* see COMMON 1

con private
4 held by or applicable to the majority of the people <*public* opinion>
syn general, popular, vulgar
rel prevalent, usual, widespread
ant private

public *n* **1** *syn* see SOCIETY 3
2 *syn* see FOLLOWING 2
rel hangers-on, suite

‖**publican** *n syn* see SALOONKEEPER

publication *n syn* see DECLARATION
rel dissemination

public house *n* **1** *syn* see HOTEL
‖2 *syn* see BAR 5

publicity *n* information with news value issued to gain public attention or support <$100,000 was allocated for new-product *publicity*>
syn advertising, buildup, hype, press⹀ agentry, promotion, puffery
rel broadcasting, promulgation, skywriting; réclame; announcement, write-up; blurb, commercial, plug, promo, puff; ballyhoo, hoopla; propaganda; hard sell

publicize *vb* to give publicity to <*publicize* a new book>
syn advertise, build up, cry, hype, press⹀ agent, puff; *compare* PROMOTE 3
rel announce, broadcast, headline, promulgate, skywrite; advance, boost, plug, push; extol; bruit, tout, trumpet; propagandize
idiom bring into the limelight, throw the spotlight on

publish *vb* **1** *syn* see DECLARE 1
rel broach, express, utter, vent, ventilate
idiom bring to public notice, lay before the public, publish (*or* noise *or* spread) abroad, put forth
2 to produce for publication and allow to be distributed and sold <*published* a newspaper>
syn get out, issue, put out
rel produce; bring out; market; distribute

puckfist *n syn* see BRAGGART

puckish *adj syn* see PLAYFUL 1

‖**pudding** *n, usu* **puddings** *pl syn* see ENTRAILS

puddle *n syn* see POOL

puddle *vb syn* see FIDDLE 2

puddy *adj syn* see ROTUND 2

pudendum *n, usu* **pudenda** *pl syn* see GENITALIA

pudgy *adj syn* see ROTUND 2
rel ‖chuffy, ‖chumpy, squab, squdgy, ‖stuggy, stumpy, thick-bodied

puerile *adj syn* see CHILDISH

puff *vb* **1** *syn* see PANT 1
idiom huff and puff, pant and blow
2 *syn* see BOAST
3 *syn* see PUBLICIZE

puff *n* **1** *syn* see DRAW 2
rel inhalation, inhaling
2 *syn* see QUILT
3 a commendatory and often extravagant publicity notice or review <this book fails to deliver what the *puff* promises>
syn blurb, plug, puffing, write-up
rel promo; boost, buildup, push; laudation, praise

puffery *n syn* see PUBLICITY

---

syn synonym(s)   *rel* related word(s)
ant antonym(s)   *con* contrasted word(s)
idiom idiomatic equivalent(s)
‖ use limited; if in doubt, see a dictionary

puffing *n syn* see PUFF 3
puffy *adj syn* see POMPOUS 1
‖**puggy** *adj syn* see SWEATY
pugilism *n syn* see BOXING
pugnacious *adj syn* see BELLIGERENT
  rel pushing, pushy, self-assertive; defiant,
rebellious; brawling
  idiom itching for a fight, itching (*or* ready)
to fight, ready to fight at the drop of a hat
  con bland, easygoing, mild; calm, peaceful;
quiet
  ant pacific
pugnacity *n syn* see ATTACK 2
puissance *n syn* see POWER 4
  rel clout, influence, sway
  con powerlessness, weakness
  ant impuissance
puissant *adj syn* see POWERFUL 2
  rel influential; commanding, ruling
  con ineffectual, inefficacious, powerless
  ant impuissant
puke *n syn* see SNOT 1
pukka *adj syn* see AUTHENTIC 2
pulchritudinous *adj syn* see BEAUTIFUL
pule *vb syn* see WHIMPER
pull *vb* 1 *syn* see EXTRACT 1
  2 to cause to move toward or after an applied force <*pull* a trunk across the floor>
  syn drag, draw, haul, lug, tow, tug
  rel strain; heave; jerk, wrench, yank; drive,
impel, push, shove
  3 *syn* see STRAIN 2
  4 *syn* see ROW
  idiom pull on the oar (*or* oars)
  5 *syn* see COMMIT 2
  idiom ‖go and do
  6 *syn* see DON 2
  7 *syn* see GET 1
pull *n* 1 *syn* see DRAW 1
  2 the power or ability to secure special favor
or partiality <had lots of *pull* with the gov-
ernment>
  syn clout, ‖drag, in, influence; *compare*
INFLUENCE 1
  rel persuasion; wire-pulling
  idiom backstairs influence
  3 *syn* see ATTRACTION 1
pullback *n syn* see DIEHARD 1
pull down *vb syn* see DESTROY 1
pull in *vb* 1 *syn* see RESTRAIN 1
  2 *syn* see ARREST 2
pull out *vb syn* see GO 2
  ant pull in
pull through *vb syn* see SURVIVE 2
pullulate *vb syn* see TEEM
pull up *vb syn* see STOP 4
pulp *vb syn* see CRUSH 2
pulpitarian *n syn* see CLERGYMAN
pulpiteer *n syn* see CLERGYMAN
pulpiter *n syn* see CLERGYMAN
pulpous *adj syn* see SOFT 6
pulpy *adj syn* see SOFT 6
pulsate *vb* to course or move with or as if
with rhythmic strokes <blood *pulsating*
through his veins>
  syn beat, palpitate, pulse, throb
  rel fluctuate, oscillate, vibrate; pump; drum,
pound, roar, thrum
pulse *vb syn* see PULSATE

pulverize *vb* 1 to reduce (as by crushing,
beating, or grinding) to minute particles
<*pulverized* the ore in a stamp mill>
  syn bray, buck, comminute, contriturate,
crush, powder, triturate; *compare* SHATTER
1
  rel break up; abrade, grate, grind; crumble,
crunch, mull; levigate; atomize, fragment,
fragmentalize, fragmentize, micronize; beat,
shatter, smash, smatter, splinter; flour, mill
  2 *syn* see DESTROY 1
pulverized *adj syn* see FINE 2
  rel pulverous, pulverulent; dusty, granular,
splintery
  ant unpulverized
pummel *vb syn* see BEAT 1
pump *vb syn* see DRAIN 1
pumpkin head *n syn* see DUNCE
‖**pumpknot** *n syn* see BUMP 2
pun *n* the humorous use of a word so as to
suggest different meanings, or of words
having the same or similar sound but different meanings <"mourning shall come with
approaching day" is a *pun*>
  syn calembour, paronomasia
  rel double entendre
  idiom play on words
punch *vb* 1 *syn* see POKE 1
  rel hit, slap, strike
  2 *syn* see PERFORATE
punch *n* 1 *syn* see CUFF
  2 *syn* see POKE 1
  3 *syn* see POINT 3
  4 *syn* see VIGOR 2
punctilious *adj syn* see CAREFUL 2
  rel conventional, formal, observant; over-
conscientious, overscrupulous
punctual *adj* 1 *syn* see CAREFUL 2
  ant unpunctual
  2 marked by exact adherence to an appointed time <a *punctual* arrival>
  syn prompt, timely
  rel quick, ready
  idiom on the dot, on time
  con late, tardy
  ant unpunctual
punctuate *vb* to mark or divide (written
matter) with punctuation marks <*punctu-
ated* the sentence>
  syn point
  rel divide, separate
puncture *n syn* see PRICK 1
  rel perforation
puncture *vb* 1 *syn* see PERFORATE
  rel riddle
  2 *syn* see DISCREDIT 2
  idiom shoot full of holes
pungent *adj* sharp and stimulating to the
mind or senses <his *pungent* wit>
  syn peppery, piquant, poignant, racy,
snappy, spicy, zesty
  rel acute, keen, salt, salty, sharp; biting,
bitter, cutting, hot, incisive, trenchant; exciting, provocative, stimulating; rich
  con banal, corny, dull, flat, hackneyed,
insipid, old hat, platitudinous, prosaic,
prosy, stale, stodgy, tasteless, unimaginative, uninteresting
  ant bland

punish *vb* **1** to inflict a penalty on in requital for a wrongdoing <*punished* the child for misbehaving>
  syn castigate, chasten, chastise, correct, discipline
  rel criticize, reprove, amerce, fine, mulct, penalize; avenge, fix, revenge; lambaste, scourge
  con overlook; absolve, acquit, exculpate, exonerate, vindicate; let off, release
  ant excuse, pardon
  2 *syn* see CONSUME 5
punishing *adj syn* see PUNITIVE
punishment *n* the act or an instance of punishing <a spanking was his *punishment*>
  syn castigation, chastisement, correction, discipline, punition, rod
  rel criticism, reproof; amercement, fine, mulct, penalty; avengement, revenge
  idiom carrot-and-stick treatment, disciplinary action, dose of strap oil, what for
  con overlooking; acquittal, exculpation, exoneration, vindication
  ant excuse, pardon
punition *n syn* see PUNISHMENT
  idiom punitive measures
punitive *adj* inflicting, involving, or constituting punishment <took *punitive* action against him>
  syn castigating, disciplinary, punishing, punitory
  rel correctional, penal
punitory *adj syn* see PUNITIVE
punk *n* **1** *syn* see NONSENSE 2
  2 *syn* see NOVICE
  3 *syn* see TOUGH
‖**punk** *adj syn* see BAD 1
puny *adj* **1** *syn* see PETTY 2
  rel feeble, weak
  2 *syn* see WEAK 1
pup *n syn* see TWERP
puppet *n syn* see TOOL 2
  rel dupe; slave
puppy *n syn* see TWERP
purblind *adj* partly blind <*purblind* with cataracts>
  syn dim-sighted, half-blind
  rel myopic, nearsighted, shortsighted; dim; blind, dark, sightless
purchasable *adj* **1** capable of being bought <*purchasable* goods>
  syn available, obtainable, on offer
  rel marketable, salable
  idiom on (or for) sale, on the market, to be had
  con rare; unavailable, unobtainable
  ant unpurchasable
  2 *syn* see VENAL 1
  rel undependable, unreliable; slippery, tricky; treacherous
purchase *vb syn* see BUY 1
  idiom make a purchase
  ant sell
purchaser *n* one to whom something is sold <instruction booklets for new-car *purchasers*>

---

  syn buyer, emptor, vendee
  rel marketer, shopper; client, customer, patron; consumer, user
  con seller, vendor
pure *adj* **1** *syn* see STRAIGHT 3
  ant impure
  2 being such and no other <his solution of the problem was *pure* genius>
  syn absolute, perfect, pure and simple, sheer, simple, unadulterated, unalloyed, undiluted, unmitigated, unmixed, unqualified; *compare* UTTER
  rel complete, plenary, total; authentic, genuine; classic; out-and-out, plain, utter
  con mixed, qualified; doubtful, dubious, questionable, uncertain
  3 *syn* see UTTER
  4 *syn* see GOOD 11
  ant impure
  5 *syn* see CHASTE
  rel fresh, inviolate, unblighted, unprofaned
  idiom as pure as the driven snow
  con contaminated, dirty, sullied
  ant immoral, impure
‖**pure** *adv syn* see VERY 1
pure and simple *adj syn* see PURE 2
pureblood *adj syn* see PUREBRED
purebred *adj* being of unmixed ancestry <a *purebred* collie>
  syn full-blooded, pedigree, pedigreed, pureblood, thoroughbred
  rel registered
  con bastard, hybrid, lowbred, mixed
  ant mongrel
‖**puredee** (*or* **pure-D**) *adj syn* see UTTER
purely *adv syn* see ALL 1
purgation *n syn* see PURIFICATION
purgative *adj* cleansing or purifying especially from sin <confession as a *purgative* ritual>
  syn expiative, expiatory, expurgatorial, expurgatory, lustral, lustratory, propitiatory, purgatorial
purgatorial *adj syn* see PURGATIVE
‖**purgatory** *n syn* see SWAMP
purge *vb* **1** *syn* see DISABUSE
  rel absolve, cleanse; clear, rid
  2 *syn* see PURIFY 2
  3 to get rid of often by exile, imprisonment, or murder <Stalin *purged* all the Party dissidents>
  syn eliminate, liquidate, remove
  rel debar, exclude, shut out; dismiss, eject, expel, oust; erase, expunge, wipe (out); exterminate
  con rehabilitate; reinstate; repatriate; accept, bear (with), tolerate
  ant depurge
purification *n* a freeing from something morally harmful, offensive, or sinful <sought *purification* through repentance>
  syn catharsis, cleansing, expurgation, lustration, purgation
  rel atonement, expiation; absolution, forgiveness; grace, redemption, salvation; rebirth, regeneration; sanctification
  con contamination, defilement
purify *vb* **1** to free from material impurities or noxious matter <*purify* the water for drinking>

---

syn clarify, clean, cleanse, depurate
rel elutriate; filter; refine
con dirty, foul, soil
ant contaminate, pollute
2 to free from guilt or moral blemish (often ceremonially) <*purify* one's heart through confession>
syn cleanse, expurgate, lustrate, purge
rel atone, expiate; absolve, remit
con defile, sully, tarnish
purist *n* one who adheres strictly and often excessively to a tradition <*purists* who believe in prescriptive grammar>
syn precisian, precisionist, traditionalist
rel Atticist, classicist; bitter-ender, conservative, diehard, Puritan
con liberal, radical, young Turk
ant revisionist
puritan *n syn* see PRUDE
puritanical *adj syn* see PRIM 1
rel rigorous, strict; bigoted, hidebound, illiberal, intolerant, narrow, narrow-minded
con liberal, tolerant; modern
purl *vb syn* see SWIRL
‖**purl** *vb syn* see SPIN 1
purlieu *n* **1** *syn* see RESORT 2
2 purlieus *pl syn* see ENVIRONS 1
3 purlieus *pl syn* see ENVIRONS 2
purloin *vb syn* see STEAL 1
purloiner *n syn* see THIEF
purloining *n syn* see THEFT
purple *adj* **1** *syn* see RISQUÉ
2 *syn* see RHETORICAL
purport *n* **1** *syn* see MEANING 1
2 *syn* see TENOR 1
rel connotation; implication
3 *syn* see SUBSTANCE 2
purported *adj syn* see ALLEGED
rel postulated, presupposed; suppositional, suppositive; academic, speculative, theoretical; reputed, rumored; suspected
purportless *adj syn* see SENSELESS 5
purpose *n* **1** *syn* see INTENTION
rel destination, direction; aim, goal, mission, objective, point; ambition, aspiration; proposal, proposition
2 *syn* see USE 4
rel mission
purpose *vb syn* see INTEND 2
rel meditate, ponder; consider; conclude, decide, determine, resolve
purposedly *adv syn* see INTENTIONALLY
purposefulness *n syn* see DECISION 2
rel certainty, confidence, sureness
con indecision, irresoluteness, irresolution, vacillation, waffling, wavering, weakness; aimlessness, indirection
ant purposelessness
purposeless *adj* **1** *syn* see FECKLESS 1
rel unhelpful, unprofitable; purportless, senseless; nonsensical
con helpful, profitable
ant purposeful
2 *syn* see RANDOM
ant purposeful
purposely *adv syn* see INTENTIONALLY
rel expressly; explicitly
con unintentionally
ant accidentally
purposively *adv syn* see INTENTIONALLY

purposiveness *n syn* see DECISION 2
purse cutter *n syn* see PICKPOCKET
pursual *n syn* see PURSUIT 2
pursuance *n syn* see PURSUIT 2
pursue *vb* **1** *syn* see FOLLOW 2
rel persevere, persist; oppress, persecute; badger, bait, hound, ride
idiom go in pursuit (of)
2 *syn* see ADDRESS 8
pursuing *n syn* see PURSUIT 2
pursuit *n* **1** *syn* see WORK 1
2 a following with a view to reach, accomplish, or obtain <the *pursuit* of happiness>
syn pursual, pursuance, pursuing, quest, search, seeking
rel following; reaching; obtaining; accomplishing, accomplishment
idiom a going all out (after)
pursy *adj syn* see FAT 2
purview *n* **1** *syn* see RANGE 2
2 *syn* see KEN
push *vb* **1** to use force so as to cause to move ahead or aside <*push* a wheelbarrow across the yard>
syn drive, propel, shove, thrust
rel launch; impel, move; force, ram
con brake, check, stay
ant pull
2 to do, effect, or accomplish by forcing aside obstacles or opposition <*pushed* her way through the crowd> <*pushed* the measure through congress>
syn bulldoze, elbow, hustle, jostle, press, ‖shog, shoulder, shove
rel dig, nudge; hunch; drive, force, thrust; bump, butt, ram
con ease, facilitate, slide (by), slip (through); expedite, speed (along)
3 *syn* see INCREASE 1
4 *syn* see PRESSURE
5 *syn* see PROMOTE 3
rel oversell
6 to engage in the illicit sale of (narcotics) <*pushing* drugs to teenagers>
syn peddle, shove
7 *syn* see PRESS 1
push *n* **1** *syn* see ENTERPRISE 4
2 *syn* see VIGOR 2
3 *syn* see STIMULUS
4 *syn* see CROWD 1
5 *syn* see SET 5
push around *vb syn* see BAIT 2
pushful *adj* **1** *syn* see AGGRESSIVE
2 *syn* see PRESUMPTUOUS
rel imposing, intrusive, obtruding, obtrusive, officious; assured, confident, self-confident
pushing *adj* **1** *syn* see AGGRESSIVE
idiom ‖not backward in going forward
2 *syn* see PRESUMPTUOUS
push off *vb syn* see GO 2
push on *vb syn* see GO 1
pushover *n syn* see SNAP 1
pushy *adj* **1** *syn* see AGGRESSIVE
‖**2** *syn* see PRESUMPTUOUS
pusillanimous *adj syn* see COWARDLY
puss *n syn* see CHILD 1
‖**puss** *n syn* see FACE 1
pussyfoot *vb* **1** *syn* see SNEAK
2 *syn* see EQUIVOCATE 2

pustule *n syn* see ABSCESS
put *vb* **1** *syn* see SET 1
  2 *syn* see FASTEN 3
  3 *syn* see PROPOSE 1
  4 *syn* see WORD
  5 *syn* see TRANSLATE 1
  6 *syn* see EXPRESS 2
  7 *syn* see ESTIMATE 3
put (back) *vb syn* see RESTORE 5
put (on) *vb syn* see GAMBLE 1
put (on *or* upon) *vb syn* see LEVY
put *n syn* see DUNCE
put about *vb syn* see INCONVENIENCE
putative *adj syn* see SUPPOSED 1
put away *vb* **1** *syn* see DIVORCE 2
  2 *syn* see CONSUME 5
  3 *syn* see MURDER 1
  4 *syn* see BURY 1
  5 *syn* see KILL 1
put by *vb syn* see SAVE 4
put down *vb* **1** *syn* see CRUSH 5
  2 *syn* see DEGRADE 1
  3 *syn* see CONSUME 5
  4 *syn* see DECRY 2
put in *vb syn* see PLANT 1
put off *vb* **1** *syn* see DELAY 2
  idiom drag one's feet
  2 *syn* see DEFER
  idiom lay on the table, let the matter stand
  3 *syn* see REMOVE 3
  ant put on
put on *vb* **1** *syn* see DON 1
  ant put off
  2 *syn* see DON 2
  rel affect, feign, sham, simulate; masquerade, pose
  idiom make as if (*or* as though)
  3 *syn* see ASSUME 4
  idiom put on a (false) front, put on an act
  4 *syn* see EMPLOY 2
  5 *syn* see STAGE
put-on *adj syn* see ARTIFICIAL 3
  rel mannered, posed; faked, sham
put-on *n* **1** *syn* see IMPOSTURE
  2 *syn* see MASK 2

put out *vb* **1** *syn* see EXERT
  2 *syn* see EXTINGUISH 1
  3 *syn* see PUBLISH 2
  4 *syn* see IRRITATE
  5 *syn* see INCONVENIENCE
  rel displease, dissatisfy; annoy, irritate
  idiom put out of the way, put to it
put over *vb syn* see DEFER
putrefy *vb syn* see DECAY
putresce *vb syn* see DECAY
putrid *adj* **1** *syn* see BAD 5
  2 *syn* see MALODOROUS 1
  3 *syn* see VICIOUS 2
putter *vb syn* see FIDDLE 2
  rel boondoggle; dawdle
‖**put to** *vb syn* see CLOSE 1
put together *vb syn* see MAKE 3
put up *vb* **1** *syn* see HARBOR 2
  2 *syn* see BUILD 1
  rel forge, make, put together, shape
  3 *syn* see ERECT 3
  4 *syn* see RAISE 9
  rel elevate, escalate
‖**puxy** *n syn* see SWAMP
puzzle *vb* to baffle and disturb mentally <a persistent fever that *puzzled* her doctor>
  syn befog, bewilder, ‖cap, confound, confuse, metagrobolize, perplex, pose, stumble;
  compare NONPLUS 1
  rel baffle, foil, frustrate; befuddle, ‖bumfuzzle, fuddle; disconcert, distract, disturb, upset; addle, muddle; mystify; amaze, dumbfound, flabbergast
  con enlighten, inform
puzzle *n syn* see MYSTERY
puzzlement *n syn* see MYSTERY
puzzle out *vb syn* see SOLVE 2
  idiom find the key to, pick the lock
pygmy *n syn* see DWARF
  ant giant
pygmy *adj syn* see TINY
pyramid *n syn* see PILE 1
Pyrrhonian *n syn* see SKEPTIC
Pyrrhonist *n syn* see SKEPTIC
pythonic *adj syn* see HUGE

Q

quack *n syn* see CHARLATAN
  rel counterfeiter, pretender, shammer, simulator
‖**quackle** *vb syn* see SUFFOCATE
quacksalver *n syn* see CHARLATAN
quackster *n syn* see CHARLATAN
quad *n syn* see COURT 1
quadrangle *n syn* see COURT 1

quadrate *adj syn* see SQUARE 1
quadrate *vb* **1** *syn* see AGREE 4
  2 *syn* see ADAPT
quadratic *adj syn* see SQUARE 1
quadratical *adj syn* see SQUARE 1
quaesitum *n syn* see AMBITION 2
quaff *vb syn* see DRINK 1
quag *n syn* see SWAMP
quaggy *adj syn* see SOFT 6
quagmire *n* **1** *syn* see SWAMP
  2 *syn* see PREDICAMENT
quail *n syn* see GIRL 1
quail *vb syn* see RECOIL

---

syn synonym(s)   *rel* related word(s)
ant antonym(s)   *con* contrasted word(s)
idiom idiomatic equivalent(s)
‖ use limited; if in doubt, see a dictionary

rel cower, cringe

quaint *adj syn* see STRANGE 4
  rel droll, funny, laughable; antiquated, antique, archaic

||**quaint** *vb syn* see INTRODUCE 4

quake *vb 1 syn* see SHAKE 2
  rel fluctuate, waver
  2 *syn* see SHAKE 1

quake *n syn* see EARTHQUAKE

||**quaker** *n syn* see EARTHQUAKE

quaking *adj syn* see TREMULOUS

quaky *adj syn* see TREMULOUS

qualification *n syn* see ABILITY 1

qualified *adj 1 syn* see ABLE
  rel disciplined, instructed, trained; catechized, examined, quizzed; proved, tested, tried
  con incapable, incompetent, unequipped, unfit
  ant disqualified, unqualified
  2 not unlimited and complete <gave only a *qualified* endorsement to the project>
  syn limited, modified, reserved
  rel circumscribed, definite, determined, fixed, restricted; partial
  con complete, entire, full, total, utter, whole; unlimited, unrestricted
  ant absolute, unqualified

qualifiedness *n syn* see ABILITY 1

qualify *vb 1 syn* see CHARACTERIZE 2
  rel ascribe, assign, attribute, impute; predicate
  2 *syn* see ENTITLE 2

quality *n 1* something inherent and distinctive <learned the special *qualities* of the native herbs>
  syn affection, attribute, character, characteristic, feature, mark, peculiarity, property, savor, trait, virtue; *compare* CHARACTERISTIC 1
  rel individuality; affirmation, predication; element, factor, parameter
  2 a usually high level of merit or superiority <merchandise of *quality*>
  syn caliber, merit, stature, value, virtue, worth
  rel arete, excellence, excellency, perfection, superbness, superiority
  con inferiority, meanness, mediocrity, poorness; inadequacy; deficiency
  3 degree of excellence <upgrading the *quality* of incoming students>
  syn caliber, class, grade
  rel capacity, character, footing, place, position, rank, situation, standing, state, station, status
  4 *syn* see STATUS 1
  5 *syn* see ARISTOCRACY
  6 *syn* see EXCELLENCE

quality *adj syn* see EXCELLENT

qualm *n* a misgiving about what one is going to do <had *qualms* about the secret meeting>
  syn compunction, conscience, demur, scruple, squeam
  rel apprehension, foreboding, misgiving, presentiment; doubt, mistrust, suspicion, uncertainty; agitation, insecurity, perturbation; objection, remonstrance; reluctance, unwillingness; impatience, nervousness, unease, uneasiness
  con aplomb, assurance, confidence, self-assurance, self-confidence, self-possession; certainty, certitude, conviction

qualmish *adj syn* see SQUEAMISH 1

qualmishness *n syn* see NAUSEA

qualmy *adj syn* see SQUEAMISH 1

quantity *n 1 syn* see BODY 5
  2 quantities *pl syn* see SCAD

quantum *n 1 syn* see BODY 5
  2 *syn* see RATION

quarrel *n* a usually verbal dispute marked by anger or discord <a *quarrel* over who would drive the car>
  syn altercation, ||barney, beef, bickering, brabble, brannigan, brawl, controversy, difficulty, dispute, dust, embroilment, falling-out, feud, fight, fracas, fuss, hassle, imbroglio, knock-down-and-drag-out, miff, ||prabble, ||pribble, rhubarb, row, ruckus, run-in, set-to, spat, squabble, squall, tiff, to-and-fro, word(s), wrangle; *compare* BRAWL 2
  rel battle royal, catfight; affray, bobbery, broil, donnybrook, fray, free-for-all, melee, ruction, rumpus, scrap, scrimmage, scuffle; conflict, contention, difference, discord, dissension, strife, variance; disagreement, misunderstanding
  idiom ||pribbles and prabbles
  con accord, concord, harmony; agreement, like-mindedness, understanding, unity

quarrel *vb* to contend noisily or captiously <with his belligerent personality he was always *quarreling* with someone>
  syn altercate, bicker, brabble, brawl, ||cast out, caterwaul, fall out, row, scrap, spat, squabble, tiff, wrangle; *compare* ARGUE 2
  rel differ, disaccord, dissent, divide, vary; bump, clash, collide, conflict, thwart; battle, contend, fight, war
  idiom have words with, pull caps
  con agree, coincide, concur

quarrelsome *adj 1 syn* see BELLIGERENT
  rel adverse, antagonistic, counter; antipathetic, hostile, inimical, rancorous
  idiom having a chip on one's shoulder
  2 apt or disposed to quarrel <when he's in a bad mood he becomes so *quarrelsome*>
  syn battlesome, brawling, brawlsome, brawly, scrappy; *compare* BELLIGERENT
  rel argumentative; disputatious; cankered, crabbed, irascible, irritable
  con conciliatory, propitiatory

quarry *n syn* see GAME 3

quarry *vb syn* see MINE

quarter *n 1* one of four equal parts <ate one *quarter* of the pie>
  syn fourth, quartern
  rel quadrant
  2 a division or part of a town or city <the market *quarter* in Paris>
  syn district, precinct, section, sector
  rel division, part; area; locality; barrio

quarter *vb 1 syn* see HARBOR 2
  2 *syn* see BILLET 1

quarterage *n syn* see SHELTER 2

quarterback *vb syn* see SUPERVISE

quartern *n syn* see QUARTER 1

quarter–witted *adj syn* see RETARDED

quartet *n* a group consisting of four individuals <a singing *quartet*>

syn four, foursome, quartetto, quaternion, quatuor, tetrad
rel quadruplet

quartetto *n syn* see QUARTET
quash *vb* **1** *syn* see ANNUL 4
2 *syn* see ABOLISH 1
3 *syn* see CRUSH 5
quashing *n syn* see REPRESSION 1
‖**quat** *vb syn* see SQUAT
quaternion *n syn* see QUARTET
quatuor *n syn* see QUARTET
quaver *vb syn* see SHAKE 1
rel falter, hesitate, vacillate, waver
‖**quawk** *vb syn* see SQUALL 1
quay *n syn* see WHARF
‖**queak** *vb syn* see SQUEAK 1
quean *n syn* see PROSTITUTE
queasiness *n syn* see NAUSEA
queasy *adj* **1** *syn* see DOUBTFUL 1
2 *syn* see SQUEAMISH 1
queer *adj* **1** *syn* see STRANGE 4
rel doubtful, dubious, questionable; droll, funny, laughable
2 *syn* see OBSESSED
‖**3** *syn* see HOMOSEXUAL
4 *syn* see SQUEAMISH 1
‖**queer** *n syn* see HOMOSEXUAL
quelch *vb syn* see SUPPRESS 2
quell *vb syn* see CRUSH 5
rel conquer, overcome, subjugate, vanquish
con abet, incite, instigate
ant foment
quench *vb* **1** *syn* see EXTINGUISH 1
2 *syn* see CRUSH 5
rel end, terminate
3 *syn* see DESTROY 1
4 to bring (as thirst) to an end with or as if with a refreshing drink <after being in the hot sun, he found it difficult to *quench* his thirst>
syn slake, ‖squench
rel appease, content, gratify, satisfy, sate, satiate; allay, alleviate, assuage, lighten, mitigate, relieve; decrease, diminish, lessen, reduce
quenching *n syn* see REPRESSION 1
quenchless *adj* **1** *syn* see INSATIABLE
2 *syn* see INDESTRUCTIBLE
querulent *adj syn* see IRRITABLE
querulential *adj syn* see IRRITABLE
querulous *adj syn* see IRRITABLE
rel blubbering, crying, wailing, weeping, whimpering; bemoaning, deploring, lamenting
query *n* **1** *syn* see INQUIRY 2
2 *syn* see UNCERTAINTY
query *vb syn* see ASK 1
quest *n* **1** *syn* see INQUIRY 1
2 *syn* see PURSUIT 2
quest *vb* **1** *syn* see HOWL 1
2 *syn* see SEEK 1
question *n* **1** *syn* see INQUIRY 2
2 *syn* see PROBLEM 2
3 *syn* see DEMUR 2
question *vb* **1** *syn* see ASK 1

syn synonym(s)   *rel* related word(s)
ant antonym(s)   *con* contrasted word(s)
idiom idiomatic equivalent(s)
‖ use limited; if in doubt, see a dictionary

2 to express doubt about <*questioned* his decision to take a new job>
syn challenge, dispute, doubt, mistrust
rel suspect, ‖suspicion; hesitate (over), puzzle (over), wonder (about)
questionable *adj* **1** *syn* see IMPROBABLE 1
ant unquestionable
2 *syn* see MOOT
rel refutable; equivocal, obscure, vague
con dependable, true, trustworthy, trusty; genuine, indubitable, real, undoubted, undubitable, veritable, very
ant authoritative; unquestionable, unquestioned
3 *syn* see UNRELIABLE 1
questioning *n syn* see INQUIRY 2
questioning *adj* **1** *syn* see INCREDULOUS
ant questionless, unquestioning
2 *syn* see INQUISITIVE 1
questionless *adj syn* see AUTHENTIC 2
queue *n syn* see LINE 5
quibble *vb* **1** to find fault with something usually on minor grounds <was a peevish critic, always ready to *quibble*>
syn cavil, chicane, hypercriticize
rel carp, criticize
idiom split hairs
con applaud, commend, compliment, recommend; approve, endorse, sanction
2 *syn* see ARGUE 2
quick *adj* **1** *syn* see FAST 3
rel agile, brisk, nimble; abrupt, impetuous
idiom quick on the trigger
con dilatory, laggard, leisurely, slow, unhasty, unhurried; comatose
ant sluggish
2 able to respond without delay or hesitation or indicative of such ability <very *quick* in perception> <his *quick* eye spotted the trouble>
syn apt, prompt, ready; compare INSTANTANEOUS
rel clever, intelligent, quick-witted, smart; adroit, deft, dexterous; acute, keen, sharp; able, capable, competent, effective, effectual
con comatose, lethargic, logy, poky, torpid; crass, dense, dull, dumb, stupid
ant slow; sluggish
3 *syn* see WISE 4
quick *adv syn* see FAST 2
quick *n syn* see CENTER 3
quicken *vb* **1** to make alive or lively <warm spring days that *quicken* the earth>
syn animate, enliven, liven, vivificate, vivify
rel activate, energize, vitalize; arouse, awaken, rouse, stir, wake
con blunt, dull; slow (down)
ant deaden
2 *syn* see PROVOKE 4
rel activate, actuate, motivate; goad, induce, spur
con check, halt, interrupt, stall, stay; curb, inhibit, restrain
ant arrest
3 *syn* see SPEED 3
con bog (down), detain, embog, hang up, mire
ant slacken
quickening *adj syn* see INVIGORATING
quick-lunch *n syn* see EATING HOUSE

quickly *adv syn* see FAST 2
quickness *n syn* see SPEED 2
ant slowness
quick-sighted *adj syn* see SHARP 4
quick-tempered *adj syn* see IRASCIBLE
quick-witted *adj* **1** *syn* see SHARP 4
2 *syn* see INTELLIGENT 2
rel apt, prompt, quick, ready
3 *syn* see WISE 4
rel acute, keen; facetious, humorous, witty
ant slow-witted
quidnunc *n* **1** *syn* see BUSYBODY
2 *syn* see GOSSIP 1
quiescence *n syn* see ABEYANCE
quiescency *n syn* see ABEYANCE
quiescent *adj syn* see LATENT
rel calm, halcyon, hushed, placid, quiet,
still, stilly, untroubled
quiet *n* **1** a period of intensified silence <the
quiet before the storm>
syn calm, hush, lull
rel cessation, stop, termination
con din, hubbub, racket, uproar
2 *syn* see SILENCE 1
quiet *adj* **1** *syn* see CALM 1
con harsh, rough; disquieted, disturbed,
perturbed, upset
ant unquiet
2 *syn* see INACTIVE
3 *syn* see STILL 3
con blatant, boisterous, clamorous, strident, vociferous
4 not showy or obtrusive <always dressed in
quiet good taste>
syn inobtrusive, restrained, subdued, tasteful, tasty, unobtrusive
rel homely, plain, simple, unpretentious
con blatant, brazen, flashy, garish, glaring,
meretricious, tawdry, tinsel; elaborate
ant gaudy, loud
quiet *n* **1** *syn* see SILENCE
rel abate, decrease, lessen
con excite, provoke, quicken, stimulate;
awaken, rally, stir
2 *syn* see CALM
con agitate; unhinge, untune
ant disquiet; excite
∥**quieten** *vb* **1** *syn* see SILENCE
2 *syn* see CALM
ant arouse; excite
quietive *adj syn* see SEDATIVE
quietness *n syn* see SILENCE 1
quietude *n syn* see SILENCE 1
quietus *n syn* see DEATH 1
∥**quiff** *n syn* see GIRL 1

quilt *n* a bed coverlet made of two layers of
cloth with a stuffing (as of cotton, wool, or
feathers) between <a warm *quilt* is nice on a
winter night>
syn ∥comfortable, comforter, pouf, puff
rel bedcover, bedspread, counterpane;
eiderdown
quinary *adj syn* see QUINTUPLE
quinta *n syn* see ESTATE 3
quintessence *n* **1** *syn* see ESSENCE 2
2 *syn* see APOTHEOSIS 1
quintessential *adj syn* see TYPICAL 1
quintessential *n syn* see ESSENCE 2
quintuple *adj* consisting of five <the problem is viewed as having *quintuple* aspects>
syn fivefold, quinary
rel quintuplicate
quip *n syn* see JOKE 1
quip (at) *vb syn* see SCOFF
quipster *n syn* see HUMORIST 2
quit *vb* **1** *syn* see CLEAR 5
2 *syn* see BEHAVE 1
3 *syn* see GO 2
4 *syn* see ABANDON 1
rel relinquish, resign, surrender
5 *syn* see STOP 3
6 to give up (as a habit, activity, or employment) especially with finality <*quit* a job>
<determined to *quit* smoking>
syn drop, leave, resign, terminate
rel retire, secede, withdraw
idiom draw one's time, give notice
con hire on, hire out
quite *adv* **1** *syn* see WELL 3
2 *syn* see ALTOGETHER 2
3 *syn* see ALL 1
4 *syn* see WELL 8
quittance *n syn* see REPARATION
quitter *n syn* see COWARD
quiver *n syn* see FLASH 1
quiver *vb syn* see SHAKE 1
rel beat, palpatate, pulsate, pulse, throb
quivering *adj syn* see TREMULOUS
quivery *adj syn* see TREMULOUS
quiz *n syn* see ECCENTRIC
quiz *vb* **1** *syn* see RIDICULE
2 *syn* see ASK 1
quizzical *adj syn* see INCREDULOUS
rel curious, inquisitive; probing, searching
∥**quod** *vb syn* see IMPRISON
quodlibetic *adj syn* see PEDANTIC
quondam *adj syn* see FORMER 2
quota *n* **1** *syn* see SHARE 1
2 *syn* see RATION
quota *vb syn* see APPORTION 2
quotidian *adj* **1** *syn* see DAILY
2 *syn* see ORDINARY 1

R

rabbity *adj syn* see SHY 1
rabble *n* 1 *syn* see MOB 2
  2 the lowest class of people <the *rabble* of
  the city>
  syn canaille, doggery, dreg(s), hoi polloi,
  mass(es), mob, other half, polloi, proletariat,
  raff, ‖ragabash, ragtag, ragtag and bobtail,
  riffraff, roughscuff, rout, scum, scurf, tag
  and rag, tagrag and bobtail, trash, unwashed
  rel bourgeoisie, commonalty, many, people,
  populace, public, rank and file
  idiom the great unwashed, the scum of the
  earth, the submerged tenth
  con aristocracy, aristoi, elite, Four Hundred, gentility, nobility, upper class, upper
  crust, upper ten, upper ten thousand
rabble-rouser *n syn* see DEMAGOGUE

rabid *adj* 1 *syn* see FURIOUS 2
  rel crazed, crazy, demented, deranged,
  insane
  2 *syn* see EXTREME 3
  rel enthusiastic, keen, obsessed, zealous
race *n syn* see CREEK 2
race *vb* 1 *syn* see RUSH 1
  2 *syn* see COURSE
race *n syn* see FAMILY 1
  rel culture, nation, nationality, people;
  breed, type, variety
rachis *n syn* see SPINE
rachitic *adj syn* see RICKETY
racial *adj syn* see ETHNIC 2
racialism *n syn* see RACISM
racism *n* racial prejudice or discrimination
  <an act of overt *racism*>
  syn racialism
  rel discrimination, prejudice; illiberality,
  unfairness; bias, one-sidedness, partiality
  con broad-mindedness, liberalism, open-
  mindedness, tolerance; indifference, neutrality
rack *vb syn* see AFFLICT
  rel distress, pain; oppress, persecute
‖**rack back** *vb syn* see REPROVE
racket *n* 1 *syn* see DIN
  ‖2 *syn* see WORK 1
racketry *n syn* see DIN
rackety *adj* 1 *syn* see NOISY
  2 *syn* see RICKETY
racking *adj syn* see EXCRUCIATING
  rel barbarous, cruel, ferocious, fierce, inhuman, savage
rack up *vb syn* see GAIN 1
racy *adj* 1 *syn* see PUNGENT
  rel fiery, gingery, mettlesome, spirited

con banal, inane, jejune
  2 *syn* see RISQUÉ
radiant *adj* 1 *syn* see BRIGHT 1
  2 *syn* see GLAD 2
radiate *vb* 1 *syn* see SHINE 1
  2 *syn* see SPREAD 2
  rel diverge
radical *adj* 1 *syn* see FUNDAMENTAL 1
  rel cardinal, essential, vital; constitutional,
  inherent, intrinsic
  ant superficial
  2 *syn* see EXTREME 3
  3 *syn* see LIBERAL 3
radical *n* one who favors rapid and sweeping
  changes <the *radicals* advocated overthrow
  of the government>
  syn extremist, revolutionary, revolutionist,
  ultraist; *compare* REACTIONARY
  rel liberal, progressive, reformer; agitator,
  insurgent, insurrectionist, rebel; anarchist,
  nihilist, red, subversive; out-and-outer;
  secessionist, separatist
  con bitter-ender, diehard, fogy, intransigent, mossback, reactionary, rightist, standpatter
  ant conservative
radius *n syn* see RANGE 2
raff *n syn* see RABBLE 2
raffish *adj syn* see WILD 7
rag *vb* 1 *syn* see SCOLD 1
  2 *syn* see BANTER
‖**ragabash** *n syn* see RABBLE 2
ragamuffin *n* a person dressed in ragged
  clothing <a poor *ragamuffin* found beg-
  ging>
  syn ragshag, scarecrow, tatterdemalion
  rel hobo, tramp, vagabond, vagrant; bum,
  loafer, wastrel; orphan, waif
  con buck, coxcomb, dandy, dude, fop
rage *n* 1 *syn* see ANGER
  rel acerbity, acrimony, asperity; frenzy,
  hysteria, mania; agitation, perturbation,
  upset
  2 *syn* see FASHION 3
  rel caprice, conceit, crotchet, fancy, freak,
  vagary, whim
rage *vb syn* see ANGER 2
ragged *adj* torn or worn to tatters <never
  saw such *ragged* clothes>
  syn frayed, frazzled, shreddy, tattered
  rel rent, torn; battered, patched; dilapidated, dingy, faded, seedy, shabby, threadbare, worn-out
raging *adj syn* see WILD 6
rags *n pl* 1 poor or ragged clothing <a beggar
  in *rags*>
  syn ‖duds, tatters
  rel odds and ends, ribbons, shreds
  2 *syn* see CLOTHES
ragshag *n syn* see RAGAMUFFIN
ragtag *n syn* see RABBLE 2
ragtag and bobtail *n syn* see RABBLE 2

---

syn synonym(s)   *rel* related word(s)
ant antonym(s)   *con* contrasted word(s)
idiom idiomatic equivalent(s)
‖ use limited; if in doubt, see a dictionary

raid n 1 syn see INVASION
 rel assault, onset, onslaught
 2 a sudden attack by officers of the law <a *raid* on a gambling joint>
 syn ‖bust

raid vb 1 to make a raid on <Indians *raided* the settlers frequently>
 syn foray, harass, harry, maraud
 rel despoil, devastate, ravage, sack, spoliate, waste; loot, plunder, rifle, rob
 2 syn see INVADE 1

raider n syn see MARAUDER

rail n syn see RAILING

rail vb syn see SCOLD 1

railing n a usually protective barrier consisting essentially of an elongated raised member <a staircase without a *railing*>
 syn balustrade, banister, rail

raillery n syn see SATIRE

railroad station n a building containing accommodations for railroad passengers or freight <an old *railroad station* fallen into disrepair>
 syn depot, station, station house

raiment n syn see CLOTHES

raiment vb syn see CLOTHE

rainbow n syn see PIPE DREAM

rainless adj syn see FAIR 2
 ant rainy

raise vb 1 syn see LIFT 1
 ant lower
 2 syn see INCITE
 3 syn see RESURRECT 1
 4 syn see ERECT 3
 5 syn see BUILD 1
 6 syn see BRING UP 1
 7 syn see GROW 1
 8 syn see GATHER 6
 9 to make larger in amount <*raised* the rent>
 syn boost, hike, increase, jack (up), jump, put up, up
 rel inflate
 idiom send through the roof
 con cut back, decrease, drop, lessen, reduce, roll back; minimize
 ant lower

raise n syn see ADDITION

raised adj 1 syn see ELEVATED 1
 2 syn see ERECT

rake vb syn see SCOUR 2

rakehell adj syn see WILD 7

raking adj syn see FAST 3

rakish adj syn see WILD 7

rally vb 1 syn see MOBILIZE 3
 2 syn see STIR 1
 rel fire; refresh, renew, restore
 3 syn see RECOVER 2
 rel brace (up), enliven, invigorate, perk (up), pick up

rally vb syn see RIDICULE 1
 rel harass, harry, tantalize, tease, worry

rallying cry n syn see BATTLE CRY

ram vb 1 syn see THRUST 2
 2 syn see CRAM 1

ramble vb 1 syn see WANDER 1
 2 syn see DIGRESS 2
 3 syn see SPRAWL 2

ramble n syn see WALK 1

rambler n syn see ROVER

rambunctious adj syn see TURBULENT 1

rampage n syn see SPREE 1
 rel turmoil, uproar

rampant adj 1 syn see RANK 1
 rel excessive, immoderate, inordinate
 con moderate, temperate; checked, curbed, restrained
 2 syn see PREVAILING

rampart n syn see BULWARK

rancid adj syn see MALODOROUS 1
 rel ‖reasty; loathsome, repulsive
 ant sweet

rancor n syn see ENMITY
 rel bitterness, vindictiveness, virulence

rancorous adj 1 syn see MALICIOUS
 2 syn see BITTER 3

rancorously adv syn see HARD 6

random adj lacking a definite plan, purpose, or pattern <a *random* choice>
 syn aimless, designless, desultory, haphazard, hit-or-miss, indiscriminate, irregular, objectless, promiscuous, purposeless, slapdash, spot, unaimed, unconsidered, unplanned; compare ACCIDENTAL
 rel contingent, fluky, fortuitous, incidental, odd
 con arranged, organized, planned; methodical, systematic; deliberate, purposeful
 ant purposive

random adv syn see ABOUT 4
 ant orderly

randomly adv syn see ABOUT 4
 ant orderly

randy adj syn see LICENTIOUS 2

range vb 1 syn see LINE 1
 rel assort, classify, sort; bias, dispose, incline, predispose
 2 syn see WANDER 1
 3 to change or differ within limits <discounts *range* from 10% to 40%>
 syn extend, go, run, vary
 rel differ, fluctuate

range n 1 syn see HABITAT
 2 sphere of action, expression, or influence <a political movement worldwide in its *range* and power>
 syn ambit, circle, compass, confine(s), dimension(s), extension, extensity, extent, length, orbit, panorama, purview, radius, reach, realm, scope, stretch, sweep, width
 rel area, space, span; domain, field, province, sphere, territory; amplitude, expanse, gamut, spread
 3 syn see KEN
 rel compass
 idiom range of comprehension
 4 syn see ORDER 4
 5 the distance or extent between possible extremes <the *range* of exhibited photographs went from the extremely good to the extremely bad>
 syn diapason, gamut, scale, spectrum
 rel compass, radius, reach, scope, stretch, sweep

rangy adj syn see GANGLING
 ant compact

rank adj 1 growing or increasing at an immoderate rate <*rank* weeds>
 syn rampant
 rel exuberant, lavish, lush, luxuriant, profuse

con scanty, sparse, thin

2 *syn* see OVERGROWN

3 *syn* see OBSCENE 2

4 *syn* see EGREGIOUS

rel conspicuous, noticeable, outstanding

5 *syn* see UTTER

6 *syn* see MALODOROUS 1

rel dank, humid; loathsome, repulsive

rank *n* **1** *syn* see LINE 5

2 *syn* see ESTATE 2

3 *syn* see STATUS 1

4 *syn* see STATUS 2

rank *vb* **1** *syn* see CLASS 2

rel arrange, order; assort, sort

2 *syn* see PRECEDE 1

rank and file *n syn* see COMMONALTY

rankle *vb* to produce continual or progressive anger, irritation, or bitterness <this decision has long *rankled* as an act of injustice>

syn fester

rel annoy, bother, irk, vex; aggravate, exasperate, irritate; harass, obsess, plague, torment

ransack *vb* **1** *syn* see SCOUR 2

2 *syn* see ROB 1

ransom *vb* to liberate by paying a price <*ransomed* the king>

syn buy, redeem

rel recover, regain, retrieve; emancipate, free, liberate; extricate, release

rant *vb* **1** *syn* see ORATE

rel bluster, huff; rage, storm

2 *syn* see SCOLD 1

rant *n syn* see BOMBAST

ran-tan *n syn* see BINGE 1

rantankerous *adj syn* see CANTANKEROUS

rap *n* **1** *syn* see HIT 1

2 *syn* see REBUKE

rap *vb* **1** *syn* see TAP 1

2 *syn* see CRITICIZE

rap *n* **1** *syn* see CHAT 2

2 *syn* see CONFERENCE 1

3 *syn* see CRITICISM 2

rapacious *adj* **1** subsisting on prey <the *rapacious* wolf seized the lamb>

syn predacious, predative, predatorial, predatory, raptorial, vulturine, vulturish, vulturous

2 *syn* see VORACIOUS

rel ferocious, fierce

rapacity *n syn* see CUPIDITY

rel claim, demand, exaction

rape *vb* to have sexual intercourse with a woman without her consent and chiefly by force or deception <*rape* a young girl>

syn defile, deflorate, deflower, force, outrage, ravish, spoil, violate

rel debauch, devirginate, dishonor, ruin; betray, deceive, mislead; entice, lure, seduce, tempt; compromise, shame, wrong

rapid *adj syn* see FAST 3

rel agile, brisk, nimble; hurried, quickened

ant deliberate; leisurely

rapidity *n syn* see SPEED 2

rapidly *adv syn* see FAST 2

rapidness *n syn* see SPEED 2

‖**rapper** *n syn* see LIE

rapport *n syn* see HARMONY 3

rapprochement *n syn* see RECONCILIATION

rapscallion *n syn* see SCAMP

rap session *n syn* see CONFERENCE 2

rapt *adj syn* see INTENT

raptorial *adj syn* see RAPACIOUS 1

rapture *n syn* see ECSTASY

rare *adj* **1** *syn* see THIN 2

2 *syn* see CHOICE

rel excellent, fine, unique

3 *syn* see INFREQUENT

con accustomed, customary, habitual, usual, wonted; abounding, profuse

4 *syn* see EXCEPTIONAL 1

rarefied *adj syn* see THIN 2

rarefy *vb syn* see THIN 2

rarely *adv* **1** *syn* see SELDOM

2 *syn* see EXTRA

raring *adj syn* see EAGER

rascal *n* **1** *syn* see VILLAIN 1

2 *syn* see SCAMP

rash *adj* **1** acting, done, or expressed with undue haste or disregard for consequences <don't do anything *rash*> <that was a very *rash* statement>

syn brash, hasty, hotheaded, ill-advised, incautious, incogitant, inconsiderate, mad=brained, madcap, reckless, thoughtless, unadvised, unconsidered, unwary; *compare* CARELESS 1

rel abrupt, headlong, impetuous, precipitate, precipitous, sudden; foolhardy, foolish, impulsive, silly; careless, heedless, imprudent, indiscreet, injudicious, unthinking, unwise

con careful, cautious, chary, circumspect, wary; advised, considered, deliberate, designed, premeditated, studied; calm, cool, level-headed

ant calculating

2 *syn* see ADVENTUROUS

rash *n syn* see EPIDEMIC

rasp *vb syn* see SCRAPE 1

raspberry *n* a sound of disapproval, contempt, or derision <the crowd gave the umpire a *raspberry*>

syn bazoo, bird, boo, ‖Bronx cheer, catcall, hiss, hoot, pooh, pooh-pooh, ‖razz

rasping *adj syn* see HARSH 3

raspish *adj syn* see IRRITABLE

raspy *adj syn* see IRRITABLE

rat *n* **1** *syn* see RENEGADE

2 *syn* see SNOT

rat *vb* **1** *syn* see DEFECT

2 *syn* see INFORM 3

rate *vb syn* see SCOLD 1

rate *n* **1** *syn* see PRICE 1

2 *syn* see DEGREE 2

rate *vb* **1** *syn* see ESTIMATE 1

2 *syn* see CLASS 2

3 *syn* see EARN 2

rather *adv* **1** *syn* see ENOUGH 2

2 *syn* see INSTEAD

3 *syn* see SOMEWHAT 2

4 *syn* see WELL 8

ratherish *adv syn* see SOMEWHAT 2

---

syn synonym(s)   *rel* related word(s)
ant antonym(s)   *con* contrasted word(s)
idiom idiomatic equivalent(s)
‖ use limited; if in doubt, see a dictionary

ratify *vb* to make something legally valid or operative usually by formal approval or sanctioning <agreed to *ratify* the treaty>
syn confirm
rel accredit, authorize, commission, license; approve, endorse, sanction; authenticate, validate
con disown, reject, repudiate

ratio *n syn* see DEGREE 2

ratiocination *n* **1** *syn* see INFERENCE 1
ant intuition
2 *syn* see INFERENCE 2

ratiocinative *adj syn* see LOGICAL 2

ration *n* an amount allotted or made available especially from a limited supply <saved up their gasoline *ration* for a vacation trip>
syn allotment, allowance, apportionment, measure, meed, part, portion, quantum, quota, share; *compare* SHARE 1
rel assignment, consignment, distribution, division

ration *vb syn* see APPORTION 2
rel allocate, allot, assign, mete (out)

rational *adj* agreeable to reason <offered a *rational* explanation>
syn consequent, intelligent, logical, reasonable, sensible, sound
rel calm, cool, level-headed, sober, stable; circumspect, judicious, prudent; lucid, normal, sane
con rash, reckless, wild; groundless, illogical, unreasonable, unreasoning, unsound; crazy, demented, deranged
ant animal, irrational; absurd

rationale *n syn* see EXPLANATION 2

rationalization *n syn* see EXPLANATION 2

rationalize *vb syn* see EXPLAIN 3

rattle *vb* **1** to make a rapid succession of short sharp noises <the window *rattled* in the wind>
syn bicker, clack, clatter, clitter, ‖ruttle, shatter
2 *syn* see CHAT 1
3 *syn* see EMBARRASS
rel addle, muddle; disturb, upset; bewilder, distract, perplex

rattlebrain *n syn* see SCATTERBRAIN

rattlebrained *adj syn* see GIDDY 1

rattlehead *n syn* see SCATTERBRAIN

rattletrap *n, usu* **rattletraps** *pl syn* see KNICKKNACK

rattletrap *adj syn* see RICKETY

rattling *adv syn* see VERY 1

ratty *adj syn* see IRASCIBLE

raucous *adj* **1** *syn* see HARSH 3
rel brusque, gruff
2 *syn* see TURBULENT 1

raunchy *adj* **1** *syn* see SLOVENLY 1
2 *syn* see OBSCENE 2

ravage *vb* to lay waste (as by plundering or destroying) <the countryside was *ravaged* by the invading soldiers>
syn deflower, depredate, desecrate, desolate, devast, devastate, devour, harry, havoc, pillage, sack, scourge, spoil, spoliate, strip, waste
rel demolish, destroy, raze; loot, plunder, ransack, rob; ruin, wreck; encroach, invade, trespass; crush, overpower, overrun, overthrow, overwhelm

idiom lay in ruins, lay waste
con build, improve, rehabilitate

ravager *n syn* see MARAUDER

rave *vb* **1** *syn* see ORATE
2 *syn* see ENTHUSE 2

ravel *vb syn* see COMPLICATE

raven *adj syn* see BLACK 1

ravening *adj syn* see VORACIOUS

ravenous *adj* **1** *syn* see VORACIOUS
2 *syn* see HUNGRY

ravine *n* a small narrow steep-sided valley <followed the *ravine* high up into the hills>
syn arroyo, chasm, cleft, clough, clove, gap, gorge, gulch
rel cut, notch; defile, pass; abyss, gulf; crevasse, crevice, fissure; ‖dry wash, gully, gutter, ‖wash; canyon

raving *adj syn* see DELIRIOUS 1

ravish *vb* **1** *syn* see TRANSPORT 2
2 *syn* see RAPE

ravisher *n syn* see MARAUDER

raw *adj* **1** not cooked <a *raw* egg>
syn uncooked
2 *syn* see UNREFINED 3
3 *syn* see RUDE 1
4 *syn* see NUDE 2
5 *syn* see INEXPERIENCED
rel untaught, untutored; unmatured, unripe
con drilled, exercised; hardened; adult, grown-up, mature, matured, ripe
6 *syn* see COARSE 3
‖**7** *syn* see OBSCENE 2

rawboned *adj syn* see LEAN

rawhider *n syn* see SLAVE DRIVER

rawness *n syn* see INEXPERIENCE

ray *n* **1** one of the lines of light that appear to radiate from a bright or luminous object <the *rays* of the sun>
syn beam, shaft, shoot
rel raylet; pencil, streak, stream; moonbeam, sunbeam
con gleam, glow, incandescence, shine
2 *syn* see PARTICLE

raze *vb syn* see DESTROY 1

razor–sharp *adj syn* see SHARP 1

‖**razz** *n syn* see RASPBERRY

razz *vb* **1** *syn* see BANTER
2 *syn* see RIDICULE

re *prep syn* see APROPOS

reach *vb* **1** *syn* see COME 1
2 *syn* see GAIN 1
3 to get into contact with especially intellectually or emotionally <there was no common ground on which she could *reach* him>
syn approach
rel affect, influence, sway; get, move, touch
idiom establish contact with, find a common denominator, get through to, get to, have a meeting of minds, make advances to, make overtures to, make up to, reach (*or* share) common ground
4 to communicate with <you can *reach* me at this number>
syn contact, get
idiom get in touch (*or* contact) with, get through to, keep in touch (*or* contact) with, maintain connections with
5 *syn* see PASS 9
6 *syn* see RUN 8

reach *n* **1** *syn* see RANGE 2

2 syn see KEN

react *vb* **1 syn** see ACT 5

2 syn see RETURN 1

reactionarist *n syn* see REACTIONARY

reactionary *adj syn* see CONSERVATIVE 1

reactionary *n* one who strongly resists change and often favors a prior condition <he is a staunch political *reactionary*>
syn Blimp, Bourbon, Colonel Blimp, diehard, reactionarist, reactionist, royalist, ultraconservative, white; *compare* DIEHARD 1, RADICAL
rel bitter-ender, conservative, intransigent, rightist, right-winger, standpatter; fogy, mossback
con extremist, radical, revolutionary, revolutionist, ultraist; liberal, progressive, reformer

reactionist *n syn* see REACTIONARY

reactivate *vb syn* see REVIVE 3

read *vb syn* see SHOW 5

readily *adv syn* see EASILY 1

readiness *n* **1 syn** see ALACRITY

2 syn see ADDRESS 1

3 the power of doing something without evidence of effort <his *readiness* in repartee>
syn ease, facility
rel eloquence, fluency, volubility
con effort, exertions, pains, trouble

reading *n syn* see INTERPRETATION 2

readjust *vb syn* see REORGANIZE

ready *adj* **1** in a state of mental or physical fitness for some experience or action <*ready* to leave at a moment's notice>
syn prepared, set
rel adjusted, fit, qualified; primed
idiom all ready, all set, champing at the bit
con unprepared, unqualified
ant unready

2 syn see WILLING 1

3 syn see QUICK 2
rel adept, expert, masterly, proficient, skilled, skillful; active, dynamic, live

ready *vb* **1 syn** see PREPARE 1

2 syn see GIRD 3

ready–made *adj* made for general sale or use rather than prepared according to individual specifications <*ready-made* clothing>
syn bought, ‖boughten, ‖off-the-peg, off-the-rack, off-the-shelf, ready-to-wear, store, store-bought, ‖store-boughten
con custom-built, made-to-order, tailor= made; handmade
ant custom-made

ready–to–wear *adj syn* see READY-MADE

ready–witted *adj syn* see INTELLIGENT 2

real *adj* **1 syn** see AUTHENTIC 2
ant bogus

2 syn see GENUINE 3

3 corresponding to known facts <discovered the *real* reason for her hasty departure>
syn actual, indisputable, true, undeniable, unfabled, veridical
rel being, existing, subsisting; certain, inevi= table, necessary; sound, valid, well= grounded

idiom deniable, disputable, doubtful, questionable; improbable, uncertain, unlikely
ant unreal; apparent; imaginary

realistic *adj* having no illusions and facing reality squarely <he made a *realistic* appraisal of his chances for advancement>
syn down-to-earth, earthy, hard, hard-boiled, hardheaded, matter-of-fact, practic, practical, pragmatic, pragmatical, sober, unfantastic, un= idealistic, unromantic, unsentimental, utilitarian
rel rational, reasonable, sane, sensible, sound; astute, prudent, shrewd; nonacademic
con dreamy, fantastic, imaginative; idealistic, impractical, irrational, romantic, visionary; theoretical
ant unrealistic; fanciful

reality *n* **1 syn** see FACT 1

2 syn see ACTUALITY 2

realize *vb* **1 syn** see GAIN 1

2 syn see THINK 1

really *adv* **1 syn** see VERY 2

2 syn see WELL 7

realm *n syn* see RANGE 2

ream *n, usu* reams *pl syn* see SCAD

ream *vb syn* see CHEAT

‖ream out *vb syn* see SCOLD 1

reanimation *n syn* see REVIVAL

reap *vb* to do the work of collecting ripened crops <storms hampered his *reaping*>
syn garner, gather, harvest, ingather
rel glean

reaping *n syn* see HARVEST 1

reappearance *n syn* see RECURRENCE

rear *vb* **1 syn** see BUILD 1

2 syn see ERECT 3

3 syn see LIFT 1

4 syn see BRING UP 1
rel foster, nurse, nurture; breed, propagate

rear *n* **1 syn** see BACK 1
ant front

2 syn see BUTTOCKS

rear *adj syn* see POSTERIOR 2
ant front

rear end *n syn* see BUTTOCKS

rearmost *adj syn* see LAST

rearrange *vb syn* see REORGANIZE

rearward *n syn* see BACK 1

reason *n* **1 syn** see EXPLANATION 2

2 syn see MOTIVE 1

3 a point or points that support something open to question <he soon gave sensible *reasons* for the proposed change>
syn argument, ground, proof, wherefore, why, whyfor
rel explanation, justification, rationalization

4 syn see CAUSE 1

5 the power of the mind by which man attains truth or knowledge <we all must use *reason* to solve this problem>
syn intellect, understanding
rel inference, ratiocination

6 syn see WIT 2

reason *vb syn* see THINK 5

reasonable *adj* **1 syn** see CONSERVATIVE 2

2 syn see MODERATE 2

3 syn see CHEAP 1
ant extravagant

4 syn see RATIONAL
ant unreasonable

reasoned adj syn see DEDUCTIVE

reasonless adj **1** syn see INSANE 1
2 syn see ILLOGICAL

reassume vb syn see RESUME 1

rebate vb syn see DECREASE

rebate n syn see DEDUCTION 1

rebel n one who breaks with or opposes constituted authority or the established order <he is a *rebel* among educators>
syn anarch, anarchist, frondeur, insurgent, insurrectionist, malcontent, mutineer, revolter
rel adversary, antagonist, opponent; assailant, attacker; extremist, radical, revolutionary, revolutionist, ultraist; debunker, iconoclast
con authoritarian, intransigent, traditionalist; conservative, reactionary, white

rebel vb syn see REVOLT 1

rebellious adj syn see INSUBORDINATE
rel alienated, disaffected, estranged
con acquiescent, resigned; submissive

rebirth n **1** syn see CONVERSION 1
2 syn see REVIVAL

rebound vb syn see RECOVER 3

rebuff vb syn see FEND (off)
idiom give the cold shoulder

rebuild vb syn see MEND 2

rebuke vb syn see REPROVE

rebuke n an expression of strong disapproval <his bad behavior earned him a sharp *rebuke*>
syn admonishment, admonition, chiding, rap, reprimand, reproach, reproof, wig, wigging
rel dressing down, earful, lecture, lesson, scolding, talking-to, tongue-lashing
idiom a flea in one's ear, slap on the wrist
con applause, compliment, praise

rebut vb **1** syn see FEND (off)
2 syn see DISPROVE 1

recalcitrance n syn see DEFIANCE 2

recalcitrant adj syn see UNRULY 1
rel obstinate, stubborn; opposing, resisting, withstanding
ant amenable

recall vb **1** syn see REMEMBER
rel educe, elicit, evoke, extract; arouse, awaken, rouse, stir, waken
2 syn see ABJURE
3 syn see REVOKE 2
4 syn see RESTORE 1

recall n syn see MEMORY 2

recant vb syn see ABJURE

recapitulation n syn see SUMMARY

recede vb **1** to move backward <they will return after the floodwaters *recede*>
syn back, fall back, retract, retreat, retrocede, retrograde
rel regress, retrogress; depart, retire, withdraw
ant proceed; advance
2 syn see DECREASE

receipts n pl syn see REVENUE

receive vb syn see TAKE 10

received adj syn see ORTHODOX 1

recension n syn see REVISION 1

recent adj **1** syn see NEW 1

2 syn see MODERN 1

recently adv syn see NEW

receptive adj **1** open to ideas, impressions, or suggestions <he has a most *receptive* mind>
syn acceptant, acceptive, influenceable, persuadable, persuasible, responsive, suasible, swayable
rel open, open-minded; accessible, amenable, suggestible
con closed, closed-minded, inhospitable
ant unreceptive
2 syn see SYMPATHETIC 2

recess vb syn see ADJOURN 2

recession n syn see DEPRESSION 3

recherché adj syn see CHOICE
rel fresh, new, novel, original; exotic, uncommon, unusual
ant commonplace

recidivate vb syn see LAPSE

reciprocal n syn see MATE 5

reciprocate vb to give back, usually in kind or quantity <they were glad of the chance to *reciprocate* her kindness>
syn recompense, requite, retaliate, return
rel exchange, interchange; compensate, repay; retort, serve out
con accept, acquire, pocket, take

recital n syn see DESCRIPTION 2
rel discourse, story; enumeration

recite vb syn see RELATE 1
rel count, enumerate, number, tell

reckless adj **1** syn see ADVENTUROUS
rel desperate, hopeless
2 syn see RASH 1
ant calculating
3 syn see IRRESPONSIBLE

reckon vb **1** syn see CALCULATE
rel count, enumerate, number; add, cast, foot, sum, total
2 syn see CONSIDER 3
rel conjecture, guess, surmise
3 syn see ESTIMATE 3
‖**4** syn see UNDERSTAND 3

reckon (on) vb syn see RELY (on *or* upon)

reckoning n **1** syn see BILL 1
2 syn see COMPUTATION

reclaim vb syn see RESTORE 3

recline vb **1** syn see SLANT 1
2 syn see REST 1

reclining adj syn see PRONE 4

recluse adj syn see SECLUDED

recluse n a person who leads a secluded or solitary life <a man who led the life of a *recluse* although living in a busy city>
syn hermit, solitary
rel anchorite, cenobite, eremite

reclusion n syn see SECLUSION

reclusive adj syn see ANTISOCIAL

recognition n **1** a learning process that relates a perception of something new to knowledge already possessed <*recognition* of a genuine diamond>
syn apperception, assimilation, identification
rel cognizance, realization; awareness, consciousness, sensibility
ant irrecognition
2 syn see CREDIT 4
ant unrecognition

recognize *vb* **1** to make out as or perceive to be something previously known <said they would *recognize* that face anywhere>
  syn know
  rel recall, recollect, remember
  2 *syn* see IDENTIFY
  3 *syn* see ACKNOWLEDGE 2
  rel note, notice, observe, remark
recoil *vb* to draw back usually through fear or disgust <*recoiled* from the snake>
  syn blanch, blench, flinch, quail, shrink, squinch, start, wince
  rel falter, hesitate, waver; balk, shy, stick, stickle; dodge, duck, swerve; quake, shake, shudder, tremble; reel (back)
  con advance, approach, near
  ant confront; defy
re—collect *vb syn* see COMPOSE 4
recollect *vb syn* see REMEMBER
  rel arouse, awaken, rally, rouse, stir, waken
recollection *n* **1** *syn* see MEMORY 2
  2 *syn* see MEMORY 1
recommence *vb syn* see RESUME 2
recommend *vb* **1** *syn* see COMMEND 2
  ant discommend
  2 *syn* see COUNSEL
recompense *vb* **1** *syn* see COMPENSATE 3
  rel accord, award, grant, vouchsafe; balance, offset
  2 *syn* see RECIPROCATE
recompense *n syn* see REPARATION
reconcile *vb* **1** *syn* see HARMONIZE 3
  idiom bury the hatchet, make peace
  ant estrange
  2 *syn* see ADAPT
reconcilement *n syn* see RECONCILIATION
reconciliate *vb syn* see HARMONIZE 3
reconciliation *n* establishment of harmony <a *reconciliation* between the two countries was effected after ten years>
  syn harmonizing, rapprochement, reconcilement
  rel appeasement, conciliation, mollification, propitiation, satisfying
  ant disagreement
recondite *adj* beyond the reach of the average intelligence <a *recondite* subject>
  syn abstruse, acroamatic, deep, esoteric, heavy, hermetic, occult, orphic, profound, secret
  rel erudite, learned, scholarly; academic, pedantic; difficult, hard; dark, enigmatic, obscure; anagogic, cabalistic, mystic, mystical; cryptic, runic, sibylline
  con easy, facile, simple, straightforward
recondition *vb* **1** *syn* see RESTORE 3
  2 *syn* see MEND 2
reconnoiter *vb syn* see SCOUT
reconsider *vb* to consider again with a view to changing or reversing <was asked to *reconsider* his decision>
  syn reevaluate, reexamine, rethink, re-treat, review, reweigh, think (over)
  rel draw off; sleep (on); amend, correct, revise

---

idiom revise one's thoughts, think better of, view in a new light
reconsideration *n syn* see REVIEW 5
reconstitute *vb syn* see REORGANIZE
reconstruct *vb* **1** *syn* see MEND 2
  2 *syn* see REORGANIZE
  3 *syn* see RESTORE 3
record *vb syn* see SHOW 5
record *n syn* see DOCUMENT 1
recount *vb syn* see RELATE 1
recountal *n syn* see DESCRIPTION 2
recounting *n syn* see DESCRIPTION 2
recoup *vb syn* see RECOVER 1
recourse *n syn* see RESOURCE 3
recover *vb* **1** to obtain again <*recover* a lost watch>
  syn get back, recoup, recruit, regain, repossess, retrieve
  rel reclaim, redeem; reacquire, recapture, retake, rewin; reoccupy, resume; rediscover; balance, compensate, offset
  con lose, mislay, misplace; forfeit, sacrifice
  2 to regain health <*recovering* from a bout of pneumonia>
  syn come round, rally
  rel convalesce, improve, mend, recuperate; perk (up), revive; heal; refresh, rejuvenate, renew, restore
  idiom get back in shape, get better, sit up and take nourishment, take a turn for the better
  con decline, fail, weaken, worsen; die, expire, perish
  3 to regain a former or normal state <the textile industry was *recovering* quickly from the depression>
  syn bounce (back), rebound, snap back
  rel rally, revive
  con decline, fail
  ant worsen
  4 *syn* see RESTORE 3
recreancy *n syn* see DEFECTION
recreant *adj syn* see FAITHLESS
recreant *n syn* see RENEGADE
recreate *vb* **1** *syn* see AMUSE
  rel refresh, rejuvenate, renew, restore
  2 *syn* see PLAY 1
recreation *n* **1** *syn* see ENTERTAINMENT
  rel ease, relaxation, repose; frolic, rollick; hilarity, jollity, mirth
  2 *syn* see PLAY 1
recreational vehicle *n syn* see TRAILER
recrementitious *adj syn* see SUPERFLUOUS
recrudesce *vb syn* see RETURN 1
  rel refurbish, renew, renovate
  con repress, suppress; cease, discontinue, stop
recruit *n syn* see NOVICE
recruit *vb syn* see RECOVER 1
  rel refresh, renew, renovate, restore; mend, rebuild, repair
rectify *vb syn* see CORRECT 1
  rel rebuild, repair
rectitude *n syn* see GOODNESS
  rel conscientiousness, justness, scrupulousness
recumbent *adj syn* see PRONE 4
  ant erect, upright
recuperate *vb syn* see IMPROVE 3
recur *vb* **1** *syn* see RETURN 1

---

rel iterate, reiterate, repeat
2 *syn* see RESORT 2

recurrence *n* **1** *syn* see DEDUCTION 1 a periodic or frequent returning <the *recurrence* of the nightmare upset him>
syn reappearance, reoccurrence, return
rel repetition, reproduction; crebrity, frequency

recurrent *adj syn* see INTERMITTENT
recurring *adj syn* see INTERMITTENT
Red *n syn* see COMMUNIST
red–blooded *adj syn* see VIGOROUS
redden *vb* **1** to make red <blood soon *reddened* the bandage>
syn incarnadine, rubify, rubric, ruby, rud, ruddle, ruddy
2 *syn* see BLUSH
redeem *vb* **1** *syn* see RANSOM
2 *syn* see FREE
3 *syn* see COMPENSATE 1
red–handed *adv* in the act of committing a misdeed <caught *red–handed*>
syn dead to rights, flagrante delicto
rel blatantly, openly
red–hot *adj* **1** *syn* see HOT 1
2 *syn* see IMPASSIONED
3 *syn* see UP-TO-DATE
red–letter *adj syn* see NOTEWORTHY
red–light district *n* a district characterized by brothels <sailors frequented the *red-light district*>
syn levee, stew(s), tenderloin
idiom street of fallen women
red–neck *n syn* see RUSTIC
redolence *n syn* see FRAGRANCE
redolent *adj* **1** *syn* see SWEET 2
2 *syn* see REMINISCENT
redouble *vb syn* see INTENSIFY
redoubt *n syn* see FORT
redoubtable *adj* **1** *syn* see FEARFUL 3
2 *syn* see FAMOUS 2
redound *vb syn* see CONTRIBUTE 2
redraft *n syn* see REVISION 1
redraft *vb syn* see REVISE
redraw *vb syn* see REVISE
redress *vb* **1** *syn* see AVENGE
2 *syn* see NEUTRALIZE
redress *n syn* see REPARATION
rel balancing, offsetting; retaliation, vengeance
reduce *vb* **1** *syn* see DECREASE
2 to decrease in amount <they decided to *reduce* prices to stimulate sales>
syn clip, cut, cut back, cut down, lower, mark down, pare, shave, slash
rel curtail, decrease, diminish, lessen; deflate, depreciate; scale (down), step down; roll back
con boost, hike, jack (up), jump, put up, raise, up
ant increase
3 *syn* see CONQUER 1
rel cripple, disable, enfeeble, undermine, weaken; debase, degrade, humble, humiliate
4 *syn* see DEGRADE 1
ant advance
5 to lose body weight especially by dieting <ate no cake while *reducing*>
syn slenderize, slim (down)
rel bant, diet

idiom lose flesh, take off weight
ant fatten
reduction *n* **1** *syn* see DEDUCTION 1
2 *syn* see DEMOTION
redundancy *n syn* see VERBIAGE 1
rel flatulence, inflatedness, inflation, tumidity, turgidity
redundant *adj syn* see WORDY
rel extra, spare, superfluous, supernumerary, surplus; iterating, reiterating, repetitious
ant concise
reduplicate *vb syn* see COPY
reduplication *n syn* see REPRODUCTION
reedy *adj syn* see THIN 1
reek *vb* **1** *syn* see SMELL 3
reeking *adj syn* see MALODOROUS 1
reeky *adj syn* see MALODOROUS 1
reel *vb* **1** *syn* see SPIN 2
2 to move uncertainly or uncontrollably (as in intoxication) <*reeled* down the street>
syn stagger, titubate, totter, wheel
rel careen, lurch, ‖swaver, sway, swing, weave, wobble; falter, ‖stammer, stumble, teeter, topple; bob, waver
reestablish *vb syn* see RESTORE 1
reevaluate *vb syn* see RECONSIDER
reexamination *n syn* see REVIEW 5
reexamine *vb syn* see RECONSIDER
refashion *vb syn* see CHANGE 1
refection *n syn* see MEAL
refer *vb* **1** *syn* see ASCRIBE
2 *syn* see SUBMIT 2
3 to call or direct attention to something <no one *referred* to his recent divorce>
syn advert, allude, bring up, point (out)
rel insert, interpolate, introduce; cite, quote; instance, mention, name, specify; glance, touch
idiom make an allusion to
4 *syn* see RESORT 2
rel advise, commune, confer, consult
referee *n syn* see JUDGE 1
referee *vb syn* see JUDGE 1
refine *vb syn* see POLISH 2
refined *adj* **1** *syn* see GENTEEL 1
ant earthy
2 *syn* see FINE 1
refinement *n syn* see CULTURE
rel finish, suavity, urbanity; civility, courtesy, politeness; dignity, elegance, grace
ant vulgarity
reflect *vb* **1** to reproduce or show as a mirror does <the trees on the shore were *reflected* in the water>
syn glass, image, mirror
rel repeat, reproduce
2 *syn* see THINK 5
rel study, weigh
reflecting *adj syn* see THOUGHTFUL 1
reflection *n* **1** *syn* see ANIMADVERSION
rel assault, attack, onset, onslaught; depreciation, derogation, disparagement
2 *syn* see THOUGHT 1
reflective *adj syn* see THOUGHTFUL 1
reformatory *n syn* see JAIL
refractory *adj syn* see OBSTINATE
ant malleable
refrain *vb* **1** to hold oneself back from doing or indulging in something <*refrained* from speaking out of turn>

syn abstain, forbear, keep, withhold
rel arrest, check, halt, interrupt, stop; curb, inhibit, restrain
2 *syn* see DENY 3
refresh *vb syn* see RENEW 1
rel animate, enliven, quicken, vivify; recover, recruit, regain; amuse, divert, recreate
con exhaust, tire
ant addle; jade
refreshed *adj* made or become fresh <awoke a *refreshed* man>
syn new, regenerated, reinvigorated, renewed, revived
rel recreated, renovated; animated, exhilarated, invigorated, stimulated
con exhausted, fagged, fatigued, jaded, tired, tuckered, wearied, worn-down, worn-out
refuge *n* **1** the state of being covered or protected <exiles seeking *refuge* in neutral countries>
syn asylum, harborage, sanctuary, shelter; *compare* SHELTER 1
rel protection, shield; immunity
con exposure, liability, openness; vulnerability
2 *syn* see SHELTER 1
3 *syn* see RESOURCE 3
refugee *n* one who flees for safety <the villagers fed and housed the *refugees* from the bombed city>
syn displaced person, DP, émigré, evacuee, fugitive
rel exile; emigrant, expatriate
idiom stateless person
refulgent *adj syn* see BRIGHT 1
refurbish *vb syn* see RENEW 1
refusal *n syn* see DENIAL 1
refuse *vb* **1** *syn* see DECLINE 4
2 *syn* see DENY 2
refuse *n* matter that is regarded as worthless and fit only for throwing away <heaps of *refuse* left by the former tenant>
syn ‖collateral, debris, dreck, ‖dust, garbage, junk, kelter, litter, ‖muck, ‖mullock, offal, outsweepings; ‖pelf, riffraff, rubbish, ‖sculch, spilth, sweepings, swill, trash, waste
rel dump, dustheap; rejectamenta, scraps; lumber; offscouring(s)
refute *vb syn* see DISPROVE 1
regain *vb syn* see RECOVER 1
rel achieve, attain, compass, gain, reach; reclaim, redeem, save; renew, restore
regal *adj syn* see KINGLY
rel august, imposing, magnificent, stately; glorious, resplendent, splendid, sublime
regale *n syn* see DINNER
regalia *n pl syn* see FINERY
regard *n* **1** *syn* see NOTICE 1
2 *syn* see CONSIDERATION 3
ant disregard
3 *syn* see INTEREST 3
4 a feeling of deferential approval and liking <held in high *regard* by his neighbors>
syn account, admiration, consideration, esteem, estimation, favor, respect

rel deference, homage, honor, reverence; appreciation, cherishing, prizing, valuing; approbation, approval, satisfaction
con deprecation, disapproval; disfavor, disgust, dislike, distaste; contempt, disdain, scorn; detestation, hate, hatred
ant despite
5 *syn* see CARE 4
regard *vb* **1** *syn* see ADMIRE 2
con reject, repudiate, scorn
ant despise
2 *syn* see CONSIDER 3
rel assay, assess, estimate, rate, value
regardful *adj* **1** *syn* see ATTENTIVE 1
2 *syn* see MINDFUL 2
3 *syn* see RESPECTFUL
regarding *prep syn* see APROPOS
regardless *adj syn* see NEGLIGENT
regardless of *prep syn* see AGAINST 4
regenerated *adj syn* see REFRESHED
region *n* **1** *syn* see AREA 1
rel neighborhood, vicinity; division, part, section, sector
2 *syn* see FIELD
register *n syn* see LIST
register *vb* **1** *syn* see ENROLL 1
2 *syn* see SHOW 5
regnant *adj* **1** *syn* see DOMINANT 1
2 *syn* see PREVAILING
regress *vb syn* see REVERT 2
regret *vb* to be very sorry for <*regrets* his mistakes> <*regret* the problems facing minorities>
syn deplore, repent, rue
rel bemoan, bewail, lament; grieve, mourn, sorrow; deprecate, disapprove
regret *n* **1** *syn* see SORROW
rel compunction, contrition, penitence, remorse, repentance; demur, qualm, scruple
2 regrets *pl syn* see APOLOGY 2
regretful *adj syn* see REMORSEFUL
regretless *adj syn* see REMORSELESS
regrettable *adj syn* see DEPLORABLE
regular *adj* **1** *syn* see GENERAL 1
rel customary, ordinary
ant irregular
2 *syn* see ORDERLY 1
rel fixed, set, settled; constant, equable, even, steady, uniform
ant irregular; sporadic
3 *syn* see UTTER
regulate *vb syn* see ADJUST 2
rel arrange, methodize, order, organize, systematize; moderate, temper
regulation *n syn* see LAW 1
rehabilitate *vb syn* see RESTORE 3
rehearse *vb* **1** *syn* see RELATE 1
rel iterate, reiterate, repeat
2 *syn* see EXERCISE 1
rel run through
reify *vb syn* see MATERIALIZE 2
reign *vb* **1** *syn* see GOVERN 1
idiom sit on the throne
2 *syn* see RULE 2
reimburse *vb syn* see COMPENSATE 3
rel recover; balance, compensate, offset
con default, dishonor, repudiate, welsh
rein *vb syn* see COMPOSE 4
reinforce *vb syn* see STRENGTHEN 2
rel augment, enlarge, increase, multiply; bolster, buttress, pillar, prop, sustain

---

syn synonym(s)　　　*rel* related word(s)
ant antonym(s)　　　*con* contrasted word(s)
idiom idiomatic equivalent(s)
‖ use limited; if in doubt, see a dictionary

ant undermine

reinstate *vb* **1** *syn* see RESTORE 5
2 *syn* see RESTORE 1

reintroduce *vb* *syn* see RESTORE 1

reinvigorated *adj* *syn* see REFRESHED

reissue *n* *syn* see EDITION

reiterate *vb* *syn* see REPEAT

reject *vb* **1** *syn* see DECLINE 4
rel debar, eliminate, exclude, shut out
ant accept; choose, select
2 *syn* see DISCARD

rejection *n* *syn* see DENIAL 1

rejoin *vb* *syn* see ANSWER 1

rejoinder *n* *syn* see ANSWER 1

rejuvenate *vb* **1** *syn* see RENEW 1
2 *syn* see RESTORE 3

rekindle *vb* *syn* see REVIVE 3

relapse *n* *syn* see LAPSE 2

relapse *vb* *syn* see LAPSE

relate *vb* **1** to tell orally or in writing the
details or circumstances of a situation <*related* the story of his life>
syn describe, narrate, recite, recount, rehearse, report, state
rel disclose, divulge, reveal, tell; detail,
itemize, particularize; depict, express, render; pronounce
idiom make public
2 *syn* see JOIN 1
rel ascribe, assign, credit, impute, refer
3 *syn* see BEAR (on *or* upon)

related *adj* connected by or as if by family
ties <persons *related* in the first degree>
<physics and mathematics are closely *re-
lated*>
syn affiliated, agnate, akin, allied, cognate,
connate, connatural, consanguine, incident,
kindred
rel associated, connected; complementary,
convertible, correlative, corresponding,
reciprocal; alike, analogous, identical; germane, pertinent, relevant
con different, dissimilar, divergent, unconnected, unlike
ant unrelated

relation *n* *syn* see RELATIVE

relative *n* a person connected with another
by blood <all of his *relatives* live out of
state>
syn kin, kinsman, kinswoman, relation
rel brother, half brother, half sister, sib,
sibling, sister; father, mother, parent; child,
daughter, son; grandfather, grandmother,
grandparent; grandchild, granddaughter,
grandson; aunt, half aunt, half uncle, uncle;
half nephew, half niece, nephew, niece;
cousin, cross-cousin, half cousin, ortho-
cousin; agnate, cognate

relative *adj* **1** *syn* see DEPENDENT 1
2 *syn* see COMPARATIVE

relax *vb* **1** *syn* see LOOSE 5
2 to become less tense or reserved <couldn't
relax in crowds>
syn ease off, loosen up, unbend, unlax,
unwind
rel calm (down), collect (oneself), compose
(oneself), cool (off), simmer down
idiom be at ease, breathe easily, feel at
home, make oneself at home
con rack (oneself), tense (up)

3 *syn* see REST 2

relaxation *n* *syn* see REST 1
rel amusement, diversion, recreation; alleviation, assuagement, mitigation, relief
ant tension

relaxed *adj* **1** *syn* see LOOSE 1
rel flexuous, sinuous; gentle, lenient, mild,
soft
ant stiff
2 *syn* see EASYGOING 3
con ascetic, austere, severe, stern
ant tense

release *vb* **1** *syn* see FREE
rel acquit, exculpate, exonerate; relinquish,
resign, surrender, yield
idiom cast loose, set at large
ant detain
2 *syn* see EMIT 2
3 *syn* see TAKE OUT (on)
ant check

relegate *vb* **1** *syn* see BANISH
2 *syn* see COMMIT 1
rel accredit, charge, credit, refer

relegation *n* **1** *syn* see EXILE 1
2 *syn* see DISPOSAL 2

relent *vb* *syn* see ABATE 4

relentless *adj* **1** *syn* see GRIM 3
rel rigorous, strict, stringent; cruel, ferocious, fierce, inhuman
con submissive, yielding
2 *syn* see INFLEXIBLE 2

relevance *n* *syn* see USE 3

relevant *adj* relating to or bearing upon the
matter in hand <*relevant* testimony>
syn ad rem, applicable, applicative, applicatory, apposite, apropos, germane, material,
pertinent, pointful
rel allied, cognate, related; appropriate, apt,
fit, fitting, proper, suitable; important, significant, weighty; admissible, allowable
idiom in point, in question, to the point
con impertinent, inadmissible, inapplicable,
inapposite, inappropriate; unallied, unas-
sociated, unconnected, unrelated; alien,
extrinsic, foreign
ant irrelevant; extraneous

reliable *adj* **1** having qualities that merit
confidence or trust <a *reliable* friend>
syn dependable, secure, tried, tried and
true, trustworthy, trusty
rel safe; inerrable, inerrant, infallible, unerring; apposite, cogent, compelling, convincing, meaningful, significant, sound, telling,
valid; attested, authenticated, circumstanti-
ated, confirmed, proven, validated, verified;
unimpeachable, unquestionable
con doubtful, dubious, problematic, questionable, suspect; independable, undependable, untried, untrustworthy; unattested,
unauthenticated, unconfirmed, unvalidated
ant unreliable
2 *syn* see CERTAIN 1

reliance *n* *syn* see TRUST 1

reliant *adj* *syn* see DEPENDENT 1

relic *n* **1** *syn* see REMEMBRANCE 3
2 *syn* see VESTIGE 1

relief *n* **1** *syn* see EASE 3
rel lightening, softening; allayment, appeasement, assuagement, mollification
ant anguish

2 syn see HELP 1

relieve vb **1** to make less grievous or more tolerable <drugs that *relieve* pain>
syn allay, alleviate, assuage, ease, lighten, mitigate, mollify
rel comfort, console, solace; appease, palliate, soften; quiet, soothe, subdue; moderate, qualify, temper; decrease, diminish, lessen, reduce; aid, benefit, help
con aggravate, enhance, heighten, sharpen; reinforce
ant intensify
2 syn see ROB 1
3 to take the place of for a time <sent to *relieve* the sentry>
syn spell, take over
rel fill in, sub, substitute; replace, supply
4 syn see EXEMPT

religion n **1** a system of religious belief <tolerant of all *religions*>
syn creed, cult, faith, persuasion
rel belief, doctrine
2 the body of persons who accept a system of religious belief <Jerusalem is a city sacred to three great *religions*>
syn church, communion, connection, creed, cult, denomination, faith, persuasion, sect

religious adj syn see DEVOUT
rel faithful, staunch, steadfast, true; ethical, moral, noble, righteous, virtuous; honest, honorable, just, upright
con godless, ungodly
ant irreligious

relinquish vb to let out of one's possession or control completely <few leaders willingly *relinquish* power>
syn abandon, cede, give up, hand over, lay down, leave, resign, surrender, ‖turn up, waive, yield; *compare* ABDICATE 1
rel lay aside; quit, throw up; abdicate, renounce; desert, forsake; abnegate, forbear, forgo, sacrifice; cast, discard, shed
ant keep

relish n **1** syn see TASTE 3
2 syn see TASTE 4
rel enjoying, liking, loving; bias, prejudice; flair, leaning, penchant, propensity
3 syn see ENJOYMENT 1

relish vb **1** syn see ENJOY 1
2 to eat or drink with pleasure <so hungry that he will *relish* plain food>
syn savor
3 syn see ADMIRE 1

relishing adj syn see PALATABLE
rel delighting, gratifying, pleasing, regaling, rejoicing, tickling
con banal, flat, inane, insipid, jejune

reluct vb syn see DISGUST

reluctant adj syn see DISINCLINED
rel calculating, cautious, chary, circumspect, wary

rely (on *or* upon) vb to place full confidence <*relied* on the doctor for an accurate diagnosis>
syn bank (on *or* upon), build (on), calculate (on *or* upon), count (on), depend (on *or*

upon), ‖lot (on *or* upon), reckon (on), trust (in *or* to)
rel commit, confide, entrust; await, expect, hope, look
idiom put faith in, swear by
con distrust, mistrust

remain vb syn see STAY 2
ant depart

remainder n a remaining group, part, or trace <he spent the *remainder* of his life in prison>
syn balance, heel, leavings, remains, remanet, remnant, residual, residue, residuum, rest
rel excess, surplus; hangover, leftover

remains n pl **1** syn see REMAINDER
2 syn see CORPSE

remanet n syn see REMAINDER

remark vb **1** syn see SEE 1
2 to make observations and pass on one's judgment <she *remarked* on the lack of modern paintings at the gallery>
syn animadvert, comment, commentate, observe
rel mention, note

remark n **1** syn see NOTICE 1
2 an expression of opinion or judgment <a *remark* that led to a vehement argument>
syn comment, commentary, note, obiter dictum, observation
rel assertion, reflection, saying, statement, utterance; clarification, elucidation, explanation, explication, exposition, interpretation; annotation, exegesis, gloss, postil, scholium

remarkable adj **1** syn see NOTICEABLE
rel exceptional; important, momentous, significant, weighty; peculiar, singular, strange, unique
2 syn see EXCEPTIONAL 1

remarkably adv syn see VERY 1

remedial adj syn see CURATIVE

remedy n **1** something used for the treatment of disease <a cold *remedy*>
syn cure, medicament, medicant, medication, medicine, pharmacon, physic
rel biologic, drug, medicinal, pharmaceutical
2 something that corrects or counteracts <no easy *remedy* for discontent>
syn antidote, corrective, counteractant, counteractive, counteragent, countermeasure, counterstep, cure
rel cure-all, elixir, panacea; nostrum

remedy vb syn see CURE

remedying adj syn see CURATIVE

remember vb to bring an image or idea from the past into the mind <*remembers* the old days>
syn bethink, cite, ‖mind, recall, recollect, remind, reminisce, retain, retrospect, revive, revoke
rel look back (on *or* upon), think (of), treasure; relive; educe, elicit, evoke, extract
con disregard, ignore, neglect, overlook; dismember, lose
ant forget

remembrance n **1** syn see MEMORY 1
2 syn see MEMORY 2

---

3 something that serves to keep a person or thing in mind <wanted to give her a small *remembrance*>
syn keepsake, memento, memorial, relic, remembrancer, reminder, souvenir, token, trophy
rel favor, gift, present

remembrancer *n syn* see REMEMBRANCE 3

remind *vb syn* see REMEMBER
rel hint, imply, intimate, suggest; admonish, advise, warn; jog, prompt
idiom put in mind

reminder *n* **1** *syn* see EXPRESSION 3
2 *syn* see REMEMBRANCE 3
rel memo, memorandum, note, notice; hint, intimation, suggestion; admonition, warning

remindful *adj syn* see REMINISCENT

reminisce *vb syn* see REMEMBER

reminiscence *n* **1** *syn* see MEMORY 1
2 *syn* see MEMORY 2

reminiscent *adj* tending to remind <shoes *reminiscent* of those worn fifty years ago>
syn redolent, remindful
rel evocative, suggestive
idiom bringing to mind

remise *vb syn* see TRANSFER 4

remiss *adj syn* see NEGLIGENT
rel faineant, indolent, lazy, slothful
ant scrupulous

remit *vb* **1** *syn* see EXCUSE 1
2 *syn* see DEFER
3 *syn* see SEND 1

remittable *adj syn* see VENIAL

remnant *n syn* see REMAINDER

remonstrance *n syn* see DEMUR 2

remonstrate *vb syn* see OBJECT 1
rel combat, fight, oppose, resist, withstand

remonstration *n syn* see DEMUR 2

remorse *n syn* see PENITENCE

remorseful *adj* motivated or marked by remorse <a *remorseful* confession>
syn apologetic, attritional, compunctious, contrite, penitent, penitential, regretful, repentant, sorry
rel mournful, rueful, sorrowful
con impenitent, regretless, unregretful; hard, obdurate
ant remorseless

remorsefulness *n syn* see PENITENCE

remorseless *adj* having no remorse <a *remorseless* villain>
syn impenitent, regretless, uncontrite, unregretful, unremorseful, unrepentant, unsorry
rel compassionless, merciless, pitiless, ruthless, uncompassionate, unmerciful
con penitent, regretful, sorry
ant remorseful

remote *adj* **1** *syn* see DISTANT 1
ant close; adjacent
2 *syn* see BACK 1
3 *syn* see OBSCURE 2
4 small in degree <a *remote* possibility>
syn ‖fat, negligible, off, outside, slender, slight, slim, small
con great, large; important, significant, weighty
5 *syn* see INDIFFERENT 2

remotest *adj syn* see EXTREME 5

remove *vb* **1** *syn* see MOVE 4

2 to take something from a place or position <*removed* the book from the shelf>
syn take away, take off, take out, withdraw
rel move, shift, transfer; extract
3 to take (as a hat) from one's person <*removed* her coat when she entered the house>
syn doff, douse, put off, take off
rel cast off, throw off
idiom off with
con don, put on, replace
4 to get rid of <*remove* the causes of poverty>
syn clear away, eliminate, take out
rel dispose (of), eradicate, exterminate, extirpate; blot out, efface, erase, expunge, obliterate
idiom do away with
5 *syn* see PURGE 3

removed *adj* **1** *syn* see DISTANT 1
ant adjoining
2 *syn* see OBSCURE 2
3 *syn* see ALONE 1

remunerate *vb* **1** *syn* see PAY 1
rel accord, award, grant, vouchsafe
2 *syn* see COMPENSATE 1

remunerative *adj syn* see ADVANTAGEOUS 1

renaissance *n syn* see REVIVAL

renascence *n syn* see REVIVAL

rencontre *n syn* see CONTEST 2

rend *vb syn* see TEAR 1
rel divide, separate

render *vb* **1** *syn* see RETURN 3
2 *syn* see REPRESENT 1
3 *syn* see TRANSLATE 3
4 *syn* see ADMINISTER 1

rendering *n* **1** *syn* see INTERPRETATION 2
2 *syn* see VERSION 1

rendezvous *n* **1** *syn* see ENGAGEMENT 3
2 *syn* see RESORT 1

rendezvous *vb syn* see GATHER 6

rendition *n* **1** *syn* see INTERPRETATION 2
2 *syn* see VERSION 1

renegade *n* a person who forsakes his faith, party, cause, or allegiance and aligns himself with another <the *renegade* derided his former beliefs>
syn apostate, defector, rat, recreant, runagate, tergiversator, turnabout, turncoat
rel iconoclast, insurgent, rebel; abandoner, deserter, forsaker; heretic, schismatic
con liege man; disciple, follower
ant adherent

renege *vb syn* see BACK DOWN

renew *vb* **1** to make like new <rested to *renew* their strength>
syn modernize, refresh, refurbish, rejuvenate, renovate, restore, update
rel make over, remodel; mend, rebuild, repair; correct, rectify, reform, revise
con bankrupt, deplete, drain, exhaust, impoverish; consume
ant wear out
2 *syn* see RESTORE 1
3 *syn* see REVIVE 3
4 *syn* see REPEAT
5 *syn* see RESUME 2

renewed *adj syn* see REFRESHED

renounce *vb* **1** *syn* see ABDICATE 1
ant arrogate
2 *syn* see ABANDON 1

idiom wash one's hands of
3 syn see DEFECT
renouncement *n syn* see RENUNCIATION
renovate *vb syn* see REVIVE 3
  2 syn see RENEW 1
  rel clean, cleanse
renown *n* **1 syn** see FAME 2
  2 syn see EMINENCE 1
renowned *adj syn* see FAMOUS 2
  rel acclaimed, extolled, lauded, praised; outstanding, signal
rent *vb syn* see HIRE 1
rent *adj syn* see LACERATED
rent *n syn* see BREACH 3
rental *n syn* see APARTMENT 1
renunciation *n* voluntary surrender or putting aside of something desired or desirable <led a life of total *renunciation* as a monk>
  syn abnegation, denial, renouncement, self= abnegation, self-denial, self-renunciation
  rel abjurement, eschewing, forbearing, forgoing, forswearing, sacrifice, self-sacrifice; rejection, repudiation, surrender, yielding
  con gripping, holding, keeping
  ant retention
reoccupy *vb syn* see RESUME 1
reoccurrence *n syn* see RECURRENCE
reopen *vb syn* see RESUME 1
reorder *vb syn* see REORGANIZE
reorganization *n syn* see SHAKE-UP
reorganize *vb* to arrange in a different way <*reorganize* a bankrupt company>
  syn readjust, rearrange, reconstitute, reconstruct, reorder, reorient, reorientate, reshuffle, retool
  rel reestablish, refound, resettle; rebuild, regenerate, renovate
  con disarrange, disorder, disorganize
reorient *vb syn* see REORGANIZE
reorientate *vb syn* see REORGANIZE
‖**rep** *n* **1 syn** see FAME 2
  2 syn see REPUTATION 2
repair *vb* **1 syn** see GO 1
  2 syn see RESORT 2
repair *vb syn* see MEND 2
repair *n* **1 syn** see ORDER 9
  2 syn see ORDER 10
reparation *n* a return for something lost or suffered, usually through the fault of another <war *reparations*>
  syn amends, compensation, indemnification, indemnity, quittance, recompense, redress, reprisal, restitution
  rel atonement, expiation; remuneration, requital, retribution, reward; adjustment, settlement
repartee *n* **1 syn** see RETORT 2
  2 syn see BANTER
  rel humor, irony, sarcasm, satire, wit; rejoinder, response, retort
repast *n syn* see MEAL
repay *vb syn* see COMPENSATE 3
  rel balance, offset; accord, award

repeal *vb syn* see REVOKE 2
  ant establish; enact
repeat *vb* to say or do again <*repeat* a command>
  syn ingeminate, iterate, reiterate, renew, reprise, resay
  rel recite, recount, rehearse, relate; hash over, recapitulate, rehash, restate, retell; chime, din, echo, harp, ring; duplicate, reproduce; copy, ditto, imitate; recrudesce, recur, return, revert
repeatedly *adv syn* see OFTEN
  idiom day after day, day by day, day in and day out
repel *vb* **1 syn** see FEND (off)
  2 syn see RESIST
  3 syn see DISGUST
  ant allure; attract
repellent *adj* **1 syn** see REPUGNANT 1
  con alluring, bewitching, captivating, charming; enticing, luring, seductive, tempting
  ant attractive; pleasing
  2 syn see OFFENSIVE
  3 syn see ANTIPATHETIC 2
repent *vb syn* see REGRET
repentance *n syn* see PENITENCE
  con complacency, self-complacency, self= satisfaction
repentant *adj syn* see REMORSEFUL
repercussion *n syn* see EFFECT 3
rephrase *vb syn* see PARAPHRASE
repine *vb syn* see COMPLAIN
replace *vb* **1 syn** see RETURN 4
  2 syn see RESTORE 5
  3 to put out of a usual or proper place or into the place of another <the old bridge was *replaced* by a new one last year>
  syn outplace, supersede, supplant
  rel renew, restore; alter, change; recoup, recover, regain, retrieve
  4 syn see CHANGE 5
replacement *n syn* see SUBSTITUTE 1
replete *adj* **1 syn** see ALIVE 5
  2 syn see FULL 1
replica *n syn* see REPRODUCTION
replicate *vb syn* see COPY
replication *n syn* see REPRODUCTION
reply *vb syn* see ANSWER 1
  con accuse, charge, impeach, indict; address, greet, salute
reply *n syn* see ANSWER 1
  con argument, dispute; greeting, salute
report *n* **1** common talk or an instance of it that spreads rapidly <spread a false *report*>
  syn buzz, cry, gossip, grapevine, hearsay, murmur, on-dit, rumble, rumor, scuttlebutt, talk, tattle, tittle-tattle, whispering, word
  rel conversation, speech; chat, chatter, chitchat, prating, small talk; canard, dirt, scandal; advice, intelligence, news, tidings
  2 syn see REPUTATION 2
  3 syn see ACCOUNT 7
  rel declaration, statement; comment, notice, review; brief, bulletin
report *vb syn* see RELATE 1
  rel communicate, impart
repose *vb syn* see REST 1
repose *n syn* see REST 1
  rel refreshment, renewal, restoration

---

syn synonym(s) **rel** related word(s)
ant antonym(s) **con** contrasted word(s)
idiom idiomatic equivalent(s)
‖ use limited; if in doubt, see a dictionary

con strain, stress; agitation, discomposure, perturbation

repository *n syn* see DEPOT 2

repossess *vb* **1** *syn* see RECOVER 1
2 *syn* see RESUME 1
3 to resume possession of (an item purchased on installment) in default of payments due <*repossessed* the car>
syn take back
rel get back, reclaim, recover, retrieve

reprehend *vb syn* see CRITICIZE
rel admonish, chide, rebuke, reprimand, reproach, reprove; berate, rate, scold, upbraid

reprehensible *adj syn* see BLAMEWORTHY

represent *vb* **1** to present an image or lifelike imitation of (as in art) <the painting *represents* a spring scene>
syn delineate, depict, describe, image, interpret, limn, picture, portray, render
rel express, realize, show; display, evince; hint, suggest; draft, outline, sketch; narrate, relate
con color, distort, falsify, garble, misinterpret, pervert, twist, warp
2 to serve as the counterpart or image of <a movie hero who *represents* the ideals of the culture>
syn body (forth), emblematize, embody, epitomize, exemplify, illustrate, mirror, personalize, personate, personify, symbolize, typify; *compare* EMBODY 1
rel denote, mean, signify; impersonate, substitute; copy, imitate, reproduce
con belie, distort, garble, twist, warp
ant misrepresent

representant *n syn* see DELEGATE

representation *n* the act of delineating <an exponent of *representation* in art>
syn delineation, depiction, description, picture, portraiture, portrayal, presentment
rel demonstration, exemplification, illustration

representative *adj syn* see TYPICAL 1
ant atypical

representative *n* **1** *syn* see INSTANCE
2 *syn* see DELEGATE

repress *vb* **1** *syn* see SUPPRESS 2
2 *syn* see COMPOSE 4

repression *n* **1** the action or process of putting down by authority or force <the *repression* of unpopular opinions>
syn choking, extinguishment, quashing, quenching, smothering, squashing, squelching, stifling, strangling, suppression, throttling
rel check, control, curb, restraint; crushing, quelling, subdual
con emboldening, encouragement, support
2 an instance of putting down by authority or force <*repressions* of racial minorities>
syn clampdown, crackdown, suppression
rel crushing, extinction, smothering; limitation, restriction

reprieve *n syn* see RESPITE 1

reprimand *n syn* see REBUKE

reprimand *vb syn* see REPROVE

reprinting *n syn* see EDITION

reprisal *n* **1** *syn* see REPARATION
2 *syn* see RETALIATION

reprise *vb syn* see REPEAT

reproach *n syn* see REBUKE
rel blame, censure, discredit

reproach *vb syn* see REPROVE

reprobate *vb* **1** *syn* see CRITICIZE
2 *syn* see DECLINE 4

reprobate *adj* **1** *syn* see ABANDONED 2
2 *syn* see WRONG 1

reprobate *n syn* see VILLAIN 1

reproduce *vb* **1** *syn* see PROCREATE 1
2 *syn* see COPY

reproduction *n* one thing which closely or essentially resembles another that has already been made, produced, or written <printed *reproductions* of the great masters>
syn carbon, carbon copy, copy, ditto, duplicate, facsimile, reduplication, replica, replication
ant original

reproof *n syn* see REBUKE

reprove *vb* to criticize adversely, especially in order to warn of or to correct a fault <*reproved* him for talking in class>
syn admonish, call down, chide, lesson, monish, ‖rack back, rebuke, reprimand, reproach, ‖sneap, tick off; *compare* CRITICIZE, LAMBASTE 3, SCOLD 1
rel counsel, warn; blame, censure, criticize, reprehend, reprobate; chasten, correct, discipline, punish
idiom haul over the coals, slap one's wrist, take to task

reptile *n syn* see SYCOPHANT

repudiate *vb* **1** *syn* see DECLINE 4
con acknowledge, admit, avow, confess, own
ant adopt
2 *syn* see DEFECT
3 *syn* see DISCLAIM
rel abandon, desert, forsake; cast, discard
con allow, concede, grant
ant own

repugnance *n syn* see ABOMINATION 2

repugnancy *n syn* see ABOMINATION 2

repugnant *adj* **1** so alien or unlikable as to arouse antagonism and aversion <the idea of moving again became *repugnant* to her>
syn abhorrent, invidious, obnoxious, repellent, revulsive
rel alien, extraneous, extrinsic, foreign; incompatible, incongruous, inconsonant, uncongenial
con acceptable, bearable, tolerable; agreeable, gratifying, pleasant, pleasing, pleasurable
ant congenial
2 *syn* see OFFENSIVE
3 *syn* see ANTIPATHETIC 2

repulse *vb* **1** *syn* see FEND (off)
2 *syn* see DISGUST
ant captivate

repulsion *n syn* see ABOMINATION 2

repulsive *adj syn* see OFFENSIVE
ant alluring

reputable *adj syn* see RESPECTABLE 1

reputation *n* **1** *syn* see FAME 2
rel authority, credit, influence, prestige, weight
2 the estimation in which one is generally held <a good *reputation*>

syn character, fame, name, ‖rep, report, repute

repute *n* **1** *syn* see FAME 2
  ant disrepute
  2 *syn* see REPUTATION 2
reputed *adj* **1** *syn* see RESPECTABLE 1
  2 *syn* see SUPPOSED 1
request *vb syn* see ASK 2
  rel appeal, petition, pray, sue
requiescence *n syn* see REST 1
require *vb* **1** *syn* see DEMAND 1
  2 *syn* see DEMAND 2
  3 *syn* see LACK
required *adj* **1** *syn* see NEEDFUL
  2 *syn* see MANDATORY
  ant optional
requirement *n* **1** something wanted or needed <production was not sufficient to satisfy *requirements* for cars>
  syn demand, need, want
  2 *syn* see ESSENTIAL 2
requisite *adj* **1** *syn* see NEEDFUL
  2 *syn* see JUST 3
requisite *n syn* see ESSENTIAL 2
requisition *vb syn* see DEMAND 1
requital *n syn* see RETALIATION
requite *vb* **1** *syn* see RECIPROCATE
  rel content, satisfy; revenge
  2 *syn* see COMPENSATE 3
resay *vb syn* see REPEAT
rescind *vb syn* see REVOKE 2
rescript *n syn* see REVISION 1
rescue *vb* to set free (as from confinement or risk) <*rescue* a drowning child>
  syn deliver, save
  rel emancipate, free, liberate, manumit, release; conserve, preserve; disembarrass, disentangle, extricate; recover, regain, retrieve; buy, ransom, redeem
research *n syn* see INQUIRY 1
resect *vb syn* see EXCISE
resemblance *n syn* see LIKENESS
  rel parallel
  ant dissemblance
resemble *vb* to be like or similar to <he *resembles* his father>
  syn favor, ‖feature, simulate
  idiom be a dead ringer for, bear a resemblance to, be the spit and image of, be the very image of, bring to mind, have all the earmarks of, look like, put one in mind of, remind one of, take after
  con differ, vary
resentfully *adv syn* see HARD 6
resentment *n syn* see OFFENSE 2
  rel animosity, animus, antagonism, antipathy, rancor; ill will, malice, malignancy, malignity, spite
reservation *n syn* see CONDITION 1
  rel circumscription
reserve *vb* **1** *syn* see KEEP 5
  2 to set or have set aside or apart <*reserve* a hotel room>
  syn bespeak, book, preengage
  rel contract, engage, retain

reserve *n* something stored or kept available for future use or need <keep a *reserve* of canned foods on hand>
  syn backlog, hoard, inventory, nest egg, reservoir, stock, stockpile, store
  rel fund, supply
  idiom something for a rainy day, something in the sock
reserved *adj* **1** inclined to cautious restraint in the expression of knowledge or opinions <too *reserved* to offer a spontaneous criticism>
  syn constrained, incommunicable, noncommittal, restrained
  rel bashful, diffident, modest, shy; ceremonious, conventional, formal
  con demonstrative, expansive, unconstrained, unrestrained; boisterous, loud, ostentatious; extroverted, open, outgoing
  ant unreserved
  2 *syn* see SILENT 3
  ant effusive
  3 *syn* see UNSOCIABLE
  ant affable
  4 *syn* see ANTISOCIAL
  5 *syn* see QUALIFIED 2
reservoir *n syn* see RESERVE
reshuffle *vb syn* see REORGANIZE
reside *vb* **1** to have as one's habitation or domicile <he *resides* in Boston>
  syn abide, bide, ‖dig, dwell, hang out, live
  rel inhabit, occupy, people, tenant; continue, endure
  2 *syn* see CONSIST 1
residence *n* **1** *syn* see HABITATION 1
  2 *syn* see HABITATION 2
residency *n syn* see HABITATION 2
resident *n syn* see INHABITANT
‖residenter *n syn* see INHABITANT
resider *n syn* see INHABITANT
residual *n syn* see REMAINDER
residue *n syn* see REMAINDER
residuum *n syn* see REMAINDER
resign *vb* **1** *syn* see RELINQUISH
  2 *syn* see ABDICATE 1
  3 *syn* see QUIT 6
resignation *n* **1** *syn* see ACQUIESCENCE
  rel humbleness, lowliness, meekness, modesty
  2 *syn* see PATIENCE
resigned *adj syn* see PASSIVE 2
  ant rebellious
resile *vb syn* see BACK DOWN
resilient *adj* **1** *syn* see ELASTIC 1
  2 *syn* see ELASTIC 2
  ant flaccid
resist *vb* to stand firm against a person or influence <the criminal *resisted* the police> <we must learn to *resist* temptation>
  syn buck, combat, contest, dispute, duel, fight, oppose, repel, traverse, withstand
  rel assail, assault, attack; contradict, contravene, gainsay, impugn; baffle, balk, foil, frustrate, thwart; check, counter, hinder, obstruct, stem
  con bow, capitulate, surrender
  ant submit, yield
resolute *adj* **1** *syn* see DECIDED 2
  rel obstinate, pertinacious, stubborn
  2 *syn* see FAITHFUL 1

syn synonym(s)   *rel* related word(s)
ant antonym(s)   *con* contrasted word(s)
idiom idiomatic equivalent(s)
‖ use limited; if in doubt, see a dictionary

resoluteness *n syn* see DECISION 2
resolution *n* 1 *syn* see ANALYSIS 1
  2 *syn* see DECISION 1
  3 *syn* see DECISION 2
  4 *syn* see COURAGE
resolve *vb* 1 *syn* see ANALYZE
  ant blend
  2 *syn* see SOLVE 1
  3 *syn* see SOLVE 2
  rel dispel, disperse, dissipate; clear, disabuse, purge, rid
  4 *syn* see DECIDE
resolve *n syn* see DECISION 2
resolved *adj syn* see DECIDED 2
resonant *adj* marked by conspicuously full and rich sounds or tones (as of speech or music) <a deep *resonant* voice rang out>
  syn consonant, fat, orotund, plangent, resounding, ringing, rotund, round, sonorant, sonorous, vibrant
  rel full, mellow, rich; deep, profound; enhanced, heightened, intensified; earsplitting, loud, powerful, stentorian, strident; beating, pulsating, pulsing, throbbing; booming, clangorous, noisy, reverberant, reverberating, sounding, thundering, thunderous; electrifying, thrilling
  con faint, low, murmurous, muted, smothered, soft, weak; flat, toneless, unmusical; cacophonous, discordant, inharmonious, off-key
resort *n* 1 *syn* see RESOURCE 3
  2 a place that is habitually frequented <a favorite *resort* of teenagers>
  syn hangout, haunt, purlieu, rendezvous, stamping ground, watering hole
  rel harbor, haven, refuge, retreat; den, nest
  3 a place providing recreation and entertainment especially to vacationers <returned to the same *resort* every year>
  syn pleasure dome, spa, watering place
  rel hotel, inn, lodge; bath(s), hot spring(s), mineral spring(s), spring(s), thermal spring(s)
resort *vb* 1 *syn* see FREQUENT
  ant avoid
  2 to betake oneself or to have recourse when in need of help or relief <they were unwilling to *resort* to her parents for aid>
  syn apply, go, recur, refer, repair run, turn
  rel address, devote, direct, employ, use, utilize
  idiom avail oneself of, fall back on (*or* upon)
resound *vb syn* see PRAISE 2
resounding *adj* 1 *syn* see RESONANT
  2 *syn* see EMPHATIC
resource *n* 1 **resources** *pl syn* see MEAN 3
  2 resources *pl syn* see WEALTH 2
  3 something to which one turns for assistance in difficulty or need in the absence of a usual means or source of supply <has exhausted every *resource* he can think of>
  syn dernier ressort, expediency, expedient, makeshift, recourse, refuge, resort, shift, stopgap, string, substitute, surrogate
  rel contraption, contrivance, device, lashup; creation, invention; fashion, manner, method, mode, system, way; means, measure, step; artifice, dodge, stratagem, subterfuge; hope, opportunity, possibility, relief

respect *n syn* see REGARD 4
  rel awe, fear, reverence; adoration, veneration, worship
  ant scorn
respect *vb syn* see ADMIRE 2
  rel revere, reverence, venerate
  ant abuse; misuse; scorn
respectable *adj* 1 worthy of esteem or deference <a *respectable* scientist>
  syn creditable, estimable, reputable, reputed, well-thought-of
  rel honorable, worthy
  ant disreputable, unrespectable
  2 *syn* see DECOROUS 1
  3 *syn* see DECENT 4
  4 *syn* see CONSIDERABLE 2
  5 acceptable in appearance or standing <wore old but *respectable* clothes>
  syn decent, presentable, tolerable; *compare* DECENT 4
  rel adequate, satisfactory; acceptable, appropriate, proper, suitable
  ant disreputable
respectful *adj* marked by or showing respect or deference <a *respectful* glance>
  syn deferential, duteous, dutiful, regardful
  rel reverent, reverential, venerating; attentive, civil, courteous, gracious, polite
  con abusive, insolent, insulting, offensive; contemptuous, impudent, irreverent, rude
  ant disrespectful
respecting *prep syn* see APROPOS
respective *adj syn* see SEVERAL 1
respire *vb syn* see BREATHE 3
respite *n* 1 a temporary suspension of the execution of a capital offender <the murderer won a *respite*>
  syn reprieve
  2 *syn* see BREAK 4
  rel intermission, lull, pause, recess; ease, leisure, rest
resplendent *adj syn* see SPLENDID 2
  rel blazing, flaming, glowing
respond *n syn* see ANSWER 1
respond *vb syn* see ANSWER 1
  rel act, behave, react
response *n syn* see ANSWER 1
responsible *adj* subject to an authority which may exact redress in case of default <she is *responsible* for the safe delivery of the goods>
  syn accountable, amenable, answerable, liable
  rel exposed, open, subject
  con clear, exempt, immune; irresponsible, unaccountable, unanswerable, unliable
  ant irresponsible
responsive *adj* 1 *syn* see RECEPTIVE 1
  ant unresponsive
  2 *syn* see SENTIENT 3
  rel answering, replying, responding
  3 *syn* see TENDER
  con cold, cool, indifferent
rest *n* 1 freedom from toil or strain <enjoyed his well-deserved *rest*>
  syn ease, leisure, relaxation, repose, requiescence
  rel deferring, intermission, suspension; quiet, silence, stillness; calm, peace, peacefulness, placidity, restfulness, serenity, tranquillity

con action, work; restlessness, strain

2 syn see BASE 1

rest *vb* **1** to dispose oneself at ease in order to relieve or avoid fatigue <she is *resting* in the bedroom after a hard day's work>
syn lie, lie down, recline, repose, stretch (out)
rel doze, nap, nod, sleep, slumber, snooze
2 to refrain from labor or exertion <planned to do nothing but *rest* during his vacation>
syn relax, rest up, unbend, unlax
rel loaf, loll, lounge; ease off, ease up, let down, let up, slacken, slack off
idiom take it easy, take life easy
con labor, toil, work; drudge, grind, slave
3 to allow an interval of rest from exertion <they *rested* for ten minutes before going back to work>
syn breathe, lay off, lie by, spell
idiom lie (*or* rest) on one's oars, stop for breath, take a break (*or* rest), take five (*or* ten), take time out

4 syn see BASE
rel depend, hang, hinge; count, rely

rest *n* **syn** see REMAINDER
rel excess, overplus, superfluity, surplus, surplusage

restart *vb* **syn** see RESUME 2

restate *vb* **syn** see PARAPHRASE

restatement *n* **syn** see VERSION 1

restitute *vb* **1** **syn** see RESTORE 3
2 syn see RETURN 4

restitution *n* **syn** see REPARATION

restive *adj* **1** **syn** see CONTRARY 3
2 syn see TENSE 1

restiveness *n* **syn** see UNREST

restless *adj* lacking rest or giving no rest <the patient was *restless* from pain> <*restless* sleep>
syn uneasy, unpeaceful, unquiet, unrestful, unsettled, untranquil
rel agitated, disturbed, perturbed, troubled; fidgety, jittery, jumpy, nervous, restive; fitful, intermittent, spasmodic
con easy, peaceful, quiet, tranquil
ant restful

restlessness *n* **syn** see UNREST

restorative *adj* **1** **syn** see CURATIVE
2 syn see TONIC 1

restore *vb* **1** to put or bring back (as into existence or use) <*restore* peace in the world>
syn recall, reestablish, reinstate, reintroduce, renew, revive
rel get back, recover, regain, retrieve, win (back)
2 syn see RENEW 1
3 to put into a previous good state <made plans to *restore* slum areas>
syn reclaim, recondition, reconstruct, recover, rehabilitate, rejuvenate, restitute
rel redeem, rescue, save; amend, reform, revise; recoup, recruit, regain, retrieve; better, improve; correct, rectify, remedy, right; return

ant deteriorate

4 to help or cause to regain signs of life and vigor <*restore* him to health>
syn resuscitate, revive, revivify
rel cure, heal, remedy; arouse, rally, rouse, stir

5 to put again in possession of something <*restore* the king to his throne>
syn give back, put (back), reinstate, replace, return

6 syn see RETURN 4

restrain *vb* **1** to prevent from or control in doing something <*restrained* the child from picking all the flowers>
syn bit, bridle, check, coarct, constrain, crimp, curb, hold back, hold down, hold in, inhibit, keep, pull in, withhold; *compare* HAMPER
rel arrest, interrupt, stop; prevent; forbear, refrain; block, hinder, impede, obstruct; gag, muzzle
idiom keep in line, put (*or* lay) under restraint
con countenance, encourage; incline, induce, move, prompt; persuade; allow, permit
ant impel; incite

2 syn see COMPOSE 4
ant abandon
3 syn see MODERATE 1

restrained *adj* **1** **syn** see QUIET 4
ant unrestrained
2 syn see UNDEMONSTRATIVE
3 syn see RESERVED 1
4 syn see CONSERVATIVE 2
ant extravagant

restraint *n* **syn** see RESTRICTION 2

restrict *vb* **syn** see LIMIT 2
rel bind, tie; shrink

restricted *adj* **syn** see DEFINITE 1

restriction *n* **1** something that restricts or restrains <they both wanted to be free of the *restriction* of the school>
syn ‖ball and chain, circumscription, cramp, limitation, stint, stricture
rel brake, check, control, curb
2 an act of restricting or the condition of being restricted <undue *restriction* of children>
syn circumscription, confinement, constrainment, constraint, cramp, restraint

rest up *vb* **syn** see REST 2

restyle *vb* **syn** see REVISE

result *n* **1** **syn** see EFFECT 1
rel close, conclusion, end, finish, termination; product, production
con origin, root, source
2 syn see ANSWER 2

resume *vb* **1** to assume or take again <*resumed* her place in society>
syn reassume, reoccupy, repossess, retake
rel reclaim, recoup, recover, regain, retrieve
2 to return to or begin again after interruption <*resumed* her work>
syn continue, pick up, recommence, renew, reopen, restart, take up
rel carry on, go on, keep up
con cease, discontinue, end, halt, postpone, quit, stop; check, intermit, interrupt

résumé *n* **syn** see SUMMARY

resurgence *n* **syn** see REVIVAL

---

syn synonym(s) *rel* related word(s)
ant antonym(s) *con* contrasted word(s)
idiom idiomatic equivalent(s)
‖ use limited; if in doubt, see a dictionary

resurrect vb **1** to restore to life <believed that his body would be literally *resurrected*>
syn raise
idiom raise from the dead
2 *syn* see REVIVE 3
resurrection n *syn* see REVIVAL
resuscitate vb **1** *syn* see RESTORE 4
2 *syn* see REVIVE 3
resuscitation n *syn* see REVIVAL
retail vb *syn* see SELL 3
retain vb **1** *syn* see HAVE 1
2 *syn* see KEEP 5
con abdicate, resign; abjure, forswear, recant, renounce, retract
3 *syn* see REMEMBER
retake vb *syn* see RESUME 1
retaliate vb *syn* see RECIPROCATE
rel avenge, revenge
idiom even the score, get back at, get even with, give in kind, give one a dose of his own medicine, give one tit for tat, pay one in his own coin, settle (*or* square) accounts, turn the tables on
retaliation n the act of inflicting or the intent to inflict injury in return for injury <they had no opportunity for *retaliation*>
syn avengement, avenging, counterblow, reprisal, requital, retribution, revanche, revenge, vengeance
rel correction, discipline, punishment; indemnification, recompense, repayment; amends, indemnity, redress, reparation, restitution
idiom an eye for an eye, blow for blow, measure for measure, tit for tat
con clemency, grace, lenity, mercy; forgiveness, pardon, remission
retard vb *syn* see DELAY 1
rel decrease, lessen, reduce; clog, fetter, hamper; baffle, balk
ant accelerate; advance
retarded adj limited in intellectual or emotional development <a *retarded* child>
syn backward, dim-witted, dull, feeble-minded, half-witted, imbecile, moronic, quarter-witted, simple, simpleminded, slow, slow-witted; *compare* SIMPLE 3, STUPID 1
rel dim, ‖dough-baked, ‖dunny, opaque; exceptional, underachieving; touched
idiom not all there, soft in the head
con bright, capable, intelligent
retch vb to make an effort to vomit <started to *retch* after drinking it>
syn gag, heave, keck
rethink vb *syn* see RECONSIDER
reticent adj *syn* see SILENT 3
con candid, open, plain
ant frank, unreticent
retinue n *syn* see ENTOURAGE
retire vb **1** *syn* see RETREAT 2
2 *syn* see GO 2
rel recede, retreat; abandon, relinquish, surrender, yield
ant advance
3 to cause to withdraw from one's position or occupation <all employees are automatically *retired* at age sixty-five>
syn pension (off), superannuate
rel discharge, dismiss; drop, leave, quit, resign, terminate, vacate

4 to go to bed <youngsters should always *retire* before midnight>
syn bed, ‖flop, pile (in), roll in, turn in
idiom go beddie-bye, go night-night, hit the hay (*or* sack)
con arise, get out, get up, pile (out), roll out, turn out, uprise
ant rise
retired adj *syn* see OBSCURE 2
retirement n *syn* see SECLUSION
retiring adj **1** *syn* see SHY 1
ant assertive
2 *syn* see UNDEMONSTRATIVE
ant forward
retool vb *syn* see REORGANIZE
retort vb *syn* see ANSWER 1
retort n **1** *syn* see ANSWER 1
2 a quick, witty, or cutting reply <he made a very clever *retort*>
syn back answer, comeback, repartee, riposte
rel reprisal, retaliation, revenge; crack, gag, jape, jest, joke, quip, sally, wisecrack, witticism
retouch vb *syn* see TOUCH UP
retract vb **1** *syn* see RECEDE 1
ant protract
2 *syn* see ABJURE
rel eliminate, exclude, rule out, suspend
retral adj **1** *syn* see POSTERIOR 2
2 *syn* see BACKWARD 1
retreat n *syn* see SHELTER 1
retreat vb **1** *syn* see RECEDE 1
rel quail, recoil, shrink
ant advance
2 to draw back from action or danger <the army *retreated* in disarray>
syn fall back, give back, retire, withdraw
rel abandon, depart, evacuate, go, leave, pull out, quit, vacate; decamp, escape, flee, fly; back down, back out, bow out, climb down
idiom beat a retreat, drop back, give ground, give way, sound a retreat
con advance, move, proceed, progress
ant attack
re-treat vb *syn* see RECONSIDER
retrench vb *syn* see SHORTEN
retribution n *syn* see RETALIATION
rel affliction, trial, tribulation, visitation
retrieve vb **1** *syn* see RECOVER 1
2 *syn* see REVIVE 3
retrocede vb *syn* see RECEDE 1
retrograde adj *syn* see BACKWARD 1
retrograde vb **1** *syn* see RECEDE 1
rel return, revert; invert, reverse; backslide, lapse, relapse
2 *syn* see DETERIORATE 1
retrogress vb *syn* see REVERT 2
retrospect n *syn* see REVIEW 5
retrospect vb *syn* see REMEMBER
retrospection n *syn* see REVIEW 5
return vb **1** to go or come back (as to a person, place, or condition) <the converted sinner soon *returned* to his old ways>
syn react, recrudesce, recur, revert, turn back
rel advert; revolve, rotate, turn; renew, restore; recover, regain; rebound, reflect, repercuss, reverberate

con abandon, depart, leave, quit
ant forsake
2 *syn* see ANSWER 1
3 to bring back (as a writ or verdict) to an office or tribunal <*return* a verdict of not guilty>
syn render
4 to bring, send, or put back to a former or proper place <*return* the gun to its holster>
syn replace, restitute, restore, take back
ant remove
5 *syn* see RESTORE 5
6 *syn* see YIELD 5
7 *syn* see RECIPROCATE
rel bestow, give
return *n* **1** *syn* see RECURRENCE
2 *syn* see ANSWER 1
3 *syn* see PROFIT
ant outlay
returnless *adj syn* see INEVITABLE
revamp *vb* **1** *syn* see MEND 2
2 *syn* see REVISE
revanche *n syn* see RETALIATION
reveal *vb* **1** to make known what has been or should be concealed <he solemnly promised he would not *reveal* the truth>
syn betray, blab (out), disclose, discover, divulge, give away, let on, ||let out, mouth, spill, tell, unbosom, unclose, uncover, uncurtain, unveil
rel break, communicate, impart; announce, blow (about or abroad), broadcast, declare, give out, publish, vent; breathe, whisper; leak; acknowledge, admit, avow, confess, let on; peach, rat, ||split, squeak, squeal (on), ||stool, talk
idiom let slip, let the cat out of the bag, spill the beans
con cover (up), hide, obscure, veil
ant conceal
2 *syn* see OPEN 2
revel *vb* **1** to be festive in a noisy or riotous manner <they *reveled* all night long>
syn carouse, frolic, hell, riot, roister, spree, wassail
idiom blow off steam, cut loose, kick up one's heels, let go, let loose, paint the town red, whoop it up
2 *syn* see WALLOW 3
revel *n syn* see MERRYMAKING
2 *syn* see REVELRY 2
revelation *n* disclosure or something disclosed by or as if by divine or preternatural means <a *revelation* closely guarded by members of the sect>
syn apocalypse, oracle, prophecy, vision
ant adumbration
reveling *n syn* see MERRYMAKING
revelment *n* **1** *syn* see MERRYMAKING
2 *syn* see REVELRY 2
revelry *n* **1** *syn* see MERRYMAKING
2 boisterous partying <they were exhausted after the night of *revelry*>
syn high jinks, revel, revelment, skylarking, wassail, whoop-de-do, whoopee, whoopla, whoop-up

syn synonym(s)   *rel* related word(s)
ant antonym(s)   *con* contrasted word(s)
idiom idiomatic equivalent(s)
|| use limited; if in doubt, see a dictionary

revenant *n syn* see APPARITION
revenge *vb syn* see AVENGE
rel defend, justify
idiom get one's own back, have one's revenge, take an eye for an eye
revenge *n syn* see RETALIATION
revengeful *adj syn* see VINDICTIVE
rel adamant, inexorable, inflexible, obdurate
revenue *n* amount received or gained usually measured in money <still holds property that yields a good *revenue*>
syn coming(s) in, income, receipts
rel earnings, gains, salary, wages; proceeds, profit, returns, yield
con expenditure, expense(s), outgoings, outlay
reverberant *adj syn* see HOLLOW 1
revere *vb* to honor and admire profoundly and respectfully <he is *revered* for his wisdom>
syn adore, reverence, venerate, worship
rel admire, esteem, regard, respect; appreciate, cherish, prize, treasure, value; exalt, magnify; enjoy, love
con contemn, despise, disdain, scorn, scout; insult, mock, scoff
ant flout
revered *adj syn* see VENERABLE 1
reverence *n* **1** *syn* see HONOR 1
rel devotion, fealty, loyalty, piety
2 the emotion inspired by what arouses one's deep respect or veneration <a deep *reverence* for honesty>
syn awe, fear
con contempt, despite, disdain, hatred, scorn; insult, mockery
reverence *vb syn* see REVERE
idiom hold in reverence
reverend *adj syn* see VENERABLE 1
reverend *n syn* see CLERGYMAN
reverential *adj syn* see VENERABLE 1
reverie *n* the condition of being lost in thought <spent the day in *reverie* before the fire>
syn brown study, muse, study, trance
rel absorption, abstraction, preoccupation; contemplation, meditation, thought; castle-building, daydreaming, dreaming
reversal *n* **1** a causing or face in an opposite direction or to appear in an inverted position <a *reversal* in policy> <the *reversal* of objects seen through a simple lens>
syn about-face, changeabout, inversion, reverse, reversement, reversion, right-about, right-about-face, turn, turnabout, turning, volte-face
rel bouleversement, overturning
2 *syn* see SETBACK
reverse *adj syn* see OPPOSITE
reverse *vb* **1** to change to the contrary or opposite side or position <the chairman *reversed* the order in which they would speak>
syn change, inverse, invert, revert, transplace, transpose, turn
rel capsize, overturn, upset; exchange, interchange; shift, transfer
2 *syn* see REVOKE 2

reverse n 1 syn see OPPOSITE
2 syn see REVERSAL 1
3 syn see SETBACK

reversement n syn see REVERSAL 1

reversion n 1 a return to an ancestral type or condition or an instance of such a return <the law was a shocking *reversion* to earlier times>
syn atavism, throwback
rel backsliding, lapse, relapse
con advance, amendment, bettering, betterment, improvement; reform
2 syn see REVERSAL 1

revert vb 1 syn see RETURN 1
2 to come or go back to a lower or worse condition <*reverted* to savagery>
syn regress, retrogress, throw back
rel backslide, lapse, relapse; decline, degenerate, deteriorate, retrograde
con advance, progress
3 syn see REVERSE 1

review n 1 syn see REVISION 1
2 syn see EXAMINATION
3 syn see CRITICISM 1
4 syn see JOURNAL
5 a retrospective view of or meditation on past events <an occurrence that in *review* did not surprise him>
syn afterlight, reconsideration, reexamination, retrospect, retrospection, revision
rel reflection, study; second thought
con anticipation, contemplation, foreseeing

review vb syn see RECONSIDER

reviewal n syn see CRITICISM 1

revile vb syn see SCOLD 1
rel asperse, calumniate, defame, libel, malign, slander, traduce, vilify
con acclaim, eulogize, extol, praise
ant laud

revisal n syn see REVISION 1

revise vb to make a new, amended, improved, or up-to-date version of <the many problems involved in *revising* a dictionary>
syn redraft, redraw, restyle, revamp, rework, rewrite, work over
rel overhaul, reorganize; perfect, polish, upgrade
con discard, disregard

revise n syn see REVISION 1

revision n 1 an act of revising <the *revision* of a manuscript>
syn recension, redraft, rescript, review, revisal, revise
rel amendment, correction, emendation, rectification
2 syn see REVIEW 5

revitalize vb syn see REVIVE 3

revival n a renewal of life, activity, or prominence <a *revival* of weaving>
syn reanimation, rebirth, renaissance, renascence, resurgence, resurrection, resuscitation, revivification, reviviscence, risorgimento
rel regeneration, rejuvenation, renewal, restoration

revive vb 1 syn see RESTORE 4
rel gain, improve, recuperate
2 syn see RESTORE 1
3 to restore from a depressed, inactive, or unused state <*revived* his hope of escape>

syn reactivate, rekindle, renew, renovate, resurrect, resuscitate, retrieve, revitalize, revivify
rel reanimate, regenerate, reinvigorate, rejuvenate; arouse, galvanize, quicken, stimulate; activate, energize, vitalize
con extinguish, put down, put out, quell, quench, suppress; inhibit
4 syn see REMEMBER

revived adj syn see REFRESHED

revivification n syn see REVIVAL

revivify vb 1 syn see REVIVE 3
2 syn see RESTORE 4

reviviscence n syn see REVIVAL

revoke vb 1 syn see REMEMBER
2 to annul by recalling or taking back <*revoke* a privilege>
syn dismantle, lift, recall, repeal, rescind, reverse
rel abrogate, annul, void; cancel, erase, expunge; invalidate, nullify; countermand, counterorder; abjure, forswear, recant, retract
ant confirm

revolt vb 1 to renounce allegiance or subjection <*revolted* against the king>
syn insurrect, mutiny, rebel, rise (against)
rel defy, oppose, resist; break, renounce, turn (against); boycott, strike; overthrow, overturn, riot
idiom kick over the traces, take up arms against
con obey, submit; aid, assist, help, succor, support; bolster, prop (up), sustain, uphold
2 syn see DISGUST

revolter n syn see REBEL

revolting adj syn see OFFENSIVE

revolute vb syn see REVOLUTIONIZE

revolution n 1 the action or an act of moving around an orbit or circular course <the *revolution* of the earth around the sun>
syn circuit, circulation, circumvolution, gyration, gyre, revolve, rotation, round, turn, wheel, whirl
rel cycle, pirouette, reel, roll, spin, twirl
2 syn see SHAKE-UP

revolution vb syn see REVOLUTIONIZE

revolutional adj syn see EXTREME 3

revolutionary adj syn see EXTREME 3

revolutionary n syn see RADICAL

revolutionist n syn see RADICAL

revolutionist adj syn see EXTREME 3

revolutionize vb to change fundamentally or completely <he *revolutionized* manufacturing processes>
syn revolute, revolution
rel alter, change, modify; recast, refashion, reform, remodel; redraw, restyle, revamp, revise; metamorphose, transfigure, transform, transmogrify; overthrow, overturn
idiom break with the past, make a clean sweep, make a radical change

revolve vb 1 syn see PONDER 2
2 syn see TURN 1

revolve n syn see REVOLUTION 1

revulsion n syn see ABOMINATION 2

revulsive adj syn see REPUGNANT 1

reward n something that is offered or given for some service or attainment <the miner received a *reward* for his hard work>

syn carrot, dividend, guerdon, meed, plum, premium, prize

rel compensation, recompense, remuneration, requital

reweigh *vb syn* see RECONSIDER

reword *vb syn* see PARAPHRASE

rework *vb syn* see REVISE

rewrite *vb syn* see REVISE

rhadamanthine *adj syn* see JUST 3

rhapsodize *vb syn* see ENTHUSE 2

rel acclaim, extol, praise

con blame, condemn, denounce; decry, derogate, detract, minimize

rhapsody *n* **1** *syn* see BOMBAST

2 *syn* see ECSTASY

rhapsody *vb syn* see ENTHUSE 2

rhetoric *n* **1** *syn* see ORATORY

2 *syn* see BOMBAST

rhetorical *adj* emphasizing style often at the expense of thought <the candidate was given to windy *rhetorical* speeches>

syn aureate, bombastic, declamatory, euphuistic, florid, flowery, grandiloquent, highfalutin, high-flown, magniloquent, ‖mouthy, oratorical, orotund, overblown, pompous, purple, sonorous, stilted, swelling, swollen, tumescent, tumid, turgid

rel chichi, orchidaceous, ostentatious, pretentious, showy; gassy, inflated, windy; exaggerated, overdone, overwrought; grand, grandiose, high-sounding, imposing; flamboyant, ornate; embellished; articulate, eloquent, fluent, glib, vocal, voluble

con homely, literal, plain, simple, unpretentious; unadorned, undecorated, unembellished, ungarnished, unornamented

ant unrhetorical

rhino *n syn* see MONEY

rhubarb *n syn* see QUARREL

rhyme *n* **1** *syn* see POETRY 1

2 *syn* see POEM

3 *syn* see RHYTHM

rhyme *vb syn* see AGREE 4

rhymer *n syn* see POETASTER

rhymester *n syn* see POETASTER

rhythm *n* the regular rise and fall in intensity of sounds that is associated chiefly with poetry and music <the *rhythm* of the music made it easy to dance to>

syn beat, cadence, cadency, measure, meter, rhyme, rhythmus, swing

rel lilt; accent

rhythmus *n syn* see RHYTHM

riant *adj syn* see MERRY

‖rib *n syn* see WIFE

rib *vb syn* see BANTER 1

ribald *n syn* see SCAMP

ribbon *n syn* see STRIP 1

rich *adj* **1** having goods, property, and money in abundance <he was a *rich* man, having accumulated his wealth in business>

syn affluent, moneyed, ‖oofy, opulent, wealthy

rel comfortable, easy, independent, prosperous, well-fixed, well-heeled, well-off, well-to-do; fat, flush

idiom flush with money, having money to burn, in the money, rich as Croesus, rolling in money

con destitute, indigent, penurious, poverty=stricken

ant poor

2 *syn* see ORNATE

3 highly seasoned and fatty, oily, or sweet <ate *rich* desserts every day>

syn heavy

rel cloying, oversweet; filling, satiating, sating; fat

con natural, simple, unseasoned

ant plain

4 *syn* see FERTILE

5 *syn* see EXPRESSIVE

richen *vb syn* see ENRICH

riches *n pl syn* see WEALTH 2

rick *n syn* see PILE 1

‖rick *vb syn* see SPRAIN

rickety *adj* likely to give way or break down <a *rickety* old chair>

syn rachitic, rackety, rattletrap, shaky, wobbly; *compare* WEAK 2

rel unsound, unsteady

con firm, rugged, solid, sturdy, substantial, well-made

ant stable

‖rickle *n syn* see PILE 1

ricochet *vb syn* see GLANCE 1

rel bound, rebound, recoil

rid *vb* to set a person or thing free of something that encumbers <*rid* himself of his troubles>

syn clear, lose, shake (off), throw off, unburden

rel free, liberate, release; disembosom, unbosom; eradicate, exterminate, extirpate, remove, uproot; abolish, extinguish

con burden, charge, clog, cumber, encumber, lade, load, lumber, saddle, task, tax, weigh, weight

ant weigh down

riddance *n syn* see DISPOSAL 2

riddle *n syn* see MYSTERY

ride *vb* **1** to travel by automobile <often *rode* out to the countryside>

syn auto, motor

idiom go for a spin

2 *syn* see DRIFT 1

3 *syn* see BAIT 1

rel oppress, persecute; torment, torture

4 *syn* see OVERLAP

ride (out) *vb syn* see SURVIVE 2

ride *n syn* see DRIVE 1

rel excursion, expedition, journey, tour, trip

rider *n syn* see APPENDIX 1

ridge *n* **1** a top or upper part especially when long and narrow <topped the mountain *ridge*>

syn chine, crest, hogback

2 *syn* see WRINKLE

‖ridge runner *n syn* see RUSTIC

ridicule *vb* to make an object of laughter <*ridiculed* him for his inability to perform the feat>

syn deride, lout, mock, quiz, rally, razz, scout, taunt, twit

rel ‖barrack, flout, gibe, jape, jeer, scoff, sneer; burlesque, caricature, mimic, travesty; haze, ride, roast

---

idiom laugh out of court, make fun (*or* game *or* sport) of, poke fun at

ridiculous *adj* **1** *syn* see LAUGHABLE
rel absurd, foolish, preposterous, silly; antic, bizarre, fantastic, grotesque
2 *syn* see INDECOROUS

riding *n* **1** *syn* see SHIVAREE
2 *syn* see HARBOR 3

rife *adj* **1** *syn* see PREVAILING
2 *syn* see ALIVE 5

riff (through) *vb* *syn* see BROWSE

riffle *vb* *syn* see RIPPLE

riffle (through) *vb* *syn* see BROWSE

riffraff *n* **1** *syn* see RABBLE 2
2 *syn* see REFUSE

rifle *n* *syn* see ROB 1

rift *n* **1** *syn* see CRACK 3
2 *syn* see BREACH 3
rel gap, hiatus, interruption, interval

rig *vb* *syn* see FURNISH 1

rig *n* *syn* see COSTUME

‖**rig** *n* **1** *syn* see IMPOSTURE
2 *syn* see PRANK

‖**rig** *vb* *syn* see DUPE

rigamajig *n* *syn* DOODAD, business, dingus, dofunny, doohickey, gadget, gizmo, thingum, thingumajig, thingumbob

rigging *n* *syn* see CLOTHES

‖**riggish** *adj* *syn* see FAST 7

right *adj* **1** *syn* see UPRIGHT 2
2 *syn* see DECOROUS 1
3 *syn* see JUST 3
4 *syn* see TRUE 3
con specious, unsound; misguided, mistaken
ant unright, wrong
5 *syn* see CORRECT 2
6 *syn* see FIT 1
7 *syn* see AUTHENTIC 2
8 *syn* see SANE 1
9 *syn* see HEALTHY 1
10 *syn* see CONSERVATIVE 1
11 *syn* see DECENT 4

right *n* **1** qualities (as adherence to duty or obedience to lawful authority) that together constitute the ideal of moral propriety or merit moral approval <the *right* is not all on one side>
syn good, straight
rel correctitude, correctness, properness, propriety, rightness
con debt, sin, wickedness; impropriety, incorrectness, unrightness
ant unright, wrong
2 something to which one has a just claim <the *right* to life, liberty, and the pursuit of happiness>
syn appanage, birthright, perquisite, prerogative, privilege
rel claim, interest, title; freedom, liberty, license
3 *usu* rights *pl* *syn* see DUE 1
4 *syn* see DIEHARD 1
‖**5** *syn* see OBLIGATION 2
‖**6** *syn* see EXCUSE 1

right *adv* **1** *syn* see JUST 1
2 *syn* see WELL 3
ant wrong, wrongly
3 *syn* see DIRECTLY 1
4 *syn* see WELL 3

5 *syn* see AWAY 3
6 *syn* see VERY 1

right *vb* **1** *syn* see CORRECT 1
‖**2** *syn* see MEND 2

right-about *n* *syn* see REVERSAL 1

right-about-face *n* *syn* see REVERSAL 1

right away *adv* *syn* see AWAY 3

righteous *adj* **1** *syn* see MORAL 1
con corrupt, flagitious, nefarious; bad, evil, immoral, reprobate, sinful, vicious, wicked, wrong
ant iniquitous, unrighteous
2 *syn* see GOOD 11
ant unrighteous

righteousness *n* *syn* see GOODNESS
ant unrighteousness

rightful *adj* **1** *syn* see JUST 3
rel equitable, fair, impartial
ant unrightful
2 *syn* see TRUE 8
ant unrightful
3 *syn* see FIT 1

right hand *n* *syn* see RIGHT-HAND MAN

right-handed *adj* having the same direction or course as the movement of the hands of a watch viewed from front <a *right-handed* propeller>
syn clockwise, dextrorotatory, positive

right-hand man *n* a reliable or indispensable person <the boss viewed his efficient assistant as his *right-hand man*>
syn girl Friday, man Friday, right hand

rightist *n* *syn* see DIEHARD 1
ant leftist

‖**rightle** *vb* *syn* see MEND 2

rightly *adv* *syn* see WELL 1

right-minded *adj* *syn* see MORAL 1

rightness *n* **1** *syn* see GOODNESS
2 *syn* see ORDER 11

right off *adv* *syn* see AWAY 3

‖**right smart** *adj* *syn* see CONSIDERABLE 2

‖**right smart** *adv* *syn* see VERY 1

right wing *n* *syn* see DIEHARD 1

right-winger *n* *syn* see DIEHARD 1
ant left-winger

rigid *adj* **1** *syn* see STIFF 1
rel firm, hard, solid
ant elastic
2 *syn* see INFLEXIBLE 2
3 extremely severe or stern <was regarded as a *rigid* disciplinarian>
syn draconian, ironhanded, rigorist, rigorous, strict, stringent, unpermissive
rel austere, severe, stern; hard-line, inflexible, tough, uncompromising, unyielding; adamant, adamantine, inexorable, obdurate
con humoring, indulgent, pampering; loose, relaxed; easy, gentle, mild
ant lax

rigor *n* *syn* see DIFFICULTY 1
rel austerity, severity, sternness; harshness, roughness; affliction, trial, tribulation, visitation
ant amenity

rigorist *adj* *syn* see RIGID 3

rigorous *adj* **1** *syn* see RIGID 3
rel inflexible, stiff; ascetic; burdensome, exacting, onerous, oppressive
con easy, effortless, facile, light, smooth
ant mild

2 syn see SEVERE 3
rel drastic
con bland, faint, lenient, smooth
3 syn see CORRECT 2
rigorously *adv syn* see HARD 5
rile *vb* **1 syn** see ROIL 1
2 syn see IRRITATE
riley *adj syn* see TURBID
rim *n syn* see BORDER 1
rim *vb syn* see BORDER 1
rima *n syn* see CRACK 3
rimation *n syn* see CRACK 3
rime *n syn* see CRACK 3
rime *vb syn* see CAKE 1
rimple *n syn* see WRINKLE
rimple *vb syn* see CRUMPLE 1
‖**rimption** *n. usu* rimptions *pl syn* see SCAD
‖**rindle** *n syn* see CREEK 2
ring *n* **1 syn** see LOOP 2
2 syn see LOOP 1
3 syn see BOXING
4 syn see CLIQUE
5 syn see COMBINATION 2
ring *vb syn* see SURROUND 1
ring *vb* to sound clearly and resonantly <the church bells were *ringing*>
syn bell, bong, chime, knell, peal, toll
rel resound, reverberate, sound
‖**ring** (up) *vb syn* see TELEPHONE
ringer *n syn* see IMAGE 1
ringing *adj syn* see RESONANT
‖**ring off** *vb syn* see SHUT UP 2
riot *n* **1 syn** see DISORDER 2
2 something or someone wildly amusing <the new comedy is a *riot*>
syn howl, ‖panic, scream, sidesplitter
rel sensation, smash, wow
riot *vb syn* see REVEL 1
riot (away) *vb syn* see WASTE 2
riotous *adj syn* see PROFUSE
rip *vb syn* see TEAR 1
rip (out) *vb syn* see SPUTTER 1
ripe *adj* **1 syn** see MATURE 1
rel seasonable, timely, well-timed; overdue
con callow, crude, raw, rude; immature, unmatured, unmellow
ant unripe; green
2 syn see CONSUMMATE 1
3 brought by aging to full flavor or the best state <*ripe* cheese>
syn aged, matured, mellow, ripened
rel ready
ant unripe
‖**ripe** *vb syn* see MATURE
ripen *vb syn* see MATURE
rel better, improve; enhance, heighten, intensify, season
ripened *adj* **1 syn** see MATURE 1
ant unripened
2 syn see RIPE 3
rip-off *n syn* see THEFT
rip off *vb syn* see ROB 1
rel abuse, exploit, impose (on *or* upon), use, bleed, fleece, gouge, skin, soak, stick
2 syn see STEAL 1

riposte *n syn* see RETORT 2
ripper *n syn* ‖DILLY, ‖corker, crackerjack, dandy, ‖dinger, humdinger, jim-dandy, ‖lulu, nifty, peach
ripping *adj syn* see MARVELOUS 2
ripple *vb* to become fretted or lightly ruffled on the surface (as water) <the pond was *rippled* by rain>
syn cockle, dimple, fret, riffle
ripsnorter *n syn* ‖DILLY, ‖corker, crackerjack, ‖daisy, dandy, ‖dinger, ‖doozer, humdinger, jim-dandy, ‖lulu
rise *vb* **1** to assume an upright or standing position <he *rose* from his chair>
syn get up, stand up, uprise, upspring
rel sit up; straighten up
idiom come to one's feet
con lie, lounge, recline, sit; loll, sprawl
2 syn see ROLL OUT
ant retire
3 syn see ADJOURN 2
ant sit
4 to move or come up from a lower to a higher level <smoke *rose* from the chimneys>
syn arise, ascend, aspire, lift, mount, soar, up, uprear
rel surge, tower; climb, scale; elevate, raise, rear
con descend, drop, lower; dip, plummet, sink
ant fall; decline
5 syn see INTENSIFY
6 syn see SURFACE
7 syn see INCREASE 2
ant abate; fall
8 syn see HAPPEN 1
9 syn see SPRING 1
rise (against) *vb syn* see REVOLT 1
rise (to) *vb syn* see APPLAUD 2
rise *n* **1 syn** see ASCENT
ant fall
2 syn see ADDITION
3 an increment in amount, number, or volume <crime is on the *rise*>
syn boost, breakthrough, hike, increase, upgrade, wax
con declension, decline, lessening, letup, reduction, slump; decrement, loss
ant drop
rise and shine *vb syn* see ROLL OUT
risible *adj syn* see LAUGHABLE
ant lachrymose, larmoyant
rising *n syn* see ASCENT
ant falling
risk *n syn* see DANGER
rel accident, chance, fortune, luck; exposedness, exposure, liability, liableness, openness
risk *vb* **1 syn** see ENDANGER
rel beard, brave, dare, defy, face; confront, encounter, meet
idiom go out of one's depth
2 syn see VENTURE 1
3 syn see GAMBLE 2
riskless *adj syn* see SAFE 2
risky *adj* **1 syn** see DANGEROUS 1
rel delicate, precarious, sensitive, ticklish, touchy; speculative
idiom on thin ice
2 syn see RISQUÉ

---

syn synonym(s)   **rel** related word(s)
ant antonym(s)   **con** contrasted word(s)
idiom idiomatic equivalent(s)
‖ use limited; if in doubt, see a dictionary

risorgimento n syn see REVIVAL

risqué adj verging on impropriety or indecency <blushed at his *risqué* stories>
syn blue, broad, off-color, purple, racy, risky, salty, sexy, shady, spicy, suggestive, wicked; *compare* OBSCENE 2
rel naughty, warm; coarse, crude, earthy, gross, lewd, obscene, raunchy, raw, ribald, vulgar; dirty, foul; indecent, indecorous, indelicate, inelegant, unrefined
con clean, decent, proper; restrained; euphemistic

‖**rissom** n syn see PARTICLE

rite n 1 syn see FORM 2
2 forms (as religious rites) appropriate to a particular event <the marriage *rites*>
syn ceremonial, ceremony, formality, liturgy, observance, ritual, service
rel celebration, occasion, solemnity; sacrament, sacramental; form

‖**rithe** n syn see CREEK 2

ritual n 1 syn see RITE 2
2 syn see FORM 2

rival n one of two or more striving for what only one can possess <political *rivals* for the nomination>
syn competition, competitor, corrival
rel contender, contestant, entrant; adversary, antagonist, opponent

rival vb 1 syn see COMPETE 1
2 to strive to equal or surpass <*rivaling* each other for the most work done>
syn compete, emulate, rivalize
rel attempt, strive, struggle, try; contend, fight
3 syn see EQUAL 3
4 syn see AMOUNT 2

rivalize vb syn see RIVAL 2

rivalry n syn see CONTEST 1

rive vb 1 syn see TEAR 1
rel divide, separate; chop, hew
2 syn see SHATTER 1

rivel n syn see WRINKLE

rivet vb 1 syn see FASTEN 1
2 syn see FASTEN 3

rivulet n syn see CREEK 2

road n 1 often **roads** pl syn see HARBOR 3
2 syn see WAY 1
3 syn see WAY 2

roadblock n syn see BAR 2

roadhouse n syn see HOTEL

roadman n syn see PEDDLER

roadstead n syn see HARBOR 3

roadster n syn see VAGABOND

roam vb syn see WANDER 1

roamer n syn see ROVER

roar vb to make a very loud and often a continuous or protracted noise <the crowd *roared* their disapproval of the speech>
syn bawl, bellow, bluster, clamor, rout; *compare* BAWL 2
rel rebound, repercuss, reverberate; shout, vociferate, yell; din
con breathe, murmur, mutter, whisper

roaring adj 1 syn see LOUD 1
2 syn see FLOURISHING

roast vb 1 syn see BURN 3
2 syn see LAMBASTE 3

rob vb 1 to take possessions unlawfully <*rob* a bank><he was mugged and *robbed*>
syn ‖knock off, knock over, loot, plunder, ransack, relieve, rifle, rip off, stick up; *compare* BURGLARIZE, HOUSEBREAK
rel ‖heist, hold up; jackroll, roll; strong-arm; filch, hijack, lift, pilfer, purloin, steal, thieve; cheat, defraud, hustle, swindle; despoil, pillage, ravage, sack
2 syn see DEPRIVE 2

robber n one who commits the crime of robbery <only one *robber* was involved in the holdup>
syn yegg; *compare* THIEF
rel hijacker, sandbagger; crook, swindler; cat burglar, cat man, housebreaker, raffles, second-story man; rifler; holdup man, stickup man; ‖bushranger, highwayman, ‖sticker-up

roborant adj syn see TONIC 1

robot n 1 a machine that looks like a human being and performs various complex acts (as walking or talking) of a human being <a *robot* that performed household chores>
syn android, automaton
rel golem
idiom bionic man
2 an efficient, insensitive, often brutalized person <working on an assembly line can often turn people into *robots*>
syn automaton, golem, machine

robust adj 1 syn see FLOURISHING
2 syn see STRONG 3

robustious adj syn see BOORISH

rock vb 1 syn see SHAKE 4
rel oscillate, sway, swing, undulate; quake, totter, tremble
2 syn see TOSS 2
3 syn see HURRY 2

rock n 1 syn see ERROR 2
2 syn see DOLLAR
3 **rocks** pl syn see MONEY

rock bottom n syn see ESSENCE 2

rock-bottom adj syn see BOTTOMMOST

rockbound adj 1 syn see ROCKY 1
2 syn see INFLEXIBLE 2

rocket vb 1 syn see SKYROCKET
rel arise, ascend, levitate, mount, surge, tower
2 syn see HURRY 2

rock pile n syn see JAIL

rock-ribbed adj 1 syn see ROCKY 1
2 syn see INFLEXIBLE 2

rocky adj 1 abounding in or consisting of rocks <a *rocky* shore>
syn rockbound, rock-ribbed
rel bebouldered, bouldery; stony
2 syn see INSENSIBLE 5

rocky adj 1 syn see UNSTABLE 2
2 syn see OBSCENE 2

‖**Rocky Mountain canary** n syn see DONKEY 1

rococo adj 1 syn see OLD-FASHIONED
2 syn see ORNATE

rod n 1 syn see BAR 1
2 syn see PUNISHMENT
idiom rod in pickle

rodomont n syn see BRAGGART

rodomontade n 1 syn see BOMBAST
rel boasting, bragging, vaunting; pride, vainglory, vanity
2 syn see BRAGGART

rodomontade *vb syn* see BOAST
rodomontade *adj syn* see BOASTFUL
rogue *n* 1 *syn* see VILLAIN 1
  rel culprit, delinquent
  2 *syn* see SWINDLER
  3 *syn* see SCAMP
roguery *n syn* see MISCHIEVOUSNESS
roguish *adj* 1 *syn* see DISHONEST
  2 *syn* see PLAYFUL 1
  3 *syn* see COY 2
roguishness *n syn* see MISCHIEVOUSNESS
roil *vb* 1 to make turbid <*roiled* the brook
with his splashings>
  syn mud, muddle, muddy, rile
  rel befoul, contaminate, dirty, pollute
  con clear, purify, settle
  2 *syn* see IRRITATE
roily *adj syn* see TURBID
roister *vb syn* see REVEL 1
role *n* 1 characteristic exterior properties and
aspects, style, and atmosphere in which
something intangible is discerned <the
moral *role* of the legislature>
  syn character, clothing
  rel appearance, face, guise, seeming, semblance, show; aspect, look
  2 *syn* see FUNCTION 1
roll *n* 1 *syn* see LIST
  2 *syn* see ROSTER 1
  ‖3 *syn* see FORTUNE 4
roll *vb* 1 *syn* see PONDER 2
  2 *syn* see SWATHE
  3 to wrap around on itself or something else
<this cloth *rolls* unevenly>
  syn furl
  4 *syn* see WALLOW 3
  5 *syn* see TURN 1
  6 *syn* see WANDER 1
  7 *syn* see POUR 2
  8 *syn* see RUMBLE
  9 *syn* see TOSS 2
roll call *n syn* see LIST
rollick *vb* 1 *syn* see GAMBOL
  2 *syn* see WALLOW 3
rollick *n syn* see ESCAPADE
rollicking *adj syn* see ANTIC 2
  rel cheerful, glad, happy, joyful, joyous,
lighthearted
roll in *vb syn* see RETIRE 4
  ant roll out
rolling stone *n syn* see ROVER
roll out *vb* to leave one's bed <*rolled* out at
dawn>
  syn arise, get up, pile (out), rise, rise and
shine, turn out, uprise
  ant roll in
roll up *vb syn* see ACCUMULATE
roly-poly *adj syn* see ROTUND 2
romance *n syn* see LOVE AFFAIR
romanesque *adj syn* see EXOTIC 2
romantic *adj syn* see EXOTIC 2
  2 *syn* see SENTIMENTAL
  rel fanciful, fantastic, imaginary, quixotic,
visionary; created, invented
  ant unromantic; matter-of-fact

Romeo *n syn* see GALLANT 2
romp *n syn* see RUNAWAY
romp *vb syn* see GAMBOL
  idiom cut capers, horse around
rondure *n syn* see BALL
roof *n syn* see TOP 1
roof *vb syn* see HARBOR 1
rook *vb syn* see FLEECE 1
rookie *n syn* see NOVICE
room *n* 1 space in a building enclosed or set
apart by a partition <the house had seven
rooms>
  syn apartment, chamber
  2 **rooms** *pl syn* see APARTMENT 1
  3 enough space or range for free movement
<no *room* for hope>
  syn elbowroom, latitude, leeway, margin,
play, scope
  rel clearance; license, range, rein, sway;
rope
room *vb syn* see HARBOR 2
room and board *n syn* see ACCOMMODA-
TIONS
roomy *adj syn* see SPACIOUS
  ant cramped
‖roose *vb syn* see COMMEND 1
roost *vb* 1 *syn* see ALIGHT
  2 *syn* see HARBOR 2
root *n* 1 *syn* see SOURCE
  rel basis, foundation, ground
  2 *syn* see BASIS 1
  3 *syn* see CENTER 3
  4 *syn* see ESSENCE 2
root *vb syn* see ENTRENCH 1
  ant uproot
root *vb syn* see APPLAUD 2
rootage *n syn* see SOURCE
rootless *adj syn* see WEAK 1
root out *vb syn* see ANNIHILATE 2
  rel demolish, destroy, raze
  ant enroot
rootstock *n syn* see SOURCE
roperipe *n syn* see VILLAIN 1
ropes *n pl syn* see INS AND OUTS
ropy *adj syn* see MUSCULAR
rose *vb syn* see BLUSH
roseate *adj syn* see HOPEFUL 2
rose-colored *adj syn* see HOPEFUL 2
rose-colored spectacles *n pl syn* see OPTI-
MISM
roster *n* 1 a list of officers or enlisted men
<an army *roster*>
  syn muster, muster roll, roll
  2 *syn* see LIST
rosy *adj syn* see HOPEFUL 2
rot *vb* 1 *syn* see DECAY
  rel corrupt, debase, vitiate
  2 *syn* see DETERIORATE 1
  3 *syn* see DEBASE 1
rot *n syn* see NONSENSE 2
rotate *vb* 1 *syn* see TURN 1
  2 to succeed or cause to succeed each other
in turn <the drivers in the car pool *rotated*
each week>
  syn alternate
  rel bandy, exchange, interchange; ensue,
follow, succeed; relieve, spell
rotation *n syn* see REVOLUTION 1
rote *n syn* see ROUTINE
rotten *adj* 1 *syn* see BAD 5

---

syn synonym(s)   *rel* related word(s)
ant antonym(s)   *con* contrasted word(s)
idiom idiomatic equivalent(s)
‖ use limited; if in doubt, see a dictionary

rel foul; tainted, touched; sour
2 syn see VICIOUS 2
3 syn see BAD 8
4 syn see BAD 1
rotter *n syn* see CAD
rotund *adj* **1 syn** see RESONANT
2 rounded or swollen with fat <a wheezing *rotund* man lumbered by>
syn chubby, plump, plumpish, plumpy, podgy, puddy, pudgy, roly-poly, round, roundabout, spuddy, tubby; *compare* FAT 2
rel beefy, chunky, dumpy, heavyset, squat, stocky, stubby, thick, thickset; paunchy, potbellied; buxom, ‖crummy
idiom on the plump side
con angular, gaunt, lank, lanky, lean, raw-boned, scrawny, skinny, spare; slender, slight, slim, thin
roturier *n syn* see UPSTART
rouge *vb syn* see BLUSH
rough *adj* **1** not smooth or even <a *rough* undressed block of stone>
syn asperous, cragged, craggy, hairy, harsh, ironbound, jagged, rugged, scabrous, scraggy, uneven, unlevel, unsmooth
rel bumpy, choppy; burred; firm, hard, solid; coarse, gross
con flat, flush, level, plain, plane
ant smooth
2 syn see WILD 6
con calm, halcyon, peaceful, placid, serene, tranquil
3 syn see TOUGH 8
4 syn see TIGHT 4
5 syn see INDECOROUS
6 syn see RUDE 1
idiom in the rough
7 syn see RUDE 3
8 syn see HARSH 3
9 syn see COARSE 3
rel discourteous, impolite, uncivil, ungracious
10 syn see BLUFF
11 syn see HARD 6
rough *n syn* see TOUGH
rough (out) *vb syn* see SKETCH
rough (up) *vb syn* see MANHANDLE
rough–and–ready *adj syn* see MAKESHIFT
rough–and–tumble *n syn* see BRAWL 2
rough–and–tumble *adj syn* see MAKESHIFT
roughhewn *adj syn* see RUDE 1
roughhouse *n syn* see HORSEPLAY
roughhouse *vb syn* see MANHANDLE
roughhousing *n syn* see HORSEPLAY
roughly *adv* **1 syn** see HARD 5
ant smoothly
2 syn see NEARLY
roughneck *n syn* see TOUGH
roughness *n syn* see INEQUALITY 1
ant smoothness
roughscuff *n syn* see RABBLE 2
round *adj* **1** having every part of the circumference equally distant from a center within <flowers crowded in stiff *round* beds>
syn circular
rel annular, globular, orbed, orbicular, rounded, spherical, spiral
2 syn see CURVED
3 syn see ROTUND 2

4 syn see OUTSPOKEN
5 syn see RESONANT
round *adv* **1 syn** see ABOUT 1
2 syn see NEARLY
3 syn see THROUGH 1
4 syn see ABOUT 6
round *prep* **1 syn** see NEAR 2
2 syn see ABOUT 4
round *n* **1 syn** see BALL
2 syn see REVOLUTION 1
3 syn see TOUR 2
4 syn see CYCLE 1
5 syn see CURVE
round *vb* **1 syn** see BALL
2 syn see SURROUND 1
3 syn see POLISH 2
4 syn see CURVE
round about *adv* **1 syn** see ABOUT 1
2 syn see ABOUT 6
3 syn see ABOUT 2
roundabout *n* **1 syn** see DETOUR
2 syn see VERBIAGE 1
3 syn see TOUR 2
4 syn see EXCURSION 1
roundabout *adj* **1 syn** see INDIRECT 1
2 syn see ROTUND 2
rounded *adj* **1 syn** see CURVED
2 syn see CURVACEOUS
rounder *n syn* see WASTREL 1
roundheel *n syn* see DOXY 1
roundly *adv* **1 syn** see WELL 3
2 syn see NEARLY
round off *vb syn* see CLIMAX
round trip *n syn* see TOUR 2
round up *vb syn* see GROUP 1
rouse *vb* **1 syn** see WAKE 1
rel animate, enliven, quicken, vivify; excite, provoke, stimulate; foment, incite, instigate
con calm, compose, lull, quiet, quieten, settle, soothe, still, tranquilize
2 syn see INTENSIFY
3 syn see PROVOKE 4
4 syn see STIR 1
rouser *n syn* see ‖DILLY
rousing *adj* **1 syn** see EXCITING
2 syn see LIVELY 1
‖**roust** *vb syn* see PROVOKE 4
roustabout *n syn* see WORKER
rout *n* **1 syn** see MOB 2
2 syn see RABBLE 2
3 syn see MULTITUDE 1
rout *vb syn* see ROAR
rout *vb syn* see RUMMAGE 3
rout *n* **1 syn** see DEFEAT 1
2 syn see RUNAWAY
rout *vb* **1** to put to precipitate flight <the army regrouped and *routed* the enemy>
syn derout, stampede
rel chase, dispel, drive, expel
idiom put to flight
2 syn see WHIP 2
route *n syn* see WAY 2
route *vb* **1 syn** see SEND 1
2 syn see GUIDE
routine *n* habitual or mechanical and sometimes monotonous performance of an established procedure <settled into the *routine* of factory work>
syn grind, groove, pace, rote, rut, treadmill
rel squirrel cage; ‖drill

idiom the beaten path, the drab monotony of habit

routine *adj* **1** *syn* see ORDINARY 1
2 *syn* see USUAL 1
rove *vb* *syn* see WANDER 1
rover *n* *syn* see PIRATE
rover *n* one who roams habitually <he spent most of his life as a *rover* always on the move>
syn drifter, meanderer, rambler, roamer, rolling stone, wanderer
rel gad, gadabout, gadder, runabout; itinerant, peripatetic; floater
idiom bird of passage
con homebody
ant stay-at-home
roving *adj* *syn* see ITINERANT
row *vb* to propel a boat by means of oars <*rowed* across the lake>
syn oar, paddle, pull
rel scull; punt; sail, scud
row *n* **1** *syn* see LINE 5
2 *syn* see SUCCESSION 2
row *n* **1** *syn* see BRAWL 2
2 *syn* see QUARREL
3 *syn* see MOUTH 1
row *vb* ‖**1** *syn* see SCOLD 1
2 *syn* see QUARREL
rowdiness *n* *syn* see HORSEPLAY
rowdy *adj* *syn* see TURBULENT 1
rowdy *n* *syn* see TOUGH
rowdydow *n* **1** *syn* see COMMOTION 4
2 *syn* see BRAWL 2
3 *syn* see BINGE 1
rowdydowdy *adj* *syn* see TURBULENT 1
rowdyish *adj* *syn* see TURBULENT 1
royal *adj* **1** *syn* see KINGLY
rel glorious, resplendent, splendid, superb; august, imposing, stately
2 *syn* see EASY 1
3 *syn* see GRAND 1
4 *syn* see EXCELLENT
royalist *n* *syn* see REACTIONARY
‖**rozzer** *n* *syn* see POLICEMAN
rub *vb* **1** *syn* see ABRADE 1
2 *syn* see CHAFE 3
rel aggravate, exasperate, nettle, peeve, provoke, rile; annoy, bother, irk, vex
3 *syn* see POLISH 1
rub *n* *syn* see OBSTACLE
rubber *n* *syn* see BUSYBODY
rubberneck *n* **1** *syn* see BUSYBODY
2 *syn* see TOURIST
rubberneck *vb* *syn* see LOOK 7
rubber stamp *n* *syn* see COMMONPLACE
rubbish *n* **1** *syn* see REFUSE
2 *syn* see NONSENSE 2
3 *syn* see PAP 2
rubbishing *adj* *syn* see CHEAP 2
rubbishly *adj* *syn* see CHEAP 2
rubbishy *adj* *syn* see CHEAP 2
rube *n* *syn* see RUSTIC
rubicund *adj* *syn* see RUDDY
rubify *vb* *syn* see REDDEN 1
rub out *vb* **1** *syn* see DESTROY 1

2 *syn* see MURDER 1
rubric *n* *syn* see NAME 1
rubric *adj* *syn* see NOTEWORTHY
rubric *vb* *syn* see REDDEN 1
ruby *vb* *syn* see REDDEN 1
ruck *n* ‖**1** *syn* see PILE 1
2 *syn* see GATHERING 2
ruck *n* *syn* see WRINKLE
ruck (up) *vb* *syn* see CRUMPLE 1
‖**ruckle** *vb* *syn* see CRUMPLE 1
rucksack *n* *syn* see BACKPACK
ruckus *n* **1** *syn* see COMMOTION 3
rel brawl, broil, melee, scrap
2 *syn* see QUARREL
ruction *n* **1** *syn* see BRAWL 2
2 *syn* see COMMOTION 4
‖**ructious** *adj* *syn* see BELLIGERENT
rud *vb* *syn* see REDDEN 1
ruddle *vb* *syn* see REDDEN 1
ruddy *adj* having a healthy reddish color <has a *ruddy* complexion after being out in the cold>
syn florid, flush, flushed, full-blooded, glowing, rubicund, sanguine
rel bronzed; blooming; blowsy
con ashen, ashy, livid, pale, pallid, wan, waxy; anemic, bloodless
ruddy *vb* *syn* see REDDEN 1
rude *adj* **1** lacking in craftsmanship or artistic finish <a *rude* sketch>
syn angular, crude, lumpy, raw, rough, roughhewn, undressed, unfashioned, unfinished, unformed, unhewn, unpolished, unworked, unwrought
rel unlicked; unprocessed; primitive, rudimental, rudimentary
con dressed, fashioned, finished, formed, hewn, polished, worked, wrought
2 *syn* see DISSONANT 1
3 hastily executed and admittedly imperfect or imprecise <*rude* estimates for the cost of building the house>
syn approximate, proximate, rough
rel crude, imperfect, imprecise, inexact
idiom ‖in the ball park
con accurate, correct; faultless, perfect; exact, precise; meticulous, scrupulous
4 *syn* see COARSE 3
5 *syn* see IGNORANT 1
6 lacking in social refinement <gave a *rude* reply to a polite question>
syn discourteous, disgracious, disrespectful, ill, ill-bred, ill-mannered, impertinent, impolite, incivil, incondite, inurbane, mannerless, ‖mismannered, uncalled-for, uncivil, uncourteous, uncouth, ungracious, unhandsome, unmannered, unmannerly, unpolished
rel brusque, crusty, curt, gruff; harsh; intrusive, meddlesome; crabbed, surly; boorish, churlish, clownish, loutish
con courteous, genteel, mannerly, polite, well-mannered; bland, diplomatic, politic, smooth, suave; affable, considerate, gracious
ant civil; urbane
7 *syn* see BARBARIAN 1
8 *syn* see INEXPERIENCED
rudely *adv* *syn* see NEARLY
rudiment *n* **1** *syn* see ESSENTIAL 1
2 rudiments *pl* *syn* see ALPHABET 2
rudimental *adj* *syn* see ELEMENTARY 1

---

syn synonym(s)   *rel* related word(s)
ant antonym(s)   *con* contrasted word(s)
idiom idiomatic equivalent(s)
‖ use limited; if in doubt, see a dictionary

rudimentary *adj syn* see ELEMENTARY 1
rue *vb syn* see REGRET
rue *n* 1 *syn* see SORROW
  2 *syn* see PENITENCE
  3 *syn* see PITY
rueful *adj* 1 *syn* see PITIFUL 1
  2 *syn* see WOEFUL 1
  3 *syn* see MELANCHOLY 2
  rel depressed, oppressed, weighed down;
piteous, pitiful; despairing, despondent,
hopeless
ruffian *n* 1 *syn* see TOUGH
  2 *syn* see THUG 1
ruffle *vb* 1 *syn* see BLOW 1
  2 *syn* see ABRADE 1
  3 *syn* see ANNOY 1
  ‖**4** *syn* see INTIMIDATE
rugged *adj* 1 *syn* see ROUGH 1
  2 *syn* see SEVERE 3
  rel arduous, difficult
  3 *syn* see HARSH 3
  4 *syn* see BOORISH
  5 *syn* see TOUGH 4
  rel brawny, burly, husky, muscular
  ant fragile
  6 *syn* see HARD 6
ruin *n* 1 *syn* see DETERIORATION 1
  2 *syn* see DOWNFALL 2
  3 the bringing about of or the results of
disaster <met *ruin* at the hands of the en-
emy>
  syn confusion, destruction, devastation,
havoc, loss, ruination
  rel crumbling, disintegration; break up,
dissolution; disrepair; wreck
  con rebuilding, reconstruction, re-creation
  4 *syn* see INJURY 1
ruin *vb* 1 *syn* see DESTROY 1
  rel deface, disfigure; maim, mangle, mutilate; depredate, desecrate, desolate, despoil,
devastate, devour, pillage, sack, spoliate,
waste
  ant restore
  2 to subject to forces that are destructive of
soundness, worth, or usefulness <in danger
of being *ruined* by prosperity>
  syn bankrupt, dilapidate, do in, shipwreck,
wreck
  rel corrupt, debase, degenerate, vitiate
  idiom play hob (or the devil) with
  con rebuild, renew, restore; reclaim, redeem, retrieve, salvage
  3 to overthrow the fortunes of <was *ruined*
during the Great Depression>
  syn bankrupt, break, bust, fold up, impoverish, pauper, pauperize
  rel beggar, clean out, deplete, drain, draw,
draw down, exhaust, use up; wipe (out);
reduce
  idiom go under, lose one's shirt (or pants),
take to the cleaners
  4 *syn* see FRUSTRATE 1
‖**ruinate** *vb syn* see DESTROY 1
ruination *n* 1 *syn* see RUIN 3
  2 *syn* see DOWNFALL 2
ruinator *n syn* see VANDAL
ruiner *n syn* see VANDAL
ruinous *adj* 1 *syn* see DESTRUCTIVE
  2 *syn* see FATAL 2
rule *n* 1 *syn* see LAW 1

  rel order; axiom, fundamental, principle;
decorum, etiquette, propriety
  2 *syn* see MAXIM
  rel fundamental, principle
rule *vb* 1 *syn* see GOVERN 1
  rel guide, lead
  2 to hold preeminence in (as by ability,
strength, or position) <an actor who right-
fully *rules* the Shakespearian stage>
  syn dominate, domineer, predominate,
preponderate, prevail, reign
  rel guide, lead; preside
  idiom be number one, take first place (in or
on)
  3 *syn* see DECIDE
  rel deduce, gather, infer, judge
rule out *vb* 1 *syn* see EXCLUDE
  2 *syn* see PREVENT 2
ruling *n syn* see EDICT 1
ruling *adj* 1 *syn* see CENTRAL 1
  con peripheral
  2 *syn* see PREVAILING
‖**rum** *adj syn* see STRANGE 4
rumble *vb* to make a low heavy rolling sound
<thunder *rumbling* in the distance>
  syn growl, grumble, roll
  rel boom, roar, thunder; peal, resound;
blast, burst, clap, crack, crash
rumble *n syn* see REPORT 1
rumble–bumble *n syn* see MISCELLANY 1
rumbustious *adj syn* see TURBULENT 1
rum–dum *adj syn* see INTOXICATED 1
rumdum *n syn* see DRUNKARD
‖**rum–hole** *n syn* see BAR 5
ruminate *vb* 1 *syn* see PONDER 2
  rel consider, excogitate, weigh
  2 *syn* see CHEW 1
ruminative *adj syn* see THOUGHTFUL 1
rummage *n syn* see CLUTTER 2
  rel conglomeration, hash, hotchpotch,
miscellany, patchwork, potpourri
rummage *vb* 1 *syn* see DISORDER 1
  2 *syn* see SCOUR 2
  3 to produce by searching <*rummaged* an
old dress out of the attic>
  syn dig out, hunt (down or out or up), rout
  rel ferret (out), find; fish, search (out), spy
(out); poke
rummery *n syn* see BAR 5
‖**rum–mill** *n syn* see BAR 5
rummy *adj syn* see STRANGE 4
rummy *n syn* see DRUNKARD
rumor *n* 1 *syn* see REPORT 1
  2 *syn* see MURMUR 1
rumor *vb syn* see GOSSIP
rumorer *n syn* see GOSSIP 1
rumormonger *n syn* see GOSSIP 1
rump *n syn* see BUTTOCKS
rumple *vb syn* see CRUMPLE 1
‖**rumpot** *n syn* see DRUNKARD
rumpus *n* 1 *syn* see COMMOTION 3
  2 *syn* see ARGUMENT 1
rumshop *n syn* see BAR 5
run *vb* 1 to move at a fast springing gait in
which both feet are momentarily off the
ground in the course of each pace <the boy
ran down the walk>
  syn dash, scamper, scoot, scurry, shin,
sprint; *compare* SCUTTLE
  rel career, course, race; bustle, hurry, hustle, rush, speed; scorch

con crawl, creep, drag, inch, mosey, poke, saunter, stroll, toddle

2 to hasten away from something that frightens or perturbs <*afraid to fight but ashamed to* run>
syn bolt, flee, fly, make off, scamper, scoot, ‖screw, skedaddle, skip, skirr
idiom beat it, make a break, run for it, show a clean pair of heels, take flight, take French leave, take to one's heels
3 *syn* see HURRY 2
idiom go all out, go like (greased) lightning
4 *syn* see RESORT 2
5 *syn* see FUNCTION 3
6 *syn* see BECOME 1
7 *syn* see LIQUEFY
8 to lie in or take a certain course <*the path* runs *along the crest of the hill*>
syn extend, go, make, reach, stretch
9 *syn* see RANGE 3
10 *syn* see HUNT 1
11 *syn* see DRIVE 3
12 *syn* see THRUST 2
13 *syn* see SMUGGLE
14 *syn* see OPERATE 3
15 *syn* see CONDUCT 3

run (through *or* over) *vb syn* see BROWSE
run (to *or* into) *vb syn* see AMOUNT 1
run *n* **1** ‖*syn* see CREEK 2
2 an uninterrupted course of occurrence or repetition especially of like things or events <*the play had a long* run>
syn continuance, continuation, duration, persistence
rel continuity, endurance, prolongation
3 *syn* see TENDENCY 1
rel course, set; bearing, direction, line, swing
4 *syn* see TRIP 1
‖**5 runs** *pl but sing or pl in constr syn* see DIARRHEA

runagate *n* **1** *syn* see RENEGADE
2 *syn* see VAGABOND
run along *vb syn* see GO 2
runaround *n* **1** *syn* see DETOUR
2 *syn* see ESCAPE 2
run away *vb syn* see ELOPE
runaway *n* a one-sided or overwhelming victory <*the game was a* runaway, *the home team winning by 30 points*>
syn cakewalk, romp, rout, walkaway, walk-over
rel breather, cinch, duck soup, pushover; setup; shutout; conquest, triumph, victory, win
con photo finish, toss-up
run down *vb syn* see DECRY 2
run-down *adj* **1** *syn* see SHABBY 1
2 *syn* see NEGLECTED
rel abandoned, derelict, deserted, desolate, forsaken, lorn
rune *n* **1** *syn* see SPELL
2 *syn* see POEM
rung *n syn* see DEGREE 1
run in *vb* **1** *syn* see ARREST 2

2 *syn* see VISIT 2
run-in *n* **1** *syn* see ENCOUNTER
2 *syn* see QUARREL
runnel *n syn* see CREEK 2
running *n syn* see OVERSIGHT 1
running *adj* **1** *syn* see ACTIVE 1
2 *syn* see EASY 9
running *adv syn* see TOGETHER 2
running mate *n syn* see ASSOCIATE 3
run-of-mine *adj* **1** *syn* see UNREFINED 3
2 *syn* see MEDIUM
run-of-the-mill *adj* **1** *syn* see MEDIUM
rel uncommon, unexceptional
2 *syn* see GENERAL 1
run on *vb syn* see CHAT 1
run out *vb* **1** *syn* see FAIL 2
2 *syn* see BANISH
run over *vb syn* see OVERFLOW 2
runt *n syn* see DWARF
runted *adj syn* see STUNTED
run through *vb syn* see GO 4
runtish *adj syn* see STUNTED
runty *adj syn* see STUNTED
run up *vb* **1** *syn* see INCREASE 2
2 *syn* see THROW UP 1
rupture *n* **1** *syn* see BREACH 3
rel division, divorce, parting
2 *syn* see SEPARATION 1
rupture *vb* **1** *syn* see OPEN 3
rel divide, divorce, part, separate, sunder; cleave, rend, rive, split
2 *syn* see SEPARATE 1
rural *adj* relating to or characteristic of the country <*a peaceful* rural *scene*>
syn agrestic, bucolic, campestral, countrified, country, out-country, outland, pastoral, provincial, rustic
rel arcadian, idyllic; natural, simple, unsophisticated
con metropolitan, municipal, oppidan; crammed, crowded, packed, populous; bustling, busy, hustling; artificial, mundane, sophisticated, worldly
ant urban; citified
ruse *n syn* see TRICK 1
rush *vb* **1** to move or cause to move quickly, impetuously, and often heedlessly <*rushed* around madly trying to get things done>
syn boil, bolt, charge, chase, dash, fling, lash, race, shoot, ‖swither, tear; *compare* COURSE, HURRY 2, PLUNGE 2, STAMPEDE 2
rel hasten, hurry, speed; dart, fly, scud; break
idiom go off half-cocked, not look before one leaps
2 *syn* see HURRY 2
3 *syn* see COURSE
rush *n* **1** *syn* see HASTE 2
2 *syn* see FLOW
rushing *adj syn* see PRECIPITATE 1
rushlight *n syn* see NONENTITY
rustic *adj syn* see RURAL
rustic *n* an inhabitant of a rural or remote area who is usually characterized by an utter lack of sophistication and cultivation <*an unbelieving* rustic *gawking at the skyscrapers*>
syn ‖apple knocker, ‖backwoodser, backwoodsman, bucolic, bumpkin, chawbacon, clodhopper, clown, country jake, countryman, greenhorn, hayseed, hick, hillbilly,

---

syn synonym(s)   *rel* related word(s)
ant antonym(s)   *con* contrasted word(s)
idiom idiomatic equivalent(s)
‖ use limited; if in doubt, see a dictionary

hillman, ‖hodge, hoosier, jake, jay, joskin, mossback, mountaineer, peasant, provincial, redneck, ‖ridge runner, rube, ‖wayback, woodsy, yap, ‖yob, yokel
rel rural; exurbanite, suburbanite; agriculturalist, farmer, granger, husbandman
con burgher, oppidan, townsman; cityite, urbanite; cosmopolitan, cosmopolite
ant city slicker
rustle *n syn* see HASTE 1
rustler *n syn* see HUSTLER 1

rusty *adj syn* see HARSH 3
‖**rusty** *adj syn* see ILL-TEMPERED
rut *n syn* see ROUTINE
ruth *n* **1** *syn* see PITY
  2 *syn* see PENITENCE
ruthful *adj syn* see WOEFUL 1
ruthless *adj syn* see GRIM 3
ruttish *adj syn* see LUSTFUL 2
‖**ruttle** *vb syn* see RATTLE 1
rutty *adj syn* see LUSTFUL 2
RV *n syn* see TRAILER

S

sable *adj syn* see BLACK 1
  rel dark, dusky, murky; gloomy, somber
sabotage *n* willful effort by indirect means to hinder, prevent, undo, or discredit (as a plan or activity) <*sabotage* of the project by disgruntled officials>
  syn subversion, undermining, wreckage, wrecking
  rel subversiveness, subversivism; damage, impairment, injury
sabotage *vb* to practice sabotage on <*sabotaged* his opponent's campaign with rumors and smears>
  syn subvert, undermine, wreck
  rel frustrate, hamper, hinder; block, obstruct; damage; break up, destroy
  idiom throw a monkey wrench into
  con assist, back, support
saccharine *adj syn* see INGRATIATING
  rel candied, cloying, honeyed, oversweet, sugar-candy, sugar-coated, sugared, sugary, sweet, syrupy
sacerdotal *adj* of, relating to, or belonging to priests or priesthood <*sacerdotal* vestments>
  syn hieratic, priestal, priestish, priestlike, priestly, sacerdotical
  rel churchly, ecclesiastical, religious; clerical, ministerial; apostolic, papal
sacerdotical *adj syn* see SACERDOTAL
sack *n syn* see BAG 1
  rel container; pocket
sack *vb syn* see DISMISS 3
  rel cashier, ship; ‖bump, ‖chuck
  idiom give one the sack, send packing
sack *vb syn* see RAVAGE
  rel forage, raid; strip
sacker *n syn* see MARAUDER
sacred *adj* **1** *syn* see HOLY 1
  rel sacramental; angelic, godly, saintly; cherished
  con lay, secular, temporal; earthly; unhallowed
  ant profane
  2 dedicated to or hallowed by association with a deity <*sacred* songs>
  syn numinous, spiritual; *compare* HOLY 1

  rel hallowed, sanctified
  3 protected (as by law, custom, or human respect) against abuse <a fund *sacred* to charity>
  syn inviolable, inviolate, sacrosanct
  rel defended, guarded, protected, shielded; immune, untouchable
Sacred Writ *n syn* see BIBLE
  idiom Good Book
sacrifice *n syn* see VICTIM 1
  rel burnt offering, oblation; sacrification; hecatomb; sin offering
sacrifice *vb* **1** to offer as a victim in sacrifice <Abraham about to *sacrifice* Isaac>
  syn immolate, victimize
  rel offer (up); consecrate, dedicate, devote; donate, give, yield
  2 *syn* see LOSE 1
  idiom kiss good-bye
  3 *syn* see FORGO
  rel cede, yield
  idiom part with
sacrilege *n syn* see PROFANATION
  rel irreverence; heresy; crime, impiety, offense, sin
sacrilegious *adj* involving or marked by debasement or defilement of what is sacred <*sacrilegious* despoilers of ancient churches>
  syn blasphemous, profane
  rel impious, irreverent, ungodly; evil, sinful, wicked; irreligious
  con godly, pious, reverent; religious
sacrosanct *adj syn* see SACRED 3
  rel esteemed, regarded, respected
sad *adj* **1** affected with or expressing sadness <was *sad* to see him go>
  syn heavyhearted, melancholy, mournful, saddened, sorry, unhappy; *compare* DOWNCAST, MELANCHOLY 2
  rel blue, dejected, dispirited, down, downbeat, downcast, drear, dumpish, dumpy; grieving, unenjoying; depressed, morose; depressing, dismal, joyless, mirthless, saddening, triste; desolate
  con happy, joyful, joyous; blithe, gay, lighthearted; exalted, fired, inspired, uplifted
  ant glad

2 causing sadness <felt miserable after listening to that *sad* song>
syn depressing, joyless, melancholic, melancholy, mournful, saddening, triste; *compare* MELANCHOLY 2
rel dismal, gloomy; afflicting, doleful, dreary, lamentable, sorrowful; pathetic, tear-jerking
con bright, gay, lively; exhilarating, heartwarming, stimulating, stirring
ant happy

sadden *vb syn* see DEPRESS 2
idiom make blue, ‖put into a funk
ant gladden

saddened *adj syn* see SAD 1

saddening *adj syn* see SAD 2

saddle *vb syn* see BURDEN
rel hamper, impede, restrict; impose, inflict
idiom hang like a millstone around one's neck

sadness *n* the quality, state, or an instance of being sad <her feelings of *sadness* and longing persisted long after he left>
syn blues, dejection, depression, dinge, (the) dismals, (the) dolefuls, dumps, dysphoria, gloom, heavyheartedness, melancholy, mopes, mournfulness, suds, unhappiness
rel dispiritedness, doldrums, downcastness, downheartedness, downs, ‖funk, listlessness, moodiness; anguish, grief, sorrow, sorrowfulness, woe; desolation, disconsolateness, disconsolation, forlornness, misery, mourning; blue devils, despondency, hopelessness, megrims, melancholia
idiom slough of despond
con happiness, joy, joyfulness, joyousness; cheerfulness, cheeriness, gayness, lightheartedness, liveliness; exhilaration, ups
ant gladness

safe *adj* **1** having been freed from risk, danger, harm, or injury <refugees who found themselves *safe* at last in a neutral country>
syn scatheless, unharmed, unscathed
rel unhurt, uninjured; intact
idiom in (or with) a whole skin, out of harm's way, safe and sound
con damaged, harmed, hurt, injured
ant unsafe
2 affording security from threat of harm, injury, risk, or loss <found a *safe* place to hide>
syn riskless, secure
rel guarding, protecting, safeguarding, sheltering, shielding; defended, guarded, protected, sheltered, shielded; unthreatened; impregnable, inviolable, invulnerable, unassailable
idiom safe as a bank vault
con insecure, undefended, unguarded, unprotected, vulnerable; threatened; hazardous, risky
ant dangerous, unsafe
3 not threatening danger <it's *safe* to go there only in the daytime>
syn healthy, uninjurious, wholesome; *compare* HARMLESS

rel innocent, innocuous, inoffensive
con hazardous, perilous, precarious, risky; harmful, injurious, unhealthy
ant dangerous, unsafe
4 *syn* see CAUTIOUS

safeguard *n syn* see DEFENSE 1
rel palladium; buffer, screen

safeguard *vb syn* see DEFEND 1
rel conserve, preserve, save; assure, ensure, insure

safekeeping *n* **1** *syn* see CUSTODY
2 *syn* see PRESERVATION 1

safeness *n syn* see SAFETY

safety *n* the quality, state, or condition of being safe <there's *safety* in numbers>
syn assurance, safeness, security
rel cover, protection, shelter; defense; impregnability, inviolability, invulnerability
con hazard, jeopardy, peril, risk, threat; instability, vulnerability
ant danger

sag *vb* **1** *syn* see SLIP 6
2 *syn* see DROOP 3
rel bend, decline; dangle, flap, flop
idiom ‖have a case of the sags
ant tauten

sag *n* **1** *syn* see DEPRESSION 2
rel settling, sinking
2 *syn* see DECLINE 3

sagacious *adj syn* see WISE 1
rel clever, intelligent, smart; far-seeing, judicious, prudent, sapient
idiom wise as an owl
con dumb, stupid, unintelligent; ignorant, unlearned, untaught; unperceptive; unwise
2 *syn* see SHREWD
rel critical, discerning, discriminating
idiom wise in the ways of the world

sagaciousness *n syn* see SAGACITY
rel judgment, wiseness

sagacity *n* intelligent application of knowledge <*sagacity* acquired from years of learning and experience>
syn insight, sagaciousness, sageness, sapience, wisdom
rel discernment, penetration, perception, perceptiveness, sensitivity; understanding; judiciousness, prudence; comprehension, grasp

sage *adj* **1** *syn* see WISE 1
rel philosophic; learned; profound
2 *syn* see WISE 2
rel acute, penetrating, probing

sage *n* one distinguished for his breadth of knowledge, experience, wisdom, and sound judgment <was one of the renowned *sages* of constitutional law>
syn savant, scholar, wise man
rel expert, master

sageness *n syn* see SAGACITY

said *adj syn* see SUCH 1

sail *vb* **1** *syn* see FLY 1
2 *syn* see FLY 4

sailor *n syn* see MARINER

sailorman *n syn* see MARINER

saintliness *n syn* see HOLINESS
rel righteousness, worthiness

saintly *adj* being of deeply religious and wholly upright character <a *saintly* old couple>

---

syn synonym(s)   *rel* related word(s)
ant antonym(s)   *con* contrasted word(s)
idiom idiomatic equivalent(s)
‖ use limited; if in doubt, see a dictionary

syn angelic, godly, holy

rel righteous, upright, upstanding, virtuous, worthy; devout, God-fearing, pious; sainted; seraph, seraphic, seraphlike

idiom pure in mind and heart

salable *adj syn* see MARKETABLE

ant unsalable

salacious *adj syn* see LICENTIOUS 2

salad *n syn* see MISCELLANY 1

salad days *n pl syn* see YOUTH 1

salary *n syn* see WAGE

salient *adj syn* see NOTICEABLE

rel important, pertinent, significant, weighty; impressive, moving, obvious, pronounced; intrusive, obtrusive

saliferous *adj syn* see SALTY 1

saline *adj syn* see SALTY 1

saliva *n* a liquid secreted into the mouth and helpful to digestion <*saliva* drooled down the baby's chin>

syn slaver, spit, spittle, water

rel sputum

salivate *vb syn* see DROOL 2

sally *n* 1 *syn* see OUTBURST 1

2 *syn* see JOKE 1

3 *syn* see EXCURSION 1

salmagundi *n syn* see MISCELLANY 1

salon *n* 1 a spacious elegant apartment or living room (as in a fashionable house) <her *salon* was decorated à la Louis XV>

syn drawing room, saloon

rel parlor; suite

2 a fashionable assemblage of notables held by custom at the home of a prominent person <was famous for her literary *salons*>

syn saloon

rel at home; reception; levee; evening, soiree

saloon *n* 1 *syn* see SALON 1

rel gallery; hall

2 *syn* see SALON 2

rel gathering, party

3 *syn* see BAR 5

saloonist *n syn* see SALOONKEEPER

saloonkeeper *n* one who owns or manages a bar <the traditional image of the fat cigar-smoking *saloonkeeper*>

syn barkeeper, boniface, innholder, innkeeper, ‖publican, saloonist, taverner; *compare* BARTENDER

rel victualler

salt *n* 1 *syn* see LIVING

2 *syn* see MARINER

salt *adj syn* see SALTY 1

saltate *vb syn* see JUMP 1

salt away *vb syn* see SAVE 4

saltimbanque *n syn* see CHARLATAN

rel impostor, pretender; cheat, fraud

salty *adj* 1 of, relating to, or containing salt <*salty* deposits>

syn saliferous, saline, salt

rel brackish, briny, saltish; salted

ant saltless

2 *syn* see RISQUÉ

3 *syn* see CAUSTIC 1

salubrious *adj syn* see HEALTHFUL

rel bracing, invigorating, stimulating

ant insalubrious

salutary *adj syn* see HEALTHFUL

rel restorative, sanative, sanatory, tonic

con debilitating, enfeebling, weakening; bad, evil

ant deleterious; unsalutary

salutation *n* 1 *syn* see GREETING

2 *syn* see ENCOMIUM

salute *vb syn* see ADDRESS 7

salute *n syn* see GREETING

salutiferous *adj syn* see HEALTHFUL

salvage *vb* to rescue and save from wreckage, destruction, or loss <*salvaged* the torpedoed vessel>

syn salve

rel deliver, redeem, rescue, save; reclaim, recover, regain, retrieve; ransom

con dump, jettison

salvation *n* 1 *syn* see PRESERVATION 1

2 *syn* see CONSERVATION 1

salve *n syn* see OINTMENT

rel emollient, lubricant; counterirritant; aid, remedy

salve *vb syn* see SALVAGE

salvo *n* 1 *syn* see BARRAGE

rel discharge; spray

2 *syn* see TESTIMONIAL 2

same *adj* 1 being one rather than another or more <went to the *same* hotel each summer>

syn exact, identical, selfsame, very

rel comparable, like, similar

ant different

2 agreeing fundamentally or absolutely <all the family have the *same* dark eyes>

syn duplicate, equal, equivalent, identic, identical, indistinguishable, tantamount; *compare* LIKE

rel comparable, like, similar; coequal

ant different

3 not changing or fluctuating <treated everyone with the *same* courtesy>

syn consistent, constant, invariable, unchanging, unfailing, unvarying

con changeable, fluctuant, inconsistent, inconstant, irregular, variable, varying

sameness *n* 1 *syn* see IDENTITY 1

rel alikeness; uniformity, uniformness, unity

2 *syn* see EQUIVALENCE

rel analogy; resemblance, similarity

sample *n syn* see INSTANCE

rel indication, sign; fragment, part, piece, portion, segment; constituent, element; individual, unit

sampling *n syn* see INSTANCE

sanative *adj syn* see CURATIVE

rel healthful, hygienic, salutary, sanitary

sanatory *adj syn* see CURATIVE

sanctified *adj syn* see HOLY 1

rel canonized, deified, sainted

ant unsanctified

sanctify *vb syn* see BLESS 1

sanctimonious *adj syn* see HYPOCRITICAL

rel deceiving, false; snuffling

ant unsanctimonious

sanctimoniousness *n syn* see HYPOCRISY

idiom odor of sanctity

ant unsanctimoniousness

sanctimony *n syn* see HYPOCRISY

sanction *n* 1 explicit authoritative permission or recognition that gives validity to acts of a subordinate <a colonial governor acting under the *sanction* of the king>

syn endorsement, fiat

rel approval, authorization, consent, permission; approbation, confirmation, encouragement, ratification, recommendation, support

con restraint; debarment; interdict, prohibition; disapprobation, disapproval, objection

ant interdiction

2 *syn* see PERMISSION

sanction *vb syn* see APPROVE 2

rel authorize, commission, license

con ban, disallow, forbid, prohibit

ant interdict

sanctioned *adj syn* see ORTHODOX 1

ant unsanctioned

sanctity *n syn* see HOLINESS

rel godliness; righteousness, uprightness

sanctorium *n syn* see SHRINE

sanctuary *n* 1 *syn* see SHRINE

2 *syn* see SHELTER 1

rel bamah; oasis

3 *syn* see REFUGE 1

sanctum *n syn* see SHRINE

sand *n syn* see FORTITUDE

rel chutzpah, gall

idiom true (*or* clear) grit

sandwich shop *n syn* see EATING HOUSE

sane *adj* 1 *syn* see HEALTHY 1

2 free from mental disorder <a thoroughly *sane* and well-balanced man>

syn all there, compos mentis, lucid, normal, right

rel balanced, oriented; levelheaded, rational, sensible, sober, sound

idiom of sound mind

con abnormal, unbalanced; neurotic, paranoid, psychopathic, psychotic, schizophrenic; balmy, crazy, ‖cuckoo, non compos, non compos mentis, nuts, screwy; deranged, lunatic, mad, wild

ant insane

3 *syn* see WISE 2

rel logical, rational, reasonable; good, right; cogent, compelling, convincing, sound

con imprudent, injudicious, unwise

saneness *n syn* see WIT 2

rel clear-mindedness, perception; comprehension, ‖smarts, understanding

sangfroid *n syn* see EQUANIMITY

rel self-containment, self-control; aloofness, coolheadedness, indifference, unconcern

sanguinary *adj* 1 *syn* see MURDEROUS

2 *syn* see BLOODY 1

ant unsanguinary

sanguine *adj* 1 *syn* see BLOODY 1

2 *syn* see MURDEROUS

3 *syn* see RUDDY

4 *syn* see CONFIDENT 1

rel expectant; hopeful, undespairing

idiom full of hope

ant hopeless

5 *syn* see OPTIMISTIC

ant unsanguine

sanguineness *n syn* see OPTIMISM

sanguineous *adj* 1 *syn* see BLOODY 1

2 *syn* see MURDEROUS

---

sanguinity *n syn* see OPTIMISM

sanity *n syn* see WIT 2

rel intelligence; comprehension

idiom sound mind

ant insanity

sans *prep syn* see WITHOUT 2

sap *n syn* see FOOL 3

sap *vb syn* see WEAKEN 1

rel deplete, drain, exhaust, knock out; ruin, wreck; destroy

saphead *n syn* see FOOL 3

rel ‖boob, jerk

sapid *adj syn* see PALATABLE

idiom fit for a king

con bland, tasteless; repulsive, unpalatable

ant insipid

sapidity *n syn* see TASTE 3

ant insipidity

sapience *n syn* see SAGACITY

sapient *adj syn* see WISE 2

rel erudite, learned, scholarly; thinking; discriminating, sapiential

sapless *adj syn* see INSIPID 3

sapor *n syn* see TASTE 3

saporous *adj syn* see PALATABLE

sappy *adj* 1 *syn* see SUCCULENT, juicy

2 *syn* see SENTIMENTAL

3 *syn* see FOOLISH 2

sarcasm *n* a savage bitter form of humor usually intended to hurt or wound <a speech full of personal jabs and *sarcasm*>

syn acerbity, causticity, corrosiveness, sarcasticness

rel humor, irony, raillery, satire, wit; jest, repartee; gibe, lampooning; mockery, ridicule, scorn, sneering; acrimony, invective; rancor, sharpness

con playfulness, waggishness, whimsicality

sarcastic *adj* marked by, expressive of, or given to sarcasm <a critic noted for his *sarcastic* comments on actors' performances>

syn acerb, acerbic, archilochian, caustic, corrosive, ‖sarky; *compare* CAUSTIC 1

rel dry; cynical, ironic, sardonic, satiric; jeering, mocking, scornful; biting, cutting, incisive; mordant, scathing, sharp, stinging; pungent, tart, trenchant

con droll, playful, sportive, waggish, whimsical

sarcasticness *n syn* see SARCASM

rel bitingness, cuttingness, incisiveness, trenchancy; derision, mocking, taunting

sardonic *adj* characterized by or expressing disdainful, skeptical humor <had a *sardonic* smile that mirrored his fixed expectation of the worst from everyone>

syn cynical, ironic, wry

rel contemptuous, disdainful, scornful; derisive, jeering, mocking, saturnine, sneering; caustic, corrosive, sarcastic, satiric

‖**sarky** *adj syn* see SARCASTIC

sash *n syn* see BELT 1

sashay *vb* to move about often self-consciously and usually in a conspicuous manner <*sashaying* around, trying to walk like a model>

syn flounce, mince, prance, ‖prink, strut

rel swagger

sass *n syn* see BACK TALK

---

syn synonym(s)　　*rel* related word(s)

ant antonym(s)　　*con* contrasted word(s)

idiom idiomatic equivalent(s)

‖ use limited; if in doubt, see a dictionary

rel impertinence, insolence, sassiness

sassy *adj* **1** *syn* see WISE 5
rel brazen, unabashed; audacious
2 *syn* see DAPPER

Satan *n* **1** *syn* see DEVIL 1
rel deuce; Mephistopheles; devil-god
idiom fallen angel, lord of the underworld, prince of darkness
2 *syn* see DEVIL 2
rel renegade, villain; beast, viper

satanic *adj* **1** of, relating to, or characteristic of Satan <*Satanic* rites>
syn devilish, diabolic, Mephistophelian
rel saturnine
2 *syn* see FIENDISH
rel evil, wicked

satanism *n* the worship of Satan usually marked by the travesty of Christian rites <interpreted *satanism* as an offshoot of the belief in two coequal and coeternal principles of good and evil>
syn diabolism
rel Black Mass

sate *vb* *syn* see SATIATE
rel overfill, overstuff, stuff
idiom have (*or* give) a bellyful of, have (*or* give) an overdose of

sated *adj* *syn* see SATIATED
ant unsated

satellite *n* *syn* see FOLLOWER
rel favorite, minion

satellite *adj* *syn* see CONCOMITANT

satiate *adj* *syn* see SATIATED
idiom stuffed to the gills
con insatiable, unsatiable
ant insatiate, unsatiate

satiate *vb* to satisfy fully or to repletion <tried to titillate rather than *satiate* his readers' interest>
syn cloy, fill, glut, gorge, jade, pall, sate, ‖stall, stodge, surfeit; *compare* SATISFY 3
rel content, fulfill, gratify, indulge, satisfy; overdose, stuff
con coax, court, invite, pique, tantalize, tempt, titillate

satiated *adj* filled to repletion <the mob, *satiated* with violence, finally dispersed>
syn full, glutted, gorged, jaded, sated, satiate, surfeited
rel fulfilled, gratified, indulged, satisfied
con avid, greedy, ravening; craving, hungering, hungry, lusting, thirsting, thirsty
ant unsatiated

satiny *adj* *syn* see SOFT 3

satire *n* humorous ridicule often used to convey rebuke or criticism or to expose folly or vice <a brilliant writer noted for her *satire*>
syn lampoonery, raillery, satiricalness
rel banter, chaffing; causticity, irony; mockery, ridicule; pasquinade, persiflage, squib; parody, spoof, spoofery, takeoff

satiric *adj* of, relating to, characterized by, or based on satire <witty, eloquent, and *satiric* plays>
syn lampooning, satirizing
rel bantering, chaffing; caustic, ironic; mocking, ridiculing; parodying, spoofing; farcical; Rabelaisian

satiricalness *n* *syn* see SATIRE

satirizing *adj* *syn* see SATIRIC

satisfactorily *adv* *syn* see WELL 4
rel competently, sufficiently
ant unsatisfactorily

satisfactory *adj* **1** *syn* see SUFFICIENT 1
ant unsatisfactory
2 *syn* see VALID
ant unsatisfactory
3 *syn* see DECENT 4
rel fair, goodish, passable
ant unsatisfactory

satisfy *vb* **1** *syn* see CLEAR 5
2 *syn* see SUIT 6
3 to satiate desires or longings <strove to *satisfy* his lust for money and power>
syn appease, content, gratify; *compare* SATIATE
rel gladden, humor, indulge, please; sate, satiate; pacify, placate
con tantalize, tease; excite, pique, provoke, stimulate; arouse
4 *syn* see ASSURE 2
rel induce, inveigle, win (over)
5 measure up to a set of criteria or requirements <courses taken to *satisfy* requirements for graduation>
syn answer, fill, fulfill, meet
rel comply (with), conform (to), serve; do, suffice
idiom fill the bill, make good

satisfying *adj* *syn* see VALID
ant unsatisfying

satisfyingly *adv* *syn* see WELL 5
rel gratifyingly, pleasingly
ant unsatisfyingly

saturate *vb* **1** *syn* see SOAK 1
rel bathe, douche, wash; imbue, infuse, suffuse
2 *syn* see PERMEATE
rel pierce, probe; inoculate, instill

saturate *adj* *syn* see WET 1

saturated *adj* *syn* see WET 1

saturnalia *n* *syn* see ORGY 2

saturnine *adj* *syn* see SULLEN
rel grave, serious, solemn, somber, staid; moping; dark, funereal; reserved, silent, taciturn, uncommunicative
con cheerful, cheery, happy; cordial, polite
ant genial

satyric *adj* **1** *syn* see LICENTIOUS 2
2 *syn* see LUSTFUL 2

sauce *n* **1** *syn* see BACK TALK
rel pertness, sauciness
‖**2** *syn* see LIQUOR 2

saucebox *n* *syn* see MINX

saucy *adj* **1** flippant and bold in manner or attitude <a saucy little flirt>
syn arch, bantam, ‖cocket, malapert, pert
rel flippant, frivolous, light-minded, volatile; bold, brash, combative; impertinent, impudent, insolent; intrusive, meddlesome, obtrusive; smart, smart-alecky, wise
con gentle, meek, mild, quiet, subdued
ant deferential
2 *syn* see INSOLENT 2

sault *n* *syn* see WATERFALL

saunter *vb* to walk slowly in an idle or leisurely manner <*sauntered* about the streets, stopping in at various shops>
syn amble, bummel, drift, linger, mope, mosey, ‖muck, stroll; *compare* WANDER 1

rel meander, ramble, roam, rove, spatiate, ||stravage, wander; loiter, tarry
con bustle, chase, hustle, scurry, tear

saunter *n syn* see WALK 1

savage *adj* **1** being undomesticated and often destructive or ferocious through lack of restraints or human control <*savage* dogs>
syn feral, vicious, wild; *compare* WILD 1
rel uncivilized, undomesticated, unsocialized; unbroken, unsubdued, untamed; bestial, brutal, brute; ferocious, fierce
con civilized, domesticated, socialized; broken, subdued, tamed; domestic, tame
2 *syn* see FIERCE 1
rel coldhearted, heartless, implacable, relentless, unrelenting; rapacious, ravenous, voracious; bloodthirsty, bloody, butcherly, murderous, rabid
3 *syn* see BARBARIAN 1
rel primeval, primitive; uncontrolled, unharnessed; harsh, rough, rugged

savant *n syn* see SAGE

save *vb* **1** *syn* see RESCUE
rel unchain, unshackle
idiom snatch from the jaws of death
con desert, leave; condemn, damn
2 *syn* see MAINTAIN 1
3 to keep secure or maintain intact from injury, decay, or loss <regular painting helps *save* the wood>
syn conserve, preserve; *compare* MAINTAIN 1
rel defend, guard, protect, safeguard, shield
con draw (out), withdraw; consume, spend, use up
4 to accumulate and store up (a supply) for future use <*saved* his money for college>
syn lay aside, lay away, lay by, lay in, lay up, put by, salt away, ||spare; *compare* HOARD
rel accumulate, cache, collect, stockpile, store (up); hoard, squirrel, stash (away); conserve, husband, manage; keep, reserve, set by; deposit, stow
idiom feather one's nest, keep as a nest egg, save for a rainy day, save to fall back on
con lose, squander, use up, waste
ant consume, spend
5 *syn* see ECONOMIZE

save *prep syn* see EXCEPT

save *conj* **1** *syn* see ONLY
2 *syn* see EXCEPT 1

save-all *adj syn* see STINGY

saving *n* **1** *syn* see PRESERVATION 1
2 *syn* see CONSERVATION 1

saving *prep syn* see EXCEPT

saving *conj syn* see EXCEPT 1

saving *adj syn* see SPARING

savoir faire *n syn* see TACT
rel manners; dignity, elegance, grace; refinement, savoir vivre, taste; aplomb, confidence, self-assurance, self-possession; blaséness, experience, sophistication
con awkwardness, clumsiness, gaucherie, ineptness, maladroitness

---

syn synonym(s)   *rel* related word(s)
ant antonym(s)   *con* contrasted word(s)
idiom idiomatic equivalent(s)
|| use limited; if in doubt, see a dictionary

savor *n* **1** *syn* see TASTE 3
rel scent, tinge
2 *syn* see QUALITY 1

savor *vb* **1** *syn* see SMACK
2 *syn* see FEEL 2
3 *syn* see RELISH 2

savorless *adj syn* see UNPALATABLE 1
rel bland; thin, watery, weak; unpleasing
con appetizing, pleasing, tempting; piquant, spicy
ant savory

savorous *adj syn* see PALATABLE

savorsome *adj syn* see PALATABLE

savory *adj* **1** *syn* see PALATABLE
rel pleasing, tempting; gustful
con acrid, sharp, strong
ant unsavory
2 *syn* see SWEET 2

||**savvy** *adj syn* see SHREWD

saw *n syn* see SAYING

||**sawbones** *n syn* see PHYSICIAN

sawbuck *n syn* see SAWHORSE

saw-edged *adj syn* see SERRATE

sawhorse *n* a rack on which something (as a board) is laid for sawing <*sawhorses* in the carpentry shop>
syn buck, horse, sawbuck, trestle, workhorse

sawtooth *adj syn* see SERRATE

saw-toothed *adj syn* see SERRATE

say *vb* **1** to express in words <learn to *say* what you mean>
syn bring out, chime in, come out (with), declare, deliver, state, tell, throw out, utter; *compare* EXPRESS 2
rel breathe; articulate, enunciate, pronounce; announce, proclaim; animadvert, comment, give, remark; cite, quote, recite, repeat; affirm, assert, aver, avow, protest
idiom out with, put in (or into) words, put it
2 *syn* see ARTICULATE 2
rel speak, talk
3 *syn* see SHOW 5

say *n syn* see VOICE 2
rel authority; decision

say *adv syn* see NEARLY

saying *n* an oft-repeated statement usually involving common experience or observation <the old *saying* that ignorance is bliss>
syn adage, byword, proverb, saw, word
rel dictum, maxim; truism

say-so *n syn* see VOICE 2

scabrous *adj syn* see ROUGH 1
rel scabby, scaly, scurfy; downy; knobby, knotty; bristly, prickly, thorny
con bald, glabrescent
ant glabrous, smooth

scad *n, usu scads pl* a great number or abundance <*scads* of opportunities>
syn gob(s), heap, jillion, load(s), million, oodles, quantities, ream(s), ||rimption(s), slather(s), slew, thousand, trillion, wad(s); *compare* MUCH, MULTITUDE 1
rel great deal, lot
con few, handful, scattering, sprinkle, sprinkling

scalawag *n syn* see SCAMP

scalding *adj syn* see HOT 1
ant freezing

scale *vb* **1** *syn* see SKIN 2

2 to shed scales or fragmentary surface matter <*scaling* skin>
   syn desquamate, exfoliate, flake (off), peel
   rel chip (off), spall (off)
scale *n* 1 *syn* see DEGREE 2
  2 *syn* see RANGE 5
scale *vb* 1 *syn* see ASCEND 1
  2 *syn* see MEASURE 2
||**scamble** *vb syn* see SPRAWL 1
scamp *n* a pleasantly mischievous person <what have those little *scamps* done now>
   syn devil, enfant terrible, limb, mischief, pixie, rapscallion, rascal, ribald, rogue, scalawag, skeezicks, slyboots, villain
   rel bird, chap, dog, ||duck; ||bleeder; joker, prankster
   con sobersides
scamper *vb* 1 *syn* see RUN 2
   rel hasten (off), hurry (away *or* off), light out, speed (away); dash (off), rush (off), shoot, tear (off), whip (off), whiz (off)
  2 *syn* see RUN 1
   rel scud, scuddle, scuttle
scan *vb syn* see BROWSE
   idiom pass one's eye over
scan *n syn* see EXAMINATION
   rel perusal; observation, reconnaissance
scandal *n syn* see DETRACTION
   rel aspersion; reproach; discredit, disrepute
||**scandal** *vb syn* see MALIGN
scandalize *vb* 1 *syn* see MALIGN
  2 *syn* see SHOCK 1
scandalizer *n syn* see GOSSIP 1
   rel blabber, blabbermouth, talker
scandalmonger *n syn* see GOSSIP 1
   rel meddler, snoop; backbiter; muckraker
scandalous *adj* 1 *syn* see LIBELOUS
  2 *syn* see OUTRAGEOUS 2
||**scant** *n syn* see SCARCITY
scant *adj* ||1 *syn* see STINGY
  2 *syn* see SHORT 3
  3 *syn* see MEAGER 2
   ant ample
scant *vb syn* see SPARE 3
scantiness *n syn* see FAILURE 3
   rel scarceness, scarcity; sparseness, sparsity
   con excess, overage, surplus
scanty *adj* 1 *syn* see MEAGER 2
   rel scarce, wanting
   con ample, enough; profuse
   ant plentiful
  2 *syn* see SHORT 3
scape *vb syn* see ESCAPE 1
||**scape** *n syn* see ESCAPE 1
scape *n syn* see VISTA
scapegoat *n* one that bears the blame for another or others <was made the *scapegoat* for his boss's errors>
   syn fall guy, goat, patsy, whipping boy
   rel mark; target; victim
scapegrace *n syn* see WASTREL 3
scar *n* a mark left by the healing of injured tissue <still had *scars* from the operation>
   syn cicatrix, scarification
   rel blemish, defect, flaw; blister, pockmark, scab; disfigurement
scar *vb* to mark with a scar <burns that had *scarred* her face>
   syn cicatrize, scarify
   rel cut, score, scratch; blemish, disfigure, flaw, mar; damage, deface

scarce *adj* 1 *syn* see SHORT 3
   rel curtailed, shortened, truncated
   con adequate, sufficient, unwanting
   ant abundant
  2 *syn* see INFREQUENT
   idiom scarce as ice water in hell, scarcer than hen's teeth, seldom met with
scarce *adv syn* see JUST 2
scarcely *adv syn* see JUST 2
   idiom just barely, only just
scarceness *n syn* see SCARCITY
scarcity *n* smallness of supply, quantity, or number in proportion to demand <a serious *scarcity* of grain>
   syn insufficiency, insufficiency, paucity, poverty, ||scant, scarceness; *compare* FAILURE 3
   rel deficiency, shortage, underage; meagerness; rareness, uncommonness; absence, dearth, lack
   con sufficiency; great deal, much; overabundance, overage, oversupply, surplus
   ant abundance
scare *vb syn* see FRIGHTEN
   rel panic, shake up; freeze, paralyze, petrify
   idiom give a scare to, strike terror into the heart of, throw a scare into
scarecrow *n syn* see RAGAMUFFIN
scared *adj syn* see AFRAID 1
   rel startled; panicked, panicky, terror-stricken
   con emboldened, heartened, reassured; aggressive, bold
   ant unafraid, unscared
scarification *n syn* see SCAR
scarify *vb* 1 *syn* see SCAR
   rel deform, disfigure, maim, mar
  2 *syn* see LAMBASTE 3
scary *adj syn* see AFRAID 1
scathe *vb syn* see LAMBASTE 3
   idiom ||give holy hell, give the business, rip (someone) up one side and down the other
scatheless *n syn* see SAFE 1
scathing *adj syn* see CAUSTIC 1
   rel brutal; burning, scorching, searing, sulphurous
scatological *adj syn* see OBSCENE 2
scatter *vb* 1 to cause to separate or break up <the rain *scattered* the crowd>
   syn dispel, disperse, dissipate
   rel break up, shatter; disband; diverge, divide, part, separate, sever
   con assemble, congregate, convene; accumulate, amass, collect, crowd
   ant gather
  2 *syn* see STREW 1
   rel dispense, distribute; cast, discard, shed; besprinkle, sprinkle
   con accumulate, amass, concentrate
   ant collect
scatterbrain *n* a flighty thoughtless person <his wife is a *scatterbrain*>
   syn birdbrain, featherbrain, featherhead, flibbertigibbet, harebrain, rattlebrain, rattlehead, shatterbrain
   rel fool, goose, silly, simpleton
scatterbrained *adj syn* see GIDDY 1
scattergood *n syn* see SPENDTHRIFT
scattering *n syn* see FEW
scene *n* 1 the total arrangement of the objects that form the scenic environment in which a

drama is enacted <spectacle plays that attempt a realistic, three-dimensional *scene*>
syn mise-en-scène, scenery, set, setting, stage set, stage setting
rel hangings, scene cloth; ‖back cloth, backdrop, background; tableau
2 **syn** see VIEW 4
3 the place of an occurrence or action <the *scene* of the crime>
syn locale, mise-en-scène, site
rel locality, location, place, spot
4 a sphere of activity, interest, or controversy <the drug *scene*>
syn arena
rel compass, field, setting, sphere; culture, environment, milieu
scenery *n* 1 **syn** see SCENE 1
rel decor, furnishings, furniture; properties, props
scent *vb* 1 **syn** see SMELL 1
2 to imbue or fill with an odor <air *scented* with herbs>
syn aromatize, odorize, perfume
scent *n* 1 **syn** see SMELL 1
rel essence, whiff
2 **syn** see FRAGRANCE
scented *adj* 1 **syn** see SWEET 2
2 **syn** see ODOROUS
ant scentless, unscented
scentless *adj* **syn** see ODORLESS
schedule *n* 1 **syn** see LIST
rel chart, table
2 **syn** see PROGRAM 1
schedule *vb* 1 to place in a schedule <*schedule* a new train>
syn card, sked
rel list, record, slate
2 **syn** see TIME 1
scheme *n* 1 **syn** see PLAN 1
rel presentation, proposal, proposition, suggestion; arrangement, order, ordering; contrivance, device, expedient
2 **syn** see PLOT 2
scheme *vb* **syn** see PLAN 1
scheme (out) *vb* **syn** see PLOT 1
schism *n* 1 **syn** see BREACH 3
2 **syn** see HERESY
3 a division of a group into two discordant groups <a *schism* within a political party>
syn chasm, cleavage, cleft, split; *compare* BREACH 3
rel divergence, division, separation; breach, break, rupture; estrangement
con unification, unity; reconciliation
schismatic *n* **syn** see HERETIC
rel protester; skeptic; radical, Young Turk
schismatic *adj* **syn** see HERETICAL
rel rebellious; unconventional
schismatist *n* **syn** see HERETIC
‖**schlemiel** *n* **syn** see FOOL 3
schlepp (or **schlepper**) *n* **syn** see OAF 2
schmo *n* **syn** see FOOL 1
schmuck *n* **syn** see FOOL 1
schnook *n* **syn** see DUNCE
schnorrer *n* **syn** see BEGGAR 1
schnozzle *n* **syn** see NOSE 1

scholar *n* **syn** see SAGE
rel pupil, student; bookman; polymath
scholarliness *n* **syn** see ERUDITION 2
ant unscholarliness
scholarly *adj* **syn** see LEARNED
rel studious; intellectual, long-hair; educated, taught, trained
con untaught, untrained
ant unscholarly
scholarship *n* 1 **syn** see EDUCATION 2
2 **syn** see ERUDITION 2
scholastic *adj* 1 **syn** see PEDANTIC
rel lettered, literary; scholarly; formal
2 **syn** see LEARNED
con conversant, versed
con unconversant, unscholarly
school *vb* **syn** see TEACH
rel inform; guide, lead, show; advance, cultivate; control, direct, manage
schooling *n* **syn** see EDUCATION 1
rel knowledge; book learning, booklore
schoolmasterish *adj* **syn** see DIDACTIC
science *n* 1 **syn** see KNOWLEDGE 2
2 **syn** see EDUCATION 2
scilicet *adv* **syn** see NAMELY
scintillate *vb* **syn** see FLASH 1
scintillating *adj* **syn** see CLEVER 5
scintillation *n* **syn** see FLASH 1
scions *n pl* **syn** see OFFSPRING
scoff *vb* to show contempt by derision or mockery <heard his tale and *scoffed* at it>
syn fleer, flout, gibe, gird, jeer, jest, quip (at), scout (at), sneer
rel pooh-pooh; deride, mock, rally, ridicule, taunt, twit; contemn, despise, disdain, scorn; boo
con accept, approve, commend; compliment; acclaim, laud, praise
scoff *n* **syn** see FOOD 1
scold *n* **syn** see VIRAGO
scold *vb* 1 to reproach angrily and abusively <loudly *scolded* him for staying out late>
syn baste, bawl out, berate, ‖bless out, ‖cample, ‖carpet, ‖chew, ‖chew out, chew down, jaw, lash, ‖mob, rag, rail, rant, rate, ‖ream out, revile, ‖row, tell off, tongue, tongue-lash, ‖tongue-walk, upbraid, vituperate, wig; *compare* CRITICIZE, LAMBASTE 3, REPROVE
rel blame, censure, criticize, denounce, reprehend, reprobate; admonish, chide, rebuke, reprimand, reproach, reprove; execrate, objurgate; brace, grill, harass, hound; blister, excoriate
idiom jump down one's throat, rake over the coals, read one the riot act, walk into
2 **syn** see GRUMBLE 1
sconce *n* **syn** see HEAD 1
scoop *n* a news story first obtained and reported by only one source (as a newspaper) <the story was a *scoop* by just a few hours>
syn beat, exclusive
scoop *vb* 1 **syn** see DIP 2
rel gather; lift, pick up
2 **syn** see DIG 2
rel gouge, grub
3 to report a news item in advance of competitors <CBS *scooped* NBC on that story>
syn beat
scoot *vb* 1 **syn** see HURRY 2

---

syn synonym(s)   **rel** related word(s)
ant antonym(s)   **con** contrasted word(s)
idiom idiomatic equivalent(s)
‖ use limited; if in doubt, see a dictionary

2 *syn* see RUN 1

3 *syn* see RUN 2

scope *n* 1 *syn* see ROOM 3

2 *syn* see RANGE 2

3 *syn* see BREADTH 2

scopic *adj syn* see EXTENSIVE 1

scopious *adj syn* see EXTENSIVE 1

scorch *vb* 1 *syn* see LAMBASTE 3

2 *syn* see BURN 3

rel seethe, simmer, stew; ‖plot

scorching *adj syn* see HOT 1

idiom scorching hot, sizzling hot

score *n* 1 scores *pl syn* see MULTITUDE 1

2 a slight cut or line made with or as if with a sharp instrument <cut *scores* on the ham before baking it>

syn scotch, scratch

rel line, mark; nick, notch, serration; cut, slit; cleft, furrow, groove, indentation; gash

3 *syn* see BILL 1

4 an obligation or injury kept in mind for future reckoning <had a *score* to settle with him>

syn account

rel grudge

5 the number of points gained by contestants in a game or contest <a record *score* of 263 for 72 holes>

syn tally

rel account, record; summary, total

idiom the final count

score *vb* 1 *syn* see LAMBASTE 3

rel ream out

idiom tear to pieces

2 *syn* see GAIN 1

3 *syn* see SUCCEED 3

scorn *n syn* see DESPITE 1

rel flouting, gibing, jeering, scoffing; derision, mockery, ridicule, taunt, taunting

con consideration, respectfulness

ant respect

scorn *vb syn* see DESPISE

rel flout, gibe, jeer, scoff; mock, ridicule, taunt

idiom hold in utter contempt

con accept, acknowledge, welcome

ant respect

scotch *n syn* see SCORE 2

Scotch *adj syn* see SPARING

scoundrel *n syn* see VILLAIN 1

scour *vb* 1 *syn* see HURRY 1

2 to make a thorough search or examination of <*scoured* the neighborhood for the lost child>

syn beat, comb, finecomb, fine-tooth-comb, forage, grub, rake, ransack, rummage, search

rel rout; look (for); seek; fan, range; rifle; ferret (out), find

idiom beat the bushes, leave no stone unturned, look high and low, look up and down, turn inside out, turn upside down

scour *vb* 1 *syn* see SCRUB 1

2 *syn* see EAT 3

scour *n, usu* scours *pl syn* see DIARRHEA

scourge *n syn* see PLAGUE 1

scourge *vb* 1 *syn* see WHIP 1

rel hit; knout; flail, whop

idiom whip to ribbons

2 *syn* see RAVAGE

3 *syn* see LAMBASTE 3

scout *vb* to explore in order to obtain information <forward observers *scouted* the terrain before the attack>

syn probe, reconnoiter

rel look (over); survey; observe; check out, examine; ‖case, inspect

idiom run reconnaissance

scout *vb* 1 *syn* see RIDICULE

2 *syn* see DESPISE

rel mock, ridicule

scout (at) *vb syn* see SCOFF

scowl *vb syn* see FROWN 1

idiom look black as thunder, pull a face (or scowl)

scrabble *vb* 1 *syn* see SCRIBBLE

2 *syn* see SCRAMBLE 1

scrag *vb* 1 *syn* see HANG 2

2 *syn* see KILL 1

3 *syn* see MURDER 1

scraggy *adj* 1 *syn* see ROUGH 1

2 *syn* see LEAN

rel gangling, spindling, spindly; skeletal; dwarfed, scrubby, stunted, undersize

scram *vb syn* see GET OUT 1

idiom ‖beat it, ‖cheese it, ‖get the hell out

scramble *vb* 1 to move or climb hastily on all fours <*scrambled* across the rocks>

syn clamber, scrabble, ‖spartle, ‖sprauchle

rel scurry, scuttle

2 *syn* see SPRAWL 2

scramble *n syn* see CLUTTER 2

rel conglomeration

scrap *n* 1 *syn* see END 4

rel chip, cutting; scrappage, waste

2 *syn* see PARTICLE

scrap *vb syn* see DISCARD

idiom consign to the scrap heap

scrap *n syn* see BRAWL 2

scrap *vb syn* see QUARREL

scrape *vb* 1 to rub or slide against something that is often harsh, rough, or sharp <chalk *scraping* on the blackboard>

syn grate, rasp, scratch

rel graze, rub, scuff; abrade, chafe, grind

2 *syn* see SCRIMP

3 to make one's way with great difficulty or succeed by a narrow margin <the student barely *scraped* through the exam>

syn shave

rel struggle; get along, get by

idiom cut it (or the corner) pretty close, have a close shave

scrape *n syn* see PREDICAMENT

rel trouble; discomfiture, embarrassment

scrapping *n syn* see DISPOSAL 2

scrappy *adj* 1 *syn* see QUARRELSOME 2

2 *syn* see BELLIGERENT

scratch *vb* 1 *syn* see SCRAPE 1

rel squeak, squeal

2 *syn* see SCRIBBLE

scratch *n* 1 *syn* see SCORE 2

‖2 *syn* see MONEY

scrawl *vb syn* see SCRIBBLE

rel inscribe; doodle

scrawny *adj syn* see LEAN

idiom just (or nothing but) skin and bones

ant brawny

screak *vb syn* see SQUEAL 2

scream *vb* **1** to voice a sudden piercing loud cry often in shock, terror, or pain <*screamed* at the sight of the accident and then fainted>
syn screech, shriek, shrill, squeal; *compare* SHOUT 1
rel screak, squeak; cry; yell; bellow, roar; caterwaul, howl, wail, ||yawl
idiom let out a scream (*or* shriek *or* screech)
2 *syn* see SQUEAL 2
3 *syn* see YELL 2
rel complain, grumble, protest; blare
idiom raise a howl
4 to produce a vivid, blatant, or startling effect <clothes and furnishings that *screamed* nouveau riche>
syn blare, shout, shriek
scream *n syn* see RIOT 2
screech *vb* **1** *syn* see SCREAM 1
rel penetrate, pierce; vent; voice
2 *syn* see SQUEAL 2
screen *vb* **1** *syn* see DEFEND 1
2 *syn* see SHADE
3 to cut off from view by interposing something resembling a screen <*screen* a view with a tall hedge>
syn block out, close, obstruct, shroud, shut off, shut out
rel conceal, hide; separate, wall off; protect, seclude; embosk
idiom throw up a screen
con bare, disclose, expose, open, reveal
4 *syn* see HIDE
rel defend, guard, protect, safeguard, shield; camouflage, cloak, cover up, disguise
5 to examine carefully and methodically in order to separate, select, or eliminate <the personnel department *screened* seventy candidates for ten jobs>
syn sieve, sift; *compare* SORT 2
rel choose, pick out, select; extract, filter (out), riddle, sort (out), winnow (out)
6 *syn* see CENSOR
||**screeve** *vb syn* see EXUDE
||**screw** *n syn* see SHAFT 3
screw *vb* **1** *syn* see CRUMPLE 1
2 *syn* see EXTORT 1
||**3** *syn* see CHEAT
4 *syn* see SCRIMP
||**5** *syn* see RUN 2
||**screw** (up) *vb syn* see BOTCH
rel confuse, muddle, snafu; spoil
screwball *n syn* see CRACKPOT
||**screwing** *n syn* see SHAFT 3
screwy *adj* ||**1** *syn* see INTOXICATED 1
2 *syn* see INSANE 1
idiom having a screw loose
scribble *vb* to write or draw hastily or roughly <*scribbled* a quick note to her on his way out>
syn scrabble, scratch, scrawl, squiggle
rel jot (down); scribe, write
scribe *vb syn* see WRITE
scrimmage *n* **1** *syn* see CLASH 2
rel scuffle; fight; free-for-all
2 *syn* see BRAWL 2

scrimp *adj syn* see MEAGER 2
scrimp *vb* to be extremely frugal and parsimonious in an effort to economize <*scrimped* all year to buy that fur coat>
syn pinch, scrape, screw, skimp, ||skinch, spare, stint; *compare* SPARE 3
rel scamp; scratch; save (up)
idiom pinch pennies
||**scrimption** *n syn* see PITTANCE
scrimpy *adj* **1** *syn* see MEAGER 2
2 *syn* see SHORT 3
3 *syn* see STINGY
scrimy *adj syn* see STINGY
script *n syn* see HANDWRITING
Scripture *n syn* see BIBLE
scrooch (down) *vb syn* see CROUCH
scrooge *n syn* see MISER
scrub *n syn* see INFERIOR
scrub *vb* **1** to clean by abrasive action <*scrubbed* the pots and pans>
syn scour
rel brush; rub; cleanse, wash; buff, polish
2 *syn* see CANCEL 2
scrubby *adj syn* see SHABBY 1
scruffy *adj syn* see SHABBY 1
scrumptious *adj syn* see DELIGHTFUL
scrunch *vb* **1** *syn* see CHEW 1
2 *syn* see CRUMPLE 1
||**scrunty** *adj syn* see STUNTED
scruple *n syn* see PARTICLE
scruple *n syn* see QUALM
rel faltering, hesitancy, hesitation, pause; reconsideration, second thought
scruple *vb syn* see DEMUR
rel question; fret, worry
scrupulous *adj* **1** *syn* see UPRIGHT 2
rel fair-minded; strict; upstanding
con questionable; shifty, slippery; dishonorable, unprincipled; dishonest
ant unscrupulous
2 *syn* see CAREFUL 2
rel critical, fastidious
con careless; undiscriminating, unparticular
ant remiss
scrutinize *vb* **1** to look at or over critically and searchingly <the jeweler *scrutinized* the diamonds to see if they were fakes>
syn canvass, ||case, check over, check up, con, examine, inspect, perlustrate, study, survey, vet, view
rel look over, overlook, peruse, pore (over), scan; consider, contemplate, weigh; penetrate, pierce, probe; analyze, dig (into), dissect; comb
idiom turn a careful (*or* heedful) eye to (*or* on)
2 *syn* see EYE 2
scrutiny *n* **1** *syn* see EXAMINATION
rel look-in, look-over, look-see
2 *syn* see EYE 3
scud *vb syn* see FLY 1
scuddle *vb syn* see SCUTTLE
scuff *vb syn* see SHUFFLE 3
scuffle *vb* **1** *syn* see WRESTLE
rel cuff, scuff
2 *syn* see SHUFFLE 3
scuffle *n syn* see BRAWL 2
||**sculch** *n syn* see REFUSE
sculp *vb syn* see SCULPTURE
sculpt *vb syn* see SCULPTURE

---

syn synonym(s)   *rel* related word(s)
ant antonym(s)   *con* contrasted word(s)
idiom idiomatic equivalent(s)
|| use limited; if in doubt, see a dictionary

sculpture vb to form an image or representation from solid material (as wood or stone) <*sculptured* a colossal statue of a horse>
syn carve, chisel, sculp, sculpt
rel cast, form; model, mold, shape

scum n 1 *syn* see RABBLE 2
idiom scum of the earth
2 *syn* see SNOT 1

‖**scumbag** n *syn* see SNOT 1

scummy adj *syn* see CONTEMPTIBLE

scurf n *syn* see RABBLE 2

scurrile adj *syn* see ABUSIVE

scurrility n *syn* see ABUSE
rel scurrilousness; maligning, traducing, vilification

scurrilous adj 1 *syn* see ABUSIVE
rel coarse, gross; filthy, foul; insulting, offending, offensive, outrageous, outraging
2 *syn* see OBSCENE 2

scurry vb 1 *syn* see SCUTTLE
2 *syn* see RUN 1
rel shoot, tear; dart, fly; scuffle, skelter

scurvy adj *syn* see CONTEMPTIBLE
rel base, low, vile

scutter vb *syn* see SCUTTLE
rel hasten, hurry, run, speed

scuttle vb to move with or as if with short rapidly alternating steps <armies of fiddler crabs *scuttled* across the road>
syn scuddle, scurry, scutter; *compare* RUN 1
rel scoot; scramble; scud

scuttlebutt n *syn* see REPORT 1

sea n *syn* see OCEAN

sea dog n *syn* see PIRATE

seal n an adhesive-backed device bearing a symbolic, pictorial, or official design <the *seal* on a diploma>
syn stamp, sticker

seam n *syn* see JOINT 1
rel bond

seaman n *syn* see MARINER

sear vb 1 *syn* see DRY 1
2 to burn or scorch with a sudden application of intense heat <*seared* the steaks in the broiler>
syn sizzle
rel parch, scorch, shrivel; burn (up)

search vb 1 *syn* see SCOUR 2
rel run down, scout (around), scrimmage, skirmish
idiom search high and low
2 to subject (a person) to a thorough check for concealed or contraband articles <police *searching* the suspects for weapons>
syn ‖fan, frisk, shake down
rel check, examine; inspect, look over, scan, scrutinize, study

search (for or out) vb *syn* see SEEK 1
rel pry (out), scout (out)

search n *syn* see PURSUIT 2

searchingly adv *syn* see HARD 4

sea robber n *syn* see PIRATE

sea rover n *syn* see PIRATE

season n a particular period of the year <the Christmas *season*>
syn time
rel period, term

season vb *syn* see HARDEN 2
rel discipline, school, train; fit, prepare; case harden, steel

seasonable adj *syn* see TIMELY 1
rel apropos, pertinent, relevant; appropriate, apt; convenient
con irrelevant; inappropriate, inapt; ill-timed, inconvenient, inopportune
ant unseasonable

seasonably adv *syn* see EARLY 1
ant unseasonably

seasoned adj *syn* see EXPERIENCED
rel acclimated, acclimatized, hardened, toughened; case-hardened, steeled
con inexperienced, unpracticed, unskilled, unversed; unacclimated, unacclimatized, unsteeled, untempered, untried
ant unseasoned

seat n 1 *syn* see BUTTOCKS
2 *syn* see CENTER 2
rel fulcrum
3 *syn* see BASE 1

seat vb to cause to be seated <an usher *seated* her in the third row>
syn sit
rel establish, place, put

seating n *syn* see BASE 1

sea wolf n *syn* see PIRATE

seclude vb to remove or separate (oneself or another) from external influences <in the convent she was *secluded* from secular life>
syn cloister, sequester
rel retire, separate, withdraw; closet, confine, enclose, immure, isolate; screen, shut off

secluded adj disposed to, living in, or characterized by seclusion <*secluded* monks> <they enjoyed *secluded* country living>
syn cloistered, hermetic, recluse, secluse, seclusive, sequestered
rel retired, withdrawn; close, hidden, private, screened, shy; alone, isolated, solitary
con communal, public

secluse adj *syn* see SECLUDED

seclusion n the act or condition of secluding or of being secluded <the queen went into *seclusion* when her husband died>
syn reclusion, retirement, sequestration; *compare* SOLITUDE
rel detachment, separation, withdrawal; reclusiveness, seclusiveness; privacy, privateness; aloneness, isolation, separateness, solitude

seclusive adj *syn* see SECLUDED

second n *syn* see INSTANT 1
idiom the flash of an eyelid

secondary adj 1 *syn* see SUBORDINATE
rel accessory, subservient
con major, prime; first, first-ranking, first-string
ant primary
2 formed from something original, primary, or basic <a *secondary* historical analysis based on original archives>
syn derivate, derivational, derivative, derived
rel borrowed, secondhand; consequent, resultant, subsequent
con basic, principle; first, firsthand, original, uncopied, underived
ant primary
3 *syn* see MINOR 2

secondary n *syn* see INFERIOR

rel second fiddle, second-in-command
second childhood *n syn* see DOTAGE
second–class *adj syn* see INFERIOR 2
second–drawer *adj syn* see INFERIOR 2
second–rate *adj syn* see INFERIOR 2
ant first-rate
secours *n syn* see HELP 1
secrecy *n* the practice or policy of keeping
secrets or maintaining concealment <*secrecy*
is an inherent feature of intelligence opera-
tions>
syn hugger-mugger, hugger-muggery, hush,
hush-hush, secretiveness, secretness, silence
rel clandestineness, covertness, furtiveness;
concealment, stealth, subterfuge; censor-
ship, suppression
ant openness
secret *adj* 1 existing or done in such a way as
to maintain concealment <was involved in
secret negotiations with the enemy>
syn clandestine, covert, furtive, hole-and=
corner, hugger-mugger, hush-hush, mystical, sneak, stealthy, sub-rosa, surreptitious,
undercover, ‖underneath, under-the-table;
compare STEALTHY 2, UNDERHAND
rel underhand, underhanded; unacknowl-
edged, unavowed, undeclared; concealed,
hidden, screened; classified, confidential,
eyes only, restricted, top secret
con acknowledged, avowed, declared, revealed; aboveboard, straightforward, unconcealed; declassified, unclassified, unrestricted; clear, evident, manifest, obvious,
patent, plain
ant open, public
2 *syn* see OBSCURE 2
3 *syn* see RECONDITE
secret *n* secrets *pl syn* see GENITALIA
secretaire *n syn* see DESK
secretary *n syn* see DESK
secrete *vb syn* see HIDE
rel deposit; withhold
secretiveness *n syn* see SECRECY
secretly *adv* in a secret manner <negotiated
secretly with both sides>
syn by stealth, clandestinely, covertly,
furtively, hugger-mugger, in camera, privately, stealthily, sub rosa, surreptitiously
rel confidentially; privatim, privily
idiom behind closed doors, on the qt, on the
quiet, under the rose, under the table
con forthrightly, plainly, publicly; mani-
festly, overtly
ant openly
secretness *n syn* see SECRECY
sect *n syn* see RELIGION 2
sectarian *adj* 1 *syn* see HERETICAL
rel splinter
con unified, united
ant nonsectarian
2 *syn* see INSULAR
sectary *n* 1 *syn* see HERETIC
rel beatnik, Bohemian, hippie; maverick;
liberal, radical, Young Turk; rebel, revolutionary

con advocate, conformist, follower
2 *syn* see FOLLOWER
rel bigot
sectator *n syn* see FOLLOWER
section *n* 1 *syn* see PART 1
rel district, locality, subdivision, vicinity;
area, belt, zone; region, tract; field, sphere,
territory
2 *syn* see QUARTER 2
section *vb* to divide into sections <*sectioned*
the class on the basis of ability>
syn sectionalize, sectionize; *compare* SEG-
MENT
rel break up, divide, separate, slice, split;
sector, segment
sectionalize *vb syn* see SECTION
sectionize *vb syn* see SECTION
sector *n syn* see QUARTER 2
secular *adj syn* see PROFANE 1
rel nonclerical, nonreligious
con clerical, ecclesiastical, ministerial,
priestly, regular; eternal
ant religious
securable *adj syn* see AVAILABLE 1
rel convenient, handy, reachable, ready
idiom at one's disposal
con unavailable, unreachable
secure *adj* 1 *syn* see CONFIDENT 1
2 *syn* see SAFE 2
rel firm, stable, strong
con open, wide-open; assailable, weak;
dangerous, precarious
ant insecure
3 *syn* see RELIABLE 1
4 *syn* see FAST 4
rel strong; iron
5 *syn* see STABLE 4
6 *syn* see SURE 1
rel established, settled; balanced
con precarious; unbalanced; unstable, wobbly
ant insecure
secure *vb* 1 *syn* see DEFEND 1
2 *syn* see ENSURE
rel underwrite
3 *syn* see CATCH 1
4 *syn* see FASTEN 2
rel batten (down), clamp, clinch, pinion,
rivet, tie down; cement
con unfasten, untie
5 *syn* see GET 1
6 *syn* see EFFECT 1
security *n* 1 *syn* see SAFETY
ant insecurity
2 *syn* see STABILITY
3 *syn* see PLEDGE 1
4 *syn* see GUARANTEE 1
rel assurance; certification; pledge
5 *syn* see DEFENSE 1
sedate *adj syn* see SERIOUS 1
rel calm, placid, serene, tranquil; collected,
composed, dispassionate, imperturbable,
unruffled; decorous, dignified, proper,
seemly
con indecorous, undignified, unseemly; airy,
flippant, light
ant flighty
sedative *n* an agent or drug that relieves
irritability, nervousness, or excitement
<took a *sedative* to help her sleep>

---

syn calmant, calmative, quietive

rel balm; pacifier, tranquilizer; sleeping pill, sleeping tablet; depressant, ||downer

con energizer; stimulant; ||upper

sediment *n* matter which settles to the bottom of a liquid <rocks hidden by *sediment* spoiled the cove for diving>

syn deposit, dreg(s), grounds, lees, precipitate, precipitation, settlings

rel bottoms, dross, recrement, scoria, slag; draff, heeltap

sedition *n* an offense against official ruling authority (as a government or sovereign) to which one owes allegiance <considered the defense industry strike to be overt *sedition*>

syn seditiousness, treason

rel alienation, disaffection, estrangement; action, protest, strike; coup, coup d'etat, putsch; insurrection, mutiny, rebellion, revolt, revolution, uprising; quislingism

con allegiance, fealty, fidelity, loyalty; duty, respect, responsibility

seditious *adj syn* see INSUBORDINATE

rel alienated, disaffected, dissident; disloyal, faithless, perfidious, traitorous, treacherous; lawless, violent

con faithful, loyal, patriotic

seditiousness *n syn* see SEDITION

seduce *vb* 1 *syn* see LURE

rel coax, tease; betray, deceive, delude, mislead; enslave, entrance; overpower, overwhelm

2 to persuade or entice into sexual partnership <his pathetic attempts to *seduce* his female coworkers>

syn debauch, undo

rel deflower; rape, ravish, violate; corrupt, degrade, pervert, ruin

seducement *n* 1 *syn* see SEDUCTION 1

rel undoing

2 *syn* see LURE 2

seduction *n* 1 the act or an instance of seducing or being seduced into a sexual relationship <his locker-room accounts of innumerable *seductions* were never taken seriously>

syn seducement

rel deflowering; rape, ravishment, violation; corruption, degradation, perversion, ruin

2 *syn* see ATTRACTION 1

rel Lorelei, siren song, temptation

seductive *adj syn* see ATTRACTIVE 1

rel desirable, mouth-watering, provocative

seductress *n syn* see SIREN

sedulous *adj syn* see ASSIDUOUS

rel active; busy; hustling, persevering, persistent, unremitting

see *vb* 1 to take cognizance of by physical or mental vision <*saw* that the boat was being driven ashore> <the only one who *saw* the truth>

syn behold, descry, discern, distinguish, espy, mark, mind, note, notice, observe, perceive, remark, twig, view

rel sight; make out; examine, inspect, scan, scrutinize; penetrate, pierce, probe; consider, study; appraise, ponder, weigh

idiom fix one's eyes (*or* mind *or* thoughts) on, occupy oneself with, pay heed (*or* attention) to, take notice of

2 to perceive something by means of the eyes <she *sees* clearly with her new glasses>

syn ||dekko, look, watch

rel gape, gaze, glare, peek, peep, peer, stare

idiom give the eye, hold in view, keep one's eye on, lay eyes on, turn one's eyes to

3 *syn* see EXPERIENCE 1

4 *syn* see DISCOVER 3

5 *syn* see THINK 1

6 *syn* see APPREHEND 1

rel discern, discriminate, recognize

7 *syn* see FORESEE

idiom see the day when

8 *syn* see LOOK 1

rel look out, watch out

idiom see to it that

9 *syn* see VISIT 2

10 *syn* see DATE

11 *syn* see GUIDE

rel accompany, go (with); attend

seeable *adj syn* see VISUAL 2

ant unseeable

seed *n* 1 *syn* see OFFSPRING

2 a beginning or source from which something (as a conception) may later develop <the growing *seeds* of suspicion in her mind>

syn bud, embryo, germ, nucleus, spark

rel rudiment; core, kernel; conceit, concept, conception, image, impression, notion

seed *vb syn* see PLANT 1

seedy *adj syn* see SHABBY 1

rel drooping, droopy, flagging, sagging, wilted, wilting; messy, slovenly, unkempt, untidy; neglected, overgrown

idiom gone to seed

con manicured, polished, shined

seeing *n syn* see EYE 2

seeing *conj syn* see BECAUSE

idiom ||being as how, in that

||**seeing glass** *n syn* see MIRROR 1

seek *vb* 1 to look for <has gone to *seek* a doctor>

syn cast about, ferret out, hunt, quest, search (for *or* out)

rel bird-dog, delve, dig, fish, mouse, nose, root, smell out, sniff

idiom go in quest (*or* search) of

2 *syn* see TRY 5

seeker *n syn* see CANDIDATE

rel bidder; petitioner; solicitant; claimant

seeking *n syn* see PURSUIT 2

seem *vb* to give the impression of being without necessarily being so in fact <things are not always the way they *seem*>

syn appear, look, sound

rel resemble, suggest; hint, imply, insinuate, intimate

idiom have (*or* show) every sign of, have the earmarks of

seeming *n* 1 *syn* see APPEARANCE 2

rel feigning, pretense, sham; facade; illusion

idiom false face (*or* front), outward show

2 *syn* see APPEARANCE 1

rel bearing, demeanor, posture; image, style; effect, impression

seeming *adj syn* see APPARENT 2

seemingly *adv syn* see OSTENSIBLY

seemliness *n* 1 *syn* see ORDER 7

2 *syn* see DECORUM 1

ant unseemliness

seemly *adj syn* see DECOROUS 1

rel compatible, congenial, congruous, consistent, consonant; pleasing
con inappropriate, unfit, unseasonable, unsuitable, untimely; incompatible, uncongenial; displeasing, unpleasing
ant unseemly

seep *vb syn* see EXUDE
rel drip; leak; flow

seer *n syn* see PROPHET

seesaw *vb* to move backward and forward or up and down from a central axis usually in a swaying often unsteady way <planes landing on the *seesawing* flight deck>
syn lurch, pitch, swag, tilt, tilter, yaw; *compare* TEETER, TOSS 2
rel cant, incline, lean, list; rock, roll, sway

seethe *vb* **1** *syn* see BOIL 2
2 *syn* see SOAK 1
3 *syn* see ANGER 2
idiom ‖do a slow burn
con calm (down), simmer (down)
ant cool (down)
4 to be in a state of internal and especially mental agitation, excitement, or turmoil <his brain *seethed* with unanswered questions>
syn boil, bubble, churn, ferment, ‖moil, simmer, smolder, stir
rel abound, swarm, teem; fret, fume, sizzle, steam; bubble over, erupt, overflow

see-through *adj syn* see TRANSPARENT 1

segment *n syn* see PART 1

segment *vb* to separate into segments <tried to *segment* the poem into understandable units>
syn segmentalize, segmentize; *compare* SECTION
rel categorize, compartmentalize; divide, separate; isolate, seclude, set off

segmentalize *vb syn* see SEGMENT

segmentize *vb syn* see SEGMENT

segregate *vb syn* see ISOLATE
rel disconnect; choose, select, single
con mix
ant desegregate

segregation *n* the quality, state, or condition of being socially or racially excluded or separated <fought against racial *segregation* in the schools>
syn apartheid, separateness, separation, separatism
rel discrimination, jim crowism; ghettoization; isolation, seclusion
ant desegregation

seity *n syn* see INDIVIDUALITY 4

seize *vb* **1** *syn* see APPROPRIATE 1
rel occupy; usurp
2 to take possession or control of usually suddenly and forcibly <the cat *seized* the fish and made off> <*seized* the rope and dragged the boat ashore>
syn catch, clutch, ‖cotch, grab, grapple, nab, ‖nail, snatch, take; *compare* CATCH 1
rel fasten (onto), grasp, catch (onto), snap (at); apprehend, arrest; capture, secure, take

over; abduct, carry off, kidnap, spirit (away or off)
idiom get into one's clutches, get one's hands (or paws) on, lay hold (on or of)
con free, loose, release
3 to affect especially as if by laying hold of <was *seized* with a coughing fit>
syn catch, strike, take
rel overtake; afflict

seizure *n syn* see ATTACK 3
rel convulsion; breakdown

seldom *adv* in few instances <she *seldom* writes home anymore>
syn hardly ever, infrequently, little, rarely, unfrequently, unoften
rel occasionally; semioccasionally; irregularly, sporadically; hardly, scarcely
idiom once in a blue moon
con regularly; frequently; usually
ant often

seldom *adj syn* see INFREQUENT

select *adj* **1** singled out from a number or group by fitness or preference <this hotel caters to a *select* clientele>
syn chosen, elect, exclusive, pick, picked, selected
rel culled, screened, weeded (out), winnowed (out); favored, preferred; best, elite
con random; indiscriminate; average, commonplace, mediocre, run-of-the-mill
2 *syn* see CHOICE
rel blue-chip, fine; best; top
3 *syn* see ECLECTIC 1

select *vb syn* see CHOOSE 1
idiom make a choice (or selection)
con ignore, pass (over); drop
ant reject

selected *adj syn* see SELECT 1
rel singled (out); appointed, tagged, tapped

selection *n syn* see CHOICE 1
rel choosing, culling, draft, drafting, picking; acumen, discernment, discrimination, insight
ant rejection

selective *adj syn* see ECLECTIC 1
rel particular, scrupulous

self-abandoned *adj syn* see ABANDONED 2

self-abnegating *adj syn* see SELF-SACRIFICING

self-abnegation *n syn* see RENUNCIATION
rel abandonment, relinquishment, resignation

self-absorbed *adj syn* see EGOCENTRIC 2
rel arrogant, cocky, self-important

self-abuse *n syn* see SELF-REPROACH

self-accusation *n syn* see SELF-REPROACH

self-admiration *n syn* see CONCEIT 2

self-asserting *adj syn* see PRESUMPTUOUS
rel aggressive, militant
con meek, modest, unassuming; docile, passive
ant self-effacing

self-assertive *adj* **1** *syn* see AGGRESSIVE
rel impertinent, intrusive, meddlesome, obtrusive, officious; audacious, bold; cocksure, sure
2 *syn* see PRESUMPTUOUS

self-assurance *n syn* see CONFIDENCE 2

---

syn synonym(s)   *rel* related word(s)
ant antonym(s)   *con* contrasted word(s)
idiom idiomatic equivalent(s)
‖ use limited; if in doubt, see a dictionary

rel collectedness, coolness, imperturbability; composure, equanimity, sangfroid
con insecurity, uncertainness

self–assured *adj syn* see CONFIDENT 1
rel self-satisfied, smug

self–assuredness *n syn* see CONFIDENCE 2

self–centered *adj* 1 *syn* see SELF-SUFFICIENT
2 *syn* see EGOCENTRIC 2
idiom wrapped up in oneself

self–centeredness *n syn* see SELFISHNESS

self–command *n syn* see WILL 3
rel self-containment, uncommunicativeness

self–complacency *n syn* see CONCEIT 2

self–complacent *adj syn* see COMPLACENT

self–composed *adj syn* see CALM 2

self–conceit *n syn* see CONCEIT 2

self–conceited *adj syn* see VAIN 3

self–concern *n syn* see SELFISHNESS

self–concerned *adj syn* see EGOCENTRIC 2

self–confidence *n syn* see CONFIDENCE 2
rel sanguineness, sureness, cockiness, overconfidence
con diffidence, shyness; self-distrust; doubt, uneasiness
ant self-doubt

self–confident *adj syn* see CONFIDENT 1

self–conscious *adj* aware of the scrutiny of others to the point of not appearing natural or spontaneous <felt *self-conscious* about wearing platform shoes>
syn affected, conscious, mannered
rel self-aware; anxious, ill at ease, uncomfortable, uneasy; formal, stiff, stilted; artificial; ||mim, prim; exhibitionist, flaunty, ostentatious
con unaware, unconcerned; blithe, easy; natural, spontaneous, unaffected

self–consequence *n syn* see CONCEIT 2

self–contained *adj syn* see SELF-SUFFICIENT

self–contemplation *n syn* see INTROSPECTION

self–contented *adj syn* see COMPLACENT

self–control *n syn* see WILL 3
rel constraint, reserve, self-containedness; balance, stability, dignity
idiom presence of mind
ant self-abandonment

self–criticism *n syn* see SELF-REPROACH

self–deceit *n syn* see SELF-DECEPTION

self–deception *n* the act or an instance of deceiving oneself or of being so deceived <to presume agreement where none exists is a dangerous form of *self-deception*>
syn self-deceit, self-delusion
rel misconception, misinterpretation, misunderstanding; deception, delusion, illusion
idiom kidding oneself

self–defense *n* an act, instance, or means of defending oneself, one's property, or a close relative <sought some measure of *self-defense* against society's lawless elements>
syn self-protection
rel self-preservation

self–delusion *n syn* see SELF-DECEPTION

self–denial *n syn* see RENUNCIATION
rel abstaining, abstemiousness, abstinence; asceticism, selflessness, self-sacrifice, self-sacrificing; self-forgetful, self-forgetting

ant self-indulgence

self–denying *adj syn* see SELF-SACRIFICING

self–dependence *n syn* see SELF-RELIANCE

self–destruction *n syn* see SUICIDE

self–discipline *n syn* see WILL 3

selfdom *n syn* see INDIVIDUALITY 4

self–educated *adj syn* see SELF-TAUGHT

self–effacing *adj syn* see SHY 1

self–esteem *n* 1 *syn* see PRIDE 2
rel self-content, self-contentment; self-satisfaction
con self-distrust, self-doubt; self-contempt
ant self-hate
2 *syn* see CONCEIT 2
rel self-flattery, self-glorification
con self-distrust, self-doubt; self-hate
ant self-contempt

self–evidencing *adj syn* see SELF-EVIDENT

self–evident *adj* evident in itself without need of argument or proof <*self-evident* truths>
syn prima facie, self-evidencing
rel clear, manifest, obvious, plain; unmistakable, unquestionable
con enigmatic, hidden, mysterious, obscure; doubtable, doubtful, questionable, uncertain

self–exaltation *n syn* see CONCEIT 2

self–examination *n syn* see INTROSPECTION

self–existent *adj* existing of or by itself and having no antecedent cause <argues backward to a first great cause, which is itself *self-existent*>
syn increate, self-existing, unbegotten, uncaused, uncreated, unoriginated
rel self-generated, self-originated, self-produced
con consequent, resultant, sequential
ant derivative

self–existing *adj syn* see SELF-EXISTENT

self–explaining *adj syn* see SELF-EXPLANATORY

self–explanatory *adj* capable of being understood without explanation <his actions are *self-explanatory*: he wants to resign>
syn self-explaining; *compare* CLEAR 5
rel clear, evident, obvious, manifest, plain, self-evident; comprehensible, understandable
con equivocal, obscure, uncertain, unclear, vague; complex; incomprehensible, mysterious; inexplicable, unexplainable

self–forgetful *adj syn* see SELFLESS

self–forgetting *adj syn* see SELFLESS

self–giving *adj syn* see SELF-SACRIFICING

self–glorifying *adj syn* see BOASTFUL

self–glory *n syn* see CONCEIT 2
rel self-aggrandizement, self-glorification

self–governing *adj syn* see DEMOCRATIC

self–government *n syn* see WILL 3

self–gratification *n* the act of pleasing oneself or of satisfying one's desires <human beings driven by unconscious forces toward *self-gratification*>
syn onanism, self-indulgence

rel self-abandonment; self-pleasing, self= satisfaction; autotheism, narcissism, self= worship

selfhood *n* **1** *syn* see INDIVIDUALITY 4
2 *syn* see SELFISHNESS

self–importance *n* **1** *syn* see CONCEIT 2
2 *syn* see EGOTISM 1
rel self-esteem, pomposity

self–important *adj syn* see POMPOUS 1

self–imposed *adj* imposed by oneself or itself <insists on working under *self-imposed* handicaps>
syn self-inflicted
rel self-generated, self-produced

self-indulgence *n* *syn* see SELF-GRATIFI= CATION
rel indulgence; excess, intemperance, over- indulgence
ant abstinence

self–indulgent *adj syn* see SYBARITIC

self–inflicted *adj syn* see SELF-IMPOSED
rel self-determined; accepted; voluntary

self–instructed *adj syn* see SELF-TAUGHT

self–interest *n* *syn* see SELFISHNESS

self–interested *adj syn* see EGOCENTRIC 2

self–involved *adj syn* see EGOCENTRIC 2

selfish *adj syn* see EGOCENTRIC 2
idiom ‖looking out for number one
con self-denying, selfless, self-sacrificing; altruistic, benevolent, charitable, generous, magnanimous
ant unselfish

selfishness *n* a concern for one's own wel- fare at the expense of or in disregard of oth- ers <his *selfishness* was consummate: he cared for no one but himself>
syn self-centeredness, self-concern, self= hood, self-interest, self-regard, self-seeking
rel egoism, egotism; self-absorption; self, selfism, selfness; autotheism, self-worship
con self-denial, selflessness, self-sacrificing; benevolence, charity, generosity
ant unselfishness

self-knowledge *n* knowledge or under- standing of one's own character, motiva- tions, and capabilities <a poet whose verse reflected deep *self-knowledge* and honesty>
syn autognosis, self-understanding
rel self-awareness; introspection, self-exam- ination, self-observation

selfless *adj* having no concern for oneself <*selfless* service to community, state, and nation>
syn self-forgetful, self-forgetting, unselfish
rel self-giving, self-sacrificing; self-renounc- ing; elevated, generous, high-minded, mag- nanimous
con self-devoted, self-loving, self-serving
ant self-centered, selfish

self–love *n* *syn* see CONCEIT 2
idiom the sixth insatiable sense
con self-abuse, self-accusation, self-re- proach; self-forgetfulness, selflessness
ant self-hate

self–mastery *n* *syn* see WILL 3

self–murder *n* *syn* see SUICIDE

selfness *n* *syn* see INDIVIDUALITY 4

self–observation *n* *syn* see INTROSPEC- TION

self–opinion *n* *syn* see CONCEIT 2

self–pleased *adj syn* see COMPLACENT

self–possessed *adj syn* see CALM 2
rel aloof, reserved; self-contained, self= controlled; self-assured

self–possession *n* *syn* see EQUANIMITY

self–pride *n* *syn* see CONCEIT 2

self–proclaimed *adj syn* see SELF-STYLED

self–protection *n* *syn* see SELF-DEFENSE

self–questioning *n* *syn* see INTROSPEC- TION

self–recrimination *n* *syn* see SELF-RE- PROACH

self–reflection *n* *syn* see INTROSPECTION

self–regard *n* **1** *syn* see SELFISHNESS
2 *syn* see PRIDE 2

self–reliance *n* reliance on one's own re- sources, efforts, and ability <a strong people characterized by bravery and *self-reliance*>
syn self-dependence
rel confidence, self-assurance, self-confi- dence; self-sufficiency, self-support

self–renouncing *adj syn* see SELF-SACRI= FICING

self–renunciation *n* *syn* see RENUNCIA- TION

self–reproach *n* an act or instance of re- proaching oneself <experienced both guilt and *self-reproach* after the quarrel>
syn self-abuse, self-accusation, self-criti- cism, self-recrimination, self-reproof
rel contrition, regret, remorse; self-castiga- tion, self-condemnation, self-flagellation, self-punishment; self-contempt
con self-contentment, self-satisfaction; self= applause
ant self-approbation

self–reproof *n* *syn* see SELF-REPROACH

self–respect *n* *syn* see PRIDE 2

self–restraining *adj syn* see ABSTEMIOUS

self–restraint *n* *syn* see WILL 3
ant abandon

self–righteous *adj syn* see HYPOCRITICAL

self–ruling *adj syn* see DEMOCRATIC

self–sacrificing *adj* sacrificing or denying oneself for others <a *self-sacrificing* love>
syn self-abnegating, self-denying, self-giv- ing, self-renouncing
rel selfless, unselfish; charitable, generous, kindly, philanthropic
con self-centered, selfish, self-seeking

selfsame *adj syn* see SAME 1
rel alike, like
idiom (the) very same
con different, unalike
ant diverse

selfsameness *n* *syn* see IDENTITY
ant diverseness

self–satisfied *adj syn* see COMPLACENT

self–scrutiny *n* *syn* see INTROSPECTION

self–searching *n* *syn* see INTROSPECTION

self–seeking *n* *syn* see SELFISHNESS

self–seeking *adj syn* see EGOCENTRIC 2

self–serving *adj syn* see EGOCENTRIC 2

self–slaughter *n* *syn* see SUICIDE

self–starter *n* *syn* see HUSTLER 1

---

syn synonym(s)   *rel* related word(s)
ant antonym(s)   *con* contrasted word(s)
idiom idiomatic equivalent(s)
‖ use limited; if in doubt, see a dictionary

self-styled *adj* given a specified designation or title by oneself often without justification <a department cluttered with *self-styled* experts>
syn self-proclaimed, soi-disant
rel self-appointed, self-created, self-given; so-called; quasi; would-be

self-sufficient *adj* maintaining or able to maintain oneself without outside aid <organisms are not *self-sufficient*, closed systems>
syn closed, independent, self-centered, self= contained, self-sufficing, self-supported, self= supporting, self-sustained, self-sustaining
rel self-dependent, self-reliant; self-subsistent, self-subsisting; individual, one-man, unit
idiom one's own man, sufficient unto oneself (*or* itself)
con dependent

self-sufficing *adj* *syn* see SELF-SUFFICIENT

self-supported *adj* *syn* see SELF-SUFFICIENT

self-supporting *adj* *syn* see SELF-SUFFICIENT

self-sustained *adj* *syn* see SELF-SUFFICIENT

self-sustaining *adj* *syn* see SELF-SUFFICIENT

self-taught *adj* having knowledge or skills acquired by one's own efforts without formal instruction <a *self-taught* painter>
syn autodidactic, self-educated, self-instructed

self-trust *n* *syn* see CONFIDENCE 2

self-understanding *n* *syn* see SELF= KNOWLEDGE

self-violence *n* *syn* see SUICIDE

self-willed *adj* *syn* see OBSTINATE
con weak, weak-willed, wishy-washy; spineless

sell *vb* 1 *syn* see BETRAY 2
2 to give up (property) to another for money or other valuable consideration <can *sell* you the house now>
syn give, market, vend
ant buy, purchase
3 to deal in or offer (articles) for sale on a regular basis <he *sells* small appliances>
syn market, merchandise, retail
rel barter, deal (in), exchange, trade, traffic; hawk, peddle; vend
ant buy
4 to command a specified price <that coat *sells* for $300>
syn bring, bring in, fetch
rel command, draw; realize, return, yield; gross, net

sell *n* *syn* see IMPOSTURE
sellable *adj* *syn* see MARKETABLE
sell off *vb* *syn* see SELL OUT 1
sell out *vb* 1 to dispose of entirely by selling <*sold out* his share of the business>
syn close out, sell off, ‖sell up
rel dump, move, unload; sacrifice
2 *syn* see DECEIVE
3 *syn* see BETRAY 3
‖**sell up** *vb* *syn* see SELL OUT 1
selvage *n* *syn* see BORDER 1

semblance *n* 1 *syn* see AIR 3
rel aspect, look
2 *syn* see LIKENESS
3 *syn* see APPEARANCE 2
rel air, pose
4 *syn* see MASK 2

semblant *adj* *syn* see APPARENT 2

seminar *n* *syn* see CONFERENCE 2

semioccasional *adj* *syn* see INFREQUENT

sempiternal *adj* *syn* see INFINITE 1

sempiternity *n* *syn* see ETERNITY 1

send *vb* 1 to cause to go or be taken from one place, person, or condition to another <*send* a messenger to the bank> <his cold *sent* him to bed>
syn address, consign, dispatch, forward, remit, route, ship, transmit
rel allocate, assign, commit, delegate; advance, launch; expedite, rush
ant receive
2 *syn* see THRILL

senectitude *n* *syn* see OLD AGE

senescence *n* *syn* see OLD AGE

senile *adj* exhibiting the weakness and loss of mental faculties often associated with old age <a *senile* professor now unable to lecture coherently>
syn doddering, doddery, ‖doted, doting
rel aging, senescent; aged, ancient, old; enfeebled, feeble, weak; decrepit, doddered, shattered
idiom in one's second childhood

senility *n* *syn* see DOTAGE
rel decline, senescence

senior *n* 1 *syn* see OLDSTER
2 one older than another <he was her *senior* by eight years>
syn elder
ant junior
3 *syn* see SUPERIOR
con inferior, subordinate, underling

senior citizen *n* *syn* see OLDSTER

sensation *n* 1 the power to respond or an act of responding to stimuli <the stage of *sensation* precedes that of rational comprehension>
syn feeling, sense, sensibility, sensitivity
rel susceptibility; consciousness; sensitiveness, sensitivity; impression, perception, response
2 *syn* see WONDER 1
rel bomb, bombshell

sensational *adj* 1 *syn* see SENSORY
2 arousing or designed to arouse a quick, intense, and usually superficial emotional response <*sensational* crime reporting>
syn livid, lurid, sensationalistic, sensationist, sultry, tabloid
rel juicy, piquant, pungent; colored, extravagant; coarse, vulgar
con exact, factual; dignified, formal, proper, restrained
3 *syn* see NOTICEABLE
rel impressive, stunning
4 *syn* see MARVELOUS 2
rel boffo, crashing, rousing, slambang, smash, smashing, superfine

sensationalistic *adj* *syn* see SENSATIONAL 2

sensationist *adj* *syn* see SENSATIONAL 2

sensatory *adj syn* see SENSORY
sense *n* **1** *syn* see MEANING 1
  rel gist, pith, substance; center, core, focus, nucleus
  2 *syn* see SUBSTANCE 2
  3 *syn* see SENSATION 1
  rel awareness, cognizance; discernment, discrimination, penetration; appreciation; recognition
  4 *usu use* pl *syn* see WIT 2
  rel consciousness
  5 *syn* see INTELLIGENCE 1
  6 ability to make intelligent choices and to reach intelligent conclusions or decisions <had enough *sense* to study something practical>
  syn common sense, good sense, gumption, horse sense, judgment, wisdom
  rel discretion, foresight, prudence; appreciation, comprehension, understanding; brains, intelligence, ‖smarts, wit
  ant folly
sense *vb syn* see FEEL 3
  rel anticipate; know, realize
senseless *adj* **1** *syn* see NUMB 1
  rel oblivious, unaware; inanimate, wooden
  2 *syn* see INSENSATE 1
  3 *syn* see INSENSIBLE 2
  4 *syn* see SIMPLE 4
  rel irrational, surd
  5 having no meaning <an ancient custom, now outdated and *senseless*>
  syn insignificant, meaningless, pointless, purportless, unmeaning
  rel purposeless; trivial, unimportant
  idiom without rhyme or reason
  con purposeful; important, meaning, meaningful, significant
senselessness *n syn* see FOOLISHNESS
  rel illogicality, stupidity
sensibility *n syn* see SENSATION 1
  rel discernment, discrimination, insight, keenness, penetration, responsiveness; affection, emotion, heart
  con apathy, indifference, insensibleness, insentience, unfeelingness, unresponsiveness
  ant insensibility
sensibilize *vb syn* see SENSITIZE
sensible *adj* **1** *syn* see MATERIAL 1
  rel concrete, solid
  con immaterial, insubstantial; unreal
  2 *syn* see PERCEPTIBLE
  rel imaginal, perceptual, sensational; weighable; evident, manifest, obvious, patent
  con imperceptible; cloudy, unclear
  ant insensible
  3 *syn* see CONSIDERABLE 2
  4 *syn* see SENTIENT 3
  5 *syn* see AWARE
  rel sensitive, susceptible; noting, observing, perceiving, remarking, seeing; appreciating, comprehending, understanding; intelligent, knowing
  con anesthetic, insensate, insensitive
  ant insensible

  6 *syn* see RATIONAL
  rel sensemaking
  7 *syn* see WISE 2
  rel rational, reasonable; down-to-earth, matter-of-fact
  con unreasonable, unsound, unwise; asinine, fatuous
  ant absurd, foolish
sensile *adj syn* see SENTIENT 3
sensitive *adj* **1** *syn* see SENTIENT 3
  rel hypersensitive, supersensitive
  con impervious, insensible, unfeeling, unimpressionable, unresponsive; wooden
  ant insensitive, unsensitive
  2 *syn* see EMOTIONAL 1
  rel high-strung, irritable, nervous, tense; insultable, oversensitive, umbrageous; unstable
  con impervious, insensate, insensible, unaffected, unemotional
  ant insensitive, unsensitive
  3 *syn* see ACUTE 3
  rel perceiving, seeing; aware, cognizant, conscious; knowing, understanding
  4 *syn* see LIABLE 2
  rel affected, impressed, influenced; disposed, inclined, predisposed
  ant insensitive
  5 *syn* see DELICATE 7
  6 *syn* see SENSORY
sensitivity *n syn* see SENSATION 1
sensitize *vb* to cause to become sensitive or more sensitive <*sensitizing* corporate officers to social and environmental problems>
  syn sensibilize
  rel animate, excite, quicken, sharpen, stimulate, whet
  ant desensitize
sensorial *adj syn* see SENSORY
sensory *adj* of or relating to sensation or the senses <*sensory* perception>
  syn sensational, sensatory, sensitive, sensorial, sensual
  rel sensate; receptive
sensual *adj* **1** *syn* see SENSORY
  2 *syn* see CARNAL 2
  rel irreligious, unspiritual
  3 *syn* see SENSUOUS
  4 *syn* see MATERIALISTIC
sensualistic *adj syn* see SENSUOUS
sensuous *adj* producing or characterized by gratification of the senses <*sensuous* pleasures>
  syn epicurean, luscious, lush, luxurious, sensual, sensualistic, voluptuous; *compare* CARNAL 2, SYBARITIC
  rel bacchic, dionysiac, Dionysian, hedonistic, pleasure-loving, pleasure-seeking; self-indulgent, sybaritic; carnal, fleshly, fleshy
  con ascetic, disciplined, restrained
sentence *vb* to decree the fate or punishment of one adjudged guilty, unworthy, or unfit <was *sentenced* to exile>
  syn condemn, damn, doom, proscribe
  rel adjudge, adjudicate, judge; ordain, rule; blame, denounce; penalize, punish; devote
  idiom pass sentence on
  con absolve, acquit, exculpate, exonerate, vindicate; discharge, free, liberate, release
sententious *adj syn* see EXPRESSIVE

---

syn synonym(s)   *rel* related word(s)
ant antonym(s)   *con* contrasted word(s)
idiom idiomatic equivalent(s)
‖ use limited; if in doubt, see a dictionary

rel aphoristic, concise, crisp, epigrammatic, piquant, pithy, terse

sentient *adj* 1 *syn* see AWARE
2 *syn* see EMOTIONAL 1
3 capable of receiving and of being readily affected by external stimuli <deeply disturbed in the most *sentient* reaches of her mind>
syn impressible, impressionable, responsive, sensible, sensile, sensitive, susceptible, susceptive
rel sensate; open, receptive, susceptive; reactive
con insensate; closed, unreceptive; unreactive

sentiment *n* 1 *syn* see LEANING 2
2 *syn* see OPINION
rel leaning, predilection, propensity; position, posture
idiom way of thinking
3 *syn* see FEELING 3
rel conception; sensation; emotionalism, sentimentality

sentimental *adj* unduly or affectedly emotional <*sentimental* love stories>
syn bathetic, drippy, gooey, lovey-dovey, maudlin, mawkish, moist, mushy, romantic, sappy, slushy, sobby, sobful, soft-boiled, ‖soppy, soupy, sticky, syrupy, tear-jerking
rel dreamy, misty-eyed, moonstruck, nostalgic, oversentimental; inane, insipid, jejune, namby-pamby, schoolgirlish, vapid; rosewater, saccharine, soft, sugar-candy, sugary, sweet; loving, tender; affectionate, demonstrative, effusive; gushing, gushy; passionate
con unaffectionate, undemonstrative; dispassionate, emotionless, unemotional, unresponsive; unfeeling, unloving; dry
ant unsentimental

sentinel *n* *syn* see GUARD 2
sentry *n* *syn* see GUARD 2
separate *vb* 1 to become or cause to become dis- united or disjoined <forces that *separate* families>
syn break up, dichotomize, disjoin, disjoint, dissect, dissever, disunite, divide, divorce, part, rupture, sever, split (up), sunder, uncombine
rel alienate, discontinue, disunify, estrange; dislink, uncouple, unjoin, unlink; disaggregate, disassemble, disgregate, dispel, disperse, dissolve, scatter; detach, disengage, disrelate, dissociate; halve, quarter
con assemble, associate, blend, mingle, mix; connect, couple, join, link; unify, unite; agglutinate, bind, cement, fuse, weld
ant combine
2 *syn* see KNOW 4
3 *syn* see SORT 2
rel compartment, compartmentalize
4 *syn* see DISCHARGE 7
5 *syn* see ISOLATE

separate *adj* 1 *syn* see SINGLE 2
rel distinctive, peculiar; detached, disconnected, disengaged
2 *syn* see FREE 1
3 *syn* see DISTINCT 1
rel free, independent

separately *adv* *syn* see APART 1

rel distinctly; solely
con conjointly, jointly
ant together

separateness *n* *syn* see SEGREGATION
ant togetherness

separation *n* 1 the act, process, or an instance of separating or of being separated <*separation* of church and state> <their *separation* was a sad occasion>
syn detachment, dissolution, disunion, division, divorce, divorcement, partition, rupture, split-up
rel disrelation, dissociation, disunity, parting, shedding; disconnection, disjointedness, disjointure; breakup, disjunction, dissection, sequestration; diffluence, dispersal; dichotomy, diremption, trichotomy
con combination; unification
ant union
2 *syn* see SEGREGATION

separatism *n* *syn* see SEGREGATION
separatist *n* *syn* see HERETIC
sepulcher *n* *syn* see GRAVE
sepulcher *vb* 1 *syn* see ENTOMB 1
2 *syn* see BURY 1
sepulchral *adj* 1 of, relating to, or serving as a sepulcher or a memorial to the dead <*sepulchral* inscriptions>
syn mortuary, tumulary
rel exequial, funebrial, funeral, funerary, funereal
2 *syn* see HOLLOW 1

sepulture *n* 1 *syn* see BURIAL 2
2 *syn* see GRAVE
sepulture *vb* 1 *syn* see ENTOMB 1
2 *syn* see BURY 1
sequel *n* 1 *syn* see SUCCESSION 2
2 *syn* see EFFECT 1
rel end, ending, termination; close, closing, finish, finishing
3 *syn* see EPILOGUE 2
rel continuation, development; aftermath, outcome, result

sequence *n* 1 *syn* see SUCCESSION 2
rel arrangement, disposition, ordering; procession
2 *syn* see ORDER 3
rel classification, grouping; placement
3 *syn* see EFFECT 1
4 *syn* see ORDER 5

sequent *adj* *syn* see CONSECUTIVE
sequential *adj* *syn* see CONSECUTIVE
sequester *vb* 1 *syn* see ISOLATE
2 *syn* see SECLUDE
rel hide, secrete
3 *syn* see APPROPRIATE 1
rel attach; impound; dispossess

sequestered *adj* *syn* see SECLUDED
rel sheltered; closeted
sequestration *n* *syn* see SECLUSION
rel retreat
sequitur *n* *syn* see INFERENCE 2
seraglio *n* *syn* see BROTHEL
sere *adj* *syn* see DRY 1
serene *adj* *syn* see CALM 1
rel noiseless, quiet, still; quiescent, resting; undisturbed
con agitated, disquieted, upset
serfage *n* *syn* see BONDAGE
serfdom *n* *syn* see BONDAGE

serial *adj syn* see CONSECUTIVE
series *n syn* see SUCCESSION 2
    rel continuance, continuation, run; category, group, set; column, tier; gradation, scale
serious *adj* **1** not light or frivolous (as in disposition, appearance, or manner) <he was disturbed by her stern, *serious* look>
    syn earnest, grave, no-nonsense, poker=faced, sedate, sober, sobersided, solemn, somber, staid, weighty
    rel businesslike, ‖dern, determined, steady, steady-going; intent, serious-minded; contemplative, meditative, pensive, reflective, thoughtful; austere, severe, stern; humorless, unhumorous; grim
    idiom serious as a judge
    con flighty, ‖flip, flippant, frivolous, volatile; casual, easy, relaxed
    ant lustful, unserious
    2 expressing, involving, or characterized by seriousness or gravity (as of consequence) <a *serious* economic situation>
    syn grave, heavy, severe, weighty
    rel important, significant; sobering; unamusing, unfunny, unhumorous; grim
    idiom no joke, no laughing matter
    con inconsequential, insignificant, unimportant, unserious
    ant trifling, trivial
    3 *syn* see HARD 6
    4 *syn* see GRAVE 3
    rel menacing, threatening
seriously *adv* **1** in a serious manner <at last settled *seriously* to work>
    syn actively, down, earnestly, for real
    rel gravely, soberly, solemnly; intently; vigorously, zealously; determinedly, purposefully, resolutely; fervently, passionately
    idiom all joking aside, in all seriousness, in earnest
    con airily, casually, flippantly, lightly, unconcernedly; carelessly, haphazardly
    2 to a serious extent <the cities are *seriously* overcrowded>
    syn gravely, intensely, severely
    rel decidedly, quite, very; dangerously; critically, deplorably, regrettably
serious–mindedness *n syn* see EARNESTNESS
    rel thoughtfulness; sober-mindedness
seriousness *n syn* see EARNESTNESS
    rel sedateness, sobriety, solemnity, staidness
    con gaiety, jollity; lightness
    ant flippancy, frivolity
sermon *n* a religious discourse delivered in public by a clergyman as part of a worship service <preached his first *sermon* on Sunday>
    syn preach, preaching, preachment, sermonizing
    rel preachification; sermonary, sermonology; sermonette; exhortation, harangue, lecture, tirade

sermonic *adj syn* see DIDACTIC
sermonize *vb* **1** *syn* see PREACH 1
    2 *syn* see DISCOURSE 1
    3 *syn* see MORALIZE
sermonizer *n syn* see CLERGYMAN
sermonizing *n syn* see SERMON
sermonizing *adj syn* see DIDACTIC
serpent *n syn* see DEVIL 1
serpentine *adj* **1** *syn* see FIENDISH
    2 *syn* see WINDING
    rel serpentiform, serpentile, serpentlike, snakelike; crooked, devious
serrate *adj* notched or toothed on the edge <jagged peaks and *serrate* ridges>
    syn denticulate, saw-edged, sawtooth, saw=toothed, serrated, serried
    rel indented, notched, scored, toothed; serrulate
serrated *adj syn* see SERRATE
serried *adj syn* see SERRATE
serve *vb* **1** *syn* see BENEFIT
    2 *syn* see ACT 4
    3 to prove adequate or sufficient <will not *serve* as a true translation>
    syn do, suffice, suit
    rel service; function, work; fit; satisfy; make
    idiom fill the bill
    4 *syn* see MINISTER (to)
    5 to put in (a term of imprisonment) <*served* ten years for armed robbery>
    syn do
    rel put in, spend; undergo
    idiom do a hitch (or stretch), serve (out) a sentence, serve time, ‖take a vacation
    6 *syn* see ADVANCE 1
    7 *syn* see TREAT 2
service *n* **1** the performance of military duty in wartime and especially in a combat zone <saw a year's *service* in Vietnam>
    syn action, combat
    rel active duty, duty; fighting
    2 *syn* see FAVOR 4
    3 *syn* see RITE 2
    4 *syn* see USE 3
serviceability *n syn* see USE 3
    rel serviceableness; durability
serviceable *adj* **1** *syn* see HELPFUL 1
    ant unserviceable
    2 *syn* see PRACTICAL 2
    ant unserviceable
serviceman *n* **1** *syn* see SOLDIER
    2 servicemen *pl syn* see TROOP 2
servile *adj* **1** *syn* see SUBSERVIENT 2
    rel obedient, submissive; passive, unresisting; bootlicking, groveling, toadyish
    con aggressive
    ant authoritative
    2 *syn* see BASE 3
servility *n syn* see BONDAGE
servitude *n syn* see BONDAGE
    con freedom, independence
set *vb* **1** to position (something) in a specified place <*set* the lamp on the table>
    syn establish, fix, lay, place, put, settle, stick
    rel bestow, deposit, park; emplace, ensconce, install; affix, anchor, wedge
    con displace, replace, supplant; remove, take (away); uproot
    2 *syn* see DIRECT 2
    idiom set one's sights on

---

syn synonym(s)   *rel* related word(s)
idiom idiomatic equivalent(s)
‖ use limited; if in doubt, see a dictionary
ant antonym(s)   *con* contrasted word(s)

3 *syn* see STATION

4 *syn* see DICTATE

rel designate, direct, instruct, specify, stipulate; establish; make, name

5 to put in order for a meal <she quickly *set* the table for dinner>

syn lay, spread

rel fix, prepare, ready; arrange

ant clear

6 *syn* see GAMBLE 1

7 *syn* see INCITE

‖8 *syn* see SIT 1

9 *syn* see BELONG 1

10 *syn* see COAGULATE

11 *of a fowl* to incubate eggs by crouching upon them <a chicken house filled with hens *setting* on eggs>

syn brood, ‖clock, cover, sit

rel hatch, incubate; hover

12 *of a celestial body* to pass below the horizon <the sun *set* at seven o'clock>

syn decline, dip, go down, sink

rel descend, drop

con ascend, climb, come up

ant rise

13 *syn* see HARDEN 1

rel crystallize, granulate; fix

set (at) *vb syn* see ESTIMATE 1

set *adj* 1 *syn* see SITUATED

2 *syn* see DECIDED 2

3 *syn* see FIRM 4

rel confirmed, entrenched, established, inveterate, rooted, well-set, well-settled; prescribed, specified

4 *syn* see LITTLE 2

rel diehard, inflexible, obstinate, pigheaded, rigid, unbending, unyielding

5 *syn* see FAST 4

rel fastened; close; sound

6 *syn* see EXPRESS 2

7 *syn* see READY 1

set *n* 1 *syn* see GIFT 2

2 *syn* see BEARING 1

3 *syn* see SCENE 1

4 *syn* see GROUP 3

rel assortment, gaggle; kit, pack

5 a number of people having something (as habit, interest, occupation, or age) in common <the horsey *set* was gathered at the bar>

syn bunch, circle, crowd, group, lot, push; *compare* CLIQUE

rel clan, clique, crew, gang, mob; cénacle; camp, faction; company

set back *vb syn* see DELAY 1

set down *vb syn* see ALIGHT

setback *n* a checking of progress <loss of his fellowship was a serious *setback* to his education>

syn backset, check, reversal, reverse; *compare* COMEDOWN

rel delay, retardation, slowdown; hindrance, impediment, obstacle, stumbling block; disappointment; rebuff; defeat; regress, regression

idiom reverse of fortune

con advancement, forwarding, progressing

set off *vb* 1 *syn* see COMPENSATE 1

2 *syn* see MOBILIZE 1

set on *vb syn* see INCITE

set out *vb* 1 *syn* see DESIGN 3

2 *syn* see HEAD 3

idiom set one's course for

setout *n* 1 *syn* see COSTUME

2 *syn* see BEGINNING

setting *n syn* see SCENE 1

setting–out *n syn* see DEPARTURE 1

settle *vb* 1 *syn* see ENSCONCE 2

2 *syn* see CALM

rel assure, reassure

ant unsettle

3 *syn* see SET 1

rel found, ground, lodge, seat

con dislodge, unseat, uproot

ant unsettle

4 *syn* see DECIDE

rel fix, seal

idiom come to a decision (*or* conclusion), form a judgment, make a decision

5 *syn* see NEGOTIATE 1

rel mediate, reconcile, straighten (out)

idiom bring to terms (*or* agreement)

6 *syn* see CLEAR 5

idiom settle the score, settle up (*or* square) accounts

7 to put in order for final disposal <waiting to *settle* an estate>

syn clean up, wind up

8 *syn* see ALIGHT

rel flop (down), plop (down)

settled *adj* 1 *syn* see FIRM 4

rel decided, determined

con uncertain, undecided

ant unsettled

2 *syn* see INVETERATE 1

3 *syn* see DECIDED 2

rel certain, fixed

con irresolute, undecided, undetermined, unresolved, vacillating, wavering

ant unsettled

settlement *n* 1 *syn* see HABITATION 1

2 *syn* see DECISION 1

rel showdown; quietus

settlings *n pl syn* see SEDIMENT

set to *vb* 1 *syn* see BEGIN 1

2 *syn* see PITCH IN 1

set–to *n* 1 *syn* see BRAWL 2

2 *syn* see QUARREL

3 *syn* see ENCOUNTER

set up *vb* 1 *syn* see ERECT 5

ant tear down

2 *syn* see ELATE

3 *syn* see ERECT 3

con disassemble, take down

4 *syn* see FOUND 2

rel generate, originate; start up; open

5 *syn* see INTRODUCE 3

6 *syn* see TREAT 3

setup *n syn* see SNAP 1

seventh heaven *n syn* see ECSTASY

rel exhilaration; bliss, paradise

con sadness, unhappiness; blues, doldrums, dumps

sever *vb* 1 *syn* see SEPARATE 1

2 *syn* see KNOW 4

3 *syn* see CUT 5

several *adj* 1 possessed by or attributed to a specific individual <the debaters expressed their *several* opinions>

syn individual, particular, respective, singular

rel independent; personal, special, specific

2 *syn* see DISTINCT 1

3 consisting of an indefinite number more than two and less than many <*several* days passed>
syn divers, some, sundry, various
rel particular, separate, single; few; considerable; many, numerous
idiom not a few
‖**4** *syn* see MANY

‖**several** *pron syn* see SUNDRY

severalize *vb syn* see KNOW 4

severally *adv syn* see APART 1
rel discretely; exclusively
idiom one at a time

severe *adj* **1** given to or characterized by strict discipline and firm restraint <treated all the students with *severe* impartiality>
syn ascetic, astringent, austere, mortified, stern
rel exacting, heavy-handed, onerous, oppressive; disciplined, iron-willed, self-disciplined; inflexible, restrictive, rigid, rigorous, strict, stringent, uncompromising, unyielding
con easy, easygoing, gentle, mild, soft; clement, forbearing, indulgent, lax, lenient, merciful
ant tender, tolerant

2 *syn* see GRIM 2
rel serious, sober, stern

3 of a kind to cause discomfort or hardship <a *severe* winter storm>
syn bitter, brutal, hard, harsh, inclement, intemperate, rigorous, rugged
rel crimpy, unpleasant; forbidding, hostile, inhospitable; bleak, disagreeable, grim; painful, raw, sharp, smart; blistering, extreme, intense, savage; blustering, blustery, stormy, wintry
con balmy, calm, equable, gentle, moderate, soft, temperate
ant mild

4 *syn* see HARD 6

5 *syn* see SERIOUS 2
rel consequential; dear, sore

severely *adv* **1** *syn* see HARD 5

2 *syn* see SERIOUSLY 2
rel markedly

‖**sew** *vb syn* see EXUDE

sew up *vb* ‖**1** *syn* see EXHAUST 4

2 *syn* see MONOPOLIZE

sexy *adj syn* see RISQUÉ

shabby *adj* **1** being ill-kept and showing signs of wear and tear <a *shabby* neighborhood full of depressing tenements>
syn bedraggled, broken-down, decrepit, dilapidated, dingy, disreputable, down-at-heel, faded, mangy, moth-eaten, run-down, scrubby, scruffy, seedy, shoddy, sleazy, slipshod, squalid, tacky, tagrag, tattered, threadbare, tired
rel disfigured, dog-eared; decaying, deteriorated, deteriorating; ramshackle, ratty, rickety; bare, miserable, neglected, poor, poverty-stricken; sordid; worm-eaten; out-

worn, worn-out; abandoned, desolate, ruined, ruinous, wrecked
idiom gone to seed
con neat, spick-and-span, tidy, trig, trim, well-kept; brand-new, fresh, new; unused
ant spruce

2 *syn* see CONTEMPTIBLE

3 *syn* see DISREPUTABLE 1

‖**shack** *n syn* see VAGABOND

shack *n syn* see HUT

shackle *n, usu* **shackles** *pl* something that confines the legs or arms so as to prevent free movement <slaves in *shackles*>
syn bond(s), chains, fetter(s), gyve(s), iron(s)
rel anklet, bilbo, leg-iron, trammel; bracelet, handcuff, manacle; straitjacket; collar, garrote

shackle *vb syn* see HAMPER
rel lash, rope, strap; chain, enchain, manacle; handcuff, pinion, secure
con unchain, unfetter, untie
ant unshackle

shade *n* **1** comparative darkness or obscurity due to interception of light rays <trees providing *shade* from the sunlight>
syn adumbration, penumbra, shadow, umbra, umbrage
rel blackness, darkness, dimness, obscuration, obscurity; cover, shelter
con brightness, brilliancy, effulgence, radiance; blaze, glare, glow

2 *syn* see APPARITION

3 *syn* see COLOR 1
rel intensity, saturation

4 *syn* see GRADATION
rel difference, distinction, variation

5 *syn* see HINT 2

shade *vb* to cast into shadow by intercepting light rays <avenues *shaded* by large trees>
syn inumbrate, screen, shadow, umbrage
rel shelter; cover
con roast, scorch, swelter; expose

shaded *adj syn* see SHADY 1
ant unshaded

shadow *n* **1** *syn* see SHADE 1

2 *syn* see APPARITION

3 *syn* see VESTIGE 1

4 *syn* see HINT 2

shadow *vb* **1** *syn* see SHADE

2 *syn* see OBSCURE

3 *syn* see TAIL

shadow (forth) *vb* **1** *syn* see SUGGEST 5

2 *syn* see ADUMBRATE 1
rel forecast, foretell, predict

shadow *adj syn* see FAINT 2

shadowed *adj syn* see SHADY 1
ant unshadowed

shadowy *adj* **1** *syn* see IMAGINARY 1

2 *syn* see GHASTLY 2

3 *syn* see FAINT 2
rel amorphous; foggy

4 *syn* see SHADY 1
ant bright

shady *adj* **1** producing, affording, or abounding in shade <a *shady* day> <cool, *shady* streets>
syn shaded, shadow, shadowed, shadowy, umbrageous, umbrous
rel bosky, screened, sheltered; dusky; dark

---

con exposed, unshaded, unshadowed; unsheltered; bright, light
ant sunny
2 *syn* see DOUBTFUL 1
3 *syn* see DISREPUTABLE 1
rel subreputable
4 *syn* see RISQUÉ
rel disreputable, shameful
shaft *n* **1** *syn* see RAY 1
2 a scornful, cutting, or pithily critical remark <the target of her latest *shaft* is the president himself>
syn barb, dart
rel cut, jab, thrust; potshot
3 harsh or unfair treatment <he really got the *shaft*: he was fired without notice>
syn ‖screw, ‖screwing
rel short end
idiom ‖a royal screwing, the dirty end of the stick, ‖the royal shaft
shake *vb* **1** to move irregularly to and fro or up and down often in a wavering or oscillating manner <was so frightened that her hands *shook*>
syn ‖didder, dither, quake, quaver, quiver, shiver, shudder, tremble, tremor, twitter
rel palpitate, quail, waver; flicker, flit, flitter, flutter; fluctuate, oscillate; chatter, shimmy, vibrate
idiom shake like an aspen leaf
2 to undergo strong vibration especially as the result of a physical blow or shock <the platform *shook* as the train passed>
syn jar, quake, tremble, tremor, vibrate
rel bounce, jounce; chatter, quiver, shimmy; rock, stagger
3 to cause to move in a quick, jerky manner <rattling and *shaking* the latch>
syn jiggle, joggle
rel bounce, ‖chounse, jounce; jostle; rattle; jerk
4 to cause to move to and fro or up and down violently <an earthquake that *shook* the whole coast>
syn agitate, concuss, convulse, rock
rel jog, jostle, rattle, ‖shog; commove, discompose, disorder, jar, jolt, unsettle; disquiet, disturb, perturb, upset; churn, roil, ruffle, stir up, whip
5 to get or keep away from (a pursuer) <tried unsuccessfully to *shake* the man tailing him>
syn lose, slip, throw off; *compare* ESCAPE 2
rel avoid, elude; outwit
idiom give the shake, give (someone) the shake (or slip), slip from under the eye of
6 *syn* see DISMAY 1
rel disturb, jar, rattle, unsettle, upset; bother, worry; unnerve, unstring
shake (off) *vb syn* see RID
shake *n* **1** *syn* see EARTHQUAKE
2 shakes *pl syn* see JITTERS
3 *syn* see INSTANT 1
4 *syn* see DEAL 2
shake down *vb* **1** *syn* see EXTORT 1
2 *syn* see SEARCH 2
shake up *vb syn* see SPEED 3
shake-up *n* an extensive and often drastic rearrangement <a personnel *shake-up* effected by new management>

syn overturn, reorganization, revolution, turnover
rel liquidation, purge; cleanout, cleanup, clearing out, clear-up; removal, riddance
idiom break with the past, clean sweep
shakiness *n syn* see INSTABILITY
shaking *adj syn* see TREMULOUS
rel unsettled, unstable, unsteady; tottering
con unshakable, unshaken
shaky *adj* **1** *syn* see WEAK 2
rel unsettled; infirm, unsound, unsteady; precarious, tottering, tottery
2 *syn* see DOUBTFUL 1
3 *syn* see TREMULOUS
4 *syn* see RICKETY
shallow *adj* **1** lacking physical depth <buried in a *shallow* grave>
syn shoal, superficial
rel shallowish; surface
idiom as deep as a mud puddle, no deeper than a heavy dew, not deep enough to float a match
con bottomless, unfathomable
ant deep
2 *syn* see SUPERFICIAL 2
rel paltry, petty, trifling, trivial; empty, hollow, idle, vain; bird-witted, feather-brained, flighty
con heavy, profound; discerning, penetrating
ant deep
shallow *n syn* see SHOAL
ant deep
sham *n* **1** *syn* see IMPOSTURE
rel facade, fakery, false front, Potemkin village
2 *syn* see HYPOCRISY
3 *syn* see MOCKERY 2
sham *vb syn* see ASSUME 4
rel ape, copy, imitate, mock; create, invent; lie, mislead
sham *adj* **1** *syn* see FICTITIOUS 2
rel affected, assumed, feigned; pseudo, so-called; make-believe, pretend
2 *syn* see COUNTERFEIT
3 *syn* see ARTIFICIAL 2
rel plaster, synthetic; adulterated; bogus
shamble *vb syn* see SHUFFLE 3
shambles *n pl but usu sing in constr syn* see MESS 3
shame *n syn* see DISGRACE
rel chagrin, embarrassment; guilt, mortification, self-reproach, self-reproof
con pride, self-admiration, self-love, self-respect
ant glory
shamed *adj syn* see ASHAMED
rel crestfallen; shamefaced, shamefast; crushed, disgraced
idiom loaded (or bowed down) with shame
ant proud
shameful *adj syn* see DISREPUTABLE 1
shameless *adj* characterized by or exhibiting boldness and a lack of shame <a *shameless* hussy>
syn arrant, barefaced, blatant, brassy, brazen, brazenfaced, impudent, overbold, unabashed, unblushing
rel audacious, bold, cheeky, presumptuous; baldfaced, high-handed; abandoned, disso-

lute, profligate; immodest, lewd; disgraceful, outrageous
idiom bold as brass, dead (*or* lost) to shame
con bashful, diffident, mousy, shy; chaste, decent, modest, pure
‖**shamus** *n* **1** *syn* see PRIVATE DETECTIVE
Shangri–la *n syn* see UTOPIA
shanty *n syn* see HUT
shape *vb syn* see MAKE 3
rel devise, plan, work up; tailor
shape *n* **1** *syn* see FORM 1
rel appearance, aspect, look, semblance
2 *syn* see ORDER 9
3 *syn* see ORDER 10
rel state, whack
shapeful *adj syn* see SHAPELY
ant shapeless
shapeless *adj syn* see FORMLESS
rel unshapely; deformed, misshapen
con proportional, proportionate, proportioned, shapeful, symmetrical
ant shapeful, shapely
shapely *adj* having a regular or pleasing shape <a *shapely* girl>
syn clean-limbed, shapeful, statuesque, trim, well-proportioned, well-turned; *compare* CURVACEOUS
rel balanced, clean-cut, proportioned, regular, symmetrical; comely, pleasing; ‖built, full-figured, rounded, ‖stacked; buxom
con dumpy, squat, stumpy; angular, lank, lean; ill-favored, ill-looking
ant shapeless, unshapely
share *n* **1** something belonging to, assumed by, or falling to one (as in division or apportionment) <wanted his *share* of the prize money>
syn allotment, allowance, bite, cut, lot, part, partage, portion, quota, slice; *compare* RATION
rel proportion, quotient, quotum; commission, percentage; divide, ‖divvy; rake-off
idiom piece of the action, slice of the melon
2 *syn* see RATION
3 *syn* see INTEREST 1
share *vb syn* see APPORTION 2
rel assign, deal (out), dispense, dole (out), give out, mete (out)
idiom ‖go snucks, share and share alike
con retain, withhold; combine, unite
2 to have, get, or use in common with another or others <she *shared* her husband's fate>
syn partake, participate
rel experience
idiom have a share (*or* part) in, have (*or* take) a hand in
shared *adj syn* see COMMON 1
ant unshared
share out *vb syn* see ADMINISTER 2
sharer *n syn* see PARTICIPANT
sharp *adj* **1** having a fine edge <a *sharp* knife makes a clean cut>
syn honed, keen, razor-sharp, unblunted, whetted

syn synonym(s)   *rel* related word(s)
ant antonym(s)   *con* contrasted word(s)
idiom idiomatic equivalent(s)
‖ use limited; if in doubt, see a dictionary

rel acute
idiom sharp as a razor blade
con blunted, dulled; unsharpened
ant blunt, dull
2 *syn* see POINTED 1
3 *syn* see INTELLIGENT 2
4 possessing or indicative of alert competence and clear understanding <people of *sharp* judgment and refined sensibilities>
syn acute, keen, penetrating, penetrative, quick-sighted, quick-witted, sharp-sighted, sharp-witted; *compare* SHREWD
rel alert, bright; clever, cute, ingenious, original, resourceful; fast, quick
idiom sharp as a knife (*or* tack)
con dull-witted; unintelligent; foolish, simple, slow, stupid
ant dull
5 *syn* see ACUTE 3
6 *syn* see WISE 4
rel adroit, nimble; clever, cute; sly, unethical
idiom nobody's fool
7 *syn* see SHORT 5
rel acrimonious, biting, double-edged, incisive, penetrating, piercing, stabbing, stinging; caustic, virulent, vitriolic
8 causing intense mental or physical distress <a *sharp* pain>
syn acute, knifelike, piercing, shooting, stabbing
rel intense, severe, smart; biting, drilling, stinging; penetrating; agonizing, excruciating; paralyzing
9 *syn* see ACRID
rel odorous; strong-scented, strong-smelling; suffocating
10 *syn* see ACUTE 4
11 *syn* see STYLISH
‖**sharp** *vb syn* see SHARPEN
sharp *adv syn* see JUST 1
sharpen *vb* to give a keen edge to <*sharpen* an ax>
syn edge, hone, ‖sharp, whet
rel dress, file, grind, stroke
idiom hone to a razor edge, hone to razor sharpness
ant blunt, dull
sharper *n syn* see SWINDLER
sharp–eyed *adj* having keen vision <the *sharp-eyed* child found all the Easter eggs>
syn eagle-eyed, hawk-eyed, lyncean, lynx-eyed, sharp-sighted
rel alert, attentive, aware, keen, lynxlike, observant, sharp, vigilant, watchful
con myopic, nearsighted, shortsighted; dim-sighted, purblind; blind
sharpie *n syn* see SWINDLER
sharply *adv syn* see HARD 4
rel intensely, penetratingly, piercingly
sharpness *n syn* see EDGE 2
ant bluntness, dullness
sharp practice *n syn* see DECEPTION 1
sharp–sighted *adj* **1** *syn* see SHARP-EYED
2 *syn* see WISE 4
sharp–witted *adj* **1** *syn* see SHARP 4
2 *syn* see WISE 4
shatter *vb* **1** to break into small pieces by or as if by a blow <*shatter* a windowpane with a rock>

syn burst, fragment, ||pash, rive, shiver, smash, ||smatter, splinter, splinterize, splitter; *compare* PULVERIZE 1

rel break, crack, rend, snap, ||spalt, split; crunch, crush; crash, dash; fragmentalize, fragmentize, pulverize; demolish, destroy, disintegrate, ruin, ||total, wreck

idiom smash to smithereens (*or* bits)

2 *syn see* DESTROY 1

3 *syn see* RATTLE 1

shatterable *adj syn see* FRAGILE 1

ant shatterproof

shatterbrain *n syn see* SCATTERBRAIN

shattering *adj syn see* DESTRUCTIVE

shattery *adj syn see* FRAGILE 1

idiom as delicate as an eggshell

shave *vb* 1 *syn see* SLIVER

2 *syn see* CUT 6

rel shingle

3 *syn see* REDUCE 2

4 *syn see* BRUSH

idiom cut (*or* shave) it close

5 *syn see* SCRAPE 3

shaveling *n syn see* BOY 1

she *n syn see* WOMAN 1

shear *vb syn see* CUT 6

rel mow; barb, barber; manicure, snip

sheath *n syn see* SKIN 3

sheathe *vb* to cover (a surface) with something that protects <a house *sheathed* with aluminum siding>

syn clad, face, side, skin

rel envelop, surround, wrap; case, cover, encase, jacket; panel

con bare, expose, strip

sheathing *n syn see* SKIN 3

shed *n* 1 *syn see* DISCARD

rel drop; divest

2 to cast off (a body covering) in a periodic process of growth or renewal <a snake *shedding* its skin>

syn exuviate, molt, slip, slough

rel cast off, discard; doff, take off

sheen *n syn see* LUSTER

rel finish; shininess

sheeny *adj syn see* LUSTROUS 1

sheepheaded *adj syn see* SIMPLE 3

sheer *adj* 1 *syn see* FILMY

rel airy, chiffon, thin; see-through

2 *syn see* UTTER

3 *syn see* PURE 2

rel arrant, bald-faced, complete, outright

4 *syn see* STEEP 1

sheer *vb* 1 *syn see* TURN 6

2 *syn see* SWERVE 1

||**shekels** *n pl syn see* MONEY

shell *n syn see* HULL

shell *vb* 1 *syn see* SHUCK

2 *syn see* BOMBARD

rel pepper; rake

idiom open fire on

shellac *vb syn see* WHIP 2

shellacking *n syn see* DEFEAT 1

rel ||clobbering, whipping

shell out *vb syn see* SPEND 1

shelter *n* 1 something (as a structure or place) that covers or affords protection <a bomb *shelter*>

syn asylum, cover, covert, harbor, harborage, haven, port, refuge, retreat, sanctuary; *compare* REFUGE 1

rel buen retiro, den, hermitage, hide, hideaway, hideout, hidey-hole, retirement, tower

2 dwellings provided for numbers of people or for a community <*shelter* for the aged>

syn housing, quarterage

rel dwellings, lodging; roof

3 *syn see* REFUGE 1

shelter *vb syn see* HARBOR 1

shelve *vb syn see* DEFER

rel dish, drop, give up

idiom put on the shelf

shenanigan *n* 1 *syn see* TRICK 1

rel fast one, game, legerdemain

2 *syn see* PRANK

rel frolic; goings-on, mischievousness; stunt

Sheol *n syn see* HELL

shepherd *vb syn see* GUIDE

Sherlock *n syn see* DETECTIVE

Sherlock Holmes *n syn see* DETECTIVE

shibboleth *n* 1 *syn see* CATCHWORD

rel platitude, truism

2 *syn see* COMMONPLACE

||**shick** *adj syn see* INTOXICATED 1

||**shicker** *adj syn see* INTOXICATED 1

||**shicker** *n syn see* DRUNKARD

shield *n syn see* DEFENSE 1

rel buffer, bumper; screen

shield *vb* 1 *syn see* HARBOR 1

idiom give cover (*or* shelter) to; take (*or* shield) under one's wing

ant expose

2 *syn see* DEFEND 1

shift *vb* ||1 *syn see* APPORTION 2

2 *syn see* CHANGE 5

3 *syn see* MOVE 4

rel alter, change, vary; budge, stir; shuffle; relocate

idiom shift place

4 *syn see* CONSUME 5

5 to carry on one's affairs independently and self-sufficiently often under difficult circumstances <after the divorce, she was forced to *shift* for herself>

syn do, fare, get along, get by, get on, ||make out, manage, muddle through, stagger (*on or* along)

rel contrive, survive; freelance; progress, succeed

idiom fend for oneself, make do, make it alone, make shift, paddle one's own canoe, stand on one's own two feet

shift *n* 1 *syn see* CONVERSION 2

2 *syn see* RESOURCE 3

rel gambit, maneuver, ploy, strategy

3 *syn see* SPELL 1

4 *syn see* TRANSITION

5 *syn see* TURN 2

shifty *adj* 1 *syn see* EVASIVE 1

rel dodging, elusive; cagey, collusive, conniving, crafty, cunning; furtive, shifty-eyed, sneaky, tricky; insidious, shady; deceitful, dishonest, fraudulent; treacherous

idiom shifty as the sand

2 *syn see* DISHONEST

3 *syn see* UNDERHAND

4 *syn see* MUTABLE 2

shill *n syn see* DECOY 2

shillaber *n syn see* DECOY 2

||**shillelagh** *n syn see* CUDGEL

shilling shocker *n syn see* DIME NOVEL

shilly–shally *adj syn* see VACILLATING 2
shilly–shally *n syn* see HESITATION
shilly–shally *vb syn* see HESITATE
shilly–shallying *adj syn* see VACILLATING 2
   rel halfhearted, lukewarm
shimmer *vb syn* see FLASH 1
shimmer *n syn* see FLASH 1
   rel blinking; spangle; spark, sparking
shin *vb syn* see RUN 1
shindig *n* 1 a large, festive, and often overly lavish party <threw the *shindig* of the year for the author>
   syn bash, ‖blowout, shindy
   rel fête, gala; ball, dance; blast, party; affair, shebang; ‖shivoo
   2 *syn* see COMMOTION 3
shindy *n* 1 *syn* see SHINDIG 1
   2 *syn* see COMMOTION 3
shine *vb* 1 to emit rays of light <the storm is over and the sun is *shining*>
   syn beam, burn, gleam, radiate
   rel glimmer, glow; incandesce, luminesce; flash, sparkle, twinkle; flare; glare
   2 *syn* see POLISH 1
shine *n* 1 *syn* see DISPLAY 2
   2 *syn* see LUSTER
   rel finish
   3 *usu* **shines** *pl syn* see PRANK
shiner *n syn* see BLACK EYE 1
shingle *vb syn* see OVERLAP
shining *adj syn* see LUSTROUS 1
shiny *adj syn* see LUSTROUS 1
ship *vb* 1 *syn* see SEND 1
   rel direct; freight; export
   ant receive
   2 *syn* see MOVE 4
shipshape *adj syn* see NEAT 2
shipwreck *vb* 1 to destroy, disable, or seriously damage a ship (as by running aground or causing to founder) <the typhoon *shipwrecked* the entire fishing fleet>
   syn beach, cast away, pile up, strand, wreck
   rel break up; scuttle; founder; capsize; go down, sink
   idiom go aground, go to the bottom (*or* Davy Jones's locker), run on the rocks
   2 *syn* see RUIN 2
shirk *vb* 1 *syn* see SNEAK
   2 *syn* see DODGE 1
   rel bilk, burke; bypass, double, eschew, get around; shuffle off, shun
shirker *n syn* see SLACKER
shirty *adj syn* see ANGRY
shivaree *n* a noisy mock serenade to a newly married couple <*shivarees* and other such disappearing rural customs>
   syn ‖belling, ‖bull band, ‖callithump, charivari, ‖horning, ‖riding, ‖skimmelton
   rel entertainment, reception, welcome
shiver *vb syn* see SHATTER 1
shiver *vb syn* see SHAKE 1
‖shivereens *n pl syn* see SMITHEREENS
shivering *adj syn* see TREMULOUS
shivers *n pl syn* see JITTERS

---

syn synonym(s)   *rel* related word(s)
ant antonym(s)   *con* contrasted word(s)
idiom idiomatic equivalent(s)
‖ use limited; if in doubt, see a dictionary

---

shivery *adj* 1 *syn* see TREMULOUS
   2 *syn* see COLD 1
shoal *adj syn* see SHALLOW 1
shoal *n* a place where a body of water (as a sea or river) is not deep <dangerous *shoals* in uncharted waters>
   syn shallow
   rel barrier, barrier reef, coral reef, fringing reef, reef, sand reef; bank, bar, sandbank, sandbar, tombolo; hook, spit; seamount
   con abyss, deep, depth
shock *n syn* see PILE 1
shock *n* 1 *syn* see IMPACT 1
   2 *syn* see EARTHQUAKE
   3 *syn* see TRAUMA
   rel prostration, stupefaction
shock *vb* 1 to offend the moral sense of <were *shocked* by pornography>
   syn scandalize
   rel astonish, astound, startle, surprise; jar, jolt, shake up; insult, offend, outrage; appall, horrify; floor, knock out; disgust, nauseate, sicken
   idiom stink in one's nostrils, turn one's stomach
   2 to cause to undergo a physical or psychological shock <his slap *shocked* her out of hysterics>
   syn jolt, startle
   rel shake; jar; electrify
shocked *adj syn* see AGHAST 2
   rel jarred, jolted, shaken up, ‖shook up; offended, outraged; appalled, horrified
shocker *n* 1 *syn* see THRILLER
   2 *syn* see DIME NOVEL
shocking *adj* 1 *syn* see FEARFUL 3
   rel heinous, monstrous
   2 *syn* see OUTRAGEOUS 2
   rel burning, glaring; disgraceful, shameful; unspeakable
shoddy *adj* 1 *syn* see CHEAP 2
   rel makeshift, scambling
   2 *syn* see SHABBY 1
   3 *syn* see DISREPUTABLE 1
shoeless *adj syn* see BAREFOOT 1
   ant shod
shoestring *adj syn* see LITTLE 3
‖shog *vb syn* see PUSH 2
shoo–in *n syn* see SURE THING
‖shool *vb syn* see SHUFFLE
shoot *vb* 1 to cause (a weapon) to drive a projectile forward <*shoot* an arrow at a target>
   syn discharge, fire, loose
   rel trigger; launch, project; expel; blast; poop
   idiom let fly
   2 *syn* see DESTROY 1
   3 *syn* see DISCREDIT 2
   ‖4 *syn* see DISCARD
   5 *syn* see VOMIT
   ‖6 *syn* see PASS 9
   7 *syn* see SHOOT UP 2
   8 *syn* see FLY 1
   9 *syn* see RUSH 1
   rel gallop, highball, hotfoot; spurt
   10 *syn* see PHOTOGRAPH
shoot *n syn* see RAY 1
shooting *adj syn* see SHARP 8
   ant stationary

shooting match *n syn* see AFFAIR 1
shoot up *vb* 1 *syn* see SKYROCKET
2 to take (a drug) by hypodermic needle <had been *shooting up* heroin for weeks>
syn ‖mainline, shoot
shop *n syn* see STORE 4
rel boutique
shoplift *vb* to steal displayed goods from a store <the manager caught them *shoplifting* records>
syn ‖boost
rel bag, cop, ‖nick, palm, pilfer, pinch, rip off, snitch, swipe
shopworn *adj syn* see TRITE
rel overused, overworked, overworn
shore *n* the land bordering a usually large body of water <watched the ships while walking along the *shore*>
syn bank, beach, coast, strand
rel coastline, shoreline, waterfront, waterside; coastland, seacoast, seashore; foreshore, littoral, shoreface, shoreside; brink, embankment, riverbank, riverside
shore (up) *vb syn* see SUPPORT 4
shore *n syn* see SUPPORT 3
short *adj* 1 having little length in space or time <a *short* visit>
syn brief
rel abbreviate, abbreviated, abridged, curtailed, decreased, diminished, lessened, shortened; curtate, decurtate
con extensive, lengthy; drawn-out, overlong; extended, prolonged, protracted
ant long
2 having small physical stature <he was the *shortest* boy present>
syn low, low-set, low-statured
rel chunky, dumpy, squat, squatty, stubby, thick, thickset
con gangling, gangly, lanky, rangy; elevated, high, lofty, spiring, towering
ant tall
3 not coming up to a measure or need <fuel was very *short* that year>
syn deficient, failing, inadequate, insufficient, scant, scanty, scarce, scrimpy, shy, skimpy, slender, unsufficient, wanting; compare MEAGER 2
rel lacking, needing; exiguous, meager, sparse
con abounding, overflowing, teeming; abundant, ample, copious, plenteous, plentiful
ant long
4 *syn* see BLUFF
ant expansive
5 lacking in graciousness or consideration <her manner was *short* and abrupt>
syn inconsiderate, sharp, thoughtless, unceremonious, ungracious
rel bluff, blunt, brusque, crusty, curt; short-spoken; gruff, irascible
con considerate, gracious, kindly; bland, smooth; ceremonious
6 readily breaking or crumbling <a rich *short* pastry>
syn brittle, crisp, crumbly, ‖crump, crunchy, friable
rel delicate, fragile
con soggy, tough

7 *syn* see CONCISE
rel compact; pointed
idiom to the point
con extended, protracted, spun-out
ant lengthy, long-drawn-out
short *adv* 1 without hesitation or delay <stopped *short*>
syn abruptly, asudden, forthwith, sudden, suddenly
con hesitantly; gradually, slowly
2 *syn* see UNAWARES
short *n syn* see SUBSTANCE 2
short *vb syn* see SPARE 3
shortage *n syn* see FAILURE 3
rel curtailment, pinch, tightness; shortfall
ant overage
short and sweet *adj syn* see CONCISE
shortcoming *n syn* see IMPERFECTION
idiom weak point
con forte, long suit
shortcut *n* a route shorter or more direct than the one ordinarily taken <they took a *shortcut* down the back roads>
syn cutoff
rel bypass
ant detour
shorten *vb* to reduce in extent (as of length or duration) <decided to *shorten* their visit> <*shorten* a skirt for summer wear>
syn abbreviate, abridge, curtail, cut, cut back, retrench, slash
rel decrease, diminish, elide, excerpt, lessen, reduce; compress, condense, contract, shrink; bobtail, clip, dock; minimize
idiom cut short
con draw out, protract
ant elongate; lengthen; extend, prolong
shorthanded *adj* short of the necessary number of people <the office was critically *shorthanded*>
syn underhanded, undermanned, understaffed
rel short, wanting
con overmanned, overstaffed
short-lived *adj syn* see TRANSIENT
rel short-haul, short-run, short-term
con long-run, long-term
ant agelong; long-lived
shortly *adv* 1 *syn* see BRIEFLY
2 *syn* see PRESENTLY 1
rel pronto, quickly
short-range *adj syn* see TACTICAL 1
ant long-range
shortsighted *adj syn* see MYOPIC
ant farsighted, longsighted
short-spoken *adj syn* see BLUFF
ant windy
shot *n* 1 *syn* see FLING 1
2 *syn* see OPPORTUNITY
3 *syn* see DRAM
‖**shot** *adj syn* see INTOXICATED 1
shotgun *vb syn* see FORCE 2
should *vb syn* see WANT 3
shoulder *vb syn* see PUSH 2
shout *vb* 1 to utter a sudden loud cry (as to express joy or triumph or to attract attention) <the mob *shouted* for a speech>
syn cry, whoop, yell; compare CALL 1, SCREAM 1
rel exclaim; howl, scream, shriek; bawl, bellow, clamor, roar, vociferate

con murmur, whisper
2 *syn* see SCREAM 4
3 *syn* see CALL 1
rel bark; bray
4 *syn* see TREAT 3

shove *vb* **1** *syn* see PUSH 1
rel cram, jam; dig, jab, poke, prod
idiom push and shove
2 *syn* see PUSH 2
3 *syn* see PUSH 6

shove (off) *vb syn* see GO 2
ant pull in

shovel *vb* **1** *syn* see DIG 1
2 *syn* see DIG 2

shovel *vb syn* see SHUFFLE

show *vb* **1** to set out or place on view for customers <we're *showing* lots of long dresses this fall>
syn display, offer
rel afford, supply; exhibit; present, proffer, submit; deal (in), sell
2 to reveal outwardly or make apparent <asked a question or two to *show* his intelligence>
syn demonstrate, evidence, evince, illustrate, manifest, mark, ostend, proclaim; *compare* LOOK 4
rel disclose, discover, divulge, lay out, reveal, unveil; present, project
con camouflage, conceal, dissemble, hide, obscure
ant disguise
3 *syn* see STAGE
4 to present in such a way as to invite notice, attention, and admiration <she loved to *show* her jewels to everyone>
syn brandish, display, disport, exhibit, expose, flash, flaunt, parade, show off, trot out
rel air, lay out, set out, spread; blazon, flourish, sport, vaunt
con belittle, deprecate, depreciate, minimize
5 to give an exact and usually automatic reading or indication of <the speedometer *shows* 70 MPH>
syn indicate, mark, read, record, register, say
rel point (to); ring up
6 *syn* see LOOK 4
rel lay out, reveal, unveil
7 *syn* see GUIDE
8 *syn* see ESTABLISH 6
rel present; plead; allege
9 *syn* see APPEAR 1
rel come, show up; materialize
10 *syn* see COME 1
idiom ‖make the scene, put in an appearance, show one's face
11 *syn* see TURN UP 3

show *n syn* see APPEARANCE 2
rel likeness; effect, impression
idiom outward show
2 *syn* see MASK 2
3 *syn* see DISPLAY 2
4 *syn* see OPPORTUNITY

5 *syn* see EXHIBITION 1
6 *syn* see EXHIBITION 2
7 *syn* see MOVIE
8 *syn* see SHOWING 1

shower *n syn* see BARRAGE
rel shatter, spatter, spray

shower *vb syn* see BATHE 1

showing *n* **1** performance in a test of skill, power, or effectiveness <he made a good *showing* in the race>
syn out, show
rel record
2 *syn* see APPEARANCE 2

show-me *adj syn* see INCREDULOUS

show off *vb syn* see SHOW 4
rel boast, brag, swagger

showpiece *n* a prime or outstanding example used or suitable for exhibition <a Fabergé Easter egg was the *showpiece* of the collection>
syn chef d'oeuvre, masterpiece, pièce de résistance
rel gem, jewel; prize
con claptrap, rubbish, trash, trivia, truck

showroom *n syn* see STORE 4

show up *vb syn* see EXPOSE 4
rel discredit; invalidate
2 *syn* see TURN UP 3
3 *syn* see COME 1

showy *adj* given to or marked by excessive outward display <*showy* decorations>
syn chichi, flamboyant, orchidaceous, ostentatious, peacockish, peacocky, pretentious, splashy, swank
rel sporty; flashy, garish, gaudy, jazzy, meretricious, tawdry; gorgeous, resplendent; luxurious, opulent, ornate, sumptuous; overdone, overwrought; sensational
con muted, quiet, restrained, subdued; elegant, graceful, restrained; appropriate, seemly
ant unshowy

shred *n syn* see PARTICLE

shred *vb syn* see SLIVER

shreddy *adj syn* see RAGGED

shrew *n syn* see VIRAGO
rel she-devil, spitfire

shrewd *adj* marked by clever discerning awareness and hardheaded acumen <the captain was a *shrewd* judge of character>
syn argute, astucious, astute, cagey, heady, perspicacious, sagacious, ‖savvy; *compare* SHARP 4, WISE 2, 4
rel canny, crafty, foxy, ingenious, ‖pawky, slick, ‖sly, tidy; clever, intelligent, knowing, quick-witted, smart; polite, smooth; judicious, prudent, sensible, wise; penetrating, piercing, probing; acute, keen, sharp; far-sighted, foresighted
con green, naive, simple, soft; foolable, gullible, slow

shrewdness *n syn* see WIT 3
rel canniness, foxiness

shriek *vb* **1** *syn* see SCREAM 1
rel squawk, ‖yarm
2 *syn* see SQUEAL 2
3 *syn* see SCREAM 4

shrill *vb syn* see SCREAM 1

shrill *adj syn* see ACUTE 4

shrine *n* a structure or place considered sacred by a religious group <pilgrims going

to the *shrine* at Lourdes hoping to be healed>
syn holy place, sanctorium, sanctuary, sanctum
rel reliquary; enshrinement

shrink *vb* **1** *syn* see CONTRACT 3
rel shrivel (up), wither
con amplify, expand
ant swell

2 *syn* see FAIL 3
idiom shrink (*or* dwindle) down to nothing

3 *syn* see RECOIL
rel cower, cringe, crouch, huddle, slink; draw (back), recede, retire, retreat, withdraw; boggle, demur, scruple
shrinking *adj* *syn* see UNDEMONSTRATIVE
shrivel *vb* *syn* see WITHER
rel parch; fossilize
shroud *vb* **1** *syn* see ENFOLD 1
2 *syn* see SCREEN 3
shrouded *adj* *syn* see ULTERIOR
shuck *n* *syn* see HULL
shuck *vb* to strip, break off, or remove the enclosing case or cover of <*shuck* corn>
syn hull, husk, shell; *compare* SKIN 2
rel decorticate, peel, skin, strip
shuck (off) *vb* *syn* see DISCARD
shudder *vb* *syn* see SHAKE 1
rel gyrate, shimmy
shuffle *vb* **1** *syn* see DISORDER 1
2 *syn* see EQUIVOCATE 2
3 to walk awkwardly in a sliding, dragging way without lifting the feet <an old drunk *shuffling* along in filthy broken slippers>
syn scuff, scuffle, shamble, ‖shool, shovel
rel drag, pad, scrape, slipper, slip-slop, slur; draggle, straggle, trail (along)
4 *syn* see STUMBLE 6
shuffle *n* *syn* see CLUTTER 2
shuffling *adj* *syn* see EVASIVE 1
shun *vb* *syn* see ESCAPE 2
rel decline, refuse, reject; snub; despise, disdain, scorn
idiom have nothing to do with, keep away from, stand aloof from, steer clear of, turn away from, turn one's back upon
con accept, adopt, welcome
shunning *n* *syn* see ESCAPE 2
shunt *vb* **1** to push or turn off to one side <*shunt* a railroad car onto a siding>
syn sidetrack, switch; *compare* TURN 6
rel change, move, shift, transfer; avert, deflect, divert, head off
idiom push aside (*or* to the side)
2 *syn* see SHUTTLE
shush *vb* **1** *syn* see SILENCE
2 *syn* see SUPPRESS 2
shut *vb* *syn* see CLOSE 1
rel lock, seal; batten (down)
ant open
‖**shut–eye** *n* *syn* see SLEEP 1
shut in *vb* *syn* see ENCLOSE 1
ant shut out
shut-in *adj* *syn* see UNSOCIABLE
shut-mouthed *adj* *syn* see SILENT 3
ant openmouthed
shut off *vb* *syn* see SCREEN 3
shut out *vb* *syn* see SCREEN 3
shuttle *vb* to travel back and forth frequently <*shuttled* between New York and Washington every week>

syn shunt
rel shuttlecock; alternate
shut up *vb* **1** *syn* see SILENCE
2 to cease speaking <told the boy to sit down and *shut up*>
syn dry up, dumb (up), ‖dummy (up), pipe down, ‖ring off
rel hush, quiet (down), shush, soft-pedal
idiom button (*or* seal) one's lips, keep quiet
shy *adj* **1** disinclined to obtrude oneself <*shy* in the presence of strangers>
syn backward, bashful, coy, demure, diffident, modest, rabbity, retiring, self-effacing, timid, unassertive, unassured
rel backhanded, hesitant, reluctant; conscious, self-conscious, self-distrustful, shamefaced, sheepish; introversive, introvert, introverted, inturned; circumspect, reserved; cautious, chary, suspicious, wary; apprehensive, fearful, nervous, skittish, timorous
con brash, forward; aggressive, audacious, intrusive, obtruding, pushing, pushy; blunt, crass
ant bold, obtrusive

2 *syn* see DISINCLINED
3 *syn* see SHORT 3
con excess, over, surplus
shy *vb* **1** *syn* see RECOIL
rel blench, quail, recoil, shrink
2 *syn* see ESCAPE 2
shy *n* *syn* see POTSHOT
Shylock *n* *syn* see LOAN SHARK
shyster *n* *syn* see PETTIFOGGER
‖**sib** *adj* *syn* see SYMPATHETIC 2
sibilate *vb* *syn* see HISS
sibylline *adj* **1** *syn* see PROPHETIC
2 *syn* see OBSCURE 3
sic *vb* *syn* see URGE
rel agitate, catalyze, inspirit, instigate; abet, aid, countenance, favor
sick *adj* **1** affected with illness or disease <was *sick* with pneumonia>
syn down, ill; *compare* UNWELL
rel diseased, disordered, fevered; ailing, ‖cronk, ‖crook, funny, indisposed, unwell; debilitated, sickly, unhealthy; rocky, tottering, wobbly; confined, laid up; lousy, mean, rotten
idiom ‖on the sick list, sick as a dog
con healthy, strong
ant well

2 *syn* see MORBID
3 *syn* see FED UP
idiom ‖up to here with
4 *syn* see FAULTY
5 *syn* see SICKLY 2
sick (up) *vb* *syn* see VOMIT
sicken *vb* **1** *syn* see UPSET 5
2 *syn* see DISGUST
sicken (with *or* of) *vb* *syn* see CONTRACT 1
sickening *adj* *syn* see OFFENSIVE
‖**sicker** *vb* *syn* see EXUDE
sickliness *n* *syn* see INFIRMITY 1
sickly *adj* **1** *syn* see UNWELL
rel ‖cranky, down
con hale, hearty; healthy, well
ant robust

2 accompanying, indicating, or suggesting sickness <a *sickly* complexion>

syn peaked, ‖peaking, peaky, sick
rel ‖pimping, puny, sickish, weak; diseased; unhealthy
con healthy, hearty
3 *syn* see UNWHOLESOME 1
4 *syn* see MORBID

sickness *n* **1** the condition of being ill <finally recovered from his *sickness*>
syn affliction, diseasedness, disorder, illness, indisposition, infirmity, unhealth; *compare* DISEASE 1, INFIRMITY 1
rel indisposedness, unhealthfulness, unhealthiness, unwellness; affection, ailment, ill
idiom ill health
con haleness, healthiness, heartiness
ant health
2 *syn* see DISEASE 1

side *n* **1** a place, space, or direction with respect to a center or a line of division <lived on the north *side* of the street> <turned to one *side*>
syn hand
rel direction, flank, sector
2 *syn* see PHASE
3 *syn* see VIEWPOINT 2
4 the attitude, position, or action of one person or group as opposed to another <could understand her *side* as well as his in the quarrel>
syn part; *compare* POSITION 1
rel attitude, disposition; posture, stance, stand; position, standpoint, viewpoint

side *vb* *syn* see SHEATHE
side (with) *vb* *syn* see SUPPORT 2
side action *n* *syn* see SIDE EFFECT
sideboards *n* *pl* *syn* see SIDE-WHISKERS
sideburns *n* *pl* *syn* see SIDE-WHISKERS
side effect *n* a secondary and usually adverse effect (as of a drug) <drowsiness is a common *side effect* of antihistamines>
syn side action, side reaction
rel effect; reaction, response
side-glance *n* a look or glance directed to one side <she shot an impatient *side-glance* at him>
syn side-look
rel glance; stare
sideling *adv* *syn* see SIDEWAYS 1
sideling *adj* *syn* see STEEP 1
‖sidelings *adv* *syn* see SIDEWAYS 1
sidelong *adv* *syn* see SIDEWAYS 1
side-look *n* *syn* see SIDE-GLANCE
side reaction *n* *syn* see SIDE EFFECT
sidereal *adj* *syn* see STELLAR 1
sidesplitter *n* *syn* see RIOT 2
sidestep *vb* **1** *syn* see EQUIVOCATE 2
2 *syn* see SKIRT 3
3 *syn* see DODGE 1
sideswipe *n* *syn* see POTSHOT
sidetrack *vb* *syn* see SHUNT 1
sideward *adv* *syn* see SIDEWAYS 1
sideways *adv* **1** to, toward, or at one side <slipped *sideways* on the ice>

syn crabwise, laterally, sideling, ‖sidelings, sidelong, sideward, sidewise; *compare* ASIDE 1
rel obliquely; indirectly
con straight; directly
2 *syn* see ASIDE 1
side-whiskers *n* *pl* the usually shaped growth of whiskers on both sides of a man's face <grew *side-whiskers* and a moustache in order to look older>
syn burnsides, dundrearies, muttonchops, sideboards, sideburns
sidewise *adv* **1** *syn* see SIDEWAYS 1
2 *syn* see ASIDE 1
sidle *vb* to move sideways or obliquely especially in an unobtrusive or furtive manner <a suspicious-looking man *sidled* up to her>
syn edge, ‖slive
rel ease, slip
siege *n* a sometimes prolonged period of disorder or stress (as of body or mind) <endured a three-week *siege* of flu>
syn bout, go; *compare* ATTACK 3
rel attack, onslaught, seizure, spell
siesta *n* *syn* see NAP
siesta *vb* *syn* see NAP
sieve *n* *syn* see GOSSIP 1
sieve *vb* *syn* see SCREEN 5
sift *vb* **1** *syn* see SCREEN 5
2 *syn* see SORT 2
3 *syn* see EXPLORE
sigh *vb* **1** to take in and let out a deep audible breath (as in weariness, grief, or relief) <flopped down in the chair and *sighed* deeply>
syn ‖sock, sough, suspire
rel breathe, respire; exhale; gasp, pant, wheeze; groan, moan; sob
idiom heave a sigh
2 to make a sound like sighing <the wind *sighed* in the branches>
syn sough
rel blow; murmur, whisper; moan; whine; whistle; howl, roar
3 *syn* see LONG
sighful *adj* *syn* see MELANCHOLY 2
sight *n* **1** *syn* see EYESORE
‖2 *syn* see MUCH
3 *syn* see EYE 2
4 *syn* see LOOK 1
5 *syn* see VIEW 4
6 *syn* see VIEW 5
sightless *adj* *syn* see BLIND 1
ant sighted
sightseer *n* *syn* see TOURIST
sign *n* **1** a motion, action, gesture, or word by which a command, thought, or wish is expressed <put a finger to her lips as a *sign* to keep quiet>
syn high sign, signal
rel gesticulation, gesture, motion; hint, indication, suggestion, warning
2 *syn* see CHARACTER 1
3 *syn* see EXPRESSION 3
rel symbolization; attestation, evidence, proof
4 *syn* see INDICATION 3
rel earmark, exponent, indicator; exhibit, show
sign *vb* **1** to affix a signature to <he refused to *sign* a confession>

---

syn synonym(s)   *rel* related word(s)
ant antonym(s)   *con* contrasted word(s)
idiom idiomatic equivalent(s)
‖ use limited; if in doubt, see a dictionary

syn autograph, ink, signature, subscribe
idiom put one's John Hancock on, put one's John Henry down (*or* on)
  2 *syn see* SIGNAL

sign (over) *vb syn see* TRANSFER 4
signal *n syn see* SIGN 1
  rel alarm, alert, tocsin; movement
signal *vb* to notify by or as if by a signal <*signaled* his wife to keep quiet>
  syn flag, gesture, motion, sign, signalize
  idiom give the high sign (to)
signal *adj syn see* NOTICEABLE
  rel characteristic, distinctive, individual, peculiar, significative; eminent, famous, illustrious, renowned
signalize *vb* 1 *syn see* CHARACTERIZE 2
  2 *syn see* SIGNAL
signature *n syn see* SIGN 1
significance *n* 1 *syn see* MEANING 1
  2 *syn see* IMPORTANCE
  rel authority, credit, influence, merit, prestige; excellence, perfection, virtue
  con indifference; triviality, unimportance, worthlessness; irrelevance
  ant insignificance
significancy *n syn see* MEANING 1
significant *adj* 1 *syn see* EXPRESSIVE
  rel cogent, compelling, convincing, sound, telling, valid; forceful, powerful; important, momentous, weighty
  con meaningless, unexpressive; unimportant
  ant insignificant
  2 *syn see* IMPORTANT 1
  con inconsequential, meaningless, unimportant
  ant insignificant
significant *n syn see* INDICATION 3
significantly *adv syn see* WELL 8
  ant insignificantly
signification *n* 1 *syn see* MEANING 1
  rel implying, signifying; construction, implication; essence, gist, substance
  ‖2 *syn see* IMPORTANCE
significative *adj syn see* INDICATIVE
signify *vb* 1 *syn see* MEAN 2
  rel bear, carry, convey; bespeak, purport
  2 *syn see* MATTER
sign on *vb syn see* ENTER 3
sign up *vb syn see* ENTER 3
silence *n* 1 absence of sound or noise <the heavy *silence* of the night>
  syn noiselessness, quiet, quietness, quietude, soundlessness, still, stillness
  rel calm, hush, lull
  con din, uproar
  ant noise
  2 *syn see* SECRECY
  3 *syn see* DEATH 1
silence *vb* to compel or reduce to silence <*silenced* the courtroom chatter by pounding her gavel>
  syn choke (off), hush, quiet, ‖quieten, shush, shut up, still
  rel dampen, deaden, dumb, lull, muffle, mute; quash, quell, squash, squelch, suppress; gag, muzzle
silent *adj* 1 *syn see* DUMB 1
  2 characterized by absence of speech <was *silent* as he faced the altar>

syn dumb, mum, ‖mumchance, speechless, wordless; *compare* DUMB 1
  rel inarticulate, muted, tongue-tied, voiceless
  con speaking, talking
  3 showing marked restraint in speaking <a stern, *silent* man>
  syn close, close-lipped, closemouthed, close-tongued, dumb, inconversable, reserved, reticent, shut-mouthed, silentious, speechless, taciturn, tight-lipped, tightmouthed, uncommunicative, wordless
  rel checked, curbed, inhibited, restrained; unconversational, unsociable; inarticulate, incoherent; mute, voiceless; mum, secretive
  con articulate, fluent, glib, vocal, voluble; babblative, garrulous, loquacious, windy; blabbering, blabbery, chattering
  ant talkative
  4 *syn see* STILL 3
  idiom silent as a post (*or* stone), silent as the grave (*or* tomb)
  ant noisy
  5 *syn see* UNSPOKEN 1
silentious *adj syn see* SILENT 3
silhouette *n syn see* OUTLINE
  rel ‖shade, shadow
silken *adj* 1 *syn see* SOFT 3
  2 *syn see* INGRATIATING
silky *adj* 1 *syn see* SOFT 3
  2 *syn see* INGRATIATING
silliness *n syn see* FOOLISHNESS
  rel illogicality
  con logic, logicality, logicalness, sanity, sensibleness; wisdom
silly *adj* 1 *syn see* SIMPLE 3
  rel empty, empty-headed, vacuous; irrational, unreasonable; ignorant, unintelligent, unwise
  ant sensible
  2 *syn see* GIDDY 1
  rel ‖balmy, crazy, ‖dippy, irrational, off, ‖wacked-out
  idiom silly as a goose
  con level-headed, practical, rational, serious
  ant sensible
  3 *syn see* FOOLISH 2
  rel funny, senseless
silvern *adj syn see* SILVERY
silver–tongued *adj syn see* GLIB
silvery *adj* relating to, containing, or resembling silver <repeated polishings gave the wood a *silvery* sheen>
  syn argent, argentate, argenteous, argentine, silvern
  rel silver; brilliant, glittering, shimmering, shining
similar *adj syn see* LIKE
  rel complementary, correlative; reciprocal
  idiom much of a muchness, much the same
  con antithetical, antonymous, contradictory, contrary, opposite
  ant dissimilar
similarity *n syn see* LIKENESS
  rel approximation; collation, correlation; association, interrelation; parallel; closeness; coincidence, synonymity
  con unlikeness, variance
  ant dissimilarity
similarly *adv syn see* ALSO 1

idiom by the same token

simile *n* **1** *syn* see ANALOGY 2

2 *syn* see LIKENESS

similitude *n* **1** *syn* see LIKENESS
rel copy, image, replica
ant dissimilitude

2 *syn* see ANALOGY 2

simmer *vb* **1** *syn* see BOIL 2

2 *syn* see SEETHE 4

simmer down *vb* *syn* see COMPOSE 4
rel quiet (down), subside
idiom ‖cool it, take it easy
con boil, seethe; explode, fulminate
ant boil over

Simon Legree *n* *syn* see SLAVE DRIVER

simon–pure *adj* *syn* see AUTHENTIC 2

simp *n* *syn* see DUNCE

simper *vb* *syn* see SMIRK

simple *adj* **1** *syn* see NATURAL 5
rel childish, childlike; amateur, green, unexperienced; trusting; ‖square

2 *syn* see PLAIN 1
ant elaborate

3 actually or apparently deficient in intelligence <a poor *simple* woman easily duped>
syn asinine, brainless, ‖buffle-headed, fatuous, foolish, insensate, mindless, nitwitted, senseless, sheepheaded, silly, soft, spoony, unintelligent, unwitty, weak-headed, weakminded, witless; *compare* RETARDED, STUPID 1
rel amateur, green, inexperienced, inexpert; credulous, gullible; childish, childlike; naive; ignorant, illiterate, uneducated, unschooled, untaught; crass, dense, dopey, dull, dumb, slow, stupid; doting, feebleminded, idiotic, retarded, simpleminded
con able, competent; alert, clever, keen; bright, intelligent, understanding
ant wise

4 *syn* see RETARDED

5 *syn* see PURE 2
rel inelaborate, stark; bald, bare, mere; fundamental, uncompounded

6 *syn* see EASY 1
rel incomplex, incomplicate
idiom simple as ABC
ant complex, complicated

simple *n* *syn* see FOOL 3

simplehearted *adj* *syn* see NATURAL 5

simpleminded *adj* *syn* see RETARDED

simplest *adj* *syn* see ELEMENTARY 1

simpleton *n* **1** *syn* see FOOL 4

2 *syn* see DUNCE
rel bungler, ‖clot

simplify *vb* to make simple or simpler <*simplify* a manufacturing process>
syn boil down, streamline
rel clarify, clean up, disentangle, disinvolve, straighten (out), unscramble; abridge, cut down, reduce, shorten; oversimplify
ant complicate

simply *adv* *syn* see JUST 3

simulacrum *n* **1** *syn* see IMAGE 1

2 *syn* see IMITATION

3 *syn* see APPEARANCE 2

simulate *vb* **1** *syn* see ASSUME 4
rel ape, copy, imitate, mimic; play-act, pose
idiom ‖make out like (or as if)

2 *syn* see RESEMBLE

simulated *adj* **1** *syn* see FICTITIOUS 2
ant genuine

2 *syn* see ARTIFICIAL 2
ant genuine

simultaneous *adj* *syn* see CONTEMPORARY 1
rel agreeing, coinciding, concurring

simultaneously *adv* *syn* see TOGETHER 1
idiom in one breath

sin *n* **1** *syn* see EVIL 3

2 *syn* see EVIL 2

3 *syn* see IMPERFECTION

sin *vb* *syn* see TRESPASS 1

since *prep* *syn* see AFTER 2
ant before

since *conj* *syn* see BECAUSE

sincere *adj* **1** genuine in feeling or expression <had a *sincere* dislike for politics>
syn heartfelt, hearty, unfeigned, wholehearted, whole-souled; *compare* GENUINE 3
rel candid, frank, frankhearted, open, plain; faithful, honest, truthful; aboveboard, forthright, pretensionless, straightforward, unpretentious; dear, devout, heartful; meant, unaffected
con affected, artificial, feigned, put-on, unmeant
ant insincere

2 *syn* see GENUINE 3
rel authentic, bona fide; serious; actual
idiom honest to God
ant insincere

sincereness *n* *syn* see GOOD FAITH

sincerity *n* *syn* see GOOD FAITH
rel heart; goodwill; singleness, straightforwardness
con cunning, deceit, guile; ill will
ant insincerity

sine qua non *n* *syn* see ESSENTIAL 2

sinew *n* **1** *syn* see POWER 4

2 *usu* **sinews** *pl* *syn* see MAINSTAY

sinewy *adj* **1** *syn* see MUSCULAR 1
rel strong, sturdy, tenacious, tough
ant flabby

2 *syn* see MUSCULAR 2

sinful *adj* **1** *syn* see WRONG 1
rel base, low, vile; disgraceful, shameful; culpable, damnable

2 *syn* see BLAMEWORTHY
ant sinless

sing *vb* **1** to utter words in musical tones and with musical inflections and modulations <children often can *sing* before they converse>
syn chant, tune, vocalize
rel descant; carol, serenade, troll, croon, hum, lull, lullaby; cantillate, hymn, intone; singsong; roar

2 *syn* see TALK 6

‖3 *syn* see INFORM 3

single *adj* **1** being without a spouse <enjoying life as a *single* girl>
syn sole, spouseless, unmarried, unwed
rel free, unattached, unfettered; celibate; maiden, virgin

---

syn synonym(s)   *rel* related word(s)
ant antonym(s)   *con* contrasted word(s)
idiom idiomatic equivalent(s)
‖ use limited; if in doubt, see a dictionary

idiom footloose and fancy-free
con attached; united; wed
ant married

2 one as distinguished from two or more or all others <a *single* instance of dishonesty has been cited>
syn lone, one, only, particular, separate, sole, solitary, unique
rel individual, singular; especial, special, specific; distinguished, singled-out; distinct
con several; manifold, many, numerous
ant multiple

3 *syn* see FRANK
4 *syn* see SOLE 4

single (out) *vb syn* see CHOOSE 1
rel screen, winnow (out); accept, admit, receive

single–eyed *adj syn* see FRANK
single–hearted *adj syn* see FRANK
single–minded *adj* **1** *syn* see FRANK
2 *syn* see INFLEXIBLE 2
rel diehard; bigoted

singleness *n* **1** *syn* see UNIQUENESS
2 *syn* see UNITY 1
ant multifariousness

singly *adv syn* see APART 1
ant together

singular *adj* **1** *syn* see SEVERAL 1
rel discrete; certain, definite; exclusive
2 *syn* see EXCEPTIONAL 1
ant usual
3 *syn* see ONLY 2
idiom first and last, one and only, one only
4 *syn* see STRANGE 4
idiom passing strange

singularity *n* **1** *syn* see INDIVIDUALITY 4
2 *syn* see INDIVIDUALITY 3
3 *syn* see UNITY 1
ant multiplicity

singularize *vb syn* see CHARACTERIZE 2·
singularness *n syn* see UNITY 1
ant multifariousness

sinister *adj* seriously threatening disaster <a *sinister* plot>
syn baleful, malefic, maleficent, malign; *compare* OMINOUS
rel fateful, ill-omened, inauspicious, ominous, portentous, unpropitious; apocalyptic, dire, doomful, ill-boding, threatening; lowering, menacing; evil, malicious
con harmless, innocent, innocuous

sink *vb* **1** to become submerged <the overloaded raft *sank* below the surface>
syn founder, go down, go under, submerge, submerse
rel capsize, overturn, tip (over); dive, plunge; scuttle; shipwreck, wreck
idiom go to Davy Jones's locker, go to the bottom, sink like a rock
con come up, rise
ant float
2 *syn* see SET 12
3 *syn* see DETERIORATE 1
ant rise
4 *syn* see STOOP 2
5 *syn* see LOWER 3
6 *syn* see THRUST 2
7 *syn* see HUMBLE
ant uplift

sink *n* **1** a place marked by a staggering amount of corruption and filth <that area of the city was a *sink* of vice and crime>
syn Augean stable, cesspit, cesspool, den, pandemonium, Sodom, sty
rel hellhole; snake-shaped
idiom Alsatian den, den of iniquity, sink of corruption
2 *syn* see DEPRESSION 2

sinkage *n syn* see DEPRESSION 2
sinkhole *n syn* see DEPRESSION 2
sinuous *adj syn* see WINDING
rel twisted; snake-shaped
idiom twisting and turning

sip *vb syn* see DRINK 1
siphon *vb* **1** *syn* see CONDUCT 4
2 *syn* see DRAIN 1
sire *n syn* see FATHER 2
sire *vb* **1** *syn* see FATHER 1
2 *syn* see GENERATE 1
siren *n* an enticingly attractive woman who lures men into dangerous or compromising situations <a slinky *siren* of the silent screen era>
syn femme fatale, Lorelei, seductress, temptress
rel charmer, vamp
siren *adj syn* see ATTRACTIVE 1
rel sirenic
siren song *n syn* see LURE 2
sissified *adj syn* see EFFEMINATE
sissy *n syn* see WEAKLING
sissy *adj syn* see EFFEMINATE
sissy–pants (*or* sissy-britches) *n pl but sing or pl in constr syn* see WEAKLING
sit *vb* **1** to rest on the buttocks or haunches <she was *sitting* in a chair>
syn ‖set
rel perch, rest; ‖plop (down), seat, sit down; squat
con arise, get up, rise, stand, stand up
2 *syn* see CONVENE 1
3 *syn* see POSE 3
4 *syn* see SET 11
5 *syn* see SEAT
rel ensconce, install, settle
sit down *vb syn* see ALIGHT
site *n* **1** *syn* see PLACE 1
2 *syn* see SCENE 3
3 a place where an archaeological excavation is made <a burial *site*>
syn dig
4 *syn* see HABITAT
sited *adj syn* see SITUATED
‖**sitfast** *adj syn* see IMMOVABLE 1
sitting duck *n syn* see TARGET 1
rel sitter
situate *vb syn* see SITUATED
situated *adj* having a site, situation, or location <a town *situated* on a hill>
syn located, placed, positioned, set, sited, situate
situation *n* **1** *syn* see PLACE 1
2 *syn* see PREGNANCY
3 *syn* see JOB 2
4 *syn* see STATUS 1
5 *syn* see STATE 1
rel bargain
sizable *adj* **1** *syn* see CONSIDERABLE 2
2 *syn* see BIG 1

rel man-sized; giant-sized

sizableness *n syn* see SIZE 2

size *n* **1** the amount of measurable space or area occupied by or comprising a thing <the *size* of the card is 3″x 5″>
syn admeasurement, dimension(s), dimensionality, extent, magnitude, measure, proportion
rel area; body, bulk, mass, volume; height; extension, length; amplitude, breadth, expanse, spread, stretch, width; measurement
2 considerable amount, proportion, volume, character, or importance <left an estate of some *size*>
syn amplitude, bigness, greatness, largeness, magnitude, sizableness
rel dimension, extent
con littleness, smallness; minuteness, tininess

sizz *vb syn* see HISS

sizzle *vb* **1** *syn* see SEAR 2
2 *syn* see HISS

sizzling *adj syn* see HOT 1

‖**skag** *n syn* see CIGARETTE

skate *n syn* see MAN 3

sked *n syn* see PROGRAM 1

sked *n syn* see SCHEDULE 1

skedaddle *vb* **1** *syn* see RUN 2
rel ‖split; cut out
2 *syn* see GET OUT 1
idiom lift them up and set them down, ‖take off like a bat out of hell

‖**skeet** *vb syn* see HURRY 2

skeezicks *n syn* see SCAMP

skein *n syn* see MAZE 1

skeletal *adj syn* see EMACIATED

skeleton *vb syn* see SKETCH

skeletonize *vb syn* see SKETCH

‖**sken** *vb syn* see SQUINT

skeptic *n* a doubting or incredulous person <people of long experience are often *skeptics*>
syn doubter, doubting Thomas, headshaker, Pyrrhonian, Pyrrhonist, unbeliever, zetetic
rel questioner; agnostic; pessimist; scoffer; cynic, misanthrope; disbeliever
con accepter; apostle, disciple, follower; devotee, diehard
ant believer

skeptical *adj syn* see INCREDULOUS
rel freethinking; dissenting; suspicious; cynical
idiom ‖from Missouri
ant believing

skeptically *adv syn* see ASKANCE 2
idiom with a grain of salt, with a note of skepticism, with a skeptical eye
con trustingly
ant gullibly

skepticism *n syn* see UNCERTAINTY
rel qualm, qualmishness
idiom question in one's mind, shadow of doubt
con belief, trust

---

syn synonym(s)   *rel* related word(s)
ant antonym(s)   *con* contrasted word(s)
idiom idiomatic equivalent(s)
‖ use limited; if in doubt, see a dictionary

ant gullibility

sketch *n syn* see COMPENDIUM 1

sketch *vb* to present succinctly <let's *sketch* our plan of action>
syn adumbrate, block (out), chalk (out), characterize, draft, outline, rough (out), skeleton, skeletonize
rel depict; diagram, diagrammatize; blueprint, delineate; line; draw, plot, trace; design, develop; detail, lay out, map (out)

sketchy *adj syn* see SUPERFICIAL 2

skew *vb* **1** *syn* see SLANT 3
2 *syn* see SWERVE 1
rel skid, slide, slip

skewer *vb syn* see IMPALE

skid *vb* **1** *syn* see SLIDE 3
rel sheer, skew, slue, veer
idiom go into a skid
2 *syn* see PLUMMET

skiddoo *vb syn* see GET OUT 1
idiom go (or take) off like a shot

skid road *n syn* see SKID ROW

skid row *n* a city street or district notorious for cheap bars, flophouses, and homeless derelicts <boozy old men wandering the *skid row*>
syn bowery, skid road

skill *n* **1** *syn* see ABILITY 2
2 *syn* see ART 1
3 *syn* see ADDRESS 1
rel ease, skillfulness

skilled *adj* **1** *syn* see PROFICIENT
con skill-less, unproficient
ant unskilled, unskillful
2 *syn* see EXPERIENCED
rel prepared, primed, trained
con unfit, unqualified, untrained
ant unskilled

skillet *n syn* see FRYING PAN

skillful *adj* **1** *syn* see PROFICIENT
rel learned, versant, well-versed
ant unskillful
2 accomplished or done with proficiency or skill <his answer was a very *skillful* evasion>
syn adroit, clever, good, pretty, ‖skilly, wicked, workmanlike, workmanly; *compare* CLEVER 4, PROFICIENT
rel expert, masterful
con clumsy; unskilled
ant inept, unskillful

‖**skilly** *adj syn* see SKILLFUL 2

‖**skimble–skamble** *n syn* see GIBBERISH 1

‖**skimmelton** *n syn* see SHIVAREE

skimp *adj syn* see MEAGER 2

skimp *vb* **1** *syn* see SCRIMP
2 *syn* see SPARE 3

skimpy *adj* **1** *syn* see MEAGER 2
2 *syn* see SHORT 3

skin *n* **1** *syn* see HIDE
2 *syn* see HULL
3 a usually thin casing forming the outside surface of a structure or thing <aircraft *skins* made of aluminum alloys>
syn sheath, sheathing

rel facing, siding; case, casing, cover, jacket; shell

4 syn see MISER

5 syn see SWINDLER

║6 syn see DOLLAR

skin *vb* **1 syn** see SHEATHE

2 to remove the surface, skin, or thin outer covering of <*skin* a Bermuda onion>
syn decorticate, excorticate, peel, scale, strip; *compare* SHUCK
rel cut off, pull off; pare, shave (off), trim; hull, husk, shuck; bark, rind; excoriate, flay, gall

3 syn see OVERCHARGE 1

4 syn see CRITICIZE

5 syn see HURRY 2

║skinch *vb* **1 syn** see SCRIMP

2 syn see SPARE 3

skinflint *n syn* see MISER

║skinhead *n syn* see BALDHEAD

skinny *adj syn* see LEAN
rel twiggy, weedy; emaciated; skeletal
idiom mere skin and bones, skinny as a rail
ant fleshy

skip *vb* **1** to move or proceed with a light bounding step <children *skipping* home from school>
syn hop, lope, skitter, spring, trip
rel caper, cavort, curvet, frisk, gambol; bounce, hippety-hop; jump; leap; bound
con hobble, shamble, shuffle; hitch, limp, stagger, totter

2 syn see GLANCE 1

3 syn see RUN 2

idiom ║split the scene

skip *n syn* see OMISSION

skirmish *n* **1 syn** see CLASH 2
rel assault, attack; ambush
con pitched battle

2 syn see ENCOUNTER

skirr *vb* **1 syn** see RUN 2

2 syn see FLY 1

skirt *n* **1 syn** see BORDER 1
rel skirting
║2 syn see WOMAN 1

skirt *vb* **1 syn** see BORDER 1

2 to make a detour or circuit (as around a congested area) <*skirted* the city to avoid traffic>
syn bypass, circumnavigate, circumvent, detour
idiom go around

3 to avoid (as a topic or question) because of difficulty, complexity, controversy, or danger <*skirted* all touchy issues>
syn burke, bypass, circumvent, ║polly-fox, sidestep; *compare* EQUIVOCATE 2, ESCAPE 2
rel avoid, dodge, duck, evade, hedge; elude, escape; ignore, skip
idiom get around
con confront, face, meet, take on

║skite *n syn* see PRANK

skitter *vb syn* see SKIP 1

skittery *adj syn* see EXCITABLE

skittish *adj* **1 syn** see GIDDY 1
rel irresponsible, undependable, unreliable
2 syn see EXCITABLE
rel restive; nervous

skive *vb syn* see CUT 6

skiver *vb syn* see IMPALE

skookum *adj syn* see EXCELLENT

skookum–house *n syn* see JAIL

skulk *vb syn* see SNEAK

skunk *n syn* see SNOT 1

skunk *vb syn* see WHIP 1

sky *n* the expanse of space surrounding the earth <blue *sky* crisscrossed with jet trails>
syn empyrean, firmament, heaven(s), welkin
rel azure; celestial sphere
idiom the wild blue yonder

sky–high *adv syn* see APART 3

sky–high *adj syn* see EXCESSIVE 1

skylarking *n* **1 syn** see HORSEPLAY
idiom ║making whoopee
2 syn see REVELRY 2

sky pilot *n syn* see CLERGYMAN
rel chaplain; padre

skyrocket *vb* to rise abruptly and rapidly (as to an unprecedented level or amount) <when the election was over taxes and prices *skyrocketed*>
syn rocket, shoot up, soar
rel climb, rise; upsoar, upspring
con slide; fall; drop
ant crash, plummet

skyscraping *adj syn* see LOFTY 6

slab *n syn* see BAR 1
rel chunk, lump

║slab *n syn* see SLIME

slabber *vb syn* see DROOL 2

slack *adj* **1 syn** see NEGLIGENT
rel dilatory, lackadaisical, lethargic, sluggish; faineant, indolent, lazy, slothful; inert, stagnant
con assiduous, busy, diligent, industrious, sedulous

2 syn see LOOSE 1
rel feeble, infirm, soft, unsteady, weak; inactive, inert, passive, supine; laggard, leisurely, slow
con tensed, tightened; constant, equable, even, steady, uniform; firm, hard
ant taut, tight

3 syn see SLOW 3

slack *vb syn* see LOOSE 5
idiom ║cut some slack, make slack
ant tighten

slack *n syn* see SLOWDOWN 1

slacken *vb* **1 syn** see DELAY 1
idiom keep back
ant quicken
2 syn see ABATE 4
3 syn see LOOSE 5
ant tighten

slackening *n syn* see SLOWDOWN 1

slacker *n* one who shirks work, responsibility, or an obligation <didn't want any *slackers* in her office>
syn goldbrick, shirker, slinker, ║spiv
rel idler, loafer; slugabed, sluggard

slack–spined *adj syn* see WEAK 4

slake *vb syn* see QUENCH 4

slam *n* **1 syn** see BLOW 1

2 syn see BANG 2

3 syn see ANIMADVERSION
rel fling, swipe; crack, potshot; rap, slap; dig, jab

slam *vb* **1** to strike with extreme force or violence <*slammed* the ball out of the park><the car *slammed* into the fence>

syn belt, blast, clobber, slug, smash, wallop; *compare* STRIKE 2
rel bang, bat, hit, knock, slap, swat, thwack; cudgel, hammer, mace; batter, beat, pound
2 *syn* see LAMBASTE 3

‖**slam** *adv* *syn* see WELL 3

slammer *n* *syn* see JAIL

slander *n* *syn* see DETRACTION
rel black wash, muckraking, mud-slinging, roorback, scandal-mongering

slander *vb* *syn* see MALIGN
rel assail, attack; damage, hurt, injure; blackwash, muckrake; belie, strumpet
idiom dish the dirt, run a smear campaign, sling the mud
ant panegyrize

slanderous *adj* *syn* see LIBELOUS
rel blackwashing, muckraking, scandal-mongering
ant panegyrical

slang *n* *syn* see DIALECT 2
rel slanginess, slanguage

slangism *n* *syn* see BARBARISM

slant *adv* *syn* see ASIDE 1

slant *vb* **1** to set or be set at an angle <*slanted* the ladder against the wall>
syn cant, heel, incline, lean, list, recline, slope, tilt, tip
rel bank, decline, descend; bend, deviate, diverge, splay, swerve, veer
2 to direct (written or spoken material) to the interests of a particular audience or group <a magazine *slanted* to farm families>
syn aim, angle
rel direct, orient, point, train; concentrate, focus; spoon-feed; bias, skew, warp
3 to orient (material) from objective presentation so as to favor a particular bias <accused the media of *slanting* the news against the president>
syn angle, bias, skew; *compare* PREJUDICE 2
rel influence, prejudice; color, distort, twist, warp
ant objectify, objectivize

slant *n* **1** *syn* see SLOPE
2 *syn* see VIEWPOINT 2
rel predilection, predisposition, prejudice

slanted *adj* *syn* see DIAGONAL

slanting *adj* *syn* see DIAGONAL

slantingly *adv* *syn* see ASIDE 1

slantingways *adv* **1** *syn* see ASIDE 1
2 *syn* see DIAGONALLY

slantly *adv* *syn* see ASIDE 1

slantways *adv* **1** *syn* see ASIDE 1
2 *syn* see DIAGONALLY

slantwise *adv* **1** *syn* see ASIDE 1
2 *syn* see DIAGONALLY

slap *n* **1** *syn* see CUFF
2 *syn* see AFFRONT
3 *syn* see FLING 1

slap *vb* **1** to strike quickly and sharply with the hand <*slapped* the hysterical girl>
syn blip, box, buffet, cuff, smack, spank, ‖wherret; *compare* STRIKE 2

rel ‖biff, ding, hit, sock, swat, whack; ‖wap, wham; bash
2 *syn* see LAMBASTE 3

‖**slap** *adv* *syn* see WELL 3

slap around *vb* *syn* see MANHANDLE

slapdash *adj* **1** *syn* see RANDOM
2 *syn* see SLIPSHOD 3

‖**slap–up** *adj* *syn* see EXCELLENT

slash *vb* **1** *syn* see CUT 1
2 *syn* see HACK
3 *syn* see LAMBASTE 3
idiom ‖light into
4 *syn* see REDUCE 2
5 *syn* see SHORTEN

slate *n* *syn* see TICKET 3

‖**slate** *vb* *syn* see LAMBASTE 3

slather *n, often* **slathers** *pl* *syn* see SCAD

slattern *n* **1** an untidy slovenly woman <two blowsy *slatterns* gossiping at the bar>
syn dowd, dowdy, drab, draggle-tail, ‖malkin, slut, ‖streel, traipse
rel frump; slob, ‖slommack, sloven; crone, gammer, hag, witch
2 *syn* see WANTON
rel prostitute, whore

slattern *adj* *syn* see SLATTERNLY

slatternly *adj* being habitually untidy and very dirty especially in dress or appearance <a filthy, *slatternly* old woman>
syn blowsy, dowdy, draggletailed, frowsy, slattern, sordid; *compare* SLOVENLY 1
rel careless, disordered, neglected, poky; bedraggled, disheveled, draggled, draggly, messy, mussy, slipshod, sloppy, slovenly, unkempt, untidy; dirty, filthy, foul, grimy, squalid
con clean, fresh, neat, tidy, trim; smart; immaculate, spotless
ant bandbox

slaughter *n* *syn* see MASSACRE
rel slaughtery; annihilation, destruction

slaughter *vb* **1** to kill (animals) for food <*slaughtered* a steer for the winter>
syn butcher, slay
rel stick
2 to kill (a person) in an especially bloody or barbarous manner <Jack the Ripper *slaughtered* his victims with a knife>
syn butcher, slay
rel kill, murder; ‖total, ‖waste; maim, mangle, mutilate, torture
3 to kill (people) in large numbers <millions *slaughtered* in death camps>
syn annihilate, decimate, exterminate, massacre, wipe (out)

‖**slaunchways** *adv* **1** *syn* see DIAGONALLY
2 *syn* see ASIDE 1

slave *n* **1** a person held in servitude or bondage <plantations worked by *slaves*>
syn bondman, bondslave, bondsman, chattel, mancipium
rel help, menial, retainer, servant; helot, serf, thrall, vassal
con freedman, freedwoman; ‖deditician
ant freeman
2 one who works at a hard, monotonous, usually menial task <*slaves* working all night for minimum wage>
syn ‖dogsbody, dray horse, drudge, galley slave, peon, slavey, toiler, workhorse

---

syn synonym(s)   *rel* related word(s)
ant antonym(s)   *con* contrasted word(s)
idiom idiomatic equivalent(s)
‖ use limited; if in doubt, see a dictionary

rel ‖coolie

slave *vb syn* see DRUDGE
idiom work like a slave

slave driver *n* a person in authority who exacts extreme effort from his subordinates <the chief proofreader was a real *slave driver*>
syn rawhider, Simon Legree, taskmaster
rel martinet
idiom a hard taskmaster

slaver *vb* **1** *syn* see DROOL 2
2 *syn* see FAWN

slaver *n syn* see SALIVA

slavery *n* **1** *syn* see WORK 2
2 *syn* see BONDAGE
idiom involuntary servitude, the yoke (*or* chains) of slavery

slavey *n* **1** *syn* see SLAVE 2
2 *syn* see HACK 2

slavish *adj* **1** *syn* see HARD 6
2 *syn* see SUBSERVIENT
rel spineless, subdued, tame; miserable, wretched
ant independent
3 copying obsequiously something superior <the painting was a *slavish* copy of an old master>
syn apish, emulative, imitative
rel uninspired; unoriginal
con fresh, new, novel, original; fanciful, imaginative, ingenious, inspired; extravagant, high-flown

slay *vb* **1** *syn* see KILL 1
2 *syn* see MURDER 1
3 *syn* see SLAUGHTER 2
4 *syn* see SLAUGHTER 1

slayer *n syn* see MURDERER

sleazy *adj* **1** *syn* see LIMP 1
rel slight, tenuous, thin; gossamery
2 *syn* see CHEAP 2
3 *syn* see SHABBY 1

sleek *vb syn* see POLISH 2

sleek *adj* having a very smooth or lustrous surface or texture <the car's *sleek* new paint job>
syn glassy, glossy, polished, ‖sleekit, sleeky, smarmy
rel smooth; glistening, lustrous

‖**sleekit** *adj syn* see SLEEK

sleeky *adj syn* see SLEEK

sleep *n* **1** the natural periodic suspension of consciousness during which the powers of the body are restored <needed eight hours of *sleep* to function efficiently>
syn ‖doss, ‖shut-eye, slumber; *compare* DOZE, NAP
rel repose, rest; slumberland
idiom the land of Nod, the arms of Morpheus
con wakefulness
2 *syn* see LETHARGY 1
3 *syn* see DEATH 1

sleep *vb* to rest in a state of sleep <*slept* for over eight hours>
syn ‖doss, slumber; *compare* DOZE, NAP
rel relax, repose, rest; oversleep, sleep in
idiom be in the land of Nod, be sunk in sleep, pound one's ear, rest in the arms of Morpheus, sleep like a top (*or* log)
con arouse, awaken, wake (up)

sleeplessness *n syn* see INSOMNIA

sleepy *adj* **1** having an inclination for or affected by sleep <was *sleepy* after the long day>
syn dozy, drowsy, nodding, ‖peepy, ‖sloomy, slumberous, slumbery, snoozy, somnolent, soporific
rel heavy, heavy-eyed, lethargic, sluggish, torpid; dazed, dopey, listless, oscitant, yawning; asleep, sleeping, slumbering; nepenthean, poppied, ‖comatose, ‖out
con awake, conscious; restless, sleepless, unsleeping; alert, wide-awake
ant wakeful
2 *syn* see INACTIVE
3 *syn* see SOPORIFIC 1

‖**sleer** *vb syn* see SNEER 1

sleight *n* **1** *syn* see ADDRESS 1
2 *syn* see TRICK 1

‖**sleighty** *adj syn* see CLEVER 4

slender *adj* **1** *syn* see THIN 1
rel slenderish, slimmish; lithe, svelte, trim
idiom slender as a reed
2 *syn* see SHORT 3
3 *syn* see REMOTE 4

slenderize *vb syn* see REDUCE 5

sleuth *n syn* see DETECTIVE

slew *n syn* see SCAD

slewed *adj syn* see INTOXICATED 1

slice *n syn* see SHARE 1
rel segment
idiom a slice of the pie (*or* melon)

slice *vb* **1** *syn* see CUT 1
2 *syn* see CUT 5

slick *vb* **1** *syn* see POLISH 2
2 *syn* see DRESS UP 1
3 *syn* see SLIDE 1

slick *adj* **1** having a glassy surface that often offers insecure footing <a floor *slick* with wax>
syn greasy, lubricious, ‖sliddery, ‖slipper, slippery, slippy, slithery
rel oily; ‖slape, smooth; soapy
idiom slick as a greased pig
con coarse, gritty, rough, uneven
2 *syn* see FULSOME
rel glossy; slippery
3 *syn* see WISE 4

slicker *n syn* see SWINDLER

‖**slidder** *vb* **1** *syn* see SLIDE 3
2 *syn* see SLITHER 2

‖**sliddery** *adj syn* see SLICK 1

slide *vb* **1** to go or progress with a smooth continuous motion <goldfish *slid* across the pool>
syn glide, glissade, slick, slip, slither
rel flow, stream
2 *syn* see SLIP 6
3 to fall or nearly fall because of loss of balance or footing <stumbled and *slid* on the ice>
syn skid, ‖slidder, slip, ‖slur
idiom take a slide (*or* a skid)
4 to shift or be shifted out of place or away from one's grasp <the packages *slid* from her arms>
syn slip
rel shift; move; fall, spill, tumble
5 *syn* see CREEP 1
6 to take a natural course <preferred to let the matter *slide* for a while>

syn coast, drift
rel glide
idiom run its course
7 *syn* see STEAL 3
8 *syn* see SNEAK
slide *n syn* see DECLINE 3
slight *adj* 1 *syn* see THIN 1
rel slightish, ‖slighty; smallish; pint-sized
2 *syn* see DELICATE 5
rel gossamery, sleazy
3 *syn* see REMOTE 4
slight *vb syn* see NEGLECT
rel skip; contemn, despise; flout, scoff
slightest *adj syn* see FIRST 4
rel ‖fat, negligible
slighting *adj syn* see DEROGATORY
slim *adj* 1 *syn* see THIN 1
rel lissome, lithe, lithesome, svelte
ant chubby
2 *syn* see CLEVER 4
3 *syn* see REMOTE 4
slim (down) *vb syn* see REDUCE 5
slime *n* a viscous and usually dirty or offensive substance <a layer of *slime* formed in
the bottom of the pool>
syn muck, ‖slab, slum
rel ooze, ‖sleech, sludge; scum
sling *vb* 1 *syn* see THROW 1
rel catapult; sock
2 *syn* see STRIDE 1
sling *vb syn* see HANG 1
slink *vb syn* see SNEAK
slink *n syn* see SNEAK
slinker *n syn* see SLACKER
slip *vb* 1 *syn* see SLIDE 1
2 *syn* see SNEAK
3 *syn* see STEAL 3
4 *syn* see SLIDE 4
5 *syn* see SLIDE 3
6 to decline gradually from a standard or
accustomed level <sales in some lines
slipped>
syn drop (off), fall (off *or* away), sag, slide,
slump
rel erode, soften; decline, go down, sink;
dip, drop; nose-dive, plummet, topple; crash
con better, gain, improve, rally, rebound;
ascend, climb, rise; skyrocket, soar
7 *syn* see SHAKE 1
8 *syn* see SHED 2
slip (on) *vb syn* see DON 1
ant slip (off)
slip *n* 1 *syn* see WHARF
2 *syn* see ESCAPE 1
3 *syn* see ERROR 2
4 *syn* see DECLINE 3
‖**slipper** *adj syn* see SLICK 1
slippery *adj* 1 *syn* see SLICK 1
2 *syn* see MUTABLE 2
slippy *adj syn* see SLICK 1
slipshod *adj* 1 *syn* see SHABBY 1
2 *syn* see SLOVENLY 1
3 marked by indifference to exactness, precision, and accuracy <a *slipshod* piece of re-
search>

syn synonym(s)   *rel* related word(s)
ant antonym(s)   *con* contrasted word(s)
idiom idiomatic equivalent(s)
‖ use limited; if in doubt, see a dictionary

syn botchy, careless, messy, slapdash,
sloppy, slovenly, unthorough, untidy
rel neglected, negligent; haphazard, slap-
happy, unmeticulous; botched-up, fouled=
up, messed-up, ‖screwed-up; faulty, imperfect, inaccurate, inexact
con fastidious, meticulous, neat; accurate,
exact, precise; methodical, orderly, systematic; thorough
slipslop *n syn* see NONSENSE 2
slipup *n syn* see ERROR 2
slit *vb syn* see CUT 1
slither *vb* 1 *syn* see SLIDE 1
rel ‖sluther
2 to walk or move in a sinuous way <the
trout *slithered* among the smooth rocks>
syn ‖slidder, snake, undulate
rel creep, glide, sidle, steal; lurk, prowl,
slink, sneak
slithery *adj syn* see SLICK 1
‖**slive** *vb syn* see SIDLE
sliver *vb* to cut into very thin slices <*slivered*
cheese>
syn shave, shred
rel carve, haggle, slice
con chop, dice, mince; comminute, powder,
pulverize; crush, mash
slobber *vb syn* see DROOL 2
slobbering *adj syn* see EFFUSIVE
slobbery *adj* 1 *syn* see EFFUSIVE
2 *syn* see SLOVENLY 1
slog *vb* 1 *syn* see STRIKE 2
2 *syn* see PLOD 1
3 *syn* see DRUDGE
slogan *n syn* see CATCHWORD
rel expression, idiom, locution
slogging *n syn* see WORK 2
‖**slommacky** *adj syn* see SLOVENLY 1
sloom *n syn* see DOZE
‖**sloom** *n syn* see DOZE
‖**sloomy** *adj syn* see SLEEPY 1
slop *n syn* see PAP 2
slop *vb* 1 *syn* see SPILL 1
2 *syn* see SPLASH
3 *syn* see GULP
4 *syn* see PLOD 1
slope *vb syn* see SLANT 1
slope *n* a natural or artificial inclined surface
<the steep *slope* of the hill>
syn grade, gradient, inclination, incline,
lean, leaning, slant, tilt
rel acclivity, ascent, rise; declivity, descent;
deflection, deviation, obliqueness, obliquity;
pitch, swag, sway, tip; bend, skew
con champaign, flat, flatland, mesa,
plain(s), plateau, tableland
ant level
sloped *adj syn* see INCLINED 3
slopeways *adv syn* see ASIDE 1
sloping *adj syn* see INCLINED 3
slopped *adj syn* see INTOXICATED 1
sloppy *adj* 1 *syn* see SLIPSHOD 3
rel amateurish; mediocre; awkward,
clumsy; poor
ant exact, precise
2 *syn* see SLOVENLY 1
3 *syn* see EFFUSIVE
rel soft; oversentimental
4 *syn* see INTOXICATED 1
slosh *n syn* see BLOW 1

slosh *vb* **1** *of a liquid* to move with a gentle lapping motion or sound <heard water *sloshing* in the bottom of the boat>
syn bubble, burble, gurgle, lap, swash, wash
rel babble; ripple; dash, plash, splash, tumble; bespatter, spatter; churn, whirl; gush, rush; roar
2 *syn* see SPLASH
3 *syn* see GULP
‖**4** *syn* see STRIKE 2
sloth *n* **1** disinclination to action or labor <a hot summer day is likely to induce *sloth* in all of us>
syn idleness, indolence, laze, laziness, slothfulness, slouch, sluggishness
rel ergophobia, faineancy, idling, lazing, loafing; apathy, heaviness, languidness, languor, lassitude, lethargy, listlessness, torpidity; shiftlessness
con assiduity, assiduousness, busyness, diligence, sedulity, sedulousness
ant industriousness, industry
2 sluggishness and apathy in the practice of virtue <the deadly sin of *sloth*>
syn acedia
rel heedlessness, inattention, inattentiveness
con assiduity
slothful *adj syn* see LAZY
con assiduous, busy, diligent, sedulous
ant industrious
slothfulness *n syn* see SLOTH 1
slouch *n* **1** *syn* see OAF 2
2 *syn* see SLUGGARD
3 *syn* see SLOTH 1
slouch *vb* to assume, have, or move with an awkwardly drooping posture, carriage, or gait <three drunks *slouched* across the room>
syn droop, loll, ‖lollop, lop, slump, trollop
rel loaf, lounge, saunter, shamble, shuffle; bend, lean, stoop; sag, wilt
con erect, straighten (up); sit up, stand up
slough *n* **1** *syn* see SWAMP
2 *syn* see INLET
‖**slough** *n syn* see HULL
slough *vb* **1** *syn* see SHED 2
2 *syn* see DISCARD
idiom ‖get shut (or shed) of
slough over *vb syn* see NEGLECT
sloven *adj syn* see SLOVENLY 1
slovenly *adj* **1** negligent of or marked by lack of neatness and order especially in appearance or dress <*slovenly* attire>
syn careless, disheveled, ill-kempt, messy, mussy, raunchy, slipshod, slobbery, ‖slommacky, sloppy, sloven, uncombed, unfastidious, unkempt, unneat, untidy; *compare* SLATTERNLY
rel down-at-heel, shabby, sleazy, sluttish, slutty; blowsy, dowdy, frowsy, frumpish
con fastidious, neat, tidy, trim; combed, groomed, well-groomed; immaculate
ant neat
2 *syn* see SLIPSHOD 3
slow *adj* **1** *syn* see RETARDED
rel limited; ‖dunch
2 moving, flowing, or proceeding at less than the usual, desirable, or required speed <a *slow* advance toward mutual understanding>

syn deliberate, dilatory, laggard, leisurely, unhasty, unhurried
rel measured, slowish, steady; unhasting, unhurrying; slow-footed, slow-going, slow≠paced; plodding, poky, rusty; dragging, flagging, halting, lagging, straggling; dawdling, delaying, postponing, procrastinating; leaden, sluggish; crawling, snaillike, snail-paced, ultra-slow
idiom as slow as a swamp turtle, as slow as molasses in January
con blitz, lightning, quick, rapid, swift; fast≠going, fast-moving, fast-paced, rapid-paced
ant fast
3 marked by reduced economic activity (as in sales or patronage) <trading was *slow* on the commodity exchange today>
syn down, off, slack, sluggish
rel moderate; reduced; low; inactive, stagnant
con active; up; heavy
slow (up *or* down) *vb syn* see DELAY 1
rel moderate, qualify, temper; abate, decrease, lessen, reduce
ant speed
slow coach *n syn* see LAGGARD
slowdown *n* **1** a slowing or gradual decrease in activity <a *slowdown* in car sales this quarter>
syn slack, slackening, slow-up
rel decline, downtrend, downturn; drop, drop-off, falloff, inactivity, stagnation; freeze
con increase, rise, upswing, upturn; acceleration, quickening
ant speedup
2 a deliberate slowing down by workers in the rate and quantity of production <air traffic snarled by a controllers' *slowdown*>
syn ‖ca' canny
rel action; protest; slow-up; sit-down; strike, walkout; stoppage
ant speedup
slowgoing *adj syn* see LAZY
slowpoke *n syn* see LAGGARD
slow-up *n syn* see SLOWDOWN 1
slow-witted *adj syn* see RETARDED
ant quick-witted
‖**slubberdegullion** *n syn* see VILLAIN 1
slue *vb syn* see SWERVE 1
slug *n syn* see SLUGGARD
rel slacker, sloven
slug *n syn* see DRAM
slug *vb syn* see SLAM 1
slugabed *n syn* see SLUGGARD
sluggard *n* an habitually lazy, shiftless, and inactive person <a *sluggard* who wanted to sleep all day>
syn bum, dolittle, do-nothing, faineant, idler, lazybones, loafer, slouch, slug, slugabed
rel lie-abed, sleepyhead; dawdler, laggard, slow coach, slowpoke; goldbrick, shirker
idiom ‖his idleship, ‖Weary Willie
con go-getter, hustler, live wire
ant dynamo
sluggish *adj* **1** *syn* see LETHARGIC
rel dragging, draggy, leaden, lumpish; costive, stiff; apathetic, stupefied
con go-getting, hustling, vigorous; expeditious

ant brisk
2 syn see SLOW 3
sluggishness *n syn* see SLOTH 1
sluice *vb syn* see POUR 2
rel flush, wash; douse, drench, soak
slum *n* a densely populated usually urban area marked by run-down housing, poverty, and social disorganization <a *slum* full of vagrants, junkies, pimps, and pushers>
syn stew
rel slumdom, slumland; tobacco road; tenderloin; skid row; ghetto; hive, kennel, rookery, warren
idiom desolation row, the wrong side of the tracks
slum *n syn* see SLIME
slumber *vb* **1** *syn* see DOZE
2 syn see SLEEP
slumber *n* **1** *syn* see SLEEP 1
2 syn see DOZE
3 syn see LETHARGY 1
slumberous *adj* **1** *syn* see SLEEPY 1
2 syn see SOPORIFIC 1
3 syn see LETHARGIC
slumbery *adj syn* see SLEEPY 1
slump *vb* **1** *syn* see FALL 2
rel droop, flag, sag
idiom come down like a rock (*or* a ton of bricks)
2 syn see SLOUCH
rel cave in, collapse
3 syn see SLIP 6
slump *n* **1** *syn* see DECLINE 3
2 syn see DEPRESSION 3
slup *vb syn* see SLURP
‖**slur** *vb syn* see SLIDE 3
slur *vb syn* see MALIGN
slur (over) *vb syn* see NEGLECT
slur *n* **1** *syn* see ANIMADVERSION
2 syn see STIGMA
slurp *vb* to eat or drink noisily <*slurping* soup with a large spoon>
syn slup
rel guzzle, lap (up), slosh, swill; suck; wolf (down); smack
con nibble, pick (at); sip
slushy *adj syn* see SENTIMENTAL
slut *n* **1** *syn* see SLATTERN 1
2 syn see WANTON
3 syn see MINX
sly *adj* **1** *syn* see CLEVER 4
rel smart; cagey; masterful
2 attaining or seeking to attain one's ends by devious means <a *sly* way of upping sales>
syn artful, astute, crafty, cunning, deep, ‖downy, foxy, guileful, insidious, subdolous, subtle, tricky, vulpine, wily; *compare* UNDERHAND
rel disingenuous, unfrank; calculating, designing, Machiavellian; scheming; cagey, devious, shady, shifty, ‖slanter, slick, slippery, smooth; clandestine, covert, furtive, stealthy; underhand, underhanded, unscrupulous; predatory; crooked, dishonest
idiom crazy like a fox, cunning as a fox (*or* serpent), sly as a fox

con candid, forthright, frank, honest, open, sincere, straightforward
sly *vb syn* see SNEAK
slyboots *n pl but sing in constr syn* see SCAMP
slyness *n syn* see CUNNING 2
smack *n* **1** *syn* see TASTE 3
2 syn see HINT 2
smack *vb* to have a trace, vestige, or suggestion of something <that plan *smacks* of radicalism>
syn savor, smell
rel resemble, suggest; reek, stink
smack *vb* **1** *syn* see KISS 1
idiom ‖plant a juicy kiss on
2 syn see SLAP 1
smack *n* **1** *syn* see CUFF
2 syn see BLOW 1
‖**smack–dab** *adv syn* see JUST 1
‖**smacker** *n syn* see DOLLAR
‖**smackeroo** *n syn* see DOLLAR
small *adj* **1** being the opposite of large <a *small* white house>
syn bantam, little, monkey, petite, smallish; *compare* TINY
rel cramped, limited, narrow, two-by-four; puny, undersized; paltry, petty, piddling, trivial
con big, great; considerable, sizable; enormous, huge, immense, vast
ant large
2 syn see MINOR 2
3 syn see LITTLE 2
4 syn see LITTLE 3
5 syn see PETTY 2
6 syn see REMOTE 4
small beer *n syn* see TRIVIA
small–beer *adj syn* see LITTLE 3
small change *n syn* see TRIVIA
smallest *adj syn* see FIRST 4
small–fry *adj syn* see MINOR 2
smallish *adj syn* see SMALL 1
ant largish
small–minded *adj syn* see ILLIBERAL
ant large-minded
small potato *n, usu* **small potatoes** *pl but sing or pl in constr syn* see TRIVIA
small talk *n* light or casual conversation <had to make *small talk* at the cocktail party>
syn bavardage, by-talk, chitchat, chitter= chatter, trifling
rel badinage, banter, repartee; babble, babbling, bibble-babble, chatter, prattle, prattling, prittle-prattle
small–time *adj syn* see MINOR 2
ant big-time
small–town *adj syn* see INSULAR
‖**smarm** *vb syn* see SMEAR 1
smarmy *adj* **1** *syn* see SLEEK
2 syn see FULSOME
smart *vb syn* see HURT 4
smart *vb* to cause or produce a sharp stinging and usually localized pain <gave him a slap that was hard enough to *smart*>
syn bite, burn, ‖stang, sting; *compare* HURT 4
rel prick; tingle; hurt
smart *adj* **1** *syn* see INTELLIGENT 2
ant stupid

---

syn synonym(s)   *rel* related word(s)
ant antonym(s)   *con* contrasted word(s)
idiom idiomatic equivalent(s)
‖ use limited; if in doubt, see a dictionary

2 *syn* see WISE 4
idiom knowing the score, on the ball
ant dull, dumb
3 *syn* see CLEVER 5
rel pert, saucy
4 *syn* see WISE 5
5 *syn* see STYLISH
rel dapper, ‖dinky, spruce
ant dowdy
‖**6** *syn* see CONSIDERABLE 2

smart aleck *n* an obnoxiously conceited and self-assertive person with pretensions to smartness or cleverness <was heckled by a *smart aleck* in the back row>
syn know-it-all, smarty, smarty-pants, wiseacre, wisecracker, wise guy, wisehead, wisenheimer
rel blowhard, boaster, braggadocio, braggart, gasbag, windbag; exhibitionist, grandstander, show-off
idiom hot-air artist

smart-alecky *adj syn* see WISE 5

smarten (up) *vb syn* see DRESS UP 1

smart set *n* ultrafashionable often international society <the *smart set* that suns in Cannes and skis in St. Moritz>
syn beautiful people, jet set, ton
rel aristocracy, aristoi, blue bloods, bon ton, elite, Four Hundred, society, upper crust, who's who

smarty *n syn* see SMART ALECK

smarty-pants *n pl but sing in constr syn* see SMART ALECK

smash *vb* **1** *syn* see SHATTER 1
2 *syn* see SLAM 1
3 *syn* see DESTROY 1

smash *n* **1** *syn* see BLOW 1
2 *syn* see BANG 2
3 *syn* see IMPACT 1
4 *syn* see CRASH 3
5 *syn* see COLLAPSE 2
6 a striking success <the new musical was a box-office *smash*>
syn bang, bell ringer, hit, succès fou, ten= strike, wow
rel sensation; knockout
idiom howling (or roaring) success, smash hit
con disaster, dud, failure
ant flop

‖**smash** *n syn* see MONEY

‖**smashed** *adj syn* see INTOXICATED 1

smashup *n* **1** *syn* see COLLAPSE 2
2 *syn* see CRASH 3

smatch *n* **1** *syn* see HINT 2
2 *syn* see FEW

smatter *vb* ‖**1** *syn* see SHATTER 1
2 *syn* see CHAT 1

smatterer *n syn* see FEW

smatterer *n syn* see AMATEUR 2

smattering *n syn* see FEW

smaze *n syn* see HAZE 1

smear *vb* **1** to overspread with something unctuous, viscous, or adhesive <*smeared* the crack with wet concrete>
syn bedaub, besmear, dab, daub, plaster, ‖smarm, smudge
rel rub; coat, cover, overlay, overspread, spread; smirch, soil
2 *syn* see TAINT 1

3 *syn* see MALIGN
idiom use smear tactics (on *or* against)
4 *syn* see WHIP 2
rel foil, frustrate; repulse
idiom mop up the floor (or earth) with

smell *vb* **1** to perceive by means of the olfactory organs <*smelled* a dead skunk>
syn nose, scent, sniff, ‖snift, snuff
rel detect, perceive, sense; whiff; ‖snaffle, snuffle
idiom get a whiff of
2 *syn* see SMACK
3 to have or emit an offensive odor <the canal *smells* today>
syn funk, reek, stench, stink
idiom offend the nostrils, smell (or stink) to high heaven

smell *n* **1** a quality that makes a thing perceptible to the olfactory sense <the *smell* of a ham cooking>
syn aroma, odor, scent
rel bouquet, fragrance, incense, perfume, redolence, spice; flavor, savor, stench, stink
2 *syn* see HINT 2

smeller *n syn* see NOSE 1

‖**smellful** *adj syn* see MALODOROUS 1
ant odorless, smell-less

smellfungus *n syn* see CRITIC

smell-less *adj syn* see ODORLESS
ant ‖smellful, smelly

smelly *adj syn* see MALODOROUS 1
con odorless, scentless, smell-less; fragrant, fresh, sweet

smidgen *n syn* see PARTICLE

smile *vb* to express amusement, satisfaction, or pleasure by brightening one's eyes and curving the corners of one's mouth upward <*smiled* as she greeted him>
syn beam, grin
rel simper, smirk
idiom break into a smile, crack a smile
con grimace; glare, glower, lower, scowl
ant frown

smirch *vb syn* see SOIL 2
rel discolor; smear

smirk *vb* to smile in an affected manner <*smirking* children imitating their teacher>
syn simper, ‖smirkle; *compare* SNEER 1
rel grin, smile; fleer, leer, sneer

‖**smirkle** *vb syn* see SMIRK

smitch *n syn* see PARTICLE

smite *vb* **1** *syn* see STRIKE 2
rel bat, belt, clobber; dash
idiom smite a blow
2 *syn* see AFFLICT

smithereens *n pl* very small particles or fragments <a house blown to *smithereens* by a bomb>
syn ‖shivereens, smithers
rel fragments, particles, pieces

smithers *n pl syn* see SMITHEREENS

smitten *adj syn* see ENAMORED 1
idiom bitten by the love bug

smoke *n syn* see CIGARETTE

smoke *vb syn* see HURRY 2

smolder *vb syn* see SEETHE 4
rel burst, erupt, explode; fulminate

smooch *vb syn* see SOIL 2

smooch *vb syn* see KISS 1
idiom ‖plant a smooch on

‖**smoodge** *vb syn* see KISS 1

smooth *adj* **1** *syn* see LEVEL
rel glossy, sleek, slick; rippleless, unbroken, unwrinkled
con harsh, rugged, scabrous, uneven
ant rough
2 *syn* see HAIRLESS
3 *syn* see EASY 9
4 *syn* see EASY 1
rel smooth-running
idiom smooth and easy
ant labored
5 *syn* see SUAVE
rel courteous, courtly, polite; smooth-faced, smooth-tongued
con bluff, blunt, brusque, crusty, curt, gruff, harsh
6 *syn* see GENTLE 1
rel agreeable, soothing

smooth *vb* **1** *syn* see EVEN 1
con corrugate; roughen; wrinkle
ant unsmooth
2 *syn* see POLISH 2

smooth *adv syn* see EVENLY 3

smoothen *vb syn* see EVEN 1

smoothly *adv* **1** *syn* see EVENLY 3
con unevenly, ununiformly
ant roughly
2 *syn* see EASILY 1
ant unsmoothly

smooth–spoken *adj syn* see VOCAL 3
ant rough-spoken

smorgasbord *n syn* see MISCELLANY 1

smother *vb* **1** *syn* see SUFFOCATE
2 *syn* see COMPOSE 4
rel hush up, muffle; cork; quash, quell, squelch; quench
3 *syn* see WHIP 2

smothering *adj syn* see STIFLING 1

smothering *n syn* see REPRESSION 1

smothery *adj syn* see STIFLING 1

‖**smouch** *vb syn* see KISS 1

smouch *vb syn* see STEAL 1

smudge *vb* **1** *syn* see SOIL 2
rel smear; blotch, splotch
2 *syn* see SMEAR 1
3 *syn* see TAINT 1

‖**smudgy** *adj syn* see STIFLING 1

smug *adj syn* see COMPLACENT
idiom pleased with oneself

smug *vb syn* see DRESS UP 1

smuggle *vb* to import or export secretly and in violation of the law <*smuggling* weapons into the country>
syn bootleg, contraband, run
idiom run contraband

smut *vb* **1** *syn* see STAIN 1
2 *syn* see TAINT 1

smutch *vb* **1** *syn* see SOIL 2
2 *syn* see TAINT 1

smutty *adj syn* see OBSCENE 2

snack *n* food served or taken informally and usually in small amounts and typically under other circumstances than a regular meal <a milk-and-cookie *snack* after school>

syn ‖bait, ‖bever, bite, ‖chack, morsel, mug≠up, nosh, ‖piece, tapa
rel collation, refreshment, tea
idiom bite to eat

snack bar (*or* **counter**) *n syn* see EATING HOUSE

‖**snaffle** *vb syn* see STEAL 1

‖**snafu** *vb syn* see CONFUSE 5

snag *n syn* see OBSTACLE
rel brake, clog, curb, drag; hold-up
idiom ‖snags and sawyers

snake *n syn* see SNOT 1

snake *vb* ‖**1** *syn* see STEAL 1
2 *syn* see CREEP 1
3 *syn* see SLITHER 2
‖**4** *syn* see SNEAK

snaky *adj syn* see WINDING

snap *vb* **1** to speak in a curt biting tone <*snapped* at his subordinates for inefficiency>
syn bark, snarl
rel growl, grumble, grunt, snort; roar, yell
idiom bite one's head off, snap off one's head (*or* nose)
2 *syn* see JERK
rel clutch, grab, grasp, seize, snaffle, snatch

snap *n* **1** something easily managed or accomplished <that exam was a *snap*>
syn breeze, child's play, cinch, duck soup, kid stuff, picnic, pie, ‖pipe, pushover, setup, ‖snip, soft touch
rel sinecure
idiom a simple twist of the wrist, simplicity itself, soft snap
con difficulty, headache, problem, trouble; bother, inconvenience, pain
ant chore
2 *syn* see PARTICLE
3 *syn* see MAN 3
4 *syn* see VIGOR 2

snap back *vb syn* see RECOVER 3

‖**snapper** *vb syn* see STUMBLE 3

snapping *adv syn* see VERY 1

snappish *adj syn* see IRRITABLE
rel curt, short, ungracious; crabbed, morose, surly

snappy *adj* **1** *syn* see IRRITABLE
2 *syn* see FAST 3
3 *syn* see PUNGENT
rel animated, lively, vivacious; prompt, quick, ready
4 *syn* see STYLISH

snare *n syn* see LURE 2
rel chicane, chicanery, deception; ensnarement, entrapment

snare *vb syn* see CATCH 3
rel seduce, tempt; involve; embrangle, enmesh, ensnarl, trammel

‖**snark** *vb syn* see SNORE

snarl *n* **1** *syn* see CONFUSION 3
rel entanglement, tangle; complexity, complication, intricacy, intricateness; labyrinth, maze; mishmash, swarm; jam
idiom tangled skein, wheels within wheels
2 *syn* see MAZE 1

snarl *vb* **1** *syn* see ENTANGLE 1
2 *syn* see COMPLICATE

snarl *vb syn* see SNAP 1

snarl up *vb syn* see CONFUSE 5

snatch *vb* **1** *syn* see SEIZE 2

---

syn synonym(s)   *rel* related word(s)
ant antonym(s)   *con* contrasted word(s)
idiom idiomatic equivalent(s)
‖ use limited; if in doubt, see a dictionary

rel jerk, wrench, yank; nip (up), whip (up)
‖**2** *syn* see KIDNAP

sneak *vb* to move or go stealthily and furtively <*sneaked* into the garage and stole the car>
  syn creep, glide, gumshoe, lurk, ‖meech, pussyfoot, shirk, skulk, slide, slink, slip, sly, ‖snake, ‖snook, steal; *compare* STEAL 3
  rel crawl, slither, worm; prowl
  idiom go on (little) cat's feet, move under cover
  con barge, strut, swagger; clump, stamp, stump; stride; march, parade

sneak *n* a person who behaves in a stealthy, furtive, or shifty manner <found out that he was a liar, a cheat, and a *sneak*>
  syn slink, sneaker, sneaksby, weasel
  rel blackguard, knave, scoundrel; cur, heel, louse, reptile, skunk, snake; toad
  idiom Jerry Sneak

sneak *adj syn* see SECRET 1
sneaker *n syn* see SNEAK
sneaking *adj syn* see UNDERHAND
  ant forthright
sneaksby *n syn* see SNEAK
sneaky *adj syn* see UNDERHAND
‖**sneap** *vb syn* see REPROVE

sneer *vb* **1** to smile with attendant facial contortions expressing scorn or contempt <*sneered* haughtily at the beggar>
  syn fleer, leer, ‖sleer; *compare* SMIRK
  rel grin, smile
  idiom curl one's lip, make a scornful (*or* mocking) face
  2 *syn* see SCOFF
  rel belittle, detract, disparage, underrate
  idiom cock a snook at, give the Bronx cheer to, give the raspberry, sneeze at, thumb one's nose at

‖**sneezer** *n syn* see NOSE 1
snicker *vb syn* see LAUGH
  idiom have a case of the snickers
snide *adj* **1** *syn* see COUNTERFEIT
  2 *syn* see CROOKED 2
sniff *vb syn* see SMELL 1
‖**snift** *vb syn* see SMELL 1
  rel ‖snifter
snifter *n syn* see DRAM
‖**sniggle** *vb syn* see LAUGH
snip *n* **1** *syn* see MINX
  ‖**2** *syn* see SNAP 1
snippety *adj syn* see BLUFF
  rel impolite, insolent, rude
snippy *adj syn* see BLUFF
snip–snap *n syn* see BANTER
snit *n* a state of agitation or excited irritation especially over a trivial matter <was in a *snit* because the bus was one minute late>
  syn fume, stew, sweat, swivet, tizzy
  rel huff, pique; conniption, fit, frenzy, seizure, taking; dither, flap, panic, ‖swither
snitch *vb syn* see INFORM 3
  2 *syn* see STEAL 1
snitch *n* ‖**1** *syn* see NOSE 1
  2 *syn* see INFORMER
snob *n* one inclined to rebuff or ignore people or things that he regards as inferior (as in culture or social status) <appeals to real lovers of music rather than musical *snobs*>
  syn high-hat, snoot, snot

rel name-dropper, snobling; bootlicker, hanger-on, lickspittle, sycophant, toady
snob *vb syn* see CUT 7
snobbish *adj* of, relating to, or characteristic of a snob <a *snobbish* group of jet-set sophisticates>
  syn ‖dicty, high-hat, potty, snobby, snooty
  rel aloof, remote; high-flown, pretentious, snotty, supercilious; haughty, hoity-toity, pompous, ritzy; condescending, patronizing; insecure, uncertain, unconfident, unself-confident, unsure
  con certain, confident, secure, self-confident
snobby *adj syn* see SNOBBISH
  rel snubbing, snubby
‖**snook** *vb* **1** *syn* see SNOOP
  2 *syn* see SNEAK
snoop *vb* to look, inquire, or search impertinently or intrusively <he knew he had no right to *snoop* into her private life>
  syn busybody, mouse, nose, ‖piroot, poke, pry, ‖snook
  rel peek, peep, peer, stare; interfere, intrude, meddle, mess
  idiom stick (*or* poke) one's nose into
snoop *n syn* see BUSYBODY
snoopy *adj syn* see CURIOUS 2
snoot *n* **1** *syn* see NOSE 1
  2 *syn* see SNOB
snooty *adj syn* see SNOBBISH
snooze *vb syn* see NAP
snooze *n syn* see NAP
‖**snoozle** *vb syn* see DOZE
snoozy *adj syn* see SLEEPY 1
snore *vb* to breathe during sleep with a rough hoarse noise due to vibration of the soft palate <driven to distraction by her sister's *snoring*>
  syn ‖snark
  rel wheeze; snuffle; snort, ‖snotter
  idiom ‖drive pigs to market, ‖saw logs (*or* wood)
snort *n syn* see DRAM
snorter *n syn* see DRAM
snot *n* **1** an utterly contemptible person <a despicable *snot* whom everyone shunned>
  syn ‖bugger, cur, dog, louse, ‖prick, puke, rat, scum, ‖scumbag, skunk, snake, sod, stinkard, stinkaroo, stinker, toad, wretch; *compare* VILLAIN 1
  rel ‖creep, ‖crumb, lowlife; knave, rogue, scoundrel, ‖skite; pig, reptile
  2 *syn* see SNOB
snout *n syn* see NOSE 1
snowball *vb syn* see INCREASE 2
snub *vb syn* see CUT 7
  rel high-hat, ‖ritz, swank; put down
  idiom look coldly upon, turn a cold shoulder (on *or* upon)
‖**snudge** *vb syn* see SNUGGLE
‖**snuff** *n syn* see OFFENSE 2
snuff *vb syn* see SMELL 1
‖**snuff** (out) *vb syn* see DIE 1
snug *adj* **1** *syn* see NEAT 2
  2 *syn* see COMFORTABLE 2
  idiom snug as a bug in a rug
  ‖**3** *syn* see PROSPEROUS 3
snug *vb syn* see SNUGGLE
snuggle *vb* to assume or be in a warm comfortable position usually near another per-

son or thing <a baby *snuggling* close to his mother>
syn burrow, ‖croodle, cuddle, nestle, nuzzle, ‖snudge, snug, ‖snuzzle
rel curl up; huddle; spoon
idiom snuggle up like a bug in a rug
con flinch, recoil, shrink

‖**snuzzle** vb *syn* see SNUGGLE

‖**sny** vb *syn* see TEEM

so *adv* 1 *syn* see ALSO 1
  2 *syn* see THUS 1
  3 *syn* see VERY 1
  4 *syn* see THEREFORE

so *conj* with the purpose that <repeated it aloud *so* there'd be no mistake>
syn as, so that
idiom in order that, to the end that, with the intent that

soak vb 1 to permeate or be permeated with or as if with water <*soak* a sponge with water> <rain *soaked* her to the skin>
syn drench, ‖drouk, impregnate, insteep, saturate, seethe, sodden, ‖sog, sop, souse, steep, waterlog; *compare* WET
rel dip, immerse, submerge; draw; infuse; infiltrate, penetrate, permeate, pervade; water-soak; drown
  2 *syn* see WET
  3 *syn* see ENGAGE 4
  4 *syn* see OVERCHARGE 1
  5 *syn* see DRINK 3
idiom ‖soak it up like a sponge

soak n 1 *syn* see DRUNKARD
  2 *syn* see BINGE 1

soaked adj *syn* see WET 1

soaker n *syn* see DRUNKARD

soaking adj *syn* see WET 1
idiom soaking wet

so-and-so adj *syn* see DAMNED 2

soapbox vb *syn* see ORATE

soapy adj *syn* see FULSOME

soar vb 1 *syn* see RISE 4
rel climb; shoot
  2 *syn* see SKYROCKET
ant plummet

soaring adj *syn* see LOFTY 6
idiom high as the sky

so as *conj* syn *syn* see SO

sob vb *syn* see CRY 2

sobby adj *syn* see SENTIMENTAL

sober adj 1 *syn* see ABSTEMIOUS
rel controlled, restrained; self-possessed
con indulgent, overindulgent; uncontrolled, unrestrained; immoderate, intemperate; excessive; profligate
  2 *syn* see SERIOUS 1
rel decorous, proper; calm, placid, serene, tranquil
con flippant, light, light-minded; unstable, volatile
ant unsober
  3 having or exhibiting self-control and avoiding extremes of behavior <his bearing was *sober*, his comments judicious>
syn moderate, temperate, unimpassioned; *compare* ABSTEMIOUS

---

syn synonym(s)   *rel* related word(s)
ant antonym(s)   *con* contrasted word(s)
idiom idiomatic equivalent(s)
‖ use limited; if in doubt, see a dictionary

rel rational, reasonable; calm, collected, composed, cool, imperturbable; constrained, disciplined, inhibited, reserved, restrained, self-controlled, self-disciplined; abstaining, forbearing, refraining; abnegating, eschewing, forgoing
con irrational, unreasonable; emotional, hotheaded, impassioned, overemotional, passionate; intemperate, uncontained, uncontrolled; excited; drunk, intoxicated; abandoned
ant unsober
  4 *syn* see SUBDUED 2
  5 *syn* see REALISTIC
rel sober-eyed, sober-minded

sobersided adj *syn* see SERIOUS 1

sobful adj *syn* see SENTIMENTAL

sobriety n *syn* see TEMPERANCE 1
rel gravity, sedateness, seriousness, soberness
con excitement; drunkenness, intoxication; abandonment
ant insobriety

sobriquet n *syn* see NICKNAME

so-called adj 1 *syn* see NOMINAL
  2 *syn* see ALLEGED

sociable adj 1 *syn* see SOCIAL 2
ant nonsocial
  2 *syn* see GRACIOUS 1
rel companionable, convivial; gregarious; close, familiar, intimate; good-natured
ant unsociable
  3 *syn* see SOCIAL 1
ant unsociable, unsocial

social adj 1 conducive to, marked by, or passed in pleasant companionship with one's friends or associates <a relaxed, *social* evening>
syn companionable, convivial, sociable
rel amusing, entertaining, pleasant, pleasurable; cordial, friendly, genial, gracious, hospitable
con unfriendly, unhospitable; eremitic, solitary
ant unsociable, unsocial
  2 inclined by nature to association or community life with others of the same species <man is a *social* animal>
syn gregarious, sociable
rel social-minded; intersocial
con eremitic, solitary, unsociable; antisocial, asocial, unsocial; remote, withdrawn
ant nonsocial

social evil n, *used with the* syn *syn* see PROSTITUTION

socialize vb to participate actively in a social group <*socializes* with her colleagues>
syn mingle
rel associate, mix

society n 1 *syn* see COMPANY 1
  2 *syn* see ASSOCIATION 2
  3 an organized aggregate of persons who are responsible for a prevailing social order <rules made in the interests of *society* rather than for the chosen few>
syn community, people, public
rel masses, populace
idiom people in general, society at large, the general public
  4 *syn* see ARISTOCRACY

idiom high society (*or* life)
sock *vb syn* see STRIKE 2
sock *n* **1** *syn* see BLOW 1
  2 *syn* see CUFF
‖**sock** *vb syn* see SIGH 1
sod *n syn* see SNOT 1
sodality *n syn* see ASSOCIATION 2
sodden *adj syn* see WET 1
sodden *vb syn* see SOAK 1
Sodom *n syn* see SINK 1
  rel Babylon
so far *adv syn* see HITHERTO 1
  idiom up till now
soft *adj* **1** *syn* see GENTLE 1
  rel moderate, temperate
  2 *syn* see SUBDUED 2
  ant loud
  3 smooth or delicate in texture, grain, or fiber <the dog's fur was *soft*>
  syn cottony, satiny, silken, silky, velvety
  rel smooth; sleek
  con coarse, rough
  ant harsh
  4 *syn* see COMFORTABLE 2
  ant rough
  5 *syn* see SIMPLE 3
  idiom ‖soft in the head
  6 giving way easily to physical touch or pressure <a *soft* cheese>
  syn mushy, pappy, pulpous, pulpy, quaggy, spongy, squashy, squelchy, squishy, squushy, yielding
  rel softish; compressible, malleable, pliable, pliant, workable; doughy, formless; flabby, fleshy
  idiom soft as butter
  con firm, solid; resistant, rigid, tough, unyielding; nail-hard, rock-hard
  ant hard
soft (on) *adj syn* see ENAMORED 1
soft-boiled *adj syn* see SENTIMENTAL
  ant hard-boiled
soften *vb syn* see DEPRECIATE 1
softened *adj syn* see SUBDUED 2
softhead *n syn* see FOOL 4
softhearted *adj syn* see TENDER
  ant hardhearted
soft-pedal *vb* to reduce the emphasis, importance, or effect of something (as an issue) <tried to *soft-pedal* military spending>
  syn de-emphasize, play (down)
  rel tone (down), tune (down); cushion, dampen, muffle, subdue; hush (up), silence, suppress; conceal, disguise
  con emphasize, play (up); focus (on), spotlight
soft-shell *adj syn* see MODERATE 4
soft soap *n syn* see FLATTERY
  rel ‖snow job
soft-soap *vb syn* see COAX
soft spot *n* **1** *syn* see APPETITE 3
  2 a vulnerable point <the major *soft spot* in the West's armor>
  syn Achilles' heel
  rel vulnerability, vulnerableness, weakness; chink, loophole
  idiom heel of Achilles, weak link (*or* point), weak link in the chain
  con impregnability, invulnerability; invincibility

soft touch *n* **1** someone who can be easily talked into giving help (as a loan) <recognized him as a *soft touch* when she was broke>
  syn easy mark
  rel softy, dupe, fool, pushover; sucker; mark, sitting duck, target
  con cynic, doubting Thomas, hard case, skeptic
  2 *syn* see SNAP 1
‖**sog** *vb syn* see SOAK 1
‖**sog** *vb syn* see DOZE
soggy *adj syn* see HUMID
soi-disant *adj syn* see SELF-STYLED
soil *vb* **1** *syn* see CONTAMINATE 1
  ant purify
  2 to make or become unclean <a shirt *soiled* with grease and grime>
  syn begrime, besoil, dirty, foul, grime, muck, ‖mucky, muddy, murk, smirch, smooch, smudge, smutch, tarnish; *compare* STAIN 1
  rel ‖becoom, ‖benasty, ‖nasty; bedaub, daub, smear; drabble, draggle; mess, spoil
  con brighten, cleanse, freshen, renew; purify
  ant clean
  3 *syn* see TAINT 1
soil *n* **1** *syn* see EARTH 2
  2 *syn* see COUNTRY
soily *adj syn* see DIRTY 1
soiree *n syn* see EVENING 1
sojourn *n* a temporary but sometimes extended stay <a summer *sojourn* in Nice>
  syn stopover, tarriance, visit
  rel stay, stop; layover
sojourn *vb syn* see VISIT 3
  rel linger; abide
Sol *n syn* see SUN 1
solace *vb syn* see COMFORT
  idiom offer (*or* give) solace to, wipe one's tears away
soldier *n* a person engaged in military service <*soldiers* fighting and dying in futile wars>
  syn fighter, fighting man, GI, man-at-arms, serviceman, swad, ‖swaddy, ‖sweat, warrior
  rel dogface, doughboy, ‖doughfoot, grunt, infantryman; trooper; guerrilla, partisan; condottiere, free companion, free lance, mercenary, soldier of fortune
soldierly *adj syn* see BRAVE 1
  rel martial; aggressive, combative, militant, pugnacious, warlike
  con unsoldierly
sole *n syn* see BOTTOM 1
sole *adj* **1** *syn* see SINGLE 1
  2 *syn* see SINGLE 2
  3 *syn* see ONLY 2
  idiom one and only
  4 belonging, granted, or attributed to the one person or group <*sole* rights of publication>
  syn exclusive, single, unshared
  con multiple; shared
solecism *n* **1** *syn* see ANACHRONISM 2
  2 *syn* see BARBARISM
  3 *syn* see FAUX PAS
solely *adv syn* see ONLY 1
solemn *adj* **1** *syn* see CEREMONIAL
  rel full, plenary; august, grand, impressive, magnificent, majestic, overwhelming; ostentatious

2 *syn* see SERIOUS 1
idiom as solemn as an owl, grave as an undertaker
solemnize *vb* 1 *syn* see KEEP 2
rel dignify, honor, solemnify, venerate
solicit *vb* 1 to seek (as advertising, orders, or votes) especially on a large scale <*solicited* contributions all over the district>
syn canvass, drum, drum up
rel ask, request; beg, beseech, implore; claim, demand, exact
2 *syn* see ASK 2
rel apply, go, refer, resort, turn
3 *syn* see DEMAND 1
solicitous *adj syn* see EAGER
solicitude *n* 1 *syn* see CARE 2
rel attention, heed, watchfulness; presentiment; compunction, qualm, scruple
con carelessness, heedlessness, indifference, neglect, negligence
ant unmindfulness
2 *syn* see CONSIDERATION 3
solid *adj* 1 *syn* see FIRM 2
rel compacted, concentrated, consolidated
con spongy; disintegrated; fluid, liquid
2 *syn* see STABLE 4
3 *syn* see VALID
rel firm, hard
ant insubstantial
4 *syn* see UNANIMOUS
solid *adv syn* see HARD 9
solidarism *n syn* see SOLIDARITY
solidarity *n* a feeling of unity (as in interests, standards, and responsibilities) that binds members of a group together <*solidarity* among union members is essential in negotiations>
syn cohesion, solidarism, togetherness
rel cohesiveness; oneness, singleness, undividedness; integrity, solidity, union, unity; esprit, esprit de corps; firmness, fixity
con separation; discord, dissension, schism; confusion, disorder, disorganization
ant division
solidify *vb syn* see HARDEN 1
rel compress, contract
idiom make (or become) hard as a rock
con soften; disintegrate, dissolve
ant liquefy
solidly *adv* 1 *syn* see HARD 9
2 *syn* see HARD 7
solitariness *n syn* see SOLITUDE
solitary *adj* 1 *syn* see ANTISOCIAL
ant gregarious
2 *syn* see UNSOCIABLE
3 *syn* see DERELICT 1
4 *syn* see LONE 1
rel companionless, unaccompanied, unattended
ant accompanied
5 *syn* see SINGLE 2
6 *syn* see ONLY 2
solitary *n syn* see RECLUSE
solitude *n* the state of one who is alone <a very social person who could not bear *solitude*>

syn aloneness, isolation, loneness, solitariness; *compare* SECLUSION
rel detachment, separateness; retirement, withdrawal; confinement, quarantine; loneliness, lonesomeness
con companionship, company
solo *adj syn* see ONLY 2
so long *interj syn* see GOOD-BYE
solution *n syn* see ANSWER 2
solve *vb* 1 to find an answer or solution for (a problem or difficulty) <mass transit partially *solved* the traffic problem>
syn fix, resolve, work, work out
rel decide, determine, settle
idiom hit upon a solution
2 to find an explanation or solution for something obscure, mysterious, or incomprehensible <the mystery of the missing cookies has been *solved*>
syn break, ||cipher, clear up, decipher, dissolve, ||dope out, figure out, puzzle out, resolve, unfold, unravel, unriddle
rel enlighten, illuminate; construe, elucidate, explain, interpret
idiom get to the bottom of, have it, put two and two together
somatic *adj syn* see BODILY
somber *adj* 1 *syn* see DARK 1
2 *syn* see GLOOMY 3
3 *syn* see SERIOUS 1
idiom as somber as an undertaker
some *adj* 1 *syn* see CERTAIN 2
2 *syn* see SEVERAL 3
some *adv* 1 *syn* see NEARLY
2 *syn* see SOMEWHAT 2
somebody *pron* one or some individual of no certain or known identity <*somebody* should be home>
syn someone
rel anybody, one
con none
ant nobody, no one
somebody *n* 1 *syn* see NOTABLE 1
ant nobody
2 *syn* see CELEBRITY 2
someday *adv syn* see YET 2
||somegate *adv syn* see SOMEHOW
somehow *adv* in some way not yet known or specified <this thing must be done *somehow*>
syn ||somegate, someway, somewise
rel anyhow, anyway, anywise
idiom by hook or by crook, in one way or another, in some such way, somehow or other (or another)
con nohow, noway, nowise
someone *pron syn* see SOMEBODY
someplace *adv syn* see SOMEWHERE 1
ant no place
something *adv syn* see SOMEWHAT 2
something *n syn* see ENTITY 1
sometime *adv syn* see YET 2
idiom one of these days
sometime *adj syn* see FORMER 2
sometimes *adv* at intervals <illustrated by beautiful and *sometimes* outstanding photographs>
syn at times, ||betimes, ever and again, ever and anon, here and there, now and again, now and then, once and again, ||otherwhile; *compare* OCCASIONALLY

---

syn synonym(s)   *rel* related word(s)
ant antonym(s)   *con* contrasted word(s)
idiom idiomatic equivalent(s)
|| use limited; if in doubt, see a dictionary

rel intermittently, periodically, recurrently; frequently; consistently, constantly
idiom every now and then (*or* again), every once in a while, every so often, from time to time
con continually, continuously, unceasingly, uninterruptedly; endlessly, ever, interminably

someway *adv syn* see SOMEHOW
somewhat *adv* **1** *syn* see WELL 8
2 to some extent or in some degree <felt *somewhat* better but not fine>
syn fairly, kind of, moderately, pretty, rather, ratherish, some, something, sort of
rel adequately, bearably, tolerably; insignificantly, slightly
idiom rather more than less
somewhen *adv syn* see YET 2
somewhere *adv* **1** to, at, or in some unknown or unspecified location <lived on a farm *somewhere* in the Midwest>
syn someplace, ‖somewheres
rel somewhither; elsewhere, otherwhere
idiom someplace or other
con anyplace, anywhere, ‖anywheres; no place, ‖nowheres
ant nowhere
2 *syn* see NEARLY
‖**somewheres** *adv syn* see SOMEWHERE 1
ant ‖nowheres
somewise *adv syn* see SOMEHOW
somnifacient *adj syn* see SOPORIFIC 1
somniferous *adj syn* see SOPORIFIC 1
somnific *adj syn* see SOPORIFIC 1
somnolent *adj* **1** *syn* see SOPORIFIC 1
2 *syn* see SLEEPY 1
rel inactive, passive, supine
somnorific *adj syn* see SOPORIFIC 1
so much as *adv syn* see EVEN 4
son *n syn* see BOY 1
rel sonny; junior
sonance *n syn* see SOUND 1
sonant *adj syn* see VOCAL 1
song *n* **1** *syn* see POETRY 1
2 music or a piece of music intended for vocal expression <played and sang a *song*>
syn aria, descant, ditty, hymn, lay, lied; *compare* MELODY
rel lyric; piece
3 *syn* see CALL 1
song and dance *n syn* see SPIEL
songful *adj syn* see MELODIOUS 2
sonorant *adj syn* see RESONANT
sonorous *adj* **1** *syn* see RESONANT
2 *syn* see RHETORICAL
3 *syn* see NOISY
‖**sonsy** *adj* **1** *syn* see LUCKY
2 *syn* see GRACIOUS 1
3 *syn* see EASYGOING 3
soon *adv* **1** *syn* see PRESENTLY 1
rel forthwith, instantly, pronto, quickly
idiom in the near future
2 *syn* see FAST 2
3 *syn* see EARLY 1
‖**soon** *adj syn* see EARLY 2
sooner *adv syn* see BEFORE 3
sooner or later *adv syn* see YET 2
soothe *vb syn* see CALM
rel comfort, console; hush, subdue

con annoy, irritate, vex
ant excite
‖**soother** *n syn* see WEAKLING
soothsay *vb syn* see FORETELL
soothsayer *n syn* see PROPHET
sop *n* **1** *syn* see WEAKLING
2 a conciliatory or propitiatory gift or advance <provided the $400 raise as a *sop*> <the new office was a *sop* to his wounded feelings>
syn sugarplum
rel douceur, gratuity; ‖baksheesh, ‖boodle, bribe, ‖palm oil
idiom sop in the pan, sop to Cerberus
sop *vb* **1** *syn* see WET
2 *syn* see SOAK 1
3 *syn* see BRIBE
sophic *adj syn* see WISE 1
sophism *n syn* see FALLACY 2
rel illogicality, irrationality; invalidity, unsoundness; claptrap
sophistic *adj syn* see ILLOGICAL
sophisticate *adj syn* see SOPHISTICATED 2
sophisticate *vb syn* see ADULTERATE
sophisticated *adj* **1** *syn* see COMPLEX 2
ant unsophisticated
2 being experienced in the ways of the world <a *sophisticated*, well-traveled man>
syn blasé, disenchanted, disentranced, disillusioned, knowing, mondaine, sophisticate, worldly, worldly-wise, world-wise; *compare* COSMOPOLITAN 1
rel adult, mature; experienced, practiced, schooled, seasoned, salty, uncelestial; couth, well-bred; smooth, suave, svelte, urbane; bored, jaded, world-weary; brittle; cynical, skeptical
con artless, gee-whiz, ingenuous, natural; green, inexperienced, unseasoned, virginal; unworldly
ant naive, unsophisticated
sophistry *n syn* see FALLACY 2
rel ambiguity, tergiversation
soporiferous *adj syn* see SOPORIFIC 1
soporific *adj* **1** tending to induce sleep <a *soporific* drug><*soporific* prose>
syn hypnotic, narcotic, opiate, sleepy, slumberous, somnifacient, somniferous, somnific, somnolent, somnorific, soporiferous, soporifical
rel calming, quietening, sedative, tranquilizing; anesthetic, deadening, numbing
con arousing, waking; invigorating, stimulating
2 *syn* see SLEEPY 1
soporifical *adj syn* see SOPORIFIC 1
sopping *adj syn* see WET 1
soppy *adj* **1** *syn* see WET 1
‖**2** *syn* see SENTIMENTAL
sorcerer *n syn* see MAGICIAN 1
sorceress *n syn* see WITCH 1
sorcerous *adj syn* see MAGIC
sorcery *n syn* see MAGIC 1
sordid *adj* **1** *syn* see DIRTY 1
2 *syn* see SLATTERNLY
3 *syn* see BASE 3
rel foul, nasty, seamy, sodden
sore *adj syn* see PAINFUL 1
sorehead *n syn* see GROUCH
sorely *adv syn* see HARD 6

sorrow *n* distress of mind <felt great *sorrow* at the loss of her friend>
syn affliction, anguish, care, ‖dole, grief, heartache, heartbreak, regret, rue, woe
rel mournfulness, sadness, sorrowfulness, unhappiness; grieving, lamentation, mourning, sorrowing; dejection, depression, melancholy; agony, distress, dolor, misery, suffering, wretchedness
con cheerfulness, gaiety, gladness, happiness, joyfulness; ecstasy
ant joy

sorrow *vb syn* SEE GRIEVE 2
rel groan, moan, sob
idiom break one's heart over, eat one's heart out
ant rejoice

sorrowful *adj* 1 *syn* SEE WOEFUL 1
rel sorrow-laden, sorrow-stricken, sorrow-struck
idiom full of (or filled with) sorrow
con sorrowless
ant joyful
2 *syn* SEE MELANCHOLY 2
ant gay

sorry *adj* 1 *syn* SEE SAD 1
rel bad, regretful, remorseful; miserable, wretched
ant glad
2 *syn* SEE REMORSEFUL
3 *syn* SEE CONTEMPTIBLE
rel inadequate, paltry, poor, trifling; cheesy, scruffy, shoddy; disgraceful

sort *n* 1 *syn* SEE TYPE
2 *syn* SEE GROUP 3

sort *vb* 1 *syn* SEE ASSORT
2 to analyze and assort (as individuals or things) to obtain those desired or required <he knew he must *sort* out facts from fancy>
syn comb, separate, sift, winnow; *compare* SCREEN 5
rel riddle, screen; choose, cull, pick, select
con consolidate, join, lump, merge; aggregate, amalgamate, blend, fuse, mix; unify

sort of *adv syn* SEE SOMEWHAT 2
SOS *n syn* SEE ALARM 1
soshed *adj syn* SEE INTOXICATED 1
so-so *adv syn* SEE ENOUGH 2
so-so *adj syn* SEE MEDIUM
sot *n syn* SEE DRUNKARD
‖**sot** *adj syn* SEE OBSTINATE
so that *conj syn* SEE SO

sotto voce *adv* in an inaudible or barely audible voice <made a snide remark to her *sotto voce*>
syn faintly, mutedly, weakly
rel low, quietly, softly; muffledly; mutteringly; aside, privately
idiom below one's breath, between one's teeth, in an aside, in an undertone, in a whisper, out of earshot, under one's breath
con aloud, out, out loud

sough *vb* 1 *syn* SEE SIGH 2
2 *syn* SEE SIGH 1

soul *n* 1 an animating essence or principle held to be inseparably associated with life or living beings <philosophers who teach that life is a manifestation of *soul*>
syn anima, animus, élan vital, pneuma, psyche, spirit, vital force
rel life, vitality
idiom breath of life
2 the immortal part of man believed to have permanent individual existence <into God's hands I commit my *soul*>
syn spirit
rel life; noumenon
idiom one's immortal soul
con flesh
ant body
3 *syn* SEE HEART 1
rel character, personality, psyche; conscience; spirit
idiom heart of hearts, heart's core, one's inmost soul (or mind), one's secret (or inner) self, (the) secret recesses of the heart
4 *syn* SEE ESSENCE 2
5 *syn* SEE HUMAN

soul-searching *n syn* SEE INTROSPECTION
soul-sick *adj syn* SEE DOWNCAST

sound *adj* 1 *syn* SEE HEALTHY 1
rel intact, unimpaired; perfect
idiom sound as a bell (or whistle), sound of mind and body
con impaired; unfit
ant unsound
2 *syn* SEE WHOLE 1
3 *syn* SEE STABLE 4
ant unsound
4 *syn* SEE VALID
rel errorless, faultless, flawless, impeccable; accurate, correct, precise; rational, reasonable; well-founded, well-grounded
con questionable, shaky; invalid
ant unsound
5 *syn* SEE ORTHODOX 1
6 *syn* SEE RATIONAL
rel right-minded, sober, sober-minded, sound-minded
ant unsound

sound *n* 1 a sensation or effect resulting from stimulation of the auditory receptors <the *sound* of thunder>
syn noise, sonance
rel vibration; resonance; sonancy; reverberation
con quiet, soundlessness
ant silence
2 *syn* SEE EARSHOT

sound *vb* 1 *syn* SEE SEEM
2 *syn* SEE DECLARE 1

sound *vb* to measure the depth of (as a body of water) typically with a weighted line <*sounding* the distance to the bottom>
syn fathom, plumb, plumb-line
idiom ‖cast (or sling) the lead, make a sounding, take soundings

sound (out) *vb syn* SEE PROBE 2
soundless *adj syn* SEE BOTTOMLESS 2
ant soundable
soundless *adj syn* SEE STILL 3
soundlessness *n syn* SEE SILENCE 1
soundness *n* 1 *syn* SEE HEALTH
ant unsoundness
2 *syn* SEE STABILITY
3 *syn* SEE WIT 2

---

syn synonym(s)   *rel* related word(s)
ant antonym(s)   *con* contrasted word(s)
idiom idiomatic equivalent(s)
‖ use limited; if in doubt, see a dictionary

rel level-headedness, sensibleness
idiom sound mind, soundness of mind
ant unsoundness

sound off *vb syn* see SPEAK UP

soup *n syn* see PREDICAMENT

soupçon *n syn* see HINT 2

soupy *adj syn* see SENTIMENTAL

sour *adj* 1 causing or characterized by the one of the basic taste sensations produced chiefly by acids <*sour* pickles>
syn acerb, acerbic, acetose, acid, acidulous, dry, tart
rel keen, sharp, tangy; ‖blinky, sourish; fermented, soured, turned; acrid, bitter, vinegary
ant sweet
2 *syn* see BAD 8

source *n* the point at which something begins its course or existence <the *source* of her wisdom was long practical experience>
syn derivation, fount, fountain, fountainhead, inception, mother, origin, provenance, provenience, root, rootage, rootstock, spring, well, wellhead, wellspring, whence
rel birthplace; beginning, commencement, dawn, dawning, onset, opening, start, starting; authorship, origination, rise, rising; antecedent, cause, determinant; parent, paternity
con end, ending, terminus
ant termination; outcome

sourpuss *n syn* see GROUCH
rel killjoy

souse *vb* 1 *syn* see DIP 1
2 *syn* see WET
3 *syn* see SOAK 1

souse *n syn* see BINGE 1

soused *adj syn* see WET 1

souvenir *n syn* see REMEMBRANCE 3
idiom token of remembrance

sovereign *adj* 1 *syn* see FREE 1
rel self-determined, self-governed
2 *syn* see DOMINANT 1
rel commanding, directing, guiding; highest, loftiest
3 *syn* see EXCELLENT
4 *syn* see KINGLY

sovereignty *n syn* see SUPREMACY

sow *vb* 1 *syn* see PLANT 1
2 *syn* see STREW 1
rel fling, toss; drill

‖**sowf** *vb syn* see HUM

sozzled *adj syn* see INTOXICATED 1

spa *n* 1 a locality featuring mineral springs or water cures <hoped a week at a *spa* would help his arthritis>
syn baths, ‖hydro, springs, watering place, wells
rel waters
idiom health spa
2 *syn* see RESORT 3

space *n* 1 *syn* see WHILE 1
rel lapse; interval, term; duration
2 *syn* see EXPANSE
rel room, roomage; spaciousness

spaced-out *adj syn* see DRUGGED

spacious *adj* larger in extent or capacity than the average <a mansion with *spacious* rooms and gardens>
syn ample, capacious, commodious, roomy, wide

rel big, generous, great, large, spacy; enormous, immense, vast; expansive, extended, extensive; boundless, spaceless
con circumscribed, confined, cramped, limited, narrow, restricted; small, tiny
ant strait

spade *vb* 1 *syn* see DIG 2
2 *syn* see DIG 1

span *n syn* see TERM 2
rel interval; space

spang *adv syn* see JUST 1

spangle *vb* 1 to adorn with small brilliant objects <a tutu *spangled* with sequins>
syn bespangle, glitter
rel adorn, decorate, ornament, trim
2 *syn* see FLASH 1

spang-new *adj syn* see BRAND-NEW

spaniel *n syn* see SYCOPHANT

spank *vb syn* see SLAP 1

spank *n syn* see CUFF
idiom a sound spank

spanking *adv syn* see VERY 1

spanking-new *adj syn* see BRAND-NEW

span-new *adj syn* see BRAND-NEW

spare *vb* 1 *syn* see EXEMPT
2 *syn* see SAVE 4
3 to refrain from the free use or consumption of <don't *spare* the syrup on my pancakes>
syn scant, short, skimp, ‖skinch, stint; *compare* SCRIMP
rel pinch
4 *syn* see SCRIMP

spare *adj* 1 *syn* see SUPERFLUOUS
idiom enough and to spare, more than enough
2 *syn* see LEAN
ant corpulent
3 *syn* see MEAGER 2
ant profuse

sparing *adj* careful in the use of money, goods, or resources <was *sparing* in his expenditures>
syn canny, chary, economical, frugal, provident, saving, Scotch, stewardly, thrifty, unwasteful, wary; *compare* STINGY
rel parsimonious, ‖scant, tight, tightfisted, ungiving
con exuberant, liberal, prodigal, profuse
ant lavish, unsparing

spark *n syn* see SEED 1

spark *n syn* see SUITOR 2

spark *vb syn* see ADDRESS 8

sparker *n syn* see SUITOR 2

sparkish *adj syn* see DAPPER

sparkle *vb syn* see FLASH 1

sparkle *n syn* see FLASH 1

sparse *adj syn* see MEAGER 2
rel dispersed, scattered; infrequent, occasional, sporadic; rare, scarce, uncommon
con close, compact, thick

‖**spartle** *vb syn* see SCRAMBLE 1

spasmodic *adj syn* see FITFUL
rel spurtive
con continual, continuous, uninterrupted

spat *n* 1 *syn* see QUARREL
‖2 *syn* see CUFF

spat *vb syn* see QUARREL

spate *n* 1 *syn* see FLOOD 2
rel progression, series, succession; rain, river, spurt

2 *syn* see FLOW
spatter *vb* **1** *syn* see SPLASH
  rel sparge
  2 *syn* see SPOT 1
  3 *syn* see MALIGN
  4 *syn* see SPUTTER 2
spatter *n* *syn* see FEW
spattering *n* *syn* see FEW
spawn *vb* *syn* see GENERATE 1
spawning *adj* *syn* see FERTILE
speak *vb* **1** to articulate words in order to
  express thoughts <always *speak* clearly>
  syn talk, utter, verbalize, vocalize, voice
  rel drawl, gasp, mouth, mumble, murmur,
  mutter, shout, splutter, spout, whisper;
  descant, dilate (on or upon), expatiate, perorate; converse, discourse; allege, assert,
  aver, convey, declare, tell
  idiom break silence, give voice (or tongue or
  utterance) to, let fall, make public (or
  known), open one's mouth (or lips), put in
  (or into) words, say one's say, speak one's
  piece
  con gabble, gibber, jabber; maunder, mumble, mutter; mispronounce, misspeak
  2 *syn* see TALK 7
  3 to have oral command of (a language) <he
  speaks fluent German>
  syn converse (in), parley, talk, use
  idiom be at ease in
  con falter, hesitate, stumble
speaker *n* *syn* see SPOKESMAN
speaking *n* *syn* see SPEECH 1
speak out *vb* *syn* see SPEAK UP
speak up *vb* to speak strongly, boldly, or
  vigorously <we'll never know how you feel if
  you don't *speak up*>
  syn sound off, speak out
  idiom come out with it, have one's say, let
  one's voice be heard, make oneself heard,
  speak one's mind, stand up and be counted
spear *vb* *syn* see IMPALE
  rel stick; bore, drill, penetrate, pierce;
  gouge, ream
special *adj* **1** of or relating to one thing or
  class <*special* soap for infants>
  syn especial, individual, particular, specific
  rel characteristic, distinctive, peculiar;
  exceptional, occasional, rare, uncommon;
  unique
  con common, familiar, ordinary; customary, habitual, usual
  2 *syn* see EXPRESS 2
  rel defined, determinate; designated, ear-
  marked
special *adv* *syn* see ESPECIALLY 1
specialize *vb* *syn* see ITEMIZE 1
specially *adv* **1** *syn* see ESPECIALLY 1
  2 *syn* see EXPRESSLY 2
species *n* *syn* see TYPE
specific *adj* **1** *syn* see SPECIAL 1
  rel limited, reserved, restricted, specialized
  con general, generic
  ant nonspecific, unspecific
  2 *syn* see EXPLICIT

con ambiguous, cloudy, indefinite, uncertain, unexplicit, unspecified, vague
  ant nonspecific, unspecific
  3 *syn* see EXPRESS 2
  ant nonspecific, unspecific
specifically *adv* **1** *syn* see EXPRESSLY 2
  2 *syn* see ESPECIALLY 1
  3 *syn* see EXPRESSLY 1
specificate *vb* *syn* see SPECIFY 3
specificize *vb* *syn* see SPECIFY 3
specify *vb* **1** *syn* see MENTION
  2 *syn* see ITEMIZE 1
  3 to make something (as a condition or
  requirement) specific <his will *specified* how
  the money would be divided>
  syn detail, particularize, specificate, specificize, stipulate; *compare* ITEMIZE 1
  rel determine, establish, fix, settle; condition, limit, set; pin (down); enumerate, list;
  precise
specimen *n* *syn* see INSTANCE
  rel sort, species, type, variety
specious *adj* *syn* see FALSE 1
  rel apparent, seeming; colorable, plausible;
  beguiling; illogical, spurious; empty, hollow,
  idle, nugatory, vain
  ant valid
speciousness *n* *syn* see FALLACY 2
  rel speciosity
  ant validity
speck *n* **1** *syn* see POINT 11
  rel pinpoint; tick
  2 *syn* see PARTICLE
speck *vb* *syn* see SPECKLE 1
speckle *vb* **1** to produce on or mark with
  small spots, speckles, or blemishes <a speckled egg>
  syn bespeckle, dot, freckle, pepper, speck,
  sprinkle, stipple; *compare* SPOT 1
  rel dapple, flake, fleck
  2 *syn* see SPOT 2
spectacle *n* *syn* see EXHIBITION 1
spectacled *adj* *syn* see BESPECTACLED
spectacular *adj* *syn* see MARVELOUS 1
  rel eye-popping, sensational, striking, thrilling; dramatic, histrionic, stagy, theatrical
  ant unspectacular
spectator *n* one who sees or looks upon
  something <sports *spectators*>
  syn beholder, by-sitter, bystander, eyewitness, looker-on, observer, onlooker, stander-
  by, viewer, watcher, witness
  rel gazer; perceiver; seer
specter *n* *syn* see APPARITION
spectral *adj* *syn* see GHASTLY 2
  rel phantom, phantomlike, shadowlike;
  disembodied, unearthly; spooky
spectrum *n* **1** *syn* see APPARITION
  2 *syn* see RANGE 5
speculate *vb* *syn* see THINK 5
  rel excogitate, review, study, weigh
  idiom beat one's brains, turn over in one's
  mind, use the gray matter
speculation *n* **1** *syn* see THOUGHT 1
  rel excogitation, review, studying, weighing
  2 *syn* see THEORY 2
speculative *adj* **1** *syn* see THEORETICAL 1
  2 *syn* see THOUGHTFUL 1
  rel musing, ruminating; curious, inquiring,
  questioning

---

syn synonym(s)	*rel* related word(s)
ant antonym(s)	*con* contrasted word(s)
idiom idiomatic equivalent(s)	
‖ use limited; if in doubt, see a dictionary	

ant unspeculative

speech *n* **1** communication, expression, or interchange of thoughts in spoken words <considered *speech* as a means of reproducing for one's listeners the images in one's mind>
syn discourse, speaking, talk, utterance, verbalization; *compare* VOCALIZATION
rel articulation, uttering, vocalization, vocalizing, voice, voicing; expressing, expression; language
idiom oral communication, vocal expression
2 a usually formal discourse delivered to an audience <a televised *speech* to the nation>
syn address, allocution, lecture, talk
rel debate, parlance, parley; declamation, harangue, oration, speechification
3 *syn see* LANGUAGE 1

speechcraft *n syn see* ORATORY

speechless *adj* **1** *syn see* DUMB 1
rel aphonic
2 *syn see* SILENT 2
3 *syn see* SILENT 3

speed *n* **1** *syn see* HASTE 1
rel alacrity, legerity; headway
con dilatoriness, tardiness
2 rate of movement, performance, or occurrence <ran through the exercise at a high *speed*>
syn ‖bat, celerity, gait, pace, quickness, rapidity, rapidness, swiftness, velocity; *compare* TEMPO
rel fastness, fleetness; clip, hickory

speed *vb* **1** *syn see* HURRY 2
idiom make haste
ant slow (up *or* down)
2 *syn see* COURSE
3 to cause to move fast or faster <*sped* our craft forward>
syn accelerate, hasten, hurry, quicken, shake up, step up, swiften
rel advance, aid, ease, encourage, expedite, facilitate, forward, further, help (along), smooth; cheer (on), drive (on), goad (on), spur (on); burn (up)
idiom ‖get the lead out
con hamper, restrain, retard; check, stay; delay, postpone, put off
ant slow (up *or* down)

speedily *adv syn see* FAST 2
idiom against the clock, hell-bent for leather, like a bat out of hell, like all forty, ‖like all get-out, on the double, to beat the band
con deliberately, languidly, leisurely; lazily, lethargically, sluggishly; crawlingly, creepingly
ant slow, slowly

speediness *n syn see* HASTE 1
ant slowness

speedy *adj syn see* FAST 3
rel agile, brisk, nimble; prompt, ready
idiom fast as greased lightning, speedy as an arrow
ant dilatory; slow

speerings *n pl syn see* NEWS

‖**spelder** *vb syn see* SPRAWL 1

spell *n* a spoken word or set of words believed to have magic power <cause death by muttering *spells* over her>
syn charm, conjuration, ‖devil-devil, incantation, rune
rel bewitching, enchanting, hexing

spell *vb syn see* BEWITCH 1

spell *vb syn see* MEAN 2

spell *vb* **1** *syn see* RELIEVE 3
2 *syn see* REST 3

spell *n* **1** a limited period or amount of activity <each *spell* of work was followed by a brief rest>
syn bout, go, shift, stint, time, tour, trick, turn
rel streak; ‖patch, period; stretch; relay
2 *syn see* WHILE 1
3 *syn see* ATTACK 3

spellbind *vb syn see* ENTHRALL 2

spell out *vb syn see* EXPLAIN 1

spend *vb* **1** to distribute or consume in payment or expenditure <*spent* fifty dollars for that dress>
syn disburse, expend, fork (out), give, lay out, outlay, pay, shell out
rel blow, drop, hand out; contribute; consume, dissipate, lavish, squander, throw away, waste
ant save
2 *syn see* GO 4
3 to cause or permit to elapse <*spent* the summer at the beach>
syn pass, while (away)

spender *n syn see* SPENDTHRIFT
ant saver

spending money *n syn see* POCKET MONEY

spendthrift *n* one who dissipates his resources foolishly and wastefully <a *spendthrift* who lost his estate through gambling>
syn high roller, prodigal, profligate, scattergood, spender, squanderer, unthrift, waster, wastethrift, wastrel
con hoarder, miser, saver

spent *adj syn see* EFFETE 2

spew *vb* **1** *syn see* VOMIT
2 *syn see* ERUPT 1
rel flood, gush

sphere *n* **1** *syn see* BALL
2 *syn see* FIELD
rel circle, jurisdiction, realm

sphere *vb syn see* BALL

spice *n* **1** *syn see* HINT 2
2 *syn see* FRAGRANCE

spick–and–span *adj* **1** *syn see* BRAND-NEW
2 *syn see* NEAT 2

spicy *adj* **1** *syn see* SWEET 2
2 *syn see* PUNGENT
rel fiery, gingery, high-spirited, spirited, zestful
3 *syn see* RISQUÉ
rel sophisticated; piquant

spider *n syn see* FRYING PAN

spiel *n* voluble, glib, or extravagant talk often intended to impress, persuade, or deceive <gave her a long sales *spiel*>
syn ‖line, pitch, song and dance
rel demagoguery; dramatics, pyrotechnics, sensationalism

‖**spieler** *n syn see* SWINDLER

spiff *vb syn see* DRESS UP 1

spiffy *adj syn see* DAPPER

‖**spiflicated** *adj syn see* INTOXICATED 1

spigot *n syn* see FAUCET
spike *vb syn* see IMPALE
spill *vb* **1** to cause or allow (something) to fall, flow, or run out and be lost or wasted <accidentally dropped the cup and *spilled* his tea>
   syn slop, squab
   rel dribble, drip, drop; spatter, splash, spray
   2 *syn* see OVERFLOW 2
   3 *syn* see REVEAL 1
spilth *n syn* see REFUSE
spin *vb* **1** to turn or cause to turn rapidly <pinwheels *spinning* in the wind>
   syn gyrate, gyre, ‖pirl, pirouette, ‖purl, twirl, whirl, whirligig; *compare* TURN 1
   rel revolve, rotate, wheel; swirl; oscillate, pendulate, vibrate
   idiom spin like a top
   2 to feel as if revolving <her head was *spinning* with figures>
   syn reel, swim, turn, whirl
   rel dizzy, giddy; fluster, mix up, muddle
   idiom be in a whirl
spin (out) *vb syn* see EXTEND 3
spin *n syn* see DRIVE 1
spinal column *n syn* see SPINE
spindling *adj syn* see GANGLING
spindly *adj syn* see GANGLING
spine *n* the articulated column of bones that is the central and axial feature of a vertebrate skeleton <fractured his *spine*>
   syn back, backbone, rachis, spinal column, vertebrae, vertebral column
   rel spinal cord
spineless *adj syn* see WEAK 4
   rel weak-kneed, weak-willed
   idiom as spineless as an amoeba
   con self-willed, strong-willed
spin-off *n syn* see OUTGROWTH 2
spinster *n* a woman who is past the common age for marrying or who seems unlikely ever to marry <a gentle *spinster*, happy in her solitary life>
   syn maiden lady, old maid, spinstress, ‖tabby
spinstress *n syn* see SPINSTER
spiny *adj syn* see THORNY
spiral *vb syn* see WIND 2
spiring *adj syn* see LOFTY 6
spirit *n* **1** *syn* see SOUL 1
   2 *syn* see APPARITION
   3 *syn* see SOUL 2
   4 *syn* see TEMPER 1
   5 a lively or brisk quality in a person or his actions <a man of great *spirit* and courage>
   syn animation, brio, dash, élan, esprit, gimp, life, oomph, verve, vim, zing; *compare* VIGOR 2
   rel ardor, briskness, enthusiasm, liveliness; drive, get-up-and-go, ginger, go, pep, snap, starch, vigor, vitality, zip; character, force, substance
   6 *syn* see COURAGE
   rel ardor, fervor, passion, zeal; energy, force, might, power, strength

   7 *often* **spirits** *pl syn* see LIQUOR
spirit (away) *vb syn* see KIDNAP
spirit (up) *vb syn* see ELATE
spirited *adj* **1** *syn* see LIVELY 1
   rel sharp; fiery, gingery, peppery
   idiom full of life (*or* go)
   ant spiritless
   2 having or manifesting a high degree of vitality, spirit, and daring <the lawyer gave a *spirited* defense of his client>
   syn beany, fiery, gingery, high-hearted, high-spirited, mettlesome, peppery, spunky
   rel game, gritty, resolute; audacious, bold, brave, courageous, dauntless, fearless, intrepid, nervy, plucky, valiant; avid, eager, hot, keen; ardent, enthusiastic, fervent, hot, passionate, peppy, zealous
   con unenthusiastic; flabby, languid, limp; boneless, spineless
   ant spiritless
spiritless *adj* **1** *syn* see DEAD 1
   2 *syn* see DOWNCAST
   idiom down in the dumps
   3 *syn* see LANGUID
   rel tame; broken, subdued, submissive
   ant spirited
spiritual *adj* **1** *syn* see IMMATERIAL 1
   rel supernatural, supramundane
   ant physical
   2 *syn* see SACRED 2
   3 *syn* see ECCLESIASTICAL
   4 appealing to, coming from, or related to the higher emotions or to the aesthetic senses <man's *spiritual* and intellectual life as opposed to his animal instincts>
   syn numinous
   rel cerebral, intellectual, mental; elevated, high, high-minded, lofty; saintly
   con low, lower; base
   ant animal
spirituous *adj* containing a considerable amount of alcohol <*spirituous* liquors>
   syn alcoholic, ardent, hard, strong
   rel spiked; inebriating, intoxicating, intoxicative; heady
   con nonalcoholic, nonintoxicating, soft
‖**spirity** *adj syn* see LIVELY 1
spit *vb syn* see IMPALE
spit *n* **1** *syn* see SALIVA
   2 *syn* see IMAGE 1
   rel counterpart; look-alike; twin
spit *vb* **1** *syn* see SPUTTER 1
   2 *syn* see SPUTTER 2
spite *n syn* see MALICE
   rel rancor; revenge, revengefulness, vengeance, vengefulness, vindictiveness
   con sympathy; affection, love, tenderness
spiteful *adj syn* see MALICIOUS
   rel antagonistic, hostile; revengeful, vengeful, vindictive
   con charitable; sympathetic; affectionate, loving
   ant spiteless
spitefulness *n syn* see MALICE
spitish *adj syn* see MALICIOUS
spitting image *n syn* see IMAGE 1
   rel mirror image
spittle *n syn* see SALIVA
spit up *vb syn* see VOMIT
‖**spiv** *n* **1** *syn* see PARASITE

---

syn synonym(s)   *rel* related word(s)
ant antonym(s)   *con* contrasted word(s)
idiom idiomatic equivalent(s)
‖ use limited; if in doubt, see a dictionary

2 *syn* see SLACKER

splash *vb* **1** *syn* to dash a liquid or semiliquid substance upon or against <*splashed* water onto her face>
syn douse, plash, slop, slosh, spatter, splatter, splosh, splurge, spurtle, swash
rel dash, throw; spray; sprinkle; ‖sprent, squirt; drench, drown, soak, sop, wet

splashy *adj syn* see SHOWY

splathering *adj syn* see CLUMSY 1

splatter *vb syn* see SPLASH

splay *adj syn* see CLUMSY 1

spleen *n syn* see MALICE
rel revenge, revengefulness, vindictiveness; wrath

splendid *adj* **1** *syn* see GRAND 2
rel baroque, flamboyant
2 extraordinarily or transcendently impressive <a *splendid* new city>
syn glorious, gorgeous, magnificent, proud, resplendent, splendiferous, splendorous, sublime, superb
rel eminent, illustrious; grand, impressive, lavish, luxurious, royal, sumptuous; divine, exquisite, lovely; incomparable, matchless, peerless, superlative, supreme, unparalleled, unsurpassed; surpassing, transcendent
con common, ordinary, run-of-the-mill
ant unimpressive

splendiferous *adj syn* see SPLENDID 2
rel dazzling, marvelous, smashing, walloping; rattling, ripping, screaming, terrific

splendorous *adj syn* see SPLENDID 2

splice *vb syn* see MARRY 2

splinter *vb syn* see SHATTER 1

splinterize *vb syn* see SHATTER 1

split *vb* **1** *syn* see CUT 5
rel crack, rive
2 *syn* see TEAR 1
‖**3** *syn* see BETRAY 2

split (up) *vb syn* see SEPARATE 1

split *n* **1** *syn* see CRACK 3
2 *syn* see SCHISM 3
3 *syn* see BREACH 3
rel alienating, estranging

split second *n syn* see INSTANT 1

splitter *vb syn* see SHATTER 1

split–up *n syn* see SEPARATION 1

‖**splodge** *vb syn* see SPLOTCH

splosh *vb syn* see SPLASH

splotch *vb* to mark or spot with irregular patches especially of contrasting color <a black horse *splotched* with white>
syn blotch, mottle, ‖splodge
rel blot, stain; dapple, fleck, marble, motley, variegate; bespot, spot; harlequin

‖**splunge** *vb syn* see PLUNGE 2

splurge *n syn* see SPREE 1
rel extravagance; splash

splurge *vb syn* see SPLASH

splurt *vb syn* see SQUIRT

splutter *vb* **1** *syn* see SPUTTER 2
2 *syn* see SPUTTER 1

spoil *n* something taken from another by force or craft <gold, jewels, and paintings are often *spoils* of war>
syn boodle, booty, loot, plunder, plunderage, prize, ‖spreaghery, ‖spulzie, swag
rel acquisition, grab, haul, take; pickings, stealings; pillage, spoliation

spoil *vb* **1** *syn* see RAVAGE
2 *syn* see INJURE 1
rel ‖snafu; ruin, wreck; demolish, destroy
3 *syn* see RAPE
4 *syn* see BABY
rel accommodate, favor, oblige
idiom spoil (one) rotten, spoil to death
5 *syn* see DECAY

spoiled *adj* **1** *syn* see DAMAGED
ant unspoiled
2 *syn* see BAD 5
rel off, tainted; putrefying, rotting
ant unspoiled

spoiler *n syn* see MARAUDER

spoken *adj* **1** *syn* see ORAL 2
ant written
2 *syn* see VOCAL 1
ant unspoken

spokesman *n* one who speaks as a representative of another <selected as *spokesman* for the party's views>
syn mouth, mouthpiece, speaker, spokesperson, spokeswoman
rel delegate, deputy, representative; champion, protagonist; prophet

spokesperson *n syn* see SPOKESMAN

spokeswoman *n syn* see SPOKESMAN

spoliate *vb syn* see RAVAGE
rel raid; maraud, gut, ravish, sweep

spoliator *n syn* see MARAUDER

sponge *n* **1** *syn* see DRUNKARD
2 *syn* see PARASITE

sponger *n syn* see PARASITE

spongy *adj syn* see SOFT 6
idiom as soft as a sponge

sponsor *n* one that accepts responsibility for another person or thing <the major *sponsor* of this project is the government>
syn angel, backer, backer-up, guarantor, patron, surety
rel advocate, champion, mainstay, supporter, upholder; preferrer, promoter; benefactor, Maecenas

sponsorship *n syn* see BACKING

spontaneity *n syn* see UNCONSTRAINT
rel extemporaneousness, offhandedness, unpremeditatedness

spontaneous *adj* acting or activated without apparent thought or deliberation <a *spontaneous* burst of applause>
syn automatic, impulsive, instinctive, involuntary, unmeditated, unpremeditated, unprompted, will-less
rel unconstrained, unforced; unreasoned, unstudied; extemporaneous, extempore, impromptu, improvised, offhand; natural, simple, unsophisticated
con deliberate, intended, intentional, planned, predetermined, preplanned, studied, thought-out, voluntary, willed, willful; forced, prompted; conventional, formal, stylized
ant premeditated

spontoon *n syn* see CUDGEL

spoof *vb syn* see DUPE

spoof *n syn* see IMPOSTURE

spook *n* ‖**1** *syn* see APPARITION
‖**2** *syn* see ECCENTRIC
3 *syn* see SPY

‖**spook** *vb* **1** *syn* see FRIGHTEN

2 *syn* see GHOSTWRITE

spooky *adj* **1** *syn* see WEIRD 1
  rel spookish; ominous
  2 *syn* see NERVOUS

‖**spoon** *n syn* see DUNCE

spoony *adj syn* see SIMPLE 3

spoony (*over or* on) *adj syn* see ENAMORED 1

spoor *n syn* see FOOTPRINT

sporadic *adj* **1** *syn* see FITFUL
  ant regular
  2 *syn* see INFREQUENT
  rel separate, single
  ant frequent

sporadically *adv syn* see OCCASIONALLY
  ant regularly

sport *vb syn* see PLAY 1

sport *n* **1** *syn* see PLAY 1
  2 sports *pl syn* see ATHLETICS
  3 *syn* see FUN 1
  rel jollification; antics, high jinks, horseplay
  4 *syn* see LAUGHINGSTOCK
  5 *syn* see CHANGE 2

sporting girl *n syn* see PROSTITUTE

sporting house *n syn* see BROTHEL

sportive *adj syn* see PLAYFUL 1

sportiveness *n syn* see MISCHIEVOUSNESS

sportsmanlike *adj syn* see FAIR 5
  ant unsporting, unsportsmanlike

sportsmanly *adj syn* see FAIR 5
  ant unsporting, unsportsmanlike

sporty *adj syn* see WILD 7

spot *n* **1** *syn* see STIGMA
  2 *syn* see DRAM
  3 *syn* see PARTICLE
  4 *syn* see PLACE
  rel scene; section, sector
  5 *syn* see JOB 2
  idiom job slot
  6 *syn* see PREDICAMENT

spot *vb* **1** to mark or stain (something) with spots <a white dress *spotted* with red mud>
  syn bespatter, bespot, spatter; *compare* SPECKLE 1
  rel blot, blotch, mottle; fleck, marble, streak, stripe; dot, pepper, speck, speckle, sprinkle, stipple; splash; dirty, soil, stain
  2 to form or appear as spots on <a bleak landscape *spotted* with cottages>
  syn dot, pimple, speckle, sprinkle, stud
  rel intersperse
  3 *syn* see IDENTIFY
  rel ascertain; see
  4 *syn* see FIND 1

spot *adj syn* see RANDOM

spotless *adj* **1** *syn* see CLEAN 1
  rel hygienic, sanitary
  2 *syn* see CHASTE
  ant spotted

spotty *adj* **1** lacking uniformity <*spotty* illumination>
  syn irregular, patchy, uneven
  rel unequal; flickering, fluctuating
  con equal, even, regular, uniform
  2 *syn* see FITFUL

---

syn synonym(s)	*rel* related word(s)
ant antonym(s)	*con* contrasted word(s)
idiom idiomatic equivalent(s)	
‖ use limited; if in doubt, see a dictionary	

spousal *n syn* see WEDDING

spousal *adj syn* see MATRIMONIAL

spouse *n* a marriage partner <consulted with her *spouse* before buying the car>
  syn consort, mate

spouseless *adj syn* see SINGLE 1
  con espoused

‖**spout** *vb syn* see PAWN

spout *n syn* see WATERFALL

spraddle *vb syn* see SPRAWL 1

sprain *vb* to injure (a joint) by a sudden twisting motion that stretches and lacerates the ligaments <*sprained* her ankle>
  syn ‖rick, turn, twist, wrench
  rel pull, strain, stretch; tear; dislocate, throw; break, fracture

sprangle *vb syn* see SPRAWL 2

sprat *n syn* see TWERP

‖**sprauchle** *vb syn* see SCRAMBLE 1

sprawl *vb* **1** to lie or sit with arms and legs stretched out carelessly and awkwardly <the dog lay *sprawled* out on the sofa>
  syn drape, ‖scamble, ‖spelder, spraddle, spread-eagle
  rel loll, lounge; slouch, slump
  2 to grow, develop, or spread irregularly and without apparent design or plan <the city *sprawls* down the whole coast>
  syn ramble, scramble, sprangle, spread=eagle, straddle, straggle
  rel extend, stretch; spread

spread *vb* **1** to extend or cause to extend over a considerable area or space <they *spread* the news far and wide> <clouds *spread* over the sky>
  syn circulate, diffuse, disperse, disseminate, distribute, propagate, radiate, strew; *compare* STREW 1
  rel deal, dispense; broadcast, communicate, pass (on), transmit; dissipate, scatter, sow; peddle, push, retail
  idiom spread abroad (*or* far and wide)
  con hold (in); contain; compress
  2 *syn* see OPEN 4
  con fold; close
  3 *syn* see SET 5

spread *n* **1** *syn* see EXPANSION 2
  rel diffusion; profusion; stretch, sweep
  2 *syn* see EXPANSE
  3 *syn* see DINNER
  4 *syn* see BEDSPREAD

spread-eagle *vb* **1** *syn* see SPRAWL 1
  2 *syn* see SPRAWL 2

‖**spreaghery** *n syn* see SPOIL

spree *n* **1** an unrestrained indulgence in or outburst of an activity <a shopping *spree*>
  syn binge, fling, orgy, rampage, splurge
  2 *syn* see BINGE 1

spree *vb syn* see REVEL 1

sprightful *adj syn* see LIVELY 1

sprightly *adj* **1** *syn* see LIVELY 1
  rel perky; breezy
  2 *syn* see ANTIC 2
  rel sportive; coltish, frisky
  3 *syn* see AGILE
  4 *syn* see CLEVER 5
  rel pungent, sharp; keen-witted, quick=witted

spring *vb* **1** to have something as a source <the primitive cultures from which civilization *springs*>

syn arise, birth, come (from), derive (from), emanate, flow, head, issue, originate, proceed, rise, stem, upspring; *compare* BEGIN 2
rel appear, emerge, come out, loom; arrive, come; begin, commence, hatch, start
2 *syn* see SKIP 1
3 *syn* see JUMP 1
4 *syn* see START 1
‖**5** *syn* see FREE

spring *n* **1** *usu* **springs** *pl syn* see SPA 1
2 *syn* see SOURCE
3 *syn* see YOUTH 1
ant autumn
4 *syn* see MOTIVE 1
rel excitant, impetus, incitement, stimulant, stimulus
5 the season between winter and summer <planting flowers in the *spring*>
syn budtime, springtide, springtime
rel ‖blackberry winter
idiom prime of the year
con autumn, fall

spring *adj syn* see VERNAL
springe *n syn* see PITFALL
springlike *adj syn* see VERNAL
springtide *n* **1** *syn* see SPRING 5
2 *syn* see YOUTH 1
ant autumn
springtime *n* **1** *syn* see SPRING 5
2 *syn* see YOUTH 1
ant autumn
springy *adj syn* see ELASTIC 1
rel rebounding, recoiling
ant rigid; springless

sprinkle *vb* **1** to scatter (something) in small drops or particles <*sprinkle* chocolate shot on whipped cream>
syn besprinkle, dust, powder, ‖strinkle; *compare* STREW 1
rel shake; scatter; pepper; sparge
2 *syn* see SPECKLE 1
3 *syn* see SPOT 2
4 *syn* see BAPTIZE
5 to rain lightly <it's only *sprinkling*, so we can still take our walk>
syn drizzle, ‖mizzle
rel mist; shower; spit
con pour, stream

sprinkling *n* **1** *syn* see HINT 2
2 *syn* see DUSTING
3 *syn* see FEW

sprint *vb syn* see RUN 1
sprit *vb syn* see SQUIRT
sprite *n syn* see FAIRY
‖**spritz** *vb syn* see SQUIRT
spruce *adj syn* see DAPPER
ant slouchy
spruce (up) *vb syn* see DRESS UP 1
sprucy *adj syn* see DAPPER
spry *adj syn* see AGILE
rel prompt, quick, ready; energetic, vigorous; healthy, robust, sound
ant doddering
spuddy *adj syn* see ROTUND 2
‖**spulzie** *n syn* see SPOIL
spume *n syn* see FOAM
spunk *n* **1** *syn* see FORTITUDE
rel bulldoggedness, doggedness
idiom clear (*or* true) grit
ant funk

2 *syn* see COURAGE
spunkless *adj syn* see COWARDLY
ant spunky
spunky *adj* **1** *syn* see BRAVE 1
idiom full of spunk
ant spunkless; funky
2 *syn* see SPIRITED 2
ant funky

spur *n syn* see STIMULUS
rel excitant; activation, actuation
ant checkrein, curb
spur *vb syn* see URGE
rel rowel; arouse, awaken, rally, rouse, stir; instigate; countenance, favor
ant curb

spurious *adj* **1** *syn* see ILLEGITIMATE 1
2 *syn* see ARTIFICIAL 2
3 of doubtful authenticity <claimed they had bought a *spurious* painting>
syn apocryphal, bastard, unauthentic, ungenuine; *compare* ARTIFICIAL 2, COUNTERFEIT
rel bogus, counterfeit, fake, phony, pseudo, sham; false, unreal
idiom not what (*or* all) it's cracked up to be
con actual, real, true; bona fide, genuine, veritable
ant authentic
4 *syn* see ARTIFICIAL 3
rel make-believe, pretend, pretended, pseudo
5 *syn* see COUNTERFEIT
spuriousness *n syn* see FALLACY 2
spurn *vb syn* see DECLINE 4
rel conspue, contemn, despise, disdain, scorn, scout; flout, scoff, sneer
con crave, desire, want
ant embrace
spur-of-the-moment *adj syn* see EXTEMPORANEOUS
spurt *vb syn* see SQUIRT
spurtle *vb syn* see SPLASH
sputter *vb* **1** to utter (words or ejaculations) hastily, explosively, and sometimes indistinctly <pompously *sputtering* his objections>
syn rip (out), spit, splutter
rel ejaculate, eject, throw (out); gibber, jabber, bluster, heckle, hector, rage, rant, rave, storm
2 to make a series of sudden short crackling or popping sounds <bacon *sputtering* in the pan>
syn spatter, spit, splutter
rel crackle, pop; hiss
spy (on *or* upon) *vb* to make furtive, stealthy, or secret observations of <had private detectives *spying* on his wife>
syn ‖stag
rel stake out; watch
spy *n* one who keeps secret watch to obtain information <was convicted on evidence produced by a *spy*>
syn agent, spook, undercover man; *compare* INFORMER
rel detective, investigator, sleuth; ‖narc; scout; beagle
idiom inside man, secret agent
spying *n syn* see ESPIONAGE
squab *adj syn* see STOCKY

‖**squab** *vb syn* see PRESS 1

squab *vb syn* see SPILL 1

squabble *n syn* see QUARREL

squabble *vb* **1** *syn* see QUARREL
  rel clash, encounter
  idiom have a squabble over
  2 *syn* see ARGUE 2
  idiom get into (*or* have) a hassle, have a verbal wrestling match

squalid *adj* **1** *syn* see DIRTY 1
  rel disheveled, slipshod, sloppy, slovenly, unkempt; frowzy, slatternly; dingy, shoddy, sleazy
  2 *syn* see SHABBY 1
  3 *syn* see BASE 3

squall *vb* **1** to make a raucous noise <angry street urchins fighting and *squalling* at each other>
  syn caw, ‖quawk, squark, squawk, yawp (*or* yaup)
  rel bellow, howl, roar, shout, yell; bark, yap, yip; croak
  2 *syn* see BAWL 2
  rel squeal; screech, shriek; yelp

squall *n syn* see QUARREL

squander *vb syn* see WASTE 2
  idiom make ducks and drakes of, play ducks and drakes with

squander *n syn* see EXTRAVAGANCE 2

squanderer *n syn* see SPENDTHRIFT

square *n* **1** *syn* see COMMON 2
  2 *syn* see FOGY

square *adj* **1** having four equal sides and four right angles <a large *square* box>
  syn foursquare, quadrate, quadratic, quadratical
  rel boxlike, boxy, squarish
  2 *syn* see EVEN 5
  3 *syn* see FAIR 4
  4 *syn* see CONVENTIONAL 1

square *vb* **1** *syn* see ADAPT
  2 *syn* see CLEAR 5
  3 *syn* see BRIBE
  4 *syn* see AGREE 4
  rel balance; coincide

square *adv syn* see JUST 1

squarehead *n syn* see DUNCE

squarely *adv* **1** *syn* see EVENLY 1
  2 *syn* see JUST 1

squark *vb syn* see SQUALL 1

squash *vb* **1** *syn* see PRESS 1
  2 *syn* see CRUSH 2
  3 *syn* see CRUSH 5
  4 *syn* see PRESS 7

squash *n* **1** *syn* see SQUELCH
  2 *syn* see CROWD 1

squashing *n syn* see REPRESSION 1

squashy *adj syn* see SOFT 6
  ant firm

squat *vb* to sit on one's haunches <they were *squatting* around the fire>
  syn hunker (down), ‖quat, ‖swat; *compare* CROUCH
  rel crouch; hunch; stoop

squat *adj syn* see STOCKY

syn synonym(s)   *rel* related word(s)
ant antonym(s)   *con* contrasted word(s)
idiom idiomatic equivalent(s)
‖ use limited; if in doubt, see a dictionary

  rel squattish, squatty
  con long, tall; twiggy
  ant lanky

‖**squaw** *n* **1** *syn* see WIFE
  2 *syn* see WOMAN 1

squawk *vb* **1** *syn* see SQUALL 1
  2 *syn* see GRIPE
  rel yap, yip

squawker *n syn* see INFORMER

squawky *adj syn* see HARSH 3
  con liquid, smooth, smooth

squdgy *adj syn* see STOCKY

squeak *vb* **1** to utter or make a short shrill cry or noise <mice *squeaking* in the barn>
  syn ‖queak; *compare* SQUEAL 2
  rel creak, grate, screak, screech, squeal; pipe; scream
  2 *syn* see TALK 6
  3 *syn* see INFORM 3

squeak *n syn* see OPPORTUNITY

‖**squeaker** *n syn* see INFORMER

squeal *vb* **1** *syn* see SCREAM 1
  idiom squeal like a stuck pig
  2 to make a harsh piercing sometimes rasping noise <tires *squealing* on wet pavement>
  syn screak, scream, screech, shriek; *compare* SQUEAK 1
  rel creak, grate, rasp
  3 *syn* see INFORM 3
  4 *syn* see TALK 6
  5 *syn* see YELL 2
  rel bitch, bleat, complain, gripe, squawk
  idiom raise a howl, scream bloody murder

squealer *n syn* see INFORMER

squeam *n syn* see QUALM

squeamish *adj* **1** inclined to become nauseated <felt *squeamish* after the heavy meal on the ship>
  syn ‖pensy, qualmish, qualmy, queasy, queer, ‖wambly; *compare* NAUSEATED
  rel unsettled, upset; dizzy, shaky, vertiginous
  2 *syn* see NAUSEATED
  idiom sick at (*or* to) one's stomach
  3 *syn* see NICE 1

squeamishness *n syn* see NAUSEA

squeamy *adj syn* see NICE 1

squeeze *vb* **1** *syn* see PRESS 1
  rel contract, ‖scruze
  2 *syn* see EMBRACE 1
  3 *syn* see EXTORT 1
  4 *syn* see EKE OUT 2
  5 *syn* see PRESS 8
  6 *syn* see PRESS 7

squeezy *adj syn* see CRAMPED

squelch *n* a sound of or as if of semiliquid matter under suction <the *squelch* of his feet in the mud>
  syn squash, squidge, squish

squelch *vb syn* see SUPPRESS 2

squelching *n syn* see REPRESSION 1

squelchy *adj syn* see SOFT 6

‖**squench** *vb* **1** *syn* see EXTINGUISH 1
  2 *syn* see QUENCH 4

squidge *n syn* see SQUELCH

squiffed *adj syn* see INTOXICATED 1

squiggle *vb* **1** *syn* see WRIGGLE
  2 *syn* see SCRIBBLE

squinch *vb* **1** *syn* see RECOIL
  2 *syn* see SQUINT

squinny *vb syn* see SQUINT
squinny *adj syn* see THIN 1
squint *vb* to look or peer with the eyes partly closed <*squinted* in the bright sunlight>
  syn ‖sken, squinch, squinny
  idiom look asquint, screw up one's eyes
  ant goggle
squirm *vb* 1 *syn* see WRIGGLE
  2 *syn* see WRITHE 1
squirrel *vb syn* see HOARD
squirt *vb* to come forth in a sudden rapid usually narrow stream <water *squirting* from the hose>
  syn jet, splurt, sprit, ‖spritz, spurt, ‖squitter
  rel pour, stream, surge; spatter; spray
  con dribble, drip, trickle
squirt *n* ‖1 **squirts** *pl syn* see DIARRHEA
  2 *syn* see TWERP
squish *n* 1 *syn* see PRESS 1
  2 *syn* see SQUELCH
squishy *adj syn* see SOFT 6
‖squit *n syn* see TWERP
‖squitter *vb syn* see SQUIRT
squush *vb syn* see PRESS 1
squushy *adj syn* see SOFT 6
stab *n* 1 *syn* see PRICK 1
  2 *syn* see POKE 1
  3 *syn* see FLING 1
stab *vb syn* see THRUST 2
  rel dagger, dirk, poniard, prong
stabbing *adj syn* see SHARP 8
stabile *adj syn* see STEADY 8
stability *vb syn* see STABILIZE
stabilitate *vb syn* see STABILIZE
stability *n* the ability to withstand force or stress without alteration of position and without material change <the structural *stability* of the bridge>
  syn firmness, security, soundness, stableness, steadiness, strength
  rel dependability, durability, reliability; solidity, solidness, sturdiness; cohesion, toughness
  con insecurity, undependability, unreliability, unsoundness, unsteadiness; weakness
  ant instability, unstability
stabilize *vb* to make or keep stable, steadfast, or firm <a policy that *stabilized* the economy>
  syn ballast, poise, stabilify, stabilitate, steady
  rel balance, counterbalance, counterpoise, equalize, equipoise; prop, support, sustain; fix, secure, set, settle
  ant unstabilize
stable *adj* 1 *syn* see SURE 1
  rel balanced, poised; fixed, set, solid, sound, steadfast
  con wobbling, wobbly
  ant instable, unstable
  2 *syn* see STEADY 2
  3 *syn* see LASTING
  rel constant, steady; safe, secure, sound; resolute, staunch, steadfast
  4 marked by solidity, firmness, and stability especially in design or construction <a *stable* foundation for the building>
  syn firm, secure, solid, sound; compare FAST 4, SURE 1
  rel strong, sturdy; unassailable, unshakable

  idiom as firm as (the rock of) Gibraltar, solid as a rock
  con insecure, shaky, unsound, weak, wobbling, wobbly
  ant instable, unstable
stableness *n syn* see STABILITY
  ant unstableness
stack *n syn* see PILE 1
stack *vb syn* see HEAP 1
‖stacked *adj* 1 *syn* see CURVACEOUS
  2 *syn* see BUXOM
stade *n syn* see STADIUM
stadium *n* a large usually unroofed structure with tiered seats enclosing a field used especially for sports <a football *stadium*>
  syn bowl, coliseum, stade
  rel arena, garden, gymnasium
‖stag *vb syn* see SPY (on or upon)
stage *n* 1 *used with the syn* see DRAMA
  2 *syn* see DEGREE 1
  rel level; phase; period
stage *vb* to present on the stage <*staged* a play>
  syn mount, produce, put on, show
  rel bring out, open; give, present; do, execute, perform, play
stage set *n syn* see SCENE 1
stage setting *n syn* see SCENE 1
stagger *vb* 1 *syn* see REEL 2
  2 *syn* see LURCH 2
  idiom pitch and plunge
  3 *syn* see TEETER
  rel ‖stiver, ‖stoit, ‖stoiter, ‖stot
  4 *syn* see HESITATE
  5 to affect with great wonder or bewilderment <a plot so bizarre as to *stagger* the imagination>
  syn boggle, dumbfound, nonplus
  rel perplex, puzzle, stump; amaze, astonish, astound, flabbergast; bowl (over), floor, knock over; devastate, overpower, overwhelm, shatter; paralyze
  idiom take (one) aback
stagger (on or along) *vb syn* see SHIFT 5
‖stagger *n syn* see FLING 1
staggering *adj syn* see MARVELOUS 1
stagnant *adj syn* see STATIC
stagnate *vb* 1 *syn* see VEGETATE
  2 *syn* see STULTIFY
stagnation *n syn* see DEPRESSION 3
staid *adj syn* see SERIOUS 1
  rel decorous, formal; collected, composed, cool; priggish, smug, starchy, stuffy
  con breezy, devil-may-care, easy, frivolous, debonair, jaunty; playful, sportive; hoydenish, rakish; fresh, irreverent; uncontrolled, unrestrained
  ant unstaid
stain *vb* 1 to soil often permanently with foreign matter <a shirt *stained* with grease>
  syn bestain, blot, discolor, smut; compare SOIL 2
  rel tinge; bedaub, daub, smear; besmirch, smirch, smudge, smutch
  2 *syn* see TAINT 1
  3 *syn* see DEBASE 1
stain *n* 1 *syn* see STIGMA
  rel blemish, defect, flaw
  idiom blot on the escutcheon
  2 *syn* see COLOR 6

stainless *adj syn* see CHASTE
 con tainted, tarnished
 ant stained
stake *n* 1 *syn* see BET
 2 *syn* see INTEREST 1
stake *vb* 1 *syn* see GAMBLE 1
 rel stake down
 2 *syn* see CAPITALIZE
stale *adj* 1 *syn* see MALODOROUS 1
 2 *syn* see TRITE
 rel dusty, fusty; dead
 ant fresh
‖**stale** *n syn* see LURE 2
stalemate *n syn* see DRAW 4
stalk *vb* 1 to pursue (game) stealthily or
 under cover <*stalk* deer>
 syn still-hunt
 rel follow, track; drive, chase, pursue; walk
 up; flush (out); ambush
 2 *syn* see STRIDE 1
stalky *adj syn* see THIN 1
stall *vb* ‖1 *syn* see SATIATE
 2 *syn* see ARREST 1
 rel brake, slow (down); hold off, put off,
 stand off; suspend; shut down
 idiom pull the checkstring
 con spur
stalwart *adj* 1 *syn* see STRONG 2
 rel athletic, brawny, husky, muscular, sinewy
 2 *syn* see BRAVE 1
stamina *n syn* see TOLERANCE 1
stammer *vb* 1 to make involuntary stops and
 repetitions in uttering syllables and words
 <the frightened child *stammered* and fell
 silent>
 syn ‖hammer, ‖stut, stutter
 rel falter, hesitate; stumble; splutter, sputter; gibber, jabber
 ‖2 *syn* see TEETER
stamp *vb* 1 *syn* see TRAMPLE 2
 rel clomp, clump, stump
 2 *syn* see IMPRESS 3
 rel etch, imprint, infix, inscribe, print
 idiom impress on the mind
stamp *n* 1 *syn* see IMPRESSION 1
 2 *syn* see TYPE
 3 *syn* see SEAL
stampede *vb* 1 *syn* see ROUT 1
 2 to take to sudden headlong flight in panic
 <cattle *stampeding* across the plain>
 syn pell-mell; *compare* RUSH 1
 rel bolt, charge, chase, crash, dash, fling,
 hurry, rush, shoot, tear
 idiom run like a pack of scalded dogs
stamping ground *n* 1 *syn* see HABITAT
 2 *syn* see RESORT 2
stance *n* 1 *syn* see POSTURE 1
 2 *syn* see POSITION 1
stanch *vb syn* see STEM
stand *vb* 1 *syn* see BEAR 10
 idiom ‖hack it, take lying down
 2 *syn* see TREAT 3
stand (on *or* upon) *vb syn* see DEPEND (on *or*
 upon) 1

idiom be contingent on
stand *n syn* see POSITION 1
standard *n* 1 *syn* see FLAG
 2 *syn* see MODEL 2
 3 a means of determining what a thing
 should be <each generation has its own
 standards of morality>
 syn benchmark, criterion, gauge, measure,
 touchstone, yardstick
 rel average, mean, median, norm, par; axiom, belief, fundamental, principle; law,
 rule; exemplar, model, pattern
 idiom rule of thumb
 4 a fixed, customary, or official measure (as
 of quantity, quality, or price) <governmen-
 tal *standards* of weights and measures>
 syn assize
 rel ‖dick
stander–by *n syn* see SPECTATOR
stand–in *n syn* see SUBSTITUTE 1
 rel second; assistant
standing *n* 1 *syn* see TERM 5
 2 *syn* see STATUS 1
 3 *syn* see STATUS 2
standoff *adj syn* see UNSOCIABLE
standoff *n syn* see DRAW 4
standoffish *adj* 1 *syn* see UNSOCIABLE
 2 *syn* see ANTISOCIAL
stand out *vb* 1 *syn* see BULGE
 2 *syn* see LOOM 3
standout *adj syn* see SUPERB 3
stand over *vb syn* see DEFER
standpat *n syn* see DIEHARD 1
standpatter *n syn* see DIEHARD 1
standpoint *n syn* see VIEWPOINT 2
standstill *n* cessation of movement <the car
 came to a *standstill* in the mud>
 syn stay, stillstand, stop
 rel arrest, check; pause; cessation, halt
 con start; movement
 ant start-up
stand up *vb syn* see RISE 1
stand–up *adj syn* see ERECT
 con lowered; flat, horizontal
‖**stang** *vb syn* see SMART
staple *n syn* see LOOP 2
staple *n syn* see BODY 3
star *adj syn* see CHIEF 2
starch *n syn* see VIGOR 2
star–crossed *adj syn* see UNLUCKY
stare *vb* 1 *syn* see LOOK 7
 idiom ‖take a gander at
 2 *syn* see GAZE 1
 idiom fix (*or* rivet) one's eyes on
stare down *vb* to overcome (someone) by or
 as if by staring <the teacher could not *stare*
 the boy *down*>
 syn look down, outstare
 rel glare; master, quell, subdue, suppress;
 overcome, overwhelm
stark *adj* 1 *syn* see UTTER
 2 *syn* see NUDE 2
 3 *syn* see EMPTY 1
‖**starkers** *adj syn* see NUDE 2
stark–naked *adj syn* see NUDE 2
 idiom bare (*or* naked) as a newborn babe,
 ‖naked as a jaybird, naked as the day one
 was born
‖**starny** *adj syn* see STELLAR 1
starry *adj syn* see STELLAR 1

---

syn synonym(s)   *rel* related word(s)
ant antonym(s)   *con* contrasted word(s)
idiom idiomatic equivalent(s)
‖ use limited; if in doubt, see a dictionary

start vb **1** to move suddenly and violently from a state of stillness or rest <*started* from his bed at the sound of shots>
syn bolt, jump, spring, startle
rel dart; bounce; bound, leap; draw (back), flinch, recoil
idiom jump out of one's skin, start aside
ant stay
2 syn see RECOIL
3 syn see BEGIN 2
rel proceed, spring
ant end
4 syn see FOUND 2
5 syn see BEGIN 1
ant stop
start n **1** syn see BEGINNING
ant finish
2 syn see ADVANTAGE 3
startle vb **1** syn see START 1
2 syn see SHOCK 2
3 syn see FRIGHTEN
rel astonish, surprise
idiom make one jump out of one's skin, ‖scare the pants off
startlish adj syn see EXCITABLE
starved adj syn see HUNGRY
rel underfed, undernourished; weakened; half-famished, half-starved
con fed, nourished; overfed
ant well-fed
starving adj syn see HUNGRY
rel craving, famishing, hungering; dying, perishing
idiom crazy for food
stash vb **1** syn see HOARD
2 syn see HIDE
rel hoard, squirrel
stasis n syn see BALANCE 1
state n **1** the way in which one manifests existence or the circumstances under which one exists or by which one is given distinctive character <remained in a weakened *state* for weeks>
syn condition, mode, posture, situation, status
rel circumstances; attitude, position, stand
idiom state of being
2 syn see STATUS 1
3 syn see STATUS 2
state vb **1** syn see RELATE 1
rel elucidate, explain, expound, interpret; set forth
2 syn see ENUNCIATE 1
3 syn see SAY 1
4 syn see EXPRESS 2
ant imply
stated adj syn see FIRM 4
stately adj **1** syn see CEREMONIAL
rel dignified, grand, noble; imperial, kingly, princely, regal, royal
2 syn see COURTLY
3 syn see GRAND 1
con lowly, poor; shabby; cheap
statement n **1** syn see EXPRESSION 1
rel outgiving; articulation, presentation, presentment, verbalization, vocalization
2 syn see WORD 1
rel description, narrative, recital
3 syn see BILL 1

static adj characterized by relatively little or no movement, progression, or change (as in conditions) <a *static* economy>
syn immobile, stagnant, stationary, unmoving; compare STEADY 2
rel constant, stabile, stable, unchanging, unfluctuating; fixed, immovable, rigid, sticky; inactive, inert; stalled, stopped, stuck
idiom at a standstill, standing still
con active, changing, mobile, moving, progressing; erratic, fluctuating, inconstant, unstable
ant dynamic
station n **1** syn see PLACE 1
2 syn see RAILROAD STATION
3 syn see STATUS 1
station vb to appoint or assign to an office or duty <*stationed* guards around the camp>
syn post, set
rel appoint, assign; place, position
stationary adj syn see STATIC
rel motionless, stock-still
ant moving
station house n syn see RAILROAD STATION
statuesque adj syn see SHAPELY
stature n **1** syn see QUALITY 2
rel prestige, standing, status; ability, capacity; competence, qualification
2 syn see STATUS 2
status n **1** rating or positioning in relation to others (as in a social order, community, class, or profession) <his *status* as a slave>
syn capacity, character, footing, place, position, quality, rank, situation, standing, state, station
rel rating
2 social or professional importance or distinction <a lawyer of international *status*>
syn cachet, consequence, dignity, position, prestige, rank, standing, state, stature
rel caliber, merit, worth; distinction, renown; eminence, prominence
con inconsequence, insignificance, unimportance
3 syn see STATE 1
rel status quo
idiom state of affairs
statute n syn see LAW 1
rel act, enactment
staunch adj **1** syn see SURE 1
2 syn see FAITHFUL 1
rel firm, strong
idiom as staunch as an oak, tried and true
con mercurial; shaky, unsteady
stave vb syn see HURRY 2
stave off vb **1** syn see FEND (off)
rel beat off, drive (off), fight (off); block, parry
2 syn see PREVENT 2
staving adv syn see VERY 1
ant barely
stay vb **1** syn see ARREST 1
rel postpone, prorogue, put off
2 to continue to be in one place for a noticeable time <*stayed* late at the office>
syn abide, bide, linger, remain, stick around, tarry, wait
rel dally, delay, dillydally, lag, procrastinate; hang around, loiter; outstay, stay out

ant go
3 *syn see* VISIT 3
rel bide, dwell, live
4 *syn see* DEFER
stay *n syn see* STANDSTILL
stay *n syn see* SUPPORT 3
stay *vb syn see* BASE
stead *vb syn see* HELP 1
steadfast *adj* **1** *syn see* IMMOVABLE 1
2 *syn see* INFLEXIBLE 2
ant unsteadfast, vacillating
3 *syn see* SURE 2
ant capricious
4 *syn see* FAITHFUL 1
rel unfaltering, unflinching, unquestioning, unwavering
steadfastly *adv syn see* HARD 7
rel staunchly, strongly
steadiness *n syn see* STABILITY
ant unsteadiness
steady *adj* **1** *syn see* SURE 2
rel unswerving; eternal, never-ending
2 being neither markedly varying nor variable in course or extent <a *steady* rain> <*steady* prices>
syn constant, equable, even, stabile, stable, unchanging, unfluctuating, uniform, unvarying; *compare* STATIC
rel steady-going; certain, changeless, fixed, set, sure, unchangeable; unflickering, unwavering; durable, reliable
con inconstant, uneven, unstable; changeable; changing, fluctuating, uncertain, undependable, undulating, unsure, varying, wavering
ant unsteady
3 *syn see* FAITHFUL 1
steady *vb syn see* STABILIZE
steady *n* **1** *syn see* BOYFRIEND 2
2 *syn see* GIRL FRIEND 2
steal *vb* **1** to take another's possession illegally and without his knowledge <*stole* a car>
syn abstract, annex, appropriate, cabbage, ‖clout, ‖cly, collar, ‖coon, ‖cop, ‖crook, filch, ‖heist, hook, lift, nab, ‖nail, ‖nick, nim, nip, pilfer, pillage, pinch, pocket, ‖prig, purloin, rip off, smouch, ‖snaffle, ‖snake, snitch, swipe, thieve, vulture
rel mooch; fleece, frisk; grab, grasp, seize, snatch, take; plagiarize; hijack, shanghai; poach, rustle; burglarize, rob; loot, plunder, rifle
idiom make off (*or* away) with, run away (*or* off) with
2 *syn see* SNEAK
3 to move or go quietly so as not to disturb <*stole* out of the sickroom on tiptoe>
syn creep, glide, mouse, slide, slip; *compare* SNEAK
rel tiptoe
con clump, stamp, stomp, stump
steal *n* **1** *syn see* THEFT
2 *syn see* BARGAIN 1
stealage *n syn see* THEFT

stealer *n syn see* THIEF
stealing *n syn see* THEFT
stealthily *adv syn see* SECRETLY
ant openly
stealthy *adj* **1** *syn see* SECRET 1
rel crafty, cunning, sly, wily; skulking, slinking, sneaking; catlike
con direct, straight, straightforward
ant open
2 being so quiet, slow, and deliberate in movement as to escape observation <the *stealthy* movements of the cat burglar>
syn catlike, catty, feline, furtive; *compare* SECRET 1
rel noiseless, pantherine, pantherish, quiet, silent; shifty, skulking, sly, sneak, sneaking, sneaky
steam *n syn see* POWER 4
steamroller *vb syn see* WHIP 2
steam up *vb syn see* ANGER 1
steel *vb* **1** *syn see* GIRD 3
rel rally; nerve; buck up; reinforce
idiom grit one's teeth, set one's jaw, take the bit in one's teeth
ant unsteel
2 *syn see* ENCOURAGE 1
steep *adj* **1** having an incline approaching the perpendicular <a *steep* trail up the mountain>
syn abrupt, arduous, precipitate, precipitous, sheer, sideling, steepdown, steep-to, steep-up, ‖stickle
rel elevated, lifted, raised; steepish; high, lofty; prerupt; perpendicular, straight-up; breakneck
con easy, gentle, gradual, moderate; shelfy, shelving, shelvy
2 *syn see* EXCESSIVE 1
steep *vb* **1** *syn see* SOAK 1
2 *syn see* INFUSE 1
steepdown *adj syn see* STEEP 1
steep–to *adj syn see* STEEP 1
steep–up *adj syn see* STEEP 1
steer *vb syn see* GUIDE
idiom steer one's course
steer *n syn see* TIP
stellar *adj* **1** of, relating to, or suggestive of a star or group of stars <*stellar* light>
syn astral, sidereal, ‖starny, starry, stellular
rel gleaming, luminous, lustrous, shining, starlike, twinkling; star-spangled
con starless
2 *syn see* CHIEF 2
stellify *vb syn see* EXALT 1
stellular *adj syn see* STELLAR 1, astral, sidereal, ‖starny, starry
stem *n syn see* SPRING 1
stem *vb* to hinder or prevent by or as if by damming <*stem* the flow of blood>
syn stanch, stop
rel arrest, check, control
stemma *n syn see* GENEALOGY
stench *vb syn see* SMELL 3
stenchful *adj syn see* MALODOROUS 1
stenchy *adj syn see* MALODOROUS 1
stentorian *adj syn see* LOUD 1
rel orotund; clamorous, vociferous; gravelly, rough; clarion-voiced, loudmouthed, loud-voiced, trumpet-tongued
stentorious *adj syn see* LOUD 1

---

stentorophonic *adj syn* see LOUD 1
step *n* 1 *syn* see FOOTPRINT
  2 *syn* see DEGREE 1
  3 *syn* see MEASURE 7
  rel act, action; motion
step *vb* 1 *syn* see WALK 1
  2 *syn* see DANCE 1
step–by–step *adj syn* see GRADUAL
step in *vb* 1 *syn* see VISIT 2
  2 *syn* see INTERPOSE 2
step up *vb syn* see SPEED 3
  ant step down
stereotyped *adj syn* see TRITE
  idiom worn thin
stereotypical *adj syn* see TRITE
  ant original
sterile *adj* 1 lacking the power to bear off-spring or produce fruit <a hybrid that is completely *sterile*>
  syn barren, effete, impotent, infecund, infertile, unfruitful
  rel sterilized; fallow, fruitless, unproductive; unprolific; arid, bare, dry; dead, desolate
  con potent, productive, rich; bearing, fruiting, fruitive, producing, turning out, yielding; fecund, fruitful, prolific, teeming
  ant fertile
  2 *syn* see UNORIGINAL
  rel flat, insipid, jejune, vapid; stale; effete, worn-out; impotent
  con fertile, fruitful, potent, producing, productive, prolific
  ant fecund
sterilize *vb* to make incapable of producing offspring <*sterilizing* animals in medical experiments>
  syn alter, castrate, change, desexualize, fix, geld, mutilate, neuter, unsex
  rel emasculate; caponize, poulardize; spay
sterling *adj syn* see HONORABLE 1
  rel pure, true
stern *adj syn* see SEVERE 1
  rel grim, implacable, unrelenting; inexorable, inflexible
  ant lenient, soft
‖**stern** *n syn* see BUTTOCKS
stew *n* 1 *syn* see BROTHEL
  2 *usu* stews *pl syn* see RED-LIGHT DISTRICT
  3 *syn* see SLUM
  4 *syn* see MISCELLANY 1
  5 *syn* see SNIT
  rel boil
  6 *syn* see COMMOTION 2
stew *vb* 1 *syn* see BOIL 2
  2 *syn* see WORRY 3
  idiom be in a stew
stewardly *adj syn* see SPARING
‖**stewed** *adj syn* see INTOXICATED 1
stick *n* 1 *syn* see BAR 1
  2 *syn* see DECOY 2
  3 sticks *pl, used with the syn* see FRONTIER 2
  idiom the middle of nowhere
stick *adv syn* see ALL 1
stick *vb* 1 *syn* see THRUST 1
  2 to become or cause to become closely and firmly attached <papers all *stuck* together>
  syn adhere, cleave, cling, cohere
  rel affix, attach, fasten, fix; glue; cement; fuse, weld; braze, solder

  idiom stick close, stick like a wet shirt, stick like the paper on the wall, stick like wax, stick to like a barnacle (*or* leech)
  con loosen; detach, disengage
  ant unstick
  3 *syn* see SET 1
  4 *syn* see NONPLUS 1
  5 *syn* see FLEECE 1
  6 *syn* see OVERCHARGE 1
  ‖7 *syn* see BEAR 10
  8 *syn* see DEMUR
stickage *n syn* see ADHERENCE 1
stick around *vb syn* see STAY 2
stick–at–nothing *adj syn* see UNSCRUPULOUS
sticker *n syn* see SEAL
sticking *n syn* see ADHERENCE 1
stick–in–the–mud *n syn* see FOGY
‖**stickle** *adj syn* see STEEP 1
stickle *vb syn* see DEMUR
  rel hold out, stall; contend, kick, object, protest
stick out *vb* 1 *syn* see BULGE
  rel outstretch, outthrust, protend, push
  2 *syn* see STRIKE 1
  3 *syn* see BEAR 10
stick up *vb syn* see ROB 1
sticky *adj* 1 having the quality of sticking by or as if by adhesion <*sticky* syrup>
  syn adhesive, ‖claggy, ‖clarty, cloggy, gluey, gooey, gummy, stodgy
  rel tacky; viscid, viscous
  2 *syn* see HUMID
  3 *syn* see HARD 6
  4 *syn* see SENTIMENTAL
‖**stickybeak** *n syn* see BUSYBODY
sticky–fingered *adj syn* see LARCENOUS
stiff *adj* 1 incapable of or highly resistant to bending or flexing <a *stiff* cardboard packing box>
  syn immalleable, impliable, incompliant, inelastic, inflexible, rigid, unbending, unflexible, unyielding; *compare* INFLEXIBLE 2
  rel stiffish; hard, resistant; hardened, petrified; stark
  idiom stiff as a board (*or* poker)
  con soft, softened; yielding; bendable, pliable, pliant; limber, supple, willowy
  ant flexible, flexile
  2 *syn* see INTOXICATED 1
  3 *syn* see OBSTINATE
  4 characterized by a lack of ease, grace, or spontaneity especially in style <a play whose dialogue and characters were *stiff* and perfunctory>
  syn buckram, cardboard, muscle-bound, stilted, wooden
  rel rigid, set, studied; machine-made, mechanical, stereotyped, stock; arid, dry, dull
  con expressive, graphic, vivid; easy, fluent, graceful, smooth
  5 *syn* see EXCESSIVE 1
stiff *n* 1 *syn* see CORPSE
  2 *syn* see DRUNKARD
  3 *syn* see MISER
stiff–necked *adj syn* see OBSTINATE
stifle *vb* 1 *syn* see SUFFOCATE
  2 *syn* see MUFFLE 2
  3 *syn* see SUPPRESS 3
  4 *syn* see STULTIFY

stifling adj 1 producing or seeming to produce suffocation <*stifling* heat>
  syn smothering, smothery, ‖smudgy, suffocating, suffocative; *compare* HUMID, STUFFY 1
  rel oppressive, overpowering; unbearable, unendurable
  2 **syn** see STUFFY 1
stifling n **syn** see REPRESSION 1
stigma n a mark of shame or discredit <the *stigma* of personal cowardice>
  syn bar sinister, black eye, blot, brand, odium, onus, slur, spot, stain
  rel besmirchment, disfigurement, smudge, smutch, taint, tainting; disgrace, dishonor, shame
  con credit, distinction, glory, honor; bay(s), crown, laurel(s)
still adj 1 **syn** see MOTIONLESS
  2 **syn** see CALM 1
  rel peaceful, unperturbed
  con roiled, roily, turbid
  3 devoid of or making no stir, sound, or noise <the streets were *still* at 3:00 A.M.>
  syn hush, hushful, noiseless, quiet, silent, soundless, stilly, whist
  rel calm, hushed, peaceful, placid, serene, tranquil; deathlike, deathly
  idiom deathly still, still as death
  ant noisy
still vb 1 **syn** see CALM
  ant agitate
  2 **syn** see SILENCE
still adv 1 **syn** see HOWEVER
  2 **syn** see YET 1
  idiom still (*or* even) more
  3 **syn** see ALSO 2
still n **syn** see SILENCE 1
still and all adv **syn** see HOWEVER
still–hunt vb **syn** see STALK 1
stillness n **syn** see SILENCE 1
stillstand n **syn** see STANDSTILL
stilly adj 1 **syn** see STILL 3
  con agitated, disturbed, noisy
  ant noiseful
  2 **syn** see CALM 1
stilted adj 1 **syn** see RHETORICAL
  2 **syn** see STIFF 4
  3 **syn** see GENTEEL 3
  rel conventional, formal; decorous; prim
stimulant n **syn** see STIMULUS
stimulate vb 1 **syn** see PROVOKE 4
  rel enliven, vivify; activate, dynamize, energize, vitalize
  idiom build a fire under, get one started (*or* moving)
  con unnerve; deaden
  2 **syn** see ELATE
stimulating adj 1 **syn** see EXCITING
  rel enlivening, lively; provocative, seminal, suggestive; incitory, stimulative, stimulatory
  2 **syn** see INVIGORATING
stimulative adj **syn** see INVIGORATING
stimulus n something that rouses the mind or spirits or incites to activity <the war proved a *stimulus* to the economy> <sought

a *stimulus* to take her mind off her own troubles>
  syn catalyst, goad, impetus, impulse, incentive, incitation, incitement, instigation, motivation, propellant, provocative, push, spur, stimulant; *compare* MOTIVE 1
  rel boost, encouragement, inducement, invitation, urging; cause, motive; excitement, piquing, provocation, stimulation
sting vb **syn** see SMART
stingy adj being unwilling or showing unwillingness to share with others <too *stingy* to tip the waiter>
  syn cheap, cheeseparing, ‖chinchy, chintzy, close, closefisted, costive, hardfisted, handhanded, ironfisted, mean, mingy, miserly, ‖narrow, narrow-fisted, narrowhearted, niggard, niggardly, parsimonious, penny=pinching, penny-wise, penurious, pinching, pinchpenny, save-all, ‖scant, scrimy, scrimpy, tight, tightfisted, ungenerous, ungiving; *compare* SPARING
  rel economical, frugal, Scotch, sparing, thrifty; scaly, screwy
  idiom as close as a vise, as close (*or* tight) as paper on a wall, near (*or* close *or* tight) as the bark on a tree
  con bountiful, giving, liberal, munificent, open-handed, philanthropic, unsparing, unstinting; prodigal
  ant generous
stink vb **syn** see SMELL 3
stinkard n **syn** see SNOT 1
stinkaroo n **syn** see SNOT 1
stinker n **syn** see SNOT 1
stinking adj 1 **syn** see MALODOROUS 1
  idiom stinking to high heaven
  ‖2 **syn** see INTOXICATED 1
‖**stinko** adj **syn** see INTOXICATED 1
stinky adj **syn** see MALODOROUS 1
stint vb 1 **syn** see SCRIMP
  2 **syn** see SPARE 3
stint n 1 **syn** see RESTRICTION 1
  2 **syn** see TASK 1
  rel amount, quantity; allotment, apportionment; participation, share
  3 **syn** see SPELL 1
stipend n **syn** see WAGE
  rel award, consideration, payment
stipple vb **syn** see SPECKLE 1
stipulate vb **syn** see SPECIFY 3
  rel designate; state; provide
stipulated adj **syn** see FIRM 3
  rel designated, pinned down
  con implied, unstated, unwritten
stipulation n **syn** see CONDITION 1
  rel specification; circumscription, limit
stir vb 1 to cause to shift from quiescence or torpor into activity <a teacher who *stirred* the minds of his most sluggish students>
  syn arouse, awaken, bestir, challenge, kindle, rally, rouse, wake, waken, whet; *compare* PROVOKE 4
  rel excite, galvanize, inspire, provoke, quicken, stimulate; agitate, foment, incite, instigate; activate, energize, vitalize, actuate, drive, impel, move; ‖roust, rout
  idiom make (*or* have) an impact on, set astir, set on fire
  2 **syn** see WAKE 1

3 *syn* see SEETHE 4

stir (up) *vb syn* see INCITE

idiom add fuel to the flame, apply the torch, feed the fire, pour oil on the fire, stir the embers

stir *n* 1 signs of excited activity, hurry, or commotion <noticed a *stir* within the crowd>

syn ado, bustle, flurry, furore, fuss, pother, whirl, whirlpool, whirlwind; *compare* COMMOTION 4

rel agitation, disquiet, stir-up; commotion, disturbance; din, hubbub, pandemonium, stirabout, tumult

con calm, peace, placidity; inaction, inactivity

ant tranquillity

2 *syn* see MOTION 1

‖**stir** *n syn* see JAIL

‖**stirra** *n syn* see MAN 3

stirring *n syn* see MOTION 1

stirring *adj syn* see EXCITING

rel heart-stirring, soul-stirring

stitch *n syn* see PAIN 1

stivy *adj syn* see STUFFY 1

stock *n* 1 *syn* see FAMILY 1

2 *syn* see ESTIMATION 1

3 *syn* see TRUST 1

4 *syn* see SUPPLY

5 *syn* see RESERVE

stock *vb* to equip, furnish, supply, or have material requisites (as for sale) <a bar that *stocks* all the best brands of liquor>

syn carry, keep

rel have; furnish, supply

idiom have (or keep) in stock, keep on hand

stockade *n syn* see JAIL

stockpile *n* 1 *syn* see PILE 1

2 *syn* see RESERVE

stockpile *vb syn* see ACCUMULATE

stock-still *adj syn* see MOTIONLESS

stocky *adj* being compact and broad in build and often short in stature <a *stocky* but quick and hard-hitting catcher>

syn ‖chuffy, ‖chumpy, chunky, dumpy, heavyset, squab, squat, squdgy, stubby, ‖stuggy, stumpy, thick, thick-bodied, thickset

rel plump, stout; bunty, low-set, short; lumpish, lumpy, pudgy; corpulent, fat

con lean, skinny, thin, wiry

stodge *vb* 1 *syn* see SATIATE

2 *syn* see PLOD 1

stodgy *adj* 1 *syn* see STICKY 1

2 *syn* see DULL 9

rel unexciting; pedantic; heavy, ponderous, weighty

3 *syn* see TACKY 2

stoic *adj syn* see IMPASSIVE 1

rel aloof, detached, indifferent, unconcerned; self-controlled, Spartan; indomitable, unassailable; long-suffering, patient, resigned

stoicism *n syn* see APATHY 1

rel backbone, fortitude, grit, guts, pluck, sand

‖**stoit** *vb syn* see LURCH 2

‖**stoiter** *vb syn* see LURCH 2

stolid *adj syn* see IMPASSIVE 1

rel blunt, dull, obtuse; dense, dull, dumb, slow, stupid; inactive, inert, passive, supine

ant sensitive

stolidity *n syn* see APATHY 1

rel dullness, dumbness, slowness, stupidity; inactiveness, inactivity, inertia, passivity

con aptness, quickness, readiness; animation, enlivening, quickening; ardor, enthusiasm, fervor, passion, zeal; fire

ant sensitivity

stomach *n* 1 *syn* see ABDOMEN

2 *syn* see APPETITE 1

stomach *vb syn* see BEAR 10

stomachache *n* abdominal pain <she has a terrible *stomachache*>

syn bellyache, colic, collywobbles, gripe(s)

rel distress, misery

‖**stomachy** *adj syn* see IRASCIBLE

stomp *vb syn* see TRAMPLE 2

stone-blind *adj syn* see BLIND 1

stone-broke *adj syn* see POOR 1

stoned *adj* 1 *syn* see INTOXICATED 1

2 *syn* see DRUGGED

stone-still *adj syn* see MOTIONLESS

stony *adj* 1 *syn* see UNFEELING 2

ant soft

2 *syn* see POOR 1

stonyhearted *adj syn* see UNFEELING 2

rel flinty, hard, stonelike

idiom as cold as marble

ant softhearted

stooge *n* 1 one who plays a subordinate or compliant role to a principal <an executive who was only a *stooge* with no real power>

syn Charlie McCarthy, dummy, yes-man

2 *syn* see TOOL 2

stool *n syn* see INFORMER

‖**stool** *vb syn* see INFORM 3

‖**stoolie** *n syn* see INFORMER

stool pigeon *n syn* see INFORMER

stoop *vb* 1 to descend from one's level (as of rank or dignity) usually to do something <a king who would not *stoop* to consider the common people>

syn condescend, deign

rel relax, thaw, unbend; accord, concede; accommodate, favor, oblige

idiom be so good as to, come (or get) down from one's high horse, lower oneself

2 to drop in status or dignity by indulgence in pettiness or unworthy behavior <a woman who would not *stoop* to tell a lie>

syn descend, sink

idiom act beneath oneself, debase (or demean) oneself, lower oneself

3 *syn* see DUCK 2

stop *vb* 1 *syn* see STEM

2 *syn* see FILL 1

rel disrupt, hinder, interrupt; cut off, shut off, turn off

ant unstop

3 to suspend or cause to suspend activity <the conversation *stopped*>

syn cease, desist, ‖deval, discontinue, give over, halt, knock off, leave off, quit, surcease; *compare* ARREST 1

rel ‖can, refrain (from); arrest, check, cut off, interrupt; stay, suspend; ‖cheese, lay off; break off, break up, end, terminate

con continue, go on, keep (on), keep up, persist

ant start

4 to come to a standstill <the car *stopped* at the intersection>
syn bring up, draw up, fetch up, halt, haul up, pull up
con start; move; pull out
ant go

stop (in *or* by) *vb syn* see VISIT 2

stop (over) *vb syn* see VISIT 3
idiom make a stopover

stop *n* 1 *syn* see END 2
ant start
2 *syn* see BAR 2
3 *syn* see STANDSTILL

stopcock *n syn* see FAUCET

stopgap *adj syn* see MAKESHIFT

stopgap *n syn* see RESOURCE 3

stopover *n syn* see SOJOURN

stopper *vb syn* see FILL 1
ant unstopper

store *vb syn* see STOW

store (up) *vb syn* see ACCUMULATE
rel deposit; cache

store *n* 1 *syn* see RESERVE
2 *syn* see SUPPLY
3 *syn* see DEPOT 2
4 a business establishment where goods are shown for sale <a food *store*>
syn market, outlet, shop, showroom
rel discounter, discount house, discount store, emporium

store *adj syn* see READY-MADE

store–bought *adj syn* see READY-MADE

‖**store–boughten** *adj syn* see READY=MADE

storehouse *n syn* see DEPOT 2

storm *n* 1 *syn* see COMMOTION 4
2 *syn* see BARRAGE

storm *vb syn* see ATTACK 1

storm and stress *n syn* see UNREST

stormful *adj syn* see WILD 6
rel threatening; dusty, murky, foul; howling, riproaring, roaring
ant calm

stormily *adv syn* see HARD 2

stormy *adj syn* see WILD 6
rel threatening; dusty, murky, foul; howling, riproaring, roaring
ant calm

story *n* 1 *syn* see ACCOUNT 7
2 a recital of real or imaginary happenings that is less elaborate than a novel <told the *story* of his escape> <a simple *story* of heart-warming devotion>
syn anecdote, narration, narrative, tale, yarn; *compare* ACCOUNT 7
rel conte; description; fable; folktale, legend, märchen; Canterbury tale, cock-and-bull story, fabrication, fairy tale, fiction
3 *syn* see LIE

storyteller *n syn* see LIAR

‖**stot** *vb syn* see LURCH 2

stout *adj* 1 *syn* see BRAVE 1
idiom bold as a lion
con irresolute; fainthearted
2 *syn* see STRONG 2

rel resolute, steadfast; hard; indomitable, invincible
idiom as strong (*or* stalwart) as an English oak
3 *syn* see FAT 2
rel thick-bodied; ‖plenitudinous
ant spare

stouthearted *adj syn* see BRAVE 1

stow *vb* to put (articles) into a storage space <*stowed* his gear belowdecks>
syn bestow, pack, store, warehouse
ant unstow

straddle *vb* 1 *syn* see BESTRIDE 2
2 *syn* see SPRAWL 2

straggle *vb* 1 *syn* see WANDER 1
2 *syn* see SPRAWL 2

straggler *n syn* see LAGGARD

straight *adv* 1 *syn* see AWAY 3
2 *syn* see DIRECTLY 1

straight *adj* 1 *syn* see DIRECT 2
idiom as straight as an arrow
ant circuitous
2 *syn* see STRAIGHTFORWARD 2
3 free from admixture or extraneous matter <a shot of *straight* liquor>
syn neat, plain, pure, unadulterated, undiluted, unmixed
rel unmodified; concentrated; strong
con adulterated, blended, mixed; watered=down; weak
4 *syn* see CONVENTIONAL 1

straight *n syn* see RIGHT 1

straightaway *adv syn* see AWAY 3

straightforward *adj syn* see DIRECT 2
2 free from all that is dishonest or secretive <a *straightforward* answer>
syn aboveboard, forthright, plain dealing, straight; *compare* FRANK
rel pretenseless; honest, honorable, just, upright, upstanding; candid, frank, open, plain, unequivocal; direct, outspoken
con equivocal, evasive, shuffling; indirect; prevaricative; dishonest, untruthful
ant devious
3 *syn* see FRANK
rel barefaced, straight-from-the-shoulder
4 *syn* see CLEAR 5

straightly *adv syn* see DIRECTLY 1

straight off *adv syn* see AWAY 3

straight-out *adj syn* see UTTER

straight-up *adj* 1 *syn* see ERECT
2 *syn* see VERTICAL

straightway *adv syn* see AWAY 3

strain *n* 1 *syn* see HINT 2
2 *syn* see MELODY
3 *syn* see MOOD 1

strain *vb* 1 *syn* see TRY 2
rel stretch
idiom put a strain on
2 to injure (as a body part) by overuse or misuse <*strained* a muscle while lifting weights>
syn pull
3 *syn* see LABOR 1
4 *syn* see EXUDE
5 *syn* see DEMUR

strain *n syn* see STRESS 1

strained *adj syn* see FORCED
rel taut, tense, tight
con unforced, unlabored; unconstrained

syn synonym(s)   *rel* related word(s)
ant antonym(s)   *con* contrasted word(s)
idiom idiomatic equivalent(s)
‖ use limited; if in doubt, see a dictionary

ant unstrained

strait n syn see JUNCTURE 2
 rel bind, squeeze; difficulty, hardship, rigor, vicissitude; bewilderment, mystification, perplexity

straitlaced adj syn see PRIM 1
 rel hidebound, intolerant, narrow, narrow-minded; rigorous, strict
 idiom prim and proper
 con easygoing, relaxed; broadminded, liberal, liberal-minded; libertine

strake vb syn see STREAK

‖**stramash** n syn see CRASH 3

strand n syn see SHORE

strand vb syn see SHIPWRECK

stranded adj syn see AGROUND
 idiom high and dry, run aground

strange adj 1 syn see EXOTIC 2
 2 syn see UNFAMILIAR 1
 rel unknown; alien
 3 syn see MARVELOUS 1
 4 deviating from what is ordinary, usual, or to be expected <a *strange*, unpredictable man>
 syn bizarre, curious, eccentric, erratic, idiosyncratic, odd, oddball, outlandish, peculiar, quaint, queer, ‖rum, rummy, singular, uncouth, unusual, weird; compare EXCEPTIONAL 1, MYSTERIOUS
 rel aberrant, abnormal, atypical, off, off-the-wall; fishy, funny; far-out, freaky, ‖kinky, kooky, offbeat, outré; ‖scatty; crazy, nutty; fantastic, grotesque
 idiom as strange as they come
 con common, ordinary, unexceptional, usual; expected, predictable
 ant familiar

stranger n a nonresident or an unknown person in a community <he felt he had become a *stranger* in a foreign land>
 syn alien, auslander, foreigner, inconnu, outcomer, outlander, outsider
 rel out-of-stater, outstater; transient; visitor; immigrant; wanderer
 idiom stranger within the gates
 con inhabitant, resident; aboriginal, aborigine, autochthon, indigene, native

strangle vb 1 syn see CHOKE 1
 2 syn see SUPPRESS 2

strangling n syn see REPRESSION 1

strapped adj syn see POOR 1

stratagem n syn see TRICK 1
 rel conspiracy, intrigue, machination, plot

strategy n syn see PLAN 1

stratospheric adj syn see EXCESSIVE 1

straw adj syn see BLOND 1
 rel strawish, strawy

straw vb syn see STREW 1

stray vb 1 syn see WANDER 1
 2 syn see ERR
 idiom stray from the straight and narrow
 3 syn see DIGRESS 2
 idiom get off the track, get sidetracked

stray adj syn see ERRATIC 1
 rel random, sporadic

streak n syn see HINT 2

streak vb to make irregular lines or stripes of contrasting colors on or in <hair *streaked* with gray>
 syn strake, striate, stripe

 rel dapple, fleck, spot; marble, variegate, vein

stream n 1 syn see CREEK 2
 2 syn see FLOW

stream vb syn see POUR 2

streamer n syn see FLAG

streamline vb syn see SIMPLIFY

‖**streel** n syn see SLATTERN 1

street n syn see WAY 1
 rel ruelle, streetlet; drive

street arab n syn see VAGABOND

street girl n syn see PROSTITUTE

streetwalker n syn see PROSTITUTE

streetwalking n syn see PROSTITUTION

strength n 1 syn see POWER 4
 rel brawn; sturdiness, toughness; healthiness, soundness
 con feebleness
 ant weakness
 2 syn see STABILITY
 3 syn see SUBSTANCE 2

strengthen vb 1 syn see ENCOURAGE 1
 2 to make strong or stronger <exercise is needed to *strengthen* the body>
 syn energize, fortify, invigorate, reinforce
 rel brace, support, undergird; anneal, ruggedize, sinew, tone (up), toughen; cheer, embolden, encourage, enhearten, ensteel, hearten, inspirit, nerve, steel
 con cripple, debilitate, disable, enfeeble, tear down, undermine; deject, discourage, dishearten, dispirit; emasculate, enervate, unman, unnerve
 ant weaken
 3 syn see GIRD 3
 idiom gather one's resources, recruit one's strength

‖**strengthy** adj syn see STRONG 1

strenuous adj 1 syn see VIGOROUS
 2 syn see HARD 6
 rel breathless, energy-consuming; mean, wicked; Herculean
 idiom a long hard pull, an uphill climb, tough going
 con comfortable, cushy, light, unburdensome
 ant effortless

stress n the action or effect of force exerted within or upon a thing <the bridge trusses slowly yielded to *stress* and buckled under the weight of the deck>
 syn pressure, strain, tension
 rel pinch; burden, weight
 2 syn see EMPHASIS
 rel import, importance

stress vb 1 syn see TRY 2
 2 syn see EMPHASIZE

stretch vb 1 syn see RUN 8
 rel range, roll
 2 syn see EXTEND 3
 con abbreviate, shorten; condense, curtail, cut, trim
 3 syn see EMBROIDER

stretch (out) vb syn see REST 1

stretch n 1 syn see RANGE 2
 2 syn see DISTANCE 1
 3 syn see EXPANSE
 rel area, region, tract
 4 syn see WHILE 1

stretch adj syn see ELASTIC 1

stretchy *adj syn* see ELASTIC 1
strew *vb* 1 to spread (something) loosely or at intervals usually over a substantial area <*strew* seed for birds>
syn bestrew, broadcast, disject, disseminate, scatter, sow, straw; *compare* SPREAD 1, SPRINKLE 1
rel dust, pepper; dissipate; cover
2 *syn* see SPREAD 1
striate *vb syn* see STREAK
strict *adj* 1 *syn* see RIGID 3
rel exacting, oppressive, unsparing; dour, forbidding, grim, hard-boiled, harsh, tough
idiom not to be trifled (*or* messed) with
con easy, easygoing; lax, loose; permissive
ant lenient
2 *syn* see TRUE 3
stricture *n* 1 *syn* see RESTRICTION 1
2 *syn* see ANIMADVERSION
‖**striddle** *vb* 1 *syn* see BESTRIDE 2
2 *syn* see STRIDE 1
stride *vb* 1 to move or walk with long often purposeful steps <*strode* to the door and slammed it>
syn march, sling, stalk, ‖striddle
rel clump, stamp, stomp, tramp, tromp
2 *syn* see BESTRIDE
strident *adj* 1 *syn* see HARSH 3
rel loud, stentorian, stertorous
2 *syn* see VOCIFEROUS
stridulent *adj syn* see HARSH 3
stridulous *adj syn* see HARSH 3
strife *n* 1 *syn* see DISCORD
rel argument, controversy, dispute; altercation, quarrel, squabble, wrangle; brawl, broil, fracas; affray, combat, fight, fray
ant accord
2 *syn* see CONTEST 1
strike *vb* 1 to engage in a temporary work stoppage to effect compliance with demands made on an employer <they *struck* for higher wages>
syn stick out, walk out
idiom go (*or* be) on strike
2 to deliver (a blow) in a strong, vigorous manner <angrily *struck* the boy>
syn ‖biff, catch, clout, ‖devel, ding, hit, ‖nail, pop, slog, ‖slosh, smite, sock, swat, whack; *compare* SLAM 1, SLAP 1
rel beat, pummel, ‖slat, ‖swap, ‖wap, whop; cudgel, hammer, mace; ‖plug, poke, ‖puck, punch; bang, bash, crash, ‖pandy, slam; ‖stoush, thrash
idiom hang one on, let one fly
3 *syn* see GIVE 10
4 *syn* see AFFLICT
5 *syn* see SEIZE 2
6 *syn* see ATTACK 1
7 *syn* see OCCUR 2
8 *syn* see AFFECT
9 *syn* see DON 2
strike *n syn* see DISCOVERY
strike out *vb syn* see HEAD 3
striker *n syn* see HELPER
striking *adj syn* see NOTICEABLE

rel showy; forceful, powerful; cogent, compelling, telling
strikingly *adv syn* see VERY 1
string *n* 1 *syn* see LINE 5
2 *syn* see RESOURCE 3
3 *syn* see SUCCESSION 2
4 **strings** *pl syn* see POWER 1
string (up) *vb syn* see HANG 2
string along *vb syn* see TRIFLE 1
idiom keep (someone) dangling
stringent *adj* 1 *syn* see RIGID 3
rel binding, confining, drawing
2 *syn* see GRIM 2
strings *n pl syn* see CONDITION 1
stringy *adj syn* see MUSCULAR 1
‖**strinkle** *vb syn* see SPRINKLE 1
strip *vb* 1 to remove the clothing of <guards *stripped* and searched the prisoners>
syn denude, disrobe, unclothe, undress
rel doff, peel, take off; bare, denudate, expose, uncover; disfrock, unfrock
idiom strip to the buff
con clothe, dress, robe; cover
2 to take something (as honors, privileges, functions, or trappings) away from <an exiled king now *stripped* of his power>
syn bankrupt, bare, denudate, denude, deprive, dismantle, disrobe, divest; *compare* DEPRIVE 2
rel bereave; deplenish, disfurnish, ‖displenish, dispossess; despoil, rob
con clothe, endow, furnish, grant, vest; install
ant invest
3 *syn* see RAVAGE
4 *syn* see SKIN 2
strip *n syn* see STRIPTEASE
strip *n* 1 a relatively long and narrow piece or section <tear old linen into *strips* for bandages>
syn band, bandeau, banding, fillet, ribbon, stripe
rel piece; section; segment; shred
2 *syn* see BAR 1
stripe *vb syn* see WHIP 1
stripe *n* 1 *syn* see STRIP 1
2 *syn* see TYPE
stripe *vb syn* see STREAK
stripling *n syn* see BOY 1
stripped *adj* 1 *syn* see NUDE 2
con attired; covered
ant clothed, dressed
2 *syn* see OPEN 2
con covered, unexposed; protected
stripper *n syn* see STRIPTEASER
stripping *n syn* see STRIPTEASE
striptease *n* entertainment in which a female performer removes her clothing piece by piece in view of an audience <a nightclub featuring *striptease*>
syn strip, stripping
idiom exotic dancing
stripteaser *n* one who performs a striptease <worked part-time as a model and *stripteaser*>
syn ecdysiast, peeler, stripper, stripteuse, teaser
idiom exotic dancer, ‖pantie peeler, ‖strip-and-shake artist, strip girl
stripteuse *n syn* see STRIPTEASER

---

syn synonym(s) *rel* related word(s)
ant antonym(s) *con* contrasted word(s)
idiom idiomatic equivalent(s)
‖ use limited; if in doubt, see a dictionary

strive *vb* 1 *syn* see LABOR 1
  2 *syn* see TRY 5
  rel labor, toil, travail, work; drive, strain
striving *n* 1 *syn* see CONTEST 1
  rel contending; combat, fight
  2 *syn* see ATTEMPT
  rel labor, toil, travail, work
stroll *vb* *syn* see SAUNTER
stroll *n* *syn* see WALK 1
strong *adj* 1 having great physical strength
  <had the *strong* hands and arms of a wres-
  tler>
  syn mighty, powerful, ‖strengthy, wieldy;
  compare MUSCULAR 2
  rel firm, robust, stark, strapping, sturdy,
  two-handed; able-bodied, tough; brawny,
  muscular, sinewy; lusty, vigorous
  idiom strong as a bull (*or* ox)
  con feeble, frail, puny, weak-bodied; forceless, impotent, powerless, strengthless
  ant weak
  2 having or manifesting great force or power
  (as in acting or resisting) <a *strong* constitu-
  tion>
  syn stalwart, stout, sturdy, tenacious, tough
  rel hardy, robust, rugged, strapping; firm,
  solid, staunch; durable, enduring; forceful,
  potent, powerful; lusty, vigorous
  con frail; forceless, impotent, powerless,
  strengthless; depleted, failing
  ant weak
  3 being rich in a characteristic ingredient
  <*strong* coffee>
  syn concentrated, full-bodied, lusty, potent,
  robust
  rel strong-flavored, strong-tasting; straight,
  undiluted, unmixed; rich; heroic, large,
  powerful
  con diluted, mixed, watered-down
  ant weak
  4 *syn* see SPIRITUOUS
  5 *syn* see SURE 1
  rel solid, substantial, unmoving, unyielding
  6 *syn* see MALODOROUS 1
strong arm *n* 1 *syn* see POWER 4
  2 *syn* see THUG 1
strong–arm *vb* *syn* see INTIMIDATE
stronghold *n* *syn* see FORT
strongly *adv* *syn* see HARD 1
  ant weakly
strong man *n* *syn* see TYRANT
strong suit *n* *syn* see FORTE
structure *n* 1 *syn* see BUILDING
  rel construction, erection, pile
  2 *syn* see EDIFICE
  3 something made up of more or less interdependent elements and having a definite
  organizational pattern <the complex bu-
  reaucratic *structure* of modern government>
  syn framework
  rel anatomy, skeleton; build, construction,
  frame; arrangement, composition, form,
  format, makeup, morphology; complex,
  network, system
struggle *vb* *syn* see TRY 5
  rel compete, vie
  idiom make a valiant attempt (*or* try)
  ant give up
struggle *n* *syn* see ATTEMPT
strum *vb* *syn* see HUM

strumpet *n* *syn* see WANTON
‖strut *vb* *syn* see STRUT 2
‖strut *n* *syn* see LIQUOR 2
strut *vb* 1 *syn* see SASHAY
  2 to walk with an air of pomposity or affected dignity <a pompous general *strutting*
  off the parade ground>
  syn ‖strunt, swagger
  rel flaunt, parade
  con cower, cringe; slink
stubborn *adj* 1 *syn* see OBSTINATE
  rel contumacious, insubordinate, rebellious;
  cantankerous, ornery; ‖stunkard, ‖stunt
  idiom set in one's ways, stubborn as a mule
  con adaptable, pliable, pliant; amenable,
  tractable
  ant docile
  2 *syn* see INFLEXIBLE 2
stubbornness *n* *syn* see DEFIANCE 2
  rel cantankerousness, orneriness
stubby *adj* *syn* see STOCKY
stube *n* *syn* see ALEHOUSE
stuck–up *adj* *syn* see VAIN 3
  idiom too big for one's breeches, wise in
  one's own conceit
stud *vb* *syn* see SPOT 2
studied *adj* *syn* see DELIBERATE 1
  rel thoughtful; intentional, voluntary, willful, willing
  con natural, offhand
  ant unstudied
studio *n* the working place of an artist (as a
  painter) <moved to a larger *studio*>
  syn atelier, bottega
  rel shop, workroom, workshop
studious *adj* *syn* see DELIBERATE 1
  ant impromptu
study *n* 1 *syn* see REVERIE
  2 *syn* see ATTENTION 1
  rel contemplation, weighing; abstraction,
  meditation, musing, pondering, rumination
  3 *syn* see EXERCISE 4
study *vb* 1 *syn* see CONSIDER 1
  idiom give careful study to
  2 *syn* see SCRUTINIZE 1
stuff *n* 1 *syn* see PERSONAL EFFECTS
  2 *syn* see MONEY
  3 *syn* see THING 5
  4 *syn* see ESSENCE 2
stuff *vb* *syn* see CRAM 1
  rel overfill, overstuff
  idiom fill to overflowing, fill to the brim
stuffed *adj* *syn* see FULL 1
stuffed shirt *n* a smug usually pompous
  person with an inflexibly conservative or
  reactionary outlook <a *stuffed shirt* with a
  starched mind>
  syn Blimp, Colonel Blimp, fuddy-duddy
  rel diehard; prig, prude, smug
  con freethinker, latitudinarian, liberal,
  libertarian, libertine; avant-garde
stuffing *n* *syn* see ENTRAILS
  rel ‖tar
stuffy *adj* 1 marked by a heavy oppressive
  quality of air <a *stuffy* room that needed
  airing>
  syn airless, breathless, close, stifling, stivy,
  suffocating, sultry; *compare* HUMID, STI-
  FLING 1
  rel heavy, oppressive, thick; stagnant; shut-
  up, unventilated

con airy, breezy; open, ventilated; bracing, invigorating, refreshing, stimulating
2 syn see PRIM 1
rel dull, humdrum, stodgy; hidebound, illiberal, narrow, narrow-minded
3 syn see POMPOUS 1

‖**stuggy** *adj syn* see STOCKY

stultify *vb* to deprive of vitality and render futile especially by enfeebling or repressive influences <artistic creativity *stultified* by the intrusion of propaganda>
syn constipate, stagnate, stifle, trammel
rel discourage, inhibit, restrain; check, stunt; enfeeble, impair, weaken; deaden, dull; repress, smother, suffocate, suppress; invalidate, nullify
con encourage, foster, nourish; pique, provoke, stimulate

stultiloquence *n syn* see CHATTER

stumble *vb* **1 syn** see WALLOW 2
rel falter, waver; trip; fall
2 syn see DEMUR
3 to move so clumsily and awkwardly as to lose one's balance or trip and fall <*stumbled* across the darkened room and fell>
syn blunder, bumble, lurch, ‖snapper; *compare* WALLOW 2
rel reel, stagger, totter; trip; pitch, topple
4 syn see LUMBER
5 syn see TEETER
rel careen, swing
6 to act, proceed, or execute in a hesitant and clumsily faltering manner <*stumbled* through his Latin translation>
syn limp, muddle, shuffle
rel falter, hesitate; wobble; blunder, bumble; botch, bungle, ‖muck
ant breeze
7 syn see HAPPEN 2
idiom come (or run) up against, fall upon, stub one's toe upon (or on)
8 syn see PUZZLE

stumblebum *n* a clumsy inept or blundering person <a staff consisting of third-raters and *stumblebums*>
syn blunderbuss, blunderer, bungler
rel incompetent
con crackerjack, ‖dab, ‖darb, expert, top-notcher, whiz; ‖natural; professional

stumbling block *n syn* see OBSTACLE

stump *vb* **1 syn** see NONPLUS 1
2 syn see LUMBER

stump *n syn* see DEFIANCE 1

stumpy *adj syn* see STOCKY

‖**stumpy** *n syn* see MONEY

stun *vb syn* see DAZE 2
rel nonplus; amaze, astound, flabbergast; knock out
idiom strike dumb (or dead)

stunner *n* **1 syn** see WONDER 1
2 syn see BEAUTY

stunning *adj* **1 syn** see EXCELLENT
2 syn see BEAUTIFUL

‖**stunpoll** *n syn* see DUNCE

‖**stunt** *adj syn* see STUNTED

stunt *vb* to hinder the normal growth and development of <the inhospitable climate had *stunted* all vegetation>
syn dwarf, suppress
rel check, curb, hold back; impair

stunt *n syn* see TRICK 3

stunted *adj* having had one's growth and development hindered or arrested <the children were *stunted* from malnutrition>
syn runted, runtish, runty, ‖scrunty, ‖stunt
rel undersized; dwarf
con able-bodied, robust well-set, well-set-up; giant, oversize; healthy, strong, sturdy, vigorous

‖**stupe** *n syn* see DUNCE

stupefy *vb* **1 syn** see DULL 5
2 syn see DAZE 2
rel addle, faze, rattle; nonplus

stupendous *adj* **1 syn** see MARVELOUS 1
2 syn see MONSTROUS 1

stupid *adj* **1** lacking in or exhibiting a lack of power to absorb ideas or impressions <a willing boy but too *stupid* to succeed in school>
syn beefheaded, beef-witted, beetleheaded, blear-eyed, blear-witted, blockheaded, blockish, chuckleheaded, dense, doltish, dull, dumb, duncical, fatheaded, goosey, hammerheaded, numskulled, pinhead, pinheaded, thick, thickheaded, thick-witted; *compare* RETARDED, SIMPLE 3
rel asinine, fatuous, foolish, silly, simple; brute, brutish, dummel, lumbering, oafish, slow, slow-witted, sluggish; ‖half-assed; crass; backward, half-witted, retarded; idiotic, imbecilic
idiom ‖dead above (or between) the ears, ‖dead from the neck up, having a block for a head, having cotton between the ears, ‖muscle-bound between the ears
con acute, alert, bright, clever, keen, knowing, quick, quick-witted, sharp, smart; sage, wise; brilliant; able, competent
ant intelligent
2 syn see LETHARGIC

stupid *n syn* see DUNCE

stupor *n syn* see LETHARGY 1
rel sopor; anesthesia, insensibility

sturdy *adj syn* see STRONG 2
rel sound, substantial
ant decrepit

Sturm und Drang *n syn* see UNREST

‖**stut** *vb syn* see STAMMER 1

stutter *vb syn* see STAMMER 1

sty *n* **1** an extremely unkempt or filthy place <the basement was a rat-infested *sty*>
syn dump, pigpen, pigsty
2 syn see SINK 1

stygian *adj syn* see INFERNAL 2

style *n* **1 syn** see VEIN 1
2 syn see NAME 1
3 syn see FASHION 3
4 an individual's characteristic attitudes and taste as expressed or indicated in his way of life <she liked the man's sophisticated *style*>
syn manner, way
rel behavior; bearing, carriage; characteristic, trait; idiosyncrasy, peculiarity

style *vb syn* see NAME 1

---

syn synonym(s)   **rel** related word(s)
ant antonym(s)   **con** contrasted word(s)
idiom idiomatic equivalent(s)
‖ use limited; if in doubt, see a dictionary

stylish *adj* being in accordance with or conforming to current fashion <she was a *stylish* dresser>
syn à la mode, chic, ‖classy, dashing, exclusive, fashionable, in, modish, posh, sharp, smart, snappy, swank, swish, tonish, tony, ‖trendy, trig, ultrafashionable, with-it; *compare* DAPPER
rel new, new-day, newfangled, new-fashioned; modern, modernistic, up-to-date; chichi, doggish, doggy, natty, rakish, sassy, swagger; ostentatious, pretentious, ritzy, showy, swell; sleek, slick
idiom in fashion, in the mode
con styleless; old-fashioned, outmoded, out-of-date; drab, tasteless
ant dowdy, unstylish

suasible *adj syn* see RECEPTIVE 1

suave *adj* being conspicuously and ingratiatingly tactful and well-mannered <a man of *suave*, well-bred equanimity>
syn bland, civilized, smooth, urbane; *compare* TACTFUL
rel affable, cordial, genial, gracious, sociable; courteous, courtly, polite; diplomatic, politic; cultivated, cultured, distingué, polished, refined, well-bred; sophisticated, worldly; ingratiating, soft, soft-spoken; fulsome, slick, unctuous
con clumsy, unpolished, unskilled; tactless, undiplomatic, untactful
ant bluff

sub *adj syn* see SUBORDINATE

sub *n syn* see SUBSTITUTE 1

subaltern *n syn* see INFERIOR 1

subaquatic *adj syn* see SUBMARINE

subaqueous *adj syn* see SUBMARINE

subaverage *adj syn* see LOW 9

subconscious *n* mental activities that occur just below the threshold of consciousness <a motive probably rooted in his *subconscious*>
syn underconsciousness, undersense
rel subconsciousness; subliminal self
idiom subconscious (*or* submerged) mind
con consciousness; awareness

subdolous *adj syn* see SLY 2

subdue *vb 1 syn* see CONQUER 1
rel extinguish, put down, quash, quell, quench, squelch, suppress

subdued *adj 1 syn* see QUIET 4
2 reduced or lacking in force, intensity, or vividness <*subdued* colors> <the child answered his questions in a timid *subdued* voice>
syn low-key, low-keyed, sober, soft, softened, toned down
rel moderated, tempered; controlled, restrained; mellow; neutral; quiet
con enlivened, intensified; bright, intense, strong; brilliant, vivid; saturated; blaring, glaring, harsh, screaming
3 *syn* see TAME
ant unsubdued

subduer *n syn* see VICTOR 1

subfusc *adj syn* see DULL 8

subitaneous *adj syn* see PRECIPITATE 1

subjacent *adj syn* see INFERIOR 1
ant superjacent

subject *n 1 syn* see CITIZEN 2
2 the basic idea or the principal object of attention in a discourse or artistic composi-

tion <the Puritan ethic was the *subject* of her paper>
syn argument, head, matter, motif, motive, point, subject matter, text, theme, topic
rel material, substance; problem, question; leitmotiv; core, meat
con elaboration, enlargement, enlarging, expatiation; development, explication

subject *adj 1 syn* see SUBORDINATE
rel servile, slavish, subservient
ant dominant, sovereign
2 *syn* see LIABLE 2
rel apt, likely

subject *vb syn* see EXPOSE 1

subjective *adj* peculiar to a particular individual as modified by individual bias and limitations <*subjective* judgments>
syn unobjective
rel biased, prejudiced; abstract, nonobjective, nonrepresentational, nonrepresentative
ant objective

subject matter *n syn* see SUBJECT 2

subjoin *vb syn* see ADD 1
rel combine, conjoin, unite
con part, separate, sever

subjugate *vb 1 syn* see CONQUER 1
rel compel, coerce, force
2 *syn* see ENSLAVE
ant liberate

subjugator *n syn* see VICTOR 1

sublease *vb syn* see SUBLET

sublet *vb* to turn over to another one's right of occupancy of (rented or leased housing) <*sublet* her apartment to a friend>
syn sublease, underlease, underlet

sublime *vb syn* see EXALT 1

sublime *adj 1 syn* see GRAND 3
2 *syn* see SPLENDID 2
rel abstract, ideal, transcendent, transcendental; divine, holy, sacred, spiritual; august, majestic, noble, stately

sublimity *n syn* see APEX 2

sublunary *adj syn* see EARTHLY 1

submarine *adj* being, acting, growing, or used under water <a *submarine* camera>
syn subaquatic, subaqueous, underwater

submerge *vb 1 syn* see DIP 1
rel drench, impregnate, saturate, soak
2 *syn* see DELUGE 1
3 *syn* see SINK 1

submerse *vb 1 syn* see DIP 1
2 *syn* see SINK 1

submission *n syn* see SURRENDER
rel bowing, submitting; acquiescence, compliance, resignation; cringing, servility; prostration
ant resistance

submissive *adj 1 syn* see TAME
rel complying, conformable, obeying; bowing down, unerect; menial, servile, slavish, subservient
ant rebellious
2 *syn* see PASSIVE 2

submit *vb 1 syn* see YIELD 2
ant resist, withstand
2 to offer or commit (something) for consideration, study, or decision <*submitted* his report directly to the general>
syn hand in, refer
rel bring, deliver, present; offer, proffer, tender; send in; provide

3 *syn* see SUGGEST 4
4 *syn* see FALL 3
   ant hold out, resist
subnormal *adj syn* see LOW 9
   rel subpar
subordinate *adj* placed in or occupying a
   lower class, rank, or status <making the
   executive *subordinate* to the legislative
   branch>
   syn collateral, dependent, secondary, sub,
   subject, tributary, under
   rel adjuvant, auxiliary, contributory, subsidiary; satellite; inferior, subaltern, subal-
   ternate; accessory, parergal, supplementary
   con chief, first, leading, main; dominant,
   master, superior
subordinate *n syn* see INFERIOR
sub rosa *adv syn* see SECRETLY
   ant aboveboard
sub–rosa *adj syn* see SECRET 1
   ant aboveboard
subscribe *vb* **1** *syn* see SIGN 1
   2 *syn* see CONTRIBUTE 1
   3 *syn* see ASSENT
   rel approve, endorse, favor, sanction
subsequent *adj* **1** being, occurring, or carried out at a time after something else <*subsequent* events disproved his predictions>
   syn after, ensuing, later, posterior, postliminary, subsequential
   rel following, next, succeeding; consequential, resultant, resulting
   con exordial, introductory, prefatory, preliminary, preludial; anterior, precedent,
   preceding, prior
   ant antecedent
   2 *syn* see CONSECUTIVE
   ant antecedent
subsequential *adj* **1** *syn* see SUBSEQUENT 1
   2 *syn* see CONSECUTIVE
   ant antecedent
subsequently *adv syn* see AFTER
   ant antecedently, priorly
subsequent to *prep syn* see AFTER 2
subservient *adj* **1** *syn* see AUXILIARY
   2 showing extreme compliance or abject
   obedience <a *subservient* minor bureaucrat>
   syn menial, obeisant, obsequious, servile,
   slavish
   rel acquiescent, compliant, resigned, submissive; cowering, cringing, fawning, truckling; abject, ignoble, mean
   idiom as obedient as a dog
   con aggressive, arrogant, haughty; rebellious; independent, irrepressible, uncontainable
   ant domineering, overbearing
subside *vb syn* see ABATE 4
   idiom dwindle down
subsidiary *adj syn* see AUXILIARY
   rel backup; minor, tributary
subsidize *vb syn* see ENDOW 2
   rel back; promote; help
subsidy *n syn* see APPROPRIATION
   rel subsidization; gift, reward

subsist *vb syn* see BE
subsistence *n syn* see LIVING
substance *n* **1** *syn* see TENOR 1
   rel import, meaning
   idiom the general drift
   2 the inner significance or central meaning of
   something written or said <just give me the
   substance of his speech>
   syn amount, body, burden, core, crux, gist,
   kernel, matter, meat, nub, nubbin, pith,
   purport, sense, short, strength, sum and
   substance, sum total, thrust, upshot; *compare* BODY 3, ESSENCE 2, MEANING 1,
   TENOR 1
   rel center, focus, heart, nucleus; point;
   import, meaningfulness
   3 *syn* see BODY 3
   rel drift, tenor
   4 *syn* see ESSENCE 2
   5 *syn* see THING 5
   6 *syn* see WEALTH 2
substantial *adj* **1** *syn* see MATERIAL 1
   con airy, ethereal
   ant unsubstantial
   2 *syn* see IMPORTANT 1
   rel key, principal; strong; serious
   3 *syn* see PROSPEROUS 3
   rel solid, solvent
substantiate *vb* **1** *syn* see EMBODY 1
   rel substantialize, substantify
   2 *syn* see CONFIRM 2
   rel demonstrate, prove, test, try
substitutable *adj syn* see INTERCHANGE-
ABLE
substitute *n* **1** a person who takes the place
   of or acts instead of another <found a *substitute* for the sick teacher>
   syn alternate, backup, fill-in, locum tenens,
   pinch hitter, replacement, stand-in, sub,
   succedaneum, surrogate
   rel relay, relief; deputy, procurator, proxy;
   supply; double, understudy
   2 *syn* see RESOURCE 3
substitute *vb syn* see EXCHANGE 2
substitute *adj* serving or fitted for use as a
   substitute <a *substitute* driver was needed
   for the long trip>
   syn alternate, alternative, backup, surrogate
   rel additional, another; other, second; reserve; supplemental, supplementary, supple-
   tory
   2 *syn* see ARTIFICIAL 2
substract *vb syn* see DEDUCT 1
substratal *adj syn* see ELEMENTAL 1
substratum *n* **1** *syn* see BASIS 1
   rel core, meat, stuff, substance
   2 *syn* see BASE 1
substruction *n syn* see BASE 1
substructure *n syn* see BASE 1
   ant superstructure
subsume *vb syn* see INCLUDE
subterfuge *n syn* see DECEPTION 1
subterrane *n syn* see CAVE
subterranean *adj* being, lying, functioning,
   or operating under the surface of the earth
   <*subterranean* hot springs that emerge as
   geysers>
   syn subterrestrial, underearth, underfoot,
   underground
   con aboveground, surface, surficial

---

syn synonym(s)   *rel* related word(s)
ant antonym(s)   *con* contrasted word(s)
idiom idiomatic equivalent(s)
‖ use limited; if in doubt, see a dictionary

subterranean *n syn* see CAVE
subterrestrial *adj syn* see SUBTERRANEAN
subtile *adj syn* see THIN 2
subtle *adj* 1 *syn* see THIN 2
  2 *syn* see FINE 1
  ant unsubtle
  3 *syn* see LOGICAL 2
  rel dexterous, skillful
  con blunt; dense
  4 *syn* see SLY 2
  ant unsubtle
subtract *vb syn* see DEDUCT 1
  ant add
subtraction *n syn* see DEDUCTION 1
  ant addition
suburbs *n pl syn* see ENVIRONS 2
  rel fringes; suburbia
subvention *n syn* see APPROPRIATION
subversion *n syn* see SABOTAGE
  rel demolishing, destroying, destruction
subvert *vb syn* see SABOTAGE
  rel overthrow, overturn, upset; demolish, destroy, ruin; corrupt, debase, deprave, pervert
  con sustain, uphold
succedaneum *n syn* see SUBSTITUTE 1
succedent *adj syn* see CONSECUTIVE
succeed *vb* 1 *syn* see FOLLOW 1
  ant precede
  2 to result favorably according to plans and desires <that advertising campaign really *succeeded*>
  syn click, come off, go, go over, pan out, prove out
  rel catch on; prevail
  idiom go over big, go over with a bang, hit the mark, make a hit, turn out well
  ant fail, flop
  3 to attain or be attaining a desired end <how to *succeed* in big business>
  syn arrive, flourish, go, make out, prosper, score, thrive
  rel ||dow; get ahead; boom; achieve, attain, gain, reach; accomplish, effect, fulfill; conquer, prevail, triumph, win (out)
  idiom do all by oneself, do well, gain one's end, get places, get somewhere, get to the top of the ladder, make a success, make it (big), make one's mark, ||make the big time, make the grade
  con dwindle, languish; fall down, flounder, founder; lose (out); bust
  ant fail
succeeding *adj syn* see CONSECUTIVE
succès fou *n syn* see SMASH 6
success *n* a succeeding fully or in accordance with one's desires <attributed his business *success* to hard work and attention to detail>
  syn arrival, ||do, flying colors, go, prosperity, successfulness
  rel accomplishment, achievement, attainment; triumph, victory
  ant failure; nonsuccess, unsuccessfulness
successful *adj* resulting in or having gained success <a *successful* business venture>
  syn prosperous, thriving; compare FLOURISHING
  rel extraordinary, notable, noteworthy, outstanding, smash, smashing

  idiom crowned (*or* blessed *or* flushed) with success, ||out front
  con failing, thriveless, unprosperous; defeated, disappointed, failed, frustrated; bankrupt, broken, destroyed, ruined
  ant successless, unsuccessful
successfully *adv syn* see WELL 5
  ant unsuccessfully
successfulness *n syn* see SUCCESS
  ant nonsuccess, unsuccessfulness
succession *n* 1 *syn* see ORDER 5
  2 a number of things that follow each other in some order <another *succession* of price hikes>
  syn alternation, chain, consecution, course, order, progression, row, sequel, sequence, series, string, suite, train; compare CYCLE 1
  rel successiveness; round, round robin
successional *adj syn* see CONSECUTIVE
successive *adj syn* see CONSECUTIVE
  rel alternating, rotating
successively *adv syn* see TOGETHER 2
succinct *adj syn* see CONCISE
  rel blunt, brusque
  idiom right to the point
  ant discursive
succinctly *adv syn* see BRIEFLY
  ant discursively
succor *n syn* see HELP 1
  rel ministration, ministry; maintenance, nourishment, sustenance
succubus *n syn* see DEVIL 2
succulent *adj* full of juice <a *succulent* roast>
  syn juicy, ||sappy
succumb *vb* 1 *syn* see YIELD 2
  rel abandon, relinquish, resign
  2 *syn* see FALL 3
  idiom hand over one's sword, meet one's Waterloo, show (*or* wave) the white flag, strike (*or* haul down) one's colors
  3 *syn* see COLLAPSE 2
  idiom bite the dust, ||take the count
  4 *syn* see DIE 1
  idiom yield one's breath
such *adj* 1 being previously characterized or specified <authorized to seize illegally parked cars and impound *such* vehicles>
  syn aforementioned, aforesaid, said
  2 being of so extreme a degree or quality <*such* nonsense as I had never heard before>
  syn that
  3 *syn* see LIKE
such *pron* 1 *syn* see SUCH A ONE
  2 *syn* see SUCHLIKE
  idiom the like
such a one *pron* someone or something that has been, is being, or will be stated, implied, or exemplified <the area is full of caverns; *such a one* may be found here>
  syn such
suchlike *adj syn* see LIKE
suchlike *pron* a person or thing of the same or similar kind <airplanes, missiles, rockets, and *suchlike*>
  syn such
||**suck** *n syn* see SYCOPHANT
sucker *n* 1 *syn* see PARASITE
  2 *syn* see FOOL 3

idiom easy pickings
sucker *vb syn* see CHEAT
suck in *vb syn* see DECEIVE
‖**suck–in** *n syn* see DECEPTION 1
suckle *vb syn* see NURSE 1
sudden *adj syn* see PRECIPITATE 1
  rel accelerated, quickened, speeded; expeditious, fast, fleet, rapid, swift
sudden *adv syn* see UNAWARES
  2 *syn* see SHORT 1
suddenly *adv* **1** *syn* see SHORT 1
  2 *syn* see UNAWARES
  idiom of (or on) a sudden, on the sudden
suds *n pl but sing or pl in constr* **1** *syn* see SADNESS
  2 *syn* see FOAM
sue *vb syn* see ADDRESS 8
  idiom make (or pay) suit to, press one's suit
sue (for *or* to) *vb syn* see PETITION
suffer *vb* **1** *syn* see BEAR 10
  rel accept, admit, receive
  idiom grin and abide
  2 *syn* see EXPERIENCE 1
  3 *syn* see LET 2
  rel countenance; accept, admit, receive; acquiesce, bow, submit, yield
  ‖**4** *syn* see HURT 4
sufferable *adj syn* see BEARABLE
  ant insufferable
sufferance *n syn* see PERMISSION
suffering *n syn* see DISTRESS
  rel adversity, misfortune
suffice *vb syn* see SERVE 3
sufficiency *n syn* see ENOUGH
  ant insufficiency
sufficient *adj* **1** being what is requisite or needed especially without superfluity <there is *sufficient* bread left for breakfast>
  syn adequate, comfortable, competent, decent, enough, satisfactory, sufficing; *compare* DECENT 4
  rel ample, plenteous, plentiful, plenty; commensurable, commensurate, due, proportionate; acceptable, agreeable, pleasing
  con inadequate, unsufficing; deficient; failing, lacking, missing, wanting
  ant insufficient
  2 *syn* see DECENT 4
  idiom fair to middling
sufficient *n syn* see ENOUGH
sufficiently *adv syn* see ENOUGH 1
  ant insufficiently
sufficing *adj syn* see SUFFICIENT 1
suffocate *vb* to stop the respiration of (as by asphyxiation) <the child was *suffocated* in an old refrigerator>
  syn asphyxiate, choke, ‖quackle, smother, stifle; *compare* CHOKE 1
  rel stive; strangle
suffocating *adj* **1** *syn* see STIFLING 1
  2 *syn* see STUFFY 1
suffocative *adj syn* see STIFLING 1
suffrage *n* the right, privilege, or power of expressing one's choice or wish (as in an election or in the determination of policy) <universal *suffrage*>

---

syn synonym(s)   *rel* related word(s)
ant antonym(s)   *con* contrasted word(s)
idiom idiomatic equivalent(s)
‖ use limited; if in doubt, see a dictionary

---

  syn ballot, franchise, vote
  rel voice
suffuse *vb syn* see INFUSE 1
  rel interject, interpose, introduce
‖**sugar** *n syn* see MONEY
sugar (over) *vb syn* see SUGARCOAT 1
sugarcoat *vb* **1** to make (something difficult or unpleasant) superficially easy or attractive <*sugarcoated* the reproach with a smile>
  syn candy, honey, sugar (over), sweeten
  rel edulcorate
  2 *syn* see PALLIATE
sugarplum *n syn* see SOP 2
suggest *vb* **1** to convey an idea indirectly <designing attractive books with jackets that truly *suggest* their contents>
  syn connote, hint, imply, insinuate, intimate; *compare* POINT 2
  rel advert, allude, refer; denote
  idiom bring to mind
  con demonstrate, display, exhibit, manifest, set out, show
  ant express
  2 *syn* see POINT 2
  rel promise
  idiom be the sign of, point in the direction of
  3 *syn* see PROPOSE 1
  4 to offer (as an idea or theory) for consideration <this, I *suggest*, is what really happened>
  syn submit, theorize
  rel conjecture; imagine
  5 to represent another thing indirectly, figuratively, and sometimes obscurely by evoking a thought, image, or conception of it <the meaning of a poem is often *suggested* in its title>
  syn adumbrate, shadow (forth); *compare* ADUMBRATE 1
  rel outline, sketch; betoken, symbolize; typify
  con display, flaunt, parade
  ant manifest
suggestion *n* **1** *syn* see PROPOSAL
  2 *syn* see HINT 1
  rel implication, innuendo
  3 *syn* see ASSOCIATION 4
  rel allusion; reminder
  con demonstration, display, exhibition, manifestation, show
  ant expression
  4 *syn* see HINT 2
suggestive *adj* **1** *syn* see EVOCATIVE
  rel significative
  2 *syn* see RISQUÉ
  rel erotic, sexy
suicide *n* the act or an instance of taking one's life voluntarily and intentionally <committed *suicide* by shooting herself>
  syn felo-de-se, hara-kiri, self-destruction, self-murder, self-slaughter, self-violence
suit *n* **1** a legal proceeding instituted for the sake of demanding justice or enforcing a right <filed a *suit* to recover her property>
  syn action, case, cause, lawsuit
  2 *syn* see PRAYER
  rel asking, request, requesting, solicitation, soliciting
suit *vb* **1** *syn* see AGREE 4

idiom be in accord with, check out to the letter

2 *syn* see SERVE 3

3 *syn* see ADAPT

4 to be suitable for or to <the right word is the one that *suits* the occasion>

syn agree (with), become, befit, fit, go (together *or* with); *compare* SUIT 6

rel harmonize (with); benefit, please, satisfy

idiom answer a need (*or* the purpose), hit the spot

con clash, conflict, disaccord, disagree

5 *syn* see FLATTER

6 to meet the needs or desires of <this arrangement *suits* me fine>

syn please, satisfy; *compare* SUIT 4

con discontent, displease, dissatisfy; disappoint, fail, let down

suitability *n syn* see ORDER 11

ant unsuitability

suitable *adj* **1** *syn* see GOOD 2

ant unsuitable

2 *syn* see JUST 3

rel reasonable; advisable, expedient, politic

ant unsuitable

3 *syn* see FIT 1

rel nice, presentable, seemly

ant unbecoming, unsuitable

4 *syn* see ELIGIBLE

ant unsuitable

suitableness *n syn* see ORDER 11

ant unsuitableness

suitably *adv syn* see WELL 4

ant unsuitably

suite *n* **1** *syn* see ENTOURAGE

2 *syn* see GROUP 3

3 *syn* see APARTMENT 1

4 *syn* see SUCCESSION 2

suited *adj syn* see ASSORTED 2

ant unsuited

suitor *n* **1** *syn* see SUPPLIANT

2 one who courts a woman or seeks to marry her <a *suitor* for the king's daughter>

syn spark, sparker, swain, wooer

rel beau, boyfriend; cavalier, gallant; lover, man, paramour

sulk *vb* to be sullen or morose in mood usually because of a grievance <*sulked* all day when he didn't call>

syn ‖dort, grump, ‖mump, pet, pout, ‖sull

rel frown, glower, lower, scowl; brood, gloom, mope, take on

idiom be in a sulk, have the sulks, ‖take the dods

sulk *n*, *often* **sulks** *pl* the state, condition, or mood of one sulking <sat in a *sulk* all day after being reprimanded>

syn ‖dods, ‖dorts, grumps, mulligrubs, mumps, pouts, sullens

rel sourness, sulkiness, surliness; glumness, grouchiness

idiom a case of the sulks

sulky *adj syn* see SULLEN

rel cranky, testy, touchy; cantankerous, irritable, querulous

idiom having the sulks

‖**sull** *vb syn* see SULK

sullen *adj* showing a forbidding or disagreeable mood <stalked out in *sullen* silence>

syn ‖chuff, ‖chuffy, crabbed, crabby, ‖dorty, dour, gloomy, glum, morose, mumpish, saturnine, sulky, surly, ugly

rel moody; tenebrific, tenebrose, tenebrous; frowning, glowering, lowering, scowling; cross, fretful, grumpy, ill-humored, peevish, petulant, pouting, pouty, sour; black, hostile, malevolent, malicious, malign, mean, ‖runty; cynical, pessimistic

con easy, gay, high-spirited, insouciant, lighthearted, smiling

sullens *n pl syn* see SULK

sully *vb syn* see TAINT 1

rel disgrace, shame

sulphurous *adj syn* see INFERNAL 1

sultry *adj* **1** *syn* see HUMID

rel smothering, smothery, ‖smudgy, stifling, suffocating

2 *syn* see STUFFY 1

3 *syn* see HOT 1

idiom hot as Hades, ‖hot as old Billy Hell

4 *syn* see SENSATIONAL 2

sum *n* **1** *syn* see WHOLE 1

2 *syn* see WHOLE 2

rel body, bulk, mass; structure

3 *syn* see SUMMARY

sum *vb* **1** *syn* see ADD 2

2 *syn* see EPITOMIZE 1

sum (to *or* into) *vb syn* see AMOUNT 1

sum and substance *n* **1** *syn* see SUBSTANCE 2

2 *syn* see MEANING 1

summarize *vb syn* see EPITOMIZE 1

rel recapitulate, résumé, retrograde

summary *adj* **1** *syn* see CONCISE

rel compact, compacted

ant circumstantial

2 done or executed on the spot and without formality <a *summary* trial and speedy execution>

syn drumhead

summary *n* a short restatement of the main points <a *summary* of the news>

syn epitome, recapitulation, résumé, sum, summation, summing-up, sum-up

rel outline; run-through; roundup; inventory

con amplification, elaboration, enlargement, expansion

summate *vb* **1** *syn* see ADD 2

2 *syn* see EPITOMIZE 1

summation *n syn* see SUMMARY

summative *adj syn* see CUMULATIVE

summer *n* the season between spring and autumn <liked to swim during the *summer*>

syn summertide, summertime

rel midsummer

summer complaint *n syn* see DIARRHEA

summerhouse *n* a covered structure in a garden or park designed to provide a shady resting place <watched the sea from the *summerhouse*>

syn alcove, belvedere, garden house, gazebo, pagoda

summertide *n syn* see SUMMER

summertime *n syn* see SUMMER

summing–up *n syn* see SUMMARY

summit *n* **1** *syn* see TOP 1

2 *syn* see APEX 2

summon *vb* **1** *syn* see CONVOKE

2 to demand or request the presence or service of <were *summoned* to the principal's office>
syn call, call in, convene, summons; *compare* CONVOKE
rel bid, command, enjoin, order; cite, subpoena
idiom bid come

summons *vb syn* see SUMMON 2

‖**sump** *n syn* see SWAMP

sumptuous *adj* **1** *syn* see LUXURIOUS 3
rel gorgeous, resplendent, splendid, superb; lavish, rich
2 *syn* see GRAND 2
rel awe-inspiring, grandiose, imposing

sum total *n* **1** *syn* see WHOLE 1
2 *syn* see SUBSTANCE 2

sum up *vb syn* see EPITOMIZE 1

sum–up *n syn* see SUMMARY

sun *n* **1** the heavenly body about which the earth rotates <up in time to see the *sun* rise>
syn daystar, phoebus, Sol
rel celestial body, luminary, orb, star
idiom old Sol
2 the radiation of the sun <enjoying the warm spring *sun*>
syn sunlight, sunshine
rel daylight; radiance, radiation

sun *vb* to expose to sunshine <*sunned* himself too long and got badly burned>
syn bask, insolate
rel sunbathe; sunburn, sun-cure, sun-dry, tan

sunbeamy *adj syn* see CHEERFUL 1

Sunday best *n syn* see FINERY
idiom Sunday-go-to-meeting clothes

sunder *vb* **1** *syn* see SEPARATE 1
rel cleave, rend, rive
2 *syn* see CUT 5

‖**sundowner** *n syn* see VAGABOND

sundries *n pl* miscellaneous small articles, details, or items <supplied such *sundries* as needles, pins, and thread>
syn etceteras, oddments, odds and ends, this and that(s)
rel notions

sundry *adj* **1** *syn* MANY, legion, multifarious, multitudinal, multitudinous, numerous, populous, ‖several, various, voluminous
idiom all and sundry
2 *syn* see SEVERAL 3
idiom all sorts of

sundry *pron, pl in constr* an indeterminate number of more than one or two <*sundry* were interviewed; a few were selected>
syn divers, many, ‖several, various
idiom all and sundry, quite a few

sunk *adj syn* see DOWNCAST

sunlight *n syn* see SUN 2

sunny *adj* **1** *syn* see FAIR 2
rel bright, brilliant
idiom bright and sunny
2 *syn* see CHEERFUL 1

sunrise *n syn* see DAWN 1

sunset *n syn* see EVENING 2

sunshine *n syn* see SUN 2

sunshine *adj syn* see FAIR 2

sunshining *adj syn* see FAIR 2

sunshiny *adj syn* see FAIR 2

sunup *n syn* see DAWN 1

sup (off *or* up) *vb syn* see DRINK 1
idiom out of this world

super *adj syn* see MARVELOUS 2
idiom out of this world

super *adv* **1** *syn* see VERY 1
2 *syn* see EVER 6

superabundant *adj* abounding to a great, abnormal, or excessive degree <*superabundant* harvests had brought down prices>
syn overabounding, overabundant, overflowing
rel abounding, abundant, cornucopian, plenteous, plentiful; excess, excessive, overmuch, surplus; crawling, teeming; overspilling; epidemic, rampant

superadd *vb syn* see ADD 1

superannuate *vb* **1** *syn* see OUTDATE
2 *syn* see RETIRE 2

superb *adj* **1** *syn* see GRAND 3
rel noble; majestic
2 *syn* see SPLENDID 2
rel imposing, stately; opulent
3 consummately impressive and supremely excellent of its kind <the writer's style is brilliant and his command of words and imagery, *superb*>
syn magnificent, outstanding, standout, superexcellent, superlative; *compare* SUPREME
rel glorious, gorgeous, marvelous, resplendent; crashing, rousing, sensational, slambang, super, superfine, wonderful; best, optimal, optimum, prime; sublime
idiom very best
con inferior, mediocre, poor, substandard; atrocious, awful, dreadful, shocking; deplorable, dismal, lamentable, pitiful, woeful; abominable, execrable, outrageous, shameful
ant wretched

superbity *n syn* see PRIDE 3

supercilious *adj syn* see PROUD 1
rel sniffish, sniffy, snifty, snippy, snuffy; sneering

superciliousness *n syn* see PRIDE 3

supererogant *adj syn* see SUPEREROGATORY

supererogative *adj syn* see SUPEREROGATORY

supererogatory *adj* given or done without compulsion, need, or warrant <people who offer *supererogatory* advice>
syn gratuitous, supererogant, supererogative, unasked, uncalled-for, wanton
rel nonessential, superfluous, supernumerary, unnecessary, unneeded
con essential, indispensable, vital; compulsory, obligatory; called-for, needful, required, requisite, sought, wanted

superexcellent *adj syn* see SUPERB 3
rel incomparable, matchless, unparalleled, unsurpassed

superficial *adj* **1** *syn* see SHALLOW 1
2 lacking in depth, solidity, and comprehensiveness <wrote only a *superficial* report on the situation>
syn cursory, depthless, shallow, sketchy, uncritical

---

syn synonym(s)   **rel** related word(s)
ant antonym(s)   **con** contrasted word(s)
idiom idiomatic equivalent(s)
‖ use limited; if in doubt, see a dictionary

rel bird's-eye, general; one-dimensional, skin-deep; smattery
con comprehensive, full, inclusive; deep, detailed, in-depth, thorough; critical
ant exhaustive

superficies *n syn* see TOP 2

superfluent *adj syn* see SUPERFLUOUS

superfluity *n* **1** *syn* see EXCESS 1
rel overflowing, swarming, teeming
2 *syn* see LUXURY

superfluous *adj* exceeding what is needed or indispensable <omitted all *superfluous* information>
syn de trop, excess, extra, recrementitious, spare, superfluent, supernumerary, surplus
rel unnecessary, unneeded, unwanted; needless, useless; dispensable, nonessential; gratuitous, supererogatory, unasked, uncalled-for
con critical, crucial, imperative; essential, fundamental, vital; consequential, important, momentous; notable, noteworthy; defective, inadequate
ant deficient

superhuman *adj* **1** *syn* see SUPERNATURAL 1
2 *syn* see SUPERNATURAL 2

superhuman *n syn* see SUPERMAN

superincumbent *adj* **1** *syn* see SUPERIOR 1
2 *syn* see ONEROUS

superintend *vb syn* see SUPERVISE

superintendence *n syn* see OVERSIGHT 1
rel direction, presidence

superintendency *n syn* see OVERSIGHT 1
rel direction, presidence

superior *adj* **1** being or regarded as being above the level of another <the new assistant received a *superior* rating for his work>
syn greater, higher, over, overlying, superincumbent, superjacent
rel major, primary, senior
con lesser, lower, nether, under
ant inferior
2 *syn* see SUPERNATURAL 1
3 *syn* see BETTER 2
ant inferior
4 being of higher quality, accomplishment, or merit <a class of *superior* students>
syn exceptional, premium; *compare* MARVELOUS 2
rel noteworthy, remarkable, unusual
con commonplace, ordinary, unexceptional, unremarkable
ant average
5 *syn* see CHOICE
6 *syn* see EXCELLENT
ant inferior
7 *syn* see PROUD 1

superior *n* one standing above another in a hierarchy of rank <was always respectful to his *superiors* in the department>
syn better, brass hat, elder, higher-up, senior
rel heavyweight
ant inferior

superiority *n syn* see BETTER 2
rel ascendancy, dominance, supremacy
ant inferiority

superjacent *adj syn* see SUPERIOR 1
ant subjacent

superlative *adj syn* see SUPERB 3
rel accomplished, consummate, finished

superman *n* a person of extraordinary power or achievement <a space program run by scientific *supermen*>
syn demigod, superhuman
idiom Triton among the minnows
con also-ran, loser, underdog
ant subhuman

supermundane *adj syn* see SUPERNATURAL 1

supernatural *adj* **1** of, relating to, or proceeding from an order of existence beyond the visible observable universe <many then believed in a *supernatural* force that directs history>
syn metaphysical, miraculous, numinous, preternatural, superhuman, supermundane, suprahuman, supramundane, supranatural, unearthly
rel paranormal, rare, unusual; spiritual; celestial, heavenly; divine
2 being much more than is natural or normal <had a *supernatural* ability to win money>
syn superhuman, supernormal, superordinary, supranormal, uncanny, unnatural
rel extraordinary, outstanding, phenomenal, remarkable; paranormal
3 *syn* see EXCESSIVE 1

supernormal *adj syn* see SUPERNATURAL 2
ant normal

supernumerary *adj syn* see SUPERFLUOUS

superordinary *adj syn* see SUPERNATURAL 2
ant ordinary

superpatriot *n syn* see PATRIOTEER

superscribe *vb syn* see ADDRESS 6

supersede *vb syn* see REPLACE 3
rel reject, repudiate; abandon, desert, forsake; discard

superseded *adj syn* see OBSOLETE

supersensible *adj syn* see PSYCHIC 1

supersensory *adj syn* see PSYCHIC 1

supertemporal *adj syn* see INFINITE 1

supervene *vb syn* see FOLLOW 1

supervenient *adj syn* see ADVENTITIOUS

supervise *vb* to have or exercise the charge, direction, and oversight of <*supervised* the construction of the new stadium>
syn boss, chaperon, overlook, oversee, quarterback, superintend, survey
rel guide, steer; administer, conduct, direct; manage, run; control; monitor, proctor

supervision *n syn* see OVERSIGHT 1

supper club *n syn* see NIGHTCLUB

supplant *vb* **1** to supersede (another) by or as if by force, trickery, or treachery <a wife who found herself *supplanted* by another woman>
syn cut out, displace, usurp
rel crowd (out), force (out); bounce, cast (out), eject, expel, oust
idiom give the bum's rush, give the old heave-ho, step into the shoes of
2 *syn* see REPLACE 3

supple *adj* **1** *syn* see ELASTIC 1
ant stiff
2 *syn* see PLASTIC

3 showing freedom and ease of bodily movement (as in bending or twisting) <the light *supple* spring of a cat>
syn limber, lissome, lithe, lithesome
rel agile, graceful, willowy, wiry, withy
con awkward, clumsy, gawky, maladroit, unhandy; ungraceful; arthritic, creaky, decrepit
ant stiff
supplement *n* **1** *syn* see COMPLEMENT 1
2 *syn* see APPENDIX 1
suppliant *n* one who asks (as for a favor or gift) humbly <a room full of *suppliants* waiting to see the king>
syn asker, beggar, petitioner, prayer, suitor, supplicant, supplicator
rel solicitant, solicitor
supplicant *n syn* see SUPPLIANT
supplicate *vb syn* see BEG
idiom ask on bended knee, ‖come down on one's marrowbones
supplication *n syn* see PRAYER
supplicator *n syn* see SUPPLIANT
supply *vb syn* see GIVE 3
rel fulfill, outfit, provision
supply *n* an accumulation of something that is a source from which things may be drawn <an unending *supply* of new talent>
syn armamentarium, fund, inventory, stock, store
rel accumulation; reserve, reservoir, stockpile, surplus; hoard
supply *adj syn* see TEMPORARY
support *vb* **1** *syn* see BEAR 10
2 to favor actively in the face of opposition <*support* an unpopular economic policy>
syn advocate, back, backstop, champion, side (with), uphold
rel applaud, approve, endorse, favor, plunk (for), pull (for), root; adopt, embrace, espouse; defend, maintain, sustain
idiom align oneself with, be on (someone's) side, take (someone's) side
con battle, combat, counter, fight, oppose; withstand
ant buck
3 to supply what is needed for sustenance <*support* his family>
syn maintain, provide (for)
idiom boil the pot, bring home the bacon, make a living for, take care of
4 to hold up in position by serving as a foundation or base for <pillars *supporting* an arch>
syn bear up, bolster, brace, buttress, carry, prop, shore (up), sustain, upbear, uphold
rel stand
5 to keep from yielding, sinking, or losing courage or stability <her friends *supported* her during the crisis>
syn bolster, buoy (up), prop, sustain, underprop, uphold; *compare* ENCOURAGE 1
rel encourage; fortify, stiffen, strengthen
support *n* **1** *syn* see HELP 1
2 *syn* see HELP 2

3 a supporting means, agency, medium, or device <girders as structural *supports*> <strong economic *support* for the government>
syn brace, buttress, column, prop, shore, stay, underpinner, underpinning, underpropping
rel base, foundation; sustentation
4 *syn* see LIVING
supportable *adj syn* see BEARABLE
ant insupportable, unsupportable
supporter *n* **1** *syn* see FOLLOWER
2 *syn* see EXPONENT
ant antagonist
supposable *adj syn* see THINKABLE 2
ant insupposable
supposal *n syn* see THEORY 1
suppose *vb* **1** *syn* see UNDERSTAND 3
rel presuppose
2 *syn* see CONJECTURE
suppose *n syn* see THEORY 2
supposed *adj* **1** accepted or advanced as true or real on the basis of less than conclusive evidence <the *supposed* efficiency of the new machine>
syn conjectural, hypothetical, putative, reputed, suppositional, suppositious, suppositious, suppositive, suppository; *compare* ALLEGED
rel assumed, postulated, postulatory, presumed, presupposed; provisional, tentative; academic, speculative, theoretical; alleged
con sure; known, proved, proven; ascertained, demonstrated, observed, recognized
ant certain
2 *syn* see ALLEGED
ant proved, proven
supposition *n* **1** *syn* see ASSUMPTION 2
2 *syn* see THEORY 2
suppositional *adj syn* see SUPPOSED 1
suppositious *adj* **1** *syn* see FICTITIOUS 1
2 *syn* see SUPPOSED 1
rel doubtful, dubious, questionable; pretended, simulated
supposititious *adj* **1** *syn* see ILLEGITIMATE 1
2 *syn* see FICTITIOUS 1
3 *syn* see SUPPOSED 1
supposititiousness *n syn* see ILLEGITIMACY 1
suppositive *adj syn* see SUPPOSED 1
suppository *adj syn* see SUPPOSED 1
suppress *vb* **1** *syn* see CRUSH 5
idiom ride roughshod over
2 to hold back more or less forcefully someone or something that seeks an outlet <management tried to *suppress* the workers' discontent> <there was no way to *suppress* her short of murder>
syn muffle, ‖quelch, repress, shush, squelch, strangle; *compare* CRUSH 5
rel curb, restrain; arrest, check, interrupt; put down, slap down; quash, quell, squash; cut off, spike; abolish, annihilate, extinguish
idiom bring to naught, crack (or clamp) down on, put the kibosh on
3 to keep from public knowledge <*suppress* all news from the front>
syn burke, hush (up), stifle
rel repress; censor; silence

idiom put the lid on
con disclose, divulge, leak, ‖let out, reveal; broadcast, circulate, diffuse, publish, spread
4 *syn* see COMPOSE 4
rel drown; swallow
5 *syn* see STUNT

suppression *n* **1** *syn* see REPRESSION 1
2 *syn* see REPRESSION 2

supra *adv syn* see ABOVE 2
ant infra

suprahuman *adj syn* see SUPERNATURAL 1

supramundane *adj syn* see SUPERNATURAL 1

supranatural *adj syn* see SUPERNATURAL 1

supranormal *adj syn* see SUPERNATURAL 2

supremacy *n* the position of being first (as in rank, power, or influence) <Britain once enjoyed *supremacy* on the seas>
syn ascendancy, ascendant, dominance, domination, dominion, masterdom, preeminence, preponderance, preponderancy, preponderation, prepotence, prepotency, sovereignty
rel authority, control, driver's seat, power, sway; mastership, mastery, principality, superiority; transcendence

supreme *adj* developed to the utmost and not exceeded by any other in degree, quality, or intensity <dying for one's principles is an example of *supreme* sacrifice>
syn incomparable, preeminent, surpassing, towering, transcendent, ultimate, unequalable, unmatchable, unsurpassable; *compare* ALONE 3, EXCELLENT, MARVELOUS 2, MAXIMUM, SUPERB 3
rel crowning, master, sovereign; unequaled, unmatched, unparalleled, unrivaled, unsurpassed; final, last; absolute, perfect

surcease *vb syn* see STOP 3

sure *adj* **1** firmly settled or established <trying to find a *sure* footing on the rugged slope>
syn fast, firm, secure, stable, staunch, strong; *compare* FAST 4, STABLE 4
2 free from doubt, hesitation, or fear <upheld a *sure* faith>
syn abiding, enduring, firm, fixed, never-failing, steadfast, steady, unfaltering, unqualified, unquestioning, unshakable, unshaken, unwavering, wholehearted
rel assured, changeless, constant, unchangeable, unchanging, uncompromising, unfailing, unvarying; certain, fixed, set
con insecure, uncertain, unreliable; feeble, infirm, shaky, unsound; doubtful, dubious, hesitant
ant unsure
3 *syn* see INFALLIBLE 1
4 *syn* see INFALLIBLE 2
5 marked by unwavering assurance especially as to the rightness of one's views or actions <was *sure* he knew the answer>
syn certain, cocksure, confident, positive
rel assured, self-assured, self-possessed, self-satisfied; arrogant, cocky, pert; decided, decisive
con doubtful, hesitant, uncertain
ant unsure

6 *syn* see POSITIVE 3
rel convincing, telling; absolute, definite; genuine, real, valid

sure–enough *adj* **1** *syn* see ACTUAL 2
2 *syn* see AUTHENTIC 2

surefire *adj syn* see INFALLIBLE 2

sureness *n syn* see CERTAINTY
ant unsureness

sure thing *n* one that is bound to be successful <was deemed a *sure thing* in the race>
syn shoo-in
rel certainty; winner

surety *n* **1** *syn* see CERTAINTY
2 *syn* see GUARANTEE 1
3 *syn* see SPONSOR

surface *n syn* see TOP 2
rel exterior, outside; cover, covering
con body, mass; inside, interior; lining

surface *vb* to come to the surface (as of water) <a submarine *surfaced* outside the harbor>
syn rise
rel come up
con go down, go under; submerge; dive

surfeit *n syn* see EXCESS 1

surfeit *vb syn* see SATIATE
rel overfill, overindulge
idiom have all one can take (*or* stand)
ant whet

surfeited *adj syn* see SATIATED
ant unsatisfied

surge *vb syn* see POUR 1

surly *adj syn* see SULLEN
rel discourteous, ill-mannered, rude, ungracious; bearish, boorish, churlish; fractious, irritable, snappish, waspish
idiom as surly as a bear
con affable, cordial, genial, gracious
ant amiable

surmise *vb syn* see CONJECTURE
rel consider, regard; hypothesize, theorize
idiom risk assuming, venture a guess

surmount *vb* **1** *syn* see OVERCOME 1
rel best, better, outdo, outstrip, outtop, outtower, surpass
idiom rise superior to
2 *syn* see CLEAR 8
3 to stand or lie at the top of <a cross *surmounts* the cupola>
syn cap, crest, crown, top
rel finish; terminate
4 *syn* see TOP

surpass *vb* **1** to be or become greater than or superior to <*surpassed* all his fellows in scholarship>
syn ‖bang, beat, best, better, cap, cob, ding, exceed, excel, outdo, outgo, outmatch, outshine, outstrip, pass, top, transcend, trump
rel distance, outdistance, outpace, outperform, outpoint, outrange, outrival, outrun, outvie; eclipse, outrank, outtop, outtower, outweigh, overshadow, overtop, rank
idiom have it all over, put to shame
2 *syn* see EXCEED 1

surpassing *adj syn* see SUPREME

surpassingly *adv syn* see VERY 1

surplus *n* **1** *syn* see EXCESS 1
ant deficiency
2 *syn* see EXCESS 2
ant shortage

surplus adj syn see SUPERFLUOUS
surplusage n 1 syn see EXCESS 2
  ant shortage, underage
  2 syn see EXCESS 1
  ant shortage
surprise vb 1 to attack unawares <hijackers *surprised* the truck driver and took his cargo>
  syn ambush, lay (for), waylay
  rel bushwhack, dry-gulch; grab, grasp, seize, take
  2 to impress forcibly through unexpectedness, startlingness, or unusualness <was *surprised* by his violent jealousy>
  syn amaze, astonish, astound, dumbfound, flabbergast
  rel startle; bewilder, confound, discomfit, disconcert, dismay, nonplus, ‖swan; faze, rattle, rock; bowl (over), floor, stagger; stun, stupefy
  idiom leave open-mouthed (*or* aghast), take aback (*or* by surprise)
surprising adj syn see MARVELOUS 1
  rel unexpected, unforeseen, unlooked-for; eye-opening, eye-popping
surrender vb 1 syn see RELINQUISH
  rel commit, consign, entrust
  2 syn see FALL 3
  rel give in, give up
  idiom haul down one's colors, strike the (*or* one's) flag
surrender n the yielding of one's person, forces, or possessions to another <the victors demanded unconditional *surrender*>
  syn capitulation, dedition, submission
  rel appeasement, Munich; relenting, succumbing, yielding; white flag
surreptitious adj syn see SECRET 1
  rel skulking, slinking, slinky, sneaking, sneaky
  con obvious, open, overt
  ant brazen
surreptitiously adv syn see SECRETLY
  con openly, overtly, plainly
  ant brazenly
surrogate n 1 syn see SUBSTITUTE
  2 syn see RESOURCE 3
surrogate adj syn see SUBSTITUTE 1
surround vb 1 to close in or as if in a ring about something <a crowd *surrounded* the accident victim>
  syn begird, beset, circle, compass, encircle, encompass, environ, gird, girdle, hem, loop, ring, round
  rel embosom, enclave, enclose, envelop; circumscribe, circumvent, confine, limit
  2 syn see BORDER 1
surroundings n pl syn see ENVIRONMENT
surveillance n 1 syn see EYE 3
  idiom peeled eye
  2 syn see LOOKOUT 3
  rel surveyance
  idiom watchful (*or* weather) eye
survey vb 1 syn see ESTIMATE 1
  rel measure, size, size up

  2 syn see SUPERVISE
  3 to view from or as if from a high place or position <*surveyed* the view from her penthouse window>
  syn overlook, oversee
  4 syn see SCRUTINIZE 1
survey n 1 syn see EXAMINATION
  2 syn see COMPENDIUM 1
‖**survigrous** adj syn see VIGOROUS
survive vb 1 syn see OUTLIVE
  2 to continue to exist or function in spite of a usually adverse condition or development <a company that managed to *survive* the recession>
  syn come through, pull through, ride (out)
  rel carry on, carry through, continue, endure, last, persist; live down, outlast, outlive; recover, revive
  idiom come out of it, live to fight again, make it through, ride out (*or* weather) the storm
  con collapse, crash, fold, fold up, go down, go under; founder, sink; close (down), close up; bankrupt, bust
  ant perish
susceptible adj 1 syn see LIABLE 2
  rel disposed, inclined, predisposed
  ant immune, unsusceptible
  2 syn see EASY 3
  rel nonresistant, soft; movable, persuadable
  ant unsusceptible
  3 syn see SENTIENT 3
  rel affected, impressed, influenced, swayed, touched; aroused, roused, stirred
  ant unsusceptible
susceptive adj syn see SENTIENT 3
suscitate vb syn see PROVOKE 4
suspect adj syn see DOUBTFUL 1
  idiom ‖a bit thin (*or* thick), open to suspicion
suspect vb 1 syn see DISTRUST
  idiom have doubts about
  2 syn see UNDERSTAND 3
  idiom be inclined to think
suspend vb 1 syn see EXCLUDE
  2 syn see DEFER
  rel arrest, check, interrupt; cease, discontinue, stop
  idiom lay on the table, put on the shelf
  3 syn see HANG 1
suspended adj hung or seeming as if hung from a support <bunches of grapes *suspended* from the vines>
  syn hanging, pendent, pendulant, pendulous, pensile
  rel dangling, swinging
suspenders n pl a pair of adjustable bands for holding up the front and rear of a pair of trousers or a skirt <every stockbroker seemed to be wearing *suspenders* and a yellow tie>
  syn braces, ‖gallows, ‖galluses
suspense n syn see SUSPENSION 2
suspension n 1 syn see ABEYANCE
  2 a temporary withholding of action or cessation of activity <asked for *suspension* of judgment until all the evidence was in>
  syn moratorium, suspense
  rel cessation, concluding, conclusion, end, ending, finish, period, termination

---

con resumption; continuance

suspicion *n* 1 *syn* see UNCERTAINTY
  rel apprehension, foreboding, misgiving, presentiment; distrust
  2 *syn* see HINT 1

‖**suspicion** *vb syn* see DISTRUST
suspicious *adj* 1 *syn* see DOUBTFUL 1
  rel questionable; queer
  2 given or prone to suspicion <was *suspicious* of everyone's motives>
  syn distrustful, jealous, mistrustful
  rel careful, cautious; leery, wary, watchful; skeptical, unbelieving
  con trustful, trusting, unsuspecting; naive; dupable, easy, exploitable, gullible
  ant unsuspicious

suspiciously *adv syn* see ASKANCE 2
  rel distrustingly, mistrustingly
  ant unsuspiciously

suspire *vb* 1 *syn* see SIGH 1
  idiom draw a long breath
  2 *syn* see LONG

sustain *vb* 1 *syn* see MAINTAIN 1
  rel nourish, support; prolong
  2 *syn* see SUPPORT 4
  rel lug, pack, tote
  3 *syn* see SUPPORT 5
  rel befriend, favor
  idiom stand by
  con abandon, forsake; ignore
  4 *syn* see BEAR 10
  5 *syn* see EXPERIENCE 1
  rel bear, endure

sustainable *adj syn* see BEARABLE
  ant unsustainable

sustenance *n* 1 *syn* see FOOD 2
  idiom bodily sustenance
  2 *syn* see LIVING

sustentation *n syn* see PRESERVATION 1
susurration *n syn* see MURMUR 1
‖**swack** *n syn* see CUFF
‖**swacked** *adj syn* see INTOXICATED 1
swad *n syn* see SOLDIER
swaddle *vb syn* see SWATHE
  rel ‖sweel
  ant unswaddle

‖**swaddy** *n syn* see SOLDIER
swag *vb* 1 *syn* see SEESAW
  2 *syn* see DROOP 3
swag *n* 1 *syn* see SPOIL
  2 *syn* see MONEY
swagger *vb* 1 *syn* see LORD
  rel swash, swashbuckle
  2 *syn* see STRUT 2
  rel bluster, brandish, flourish
  con blench, quail; shrink, wince; truckle
‖**swagger** *n syn* see VAGABOND
‖**swagman** *n syn* see VAGABOND
swain *n* 1 *syn* see BOYFRIEND 1
  2 *syn* see SUITOR 1
swainish *adj syn* see BOORISH
swallow *vb* 1 to receive through the esophagus into the stomach <*swallowed* the pills easily with a sip of water>
  syn down, take
  rel drop, gulp, ‖quilt, toss; ingest, ingurgitate
  2 *syn* see DRINK 1
  3 *syn* see BELIEVE 1
  idiom swallow (something) hook, line, and sinker

4 *syn* see BEAR 10
5 *syn* see ACCEPT 2
6 *syn* see MUMBLE
swamp *n* wet spongy land saturated and sometimes partially covered with water <hunted alligators in the Florida *swamps*>
  syn baygall, bog, fen, marsh, marshland, mire, morass, ‖moss, muskeg, ‖purgatory, ‖puxy, quag, quagmire, slough, ‖sump, swampland, ‖swang, ‖vlei
  rel bottoms, ‖holm; ‖glade; ‖jheel; quake ooze; shaking prairie, trembling prairie
swamp *vb* 1 *syn* see DELUGE 1
  2 *syn* see DELUGE 3
swampland *n syn* see SWAMP
‖**swang** *n syn* see SWAMP
swank *vb syn* see LORD
swank *adj* 1 *syn* see SHOWY
  2 *syn* see STYLISH
swap *vb* 1 *syn* see EXCHANGE 2
  2 *syn* see TRADE 1
  idiom ‖swap horses, swap out of
‖**swap** *n syn* see BLOW 1
‖**swapping** *adj syn* see HUGE
‖**swart** *vb syn* see FAINT
swarm *vb syn* see TEEM
  idiom gather (or swarm) like bees
swarming *adj syn* see ALIVE 5
swart *adj syn* see DARK 3
swarth *adj syn* see DARK 3
swarthy *adj syn* see DARK 3
swash *vb* 1 *syn* see SLOSH 1
  2 *syn* see SPLASH
swashy *adj syn* see INSIPID 3
swat *vb* ‖1 *syn* see SQUAT
  2 *syn* see STRIKE 2
  rel blip, box, buffet, cuff, smack; belt, clobber, slug, smash, wallop
swat *n syn* see HIT 1
swathe *vb* to cover or bind completely with clothing or material <legs *swathed* in bandages> <the baby was *swathed* in a warm shawl>
  syn drape, enswathe, envelop, enwrap, roll, swaddle, wrap (up); *compare* ENFOLD 1
  rel enfold; encase; cover
  con bare, denude, expose, strip, uncover, unswaddle, unwrap
  ant unswathe
sway *vb* 1 *syn* see SWING 1
  2 *syn* see LURCH 2
  3 *syn* see GOVERN 1
  4 *syn* see AFFECT
  rel bias, dispose, incline, predispose; conduct, control, direct, manage; govern, rule
sway *n syn* see POWER 1
  rel range, reach, scope, sweep; amplitude, expanse, spread, stretch
swayable *adj syn* see RECEPTIVE 1
swear *vb* 1 *syn* see VOW
  idiom swear on a stack of Bibles, swear to God, swear up and down
  2 *syn* see TESTIFY 2
  3 to use profane, blasphemous, or obscene language <*swore* when the horse threw him>
  syn bedamn, curse, cuss, damn, execrate, imprecate
  rel blaspheme; rail, rant; abuse, revile, vilify, vituperate
  idiom ‖chew the dirty rag, curse and swear, fall a-cursing, ‖let out religion, make the air

blue, rip (*or* rap) out an oath, swear like a
sailor (*or* trooper), use language
swear *n syn* see SWEARWORD
swearing *n syn* see BLASPHEMY 1
swearword *n* a profane, blasphemous, or
obscene word <let loose with a string of
swearwords>
   syn curse, cuss, cussword, expletive, oath,
swear
   rel four-letter word, obscenity, scurrility
   idiom blue word, one-horse oath, raw one,
ripe (*or* juicy) word, sailor's blessing, six=
cornered oath, strong word
sweat *vb* **1** *syn* see EXUDE
   2 *syn* see FLEECE 1
sweat *n* **1** *syn* see WORK 2
   2 *syn* see SNIT
   ‖**3** *syn* see SOLDIER
sweatful *adj syn* see SWEATY
sweating *adj syn* see SWEATY
sweat out *vb syn* see BEAR 10
sweaty *adj* producing, accompanied by, or
characterized by sweat <he still held the
racket tight in *sweaty* hands>
   syn asweat, perspiring, perspiry, ‖puggy,
sweatful, sweating
   rel clammy; sticky; wet
   idiom bathed in sweat, covered with sweat,
drenched with (*or* in) sweat, in a muck of a
sweat, wet with sweat (*or* perspiration)
sweep *vb syn* see FLY 4
sweep *n syn* see RANGE 2
sweeping *n sweepings pl syn* see REFUSE
sweeping *adj* **1** *syn* see ALL-AROUND 2
   rel all-embracing, all-encompassing
   2 *syn* see INDISCRIMINATE 1
   rel all-out, out-and-out, whole-hog; across=
the-board, blanket
sweet *adj* **1** distinctly pleasing or charming
<a *sweet* smile>
   syn dulcet, engaging, winning, winsome
   rel agreeable, pleasant, pleasing; beautiful,
fair, lovely; delectable, delicious, delightful,
luscious; angelic, heavenly
   con disagreeable, unpleasant; displeasing,
obnoxious, repulsive
   ant bitter
   2 having a pleasant smell <the *sweet* odor of
flowers and incense>
   syn ambrosial, aromal, aromatic, balmy,
fragrant, perfumed, perfumy, redolent,
savory, scented, spicy; *compare* ODOROUS
   rel clean, fresh; sweetish
   con funky, fusty, musty, noisome, putrid,
rancid, rotten, stale, stinking, strong, whiffy;
fetid, foul, olid, rank, smelly
   ant malodorous
   3 *syn* see MELODIOUS 1
sweet *n syn* see SWEETHEART 1
sweeten *vb* **1** *syn* see PACIFY
   2 *syn* see SUGARCOAT 1
sweetheart *n* **1** one who is dearly beloved —
often used as a term of endearment <was her
childhood *sweetheart*> <*sweetheart*, you
know I'll wait>

   syn beloved, darling, dear, flame, heartthrob, honey, honeybunch, love, loveling,
sweet, sweeting, turtledove
   rel ‖cutie pie, deary, pigsney; pet, puggy
   2 *syn* see GIRL FRIEND 2
   rel doll baby, lovey-dovey, ‖tootsie
   3 *syn* see BOYFRIEND 2
   rel paramour; ‖dreamboat
sweetheart *vb syn* see ADDRESS 8
sweetie *n syn* see GIRL FRIEND 2
   rel sweetie pie
sweetling *n syn* see SWEETHEART 1
sweetness and light *n syn* see AMENITY 1
sweet-talk *vb syn* see COAX
swell *vb* **1** *syn* see EXPAND 3
   rel balloon, belly, bloat, blow up, bosom;
pouch, pout; overblow
   con compress, condense, constrict, contract
   ant shrink
   2 *syn* see LORD
   rel puff
   idiom act the grand seigneur, swell it
swell *n syn* see EXPERT
swell *adj syn* see MARVELOUS 2
swelled head *n syn* see CONCEIT 2
swellheadedness *n syn* see CONCEIT 2
swelling *adj syn* see RHETORICAL
‖**swelt** *vb* **1** *syn* see DIE 1
   2 *syn* see FAINT
swelter *vb syn* see BURN 3
sweltering *adj syn* see HOT 1
   idiom ‖hot as the hinges of hell
   ant frigid
sweltry *adj syn* see HOT 1
swerve *vb* **1** to turn or be turned away
abruptly from a straight line or course
<*swerved* the car to avoid collision>
   syn dip, sheer, skew, slue, train off, veer
   2 to be deflected from a fixed or right course
of action or conduct <never *swerved* from
the concept of duty, honor, country>
   syn depart, deviate, digress, diverge
   rel shift; waver; err, stray, wander
   idiom deviate from the straight and narrow,
get off the proper course (*or* path)
swift *adj syn* see FAST 3
   rel headlong, precipitate, sudden; double=
quick; supersonic
   ant sluggish
swift *adv syn* see FAST 2
   ant sluggishly
swiften *vb syn* see SPEED 3
swiftly *adv syn* see FAST 2
   con slowly
   ant sluggishly
swiftness *n* **1** *syn* see SPEED 2
   ant sluggishness
   2 *syn* see HASTE 1
   ant slowness
swig *n syn* see DRINK 3
swig *vb syn* see DRINK 3
swill *vb* **1** *syn* see DRINK 3
   2 *syn* see CONSUME 5
swill *n* **1** *syn* see REFUSE
   2 *syn* see DRINK 3
swillbowl *n syn* see DRUNKARD
swiller *n syn* see DRUNKARD
swim *vb syn* see SPIN 2
   idiom have one's head swim
swimming *adj syn* see DIZZY 2

---

syn synonym(s)   *rel* related word(s)
ant antonym(s)   *con* contrasted word(s)
idiom idiomatic equivalent(s)
‖ use limited; if in doubt, see a dictionary

rel fluctuating, swaying, wavering

swimmingly *adv syn* see WELL 5

swimmy *adj syn* see DIZZY 2

swindle *vb syn* see CHEAT
 rel rogue; victimize
 idiom sell one a bill of goods, take for a ride, take for a sucker

swindle *n syn* see IMPOSTURE

swindler *n* one who defrauds usually of money and especially by imposture or by gaining the victim's confidence <lost their savings to *swindlers* in a get-rich-quick scheme>
 syn bunco steerer, cheat, cheater, chiaus, come-on, confidence man, con man, defrauder, diddler, double-dealer, flimflammer, ‖grifter, gyp, gypper, ‖mace, mountebank, Peter Funk, rogue, sharper, sharpie, skin, slicker, ‖spieler, trickster
 rel bilk, bilker, blackleg, charlatan, chiseler, crook, deceiver, dodger, fraud, gouger, harpy, highbinder, hoaxer, operator, rook, shark, sharp, sharpster, tricker; scoundrel

swing *vb* 1 *syn* see HANDLE 2
 2 to move rhythmically to and fro, up and down, or back and forth <the clock's pendulum *swung* slowly>
 syn oscillate, pendulate, sway
 rel undulate, wave; rock, roll; revolve, rotate, switch, wheel; jiggle, wag, waggle, wiggle, wigwag
 3 *syn* see TURN 6
 4 *syn* see LURCH 2

swing *n* 1 *syn* see RHYTHM
 2 *syn* see HANG

‖**swingeing** *adj syn* see EXCELLENT

swinish *adj syn* see BRUTISH

swipe *n* 1 *syn* see HIT 1
 2 *syn* see CRITICISM 2

swipe *vb syn* see STEAL 1

swirl *vb* to move swiftly in circles, eddies, or undulations <water *swirled* into the storm drains>
 syn eddy, gurge, purl, swoosh, whirl, whirlpool, whorl
 rel boil, roil; gush, surge

swish *vb syn* see HISS

swish *adj syn* see STYLISH

switch *vb* 1 *syn* see WAG
 2 *syn* see EXCHANGE 2
 3 *syn* see SHUNT 1

‖**swither** *vb syn* see RUSH 1

swivet *n syn* see SNIT

swizzle *vb syn* see DRINK 3

swollen *adj syn* see RHETORICAL

swoon *vb syn* see FAINT
 rel die away, drown

swoon *n syn* see FAINT

swoosh *vb syn* see SWIRL

sworn *adj syn* see INVETERATE 1

sybarite *n syn* see HEDONIST

sybaritic *adj* marked by or given to luxury or voluptuous living <the *sybaritic* grandeur of a sultan's harem> <a man of *sybaritic* and self-indulgent habits>
 syn hedonistic, onanistic, self-indulgent, sybarital, sybaritish; *compare* SENSUOUS
 rel apolaustic, pleasure-loving; epicurean, luxurious; carnal, sensual, voluptuous

sybaritical *adj syn* see SYBARITIC

sybaritish *adj syn* see SYBARITIC

sycophancy *n syn* see DETRACTION

sycophant *n* a base or servilely attentive flatterer and self-seeker <*sycophants* who slavishly curried favor with the king>
 syn apple-polisher, bootlick, bootlicker, ‖brownnose, ‖brownnoser, ‖clawback, creature, ‖easy rider, footlicker, groveler, lickspit, lickspittle, minion, reptile, spaniel, ‖suck, toad, toadeater, toadier, toady, truckler, yes-man; *compare* PARASITE
 rel flunky, gopher, lackey, slave, stooge; flatterer, self-seeker; snob, tuft-hunter

sycophant *adj syn* see FAWNING

sycophantic *adj syn* see FAWNING

sycophantical *adj syn* see FAWNING

sycophantish *adj syn* see FAWNING

syllable *n syn* see PARTICLE

syllabus *n syn* see COMPENDIUM 1

sylloge *n syn* see COMPENDIUM 1

symbol *n* 1 something that stands for something else by reason of relationship, association, convention, or accidental resemblance <the lion is often used as a *symbol* of courage>
 syn attribute, emblem; *compare* INDICATION 3
 rel indication, token, type; badge, mark, note, sign, stamp; character, design, device, figure, motif, pattern; representation
 2 *syn* see CHARACTER 1

symbolism *n syn* see ALLEGORY 1

symbolization *n syn* see ALLEGORY 1

symbolize *vb syn* see REPRESENT 2

symmetrical *adj syn* see PROPORTIONAL

symmetry *n* beauty of form or arrangement arising from balanced proportions <the superb *symmetry* of the design>
 syn balance, harmony, proportion
 rel arrangement, order; agreement, conformity; equality, evenness, regularity; rhythm; finish
 con asymmetry, dissymmetry; disproportion, imbalance, irregularity, unbalance

sympathetic *adj* 1 *syn* see CONSONANT 1
 ant unsympathetic
 2 favorably inclined <found his hearers *sympathetic* to his proposal>
 syn friendly, receptive, ‖sib, well-disposed
 rel agreeable, congenial, favorable; amenable, open, open-minded, receptive, responsive
 con ill-disposed, unfriendly, unreceptive; cool, indifferent, lukewarm; neutral
 ant unsympathetic
 3 *syn* see TENDER
 rel benign, benignant, kind, kindly; appreciating, comprehending, understanding
 ant unsympathetic

sympathize (with) *vb syn* see COMPASSIONATE
 rel appreciate, comprehend, understand

sympathy *n* 1 *syn* see ATTRACTION 2
 ant antipathy
 2 a feeling for or a capacity for sharing in the interests of another <he was in *sympathy* with her desire to succeed>
 syn compassion, empathy, fellow feeling
 rel responsiveness, sensitivity; feelings, heart; tenderness, warmheartedness,

warmth; benignancy, benignness, kindliness, kindness
con disinterest, unconcern
3 syn see PITY
symphonic adj syn see HARMONIOUS 1
symphonious adj syn see HARMONIOUS 1
symphonize vb syn see HARMONIZE 4
symphony n syn see ORCHESTRA
rel concert band, symphony band; symphony orchestra
symptom n syn see INDICATION 3
synchronal adj syn see CONTEMPORARY 1
synchronic adj syn see CONTEMPORARY 1
synchronous adj syn see CONTEMPORARY 1
syncope n syn see FAINT
syndicate n a combination of interlocked companies or enterprises <a large newspaper *syndicate*>
syn cartel, chain, combine, conglomerate, group, pool, trust
rel association, organization; partnership, union
syndrome n syn see DISEASE 1
synergetic adj syn see COOPERATIVE
ant counteractive
synergic adj syn see COOPERATIVE
ant counteractive
synopsis n syn see ABRIDGMENT
synopsize vb syn see EPITOMIZE 1
idiom hit the high spots, put it in a nutshell

synthesize vb syn see HARMONIZE 4
synthetic adj formed or developed by human art, skill, or effort and not by natural processes <*synthetic* plastics>
syn artificial, factitious, man-made; compare ARTIFICIAL 2
rel manufactured; constructed, fabricated, made
con natural
syrupy adj syn see SENTIMENTAL
system n 1 an organized integrated whole made up of diverse but interrelated and interdependent parts <the capitalist *system*>
syn complex; compare WHOLE 2
rel aggregation, array; mesh, network; arrangement, disposition, scheme, setup; order, pattern
con disorganization; chaos
2 syn see WHOLE 2
3 syn see ORDER 8
rel procedure, proceeding, process
4 syn see METHOD 1
systematic adj syn see ORDERLY 1
rel arranged, ordered, organized, systematized; analytical, logical
con disorganized; chaotic
ant unsystematic
systematize vb syn see ORDER 1
rel contrive, frame
con confuse, disorder, jumble

T

tab n 1 syn see EYE 3
2 syn see BILL 1
3 syn see CHECK 2
4 syn see PRICE 1
tabby n 1 syn see GOSSIP 1
‖2 syn see SPINSTER
tabernacle n syn see HOUSE OF WORSHIP
table n 1 a piece of furniture on which food is customarily served <a feast on the *table*>
syn board, dining table, dinner table, mahogany, ‖table-board
rel bar, buffet, counter, sideboard
2 a condensed ordered enumeration of items usually arranged in columns <a *table* of weights and measures>
syn chart, tabulation
rel list; diagram
3 syn see PLATEAU
‖**table–board** n syn see TABLE 1
tableland n syn see PLATEAU
tabloid adj syn see SENSATIONAL 2
taboo n a restraint imposed by social usage or as a protective measure <a society rife with antiquated moral *taboos*>

syn ban, forbiddance, interdiction, prohibition, proscription
rel inhibition, limitation, reservation, restraint, restriction; regulation, sanction; don't
con acceptance, toleration; approval, authorization, permission, permit, permittance
taboo vb syn see FORBID
tabulation n syn see TABLE 2
tacit adj 1 expressed or conveyed without words, speech, or forthright reference <they made a *tacit* agreement to work together>
syn implicit, implied, inarticulate, inferred, undeclared, understood, unexpressed, unsaid, unspoken, unuttered, wordless
rel alluded (to), hinted (at), intimated, suggested; assumed
con expressed, spoken, verbal; categorical, explicit, express, unequivocal
2 syn see UNSPOKEN 1
taciturn adj syn see SILENT 3
rel laconic, unexpressive; brooding, dour
con chatty, communicative, loquacious, talkative; convivial, uninhibited, unreserved, unrestrained
ant garrulous
tack n syn see TURN 2
rel alteration; digression, tangent; swerve, zigzag

syn synonym(s)   rel related word(s)
ant antonym(s)   con contrasted word(s)
idiom idiomatic equivalent(s)
‖ use limited; if in doubt, see a dictionary

tackle *n syn* see EQUIPMENT

tackle *vb syn* see ATTACK 2
rel take on, undertake; plunge into, set about
idiom get on the job, put one's shoulder to the wheel, start the ball rolling
con avoid, delay, hesitate, put off

tackling *n syn* see EQUIPMENT

tacky *adj* **1** *syn* see SHABBY 1
rel dowdy, outmoded, unstylish; messy, sloppy, slovenly, unkempt, untidy; blowsy, frowsy, frumpish
idiom gone to seed
2 marked by a lack of style or good taste <an old *tacky* scarf spoiled her outfit>
syn dowdy, frumpish, frumpy, outmoded, out-of-date, stodgy, unstylish
rel unbecoming; crude, inelegant, tasteless; incorrect, unsuitable; cheap, gaudy
con ‖mod, modern, modish, smart, stylish, tasteful; elegant

tact *n* skill and grace in dealing with others <handled the embarrassing situation with great *tact*>
syn address, delicatesse, diplomacy, poise, savoir faire, tactfulness; *compare* ADDRESS 1
rel control, head, presence, repose; amenity, courtesy, gallantry; policy, politicness, smoothness, suavity, urbanity; adroitness, deftness, skill; acumen, finesse, perception, sensitivity
con abruptness, bluntness, coarseness, discourtesy, rudeness
ant tactlessness

tactful *adj* marked by or exhibiting tact <his *tactful* skill in handling negotiations>
syn delicate, diplomatic, politic, tactical; *compare* SUAVE
rel polished, suave, urbane; adroit, deft, skilled, skillful; perceptive, sensitive
con clumsy, unpolished, unskilled; discourteous, impolite, rude; undiplomatic
ant blunt, tactless, untactful

tactfulness *n syn* see TACT
rel civility, civilness, politeness; polish
ant tactlessness

tactic *adj syn* see TACTILE 2

tactical *adj* **1** made or carried out with only a limited or immediate end in view <had time only for *tactical* decisions and not strategic planning>
syn short-range
con long-range
ant strategic
2 *syn* see EXPEDIENT
3 *syn* see TACTFUL

tactile *adj* **1** *syn* see TANGIBLE 1
2 of or relating to the sense of touch <*tactile* responses>
syn tactic, tactual

tactility *n syn* see TOUCH 3

taction *n syn* see TOUCH 2

tactless *adj* marked by a lack of tact <his *tactless* remark hurt her>
syn brash, impolitic, maladroit, undiplomatic, unpolitic, untactful
rel impolite, inconsiderate, indelicate, rude; bungling, inept
con diplomatic, polite, tactical
ant tactful

tactual *adj syn* see TACTILE 2

tad *n syn* see BOY 1

tag *n* **1** *syn* see COMMONPLACE
2 *syn* see TICKET 2

tag *vb syn* see TAIL

tag and rag *n syn* see RABBLE 2

tag end *n syn* see TAIL END 2

tagrag *adj syn* see SHABBY 1

tagrag and bobtail *n syn* see RABBLE 2

tail *n syn* see BUTTOCKS

tail *vb* to follow (someone) for purposes of surveillance <detectives *tailing* the suspects>
syn bedog, dog, shadow, tag, trail; *compare* EYE 2, FOLLOW 2
rel hound, pursue

tail end *n* **1** *syn* see BUTTOCKS
2 the hindmost part of something <watched the *tail end* of the parade march off>
syn tag end

tailor *vb syn* see ADAPT
rel style; dovetail; shape up

tailor–made *adj syn* see CUSTOM-MADE

tailor–make *vb syn* see ADAPT

taint *vb* **1** to touch or affect with something bad or undesirable <his good reputation was *tainted* by the scandal>
syn besmear, besmirch, blur, cloud, defile, dirty, discolor, smear, smudge, smut, smutch, soil, stain, sully, tar, tarnish; *compare* CONTAMINATE 1
rel discredit; brand, stigmatize; blacken; damage, harm, hurt
idiom cast a slur upon; give a bad name to, give a black mark to
con brighten, cleanse, clear
2 *syn* see DECAY
rel befoul, contaminate, foul
3 *syn* see CONTAMINATE 1

taintless *adj syn* see CLEAN 1
ant tainted

take *vb* **1** *syn* see CATCH 1
2 *syn* see SEIZE 2
idiom make off with
con drop, dump, give up, relinquish, surrender
3 *syn* see APPROPRIATE 1
con relinquish, yield
4 to lay hold of (as with the hands or an instrument) <*took* the ax by the handle>
syn clasp, grasp, grip
rel hold; handle
idiom take hold of
con drop, release
5 *syn* see SEIZE 3
rel contract, get; harrow, reach, torment
6 *syn* see CATCH 1
7 *syn* see ATTRACT 1
8 *syn* see SWALLOW 1
9 *syn* see EAT 1
10 to bring into and accept in a particular capacity or relationship <*took* his son as a member of the firm>
syn admit, receive, take in
rel bring; accept; have, include
11 *syn* see BUY 1
12 *syn* see CHOOSE 1
13 *syn* see DEMAND 1
14 to obtain from another source by means of derivation <*takes* his name from his father's>

syn derive, draw
rel get, obtain; borrow
15 syn see BEAR 10
rel withstand; undergo; ‖hack
idiom take it lying down, take it on the chin
16 syn see CONTRACT 1
idiom take sick with
17 syn see APPREHEND 1
18 syn see UNDERSTAND 3
19 syn see DEDUCT 1
20 syn see TREAT 2
21 syn see CHEAT
rel bamboozle, hoodwink
idiom take for a ride
22 syn see ACT 2
take (from) *vb syn* see DECRY 2
take (to) *vb syn* see HABITUATE 2
rel enjoy, fancy, favor, like
idiom get used to
take away *vb* **1 syn** see REMOVE 2
rel separate
2 syn see DEDUCT 1
3 syn see DECRY 2
take back *vb* **1 syn** see RETURN 4
2 syn see REPOSSESS 3
3 syn see ABJURE
take down *vb syn* see DISMOUNT
take in *vb* **1 syn** see TAKE 10
2 syn see INCLUDE
3 syn see APPREHEND 1
rel perceive; ‖savvy; absorb, assimilate, digest
4 syn see DECEIVE
rel flimflam, take; trick
take off *vb* **1 syn** see REMOVE 2
2 syn see REMOVE 3
3 syn see DEDUCT 1
4 syn see KILL 1
5 syn see MIMIC
idiom do a takeoff on
6 syn see GET OUT 1
7 syn see HEAD 3
idiom hit the road (*or* trail)
8 syn see GO 2
takeoff *n syn* see CARICATURE 2
take on *vb* **1 syn** see DON 2
2 syn see ADD 1
3 to proceed to deal with <*took on* a new job with more responsibilities>
syn take up, undertake
rel begin, commence, enter (upon); attempt, endeavor, try; launch, venture
idiom set about, take upon oneself
con abandon, drop, forsake
ant give up
4 syn see ENGAGE 5
5 syn see EMPLOY 2
6 syn see ADOPT
ant give up
take out *vb* **1 syn** see REMOVE 2
2 syn see REMOVE 4
3 syn see DEDUCT 1
4 syn see DATE
take out (on) *vb* to find release for (as emotions) <*took out* her anger on the dog>

syn loose, release, unleash, vent
idiom give vent to, let loose (*or* fly)
con control, govern, restrain; bottle (up), check, keep down, quell, smother; repress, suppress
take over *vb* **1 syn** see RELIEVE 3
take up *vb* **1 syn** see LIFT 1
2 syn see BEGIN 1
3 syn see TAKE ON 3
rel assume; tackle
idiom address oneself to
4 syn see ADOPT
rel support; affiliate
5 syn see RESUME 2
taking *adj syn* see INFECTIOUS 3
tale *n* **1 syn** see STORY 2
rel myth, saga
2 syn see DETRACTION
3 syn see LIE
rel fiction; yarn
4 syn see WHOLE 1
tale *vb syn* see COUNT 1
talebearer *n* **1 syn** see INFORMER
2 syn see GOSSIP 1
talent *n syn* see GIFT 2
rel art, craft, skill; endowment; expertise, forte
talisman *n syn* see CHARM 2
idiom good-luck piece, lucky piece (*or* charm)
talk *vb* **1 syn** see SPEAK 3
2 syn see SPEAK 1
3 syn see CONVERSE
4 syn see CHAT 1
rel palaver; spout off
idiom talk one's arm (*or* ear *or* leg) off, flap (*or* wag) the (*or* one's) tongue
5 syn see GOSSIP
6 to reveal secret or confidential information usually concerning illegal acts <at last the suspect *talked* to the police>
syn sing, squeak, squeal; *compare* INFORM 3
rel inform (on); divulge, reveal; confess
idiom spill one's guts, spill the beans, tell all
7 to give a talk <he *talks* to community groups on ecology>
syn address, lecture, prelect, speak
rel declaim, harangue, hold forth, perorate, speechify, spout
talk (into) *vb syn* see INDUCE 1
talk *n* **1 syn** see SPEECH 1
2 syn see CONVERSATION 2
3 syn see CHAT 2
4 a formal or prearranged discussion, exchange, or negotiation usually of a political nature <summit *talks* on nuclear arms>
syn conference, meeting, parley, powwow
rel dialogue, discussion, exchange; negotiation; deliberation
5 syn see REPORT 1
6 syn see SPEECH 2
rel spiel; conference, discussion
talkative *adj* given to talk or talking <a *talkative*, sociable man>
syn babblative, chatty, gabby, garrulous, loose-lipped, loose-tongued, loquacious, mouthy, multiloquent, multiloquious, talky, tonguey; *compare* GLIB
rel articulate, eloquent, fluent; vocal, voluble; buzzy, gossipy

---

syn synonym(s)   *rel* related word(s)
ant antonym(s)   *con* contrasted word(s)
idiom idiomatic equivalent(s)
‖ use limited; if in doubt, see a dictionary

con closemouthed, laconic, reserved, reticent, uncommunicative; speechless
ant silent

talkee–talkee *n syn* see CHATTER

talky *adj syn* see TALKATIVE

tall *adj syn* see HIGH 1
rel high-reaching, sky-high, skyscraping
idiom higher than a cat's back
con abbreviated, truncated; low
ant short

tally *n syn* see SCORE 5

tally *vb* 1 *syn* see INVENTORY
2 *syn* see COUNT 1
3 *syn* see AGREE 4
rel equal, match; balance, complement
con conflict (with), differ (from), disagree (with)

tame *adj* docilely tractable <a *tame* lion>
syn domestic, domesticated, domitae naturae, subdued, submissive
rel broken (in), ‖busted, housebroken, trained; amenable, biddable, docile, obedient, tractable; pliable, pliant; meek, mild
idiom gentle as a lamb
con fierce, savage, tameless; undomesticated, untrained; unbridled, unbroken
ant untamed, wild

tame *vb syn* see DOMESTICATE

tamp *vb syn* see CRAM 1
rel fill up (or in), plug up; concentrate

tamper (with) *vb* 1 *syn* see BRIBE
2 *syn* see MEDDLE
rel interpose, intervene; doctor, manipulate

tang *n syn* see TASTE 3
rel bite, nip, piquancy, twang; aroma, pungency; spiciness, tanginess

tangible *adj* 1 capable of being perceived especially by the sense of touch <a stuffed animal that provides *tangible* as well as visual stimulation for infants>
syn palpable, tactile, touchable; *compare* PERCEPTIBLE
rel corporeal, physical; embodied, material, real, substantial
con ethereal, spiritual, unreal
ant intangible
2 *syn* see MATERIAL 1
3 *syn* see PERCEPTIBLE
rel distinct, evident, manifest, obvious, patent, plain
con clouded, cloudy, imperceptible, indistinct, unclear
ant intangible

tangle *vb* 1 *syn* see INVOLVE 1
idiom make a party to
ant untangle
2 *syn* see CATCH 3
ant untangle
3 *syn* see ENTANGLE 1
rel foul up, mix up
4 *syn* see COMPLICATE
ant untangle

tangle *n syn* see MAZE 1

tanked *adj syn* see INTOXICATED 1

tank town *n syn* see BURG

tank up *vb syn* see DRINK 3

tantalize *vb syn* see WORRY 1
rel badger, bait; frustrate

tantamount *adj syn* see SAME 2
rel alike, like, uniform; selfsame, very

idiom as much as to say

tap *n* 1 *syn* see FAUCET
2 *syn* see BAR 5

tap *vb syn* see DRAIN 1

tap *vb* 1 to strike or hit audibly and usually lightly <*tapped* her pencil on the desk>
syn bob, knock, rap, tunk
rel bang, beat, hammer, hit, pound, smite, strike, thud, thump
2 *syn* see DESIGNATE 2

tapa *n syn* see SNACK

taper *vb syn* see DECREASE

taper off *vb syn* see DECREASE

taproom *n syn* see BAR 5

tapster *n syn* see BARTENDER

tar *n syn* see MARINER

tar *vb syn* see TAINT 1

taradiddle *n syn* see LIE

tardy *adj* not arriving, occurring, or done at the set, due, or expected time <be *tardy* for school>
syn behindhand, belated, late, lated, overdue, unpunctual
rel delayed, detained; dilatory, laggard, slow; delinquent
con beforehand, early; convenient, opportune, seasonable, timely; precise, punctilious
ant prompt, punctual

target *n* 1 an object of ridicule, attack, or abuse <made him the chief *target* of political satire>
syn butt, mark, sitting duck
rel victim; fall guy, scapegoat, whipping boy
2 *syn* see AMBITION 2
3 *syn* see USE 4

tariff *n* 1 *syn* see TAX 1
2 *syn* see PRICE 1

‖**tarnation** *adj syn* see UTTER

tarnish *vb syn* see DULL 1
2 *syn* see SOIL 2
rel contaminate, defile, pollute, stain, taint
con clean, cleanse; shine (up)
ant polish
3 *syn* see INJURE 1
4 *syn* see TAINT 1
rel defame, disgrace, embarrass; slander

tarpaulin *n syn* see MARINER

tarriance *n syn* see SOJOURN

tarry *vb* 1 *syn* see DELAY 2
rel falter, flag
2 *syn* see STAY 2
rel dawdle; sojourn
3 *syn* see VISIT 3

tart *adj syn* see SOUR 1
rel piquant, pungent
ant flat

tart *n syn* see DOXY 1

Tartarean *adj syn* see INFERNAL 1

Tartuffe *n syn* see HYPOCRITE

Tartuffery *n syn* see HYPOCRISY

Tartuffism *n syn* see HYPOCRISY

task *n* 1 a piece of work assigned or to be done <laboratory *tasks* assigned to chemistry students>
syn assignment, chare, chore, devoir, duty, job, stint
rel enterprise, project, undertaking; errand, labor, toil, work; charge, function, mission, office, province; business, calling, employment, occupation, vocation

2 a necessary undertaking that is usually difficult, dull, disagreeable, or problematic <deciphering his handwriting is a real *task*>
syn chore, effort, job, taskwork
rel burden, onus, strain, tax; bother, headache, nuisance, pain, trouble
idiom a hard (or long) row to hoe
con child's play, cinch, duck soup, picnic, ‖pipe, sinecure, snap
3 syn see LOAD 3
task vb syn see BURDEN
taskmaster n syn see SLAVE DRIVER
taskwork n syn see TASK 2
taste vb syn see FEEL 2
idiom be exposed to, run up against
taste n 1 syn see HINT 2
rel bit, sample, sampling
2 syn see APPETITE 1
3 the property of a substance which makes it perceptible to the gustatory sense <children often dislike the *taste* of olives>
syn flavor, relish, sapidity, sapor, savor, smack, tang
4 a liking for or enjoyment of something because of the pleasure it gives <had a *taste* for fast cars>
syn gusto, heart, palate, relish, zest
rel appreciation, comprehension, understanding; partiality, predilection, prepossession; disposition, inclination, predisposition
con dislike, disrelish; allergy, aversion, repugnance, repulsion
ant antipathy; distaste
5 syn see APPETITE 3
ant distaste
6 the power or practice of discerning and enjoying whatever constitutes excellence (as in the fine arts) <a room whose decoration reflected her exquisite *taste*>
syn tastefulness
rel correctness; finesse, polish, refinement; elegance, grace
con gracelessness, inelegance, unrefinement; incorrectness, vulgarity
ant tastelessness
tasteful adj 1 syn see PALATABLE
rel rich
ant savorless, tasteless
2 syn see QUIET 4
ant tasteless
tastefulness n syn see TASTE 6
ant tastelessness
tasteless adj 1 syn see UNPALATABLE 1
rel bland, dull, stale, vapid; unflavored; uninteresting
con flavorful, pleasing
ant tasteful, tasty
2 syn see BARBARIC 1
rel inelegant, unpolished, unrefined
idiom in bad taste
ant tasteful, tasty
tasty adj 1 syn see PALATABLE
idiom fit for a king
con unsavory; bland, flavorless, unpalatable
ant savorless, tasteless

---

syn synonym(s)   rel related word(s)
ant antonym(s)   con contrasted word(s)
idiom idiomatic equivalent(s)
‖ use limited; if in doubt, see a dictionary

---

2 syn see QUIET 4
ant tasteless
‖**tats** n pl syn see DICE
‖**tatter** vb syn see HURRY 2
tatterdemalion n syn see RAGAMUFFIN
tattered adj 1 syn see RAGGED
2 syn see SHABBY 1
tatters n pl syn see RAGS 1
tattle vb syn see GOSSIP
idiom tell tales out of school
tattle n syn see REPORT 1
tattler n syn see INFORMER
tattletale n syn see INFORMER
tatty adj syn see CHEAP 2
taunt vb syn see RIDICULE
rel banter, chaff; provoke; upbraid; disdain, scorn; affront, insult, offend, outrage
taut adj syn see TIGHT 3
rel firm, trim; stretched
con flabby; relaxed
ant slack
tautology n syn see VERBIAGE 1
rel reiteration, repetition, repetitiousness; padding
tavern n 1 syn see BAR 5
2 syn see HOTEL
tavern car n syn see PARLOR CAR
taverner n syn see SALOONKEEPER
tawdry adj syn see GAUDY
rel common, sleazy; flaring, screaming
tax vb 1 syn see BURDEN
rel overtax
idiom press hard upon, tax the strength of, weigh heavy on (or upon)
2 syn see ACCUSE
tax n 1 a charge usually of money imposed by authority upon persons or property for public purposes <federal, state, and local *taxes* bear heavily on the thrifty>
syn assessment, ‖cess, duty, impost, levy, tariff
rel tithe, tribute; boodle, boondoggle, giveaway, pork barrel
2 syn see LOAD 3
rel difficulty, strain; demand, imposition
taxi n syn see TAXICAB
taxicab n an automobile that carries passengers for a fare <took a *taxicab* from the airport to his hotel>
syn cab, hack, taxi
rel ‖crawler, nighthawk
taxing adj syn see ONEROUS
rel wearing; tedious, troublesome
TB n syn see TUBERCULOSIS
‖**tea** n syn see MARIJUANA
teach vb to cause to acquire knowledge or skill <*teach* a child to read>
syn discipline, educate, instruct, school, train
rel communicate, impart; implant, inculcate, instill; edify, enlighten, indoctrinate; fit, ground, prepare, rear; drill, exercise, practice; coach, tutor; lesson
idiom give instruction
teaching n syn see EDUCATION 1
teachy adj syn see DIDACTIC
tear vb 1 to separate (one part of a substance or object from another) forcibly <*tore* a chunk from the loaf on the table>
syn cleave, rend, rip, rive, split

rel cut, gash, incise, slash, slit; devil, pull (apart), rift, sever, sunder; ribbon, shred; break, crack, rupture; damage, impair, injure

2 *syn* see EXTRACT 1

3 *syn* see RUSH 1

4 *syn* see COURSE

tear *n syn* see BINGE 1

tear down *vb* **1** *syn* see DESTROY 1
ant build up

2 *syn* see MALIGN
ant build up

teardrops *n pl syn* see TEARS

tearful *adj* flowing with or accompanied by tears <*tearful* entreaties>
syn lachrymose, teary, weeping, weepy
rel lamenting, mournful; sniveling; bawling, blubbering, crying, sobbing
con dry-eyed
ant tearless

tearing *adj syn* see EXCRUCIATING

tear-jerking *adj syn* see SENTIMENTAL

tears *n pl* a profuse secretion of saline fluid that overflows the eyelids and dampens the face <a blow that brought *tears* to his eyes>
syn teardrops, water

teary *adj syn* see TEARFUL
ant tearless

tease *vb syn* see WORRY 1
rel disturb, importune
idiom give a bad time

teaser *n syn* see STRIPTEASER

tease up *vb syn* see TOUCH UP

‖tec *n syn* see DETECTIVE

teched *adj syn* see INSANE 1

technique *n syn* see METHOD 1

tedious *adj* **1** *syn* see IRKSOME

2 *syn* see ARID 2
rel dragging, mortal, slow, tiresome

tedium *n* a state of dissatisfaction and weariness <incessant routine without variety breeds *tedium*>
syn boredom, doldrums, ‖dullsville, ennui, yawn
rel irksomeness, tediousness, tiresomeness, wearisomeness; dullness, monotony
con enlivenment, interest, invigoration, refreshment

teem *vb* to be abundantly stocked or provided <rivers *teeming* with fish>
syn abound, crawl, flow, pullulate, ‖sny, swarm
rel bristle, bustle; cram, crowd, jam, pack; overbrim, overflow, overrun
con lack, want

teem *vb syn* see POUR 3

teeming *adj syn* see ALIVE 5
rel multitudinous, populous, pregnant; bristling
con rare, sparse, uncommon; empty, lacking, void, wanting

teensy *adj syn* see TINY

teensy-weensy *adj syn* see TINY

teenty *adj syn* see TINY

teeny *adj syn* see TINY

teeny-weeny *adj syn* see TINY

tee off *vb syn* see BEGIN 1

teeter *vb* to progress (as by walking) unsteadily <*teetered* along on 4-inch heels>

syn falter, lurch, stagger, ‖stammer, stumble, topple, totter, wobble; *compare* LURCH 2, SEESAW
rel sway, weave

teethy *adj syn* see TOOTHY 1

teetotal *adj syn* see DRY 3

tehee *vb syn* see LAUGH

telephone *vb* to communicate with (a person) by telephone <*telephoned* him yesterday>
syn ‖buzz, call, phone, ‖ring (up)
idiom ‖get (one) on the horn, give (one) a buzz (or ring)

telestic *adj syn* see MYSTICAL 1

television *n* a medium of communication involving the transmission and reproduction of images by radio waves <it's fashionable to put down *television*>
syn boob tube, box, ‖idiot box, ‖telly, tube, TV, video

tell *vb* **1** *syn* see COUNT 1

2 *syn* see SAY 1
rel communicate, convey, impart

3 *syn* see REVEAL 1
rel recite, recount, rehearse, relate; acquaint, apprise, inform

4 *syn* see INFORM 2

5 *syn* see COMMAND

6 *syn* see WEIGH 3

telling *adj syn* see VALID
rel power-packed; influential, weighty; significant, striking

tell off *vb syn* see SCOLD 1
rel call down; denounce
idiom give (one) a piece of one's mind, tell (one) a thing or two, tell (one) where to get off

telltale *n* **1** *syn* see GOSSIP 1

2 *syn* see HINT 1

tellurian *adj syn* see EARTHLY 1

telluric *adj syn* see EARTHLY 1

‖telly *n syn* see TELEVISION

temblor (*or* **tremblor**) *n syn* see EARTHQUAKE

temerarious *adj syn* see ADVENTUROUS
rel heedless, imprudent, incautious, injudicious

temerity *n* conspicuous or flagrant boldness (as in speech, behavior, or action) <had the *temerity* to order an attack when hopelessly outnumbered>
syn assurance, audacity, brashness, hardihood, hardiness, nerve
rel daring, foolhardiness, heedlessness, rashness, recklessness, venturesomeness; impetuosity, precipitateness; impertinence, intrusiveness
con deliberation, judgment, judiciousness, prudence; heed, heedfulness
ant caution

temper *vb syn* see MODERATE 1
rel dilute, season; ease, pacify, soften; adjust, modify; curb, tone (down)
idiom take the edge off

temper *n* **1** a general or prevailing quality or characteristic (as of moral or social attitudes and behavior) <the wild fashions reflected the *temper* of the times>
syn mood, spirit, timbre, tone

rel atmosphere, aura, climate; orientation, outlook; disposition, drift, leaning, tendency, trend; character, nature, peculiarity
2 *syn* see DISPOSITION 3
rel condition, posture, state; attribute, property, quality; style, type, way
idiom turn of mind
3 *syn* see MOOD 1
idiom frame (*or* state) of mind
4 an outbreak or display of anger <a childish fit of *temper*>
syn passion
rel anger, fury, ire, rage; conniption, fit, outburst, tantrum

temperament *n syn* see DISPOSITION 3
rel mentality, mind; kind, type, way
idiom inner nature

temperamental *adj* **1** *syn* see MOODY
2 *syn* see INCONSTANT 1
ant steady

temperance *n* **1** an avoidance of extremes (as in action, thought, or feeling) <a man who knew no *temperance* in his opinions>
syn measure, moderateness, moderation
rel reasonableness; constraint, restraint
idiom happy medium
con extremeness, radicalness; excess, excessiveness; immoderateness, immoderation, unconstraint, unreasonableness, unrestraint
ant intemperance, intemperateness
2 strict habitual and usually complete self≈denial in the gratification of appetites or passions <an ascetic who practiced complete *temperance*>
syn abstinence, continence, sobriety
rel abnegation, eschewal, forbearance, forgoing, refrainment, sacrifice, self-denial, self-deprivation; control, restraint, self≈control, self-discipline; asceticism, austerity, mortification
con intemperance, intemperancy, intemperateness, prodigality
ant excess

temperate *adj* **1** *syn* see MODERATE 2
rel constant, equable, even, steady; checked, curbed, regulated, restrained
ant intemperate
2 *syn* see ABSTEMIOUS
rel indulgent; self-indulgent
con intemperate; dissipated, prodigal, profligate
ant excessive
3 *syn* see CONSERVATIVE 2
4 *syn* see SOBER 3

temperish *adj syn* see IRASCIBLE
tempersome *adj syn* see ILL-TEMPERED
tempestuous *adj syn* see WILD 6
rel tumultuous, unbridled, unrestrained, violent
ant calm, quiet

temple *n syn* see HOUSE OF WORSHIP
tempo *n* rate of performance or delivery <increased sales and production *tempo*>
syn pace, time; *compare* SPEED 2
rel speed; momentum

temporal *adj* **1** *syn* see MATERIALISTIC
ant nontemporal
2 *syn* see PROFANE 1
rel material, physical; nonsacred, nonspiritual, unhallowed, unsanctified, unspiritual
con celestial, heavenly
ant spiritual

temporary *adj* lasting, continuing, or serving for a limited time <was *temporary* president of the company for nine months>
syn acting, ad interim, interim, pro tem, pro tempore, supply; *compare* TRANSIENT
rel alternate, substitute; interimistic, provisional, provisory; jackleg, make-do, makeshift, stopgap
ant permanent

tempt *vb syn* see LURE
rel provoke, rouse; court, invite, solicit, vamp, woo
idiom whet the appetite
con discourage; dissuade; repel, repulse, revolt

temptation *n syn* see LURE 2
tempting *adj syn* see ENTICING
rel appetizing, mouth-watering; provoking, rousing, tantalizing
con repellent, repulsive
ant untempting

temptress *n syn* see SIREN
ten *n syn* see BREAK 4
tenable *adj* **1** capable of being defended against attack <the platoon's position was no longer *tenable*>
syn defendable, defensible
rel impregnable, secure
con insecure, vulnerable; defenseless, helpless, unprotected; dangerous, precarious, risky
ant untenable
2 *syn* see JUSTIFIABLE
rel believable, credible, maintainable, plausible
con indefensible, inexcusable, unbelievable, unjustifiable
ant untenable

tenacious *adj* **1** *syn* see STRONG 2
rel bulldogged, bulldoggish, bulldoggy, dogged, obstinate, pertinacious, stubborn; resolute, steadfast, true; persevering, persisting
2 *syn* see VISCOUS
rel cohesive; tacky; sticky
3 *syn* see FAST 4
con lax, slack

tenant *n syn* see INHABIT
tenantable *adj syn* see LIVABLE 1
idiom fit to live in
con uninhabitable

tend *vb* **1** *syn* see TILL
2 to supervise or take charge of <employed a girl to *tend* the children each day>
syn attend, care (for), mind, watch
rel cherish, cultivate, foster, minister, nurse, nurture, serve; defend, guard, shield; safeguard, shield; supervise
idiom look after, see after, see to, take care of, take under one's wing
con disregard, ignore, neglect

---

syn synonym(s)   *rel* related word(s)
ant antonym(s)   *con* contrasted word(s)
idiom idiomatic equivalent(s)
‖ use limited; if in doubt, see a dictionary

tend vb **1** to have or exhibit an inclination or tendency <he *tends* to praise people too highly>
syn incline, lean, look; *compare* INCLINE 3
idiom be disposed
2 *syn* see CONTRIBUTE 2

tendency n **1** a movement or course having a particular direction and character <a growing *tendency* to underestimate the potential strength of that nation>
syn current, drift, run, tenor, trend
rel curve, inclination, leaning, propensity; turn; shift; custom, habit, usage, way
2 *syn* see LEANING 2

tendentious *adj syn* see BIASED 2

tender *adj* showing or expressing affectionate interest in another <his mother was very *tender* with her wayward son>
syn compassionate, kindhearted, responsive, softhearted, sympathetic, warm, warmhearted
rel gentle, lenient, mild, soft, yielding; considerate, solicitous, thoughtful; affectionate, fond, loving; benevolent, charitable, humane, mild; commiserative; forgiving, merciful, tolerant
con callous, hard, harsh; inhumane, uncharitable, unfeeling
ant rough, severe

tender *vb syn* see OFFER 1
rel propose, purpose, submit, suggest

tenderfoot n *syn* see NOVICE

tenderloin n *syn* see RED-LIGHT DISTRICT

tenebrific *adj syn* see GLOOMY 3

tenebrous *adj* **1** *syn* see DARK 1
2 *syn* see OBSCURE 3

tenement n *syn* see APARTMENT 1

tenet n *syn* see DOCTRINE
rel belief, conviction, persuasion, view

tenor n **1** the course of thought that is retained through something spoken or written <the *tenor* of the book is first expressed in the introduction>
syn drift, purport, substance; *compare* BODY 4, MEANING 1, SUBSTANCE 2
rel intent; inclination, trend; mood, tone; core, gist, meat, stuff
2 *syn* see TENDENCY 1

tense *adj* **1** *syn* see TIGHT 3
rel strained, stretched
ant relaxed
2 feeling or showing nervous tension <the soldiers were *tense* as they waited for the order to advance>
syn edgy, nervy, restive, uneasy, uptight
rel queasy, jittery, rusty, unquiet; anxious, concerned, overanxious
con easy; calm, placid, ||loose, placid, unconcerned; firm, nerveless, unshaken
ant relaxed

tension n **1** *syn* see STRESS 1
rel tautness, tenseness, tightness
idiom stress and strain
ant relaxation
2 emotional strain <was suffering from nervous *tension*>
syn unease, uptightness
rel strain, stress; anxiety, nerves, nervousness, uneasiness; agitation, discomfort, disquiet, misease

ten-strike n *syn* see SMASH 6

tent *vb syn* see CAMP

tentative *adj* **1** *syn* see CONDITIONAL 1
rel acting, ad interim, makeshift, temporary; probationary; experimental, test, trial
con conclusive, decisive, definitive
ant final
2 *syn* see VACILLATING 2
rel disinclined, reluctant

tenue n *syn* see BEHAVIOR

tenuous *adj* **1** *syn* see THIN 2
2 *syn* see THIN 1
rel aerial, airy, ethereal, fine
con abundant
ant dense
3 having little substance or strength and usually not firmly based <only a *tenuous* link in the chain of evidence>
syn feeble, insubstantial, unsubstantial; *compare* IMPLAUSIBLE
rel flimsy, weak; insignificant
con significant, sound, strong
ant substantial

tenure n *syn* see HOLD

tepid *adj* **1** moderately warm <a *tepid* bath>
syn lukewarm, milk-warm, warmish
rel mild, temperate, warm
con cold, cool, freezing, frozen; heated, hot, steaming
2 lacking in animation, force, passion, conviction, or commitment <gave only a *tepid* endorsement to the candidate>
syn halfhearted, lukewarm, unenthusiastic; *compare* ARID 2
rel indifferent; colorless, dull, lifeless, unlively; feeble, marrowless, pithless, sapless, spiritless; dim, faint, forceless, weak
con animated, forceful; fiery, impassioned, passionate, spirited

tergiversate *vb* **1** *syn* see DEFECT
idiom fall away from
2 *syn* see EQUIVOCATE 2
idiom beg the question

tergiversation n **1** *syn* see DEFECTION
rel about-face, reversal, reverse; denial, disavowal, forswearing, renunciation, repudiation
2 *syn* see AMBIGUITY

tergiversator n *syn* see RENEGADE

tergiverse *vb* **1** *syn* see DEFECT
2 *syn* see EQUIVOCATE 2

term n **1** *syn* see LIMIT 1
rel terminus
2 a limited, definite, or measurable extent of time during which something exists, lasts, or is in progress <the office has a *term* of four years>
syn duration, span, time
rel phase; go, period, spell, stretch; hitch, tour, turn; standing
3 *syn* see WORD 2
4 terms pl *syn* see CONDITION 1
rel detail, item, particular, point; limit
5 terms pl mutual social relationship or relative position <fight on equal *terms*> <the two were on *terms* of great intimacy>
syn footing, standing
rel coequality, equipollence, status; equality, equivalence, par, parity; balance

term *vb syn* see NAME 1

termagant *n syn* see VIRAGO

termagant *adj syn* see TURBULENT 1

terminable *adj* liable to be terminated or subject to termination <marriage is a *terminable* institution>
syn determinable, endable
rel finite, limited; limitable

terminal *adj syn* see LAST
con beginning, starting
ant initial

terminate *vb* **1** *syn* see CLOSE 3
rel abolish, extinguish; discontinue, wind down
idiom put the lid on
ant initiate
2 *syn* see ADJOURN 2
3 *syn* see DISMISS 3
4 *syn* see QUIT 6

terminated *adj syn* see COMPLETE 4

terminating *adj syn* see LAST
ant initial

termination *n syn* see END 2
rel issue, outcome, ‖pay-off, result
con source; beginning, start
ant initiation

terminology *n* the specialized or technical terms and expressions peculiar to a field, subject, or trade <the *terminology* of the plastics industry>
syn cant, dictionary, jargon, language, lexicon, palaver, vocabulary; *compare* DIALECT 2
rel shoptalk; gibberish, gobbledygook

terminus *n syn* see END 2

terra firma *n syn* see EARTH 2

terrain *n* **1** the physical configuration and features of a tract of land <made an analysis of the *terrain* via aerial photos>
syn topography
rel contour, form, profile, shape
2 an area devoted to a specified activity <the whole county had become breeding and racing *terrain*>
syn territory, turf
3 *syn* see FIELD

terrene *adj* **1** *syn* see EARTHLY 1
2 *syn* see EARTHY 1

terrestrial *adj* **1** *syn* see EARTHLY 1
rel earthbound, prosaic; profane, secular, unspiritual
ant empyreal
2 *syn* see EARTHY 1

terrible *adj* **1** *syn* see FEARFUL 3
2 *syn* see HARD 6
3 *syn* see INTENSE 1
4 *syn* see GHASTLY 1

terribly *adv syn* see VERY 1

terrific *adj* **1** *syn* see FEARFUL 3
rel terrorizing; agitating, disquieting, upsetting
2 *syn* see MARVELOUS 2
rel magnificent, superb; rattling, screaming

terrified *adj syn* see AFRAID 1
rel horrified, shocked; terrorized; frozen, paralyzed

con unfearful, unfearing, unfrightened
ant unafraid

terrify *vb syn* see FRIGHTEN
rel freeze, paralyze, petrify, stun, stupefy
idiom put the fear of God into, strike fear into the heart of

terrifying *adj syn* see GHASTLY 1
ant unterrifying

territory *n* **1** *syn* see AREA 1
2 *syn* see FIELD
3 *syn* see TERRAIN 2

terror *n syn* see FEAR 1
rel awe, fearfulness

terroristic *adj* characterized by or practicing terror as a means of coercion <used torture and other *terroristic* tactics to extract confessions>
syn gestapo
rel coercive, strong-arm; brutal, cruel, merciless; immoral, improper, unsanctioned

terrorize *vb* **1** *syn* see FRIGHTEN
idiom scare to death
2 *syn* see INTIMIDATE
idiom use gestapo tactics on

terse *adj syn* see CONCISE
rel close, compact; lean, precise; clear-cut, crisp, incisive; taut
con circuitous; pleonastic, redundant, repetitious

tersely *adv syn* see BRIEFLY
rel closely, compactly; crisply, incisively, precisely; abruptly, curtly
idiom in as few words as possible
ant prolixly

test *n syn* see EXPERIMENT
rel inspection, scrutiny; confirmation, corroboration, substantiation, verification

test *vb* **1** *syn* see TRY 1
rel assay, essay; confirm, substantiate, verify
idiom bring to test
2 *syn* see PROVE 1

test (out) *vb syn* see EXPERIMENT

test *adj syn* see EXPERIMENTAL
rel proving, testing, trying; probational, speculative

testament *n syn* see TESTIMONY

testify *vb* **1** to serve as evidence of <present conditions *testify* to the accuracy of his predictions>
syn attest, point (to)
rel affirm; demonstrate, show; prove
con discredit, disprove, invalidate; confute, refute
2 to make a solemn declaration under oath for the purpose of establishing a fact (as in court) <*testified* against the defendant>
syn depone, depose, ‖mount, swear
idiom give testimony
3 *syn* see INDICATE 2

testimonial *n* **1** *syn* see TESTIMONY
rel indication, manifestation, show, sign, symbol, token
2 an expression of great approval and high esteem <a dinner was planned as a *testimonial* in her honor>
syn appreciation, salvo, tribute
rel salute; triumph; jubilee; commemoration, memorialization, remembrance
3 *syn* see MONUMENT 2

---

syn synonym(s) *rel* related word(s)
ant antonym(s) *con* contrasted word(s)
idiom idiomatic equivalent(s)
‖ use limited; if in doubt, see a dictionary

testimony *n* something that serves as tangible verification <the results are remarkable *testimony* to the accuracy of his predictions>
syn attestation, confirmation, evidence, proof, testament, testimonial, witness; *compare* INDICATION 3
rel demonstration, illustration; affirmation, corroboration, documentation, substantiation, verification

testy *adj syn* see IRASCIBLE
rel annoyed, exasperated, grouchy, irritable

tetchy *adj syn* see IRASCIBLE
rel ill-humored; cantankerous

tête-à-tête *n* a private conversation between two people <had a *tête-à-tête* with her in a quiet corner>
syn vis-à-vis
rel causerie, chat, coze; conversation, talk; argument, discussion

tetrad *n syn* see QUARTET

‖**tew** *vb syn* see WORRY 3

text *n syn* see SUBJECT 2
rel consideration, issue; fundamentals; idea

texture *n* 1 *syn* see ESSENCE 1
2 a thing often highly complex underlying scheme, structure, or pattern <war destroys the very *texture* of a society>
syn fabric, fiber, web
rel framework, structure; composition, constitution, makeup; pattern, scheme

thalassic *adj syn* see MARINE 1

thankful *adj syn* see GRATEFUL 1
con unappreciative, ungrateful
ant thankless, unthankful

thankless *adj* 1 not inclined to give thanks <a *thankless* guest>
syn unappreciative, ungrateful, unthankful
rel self-centered; careless, heedless, thoughtless; unappreciative, ungrateful, unmindful
con appreciative, grateful, mindful; careful, heedful, thoughtful
ant thankful
2 not likely to obtain thanks <a *thankless* job>
syn unappreciated, ungrateful, unthankful
rel disagreeable, distasteful, unpleasant; miserable, wretched
con thankworthy

thanks *n pl syn* see GRACE 1

thanksgiving *n syn* see GRACE 1

thankworthy *adj syn* see WORTHY 1

thank-you-ma'am *n syn* see BUMP 3

that *adj* 1 being the other <we argued it this way and we argued it *that* way>
syn another
ant this
2 *syn* see SUCH 2

thaumaturgic *adj syn* see MAGIC 1

thaumaturgy *n syn* see MAGIC 1

thaw *vb syn* see LIQUEFY

theater *n syn* see DRAMA

theatral *adj syn* see DRAMATIC 1

theatric *adj syn* see DRAMATIC 1

theatrical *adj* 1 *syn* see DRAMATIC 1
2 having qualities resembling a stage play or an actor's performance <he slowly made an exaggerated *theatrical* bow>
syn dramatic

rel histrionic, melodramatic, staged; affected, artificial, exaggerated, mannered, unnatural

theft *n* the unlawful taking and carrying away of property without the consent of its owner <was found guilty of auto *theft*>
syn larceny, lift, pinch, purloining, rip-off, steal, stealage, stealing, thievery, thieving, ‖touch
rel filching, pilferage, pilfering, swiping; robbery, robbing, ‖stouth, ‖stouthrief; ‖score

theme *n* 1 *syn* see SUBJECT 2
2 *syn* see ESSAY 2

then *adv* 1 at another time <science as it was taught *then*>
syn again, anon, when; *compare* BEFORE 2
rel before, formerly
2 *syn* see AGAIN 4
3 *syn* see THEREFORE

thence *adv* 1 *syn* see AWAY 1
2 *syn* see THEREFROM

thenceforth *adv* from that time forward <the island which was *thenceforth* to be their home>
syn thenceforward, thereafter; *compare* HENCEFORTH
idiom from then on

thenceforward *adv syn* see THENCEFORTH

theorem *n syn* see PRINCIPLE 1

theoretical *adj* 1 concerned principally with abstractions and theories <*theoretical* versus applied physics>
syn academic, closet, speculative
rel conjectural, hypothetical, notional, suppositional, unproved; analytical, problematical
con practical; factual; proved
ant applied
2 *syn* see ABSTRACT 1
rel idealized, ivory-tower
ant concrete

theorize *vb syn* see SUGGEST 4

theory *n* 1 a belief, policy, or procedure proposed or followed as the basis of action <an educational system that was based on the *theory* that men learn best by experience>
syn hypothesis, supposal; *compare* ASSUMPTION 2
rel base, basis, grounds, position, premise, understanding
ant practice
2 something taken for granted especially on trivial or inadequate grounds <her *theory* that the house was haunted>
syn conjecture, perhaps, speculation, suppose, supposition
rel guess, guesswork, surmise; feeling, hunch, impression, presentiment, suspicion
con assurance, certainty, knowledge

there *adv* to or into that place <they seldom go *there* anymore>
syn thither, thitherward, yon
rel yonder
ant here

thereafter *adv syn* see THENCEFORTH

thereby *adv* in consequence of that <lied to the jury, *thereby* negating his testimony>
syn therethrough; *compare* THEREFROM

therefore *adv* for this or that reason <I think, *therefore* I am>

syn accordingly, consequently, ergo, hence, so, then, thereupon, thus
rel thence, therefrom

therefrom *adv* from that thing, fact, or circumstance <public opinion and a policy deriving *therefrom*>
syn thence, thereof; *compare* THEREBY

thereof *adv syn* see THEREFROM

thereon *adv* on or upon that <knew both the text and commentary *thereon*>
syn thereupon
rel therein, thereof, thereto

therethrough *adv syn* see THEREBY

theretofore *adv* up to that time <*theretofore* obscure communities>
syn thereuntil
rel ‖afore, before, previously
idiom before then

thereuntil *adv syn* see THERETOFORE
idiom until then

thereupon *adv* **1** *syn* see THEREON
2 *syn* see THEREFORE

thesis *n* **1** a position assumed or a point made especially in controversy <her *thesis* about the assassination was arguable>
syn contention, contestation
rel point, position; argument; belief, opinion, sentiment(s), view(s)
2 *syn* see ASSUMPTION 2
3 *syn* see DISCOURSE 2
rel exposition; argument, argumentation

thespian *adj syn* see DRAMATIC 1

thespian *n syn* see ACTOR 1

thew *n syn* see MUSCLE 1

thick *adj* **1** *syn* see STOCKY
rel broad, wide; bulky, burly, husky; blubber, blubbery, massive; obese
con slender, slight, slim; lanky, spare; skeletal
2 *syn* see CLOSE 4
rel concentrated, crammed; localized
con dispersed, scattered
ant diffuse
3 *syn* see STUPID 1
4 *syn* see FAMILIAR 3
idiom hand in glove, thick as thieves
5 *syn* see IMPLAUSIBLE
idiom a little too thick

thick–bodied *adj syn* see STOCKY

thickhead *n syn* see DUNCE
rel ‖clot

thickheaded *adj syn* see STUPID 1

thickset *adj syn* see STOCKY
rel fleshy, portly

thickskull *n syn* see DUNCE
rel lout

thick–witted *adj syn* see STUPID 1

thief *n* one who steals <a *thief* took her money>
syn filcher, larcener, larcenist, nimmer, pilferer, prig, purloiner, stealer; *compare* ROBBER
rel burglar, cat burglar, cat man, housebreaker; hijacker, robber; ‖booster, ‖dip, lifter, shoplifter; nip, pickpocket

thieve *vb syn* see STEAL 1

thievery *n syn* see THEFT

thieving *adj syn* see LARCENOUS

thieving *n syn* see THEFT

thievish *adj syn* see LARCENOUS

thin *adj* **1** not thick, heavy, or broad (as in configuration or physique) <a *thin* body>
syn attenuate, reedy, slender, slight, slim, squinny, stalky, tenuous, twiggy; *compare* LEAN
rel lank, lanky, lathy, lean, macilent, spare; cadaverous, gaunt, pinched, skeletal, wasted; meager, puny, small, twiglike
con broad, wide; compact, dense, solid; heavy, massive; corpulent, fat, obese
ant thick
2 characterized by wide separation of component particles <thin air at high altitudes>
syn attenuate, attenuated, rare, rarefied, subtile, subtle, tenuous
rel diffuse, diluted, dispersed; fine, refined
con heavy, thick
ant dense
3 *syn* see DILUTE
4 *syn* see ACUTE 4
rel high-pitched
con low, low-pitched; guttural; deep
5 *syn* see IMPLAUSIBLE
rel vapid; transparent; questionable; untenable
idiom a bit thin
con believable, convincing, sound, substantial

thin *vb* **1** to make thin or thinner <a once powerful frame *thinned* by privation>
syn attenuate, extenuate, wiredraw
rel diminish, reduce; weaken
con broaden, enlarge; strengthen
ant thicken
2 to make or become less dense <the air *thinned* at high altitudes>
syn attenuate, rarefy
ant densify
3 *syn* see DILUTE

thing *n* **1** *syn* see AFFAIR 1
2 *syn* see OCCURRENCE
3 *syn* see ACTION 1
rel exploit, feat, stunt
4 whatever is apprehended as having actual, distinct, and demonstrable existence <there is a place for each *thing* in the lab>
syn article, object
rel entity, item
5 that which can be known as having existence in space or time <virtue is not a *thing*, but an attribute of a *thing*>
syn being, entity, individual, material, matter, object, stuff, substance
rel item, particular
con attribute, characteristic, property, quality
6 *syn* see ENTITY 1
ant nonentity, nonexistence
7 things *pl syn* see POSSESSION 2
8 things *pl syn* see PERSONAL EFFECTS
9 things *pl syn* see CLOTHES
10 *syn* see POINT 1
11 *syn* see FASHION 3
12 *syn* see FETISH 2

thingum *n syn* see DOODAD

---

syn synonym(s)   *rel* related word(s)
ant antonym(s)   *con* contrasted word(s)
idiom idiomatic equivalent(s)
‖ use limited; if in doubt, see a dictionary

thingumajig *n syn* see DOODAD

thingumbob *n syn* see DOODAD

thingummy *n syn* see DOODAD

think *vb* 1 to form an idea of something in the mind <try to *think* exactly how the accident happened>
syn conceive, envisage, envision, fancy, feature, image, imagine, project, realize, see, vision, visualize
rel consider, contemplate, study, weigh; appreciate, comprehend, understand; cerebrate, ideate; conjecture, guess, surmise
2 *syn* see UNDERSTAND 3
3 *syn* see CONJECTURE
4 *syn* see FEEL 3
rel estimate; regard
5 to use one's powers of conception, judgment, or inference <the power to *think* sets humans apart from other animals>
syn cerebrate, cogitate, deliberate, reason, reflect, speculate
rel consider, contemplate; brood, meditate, mull, muse, ponder, ruminate; intellectualize, logicalize, logicize, rationalize; conclude, deduce, infer, judge
idiom put on one's thinking cap, set one's brain to work, use one's head, use the old bean

think (out *or* over) *vb syn* see CONSIDER 1

think (over) *vb syn* see RECONSIDER

thinkable *adj* 1 capable of being thought about <concepts that are easy enough to be *thinkable*>
syn cogitable
rel imaginable, presumable, supposable; comprehendible, comprehensible
con unimaginable; incomprehensible, uncomprehensible
ant unthinkable
2 capable of being made actual <nationalism at this time would be scarcely *thinkable*>
syn conceivable, imaginable, supposable
rel likely, possible; convincing, plausible; feasible, practicable, practical
con inconceivable, unimaginable; impossible, unlikely; implausible; impractical, unfeasible
ant unthinkable

thinking *adj syn* see THOUGHTFUL 1
ant unthinking

third degree *n syn* see CROSS-EXAMINATION

third estate *n syn* see COMMONALTY

thirst *vb syn* see LONG
rel covet; desire, wish

thirsting *adj syn* see THIRSTY 1

thirsty *adj* 1 experiencing a desire for drink <the long hot walk had made him *thirsty*>
syn athirst, dry, thirsting
rel juiceless, parched, sapless
2 *syn* see DRY 1
3 *syn* see EAGER
idiom hungry for, itching for, wild for
ant sated, satiated

this and that *n, often* this and thats *pl syn* see SUNDRIES

thither *adv syn* see THERE
ant hither

thitherward *adv syn* see THERE
ant hitherward

thorny *adj* bristling with perplexities, points of controversy, or other conflicting elements <the *thorny* question of states' rights>
syn nettlesome, prickly, spiny
rel troublesome, vexatious; difficult; tricky

thorough *adj* 1 *syn* see EXHAUSTIVE
rel absolute
2 *syn* see CIRCUMSTANTIAL

thoroughbred *adj syn* see PUREBRED
con mixed, mongrel

thoroughfare *n syn* see WAY 1

thoroughgoing *adj* 1 *syn* see EXHAUSTIVE
2 *syn* see UTTER

thoroughly *adv* 1 *syn* see WELL 3
2 in a detailed and complete manner <*thoroughly* investigated the accusations>
syn completely, detailedly, exhaustively, in and out, inside out, up and down
idiom item by item, to the last detail
con casually, offhandedly, sketchily, superficially
ant cursorily
3 *syn* see VERY 1
4 *syn* see HARD 3

though *adv syn* see HOWEVER

though *conj* in spite of the fact that <*though* they know the war is lost, they continue to fight>
syn albeit, although, howbeit, much as, when, whereas, while

thought *n* 1 the act or process of thinking <sat immersed in deep *thought*>
syn brainwork, cerebration, cogitation, deliberation, reflection, speculation
rel contemplation; meditation, musing, pondering, rumination
2 *syn* see IDEA

thoughtful *adj* 1 characterized by or exhibiting the power to think <the doctor had a shrewd rather than a *thoughtful* face>
syn cogitative, contemplative, meditative, pensive, ‖pensy, pondering, reflecting, reflective, ruminative, speculative, thinking
rel analytical, calculating, logical, rational; earnest, grave, melancholy, serious, sober, studious; brainy, intellectual; deep, inseeing, introspective
con irrational; dull, slow, stupid, unthinking; empty-headed, shallow, vacuous
ant thoughtless
2 *syn* see MINDFUL 2
3 mindful of others <the thank-you note was a *thoughtful* gesture>
syn attentive, considerate
rel anxious, careful, concerned, heedful, mindful, solicitous; chivalrous, civil, courteous, gallant, gracious, polite, well-bred
con careless, heedless, inattentive, negligent, remiss, unconcerned, unmindful, unthinking; inconsiderate; discourteous, impolite
ant thoughtless, unthoughtful

thoughtfully *adv syn* see WELL 2
rel courteously, politely, solicitously
con discourteously, impolitely; inconsiderately, heedlessly, unkindly
ant thoughtlessly, unthoughtfully

thoughtless *adj* 1 *syn* see RASH 1
2 *syn* see CARELESS 1
con mindful

ant thoughtful
3 *syn* see SHORT 5
rel discourteous, impolite, rude; selfish
ant thoughtful

thought–out *adj syn* see DELIBERATE 1
rel investigated; analyzed
idiom thought over (*or* through)

thousand *n syn* see SCAD

thrall *n syn* see BONDAGE

thralldom *n syn* see BONDAGE

thrash *vb* 1 *syn* see BEAT 1
2 *syn* see WHIP 2
3 *syn* see WHIP 1
rel strike; paddywhack, ‖pail

thrashing *n syn* see DEFEAT 1

thrash out *vb syn* see DISCUSS 1

threadbare *adj* 1 *syn* see SHABBY 1
rel damaged, impaired, injured; frayed,
ragged; shopworn, timeworn, worn
idiom the worse for wear, worn to rags (*or*
threads)
2 *syn* see TRITE
rel common, familiar; imitative, uncreative;
set, stock; banal, corny
con fresh, new; different, novel, original,
unconventional, unusual; memorable

threaten *vb* to announce or forecast impending danger or evil <bullies *threatening* the
child with a beating>
syn menace
rel browbeat, bulldoze, cow, intimidate;
augur, forebode, portend, presage; caution,
forewarn, warn
idiom make (*or* utter) threats against

threatening *adj* 1 *syn* see IMMINENT 2
rel impending; forthcoming, upcoming,
close, near
2 *syn* see OMINOUS

threesome *n syn* see TRIAD

threshold *n syn* see VERGE 2

thrift *n syn* see ECONOMY
rel austerity, economizing; saving; parsimony
ant waste

thriftiness *n syn* see ECONOMY
ant thriftlessness

thriftless *adj syn* see IMPROVIDENT
ant thrifty

thrifty *adj* 1 *syn* see FLOURISHING
rel blooming, burgeoning; growing
2 *syn* see SPARING
rel foresighted, prudent; conserving, preserving
con extravagant, improvident
ant wasteful

thrill *vb* to fill with emotions that stir or
excite or to be so excited <an audience
thrilled by the brilliant spectacle>
syn electrify, enthuse, send
rel animate, excite, galvanize, move,
quicken, stimulate; arouse, inspire, rally,
rouse, stir
idiom thrill to pieces (*or* to bits)
con bore, ennui, weary

thrill *n* sudden emotional stimulation, excitement, or enjoyment <they both got a *thrill*
out of small-boat racing>
syn bang, boot, kick, wallop
rel excitement, lift, stimulation, titillation

thriller *n* a work of fiction or drama designed to hold the interest by use of a high
degree of intrigue, adventure, or suspense
<wrote cheap detective *thrillers*>
syn chiller, shocker, thriller-diller
rel gothic, mystery; dime novel, penny
dreadful, shilling shocker

thriller–diller *n syn* see THRILLER

thrive *vb* 1 *syn* see BOOM
rel come on, develop, grow; increase; prosper
con stagnate; fail; bust
2 *syn* see SUCCEED 3
rel advance, progress
idiom make a go, turn out well

thriving *adj* 1 *syn* see FLOURISHING
rel blooming, growing; advancing, progressing
idiom going strong
con shriveling; dying
2 *syn* see SUCCESSFUL

thriving *n syn* see PROSPERITY 2

throb *vb syn* see PULSATE
rel thump; resonate

throe *n* 1 *syn* see ATTACK 3
rel convulsion
2 *syn* see PAIN 1
rel stab

throne *n syn* see TOILET

throng *n syn* see CROWD 1
rel assemblage, assembly, collection, congregation, gathering; bunch, flock, group,
pack

thronged *adj syn* see ALIVE 5
rel crawling

throttle *vb syn* see CHOKE 1
rel garrote

throttling *n syn* see REPRESSION 1

through *prep* 1 *syn* see VIA 1
2 *syn* see VIA 2
3 *syn* see OVER 6
4 *syn* see ABOUT 4
idiom clear through

through *adv* 1 from beginning to end <the
region has a mild climate the whole year
through>
syn around, over, round, throughout
2 *syn* see OVER 5

through *adj* 1 *syn* see DIRECT 2
con obstructed; interrupted
2 *syn* see COMPLETE 4
3 having no further value, strength, or resources <when he lost his voice, his singing
career was *through*>
syn done for, finished, washed-up
rel ended; over
4 being at the very end of a course, concern,
or relationship <was *through* with his wife>
syn done, washed-up
rel finished

through–and–through *adv syn* see DOWN
2

throughout *adv* 1 *syn* see EVERYWHERE 1
2 *syn* see THROUGH 1

throughout *prep* 1 *syn* see ABOUT 4

---

syn synonym(s)   *rel* related word(s)
ant antonym(s)   *con* contrasted word(s)
idiom idiomatic equivalent(s)
‖ use limited; if in doubt, see a dictionary

2 *syn* see DURING

throw *vb* **1** to cause to move swiftly through space by a propulsive movement or a propelling force <*throw* a ball to first base>
syn ‖bung, cast, chuck, fire, fling, heave, hurl, launch, pitch, sling, toss
rel ding, drive, impel, precipitate, shoot; project, propel, push, shove, thrust; flick, flip; shy, tumble; lift, lob
2 to dislodge from one's seat especially in horseback riding <was *thrown* while taking a fence>
syn buck (off), pitch, unhorse, unseat
rel ding (off), fling (off)
3 *syn* see OVERCOME 1
4 *syn* see DON 1
5 *syn* see EXERT
6 *syn* see ADDRESS 3

throw away *vb* **1** *syn* see DISCARD
ant salvage
2 *syn* see WASTE 2
con lay away, lay by, lay up

throw back *vb* *syn* see REVERT 2

throwback *n syn* see REVERSION 1

throw down *vb syn* see FELL 1
rel cast down

throw in *vb syn* see INTRODUCE 6
rel contribute

throwing away *n syn* see DISPOSAL 2
ant salvaging

throw off *vb* **1** *syn* see RID
2 *syn* see SHAKE 5
3 *syn* see EMIT 2
rel disgorge, eject, exhaust, expel
4 *syn* see CONFUSE 2

throw out *vb* **1** *syn* see EJECT 1
2 *syn* see DISCARD
3 *syn* see SAY 1
4 *syn* see CONFUSE 2

throw over *vb syn* see ABANDON 1

throw up *vb* **1** to construct or erect hastily and often carelessly <makeshift buildings *thrown up* almost overnight>
syn jerry-build, run up
rel roughcast, roughhew
idiom slap together, throw together
2 *syn* see VOMIT

thrum *vb syn* see HUM
rel ‖birr, purr

thrust *vb* **1** *syn* see PUSH 1
rel crowd, jam; bump, elbow, jostle, nudge, prod, shoulder
2 to cause (as a pointed instrument) to penetrate forcibly <*thrust* the dagger through her heart>
syn dig, drive, plunge, ram, run, sink, stab, stick
rel jab, shove; impale; pierce; embed; put

thrust *n syn* see SUBSTANCE 2

thud *vb* to make a dull sound by or as if by striking a surface with something thick and heavy <heard footsteps *thudding* down the hall>
syn clonk, clunk, thump
rel tunk; hit, smite, strike; beat, pound

thug *n* **1** a person inclined or hired to treat another roughly, brutally, or murderously <was beaten and robbed by *thugs*>
syn ‖gorilla, ‖hood, hoodlum, hooligan, ruffian, strong arm; *compare* TOUGH

rel bully, ‖larrikan, plug-ugly, roughneck, rowdy, tough; punk; cutthroat, gangster, gunman, mobster; goon, hatchet man
2 *syn* see TOUGH

thumb *vb syn* see HITCHHIKE
idiom thumb a ride

thumb (through) *vb syn* see BROWSE

thump *vb syn* see THUD
rel hammer, knock

thunder *n* the sound that follows a flash of lightning and is caused by sudden expansion of the air in the path of the electrical discharge <he was more afraid of *thunder* than of lightning>
syn thunderclap, thundercrack, thundering
rel fulmination

thunderbolt *n* a single discharge of lightning with the accompanying thunder <she was startled by the *thunderbolt*>
syn bolt, thunderstroke

thunderclap *n syn* see THUNDER

thundercrack *n syn* see THUNDER

thundering *n syn* see THUNDER

thunderstroke *n syn* see THUNDERBOLT

thunderstruck *adj syn* see AGHAST 2
rel bewildered, staggered; breathless, stunned
idiom struck dumb

thus *adv* **1** in this or that manner <summoned his counselors and spoke *thus* to them>
syn so, thus and so, thus and thus, thusly
2 *syn* see THEREFORE

thus and so *adv syn* see THUS 1

thus and thus *adv syn* see THUS 1

thus far *adv syn* see HITHERTO 1

thusly *adv syn* see THUS 1

thwack *n syn* see BLOW 1

thwart *adj syn* see TRANSVERSE

thwart *vb syn* see FRUSTRATE
rel curb, restrain, scotch; cross; foul up, gum up, queer; stymie; counter, match, oppose, pit, play(off), vie
con aid, assist, help, support; abet, encourage

‖**tick** *n syn* see INSTANT 1

ticket *n* **1** a slip giving information (as of ownership, identity, or price) <the price of the iron is on the *ticket*>
syn label, tag
rel card; slip; sticker
2 a card of admission <theater *tickets*>
syn carte d'entrée
rel pass
3 a list of candidates for appointment, nomination, or election <vote the party *ticket*>
syn slate
rel choice; lineup; list
4 *syn* see BALLOT 1
5 *syn* see PASSPORT

ticklish *adj* **1** *syn* see UNSTABLE 2
2 *syn* see DELICATE 7
rel critical
3 *syn* see INCONSTANT 1

tick off *vb* **1** *syn* see ENUMERATE 2
2 *syn* see REPROVE

tidbit (or **titbit**) *n syn* see DELICACY

‖**tiddly** *adj syn* see INTOXICATED 1

tide *n syn* see FLOW

tidings *n pl syn* see NEWS

tidy *adj syn* see NEAT 2
  rel sleek, spruce
  ant untidy

tie *n* **1** *syn* see BOND 3
  rel fastener, fastening; attachment
  2 *syn* see DRAW 4

tie *vb* **1** to make fast and secure <*tie* a bundle with strong cord>
  syn bind, tie up
  rel attach, fasten; connect, join, link; anchor, moor, rivet, secure; lash, truss (up); band, cinch, gird, rope
  con loose, loosen; disconnect
  ant untie
  2 *syn* see MARRY 2
  3 *syn* see HAMPER
  idiom tie hand and foot, tie one's hands
  ant untie
  4 *syn* see EQUAL 3

tier *n* **1** *syn* see LINE 5
  rel layer
  2 *syn* see CLASS 1

tie up *vb* **1** *syn* see TIE 1
  2 *syn* see HAMPER

tie-up *n* *syn* see ASSOCIATION 1
  rel linkup

tiff *n* *syn* see QUARREL

tiff *vb* *syn* see QUARREL

tiffany *adj syn* see FILMY

tight *adj* **1** *syn* see FAST 4
  rel clasped; solid, steadfast
  con lax, limp; shaky
  ant loose
  2 *syn* see CLOSE 4
  ant loose
  3 fitting, drawn, or stretched so that there is no slackness or looseness <a *tight* drumhead>
  syn close, taut, tense
  rel skintight; constricted, contracted, drawn, tightened; inflexible, rigid, stiff
  con loosened, slack, unconstricted
  ant loose
  4 difficult to cope with, get through, or circumvent <a very *tight* diplomatic situation>
  syn arduous, rough, tricksy, trying
  rel difficult; exacting; tense; critical; punishing; distressing, disturbing, upsetting
  5 *syn* see STINGY
  6 *syn* see INTOXICATED 1
  idiom tight as a tick

tight *adv syn* see HARD 7

tightfisted *adj syn* see STINGY
  rel grudging, mean, shabby

tight-laced *adj syn* see PRIM 1

tight-lipped *adj syn* see SILENT 3
  idiom with one's lips sealed

tightly *adv syn* see HARD 7

tight-mouthed *adj syn* see SILENT 3

tightwad *n syn* see MISER

till *prep syn* see UNTIL

till *conj* up to the time when <be sure to wait *till* I come>
  syn until

till *vb* to prepare (soil) for the raising of crops <*till* the soil>

syn cultivate, dress, ‖labor, tend, work
  rel harrow, hoe, mulch, plow, turn; plant, sow

tillable *adj syn* see ARABLE
  ant untillable

tilt *vb* **1** *syn* see SLANT 1
  2 *syn* see SEESAW

tilt *n syn* see SLOPE

tilted *adj syn* see INCLINED 3

tilter *vb syn* see SEESAW

tilting *adj syn* see INCLINED 3

timber *n* **1** *syn* see FOREST
  2 a large squared or dressed piece of wood <roof *timbers*>
  syn balk, beam
  rel girder, rafter

timberland *n syn* see FOREST

timbre *n syn* see TEMPER 1

time *n* **1** *syn* see WHILE 1
  rel season
  2 *syn* see OCCASION 5
  3 *syn* see OPPORTUNITY
  idiom the proper moment
  4 *syn* see PERIOD 2
  5 *syn* see TERM 2
  6 *syn* see SEASON
  7 *syn* see TEMPO
  8 *syn* see SPELL 1
  ‖**9** *syn* see BINGE 1

time *vb* **1** to arrange or set the time of <*timed* his visits to coincide with her vacations>
  syn book, schedule
  rel plan, program, set up
  2 to ascertain or record the time, duration, or rate of <*timed* the car at 100 mph>
  syn clock
  idiom hold the clock on

time and again *adv syn* see OFTEN

timeless *adj* **1** *syn* see CONTINUAL
  2 *syn* see ETERNAL 4

timely *adv syn* see EARLY 1

timely *adj* **1** done or occurring at a suitable time <await a more *timely* moment>
  syn auspicious, favorable, opportune, propitious, prosperous, seasonable, timeous, well-timed
  rel appropriate, fit, fitting, meet, proper, suitable; likely, promising
  con improper, inappropriate, unfitting; inauspicious, inopportune, unfavorable, unpropitious, unsuitable; ill-timed
  ant untimely
  2 *syn* see PUNCTUAL 2

timeous *adj syn* see TIMELY 1

timetable *n syn* see PROGRAM 1
  rel table; plan

timeworn *adj* **1** *syn* see ANCIENT 1
  2 *syn* see TRITE

timid *adj* **1** *syn* see SHY 1
  rel humble; shrinking
  ant bold
  2 marked by or exhibiting a lack of boldness, courage, or determination <was too *timid* to ski>

syn timorous, ‖timorsome, undaring
  rel gentle, mild, milk-toast, milky; cautious, chary, wary; jumpy, nervous, skittish; afraid, apprehensive, fainthearted, fearful; chicken, chickenhearted, henhearted,

---

syn synonym(s)   *rel* related word(s)
ant antonym(s)   *con* contrasted word(s)
idiom idiomatic equivalent(s)
‖ use limited; if in doubt, see a dictionary

mouselike, mousy, pigeonhearted; cowardly, yellow; funky, panicky
con audacious, brave, courageous, daring, doughty, fearless, intrepid, lionhearted, unafraid, valiant, valorous
ant bold
3 syn see VACILLATING 2

timorous *adj syn* see TIMID 2
rel quailing, recoiling, shrinking; quivering, shivering, shuddering, trembling
ant assured

‖**timorsome** *adj syn* see TIMID 2

tincture *n* **1 syn** see COLOR 6
2 syn see HINT 2
rel smattering

tincture *vb syn* see TINT
rel pigment; stain

ting *vb syn* see TINKLE 1

tinge *vb syn* see TINT
rel streak

tinge *n* **1 syn** see COLOR 1
rel coloration, coloring, tincture; stain
2 syn see HINT 2

tingle *vb* **1 syn** see TINKLE 1
rel chime
2 syn see JINGLE

tinker *vb syn* see FIDDLE 2
idiom play around

tinkle *vb* **1** to make a repeated light high-pitched ringing sound <wind-bells *tinkling* in the breeze>
syn plink, ting, tingle
rel clink, jangle, jingle
2 syn see JINGLE
3 syn see CHAT 1

tinsel *adj syn* see GAUDY

tint *n syn* see COLOR 1
rel tincture, touch; coloration, pigmentation; dye, stain, wash

tint *vb* to color with a slight shade or stain <white blossoms *tinted* with pale pink>
syn complexion, tincture, tinge
rel color, dye; shade, touch (up); stain, wash

tintamarre *n syn* see DIN

tiny *adj* exceptionally or remarkably small <the first *tiny* buds of spring flowers>
syn ‖bitsy, diminutive, dwarf, dwarfish, itsy-bitsy, itty-bitty, lilliputian, midget, miniature, minikin, minute, peewee, pint-size, pocket, pocket-size, pygmy, teensy, teensy-weensy, teenty, teeny, teeny-weeny, wee, weeny, weeny; *compare* SMALL 1
rel minuscular, minuscule; infinitesimal, microscopic, minim
con colossal, enormous, gigantic, immense, mammoth, vast
ant huge

tip *n syn* see POINT 9

tip *vb syn* see SLANT 1

tip *vb syn* see TIPTOE
rel creep, mince, pussyfoot, steal

tip (over) *vb syn* see OVERTURN 1
idiom turn upside down

tip *n syn* see GRATUITY

tip *n* a piece of advice or confidential information given by one thought to have access to special or inside sources <gave him a *tip* on which horse would win>
syn point, pointer, steer, tip-off
rel advice; information; clue, cue, hint; forecast, prediction

idiom a bit of inside advice, a bug in the ear, a word to the wise

tip–off *n syn* see TIP

tipped *adj syn* see INCLINED 3

tipple *vb syn* see DRINK 3
idiom drown one's cares (*or* sorrows)

tipple *n syn* see LIQUOR 2

tippler *n syn* see DRUNKARD

tipster *n syn* see INFORMER

tipsy *adj syn* see INTOXICATED 1
rel dazed, unsteady

tiptoe *vb* to walk or proceed quietly on or as if on the ends of the toes <*tiptoed* through the dark house>
syn tip, toe
rel creep, gumshoe, pussyfoot, steal
con clomp, clump, stamp, stomp, stump

tirade *n* a violent, often protracted, and usually denunciatory speech or writing <lashed out with a vicious *tirade* of angry protest>
syn diatribe, harangue, jeremiad, philippic
rel rant, rodomontade, screed; abuse, invective, revilement, vituperation; censure, condemnation, denunciation; berating, tongue-lashing; lecture, sermon

tire *vb* **1** to deplete the strength and energy of <the plane trip *tired* him>
syn drain, fatigue, jade, wear, wear down, weary; *compare* EXHAUST 4
rel debilitate, enervate, enfeeble, sap, weaken; exhaust, wear out
con brace (up), invigorate, strengthen; animate, energize, enliven, pep (up), quicken, stimulate, vitalize
2 syn see BORE
rel jade, wear; irk; disgust, nauseate, sicken
idiom make one tired, put one to sleep

tired *adj* **1** being depleted of strength and energy <was too *tired* to go on>
syn ‖clapped-out, fatigued, jaded, wearied, weary, worn, worn-down, worn-out
rel overtaxed, overworked; drained, run-down; ‖beat, ‖bushed, dog-tired, exhausted, fagged, frazzled, overworn, ‖pooped, ‖tucked up, tuckered; collapsing, consumed, knocked out, prostrate, spent
idiom worn to a frazzle
con active, energetic, lively, strong, tireless
ant rested; fresh, untired
2 syn see SHABBY 1
3 syn see FED UP
rel annoyed, bothered, displeased, irked
idiom having a bellyful of, having about enough of
4 syn see TRITE

tiredness *n syn* see FATIGUE
rel collapse, prostration

tireless *adj syn* see INDEFATIGABLE
rel active, enthusiastic
con inactive, listless, tired, unenergetic, unenthusiastic, weak

tiresome *adj syn* see IRKSOME
rel dull; jading; burdensome, onerous, oppressive; difficult, hard

tiring *adj syn* see IRKSOME

Titan *n syn* see HUGE

titanic *adj syn* see HUGE

title *n* **1 syn** see CLAIM 1
rel argument, ground, justification, proof, reason; desert, due, merit

2 *syn* see NAME 1
title *vb syn* see NAME 1
titter *vb syn* see LAUGH
  rel twitter
  idiom laugh behind (*or* in) one's hand, laugh in one's beard
tittle *n syn* see PARTICLE
  rel fleck, flyspeck, speck; crumb, grain, scrap, snippet
tittle–tattle *n* 1 *syn* see CHATTER
  2 *syn* see REPORT 1
titubate *vb syn* see REEL 2
titular *adj syn* see NOMINAL
tizzy *n syn* see SNIT
to *prep* 1 in the direction of and as far as <was driving *to* the city>
  syn into
  rel toward
  ant from
  2 *syn* see AGAINST 2
  rel on, over, upon
  3 *syn* see BEFORE 1
  4 *syn* see UNTIL
  5 for the particular purpose of <a market study tailored *to* your needs>
  syn for
  idiom in contemplation (*or* consideration) of, with an eye to, with a view to
  6 in complement to <played Romeo *to* her Juliet>
  syn opposite
toad *n syn* see SNOT
toad *n syn* see SYCOPHANT
toadeater *n syn* see SYCOPHANT
toadier *n syn* see SYCOPHANT
toady *n syn* see SYCOPHANT
toady *vb syn* see FAWN
  rel follow, tag, tail, trail
toadying *adj syn* see FAWNING
toadyish *adj syn* see FAWNING
to–and–fro *n syn* see HESITATION
  2 *syn* see QUARREL
toast *n syn* see DRINK 2
to–be *n syn* see FUTURE
tocsin *n syn* see ALARM 1
  rel sign, signal
today *adv* at the present time <youth *today* do not know what poverty is>
  syn now, nowadays, presently
  idiom in this day and age, these days
  con then, yesteryear
today *n syn* see PRESENT
todayish *adj syn* see PRESENT
to–do *n* 1 *syn* see COMMOTION 4
  2 *syn* see COMMOTION 3
toe *vb syn* see TIPTOE
tog (out *or* up) *vb syn* see DRESS UP 1
together *adv* 1 at one and the same time <events that occurred *together*>
  syn at once, coincidentally, coincidently, coinstantaneously, concurrently, simultaneously
  idiom all at once, all together
  ant separately
  2 in succession usually without intermission <was moody for days *together*>

syn consecutively, continually, continuously, hand running, night and day, running, successively, unintermittedly, uninterruptedly
  idiom on end
  3 in or by combined action or effort <students and faculty protested *together*>
  syn conjointly, jointly, mutually
  rel collectively, concertedly, unanimously
  idiom in one breath, in the same breath, with one accord, with one voice
  ant separately
togetherness *n* 1 *syn* see ASSOCIATION 1
  2 *syn* see SOLIDARITY
‖**toggle** *vb syn* see DRESS UP 1
togs *n pl syn* see CLOTHES
toil *n syn* see WORK 2
  idiom sweat of one's brow, toil and trouble
toil *vb* 1 *syn* see LABOR 1
  2 *syn* see DRUDGE
  3 *syn* see PLOD 1
toil *n*, *usu* **toils** *pl syn* see WEB 2
toiler *n syn* see SLAVE 2
toilet *n* a fixture for defecation and urination
  syn ‖can, convenience, ‖donicker, head, john, johnny, latrine, lavatory, ‖loo, ‖pot, ‖potty, privy, ‖throne, water closet
  rel hopper
toilful *adj syn* see HARD 6
toilsome *adj syn* see HARD 6
toilsomely *adv syn* see HARD 8
token *n* 1 *syn* see INDICATION 3
  rel harbinger, omen, portent; characteristic, earmark; indicator, smack
  2 *syn* see REMEMBRANCE 3
  3 *syn* see EXPRESSION 3
  4 *syn* see PLEDGE 1
‖**tokus** *n syn* see BUTTOCKS
tolerable *adj* 1 *syn* see BEARABLE
  ant intolerable
  2 *syn* see RESPECTABLE 5
  3 *syn* see DECENT 4
  rel fair, goodish, OK, tidy
  idiom better than nothing, good enough
  ant intolerable
tolerably *adv syn* see ENOUGH 2
tolerance *n* 1 the capacity to bear something unpleasant, painful, or difficult <had always had a high *tolerance* to pain>
  syn endurance, stamina, toleration
  rel fortitude, grit, guts; strength, vigor; long-suffering, patience, sufferance; steadfastness, steadiness; opposition, resistance
  ant intolerance
  2 *syn* see FORBEARANCE 2
  rel liberality, liberalness, open-mindedness, permissiveness
  con narrow-mindedness; prejudice; dogmatism; bigotry
  ant intolerance
tolerant *adj* 1 *syn* see LIBERAL 3
  rel open-minded; permissive
  con narrow, narrow-minded; prejudiced; dogmatic; bigoted
  ant intolerant
  2 *syn* see FORBEARING
  rel benevolent, humane; condoning, excusing, forgiving, sympathetic, understanding
  con severe, stern; uncompromising, unforgiving, unsympathetic

---

syn synonym(s)   *rel* related word(s)
ant antonym(s)   *con* contrasted word(s)
idiom idiomatic equivalent(s)
‖ use limited; if in doubt, see a dictionary

ant intolerant

tolerate *vb* 1 *syn* see ACCEPT 2
  rel condone, countenance; allow, consent (to), permit; have, hear (to)
  2 *syn* see BEAR 10
  rel sustain

toleration *n* 1 *syn* see FORBEARANCE 2
  2 *syn* see TOLERANCE 1

toll *n* *syn* see EXPENSE 2

toll *vb* *syn* see LURE

toll *vb* *syn* see RING

‖**tomato** *n* *syn* see PROSTITUTE

tomb *n* *syn* see GRAVE
  rel box, coffin, ‖trough

tomb *vb* 1 *syn* see BURY 1
  ant untomb
  2 *syn* see ENTOMB 1
  ant disentomb, untomb

tomboy *n* a girl exhibiting boyish behavior <a *tomboy* who still rode, fished, and fought with her brothers>
  syn gamine, hoyden
  rel romp

tombstone *n* an inscribed memorial stone set at a place of interment <read the epitaph on the *tombstone* of her ancestor>
  syn footstone, grave marker, gravestone, headstone, ledger, monument
  rel memorial; cenotaph

tome *n* *syn* see BOOK 1

tomfool *n* *syn* see FOOL 1

tomfool *adj* *syn* see FOOLISH 2

tomfoolery *n* 1 *syn* see NONSENSE 2
  2 *syn* see PRANK

tommyrot *n* *syn* see NONSENSE 2

Tom o' Bedlam *n* *syn* see LUNATIC 1

Tom Thumb *n* *syn* see DWARF

ton *n* 1 *syn* see FASHION 3
  2 *syn* see SMART SET

tone *n* 1 *syn* see INFLECTION
  2 *syn* see VEIN 1
  3 *syn* see COLOR 1
  rel blend
  4 the state of a living body or any of its organs or parts in which the functions are healthy and performed with due vigor <diet and exercise contributed to her good muscle *tone*>
  syn tonicity, tonus
  rel health, healthiness; elasticity, resiliency; strength, vigor
  5 *syn* see TEMPER 1
  rel current, movement
  idiom (the) state of things
  6 *syn* see MOOD 1

toned down *adj syn* see SUBDUED 2

tongue *n* *syn* see LANGUAGE 1

tongue *vb* *syn* see SCOLD 1

tongue–lash *vb* *syn* see SCOLD 1
  idiom give one the rough side of one's tongue

tongue–tied *adj syn* see INARTICULATE 3
  con loose-lipped, loose-tongued

‖**tongue–walk** *vb* *syn* see SCOLD 1
  idiom give one the rough side of one's tongue

tonguey *adj syn* see TALKATIVE

tonic *adj* 1 increasing or restoring physical or mental tone <the *tonic* effect of a vacation>
  syn astringent, restorative, roborant

rel invigorating, refreshing, renewing, strengthening; bracing, sharp
  con debilitating, enfeebling, weakening; enervating; exhausting, grueling, sapping
  2 *syn* see INVIGORATING

tonicity *n* *syn* see TONE 4

tonish *adj syn* see STYLISH

tonus *n* *syn* see TONE 4

tony *adj syn* see STYLISH

too *adv* 1 *syn* see ALSO 2
  2 *syn* see EVER 6
  rel exorbitantly, immoderately, unconscionably, unmeasurably
  3 *syn* see VERY 1

‖**toodle–oo** *interj syn* see GOOD-BYE

tool *n* 1 *syn* see IMPLEMENT
  rel machine, mechanism
  2 one used or manipulated by another to accomplish his purposes <had no intention of being used as a *tool* by either faction>
  syn cat's-paw, pawn, puppet, stooge
  rel agent, hireling, vehicle; chump, sucker

tool *vb syn* see DRIVE 5

toot *vb syn* see DECLARE 1

toot *n syn* see BINGE 1

toothful *n syn* see DRAM

toothsome *adj syn* see PALATABLE
  rel agreeable, pleasant, pleasing

toothy *adj* 1 having or showing prominent teeth <a wide *toothy* grin>
  syn teethy
  2 *syn* see PALATABLE

too–too *adj syn* see GENTEEL 3
  rel chichi

‖**tootsie** *n syn* see DOXY 1

top *n* 1 the highest point <hiked to the *top* of the mountain>
  syn apex, crest, crown, fastigium, peak, roof, summit, vertex
  rel acme, climax, culmination, height, pinnacle; cusp, head, point, tip
  con base, foot, sole; nadir
  ant bottom
  2 the outer or upper part <the *top* of the table>
  syn face, superficies, surface
  3 *syn* see BEST
  ant bottom

top *vb* 1 to remove or cut back the top of <*top* a tree>
  syn crop, detruncate, pollard, truncate
  rel clip, dock, prune, trim; curtail, shorten
  2 *syn* see SURPASS 1
  3 *syn* see SURMOUNT 3

top *adj* 1 of, relating to, or being at the top <the *top* floor of the house>
  syn apical, highest, loftiest, topmost, uppermost
  con bottommost, lowest
  ant bottom
  2 *syn* see EXCELLENT
  3 *syn* see MAXIMUM

top–drawer *adj syn* see EXALTED 1

tope *vb syn* see DRINK 3

toper *n syn* see DRUNKARD

Tophet *n syn* see HELL

topic *n syn* see SUBJECT 2
  rel proposition; issue

topless *adj syn* see LOFTY 6

toploftical *adj syn* see PROUD 1

toplofty *adj syn* see PROUD 1
 rel inflated, puffed; egotistic
 con crestfallen
topmost *adj* **1** *syn* see TOP 1
 ant bottommost
 2 *syn* see MAXIMUM
top–notch *adj syn* see EXCELLENT
top off *vb* **1** *syn* see CLIMAX
topography *n syn* see TERRAIN 1
topple *vb* **1** *syn* see FALL 2
 2 *syn* see TEETER
 3 *syn* see OVERTURN 1
 4 *syn* see OVERTHROW 2
top–ranking *adj syn* see EXALTED 1
topsy–turviness *n syn* see CONFUSION 3
topsy–turvy *adj* **1** *syn* see UPSIDE-DOWN 1
 2 *syn* see UPSIDE-DOWN 2
 rel cockeyed, disarranged, disjointed, disordered, unhinged
torch *n syn* see INCENDIARY
toreador *n syn* see BULLFIGHTER
torero *n syn* see BULLFIGHTER
torment *n syn* see AFFLICT
 rel distress, trouble; hurt, pain, punish
 2 *syn* see MOLEST
tormented *adj syn* see DISTRAUGHT
tormenting *adj syn* see EXCRUCIATING
torn *adj syn* see LACERATED
tornado *n* a violent destructive whirling wind accompanied by a funnel-shaped cloud extending downward from a cumulonimbus cloud <the *tornado* caused extensive destruction>
 syn cyclone, twister; *compare* HURRICANE, WHIRLWIND 1
torpedo *n syn* see ASSASSIN
torpid *adj syn* see LETHARGIC
 rel dull, leaden, sodden; motionless, static; numb
 con lively; frisky, sprightly, vigorous; fast
 ant active
torpidity *n syn* see LETHARGY 1
 rel listlessness, passivity, stagnation
torpidness *n syn* see LETHARGY 1
 ant activeness
torpor *n syn* see LETHARGY 1
 rel stolidity; passivity
 ant activity; animation
torrent *n syn* see FLOOD 2
 rel flux, rush
torrid *adj syn* see HOT 1
 idiom burning hot, hot enough to roast an ox
 ant arctic
 2 *syn* see IMPASSIONED
 rel sultry
 ant frigid
tort *n syn* see EVIL 3
tortuous *adj syn* see WINDING
 rel involute, vermiculate; cranky; involved
torture *vb* **1** *syn* see AFFLICT
 rel oppress, persecute, wrong; hurt; maim, mangle, mutilate
 idiom put on the rack, put to torture
 2 *syn* see DEFORM

torturing *adj syn* see EXCRUCIATING
torturous *adj syn* see EXCRUCIATING
tory *n syn* see DIEHARD 1
 rel loyalist, traditionalist
tory *adj syn* see CONSERVATIVE 1
tosh *n syn* see NONSENSE 2
toss *vb* **1** *syn* see THROW 1
 2 to rise and fall often rhythmically or with alternate motions <a small boat *tossing* in heavy seas>
 syn heave, pitch, rock, roll; *compare* SEE-SAW
 rel bob; sway
 3 *syn* see DRINK 1
 4 *syn* see WRITHE 1
 idiom toss and turn
toss (around) *vb syn* see DISCUSS 1
 rel bandy (about)
tosspot *n syn* see DRUNKARD
tot *n syn* see DRAM
tot *vb syn* see ADD 2
total *adj* **1** *syn* see WHOLE 4
 rel overall; comprehensive, full, inclusive, plenary; teetotal
 ant partial
 2 *syn* see UTTER
 3 *syn* see TOTALITARIAN 1
 rel authoritative; absolute, arbitrary, despotic; omnipotent
 4 *syn* see TOTALITARIAN 2
 rel monopolistic
 5 concentrating and employing all resources on a single objective <a *total* offensive>
 syn all-out, full-blown, full-out, full-scale, totalitarian, unlimited
 rel out-and-out, unreserved, unrestricted
 con hampered, impeded, trammeled; restrained, restricted; stinted
 ant limited
total *n* **1** *syn* see WHOLE 1
 2 *syn* see BODY 5
total *vb* **1** *syn* see ADD 2
 2 *syn* see AMOUNT 1
 rel comprise, consist (of); stack up; equal, result (in), yield
 idiom mount up to, pile up to
 3 to make a total wreck of <*totaled* his car when he hit the wall>
 syn demolish, wreck; *compare* DESTROY 1
 rel crack up, smash
totalistic *adj syn* see TOTALITARIAN 1
 con democratic; individualistic
totalitarian *adj* **1** of or relating to centralized control by one autocratic leader or party considered to be infallible <Nazi Germany was a *totalitarian* state>
 syn authoritarian, total, totalistic; *compare* ABSOLUTE 4, DICTATORIAL
 con democratic, popular; constitutional
 2 having or exercising dictatorial powers often tending toward monopoly <antitrust legislation reversing the trend toward the *totalitarian* collectivism of big business>
 syn total
 3 *syn* see TOTAL 5
totalitarianism *n syn* see TYRANNY
totality *n* **1** *syn* see WHOLE 1
 2 *syn* see ENTIRETY 1
 3 *syn* see WHOLE 2
 rel configuration, form

---

syn synonym(s) **rel** related word(s)
ant antonym(s) **con** contrasted word(s)
idiom idiomatic equivalent(s)
‖ use limited; if in doubt, see a dictionary

totalize *vb syn* see ADD 2

totally *adv syn* see ALL 1

tote *vb syn* see CARRY 1
rel cart, haul; shoulder

‖**tote** *n syn* see WHOLE 1

tote *vb syn* see ADD 2

totter *vb* 1 *syn* see TEETER
rel shimmy
2 *syn* see REEL 2
rel blunder, stumble, trip; dodder, ‖dotter; flounder

touch *vb* 1 to probe with a sensitive part of the body (as a finger) so as to get or produce a sensation often in the course of examining or exploring <*touch* an iron to test its temperature>
syn feel, finger, handle, palpate, paw
rel brush, graze; caress, fondle, rub, stroke, toy (with); palm, thumb; examine, inspect, probe, scrutinize; investigate
2 *syn* see ADJOIN
3 *syn* see EQUAL 3
4 *syn* see AFFECT
rel arouse, stir; excite, quicken, stimulate
idiom touch a chord
5 *syn* see AMOUNT 2
rel come (to), come (on)

touch *n* 1 *syn* see CONTACT 1
rel junction; communication
2 an act of touching or feeling <woke her with a light *touch* on her hand>
syn palpation, taction
rel brush, pat, stroke; contact
3 tactile sensitivity <a blanket soft to the *touch*>
syn feel, tactility
rel feeling
4 a specified sensation conveyed through the tactile receptors <the velvety *touch* of a fabric>
syn feel, feeling
5 *syn* see HINT 2
6 distinctive manner or method <this house needs a woman's *touch*>
syn hand
rel manner, style, way
‖7 *syn* see THEFT

touchable *adj syn* see TANGIBLE 1
ant untouchable

touch down *vb syn* see ALIGHT

touching *prep* 1 *syn* see AGAINST 2
idiom up against
2 *syn* see APROPOS

touching *adj* 1 *syn* see ADJACENT 3
rel meeting; impinging; overlapping
2 *syn* see MOVING 2
rel compassionate, responsive, sympathetic, tender; piteous, pitiable, pitiful, tear-jerking

touch-me-not-ish *adj syn* see UNSOCIABLE

touchstone *n syn* see STANDARD 3
rel check, test, trial; barometer, scale; demonstration, proof

touch up *vb* to improve or perfect by small additional strokes or alterations <*touch up* a picture>
syn brush up, retouch, tease up
rel improve, perfect, polish; do (up), fix (up)
idiom put finishing touches on

touchy *adj* 1 *syn* see IRASCIBLE

rel hypersensitive, oversensitive, sensitive, thin-skinned; temperamental, volatile, miffy
ant imperturbable
2 *syn* see DELICATE 7
rel dicey, risky, unpredictable; harmful, hazardous, unsafe

tough *adj* 1 *syn* see STRONG 2
rel flinty, hard, unyielding; resistant, unbreakable, withstanding
idiom tough as leather (*or* nails)
con breakable; brittle; yielding
ant fragile
2 *syn* see VISCOUS
3 advocating a persistently firm course of action <a *tough* foreign policy>
syn hard-line, inflexible, uncompromising, unyielding
rel stiff, taut; fixed, confirmed, hard-shell, narrow, rigid; arbitrary, immutable, unalterable; hard-boiled, hardened, obdurate; harsh, procrustean, rigorous, severe, strict; drastic
con liberal, relaxed; compromising, flexible, laissez-faire, yielding
ant soft
4 having or exhibiting great physical endurance (as to strain, hardship, or labor) <the rigorous climate created a *tough* people>
syn hardy, rugged
rel conditioned, hard-bitten, hardened, seasoned, steeled; fit, healthy, lusty, robust, vigorous; stalwart, strong, sturdy
con delicate, fragile, frail, tender; half-hardy, puny; weakened
ant weak
5 *syn* see OBSTINATE
rel hardfisted, hardhanded, hardheaded, tough-minded
6 *syn* see HARD 6
ant soft
7 *syn* see ONEROUS
ant soft
8 frequented by rowdy or criminal elements <lived in a *tough* neighborhood>
syn bad, rough
rel disorderly, rowdy; dangerous, unsafe; ghetto, inner-city, underprivileged
con orderly, quiet, safe

tough (out) *vb syn* see ACCEPT 2

tough *n* a rough or unruly person often taking part in bullying or violent behavior <attacked by a gang of *toughs*>
syn ‖b'hoy, bullyboy, mucker, mug, plug-ugly, punk, rough, roughneck, rowdy, ruffian, thug, toughie, yahoo; *compare* BULLY 1, THUG 1
rel goon, hood, hoodlum, hooligan

toughen *vb syn* see HARDEN 2
rel develop, strengthen
ant weaken

toughie *n syn* see TOUGH
rel ‖heavy

tour *n* 1 *syn* see SPELL
2 a journey in which one eventually returns to the starting point <made a quick *tour* of all the bars>
syn circuit, round, roundabout, round trip; *compare* TRIP 1
rel turn; circle tour

tour de force *n* 1 *syn* see FEAT 2

2 *syn* see MASTERPIECE 1

tourist *n* one who makes a tour for pleasure or culture <*tourists* going through the castle>
syn rubberneck, sightseer, ‖tripper
rel day-tripper, excursionist; traveler; visitor

tout *vb* 1 *syn* see LOOKOUT 3

tout *vb* to overly publicize <was *touted* as the world's most modern shopping center>
syn ballyhoo, herald, trumpet
rel proclaim, publicize; plug, promote; acclaim, laud, praise
idiom praise to the skies

tow *vb* *syn* see PULL 2
rel propel; push
idiom take in tow

toward *adj* *syn* see GOOD 1
ant untoward

toward *prep* 1 *syn* see APROPOS
2 *syn* see AGAINST 1

tower (above *or* over) *vb* *syn* see OVERLOOK 2

towering *adj* 1 *syn* see LOFTY 6
rel altitudinous, high, tall; stratospheric
2 *syn* see SUPREME
3 *syn* see MONSTROUS 1
4 reaching a high point of greatness, intensity, or violence <a *towering* rage>
syn monumental, overwhelming
rel ‖crashing; overpowering; mind-blowing
con minor, petty, piddling, puny, trivial
5 *syn* see EXCESSIVE 1

towery *adj* *syn* see LOFTY 6

to wit *adv* *syn* see NAMELY

towner *n* *syn* see TOWNSMAN

townish *adj* of, relating to, or characteristic of a town or of urban life <enjoyed a fast-paced, competitive, *townish* life-style>
syn towny
rel city, metropolitan, urban
con bucolic, rural; isolated, lonely, solitary

townman *n* *syn* see TOWNSMAN

townsman *n* a town dweller <population composed mostly of *townsmen* and a few countrymen>
syn burgher, cit, citizen, towner, townman, towny

towny *n* *syn* see TOWNSMAN

towny *adj* *syn* see TOWNISH

tow-row *n* *syn* see COMMOTION 4

toxic *adj* *syn* see POISONOUS
ant nontoxic

toxicant *adj* *syn* see POISONOUS

toy *n* 1 *syn* see KNICKKNACK
2 something for a child to play with <games, dolls, and other *toys*>
syn ‖die, ‖play-pretty, plaything, ‖pretty

toy *vb* *syn* see TRIFLE 1
rel disport, frolic, play, sport; fiddle (with), tease; caress, cosset, cuddle, dandle, pet
idiom fool (or mess) around with

trace *n* 1 *syn* see TRACK 1
rel evidence, proof
2 *syn* see VESTIGE 1

rel mark, token
3 *syn* see HINT 2

trace *vb* *syn* see TRACK 1

track *n* 1 detectable evidence that something has passed <the *track* of a sleigh in the snow>
syn trace, tread
rel impress, imprint, mark, print; sign, vestige
2 *syn* see TRAIL
rel footpath, footway, walk
idiom beaten path
3 *syn* see WAY 1
rel roadway, trackway
4 *syn* see FOOTPRINT
rel scent, slot

track *vb* 1 to follow the tracks or traces of <*track* a wounded deer>
syn trace, trail
rel follow; dog, shadow, tail; chase, pursue; find, hunt (down), smell (out)
idiom be hot on the trail of
2 *syn* see TRAVEL 2

tract *n* 1 *syn* see AREA 1
rel amplitude, spread, stretch; part, portion, section, sector
2 *syn* see LOT 3
3 *syn* see FOOTPRINT

tractable *adj* *syn* see OBEDIENT
rel flexible, pliable, pliant; manageable; subdued
con headstrong, unmanageable, willful; obstinate, refractory, stubborn
ant intractable, unruly

tractate *n* *syn* see DISCOURSE 2

trade *n* 1 a pursuit followed as an occupation or means of livelihood and requiring technical knowledge and skill <the *trade* of a carpenter>
syn art, calling, craft, handicraft, métier, profession, vocation
rel employment, occupation, pursuit, work
con avocation, hobby
2 *syn* see BUSINESS 4
rel market
3 *syn* see PATRONAGE 2

trade *vb* 1 to give one thing in return for another with an expectation of gain <*traded* furs for beads and cloth>
syn bargain, barter, exchange, swap, traffic, truck; *compare* EXCHANGE 2
rel market, merchandise, sell; deal; argue, chaffer, dicker, haggle, wrangle
idiom make (or strike) a bargain, make a deal
2 *syn* see EXCHANGE 2

trademark *n* *syn* see MARK 7

trader *n* *syn* see MERCHANT

tradesman *n* *syn* see MERCHANT

tradition *n* 1 an inherited or established way of thinking, feeling, or doing <America's puritanical *tradition* is still very much alive>
syn heritage
rel culture; convention, custom, ethic, form; birthright, inheritance, legacy
2 *syn* see LORE 2

traditional *adj* 1 of or relating to tradition <a *traditional* interpretation of the Bible>
syn conventional, tralatitious; *compare* CONVENTIONAL 1

---

syn synonym(s)   *rel* related word(s)
ant antonym(s)   *con* contrasted word(s)
idiom idiomatic equivalent(s)

‖ use limited; if in doubt, see a dictionary

rel ancestral, immemorial, old; customary, habitual, usual; acknowledged, established, establishmentarian, fixed; common, popular
con new; unconventional, unusual; individualistic, original, personal
2 syn see ORAL 2

traditionalist *n syn* see PURIST

traditionalistic *adj syn* see CONSERVATIVE 1

traduce *vb* **1 syn** see MALIGN
rel mock; disgrace; betray; violate

traducing *adj syn* see LIBELOUS

traffic *n* **1 syn** see BUSINESS 4
2 syn see COMMERCE 2
rel relations, relationship; closeness, connection, familiarity, intimacy
3 syn see PATRONAGE 2
4 the number or volume of vehicles or pedestrians moving along a route <freeway *traffic* is heavy during the rush hour>
syn travel

traffic *vb* **1 syn** see TRADE 1
2 to engage in illegal or disreputable business or activity <*trafficked* in drugs>
syn truck
rel deal (in), push, shove; black-market; bootleg, moonshine; fence
idiom handle (or deal in) under the counter

trafficable *adj syn* see MARKETABLE

trafficker *n syn* see MERCHANT

tragedy *n* **1 syn** see DISASTER
rel blow, shock
2 syn see MISFORTUNE
rel unluckiness; curse, lot; woe(s)
con prosperity, success
ant triumph

trail *vb* **1 syn** see DRAG 3
2 syn see DELAY 2
rel plod, trudge; falter, flag; halt
3 syn see TRACK 1
rel nose (out), sniff (out)
idiom follow a scent
4 syn see TAIL
5 syn see FOLLOW 2

trail *n* a rough course or way formed by or as if by repeated chance footsteps <an old Indian *trail*>
syn path, pathway, track, ‖trod
rel footpath, footwalk, footway

trailer *n* a motor-equipped or motor-drawn highway vehicle designed to serve as a place for dwelling or business <toured the country in a *trailer*>
syn camper, ‖caravan, house trailer, mobile home, motor home, recreational vehicle, RV
rel van

train *vb syn* see LURE

train *n* **1 syn** see ENTOURAGE
2 syn see SUCCESSION 2
rel course, run; line, thread; gradation, scale, tier

train *vb* **1 syn** see TEACH
rel cultivate, develop, shape; accustom, habituate; harden, season
2 syn see DIRECT 2

training *n syn* see EDUCATION 1

train off *vb syn* see SWERVE 1

traipse *vb* **1 syn** see WANDER 1
2 syn see WALK 1
3 syn see DRAG 3

traipse *n syn* see SLATTERN 1

trait *n* **1 syn** see QUALITY 1
2 syn see CHARACTERISTIC 1
rel denominator; attribute, quality

traitorous *adj syn* see FAITHLESS
rel apostate, renegade; mutinous, rebellious, seditious; alienated, disaffected, estranged; unpatriotic
con faithful; patriotic

traject *vb syn* see CONDUCT 4

tralatitious *adj syn* see TRADITIONAL 1
idiom handed down from time immemorial

tralucent *adj syn* see TRANSLUCENT 1

trammel *vb* **1 syn** see ENTANGLE 3
2 syn see HAMPER
rel circumscribe, confine, limit; bind, enchain, handcuff, manacle
3 syn see STULTIFY

tramp *vb* **1** to walk, tread, or step especially heavily <heard hobnailed boots *tramping* across the square>
syn trample, tromp; *compare* PLOD 1
rel march; thud; footslog, stodge, trudge; stamp, stomp
2 syn see HIKE 1
3 syn see TRAMPLE 2

tramp *n* **1 syn** see VAGABOND
2 syn see WANTON
3 a journey on foot or a walking trip <took a long *tramp* through the woods>
syn hike, walkabout
rel ramble, saunter, stroll, walk; traipse

tramper *n syn* see VAGABOND

trample *vb* **1 syn** see TRAMP 1
2 to tread on forcibly and repeatedly so as to crush or injure <was *trampled* to death by his horse>
syn stamp, stomp, tramp, tromp
rel ‖stoach, ‖stramp, ‖stunt; pound; tread (on); override

trance *vb syn* see TRANSPORT 2

trance *n syn* see REVERIE

tranquil *adj syn* see CALM 2
rel irenic, pacific, peaceful; quiet, still; stable, steady
con stirred up, troubled
ant agitated

tranquilize *vb syn* see CALM
rel hush; sedate; subdue
idiom pour oil on troubled waters
ant agitate

transaction *n syn* see CONTRACT

transcend *vb syn* see SURPASS 1
idiom go beyond, rise above

transcendent *adj* **1 syn** see SUPREME
rel accomplished, consummate, finished; entire, intact, perfect, whole
2 syn see ABSTRACT 1
rel absolute, ultimate; boundless, eternal, infinite

transcendental *adj* **1 syn** see OTHERWORLDLY 1
2 syn see ABSTRACT 1
rel supernatural, supranatural, ultimate

transfer *vb* **1 syn** see MOVE 4
rel carry, convey; relocate
2 syn see GIVE 3
rel convey, transmit
3 syn see TRANSFORM

4 to shift the title of (property) from one owner to another <to preserve the farm intact he *transfers* it to a single heir>
syn abalienate, alien, alienate, assign, cede, convey, deed, make over, remise, sign (over)
transfigure *vb syn* see TRANSFORM
transfix *vb syn* see IMPALE
transform *vb* to make over to a radically different form, composition, state, or disposition <the interaction of social forces *transforms* custom and produces a new tradition>
syn change, commute, convert, metamorphize, metamorphose, mutate, transfer, transfigure, translate, transmogrify, transmute, transpose, transubstantiate; *compare* CHANGE 1
rel alter; denature
transformation *n syn* see CONVERSION 2
transfuse *vb syn* see PERMEATE
transgress *vb* **1** *syn* see VIOLATE 1
2 *syn* see TRESPASS 1
transgression *n syn* see BREACH 1
rel erring, error, lapse, slip; overstepping; misbehavior, misstepping
transient *adj* lasting or staying only a short time <features of a *transient* culture now extinct>
syn ephemeral, evanescent, fleeting, fugacious, fugitive, impermanent, momentaneous, momentary, passing, short-lived, transitory, volatile; *compare* TEMPORARY 1
rel deciduous, flitting, unstable; temporal, temporary; insubstantial
idiom as transient as the clouds, here today and gone tomorrow
con lasting, perdurable, permanent, substantial; durable, stable
ant perpetual
transit *n* **1** *syn* see PASSAGE 1
2 *syn* see TRANSITION
3 *syn* see TRANSPORTATION 1
4 public conveyance of passengers or goods as a commercial enterprise <mass *transit*>
syn transport, transportation
transition *n* passage from one state or condition to another <the *transition* from boyhood to manhood>
syn alteration, passage, shift, transit
rel change, conversion, metamorphosis, transformation; development, evolution; growth, progress
transitional *adj* involving or characterized by passage from one stage, condition, or state to another <a *transitional* phase of social development>
syn transitive, transitory
rel developing, evolving; altering, changing, shifting
idiom being in a state of flux
transitive *adj syn* see TRANSITIONAL
transitory *adj* **1** *syn* see TRANSIENT
rel changeable; nonpermanent, unenduring; brief, short-term
2 *syn* see TRANSITIONAL

translate *vb* **1** to make a version of in another language <*translated* many secret documents from French to English>
syn put, render, turn
rel transliterate; transcribe; interpret; metaphrase, paraphrase
2 *syn* see TRANSFORM
translate (into) *vb syn* see PARAPHRASE
translation *n syn* see VERSION 1
translucent *adj* **1** *syn* see TRANSPARENT 1
2 *syn* see CLEAR 4
rel apparent, obvious, unmistakable
3 admitting and diffusing light so that objects beyond cannot be clearly distinguished <*translucent* amber>
syn clear, tralucent, translucid, transparent; *compare* TRANSPARENT 1
rel lucent, lucid
translucid *adj syn* see TRANSLUCENT 3
transmarine *adj syn* see OVERSEAS
transmigrate *vb syn* see MIGRATE
transmigratory *adj syn* see MIGRATORY
transmit *vb* **1** *syn* see SEND 1
rel convey, transport
2 *syn* see COMMUNICATE 1
3 *syn* see HAND DOWN
rel instill; transfuse, translate
4 *syn* see CONDUCT 4
transmogrify *vb syn* see TRANSFORM
transmundane *adj* *syn* see OTHERWORLDLY 1
transmute *vb syn* see TRANSFORM
transparent *adj* **1** admitting light without appreciable diffusion or distortion so that objects beyond are entirely visible <a sheet of *transparent* plastic>
syn clear, limpid, pellucid, see-through, translucent; *compare* TRANSLUCENT 3
rel crystal, crystalline, glassy; diaphanous
idiom clear as glass (or crystal)
con dark, smoky; cloudy, foggy hazy, misty, nubilous
ant opaque
2 *syn* see FILMY
3 *syn* see TRANSLUCENT 3
4 *syn* see CLEAR 4
rel distinguishable, recognizable; articulate, distinct, plain; unambiguous, unequivocal
con muddy, turbid
transpicuous *adj syn* see CLEAR 4
transpierce *vb syn* see IMPALE
transpire *vb* **1** *syn* see GET OUT 2
2 *syn* see HAPPEN 1
rel eventuate, result
transplace *vb syn* see REVERSE 1
rel remove; rearrange
transport *vb* **1** *syn* see CARRY 1
2 to carry away by strong and usually pleasant emotion <*transported* with ecstasy>
syn enrapture, enravish, entrance, ravish, trance
rel excite, move, provoke, quicken, stimulate; agitate, inflame, stir (up); elevate, uplift; carry away, delight, imparadise; ‖send, slay, thrill, ‖wow
3 *syn* see BANISH
transport *n* **1** *syn* see TRANSPORTATION 1
2 *syn* see ECSTASY
rel ardor, enthusiasm, fervor, passion; happiness

3 *syn* see VEHICLE 3

4 *syn* see TRANSIT 4

transportable *adj syn* see PORTABLE

transportation *n* 1 an act, process, or instance of transporting or being transported <arranged for the *transportation* of his luggage>

syn carriage, carrying, conveyance, transit, transport, transporting

rel hauling, moving

2 *syn* see VEHICLE 3

3 *syn* see TRANSIT 4

transporting *n syn* see TRANSPORTATION 1

transpose *vb* 1 *syn* see TRANSFORM

2 *syn* see TRANSLATE 1

3 *syn* see REVERSE 1

transubstantiate *vb syn* see TRANSFORM

transude *vb syn* see EXUDE

transversal *adj syn* see TRANSVERSE

rel bent; intersecting

transverse *vb syn* see TRAVERSE 4

transverse *adj* extended or lying in a direction across something else <the *transverse* arches of the cathedral ceiling>

syn crossing, crosswise, thwart, transversal, traverse

rel diagonal, oblique; across, crossed

con perpendicular

ant longitudinal

transversely *adv syn* see OVER 1

transversely *adv syn* see OVER 1

trap *n* 1 *syn* see LURE 2

rel artifice, feint, gambit, maneuver, ploy, ruse, stratagem, wile; birdlime, net; ambuscade, ambush; conspiracy, intrigue, machination, plot

2 *syn* see POLICEMAN

3 *syn* see MOUTH 1

trap *vb syn* see CATCH 3

rel mousetrap, snag

trapfall *n syn* see PITFALL

traps *n pl syn* see PERSONAL EFFECTS

trash *n* 1 *syn* see REFUSE

rel leavings

2 *syn* see NONSENSE 2

3 *syn* see RABBLE 2

trash *vb syn* see VANDALIZE

trash *vb syn* see PLOD 1

trashy *adj syn* see CHEAP 2

rel third-rate

trauma *n* intense mental, emotional, or physical disturbance resulting from stress <a broken home may produce persistent *trauma* in children>

syn shock, traumatism

rel blow, stress; traumatization; derangement, disturbance, upset; collapse

traumatism *n syn* see TRAUMA

travail *n* 1 *syn* see WORK 2

rel task; struggle

idiom toil and trouble

con relaxation, rest

2 *syn* see LABOR 2

rel contractions, pains

idiom birth throe

travel *vb* 1 *syn* see GO 1

rel move (on); voyage; roam, trek; explore

2 to journey over (as by conveyance) <certain roads can be *traveled* only on horseback>

syn cover, do, pass (over), track, traverse

rel cross

travel *n* 1 *syn* see PASSAGE 1

2 often **travels** *pl syn* see JOURNEY

3 *syn* see TRAFFIC 4

travelable *adj syn* see PASSABLE

traveler *n syn* see VAGABOND

traverse *n syn* see OBSTACLE

traverse *vb* 1 *syn* see RESIST

2 *syn* see DENY 4

rel oppose; dismiss; squash, squelch

3 *syn* see TRAVEL 2

4 to extend or lie across (something) <a highway *traversing* the entire state>

syn cross, track

rel crisscross, intersect, quarter

idiom cut across

5 to pass over, along, or to and fro especially on foot <deep in thought he *traversed* the terrace again and again>

syn perambulate, walk

rel peregrinate; track, tread; pace

traverse *adj syn* see TRANSVERSE

travesty *n* 1 *syn* see CARICATURE 2

rel mimicry; distortion, exaggeration; ridicule

2 *syn* see MOCKERY 2

travesty *vb syn* see MIMIC

treacherous *adj* 1 *syn* see FAITHLESS

rel undependable, unreliable, untrustworthy; betraying, deceptive, double-crossing, falsehearted, misleading, Punic

ant dependable; trustworthy

2 *syn* see DANGEROUS 1

rel deceptive, ticklish, tricky; precarious

treacherousness *n syn* see TREACHERY

ant dependability; trustworthiness

treachery *n* betrayal of a trust or confidence <corruption in public office is little short of *treachery*>

syn disloyalty, faithlessness, perfidiousness, perfidy, treacherousness, treason; *compare* INFIDELITY

rel falseheartedness, falseness; double cross, double-dealing; sellout

idiom dirty pool, dirty work at the crossroads

con incorruptibility, reliability; probity, rectitude, uprightness; constancy, fidelity, loyalty, staunchness

ant dependability; trustworthiness

tread *vb* 1 *syn* see DANCE 1

2 *syn* see WALK 1

rel march, stride; tromp

tread *n syn* see TRACK 1

treadmill *n syn* see ROUTINE

treason *n* 1 *syn* see TREACHERY

rel deceit, deceitfulness; duplicity; Machiavellianism

idiom breach of trust (or faith)

con allegiance, loyalty

ant staunchness

2 *syn* see SEDITION

rel disloyalty, treacherousness, treachery; high treason; misprision

ant allegiance

treasure *n syn* see FIND 1

rel catch, plum, prize; pearl

treasure *vb syn* see APPRECIATE 1

rel conserve, guard, preserve, save; idolize, revere, reverence, venerate, worship *idiom* hold dear

treasure–house *n* **1** *syn* see TREASURY 1
  2 *syn* see BONANZA
treasure trove *n* **1** *syn* see FIND 1
  2 *syn* see BONANZA
treasury *n* **1** a place (as a room or building) where valuables are kept <priceless gold candlesticks kept in the *treasury* of the cathedral>
  syn treasure-house
  rel archive(s), gallery, museum; depository, repository, storehouse
  idiom treasure room
  2 the place of deposit, retention, and disbursement of collected funds <the union *treasury* held emergency strike funds>
  syn chest, coffer, exchequer, war chest
  rel depositary, depository
  3 *syn* see BONANZA
treat *vb* **1** *syn* see CONFER 2
  rel consider, study, weigh; deliberate, reason, think
  2 to have to do with or behave toward (a person or thing) in a specified manner <*treat* all employees fairly and impartially>
  syn deal (with), handle, play, serve, take, use
  rel conduct, do with, manage, ‖wield; regard, respect; account, consider, hold; appraise, estimate, evaluate, rate, value
  idiom act with regard to, conduct oneself toward, do by
  3 to pay for another's entertainment <*treated* her to a few drinks>
  syn blow, set up, ‖shout, stand
  rel stake
  idiom go treat, pick up the tab for, stand treat
  4 to give medical treatment to <was *treated* by an eye specialist>
  syn doctor
  rel attend, care (for), minister (to), nurse
treat *n* *syn* see DELICACY
treatise *n* *syn* see DISCOURSE 2
  rel writing; book; argument, discussion, exposition
treaty *n* a formal, usually written, arrangement made by negotiation between two or more political authorities <the two nations finally signed an arms-limitation *treaty*>
  syn agreement, concord, convention, pact; *compare* CONTRACT
  rel arrangement, entente, understanding; bargain, contract; charter, compact, concordat, covenant; alliance, cartel, league; accord, reconciliation, settlement
treble *adj* *syn* see ACUTE 4
  ant bass
tree *vb* *syn* see CORNER
trek *n* *syn* see JOURNEY
tremble *vb* **1** *syn* see SHAKE 1
  rel shrink, wince
  idiom tremble like a leaf
  2 *syn* see SHAKE 2
trembling *adj* *syn* see TREMULOUS

---

syn synonym(s)   *rel* related word(s)
ant antonym(s)   *con* contrasted word(s)
idiom idiomatic equivalent(s)

‖ use limited; if in doubt, see a dictionary

---

  ant steady
tremendous *adj* **1** *syn* see FEARFUL 3
  2 *syn* see MONSTROUS 1
  3 *syn* see HUGE
  rel amazing, astounding, flabbergasting; terrific
  idiom great big
  ant minute
tremendousness *n* *syn* see ENORMITY 2
  rel bigness, largeness
tremor *n* *syn* see EARTHQUAKE
tremor *vb* **1** *syn* see SHAKE 1
  2 *syn* see SHAKE 2
tremorous *adj* *syn* see TREMULOUS
tremulant *adj* *syn* see TREMULOUS
tremulous *adj* characterized by or affected with trembling or tremors <her *tremulous* hands could scarcely hold the book>
  syn aquake, aquiver, ashake, ashiver, quaking, quaky, quivering, quivery, shaking, shaky, shivering, shivery, trembling, tremorous, tremulant
  rel aguish; aspen; palpitating; vibrating
  idiom having the shakes
  con firm, settled, stable, steady, unmoving
trench *n* a long narrow furrow in the ground <dig a *trench* for a sewer pipe>
  syn cut, ditch
  rel gully; drill, furrow; fosse; trough; drain, sink
trench *vb* *syn* see BORDER 3
trenchant *adj* **1** *syn* see INCISIVE
  rel piercing, probing, razor-sharp; sarcastic, sardonic, satiric; acrid; piquant, poignant, pungent
  2 *syn* see CAUSTIC 1
  rel scalding, scorching
trend *n* **1** *syn* see TENDENCY 1
  rel movement; flow; direction, orientation; swing, wind; progression
  2 *syn* see FASHION 3
‖**trendy** *adj* *syn* see STYLISH
  rel ultramodern
  con dated, outmoded
trepidation *n* *syn* see FEAR 1
  ant unapprehensiveness
trepidity *n* *syn* see FEAR 1
  ant intrepidity, intrepidness
trespass *n* *syn* see BREACH 1
  rel encroachment, entrenchment, invasion; intrusion, obtrusion
trespass *vb* **1** to commit an offense <exhibited scrupulous fairness even to those who *trespassed* against him>
  syn offend, sin, transgress
  rel deviate, err, lapse
  idiom do wrong by
  2 to make inroads on the property, territory, or rights of another <warned the hunters not to *trespass* on his land>
  syn encroach, entrench, infringe, invade
  rel enter, penetrate, pierce, probe; interlope, intermeddle, intrude; transgress
  idiom crash the gate
trestle *n* *syn* see SAWHORSE
triad *n* a union or group of three often closely related individuals or things <a *triad* of deities>
  syn threesome, trine, trinity, trio, triple, triumvirate, triune, troika; *compare* TRIUMVIRATE 1

trial *n* **1** the state or fact of being tested (as by suffering) <the Vietnam war period was a time of great national *trial*>
syn affliction, calvary, cross, crucible, ordeal, tribulation, visitation
rel agony, distress, misery, suffering; anguish, grief, heartbreak, sorrow, woe; adversity, misfortune; difficulty, hardship, rigor, vicissitude
idiom crown of thorns, fiery ordeal, trial and tribulation
2 a source of vexation or annoyance <living in a crowded hotel is a real *trial*>
syn care, trouble, worry
rel complication, difficulty; annoyance, distress, misfortune; ordeal
3 *syn* see EXPERIMENT
4 *syn* see ATTEMPT
trial *adj syn* see EXPERIMENTAL 2
trial and error *n syn* see EXPERIMENT
trial balloon *n syn* see FEELER
rel trial
trial run *n syn* see EXPERIMENT
tribe *n syn* see FAMILY 1
tribulation *n syn* see TRIAL 1
rel oppression, persecution, wronging
tribunal *n syn* see COURT 2
tributary *adj syn* see SUBORDINATE
rel conquered, subdued, subjugated, vanquished; accessory, minor; satellite
tribute *n* **1** *syn* see TESTIMONIAL 2
rel recognition; monument
2 *syn* see ENCOMIUM
trice *n syn* see INSTANT 1
trick *n* **1** an indirect, ingenious, and often cunning means to gain an end <used every *trick* in the bag to cover up the scandal>
syn artifice, chouse, device, feint, gambit, gimmick, jig, maneuver, play, ploy, ‖prat, ruse, shenanigan, sleight, stratagem, whizzer, wile; *compare* PRANK
rel contrivance, craft, expediency; blind, bluff, diversion, dodge, dodgery, red herring; curve, deception, sham, stall; fraud, ‖rort, scheme, shift, skin game
2 *syn* see PRANK
rel boutade; escapade; practical joke
3 an ingenious or dexterous act or procedure designed to puzzle or amuse <a juggler's *trick*>
syn feat, stunt
rel accomplishment
4 tricks *pl syn* see PERSONAL EFFECTS
5 *syn* see HANG
6 *syn* see HABIT 1
7 *syn* see SPELL
trick *adj* somewhat defective and inclined to function abnormally on occasion <a *trick* lock that doesn't always catch>
syn tricky, undependable
rel catchy, touchy; unreliable, untrustworthy; insecure, shaky, unstable; defective, dysfunctioning, malfunctioning
trick *vb syn* see DUPE
rel outtrick, outtrump, outwit; have
idiom take (someone) for a ride
trick (off, out, *or up*) *vb syn* see DRESS UP 1
trickery *n syn* see DECEPTION 1
rel double-cross; underhandedness
idiom underhand dealing

trickle *vb syn* see DRIP
ant gush
trickster *n* **1** *syn* see SWINDLER
idiom gyp artist
2 *syn* see MAGICIAN 2
tricksy *adj syn* see TIGHT 4
tricky *adj* **1** *syn* see SLY 2
rel deceptive, delusive; delusory, misleading; deceitful, dishonest
2 *syn* see UNSTABLE 2
rel catchy, difficult, trappy; quirky
3 *syn* see DELICATE 7
4 *syn* see TRICK
tried *adj syn* see RELIABLE 1
rel constant, faithful, staunch, steadfast; demonstrated, proved, tested; approved, certified
ant untried
tried and true *adj syn* see RELIABLE 1
trifle *n* **1** *syn* see KNICKKNACK
rel rope yarn
2 *syn* see HINT 2
trifle *vb* **1** to behave amorously without serious intent <was interested only in *trifling* with her, not marrying her>
syn coquet, dally, flirt, fool, lead on, string along, toy, wanton
rel play (with); mess around, ‖muck, mucker; philander; mash
2 *syn* see FIDDLE 1
trifle (away) *vb syn* see WASTE 2
rel misuse; burn (up); use up
con retain, save
trifling *n syn* see SMALL TALK
trifling *adj syn* see PETTY 2
rel banal, inane, insipid, jejune, vapid; empty, frivolous, hollow, idle, nugatory, otiose, vain; insignificant, unimportant
trig *adj* **1** *syn* see NEAT 2
2 *syn* see STYLISH
‖**3** *syn* see FULL 1
triggerman *n syn* see ASSASSIN
trill *vb syn* see DRIP
trillion *n syn* see SCAD
trim *vb* **1** *syn* see ADORN
2 *syn* see WHIP 2
rel ‖skin
3 *syn* see CUT 6
trim *adj* **1** *syn* see NEAT 2
rel clean, clean-cut, fit, spruce; shapely, streamlined, symmetrical
con disordered, shapeless, straggly
ant frowsy
2 *syn* see SHAPELY
trim *n syn* see ORDER 10
rel commission; whack
trine *n syn* see TRIAD
trinity *n syn* see TRIAD
trinket *n syn* see KNICKKNACK
rel plaything, frippery, showpiece; tinsel; trinketry, trinkums
trio *n syn* see TRIAD
trip *vb syn* see SKIP 1
trip *n* **1** a single passage of a vehicle between two points or to a point and return <a regular bus *trip* to and from the city>
syn run; *compare* DRIVE 1, JOURNEY, TOUR 2
rel drive; progress
2 *syn* see JOURNEY

rel run

3 *syn* see ERROR 2

tripes *n pl syn* see ENTRAILS

triple *n syn* see TRIAD

tripped out *adj syn* see DRUGGED

‖**tripper** *n syn* see TOURIST

triste *adj syn* see SAD 2

trite *adj* used or occurring so often as to have lost interest, freshness, or force <unrequited love has become a *trite* theme>
syn bathetic, chain, cliché, clichéd, commonplace, corny, hack, hackneyed, musty, old hat, shopworn, stale, stereotyped, stereotypical, threadbare, timeworn, tired, twice-told, warmed-over, well-worn, worn-out
rel common, ordinary; banal, dull, flat, jejune, mildewed, vapid; bedridden, drained, exhausted, used-up; bromidic, platitudinous, prosaic, ready-made, set, stock
con first, new, seminal; novel, unique; creative, imaginative; uncopied; memorable; distinctive
ant fresh, original

triturate *vb syn* see PULVERIZE 1

triumph *n* **1** *syn* see VICTORY 1
rel ascendancy, gain; surmounting, vanquishing, vanquishment
ant defeat
2 *syn* see EXULTATION
rel joy; festivity, merriment, reveling

triumph *vb* **1** *syn* see EXULT
rel gloat
2 *syn* see WIN 1
rel prosper, succeed; conquer, surmount
idiom get the best (*or* better) of
con lose
ant fail
3 *syn* see CONQUER 2

triumphal *adj syn* see EXULTANT

triumphant *adj syn* see EXULTANT
rel rejoicing, triumphing

triumvirate *n* **1** an administrative or ruling body of three <a monarchy replaced by a *triumvirate* of generals>
syn troika; compare TRIAD
rel junta
2 *syn* see TRIAD

triune *n syn* see TRIAD

trivia *n pl but sometimes sing in constr* unimportant matters <they became bored with the *trivia* of everyday life>
syn minutia(e), small beer, small change, small potato(es), triviality

trivial *adj* **1** *syn* see LITTLE 3
rel slight; negligible
idiom no great shakes
con considerable
ant momentous, weighty
2 *syn* see PETTY 2
rel captious, fribbling, frivolous; shallow, superficial

triviality *n syn* see TRIVIA
rel shallowness, superficiality, unimportance

con basic(s), essential(s), fundamental(s)

‖**trod** *n syn* see TRAIL

troika *n* **1** *syn* see TRIUMVIRATE 1
2 *syn* see TRIAD

trollop *n syn* see WANTON
idiom (a) fast number

trollop *vb syn* see SLOUCH

tromp *vb* **1** *syn* see TRAMP 1
2 *syn* see HIKE 1
rel slog, trudge
3 *syn* see TRAMPLE 2
4 *syn* see BEAT 1

troop *n* **1** *syn* see COMPANY 4
rel assemblage, assembly, collection, gathering; army, host, legion, multitude
2 *troops* *pl* members of a nation's military units <Marines, GI's, and Seabees were among the *troops* sent to war>
syn armed forces, forces, military, servicemen
rel combatants; soldiers, troopers
idiom fighting men

troop *vb syn* see WALK 1

trophy *n syn* see REMEMBRANCE 3

tropic *adj syn* see TROPICAL
rel baking, broiling, scorching, sweltering
con arctic

tropical *adj* of, relating to, or occurring in the tropics <*tropical* fruits>
syn tropic
rel equatorial, semitropical, subtropical; warm; hot, sultry, torrid
con temperate

tropical cyclone *n syn* see HURRICANE

tropical storm *n syn* see HURRICANE

trot *n* **1** *syn* see HAG 2
2 *syn* see PONY
‖**3** *trots* *pl* *syn* see DIARRHEA

troth *n syn* see ENGAGEMENT 2

trot out *vb syn* see SHOW 4

troubadour *n syn* see BARD 1
rel balladist; rhymer, rhymester

trouble *vb* **1** to cause to be uneasy or upset <sorrows that *trouble* the strongest of men>
syn ail, cark, distress, upset, worry
rel agitate, concern, discompose, disquiet, disturb, perturb, rowel, ‖worrit; annoy, bother, fret, irk, vex; ‖destroy, haunt
2 *syn* see TRY 2
rel upset, worry; discompose, disconcert, disturb; harry, irritate; afflict, torment
3 *syn* see INCONVENIENCE
rel annoy, pester, plague, worry; impose (on *or* upon), intrude

trouble *n* **1** *syn* see TRIAL 2
2 *syn* see EFFORT 1
rel ado, bustle, flurry, fuss, pother; bother, inconvenience; difficulty, hardship, rigor; strain, stress
3 a condition of annoyance, disturbance, or distress <got him into *trouble* by repeating gossip>
syn Dutch, hot water
rel bind, difficulty, predicament

troubled *adj syn* see DISTRAUGHT

troublemaker *n* a person who consciously or unconsciously causes trouble <a *troublemaker* who set father against daughter>
syn bad actor, mischief-maker
rel agitator, inciter, inflamer, instigator

---

syn synonym(s)   *rel* related word(s)
ant antonym(s)   *con* contrasted word(s)
idiom idiomatic equivalent(s)
‖ use limited; if in doubt, see a dictionary

troublesome *adj* giving trouble or anxiety
<a *troublesome* infection>
syn mean, pesky, troublous, ugly, vexatious, wicked
rel annoying, bothersome, vexing; alarming, disquieting, disturbing, upsetting; infestive; painful
con untroublesome
ant innocuous

troublesomeness *n syn* see INCONVENIENCE
rel difficulty; irritation, vexation

troublous *adj syn* see TROUBLESOME
rel troubling

trounce *vb syn* see WHIP 2
idiom walk all over

trouncing *n syn* see DEFEAT 1

troupe *n syn* see COMPANY 4

trouper *n syn* see ACTOR 1
rel entertainer; artiste

trove *n syn* see ACCUMULATION

truce *n* a suspension of or an agreement for suspending hostilities <the high command ordered a *truce* for the holidays>
syn armistice, cease-fire
rel break, ‖breather, letup, lull, pause, respite; de-escalation, ‖wind-down; accord, reconciliation; peace

truck *vb* 1 *syn* see TRADE 1
rel handle; peddle, retail
2 *syn* see TRAFFIC 2
idiom have truck with

truck *n syn* see COMMERCE 2

truckle *vb syn* see FAWN
rel knuckle down, knuckle under, succumb; follow, tag, tail, trail
idiom kiss (*or* lick) one's boots, lick the feet of, make a doormat of oneself

truckler *n syn* see SYCOPHANT

truckling *adj syn* see FAWNING

truculent *adj* 1 *syn* see FIERCE 1
rel browbeating, bullying, cowing, intimidating; frightening, terrifying, terrorizing
2 *syn* see ABUSIVE
rel caustic, mordacious, mordant, scathing, sharp, trenchant; harsh, rough, severe; vitriolic
3 *syn* see BELLIGERENT

trudge *vb syn* see PLOD 1

true *adj* 1 *syn* see FAITHFUL 1
rel sincere, unfeigned, whole-hearted, whole-souled
ant false, fickle
2 *syn* see UPRIGHT 2
rel creditable, estimable, worthy; high-principled, right-minded, truehearted
3 conformable to fact or to a standard, rule, or model <gave a *true* account of the accident>
syn faithful, just, right, strict, undistorted, veracious, veridical
rel careful, conscientious, meticulous, punctilious, scrupulous; finicky, fussy, overnice; accurate, precise; absolute, mathematical
idiom true to the letter
con imprecise, inaccurate, incorrect, inexact; erroneous, false
ant untrue
4 *syn* see GENUINE 3
con deceitful

5 *syn* see AUTHENTIC 2
rel genuine, kosher; sincere, unfaked, unfeigned
con artificial, fake, faked, feigned; insincere
ant false
6 *syn* see REAL 3
rel natural, normal, regular, typical
ant false
7 being such as it should be <meanings presented in their *true* relationship>
syn appropriate, desired, fitting, proper
rel acceptable; applicable, befitting, likely, suitable
con inappropriate, unfitting
8 being such by right <the *true* heir>
syn legitimate, rightful
rel lawful, legal, proper
con illegitimate, spurious, suppositious
ant false
9 that can be relied on <polls can provide a *true* projection of public sentiment>
syn authoritative, dependable, trustable, trustworthy
rel meaningful, significant; expressive, indicative, suggestive
con independable, undependable, untrustworthy; doubtful, questionable

truelove *n* 1 *syn* see GIRL FRIEND 2
2 *syn* see BOYFRIEND 2
idiom one and only

true–tongued *adj syn* see TRUTHFUL

truism *n* 1 *syn* see VERACITY 2
2 *syn* see MAXIM
3 *syn* see COMMONPLACE

trull *n syn* see WANTON

truly *adv* 1 *syn* see VERY 2
rel absolutely, positively
2 *syn* see EVEN 3
rel confidently, really
3 *syn* see WELL 7
rel probably; surely

trump *n syn* see TRUMP CARD

trump *vb syn* see SURPASS 1

trump card *n* something decisive or telling often held in reserve <kept a political *trump card* up her sleeve till election eve>
syn clincher, trump
rel ace; coup, coup de grace, coup de main
idiom ace in the hole

trumpery *n syn* see NONSENSE 2

trumpery *adj syn* see CHEAP 2

trumpet *vb syn* see TOUT

truncate *vb syn* see TOP 1
rel abbreviate, abridge; cut off, lop; shear

truncheon *n syn* see CUDGEL

trust *n* 1 complete assurance and certitude regarding the character, ability, strength, or truth of someone or something <they continue to have *trust* in his judgment>
syn confidence, dependence, faith, hope, reliance, stock
rel assurance, certainty, certitude, conviction; belief, credence, credit; positiveness, sureness; entrustment; overconfidence, oversureness
con doubt, dubiety, dubiosity, skepticism, suspicion, uncertainty
ant mistrust
2 *syn* see SYNDICATE
3 *syn* see CUSTODY

trust *vb syn* see ENTRUST 1
  rel commit, consign, hand over
trust (in *or* to) *vb syn* see RELY (on *or* upon)
  rel assume, imagine, presume
  idiom have no reservations
trustable *adj syn* see TRUE 9
  ant trustless
trustless *adj syn* see UNRELIABLE 1
  rel unworthy; unfaithful; suspect, suspicious; dishonest; deceitful; treacherous
  ant trustable, trustworthy
trustworthy *adj* 1 *syn* see RELIABLE 1
  rel truthful, veracious; honest, scrupulous, upright
  con deceitful; dishonest
  ant untrustworthy
  2 *syn* see TRUE 9
  rel accurate, exact; valid; realistic
  con inaccurate, inexact; invalid; unrealistic; suspect
  ant untrustworthy
  3 *syn* see AUTHENTIC 1
trusty *adj* 1 *syn* see RELIABLE 1
  rel predictable, stable; firm, sound; responsible, ‖straight
  con capricious
  ant untrusty
  2 *syn* see AUTHENTIC 1
  ant untrusty
truth *n* 1 *syn* see VERACITY 1
  rel precision, rightness, trueness; authenticity, genuineness, veritableness; candor
  idiom unvarnished truth (*or* truthfulness)
  con equivocation, evasion, hedging; deception, deceptiveness, falseness
  ant falsity, untruth
  2 *syn* see VERACITY 2
  rel reality
  idiom (the) gospel truth, (the) truth of the matter
  ant lie, untruth
truthful *adj* observant of *or* telling the truth <a *truthful* witness>
  syn true-tongued, truth-speaking, truthtelling, veracious, veridical
  rel candid, frank, honest, sincere; accurate, factual; real, realistic
  con false, insincere, truthless, uncandid; inaccurate; unrealistic
  ant untruthful
truthfulness *n syn* see VERACITY 1
  ant untruthfulness
truthlessness *n syn* see MENDACITY
truth-speaking *adj syn* see TRUTHFUL
truth-telling *adj syn* see TRUTHFUL
try *vb* 1 to subject to testing <*try* the door to be sure it's locked>
  syn check, examine, prove, test
  rel inspect, scrutinize; appraise, judge, weigh
  idiom make trial of, put to proof, put to the test
  2 to subject to stress <the fine print *tried* her eyes>
  syn distress, harass, irk, pain, strain, stress, trouble

  rel annoy, bother, vex
  3 *syn* see AFFLICT
  4 *syn* see PROVE 1
  5 to make an effort to do or accomplish something <the baby is *trying* to walk>
  syn assay, attempt, endeavor, essay, offer, seek, strive, struggle, undertake
  rel aim, aspire, hope, strike
  idiom do one's best (*or* utmost) to, have a go at
try (out) *vb syn* see EXPERIMENT
  rel examine, inspect, scrutinize; demonstrate, prove
  idiom cut and try, put to trial, try for size
try *n* 1 *syn* see ATTEMPT
  2 *syn* see FLING 1
  rel dab, jab
trying *adj* 1 *syn* see TIGHT 4
  rel annoying, bothersome, irksome, irritating, troublesome, vexing; strenuous; sticky, tricky
  2 *syn* see ONEROUS
try on *vb syn* see EXPERIMENT
tryst *n syn* see ENGAGEMENT 3
‖**tub** *n syn* see FATTY
tub *vb syn* see BATHE 1
tubby *adj syn* see ROTUND 2
  idiom plump as a dumpling (*or* partridge)
tube *n syn* see TELEVISION
tuberculosis *n* a communicable bacterial disease typically marked by wasting, fever, and formation of cheesy tubercles often in the lungs <Victorian heroines fading away with *tuberculosis*>
  syn consumption, phthisis, TB, white plague
tuck (in) *vb syn* see BED
  rel snug (down *or* up), snuggle
‖**tuck** *n syn* see FOOD 1
tuck *n syn* see ENERGY 1
‖**tucked up** *adj syn* see CRAMPED
tucker *vb syn* see EXHAUST 3
  rel gruel; wilt; drop
  idiom take the tuck out of
tug *vb* 1 *syn* see CONTEND 1
  2 *syn* see LABOR 1
  3 *syn* see PULL 2
tug-of-war *n syn* see CONTEST 1
tuition *n syn* see EDUCATION 1
tumble *vb* 1 *syn* see FALL 2
  rel trip; come (down), descend
  2 *syn* see PLUMMET
  rel depreciate; sag, slump
  idiom take a downward spiral, take a nosedive
  3 *syn* see HAPPEN 2
  4 *syn* see DISCOVER 3
  5 *syn* see OVERTHROW 2
  6 *syn* see FELL 1
  7 *syn* see CONFUSE 5
  8 *syn* see DISORDER 1
tumble (to) *vb syn* see APPREHEND 1
tumble *n syn* see CLUTTER 2
tumescent *adj* 1 *syn* see INFLATED
  rel bloated; bulging
  2 *syn* see RHETORICAL
tumid *adj* 1 *syn* see INFLATED
  rel dilated, distended, expanded, swollen
  2 *syn* see RHETORICAL
tummy *n syn* see ABDOMEN

---

syn synonym(s)   *rel* related word(s)
ant antonym(s)   *con* contrasted word(s)
idiom idiomatic equivalent(s)
‖ use limited; if in doubt, see a dictionary

tumulary *adj syn* see SEPULCHRAL 1

tumult *n* **1** *syn* see COMMOTION 1
  rel disturbance, turmoil, uproar
  2 *syn* see COMMOTION 2
  rel babel, din, hullabaloo, pandemonium, racket
  con calm, hush, lull, quietude
  3 *syn* see COMMOTION 2
  rel seething; disorder, unsettlement; ferment, maelstrom, paroxysm
  4 *syn* see DIN
  rel noise; ‖corroboree
  idiom ‖all hell broken loose

tumultuous *adj syn* see TURBULENT 1

tumultuously *adv syn* see HARD 2

tun *n syn* see CASK
  rel vat

tune *n* **1** *syn* see MELODY
  rel carol; composition, number, piece
  2 *syn* see HARMONY 1
  3 *syn* see HARMONY 2
  4 *syn* see ORDER 4

tune *vb* **1** *syn* see SING 1
  2 *syn* see HARMONIZE 3
  rel fix, regulate
  3 to adjust with respect to resonance <*tune* a TV set to a local station>
  syn dial

tune (up) *vb syn* see ADJUST 2

tuned *adj syn* see MELODIOUS 2

tuneful *adj* **1** *syn* see MELODIOUS 2
  2 *syn* see MELODIOUS 1
  ant tuneless

tunk *vb syn* see TAP 1

turbid *adj* clouded with or as if with roiled sediment <a *turbid* stream>
  syn muddy, riley, roily
  rel dark, dense, obscure; mucky, thick; clouded, cloudy, murky, opaque, smoky; dull
  con translucent; lucid, pellucid, transparent; crystal, crystalline; clean, pure, undefiled
  ant clear, limpid

turbulence *n syn* see COMMOTION 2
  rel babel, din, pandemonium, uproar; unruliness; fight, fracas
  con calmness, composure, placidity, quiet

turbulent *adj* **1** given to insubordination and disorder <a *turbulent* and irresponsible group>
  syn boisterous, disorderly, rambunctious, raucous, rowdy, rowdydowdy, rowdyish, rumbustious, termagant, tumultuous, unruly; *compare* UNRULY 1
  rel mutinous; fast, roisterous, uncontrollable, uninhibited, wild; clamorous, loudmouthed; brawling, quarrelsome, rough, roughhouse; hell-for-leather, rip-roaring, tempestuous
  con calm, placid, quiet, tranquil; controlled, orderly, peaceful, restrained
  2 *syn* see WILD 6
  rel agitated, convulsed, moiling, stirred up; boiling, roily, ruffled, swirling; howling, riotous, roaring; tempest-tossed

turbulently *adv syn* see HARD 2
  rel blusteringly

turf *n syn* see TERRAIN 2
  rel area, region, sphere

turgid *adj* **1** *syn* see INFLATED 1
  rel swelling, turgescent
  2 *syn* see RHETORICAL

turmoil *n* **1** *syn* see COMMOTION 2
  rel jitteriness, nervousness, restlessness, unease, uneasiness; disorder, disruption; moil; riot, strife, uproar
  2 *syn* see UNREST
  rel distress; anxiety, anxiousness
  ant tranquillity
  3 *syn* see COMMOTION 4

turn *vb* **1** to move or cause to move in a curved or circular path on or as if on an axis <*turned* the wheel sharply to avoid a collision>
  syn circle, circumduct, gyrate, gyre, revolve, roll, rotate; *compare* SPIN 1
  rel orbit; pirouette, spin, twirl, whirl; twist, weave, wind; circulate, eddy, oscillate, sway, swing, vibrate
  2 *syn* see SPRAIN
  3 *syn* see REVERSE 1
  4 *syn* see PLOW
  5 *syn* see UPSET 5
  rel discompose, undo; unbalance
  6 to change or cause to change course or direction <*turned* his car down a side road>
  syn avert, deflect, divert, pivot, sheer, swing, veer, volte-face, wheel, whip, whirl; *compare* SHUNT 1
  rel depart, detract, deviate, digress, diverge; move, shift; switch, swivel, twist, zigzag; call off, double (back), reverse, shunt, sidetrack; bend, curve, sway; detour, rechannel, turn away
  7 *syn* see DIRECT 2
  con call off, detract (from), distract, divert (from), draw (away)
  8 *syn* see ADDRESS 3
  rel employ, use; plunge (into), undertake
  idiom turn one's hand (or energies) to
  con avoid, dodge, shy (away)
  9 *syn* see CURDLE
  10 *syn* see DECAY
  11 *syn* see CHANGE 1
  12 *syn* see TRANSLATE 1
  13 *syn* see DULL 3
  14 *syn* see SPIN 2
  15 *syn* see DEFECT
  16 *syn* see RESORT 2
  17 *syn* see BECOME 1
  rel change (into), pass (into)

turn (on *or* upon) *vb syn* see DEPEND (on *or* upon) 1

turn *n* **1** *syn* see REVOLUTION 1
  2 an often sudden change in course or trend <his health took a *turn* for the better>
  syn bend, deflection, deviation, double, shift, tack, yaw
  rel course, drift, trend
  3 *syn* see REVERSAL 1
  4 a point at which a change of course takes place <hidden by a *turn* in the road>
  syn angle, bend, bow, flection, flexure, turning
  rel curve, twist; corner
  5 *syn* see WALK 1
  6 *syn* see DRIVE 1
  7 *syn* see SPELL 1
  8 *syn* see CHANGE 1

9 *syn* see GIFT 2
rel bias, disposition, predisposition
10 an unusual, unexpected, or special interpretation or construction <gave a new *turn* to the old joke>
syn twist
rel construction, interpretation; device, gimmick, trick
11 *syn* see ATTACK 3

turnabout *n* **1** *syn* see REVERSAL 1
2 *syn* see RENEGADE
rel backslider, coward, quitter, turnback

turn back *vb syn* see RETURN 1

turncoat *n syn* see RENEGADE
rel deserter, straggler; betrayer, quisler, quisling, traitor; spy

turn down *vb syn* see DECLINE 4

turned on *adj syn* see DRUGGED

turn in *vb syn* see RETIRE 4
ant turn out

turning *n* **1** *syn* see TURN 4
2 *syn* see DEVIATION 1
rel detour
3 *syn* see REVERSAL 1

turning point *n syn* see JUNCTURE 2
rel climax, culmination, peak
idiom moment of truth

turnip *n syn* see DUNCE

turn off *vb* **1** *syn* see DISMISS 3
2 *syn* see HANG 2

turn out *vb* **1** *syn* see FURNISH 1
rel deck, dress (out)
2 *syn* see BEAR 9
3 *syn* see ROLL OUT

turnout *n* **1** *syn* see COSTUME
2 *syn* see OUTPUT

turn over *vb* **1** *syn* see OVERTURN 1
2 *syn* see PLOW
3 *syn* see PONDER 2
idiom turn over in one's mind
4 *syn* see GIVE 3
rel assign, confer, consign, convey, delegate, relegate; give up, relinquish, ‖turn up
idiom come across with, put into the hands of
con get back, reclaim, recover, regain, retrieve, take back
5 *syn* see COMMIT 1

turnover *n syn* see SHAKE-UP

turn up *vb* **1** *syn* see FIND 1
rel see; uncover, unearth; track (down)
idiom come across
‖**2** *syn* see RELINQUISH
3 to arrive when or where expected <*turned* up for dinner promptly at seven o'clock>
syn show, show up
rel appear, arrive, come, materialize; blow in, pop (in), punch in, roll (in), weigh in
idiom make one's appearance, put in an appearance
4 *syn* see COME 1

turtledove *n syn* see SWEETHEART 1

tussle *vb syn* see WRESTLE
rel scrap, skirmish, spar; hassle
idiom get into a tussle

---

tutelage *n syn* see EDUCATION 1

TV *n syn* see TELEVISION

twaddle *n syn* see NONSENSE 2
rel gabble; wish-wash

twaddle *vb* **1** *syn* see BABBLE 2
2 *syn* see CHAT 1

twang *n syn* see HINT 2

‖**twat** *n syn* see BUTTOCKS

tweedle *vb syn* see CHIRP

tween *prep syn* see BETWEEN 2

tweet *vb syn* see CHIRP

twerp *n* a usually young or insignificant upstart who meddles beyond his competence or concern <ignored the protests of that insolent *twerp*>
syn pup, puppy, sprat, squirt, ‖squit
rel upstart; ‖squib; fool, jerk, ‖twit; brat
idiom small-time big shot

twice-told *adj syn* see TRITE

twiddle *vb syn* see FIDDLE 1
rel finger, manipulate, palpate; monkey (with), toy (with)
idiom twiddle around with

twiddle *vb syn* see CHAT 1

twig *vb* **1** *syn* see SEE 1
2 *syn* see APPREHEND 1

‖**twig** *n syn* see FASHION 3

twiggy *adj syn* see THIN 1

twilight *n* **1** *syn* see EVENING 1
rel afterglow, afterlight
2 *syn* see EVENING 1
rel decline; end

twin *adj* made up of two very closely matched or identical aspects, elements, individuals, or parts <the *twin* threats of inflation and recession>
syn double, dual, paired
rel bifold, binary, twofold; identical, matched, matching; like, similar
con independent, separate; dissimilar, unlike

twin *n syn* see MATE 5

twine *vb syn* see WIND 2
rel interweave; undulate; enmesh, entangle, tangle

twinge *n syn* see PAIN 1

twinkle *vb* **1** *syn* see BLINK 2
rel illuminate, light, light up; shine
2 *syn* see FLASH 1
3 *syn* see WINK

twinkle *n* **1** *syn* see INSTANT 1
2 *syn* see FLASH 1

twinkling *n syn* see INSTANT 1
idiom the twinkling of an eye

twirl *vb syn* see SPIN 1

twist *vb* **1** *syn* see SPRAIN
2 *syn* see MISREPRESENT
3 *syn* see WIND 2
ant untwist

twist *n syn* see TURN 10

twister *n syn* see TORNADO

twisting *adj syn* see CROOKED 1

twit *vb syn* see RIDICULE
rel jive, josh, tease; chide, reproach, reprove; blame, censure, reprehend

twitch *vb syn* see JERK
rel clutch, grasp, pluck, snatch; nip, pinch

twitter *vb* **1** *syn* see CHIRP
2 *syn* see CHAT 1
3 *syn* see SHAKE 1

---

syn synonym(s)   *rel* related word(s)
ant antonym(s)   *con* contrasted word(s)
idiom idiomatic equivalent(s)
‖ use limited; if in doubt, see a dictionary

twittery adj syn see NERVOUS
  rel flustered; twittering
  idiom all atwitter, all fluttery, all of a twitter
twitty adj syn see IRRITABLE
twixt prep syn see BETWEEN 2
twofold adj 1 having two parts, elements, or aspects <the problem is *twofold*: to find gasoline and to be able to pay for it>
  syn bifold, binary, double, double-barreled, dual, dualistic, duple, duplex
  rel dyadic; paired, twin
  con distinct, separate
  2 being twice as large, as great, or as many <a *twofold* increase in enrollment>
  syn double, double-barreled
  idiom twice over
two-handed adj 1 designed for or requiring the use of both hands <a *two-handed* sword>
  syn bimanual
  2 having or being efficient with two hands <*two-handed* tennis players are rare>
  syn ambidextrous, bimanual
twosome n syn see COUPLE
two-time vb syn see DECEIVE
two-wheeler n syn see BICYCLE
tycoon n syn see MAGNATE
tyke n syn see DOG 1
type n a number of individuals thought of as a group because of a common quality or qualities <political radicals of whatever *type*>
  syn breed, cast, character, class, cut, description, feather, ilk, kidney, kind, lot, mold, nature, order, persuasion, sort, species, stamp, stripe, variety, way
  rel blazon, brand, form; sample, specimen; category, group, rubric
typhoon n syn see HURRICANE
typic adj syn see GENERAL 1
  rel average, ordinary
typical adj 1 constituting or having the nature of a type <a *typical* instance of guilt by association>
  syn archetypal, classic, classical, exemplary, ideal, model, paradigmatic, prototypal,

prototypical, quintessential, representative
  rel characteristic; emblematic, symbolic; absolute, consummate, perfect
  con uncharacteristic; unusual
  ant atypical, untypical
  2 syn see GENERAL 1
  rel old hat, unexceptional; collective, quintessential, representative; characteristic, specific
  idiom being the rule and not the exception
  con distinctive; exceptional, extraordinary, unusual; abnormal
  ant atypical, untypical
typification n syn see ALLEGORY 1
typify vb 1 syn see REPRESENT 2
  2 syn see EPITOMIZE 2
  rel model
tyrannical adj syn see ABSOLUTE 4
  rel brutal, harsh, oppressive; roughshod
tyrannize vb to exercise arbitrary power over often with unjust and oppressive severity <a country *tyrannized* by a dictator and his secret police>
  syn despotize
  rel dictate, dominate, domineer, overlord; crush, oppress, trample; shackle; terrorize
tyrannous adj syn see ABSOLUTE 4
  rel lordly; fascistic, totalitarian
tyranny n absolute government in which unlimited power is vested in a single usually severe and oppressive ruler <the *tyranny* of Hitler>
  syn autocracy, despotism, dictatorship, totalitarianism
  rel monocracy; absolutism, authoritarianism, fascism; domination, oppression, totality; terrorism
  idiom iron heel (or boot)
  con democracy; freedom; anarchy
tyrant n a ruler who exercises absolute power oppressively and brutally <Hitler and Stalin as twentieth-century *tyrants*>
  syn despot, dictator, duce, oppressor, strong man
  rel autocrat, totalitarian
  idiom man on horseback
tyro n 1 syn see AMATEUR 2
  2 syn see NOVICE

U

uberrima fides n syn see GOOD FAITH
ubiquitous adj syn see OMNIPRESENT
ugly adj 1 syn see GRAVE 3
  2 unpleasing to the sight <an *ugly* decaying neighborhood>
  syn hideous, ill-favored, ill-looking, unbeautiful, uncomely, unsightly
  rel homely, plain; bizarre, grotesque; repelling, repugnant, repulsive; unattractive, uninviting, unpleasing, unprepossessing
  idiom homely as a mud (or hedge) fence, not

much to look at, short on looks
  con comely, fair, good-looking, handsome, lovely, pretty; attractive, prepossessing
  ant beautiful
  3 syn see BASE 3
  4 syn see TROUBLESOME
  5 syn see SULLEN
ukase n syn see EDICT 1
ulterior adj lying behind what is manifest or avowed <an *ulterior* motive>
  syn buried, concealed, covert, guarded, hidden, obscured, privy, shrouded

rel ambiguous, cryptic, dark, enigmatic, equivocal, obscure
idiom hidden under the rug, kept behind a screen, under cover, under wraps
con clear, open, overt, plain, straightforward; explicit, expressed

ultimate *adj* 1 *syn* see LAST
2 *syn* see SUPREME
3 being so fundamental as to stand at the extreme limit of the actually or conceivably knowable <*ultimate* realities>
syn absolute, categorical
rel empyreal, empyrean, sublime, transcendental; exalted, grand, lofty

ultimate *n* 1 *syn* see APOTHEOSIS 1

ultimate *vb* *syn* see CLOSE 3

ultimately *adv* *syn* see YET 2

ultra *adj* 1 *syn* see EXTREME 3
2 *syn* see OUTLANDISH 3

ultraconservative *n* *syn* see REACTIONARY

ultrafashionable *adj* *syn* see STYLISH

ultraist *n* *syn* see RADICAL

ultraist *adj* *syn* see EXTREME 3

ultramarine *adj* *syn* see OVERSEAS

ululate *vb* *syn* see HOWL 1
rel bewail, lament

umbra *n* 1 *syn* see APPARITION
2 *syn* see SHADE 1

umbrage *n* 1 *syn* see SHADE 1
2 *syn* see FOLIAGE
3 *syn* see OFFENSE 2
rel annoyance, irking, vexation; exasperation, irritation, nettling, provoking; fury, ire, rage, wrath

umbrage *vb* 1 *syn* see SHADE
2 *syn* see ANGER 2

umbrageous *adj* *syn* see SHADY 1

umbrous *adj* *syn* see SHADY 1

umpire *n* *syn* see JUDGE 1

umpire *vb* *syn* see JUDGE 1

unabashed *adj* *syn* see SHAMELESS
ant abashed

unabbreviated *adj* *syn* see UNABRIDGED
ant abbreviated

unabridged *adj* not shortened by omission of parts (as words) <published an *unabridged* edition of Shakespeare's plays>
syn complete, unabbreviated, uncondensed, uncut, undocked, whole-length
rel entire, intact, whole
con condensed, cropped, curtailed, cut, incom-pleted, shortened, trimmed
ant abridged

unacceptable *adj* *syn* see OBJECTIONABLE
ant acceptable

unaccompanied *adj* *syn* see ALONE 1
ant accompanied, companioned

unaccomplished *adj* *syn* see AMATEURISH
ant accomplished, skilled

unaccountable *adj* 1 *syn* see INEXPLICABLE
ant accountable
2 *syn* see MYSTERIOUS

unaccustomed *adj* *syn* see UNFAMILIAR 1

ant accustomed, familiar

unacquaintance *n* *syn* see IGNORANCE 2
ant acquaintance

unacquainted *adj* *syn* see IGNORANT 2
ant acquainted

unacquaintedness *n* *syn* see IGNORANCE 2
ant acquaintance

unacquired *adj* *syn* see INNATE 1
ant acquired

unadorned *adj* *syn* see PLAIN 1
ant adorned

unadulterated *adj* 1 *syn* see PURE 2
2 *syn* see STRAIGHT 3
ant adulterated

unadvisable *adj* *syn* see INADVISABLE
ant advisable

unadvised *adj* *syn* see RASH 1
ant advised, thought-out

unaffable *adj* *syn* see UNDEMONSTRATIVE
ant affable

unaffected *adj* *syn* see NATURAL 5
ant affected, artificial

unafraid *adj* *syn* see BRAVE 1
rel composed, cool, imperturbable; assured, confident, sure
con apprehensive, fearful
ant afraid

unaimed *adj* *syn* see RANDOM

unalert *adj* *syn* see INCAUTIOUS 1
ant alert

unalike *adj* *syn* see DIFFERENT 1
ant alike

unalloyed *adj* *syn* see PURE 2

unalluring *adj* *syn* see PLAIN 5
ant alluring, attractive

unalterable *adj* *syn* see INFLEXIBLE 3
ant alterable

unambiguous *adj* 1 *syn* see CLEAR 4
ant ambiguous, obscure
2 *syn* see EXPLICIT
ant ambiguous
3 *syn* see CLEAR 5

unanimated *adj* *syn* see DEAD 1

unanimous *adj* being of one mind <they were *unanimous* in their determination to win>
syn consentaneous, consentient, solid
rel agreed, agreeing, concordant, concurrent, harmonious
idiom of one accord, of one (*or* the same) mind, with one voice
con differing, disagreed, disagreeing, discordant, inharmonious

unanticipatedly *adv* *syn* see UNAWARES

unapparent *adj* *syn* see IMPERCEPTIBLE
ant apparent, detectable

unappeasable *adj* 1 *syn* see INSATIABLE
ant appeasable
2 *syn* see GRIM 3
ant appeasable, placable

unappetizing *adj* *syn* see UNPALATABLE 1
ant appetizing

unappreciable *adj* *syn* see IMPERCEPTIBLE
ant appreciable

unappreciated *adj* *syn* see THANKLESS 2
ant appreciated

unappreciative *adj* *syn* see THANKLESS 1
ant appreciative

unapproachable *adj* 1 *syn* see INACCESSIBLE

---

syn synonym(s)   *rel* related word(s)
ant antonym(s)   *con* contrasted word(s)
idiom idiomatic equivalent(s)
‖ use limited; if in doubt, see a dictionary

ant approachable, attainable

2 *syn* see UNSOCIABLE

ant accessible, approachable

unapt *adj* **1** *syn* see IMPROPER 1

2 *syn* see UNSKILLFUL 1

ant apt

unarm *vb* *syn* see DISARM 2

unartful *adj* *syn* see NATURAL 5

ant artful

unarticulate *adj* *syn* see DUMB 1

ant articulate

unartificial *adj* *syn* see NATURAL 5

ant affected, artificial

unasked *adj* **1** not asked or invited <annoyed by his *unasked* advice>

syn unbidden, uninvited, unrequested, unsought

rel arrogant, impudent, overbearing, presumptuous; spontaneous, voluntary; unacceptable, unwanted, unwelcome

con desired, invited, sought, wanted; acceptable, welcome

ant asked

2 *syn* see SUPEREROGATORY

unassailable *adj* *syn* see INVINCIBLE 1

rel stalwart, stout, strong, sturdy, tenacious, tough

ant assailable

unassertive *adj* *syn* see SHY 1

ant aggressive, assertive

unassorted *adj* *syn* see MISCELLANEOUS

unassuming *adj* *syn* see HUMBLE 1

ant assuming, presumptuous

unassured *adj* **1** *syn* see UNSAFE

2 *syn* see SHY 1

ant assured

3 *syn* see INSECURE 1

unattainable *adj* **1** *syn* see INACCESSIBLE

ant attainable

2 *syn* see IMPOSSIBLE 1

unattractive *adj* *syn* see PLAIN 5

ant alluring, attractive

unauthentic *adj* *syn* see SPURIOUS 3

ant authentic, genuine

unavailable *adj* *syn* see FUTILE

unavailing *adj* *syn* see FUTILE

unavoidable *adj* *syn* see INEVITABLE

ant avoidable

unavoidably *adv* *syn* see WILLY-NILLY

unaware *adv* *syn* see UNAWARES

unaware *adj* *syn* see IGNORANT 2

ant aware, conscious

unawaredly *adv* *syn* see UNAWARES

unawareness *n* *syn* see IGNORANCE 2

ant awareness, consciousness

unawares *adv* without warning <caught *unawares* by company>

syn aback, short, sudden, suddenly, unanticipatedly, unaware, unawaredly, unexpectedly

rel unprepared, unready

idiom like a bolt from the blue, off base, out of a clear sky, out of the blue

unbalance *vb* *syn* see MADDEN 1

unbalance *n* *syn* see INSANITY 1

rel disorientation, instability

unbalanced *adj* **1** *syn* see LOPSIDED

ant balanced

2 *syn* see INSANE 1

unbearable *adj* *syn* see INSUFFERABLE

ant bearable, supportable

unbearing *adj* *syn* see BARREN 2

unbeatable *adj* *syn* see INVINCIBLE 1

ant beatable, defeatable

unbeauteous *adj* *syn* see PLAIN 5

ant beauteous

unbeautified *adj* *syn* see PLAIN 1

ant beautified, embellished

unbeautiful *adj* **1** *syn* see PLAIN 5

ant beautiful

2 *syn* see UGLY 2

ant beautiful

unbecoming *adj* **1** *syn* see INDECOROUS

rel awkward, clumsy, gauche, inept, maladroit

ant becoming, seemly

2 *syn* see IMPROPER 1

unbecomingness *n* *syn* see IMPROPRIETY 1

ant becomingness, seemliness

unbefitting *adj* *syn* see IMPROPER 1

ant apropos, befitting

unbegotten *adj* *syn* see SELF-EXISTENT

unbelief *n* the attitude or state of mind of one who does not believe <after so much deception, so many lies, she could offer nothing but *unbelief* to his words>

syn disbelief, incredulity, unbelievingness, unfaith

rel doubt, dubiety, dubiosity, skepticism, uncertainty; distrust, mistrust, suspicion; apprehension, misgiving, qualm

con assurance, certitude, security, trust; dependence, reliance, stock, store

ant belief

unbelievable *adj* **1** *syn* see INCREDIBLE 1

ant believable, credible

2 *syn* see IMPLAUSIBLE 1

ant believable, credible

unbelieve *vb* *syn* see DISBELIEVE

ant believe, credit

unbeliever *n* *syn* see SKEPTIC

ant believer

unbelieving *adj* *syn* see INCREDULOUS

ant believing

unbelievingness *n* *syn* see UNBELIEF

unbend *vb* **1** *syn* see RELAX 2

2 *syn* see REST 2

unbendable *adj* *syn* see INFLEXIBLE 2

ant bendable

unbending *adj* **1** *syn* see STIFF 1

ant bendable

2 *syn* see INFLEXIBLE 2

3 *syn* see UNSOCIABLE

unbiased *adj* *syn* see FAIR 4

rel aloof, uninterested

ant biased

unbidden *adj* *syn* see UNASKED

unbind *vb* **1** *syn* see LOOSE 3

ant bind

2 *syn* see FREE

ant bind

unblamable *adj* *syn* see GOOD 11

ant blamable, blameworthy

unblemished *adj* **1** *syn* see WHOLE 1

ant blemished, flawed

2 *syn* see CHASTE

unblenched *adj* *syn* see BRAVE 1

unblenching *adj* *syn* see BRAVE 1

unblock *vb* *syn* see OPEN 1

ant block

unblunted *adj syn* see SHARP 1
ant blunt, blunted
unblurred *adj syn* see CLEAR 4
ant blurred
unblushing *adj syn* see SHAMELESS
unbodied *adj syn* see IMMATERIAL 1
ant bodied, incarnate
unbookish *adj syn* see UNSCHOLARLY
ant bookish
unbosom *vb syn* see REVEAL 1
unbounded *adj syn* see LIMITLESS
ant bounded, limited
unbrace *vb syn* see WEAKEN 1
ant brace, reinforce
unbroken *adj syn* see WHOLE 1
ant broken
unbrookable *adj syn* see INSUFFERABLE
unbuild *vb syn* see DESTROY 1
ant build
unburden *vb syn* see RID
rel discharge, disencumber, unload
con encumber, lade, load, saddle, tax,
weight
ant burden
unbury *vb syn* see EXHUME
ant bury
uncalled-for *adj* 1 *syn* see UNNECESSARY
ant required
2 *syn* see SUPEREROGATORY
3 *syn* see BASELESS
rel absurd, foolish, preposterous, silly;
impertinent, intrusive, officious
ant well-founded
4 *syn* see RUDE 6
uncandid *adj syn* see DISINGENUOUS
ant candid
uncanny *adj* 1 *syn* see WEIRD 1
2 *syn* see SUPERNATURAL 2
uncared-for *adj syn* see NEGLECTED
ant cared-for
uncareful *adj syn* see IRRESPONSIBLE
ant careful
uncaring *adj syn* see CARELESS 1
ant careful
uncaused *adj syn* see SELF-EXISTENT
unceasing *adj syn* see CONTINUAL
uncelebrated *adj syn* see OBSCURE 5
ant celebrated, noted
uncelestial *adj syn* see EARTHLY 1
ant celestial
unceremonious *adj* 1 *syn* see INFORMAL 1
ant ceremonious
2 *syn* see SHORT 5
uncertain *adj* 1 not stable, consistent, or
predictable <was in very *uncertain* health>
syn capricious, chancy, dicey, erratic, fluctuant, iffy, incalculable, unpredictable,
whimsical; *compare* INCONSTANT 1
rel questionable, undependable, unsettled;
fickle, inconstant, insecure, unstable, unsure; changeable, mutable, protean, variable; unexpectable, unforeseeable
idiom in a state of uncertainty, in suspense
2 *syn* see INCONSTANT 1
3 *syn* see MUTABLE 2

syn synonym(s)   *rel* related word(s)
ant antonym(s)   *con* contrasted word(s)
idiom idiomatic equivalent(s)
‖ use limited; if in doubt, see a dictionary

4 *syn* see DOUBTFUL 1
ant certain
5 *syn* see MOOT
ant certain
6 *syn* see OBSCURE 3
7 *syn* see VACILLATING 2
idiom at a loss
ant certain, set
uncertainty *n* a feeling of unsureness about
someone or something <troubled by a growing *uncertainty* about the future>
syn concern, doubt, doubtfulness, dubiety,
dubiosity, dubitancy, incertitude, mistrust,
query, skepticism, suspicion, uncertitude,
wonder
rel anxiety, bother, disquiet, trouble, worry;
agitation, distress, perturbation, uneasiness;
disfaith, distrust; hesitation, reserve, salt
con assurance, certitude, confidence, conviction; complacency, content, satisfaction
ant certainty
uncertitude *n syn* see UNCERTAINTY
ant certitude
unchain *vb syn* see FREE
ant chain
unchangeable *adj syn* see INFLEXIBLE 3
ant changeable
unchanging *adj* 1 *syn* see STEADY 2
2 *syn* see SAME 3
ant changeable, changing
uncharnel *vb syn* see EXHUME
unchaste *adj* 1 *syn* see IMPURE 1
ant chaste
2 *syn* see FAST 7
ant chaste
unchristian *adj syn* see OUTRAGEOUS 1
ant ‖Christian
uncivil *adj* 1 *syn* see BARBARIAN 1
2 *syn* see RUDE 6
rel coarse, crass, crude
con polished, smooth, urbane
ant civil
uncivilized *adj* 1 *syn* see BARBARIAN 1
ant civilized
2 *syn* see BOORISH
ant civilized
3 *syn* see OUTRAGEOUS 1
unclad *adj syn* see NUDE 2
unclean *adj* 1 *syn* see IMPURE 1
ant clean, pure
2 *syn* see DIRTY 1
ant clean, cleanly
3 *syn* see IMPURE 3
ant clean; purified
uncleanly *adj* 1 *syn* see IMPURE 1
ant cleanly
2 *syn* see DIRTY 1
ant clean, cleanly
unclear *adj* 1 *syn* see OBSCURE 3
ant clear
2 *syn* see FAINT 2
ant clear, distinct
3 *syn* see DOUBTFUL 1
ant clear
uncloak *vb syn* see EXPOSE 4
ant cloak
unclose *vb* 1 *syn* see OPEN 1
ant close
2 *syn* see REVEAL 1
unclosed *adj syn* see OPEN 1

unclothe vb 1 syn see STRIP 1
ant closed
2 syn see OPEN 2
ant dress

unclothed adj syn see NUDE 2
ant clothed, dressed

unclouded adj syn see FAIR 2
ant clouded, cloudy

uncluttered adj syn see NEAT 2
ant cluttered

uncolored adj syn see FAIR 4
ant colored, partial

uncombed adj syn see SLOVENLY 1

uncombine vb syn see SEPARATE 1
ant combine

un–come-at-able adj syn see INACCESSI-
BLE
ant come-at-able

uncomely adj 1 syn see IMPROPER 1
2 syn see PLAIN 5
ant comely
3 syn see UGLY 2
ant comely

uncomfortable adj causing or likely to
cause discomfort <kept an *uncomfortable*
chair for uninvited callers>
syn comfortless, discomforting, harsh,
uncomforting, uncomfy
rel distressing, easeless, uneasy
con comforting, easy, soothing
ant comfortable

uncomforting adj syn see UNCOMFORT-
ABLE
ant comforting

uncomfy adj syn see UNCOMFORTABLE
ant comfy

uncommon adj 1 syn see INFREQUENT
con commonplace, everyday, ordinary
ant common
2 syn see EXCEPTIONAL 1
ant common, commonplace

||*uncommon* adv syn see EXTRA

uncommonly adv 1 syn see OCCASION-
ALLY
ant commonly
2 syn see EXTRA

uncommunicative adj syn see SILENT 3
ant communicative
2 syn see UNSOCIABLE

uncompanionable adj syn see UNSOCIA-
BLE
ant companionable

uncompassionate adj syn see UNFEELING
2
ant compassionate

uncompensated adj syn see UNPAID 1
ant compensated

uncomplainingness n syn see PATIENCE
ant complainingness, discontent

uncomplete adj syn see DEFICIENT 1
ant complete

uncompliant adj syn see INFLEXIBLE 2
ant compliant

uncomplimentary adj syn see DEROGA-
TORY
ant complimentary

uncomprehensible adj syn see INCOMPRE-
HENSIBLE 1
ant comprehensible, graspable

uncompromising adj 1 syn see INFLEXI-
BLE 2

2 syn see TOUGH 3

unconcealed adj syn see FRANK

unconceivable adj syn see IMPLAUSIBLE
ant conceivable

unconcern n syn see APATHY 2
ant concern

unconcerned adj syn see INDIFFERENT 2
rel collected, composed, cool, nonchalant
con anxious, careful, solicitous, worried
ant concerned

uncondensed adj syn see UNABRIDGED
ant condensed

unconfident adj syn see INSECURE 1
ant confident

unconfined adj syn see FREE 2
ant confined

uncongenial adj 1 syn see ANTIPATHETIC 2
rel displeasing, unattractive, unlikable,
unpleasing
ant congenial
2 syn see INHARMONIOUS 2

unconnected adj syn see INCOHERENT 2
ant connected, ordered

unconquerable adj 1 syn see INVINCIBLE 1
rel insuperable, unsurmountable; proof,
resistant, secure, tight
idiom more than a match for
con beatable, vincible; expugnable, pregna-
ble, vulnerable; insecure, open, unprotected
ant conquerable
2 syn see INSUPERABLE
ant conquerable

unconscionable adj 1 syn see UNSCRUPU-
LOUS
ant conscientious, consciable
2 syn see EXCESSIVE 1
3 syn see UNREASONABLE 2
4 syn see OUTRAGEOUS 1

unconscious adj syn see INSENSIBLE 2
ant conscious

unconsequential adj syn see PETTY 2
ant consequential

unconsidered adj 1 syn see PETTY 2
2 syn see RANDOM
ant considered, planned
3 syn see RASH 1
ant considered

unconsolable adj syn see INCONSOLABLE
ant consolable

unconspicuous adj syn see INCONSPICU-
OUS
ant conspicuous

unconstrained adj 1 syn see EASYGOING 3
2 syn see DEMONSTRATIVE
ant constrained

unconstraint n freedom from constraint or
pressure <had always been used to the *unconstraint* of a happy affectionate family>
syn abandon, ease, naturalness, spontaneity, unrestraint; *compare* ABANDON 2
rel impulsiveness, instinctiveness; ingenuousness, naiveté, simplicity, unsophistication
con pressure, strain, stress, tension; formality, rigidity; sophistication
ant constraint

uncontainable adj syn see IRREPRESSIBLE

uncontent adj syn see DISCONTENTED
ant content, contented

uncontented adj syn see DISCONTENTED

ant content, contented

uncontestable *adj syn see* POSITIVE 3
 ant contestable

uncontinuous *adj syn see* INCOHERENT 2

uncontrite *adj syn see* REMORSELESS
 ant contrite

uncontrollable *adj* 1 *syn see* UNRULY 1
 ant controllable
 2 *syn see* IRREPRESSIBLE
 ant controllable

uncontrovertible *adj syn see* POSITIVE 3
 ant controvertible, disputable

unconversant *adj syn see* INEXPERIENCED
 ant conversant, versed

unconvincing *adj syn see* IMPLAUSIBLE
 ant convincing

uncooked *adj syn see* RAW 1
 ant cooked

‖**uncorporal** *adj syn see* IMMATERIAL 1

uncorrectable *adj syn see* HOPELESS 2
 ant correctable

uncostly *adj syn see* CHEAP 1
 ant costly

uncountable *adj* 1 *syn see* INNUMERABLE
 ant countable
 2 *syn see* INCALCULABLE 1

uncounted *adj syn see* INNUMERABLE

uncouple *vb syn see* DETACH
 ant couple

uncourteous *adj syn see* RUDE 6
 ant courteous

uncouth *adj* 1 *syn see* STRANGE 4
 2 *syn see* DERELICT 1
 3 *syn see* COARSE 3
 ant couth
 4 *syn see* RUDE 6

uncover *vb* 1 *syn see* REVEAL 1
 2 *syn see* EXPOSE 1
 3 *syn see* OPEN 2
 ant cover

uncovered *adj syn see* OPEN 2

uncreate *vb syn see* ANNIHILATE 2

uncreated *adj syn see* SELF-EXISTENT
 ant created

uncreative *adj syn see* UNORIGINAL
 ant creative

uncritical *adj syn see* SUPERFICIAL 2
 rel imprecise, inaccurate, inexact; careless, casual, offhand, perfunctory; slipshod
 con accurate, exact, precise; careful; discerning, discriminating, penetrating
 ant critical

uncrown *vb syn see* DEPOSE 1
 ant coronate, crown

unction *n syn see* OINTMENT

unctious *adj syn see* FULSOME

unctuous *adj* 1 *syn see* FATTY 2
 2 *syn see* FULSOME

uncultivated *adj* 1 *syn see* COARSE 3
 ant cultivated
 2 *syn see* BARBARIAN 1
 ant cultivated
 3 *syn see* WILD 1
 ant cultivated

uncultured *adj* 1 *syn see* BOORISH

 ant cultured
 2 *syn see* COARSE 3

uncurable *adj syn see* HOPELESS 2
 ant curable

uncurbed *adj syn see* AUDACIOUS 4
 ant curbed

uncurious *adj syn see* INDIFFERENT 2
 ant curious

uncurtain *vb syn see* REVEAL 1

uncustomary *adj syn see* EXCEPTIONAL 1
 ant customary

uncut *adj syn see* UNABRIDGED
 ant cut

undamaged *adj syn see* WHOLE 1
 ant damaged

undaring *adj syn see* TIMID 2
 ant daring

undarkened *adj syn see* FAIR 2

undauntable *adj syn see* BRAVE 1

undaunted *adj syn see* BRAVE 1
 ant daunted

undear *adj syn see* CHEAP 1
 ant dear

undeceive *vb syn see* DISABUSE
 ant deceive

undecided *adj* 1 *syn see* PENDING
 ant decided
 2 *syn see* DOUBTFUL 1

undecipherable *adj syn see* ILLEGIBLE
 ant decipherable

undecisive *adj syn see* VACILLATING 2
 ant decisive

undeclared *adj syn see* TACIT 1

undecorated *adj syn see* PLAIN 1
 ant decorated

undecorous *adj syn see* INDECOROUS
 ant decorous

undefeatable *adj syn see* INVINCIBLE 1
 ant defeatable

undefiled *adj syn see* CHASTE

undefined *adj syn see* FAINT 2
 ant defined

undeflowered *adj syn see* VIRGIN 1
 ant deflowered

undelude *vb syn see* DISABUSE
 ant delude

undemonstrated *adj syn see* UNTRIED 1
 ant demonstrated

undemonstrative *adj* not socially outgoing
 <a shy *undemonstrative* person yet capable
 of deep feeling>
 syn aseptic, restrained, retiring, shrinking,
 unaffable, unexpansive, withdrawn; *compare*
 UNSOCIABLE
 rel chill, cold, frigid, glacial, icy; emotionless, indifferent, unemotional, uninterested;
 aloof, distant, reserved, standoffish
 con free and easy, hail-fellow-well-met,
 outgiving, outgoing, palsy-walsy; sociable
 ant demonstrative

undeniable *adj* 1 *syn see* POSITIVE 3
 ant deniable
 2 *syn see* REAL 3

undenominational *adj syn see* NONSEC-
TARIAN
 ant denominational

undependable *adj* 1 *syn see* UNRELIABLE 1
 ant dependable
 2 *syn see* UNSAFE
 ant dependable

---

syn synonym(s)   *rel* related word(s)
ant antonym(s)   *con* contrasted word(s)
idiom idiomatic equivalent(s)
‖ use limited; if in doubt, see a dictionary

3 *syn* see TRICK
ant dependable

under *adv syn* see BELOW 1
ant above, over

under *prep syn* see BELOW 1
ant over

under *adj* 1 *syn* see INFERIOR 1
2 *syn* see SUBORDINATE

underage *n syn* see FAILURE 3
ant overage

underconsciousness *n syn* see SUBCON-
SCIOUS

undercover *adj syn* see SECRET 1

undercover man *n syn* see SPY

undercroft *n syn* see CRYPT

underdeveloped *adj syn* see BACKWARD 6

underdog *n syn* see VICTIM 2
ant overdog, top dog

underearth *adj syn* see SUBTERRANEAN

underfoot *adj* 1 *syn* see SUBTERRANEAN
2 *syn* see DOWNTRODDEN

undergo *vb syn* see EXPERIENCE 1
rel abide, bear, endure, tolerate; bow, defer,
submit, yield

underground *adj syn* see SUBTERRANEAN

underhand *adj* characterized by sly unobtrusive craft or deceit <ready to use the most
underhand methods to gain his ends>
syn devious, duplicitous, guileful, indirect,
shifty, sneaking, sneaky, underhanded;
compare SECRET 1, SLY 2
rel dishonest, dishonest; crooked, oblique;
crafty, cunning, insidious, sly, tricky, wily;
furtive, hangdog
con candid, frank, open, plain; forthright,
straightforward
ant aboveboard

underhanded *adj* 1 *syn* see UNDERHAND
ant aboveboard
2 *syn* see SHORTHANDED

underivative *adj syn* see PRIMARY 5
ant derivative

underived *adj syn* see PRIMARY 5
ant derived

underlease *vb syn* see SUBLET

underlet *vb syn* see SUBLET

underline *vb syn* see EMPHASIZE

underline *n syn* see CAPTION

underling *n syn* see INFERIOR

underlying *adj* 1 *syn* see FUNDAMENTAL 1
rel cardinal, essential, vital; critical, crucial,
indispensable, necessary, needful
2 *syn* see ELEMENTAL 1

undermanned *adj syn* see SHORTHANDED
ant overmanned

undermine *vb* 1 *syn* see WEAKEN 1
rel ruin, wreck; foil, frustrate, thwart
idiom bore from within
ant reinforce
2 *syn* see SABOTAGE

undermining *n syn* see SABOTAGE

undermost *adj syn* see BOTTOMMOST
ant uppermost

underneath *prep syn* see BELOW 1

underneath *adv syn* see BELOW 1

‖**underneath** *adj syn* see SECRET 1

underneath *n syn* see BOTTOM 1

underpinner *n syn* see SUPPORT 3

underpinning *n* 1 *syn* see BASIS 1
2 *syn* see BASE 1

3 *syn* see SUPPORT 3

underprivileged *adj* deficient in basic economic and social resources <the role of the
school in bettering the lot of *underprivileged*
children>
syn depressed, deprived, disadvantaged
rel handicapped; hapless, ill-fated, ill-
starred, unfortunate, unlucky; impoverished, needy, poor
idiom badly off, in adverse circumstances,
out of luck
con advantaged, fortunate, privileged;
coddled, indulged, spoiled

underprize *vb syn* see DEPRECIATE 1
ant overprize

underprop *vb syn* see SUPPORT 5

underpropping *n syn* see SUPPORT 3

underrate *vb syn* see DEPRECIATE 1
ant overrate

underscore *vb syn* see EMPHASIZE

undersense *n syn* see SUBCONSCIOUS

undersexed *adj syn* see FRIGID 3
ant oversexed

underside *n syn* see BOTTOM 1

understaffed *adj syn* see SHORTHANDED
ant overstaffed

understand *vb* 1 *syn* see APPREHEND 1
idiom get the drift
ant misunderstand
2 *syn* see KNOW 1
idiom get the hang of
3 to view as plausible or likely <I *understand*
he is expected home soon>
syn assume, believe, ‖conceit, conceive,
expect, gather, imagine, ‖reckon, suppose,
suspect, take, think, ‖wit; *compare* CONJEC-
TURE
rel conclude, deduce, infer; conjecture,
guess, presume, surmise; fancy; consider
con know; challenge, doubt, question

understandable *adj* of a kind to be readily
understood <her style was smooth and easy,
her language *understandable*>
syn apprehensible, comprehendible, comprehensible, fathomable, graspable, intelligible, knowable, lucid, luminous; *compare*
CLEAR 4, 5
rel clear-cut, unambiguous, unblurred;
plain, simple, straightforward; exoteric, lay,
popular
con mysterious, obscure, strange, vague;
cryptic, esoteric, hidden

understanding *n* 1 *syn* see REASON 5
rel discernment, discrimination, insight,
penetration; awareness, intuition; apprehension, comprehension, grasp
2 *syn* see AGREEMENT 2
3 *syn* see MEANING 1

understood *adj syn* see TACIT 1

understrapper *n syn* see INFERIOR

understructure *n syn* see BASE 1
ant superstructure

undersurface *n syn* see BOTTOM 1

undertake *vb* 1 *syn* see TRY 5
rel begin, commence, start
idiom put (or set) one's hand to
2 *syn* see TAKE ON 3
3 *syn* see PROMISE 1
rel certify, warrant
idiom stand back of (or behind)

undertaker n 1 syn see ENTREPRENEUR 1
  2 syn see MORTICIAN
undertaking n 1 syn see ATTEMPT
  2 syn see PROJECT 2
under–the–table adj syn see SECRET 1
  ant aboveboard
undertone n 1 syn see MURMUR 1
  2 syn see ASSOCIATION 4
undervalue vb syn see DEPRECIATE 1
  ant overvalue
underwater adj syn see SUBMARINE
underwit n syn see FOOL 4
underworld n syn see HELL
undescribable adj syn see UNUTTERABLE
  ant describable
undesignated adj syn see ANONYMOUS
undesigned adj syn see UNINTENTIONAL
  ant designed
undesigning adj syn see GENUINE 3
  ant designing
undesirable adj syn see OBJECTIONABLE
  ant desirable
undesired adj syn see UNWELCOME 1
  ant desired
undestroyable adj syn see INDESTRUCTI-
  BLE
  ant destroyable, destructible
undeterminable adj syn see INDEFINITE 1
  ant determinable
undetermined adj 1 syn see PENDING
  ant determined
  2 syn see FAINT 2
undeveloped adj 1 syn see BACKWARD 6
  ant developed
  2 syn see PRIMITIVE 3
  ant advanced
undeviatingly adv syn see DIRECTLY 1
undevised adj syn see UNINTENTIONAL
  ant devised
undexterous adj syn see UNSKILLFUL 1
  ant dexterous
undifferenced adj syn see LIKE
undifferentiated adj syn see LIKE
  ant differentiated
undiluted adj 1 syn see STRAIGHT 3
  ant diluted
  2 syn see PURE 2
undiplomatic adj syn see TACTLESS
  ant diplomatic
undiscernible adj syn see IMPERCEPTIBLE
  ant discernible
undisciplinable adj syn see UNRULY 1
undisciplined adj syn see UNRULY 1
  ant disciplined
undiscriminated adj syn see INDISCRIMI-
  NATE 1
  ant discriminate, discriminated
undiscriminating adj syn see INDISCRIMI-
  NATE 1
undisguised adj syn see FRANK
undisputable adj syn see POSITIVE 3
  ant controvertible, disputable
undissembled adj 1 syn see GENUINE 3
  ant dissembled, feigned
  2 syn see FRANK

undissembling adj syn see FRANK
  ant dissembling
undistinct adj syn see FAINT 2
  ant clear, distinct
undistinctive adj syn see FAIR 4
undistinguishing adj syn see INDISCRIMI-
  NATE 1
undistorted adj syn see TRUE 3
  ant distorted
undistracted adj syn see WHOLE 5
undivided adj syn see WHOLE 5
  ant divided
undo vb 1 syn see LOOSE 3
  2 syn see OPEN 1
  rel loose, untie
  3 syn see ABOLISH 1
  4 syn see DESTROY 1
  5 syn see OUTWIT
  idiom bring down (or low), bring to naught
  6 syn see SEDUCE 2
undocked adj syn see UNABRIDGED
  ant docked
undoing n syn see DOWNFALL 2
undomesticated adj syn see WILD 1
  ant domesticated
undoubtable adj syn see POSITIVE 3
  ant doubtable, questionable
undoubted adj syn see AUTHENTIC 2
  ant doubtful, questionable
undoubtedly adv syn see WELL 7
undoubtful adj syn see CONFIDENT 1
  ant doubtful
undress vb 1 syn see STRIP 1
  ant dress
  2 syn see EXPOSE 4
  ant dress up
undressed adj 1 syn see NUDE 2
  ant dressed
  2 syn see RUDE 1
  ant dressed, finished
undubitable adj syn see AUTHENTIC 2
  ant dubitable
undue adj 1 syn see IMPROPER 1
  2 syn see EXCESSIVE 2
  3 syn see UNREASONABLE 2
undulate vb syn see SLITHER 2
unduly adv syn see EVER 6
  ant duly
unduteous adj syn see IMPIOUS 2
  ant duteous
undutiful adj syn see IMPIOUS 2
  ant dutiful
undying adj syn see IMMORTAL 1
  rel continuing, persistent; interminable,
  unceasing; inextinguishable, unquenchable
  ant mortal
uneager adj syn see DISINCLINED
  ant eager
unearth vb syn see DISCOVER 3
  rel exhibit, expose, show; disclose, reveal;
  delve, dig
unearthing n syn see DISCOVERY
unearthly adj 1 syn see SUPERNATURAL 1
  2 syn see WEIRD 1
  3 syn see FOOLISH 2
unease n 1 syn see CARE 2
  2 syn see TENSION 4
  3 syn see EMBARRASSMENT
  ant ease, easiness
uneasiness n 1 syn see CARE 2

---

syn synonym(s)   rel related word(s)
ant antonym(s)   con contrasted word(s)
idiom idiomatic equivalent(s)
‖ use limited; if in doubt, see a dictionary

2 **syn** see EMBARRASSMENT
ant ease, easiness
uneasy *adj* 1 **syn** see TENSE 2
rel anxious, careful, concerned, solicitous, worried; agitated, disquieted, disturbed, perturbed
idiom on pins and needles
ant easy
2 **syn** see RESTLESS
3 **syn** see DOUBTFUL 1
uneatable *adj syn* see INEDIBLE
ant eatable
uneducated *adj syn* see IGNORANT 1
ant educated, lettered
unelaborate *adj syn* see PLAIN 1
ant elaborate
unembellished *adj syn* see PLAIN 1
ant embellished
unembodied *adj syn* see IMMATERIAL 1
unembroidered *adj syn* see PLAIN 1
unemotional *adj syn* see COLD 2
rel dispassionate; unfeeling; impassive
con affective, feeling; affectionate, demonstrative
ant emotional
2 **syn** see UNFEELING 2
unemphatic *adj syn* see INCONSPICUOUS
unemployed *adj* lacking a gainful occupation <the problems of *unemployed* workers>
syn jobless, workless
rel free, unengaged, unoccupied; underemployed; fired, laid off
idiom at liberty, let go, on layoff, out of work
ant employed
unending *adj* 1 **syn** see EVERLASTING 1
2 **syn** see CONTINUAL
unendurable *adj syn* see INSUFFERABLE
ant endurable
unenlarged *adj syn* see ILLIBERAL
unenlightened *adj syn* see BACKWARD 5
ant enlightened
unennobled *adj syn* see IGNOBLE 1
ant ennobled, noble
unentangle *vb syn* see EXTRICATE 2
ant entangle
unenthusiastic *adj syn* see TEPID 2
ant enthusiastic
unequal *adj* 1 **syn** see DIFFERENT 1
2 **syn** see LOPSIDED
unequalable *adj syn* see SUPREME
unequaled *adj syn* see ALONE 3
ant equaled
unequipped *adj syn* see UNFIT 2
unequitable *adj syn* see INEQUITABLE
ant equitable
unequivocal *adj* 1 **syn** see CLEAR 5
ant equivocal
2 **syn** see POSITIVE 1
ant equivocal
3 **syn** see POSITIVE 3
unequivocally *adv syn* see EASILY 2
uneradicable *adj syn* see INDELIBLE
ant eradicable
unerasable *adj syn* see INDELIBLE
ant erasable
unerring *adj syn* see INFALLIBLE 1
unescapable *adj syn* see INEVITABLE
ant escapable
unessential *adj* 1 **syn** see UNNECESSARY

ant essential
2 **syn** see DISPENSABLE
ant essential
unethical *adj syn* see CORRUPT 2
ant ethical
unevadable *adj syn* see INEVITABLE
ant evadable
uneven *adj* 1 **syn** see ROUGH 1
ant even
2 **syn** see LOPSIDED
ant even
3 **syn** see SPOTTY 1
rel differing, disparate, unequal; discrepant, inconsistent
con consistent, equal, regular
unevenness *n* 1 **syn** see DISPARITY
2 **syn** see INEQUALITY 1
uneventful *adj syn* see COMMON 6
ant eventful
unevolved *adj syn* see PRIMITIVE 3
ant advanced, evolved
unexaminable *adj syn* see MYSTERIOUS
unexampled *adj syn* see ONLY 2
unexceptionable *adj syn* see DECENT 4
ant exceptionable
unexceptional *adj* 1 **syn** see DECENT 4
2 **syn** see COMMON 6
ant exceptional
unexcessive *adj syn* see CONSERVATIVE 2
ant excessive
unexpansive *adj syn* see UNDEMONSTRATIVE
ant expansive
unexpectedly *adv syn* see UNAWARES
unexpedient *adj syn* see INADVISABLE
ant expedient
unexperienced *adj* see INEXPERIENCED
ant experienced
unexpert *adj syn* see INEFFICIENT 2
ant expert
unexplainable *adj syn* see INEXPLICABLE
ant explainable, explicable
unexplicit *adj syn* see OBSCURE 3
ant explicit
unexpressed *adj* 1 **syn** see UNSPOKEN 1
ant expressed
2 **syn** see TACIT 1
ant expressed
unexpressible *adj syn* see UNUTTERABLE
ant expressible
unexpressive *adj syn* see EXPRESSIONLESS
ant expressive
unextreme *adj syn* see CONSERVATIVE 2
unfabled *adj syn* see REAL 3
ant fabled
unfacile *adj syn* see UNSKILLFUL 1
unfailing *adj* 1 **syn** see SAME 3
2 **syn** see INFALLIBLE 2
ant fallible
unfair *adj syn* see INEQUITABLE
ant fair
unfairness *n syn* see INJUSTICE 1
ant fairness
unfaith *n syn* see UNBELIEF
ant faith
unfaithful *adj syn* see FAITHLESS
ant faithful
unfaithfulness *n syn* see INFIDELITY
ant faithfulness

unfaltering *adj syn* see SURE 2
unfamed *adj syn* see OBSCURE 5
ant famed
unfamiliar *adj* **1** not well known <trying to find her way about the *unfamiliar* room in the dark>
syn new, strange, unaccustomed
rel exotic, foreign; curious, peculiar, remarkable; unknown
con accustomed, commonplace, customary, ordinary, usual, wonted
ant familiar
2 *syn* see IGNORANT 2
ant familiar
unfamiliarity *n syn* see IGNORANCE 2
unfantastic *adj syn* see REALISTIC
ant fantastic
unfashioned *adj syn* see RUDE 1
unfasten *vb syn* see LOOSE 3
ant fasten
unfastidious *adj syn* see SLOVENLY 1
ant fastidious
unfathered *adj syn* see ILLEGITIMATE 1
unfathomable *adj* **1** *syn* see BOTTOMLESS 2
ant fathomable
2 *syn* see INCOMPREHENSIBLE 1
ant fathomable
unfathomed *adj syn* see HUGE
unfavorable *adj* **1** *syn* see ADVERSE 2
ant favorable
2 *syn* see EVIL 5
unfavorably *adv syn* see AMISS 2
unfearful *adj syn* see BRAVE 1
ant fearful
unfearing *adj syn* see BRAVE 1
ant fearing
unfeasible *adj syn* see IMPOSSIBLE 1
ant feasible, practicable
unfeeling *adj* **1** *syn* see INSENSATE 1
ant feeling
2 lacking in normal human sympathy <an *unfeeling* response to a plea for help>
syn callous, cold-blooded, coldhearted, compassionless, hard-boiled, hardened, hardhearted, heartless, ironhearted, marblehearted, obdurate, stony, stonyhearted, uncompassionate, unemotional, unsympathetic; *compare* PITILESS
rel brutal, cruel, indurated, merciless, roughnatured, ruthless, tough; exacting, severe; unamiable, uncordial, unkind; cantankerous, churlish, crotchety, curmudgeonly, surly
idiom hard of heart
con considerate, gentle, thoughtful; kind, merciful; compassionate, sympathetic, warmhearted
ant feeling
3 *syn* see NUMB 1
unfeigned *adj* **1** *syn* see SINCERE 1
ant feigned
2 *syn* see GENUINE 3
ant dissembled, feigned
unfertile *adj syn* see BARREN 2
ant fertile

unfinished *adj* **1** *syn* see RUDE 1
ant dressed, finished
2 *syn* see AMATEURISH
ant finished
unfit *adj* **1** not adapted or appropriate to a particular end <land *unfit* for farming>
syn ill-adapted, ill-suited, inappropriate, inapt, unfitted, unmeet, unsuitable, unsuited
rel discordant, inharmonious; improper, infelicitous, unbecoming; incompatible, incongruous, uncongenial
idiom out of drawing, out of one's element, out of place
con adapted, appropriate, apt, suitable, suited; congruous, harmonious
ant fit
2 lacking essential qualifications <politicians *unfit* to govern>
syn disqualified, incapable, incompetent, ineligible, unequipped, unfitted, unqualified
rel awkward, blundering, bungling; butterfingered, heavy-handed, maladjusted, maladroit, unhandy; inefficient, inexpert, unproficient, unskillful
con capable, competent, qualified; adroit, dexterous, handy; expert, skilled
unfitted *adj* **1** *syn* see UNFIT 1
2 *syn* see UNFIT 2
ant fitted
unfitting *adj syn* see IMPROPER 1
ant fitting
unfix *vb* **1** *syn* see LOOSE 3
ant fix
2 *syn* see DETACH
unfixedness *n syn* see INSTABILITY
unflagging *adj syn* see INDEFATIGABLE
rel constant, steady
ant flagging
unflappable *adj syn* see COOL 2
rel easy, relaxed
unflawed *adj syn* see PERFECT 2
ant flawed
unfledged *adj syn* see YOUNG 1
ant fledged
unfleshed *adj syn* see INEXPERIENCED
unfleshly *adj syn* see IMMATERIAL 1
ant fleshly
unflexible *adj syn* see STIFF 1
ant flexible
unflinching *adj syn* see GRIM 3
unfluctuating *adj syn* see STEADY 2
ant fluctuant, fluctuating
unfold *vb* **1** *syn* see OPEN 4
ant fold
2 *syn* see SOLVE 2
3 to disclose by degrees to the sight or understanding <shyly she *unfolded* her hopes for the future>
syn develop, elaborate, evolve
rel demonstrate, evidence, evince, manifest, show; disclose, display, exhibit, expose, reveal
unfolding *n syn* see DEVELOPMENT
unforbearing *adj syn* see INTOLERANT 1
ant forbearing
unforced *adj syn* see VOLUNTARY
ant forced
unforgivable *adj syn* see INEXCUSABLE
ant forgivable
unformed *adj* **1** *syn* see FORMLESS

---

syn synonym(s)   *rel* related word(s)
ant antonym(s)   *con* contrasted word(s)
idiom idiomatic equivalent(s)
‖ use limited; if in doubt, see a dictionary

rel unfinished
ant formed

2 *syn see* RUDE 1

unfortunate *adj* **1** *syn see* UNLUCKY
rel infelicitous; deplorable, miserable, sad, wretched; malefic
con auspicious, favorable, propitious
ant fortunate

2 *syn see* INFELICITOUS

3 *syn see* DEPLORABLE

unfounded *adj syn see* BASELESS
rel deceptive, misleading; dishonest, mendacious, untruthful
ant well-founded

unframe *vb syn see* DESTROY 1

unfrank *adj syn see* DISINGENUOUS
ant frank

unfrequent *adj syn see* INFREQUENT
ant frequent

unfrequently *adv syn see* SELDOM
ant frequently

unfriendly *adj syn see* HOSTILE 1
ant friendly

unfruitful *adj syn see* STERILE 1
con fecund, fertile
ant fruitful, prolific

unfunctional *adj syn see* IMPRACTICABLE 2
ant functional

unfussy *adj syn see* EASYGOING 3
ant fussy

ungainly *adj syn see* CLUMSY 1
rel blundering, lubberly, maladroit
con graceful, supple, willowy; gainly

ungarnished *adj syn see* PLAIN 1
ant garnished

ungenerous *adj* **1** *syn see* PETTY 2
ant generous

2 *syn see* STINGY
ant generous

ungenial *adj syn see* ANTIPATHETIC 2
ant genial

ungenuine *adj syn see* SPURIOUS 3
ant genuine

ungetatable *adj syn see* INACCESSIBLE
ant getatable

ungifted *adj syn see* AMATEURISH
ant gifted

ungiving *adj syn see* STINGY

ungodly *adj* **1** *syn see* IMPIOUS 1
ant godly

2 *syn see* INDECOROUS

3 *syn see* OUTRAGEOUS 1

ungovernable *adj syn see* UNRULY 1
ant governable

ungoverned *adj syn see* AUDACIOUS 4

ungracious *adj* **1** *syn see* RUDE 6
ant gracious

2 *syn see* SHORT 5
ant gracious

ungraded *adj syn see* UNREFINED 3

ungraspable *adj syn see* INCOMPREHENSIBLE 1
ant comprehensible, graspable

ungrateful *adj* **1** *syn see* THANKLESS 1
ant grateful

2 *syn see* THANKLESS 2

3 *syn see* OFFENSIVE

ungratified *adj syn see* DISCONTENTED
ant gratified

ungrounded *adj syn see* BASELESS

unguarded *adj syn see* INCAUTIOUS 1
ant guarded

unguent *n syn see* OINTMENT

unguessed *adj syn see* MYSTERIOUS

unguilty *adj syn see* INNOCENT 2
ant guilty

unhallowed *adj* **1** *syn see* IMPIOUS 1

2 *syn see* FIENDISH

unhampered *adj syn see* AUDACIOUS 4
ant hampered

unhandsome *adj* **1** *syn see* PLAIN 5
ant handsome

2 *syn see* RUDE 6

unhandy *adj* **1** *syn see* UNWIELDY

2 *syn see* UNSKILLFUL 1
ant handy

3 *syn see* AWKWARD 2
ant handy

unhappiness *n* **1** *syn see* MISERY 1
ant happiness

2 *syn see* SADNESS
ant happiness

unhappy *adj* **1** *syn see* UNLUCKY
ant happy

2 *syn see* INFELICITOUS
ant happy

3 *syn see* AWKWARD 2

4 *syn see* SAD 1
ant happy

5 *syn see* BAD 8

6 *syn see* GLOOMY 3

unharmed *adj syn see* SAFE 1

unharmonious *adj* **1** *syn see* DISSONANT 1
ant harmonious

2 *syn see* INHARMONIOUS 2
ant harmonious

unhasty *adj syn see* SLOW 2
ant hasty

unhealth *n syn see* SICKNESS 1
ant health

unhealthful *adj syn see* UNWHOLESOME 1
ant healthful

unhealthiness *n syn see* INFIRMITY 1
ant healthiness

unhealthy *adj* **1** *syn see* UNWHOLESOME 1
ant healthy

2 *syn see* DANGEROUS 1

3 *syn see* VICIOUS 2

unheard-of *adj syn see* OBSCURE 5

unheavy *adj syn see* LIGHT 1
ant heavy

unheeding *adj* **1** *syn see* INATTENTIVE
ant heedful, heeding

2 *syn see* CARELESS 1
ant heedful, heeding

unhewn *adj syn see* RUDE 1

unhinge *vb* **1** *syn see* UPSET 5

2 *syn see* MADDEN 1

3 *syn see* DISCOMPOSE 1

unholy *adj* **1** *syn see* IMPIOUS 1
ant holy

2 *syn see* BLAMEWORTHY

3 *syn see* OUTRAGEOUS 1

unhonest *adj syn see* DISHONEST
ant honest

unhorse *vb* **1** *syn see* THROW 2

2 *syn see* OVERTHROW 2

unhurried *adj syn see* SLOW 2
ant hurried

unhurt *adj syn* see WHOLE 1
unicity *n syn* see UNIQUENESS
unidealistic *adj syn* see REALISTIC
  ant idealistic
unification *n* a bringing together or being
  brought together into an integrated whole
  <*unification* of mass transit facilities is increasingly needed>
  syn coadunation, coalition, combination,
  consolidation, melding, mergence, merger,
  merging, union; *compare* ALLIANCE 2
  rel affiliation, connection, interlocking,
  joining, linkage; coupling, hookup
  con dissociation, disunion, division, parting, partition, separation
  ant disunification
uniform *adj* 1 *syn* see LIKE
  ant various
  2 *syn* see STEADY 2
  rel compatible, consistent, consonant;
  ordered, orderly, regular
  ant multiform
uniformly *adv syn* see EVENLY 3
  ant variably
unify *vb* 1 to gather or combine parts or
  elements into a close mass or a coherent
  whole <minorities that are *unified* by perse-
  cution>
  syn compact, concentrate, consolidate,
  integrate; *compare* UNITE 2
  rel articulate, concatenate; order, organize,
  systematize; bind, tie
  idiom make one
  con divide, part, scatter; disorder, disorganize; disunite, divide, separate
  ant break up, disunify
  2 *syn* see HARMONIZE 4
  ant disunify
unifying *adj syn* see INTEGRATIVE
  ant disunifying
unilluminated *adj syn* see DARK 1
  ant illuminated
unimaginable *adj* 1 *syn* see INCONCEIV-
  ABLE 1
  ant imaginable
  2 *syn* see EXCEPTIONAL 1
  3 *syn* see INCREDIBLE 1
unimpaired *adj syn* see WHOLE 1
  ant impaired
unimpassioned *adj* 1 *syn* see MATTER-OF-
  FACT 3
  ant impassioned
  2 *syn* see SOBER 3
  rel impassive, phlegmatic, stoic, stolid;
  calm, placid, tranquil
  con ardent, fervent, fervid, heated, keen
  ant impassioned, passionate
unimpeachable *adj syn* see DECENT 4
unimportant *adj syn* see LITTLE 3
  ant important
unimpressible *adj syn* see INSUSCEPTIBLE
  ant impressible
unimpressionable *adj syn* see INSUSCEPTI-
  BLE
  ant impressionable

unindifferent *adj syn* see BIASED 2
  ant indifferent
unindulgent *adj syn* see INTOLERANT 1
  ant indulgent
uninflammable *adj syn* see NONCOMBUS-
  TIBLE
  ant flammable, inflammable
uninformed *adj syn* see IGNORANT 2
  ant informed
uninhibited *adj syn* see AUDACIOUS 4
  ant inhibited
uninhibitedness *n syn* see ABANDON 2
uninitiate *n syn* see AMATEUR 2
uninjured *adj syn* see WHOLE 1
  ant injured
uninjurious *adj syn* see SAFE 3
uninspired *adj* 1 *syn* see UNORIGINAL
  ant inspired
  2 *syn* see PONDEROUS 2
  ant inspired
uninstructed *adj* 1 *syn* see IGNORANT 2
  2 *syn* see IGNORANT 1
unintelligent *adj syn* see SIMPLE 3
  ant intelligent
unintelligible *adj* 1 *syn* see INCOMPRE-
  HENSIBLE 1
  ant intelligible
  2 *syn* see OBSCURE 3
  ant intelligible
unintended *adj syn* see UNINTENTIONAL
  ant intended
unintentional *adj* not the result of intent or
  design <her slight of the newcomer was
  quite *unintentional*>
  syn inadvertent, undesigned, undevised,
  unintended, unplanned, unpremeditated,
  unpurposed, unthought; *compare* ACCIDEN-
  TAL, EXTEMPORANEOUS
  rel causeless, chance, haphazard, purposeless, random; unanticipated, unexpected,
  unforeseen, unlooked-for; unthinking, unwitting
  con deliberate, designed, devised, intended,
  planned, premeditated, purposed
  ant intentional
uninterested *adj syn* see INDIFFERENT 2
  ant interested
uninteresting *adj syn* see ARID 2
  ant interesting
unintermitted *adj syn* see CONTINUAL
  ant intermitted, intermittent
unintermittedly *adv syn* see TOGETHER 2
  ant intermitted, intermittent
unintermittent *adj syn* see CONTINUAL
  ant intermitted, intermittent
uninterrupted *adj* 1 *syn* see CONTINUAL
  ant interrupted
  2 *syn* see DIRECT 2
uninterruptedly *adv syn* see TOGETHER 2
  ant interruptedly
uninventive *adj syn* see UNORIGINAL
  ant inventive
uninvited *adj syn* see UNASKED
  ant invited
union *n* 1 *syn* see UNIFICATION
  ant disunion
  2 *syn* see ASSOCIATION 2
  3 *syn* see JOINT 1
  4 *syn* see ALLIANCE 2
unique *adj* 1 *syn* see ONLY 2
  2 *syn* see SINGLE 2

---

syn synonym(s)   *rel* related word(s)
ant antonym(s)   *con* contrasted word(s)
idiom idiomatic equivalent(s)
‖ use limited; if in doubt, see a dictionary

3 *syn* see ALONE 3

4 *syn* see EXCEPTIONAL 1

uniqueness *n* the quality or state of standing alone and without a peer — *she time she rode in an old-time sleigh* <never would she forget the *uniqueness* of that experience>

syn oneness, singleness, unicity, uniquity

rel curiousness, oddity, peculiarity, quaintness, singularity, strangeness; import, mark, moment, note, significance; memorability, notability, remarkableness, unusualness

con commonness, commonplaceness, ordinariness; routineness; monotony, sameness, tediousness

uniquity *n syn* see UNIQUENESS

unite *vb* 1 *syn* see JOIN 1

rel amalgamate, blend, merge, mix

ant alienate; disunite, divide

2 to join forces especially in order to act more effectively <citizen groups *uniting* to further the fight against crime>

syn band, coadjute, combine, concur, conjoin, cooperate, league; *compare* UNIFY 1

rel affiliate, ally, associate, confederate; coalesce, commingle, fuse, mingle, weld

idiom draw together, hook up with, join forces (with), make common cause (with), throw in with

con break up, disband, separate, split (up)

ant disunite, part

unity *n* 1 the condition of being or consisting of one <*unity* — the idea conveyed by whatever we visualize as one thing>

syn individuality, oneness, singleness, singularity, singularness

rel identity, selfsameness, soleness, uniqueness, uniquity

ant multiplicity

2 *syn* see HARMONY 3

rel agreement, identity, oneness, union; solidarity; conformance, congruity

ant disunity

universal *adj* 1 *syn* see OMNIPRESENT

2 present or significant throughout the world <*universal* aspirations for a better world>

syn catholic, cosmic, cosmopolitan, ecumenical, global, planetary, worldwide

rel all-embracing, all-inclusive; broad, extensive, sweeping; all, entire, total, whole

con narrow, petty, provincial

ant parochial

3 *syn* see GENERAL 2

ant particular

universe *n* the totality of physical entities <theories of the expanding *universe*>

syn cosmos (*or* kosmos), creation, macrocosm, macrocosmos, megacosm, nature, world

univocal *adj syn* see CLEAR 5

ant ambiguous

unjust *adj syn* see INEQUITABLE

ant just

unjustifiable *adj* 1 *syn* see UNREASONABLE 2

ant justifiable

2 *syn* see INEXCUSABLE 1

ant justifiable

unjustness *n syn* see INJUSTICE 1

ant justice, justness

unkempt *adj syn* see SLOVENLY 1

ant kempt

unknow *vb syn* see FORGET 1

unknowable *adj* 1 *syn* see INCOMPREHENSIBLE 1

ant knowable

2 *syn* see INCONCEIVABLE 1

ant knowable

3 *syn* see MYSTERIOUS

unknowing *adj syn* see IGNORANT 2

ant knowing

unknowingness *n syn* see IGNORANCE 2

ant knowingness

unknown *adj syn* see OBSCURE 5

ant well-known

unlade *vb syn* see UNLOAD

ant lade, load

unlawful *adj* contrary to or prohibited by law <the spread of *unlawful* wiretapping>

syn criminal, illegal, illegitimate, illicit, lawless, wrongful

rel flagitious, iniquitous, nefarious; black-market, bootleg, under-the-counter; exceptionable, improper, intolerable, objectionable

idiom against the law

con condign, due, rightful; allowable, justifiable, permissible

ant lawful

unlawfulness *n syn* see ILLEGALITY

ant lawfulness

unlax *vb* 1 *syn* see RELAX 2

2 *syn* see REST 2

unlearned *adj syn* see UNSCHOLARLY

ant erudite, learned

unleash *vb syn* see TAKE OUT (on)

unless *conj syn* see EXCEPT 1

unlettered *adj syn* see IGNORANT 1

ant educated, lettered

unlevel *adj syn* see ROUGH 1

ant level

unlike *adj syn* see DIFFERENT 1

ant like

unlikely *adj syn* see IMPROBABLE 1

ant likely

unlikeness *n syn* see DISSIMILARITY

rel incompatibility, incongruousness, inconsistence

ant likeness

unlimited *adj* 1 *syn* see LIMITLESS

ant limited, measured

2 *syn* see TOTAL 5

ant limited

unload *vb* to remove cargo or the cargo of <*unload* cattle from a truck>

syn disburden, discharge, off-load, unlade, unship, unstow

rel disencumber, dump, jettison, lighten; stevedore; debark, disembark, land

idiom break bulk

ant lade, load

unloose *vb syn* see LOOSE 3

unloosen *vb syn* see LOOSE 3

unloyal *adj syn* see FAITHLESS

ant loyal

‖**unluck** *n syn* see MISFORTUNE

ant luck

unlucky *adj* 1 *syn* see OMINOUS

2 involving or suffering misfortune that results from chance <in spite of careful

planning the expedition was *unlucky* from the start>
  syn hapless, ill-fated, ill-starred, luckless, misfortunate, star-crossed, unfortunate, unhappy, untoward
  rel calamitous, cataclysmic, catastrophic, dire, disastrous, tragical
  idiom down on one's luck, out of luck
  con fortunate, happy, providential; prosperous, successful; coming, made
  ant lucky

unmake *vb* **1 syn** see DESTROY 1
  2 syn see DEPOSE 1
  ant make

unman *vb* **syn** see UNNERVE
  rel deplete, drain, exhaust, impoverish; abase, degrade; disqualify, paralyze, prostrate, unfit
  idiom knock the bottom (*or* stuffing) out of
  con brace, fortify
  ant man

unmanageable *adj* **syn** see UNRULY 1
  ant manageable

unmanly *adj* **1 syn** see COWARDLY
  ant manly
  2 syn see EFFEMINATE
  ant manly

unmannered *adj* **1 syn** see RUDE 6
  2 syn see FRANK

unmannerly *adj* **syn** see RUDE 6
  ant mannerly

unmarred *adj* **syn** see WHOLE 1
  ant marred

unmarried *adj* **syn** see SINGLE 1
  ant married, wed

unmarry *vb* **syn** see DIVORCE 2

unmask *vb* **syn** see EXPOSE 1

unmatchable *adj* **syn** see SUPREME

unmatched *adj* **1 syn** see ALONE 3
  2 syn see ODD 1
  ant matched

unmaterial *adj* **syn** see IMMATERIAL 1
  ant material

unmeaning *adj* **syn** see SENSELESS 5
  ant meaningful

unmeasurable *adj* **1 syn** see INCALCULABLE 1
  ant measurable
  2 syn see EXCESSIVE 1

unmeasured *adj* **1 syn** see INCALCULABLE 1
  ant measurable
  2 syn see LIMITLESS
  ant limited, measured

unmeditated *adj* **syn** see SPONTANEOUS
  ant meditated

unmeet *adj* **syn** see UNFIT 1
  ant meet

unmeetness *n* **syn** see IMPROPRIETY 1

unmellowed *adj* **syn** see YOUNG 1
  con developed, matured, ripened
  ant mellow, mellowed

unmerciful *adj* **syn** see PITILESS
  ant merciful

unmindful *adj* **syn** see FORGETFUL

con anxious, careful, concerned
  ant mindful; solicitous

unmindfulness *n* **syn** see APATHY 2
  ant mindfulness

unmistakable *adj* **syn** see CLEAR 5
  ant mistakable

unmitigated *adj* **1 syn** see PURE 2
  2 syn see UTTER

unmixable *adj* **syn** see INCONSONANT 1

unmixed *adj* **1 syn** see STRAIGHT 3
  ant blended, mixed
  2 syn see PURE 2

unmodern *adj* **syn** see OLD-FASHIONED
  ant modern

unmodifiable *adj* **syn** see INFLEXIBLE 3
  ant modifiable

unmovable *adj* **1 syn** see IMMOVABLE 1
  ant mobile, movable
  2 syn see INFLEXIBLE 3

unmoving *adj* **syn** see STATIC
  ant mobile

unmusical *adj* **syn** see DISSONANT 1
  ant musical

unnamed *adj* **syn** see ANONYMOUS

unnatural *adj* **1 syn** see IRREGULAR 1
  2 syn see SUPERNATURAL 2
  ant natural

unneat *adj* **syn** see SLOVENLY 1
  ant neat

unnecessary *adj* not needed <*unnecessary* loss of life>
  syn inessential, needless, uncalled-for, unessential, unneeded, unneedful, unrequired
  rel excess, redundant, superfluous, surplus; lavish, prodigal, profuse; gratuitous, supererogatory
  con essential, needed, required, vital; inevitable, unescapable
  ant necessary; unavoidable

unneeded *adj* **syn** see UNNECESSARY
  ant needed; unavoidable

unneedful *adj* **syn** see UNNECESSARY
  ant needful; unavoidable

unnerve *vb* to deprive of strength, spirit, and vigor <a man so *unnerved* as to be bereft of sense and judgment>
  syn castrate, emasculate, enervate, unman, unstring
  rel enfeeble, sap, undermine, weaken; bewilder, confound, distract; agitate, perturb, upset
  con brace (up), inspirit, invigorate, reinforce, strengthen; encourage, hearten, steel
  ant nerve

unneutral *adj* **syn** see BIASED 2
  ant neutral

unnoted *adj* **syn** see OBSCURE 5
  rel unconsidered, unobserved, unremarked
  ant noted

unnoteworthy *adj* **syn** see COMMON 6
  ant noteworthy

unnoticeable *adj* **syn** see INCONSPICUOUS
  ant noticeable

unnoticing *adj* **syn** see INATTENTIVE
  ant noticing

unnumberable *adj* **syn** see INNUMERABLE

unnumbered *adj* **syn** see INNUMERABLE
  ant numbered

unobjectionable *adj* **syn** see DECENT 4
  ant objectionable

---

syn synonym(s)   **rel** related word(s)
ant antonym(s)   **con** contrasted word(s)
idiom idiomatic equivalent(s)
|| use limited; if in doubt, see a dictionary

unobjective adj syn see SUBJECTIVE
    ant objective
unobservable adj syn see IMPERCEPTIBLE
unobservant adj syn see INATTENTIVE
    ant observant, observing
unobserving adj syn see INATTENTIVE
    ant observant, observing
unobstructed adj syn see OPEN 1
    con clogged, plugged
    ant obstructed
unobtainable adj syn see INACCESSIBLE
unobtrusive adj syn see QUIET 4
    ant obtrusive
unoffending adj syn see HARMLESS
    ant offending
unoffensive adj syn see HARMLESS
    ant offensive
unofficial adj syn see INFORMAL 1
unoften adv syn see SELDOM
    ant often
unordinary adj syn see EXCEPTIONAL 1
    ant ordinary
unorganized adj syn see INCOHERENT 2
    ant organized
unoriginal adj lacking or manifesting a lack
    of capacity for originality <a good man but
    with a mind stolid and *unoriginal*>
    syn noncreative, sterile, uncreative, unin-
    spired, uninventive, unoriginative; *compare*
    ARID 2
    rel arid, barren, dry; dull, prosaic, staid,
    stodgy, stuffy, unfired
    con creative, inspired, inventive, originative;
    alert, aware, keen; constructive, productive
    ant original
unoriginated adj syn see SELF-EXISTENT
unoriginative adj syn see UNORIGINAL
    ant originative
unornamented adj syn see PLAIN 1
unorthodox adj syn see HERETICAL
    ant orthodox
unorthodoxy n syn see HERESY
    ant orthodoxy
unostentatious adj syn see PLAIN 1
    ant ostentatious
unpaid adj 1 serving without pay <a charity
    manned by *unpaid* assistants>
    syn uncompensated, unrecompensed, un-
    remunerated
    rel freewill, gratuitous, voluntary, volunteer
    con compensated, recompensed, remuner-
    ated
    ant paid
    2 not cleared by payment <an *unpaid* bill>
    syn due, mature, outstanding, overdue,
    owing, payable, unsettled
    idiom in arrears
    con cleared, discharged, liquidated, settled
    ant paid
unpaired adj syn see ODD 1
    ant paired
unpalatable adj 1 lacking appeal to the
    sense of taste <threw together a greasy *un-
    palatable* meal>
    syn distasteful, flat, flavorless, ill-flavored,
    insipid, savorless, tasteless, unappetizing,
    unsavory
    rel loathsome, nauseous, sickening; thin,
    washy, watery, weak
    con appetizing, delectable, delicious, flavor-
    some, sapid, savory, tasty

    ant palatable
    2 syn see BITTER 2
unparagoned adj syn see ALONE 3
    ant paragoned
unparalleled adj syn see ALONE 3
    ant paralleled
unpardonable adj syn see INEXCUSABLE
    ant pardonable
unparented adj syn see ORPHAN
unpassioned adj syn see NEUTRAL
    ant impassioned, passionate
unpatient adj syn see IMPATIENT 1
    ant patient
unpeace n syn see DISCORD
    ant peace
unpeaceful adj syn see RESTLESS
    ant peaceful
unpedantic adj syn see LIVELY 1
    ant pedantic
unperceivable adj syn see IMPERCEPTIBLE
unperceiving adj 1 syn see IMPERCEPTIVE
    ant perceiving, perceptive, percipient
    2 syn see INATTENTIVE
unperceptive adj syn see IMPERCEPTIVE
    ant perceiving, perceptive, percipient
unperishable adj syn see INDESTRUCTIBLE
    ant perishable
unpermissive adj syn see RIGID 3
    ant permissive
unphysical adj syn see IMMATERIAL 1
    ant physical
unpierceable adj syn see IMPASSABLE 1
    ant pierceable
unpitying adj syn see PITILESS
    ant pitying
unplanned adj 1 syn see RANDOM
    ant planned
    2 syn see UNINTENTIONAL
    ant planned
unpleasant adj syn see BAD 8
unpliable adj syn see OBSTINATE
    ant pliable, pliant
unpliant adj syn see OBSTINATE
    ant pliable, pliant
unpolished adj 1 syn see RUDE 1
    idiom in the rough
    ant polished
    2 syn see RUDE 6
    3 syn see BOORISH
    ant polished
unpolitic adj syn see TACTLESS
    ant politic
unpractical adj syn see IMPRACTICAL 1
    ant practical
unpracticed adj 1 syn see UNTRIED 1
    2 syn see INEXPERIENCED
    ant practiced
unpredictable adj syn see UNCERTAIN 1
    ant predictable
unprejudiced adj syn see FAIR 4
    ant prejudiced
unpremeditated adj 1 syn see SPONTANE-
    OUS
    2 syn see UNINTENTIONAL
    ant premeditated
unprepossessed adj syn see FAIR 4
    ant prepossessed
unprescribed adj syn see VOLUNTARY
    ant prescribed
unpretentious adj syn see PLAIN 1

ant pretentious
unpretty *adj syn see* PLAIN 5
  ant pretty
unprevailing *adj syn see* FUTILE
unprincipled *adj* **1** *syn see* UNSCRUPULOUS
  ant principled
  2 *syn see* ABANDONED 2
  rel corrupt, crooked, unscrupulous; dishonest, unconscientious, unethical
  3 *syn see* CORRUPT 2
  ant principled
unproductive *adj* **1** *syn see* BARREN 2
  rel impotent, infecund, unprolific
  ant productive
  2 *syn see* FUTILE
  ant productive
unprofane *adj syn see* HOLY 1
  ant profane
unproficient *adj syn see* UNSKILLFUL 1
  ant proficient, skilled
unprogressive *adj* **1** *syn see* BACKWARD 6
  ant progressive
  2 *syn see* BACKWARD 5
  ant progressive
unprompted *adj syn see* SPONTANEOUS
unpropitious *adj syn see* OMINOUS
  rel adverse, antagonistic, counter
  con cheering, encouraging, reassuring
  ant propitious
unproportionate *adj syn see* LOPSIDED
  ant proportionate
unprosperous *adj syn see* POOR 1
  ant prosperous
unprosperousness *n syn see* POVERTY 1
  ant prosperousness
unprotected *adj syn see* HELPLESS 1
  rel undefended, unguarded, unsheltered, unshielded; insecure, unsafe
  ant protected
unproved *adj syn see* UNTRIED 1
  ant proved
unpunctual *adj syn see* TARDY
  ant punctual
unpurposed *adj* **1** *syn see* UNINTENTIONAL
  2 *syn see* FECKLESS 1
unqualified *adj* **1** *syn see* UNFIT 2
  rel unskilled; unsuitable
  ant qualified
  2 *syn see* SURE 2
  rel unconditional, unlimited, unreserved; clear, explicit, express; entire, perfect, utter
  ant qualified
  3 *syn see* UTTER
  4 *syn see* PURE 2
unquenchable *adj syn see* INSATIABLE
  ant quenchable
unquestionable *adj* **1** *syn see* AUTHENTIC 2
  ant doubtable, questionable
  2 *syn see* POSITIVE 3
  rel dependable, reliable; established, well-founded, well-grounded
  ant doubtable, questionable
  3 *syn see* DOWNRIGHT 2
unquestionably *adv syn see* EASILY 2

ant questionably
unquestioning *adj syn see* SURE 2
  ant questioning
unquiet *adj syn see* RESTLESS
  ant quiet
unravel *vb syn see* SOLVE 2
  rel disentangle, extricate, untangle
unreachable *adj syn see* INACCESSIBLE
  ant reachable
unreadable *adj syn see* ILLEGIBLE
  ant legible, readable
unreal *adj syn see* FICTITIOUS 1
  ant real
unrealistic *adj syn see* IMPRACTICAL 1
  ant realistic
unrealizable *adj syn see* IMPOSSIBLE 1
  ant realizable
unreasonable *adj* **1** *syn see* ILLOGICAL
  rel incongruous, loose, self-contradictory
  ant reasonable
  2 exceeding the bounds of reason or right <the constitutional guarantees against *unreasonable* searches and seizures>
  syn unconscionable, undue, unjustifiable, unwarrantable, unwarranted
  rel arbitrary, peremptory; excessive, immoderate, inordinate, overmuch; improper, unlawful, unrightful, wrongful
  con lawful, licit; proper, right, tolerable
  ant reasonable
unreasoned *adj syn see* ILLOGICAL
  ant reasoned
unrecking *adj syn see* CARELESS 1
unreckonable *adj syn see* INCALCULABLE 1
unrecompensed *adj syn see* UNPAID 1
  ant recompensed
unrecoverable *adj syn see* HOPELESS 2
unrefined *adj* **1** *syn see* BOORISH
  ant refined
  2 *syn see* COARSE 3
  ant refined
  3 not freed from unwanted material <shipped the *unrefined* ore>
  syn crude, impure, native, raw, run-of-mine, ungraded, unsorted
  rel rough, roughcast, roughhewn; coarse, natural, undressed, unprocessed
  idiom in the rough
  con dressed, processed
  ant refined
unreflective *adj syn see* CARELESS 1
unregretful *adj syn see* REMORSELESS
  ant regretful
unregular *adj syn see* IRREGULAR 1
  ant regular
unrehearsed *adj syn see* EXTEMPORANEOUS
  ant rehearsed
unrelenting *adj syn see* GRIM 3
  ant relenting
unreliable *adj* **1** not to be counted on <it is certain that much of the testimony was *unreliable*>
  syn dubious, fly-by-night, questionable, trustless, undependable, unsure, untrustworthy, untrusty
  rel fickle, inconstant, unstable, vacillating; faithless, false, untrue; falsehearted, perfidious; shifty, slick, slippery, tricky; inaccurate, inexact, unfaithful

---

syn synonym(s)   *rel* related word(s)
ant antonym(s)   *con* contrasted word(s)
idiom idiomatic equivalent(s)
‖ use limited; if in doubt, see a dictionary

idiom not to be depended (*or* relied) on
con dependable, trustworthy, trusty; constant; faithful, true
ant reliable
2 *syn* see UNSAFE
ant reliable
unreligious *adj syn* see IRRELIGIOUS
ant religious
unremarkable *adj syn* see ORDINARY 1
unremitting *adj syn* see CONTINUAL
unremittingly *adv syn* see HARD 3
unremorseful *adj syn* see REMORSELESS
ant remorseful
unremunerated *adj syn* see UNPAID 1
ant remunerated
unrenowned *adj syn* see OBSCURE 5
ant renowned
unrepealable *adj syn* see IRREVOCABLE
ant repealable
unrepeatable *adj syn* see ONLY 2
unrepentant *adj syn* see REMORSELESS
ant repentant
unrepresentative *adj syn* see ABNORMAL 1
unrequested *adj syn* see UNASKED
unrequired *adj* **1** *syn* see UNNECESSARY
ant required
2 *syn* see DISPENSABLE
ant required
unreserved *adj* **1** *syn* see FRANK 1
ant reserved
2 *syn* see DEMONSTRATIVE
ant reserved
3 *syn* see EASYGOING 3
unresistant *adj syn* see PASSIVE 2
ant resistant, resisting
unresisting *adj syn* see PASSIVE 2
ant resistant, resisting
unresolved *adj syn* see VACILLATING 2
ant resolved
unrespectable *adj syn* see DISREPUTABLE 1
ant respectable
unresponsive *adj* **1** *syn* see INSUSCEPTIBLE
ant responsive
2 *syn* see FRIGID 3
unresponsiveness *n syn* see APATHY 1
ant responsiveness
unrest *n* a disturbed uneasy state <that popular *unrest* that, unchecked, can lead to insurrection and anarchy>
syn ailment, disquiet, disquietude, ferment, inquietude, restiveness, restlessness, storm and stress, Sturm und Drang, turmoil
rel agitation, commotion, confusion, convulsion, tumult, turbulence, upheaval; anarchy, chaos, disorder
con calm, easiness, peace, quiet
unrestful *adj* **1** *syn* see RESTLESS
ant restful
2 *syn* see NERVOUS
unrestrainable *adj syn* see IRREPRESSIBLE
ant restrainable
unrestrained *adj* **1** *syn* see EXCESSIVE 2
2 *syn* see FREE 2
ant restrained
3 *syn* see AUDACIOUS 4
rel candid, frank, open; forthright, plainspoken, straightforward; bluff, blunt, brusque

ant restrained
4 *syn* see DEMONSTRATIVE
ant restrained
unrestraint *n* **1** *syn* see UNCONSTRAINT
ant restraint
2 *syn* see ABANDON 2
unrestricted *adj syn* see OPEN 4
unriddle *vb syn* see SOLVE 2
unrighteous *adj syn* see INEQUITABLE
ant righteous
unripe *adj syn* see YOUNG 1
unrivaled *adj syn* see ALONE 3
unromantic *adj syn* see REALISTIC
ant romantic
unruffled *adj syn* see COOL 2
ant discomposed, ruffled
unruly *adj* **1** resistant to discipline or control <a stubborn *unruly* boy>
syn fractious, indocile, indomitable, intractable, recalcitrant, uncontrollable, undisciplinable, undisciplined, ungovernable, unmanageable, untoward, wild; *compare* OBSTINATE, TURBULENT 1
rel contumacious, incorrigible, insubordinate, rebellious; contrary, froward, perverse, wayward; boisterous, obstreperous, rampageous; disorderly, raffish, rambunctious, rowdy, turbulent
idiom out of hand
con controlled, easy, mild, restrained; disciplined, governable, manageable; amenable, biddable, obedient; correct, proper
ant docile, tractable
2 *syn* see TURBULENT 1
rel hard, ruffianly, tough
3 *syn* see DISOBEDIENT
unsacred *adj syn* see PROFANE 1
ant sacred
unsafe *adj* not to be depended on or trusted <an *unsafe* investment>
syn unassured, undependable, unreliable, untrustworthy
rel insecure, shaky, tottery, unsound, unstable; chancy, hazardous, risky; dangerous, jeopardous, perilous; erratic, uncertain
con dependable, trustworthy; secure, sound, stable, substantial
ant safe
unsaid *adj syn* see TACIT 1
unsalutary *adj syn* see UNWHOLESOME 1
ant salutary
unsandaled *adj syn* see BAREFOOT 1
ant sandaled
unsane *adj syn* see INSANE 1
ant sane
unsatiate *adj syn* see INSATIABLE
ant satiate, satiated
unsatisfactory *adj syn* see BAD 1
ant satisfactory
unsatisfiable *adj syn* see INSATIABLE
ant satisfiable
unsavory *adj syn* see UNPALATABLE 1
ant savory
unsay *vb syn* see ABJURE
unscathed *adj syn* see SAFE 1
unscholarly *adj* not devoted to scholarly pursuits <*unscholarly* concerns>
syn inerudite, unbookish, unlearned, unstudious
rel unenlightened, uninformed, uninitiated; callow, green, unripe; inexperienced, naive

con bookish, erudite, learned; enlightened, informed; experienced
ant scholarly

unschooled *adj* **1** *syn* see IGNORANT 1
2 *syn* see NATURAL 5

unscramble *vb syn* see EXTRICATE 2

unscrupulous *adj* **1** lacking in moral scruples <*unscrupulous* conduct of political leaders>
syn conscienceless, stick-at-nothing, unconscionable, unprincipled
rel crafty, deceitful, scheming; improper, unseemly, wrongful; corrupt, crooked, dishonest; questionable, shady, sinister, underhand
con conscientious, dutiful, proper, upright; dependable, reliable, responsible
ant scrupulous
2 *syn* see CORRUPT 2
con meticulous, particular, punctilious, strict
ant scrupulous

unseasonable *adj* **1** involving or occurring at an inappropriate or unexpected time <his wife's sudden return proved most *unseasonable*>
syn ill-seasoned, ill-timed, inopportune, malapropos, mistimed, untimely
rel deplorable, inappropriate, inconvenient, unsuitable; inauspicious, infelicitous, undesirable, unfavorable, unfortunate
con apropos, opportune, timely, well-timed
ant seasonable
2 *syn* see IMPROPER 1

unseasoned *adj syn* see INEXPERIENCED
ant seasoned

unseat *vb syn* see THROW 2

unsectarian *adj syn* see NONSECTARIAN
ant sectarian

unseemliness *n syn* see IMPROPRIETY 1
ant propriety, seemliness

unseemly *adj* **1** *syn* see INDECOROUS
rel coarse, crude, inelegant, unrefined; raffish, rowdy, ruffianly
con prim, restrained, starchy, stiff, stilted; elegant, gracious, polished, refined
ant seemly
2 *syn* see IMPROPER 1
ant seemly

unselfish *adj syn* see SELFLESS
ant selfish

unsentimental *adj syn* see REALISTIC
ant sentimental

unserviceable *adj syn* see IMPRACTICABLE 2
ant serviceable

unsettle *vb* **1** *syn* see DISORDER 1
rel agitate, disquiet, perturb; discommode, incommode, trouble
con calm, ease, quiet, stabilize, steady
ant settle
2 *syn* see UPSET 5
ant settle
3 *syn* see DISCOMPOSE 1

unsettled *adj* **1** *syn* see RESTLESS

2 *syn* see CHANGEABLE 1
ant settled
3 *syn* see DOUBTFUL 1
4 *syn* see PENDING
ant settled
5 *syn* see BACK 1
6 *syn* see UNPAID 2
ant settled

unsettledness *n syn* see INSTABILITY

unsex *vb syn* see STERILIZE

unshackle *vb syn* see FREE
ant shackle

unshakable *adj syn* see SURE 2
ant shakable

unshaken *adj syn* see SURE 2
ant shaken

unshaped *adj syn* see FORMLESS
ant shaped

unshared *adj syn* see SOLE 4
ant shared

unship *vb syn* see UNLOAD

unshod *adj syn* see BAREFOOT 1
ant shod

unshroud *vb syn* see EXPOSE 4
ant shroud

unshut *vb syn* see OPEN 1
ant shut

unsightly *adj syn* see UGLY 2
rel ill-shaped, unshapely; unesthetic, drab, dull, lackluster
ant sightly

unsimilar *adj syn* see DIFFERENT 1
ant similar

unskilled *adj* **1** *syn* see AMATEURISH
ant skilled
2 *syn* see INEFFICIENT 2
ant skilled

unskillful *adj* **1** lacking in skill or proficiency <an ardent but *unskillful* home mechanic>
syn inadept, inapt, inept, inexpert, unapt, undexterous, unfacile, unhandy, unproficient
rel incapable, incompetent; unfitted, unqualified, unready
con adept, apt, dexterous, expert, handy, proficient
ant skillful
2 *syn* see INEFFICIENT 2

unsleeping *adj syn* see WATCHFUL
ant sleeping

unsmooth *adj syn* see ROUGH 1
ant smooth

unsober *adj syn* see INTOXICATED 1
ant sober

unsociable *adj* disinclined to active social intercourse <tried to hide his basically shy *unsociable* nature under a professional heartiness of manner>
syn aloof, cool, distant, insociable, offish, reserved, shut-in, solitary, standoff, standoffish, touch-me-not-ish, unapproachable, unbending, uncommunicative, uncompanionable, withdrawn; *compare* INDIFFERENT 2, UNDEMONSTRATIVE
rel self-contained, self-sufficient; exclusive, inaccessible, remote; prickly, sensitive; brooding, secretive; diffident, shy, timid
con cordial, genial, hearty, outgoing; companionable, friendly, gregarious
ant sociable, social

---

syn synonym(s)   *rel* related word(s)
ant antonym(s)   *con* contrasted word(s)
idiom idiomatic equivalent(s)
‖ use limited; if in doubt, see a dictionary

unsoiled *adj syn* see CLEAN 1
ant soiled, sullied

unsoluble *adj syn* see INSOLUBLE
ant soluble, solvable

unsolvable *adj syn* see INSOLUBLE
ant soluble, solvable

unsophisticated *adj syn* see NATURAL 5
rel authentic, bona fide, genuine; callow, crude, green, uncouth
con finished, polished, smooth, suave
ant sophisticated

unsorry *adj syn* see REMORSELESS
ant sorry

unsorted *adj* 1 *syn* see MISCELLANEOUS
2 *syn* see UNREFINED 3
ant sorted

unsought *adj* 1 *syn* see UNASKED
2 *syn* see UNWELCOME 1

unsound *adj* 1 *syn* see INSANE 1
ant sound
2 *syn* see WEAK 1
rel damaged, faulty, flawed, imperfect
con solid, strong, substantial
ant sound
3 *syn* see FALSE 1
ant sound
4 *syn* see DANGEROUS 1

unsparing *adj syn* see LIBERAL 1
ant close, sparing

unspeakable *adj syn* see UNUTTERABLE
rel loathsome, offensive, repulsive, revolting; abominable, detestable, hateful, odious; distasteful, obnoxious, repellent, repugnant; atrocious, disgusting, outrageous

unspoiled *adj syn* see VIRGIN 2

unspoken *adj* 1 not put into words <met regularly by a sort of *unspoken* agreement>
syn silent, tacit, unexpressed, unuttered, unvoiced, wordless
rel implicit, implied, understood; hinted, intimated, suggested; mute, unsaid, unstated
con mentioned, said, stated, told, voiced
ant spoken
2 *syn* see TACIT 1
ant spoken

unstability *n syn* see INSTABILITY
ant stability

unstable *adj* 1 *syn* see MOVABLE
ant stable
2 difficult to manage because of lack of physical steadiness <the canoe is an inherently *unstable* craft>
syn rocky, ticklish, tricky
rel insecure, uncertain, unsteady
con secure, steady
ant stable
3 *syn* see WEAK 2
ant stable
4 *syn* see INCONSTANT 1
rel buoyant, effervescent, elastic, resilient; freakish
ant stable
5 *syn* see CHANGEABLE 1
ant stable
6 *syn* see MUTABLE 2
ant stable
7 *syn* see DOUBTFUL 1

unstableness *n syn* see INSTABILITY
ant stability, stableness

unsteadfast *adj syn* see MOVABLE

ant steadfast

unsteadfastness *n syn* see INSTABILITY
ant steadfastness

unsteadiness *n syn* see INSTABILITY
ant steadiness

unsteady *adj* 1 *syn* see MOVABLE
2 *syn* see CHANGEABLE 1
ant steady
3 *syn* see MUTABLE 2
ant steady

unsteel *vb syn* see DISARM 2

unstop *vb syn* see OPEN 1
ant stop

unstow *vb syn* see UNLOAD

unstrengthen *vb syn* see WEAKEN 1
ant strengthen

unstring *vb syn* see UNNERVE

unstudied *adj* 1 *syn* see NATURAL 5
ant studied
2 *syn* see EXTEMPORANEOUS
ant studied

unstudious *adj syn* see UNSCHOLARLY
ant studious

unstylish *adj syn* see TACKY 2
ant stylish

unsubstantial *adj* 1 *syn* see TENUOUS 3
ant substantial
2 *syn* see IMPLAUSIBLE
3 *syn* see IMMATERIAL 1
ant substantial
4 *syn* see WEAK 1
rel insecure, shaky, undependable
ant substantial

unsuccess *n syn* see FAILURE 2
ant success, successfulness

unsuccessfulness *n syn* see FAILURE 2
ant success, successfulness

unsufferable *adj syn* see INSUFFERABLE
ant sufferable

unsufficient *adj syn* see SHORT 3
ant sufficient

unsuitable *adj* 1 *syn* see UNFIT 1
rel undesirable, unhappy
ant suitable
2 *syn* see IMPROPER 1
ant suitable

unsuited *adj* 1 *syn* see UNFIT 1
rel inadmissible, objectionable, unacceptable; disappointing, inadequate
ant suited

unsullied *adj* 1 *syn* see CHASTE
ant sullied
2 *syn* see CLEAN 1
ant soiled, sullied

unsupportable *adj syn* see INSUFFERABLE
ant bearable, supportable

unsure *adj* 1 *syn* see INSECURE 1
ant sure
2 *syn* see WEAK 2
3 *syn* see DOUBTFUL 1
ant sure
4 *syn* see UNRELIABLE 1

unsurmountable *adj syn* see INSUPERABLE
ant surmountable

unsurpassable *adj syn* see SUPREME
ant surpassable

unsusceptible *adj syn* see INSUSCEPTIBLE
ant susceptible

unsuspecting *adj syn* see CREDULOUS
ant suspecting, suspicious

unsuspicious *adj syn* see CREDULOUS
  ant suspecting, suspicious
unswayable *adj syn* see INFLEXIBLE 2
  ant suasible
unswerving *adj syn* see WHOLE 5
  rel constant, steadfast, steady, unremitting;
  firm, unfaltering, unwavering
unsymmetrical *adj syn* see LOPSIDED
  ant symmetrical
unsympathetic *adj* **1** *syn* see ANTIPA-
  THETIC
  rel dislikable, unlikable; displeasing, unpleasant, unpleasing
  con appealing, congenial, likable; pleasant,
  pleasing
  ant sympathetic
  2 *syn* see UNFEELING 2
  rel cold, cool, frigid; disinterested, halfhearted, indifferent, lukewarm
  ant sympathetic
untactful *adj syn* see TACTLESS
  ant tactful
untangle *vb syn* see EXTRICATE 2
  ant entangle, tangle
untapped *adj syn* see VIRGIN 2
untaught *adj syn* see IGNORANT 1
untellable *adj syn* see UNUTTERABLE
  ant expressible
untempered *adj syn* see EXCESSIVE 2
  ant temperate, tempered
untenable *adj syn* see INEXCUSABLE
  ant tenable
untended *adj syn* see NEGLECTED
untested *adj syn* see UNTRIED 1
  ant tested, tried
unthankful *adj* **1** *syn* see THANKLESS 2
  2 *syn* see THANKLESS 1
  ant thankful
unthinkable *adj* **1** *syn* see EXCEPTIONAL 1
  2 *syn* see INCREDIBLE 1
  ant thinkable
unthinking *adj syn* see CARELESS 1
unthorough *adj syn* see SLIPSHOD 3
  ant thorough
unthought *adj syn* see UNINTENTIONAL
  ant aforethought
unthrift *n* **1** *syn* see EXTRAVAGANCE 2
  ant thrift
  2 *syn* see SPENDTHRIFT
unthrift *adj syn* see IMPROVIDENT
unthrifty *adj syn* see IMPROVIDENT
  ant thrifty
untidy *adj* **1** *syn* see SLOVENLY 1
  ant tidy
  2 *syn* see SLIPSHOD 3
untie *vb syn* see EXTRICATE 2
untighten *vb syn* see LOOSE 5
  ant tighten
until *prep* up to a stipulated time <we never
  met him *until* last night>
  syn before, in advance of, prior to, till, to,
  up till, up to; *compare* BEFORE 1
until *conj syn* see TILL
untimely *adj* **1** *syn* see EARLY 2
  ant timely
  2 *syn* see UNSEASONABLE 1

  con opportune, pat, seasonable, well-timed
  ant timely
  3 *syn* see IMPROPER 1
  ant timely
untiring *adj syn* see INDEFATIGABLE
  con casual, disinterested, intermittent
untold *adj* **1** *syn* see HUGE
  2 *syn* see INNUMERABLE
untouchable *n syn* see OUTCAST
  rel déclassé, outcaste, outsider
untouched *adj* **1** *syn* see WHOLE 1
  2 *syn* see VIRGIN 2
untoward *adj* **1** *syn* see UNRULY 1
  2 *syn* see UNLUCKY
  3 *syn* see INDECOROUS
untowardness *n syn* see IMPROPRIETY 1
untrammeled *adj syn* see AUDACIOUS 4
untranquil *adj syn* see RESTLESS
untried *adj* **1** not subjected to test or proof
  (as by experience or use) <the fledgling's
  untried wings>
  syn undemonstrated, unpracticed, unproved, untested
  rel inexperienced, unseasoned; callow,
  green, immature; fresh, half-baked, unripe
  con practiced, proven, tested; accomplished, finished, skilled; initiated
  ant tested, tried
  2 *syn* see INEXPERIENCED
untroubled *adj syn* see CALM 1
  ant troubled
untroublesome *adj syn* see EASY 1
untrue *adj* **1** *syn* see FAITHLESS
  ant true
  2 *syn* see FALSE 1
  rel imprecise, inexact, unprecise; forsworn,
  perjured
  con exact, precise
  ant true
untruism *n syn* see LIE
  ant truism
untrustworthy *adj* **1** *syn* see UNRELIABLE
  1
  ant trustworthy
  2 *syn* see UNSAFE
  ant trustworthy
untrusty *adj syn* see UNRELIABLE 1
  ant trusty
untruth *n* **1** *syn* see FALLACY 1
  ant truth
  2 *syn* see LIE
  ant truth
untruthful *adj syn* see DISHONEST
  rel deceptive, delusive, delusory, misleading; false, wrong; inaccurate, incorrect
  ant truthful
untruthfulness *n syn* see MENDACITY
  ant truthfulness
untune *vb syn* see DISCOMPOSE 1
untutored *adj* **1** *syn* see IGNORANT 1
  2 *syn* see NATURAL 5
untwine *vb syn* see EXTRICATE 2
untypical *adj syn* see ABNORMAL 1
  ant typical
ununderstandable *adj syn* see INCONCEIV-
  ABLE 1
  ant understandable
unusable *adj syn* see IMPRACTICABLE 2
  ant usable
unused *adj syn* see VACANT 4

---

syn synonym(s)   *rel* related word(s)
ant antonym(s)   *con* contrasted word(s)
idiom idiomatic equivalent(s)
‖ use limited; if in doubt, see a dictionary

unusual adj 1 syn see EXCEPTIONAL 1
  idiom the exception rather than the rule
  ant usual
  2 syn see STRANGE 4
  ant usual
unusually adv syn see EXTRA
unutterable adj being beyond human power to tell or describe <*unutterable* spiritual bliss>
  syn incommunicable, indefinable, indescribable, ineffable, inenarrable, inexpressible, undescribable, unexpressible, unspeakable, untellable
  rel inconceivable, incredible, unbelievable, unimaginable; awesome, awful, marvelous, prodigious, wonderful, wondrous
  idiom beyond expression
  con commonplace, humdrum, ordinary; monotonous, samely, unvarying
unuttered adj 1 syn see UNSPOKEN 1
  ant uttered
  2 syn see TACIT 1
  ant uttered
unvarnished adj syn see FRANK
unvarying adj 1 syn see STEADY 2
  ant varying
  2 syn see SAME 3
  ant variable, varying
unveil vb 1 syn see OPEN 2
  ant veil
  2 syn see REVEAL 1
  ant veil
unveracity n syn see MENDACITY
  ant veracity
unversed adj syn see INEXPERIENCED
  ant versed
unvigilant adj syn see INCAUTIOUS 1
  ant vigilant
unvital adj syn see PETTY 2
  ant vital
unvocal adj syn see INARTICULATE 3
  ant vocal
unvoiced adj syn see UNSPOKEN 1
  ant voiced
unwanted adj 1 syn see UNWELCOME 1
  ant wanted
  2 syn see OBJECTIONABLE
unwarrantable adj syn see UNREASONABLE 2
  ant warrantable
unwarranted adj 1 syn see BASELESS
  2 syn see UNREASONABLE 2
unwary adj 1 syn see INCAUTIOUS 1
  ant wary
  2 syn see CREDULOUS
  3 syn see RASH 1
  ant wary
unwashed adj syn see IGNOBLE 1
unwashed n syn see RABBLE 2
unwasteful adj syn see SPARING
  ant wasteful
unwatchful adj 1 syn see INATTENTIVE
  ant watchful
  2 syn see INCAUTIOUS 1
  ant watchful
unwatered adj syn see DRY 1
  ant watered
unwavering adj syn see SURE 2
  ant wavering
unweariable adj syn see INDEFATIGABLE

  ant weariable
unwearying adj syn see INDEFATIGABLE
  rel constant, steady; interminable, unceasing
unwed adj syn see SINGLE 1
  ant married, wed
unwelcome adj 1 not of a kind to be welcome <an *unwelcome* interruption that scattered his train of thought>
  syn undesired, unsought, unwanted, unwished
  rel distasteful, obnoxious, repellent; unasked; undesirable, unpleasant, unpleasing
  con desired, sought, wanted; agreeable, desirable, pleasant, pleasing
  ant welcome
  2 syn see OBJECTIONABLE
  ant welcome
unwell adj somewhat disordered in health <had felt *unwell* from the moment she got up>
  syn ailing, ‖donsie, indisposed, low, mean, off-color, offish, poorly, sickly; *compare* SICK 1
  rel rocky, shaky, wobbly; feeble, frail, infirm, weakly; ill, sick; qualmish, queasy, squeamish
  idiom out of sorts, under the weather
  ant well
unwholesome adj 1 likely to be detrimental to physical, mental, or moral health <an *unwholesome* crime-ridden neighborhood>
  syn insalubrious, insalutary, noisome, noxious, sickly, unhealthful, unhealthy, unsalutary
  rel baneful, deleterious, detrimental, pernicious; harmful, hurtful, injurious, mischievous
  con healthful, hygienic, salubrious, salutary
  ant wholesome
  2 syn see OFFENSIVE
  ant wholesome
unwieldy adj clumsy and difficult to handle usually because of excessive weight and awkward form <a massive *unwieldy* sledgehammer>
  syn cumbersome, cumbrous, ponderous, unhandy; *compare* HEAVY 1
  rel awkward, inconvenient; uncontrollable, unmanageable; bulky, clumsy, lumbering, massive; burdensome, encumbering, onerous
  con compact, neat, trig, trim; adaptable, convenient, handy; easy, facile, light
  ant wieldy
unwilling adj syn see DISINCLINED
  ant willing
unwind vb syn see RELAX 2
unwise adj not marked by or according with good sense or sound judgment <his decision to quit school was most *unwise*>
  syn ill-advised, ill-judged, impolitic, imprudent, indiscreet, injudicious
  rel senseless, thoughtless, witless; impractical, unsound; fatuous, inane, inept; inappropriate, undesirable, unfortunate; foolish, misguided, unintelligent; childish, immature, naive
  idiom penny-wise and pound-foolish
  con discreet, judicious, prudent; sane, sensible, sound; appropriate, apt, desirable

ant wise
unwished *adj syn see* UNWELCOME 1
unwishful *adj syn see* DISINCLINED
ant wishful
unwitting *adj* **1** *syn see* FORGETFUL
ant witting
  2 *syn see* IGNORANT 2
  ant witting
unwitty *adj syn see* SIMPLE 3
ant ‖witty
unwonted *adj syn see* EXCEPTIONAL 1
ant wonted
unworkable *adj* **1** *syn see* IMPOSSIBLE 1
  2 *syn see* IMPRACTICABLE 2
  ant workable
unworked *adj syn see* RUDE 1
ant worked, wrought
unworkmanlike *adj syn see* INEFFICIENT 2
ant workmanlike, workmanly
unworldly *adj* **1** *syn see* DREAMY 1
  2 *syn see* NATURAL 5
  ant worldly
unworthy *adj syn see* WORTHLESS 1
ant worthy
unwritten *adj syn see* ORAL 2
ant written
unwrought *adj syn see* RUDE 1
ant worked, wrought
unyielding *adj* **1** *syn see* STIFF 1
  ant yielding
  2 *syn see* OBSTINATE
  rel firm, fixed, rigid
  ant yielding
  3 *syn see* GRIM 3
  4 *syn see* TOUGH 3
  ant yielding
  5 *syn see* INFLEXIBLE 2
up *adj* **1** *syn see* BAD 1
  2 *syn see* FAMILIAR 3
  3 *syn see* UP-TO-DATE
up *vb* **1** *syn see* RISE 4
  2 *syn see* RAISE 9
up-and-coming *adj syn see* ENTERPRIS-ING 2
  rel alert, eager, keen, ready
up and down *adv syn see* THOROUGHLY 2
up-and-down *adj syn see* DOWNRIGHT 2
upbear *vb syn see* SUPPORT 4
upbeat *adj syn see* OPTIMISTIC
upbraid *vb syn see* SCOLD 1
upchuck *vb syn see* VOMIT
upclimb *vb syn see* ASCEND 1
upcoming *adj syn see* FORTHCOMING
  rel foreseen, prospective
  idiom in prospect, on the horizon
up-country *n syn see* FRONTIER 2
update *vb syn see* RENEW 1
upend *vb syn see* WHIP 2
upgo *vb syn see* ASCEND 1
upgrade *vb syn see* ADVANCE 2
  ant downgrade
upgrade *n syn see* RISE 3
upgrading *n syn see* ADVANCEMENT 1
  ant downgrading
upgrowth *n syn see* DEVELOPMENT

upheaval *n syn see* COMMOTION 1
  rel cataclysm, catastrophe, disaster; alteration, change; churning, heaving, stirring
upheaved *adj syn see* ELEVATED 1
  ant downthrown
uphill *adj syn see* HARD 6
uphold *vb* **1** *syn see* SUPPORT 5
  rel defend, justify, maintain, vindicate; aid, assist, help
  ant contravene; subvert
  2 *syn see* SUPPORT 2
  3 *syn see* SUPPORT 4
  4 *syn see* LIFT 1
upholstered *adj* **1** *syn see* LUXURIOUS 3
  2 *syn see* FAT 2
upland *n syn see* PLATEAU
uplay *vb syn see* ACCUMULATE
uplift *vb* **1** *syn see* LIFT 1
  2 *syn see* ILLUMINATE 2
  ant degrade
uplifted *adj syn see* ELEVATED 1
upon *prep* **1** *syn see* OVER 3
  2 *syn see* OVER 4
upper class *n syn see* ARISTOCRACY
upper crust *n syn see* ARISTOCRACY
  rel (the) Four Hundred
upper hand *n syn see* BETTER 2
uppermost *adj syn see* TOP 1
  ant lowermost
‖**upper story** *n syn see* MIND 1
‖**upperworks** *n pl syn see* MIND 1
uppish *adj syn see* PRESUMPTUOUS
uppity *adj syn see* PRESUMPTUOUS
upraise *vb* **1** *syn see* LIFT 1
  2 *syn see* COMFORT
  ant depress
upraised *adj syn see* ELEVATED 1
uprear *vb* **1** *syn see* LIFT 1
  2 *syn see* BUILD 1
  3 *syn see* EXALT 1
  con bust, demote, downgrade
  ant degrade
  4 *syn see* RISE 4
upright *adj* **1** *syn see* ERECT
  2 having or manifesting a strict regard for what is morally right <an *upright* man ready to give even the devil his due>
  syn conscientious, honest, honorable, just, right, scrupulous, true
  rel ethical, moral, principled, righteous, virtuous; equitable, fair, impartial; elevated, high-minded, noble; blameless, exemplary, good, pure
  con crooked, devious, oblique; depraved; base, low, vile; ignoble, mean
  ant corrupt
uprightness *n syn see* GOODNESS
  rel nobility, reputability, worthiness; honesty, integrity
  ant corruption
uprise *vb* **1** *syn see* RISE 1
  2 *syn see* ROLL OUT
uprisen *adj syn see* ELEVATED 1
uproar *n* **1** *syn see* DIN
  rel chaos, confusion, disorder; brawl, broil, fracas, melee; commotion, confusion, turbulence, turmoil
  con calm, peace, quiet
  2 *syn see* COMMOTION 4
  3 *syn see* COMMOTION 3

---

syn synonym(s)   *rel* related word(s)
ant antonym(s)   *con* contrasted word(s)
idiom idiomatic equivalent(s)
‖ use limited; if in doubt, see a dictionary

uproarious *adj syn* see NOISY

uproot *vb syn* see ANNIHILATE 2

rel demolish, destroy; overthrow, overturn, subvert; displace, replace, supersede, supplant; move, shift, transplant

ant establish; inseminate

upset *vb 1 syn* see OVERTURN 1

rel invert, reverse; bend, curve, turn

2 *syn* see DISCOMPOSE 1

rel bewilder, confound, distract; unman, unnerve

idiom rock the boat

3 *syn* see TROUBLE 1

4 *syn* see DISORDER 1

5 to disturb the normal functioning especially of body or mind <her stomach was badly *upset* by too many sweets>

syn derange, disorder, sicken, turn, unhinge, unsettle

rel afflict, indispose, lay up; ail, suffer; debilitate, incapacitate, invalid

upshot *n 1 syn* see EFFECT 1

rel ending, termination; climax, culmination; completion, conclusion, finish

2 *syn* see SUBSTANCE 2

upside–down *adj 1* having the upper and lower parts reversed in position <*upside down* letters>

syn inverted, topsy-turvy

rel reversed

2 confused utterly even to the point of inversion of the normal or reasonable <*upside down* logic that confused cause with effect>

syn arsy-varsy, downside-up, topsy-turvy

rel inverted, reversed; chaotic, confused, helter-skelter, jumbled, mixed-up; fouled-up, haywire, ‖snafu

con orderly, well-ordered; logical, reasonable, sensible, sound; legitimate, plausible

upspring *vb syn* see SPRING 1

2 *syn* see RISE 1

upstanding *adj syn* see ERECT

upstart *n* a usually crude and pushing person who has recently reached a position of prominence, power, or wealth <declared the new executive an *upstart* lacking all breeding and culture>

syn arriviste, nouveau riche, parvenu, roturier

rel bounder, cad, outsider; guttersnipe, mucker, slob, vulgarian; boor, lout, roughneck, rowdy; comer; social climber

upsurge *vb syn* see INCREASE 2

uptight *adj syn* see TENSE 2

uptightness *n syn* see TENSION 2

up till *prep syn* see UNTIL

up to *prep syn* see UNTIL

up-to-date *adj* completely modern (as in style or outlook) <using *up-to-date* methods of study>

syn abreast, au courant, contemporary, down-to-date, red-hot, up, up-to-the-minute

rel convenient, opportune, timely; expedient, fitting, suitable; advanced, modern, stylish; à la mode, dashing, modish

idiom abreast of the times

con dusty, rusty, stale, timeworn; antiquated, outmoded, superannuated

ant out-of-date; archaic

up-to-the-minute *adj syn* see UP-TO-DATE

upturn *n syn* see COMMOTION 1

uranian *adj syn* see HOMOSEXUAL

uranian *n syn* see HOMOSEXUAL

uranist *n syn* see HOMOSEXUAL

urban *adj* of, relating to, or characteristic of a city <*urban* disorders>

syn burghal, city, municipal

rel inner city; metropolitan; civic, popular, public; oppidan, town, village

ant rural

urbane *adj 1 syn* see COSMOPOLITAN 1

2 *syn* see SUAVE

rel balanced, poised

ant bucolic, clownish

3 *syn* see GENTEEL 1

rel affable, civil, courteous, gracious, obliging

ant rude

urchin *n* a pert or roguish youngster <*urchins* pilfering apples on their way to school>

syn gamin, imp, monkey

rel brat, bratling, cub, dickens, pup, whelp, whippersnapper; guttersnipe, mudlark, ragamuffin, street arab; hobbledehoy

urge *vb* to press or impel to action, effort, or speed <his conscience *urged* him to tell the truth>

syn egg (on), exhort, goad, prick, prod, prompt, propel, sic, spur

rel hurry, hustle, push, rush, shove; blandish, cajole, coax, encourage, incite, needle, solicit, wheedle; constrain, drive, high-pressure, press, pressure; provoke, set (on), tar (on)

idiom bring pressure to bear on, twist one's arm

con brake, check, constrain, curb, hold back, inhibit, restrain

urge *n syn* see DESIRE 1

rel goad, incentive, motive, spring, spur

urgent *adj syn* see PRESSING

rel driving, impelling; demanding

usable *adj syn* see OPEN 5

ant unusable

usage *n 1 syn* see HABIT 1

rel choice, preference; procedure, proceeding, process; guidance, guiding, lead

2 *syn* see FORM 3

rel ceremony, formality

usance *n syn* see USE 1

use *n 1* the act or practice of using something or the state of being used <all tools must be kept ready for instant *use*>

syn appliance, application, employment, operation, play, usance; *compare* EXERCISE 1

con desuetude, disuse

ant nonuse

2 *syn* see EXERCISE 1

3 the quality of being appropriate or valuable to some end <even the scraps had some *use*>

syn account, advantage, applicability, appropriateness, avail, fitness, relevance, service, serviceability, usefulness, utility

rel adaptability, availability, benefit, efficacy; profit, value, worth

con inadequacy, inapplicability, inappropriateness, insufficiency, unfitness, unserviceability, uselessness, worthlessness

4 a particular service or end <industrial *uses* of atomic energy>
syn duty, function, goal, mark, object, objective, purpose, target
5 *syn* see HABIT 1
rel ceremony, formality
6 *syn* see NEED 3

use *vb* **1** *syn* see ACCUSTOM
2 to put into action or service <it is necessary to *use* resources wisely>
syn apply, bestow, employ, exercise, exploit, handle, utilize
rel manipulate, operate, ply, wield; control, govern, manage, regulate
idiom avail oneself of, bring into play, fall back (on *or* upon), make use of, press into service, put into action, put to use
con dissipate, exhaust, use up; waste
3 *syn* see OPERATE 3
4 *syn* see SPEAK 3
5 *syn* see EXPLOIT 2
idiom make the most of, make use of
6 *syn* see TREAT 2

used up *adj syn* see EFFETE 2

useful *adj* **1** *syn* see PRACTICAL 2
2 *syn* see GOOD 1
ant useless
3 *syn* see GOOD 2
ant useless

usefulness *n syn* see USE 3
ant uselessness

useless *adj* **1** *syn* see FUTILE 1
ant useful
2 *syn* see IMPRACTICABLE 2
ant useful
3 *syn* see FECKLESS 1

use up *vb* **1** *syn* see CONSUME 1
2 *syn* see GO 4
3 *syn* see DEPLETE

usher *vb syn* see PRECEDE 3

usher in *vb syn* see INTRODUCE 3

usual *adj* **1** familiar through frequent or regular repetition <the sort that would perform her *usual* chores while waiting for the end of the world>
syn accepted, accustomed, chronic, customary, habitual, routine, wonted
rel natural, normal, regular, typical; common, familiar, ordinary; current, prevailing, prevalent, rife
idiom that make up one's daily round
con exceptional, rare, unaccustomed; remarkable, strange, unexpected
ant unusual
2 *syn* see GENERAL 1
3 *syn* see ORDINARY 1

usually *adv* **1** by or in accord with habit or custom <establishments of a kind *usually* restricted to back streets>
syn as usual, consistently, customarily, habitually, wontedly
2 more often than not <he is *usually* late for work>
syn as a rule, by ordinary, commonly, frequently, generally, ordinarily

rel now and again (*or* now and then), occasionally, once and again, sometimes
idiom for the most part, in the main
con infrequently, seldom, uncommonly
ant rarely

usurer *n syn* see LOAN SHARK

usurp *vb* **1** *syn* see ARROGATE 1
ant abdicate
2 *syn* see SUPPLANT 1

utensil *n syn* see IMPLEMENT

utile *adj syn* see PRACTICAL 2
ant inutile

utilitarian *adj syn* see REALISTIC

utility *n syn* see USE 3
ant inutility

utilize *vb syn* see USE 2
rel advance, forward, further, promote

utmost *adj* **1** *syn* see EXTREME 5
2 *syn* see MAXIMUM
3 *syn* see EXTREME 1

utopia *n* an often imaginary place or situation of perfection and order <as far back as Plato, writers have attempted to portray their notion of *utopia*>
syn arcadia, Cockaigne, fairyland, heaven, lubberland, paradise, promised land, Shangri-la, wonderland, Zion
rel dreamland, dreamworld, never-never land

utopian *adj* **1** *syn* see IDEALISTIC
rel abstract, ideal, transcendental
2 *syn* see AMBITIOUS 2
rel impossible, impracticable, unfeasible; arcadian, edenic, millennial, otherworldly

utopian *n syn* see DREAMER

utter *adj* being such without qualification — used especially to intensify the noun modified <acted like an *utter* idiot>
syn absolute, all-fired, arrant, black, blamed, blank, blankety-blank, blasted, bleeding, blessed, blighted, blinding, ‖blinking, blithering, ‖blooming, blue, complete, confounded, ‖consarned, consummate, crashing, dad-blamed, dad-blasted, dad=burned, damned, dang, darn (*or* durn), dashed, deuced, doggone, double-dyed, double-dyed, downright, flat-out, goldarn, gross, hell-fired, infernal, out-and-out, outright, perfect, positive, ‖proper, pure, ‖puredee (*or* pure-D), rank, regular, sheer, stark, straight-out, ‖tarnation, thoroughgoing, total, unmitigated, unqualified; *compare* PURE 1

utter *vb* **1** *syn* see SPEAK 1
idiom give utterance to
2 *syn* see SAY 1

utterance *n* **1** *syn* see WORD 1
2 *syn* see VOCALIZATION
3 *syn* see EXPRESSION 1
4 *syn* see SPEECH 2

uttering *n syn* see VOCALIZATION

utterly *adv* **1** *syn* see WELL 3
2 *syn* see ALL 1

uttermost *adj* **1** *syn* see EXTREME 5
2 *syn* see EXTREME 1

---

syn synonym(s)   *rel* related word(s)
ant antonym(s)   *con* contrasted word(s)
idiom idiomatic equivalent(s)
‖ use limited; if in doubt, see a dictionary

V

vacancy *n syn* see VACUITY 2
 rel desertedness
 ant occupancy
vacant *adj* **1** *syn* see EMPTY 1
 rel tenantless, unfilled, unoccupied, untaken
 con inhabited, tenanted
 ant occupied
 2 *syn* see VACUOUS 2
 3 *syn* see EXPRESSIONLESS
 rel empty-headed, inane, thoughtless, witless
 4 not being put to normal or appropriate use <*vacant* land>
 syn idle, unused
 rel bare, empty; unfilled, unoccupied
 con filled; used
 ant occupied
vacate *vb* **1** *syn* see ANNUL 4
 rel repeal, rescind, retract, reverse, revoke
 idiom declare null and void
 2 to make something (as an office, post, or dwelling) vacant or empty <*vacate* a house>
 syn clear, empty, void
 rel abandon, give up, part (with *or* from), relinquish; leave, quit
vacation *n* a period spent away from one's usual activity or work often in travel or recreation <took a two-week *vacation* to Florida>
 syn holiday, leave
 rel break, breathing space (*or* breathing spell), intermission, recess; time off; respite, rest; furlough
vacillant *adj syn* see VACILLATING 2
vacillate *vb syn* see HESITATE
 rel swag, sway, ‖swither; alternate, seesaw, teeter, teeter-totter, wag, waggle, wigwag, wobble; dally, dawdle, fiddle-faddle
 idiom blow hot and cold, hem and haw, swing from one thing to another
 con decide, resolve, settle
vacillating *adj* **1** *syn* see WEAK 2
 rel unfixed; unsettled, unsteady; changeable, fickle, inconstant; eccentric, erratic, mercurial, volatile
 con constant, steady, unchanging; strong
 2 given to or manifesting hesitation or vacillation <a *vacillating* witness>
 syn double-minded, faltering, halting, hesitant, hesitating, indecisive, irresolute, pendulous, shilly-shally, shilly-shallying, tentative, timid, uncertain, undecisive, unresolved, vacillant, vacillatory, wavering, weak-kneed, whiffling, wiggle-waggle, wobbly
 rel doubtful, doubting, unsure; fluctuating, oscillating, shifting; dallying, dawdling, demurring, dillydallying, stalling
 con certain, decisive, resolute, resolved, sure; definite, positive
vacillation *n syn* see HESITATION

 rel dallying, demurral, dillydallying, stalling
vacillatory *adj syn* see VACILLATING 2
 rel alternating, seesawing, varying; indecisive, irresolute, uncertain
vacuity *n* **1** *syn* see HOLE 3
 2 the condition, fact, or quality of being vacuous <the utter *vacuity* of his expression>
 syn blankness, emptiness, vacancy, vacuousness, voidness
 rel bareness, barrenness, bleakness, desolateness, hollowness; dullness, inaneness, inanity, stupidity
 3 *syn* see NOTHINGNESS
vacuous *adj* **1** *syn* see EMPTY 1
 2 characterized by a lack of substance, thought, or intellectual content <a *vacuous* mind>
 syn empty-headed, vacant; *compare* STUPID 1
 rel shallow, superficial; blank, empty; dull, foolish, inane, silly
vacuousness *n syn* see VACUITY 2
vade mecum *n syn* see HANDBOOK
vag *n syn* see VAGABOND
vagabond *adj syn* see ITINERANT
 rel vagabondish
vagabond *n* a person who wanders at will or as a habit <a park full of *vagabonds* sleeping on benches>
 syn arab, ‖bindle stiff, bum, canter, clochard, derelict, drifter, floater, ‖gangrel, hobo, piker, roadster, runagate, ‖shack, street arab, ‖sundowner, ‖swagger, ‖swagman, tramp, tramper, ‖traveler, vag, vagrant, Weary Willie
 rel roamer, rover, wanderer; boomer, migrant, runabout, straggler, stray, transient; bohemian, gypsy, picaro, picaroon; ‖casual; stiff; beggar, rogue
 idiom knight of the road
vagabond *vb syn* see WANDER 1
vagabondage *n syn* see VAGRANCY
vagabondia *n syn* see VAGRANCY
vagabondism *n syn* see VAGRANCY
vagabondize *vb syn* see WANDER 1
vagarious *adj syn* see ARBITRARY 1
 rel unreasonable; kinky
vagary *n syn* see CAPRICE
 rel daydream, dream, fantasy; kink, quirk
 idiom passing fancy
vagrancy *n* the act or state of wandering from place to place usually with no means of support <dropped out of society and lived a life of *vagrancy*>
 syn hoboism, vagabondage, vagabondia, vagabondism
 rel itineracy, itinerancy, nomadism; rambling, roaming, roving, wandering
vagrant *n syn* see VAGABOND

vagrant *adj syn* see ITINERANT
rel aimless, errant, erratic; straying; saun-
tering, strolling
vague *adj* **1** *syn* see OBSCURE 3
rel indeterminate, indistinct, unplain;
cloudy, dim, hazy, nebulous; muddy
con clear, distinct
ant express
2 *syn* see FAINT 2
rel nebulous, unsubstantial; indefinite,
unplain; uncertain, unrecognizable; dream-
like, dreamy
3 *syn* see HAZY
rel bleared, bleary, blurry
vain *adj* **1** devoid of worth or significance
<the *vain* pursuits of a luxurious life>
syn empty, hollow, idle, nugatory, otiose
rel profitless, unprofitable, useless, valueless, void, worthless; ineffective, ineffectual,
inefficacious; bootless, fruitless; abortive,
futile
con useful, valuable, worthy; effective,
effectual, efficacious
2 *syn* see FUTILE
rel paltry, petty, puny, trifling, trivial; delusive, delusory, misleading
3 having or exhibiting undue or excessive
pride especially in one's appearance or
achievements <was *vain* about his clothes>
syn conceited, ‖conceity, narcissistic, self=
conceited, stuck-up, vainglorious; *compare*
PROUD 1
rel arrogant, egocentric, egoistic, haughty,
‖pensy, proud, self-important, swollen=
headed; boastful, self-exalting; coxcombical,
dandyish, foppish
idiom stuck on oneself
con humble, meek, modest; bashful, diffident, retiring, shy
vainglorious *adj syn* see VAIN 3
rel boastful, bragging, vaunting; disdainful,
insolent, supercilious
vainglory *n syn* see CONCEIT 2
rel arrogance, haughtiness; boastfulness,
bombast; exhibition, flaunting, parading
con lowliness, meekness; bashfulness, diffidence, self-effacement, shyness; modesty
ant humility
vainness *n syn* see CONCEIT 2
vale *n syn* see VALLEY
valedictory *adj syn* see PARTING
valiance *n syn* see HEROISM
con feebleness, ineffectiveness; fear
valiancy *n syn* see HEROISM
con feebleness, ineffectiveness; fear
valiant *adj syn* see BRAVE 1
ant pusillanimous
valid *adj* having the power to impress others
as right and well-founded <a *valid* conclu-
sion>
syn cogent, convincing, satisfactory, satisfying, solid, sound, telling
rel persuasive, potent, strong; attested,
confirmed, corroborated, demonstrated,
determined, established, substantiated,
validated, verified; lawful, legal, licit; effec-

tive, effectual; conclusive, decisive, definitive, determinative; acceptable
con groundless, shaky, unconvincing, unfounded, unsound; fallacious, false, misleading, sophistical; counterfeit, fictitious
ant invalid
validate *vb syn* see CONFIRM 2
rel approve, endorse, legalize, ratify, rub-
ber-stamp, sanction
con abolish, abrogate, annul, cancel, repeal;
void
ant invalidate
validity *n syn* see POINT 3
rel efficacy, gravity, soundness; persuasiveness, potency
con inconsistency; unsoundness; fallacy,
falsity
ant invalidity, invalidness
validness *n syn* see POINT 3
ant invalidity, invalidness
valley *n* an elongate depression of the earth's
surface commonly situated between ranges
of hills or mountains <small farms dotted
the floor of the *valley*>
syn ‖combe, dale, glen, vale
rel dell, dingle, hollow; ‖rincon; canyon
valor *n syn* see HEROISM
rel mettle, resolution, spirit, tenacity; in-
domitableness, invincibility, unconquerable-
ness; backbone, fortitude, guts, sand
con cowardliness, fear
ant pusillanimity, pusillanimousness
valorous *adj syn* see BRAVE 1
ant pusillanimous
valorousness *n syn* see HEROISM
rel chivalrousness, chivalry; manliness
con cowardliness
ant pusillanimity, pusillanimousness
valuable *adj syn* see PRECIOUS 1
rel dear, expensive; appreciated, prized,
treasured, valued; admired, esteemed, respected
idiom of great value
con cheap, inexpensive, trashy; unmarketable, unsalable; unworthy
ant valueless, worthless
valuate *vb syn* see ESTIMATE 1
valuation *n* **1** *syn* see ESTIMATE 1
rel judgment, opinion, rating
2 *syn* see WORTH 1
rel charge, cost, price
value *n* **1** *syn* see WORTH 1
rel appraisal, assessment; charge, cost,
expense, price
2 *syn* see QUALITY 2
value *vb* **1** *syn* see ESTIMATE 1
rel compute, figure, gauge, reckon
idiom place a value (or price) on
2 *syn* see APPRECIATE 1
rel care (for); revere, reverence, venerate
idiom set much by
valueless *adj syn* see WORTHLESS 1
ant valuable
valve *n syn* see FAUCET
rel shutoff
‖**vamoose** *vb syn* see GET OUT 1
vamp *vb syn* see MEND 2
rel brush up, fix up, touch up; furbish, refurbish
vamp (up) *vb syn* see CONTRIVE 2

---

syn synonym(s)　　　*rel* related word(s)
ant antonym(s)　　　*con* contrasted word(s)
idiom idiomatic equivalent(s)
‖ use limited; if in doubt, see a dictionary

vamp *n syn* see FLIRT
rel charmer, enchantress, enticer, femme fatale, gold digger, inveigler, seductress, siren, temptress

vandal *n* one who willfully destroys or mars something valuable <*vandals* had knocked off the head of the statue>
syn defacer, despoiler, destroyer, ruinator, ruiner, wrecker
rel hoodlum, hooligan, lout, ruffian; devastator, ravager, spoiler, spoliator; looter, pillager, plunderer; iconoclast

vandalize *vb* to destroy or deface (as public or private property) willfully or maliciously <youths *vandalized* the shop>
syn ‖trash, wreck
rel ‖rip off; destroy, tear up

vanish *vb* to pass from view or out of existence <the moon *vanished* behind a cloud>
syn clear, disappear, evanesce, evanish, evaporate, fade
rel dematerialize, dissolve, melt (away); die
idiom do the vanishing act, vanish from sight, vanish into thin air, vanish like a dream
con arise, break out (*or* through), come (forth *or* out), emerge, issue, loom (up), materialize, show (up)
ant appear

vanished *adj syn* see EXTINCT 2
rel expired, passed away; annihilated, no more, perished

vanity *n syn* see CONCEIT 2
rel autotheism, self-worship

vanquish *vb syn* see CONQUER 1
rel surmount; overturn, subvert; humble, trample

vanquisher *n syn* see VICTOR 1
rel champ, champion
con loser

vanquishment *n syn* see DEFEAT 1
rel mastery, subdual, subjugation

vantage *n syn* see ADVANTAGE 3
ant disadvantage

vapid *adj syn* see INSIPID 3
rel flavorless, milk-toast, tasteless, weak; dull, unimaginative, uninteresting
idiom neither hot nor cold, neither one thing nor the other
con brisk, lively, tangy, zesty; crisp, forceful, incisive, trenchant; expressive, meaningful, pregnant, significant, telling

vaporous *adj* 1 *syn* see HAZY
2 *syn* see AIRY 3
rel unsubstantial, wispy; illusory, unreal

vapory *adj* 1 *syn* see HAZY
2 *syn* see AIRY 3
rel gaseous

variable *adj* 1 *syn* see CHANGEABLE 1
rel fitful, spasmodic; irregular, unequable, unequal, uniniform
con unchanging, unvarying; immobile, stable, unmoving; equable, equal, uniform
ant constant, invariable
2 *syn* see MUTABLE 2
3 *syn* see INCONSTANT 1

variance *n* 1 the quality, state, or fact of being variable <a daily *variance* of 1°F.>
syn difference, variation
rel change, deviation, fluctuation

ant invariance
2 *syn* see DISCORD
rel division, separation, severing, sundering

variation *n* 1 *syn* see CHANGE 1
rel difference, dissimilarity; deflection, discrepancy
con stability, unchangeableness
2 *syn* see VARIANCE 1
rel shift; divergence; discrepancy, disparity
con uniformity

varicolored *adj syn* see VARIEGATED
ant solid

varied *adj syn* see MISCELLANEOUS

variegated *adj* having a pattern involving different colors or shades of color <*variegated* leaves>
syn dappled, discolor, motley, multicolor, multicolored, multihued, parti-color, parti≠colored, polychromatic, polychrome, varicolored, versicolor, versicolored
rel checked, checkered; piebald, pied, skewbald; freaked, streaked; flecked; stippled; marbled; mottle, mottled, spattered, speckled, spotted; calico; pinto
ant solid

variety *n* 1 the quality or state of being composed of different parts, elements, or individuals <the *variety* of the city's cultural life>
syn diverseness, diversity, multeity, multifariousness, multiformity, multiplicity, variousness
rel diversification, heterogeneity, variation
2 a collection of different things, forms, or qualities especially of a particular class <had a great *variety* of jobs in his lifetime>
syn assortment
rel conglomeration, medley, miscellany
3 *syn* see TYPE
rel classification; grade, rank

various *adj* 1 *syn* see MANY
rel assorted, heterogeneous, miscellaneous, omnifarious, omnigenous
2 *syn* see DIFFERENT 1
rel changing, variant, varied, varying; distinct, separate; distinctive, individual, peculiar
ant uniform
3 *syn* see SEVERAL 3
ant many, numerous
4 *syn* see DISTINCT 1
5 *syn* see CERTAIN 1

various *pron, pl in constr syn* see SUNDRY

variously *adv syn* see OTHERWISE 1

variousness *n syn* see VARIETY 1

varnish *vb syn* see PALLIATE

vary *vb* 1 *syn* see CHANGE 1
rel modulate, qualify
2 *syn* see DIFFER 1
3 *syn* see DIFFER 2
rel depart, deviate, digress, diverge; divide, part, separate
ant agree
4 *syn* see RANGE 3

vast *adj syn* see HUGE
rel big, large; ample, capacious, spacious; broad, expansive, far-flung, wide, widespread; astronomical, cosmic
con confined, limited, narrow, restricted

vastness *n syn* see ENORMITY 2

vatic *adj syn* see PROPHETIC
vaticinal *adj syn* see PROPHETIC
vaticinate *vb syn* see FORETELL
vault *n syn* see CRYPT
vault *vb* 1 *syn* see JUMP 1
  rel upleap, upspring; overjump, overleap; clear; rise, soar; ascend, mount; surmount
  2 *syn* see CLEAR 8
vaulting *adj syn* see AMBITIOUS 1
  rel enthusiastic; opportunistic
vaunt *vb syn* see BOAST
  rel brandish, display, exhibit, expose, flaunt, parade, show off
  idiom puff oneself
vaunter *n syn* see BRAGGART
vaunting *adj syn* see BOASTFUL
vector *n* an agent capable of transmitting a pathogen from one organism to another <fleas are *vectors* of bubonic plague>
  syn carrier, vehicle
veer *vb* 1 *syn* see TURN 6
  2 *syn* see SWERVE 1
  rel depart, deviate, digress, diverge; angle off, bear off; twist; pivot, turn, wheel
vegetate *vb* to lead a passive existence without exertion of body or mind <he never really lived his life—he merely *vegetated*>
  syn stagnate
  rel idle; languish; hibernate
  idiom idle life away, live the life of a clam, pass the time
vehement *adj syn* see INTENSE 1
  rel emphatic, pronounced; energetic, hearty, lively, zealous; forceful, potent, powerful; ardent, fervent, fervid, heated, impassioned, passionate, perfervid; delirious, frantic, furious, rabid, wild
vehicle *n* 1 *syn* see VECTOR
  rel agent
  2 *syn* see MEAN 2
  rel implement, tool
  3 a means of transporting goods or passengers <his *vehicle* was an old battered coupe>
  syn conveyance, transport, transportation
veil *n syn* see MASK 2
veil *vb syn* see ENFOLD 1
  rel mantle, overspread, spread (over); blanket, curtain; camouflage, cloak, cover (up), disguise, mask; conceal, hide, screen, secrete
  con exhibit, lay (open), open up, reveal, uncover, unmask; bare, expose, show
  ant unveil
vein *n* 1 a distinctive method of expression <wrote her speech in the proper *vein* for a very sophisticated audience>
  syn fashion, manner, mode, style, tone
  rel way; line; mood, tenor
  2 *syn* see HINT 1
  3 *syn* see MOOD 1
  rel complexion, disposition, fettle, temperament; character, nature, spirit
velitation *n syn* see ENCOUNTER
velleity *n syn* see WILL 1
  rel volition; wish
vellicate *vb syn* see JERK

  rel nip, pinch; fidget, jig, jiggle
velocipede *n syn* see BICYCLE
velocity *n syn* see SPEED 2
  rel headway, impetus, momentum; dispatch, expedition, haste, hurry
velutinous *adj syn* see VELVETY
velvetlike *adj syn* see VELVETY
  idiom soft as velvet
velvety *adj* 1 having the extreme softness associated with the surface or appearance of velvet <wore a *velvety* red flower in her hair>
  syn velutinous, velvetlike
  rel plush, plushy, smooth, soft; glossy, sleek, slick; satiny, silken, silky
  2 *syn* see SOFT 1
venal *adj* 1 open to corrupt influence and especially bribery <a *venal* legislator>
  syn bribable, buyable, corruptible, purchasable; *compare* CORRUPT 2, CROOKED 2
  rel corrupt, flagitious, infamous, iniquitous, nefarious, vicious; hack, hireling, mercenary, paid; ignoble, sordid; unethical, unprincipled, unscrupulous
  2 *syn* see CORRUPT 2
vend *vb* 1 *syn* see SELL 2
  2 *syn* see PEDDLE 2
  3 *syn* see DECLARE 1
vendee *n syn* see PURCHASER
vendetta *n* a prolonged mutual enmity marked by bitter hostility and conflict <a long-standing *vendetta* between two rival gangs>
  syn feud
  rel dispute, quarrel; rhubarb, row, wrangle; conflict, fight, set-to; blood feud, blood vengeance
vendible *adj syn* see MARKETABLE
  ant unvendible
vendible *n, usu* **vendibles** *pl syn* see MERCHANDISE
vendor *n syn* see PEDDLER
veneer *n syn* see MASK 2
veneer *vb syn* see PALLIATE
venerable *adj* 1 deserving to be venerated usually by reason of prolonged testing (as of character) <a *venerable* judge with an impressive knowledge of the law>
  syn patriarchal, revered, reverend, reverential; *compare* HONORABLE 1
  rel dignified, imposing, stately; admirable, estimable; honored, reverenced; worshipful; sacred
  ant unvenerable
  2 *syn* see ANCIENT 1
  rel elderly; patriarchal, reverenced, reverend, venerated
  con contemporary, current; fresh, inexperienced, new, untried, unused
venerate *vb syn* see REVERE
  rel honor; idolize
  idiom put on a pedestal
venery *n syn* see HUNTING
venge *vb syn* see AVENGE
  idiom even (up) the score, repay in kind, settle accounts (*or* an account)
vengeance *n syn* see RETALIATION
  rel return; repayment; revengefulness, vengefulness
vengeful *adj syn* see VINDICTIVE

---

syn synonym(s)   *rel* related word(s)
ant antonym(s)   *con* contrasted word(s)
idiom idiomatic equivalent(s)

‖ use limited; if in doubt, see a dictionary

rel antagonistic, hostile, inimical, rancorous
con charitable, forgiving, kind; benevolent, benign, inoffensive

venial *adj* of a kind that can be remitted and that does not warrant punishment or penalty <the *venial* indiscretions of youth>
syn excusable, forgivable, pardonable, remittable
rel allowable, unobjectionable; insignificant, minor, trifling, trivial; harmless, tolerable
con criminal, damning, deadly, mortal; grievous, outrageous, serious; inexcusable, unforgiv- able, unpardonable, unremittable
ant heinous

venom *n* *syn* see POISON
rel ill will, malignity, rancor, venomousness, virulence, vitriol
con antidote, remedy

venomous *adj* *syn* see POISONOUS
rel malevolent, malign, malignant; baleful, malefic, maleficent; viperish, viperlike, viperous

vent *vb* 1 *syn* see EMIT 2
rel cast out, discharge, exhaust
2 *syn* see EXPRESS 2
rel utter, voice; assert, declare
idiom come out with, give vent to
con check, curb, inhibit, restrain; repress, suppress
3 *syn* see TAKE OUT (on)

vent *n* 1 *syn* see APERTURE
2 *syn* see EXPRESSION 1
rel articulation, verbalization, vocalization

venter *n* *syn* see ABDOMEN

ventilate *vb* 1 *syn* see BROACH
2 *syn* see EXPRESS 2
rel go into, take up; debate, deliberate, discourse (about), discuss, ||rap (about), talk over (or of or about), thresh out; advertise, broadcast, publish
idiom chew the fat (or the rag)

ventilation *n* *syn* see CONFERENCE 1

venture *vb* 1 to expose to risk or loss <*ventured* their capital in foreign trade>
syn adventure, chance, hazard, risk, wager; *compare* GAMBLE 1
rel endanger, imperil, jeopard, jeopardize, jeopardy, peril; expose, lay (open)
idiom take chances (or risks) on (or with)
2 *syn* see GAMBLE 2
rel bet, operate, play (for), speculate, stake; jeopard, jeopardize, jeopardy
idiom luck it
3 *syn* see FACE 3

venture *n* *syn* see ADVENTURE
rel attempt, undertaking; crack, fling; dare, gamble, fling, speculation
idiom leap in the dark

venturesome *adj* *syn* see ADVENTUROUS
rel stalwart, stout, sturdy; brave; overbold
con timid, timorous; afraid, apprehensive, fearful

venturous *adj* *syn* see ADVENTUROUS
rel aggressive, enterprising, hustling

veracious *adj* 1 *syn* see TRUTHFUL
rel direct; undeceitful, undeceptive
con equivocal; deceitful, dishonest, insincere; false, untruthful
ant unveracious

2 *syn* see TRUE 3
rel unquestionable, valid
con illusory, invalid, wrong
ant unveracious

veraciousness *n* *syn* see VERACITY 1
rel artlessness, openness; trustworthiness
con falseness, insincerity

veracity *n* 1 the quality or state of keeping close to fact and avoiding distortion or misrepresentation <questions the *veracity* of that witness>
syn truth, truthfulness, veraciousness, veridicality, verity
rel accuracy, correctness, exactness, factualness; frankness, honesty
con inaccuracy, incorrectness; deception, dishonesty, untruth, untruthfulness
ant unveracity
2 something that is true <can make lies sound like *veracities*>
syn gospel, truism, truth, verity
rel verisimilitude; actuality; fact
con lie, untruth
ant unveracity

verbal *adj* 1 *syn* see ORAL 2
2 *syn* see VERBATIM

verbalism *n* 1 *syn* see WORDING
rel styling
2 *syn* see VERBOSITY

verbality *n* *syn* see VERBIAGE 1
rel verbalism, verboseness, verbosity, wordiness

verbalization *n* *syn* see SPEECH 1

verbalize *vb* *syn* see SPEAK 1
rel air, express, give, say, state, vent, ventilate, word
idiom couch in terms, find words to express

verbatim *adv* in the same words <repeated their earlier conversation *verbatim*>
syn direct, directly, literally, literatim, word for word
rel accurately, exactly, precisely
idiom to the letter
con basically, essentially, in essence; carelessly, imprecisely, inaccurately, inexactly

verbatim *adj* using the same words <court stenographers took down the *verbatim* testimony>
syn literal, verbal, word-for-word
rel close, faithful, strict; exact, precise
idiom following the letter, true to the letter
con careless, imprecise, inaccurate, inexact

verbiage *n* 1 a stylistic fault involving excessive wordiness that obscures or unduly complicates expression <the florid *verbiage* of the dissertation>
syn circumambages, circumbendibus, circumlocution, periphrase, periphrasis, pleonasm, redundancy, roundabout, tautology, verbality; *compare* VERBOSITY
rel nimiety; repetition; expansiveness, floridity, floridness; longiloquence, long-windedness
idiom purple prose
con breviloquence, brevity, briefness, terseness
ant concision
2 *syn* see WORDING

verbose *adj* *syn* see WORDY

rel flowery, grandiloquent, magniloquent; circumlocutory, periphrastic, pleonastic, tautologous

con precise; close, compact, lean, tight

ant concise; laconic

verboseness *n syn* see VERBOSITY

ant conciseness

verbosity *n* the quality or state or an instance of being wordy <his two-hour lecture was the epitome of *verbosity*> <flowery *verbosities* weakened his speech>

syn prolixity, prolixness, verbalism, verboseness, windiness, wordiness; *compare* VERBIAGE 1

rel bombast, grandiloquence; long-windedness; redundancy

con conciseness, preciseness, succinctness, terseness; leanness, tightness

verboten *adj syn* see FORBIDDEN

rel disallowed, disapproved; unauthorized, unlicensed, unsanctioned; outlawed, taboo

con allowed, permitted; authorized, licensed; approved, endorsed, sanctioned

verdure *n syn* see FOLIAGE

verge *n* 1 *syn* see BORDER 1

2 a time interval or set of circumstances marking the imminent beginning of a new state, condition, or action <on the *verge* of war>

syn brink, edge, point, threshold

rel border line

verge *vb* 1 *syn* see BORDER 1

rel approach; incline, lean, tend (to *or* toward); touch (on *or* upon)

2 *syn* see ADJOIN

3 *syn* see BORDER 3

veridical *adj* 1 *syn* see TRUTHFUL

2 *syn* see REAL 3

3 *syn* see TRUE 3

rel uncolored, undistorted, unvarnished; actual, real

con invalid; illusory, unreal

veridicality *n syn* see VERACITY 1

rel genuineness

verificatory *adj syn* see CORROBORATIVE

verify *vb syn* see CONFIRM 2

rel demonstrate, prove, test, try; document, establish, settle

verily *adv syn* see EVEN 3

verisimilitude *n* the quality of a representation that causes it to appear true <her characters are too stilted for *verisimilitude*>

syn color, plausibility, verisimility

rel authenticity, genuineness, veritableness; likeness, resemblance, similarity

verisimility *n syn* see VERISIMILITUDE

veritable *adj syn* see AUTHENTIC 2

rel undenied, unrefuted; actual, factual

con doubtful, questionable; imaginary, unreal, untrue; artificial, factitious; counterfeit, false, spurious

veritably *adv syn* see VERY 2

verity *n* 1 *syn* see VERACITY 2

ant falsity

2 *syn* see VERACITY 1

vernacular *adj* of or relating to everyday speech <*vernacular* Welsh differs greatly from literary Welsh>

syn colloquial, vulgar, vulgate

vernacular *n* 1 *syn* see LANGUAGE 1

rel mother tongue

idiom native tongue

2 *syn* see DIALECT 2

3 a commonly spoken as opposed to a prestige variety of a language <literary Chinese and the various *vernaculars*>

syn colloquial, patois, vulgate; *compare* DIALECT 2

rel dialect, lingo, slang

vernacularism *n syn* see BARBARISM

vernacularity *n syn* see BARBARISM

vernal *adj* of, relating to, or resembling the spring of the year <*vernal* sunshine>

syn spring, springlike

versant *adj syn* see FAMILIAR 3

ant unversed

versatile *adj* having a wide range of skills, aptitudes, or interests <a *versatile* artist, who is at home in any medium>

syn adaptable, all-around, ambidextrous, many-sided, mobile, myriad-minded

rel elastic, flexible, plastic, pliable; adroit, dexterous, facile; able, skilled, skillful; accomplished, conversant; gifted, talented; well-rounded

con inadequate, limited

verse *n* 1 *syn* see POETRY 1

2 *syn* see POEM

rel jingle; ballad, lay; sonnet; lyric; ode; epic

versed *adj* 1 *syn* see EXPERIENCED

rel competent

con incompetent

ant unversed

2 *syn* see FAMILIAR 3

ant unversed

verseman *n syn* see POETASTER

versemonger *n syn* see POETASTER

verser *n syn* see POETASTER

versesmith *n syn* see POETASTER

versicolor *adj syn* see VARIEGATED

versicolored *adj syn* see VARIEGATED

versificator *n syn* see POETASTER

versifier *n syn* see POETASTER

version *n* 1 a restating often in simpler language of something previously stated or written <a simple *version* of "Tom Sawyer" for the use of children>

syn paraphrase, rendering, restatement, translation

rel rendition; clarification, interpretation; condensation, simplification; rewording; restipulation

2 *syn* see ACCOUNT 7

rel tale

3 *syn* see INTERPRETATION 2

versus *prep* 1 in conflict with <the case of John Doe *versus* Richard Roe>

syn against

rel con, contra

idiom at cross-purposes with (*or* to), at odds with, at outs with, at variance with, on the outs with

2 in contrast with <the age-old argument about free trade *versus* protection>

syn over against, vis-à-vis

---

syn synonym(s)   *rel* related word(s)
ant antonym(s)   *con* contrasted word(s)
idiom idiomatic equivalent(s)
‖ use limited; if in doubt, see a dictionary

idiom as opposed to

vertebrae *n syn* see SPINE

vertebral column *n syn* see SPINE

vertex *n syn* see TOP 1
  rel cap; tip-top; apogee, zenith
  idiom upper extremity

vertical *adj* situated at right angles to the plane of the horizon or extending from that plane at such an angle <*vertical* walls>
  syn perpendicular, plumb, straight-up
  rel erect, upright; steep, up-and-down
  con flat, plane
  ant horizontal

verticalism *n syn* see VERTICALITY

verticality *n* the quality or state of being vertical <the soaring *verticality* of the spires>
  syn perpendicularity, plumbness, verticalism, verticalness
  rel erectness, uprightness
  con flatness, lowness
  ant horizontality

verticalness *n syn* see VERTICALITY

vertiginous *adj syn* see DIZZY 2

verve *n syn* see SPIRIT 5
  rel liveliness, vivacity; bounce, buoyancy, elasticity, resiliency, spring; fire, gusto, zest

very *adj* **1** *syn* see AUTHENTIC 2
  rel hundred-percent, perfect; correct, exact, right
  con fake, fraudulent, mock, sham
  2 *syn* see PRECISE 4
  rel especial, express, special
  3 *syn* see PERFECT 3
  4 being as stated without addition or superfluity <the *very* thought of it makes me ill>
  syn bare, mere
  5 *syn* see SAME 1
  idiom (the) very same

very *adv* **1** to a high or exceptional degree <a *very* successful meeting>
  syn ║awful, awfully, ║big, ║crazy, damned, ║dreadful, dreadfully, eminently, exceedingly, exceptionally, extremely, greatly, highly, hugely, insatiably, ║larruping, ║main, mightily, mighty, ║monstrous, ║mortacious, mortally, most, much, notably, parlous, pesky, ║pure, rattling, remarkably, right, ║right smart, snapping, so, spanking, staving, strikingly, super, surpassingly, terribly, thoroughly, too, vitally, whacking, whopping
  rel passing, quite, somewhat; perfectly, seriously, significantly, tellingly
  idiom nothing if not
  con inconsiderably, little, scarcely, slightly
  2 in actual fact <told the *very* same story>
  syn actually, de facto, genuinely, really, truly, veritably
  rel exactly, precisely; almost, nearly, practically, well-nigh
  idiom in point of fact, in truth
  con apparently, ostensibly, outwardly, seemingly

vest *vb* **1** *syn* see INVEST 2
  2 *syn* see BELONG 2

vestibule *n* an entrance chamber between the outer door and the interior of a building <the *vestibule* of a theater>
  syn foyer, lobby

  rel entrance hall, entry, entryway; portal, portico; antechamber, anteroom; narthex

vestige *n* **1** something (as a mark or visible sign) left by a material thing formerly present but now lost or unknown <digging for the *vestiges* of past civilizations>
  syn memento, relic, shadow, trace
  rel remainder, remains; rag, remnant, scrap, tag
  2 *syn* see FOOTPRINT
  rel path; trail

vet *vb syn* see SCRUTINIZE 1
  idiom go over with a fine-tooth comb

vet *adj syn* see EXPERIENCED

vet *n syn* see VETERAN

veteran *n* one having knowledge or ability gained through long experience <was a political campaign *veteran* of long standing>
  syn longtimer, old hand, old-timer, vet
  rel expert, master, past master
  con amateur, freshman, youngster
  ant novice

veteran *adj syn* see EXPERIENCED
  rel wise; sophisticated, worldly
  idiom dry behind the ears, not born yesterday, wise in the ways of the world
  con inexperienced, unpracticed, unversed; unqualified, unskilled, untrained

veto *vb* to refuse to admit or approve <the President *vetoed* the bill>
  syn kill, negative, ║nix, non-placet
  rel decline, deny, disallow, forbid, prohibit, refuse, reject; defeat
  idiom put one's veto on
  con admit, approve, assent (to); pass

vex *vb syn* see ANNOY 1
  rel ║chaw, embarrass; plague; anger, infuriate
  con appease, mollify, pacify, propitiate, smooth (over); please, regale
  ant soothe

vexation *n syn* see ANNOYANCE 1
  rel aggravation, irritation

vexatious *adj syn* see TROUBLESOME

vexing *n syn* see ANNOYANCE 1

via *prep* **1** over a route that passes through <shipped to New York *via* the Panama Canal>
  syn by, by way of, through
  rel along; over
  2 using as a means of approach or action <reached the voters *via* mass-media advertising>
  syn by, by dint of, by means of, by virtue of, by way of, per, through, with
  idiom through the medium of

viable *adj syn* see POSSIBLE 1

viands *n pl syn* see FOOD 1
  rel fare

vibrant *adj syn* see RESONANT

vibrate *vb syn* see SHAKE 2

vice *n* **1** degrading or immoral habits and practices <an exposé of *vice* and crime in the city>
  syn corruption, depravity, immorality, wickedness
  rel decay, rot, squalor; evil, ill, sin, wrong; indecency, unchastity; debasement, debauchery, licentiousness, perversion
  con morality; respectability; uprightness

ant virtue
2 *syn* see FAULT 2
rel shortcoming
idiom weak point
3 *syn* see BLEMISH

vice versa *adv syn* see AGAIN 5
vicinage *n syn* see LOCALITY 1
vicinity *n* **1** *syn* see LOCALITY 1
2 *syn* see ORDER 4
vicious *adj syn* see WRONG 1
2 highly offensive or reprehensible in character, nature, or conduct <*vicious* parents who were a bad influence on their children>
syn corrupt, degenerate, depraved, flagitious, infamous, miscreant, nefarious, perverse, putrid, rotten, unhealthy, villainous
rel bad, faulty, poor, unsound; opprobrious, reprehensible; contaminated, obnoxious, septic
con good, moral, righteous, right-minded
ant virtuous
3 *syn* see SAVAGE 1
rel brutish; bloodthirsty
4 *syn* see MALICIOUS
5 *syn* see INTENSE 1
rel severe
vicissitude *n* **1** *syn* see CHANGE 2
rel alternation; reversal; transposition; progression; diversity, variety
2 *syn* see DIFFICULTY 1
rel chop and change, ups and downs; adversity, mischance, misfortune; affliction, trial, tribulation
victim *n* **1** a living being sacrificed (as in a religious rite) <offered up human *victims* to appease their bloodthirsty gods>
syn offering, sacrifice
2 one subjected to oppression, loss, or suffering <*victims* of social injustice>
syn bottom dog, casualty, prey, underdog
rel quarry
3 *syn* see FOOL 3
idiom easy mark, easy pickings
victimize *vb* **1** *syn* see SACRIFICE 1
2 *syn* see DUPE
victor *n* **1** one that defeats an enemy <the Allies were the *victors* of World War II>
syn conqueror, defeater, master, subduer, subjugator, vanquisher
rel winner
con conquered, defeated, subjugated; loser
ant vanquished
2 a successful contender <emerged as *victor* in the swimming meet>
syn winner
rel champ, champion; first, top
idiom conquering hero
ant loser
Victorian *adj syn* see PRIM 1
rel old-fashioned, old-maidish; hidebound; starchy
con easy going; trendy, with-it
victory *n* **1** the overcoming of an opponent <won a knockout *victory* in the first round>
syn conquest, triumph, win

rel command, control, dominion, mastery, subjugation; superiority, supremacy; walkaway, walkover
idiom a feather in one's cap
con loss; bust, failure, fizzle, flop, ‖floperoo, washout; comedown, cropper
ant defeat
2 *syn* see BETTER 2
victuals *n pl syn* see FOOD 1
videlicet *adv syn* see NAMELY
video *n syn* see TELEVISION
vie *vb* **1** *syn* see COMPETE 1
rel challenge; match; outvie
2 *syn* see OPPOSE 1
view *n* **1** *syn* see LOOK 1
rel examination, inspection, scan, scrutiny
2 *syn* see EXAMINATION
3 *syn* see EYE 4
4 what is revealed to the vision or can be seen <the *view* from the window>
syn outlook, scene, sight
rel panorama, picture, prospect, vista
5 extent or range of vision <there were still no ships in *view*>
syn sight
rel look; apprehension, scan
6 something (as an aim, end, or motive) to or by which the mind is directed <kept this *view* in mind while negotiating>
syn object
rel intent, intention, purpose; aim, ambition, goal, objective; design, plan, project; consideration, notion; expectation
7 *syn* see OPINION
rel concept, conception; deduction, inference
view *vb* **1** *syn* see SCRUTINIZE 1
2 *syn* see EYE 1
rel observe
3 *syn* see SEE 1
4 *syn* see CONSIDER 3
viewable *adj syn* see VISUAL 2
viewer *n syn* see SPECTATOR
viewpoint *n* **1** *syn* see EYE 4
2 the position or attitude that determines how something is seen, presented, or evaluated <from this *viewpoint* the picture looks askew> <consider totalitarianism from the German *viewpoint*>
syn angle, direction, outlook, side, slant, standpoint; *compare* EYE 4
rel estimation; attitude, position, posture, stand; long view, perspective
idiom frame of reference, point of view, vantage point
viewy *adj syn* see IMPRACTICAL 1
vigil *n syn* see LOOKOUT 3
vigilance *n syn* see LOOKOUT 3
vigilant *adj syn* see WATCHFUL
rel agog, anxious, avid, eager, keen; acute, sharp, sharp-eyed; attentive
idiom on one's guard, with a weather eye open
con lax, neglectful, negligent, remiss, slack; forgetful, oblivious, unmindful
vigor *n* **1** *syn* see POWER 4
2 a quality of physical or mental force or forcefulness <the *vigor* of youth>
syn bang, drive, getup, get-up-and-go, go, pep, punch, push, snap, starch, vitality;

---

syn synonym(s)   *rel* related word(s)
ant antonym(s)   *con* contrasted word(s)
idiom idiomatic equivalent(s)
‖ use limited; if in doubt, see a dictionary

compare ENERGY 2, ENTERPRISE 4, SPIRIT 5

rel bounce, energy, force, might, muscularity, power, strength; healthiness, soundness; lustiness, manliness, virility

con slowness, sluggishness

ant weakness

3 syn see ENERGY 2

rel dash, drive, dynamism, fire, punch, starch, steam, vim, zing, zip; ability, capability, capacity

con ineffectiveness; impotence; incompetence, uselessness, worthlessness

vigorous *adj* having or manifesting great vitality and force <seemed as *vigorous* as a youth half his age>

syn dynamic, energetic, lusty, red-blooded, strenuous, ‖survigrous, vital

rel brisk, dashing, lively, slashing; exuberant, mettlesome, proud, spirited; driving, hard-driving, hard-hitting, robust, rough-and-ready, zealous; bouncing, hardy, healthy, hearty, masterful, potent, powerful, strong, tough; rude, stout, sturdy; athletic, husky, muscular, sinewy

con languorous, unenergetic; decrepit, feeble, infirm, weak; impotent

ant lethargic

vigorously *adv syn* see HARD 1

rel alertly, eagerly; boldly, firmly, purposefully, resolutely, unfalteringly, zealously; lustily, robustly

con aimlessly, languorously; falteringly, indecisively; impotently

vile *adj* **1 syn** see BASE 3

rel corrupted, debased, debauched, depraved, perverted; coarse, gross, obscene, vulgar; disgusting, foul, nasty; abhorrent, contemptible, loathsome, offensive, repulsive, revolting

2 syn see OFFENSIVE

vilify *vb syn* see MALIGN

rel abuse, mistreat, misuse, outrage; assail, attack, berate; denounce

con commend, compliment; acclaim, exalt; celebrate, glorify, honor; adore, worship

ant eulogize

vilifying *adj syn* see LIBELOUS

villa *n syn* see MANSION

villain *n* **1** a low, mean, reprehensible person utterly lacking in principle <was an insufferable bully, a tyrant, and a *villain* in general>

syn blackguard, heel, knave, lowlife, miscreant, rascal, reprobate, rogue, roperipe, scoundrel, ‖slubberdegullion; *compare* SNOT 1, DEVIL 2

rel meanie; evildoer, offender, sinner; criminal, malefactor

2 syn see SCAMP

villainize *vb syn* see MALIGN

ant eulogize

villainous *adj syn* see VICIOUS 2

rel contrary, detestable, objectionable, offensive; debased, perverted; atrocious, heinous, outrageous; abandoned, dissolute, profligate

villenage *n syn* see BONDAGE

vim *n syn* see SPIRIT 5

rel pepper; kick, push

vinculum *n syn* see BOND 3

vindicable *adj syn* see JUSTIFIABLE

rel inoffensive, unobjectionable, venial

con indefensible, unjustifiable; inexcusable, unforgivable; heinous, mortal

vindicate *vb* **1 syn** see AVENGE

2 syn see MAINTAIN 2

rel advocate, plead (for), second, support, uphold; rationalize; bear out, prove

3 syn see EXCULPATE

rel confute, disprove, refute; defend, guard, protect, shield

con accuse, attack, calumniate

ant convict

vindictive *adj* showing or motivated by a desire for vengeance <*vindictive* hatred for his brother>

syn revengeful, vengeful, wreakful

rel grim, implacable, merciless, relentless, unrelenting; malicious, malign, malignant, spiteful

con charitable, forgiving, merciful, relenting

ant unvindictive

vinegarish *adj syn* see CANTANKEROUS

vinegary *adj syn* see CANTANKEROUS

vintage *adj* **1** being of old, recognized, and enduring interest, importance, or quality <a *vintage* comedy from the silent movie era>

syn classic, classical

2 syn see OLD-FASHIONED

violate *vb* **1** to fail to keep <people who thoughtlessly *violate* the law>

syn breach, break, contravene, infract, infringe, offend, transgress

rel disregard, trample (on *or* upon); err, sin; overpass, trespass

con abide by, carry out, fulfill, submit (to); heed, keep, mind

ant observe; obey

2 syn see RAPE

violation *n* **1 syn** see BREACH 1

rel break; encroachment; illegality, misdemeanor, offense, wrong

ant observance

2 syn see PROFANATION

rel defacement, defacing

violence *n syn* see FORCE 4

rel frenzy, fury, savagery; assault, attack, clash, foul play, onslaught, rampage, struggle, tumult, uproar

con passiveness, passivity; peace, peacefulness

ant nonviolence

violent *adj syn* see INTENSE 1

rel forceful, forcible, mighty, potent, powerful, strong; extreme, immoderate, inordinate; acute, cutting, piercing, splitting

con calm, moderate, peaceful

ant nonviolent

violently *adv syn* see HARD 2

rel combatively; destructively, ruinously

idiom like fury, with a vengeance

VIP *n syn* see NOTABLE 1

virago *n* a woman of extremely pugnacious temperament <an overbearing *virago* who screamed at her children and squabbled with her neighbors>

syn amazon, fishwife, harpy, ogress, scold, shrew, termagant, vixen, Xanthippe

rel cat; dragon; fury

virgin *adj* **1** never having had sexual relations <*virgin* girls were sacrificed>

syn intact, maiden, undeflowered, virginal
rel innocent, untouched; single, spouseless, unmarried, unwed; abstinent, celibate
2 not marred or altered from a natural or original state <a *virgin* forest>
syn unspoiled, untapped, untouched, virginal
rel primeval, pristine; fresh, new; unmarred, unsullied

virginal *adj* 1 *syn* see VIRGIN 1
2 *syn* see VIRGIN 2

virginity *n* the quality or state of being a virgin <lost her *virginity*>
syn ‖cherry, maidenhead, maidenhood
rel chasteness, chastity, purity

virile *adj* 1 *syn* see POTENT 3
2 characterized by the energy and drive considered typical of a man or of men <developed a strong *virile* prose style>
syn manlike, manly, masculine
rel macho, manful, mannish; decisive, driving, forceful; energetic, potent, robust; ultramasculine
con effeminate, womanish; emasculated, weak, weakened; impotent

virility *n* the vigor or agressiveness held to be typical of males <pundits decided that the candidate's conspicuous *virility* appealed to voters>
syn maleness, manfulness, manliness, masculinity
rel courage, dauntlessness, guts, machismo, macho, mettle, ‖moxie, pluck, resolution, spirit, spunk
con effeminacy, unmanliness; impotence, weakness; prissiness, sissiness

virtual *adj* *syn* see IMPLICIT 2
rel basic, essential, fundamental
ant actual

virtuality *n* *syn* see ESSENCE 2

virtually *adv* not absolutely or actually, yet so nearly so that the difference is negligible <that request is *virtually* an order>
syn in essence, morally, practically; *compare* ALMOST 2
rel basically, essentially, fundamentally; absolutely, actually
idiom for all practical purposes, in effect, in substance, to all intents and purposes

virtue *n* 1 *syn* see GOODNESS
rel fealty, fidelity, loyalty, piety; virtuousness
con dishonesty; disloyalty, infidelity; evil; immorality; depravity
ant vice
2 *syn* see EXCELLENCE
rel attribute, characteristic, feature, property; effectiveness, effectualness, efficacy; force, might, power, strength
3 *syn* see QUALITY 1
4 *syn* see QUALITY 2
5 *syn* see POWER 4

virtuosic *adj* *syn* see CONSUMMATE 1

virtuoso *n* 1 *syn* see EXPERT
2 *syn* see MUSICIAN

virtuous *adj* 1 *syn* see EFFECTIVE
ant virtueless
2 *syn* see MORAL 1
rel spotless, unsullied, untainted, untarnished; worthy
con dishonest; unjust; unworthy; impure, tainted; immodest, immoral, indecent; vicious, wicked
ant unvirtuous, virtueless
3 *syn* see GOOD 1
rel faultless, sinless
idiom innocent as a lamb, in the clear, without reproach
con bad, impure, unrighteous
ant unvirtuous, virtueless; vicious

virulent *adj* 1 *syn* see POISONOUS
rel malign, malignant
2 *syn* see BITTER 3
rel biting, cutting, scathing, sharp, stabbing; hateful, spiteful, unfriendly

virus *n* *syn* see POISON
rel corruption, taint

visage *n* 1 *syn* see FACE 1
2 *syn* see LOOK 2

vis-à-vis *n* 1 *syn* see OPPOSITE NUMBER
2 *syn* see TÊTE-À-TÊTE

vis-à-vis *prep* 1 *syn* see AGAINST 1
rel opposite
2 *syn* see VERSUS 2

viscera *n pl syn* see ENTRAILS

visceral *adj* 1 *syn* see INNER 2
2 *syn* see INSTINCTIVE 1

viscerous *adj* *syn* see INNER 2

viscid *adj* *syn* see VISCOUS
rel jellylike, slabby

viscose *adj* *syn* see VISCOUS
rel smeary

viscous *adj* having a glutinous adhesive consistency or quality <a *viscous* scum covered the surface of the platter>
syn tenacious, tough, viscid, viscose
rel ‖slab, slimy, thick; glutinous, gummy, ropy, sticky; semifluid; stiff

visibility *n* the quality or state of being visible <very poor *visibility* due to fog>
syn visuality

visible *adj* *syn* see VISUAL 2
rel seen

vision *n* 1 *syn* see REVELATION
rel apparition, phenomenon, presence
2 *syn* see FANCY 4
rel muse
idiom phantom of the mind
3 *syn* see EYE 2

vision *vb syn* see THINK 1

visional *adj* *syn* see VISUAL 1

visionary *adj* 1 *syn* see DREAMY 1
rel abstracted, introspective, musing; impractical
idiom out of this world, up in the clouds
2 *syn* see IDEALISTIC
rel exalted, grandiose, lofty, noble, pretentious
ant pragmatic, pragmatical
3 *syn* see AMBITIOUS 2
rel radical

visionary *n syn* see DREAMER
ant pragmatist

visionless *adj* *syn* see BLIND 1

visit *vb* 1 *syn* see INFLICT 2

---

syn synonym(s)   *rel* related word(s)
ant antonym(s)   *con* contrasted word(s)
idiom idiomatic equivalent(s)
‖ use limited; if in doubt, see a dictionary

rel afflict, bother, pain, trouble; avenge, punish
idiom bring down upon
2 to make a social call upon <*visited* friends briefly in the evening>
syn call, come by, come over, drop (in *or* by), look in, look up, pop (in), run in, see, step in, stop (in *or* by)
3 to reside with temporarily as a guest <*visited* with friends in the country for a few weeks>
syn sojourn, stay, stop (over), tarry
rel frequent; reside
4 *syn* see CONVERSE
visit *n* 1 a coming to stay with another temporarily and usually briefly <pay a *visit* to friends>
syn call, visitation
2 *syn* see SOJOURN
visitant *n syn* see VISITOR 1
visitation *n* 1 *syn* see VISIT 1
2 *syn* see TRIAL 1
rel mischance; calamity, catastrophe, disaster
visitor *n* 1 one who visits another <there are *visitors* in the living room>
syn caller, guest, visitant; *compare* COMPANY 2
rel invitee
2 *visitors* *pl syn* see COMPANY 2
visor *n* 1 a projecting front brim on a cap or hat for shading the eyes <the *visor* kept out the sun>
syn bill, peak
rel eyeshade
2 *syn* see MASK 1
vista *n* an extensive or distant view <a long flat tree-lined *vista*>
syn lookout, outlook, perspective, prospect, scape
rel panorama, scene, sight, view; range, scope, survey
idiom long view
visual *adj* 1 of or relating to or used in vision <the *visual* sense>
syn ocular, optic, optical, visional
2 capable of being seen <*visual* objects>
syn ocular, seeable, viewable, visible
rel discernible, perceivable, perceptible
visuality *n syn* see VISIBILITY
visualize *vb* 1 *syn* see THINK 1
rel picture, view; objectify; call up, conjure (up)
idiom bring (*or* call) to mind, conjure up a mental image (*or* picture) of, see in the mind's eye
2 *syn* see FORESEE
vital *adj* 1 *syn* see LIVING 1
rel breathing
2 *syn* see VIGOROUS
3 *syn* see ESSENTIAL 2
rel indispensable, needed, needful, required, requisite, integral, prerequisite
vital force *n syn* see SOUL 1
vitality *n syn* see VIGOR 2
rel animation, life, liveliness, pulse; endurance, energy, spirit, vim
vitalize *vb* to arouse to activity, animation, or life <atomic energy is a force that can *vitalize* or destroy human civilization>

syn actify, activate, activize, energize
rel animate, enliven, invigorate, quicken, vivify; dynamize, excite, galvanize, provoke, stimulate; pep up, strengthen
idiom put life into
con eviscerate, weaken
ant atrophy; devitalize
vitalizing *adj syn* see INVIGORATING
ant devitalizing
vitally *adv syn* see VERY 1
vitiate *adj syn* see DEBASED
ant purified
vitiate *vb* 1 *syn* see INJURE 1
rel twist, warp
2 *syn* see DEBASE 1
rel defile, soil, sully, taint; prostitute; contaminate
idiom drive to the dogs
ant purify
3 *syn* see ABOLISH 1
vitiated *adj syn* see DEBASED
rel contaminated, defiled, polluted, tainted; impaired, injured, spoiled
ant purified
vitriolic *adj syn* see BITTER 3
vituperate *vb syn* see SCOLD 1
rel condemn, lambaste; asperse, calumniate, malign, traduce; bark (at), growl (at), yell (at); abuse, curse
idiom rip into
con applaud, commend, compliment; eulogize, extol, praise
ant acclaim
vituperation *n syn* see ABUSE
rel blame, censure, revilement, scolding, tongue-lashing
con eulogy, extolment
ant acclaim, praise
vituperative *adj syn* see ABUSIVE
rel censorious, critical; severe; railing, scolding
vituperatory *adj syn* see ABUSIVE
rel censorious, critical; severe; railing, scolding
vituperous *adj syn* see ABUSIVE
rel censorious, critical; severe; railing, scolding
vivacious *adj* 1 *syn* see LIVELY 1
rel breezy, vibrant, zesty; froliclesome, playful, sportive
idiom gay as a lark
ant languid
2 *syn* see EXUBERANT 1
viva voce *adj syn* see VOCAL 1
vivid *adj* 1 *syn* see COLORFUL
2 *syn* see GRAPHIC 1
rel acute, intense, keen, sharp; dramatic, dramaturgic, theatrical; eloquent, expressive, meaningful, rich; animated, lively, spirited, vigorous
vivificate *vb syn* see QUICKEN 1
rel revive
vivify *vb syn* see QUICKEN 1
rel refresh, renew, restore; excite, galvanize
idiom give life to, imbue with life, put new life into
vivres *n pl syn* see FOOD 1
vixen *n syn* see VIRAGO
vizard *n syn* see MASK 1
‖**vlei** *n syn* see SWAMP

vocable *n syn* see WORD 2
　rel verbalism
vocabulary *n* **1** the sum or set of words employed by a language, group, individual, or work or in relation to a subject <Latin contributes heavily to the *vocabulary* of English>
　syn lexicon, word-hoard, word-stock
　idiom stock of words
　2 *syn* see TERMINOLOGY
　rel phraseology
vocal *adj* **1** uttered by the voice or having to do with such utterance <the infant's primitive *vocal* sounds from which language develops>
　syn articulate, oral, sonant, spoken, viva voce, voiced
　rel intonated; expressed, uttered
　con unexpressed, unuttered, unvoiced
　ant nonvocal
　2 *syn* see VOCALIC
　ant consonantal
　3 being able to express oneself clearly or easily <he was hardly *vocal*: he could scarcely express the simplest concepts>
　syn articulate, eloquent, fluent, smooth‐spoken
　rel expressing, voicing; expressive; outspoken, stentorian, venting
　con faltering, halting, hesitant, stumbling
　4 *syn* see OUTSPOKEN
vocalic *adj* marked by, consisting of, or functioning as a vowel or vowels <*vocalic* and consonantal sounds>
　syn vocal, vowel, vowely
　rel vowellike
vocalism *n syn* see VOCALIZATION
vocalization *n* the exercise of the vocal organs in song or speech <her *vocalization* of a previously unstated thought>
　syn articulation, utterance, uttering, vocalism; *compare* SPEECH 1
　rel mouth, mouthing; sounding, voice, voicing; diction, enunciation, verbalization; speaking, speech
vocalize *vb* **1** *syn* see SPEAK 1
　rel emit, let out; express; enunciate, pronounce; communicate, convey, impart
　idiom execute vocally
　2 *syn* see SING 1
vocation *n* **1** *syn* see TRADE 1
　2 *syn* see MISSION
vocative *adj syn* see GLIB
　rel chatty, garrulous, loquacious, talkative, windy; slick, smooth
vociferant *adj syn* see VOCIFEROUS
vociferate *vb syn* see CALL 1
vociferous *adj* so loud, noisy, and insistent as to compel attention <the crowd made *vociferous* protests against the speaker's statement>
　syn blatant, boisterous, clamorous, ‖dinsome, loudmouthed, multivocal, obstreperous, openmouthed, strident, vociferant
　rel distracting; loud, noisy, shrill

　con close-lipped, reserved, silent, uncommunicative; noiseless, quiet, still
vogue *n syn* see FASHION 2
　rel bon ton, fashionableness, stylishness
voice *n* **1** *syn* see EXPRESSION 1
　rel speech
　2 the right to express a wish, choice, or opinion or to influence a situation <even the youngest had a *voice* in planning the party>
　syn say, say-so
voice *vb syn* see SPEAK 1
　rel sound; articulate, enunciate, pronounce; formulate, phrase, present, put; recount, tell
voiced *adj syn* see VOCAL 1
voiceless *adj syn* see DUMB 1
void *adj* **1** *syn* see EMPTY 1
　ant full
　2 *syn* see DEVOID
　rel scant, short, shy; bare, bereft, denuded, deprived
　3 *syn* see NULL
　rel negated
void *n syn* see HOLE 3
void *vb* **1** *syn* see VACATE 2
　rel evacuate; deplete, drain, eliminate; eject, remove, throw out
　2 *syn* see DISCHARGE 5
void *vb syn* see ANNUL 4
　idiom declare (*or* make) null and void
voidness *n syn* see VACUITY 2
　ant fullness
volage *adj syn* see GIDDY 1
volant *adj syn* see AGILE
volatile *adj* **1** *syn* see ELASTIC 2
　rel capricious, fickle, inconstant, mercurial, unstable; flighty, flippant, frivolous, light‐minded; changeable, protean, variable
　2 *syn* see EXCITABLE
　rel explosive
　3 *syn* see INCONSTANT 1
　4 *syn* see TRANSIENT
volatility *n syn* see LIGHTNESS
　rel animation, sprightliness; inconstancy, instability, mercurialness; changeability, variability
volition *n syn* see WILL 2
　rel choice, election, option, selection; desire, preference
　con coercion, compulsion, duress, force
volley *n syn* see BARRAGE
volte-face *n syn* see REVERSAL 1
volte-face *vb syn* see TURN 6
　rel about-face, face (about), right-about‐face
voluble *adj syn* see GLIB
volume *n* **1** *syn* see BOOK 1
　2 *syn* see BULK 1
　rel amount, content, quantity
　3 *syn* see BODY 4
voluminous *adj syn* see MANY
voluntary *adj* consisting of or proceeding from an exercise of free will <the law requires that a confession be *voluntary*>
　syn deliberate, intentional, unforced, unprescribed, willful, willing, witting
　rel chosen, elected, opted, volitional; autonomous, free, independent
　con coerced, compelled, forced; unintentional, unplanned, unwilling, unwitting
　ant involuntary

---

syn synonym(s)　　*rel* related word(s)
ant antonym(s)　　*con* contrasted word(s)
idiom idiomatic equivalent(s)
‖ use limited; if in doubt, see a dictionary

voluptuous *adj syn* see SENSUOUS
rel indulgent, self-gratifying; abandoned, dissipated, dissolute, excessive, wanton
con self-contained, self-denying
ant ascetic

vomit *vb* to discharge the contents of the stomach through the mouth <the churning seas made several passengers *vomit*>
syn barf, bring up, ||cack, ||cascade, ||cast, ||cat, disgorge, ||heave, shoot, sick (up), spew, spit up, throw up, upchuck
rel gag, regurgitate, retch; keck; eject, expel
idiom ||blow one's lunch, holler New York, lose one's cookies

voodoo *n* 1 *syn* see MAGICIAN 1
2 *syn* see JINX

voodoo *vb syn* see BEWITCH 1

voodooist *n syn* see MAGICIAN 1

voracious *adj* excessively greedy (as in appetite, reactions, or behavior) <the wolverine is an extremely *voracious* eater>
syn edacious, gluttonous, rapacious, ravening, ravenous
rel acquisitive, covetous, grasping, greedy; devouring, gorging, satiating, sating, surfeiting; avid, insatiable

vortex *n syn* see EDDY
rel spiral, spout

votary *n* 1 *syn* see ADDICT
rel disciple; freak
2 *syn* see AMATEUR 1
rel hound

vote *n* 1 *syn* see BALLOT 1
2 *syn* see SUFFRAGE

vote (in *or* into) *vb syn* see ELECT 2
rel choose, decide
idiom cast one's vote for

vouch *vb syn* see CERTIFY 1
rel support, uphold; confirm, corroborate, prove, substantiate, verify; assure, guarantee

vouchsafe *vb syn* see GRANT 1
rel condescend, deign, stoop; accommodate, favor, oblige

vow *vb* to promise solemnly <*vowed* never to leave each other>
syn covenant, pledge, plight, swear; *compare* PROMISE 1
rel assert, declare, ||swan; promise
idiom give (*or* make) a solemn promise, give one's word of honor

vowel *adj syn* see VOCALIC

vowely *adj syn* see VOCALIC

voyage *n* a journey by water <took the new ship on a long *voyage*>
syn cruise
rel journey, tour, trip

voyeur *n syn* see PEEPING TOM

vulgar *adj* 1 *syn* see VERNACULAR
rel conversational, spoken; idiomatic
2 *syn* see PUBLIC 4
3 *syn* see COARSE 3
4 *syn* see OBSCENE 2
rel base, low, vile; loathsome, offensive, repulsive, revolting; indecorous, indelicate, uncouth
con decent, delicate, refined; high-minded, lofty, noble
5 *syn* see BARBARIC 1
rel inelegant, ungraceful; improper, incorrect, unseemly; uncouth, unpolished, unrefined
idiom in very poor taste
con elegant, graceful; correct, proper, seemly

vulgarism *n syn* see BARBARISM

vulgate *adj syn* see VERNACULAR

vulgate *n syn* see VERNACULAR 3

vulnerability *n syn* see EXPOSURE
rel vincibility

vulnerableness *n syn* see EXPOSURE
rel weakness

vulnerary *adj syn* see CURATIVE

vulpine *adj syn* see SLY 2

vulture *vb syn* see STEAL 1

vulturine *adj syn* see RAPACIOUS 1

vulturish *adj syn* see RAPACIOUS 1

vulturous *adj syn* see RAPACIOUS 1

W

||wack *n syn* see ECCENTRIC

wacky *adj* 1 *syn* see FOOLISH 2
2 *syn* see INSANE 1

wad *n* 1 *syn* see LUMP 1
2 *often* **wads** *pl syn* see SCAD
3 *syn* see FORTUNE 4

wade (in *or* into) *vb syn* see PITCH IN 1

||waffle *vb syn* see BABBLE 2

wag *vb* to move to and fro <the dog *wagged* his tail briskly>
syn beat, lash, switch, waggle, wave, woggle
rel shake, twitch, wiggle; oscillate; wigwag

wag *n* 1 a person full of sportive humor <a gay young *wag*, always full of fun>
syn card, comedian, humorist, joker, zany
rel clown, cutup, madcap, prankster, show-off; jester, kidder, quipster, wisecracker, wit
idiom life of the party
2 *syn* see ZANY 1
3 *syn* see HUMORIST 2

wage *n, often* **wages** *pl* the price paid a person for his labor or services <high *wages* are often seen as a factor in inflation>
syn emolument, fee, hire, pay, pay envelope, salary, stipend
rel compensation, recompense, remuneration, reward; earnings, income, receipts, return(s), take

wager *n syn* see BET

wager *vb* 1 *syn* see VENTURE 1

2 syn see GAMBLE 1
  idiom lay a wager
waggery *n* **1** syn see MISCHIEVOUSNESS
  2 syn see JOKE 1
waggish *adj* syn see PLAYFUL 1
  rel facetious, humorous, jocose, jocular, witty; comic, comical, droll, funny, laughable, ludicrous; arch, pert, saucy
  con earnest, grave, sedate, serious, sober, staid
waggishness *n* syn see MISCHIEVOUSNESS
waggle *vb* syn see WAG
  rel sway, waddle, wobble
wail *vb* **1** syn see CRY 2
  idiom make an outcry
  2 syn see HOWL 1
  3 syn see BAWL 2
  4 syn see COMPLAIN
wailful *adj* syn see MELANCHOLY 2
waistband *n* syn see BELT 1
wait *vb* syn see STAY 2
  rel anticipate, foresee; await, expect
  idiom bide one's time, cool one's heels, look forward to, mark time
  con depart, go, leave
wait (on) *vb* syn see MINISTER (to)
waive *vb* **1** syn see RELINQUISH
  rel allow, concede, grant
  con claim, demand, exact, require; assert, defend, maintain
  2 syn see DEFER
wake *vb* **1** to stop sleeping <she usually *woke* before dawn>
  syn awake, awaken, rouse, stir, waken
  rel freshen, renew
  con catnap, doze, drowse, nap, nod, snooze; sleep, slumber
  2 syn see STIR 1
  rel freshen, renew
  con calm, ease, mollify, relax
waken *vb* **1** syn see STIR 1
  rel freshen, renew
  con calm, ease, mollify, relax
  2 syn see WAKE 1
wale *n* syn see WHEAL
walk *vb* **1** to advance on foot step by step <often *walked* to work on pleasant mornings>
  syn ambulate, foot (it), hoof, pace, step, traipse, tread, troop
  rel circumambulate, perambulate, promenade, ramble, stroll; hike, tramp; lumber, plod, slog, stride, stump, trudge; leg, race, run
  idiom beat one's feet, heel and toe it, ride shanks' mare
  con drive, ride
  2 syn see TRAVERSE 5
walk *n* **1** a usually brief journey on foot for pleasure or exercise <always took a *walk* before breakfast>
  syn constitutional, ramble, saunter, stroll, turn
  rel hike, march, tramp; deambulation, parade, promenade; airing, stretch

2 syn see FIELD
walkabout *n* syn see TRAMP 3
walkaway *n* syn see RUNAWAY
walk out *vb* syn see STRIKE 1
walkover *n* syn see RUNAWAY
wall *n* syn see BAR 2
wall *vb* syn see ENCLOSE 1
wallop *n* **1** syn see BLOW 1
  2 syn see IMPACT 1
  3 syn see THRILL
wallop *vb* **1** syn see BEAT 1
  2 syn see WHIP 2
  3 syn see SLAM 1
walloping *adj* syn see HUGE
wallow *vb* **1** to roll or move in an indolent and ungainly yet comfortable fashion <hogs *wallowing* in a cool mudhole>
  syn welter
  rel flounder, roll, tumble; cuddle, nestle, snuggle
  2 to move or progress unsteadily and clumsily as if beset by obstacles <*wallowed* through the mire for miles trying to get help>
  syn blunder, flounder, lurch, stumble; *compare* STUMBLE 3
  rel reel, stagger, sway, totter, wamble, welter
  idiom make heavy weather (of)
  3 to become deeply or excessively involved in or with something subjectively felt as pleasant <*wallowing* in luxury>
  syn bask, indulge, luxuriate, revel, roll, rollick, welter
  rel baby, humor, pamper, spoil; appreciate, delight (in), enjoy, relish
  con abstain, refrain; avoid, eschew, shun
waltz *vb* syn see BREEZE
wambly *adj* syn see SQUEAMISH 1
wampum *n* syn see MONEY
wan *adj* **1** syn see PALE 1
  rel cadaverous, haggard, worn; blanched, bleached, washed-out; anemic, bloodless
  2 syn see WEAK 4
wander *vb* **1** to move about from place to place more or less aimlessly and without obvious plan <*wandering* through the forest>
  syn bat, circumambulate, drift, gad, gallivant, maunder, meander, mooch, ‖project, ramble, range, roam, roll, rove, straggle, stray, traipse, vagabond, vagabondize; *compare* SAUNTER
  rel amble, saunter, stroll; divagate, diverge; trail; boom, bum, tramp
  2 syn see DIGRESS 2
  3 syn see ERR
wanderer *n* syn see ROVER
wandering *adj* **1** syn see ITINERANT
  2 syn see ERRATIC 1
  3 syn see DELIRIOUS 1
wane *vb* **1** syn see ABATE 4
  ant wax
  2 syn see FAIL 3
  ant wax
wangle *vb* syn see ENGINEER
  rel outflank, outgeneral, outmaneuver, overreach
waning *n* syn see FAILURE 4
  ant waxing

---

syn synonym(s)   *rel* related word(s)
ant antonym(s)   *con* contrasted word(s)
idiom idiomatic equivalent(s)
‖ use limited; if in doubt, see a dictionary

‖**wanky** *adj syn* see WEAK 1

want *vb* 1 *syn* see LACK
 idiom be found wanting, fall short, feel the want of
2 *syn* see DESIRE 1
 rel choose, prefer
 idiom could do with, have a mind (*or* an eye) to
3 to have as a duty or responsibility <you *want* to behave yourself>
 syn must, ought, should
 rel become, befit, behoove; need (to)
 idiom be wise to, had better (*or* best)

want *n* **1** *syn* see ABSENCE
 rel exigency, necessity, need
 con sufficiency
2 *syn* see POVERTY 1
 rel exiguousness, meagerness, scantiness, skimpiness; inadequacy, insufficiency
 con riches
3 *syn* see REQUIREMENT 1

wanting *adj syn* see ABSENT 1
2 *syn* see SHORT 3
3 *syn* see DEFICIENT 1

wanting *prep syn* see WITHOUT 2

wanton *adj* **1** *syn* see FAST 7
 rel lax, slack, wayward
 idiom of easy virtue, of loose morals
 con austere, puritanical, restrained, self=restrained
 ant chaste
2 *syn* see SUPEREROGATORY
 rel malevolent, malicious, spiteful; contrary, perverse, wayward

wanton *n* a woman who engages in lewd unseemly conduct <giddy *wantons* flaunting themselves in bars>
 syn baggage, ‖bim, ‖bimbo, cyprian, hussy, jade, jezebel, ‖pig, slattern, slut, strumpet, tramp, trollop, trull, wench; *compare* DOXY, HARLOT 1, PROSTITUTE
 idiom loose woman

wanton *vb syn* see TRIFLE 1
wantwit *n syn* see DUNCE
war *vb syn* see CONTEND 1
 rel attempt, endeavor, essay, strive, struggle; challenge, engage, take on
 idiom draw the sword against, lift one's hand against, take up the cudgels

warble *n syn* see MELODY
war chest *n syn* see TREASURY 2
war club *n syn* see CUDGEL
war cry *n syn* see BATTLE CRY
ward *n* **1** *syn* see GUARD 2
2 *syn* see DEFENSE 1
3 *syn* see CUSTODY

ward *vb* **1** to cause to miss an objective by or as if by turning aside <*warded* the stroke of his enemy's sword with his shield>
 syn deflect, fend, parry
 rel block, check, halt, stay, stymie; avert, divert, turn
 idiom keep at arm's length, turn aside
2 *syn* see PREVENT 2
 rel balk, foil, frustrate, thwart; check, interrupt
 ant conduce (to)

ward (off) *vb syn* see FEND (off)
 ant bring on

warden *n syn* see CUSTODIAN

ware *adj syn* see AWARE
warehouse *vb syn* see STOW
 rel accommodate; guard, protect, shelter
wares *n pl syn* see MERCHANDISE
warfare *n syn* see CONTEST 1
warhorse *n syn* see COURSER
warlike *adj* **1** *syn* see BELLIGERENT
 ant peaceable
2 *syn* see MARTIAL
 rel battling, contending, fighting, warring
 ant unwarlike

warlock *n syn* see MAGICIAN 1
warm *adj* **1** *syn* see ENTHUSIASTIC
2 *syn* see TENDER
 rel ardent, fervent, passionate; affable, cordial, gracious; heartfelt, hearty, sincere, wholehearted
 ant cool; austere

warmed–over *adj syn* see TRITE
warmhearted *adj syn* see TENDER
 rel benign, benignant, kind, kindly, outgoing
 con austere, cold, cool, frigid, frosty, severe, stern
 ant coldhearted

warming *n syn* see DEFEAT 1
warmish *adj syn* see TEPID 1

warn *vb* **1** to let one know of approaching danger or risk <police and the weather service join to *warn* travelers of hazardous road conditions>
 syn caution, forewarn
 rel advise, alert, apprise, inform, notify, tip; counsel, direct, guide
 idiom address a warning to, give warning, put a flea in one's ear, put one on guard
2 *syn* see INFORM 2
3 *syn* see COMMAND

warning *n* something and especially a statement that warns or is intended to warn <gave them *warning* that disobedience would lead to punishment>
 syn admonition, caution, caveat, commonition, forewarning, monition
 rel advice, counsel, guidance, recommendation; hint, suggestion, tip
 idiom flea (*or* word) in the ear, word to the wise

warning *adj syn* see MONITORY
warp *vb* **1** *syn* see DEBASE 1
 rel contort, crook, distort, twist
 con disentangle, rectify, straighten, unkink
2 *syn* see DEFORM
 rel bend, crook, kink, twist
3 *syn* see MISREPRESENT

war paint *n* **1** *syn* see FINERY
2 *syn* see MAKEUP 3

warped *adj syn* see BIASED 2
 ant unwarped

warrant *n* **1** *syn* see PLEDGE 1
2 *syn* see BASIS 3
3 *syn* see WORD 8

warrant *vb* **1** *syn* see MAINTAIN 2
 rel state; assure, ensure, insure
2 to give assurance of the worth of something especially in respect to quality, quantity, or condition <*warranted* the merchandise to be exactly as described in the catalog>
 syn certify, guarantee, guaranty

rel assure, insure, secure; back, sponsor, stipulate; affirm, claim, state
idiom stand behind
3 *syn* see JUSTIFY 4
rel endorse; call (for); need, require
warrantable *adj syn* see JUSTIFIABLE
ant unwarrantable
warranty *n syn* see GUARANTEE 1
warrior *n syn* see SOLDIER
wary *adj* **1** *syn* see CAUTIOUS
rel distrustful, doubting, leery, suspicious; vigilant, watchful
idiom on one's guard
con careless, heedless, thoughtless; devil=may-care, reckless, venturesome
ant foolhardy; unwary
2 *syn* see SPARING
wash *vb* **1** *syn* see BATHE 1
2 *syn* see BATHE 2
3 *syn* see DRIFT 1
4 *syn* see SLOSH 1
washed–out *adj syn* see EFFETE 2
washed–up *adj* **1** *syn* see THROUGH 3
2 *syn* see THROUGH 4
wash out *vb* **1** *syn* see FAIL 4
2 *syn* see DISCARD
wash up *vb syn* see GO 4
washy *adj syn* see DILUTE
waspish *adj* **1** *syn* see IRRITABLE
rel contrary, impatient, perverse; malicious, sharp, spiteful; crabbed, cross-grained
2 *syn* see CANTANKEROUS
waspy *adj* **1** *syn* see IRRITABLE
rel contrary, impatient, perverse; malicious, sharp, spiteful; crabbed, cross-grained
2 *syn* see CANTANKEROUS
wassail *n* **1** *syn* see BINGE 1
2 *syn* see REVELRY 2
wassail *vb syn* see REVEL 1
waste *n* **1** an area of the earth unsuitable for cultivation or general habitation <the scattered dwellers of southern Africa's dry *wastes*>
syn badland, barren, desert, wasteland, wild, wilderness, wild land, wildness
rel brush, brushland, bush; jungle
2 *syn* see EXTRAVAGANCE 2
3 *syn* see REFUSE
rel rubble, rummage
waste *vb* **1** *syn* see RAVAGE
idiom reduce to a shambles
ant conserve

2 to spend or expend freely and usually foolishly or futilely <*wasted* his inheritance on women and gambling> <*waste* one's time on trifles>
syn blow, blunder (away), cast away, consume, dissipate, dribble (away), drivel, fool (away), fritter, frivol away, muddle (away), ‖piss away, potter (away), prodigalize, riot (away), squander, throw away, trifle (away)
rel disburse, expend, spend; dispense, distribute; deplete, drain, exhaust, impoverish; dispel, disperse, scatter; misspend

idiom let slip through one's fingers, pour down the drain, throw good money after bad
ant save; conserve
waste (away) *vb syn* see FAIL 3
wasted *adj syn* see EMACIATED
rel meager; shriveled, withered, wizened
con healthy, robust; stalwart, stout, strong, sturdy
wastefulness *n syn* see EXTRAVAGANCE 2
ant frugality
wasteland *n syn* see WASTE 1
waster *n* **1** *syn* see SPENDTHRIFT
rel dissipater, fritterer; idler, loafer, lounger
2 *syn* see WASTREL 1
wastethrift *n syn* see SPENDTHRIFT
wastrel *n* **1** a worthless, self-indulgent, and reprehensible person <loafers and other *wastrels* lounging on the corner>
syn ‖bad lot, good-for-nothing, ne'er-do=well, no-good, profligate, rounder, scapegrace, waster
rel lecher, libertine, rake, rip, roué; blackguard, black sheep, knave, rascal, rogue, scoundrel; rapscallion, scalawag, scamp
idiom sad case
2 *syn* see SPENDTHRIFT
rel dissipater, fritterer; idler, loafer, lounger
watch *vb* **1** *syn* see SEE 2
rel examine, follow, inspect, scan, scrutinize
idiom keep an eye on, keep tabs on
2 *syn* see EYE 2
3 *syn* see TEND 1
idiom keep watch over
4 *syn* see LOOK 1
watch *n* **1** *syn* see LOOKOUT 3
2 *syn* see GUARD 2
3 *syn* see EYE 3
watch and ward *n syn* see LOOKOUT 3
watchdog *n syn* see CUSTODIAN
watcher *n syn* see SPECTATOR
watchfire *n syn* see BEACON 1
watchful *adj* paying close attention usually with a view to anticipating approaching danger or opportunity <adopted a policy of *watchful* waiting>
syn alert, open-eyed, unsleeping, vigilant, wakeful, wide-awake
rel cautious, chary, circumspect, wary; prompt, quick, ready
idiom keeping one's eyes peeled (or open), on the watch (or lookout)
con careless, heedless, thoughtless; inadvertent; absentminded, abstracted, faraway
ant unwatchful
watchman *n syn* see GUARD 2
watch out *vb syn* see BEWARE
watchword *n* **1** *syn* see PASSWORD 1
2 *syn* see PASSWORD 3
3 *syn* see CATCHWORD
water *n* **1** *syn* see TEARS
2 *syn* see SALIVA
water *vb syn* see DROOL 1
water closet *n syn* see TOILET
watercourse *n syn* see CHANNEL 1
watered–down *adj syn* see DILUTE
waterfall *n* a precipitous descent of water or the site of this <heard the roar of the *waterfall*>
syn cascade, cataract, chute, fall(s), ‖force, sault, spout

---

syn synonym(s)   *rel* related word(s)
ant antonym(s)   *con* contrasted word(s)
idiom idiomatic equivalent(s)
‖ use limited; if in doubt, see a dictionary

rel rapid(s), riffle, shoot; eddy, surge, vortex, whirlpool

watering hole *n* **1** *syn* see RESORT 2

2 *syn* see BAR 5

3 *syn* see NIGHTCLUB

watering place *n* **1** *syn* see SPA 1

2 *syn* see RESORT 3

3 *syn* see BAR 5

4 *syn* see NIGHTCLUB

waterish *adj* **1** *syn* see DILUTE

2 *syn* see PALE 2

3 *syn* see INSIPID 3

waterless *adj* *syn* see DRY 1

ant watered

waterlog *vb* *syn* see SOAK 1

watery *adj* **1** *syn* see DILUTE

2 *syn* see PALE 2

3 *syn* see INSIPID 3

wave *vb* *syn* see WAG

waver *vb* *syn* see HESITATE

rel palter, shift, trim; seesaw, teeter

idiom back and fill, hem and haw

wavering *n* *syn* see HESITATION

wavering *adj* **1** *syn* see VACILLATING 2

ant unwavering

2 *syn* see WEAK 2

wax *vb* **1** *syn* see INCREASE 2

ant wane

2 *syn* see BECOME 1

wax *n* *syn* see RISE 3

ant wane

waxen *adj* *syn* see PALE 1

waxy *adj* *syn* see ANGRY

way *n* **1** a public and unobstructed passage leading from one place to another <tracing the remains of an old lumberman's *way*>

syn artery, avenue, boulevard, ‖drag, highway, path, road, street, thoroughfare, track

rel course, line, passage, route; alley, byway, lane, ride, row

2 that along which one passes in going from one place to another <his *way* led through wooded hills>

syn course, line, passage, path, road, route

3 *syn* see DOOR 1

4 *syn* see METHOD 1

rel custom, habit, habitude, practice, usage, use, wont

5 *syn* see STYLE 4

6 *syn* see HABIT 1

7 *syn* see DISTANCE 2

8 *syn* see TYPE

‖**wayback** *n* *syn* see RUSTIC

wayfaring *adj* *syn* see ITINERANT

waylay *vb* *syn* see SURPRISE 1

rel lurk, prowl, skulk, slink

idiom lay wait for, lie in wait for

ways *n pl but sing in constr syn* see DISTANCE 2

wayward *adj* **1** *syn* see CONTRARY 3

rel capricious, fickle, inconstant, unstable, variable

con complaisant, good-natured

2 *syn* see ARBITRARY 1

weak *adj* **1** lacking physical, mental, or moral strength <a *weak* spirit in a *weak* body>

syn decrepit, feeble, flimsy, fragile, frail, infirm, insubstantial, puny, unsound, unsubstantial, ‖wanky, weakly

rel debilitated, enfeebled, sickly, spindly, weakened; forceless, impotent, impuissant, powerless

con stalwart, stout, sturdy, tenacious, tough; dynamic, energetic, forceful, vigorous

ant strong

2 deficient in stability <a love too *weak* to bear the trials of daily life>

syn dickey, fluctuant, insecure, rootless, shaky, unstable, unsure, vacillating, wavering, wobbly; *compare* RICKETY

rel hesitant, irresolute, trimming, uncertain; insubstantial, undependable, unreliable

con certain, secure, solid, stable, sure; dependable, reliable, substantial

ant strong

3 *syn* see IMPLAUSIBLE

4 not equal to the requirements and demands of a situation <a *weak* executive>

syn boneless, emasculate, forceless, impotent, inadequate, ineffective, ineffectual, invertebrate, slack-spined, spineless, wan

rel unfit, unqualified, unsuitable; bungling, incompetent, inept

con able, competent, effective, efficient; adequate, fit, qualified, satisfactory, sufficient, suitable; manly, masculine, virile

ant strong

5 *syn* see DILUTE

ant strong

weaken *vb* **1** to lose or cause to lose strength, vigor, or energy <his hesitation *weakened* the force of his argument>

syn attenuate, blunt, cripple, debilitate, disable, enfeeble, sap, unbrace, undermine, unstrengthen; *compare* PARALYZE 1

rel emasculate, enervate, incapacitate, unman, unnerve; damage, impair, injure; lessen, minimize, reduce; dilute, thin

con better, improve; activate, energize, invigorate, vitalize

ant strengthen

2 *syn* see FAIL 1

3 *syn* see FAIL 3

4 *syn* see DILUTE

weak-headed *adj* *syn* see SIMPLE 3

weak-kneed *adj* *syn* see VACILLATING 2

weakling *n* a person lacking in stamina and character <her speech deplored the characterless *weaklings* in critical positions>

syn baby, doormat, invertebrate, jellyfish, milksop, Milquetoast, ‖molly, mollycoddle, namby-pamby, nebbish, pantywaist, sissy, sissy-pants (or sissy-britches), sop, wimp

rel butt, mark, pushover, sucker; drip, mama's boy, misfit, mother's boy, nerd, sad sack, weak sister

idiom shrinking violet

weakly *adv* *syn* see SOTTO VOCE

ant strongly

weakly *adj* *syn* see WEAK 1

weak-minded *adj* *syn* see SIMPLE 3

weakness *n* *syn* see APPETITE 3

weal *n* *syn* see WHEAL

weald *n* *syn* see FOREST

wealth *n* **1** *syn* see MEAN 3

2 one's worldly possessions <at that point his *wealth* consisted of the clothes he stood in and a solitary quarter>

syn fortune, property, resources, riches, substance, worth *rel* assets, estate, goods, holdings, possessions

wealthy *adj syn* see RICH 1
con impoverished, penniless, poor
ant indigent

wean *vb syn* see ESTRANGE
ant addict

wear *vb* 1 *syn* see ABRADE 1
2 *syn* see TIRE 1

wear (away) *vb syn* see EAT 3

wear down *vb syn* see TIRE 1

wearied *adj syn* see TIRED 1
ant refreshed; unwearied, unweary

weariful *adj syn* see ARID 2

weariless *adj syn* see INDEFATIGABLE

weariness *n syn* see FATIGUE

wearisome *n syn* see ARID 2

wear out *vb* 1 *syn* see EXHAUST 4
‖2 *syn* see WHIP 1

weary *vb* 1 *syn* see TIRE 1
rel debilitate, enfeeble, weaken; depress, oppress, weigh
con animate, energize, vitalize; enliven, quicken, vivify
ant refresh
2 *syn* see BORE

weary *adj* 1 *syn* see TIRED 1
ant refreshed, unwearied, unweary
2 *syn* see FED UP

Weary Willie *n syn* see VAGABOND

weasel *n syn* see SNEAK

weasel *vb syn* see EQUIVOCATE 2

weathery *adj syn* see CHANGEABLE 1

weave *vb syn* see LURCH 2

web *n* 1 *syn* see TEXTURE 2
2 something by which one is ensnared, held fast, or inextricably involved <diplomacy caught in its own *web* of double-dealing>
syn cobweb, entanglement, mesh(es), toil(s); *compare* ENTANGLEMENT
rel complexity, complication; labyrinth, maze, morass, skein, snarl, tangle; embroilment, enmeshment, ensnarement, entrapment, involvement
idiom a tangled web
3 *syn* see MAZE 1

wed *vb* 1 *syn* see MARRY 1
2 *syn* see MARRY 2
3 *syn* see JOIN 1

wedded *adj syn* see MATRIMONIAL
con unwed, unwedded

wedding *n* the marriage ceremony usually with its accompanying festivities <one of the most elaborate *weddings* of the social season>
syn bridal, espousal(s), marriage, nuptial(s), spousal

wedlock *n syn* see MARRIAGE 1

wee *adj syn* see TINY

weed *n syn* see MARIJUANA

weensy *adj syn* see TINY

weeny *adj syn* see TINY

weep *vb* 1 *syn* see DEPLORE 1
2 *syn* see EXUDE
3 *syn* see CRY 2

4 *syn* see DRIP

weeping *adj syn* see TEARFUL

weepy *adj syn* see TEARFUL

weigh *vb* 1 *syn* see CONSIDER 1
rel appraise, evaluate, rate
2 *syn* see BURDEN
3 to carry intellectual weight <this evidence *weighed* heavily against him>
syn count, militate, tell
rel import, matter, register, signify
idiom amount to some shucks, be something, carry weight, cut (some) ice
4 *syn* see MATTER

weigh down *vb syn* see DEPRESS 2
ant raise (one's spirits)

weight *n* 1 *syn* see LOAD 2
2 *syn* see IMPORTANCE
3 *syn* see INFLUENCE 1
rel effectiveness, efficacy; forcefulness, forcibleness, potency, powerfulness
4 *syn* see LOAD 3

weight *vb* 1 *syn* see ADULTERATE
rel burden, cumber, encumber; contaminate, corrupt, foul up, spoil
2 *syn* see BURDEN

weightiness *n syn* see IMPORTANCE

weightless *adj syn* see LIGHT 1
ant weighty

weighty *adj* 1 *syn* see IMPORTANT 1
2 *syn* see SERIOUS 1
3 *syn* see SERIOUS 2
4 *syn* see HEAVY 1
ant weightless
5 *syn* see FAT 2
6 *syn* see ONEROUS

weird *n* 1 *syn* see FATE
2 *syn* see PREDICTION

weird *adj* 1 fearfully and mysteriously strange or fantastic <shuddered at the *weird* unearthly glow that swept across the sky>
syn eerie, spooky, uncanny, unearthly
rel creepy, haunting, unnatural; preternatural, supernatural; supernal; curious, odd, peculiar, queer, strange; inscrutable, mysterious; awe-inspiring, awful, dreadful, fearful, horrific
con common, commonplace, everyday, quotidian; natural, normal, ordinary
2 *syn* see STRANGE 4

welcome *adj syn* see PLEASANT 1
rel congenial, cordial, genial, sympathetic; contenting, satisfying
ant unwelcome

welfare *n* a state of thriving and progress <parents who seek their children's *welfare*>
syn advantage, benefit, good, interest, prosperity, well-being
rel fortune, luck, success; contentment, felicity, happiness, satisfaction
ant illfare

welkin *n syn* see SKY

well *n* 1 **wells** *pl syn* see SPA 1
2 *syn* see SOURCE

well *adv* 1 in a good, proper, or acceptable manner <the children behaved very *well* at the party>
syn aright, befittingly, correctly, decorously, fitly, fittingly, justly, nicely, properly, rightly

syn synonym(s)   *rel* related word(s)
ant antonym(s)   *con* contrasted word(s)
idiom idiomatic equivalent(s)
‖ use limited; if in doubt, see a dictionary

rel bearably, passably, tolerably, unobjectionably; considerably, pleasantly, thoughtfully, white; appropriately
con badly, improperly, objectionably, obnoxiously, outrageously
ant ill
2 in a pleasant, cooperative, or thoughtful manner <he speaks *well* of your new proposal>
syn considerately, generously, heedfully, kindly, thoughtfully
rel concernedly, interestedly; approvingly
con contemptuously, disdainfully, scornfully
3 to a full extent or degree <you are *well* aware of the problems we face>
syn à fond, altogether, clear, ‖cleverly, completely, entirely, fully, perfectly, ‖plumb, quite, right, roundly, ‖slam, ‖slap, thoroughly, utterly, wholly
rel certainly, obviously, surely, undoubtedly, unquestionably; sublimely
idiom all the way
con barely, hardly, scarcely
4 in an adequate or appropriate manner <any large box will answer our need very *well*>
syn acceptably, adequately, amply, appropriately, becomingly, fittingly, properly, right, satisfactorily, suitably
5 in a desirable or pleasing manner <everything went *well* on the trip>
syn favorably, fortunately, happily, prosperously, satisfyingly, successfully, swimmingly
rel comfortably, easily, smoothly
con amiss, wrong
ant badly
6 *syn* see EASILY 1
7 in all likelihood <the fighting may *well* continue for years>
syn doubtlessly, easily, indeed, really, truly, undoubtedly
rel conceivably, perhaps, possibly; likely, probably
8 to a considerable extent or degree <they landed *well* beyond the wharf>
syn considerably, far, quite, rather, significantly, somewhat
idiom by a long way, by a wide margin
well *adj* **1** *syn* see PROSPEROUS 3
2 *syn* see HEALTHY 1
ant ill, unwell
3 *syn* see LUCKY
well–behaved *adj syn* see GOOD 13
well–being *n* **1** *syn* see PROSPERITY 2
ant ill-being
2 *syn* see WELFARE
ant ill-being
well–bred *adj syn* see GENTEEL 1
ant ill-bred
well–conditioned *adj syn* see HEALTHY 1
well–developed *adj syn* see CURVACEOUS
well–disposed *adj syn* see SYMPATHETIC 2
ant ill-disposed
well–favored *adj syn* see BEAUTIFUL
ant ill-favored
well–fixed *adj syn* see PROSPEROUS 3
ant badly off

well–founded *adj* having a firm foundation in fact or logic <offered *well-founded* arguments to support his position>
syn cogent, good, just, justified, well≈ grounded
rel sound, substantial, telling, valid; rational, reasonable, reasoned; fundamental, meaty, pithy
con unjustified; insubstantial, invalid, unsound; irrational, unreasonable
well–groomed *adj* **1** *syn* see NEAT 2
2 *syn* see DAPPER
well–grounded *adj* *syn* see WELL≈ FOUNDED
wellhead *n syn* see SOURCE
well–heeled *adj syn* see PROSPEROUS 3
ant badly off
well–hung *adj syn* see GLIB
well–known *adj* much talked about <a *well≈ known* hospital>
syn famous, leading, noted, notorious, popular, prominent; *compare* FAMOUS 2
rel conspicuous, important, outstanding
idiom on everyone's tongue
con inconspicuous, obscure, unheard-of, unimportant, unnoted, unpopular
ant unknown
well–liked *adj syn* see FAVORITE 2
well–liking *adj syn* see HEALTHY 1
well–mannered *adj syn* see CIVIL 2
ant ill-mannered
well–nigh *adv* **1** *syn* see NEARLY
2 *syn* see ALMOST 1
well–off *adj syn* see PROSPEROUS 3
ant badly off
well over *vb syn* see OVERFLOW 2
well–paying *adj syn* see ADVANTAGEOUS 1
well–proportioned *adj syn* see SHAPELY
wellspring *n syn* see SOURCE
well–thought–of *adj syn* see RESPECTABLE 1
well–timed *adj syn* see TIMELY 1
con premature, untimely; behindhand, late, tardy
ant ill-timed
well–to–do *adj syn* see PROSPEROUS 3
ant badly off
well–turned *adj syn* see SHAPELY
well–worn *adj syn* see TRITE
welsh *vb syn* see BACK DOWN
welt *n* **1** *syn* see WHEAL
‖**2** *syn* see BLOW 1
weltanschauung *n syn* see IDEOLOGY
welter *vb* **1** *syn* see WALLOW 1
rel strive, struggle; toss, tumble, writhe; grovel
2 *syn* see WALLOW 3
welter *vb syn* see WITHER
wench *n* **1** *syn* see GIRL 1
2 *syn* see WANTON
wend *vb syn* see GO 1
western *n* a motion picture or radio or television play with its scene laid in the western U.S. and having cowboys as its main characters <young boys delighting in Saturday morning *westerns*>
syn horse opera, oater
rel shoot-'em-up
wet *vb* to make wet by or as if by saturating with water <they were *wet* thoroughly by the pouring rain>

syn deluge, douse, drench, drown, soak, sop, souse; *compare* SOAK 1
rel damp, dampen, moisten; humidify, humify; fill, impregnate, saturate; irrigate; lave, rinse, wash
ant desiccate, dry

wet *adj* **1** containing or impregnated with liquid <change *wet* clothing for dry>
syn drenched, dripping, madid, saturate, saturated, soaked, soaking, sodden, sopping, soppy, soused, wringing-wet
rel soggy, water-logged; damp, dank, moist, wettish
idiom dripping (*or* soaking *or* sopping) wet
con bone-dry, dehydrated, desiccated, parched, sere, waterless
ant dry

2 *syn* see INTOXICATED 1

‖**wet** *n syn* see DRAM

wettish *adj syn* see DAMP

whack *vb syn* see STRIKE 2

whack *n* **1** *syn* see BLOW 1
2 *syn* see FLING 1

whacking *adj syn* see HUGE

whacking *adv syn* see VERY 1

whale *n syn* see GIANT

whale *vb syn* see WHIP 1

whaling *adj syn* see HUGE

wham *n syn* see BANG 2

whammy *n syn* see JINX

whangdoodle *n syn* see NONSENSE 2

wharf *n* a structure used by boats and ships for taking on or landing cargo and passengers <brought the boat alongside the *wharf* and moored her>
syn berth, dock, jetty, levee, pier, quay, slip

what–do–you–call–it *n* a thing or person that the speaker cannot (as from not knowing or from forgetting) name <hand me one of those little *what-do-you-call-its*> <went to *what-do-you-call-her's* house last week>
syn what-is-it, whatsis, what's its name, what-you-call-it, what-you-may-call-it, whatyoumayjigger; *compare* DOODAD, GADGET 1

what–is–it *n syn* see WHAT-DO-YOU-CALL-IT

whatnot *n syn* see KNICKKNACK

whatsis *n syn* see WHAT-DO-YOU-CALL-IT

what's its name *n syn* see WHAT-DO-YOU-CALL-IT

what–you–call–it *n syn* see WHAT-DO-YOU-CALL-IT

what–you–may–call–it *n syn* see WHAT-DO-YOU-CALL-IT

whatyoumayjigger *n syn* see WHAT-DO-YOU-CALL-IT

wheal *n* a ridge raised on the skin by or as if by a stroke of a lash <the convict's back was covered with *wheals* and old scars>
syn wale, weal, welt, whelk, ‖whelp
rel strake, streak, stripe

wheedle *vb syn* see COAX

wheel *n* **1** *syn* see CYCLE 1
2 *syn* see REVOLUTION 1

3 *syn* see LEAGUE 4

wheel *vb* **1** *syn* see REEL 2
2 *syn* see DRIVE 5
3 *syn* see TURN 6

wheeze *vb syn* see HISS

wheeze *n syn* see PRANK

whelk *n syn* see WHEAL

whelm *vb* **1** *syn* see DELUGE 1
2 *syn* see DELUGE 3
3 *syn* see OVERWHELM 4

‖**whelp** *n syn* see WHEAL

when *adv syn* see THEN 1

when *conj syn* see THOUGH

whence *n syn* see SOURCE

where *adv* **1** *syn* see WHEREVER
2 *syn* see WHITHER 2

where *n syn* see PLACE 1

whereabouts *adv syn* see WHITHER 1
con hereabouts, thereabouts

whereas *conj* **1** *syn* see BECAUSE
2 *syn* see THOUGH

‖**whereaway** *adv syn* see WHITHER 1

wherefore *n syn* see REASON 3

whereto *adv syn* see WHITHER 2

whereunto *adv syn* see WHITHER 2

wherever *adv* at, in, or to any or every place in or to which <he goes *wherever* he is needed>
syn everywhere, where
con here, there

‖**wherret** *vb syn* see SLAP 1

‖**wherret** *vb syn* see WORRY 1

whet *vb* **1** *syn* see SHARPEN
2 *syn* see STIR 1

whet *n* ‖**1** *syn* see WHILE 1
2 *syn* see APPETIZER

whether or no *adv syn* see WILLY-NILLY

whetted *adj syn* see SHARP 1

whicker *vb syn* see NEIGH

whiff *n syn* see HINT 2

whiffet *n syn* see NONENTITY

whiffle *vb syn* see HESITATE

whiffling *adj syn* see VACILLATING 2

whiffy *adj syn* see MALODOROUS 1

whigmaleerie *n* **1** *syn* see CAPRICE
2 *syn* see KNICKKNACK

while *n* **1** a somewhat indefinite period of time <sat down to rest for a *while*>
syn bit, space, spell, stretch, time, ‖whet
2 *syn* see OCCASION 5
3 *syn* see EFFORT 1

while *conj syn* see THOUGH

while *vb* to pass time and especially leisure time without boredom or in pleasant ways <*whiled* odd hours away in dreaming>
syn beguile, fleet, wile
rel amuse, divert, entertain; brighten, enliven, lighten

while (away) *vb syn* see SPEND 3

whilom *adj syn* see FORMER 2

whim *n syn* see CAPRICE
rel idea; disposition, inclination, thought; dream, fantasy, vision

whimper *vb* to cry feebly and often plaintively or peevishly <a baby *whimpering* in his sleep>
syn pule, whine; *compare* CRY 2

whimsical *adj* **1** *syn* see ARBITRARY 1
2 *syn* see UNCERTAIN 1

whimsied *adj syn* see ARBITRARY 1

---

syn synonym(s) *rel* related word(s)
ant antonym(s) *con* contrasted word(s)
idiom idiomatic equivalent(s)
‖ use limited; if in doubt, see a dictionary

whimsy *n syn* see CAPRICE
 rel idea; disposition, inclination, thought; dream, fantasy, vision
whim–whams *n pl syn* see JITTERS
whine *vb* 1 *syn* see WHIMPER
 2 *syn* see COMPLAIN
‖whinner *vb syn* see NEIGH
whinny *vb syn* see NEIGH
whiny *adj syn* see IRRITABLE
whip *vb* 1 to strike repeatedly with or as if with a lash or rod <*whip* a dog for stealing from the table>
 syn flagellate, flog, hide, ‖larrup, lash, lather, scourge, stripe, thrash, ‖wear out, whale, ‖yerk
 rel beat, belabor, drub, wallop; bastinado, birch, bludgeon, cane, cudgel, quirt, switch
 2 to defeat utterly <*whipped* their traditional rival by a score of 40 to 7>
 syn beat, blast, ‖bowl (down *or* out), ‖clean up (on), ‖clobber, ‖cream, curry, drub, dust, lambaste, ‖larrup, lick, mop (up), overrun, overwhelm, rout, shellac, skunk, smear, smother, steamroller, thrash, trim, trounce, upend, wallop, whomp; *compare* CONQUER 1, DEFEAT 2
 rel conquer, defeat, overcome, subdue, vanquish
 idiom cook one's goose, deal a crushing defeat, settle one's hash, snow one under
 3 to agitate with an instrument so as to stiffen and increase the bulk of by incorporation of air <*whip* cream for a shortcake>
 syn beat, whisk
 4 *syn* see TURN 6
whip (up) *vb syn* see INCITE
 ant calm (down)
whip hand *n syn* see BETTER 2
whippersnapper *n syn* see NONENTITY
whipping boy *n syn* see SCAPEGOAT
whippy *adj syn* see ELASTIC 1
whipster *n syn* see NONENTITY
whirl *vb* 1 *syn* see SPIN 1
 2 *syn* see SWIRL
 3 *syn* see TURN 6
 4 *syn* see HURRY 2
 5 *syn* see SPIN 2
whirl *n* 1 *syn* see REVOLUTION 1
 2 *syn* see EDDY
 3 *syn* see COMMOTION 4
 4 *syn* see STIR 1
 5 *syn* see FLING 1
whirlblast *n syn* see WHIRLWIND 1
whirligig *vb syn* see SPIN 1
whirlpool *n* 1 *syn* see EDDY
 2 *syn* see STIR 1
whirlpool *vb syn* see SWIRL
‖whirlpuff *n syn* see WHIRLWIND 1
whirlwind *n* 1 a rotating windstorm of limited extent that is often accompanied by a column of dust or vapor <*whirlwinds* moved across the plowed land>
 syn whirlblast, ‖whirlpuff, whirly; *compare* HURRICANE, TORNADO
 rel dust devil, rainspout, sand column, sand spout, waterspout
 2 *syn* see STIR 1
whirly *n syn* see WHIRLWIND 1
whish *vb* 1 *syn* see HISS
 2 *syn* see HURRY 2

whisk *vb* 1 *syn* see HURRY 2
 2 *syn* see WHIP 3
whisker *n syn* see HAIR
whiskered *adj* 1 *syn* see BEARDED
 2 *syn* see HAIRY 1
whiskers *n pl syn* see BEARD
whisper *vb* 1 *syn* see HISS
 2 *syn* see CONFIDE 1
whisper *n* 1 *syn* see MURMUR 1
 2 *syn* see HINT 2
whispering *n syn* see REPORT 1
whist *adj syn* see STILL 3
whistle–stop *n syn* see BURG
whit *n syn* see PARTICLE
white *adj syn* see FAVORABLE 5
 ant black
white *n syn* see REACTIONARY
 ant red
white *vb* 1 *syn* see WHITEN 1
 2 *syn* see WHITEN 1
whited sepulcher *n syn* see HYPOCRITE
white–haired *adj syn* see FAVORITE 1
white–headed *adj syn* see FAVORITE 1
white–hot *adj* 1 *syn* see HOT 1
 2 *syn* see IMPASSIONED
white lightning *n syn* see MOONSHINE 2
white–livered *adj syn* see COWARDLY
whiten *vb* 1 to free from color and make white or whiter <*whiten* linen in the sun>
 syn blanch, bleach, blench, decolor, decolorize, white
 rel dim, dull, fade, lighten, pale; etiolate; frost, grizzle, silver
 con color, darken
 ant blacken
 2 *syn* see PALLIATE
white plague *n syn* see TUBERCULOSIS
whitewash *vb syn* see PALLIATE
whither *adv* 1 to what place <*whither* did they go?>
 syn where, whereabouts, ‖whereaway
 2 to what point, conclusion, or end <*whither* is our nation drifting?>
 syn whereto, whereunto
whiz *vb* 1 *syn* see HISS
 2 *syn* see HURRY 2
whiz *n syn* see EXPERT
 ant dub, duffer
whiz–bang *adj syn* see EXCELLENT
whizzer *n syn* see TRICK 1
whole *adj* 1 free from damage, defect, or flaw <feared the eggs were broken but found them *whole*>
 syn entire, flawless, good, intact, perfect, sound, unblemished, unbroken, undamaged, unhurt, unimpaired, uninjured, unmarred, untouched
 rel complete, plenary; healthy, well
 con broken, damaged, defective, impaired, injured, marred
 2 *syn* see HEALTHY 1
 3 lacking nothing that properly belongs to it <the effect of the *whole* mural>
 syn choate, complete, entire, full, integral, perfect
 rel orbicular, rounded, well-rounded
 ant partial
 4 including every constituent element or individual <the *whole* community rose to his defense>

syn all, complete, entire, gross, outright, total

ant partial

5 not scattered or dispersed <gave the matter her *whole* attention>

syn concentrated, exclusive, fixed, undistracted, undivided, unswerving

whole *n* **1** the total supply or amount <the *whole* of our creative literature>

syn aggregate, all, be-all and end-all, entirety, gross, sum, sum total, tale, total, totality, ||tote

rel amount, supply; result, resultant, summation; bulk, mass, quantity, quantum

con detail, division, fraction, fragment, portion, section, segment, share

ant part

2 an organized array of parts or elements forming or functioning as a unit <stars, planets, galaxies — all but parts of one stupendous *whole*, the universe>

syn entity, integral, integrate, sum, system, totality; *compare* SYSTEM 1

rel being, organism, organization; coherence, cohesion, linkage; unity

con accumulation, aggregation, heap, pile, mass; section, segment; selection

ant part; agglomeration

wholehearted *adj* **1** *syn* see SURE 2

2 *syn* see SINCERE 1

rel ardent, fervent, impassioned, passionate; earnest, serious; authentic, bona fide, genuine

whole-hog *adj syn* see EXHAUSTIVE

whole-length *adj syn* see UNABRIDGED

wholeness *n* **1** *syn* see HEALTH

rel integrity, heartiness, robustness, vigor

2 *syn* see ENTIRETY 1

3 *syn* see INTEGRITY 2

whole number *n syn* see NUMBER

wholesale *adj syn* see INDISCRIMINATE 1

wholesome *adj* **1** *syn* see HEALTHFUL

ant noxious; unwholesome

2 *syn* see CURATIVE

3 *syn* see HEALTHY 1

4 *syn* see SAFE 3

ant noxious

whole-souled *adj syn* see SINCERE 1

rel ardent, fervent, impassioned; earnest, intense, serious

wholly *adv* **1** *syn* see WELL 3

2 *syn* see ALL 1

whomp *vb syn* see WHIP 2

whoop *vb syn* see SHOUT 1

whoop *n syn* see PARTICLE

whoop-de-do *n syn* see REVELRY 2

whoopee *n* **1** *syn* see REVELRY 2

2 *syn* see MERRYMAKING

whoopla *n* **1** *syn* see COMMOTION 4

2 *syn* see REVELRY 2

whoop-up *n syn* see REVELRY 2

whoosh *vb syn* see HISS

whop *vb syn* see BEAT 1

whop *n syn* see BLOW 1

whopping *adj syn* see HUGE

whopping *adv syn* see VERY 1

whore *n* **1** *syn* see HARLOT 1

2 *syn* see PROSTITUTE

whoredom *n syn* see PROSTITUTION

whorehouse *n syn* see BROTHEL

whoreson *n syn* see BASTARD 1

whorish *adj syn* see FAST 7

whorl *vb syn* see SWIRL

who's who *n syn* see ARISTOCRACY

why *n* **1** *syn* see REASON 3

2 *syn* see MYSTERY

whyfor *n syn* see REASON 3

wicked *adj* **1** *syn* see WRONG 1

ant upright

2 *syn* see PLAYFUL 1

3 *syn* see RISQUÉ

4 *syn* see MALICIOUS

5 *syn* see DANGEROUS 1

6 *syn* see TROUBLESOME

7 *syn* see OUTRAGEOUS 1

8 *syn* see SKILLFUL 2

9 *syn* see ABLE

wickedness *n* **1** *syn* see EVIL 2

2 *syn* see VICE 1

wide *adj* **1** *syn* see SPACIOUS

2 *syn* see EXTENSIVE 1

3 *syn* see LIBERAL 3

wide-awake *adj syn* see WATCHFUL

rel alive, awake, aware, conscious, sensible

widen *vb syn* see BROADEN

wideness *n syn* see BREADTH 2

widespread *adj syn* see PREVAILING

widget *n syn* see GADGET 1

width *n syn* see RANGE 2

wield *vb* **1** *syn* see HANDLE 2

rel conduct, control

2 *syn* see EXERT

wieldy *adj syn* see STRONG 1

wiener *n syn* see FRANKFURTER

wienerwurst *n syn* see FRANKFURTER

||**wienie** *n syn* see FRANKFURTER

wife *n* the female partner in a marriage <a sense of humor is a requirement for his potential *wife*>

syn ||ball and chain, lady, ||little woman, ||missus, Mrs., ||old lady, ||old woman, ||rib, ||squaw, ||woman

rel consort, helpmate, helpmeet, mate, other half, spouse; bride, dowager, matron; concubine

idiom better half

con maid, maiden; widow

wig *n syn* see REBUKE

wig *vb syn* see SCOLD 1

wigging *n syn* see REBUKE

wiggle *vb syn* see WRIGGLE

wiggle-waggle *adj syn* see VACILLATING 2

wiggle-waggle *vb syn* see HESITATE

wiggy *adj syn* see POMPOUS 1

wight *n syn* see HUMAN

wild *adj* **1** living and growing in a state of nature and without human intervention <lived on *wild* plants and game animals>

syn agrarian, agrestal, native, natural, uncultivated, undomesticated; *compare* SAVAGE 1

rel escaped, feral; unsubdued, untamed

ant cultivated, domesticated

2 *syn* see SAVAGE 1

ant tame, tamed

---

syn synonym(s)   *rel* related word(s)
ant antonym(s)   *con* contrasted word(s)
idiom idiomatic equivalent(s)
|| use limited; if in doubt, see a dictionary

3 *syn* see IRRESPONSIBLE
rel adventurous, audacious, daring, dashing; brash, cocksure, rash
4 *syn* see FURIOUS 2
rel bewildered, distracted, upset; agitated, perturbed, upset; addled, confused, muddled; crazy, demented, deranged, mad
con easy, relaxed
5 *syn* see UNRULY 1
6 marked by turmoil and fury especially of natural elements <a *wild* night of howling winds and driving snow>
syn blustering, blustery, ‖coarse, dirty, furious, raging, rough, stormful, stormy, tempestuous, turbulent
rel blatant, boisterous, clamorous, ungovernable, unruly; brutal, harsh, severe
con calm, peaceful, placid, quiet, stormless; halcyon, irenic, serene
7 given to unrestrained self-indulgence and pursuit of pleasure <her son got in with a *wild* bunch and took to drink>
syn devil-may-care, fast, gay, raffish, rakehell, rakish, sporty
rel boisterous, roisterous, rollicking, swaggering; careless, heedless, irresponsible, thoughtless; lewd, loose, unchaste, wanton
con moderate, restrained, sober, sparing, temperate; bridled, controlled, curbed; self-controlled
8 *syn* see EXTRAVAGANT 1
9 *syn* see BARBARIAN 1
ant cultivated, cultured
10 *syn* see BARBARIC 1
wild *n syn* see WASTE 1
wilderness *n syn* see WASTE 1
rel backcountry, backland(s), hinterland
idiom back of beyond
wild land *n syn* see WASTE 1
wildly *adv syn* see HARD 2
wildness *n syn* see WASTE 1
wile *n syn* see TRICK 1
rel chicane, chicanery, trickery; cunning, deceit, dissimulation, guile
con candor, frankness, openness, plain dealing, straightforwardness, unconstraint; artlessness, naturalness, sincerity
wile *vb* **1** *syn* see ATTRACT 1
2 *syn* see WHILE
wiliness *n syn* see CUNNING 2
will *vb* to be inclined <you may decide whichever way you *will*>
syn choose, elect, like, please, wish
rel crave, desire, want
idiom have a mind to, see (*or* think) fit
will *n* **1** a desire to act in a particular way or have a particular thing <I've no *will* to be sociable tonight>
syn fancy, inclination, liking, mind, pleasure, velleity
rel appetite, desire, passion, urge; hankering, longing, pining, yearning
idiom heart's desire
con aversion, dislike, distaste, repugnance, repulsion, revulsion
2 the aspect of mind involved in choosing or deciding <problems arise when one's *will* and judgment come in conflict>
syn volition
rel design, intent, purpose, wishes; character, disposition, temper

3 power of controlling one's actions, impulses, or emotions <a self-indulgent man of feeble character and little *will*>
syn discipline, self-command, self-control, self-discipline, self-government, self-mastery, self-restraint, willpower
rel aplomb, assurance, confidence, poise, self-possession; control, discretion, restraint
con gratification, indulgence, self-indulgence
will *vb* to give to another by will <*will* family treasures to a relative>
syn bequeath, devise, leave, legate
willful *adj* **1** *syn* see OBSTINATE
rel contumacious, factious
idiom having the bit in one's teeth, not yielding an inch
con amenable, docile, obedient, tractable
ant biddable
2 *syn* see VOLUNTARY
rel intentional, purposive; decided, determined, resolved; dogged, obstinate, pertinacious, stubborn
con accidental, chance, involuntary, unintentional, unplanned
willies *n pl syn* see JITTERS
willing *adj* **1** prepared in mind or by disposition <*willing* to help>
syn disposed, fain, inclined, minded, predisposed, prone, ready
rel agreeable, compliant, favorable; forward, game, prompt
idiom in the mood
con averse, disinclined, indisposed, loath, reluctant, unminded
ant unwilling
2 *syn* see VOLUNTARY
rel disposed, inclined, predisposed; open, prone
will–less *adj syn* see SPONTANEOUS
willpower *n syn* see WILL 3
willy–nilly *adv* surely and without regard to plans or inclination <it seems that we must drift *willy-nilly* toward disaster>
syn helplessly, inescapably, inevitably, perforce, unavoidably, whether or no
idiom as a matter of course, come what may, of necessity, without let or choice
‖**willy–willy** *n syn* see HURRICANE
wilt *vb* **1** *syn* see WITHER
2 *syn* see COLLAPSE 2
3 *syn* see DROOP 3
wily *adj syn* see SLY 2
rel sagacious, shrewd; clever, knowing
con aboveboard, forthright, straightforward; guileless, open, trusting
wimp *n syn* see WEAKLING
win *vb* **1** to gain the victory <the home team *won* by a wide margin>
syn beat, overcome, prevail, triumph; *compare* CONQUER 1
idiom bear off the palm (*or* prize), bring home the bacon, carry the day, come out first (*or* ahead), finish in front
ant lose
2 *syn* see GAIN 1
3 *syn* see EARN 1
rel produce, yield
4 *syn* see GET 1
ant lose

win (over) *vb* **1** *syn* see DISARM 2
   2 *syn* see INDUCE 1
win *n* *syn* see VICTORY 1
wince *vb* *syn* see RECOIL
   rel dodge, duck, jib, sheer, swerve, turn; cower, cringe
wind *n* **1** *syn* see NOTHING 1
   2 *syn* see HINT 1
wind *vb* *syn* see BLOW 1
wind *vb* **1** *syn* see DEFORM
   2 to follow a circular, spiral, or writhing course <the vine *wound* its way up the pillar>
   syn coil, corkscrew, curl, entwine, spiral, twine, twist, wreathe; *compare* CURVE
   rel bend, curve, meander, weave; circle, encircle, enlace, gird, girdle, surround; enclose, envelop
windbaggery *n* *syn* see NONSENSE 2
windiness *n* *syn* see VERBOSITY
winding *adj* curving repeatedly first one way then another <a *winding* country road>
   syn anfractuous, convoluted, flexuous, meandering, meandrous, serpentine, sinuous, snaky, tortuous; *compare* CROOKED 1
   rel bending, curving, twisting; crooked, devious; circuitous, indirect, roundabout
   con direct, straight
window dressing *n* *syn* see MASK 2
windrow *n* *syn* see PILE 1
wind up *vb* **1** *syn* see CLOSE 3
   2 *syn* see SETTLE 7
windup *n* *syn* see FINALE
windy *adj* **1** marked by more wind than usual <a *windy* March day>
   syn airy, blowy, breezy, gusty
   rel brisk, fresh; drafty
   con breathless, motionless, still
   ant windless
   2 *syn* see INFLATED
   3 *syn* see WORDY
wing *n* *syn* see ANNEX
   rel expansion, prolongation; bulge, projection, protrusion, protuberance
wing *vb* *syn* see FLY 4
wink *vb* to close and open the eyelids quickly <*winking* involuntarily as the light struck his eyes>
   syn bat, blink, nictate, nictitate, twinkle
   rel squinch, squinny, squint; flutter
wink (at) *vb* *syn* see CONNIVE 1
wink *n* **1** *syn* see INSTANT 1
   2 *syn* see HINT 1
winker *n* *syn* see EYE 1
winner *n* *syn* see VICTOR 1
   ant loser
winning *adj* *syn* see SWEET 1
winnow *vb* **1** *syn* see BLOW 1
   2 *syn* see SORT 2
winsome *adj* *syn* see SWEET 1
   rel adorable, lovable, lovesome
wipe (out) *vb* **1** *syn* see ERASE

   2 *syn* see HANDKERCHIEF
‖**wiped out** *adj* *syn* see DRUGGED
‖**wiper** *n* *syn* see HANDKERCHIEF
‖**wire** *n* *syn* see PICKPOCKET
wiredraw *vb* *syn* see THIN 1
wiry *adj* *syn* see MUSCULAR 1
wisdom *n* **1** *syn* see KNOWLEDGE 2
   2 *syn* see SAGACITY
   3 *syn* see SENSE 6
   rel judiciousness, sageness, saneness, sapience; perspicacity, sagacity, shrewdness
   ant folly
wise *n* *syn* see METHOD 1
wise *adj* **1** having or exhibiting a capacity for discernment and the intelligent application of knowledge <to be *wise* is to use knowledge well>
   syn discerning, gnostic, insighted, insightful, knowing, knowledgeable, perceptive, sagacious, sage, sophic, wisehearted
   rel aware, grasping, intuitive, sensing; acute, keen, perspicacious; cogitative, contemplative, reflective, thoughtful; astute, sharp, shrewd
   con dull, obtuse, slow, slow-witted; insensitive, unaware, unknowing
   ant unwise
   2 exercising or involving sound judgment <*wise* management of scarce resources>
   syn judgmatic, judicious, prudent, sage, sane, sapient, sensible; *compare* SHREWD
   rel canny, discreet, foresighted, provident; astute, perspicacious, sagacious, shrewd; alert, bright, intelligent, keen, smart
   con careless, heedless, injudicious; improvident, imprudent, indiscreet, short-sighted
   ant foolish, unwise
   3 *syn* see EXPEDIENT
   4 shrewdly aware and subtly resourceful <a *wise* operator with his eye always on the main chance>
   syn canny, hep, knowing, nimble-witted, quick, quick-witted, sharp, sharp-witted, slick, smart; *compare* INTELLIGENT 2, SHREWD
   rel cagey, foresighted, shrewd; artful, crafty, cunning, slippery, smooth, tricky, wily; steel-trap
   idiom in the groove, not born yesterday, on the beam
   con narrow, prim, puritanical, straitlaced; conservative, plodding, ‖square
   5 presumptuously confident and self-assured <a bunch of *wise* kids tearing up the neighborhood>
   syn ‖biggety, bold, bold-faced, cheeky, forward, fresh, impudent, nervy, pert, procacious, sassy, smart, smart-alecky
   rel arrogant, brash, cocky, insolent; flip, flippant, impertinent, lippy, saucy
   con demure, mannerly, modest, proper; dull, priggish, stuffy
wise (up) *vb* *syn* see INFORM 2
wiseacre *n* *syn* see SMART ALECK
wisecrack *n* *syn* see JOKE 1
wisecracker *n* *syn* see SMART ALECK
wise guy *n* *syn* see SMART ALECK
wisehead *n* *syn* see SMART ALECK
wisehearted *adj* *syn* see WISE 1
wise man *n* *syn* see SAGE

---

wisenheimer *n syn* see SMART ALECK
wish *vb* **1** *syn* see DESIRE 1
  rel expect, hope; fancy
  2 *syn* see WILL
  3 *syn* see IMPOSE 4
wishy–washy *adj* **1** *syn* see INSIPID 3
  rel enervated, languid, listless; spiritless;
  flavorless, savorless
  idiom neither flesh, fowl, nor good red
  herring, neither one thing nor the other
  2 *syn* see CHARACTERLESS
wistful *adj syn* see PENSIVE 2
‖**wit** *vb syn* see UNDERSTAND 3
wit *n* **1** *syn* see MIND 1
  rel perspicacity, sagacity; apprehension,
  awareness, comprehension
  2 *often* **wits** *pl* mental soundness and health
  <frightened nearly out of her *wits*>
  syn lucidity, ‖marbles, mind, reason, saneness, sanity, sense(s), soundness
  rel balance, rationality
  con aberration; craziness; derangement,
  insanity, lunacy, madness, mania
  ant witlessness
  3 acuteness of perception or judgment <had
  the *wit* to know that he was out of his depth
  in such a discussion>
  syn acumen, astucity, astuteness, clear-
  sightedness, discernment, discrimination,
  keenness, penetration, percipience, perspicacity, shrewdness; *compare* PRUDENCE 1
  rel awareness, comprehension, grasp, insight, perception, understanding; prudence,
  sagaciousness, sagacity, sageness, sapience,
  wisdom; clairvoyance, divination, ESP,
  sensing
  con aridity, dullness, prosaicness, unimaginativeness; fatuity, foolishness, inanity, silliness; stupidity
  4 *syn* see INTELLIGENCE 1
  5 a talent for banter or persiflage <a jolly
  man, noted for his kindly *wit*>
  syn esprit, humor
  rel alertness, keenness, quick-wittedness;
  brilliance, cleverness, intelligence, smartness
  6 *syn* see HUMOR 5
  7 *syn* see HUMORIST 2
witch *n* **1** a woman who practices the black
  arts <ancient laws against *witches*>
  syn bruja, enchantress, hag, hex, lamia,
  sorceress, witchwoman; *compare* MAGICIAN
  1
  2 *syn* see HAG 2
witch *vb syn* see BEWITCH 1
witchcraft *n* **1** *syn* see MAGIC 1
  2 *syn* see CHARM 3
witchery *n* **1** *syn* see MAGIC 1
  2 *syn* see CHARM 3
witching *n syn* see MAGIC 1
witchwoman *n syn* see WITCH 1
witchy *adj syn* see MAGIC
with *prep* **1** *syn* see OVER 3
  2 *syn* see FOR 2
  3 *syn* see VIA 2
withal *adv* **1** *syn* see ALSO 2
  2 *syn* see HOWEVER
withdraw *vb* **1** *syn* see REMOVE 2
  ant deposit
  2 *syn* see ABJURE
  3 *syn* see GO 2

  rel quail, recoil, retreat, shrink; recede
  idiom give ground, give way
  con advance, progress; arrive, come
  4 *syn* see RETREAT 2
  ant advance
withdrawal *n syn* see DEPARTURE 1
  ant approach
withdrawn *adj* **1** *syn* see UNDEMONSTRA-
TIVE
  ant outgiving
  2 *syn* see INDIFFERENT 2
  3 *syn* see UNSOCIABLE
  ant outgoing
wither *vb* to lose substance and freshness by
  or as if by loss of natural moisture <projects
  that *wither* and die from lack of popular
  interest>
  syn dry up, mummify, mummy, shrivel,
  welter, wilt, wizen
  rel cave in, collapse, deflate, fold; constrict,
  contract, shrink; decline, wane
  con freshen, revive, revivify; develop, grow,
  increase, wax
  ant flourish
withhold *vb* **1** *syn* see RESTRAIN 1
  2 *syn* see KEEP 5
  con award, concede, grant, vouchsafe
  ant accord
  3 *syn* see DENY 2
  4 *syn* see REFRAIN 1
within *adv syn* see INDOORS
  ant without
within *n syn* see INTERIOR
  ant without
withindoors *adv syn* see INDOORS
  ant withoutdoors
withinside *adv syn* see INDOORS
  ant withoutside
with–it *adj syn* see STYLISH
without *prep* **1** *syn* see BEYOND 1
  2 not having <living *without* decent housing
  or adequate food>
  syn awanting, lacking, minus, sans, wanting
without *adv syn* see OUTDOORS
  ant within
without *n syn* see OUTDOORS
‖**without** *conj syn* see EXCEPT 1
withoutdoors *adv syn* see OUTDOORS
  ant indoors, withindoors
with respect to *prep syn* see APROPOS
withstand *vb syn* see RESIST
  rel bear, endure, stand, suffer, tolerate
  con capitulate, submit, yield
witless *adj* **1** *syn* see SIMPLE 3
  2 *syn* see INSANE 1
witlessness *n syn* see FOOLISHNESS
witness *n* **1** *syn* see TESTIMONY
  2 *syn* see SPECTATOR
witness *vb* **1** *syn* see CERTIFY 1
  rel affirm; endorse, subscribe
  2 *syn* see INDICATE 2
witticism *n syn* see JOKE 1
wittiness *n syn* see HUMOR 4
witting *adj* **1** *syn* see AWARE
  ant unwitting
  2 *syn* see VOLUNTARY
  ant unwitting
witty *adj* provoking or intended to provoke
  mirth <a whimsical *witty* discussion on the
  foreignness of honesty to politics>

syn facetious, humorous, jocose, jocular
rel amusing, diverting, entertaining; scintillating, sparkling; penetrating, piercing, probing; funny, ridiculous, risible
con foolish, senseless, silly; brash, cheeky, fresh; earnest, serious, sober, solemn
ant unwitty

wiz *n* *syn* see EXPERT
ant dub, dud, duffer

wizard *n* **1** *syn* see MAGICIAN 1
2 *syn* see EXPERT
ant dub, dud, duffer

wizardly *adj* *syn* see MAGIC

wizardry *n* *syn* see MAGIC 1

wizen *vb* *syn* see WITHER
rel decrease, diminish, dwindle, reduce

wobble *vb* **1** *syn* see LURCH 2
2 *syn* see TEETER
3 *syn* see SHAKE

wobbly *adj* **1** *syn* see RICKETY
2 *syn* see WEAK 2
3 *syn* see VACILLATING 2

woe *n* **1** *syn* see SORROW
rel bemoaning, bewailing, deploring, lamentation
con bliss, felicity, happiness
2 *syn* see MISERY 1
3 *usu* woes *pl* *syn* see DISASTER

woebegone *adj* **1** *syn* see DOWNCAST
rel lugubrious, melancholy
con alert, concerned, interested, spirited; lively, vigorous; avid, eager, keen
2 *syn* see GLOOMY 3
rel dilapidated, outworn, shabby, worn
con bright, crisp, fresh, gay

woeful *adj* **1** full of or expressive of woe <a *woeful* countenance>
syn afflicted, doleful, dolent, dolorous, miserable, rueful, ruthful, sorrowful, wretched
rel harrowed, racked, tortured, wrung; crushed, overcome, stricken; disconsolate, heartsick, inconsolable; dejected, depressed, dispirited, downcast, downhearted, low-spirited
idiom cut to the heart, cut up, in the dumps (*or* depths *or* doldrums), on the rack
con content, satisfied; easy, peaceful, quiet; cheerful, gay, lighthearted
ant joyful
2 *syn* see MELANCHOLY 2
3 *syn* see DEPLORABLE
rel dismal, grave, sad; unprecedented

woggle *vb* *syn* see WAG

wolf *n* a man forward, direct, and zealous in amorous pursuit of women <known far and wide as a lecherous old *wolf*>
syn Casanova, chaser, Don Juan, ladies' man, lady-killer, masher, philander, philanderer, womanizer
rel amorist; lecher, libertine, Lothario, profligate, rip, roué, rounder
idiom man on the make, skirt chaser

wolf *vb* **1** *syn* see GULP
2 *syn* see PHILANDER

wolfish *adj* *syn* see FIERCE 1

woman *n* **1** a female human being <a health club that caters to *women*>
syn ‖babe, ‖broad, ‖dame, ‖doll, female, gal, gentlewoman, ‖girl, lady, she, ‖skirt, ‖squaw
rel ‖bird, ‖chick; milady
‖**2** *syn* see WIFE
3 *syn* see MISTRESS

womanish *adj* *syn* see FEMININE

womanize *vb* *syn* see PHILANDER

womanizer *n* *syn* see WOLF

womanlike *adj* *syn* see FEMININE

womanly *adj* *syn* see FEMININE

wonder *n* **1** something that causes fascinated astonishment or admiration <the seven *wonders* of the ancient world>
syn marvel, miracle, phenomenon, portent, prodigy, sensation, stunner
rel curiosity, cynosure, gazingstock, spectacle
idiom one for the book(s), something to shout (*or* write home) about
2 the complex emotion aroused by the strange and incomprehensible and especially the awe-inspiring <stood gazing in wide-eyed *wonder* at the scene unveiled before her>
syn admiration, amaze, amazement, marveling, wonderment
rel awe, fear, reverence; bewilderment, perplexity, puzzlement; astonishment, marvel, shock
con disinterest, incuriosity, indifference, unconcern; dispassion, impassivity; casualness, offhandedness; boredom, ennui
3 *syn* see UNCERTAINTY
rel assailability, vulnerability
con unconcern

wonderful *adj* **1** *syn* see MARVELOUS 1
2 *syn* see MARVELOUS 2
ant lousy

wonderland *n* *syn* see UTOPIA

wonderment *n* *syn* see WONDER 2

wondrous *adj* *syn* see MARVELOUS 1

wont *n* *syn* see HABIT 1

wont *vb* *syn* see ACCUSTOM

wonted *adj* *syn* see USUAL 1
ant unwonted

wontedly *adv* *syn* see USUALLY 1
ant unwontedly

woo *vb* *syn* see ADDRESS 8
idiom bill and coo, pitch woo

wood *n,* often woods *pl* but sing or pl in constr
syn see FOREST

wooden *adj* **1** *syn* see STIFF 4
rel awkward, clumsy; heavy, ponderous, weighty
con limber, supple; plastic, pliable, pliant
2 *syn* see AWKWARD 2

woodenhead *n* *syn* see DUNCE

woodland *n* *syn* see FOREST

woods colt *n* *syn* see BASTARD 1

woodsy *adj* *syn* see RUSTIC

wooer *n* *syn* see SUITOR 2

woolly *adj* *syn* see HAIRY 1

word *vb* to convey (as an impression, a thought, or a need) in words <seemed scarcely to know how to *word* her appeal>
syn couch, express, formulate, phrase, put;
compare EXPRESS 2

---

syn synonym(s)   *rel* related word(s)
ant antonym(s)   *con* contrasted word(s)
idiom idiomatic equivalent(s)
‖ use limited; if in doubt, see a dictionary

rel convey, offer, submit; say, state, tell

word *n* **1** something that is said <didn't tell a *word* about his plans>
syn statement, utterance
rel announcement, declaration, pronouncement

2 a pronounceable sound or combination of sounds that expresses and symbolizes an idea <be sure you learn the meaning of each *word*>
syn term, vocable
rel expression, idiom, locution, phrase
3 *syn* see COMMAND 1
4 *syn* see NEWS
5 *syn* see REPORT 1
6 *syn* see MESSAGE 1
7 *syn* see SAYING
8 a statement whose weight or worth depends on the truthfulness or authority of its maker <had the doctor's *word* that no operation would be needed>
syn assurance, guarantee, pledge, warrant; *compare* PROMISE
rel commitment, engagement, undertaking; oath; vow; promise
9 *syn* see PROMISE
10 *usu* **words** *pl syn* see QUARREL
11 *syn* see PASSWORD 3
12 *syn* see PASSWORD 1

wordage *n syn* see WORDING
word for word *adv syn* see VERBATIM
word-for-word *adj syn* see VERBATIM
word-hoard *n syn* see VOCABULARY 1
wordiness *n syn* see VERBOSITY
con crispness, pithiness, trenchancy
ant laconicism, laconism

wording *n* manner or style of verbal expression <take care with the *wording* of a formal invitation>
syn diction, parlance, phrase, phraseology, phrasing, verbalism, verbiage, wordage
rel language, mode, style

wordless *adj* **1** *syn* see TACIT 1
2 *syn* see SILENT 2
3 *syn* see SILENT 3
4 *syn* see UNSPOKEN 1
ant wordy

word-of-mouth *adj syn* see ORAL 2
word-stock *n syn* see VOCABULARY 1
wordy *adj* using or marked by the use of more words than are needed to express an idea <tired of dull *wordy* editorials>
syn diffuse, long-winded, palaverous, prolix, redundant, verbose, windy
rel flatulent, inflated, tumid, turgid; garrulous, glib, loquacious, talkative, voluble; bombastic, highfalutin, rhetorical
con compendious, concise, pithy, succinct, summary, terse; lean, taut
ant laconic

work *n* **1** the activity that affords one his livelihood <laborers hurrying to *work* at dawn>
syn business, calling, employment, job, line, occupation, pursuit, ‖racket; *compare* JOB 2
rel art, craft, handicraft, métier; profession, trade, vocation, walk

2 strenuous activity that involves difficulty and effort and usually affords no pleasure <had done much hard *work* during her life>

syn bullwork, donkeywork, drudge, drudgery, grind, labor, moil, plugging, slavery, slogging, sweat, toil, travail
rel effort, exertion, pains, trouble; chore, duty, job; elucubration; striving; spadework
ant play

3 **works** *pl syn* see FACTORY
work *vb* **1** *syn* see OPERATE 3
2 *syn* see TILL
3 *syn* see SOLVE 1
4 *syn* see LABOR 1
5 *syn* see FUNCTION 3
6 *syn* see ACT 5

work (for) *vb syn* see BENEFIT
workable *adj syn* see POSSIBLE 1
rel applicable, exploitable, usable
ant unworkable

workaday *adj* **1** *syn* see PROSAIC 3
2 *syn* see ORDINARY 1
workday *adj syn* see PROSAIC 3
worker *n* one who earns a living by labor and especially by manual labor <weary *workers* straggling home each night>
syn hand, laborer, ‖mozo, operative, roustabout, workhand, workingman, workman
rel artisan, craftsman, handicraftsman, mechanic; employee
ant idler

workhand *n syn* see WORKER
workhorse *n syn* see SLAVE 2
2 *syn* see SAWHORSE
work in *vb syn* see INSINUATE 3
working *adj* **1** *syn* see ACTIVE 1
2 *syn* see BUSY 1
workingman *n syn* see WORKER
workless *adj syn* see UNEMPLOYED
workman *n syn* see WORKER
workmanlike *adj syn* see SKILLFUL 2
ant unworkmanlike
workmanly *adj syn* see SKILLFUL 2
work off *vb syn* see FOIST 3
work out *vb syn* see SOLVE 1
work over *vb syn* see REVISE
work-shy *adj syn* see LAZY
work up *vb syn* see GENERATE 3
world *n* **1** *syn* see EARTH 1
2 *syn* see UNIVERSE
worldly *adj* **1** *syn* see EARTHLY 1
ant otherworldly
2 *syn* see MATERIALISTIC
ant otherworldly, unworldly
3 *syn* see SOPHISTICATED 2
ant unworldly
worldly-wise *adj syn* see SOPHISTICATED 2
rel callous, hard-boiled, hardened
con naive, unsophisticated, unworldly
worldwide *adj syn* see UNIVERSAL 2
con parochial
world-wise *adj syn* see SOPHISTICATED 2
world-without-end *adj syn* see EVERLASTING 1
world-without-end *n syn* see ETERNITY 2
worm *n syn* see WRETCH 1
worm *vb* **1** *syn* see INSINUATE 3
2 *syn* see WRIGGLE
wormling *n syn* see WRETCH 1
worn *adj* **1** *syn* see TIRED 1
2 *syn* see HAGGARD
worn-down *adj syn* see TIRED 1

worn-out adj **1** syn see EFFETE 2
  2 syn see TIRED 1
  3 syn see TRITE
worried adj syn see DISTRAUGHT
  ant unworried
worry vb **1** to disturb one or destroy one's
  peace of mind by repeated or persistent
  tormenting attacks <vain regrets that *worry*
  his spirit>
    syn annoy, bedevil, beleaguer, dun, gnaw,
    hagride, harass, harry, hassle, needle, pester,
    plague, tantalize, tease, ‖wherret
    rel beset, bother, fret, pelt, trouble, vex;
    goad, test, try; afflict, torment, torture;
    aggrieve, oppress, persecute, wrong
    idiom give one gyp
    con comfort, console, solace; alleviate,
    assuage, ease, relieve
  2 syn see TROUBLE 1
  3 to experience concern, disquietude, or
  anxiety <*worrying* over his children's
  health>
    syn cark, fret, fuss, pother, stew, ‖fume
    rel carry on, take on; despair, give up;
    bother, concern (oneself); agitate, disquiet,
    disturb, trouble
    idiom be upset, bite one's nails
    con accept, submit; abide, bear, endure,
    stand, support; disregard, ignore, overlook,
    pass over
worry n **1** syn see CARE 2
    rel presentiment; doubt, mistrust, uncer-
    tainty; anguish, heartache, woe
    con composure, equanimity, sangfroid;
    assurance, certainty, certitude, confidence,
    security
  2 syn see TRIAL 1
worrywart n syn see PESSIMIST
worsen vb syn see DETERIORATE 1
    rel blast, blight, debase, degrade, humble,
    lower; corrupt, foul, taint
    idiom get worse, grow worse
    ant better
worship n syn see ADORATION
worship vb **1** syn see REVERE
    con contemn, despise, disdain, flout, scorn;
    curse, execrate, vilify
  2 syn see ADORE 3
    ant abominate; scorn
  3 syn see LOVE 2
worst vb syn see DEFEAT 2
worth n **1** equivalence in good qualities (as
  utility, importance, or desirability) express
  or implied <impossible to estimate the *worth*
  of such a man to the community>
    syn account, valuation, value
    rel class, excellence, merit, perfection, qual-
    ity, virtue; rate; use, usefulness, utility; con-
    sequence, importance, mark, moment, note,
    significance, weight
    con baseness, meanness, paltriness, poor-
    ness
    ant worthlessness
  2 syn see QUALITY 2
  3 syn see WEALTH 2

worthless adj **1** lacking all excellence or
  value <gave me a *worthless* check>
    syn draffy, drossy, good-for-nothing, in-
    utile, ‖no-account, no-good, nothing, un-
    worthy, valueless
    rel inferior, mediocre, poor, second-rate;
    defective, flawed, imperfect; bootless, inef-
    fectual, unavailing, useless; contemptible,
    dusty, mean, sad, sorry
    idiom dear at any price, of no earthly value
    (or worth)
    con esteemed, precious; useful, valuable,
    worthwhile; invaluable, priceless
    ant worthful
  2 syn see FECKLESS 1
    rel incapable, incompetent, unqualified
worthwhile adj syn see ADVANTAGEOUS 1
worthy adj **1** having worth or merit <a *worthy* custom handed down from our ances-
  tors>
    syn admirable, commendable, deserving,
    estimable, laudable, meritable, meritorious,
    praisable, praiseworthy, thankworthy
    rel invaluable, precious, priceless; desirable,
    pleasing, satisfying; divine
    con good-for-nothing, ‖no-account, no-
    good, valueless; contemptible, sad, sorry
    ant worthless
  2 syn see HONORABLE 1
    ant unworthy
wound vb syn see INJURE 3
wow n syn see SMASH 6
‖**wowser** n syn see PRUDE
wrack vb syn see DESTROY 1
wrackful adj syn see DESTRUCTIVE
wraith n syn see APPARITION
wrangle vb **1** syn see QUARREL
  2 syn see ARGUE 2
wrangle n syn see QUARREL
wrap vb syn see ENFOLD 1
    rel camouflage, cloak, mask
    ant unwrap
wrap (up) vb **1** syn see BUNDLE UP
  2 syn see SWATHE
wrapped adj syn see INTENT
wrapped up adj syn see INTENT
wrap up vb syn see CLOSE 3
wrath n syn see ANGER
    rel acerbity, acrimony, asperity; offense,
    resentment
wrathful adj syn see ANGRY
wrathy adj syn see ANGRY
‖**wraxle** vb syn see WRESTLE
wreak vb syn see INFLICT 2
wreakful adj syn see VINDICTIVE
wreath n a circlet of intertwined leaves or
  flowers worn upon the head as an ornament
  or as a mark of honor or esteem <received
  the laurel *wreath* of victory from the emper-
  or's own hand>
    syn chaplet, coronal, coronet, crown, gar-
    land
    rel bay(s), laurel
wreathe vb syn see WIND 2
wreck n **1** syn see CRASH 3
  2 syn see COLLAPSE 2
  3 syn see JALOPY
wreck vb **1** syn see VANDALIZE
  2 syn see DESTROY 1
    rel despoil, loot, plunder, ravage; cripple,
    disable

---

syn synonym(s)   rel related word(s)
ant antonym(s)   con contrasted word(s)
idiom idiomatic equivalent(s)
‖ use limited; if in doubt, see a dictionary

3 *syn* see TOTAL 3
4 *syn* see SABOTAGE
5 *syn* see SHIPWRECK 1
6 *syn* see RUIN 2
7 *syn* see INFLICT 2
wreckage *n* 1 *syn* see SABOTAGE
2 *syn* see DRIFTWOOD
wrecker *n syn* see VANDAL
wreckful *adj syn* see DESTRUCTIVE
wrecking *n syn* see SABOTAGE
wrench *vb* 1 to shift the position of or move by or as if by vigorous twisting <suddenly *wrenched* her around to face him>
syn wrest, wring, wry
rel bend, twist; coerce, compel, constrain, force; drag, rend, tear; contort, distort
2 *syn* see SPRAIN
3 *syn* see MISREPRESENT
4 *syn* see EXTORT 1
wrest *vb* 1 *syn* see WRENCH 1
rel arrogate, confiscate, usurp; elicit, extort, extract
2 *syn* see EXTORT 1
3 *syn* see MISREPRESENT
wrestle *vb* to struggle with an opponent at close quarters <determined to solve the problem if he had to *wrestle* with it all night>
syn grapple, scuffle, tussle, ‖wraxle
rel contend, fight, struggle; endeavor, essay; labor, moil, toil, travail, work; exert, strain, stretch, strive
wretch *n* 1 a worthless and often vicious or contemptible person <a treacherous drink-sodden *wretch*>
syn ‖blighter, lowlife, mucker, no-good, worm, wormling
rel good-for-naught, good-for-nothing, ne'er-do-well; blackguard, caitiff, devil, knave, rapscallion, rascal, rogue, rotter, scalawag, scoundrel, villain
idiom sad case
2 *syn* see SNOT 1
wretched *adj* 1 *syn* see WOEFUL 1
rel melancholy; abject, mean, sordid; piteous, pitiable, pitiful; despairing, despondent, forlorn, hopeless
con animated, gay, lively; content, contented, satisfied; gratified, pleased
2 *syn* see BASE
wretchedness *n syn* see MISERY 1
wriggle *vb* to move or advance with worm-like motions <the attackers *wriggled* stealthily through the underbrush>
syn squiggle, squirm, wiggle, worm, writhe
rel flow, glide, ooze, slide, slip
wring *vb* 1 *syn* see EXTORT 1
2 *syn* see WRENCH 1
rel press, squeeze
3 *syn* see AFFLICT
wringing-wet *adj syn* see WET 1
wrinkle *n* a small linear prominence or depression on a surface <a benign old face netted with *wrinkles*>
syn corrugation, crease, crinkle, fold, furrow, plica, ridge, rimple, rivel, ruck
rel crow's foot; pleat, pucker
wrinkle *vb syn* see CRUMPLE 1
write *vb* to form characters or words on a surface (as of paper) usually with pen or pencil <learned to *write* at an early age>

syn engross, indite, inscribe, scribe
rel dot (down), jot, note; chalk, pen, pencil; scratch, scrawl, scribble; draft, draw, make out; write down, write up
idiom push one's pen, put in writing, take down
write down *vb syn* see DEPRECIATE 1
ant write up
write off *vb* 1 *syn* see DEPRECIATE 1
2 *syn* see DECRY 2
write-up *n syn* see PUFF 3
writhe *vb* 1 to twist and turn in physical or mental distress <*writhing* in anguish with a throbbing toothache>
syn agonize, squirm, toss
rel blench, flinch, recoil, shrink, wince; contort, distort; bend, twist; thrash, tumble
2 *syn* see WRIGGLE
writing *n syn* see PRINT 2
writing desk *n syn* see DESK
wrong *n* 1 *syn* see INJUSTICE 2
2 *syn* see EVIL 2
3 *syn* see EVIL 3
4 *syn* see INJUSTICE 1
wrong *adj* 1 rejecting or deviating from the dictates of moral or divine law <had a *wrong* outlook on life> <*wrong* principles of conduct>
syn bad, evil, immoral, iniquitous, reprobate, sinful, vicious, wicked
rel blamable, blameworthy, censurable, reprehensible; corrupt, debauched, depraved; abandoned, dissolute, infamous, villainous; blasphemous, unholy, unrighteous; accursed, unblessed
con ethical, high-principled, moral, righteous, upright; chaste, innocent, pure, virtuous
ant right
2 *syn* see FALSE 1
idiom at fault, barking up the wrong tree, in error, on the wrong track
con exact, precise
ant right
3 *syn* see BAD 1
rel improper, inappropriate, inapt, infelicitous, unfit, unfitting, unhappy, unsuitable
con appropriate, fit, fitting, proper, suitable
4 *syn* see MISTAKEN
ant right
5 *syn* see INSANE 1
wrong *adv syn* see AMISS 2
ant right
wrong *vb* to inflict injury on another without justification <these men who have *wronged* the public trust deserve no consideration>
syn aggrieve, oppress, outrage, persecute
rel abuse, ill-treat, maltreat, mistreat; harm, hurt, injure; offend
idiom do wrong to (or by)
con guard, protect, safeguard; care (for), cherish; honor, love, respect
wrongdoing *n* 1 *syn* see EVIL 3
2 *syn* see MISCONDUCT
wrongful *adj syn* see UNLAWFUL
ant rightful
wrongheaded *adj* 1 *syn* see OBSTINATE
2 *syn* see CONTRARY 3
wrongly *adv syn* see AMISS 1
ant rightly

wroth *adj syn* see ANGRY
wrothful *adj syn* see ANGRY
wrothy *adj syn* see ANGRY

wry *vb syn* see WRENCH 1
wry *adj syn* see SARDONIC

X Y Z

x *n syn* see ERROR 1
x (out) *vb syn* see ERASE
Xanthippe *n syn* see VIRAGO
Xmas *n syn* see CHRISTMAS
yahoo *n syn* see TOUGH
yak *n syn* see CHATTER
yak *vb syn* see CHAT 1
‖**yak** *n syn* see JOKE 1
yakety–yak *n syn* see CHATTER
yakety–yak *vb syn* see CHAT 1
yak–yak *n syn* see CHATTER
yak–yak *vb syn* see CHAT
yammer *vb* 1 *syn* see GRIPE
 2 *syn* see CHAT 2
yank *vb* 1 *syn* see JERK
 rel tug; clutch, grab, snatch
 2 *syn* see EXTRACT 1
yap *n* 1 *syn* see RUSTIC
 ‖2 *syn* see MOUTH 1
yard *n syn* see COURT 1
yardstick *n syn* see STANDARD 3
yare *adj syn* see AGILE
yarn *n* 1 *syn* see STORY 2
 2 *syn* see CHAT 2
yarn *vb syn* see CONVERSE
yatter *n syn* see CHATTER
yatter *vb syn* see CHAT 1
yaw *n syn* see TURN 2
yaw *vb syn* see SEESAW
yaw *vb syn* see YAWN
yawn *vb* to breathe deeply with jaws widespread usually in reaction to fatigue or boredom <*yawned* again and again in the stuffy room>
 syn gape, yaw
 rel doze, drowse, nap, snooze
yawn *n syn* see TEDIUM
yawning *adj syn* see CAVERNOUS 1
yawp (or **yaup**) *vb* 1 *syn* see SQUALL 1
 2 *syn* see GRIPE
yea *adv* 1 *syn* see ALSO 2
 2 *syn* see YES 1
 3 *syn* see EVEN 3
yearbook *n* a book issued yearly to chronicle a particular part of the preceding year's activities <sports editor of his school *yearbook*>
 syn annual, annuary
yearn *vb syn* see LONG
 rel covet, desire, wish; pant
 ant dread

years *n pl syn* see OLD AGE
yeast *n syn* see FOAM
yeasty *adj syn* see GIDDY 1
yegg *n syn* see ROBBER
yell *vb* 1 *syn* see SHOUT 1
 2 to complain vigorously or vociferously <let the opposition *yell*; we got the vote>
 syn howl, scream, squeal, yip, yowl
 rel cry, lament, squall, wail, weep; bemoan, bewail, deplore
 idiom beat one's breast, make an outcry, tear one's hair, yell to high heaven
 con acclaim, applaud, cheer, hail
 3 *syn* see CALL 1
yellow *adj syn* see COWARDLY
yellowback *n syn* see DIME NOVEL
yellowbelly *n syn* see COWARD
 rel fink, rat, stinker
yellow dog *n syn* see CAD
yen *vb syn* see LONG
‖**yep** *adv syn* see YES 1
 ant ‖nope
‖**yerk** *vb syn* see WHIP 1
yes *adv* 1 —used as a function word to express assent, understanding, or acceptance <*yes*, I can do that>
 syn agreed, all right, aye, OK (or okay), ‖okeydoke, yea, ‖yep
 rel assuredly, certainly, gladly, willingly; undoubtedly, unquestionably
 idiom beyond a doubt, beyond any shade (or shadow) of doubt, with all my heart, without the least doubt
 2 *syn* see EXACTLY 3
yes *vb syn* see ASSENT
yes–man *n* 1 *syn* see STOOGE 1
 2 *syn* see SYCOPHANT
yesterday *n syn* see PAST
 ant tomorrow
yesteryear *n syn* see PAST
yet *adv* 1 beyond this — used as an intensive to stress the comparative degree <in spite of her protest he went *yet* faster>
 syn even, still
 2 at some future time <just wait, we'll get there *yet*>
 syn eventually, finally, someday, sometime, somewhen, sooner or later, ultimately
 idiom after a while, in due course, in the course of time
 3 *syn* see ALSO 2
 4 *syn* see HITHERTO 1
 5 *syn* see HOWEVER
yet *conj syn* see ONLY
yield *vb* 1 *syn* see RELINQUISH

---

syn synonym(s) *rel* related word(s)
ant antonym(s) *con* contrasted word(s)
idiom idiomatic equivalent(s)
‖ use limited; if in doubt, see a dictionary

con appropriate, arrogate, confiscate
2 to give way before a force that one can no longer resist <*yielded* to temptation>
syn bow, buckle (under), capitulate, cave, defer, knuckle, knuckle under, submit, succumb
rel accord, award, concede, grant; cede, surrender, waive; break, fail
idiom give ground, give place, give way
con bear up, hold out, resist
ant withstand
3 syn see BEAR 9
4 syn see GIVE 7
rel discharge, eject, emit, vent
5 to produce as return or revenue <an investment that *yields* 10 percent>
syn bring in, pay, return
rel afford, furnish, provide, supply; hold out, offer, proffer, tender
idiom afford (or give or provide) a return of, put at one's disposal
6 syn see GIVE 12
yield n syn see OUTPUT
yielding adj **1** syn see SOFT 6
ant unyielding
2 syn see PASSIVE 2
yip vb syn see YELL 2
‖**yob** n syn see RUSTIC
yoke n **1** syn see BONDAGE
2 syn see BOND 3
yoke vb **1** syn see HITCH 2
2 syn see JOIN 1
yokel n syn see RUSTIC
yon adv **1** syn see BEYOND 1
2 syn see THERE
yonder adv syn see BEYOND 1
yore n syn see PAST
young adj **1** being in an early stage of life, growth, or development <interested in molding *young* minds>
syn callow, green, immature, infant, juvenile, unfledged, unripe, youthful
rel fresh, new; crude, raw, unfinished, unformed
con full-grown, grown-up, mature, ripe; aged, elderly, superannuated
ant old; old
2 syn see INEXPERIENCED
youngling n syn see CHILD 1
young man n syn see BOYFRIEND 1
young one n syn see CHILD 1
youngster n syn see CHILD 1
youth n **1** the period of life in which one passes from childhood to maturity <the thought of regaining one's *youth*>
syn adolescence, greenness, juvenility, prime, puberty, pubescence, salad days, spring, springtide, springtime, youthfulness, youthhood
rel callowness, immaturity, inexperience, unripeness; dewiness
idiom awkward age, flower (or springtime or May) of life
ant age
2 syn see CHILD 1
youthful adj syn see YOUNG 1
rel beardless, boyish, puerile; maiden, virgin, virginal
con adult, matured
ant aged, elderly

youthfulness n syn see YOUTH 1
youthhood n syn see YOUTH
yowl vb **1** syn see YELL 2
2 syn see BAWL 2
yule n syn see CHRISTMAS
yuletide n syn see CHRISTMAS
yummy adj syn see DELIGHTFUL
zakuska n syn see APPETIZER
zany n **1** syn see CLOWN 1
rel comic, farceur, funnyman
2 one who makes an exhibition of himself for the amusement of others <tired of having her parties spoiled by drunken *zanies*>
syn clown, cutup, farceur, joker, jokester, wag
rel practical joker, pranker, prankster, trickster; exhibitionist, show-off
3 syn see WAG 1
4 syn see FOOL 4
zany adj syn see FOOLISH 2
zeal n syn see PASSION 6
rel energy, gusto, spirit, zest; fierceness, intensity, vehemence; avidity, keenness, readiness, urgency; earnestness, seriousness, sincerity
con coolness, halfheartedness, indifference, lukewarmness; carelessness, heedlessness, insouciance; negligence, unmindfulness; disinterest, lackadaisy, unconcern
ant apathy
zealot n syn see ENTHUSIAST
rel adherent, disciple, follower, partisan, sectary
zealous adj syn see ENTHUSIASTIC
rel afire, ardent, fervent, fervid, fired; avid, eager, dedicated, fanatic, frenetic, rabid, wild-eyed; infatuated, obsessed, possessed
con cool, halfhearted, indifferent, lukewarm; careless, heedless, insouciant, negligent, unmindful; disinterested, lackadaisical, uninterested
ant apathetic
zemi n syn see CHARM 2
zenith n syn see APEX 2
ant nadir
zero n **1** a numerical symbol 0 denoting the absence of all magnitude or quantity <wrote a row of *zeros* after the decimal point>
syn aught (or ought), cipher, goose egg, naught (or nought), nothing, zilch
rel blank, nil, void
2 syn see NONENTITY
zero (in) vb syn see DIRECT 2
zero hour n syn see JUNCTURE 2
zest n syn see TASTE 4
rel ardor, eagerness, enthusiasm, fervor, passion, zeal; delectation, delight, enjoyment, pleasure, satisfaction; bliss, ecstasy, elation
zesty adj syn see PUNGENT
zetetic n syn see SKEPTIC
zilch n **1** syn see ZERO 1
2 syn see NONENTITY
zing n **1** syn see EAGERNESS
2 syn see SPIRIT 5
Zion n **1** syn see HEAVEN 2
2 syn see UTOPIA
zip vb **1** syn see BREEZE
2 syn see HURRY 2
zippy adj syn see AGILE

rel alert, keen, ready; dynamic, forceful, intense
zoetic *adj syn* see LIVING 1
Zoilus *n syn* see CRITIC
zombie *n* **1** *syn* see DUNCE

2 *syn* see ECCENTRIC
zone *n syn* see AREA 1
rel section, sector, segment
zonked *adj* **1** *syn* see INTOXICATED 1
2 *syn* see DRUGGED

syn synonym(s)   *rel* related word(s)
ant antonym(s)   *con* contrasted word(s)
idiom idiomatic equivalent(s)
‖ use limited; if in doubt, see a dictionary